W9-CDF-885

NOTE TO STUDENTS

LEARNING AID

Make reviewing a snap! Put marketing concepts to work! A comprehensive study guide, entitled *Learning Aid for Use with Basic Marketing*, Seventh Canadian Edition, by E. Jerome McCarthy, Stanley J. Shapiro, and William D. Perreault, Jr., is available from your campus bookstore.

It's specially designed for this text and puts key chapter material at your fingertips. Sample exam questions and interesting application exercises make your study time count.

Check your campus bookstore or ask the manager to place an order today.

APPLICATIONS IN BASIC MARKETING

A free book offered in annual editons—*Applications in Basic Marketing*, by E. Jerome McCarthy and William D. Perreault, Jr.—is shrinkwrapped with all *new* texts. It features clippings from the popular business press. Separate copies may be purchased through your local campus bookstore.

Seventh Canadian Edition

Basic Marketing
A Global-Managerial Approach

E. Jerome McCarthy, PhD
Michigan State University

Stanley J. Shapiro, PhD
Simon Fraser University

William D. Perreault, Jr., PhD
University of North Carolina

Burr Ridge, Illinois
Boston, Massachusetts
Sydney, Australia

© RICHARD D. IRWIN, INC., 1975, 1979, 1983, 1986, 1989, 1992, and 1994

Sponsoring editor: Evelyn Veitch
Project editor: Mary Conzachi
Product manager: Murray Moman
Production manager: Bob Lange
Designer: Keith McPherson
Art coordinator: Mark Malloy
Art studio: Jay Benson Studios
Photo research coordinator: Patricia A. Seefelt
Compositor: Carlisle Communications, Ltd.
Typeface: 10.5/12 Goudy
Printer: Von Hoffmann Press
Library of Congress Catalog Card No.: 93–79781

Printed in the United States of America

1 2 3 4 5 6 7 8 9 0 VH 1 0 9 8 7 6 5 4

To Roberta,
previously, now, and forever.

S.J.S.

Preface

Ⓦ e're excited about the seventh Canadian edition of *Basic Marketing,* and we hope you will be as well. This edition introduces a number of important innovations, while simultaneously building on the traditional strengths of the text and all of the supporting materials that accompany it. We planned this revision based on the most extensive and detailed user feedback we've ever had. That feedback gave us hundreds of ideas for big and small additions, changes, and improvements. We'll highlight some of those changes in this Preface, but first it's useful to put this newest edition in a longer-term perspective.

The first American edition of *Basic Marketing* pioneered an innovative structure—using the four Ps with a managerial approach—for the introductory marketing course. In the 33 years since publication of that first edition, there have been constant changes in marketing management. Some of the changes have been dramatic, and others have been subtle. Throughout all of these changes, *Basic Marketing*—and the supporting materials to accompany it—have been more widely used than any other teaching package for introductory marketing. It is gratifying that the four Ps concept has proved to be an organizing structure that has worked well for millions of students and teachers.

Of course, this position of leadership is not the result of a single strength or of one long-lasting innovation. With each new edition of *Basic Marketing,* we have seized the opportunity to introduce innovations—and to better meet the needs of students and faculty. We believe that attention to quality in every aspect of the text and support materials does make a difference, a belief consistently reaffirmed by the enthusiastic response of students and teachers alike.

We believe that the seventh Canadian edition of *Basic Marketing* is the highest quality teaching and learning resource ever available for the introductory course. The whole text and all the supporting materials have been critically revised, updated, and rewritten. As in past editions, clear and interesting communication has been a priority. Careful explanations provide a crisp focus on the important basics of marketing strategy planning. At the same time, we have researched and introduced new concepts and integrated hundreds of new examples that bring the concepts alive.

The seventh Canadian edition focuses special attention on changes taking place in today's dynamic markets. For example, we have integrated international perspectives throughout *every* chapter of the text. Similarly, each chapter features carefully integrated discussion of the ethical issues that all marketers face. These two factors alone have made this the most significant Canadian revision ever published. We've also integrated new material on topics such as total quality management (with special emphasis on customer service quality), just-in-time relationships, competitor analysis, value pricing, environmental concerns, information technologies, brand extensions, and direct marketing.

Throughout the seventh Canadian edition, we have focused more attention on the importance of competitive advantage in strategy planning. You'll learn about the changing relationships in channels of distribution—ranging from coordination of logistics efforts among firms to the increasing conflict between producers and large retail chains. You'll see how intense competition—both in North America and around the world—is affecting marketing strategy planning. You'll see why rapid response in new-product development is so critical.

Some other marketing texts have attempted to describe such changes. But what sets *Basic Marketing* apart is that the explanations and examples not only highlight the changes taking place today but also equip students to see *why* these changes are taking place—and what changes to expect in the future. That is an important distinction, because marketing is dynamic. Our objective is to equip students to analyze marketing situations and develop workable marketing strategies—not just recite some list of terms or ideas.

Along with the new content, we've given the text a fresh design. The changes range from a new typeface and open page layout to new artwork and illustrations. By using the latest advances in computer-aided design, we were able to research and evaluate hundreds of combinations of design elements to arrive at an overall redesign that makes important concepts and points even clearer to students.

The aim of all this revising, refining, editing, and illustrating is to make sure that each student really does get a good feel for a market-directed system and how he or she can help it—and some company—run better. We believe marketing is important and interesting, and we want every student who reads *Basic Marketing* to share our enthusiasm.

A new and exciting approach has also been taken to the task of Canadianization. The Canadian vignettes that open most chapters, the increased number of Canadian marketing demos, the 12 new Canadian cases, the many Canadian advertisements and pictures all make a significant addition to the Canadian content of this edition. The most up-to-date Canadian statistics available at the time of publication—many drawn from just released 1991 census data—are found throughout the text.

The emphasis of the seventh Canadian edition of *Basic Marketing* is on marketing strategy planning. Twenty-two chapters introduce the important concepts in marketing management and help students see marketing through the eyes of marketing managers. The organization of the chapters and topics was carefully planned. But we took special care in writing so that it is possible to rearrange and use the chapters in many different sequences, and to fit different needs.

The first two chapters deal with the nature of marketing—focusing both on its macro role in a global society and its micro role in businesses and other organizations. The first chapter stresses that the effectiveness of our macromarketing system depends on the decisions of many producers and consumers. That sets the stage for the second chapter—and the rest of the book—which focuses on how businesspeople and marketing managers, in particular, develop marketing strategies to satisfy specific target markets.

Chapter 3 introduces a strategic planning view of how managers can find new market opportunities. The emphasis is on identifying target markets with market segmentation and positioning approaches. This strategic view alerts students to the importance of evaluating opportunities in the external environments affecting marketing—and these are discussed in Chapter 4. Chapter 5 is a contemporary view of getting information, from marketing information systems and marketing research, for marketing management planning.

The next three chapters take a closer look at customers so students will better understand how to segment markets and satisfy target market needs. Chapter 6 and its accompanying addendum introduce the demographic dimensions of both the Canadian and global consumer markets. The following two chapters study the behavioral features of the consumer market and how business and organizational customers like manufacturers, channel members, and government purchasers are similar to and different from final consumers.

The next group of chapters—Chapters 9 through 19—is concerned with developing a marketing mix out of the four Ps: Product, Place (involving channels of distribution, logistics, and distribution customer service), Promotion, and Price. These chapters are concerned with developing the "right" Product and making it available at the "right" Place with the "right" Promotion and the "right" Price—to satisfy target customers and still meet the objectives of the business. These chapters are presented in an integrated, analytical way, so students' thinking about planning marketing strategies develops logically.

Chapter 20 ties the four Ps into planning for whole marketing programs and discusses how total quality management approaches can guide implementation of the marketing plan. Chapter 21 discusses marketing control—a topic becoming even more important now that more control-related information is available faster. The final chapter considers how efficient the marketing process is. Here, we evaluate the effectiveness of both micro- and macro-marketing—and consider the competitive, ethical, and social challenges facing marketing managers now and in the future. After this chapter, the student might want to look at the newly introduced Appendix E, which covers career opportunities in marketing.

Some textbooks treat special topics—like international marketing, marketing ethics, environmental concerns, services marketing, marketing for nonprofit organizations, and business-to-business marketing—in separate chapters. We have not done that because we are convinced that treating such topics separately leads to an unfortunate compartmentalization of ideas. We think they are too important to be isolated that way. Instead, they are interwoven and illustrated throughout the text to emphasize that marketing thinking is crucial in all aspects of our society and economy. However, a new appendix on social marketing has been added to provide additional information on this important topic.

Really understanding marketing and how to plan marketing strategies can build self-confidence—and it can help prepare students to take an active part in the business world. To move students in this direction, we deliberately include a variety of frameworks, models, classification systems, and how-to-do-it techniques that should speed the development of "marketing sense"—and enable students to analyze marketing situations in a confident and meaningful way. Taken seriously, they are practical and they work. In addition, because they are interesting and understandable, they equip students to see marketing as the challenging and rewarding area it is.

So students will see what is coming in each *Basic Marketing* chapter, behavioral objectives are included on the first page of each chapter and, to speed student understanding, important new terms are shown in blue and defined immediately. Further, a glossary of these terms is presented at the end of the book. Within chapters, major section headings and second-level headings (placed in the margin for clarity) immediately show how the material is organized *and* summarize key points in the text. Further, we have placed annotated photos and advertisements near the concepts they illustrate to provide a visual reminder of the ideas. All of these aids help the student understand important concepts and speed review before exams. End-of-chapter questions and problems offer additional opportunities. They encourage students to investigate the marketing process and develop their own ways of thinking about it. They can be used for independent study or as a basis for written assignments or class discussion.

Understanding of the text material can be deepened by analysis and discussion of specific examples. *Basic Marketing* features several different types of illustrations. Each chapter starts with an in-depth vignette developed specifically to highlight that chapter's teaching objectives. In addition, every chapter contains Canadian marketing demos. Each demo illustrates how a particular company has developed its marketing strategy, with emphasis on a topic covered in that chapter. Because all of these demos provide an excellent basis for critical evaluation and discussion, they should be considered an essential part of the chapter.

In addition, there are several suggested cases listed at the end of each chapter. The focus of these cases is on problem solving. They encourage students to apply—and really get involved with—the concepts developed in the text. Case-based assignments stimulate a problem-solving approach to marketing strategy planning and give students hands-on experience that shows how logical analysis of alternative strategies can lead to improved decision making. Of the 37 cases found at the end of the text, 19 did not appear in the preceding sixth edition and another 4 have been substantially modified.

Some professors and students want to follow up on text readings. Each chapter is supplemented with detailed references to both classic articles and current readings in business publications. These references, which are located at the end of the book, can guide more detailed study of the topics covered in a chapter.

Our publisher will also provide a new edition of *Applications in Basic Marketing* free of charge shrinkwrapped with each new copy of the seventh Canadian edition of *Basic Marketing!* This annually updated collection of marketing clippings—from publications such as *The Wall Street Journal, Fortune,* and *Business Week*—provides convenient access to short, interesting, and current discussions of marketing issues. The 1993–1994 edition features more than 100 new articles. There are a variety of short clippings related to each chapter in *Basic Marketing.* In addition, because we revise this collection *each year,* it can include timely material that is available in no other text.

A separate *Learning Aid* provides several more teaching units and offers further opportunities to obtain a deeper understanding of the material. That *Learning Aid* can be used by the student alone or with teacher direction. Portions of the *Learning Aid* help students review what they have studied. For example, there is a brief introduction to each chapter, a list of the important new terms (with page numbers for easy reference), true-false questions (with answers) that cover *all* the important terms and concepts, and multiple-choice questions (with answers) illustrating the kinds of questions that may appear in examinations. In addition, the *Learning Aid* has cases, exercises, and problems—with clear instructions and worksheets for the student to complete. The *Learning Aid* exercises can be used as classwork or homework—to drill on certain topics and to deepen understanding of others by motivating application and then discussion. In fact, reading *Basic Marketing* and working with the *Learning Aid* can be the basic activity of the course.

Another element is *The Marketing Game!*, a microcomputer-based competitive simulation. It was developed specifically to reinforce the target marketing and marketing strategy planning ideas discussed in *Basic Marketing*. Students make marketing management decisions, blending the four Ps to compete for the business of different possible target markets. The innovative design of *The Marketing Game!* allows the instructor to increase the number of decision areas involved as students learn more about marketing. In fact, many instructors use the advanced levels of the game as the basis for a second course.

A detailed *Instructor's Manual* provides chapter by chapter lecture outlines, transparency masters, and answers to all questions, cases, and learning aid material.

To complete the pedagogical package, thousands of objective test questions—written by the authors to really work with the text—give instructors a high-quality resource.

In closing, we return to a point raised at the beginning of this preface: *Basic Marketing* has been the leading textbook in marketing for more than three decades. We take the responsibilities of that leadership seriously. We know that you want and deserve the very best teaching and learning materials possible. It is our commitment to bring you those materials—today with this edition and in the future with subsequent editions. We recognize that fulfilling this commitment requires a process of continuous improvement. Improvements, changes, and development of new elements must be ongoing—because needs change. You are an important part of this evolution, of this leadership. We encourage your feedback. Thoughtful criticisms and suggestions from students and teachers alike have helped to make *Basic Marketing* what it is. We hope that you will help make it what it will be in the future.

Stanley J. Shapiro

Acknowledgments

The seventh Canadian edition of *Basic Marketing* could not have been prepared without the support and assistance of numerous friends and associates. I am most grateful to all of these individuals—not only those identified below but also anyone who, because of an error or oversight on my part, may not be adequately acknowledged in the paragraphs that follow.

How this Canadian edition differs from its predecessors is discussed in the accompanying Preface. However, each succeeding edition of any text builds on and refines what has preceded it. Consequently, all those who assisted in the preparation of previous Canadian editions are again deserving of thanks, for they have contributed as well to this latest effort. A complete listing of those individuals is found in preceding acknowledgment sections.

Contributions by professional colleagues to the successful completion of this text took two forms—preparing material that was included in the text and critically evaluating both this volume and its immediate predecessor. Important contributions to the text itself and to the accompanying appendixes were made by Professors P. Lane of Western Michigan University and C. Kaufman of Rutgers University, Mr. B. Canzer of John Abbot College and Concordia University, and Ms. Tanya Stastny of Just the Facts Research Inc. Despite their very busy schedules, Professors Lane and Kaufman found time to write the new section on the different aspects of time that provides such a useful addition to Chapter 7's treatment of consumer behavior. Mr. Canzer, who also provided a case, wrote the very insightful appendix on social marketing that follows Chapter 20. Ms. Stastny prepared Appendix B, which deals with Canadian sources of marketing information.

Two thirds of the cases appearing in this seventh edition have been prepared by Canadian marketing professors. Because they held up so well in classroom use, I have again included 13 cases originally provided for a previous edition by D. Aronchik of Ryerson Polytechnical Institute, P. Banting of McMaster University, M. Borts of McGill University, K. Hardy of the University of Western Ontario, V. H. Kirpalani and H. Simpkins of Concordia University, J. Kyle of Mount Saint Vincent University, M. Ryder of McMaster University, F. Saleh of the University of Saskatchewan, R. Tamilia of the University of Quebec at Montreal, and E. Weymes, formerly of the University of Regina. An additional 12 Canadian cases appear for the first time in *Basic Marketing*. Two of these cases were provided by W. Good of the University of Manitoba and another pair by T. Funk of the University of Guelph. Five of the case authors or case writing teams whose previous contributions were held over and who provided additional material are P. Banting, V. H. Kirpalani and H. Simpkins, L. Meredith, M. Ryder, and M. Borts, this time in conjunction with J. Mintz and J. Laporte of Health and Welfare Canada. Other authors contributing cases new to the text include Mr. B. Canzer of John Abbot College and Concordia University, C. Weinberg of the University of British Columbia, and R. Wyckham of Simon Fraser University.

In the area of manuscript evaluation, truly exemplary assistance was provided by Paulette Padanyi of Ryerson Polytechnic University, Yiming Tang of York University, Stephen Turnbull of the British Columbia Institute of Technology, Vivian Vaupshas of McGill University, and Janice Shearer, Brad Berry, and Bill Lucas of Mohawk College, all of whom carefully reviewed the predecessor sixth edition and indicated areas where improvement, enhancement, or updating were in order. Many of their suggestions were incorporated into this edition and none were dismissed without very careful consideration. Thanks are also due to George Jacob of the British Columbia Institute of Technology, Peter Popkowski Leszczyc of the University of Alberta, and Gordon Thomas of the University of Manitoba for reviewing a first draft of some of the most significantly revised chapters in this edition. Last but not least, I am especially grateful to Paulette Padanyi of Ryerson Polytechnic University for her careful review of the accompanying *Learning Aid*, *Instructor's Manual*, and Test Bank.

The various marketing demos found throughout the text also made a significant collective contribution in both volume and quality. I wish to thank all those furnishing such material for providing an exciting, contemporary, "real world" feel to this text. I am equally obligated to all those who allowed me to reproduce the pictures and illustrations that so greatly heighten this edition's Canadian imagery.

Next to be recognized are those at Simon Fraser University who contributed so much to this revision. Ms. Heather Fox, then a marketing major in our MBA program, both helped in the selection of marketing demos and contributed immeasurably to the revision of the opening chapters of the text. She was soon joined in this effort by her colleague, Ms. Roberta Hupman, who became increasingly involved through completion after Heather signed off so that she might finish her MBA research paper. Since both Heather and Roberta had been teaching assistants in SFU's introductory marketing course, they had a unique feel for what would be well received in the "real classroom." Together they made an indispensable contribution to the successful completion of the project.

The Dean's office at the SFU Faculty of Business Administration is staffed with truly remarkable individuals. Their job descriptions say nothing about the periodic revision of a marketing textbook. Nevertheless, Margaret Oxnard, Diane Lesack, Carol Roche, and Linda Wetzel cheerfully and skillfully provided the extensive administrative and clerical support this type of project requires. The initiative they, along with Helene Michaels and Carole Murrell, showed in many other areas also helped me free up the time a revision of this magnitude requires.

The "Porter contribution" must also be recognized. Ann and Abe Porter have now become old hands at providing the mix of research and clerical support needed to convert the 11th American edition to its seventh Canadian counterpart. They were also responsible for the many associated changes in the accompanying *Learning Aid* and *Instructor's Manual*. Of course, wrestling footnotes to the ground also remains a specialty of that household.

Finally, the patience shown and support provided by Roberta Shapiro during 10 successive efforts at Canadianization (7 *Basic* and 3 *Essentials*) must also be acknowledged. She is always there for me and with me whether the particular issue at hand involves publishing, politics, or academic administration. Now, if Robert were only prepared to show more patience and to demonstrate less dogged determination.

Contents

Seventh Canadian Edition

Basic Marketing

A Global-Managerial Approach

Marketing's Role in the Global Economy

When You Finish This Chapter, You Should

❶
Know what marketing is and why you should learn about it.

❷
Understand the difference between micro-marketing and macro-marketing.

❸
Know why and how macro-marketing systems develop.

❹
Understand why marketing is crucial to economic development and our global economy.

❺
Know why marketing specialists—including middlemen and facilitators—develop.

❻
Know the marketing functions and who performs them.

❼
Understand the important new terms (shown in blue).

(T) he quality of life for Canadians has never been better. The Organization for Economic Cooperation and Development (OECD) ranks the world's richest nations on a scale of 1 to 100, with the United States at 100. In 1970, Canada placed third on this list, behind the United States and Switzerland, with a ranking of 79 out of 100. Two decades later, Canada has closed the gap with the United States and overtaken Switzerland to place second on the list, with a ranking of 95.[1]

Based on this ranking, Canada would appear to be a highly desirable place to live. However, is there a problem brewing due to the nation's level of competitiveness?

The World Competitiveness Report presents a more disturbing portrait of Canada's position in the global marketplace. In the early 1990s, Canada's competitive position dropped from 5th to 11th. That competitiveness is measured on eight factors:[2]

1. **Domestic economic strength**—a macroeconomic evaluation of the domestic economy overall.
2. **Internationalization**—the extent to which the country participates in international trade and investment flows.
3. **Government**—the extent to which government policies are conducive to competitiveness.
4. **Finance**—the performance of capital markets and the quality of financial services.
5. **Infrastructure**—the extent to which resources and systems are adequate to serve the basic needs of business.
6. **Management**—the extent to which enterprises are managed in an innovative, profitable, and responsible manner.

7. *Science and technology*—scientific and technological capacity, together with the success of basic and applied research.
8. *People*—the availability and qualifications of human resources.

Canada's ability to retain its high standard of living will depend on its ability to compete in the global market. Remaining competitive will require the joint effort of business, government, and labor.

Within this context, marketing has a significant role to play. Marketing is an important tool for reaching the world with Canadian products and services. This chapter will explore how marketing does this and why it is crucial to our continued economic development and our global impact.

MARKETING—WHAT'S IT ALL ABOUT?

Marketing is more than selling or advertising

If forced to define marketing, most people, including some business managers, say that marketing means "selling" or "advertising." It's true that these are parts of marketing. But *marketing is much more than selling and advertising*.

To illustrate some of the other important things that are included in marketing, think about all the different types of skis that are available to downhill and cross-country skiers, beginners and pros. Most of us weren't born with skis on our feet. Nor do we make our own skis. Instead, they are made by firms like Rossignol, Dynastar, K2, and Salomon.

Most skis are intended to do the same thing—get the skier down the mountain or across the field. But a skier can choose from a wide assortment of skis. There are different shapes, materials, weights, and lengths. You can buy a pair of skis for as low as $100 or spend over $600!

This variety in sizes and materials complicates the production and sale of skis. The following list shows some of the many things a firm should do before and after it decides to produce skis.

1. Analyze the needs of people who ski and decide if consumers want more or different types of skis.
2. Predict what types of skis—lengths, weights, shapes—different skiers will want and decide which of these people the firm will try to satisfy.
3. Estimate how many of these people will be skiing over the next several years and how many skis they'll buy.
4. Predict exactly when these skiers will want to buy skis.
5. Determine where in the world these skiers will be and how to get the firm's skis to them.
6. Estimate what price they are willing to pay for their skis and if the firm can make a profit selling at that price.
7. Decide which kinds of promotion should be used to tell potential customers about the firm's skis.
8. Estimate how many competing companies will be making skis, how many skis they'll produce, what kind, and at what prices.

The above activities are not part of **production**—actually making goods or performing services. Rather, they are part of a larger process—called **marketing**—

All skis can get you down the mountain—but there are many variations to meet the needs of different people.

that provides needed direction for production and helps make sure that the right goods and services are produced and find their way to consumers.

Our ski example shows that marketing includes much more than selling or advertising. We'll describe marketing activities in the next chapter. And you'll learn much more about them before you finish this book. For now, it's enough to see that marketing plays an essential role in providing consumers with need-satisfying goods and services.

HOW MARKETING RELATES TO THE PRODUCTION OF GOODS AND SERVICES

Production is a very important economic activity. Whether for lack of skill and resources or just lack of time, most people don't make most of the products they use. Picture yourself, for example, building a mountain bike, a compact disc player, or a digital watch—starting from scratch! We also turn to others to produce services such as health care, air transportation, and entertainment. Clearly, the high standard of living that most people in advanced economies enjoy is made possible by specialized production.

Skis, like mousetraps, don't sell themselves

Although production is a necessary economic activity, some people overrate its importance in relation to marketing. Their attitude is reflected in the old saying: "Make a better mousetrap and the world will beat a path to your door." In other words, they think that if you just have a good product, your business will be a success.

The better mousetrap idea probably wasn't true in Grandpa's time, and it certainly isn't true today. In modern economies, the grass grows high on the path to the Better Mousetrap Factory—if the new mousetrap isn't properly marketed. We have already seen, for example, that there's a lot more to marketing skis than just making them. This is true for most goods and services.

The point is that production and marketing are both important parts of a total business system aimed at providing consumers with need-satisfying goods and services. Together, production and marketing supply five kinds of economic utility—form, task, time, place, and possession utility—that are needed to provide consumer satisfaction. Here, **utility** means the power to satisfy human needs. See Exhibit 1–1.

Skis do not automatically provide utility

Form utility is provided when someone produces something tangible—for instance, a pair of skis. **Task utility** is provided when someone performs a task for someone else—for instance, when a bank handles financial transactions. But just producing skis or handling bank accounts doesn't result in consumer satisfaction. The product must be something that consumers want or there is no need to be satisfied—and no utility.

This is how marketing thinking guides the production side of goods and services. Marketing decisions focus on the customer and include decisions about what goods and services to produce. It doesn't make sense to provide goods and services consumers don't want when there are so many things they do want or need. Let's take our mousetrap example a step further. Some customers don't want *any kind* of mousetrap. They may want someone else to produce a service and exterminate the mice for them, or they may live where mice are not a problem. Marketing is concerned with what customers want—and it should guide what is produced and offered. This is an important idea that we will develop more completely later.

Even when marketing and production combine to provide form or task utility, consumers won't be satisfied until possession, time, and place utility are also provided. **Possession utility** means obtaining a good or service and having the

Exhibit 1–1   Types of Utility and How They Are Provided

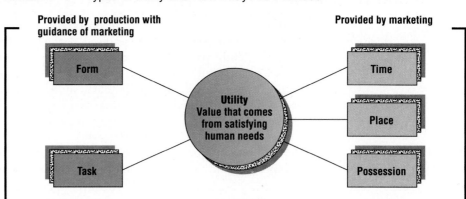

right to use or consume it. Customers usually exchange money or something else of value for possession utility.

Time utility means having the product available *when* the customer wants it. And **place utility** means having the product available *where* the customer wants it. Skis that stay at a factory don't do anyone any good. Time and place utility are very important for services, too. For example, neighborhood emergency care health clinics have recently become very popular. People just walk in as soon as they feel sick, not a day later when their doctor can schedule an appointment.

Stated simply, marketing provides time, place, and possession utility. It should also guide decisions about what goods and services should be produced to provide form utility and task utility. We'll look at how marketing does this later in this chapter. First, we want to discuss why you should study marketing, and then we'll define marketing.

MARKETING IS IMPORTANT TO YOU

Marketing is important to every consumer

Marketing affects almost every aspect of your daily life. All the goods and services you buy, the stores where you shop, and the radio and TV programs paid for by advertising are there because of marketing. This process doesn't come cheap. In advanced economies, marketing costs about 50 cents of each consumer's dollar. For some goods and services, the percentage is much higher.

Marketing is something you are exposed to all the time. Even your job résumé is part of a marketing campaign to sell yourself to some employer! Some courses are interesting when you take them but never relevant again once they're over. Not so with marketing—you'll be a consumer dealing with marketing for the rest of your life.

Marketing provides many interesting career opportunities.

Source: *The Financial Post*, June 9, 1992, p. B42.

Marketing will be important to your job	Another reason for studying marketing is that there are many exciting and rewarding career opportunities in marketing. Marketing is often the route to the top. Throughout this book you will find information about opportunities in different areas of marketing—in sales, advertising, product management, marketing research, distribution, and other areas. And Appendix E is all about career planning in marketing.

Even if you're aiming for a nonmarketing job, you'll be working with marketing people. Knowing something about marketing will help you understand them better. It will also help you do your own job better. Marketing is important to the success of every organization. Remember, a company that can't successfully sell its products doesn't need accountants, financial managers, production managers, personnel managers, computer programmers, or credit managers.

Marketing concepts and techniques apply to nonprofit organizations, too. Many nonprofit organizations have a marketing manager. And the same basic principles used to sell soap are also used to "sell" ideas, politicians, mass transportation, health care services, conservation, museums, and even colleges. Think about the school where you take this course. If you didn't know about its offerings—or if they didn't interest you—you probably would have picked some other school.[3]

Marketing affects economic growth	An even more basic reason for studying marketing is that marketing plays a big part in economic growth and development. Marketing stimulates research and new ideas—resulting in new goods and services. Marketing gives customers a choice among products. If these products satisfy customers, fuller employment, higher incomes, and a higher standard of living can result. An effective marketing system is important to the future of all nations.[4]

HOW SHOULD WE DEFINE MARKETING?

As we said earlier, some people think of marketing too narrowly as "selling and advertising." On the other hand, one authority defined marketing as the "creation and delivery of a standard of living."[5] That definition is too broad.

An important difference between the two definitions may be less obvious. The first definition is a *micro*-level definition. It focuses on activities performed by an individual organization. The second is a *macro*-level definition. It focuses on the economic welfare of a whole society.

Micro- or macro-marketing?	Which view is correct? Is marketing a set of activities done by individual firms or organizations? Or is it a social process?

To answer this question, let's go back to our ski example. We saw that a producer of skis has to perform many customer-related activities besides just making skis. The same is true for an insurance company, an art museum, or a family-service agency. This supports the idea of marketing as a set of activities done by individual organizations.

On the other hand, people can't live on skis and art museums alone! In advanced economies, it takes thousands of goods and services to satisfy the many needs of society. For example, a typical Eaton's department store carries 200,000 different items. A society needs some sort of marketing system to organize the efforts of all the producers and middlemen needed to satisfy the varied needs of all its citizens. So marketing is also an important social process.

The answer to our question is that *marketing is both a set of activities performed by organizations and a social process.* In other words, marketing exists at both the micro and macro levels. Therefore, we will use two definitions of marketing—one for micro-marketing and another for macro-marketing. The first looks at customers and the organizations that serve them. The second takes a broad view of our whole production-distribution system.

MICRO–MARKETING DEFINED

Micro-marketing is the performance of activities that seek to accomplish an organization's objectives by anticipating customer or client needs and directing a flow of need-satisfying goods and services from producer to customer or client. Let's look at this definition.[6]

Applies to profit and nonprofit organizations

To begin with, this definition applies to both profit and nonprofit organizations. Profit is the objective for most business firms. But other types of organizations may seek more members—or acceptance of an idea. Customers or clients may be individual consumers, business firms, nonprofit organizations, government agencies, or even foreign nations. While most customers and clients pay for the goods and services they receive, others may receive them free of charge or at a reduced cost through private or government support.

More than just persuading customers

You already know that micro-marketing isn't just selling and advertising. Unfortunately, many executives still think it is. They feel that the job of marketing is to "get rid of" whatever the company happens to produce. In fact, the aim of marketing is to identify customers' needs—and meet those needs so well that the product almost "sells itself." This is true whether the product is a physical good, a service, or even an idea. If the whole marketing job has been done well, customers don't need much persuading. They should be ready to buy. Northern Telecom understands this and has moved its people from thinking of sales as marketing to thinking of marketing as meeting customer needs. As a result, it understands its competition better. It also understands its customer requirements better and can translate them into fuctions and features in its products. It realizes that this is a necessary step to achieving the goal of becoming the preferred telecommunications company of customers, suppliers, and professional talent around the world.[7]

The aim of marketing is to identify customers' needs—and to meet these needs so well that the product almost sells itself.

Northern Telecom uses much of its advertising to show how it satisfies corporate needs.

Begins with customer needs

Northern Telecom knows that *marketing should begin with potential customer needs*—not with the production process. Marketing should try to anticipate needs. And then marketing, rather than production, should determine what goods and services are to be developed—including decisions about product design and packaging; prices or fees; credit and collection policies; use of middlemen; transporting and storing policies; advertising and sales policies; and, after the sale, installation, customer service, warranty, and perhaps even disposal policies.

Marketing does not do it alone

This does not mean that marketing should try to take over production, accounting, and financial activities. Rather, it means that marketing—by interpreting customers' needs—should provide direction for these activities and try to coordinate them. After all, the purpose of a business or nonprofit organization is to satisfy customer or client needs. It is not to supply goods and services that are convenient to produce and *might* sell or be accepted free.

THE FOCUS OF THIS TEXT—MANAGEMENT–ORIENTED MICRO-MARKETING

Since most of you are preparing for a career in management, the main focus of this text will be on micro-marketing. We will see marketing through the eyes of the marketing manager.

It is important to keep in mind that the micro-marketing ideas and decision areas we will be discussing throughout this text apply to a wide variety of marketing management situations. They are important not only for large and small business firms but also for all types of public sector and nonprofit organizations. They are useful in domestic markets and international markets, and regardless of whether the organization focuses on marketing physical goods, services, or an idea or cause. They are equally critical whether the relevant customers or clients are individual consumers, businesses, or some other type of organization. In short, every organization needs to think about its markets and how effectively it meets its customers' and clients' needs. For editorial convenience, and to reflect the fact that most readers will work in business settings, when we discuss marketing concepts, we will sometimes use the term *firm* as a shorthand way of referring to any type of organization, whether it is a political party, a religious organization, a government agency, or the like. However, to reinforce the point that the ideas apply to all types of organizations, throughout the book we will illustrate marketing management concepts with examples that represent a wide variety of marketing situations.

Although micro-marketing is the primary focus of the text, marketing managers must remember that their organizations are just small parts of a larger macro-marketing system. Therefore, the rest of this chapter will look at the macro-view of marketing. Let's begin by defining macro-marketing and reviewing some basic ideas. Then, in Chapter 2, we'll explain the marketing management decision areas we will be discussing in the rest of the book.

MACRO–MARKETING DEFINED

Macro-marketing is a social process that directs an economy's flow of goods and services from producers to consumers in a way that effectively matches supply and demand and accomplishes the objectives of society.

Emphasis is on whole system

Like micro-marketing, macro-marketing is concerned with the flow of need-satisfying goods and services from producer to consumer. However, the emphasis with macro-marketing is not on the activities of individual organizations. Instead, the emphasis is on *how the whole marketing system works*. This includes looking at how marketing affects society, and vice versa.

Every society needs a macro-marketing system to help match supply and demand. Different producers in a society have different objectives, resources, and skills. Likewise, not all consumers share the same needs, preferences, and wealth. In other words, within every society there are both heterogeneous supply capabilities and heterogeneous demands for goods and services. The role of a macro-marketing system is to effectively match this heterogeneous supply and demand *and* at the same time accomplish society's objectives. See Marketing Demo 1–1 for a more complete treatment of the scope of macro-marketing.

Is it effective and fair?

The effectiveness and fairness of a particular macro-marketing system must be evaluated in terms of that society's objectives. Obviously, all nations don't share the same objectives. For example, Swedish citizens receive many "free" services—like health care and retirement benefits. Goods and services are fairly evenly distributed among the Swedish population. By contrast, at least until the Gulf War, Iraq placed little emphasis on producing goods and services for individual consumers—and more on military spending. In India, the distribution of goods and services is very uneven—with a big gap between the "have-nots" and the

---

MARKETING DEMO 1–1
Categories of Macro-Marketing Phenomena

Effect of Marketing on Society

This describes what has been referred to as social consequences, secondary or tertiary effects, externalities (not in the precise economics usage), and so forth.

    Economic Development

The effect of marketing institutions, behaviors, and systems on the economic development of a geographical or political entity. This includes both developing and developed areas.

    Stakeholder Welfare

Every society is made up of numerous stakeholder groups that are affected differentially by markething actions.

    Consumption Patterns

Marketing actions affect consumption choices in society and therefore the aggregate patterns of consumption. Included are a whole range of social and cultural effects.

    Environmental Effects

Every marketing action and transaction has some level of effect on the physical environment. Some marketing actions individually or collectively have substantial effects on the air, water, land, and habitat.

Effect of Society on Marketing

Societal institutions, processes, and culture, through all their diverse levels and facets, affect marketing and markets.

    Public Policies

The intended and unintended effects of laws and governmental rules and administrative actions affect almost every facet of marketing. The structure of markets and competitive dynamics are shaped by public policy.

    Nongovernmental Sanction Systems

A wide diversity of nongovernmental forces also affect marketing behaviors. These range from trade associations to religious organizations. They come in the form of voluntary acceptance and are enforced through social processes. Values, ethics, and norms are established through acculturation or socialization processes.

Marketing Systems

The understanding of marketing systems allows the effective analysis of marketing actions on society, and vice versa. Marketing systems are built by individual and organizational behaviors within their environments, resulting in marketing structures and processes. Key elements are channels of distribution, marketing institutions, system linkages, and generally accepted decision rules.

Source: Robert W. Nason, "Macromarketing in an Era of Global Change," *Canadian Journal of Administrative Sciences* 9, no. 2, p. 99.

---

elite "haves." Whether each of these systems is judged fair or effective depends on the objectives of the society.

    Let's look more closely at macro-marketing.[8] And to make this more meaningful to you, consider (1) what kind of a macro-marketing system you have and (2) how effective and fair it is.

Consumers in Moscow wait in a three-hour line to buy a rare delicacy—a Chiquita banana. Things are easier for most consumers in Canada, the United States, and Western Europe.

EVERY SOCIETY NEEDS AN ECONOMIC SYSTEM

All societies must provide for the needs of their members. Therefore, every society needs some sort of **economic system**—the way an economy organizes to use scarce resources to produce goods and services and distribute them for consumption by various people and groups in the society.

How an economic system operates depends on a society's objectives and the nature of its political institutions.[9] But regardless of what form these take, all economic systems must develop some method—along with appropriate economic institutions—to decide what and how much is to be produced and distributed by whom, when, to whom, and why. How these decisions are made may vary from nation to nation. But the macro-level objectives are basically similar: to create goods and services and make them available when and where they are needed—to maintain or improve each nation's standard of living or other socially defined objective.

HOW ECONOMIC DECISIONS ARE MADE

There are two basic kinds of economic systems: planned systems and market-directed systems. Actually, no economy is entirely planned or market-directed. Most are a mixture of the two extremes.

Government planners
may make the decisions

In a **planned economic system**, government planners decide what and how much is to be produced and distributed by whom, when, to whom, and why. Producers generally have little choice about what goods and services to produce. Their main task is to meet their assigned production quotas. Prices are set by government planners and tend to be very rigid—not changing according to supply and demand. Consumers usually have some freedom of choice—it's impossible to control every single detail! But the assortment of goods and services may be quite limited. Activities such as market research, branding, and advertising usually are neglected. Sometimes they aren't done at all.

Government planning may work fairly well as long as an economy is simple and the variety of goods and services is small. It may even be necessary under certain conditions—during wartime, drought, or political instability, for example. However, as economies become more complex, government planning becomes more difficult. It may even break down. Planners may be overwhelmed by too many complex decisions. And consumers may lose patience if the planners don't respond to their needs.

The collapse of communism in Eastern Europe dramatically illustrates this. Citizens of what was the Soviet Union were not satisfied with the government's plan—because products consumers wanted and needed were not available. To try to reduce consumer dissatisfaction, government planners tried to put more emphasis on making consumer goods available, but they were not able to produce the results consumers wanted. In short, it was consumer dissatisfaction with decisions made by government planners that brought about a revolution—one that is leading to the development of market-directed economies in the new, independent republics of Eastern Europe.[10] For an example of how this is happening, see Marketing Demo 1–2.

A market-directed economy adjusts itself

In a **market-directed economic system,** the individual decisions of the many producers and consumers make the macro-level decisions for the whole economy.

MARKETING DEMO 1–2
The Marketing System Improves in a United Germany

Prior to the fall of the Berlin Wall, consumers in East Germany often had to wait in long lines to make purchases at government-controlled stores. There were frequent shortages of the products consumers wanted and needed—including basic foods. The Berlin Wall was more than just a symbol of political differences between East and West. Trade with the market-directed economy of the West was very limited, and the macro-marketing system in the East was not effective in meeting consumer needs. The failure of the economic system prompted political change.

With the reunification of Germany, the political limits on trade were gone. Yet there were still problems. Even in a market-directed economy, it takes time for new middlemen and facilitators to develop. For example, eastern Germany had no efficient wholesalers to supply the chain of 170 Konsum retail stores, which were previously state-owned. And it was expensive for producers in the West who wanted to reach the market in the East to do it without help.

However, the Tegut grocery chain in the West saw the opportunity and quickly did something about

it. Tegut established an automated warehouse in the East to supply the Konsum stores. The warehouse made it economical to assemble needed assortments of products from many different producers. Even so, information about which Konsum stores needed what products was bad because telecommunications systems in the East were so poor. With the help of Tandem computer company, Tegut set up a computer network to link the stores to the new warehouse. The computer system provided for timely reordering from the warehouse, on-line management of inventories and distribution, and even payment control.

With the help of middlemen like Tegut, both local and foreign producers are better able to meet consumer needs.

Source: Tandem, 1990 Annual Report; "The New Germany's Glowing Future," *Fortune,* December 3, 1990, pp. 146–54; "Berlin Tries to Raze Its Great Divide," *Insight,* October 15, 1990, pp. 8–17; "West Brands Rain on East's Parade," *Advertising Age,* October 1, 1990, p. 15ff.; "Speeding over the Bumps," *Time,* July 30, 1990, pp. 30–31; "A New Germany," *Newsweek,* July 9, 1990, pp. 28–36; "One Germany," *Business Week,* April 2, 1990, pp. 46–54; "Dealmakers Are Pouring thorugh the Brandenburg Gate," *Business Week,* February 12, 1990, pp. 42–43; "Freedom!" *Time,* November 20, 1989, pp. 24–33; "The Wall Comes Down," *Newsweek,* November 20, 1989, pp. 24–30.

In a pure market-directed economy, consumers make a society's production decisions when they make their choices in the marketplace. They decide what is to be produced and by whom—through their dollar "votes."

Price is a measure of value

Prices in the marketplace are a rough measure of how society values particular goods and services. If consumers are willing to pay the market prices, then apparently they feel they are getting at least their money's worth. Similarly, the cost of labor and materials is a rough measure of the value of the resources used in the production of goods and services to meet these needs. New consumer needs that can be served profitably—not just the needs of the majority—will probably be met by some profit-minded businesses.

In summary, in a market-directed economic system, the prices in both the production sector (for resources) and the consumption sector (for goods and services) vary to allocate resources and distribute income according to consumer preferences. Over time, the result is a balance of supply and demand and the coordination of the economic activity of many individuals and institutions.

Greatest freedom of choice

Consumers in a market-directed economy enjoy great freedom of choice. They are not forced to buy any goods or services, except those that must be provided for the good of society—things such as national defense, schools, police and fire protection, highway systems, and public-health services. These are provided by the community—and citizens are taxed to pay for them.

Similarly, producers are free to do whatever they wish—provided that they stay within the rules of the game set by government *and* receive enough dollar votes from consumers. If they do their job well, they earn a profit and stay in business. But profit, survival, and growth are not guaranteed.

Conflicts can result

Producers and consumers making free choices can cause conflicts and difficulties. This is called the **micro-macro dilemma**: What is "good" for some producers and consumers may not be good for society as a whole.

Consider for a minute problems related to the sale of alcohol. Each year, thousands of people die or are hospitalized as an indirect or direct result of liquor

Many consumers want convenient packaging, but it can be an environmental problem. International Paper and McDonald's have started recycling programs that both satisfy consumers and meet social needs.

consumption. The cost to society is high, yet the sale of alcohol is not banned. Alcohol consumption is an accepted practice in Canada, and producers profit by selling it. Should society limit its availability to certain segments of the population or allow it to be freely available to anyone who wants to purchase it regardless of social cost?

Such decisions don't have to involve a matter of life and death to be important. Many Canadians want the convenience of disposable products and products in easy-to-use, small-serving packages. But these same "convenient" products and packages often lead to pollution of the environment and inefficient use of natural resources. Should future generations be left to pay for the consequences of pollution that is the result of free choice by today's consumers?

Questions like these are not easy to answer. The basic reason is that many different people may have a stake in the outcomes—and social consequences—of the choices made by individual managers *and* consumers in a market-directed system. As you read this book and learn more about marketing, you will also learn more about social responsibility in marketing—and why it must be taken seriously.

The role of government

The Canadian economy and most other Western economies are mainly market-directed—but not completely. Society assigns supervision of the system to the government. For example, besides setting and enforcing the "rules of the game," government agencies control interest rates and the supply of money. They also set import and export rules that affect international competition, regulate radio and TV broadcasting, and sometimes control wages and prices, and so on. Government also tries to be sure that property is protected, contracts are enforced, individuals are not exploited, no group unfairly monopolizes markets, and producers deliver the kinds and quality of goods and services they claim to be offering.

You can see that we need some of these government activities to make sure the economy runs smoothly. However, some people worry that too much government guidance threatens the survival of a market-directed system—and the economic and political freedom that goes with it. For example, in the past decade, the Canadian government has done much less interfering—especially in markets for services such as banking, transportation, and communications. The vigorous competition among airlines is a good example of what follows. A few years ago, a U.S. government agency controlled airline prices and routes. Now that agency doesn't exist, and these decisions are made by marketing managers—and consumers.[11] However, vigorous competition in the airline industry has driven a number of these airlines into bankruptcy and encouraged a series of mergers.

ALL ECONOMIES NEED MACRO–MARKETING SYSTEMS

At this point, you may be saying to yourself: All this sounds like economics—where does marketing fit in? Studying a macro-marketing system is a lot like studying an economic system except we give more detailed attention to the "marketing" components of the system—including consumers and other customers, middlemen, and marketing specialists. We focus on the activities they perform—and how the interaction of the components affects the effectiveness and fairness of a particular system.

In general, we can say that no economic system, whether centrally planned or market-directed, can achieve its objectives without an effective macro-marketing system. To see why this is true, we will look at the role of marketing in primitive economies. Then we will see how macro-marketing tends to become more and more complex in advanced economic systems.

Marketing
involves exchange

In a **pure subsistence economy**, each family unit produces everything it consumes. There is no need to exchange goods and services. Each producer-consumer unit is totally self-sufficient, although usually its standard of living is relatively low. No marketing takes place because *marketing doesn't occur unless two or more parties are willing to exchange something for something else.*

What is a market?

The term *marketing* comes from the word **market**—which is a group of potential customers with similar needs who are willing to exchange something of value with sellers offering various goods and/or services—that is, ways of satisfying those needs. Of course, some negotiation may be needed. This can be done face-to-face at some physical location (for example, a farmers' market). Or it can be done indirectly—through a complex network of middlemen who link buyers and sellers living far apart.

In primitive economies, exchanges tend to occur in central markets. **Central markets** are convenient places where buyers and sellers can meet face-to-face to exchange goods and services. We can understand macro-marketing better by seeing how and why central markets develop. We'll start with a very simple case, but thinking about it will clarify what happens when a more complex system is involved.

Central markets
help exchange

Imagine a small village of five families—each with a special skill for producing some need-satisfying product. After meeting basic needs, each family decides to specialize. It's easier for one family to make two pots and for another to make two baskets than for each one to make one pot and one basket. Specialization makes labor more efficient and more productive. It can increase the total amount of form utility created. Specialization also can increase the task utility in producing services, but for the moment we'll focus on products that are physical goods.

If these five families each specialize in one product, they will have to trade with each other. As Exhibit 1–2A shows, it will take the five families 10 separate exchanges to obtain some of each of the products. If the families live near each other, the exchange process is relatively simple. But if they are far apart, travel back and forth will take time. Who will do the traveling—and when?

Faced with this problem, the families may agree to come to a central market and trade on a certain day. Then each family makes only one trip to the market to trade with all the others. This reduces the total number of trips to five, which makes exchange easier, leaves more time for producing and consuming, and also provides for social gatherings.

A money system
simplifies trading

While a central meeting place simplifies exchange, the individual bartering transactions still take a lot of time. Bartering only works when someone else wants what you have, and vice versa. Each trader must find others who have products of about equal value. After trading with one group, a family may find itself with extra baskets, knives, and pots. Then it has to find others willing to trade for these products.

A common money system changes all this. Sellers only have to find buyers who want their products and agree on the price. Then the sellers are free to spend this income to buy whatever they want. (Note that if some buyers and sellers use

Exhibit 1–2   The Benefits of Having a Central Market and Middleman

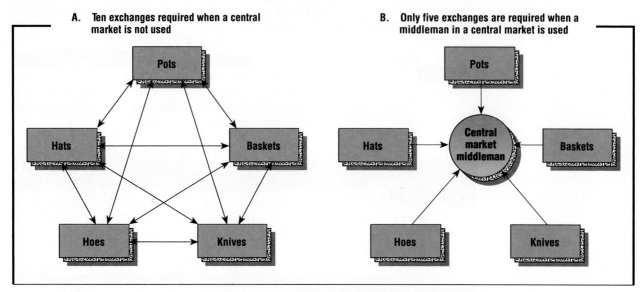

A. Ten exchanges required when a central market is not used

B. Only five exchanges are required when a middleman in a central market is used

different money systems—some use dollars and others use yen—they must also agree on the rate at which the money will be exchanged.)

Middlemen help exchange even more

The development of a central market and a money system simplifies the exchange process among the five families in our imaginary village. But they still need to make 10 separate transactions. So it still takes a lot of time and effort for the five families to exchange goods.

This clumsy exchange process is made much simpler by the appearance of a **middleman**—someone who specializes in trade rather than production. A middleman is willing to buy each family's goods and then sell each family whatever it needs. Of course, there is a charge for this service, but this charge may be more than offset by savings in time and effort.

In our simple example, using a middleman at a central market reduces the necessary number of exchanges for all five families from 10 to 5. See Exhibit 1–2B. Each family has more time for production, consumption, and leisure. Also, each family can specialize in producing what it produces best, creating more form and task utility. Meanwhile, by specializing in trade, the middleman provides additional time, place, and possession utility. In total, all the villagers may enjoy greater economic utility—and greater consumer satisfaction—by using a middleman in the central market.

Note that the reduction in transactions that results from using a middleman in a central market becomes more important as the number of families increases. For example, if the population of our imaginary village increases from 5 to 10 families, 45 transactions are needed without a middleman. Using a middleman requires only one transaction for each family.

Today, such middlemen—offering permanent trading facilities—are known as *wholesalers* and *retailers*. The advantages of working with middlemen increase with increases in the number of producers and consumers, their distance from each other, and the number and variety of competing products. That is why there are so many wholesalers and retailers in modern economies.

THE ROLE OF MARKETING IN ECONOMIC DEVELOPMENT

Most modern economies have advanced well beyond the five-family village, but the same ideas still apply. The main purpose of markets and middlemen is to make exchange easier and allow greater time for production, consumption, and other activities—including recreation.

Effective marketing system is necessary

Although it is tempting to conclude that more effective macro-marketing systems are the result of greater economic development, just the opposite is true. *An effective macro-marketing system is necessary for economic development.* Improved marketing is often the key to growth in less-developed nations.

Breaking the vicious circle of poverty

Without an effective macro-marketing system, the less-developed nations may not be able to escape the "vicious circle of poverty." Many people in these nations can't leave their subsistence way of life to produce for the market because there are no buyers for what they produce. And there are no buyers because everyone else is producing for their own needs. As a result, distribution systems and middlemen do not develop.

Breaking this vicious circle of poverty may require major changes in the inefficient micro- and macro-marketing systems that are typical in less-developed nations. At the least, more market-oriented middlemen are needed to move surplus output to markets—including foreign markets—where there is more demand.[12] You can see how this works, and why links between the macro-marketing systems of different countries are so important, by considering the differences in markets that are typical at different stages of economic development.

Mexico hopes to attract investment from other countries to help speed economic development.

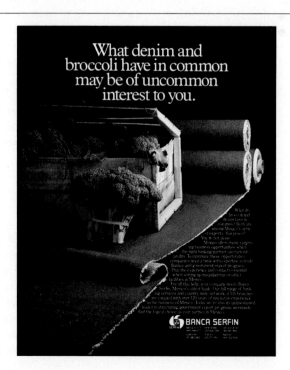

STAGES OF ECONOMIC DEVELOPMENT

Some markets are more advanced and/or growing more rapidly than others. And some countries—or parts of a country—are at different stages of economic development. This means their demands—and their marketing systems—vary.

To get some idea of the many possible differences in potential markets, we'll discuss six stages of economic development. These stages are helpful, but they greatly oversimplify the real world for two reasons. First, different parts of the same country may be at different stages of development, so it isn't possible to identify a single country or region with only one stage. Second, some countries skip one or two stages due to investments by foreign firms or investments by their own eager governments. For example, the building of uneconomical steel mills to boost national pride—or the arrival of multinational car producers—might lead to a big jump in stages. This stage-jumping does not destroy the six-stage process—it just explains why more rapid movements take place in some situations.

Stage 1—Self-supporting agriculture

In this stage, most people are subsistence farmers. A simple marketing system may exist, but most of the people are not part of a money economy. Some parts of Africa and New Guinea are in this stage. In a practical sense, these people are not a market because they have no money to buy products.

Stage 2—Preindustrial or commercial

Some countries in sub-Saharan Africa and the Middle East are in this second stage. During this stage, we see more market-oriented activity. Raw materials such as oil, tin, and copper are extracted and exported. Agricultural and forest crops such as sugar, rubber, and timber are grown and exported. Often this is done with the help of foreign technical skills and capital. A commercial economy may develop along with—but unrelated to—the subsistence economy. These activities may require the beginnings of a transportation system to tie the extracting or growing areas to shipping points. A money economy operates in this stage.

Such countries import industrial machinery and equipment—and component materials and supplies for huge construction projects. They also need imports—including luxury products—to meet the living standards of technical and supervisory people.

The few large landowners—and those who benefit by this new business activity—may develop expensive tastes. The few natives employed by these larger firms—and the small business managers who serve them—may form a small, middle-income class. But most of the population has no money. For practical purposes, they are not in the market. The total market in Stage 2 may be so small that local importers can easily handle the demand. There is little reason for local producers to even try.

Stage 3—Primary manufacturing

In this third stage, a country may do some processing of metal ores or agricultural products it once exported in raw form. Sugar and rubber, for example, are both produced and processed in Indonesia. Companies based elsewhere in the world may set up factories to take advantage of low-cost labor. Most of the output from these factories is exported, but the income earned by the workers stimulates economic development. In addition, a growing group of professionals and technicians is needed to run the developing agricultural-industrial complex.

The demands of this group—and the growing number of wealthy natives—differ dramatically from the needs of the lower class and the emerging middle class. Even though the local market expands in this third stage, a large part of the population continues to be almost entirely outside the money economy—and local producers are likely to have trouble finding enough demand to keep them in business.

Stage 4—Nondurable and semidurable consumer products manufacturing

At this stage, small local manufacturing begins—especially in those lines that need only a small investment to get started. Often, these industries grow from the small firms that supplied the processors dominating the last stage. For example, plants making explosives for extracting minerals might expand into soap manufacturing. Multinational firms speed development of countries in this stage by investing in promising opportunities.

Paint, drug, food and beverage, and textile industries develop in this stage. Because clothing is a necessity, the textile industry is usually one of the first to develop. This early emphasis on the textile industry in developing nations is one reason the world textile market is so competitive.

As some of the small producers become members of the middle- or even upper-income class, they help to expand the demand for imported products. As this market grows, local businesses begin to see enough volume to operate profitably. So there is less need for imports to supply nondurable and semidurable products. But most consumer durables and capital equipment are still imported.

Stage 5—Capital equipment and consumer durable products manufacturing

In this stage, the production of capital equipment and consumer durable products begins—including cars, refrigerators, and machinery for local industries. Such manufacturing creates other demands—raw materials for the local factories, and food and clothing for the rural population entering the industrial labor force. Industrialization begins, but the economy still depends on exports of raw materials—either wholly unprocessed or slightly processed. The country may still have to import special heavy machinery and equipment in this stage, and imports of consumer durables may still compete with local products.

Stage 6—Exporting manufactured products

Countries that haven't gone beyond the fifth stage are mainly exporters of raw materials. They import manufactured products to build their industrial base. In the sixth stage, countries begin exporting manufactured products. Countries often specialize in certain types of manufactured products—iron and steel, watches, cameras, electronic equipment, and processed food.

These countries have grown richer. They have needs—and the purchasing power—for a wide variety of products. In fact, countries in this stage often carry on a great deal of trade with each other. Each trades those products in which it has production advantages. In this stage, almost all consumers are in the money economy. And there may be a large middle-class. Canada, the United States, most of the Western European countries, and Japan are at this last stage.[13]

NATIONS' MACRO–MARKETING SYSTEMS ARE CONNECTED

As a nation grows, its international trade grows

All countries trade to some extent—we live in an interdependent world. We saw above how trade expands as a country develops and industrializes. In fact, the largest changes in world trade are usually seen in rapidly developing economies. Over the last decade, for example, exports from Hong Kong, Taiwan, and Singapore have risen dramatically.

Exhibit 1–3   Canadian Exports by Country—Top 15, 1992 (in thousands of dollars)

United States	$118,421,831
Japan	7,412,842
United Kingdom	3,012,401
Germany	2,161,367
People's Republic of China	2,132,796
Netherlands	1,425,092
South Korea	1,405,155
France	1,339,359
Former USSR	1,263,862
Switzerland	1,126,271
Italy	1,084,504
Belgium	1,072,466
Taiwan	952,931
Mexico	770,570
Hong Kong	757,120

Source: Statistics Canada, *Summary of Canadian International Trade,* December 1992, Cat. 65-001.

Even so, the largest traders are highly developed nations. For example, imports of manufactured goods into Japan have increased at an annual average of 30 percent since 1986. As shown in Exhibits 1–3 and 1–4, Japan is Canada's second largest trading partner, with trade between the two countries totaling just over $18 billion.[14]

Because trade among nations is important in economic development, most countries are eager to be able to sell their goods and services in foreign markets. Yet at the same time, they often don't want their local customers to spend cash on foreign-made products. They want the money—and the opportunities for jobs and economic growth—to stay in the local economy.

Tariffs and quotas
may reduce trade

Taxes and restrictions at national or regional borders greatly reduce the free flow of goods and services between the macro-marketing systems of different

Exhibit 1–4   Canadian Imports by Country—Top 15, 1992 (in thousands of dollars)

United States	$96,397,743
Japan	10,757,825
United Kingdom	4,102,501
Germany	3,531,435
Mexico	2,751,069
Canada	2,746,718
France	2,688,734
Taiwan	2,469,647
People's Republic of China	2,447,155
South Korea	2,008,543
Italy	1,744,624
Norway	1,510,397
Hong Kong	1,134,665
Sweden	791,745
Australia	750,989

Source: Statistics Canada, *Summary of Canadian International Trade,* December 1992, Cat. 65-001.

countries. **Tariffs**—taxes on imported products—vary, depending on whether a country is trying to raise revenue or limit trade. Restrictive tariffs often block all movement. But even revenue-producing tariffs cause red tape, discourage free movement of products, and increase the prices consumers pay.

Quotas act like restrictive tariffs. **Quotas** set the specific quantities of products that can move into or out of a country. Great market opportunities may exist in the markets of a unified Europe, for example, but import quotas (or export controls applied against a specific country) may discourage outsiders from entering.

Trade restrictions can be a potential source of conflict between nations. For example, Canada charged the United States with unfair trading practices when a tariff was placed on Canadian softwood lumber shipments. The US timber interests argue that Canadian provinces subsidize their lumber companies, in part by charging low stumpage prices for government-owned trees. Needless to say, Canadian timber firms disagree. They are fighting to have the penalty tariff removed in order to protect a $3 billion a year US market.[15] Marketing Demo 1–3's discussion of Ontario's "environmental fee" on canned beer provides an example of the complexities inherent in trade disputes.

Markets may rely on international countertrade

To overcome the problems of trade restrictions, many firms have turned to **countertrade**—a special type of bartering in which products from one country are traded for products from another country. For example, Russia has recently traded diamonds, timber, and cotton for Canadian grain. This is described in more detail in Marketing Demo 1–4. The Canadian Wheat Board is not alone in using countertrade. However, less than 1 percent of all Canadian exports rely on countertrade.[16]

MARKETING DEMO 1–3
Trade Disputes Can Be Complex

In the early 1990s, Ontario added an environmental fee of 10 cents per can to beer produced in Canada and the United States. This levy on cans of beer produced in the United States represented an increase of more than 50 percent on the tax in place before the budget. No such levy had previously been slapped on Canadian canned beer.

US brewers noted that the effect of the new tax was to make their beer more expensive than Canadian bottled beer. Previously, they had enjoyed a price advantage. Since almost all the 6 million cases of US beer shipped to Canada annually came in cans and almost 80 percent of the beer brewed in Ontario and other provinces was sold in bottles, the US claimed that this new tax gave Canadian brewers an advantage over their US counterparts.

The Ontario government denied this claim and noted that the new environmental levy was imposed at the same rate on both Canadian and US canned beer. The tax was said to be part of the government's policy of encouraging the three Rs of environmentalism—reduce, reuse, and recycle.

According to that policy, reusing products was preferable to recycling, and the rationale for this environmental tax was to favor refillable bottles. The Canadian position was considerably weakened by the fact that no such levies were imposed on cans of soft drinks.

Source: "Trade Battle Heats Up," *The Globe and Mail*, May 2, 1992, p. 19.

MARKETING DEMO 1–4
Russia in Trading Game for Grain

Cash-strapped Russia is bartering diamonds, timber, and cotton in exchange for Canadian grain. The result is cold cash for Canadian farmers and grain sales that would not otherwise have been possible, according to Canadian Wheat Board representative Brian Stacey.

It will also mean more business for the Port of Vancouver, which has shipped almost no grain to Russia since exports were halted in 1992 after Moscow reached its limit on a $2 billion revolving line of credit. Russia contracted to take 1 million metric tons in January 1992 and still had 477,000 tons to collect when it was cut off for being more than $400 million in arrears on scheduled payments and interest.

Stacey said bartering is one of the ways the Board came up with to get grain moving back to Russia. "Because of the credit situation, we were unable to ship to them. But we have been successful in working out some arrangements where a third party would pay cash, we would give grain to the

Russians, and the Russians would barter commodities to the third party for payment for the grain."

The bartering had to be done through international trading companies, because under Canadian law, the Wheat Board can only sell for cash or credit. He said one shipment of 38,000 tons of feed grain has already left Canada for Uzbekistan in exchange for cotton, and other shipments are being arranged involving timber and diamonds.

"The fact that we are successful in doing business into Russia gives us a competitive advantage to some extent," Stacey said. The barter sales are separate from any Canadian foreign aid, and all sales are for cash at "commercial grain values." "We would consider other things if it enables business to be done. As a result, our salespeople are getting calls from all sorts of people that we would not normally deal with," says Stacey.

Source: Alan Daniels, "Russia in Trading Game for Grain," *The Vancouver Sun*, April 14, 1993, p. D1.

CAN MASS PRODUCTION SATISFY A SOCIETY'S CONSUMPTION NEEDS?

Urbanization brings together large numbers of people. They must depend on others to produce most of the goods and services they need to satisfy their basic needs. Also, in advanced economies, many consumers have higher discretionary incomes. They can afford to satisfy higher-level needs as well. A modern economy faces a real challenge to satisfy all these needs.

Economies of scale mean lower cost

Fortunately, advanced economies can often take advantage of mass production with its **economies of scale**—which means that as a company produces larger numbers of a particular product, the cost for each of these products goes down. You can see that a one-of-a-kind, custom-built car would cost much more than a mass-produced standard model.

Of course, even in advanced societies, not all goods and services can be produced by mass production—or with economics of scale. Consider medical care. It's difficult to get productivity gains in labor-intensive medical services—like brain surgery. Nevertheless, from a macro-marketing perspective, it is clear that we are able to devote resources to meeting these "quality-of-life" needs because we are achieving efficiency in other areas.

Thus, modern production skills can help provide great quantities of goods and services to satisfy large numbers of consumers. But mass production alone does not solve the problem of satisfying consumers' needs. We also need effective marketing.

Any large potato chip factory takes advantage of mass production, but effective marketing is also needed to satisfy consumer needs.

Effective marketing is needed to link producers and consumers

Effective marketing means delivering the goods and services that consumers want and need. It means getting products to them at the right time, in the right place, and at a price they're willing to pay. That's not an easy job—especially if you think about the variety of goods and services a highly developed economy can produce and the many kinds of goods and services consumers want.

Effective marketing in an advanced economy is more difficult because producers and consumers are separated in several ways. As Exhibit 1–5 shows, exchange between producers and consumers is hampered by spatial separation, separation in time, separation in information and values, and separation of ownership. "Discrepancies of quantity" and "discrepancies of assortment" further complicate exchange between producers and consumers. That is, each producer specializes in producing and selling large amounts of a narrow assortment of goods and services, but each consumer wants only small quantities of a wide assortment of goods and services.[17]

Marketing functions help narrow the gap

The purpose of a macro-marketing system is to overcome these separations and discrepancies. The universal functions of marketing help do this.

The **universal functions of marketing** are: buying, selling, transporting, storing, standardization and grading, financing, risk taking, and market information. They must be performed in all macro-marketing systems. *How* these functions are performed—and *by whom*—may differ among nations and economic systems. But they are needed in any macro-marketing system. Let's take a closer look at them now.

Exhibit 1–5   Marketing Facilitates Production and Consumption

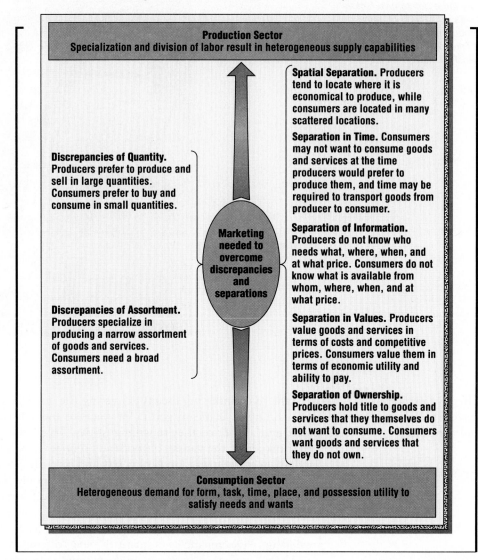

Exchange usually involves buying and selling. The **buying function** means looking for and evaluating goods and services. The **selling function** involves promoting the product. It includes the use of personal selling, advertising, and other mass-selling methods. This is probably the most visible function of marketing.

The **transporting function** means the movement of goods from one place to another. The **storing function** involves holding goods until customers need them.

Standardization and grading involve sorting products according to size and quality. This makes buying and selling easier because it reduces the need for inspection and sampling. **Financing** provides the necessary cash and credit to produce, transport, store, promote, sell, and buy products. **Risk taking** involves bearing the uncertainties that are part of the marketing process. A firm can never be sure that customers will want to buy its products. Products can also be damaged, stolen, or outdated. The **market information function** involves the collection, analysis, and distribution of all the information needed to plan, carry out, and control marketing activities whether in the firm's own neighborhood or in a market overseas.

WHO PERFORMS MARKETING FUNCTIONS?

Producers, consumers, and marketing specialists

From a macro-level viewpoint, these marketing functions are all part of the marketing process—and must be done by someone. None of them can be eliminated. In a centrally planned economy, some of the system functions may be performed by government agencies. Others may be left to individual producers and consumers. In a market-directed system, marketing functions are performed by producers, consumers, and a variety of marketing specialists (see Exhibit 1–6). Regardless of who perfoms the marketing functions, in general they must be performed effectively or the performance of the whole macro-marketing system will suffer. Keep in mind that the macro-marketing systems for different nations may interact. For example, producers based in one nation may serve consumers in another country, perhaps with help from middlemen and other specialists from both countries.

Specialists perform some functions

Earlier in this chapter, you saw how producers and consumers benefitted when marketing specialists (middlemen) took over some buying and selling. Producers and consumers also benefit when marketing specialists perform the other marketing functions. So we find marketing functions being performed not only by marketing middlemen but also by a variety of other **facilitators**—firms that provide one or more of the marketing functions other than buying or selling.

Exhibit 1–6   Model of a Market-Directed Macro-Marketing System

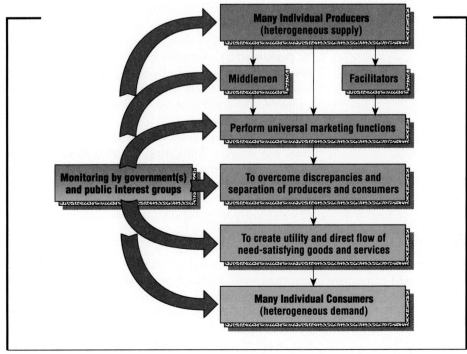

*Facilitators—including
transportation firms and
advertising specialists—may
help a marketing manager
with one or more of the
marketing functions.*

These include advertising agencies, marketing research firms, independent product-testing laboratories, public warehouses, transporting firms, communications companies, and financial institutions (including banks). Through specialization or economies of scale, marketing middlemen and facilitators are often able to perform the marketing functions better—and at a lower cost—than producers or consumers can. This allows producers and consumers to spend more time on production and consumption.

**Functions can be shifted
and shared**

Taking a macro perspective, we see that all of the marketing functions must be performed by someone. But, *from a micro viewpoint, not every firm must perform all of the functions. Further, not all goods and services require all the functions at every level of their production.* "Pure services"—like a plane ride—don't need storing, for example. But storing is required in the production of the plane and while the plane is not in service.

Some marketing specialists perform all the functions. Others specialize in only one or two. Marketing research firms, for example, specialize only in the market information function. The important point to remember is this: *Responsibility for performing the marketing functions can be shifted and shared in a variety of ways, but no function can be completely eliminated.*

HOW WELL DOES OUR MACRO–MARKETING SYSTEM WORK?

**It connects remote
producers and consumers**

A macro-marketing system does more than just deliver goods and services to consumers—it allows mass production with its economies of scale. Also, mass communication and mass transportation allow products to be shipped where they're needed. Coconuts from the tropics can be found in Canadian stores almost year-round, and electronic parts from Taiwan are used in making products all over the world.[18]

It encourages growth and new ideas	In addition to making mass production possible, a market-directed, macro-marketing system encourages **innovation**—the development and spread of new ideas and products. Competition for consumers' money forces firms to think of new and better ways to satisfying consumer needs.

It has its critics

In explaining marketing's role in society, we described some of the benefits of a market-directed, macro-marketing system. We can see this in Canada's macro-marketing system. That system provides—at least in material terms—one of the highest standards of living in the world. It seems to be effective and fair in many ways.

We must admit, however, that marketing—as it exists in Canada and other developed societies—has many critics! Marketing activity is especially open to criticism because it is the part of business most visible to the public. There is nothing like a pocketbook issue for getting consumers excited!

Typical complaints about marketing include:

Advertising is too often annoying, misleading, and wasteful.

Products are not safe—or the quality is poor.

Marketing makes people too materialistic—it motivates them toward "things" instead of social needs.

Easy consumer credit makes people buy things they don't need and really can't afford.

Packaging and labelling are often confusing and deceptive.

Middlemen add to the cost of distribution—and raise prices without providing anything in return.

Marketing creates interest in products that pollute the environment.

Too many unnecessary products are offered.

Marketing serves the rich and exploits the poor.

Such complaints cannot and should not be taken lightly. They show that many people aren't happy with some parts of the marketing system. Certainly, the strong public support for consumer protection laws proves that not all consumers feel they are being treated like royalty.

As you consider the various criticisms of marketing, keep in mind that some of them deal with the marketing practices of specific firms and are micro-marketing oriented. Others are really criticisms of the whole macro-marketing system. This is an important distinction.

? Is it an ethical issue?

Certainly some complaints about marketing arise because some individual firm or manager was intentionally unethical and cheated the market. But at other times, problems and criticism may arise because a manager did not fully consider the ethical implications of a decision. In either case, there is no excuse for sloppiness when it comes to **marketing ethics**—the moral standards that guide marketing decisions and actions. Each individual develops moral standards based on his or her own values. That helps explain why opinions about what is right or wrong often vary from one person to another, from one society to another, and among different groups within a society. It is sometimes difficult to say whose opinions are "correct." Even so, such opinions may have a very real influence on whether an individual's (or a firm's) marketing decisions and actions are accepted or rejected. So marketing ethics are not only a philosophical issue, but also a pragmatic concern. Throughout the text we will be discussing the types of ethical issues individual marketing managers face. In fact, these issues are so important that we will highlight them with the special symbol used in the heading for this section. But we won't be moralizing and trying to tell you how you should think on any given issue. Rather, by the end of the course we hope that *you* will have some firm personal opinions about what is and is not ethical in micro-marketing activities.

Keep in mind, however, that not all criticisms of marketing focus on ethical issues; fortunately, the prevailing practice of most businesspeople is to be fair and honest. Moreover, not all criticisms are specific to the micro-marketing activities of individual firms. Some of the complaints about marketing really focus on the basic idea of a market-directed macro-marketing system—and these criticisms often occur because people don't understand what marketing is—or how it works. As you go through this book, we'll discuss some of these criticisms. Then in our final chapter, we will return to a more complete appraisal of marketing in our consumer-oriented society.

CONCLUSION

In this chapter, we defined two levels of marketing: micro-marketing and macro-marketing. Macro-marketing is concerned with the way the whole global economy works. Micro-marketing focuses on the activities of individual firms. We discussed the role of marketing in economic development—and the functions of marketing and who performs them. We ended by raising some of the criticisms of marketing—both of the whole macro system and of the way individual firms work.

We emphasized macro-marketing in this chapter, but the major thrust of this book is on micro-marketing. By learning more about market-oriented decision making, you will be able to make more efficient and socially responsible decisions. This will help improve the performance of individual firms and organizations (your employers). And eventually it will help our macro-marketing system work better.

We'll see marketing through the eyes of the marketing manager—maybe *you* in the near future. And we will show how you can contribute to the marketing process. Along the way, we'll discuss the impact of micro-level decisions on society, and the ethical issues that marketing managers face. Then in Chapter 22—after you have had time to understand how and why producers and consumers think and behave the way they do—we will evaluate how well both micro-marketing and macro-marketing perform in a market-directed economic system.

QUESTIONS AND PROBLEMS

1. List your activities for the first two hours after you woke up this morning. Briefly indicate how marketing affected your activities.

2. It is fairly easy to see why people do not beat a path to a mousetrap manufacturer's door, but would they be similarly indifferent if some food processor developed a revolutionary new food product that would provide all necessary nutrients in small pills for about $100 per year per person?

3. Distinguish between macro- and micro-marketing. Then explain how they are interrelated, if they are.

4. Distinguish between how economic decisions are made in a planned economic system and how they are made in a market-directed economy.

5. A committee of the American Marketing Association defined marketing as "the process of planning and executing the conception, pricing,

promotion, and distribution of ideas, goods, and services to create exchanges that satisfy individual and organizational objectives." Does this definition consider macro-marketing? Explain your answer.

6. Identify a "central market" in your city and explain how it facilitates exchange.

7. Explain why tariffs and quotas affect international marketing opportunities.

8. Discuss the prospects for a group of Latin American entrepreneurs who are considering building a factory to produce machines that make cans for the food industry. Their country is in Stage 4—the nondurable and semidurable consumer products manufacturing stage. The country's population is approximately 20 million, and there is some possibility of establishing sales contacts in a few nearby countries.

9. Discuss the nature of marketing in a socialist economy. Would the functions that must be provided and the development of wholesaling and retailing systems be any different than in a market-directed economy?

10. Discuss how the micro-macro dilemma relates to each of the following products: air bags in cars, nuclear power, bank credit cards, and pesticides that improve farm production.

11. Describe a recent purchase you made, and indicate why that particular product was available at a store—in particular, at the store where you bought it.

12. Refer to Exhibit 1–5, and give an example of a purchase you recently made that involved separation of information and separation in time between you and the producer. Briefly explain how these separations were overcome.

13. Define the functions of marketing in your own words. Using an example, explain how they can be shifted and shared.

14. Explain, in your own words, why this text emphasizes micro-marketing.

15. Explain why a small producer might want a marketing research firm to take over some of its information-gathering activities.

16. Explain why a market-directed macro-marketing system encourages innovation. Give an example.

SUGGESTED CASES

1. The Yaka-Boochee

2. Canbank

Marketing's Role within the Firm or Nonprofit Organization

Chapter 2

When You Finish This Chapter, You Should

❶

Know what the marketing concept is—and how it should affect strategy planning in a firm or nonprofit organization.

❷

Understand what a marketing manager does.

❸

Know what marketing strategy planning is—and why it will be the focus of this book.

❹

Understand target marketing.

❺

Be familiar with the four Ps in a marketing mix.

❻

Know the difference between a marketing strategy, a marketing plan, and a marketing program.

❼

Understand the important new terms (shown in blue).

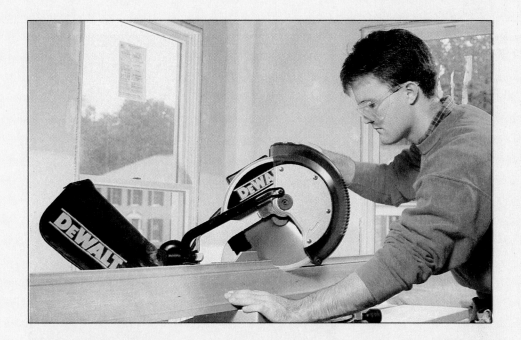

In the winter of 1992, marketing managers in the power tool division at Black & Decker (B&D) were looking forward to improved profits because of a new marketing plan they had developed. Black & Decker tools were well known among consumers and dominated the do-it-yourself market. However, they were capturing only about 10 percent of the sales to professionals who bought power tools for commercial work. There was a good opportunity for profitable growth with these customers, but B&D needed a special marketing effort targeted at their needs. Makita (a Japanese producer) already had a strong reputation with these customers. And other competitors—including Sears (with its Craftsman brand), Snap-On, and producers from Japan and Germany—were likely to join the battle for this business. To come out on top in these "saw wars," B&D's managers had to make many decisions.

B&D marketing managers spent three months visiting more than 200 tool stores and job sites to get feedback from professionals about their interests and needs. Some of the details were simple but useful: "paint it yellow to make it easy to see and to signify safety." Other concerns also surfaced. For example, the well-regarded Black & Decker brand name did not have as favorable an image with these professionals as it did with consumers. The professionals thought of it as a good "consumer brand" that had no particular advantage for their needs. They wanted very reliable tools—ones that would stand up to their demanding applications.

Working with people in research and development and manufacturing, B&D marketing managers developed a special line of 33 tools for this target market. Tests showed that all but two of the tools would satisfy professional customers better than competing products from Makita; the two that didn't were redesigned. Going even further to meet the target customers' reliability needs, B&D set up 117 service centers and offered a 48-hour repair guarantee. B&D even promised a free loaner tool during the repair. Marketing managers also decided that it would be better to use the firm's less widely known DeWalt brand name rather than try

Services can be advertised as effectively as goods.

to change the target customers' beliefs about the Black & Decker brand. Marketing research showed that the professional target market already respected the DeWalt name.

Marketing managers also had to decide the best way to reach the target market. Should they start in some introductory regions or distribute the new products in as many countries as possible all at once? Should they focus on middlemen who had sold their other products in the past? Or should they put special emphasis on working closely with middlemen, like the Home Hardware chain, who already had a strong relationship with the professional target market?

B&D also had to decide how to promote the new line of DeWalt tools. Marketing managers had to decide how many salespeople would be needed to work with middlemen. They also had to develop plans for advertising to the target customers—including deciding on an advertising theme and determining how much to spend and where to spend it.

They had other decisions to make. The price on their consumer products had been set low to attract price-sensitive buyers. Should they stick with a low beat-the-competition price on the DeWalt line, or would a premium price be more profitable with professionals who were more concerned about long-term reliability? Should they offer introductory price rebates to help attract customers from Makita and other brands? Should they offer middlemen special discounts for large orders?

Black & Decker managers did a good job with all of these decisions. Their marketing plan is so promising that they hope to achieve $180 million in sales by 1996. Of course, they can't afford to be complacent as they implement the plan and check progress against their objectives. Competitors will also be making changes. Ultimately, if Black & Decker is to come out on top, it must continue to do the best job of satisfying customers.[1]

We've mentioned only a few of many decisions Black & Decker marketing managers had to make, but you can see that each of these decisions affects the others. Making marketing decisions is never easy. But knowing what basic decision areas have to be considered helps you to plan a better, more successful strategy. This chapter will get you started by giving you a framework for thinking about all the marketing management decision areas.

Marketing and marketing management are important in our society—and in business firms and nonprofit organizations. As you saw in Chapter 1, marketing is concerned with anticipating needs and directing the flow of goods and services from producers to consumers. This is done to satisfy the needs of consumers and achieve the objectives of the firm (the micro view) and of society as a whole (the macro view).

To get a better understanding of marketing, we are going to look at things from the viewpoint of the marketing manager—the one who makes an organization's important marketing decisions.

MARKETING'S ROLE HAS CHANGED A LOT OVER THE YEARS

From our Black & Decker example, it's clear that marketing decisions are very important to a firm's success. But marketing hasn't always been so complicated. In fact, it's only in the last 30 years or so that an increasing number of producers, wholesalers, retailers, and nonprofit organizations have adopted modern marketing thinking. Instead of just focusing on producing or selling *products*, these organizations focus on *customers*—and try to integrate an organizationwide effort to satisfy them.

We will discuss five stages in marketing evolution: (1) the simple trade era, (2) the production era, (3) the sales era, (4) the marketing department era, and (5) the marketing company era. We'll talk about these eras as if they applied generally to all firms—but keep in mind that *some managers still have not made it to the final stages*. They are stuck in the past with old ways of thinking.

Specialization permitted trade—and middlemen met the need

When societies first moved toward some specialization of production and away from a subsistence economy where each family raised and consumed everything it produced, traders played an important role. Early "producers for the market" made products that were needed by themselves and their neighbors. (Recall the five-family example in Chapter 1.) As bartering became more difficult, societies moved into the **simple trade era**—a time when families traded or sold their "surplus" output to local middlemen. These specialists resold the goods to other consumers or distant middlemen. This was the early role of marketing—and it is still the focus of marketing in many of the less-developed areas of the world. In fact, even in North America, the United Kingdom, and other more advanced economies, marketing didn't change much until the Industrial Revolution brought larger factories a little over a hundred years ago.

From the production to the sales era

From the Industrial Revolution until the 1920s, most companies were in the production era. The **production era** is a time when a company focuses on production of a few specific products—perhaps because few of these products are available in the market. "If we can make it, it will sell" is management thinking characteristic of the production era. Because of product shortages, many nations, including many of the newly independent republics of Eastern Europe, continue to operate with production era approaches.

By about 1930, most companies in the industrialized Western nations had more production capability than ever before. Now the problem wasn't just to produce—but to beat the competition and win customers. This led many firms to enter the sales era. The **sales era** is a time when a company emphasizes selling because of increased competition.

To the marketing department era

For most firms in advanced economies, the sales era continued until at least 1950. By then, sales were growing rapidly in most areas of the economy. The problem was deciding where to put the company's effort. Someone was needed to tie together the efforts of research, purchasing, production, shipping, and sales. As this situation became more common, the sales era was replaced by the marketing department era. The **marketing department era** is a time when all marketing activities are brought under the control of one department to improve short-run policy planning and to try to integrate the firm's activities.

To the marketing company era

Since 1960, most firms have developed at least some staff with a marketing management outlook. Many of these firms have even graduated from the marketing department era into the marketing company era. The **marketing company era** is a time when, in addition to short-run marketing planning, marketing people develop long-range plans—sometimes 10 or more years ahead—and the whole company effort is guided by the marketing concept.

In 1896, a firm could easily sell all the typewriters it could produce because there were few available in the market.

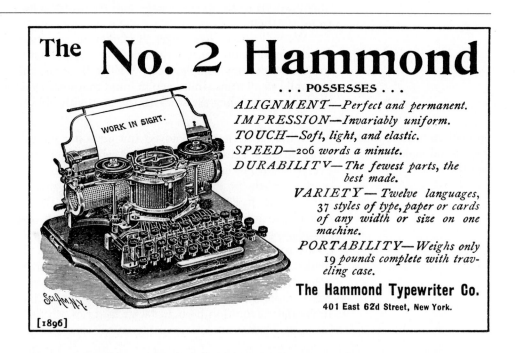

WHAT DOES THE MARKETING CONCEPT MEAN?

The **marketing concept** means that an organization aims *all* its efforts at satisfying its *customers*—at a profit. The marketing concept is a simple but very important idea. See Exhibit 2–1.

It is not really a new idea—it's been around for a long time. But some managers act as if they are stuck at the beginning of the production era, when there were shortages of most products. They show little interest in customers' needs. These managers still have a **production orientation**—making whatever products are easy to produce and *then* trying to sell them. They think of customers existing to buy the firm's output rather than of firms existing to serve customers and—more broadly—the needs of society.

Well-managed firms have replaced this production orientation with a marketing orientation. A **marketing orientation** means trying to carry out the marketing concept. Instead of just trying to get customers to buy what the firm has produced, a marketing-oriented firm tries to produce what customers need.

Three basic ideas are included in the definition of the marketing concept: (1) customer satisfaction, (2) a total company effort, and (3) profit—not just sales—as an objective. These ideas deserve more discussion.

Customer satisfaction guides the whole system

"Give the customers what they need" seems so obvious that it may be hard for you to see why the marketing concept requires special attention. However, people don't always do the logical and obvious—especially when it means changing what they've done in the past. In a typical company 30 years ago, production managers thought mainly about getting out the product. Accountants were interested only in balancing the books. Financial people looked after the company's cash position. And salespeople were mainly concerned with getting orders. Each department thought of its own activity as the center of the business—with others working around "the edges." No one was concerned with the whole system. As long as the company made a profit, each department went merrily on—doing its

Exhibit 2–1 Organizations with a Marketing Orientation Carry Out the Marketing Concept

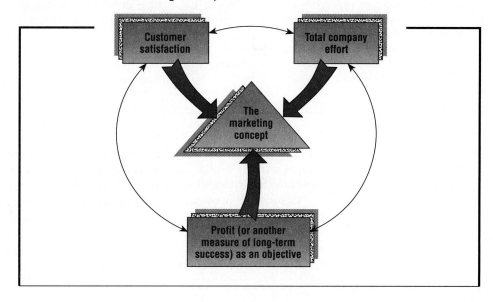

MARKETING DEMO 2–1
What Nabob Believes

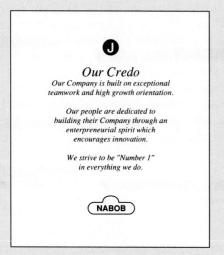

J

Our Credo

*Our Company is built on exceptional
teamwork and high growth orientation.*

*Our people are dedicated to
building their Company through an
enterpreneurial spirit which
encourages innovation.*

*We strive to be "Number 1"
in everything we do.*

NABOB

Our principles have given shape to a corporate strategy that places extraordinary emphasis on relationships with *people*:

The Customer Comes First

Because the consumer holds the ultimate key to the company's success, changing tastes and trends must be anticipated to satisfy the world's demand for the right product, in the right place, at the right time. The "right place and time" are essential to consumer satisfaction, and to realize both, outstanding customer service must pervade the entire organization. It *does*. From the way we answer telephones to the moment our products reach our customers, the "service chain" is deeply ingrained into the attitudes and actions of every Nabob employee.

An Entrepreneurial Spirit

People who have a compulsion to succeed as entrepreneurs—by originating and taking responsibility for individual initiatives in an environment of cohesive teamwork—flourish in the Nabob organization. And have a surprisingly good time in the process. Excellence and continuous personal growth are fostered through high performance standards and equally high leadership, motivation and training standards. A lot is expected—and a lot is offered.

Nabob and The Community

Nabob also believes it has responsibilities toward a wider circle of people: the communities within which we live and work. As official sponsor of Wheelchair Track And Field in Canada, the company has assumed national leadership in the campaign to promote public recognition of a sport that is offering new opportunities for self-realization to many Canadian athletes. Nabob also offers direct donations to such essential humanitarian organizations as the United Way, Canada's Food Banks and Ronald McDonald House.

Insofar as possible, we are determined to assist in preserving the fragile world environment and are active participants in the International Research Centre's efforts to develop more environmentally friendly packaging and safer processing systems. Through Nabob's patented Swiss Water Decaffeinating process, we have been producing 100 percent chemical-free decaffeinated coffee in the Vancouver facility since 1987.

Source: Nabob Inc. "The Enterprise of Entrepreneurs," company publication.

own thing. Unfortunately, this is still true in many companies today. Nabob is one company that's striving to make customer needs the first priority throughout the company. See Marketing Demo 2–1 for this statement.

Ideally, all managers should work together because the output from one department may be the input to another. But some managers tend to build "fences" around their own departments, as seen in Exhibit 2–2A. There may be meetings to try to get them to work together—but they come and go from the meetings worried only about protecting their own turf.

Exhibit 2–2   Contrasting Views of a Business

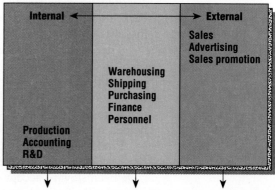

A.   A business as a box
   (most departments have high fences)

Sales · Inventory control · Sales promotion · R&D · Warehousing · Personnel · Accounting · Purchasing · Production · Shipping · Advertising · Finance

Each department sees its activities as what is most important.

B.   Total system view of a business
   (implementing marketing concept; still have
   departments but all guided by what customers want)

Internal ← → External

Sales
Advertising
Sales promotion

Warehousing
Shipping
Purchasing
Finance
Personnel

Production
Accounting
R&D

All departments work together to provide customer satisfaction.

We use the term *production orientation* as a shorthand way to refer to this kind of narrow thinking—and lack of a central focus—in a business firm. But keep in mind that this problem may be seen in sales-oriented sales representatives, advertising-oriented agency people, finance-oriented finance people, directors of nonprofit organizations, and so on. It is not just a criticism of people who manage production. They aren't necessarily any more guilty of narrow thinking than anyone else.

The "fences" come down in an organization that has accepted the marketing concept. There are still departments, of course, because specialization makes sense. But the total system's effort is guided by what customers want—instead of what each department would like to do.

In such a firm, it is more realistic to view the business as a box with both internal and external activities as shown in Exhibit 2–2B. Some internal departments—production, accounting, and research and development (R&D)—are mainly concerned with affairs inside the firm. The external departments are concerned with outsiders—sales, advertising, and sales promotion. Finally, some departments—warehousing, shipping, purchasing, finance, and personnel—work with both insiders and outsiders.

The important point is to have a guiding focus that *all* departments adopt. It helps the organization work as a total "system" rather than a lot of separate parts. The marketing concept, however, is more complete than many systems-oriented ideas. It actually specifies a high-level objective—customer satisfaction—that is logical for each and every part of the system. It also specifies a profit objective, which is necessary for the system's survival.

Survival and success
require a profit

Firms must satisfy customers, or the customers won't continue to "vote" for the firm's survival and success with their money. But firms must also keep in mind that sales revenue from customers comes at a cost. It may cost more to satisfy some needs than any customers are willing to pay. So profit—the difference between a firm's revenue and its total costs—is the bottom-line measure of the firm's success and ability to survive. It is the balancing point that helps the firm determine what needs it will try to satisfy with its total (sometimes costly!) effort.

ADOPTION OF THE MARKETING CONCEPT HAS NOT BEEN EASY OR UNIVERSAL

The marketing concept seems so logical that you would think most firms would quickly adopt it. But this isn't the case. Most firms are still production-oriented. In fact, the majority are either production-oriented—or regularly slip back that way—and must consciously refocus their planning on customers' interests.

The marketing concept was first accepted by consumer products companies such as General Electric and Procter & Gamble. Competition was intense in some of their markets—and trying to satisfy customers' needs more fully was a way to win in this competition. Widespread publicity about the success of the marketing concept at companies like General Electric and Procter & Gamble helped spread the message to other firms.[2]

Producers of industrial commodities—steel, coal, paper, glass, chemicals—have accepted the marketing concept slowly if at all. Similarly, many retailers have been slow to accept the marketing concept, in part because they are so close to final consumers that they think they really know their customers.

Service industries are catching up

Service industries, including airlines, banks, investment firms, lawyers, physicians, accountants, and insurance companies, were slow to adopt the marketing concept, too. But this has changed dramatically in the last decade, partly due to government regulation changes that forced many of these businesses to be more competitive.[3]

In response to an increasingly competitive business environment, Canadian law firms are beginning to hire marketers! Clients are becoming more savvy and less loyal. Rather than return to the same firm or have that firm handle all their legal business, they are more likely to shop around for a better price and the best service. In order to keep clients and attract new ones, law firms are finding that they need to develop a marketing orientation.[4]

It's easy to slip into a production orientation

The marketing concept may seem obvious, but it's very easy to slip into a production-oriented way of thinking. For example, a retailer might prefer only weekday hours—avoiding nights, Saturdays, and Sundays, when many customers would prefer to shop. Or a company might rush to produce a clever new product developed in its lab—rather than first finding if it will fill an unsatisfied need. Many firms in high-technology businesses fall into this trap. They think that

Many service industries have begun to apply the marketing concept.

technology is the source of their success, rather than realizing that technology is only a means to meet customer needs.

Take a look at Exhibit 2–3. It shows some differences in outlook between adopters of the marketing concept and typical production-oriented managers. As the exhibit suggests, the marketing concept—if taken seriously—is really very powerful. It forces the company to think through what it is doing—and why. And it motivates the company to develop plans for accomplishing its objectives.

Where does competition fit?
Some critics say that the marketing concept doesn't go far enough in today's highly competitive markets. They think of marketing as "warfare" for customers— and argue that a marketing manager should focus on competitors, not customers. That viewpoint, however, misses the point. The marketing concept idea isn't just to satisfy customers—but to do it at a profit through an integrated, whole company effort. Customers, competitors, and profits must be considered simultaneously. Profit opportunities depend not only on outdoing some other firm—but also on doing the right thing. In fact, often the best way to beat the competition is to be first to find and satisfy a need that others have not even considered. The competition between Pepsi and Coke illustrates this.

Coke and Pepsi were spending millions of dollars on promotion—fighting head-to-head for the same cola customers. They put so much emphasis on the competitor that they missed opportunities. Then, Pepsi recognized consumer interest in a potential new product idea: a soft drink based on fruit juice. Pepsi's Slice brand soft drink was first on the market, and that helped Slice win loyal customers and space on retailers' shelves.

Exhibit 2–3   Some Differences in Outlook between Adopters of the Marketing Concept and the Typical Production-Oriented Managers

Topic	Marketing Orientation	Production Orientation
Attitudes toward Customers	Customer needs determine company plans	They should be glad we exist, trying to cut costs and bringing out better products
Product Offering	Company makes what it can sell	Company sells what it can make
Role of Marketing Research	To determine customer needs and how well company is satisfying them	To determine customer reaction, if used at all
Interest in Innovation	Focus on locating new opportunities	Focus is on technology and cost-cutting
Importance of Profit	A critical objective	A residual, what's left after all costs are covered
Role of Customer Credit	Seen as a customer service	Seen as a necessary evil
Role of Packaging	Designed for customer convenience and as a selling tool	Seen merely as protection for the product
Inventory Levels	Set with customer requirements and costs in mind	Set to make production more convenient
Transportation arrangements	Seen as a customer service	Seen as an extension of production and storage activities, with emphasis on cost minimization
Focus of Advertising	Need-satisfying benefits of products and services	Product features and how products are made
Role of Sales Force	Help the customer to buy if the product fits his or her needs, while coordinating with rest of firm	Sell the customer, don't worry about coordination with other promotion efforts or rest of firm

THE MARKETING CONCEPT APPLIES IN NONPROFIT ORGANIZATIONS

Newcomers to marketing thinking

The marketing concept is as important for nonprofit organizations as it is for business firms. However, prior to 1970, few people paid attention to the role of marketing in facilitating the types of exchanges that are typical of nonprofits. Now, marketing is widely recognized as applicable to all sorts of public and private nonprofit organizations—ranging from government agencies, health care organizations, educational institutions, and religious groups to charities, political parties, and fine arts organizations.

Some nonprofit organizations operate just like a business. For example, there may be no practical difference between the gift shop at a museum and a for-profit shop located across the street. On the other hand, some nonprofits differ from business firms in a variety of ways.

Support may not come from satisfied "customers"

As with any business firm, a nonprofit organization needs resources and support to survive and achieve its objectives. Yet support often does not come directly from those who receive the benefits the organization produces. For example, the World Wildlife Fund protects animals. If supporters of the World Wildlife Fund are not satisfied with its efforts—don't think the benefits are worth what it costs to provide them—they will, and should, put their time and money elsewhere.

Just as most firms face competition for customers, most nonprofits face competition for the resources and support they need. A sorority will falter if potential members join other organizations. A shelter for the homeless may fail if supporters decide to focus on some other cause, such as AIDS education. A community theatre group that decides to do a play that the actors and the director like—never stopping to consider what the audience might want to see—may find that the audience goes somewhere else.

What is the bottom line?

As with a business, a nonprofit must take in as much money as it spends or it won't survive. However, a nonprofit organization does not measure profit in the same way as a firm. And its key measures of long-term success are also different. The YMCA, colleges, symphony orchestras, and the post office, for example, all seek to achieve different objectives—and need different measures of success.

Profit guides business decisions because it reflects both the costs and benefits of different activities. In a nonprofit organization, it is sometimes more difficult to be objective in evaluating the benefits of different activities relative to what they cost. However, if everyone in an organization agrees to *some* measure of long-run success, it helps serve as a guide to where the organization should focus its efforts.

May not be organized for marketing

Some nonprofits face other challenges in organizing to adopt the marketing concept. Often, no one has overall responsibility for marketing activities. A treasurer or accountant may keep the books, and someone may be in charge of "operations"—but marketing may somehow seem less crucial, especially if no one understands what marketing is all about. Even when some leaders do the marketing thinking, they may have trouble getting unpaid volunteers with many different interests to all agree with the marketing strategy. Volunteers tend to do what they feel like doing!

The marketing concept provides focus

We have been discussing some of the differences between nonprofit and business organizations. However, the marketing concept is helpful in *any* type of organization. Success is unlikely if everyone doesn't pull together to strive for common objectives that can be achieved with the available resources. Adopting

Marketing is being more widely accepted by nonprofit organizations.

the marketing concept helps to bring this kind of focus. After all, each organization is trying to satisfy some group of consumers in some way.[5] Marketing Demo 2–2 shows how a firm can focus its efforts on identifying and satisfying customer needs.

Nonprofits achieve objectives by satisfying needs

A simple example shows how marketing concept thinking helped one nonprofit service organization do a better job of achieving its objectives. A police chief in a small town was trying to fight increased robberies in residential areas. He asked the town manager for a larger budget—for more officers and cars to patrol neighborhoods. The town manager wasn't convinced a bigger police budget would solve the problem. Instead, she tried a different approach. One police officer was taken off the beat and put in charge of a community watch program. This officer helped neighbors organize to look after each others' property and notify the police of any suspicious situations. The officer also set up a program to engrave ID numbers on belongings and installed signs warning thieves that a community watch was in effect. Break-ins all but stopped—without increasing the police budget. What the town's citizens *really* needed was more effective crime prevention—not just more police officers.

Throughout this book, we'll be discussing the marketing concept and related ideas as they apply in many different settings. Often, we'll simply say "in a firm" or "in a business"—but remember that most of the ideas can be applied in *any* type of organization.

MARKETING DEMO 2–2
Wise Marketer Knows Customer's Needs

(M) arketing isn't fancy jargon strung together pretending to be a plan; it's as simple, and as complicated, as selling stuff to folks. The key is to never forget there is another living human being on the other end of the marketing chain.

The only time your bell rings is when the customer pulls. It's your job to get him to love that chain so much he never wants to let go.

We need to keep that same simple focus when we try to measure our customer-service efforts. Often we forget the basics:

1. Define the customer. Every business really only has two assets—employees and clients. Organizations that are truly dedicated to quality and service take both external and internal customer relationships into account.

2. Let the customer define his or her service needs. Many organizations assume a great deal about their customers' needs without really asking them what they want.

3. Service goals need to be specific and measurable.

4. Measure only what you're prepared to fix. Many organizations ask for feedback on issues they are not willing to change and just further annoy their customers.

5. Use impartial measurement and evaluation. The potential for political maneuvering and posturing is significant in most large organizations. The need for truly unbiased and unfil-

tered data is clear. Third-party collection and evaluation do add cost, but it may also help get your service enhancement program off to a good start.

Once everyone is working in true team fashion, rivalries subside and internal data collection and evaluation can begin.

6. Expect tons of initial fingerpointing. Since most organizations have never installed effective measurement systems (except for financial reporting), measuring other performance criteria is very disconcerting for most employees and especially management.

7. Expect customer complaints to increase substantially.

Given the opportunity for feedback, more customers will take the time to complain. When you realize that 25 percent of any company's customers are considering moving to the competition at any given time, getting another chance to make them happy is like winning a lottery!

8. Balance people and systems. Your level of service can be mapped on two axes—systems and people. The ideal spot is to have high and equal emphasis on both. More importantly, deliver both. Customers then walk away feeling you care and it shows.

Source: Tom Stirr, "Wise Marketer Knows Customer's Needs," *Marketing*, May 4, 1992, p. 43.

THE MARKETING CONCEPT, SOCIAL RESPONSIBILITY, AND MARKETING ETHICS

Society's needs must be considered

The marketing concept is so logical that it's hard to argue with it. Yet when a firm focuses its efforts on satisfying some consumers—to achieve its objectives—there may be negative effects on society. (Remember that we discussed this micro-macro dilemma in Chapter 1.) This means that marketing managers should be concerned with **social responsibility**—a firm's obligation to improve its positive effects on society and reduce its negative effects. Being socially responsible sometimes requires difficult trade-offs.

Consider, for example, the environmental problems created by CFCs (chlorofluorocarbons), chemicals used in hundreds of critical products including fire extinguishers, refrigerators, cooling systems for skyscrapers, insulation, and electronic circuit boards. We now know that CFCs deplete the earth's ozone layer. The result is a possible global warming and exposure to cancer-causing ultraviolet radiation. Yet it was not possible to immediately stop producing and using all CFCs. For many products critical to society, there was no feasible short-term substitute for CFCs. Imperial Chemical Industries of the United Kingdom and Elf Atochem of France are now producing a feasible substitute for CFC, called HFC-134A. Du Pont and Allied Signal will also be producing HFC-134A by 1996, the date set for the total ban on CFCs according to the 1992 Montreal protocal.[6]

The issue of social responsibility in marketing also raises other important questions—for which there are no easy answers.

Should all consumer needs be satisfied?

Some consumers want products that may not be safe or good for them in the long run. Some critics argue that businesses should not offer cigarettes, high-heeled shoes, alcoholic beverages, sugar-coated cereals, soft drinks, and many processed foods because they aren't "good" for consumers in the long run.

Similarly, motorcycles are one of the most dangerous products identified by the Consumer Product Safety Commission. Should Harley-Davidson stop production? What about skis, mopeds, and scuba equipment? Who should decide if these products will be offered to consumers? Is this a micro-marketing issue or a macro-marketing issue?

What if it cuts into profits?

Being more socially conscious often seems to lead to positive customer response. For example, Gerber had great success when it improved the nutritional quality of its baby food. And many consumers have been eager to buy products that are friendly to the environment (even at a higher price).

Yet as the examples above show, there are times when being socially responsible conflicts with a firm's profit objective. Concerns about such conflicts have prompted critics to raise the basic question: Is the marketing concept really desirable?

Many marketing managers and socially conscious marketing companies are trying to resolve this problem. Their definition of customer satisfaction includes long-range effects—as well as immediate customer satisfaction. They try to balance consumer, company, *and* social interests.

You too will have to make choices that balance these social concerns—either in your role as a consumer or as a manager in a business firm. So throughout the text we will be discussing many of the social issues faced by marketing management.

The marketing concept guides marketing ethics

Organizations that have adopted the marketing concept are concerned about marketing ethics as well as broader issues of social responsibility. It is simply not possible for a firm to be truly consumer-oriented and at the same time intentionally unethical in decisions or actions that affect customers.

Individual managers in an organization may have different values. As a result, problems may arise when someone does not share the same marketing ethics as others in the organization. One person operating alone can damage a firm's reputation and even survival. Because the marketing concept involves a companywide focus, it is a foundation for marketing ethics common to everyone in a firm—and helps to avoid such problems.

To be certain that standards for marketing ethics are as clear as possible, many organizations have developed their own written codes of ethics. Consistent with the marketing concept, these codes usually state, at least at a general level, the ethical standards that everyone in the firm should follow in dealing with customers and other people. Many professional societies have also adopted such codes. For example, the American Marketing Association's code of ethics—see Exhibit 2–4—sets specific ethical standards for many aspects of the management job in marketing.[7]

Exhibit 2–4   Code of Ethics, American Marketing Association

CODE OF ETHICS

Members of the American Marketing Association (AMA) are committed to ethical professional conduct. They have joined together in subscribing to this Code of Ethics embracing the following topics:

Responsibilities of the Marketer

Marketers must accept responsibility for the consequences of their activities and make every effort to ensure that their decisions, recommendations, and actions function to identify, serve, and satisfy all relevant publics: customers, organizations and society.

Marketers' professional conduct must be guided by:

1. The basic rule of professional ethics: not knowingly to do harm;
2. The adherence to all applicable laws and regulations;
3. The accurate representation of their education, training and experience; and
4. The active support, practice and promotion of this Code of Ethics.

Honesty and Fairness

Marketers shall uphold and advance the integrity, honor, and dignity of the marketing profession by:

1. Being honest in serving consumers, clients, employees, suppliers, distributors and the public;
2. Not knowingly participating in conflict of interest without prior notice to all parties involved; and
3. Establishing equitable fee schedules including the payment or receipt of usual, customary and/or legal compensation for marketing exchanges.

Rights and Duties of Parties in the Marketing Exchange Process

Participants in the marketing exchange process should be able to expect that:

1. Products and services offered are safe and fit for their intended uses;
2. Communications about offered products and services are not deceptive;
3. All parties intend to discharge their obligations, financial and otherwise, in good faith; and
4. Appropriate internal methods exist for equitable adjustment and/or redress of grievances concerning purchases.

It is understood that the above would include, *but is not limited to,* the following responsibilities of the marketer:

In the area of product development and management,

- disclosure of all substantial risks associated with product or service usage;
- identification of any product component substitution that might materially change the product or impact on the buyer's purchase decision;
- identification of extra-cost added features.

In the area of promotions,

- avoidance of false and misleading advertising;
- rejection of high pressure manipulations, or misleading sales tactics;
- avoidance of sales promotions that use deception or manipulation.

In the area of distribution,

- not manipulating the availability of a product for purpose of exploitation;
- not using coercion in the marketing channel;
- not exerting undue influence over the reseller's choice to handle a product.

In the area of pricing,

- not engaging in price fixing;
- not practicing predatory pricing;
- disclosing the full price associated with any purchase.

In the area of marketing research,

- prohibiting selling or fund raising under the guise of conducting research;
- maintaining research integrity by avoiding misrepresentation and omission of pertinent research data;
- treating outside clients and suppliers fairly.

Organizational Relationships

Marketers should be aware of how their behavior may influence or impact on the behavior of others in organizational relationships. They should not demand, encourage or apply coercion to obtain unethical behavior in their relationships with others, such as employees, suppliers or customers.

1. Apply confidentiality and anonymity in professional relationships with regard to privileged information;
2. Meet their obligations and responsibilities in contracts and mutual agreements in a timely manner;
3. Avoid taking the work of others, in whole, or in part, and represent this work as their own or directly benefit from it without compensation or consent of the originator or owner;
4. Avoid manipulation to take advantage of situations to maximize personal welfare in a way that unfairly deprives or damages the organization or others.

Any AMA members found to be in violation of any provision of this Code of Ethics may have his or her Association membership suspended or revoked.

THE MANAGEMENT JOB IN MARKETING

Now that you know about the marketing concept—a philosophy to guide the whole firm—let's look more closely at how a marketing manager helps a firm to achieve its objectives. The marketing manager is a manager, so let's look at the marketing management process.

The **marketing management process** is the process of (1) *planning* marketing activities, (2) directing the *implementation* of the plans, and (3) *controlling* these plans. Planning, implementation, and control are basic jobs of all managers, but here we will emphasize what they mean to marketing managers.

Exhibit 2–5 shows the relationships among the three jobs in the marketing management process. The jobs are all connected to show that the marketing management process is continuous. In the planning job, managers set guidelines for the implementing job—and specify expected results. They use these expected results in the control job—to determine if everything has worked out as planned. The link from the control job to the planning job is especially important. This feedback often leads to changes in the plans—or to new plans.

Marketing managers should seek new opportunities

Exhibit 2–5 shows that marketing managers must seek attractive new opportunities—as customers' needs change or as the organization's ability to meet customers' needs changes. In the next two chapters, we will discuss how marketing managers seek and evaluate opportunities. For now, however, note that marketing managers cannot be satisfied just planning present activities. Markets are dynamic. Consumers' needs, competitors, and the environment keep changing.

Consider Parker Brothers, a company that seemed to have a "Monopoly" in family games. While it continued selling board games, firms like Atari and Nintendo zoomed in with video game competition. Of course, not every opportunity is good for every company. Really attractive opportunities are those that fit with what the whole company wants—and is able to do.

Exhibit 2–5   The Marketing Management Process

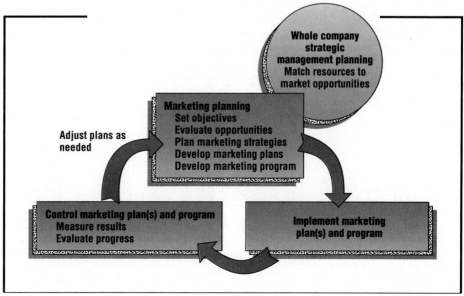

Strategic management planning concerns the whole firm

The job of planning strategies to guide a whole company is called **strategic (management) planning**—the managerial process of developing and maintaining a match between an organization's resources and its market opportunities. This is a top-management job that includes planning not only for marketing activities but also for production, research and development, and other functional areas. We won't discuss whole company planning in this text, but you need to understand that marketing department plans are not whole company plans.

On the other hand, company plans should be market-oriented. And the marketing manager's plans can set the tone and direction for the whole company. So we will use *strategy planning* and *marketing strategy planning* to mean the same thing.[8]

WHAT IS MARKETING STRATEGY PLANNING?

Marketing strategy planning means finding attractive opportunities and developing profitable marketing strategies. But what is a "marketing strategy"? We have used these words rather casually so far. Now let's see what they really mean.

What is a marketing strategy?

A **marketing strategy** specifies a target market and a related marketing mix. It is a "big picture" of what a firm will do in some market. Two interrelated parts are needed:

1. A **target market**—a fairly homogeneous (similar) group of customers to whom a company wishes to appeal.
2. A **marketing mix**—the controllable variables the company puts together to satisfy this target group.

The importance of target customers in this process can be seen in Exhibit 2–6, where the customer—the "C"—is at the center of the diagram. The customer is surrounded by the controllable variables that we call the *marketing mix*. A typical marketing mix includes some product, offered at a price, with some promotion to tell potential customers about the product, and a way to reach the customer's place.

Exhibit 2–6
A Marketing Strategy

VIA Rail is targeting its new class of rail service, Silver and Blue, to the American tourist interested in a first-class travel experience. In order to reach this segment, VIA has paid careful attention to the needs of its customers and translated those needs into product changes. Showers have been installed in each compartment, comfortable armchairs that convert into sleeping facilities have been added, and designer label toiletries can be found in the bathrooms. The dining service has been improved to offer an extensive choice of appetizers, entrees, and desserts served on china, crystal, and silver. Plans are in the works to introduce a frequent traveler program in response to customer demand. Promotion includes an ad campaign in a US travel and leisure magazine as well as a sales force blitz of the US travel agent sector. Prices are set at a level that attracts the recession-shocked traveler looking for a transportation alternative to car or air travel.[9]

SELECTING A MARKET–ORIENTED STRATEGY IS TARGET MARKETING

Target marketing is not mass marketing

Note that a marketing strategy specifies some *particular* target customers. This approach is called *target marketing*, to distinguish it from *mass marketing*. **Target marketing** says that a marketing mix is tailored to fit some specific target customers. In contrast, **mass marketing**—the typical production-oriented approach—vaguely aims at "everyone" with the same marketing mix. Mass marketing assumes that everyone is the same—and considers everyone a potential customer. It may help to think of target marketing as the "rifle approach" and mass marketing as the "shotgun approach."

Mass marketers may do target marketing

Commonly used terms can be confusing here. The terms *mass marketing* and *mass marketers* do not mean the same thing. Far from it! Mass marke*ting* means trying to sell to "everyone," as we explained above. Mass marke*ters* like General Foods and Eaton's are aiming at clearly defined target markets. The confusion with mass marketing occurs because their target markets usually are large and spread out.

Target marketing can mean big markets and profits

Target marketing is not limited to small market segments—only to fairly homogeneous ones. A very large market—even what is sometimes called the mass market—may be fairly homogeneous, and a target marketer will deliberately aim at it. For example, a very large group of parents of young children are homogeneous on many dimensions—including their attitudes about changing baby diapers. In the United States alone, this group spends about $3.5 billion a year on disposable diapers—so it should be no surprise that it is a major target market for companies like Kimberly-Clark (Huggies) and Procter & Gamble (Pampers). These days, so many customers in this target market buy disposable diapers that the challenge isn't just offering them a product they want, but in finding an ecologically sound way to dispose of it!

The basic reason for a marketing manager to focus on some specific target customers is to gain a competitive advantage—by developing a more satisfying marketing mix that should also be more profitable for the firm. Toshiba, for example, established a competitive advantage with traveling business computer users by being first to offer a powerful laptop computer. Charles Schwab, the discount stock brokerage firm, targets knowledgeable investors who want a convenient, low-cost way to buy and sell stocks by phone without a lot of advice (or pressure) from a salesperson.

DEVELOPING MARKETING MIXES FOR TARGET MARKETS

There are many marketing mix decisions

There are many possible ways to satisfy the needs of target customers. A product can have many different features and quality levels. Service levels can be adjusted. The package can be of various sizes, colors, or materials. The brand name and warranty can be changed. Various advertising media—newspapers, magazines, radio, television, billboards—may be used. A company's own sales force or other sales specialists can be used. Different prices can be charged. Price discounts may be given, and so on. With so many possible variables, is there any way to help organize all these decisions and simplify the selection of marketing mixes? The answer is yes.

The four Ps make up a marketing mix

It is useful to reduce all the variables in the marketing mix to four basic ones:

Product.   Promotion.

Place.   Price.

Exhibit 2–7
A Marketing Strategy—
Showing the Four Ps
of a Marketing Mix

Product—the good
or service for the
target's needs

Place—reaching
the target

It helps to think of the four major parts of a marketing mix as the "four Ps." Exhibit 2–7 emphasizes their relationship and their common focus on the customer—"C".

Customer is not part of the marketing mix

The customer is shown surrounded by the four Ps in Exhibit 2–7. Some students assume that the customer is part of the marketing mix—but this is not so. The customer should be the *target* of all marketing efforts. The customer is placed in the center of the diagram to show this. The C stands for some specific customers—the target market.

Exhibit 2–8 shows some of the strategy decision variables organized by the four Ps. These will be discussed in later chapters. For now, let's just describe each P briefly.

The Product area is concerned with developing the right product for the target market. This offering may involve a physical good, a service, or a blend of both. Keep in mind that Product is not limited to physical goods. For example, the product of H & R Block is a completed tax form. The product of a political party is the set of causes it will work to achieve. The important thing to remember is that your good and/or service should satisfy some customers' needs.

Along with other Product-area decisions shown in Exhibit 2–8, we will talk about developing and managing new products and whole product lines. We will also discuss the characteristics of various kinds of products so that you will be able to make generalizations about product classes. This will help you to develop whole marketing mixes more quickly.

Place is concerned with all the decisions involved in getting the *right* product to the target market's Place. A product isn't much good to a customer if it isn't available when and where it's wanted.

A product reaches customers through a channel of distribution. A **channel of distribution** is any series of firms (or individuals) from producer to final user or consumer.

Exhibit 2–8   Strategy Decision Areas Organized by the Four Ps

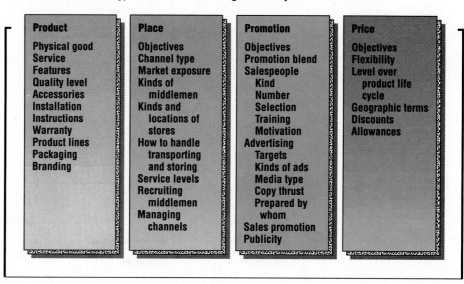

Sometimes, a channel system is quite short. It may run directly from a producer to a final user or consumer. This is especially common in business markets and in the marketing of services. Often, the system is more complex—involving many different kinds of middlemen and specialists. See Exhibit 2–9 for some examples. And if a marketing manager has several different target markets, several different channels of distribution might be needed.

We will also see how physical distribution service levels and decisions concerning logistics (transporting and storing) relate to the other Place decisions and the rest of the marketing mix.

Promotion—telling and selling the customer

The third P—Promotion—is concerned with *telling* the target market about the right product. Promotion includes personal selling, mass selling, and sales promotion. It is the marketing manager's job to blend these methods.

Personal selling involves direct communication between sellers and potential customers. Personal selling usually happens face-to-face, but sometimes the communication occurs over the telephone. Personal selling lets the salesperson adapt the firm's marketing mix to each potential customer. But this individual attention comes at a price; personal selling can be very expensive. Often, this personal effort has to be blended with mass selling and sales promotion.

Mass selling is communicating with large numbers of customers at the same time. The main form of mass selling is **advertising**—any *paid* form of nonpersonal presentation of ideas, goods, or services by an identified sponsor. **Publicity**—any *unpaid* form of nonpersonal presentation of ideas, goods, or services—is another important form of mass selling.

Sales promotion refers to those promotion activities—other than advertising, publicity, and personal selling—that stimulate interest, trial, or purchase by final customers or others in the channel. This can involve use of coupons, point-of-

Exhibit 2–9 Four Examples of Basic Channels of Distribution for Consumer Products

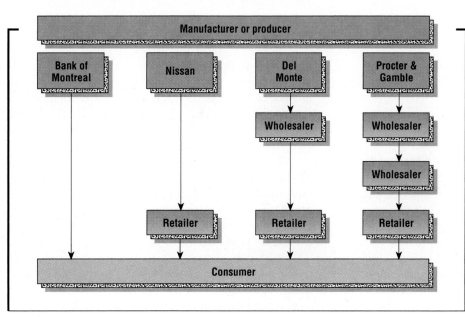

A firm's product may involve a service (like a stay in a hotel), a physical food (like cereal), or a combination of both.

purchase materials, samples, signs, catalogues, novelties, and circulars. Sales promotion specialists work with the personal-selling and mass-selling people.

Price—making it right

In addition to developing the right Product, Place, and Promotion, marketing managers must also decide the right Price. In setting a price, they must consider the kind of competition in the target market—and the cost of the whole marketing mix. They must also try to estimate customer reaction to possible prices. Besides this, they also must know current practices as to markups, discounts, and other terms of sale. Further, they must be aware of legal restrictions on pricing.

If customers won't accept the Price, all of the planning effort will be wasted. So you can see that Price is an important area for a marketing manager.

Each of the four Ps contributes to the whole

All four Ps are needed in a marketing mix. In fact, they should all be tied together. But is any one more important than the others? Generally speaking, the answer is no—all contribute to one whole. When a marketing mix is being developed, all (final) decisions about the Ps should be made at the same time. That's why the four Ps are arranged around the customer (C) in a circle—to show that they all are equally important.

Let's sum up our discussion of marketing mix planning thus far. We develop a *Product* to satisfy the target customers. We find a way to reach our target customers' *Place*. We use *Promotion* to tell the target customers (and middlemen) about the product that has been designed for them. And we set a *Price* after estimating expected customer reaction to the total offering and the costs of getting it to them.

Strategy jobs must be done together

It is important to stress—it cannot be overemphasized—that selecting a target market *and* developing a marketing mix are interrelated. Both parts of a marketing strategy must be decided together. It is *strategies* that must be evaluated against the company's objectives, not alternative target markets or alternative marketing mixes.

Understanding target markets leads to good strategies

A target market's needs virtually determine the nature of an appropriate marketing mix. So marketers must analyze their potential target markets with great care. This book will explore ways to identify attractive market opportunities and develop appropriate strategies. These ideas can be seen more clearly with an example in the home financing market.

The Royal Bank was interested in capturing more of the market looking for financing to purchase a new home. Its strategy planning process involved recognizing the target market's wide ranges of housing needs and of incomes available to meet those needs.

As Exhibit 2–10 shows, the typical home owner owns three different homes during a lifetime. First-time buyers are usually in their 20s. The home they tend to buy is no-frills and functional. A few years later, these people become move-up buyers. Financially better off and with hefty equities from their first homes, they buy larger, more expensive dwellings—usually single-family houses. As years go by, they become empty nesters and move again—often to smaller, more easily maintained dwellings such as bungalows, townhouses, or condominiums.

Each group of home buyers seeks out different qualities in homes. But, more important to the Royal Bank, each group requires different banking services. Understanding their needs allows the bank to design services for them throughout their lives. For first-time home buyers, the Royal provides a series of publications that introduce them to the issues they must be aware of before they invest, including types of mortgages and interest rates. For those planning their move up, the Royal provides a variety of ways they can pay off their mortgages and buy up. And for those selling their empty nest to purchase something more manageable, the bank provides savings accounts that offer high interest for the money they'll have to invest.

Many firms identify several potential target markets for their products but plan their marketing mix around one target market. The Royal Bank chose to concentrate its efforts on selling three markets a particular product that was modified to meet all of their needs. Knowing what it did about each group, the bank offered financing for home purchases (Product) made widely available through all of their branches (Place) aimed at low-, middle-, and high-income purchasers through personal consultation and informative brochures (Promotion), of course, on terms they could live with (Price).[10]

Exhibit 2–10   The Home Financing Market

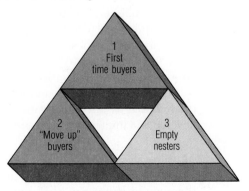

THE MARKETING PLAN IS A GUIDE TO IMPLEMENTATION AND CONTROL

Now that the key ideas of marketing strategy planning have been introduced, we can return to our overview of the marketing management process. You will see how a marketing strategy leads to a marketing plan and ultimately to implementation and control. (see Exhibit 2–5).

Marketing plan fills out marketing strategy

A marketing strategy sets a target market and a marketing mix. It is a "big picture" of what a firm will do in some market. A marketing plan goes further. A **marketing plan** is a written statement of a marketing strategy *and the time-related details for carrying out the strategy.* It should spell out the following in detail: (1) what marketing mix will be offered, to whom (that is, the target market), and for how long; (2) what company resources (shown as costs) will be needed at what rate (month by month, perhaps); and (3) what results are expected (sales and profits, perhaps monthly or quarterly). The plan should also include some control procedures—so that whoever is to carry out the plan will know if things are going wrong. This might be something as simple as comparing actual sales against expected sales—with a warning flag to be raised whenever total sales fall below a certain level.

Implementation puts plans into operation

After a marketing plan is developed, a marketing manager knows *what* needs to be done. Then the manager is concerned with **implementation**—putting marketing plans into operation.

Strategies work out as planned only when they are effectively implemented. Many **operational decisions**—short-run decisions to help implement strategies—may be needed.

Managers should make operational decisions within the guidelines set down during strategy planning. They develop Product policies, Place policies, and so on as part of strategy planning. Then operational decisions within these policies probably will be necessary—while carrying out the basic strategy. Note, however, that as long as these operational decisions stay within the policy guidelines, managers are making no change in the basic strategy. If the controls show that operational decisions are not producing the desired results, however, the managers may have to reevaluate the whole strategy—rather than just working harder at implementing it.

It's easier to see the difference between strategy decisions and operational decisions if we illustrate these ideas using a shoe company example. Possible four-P or basic strategy policies are shown in the left-hand column in Exhibit 2–11, and likely operational decisions are shown in the right-hand column.

It should be clear that some operational decisions are made regularly—even daily—and such decisions should not be confused with planning strategy. Certainly, a great deal of effort can be involved in these operational decisions. They might take a good part of the sales or advertising manager's time. But they are not the strategy decisions that will be our primary concern.

Our focus has been—and will continue to be—on developing marketing strategies. But it is also important to see that eventually, marketing managers must develop and implement marketing plans. We discuss this more fully in Chapter 20.[11]

Several plans make a whole marketing program

Most companies implement more than one marketing strategy—and related marketing plan—at the same time. They may have several products—some of them quite different—that are aimed at different target markets. The other

Exhibit 2–11   Relation of Strategy Policies to Operational Decisions
for Baby Shoe Company

Marketing Mix Decision Area	Strategy Policies	Likely Operational Decisions
Product	Carry as limited a line of colors, styles, and sizes as will satisfy the target market.	Add, change, or drop colors, styles, and/or sizes as customer tastes dictate.
Place	Distribute through selected "baby products" retailers who will carry the full line and provide good in-store sales support and promotion.	In market areas where sales potential is not achieved, add new retail outlets and/or drop retailers whose performance is poor.
Promotion	Promote the benefits and value of the special design and how it meets customer needs	When a retailer hires a new salesperson, send current training package with details on product line; increase use of local newspaper print ads during peak demand periods (before holidays, etc.).
Price	Maintain a "premium" price, but encourage retailers to make large-volume orders by offering discounts on quantity purchases.	Offer short-term introductory price "deals" to retailers when a new style is first introduced.

elements of the marketing mix may vary, too. Gillette's Right Guard deodorant, its Atra Plus razor blades, and its Liquid Paper correction fluid all have different marketing mixes. Yet the strategies for each must be implemented at the same time.[12]

A **marketing program** blends all of the firm's marketing plans into one big plan. See Exhibit 2–12. This program, then, is the responsibility of the whole company. Typically, the whole *marketing program* is an integrated part of the whole company strategic plan we discussed earlier.

Ultimately, marketing managers plan and implement a whole marketing program. In this text, however, we will emphasize planning one marketing strategy at a time, rather than planning—or implementing—a whole marketing program.

Exhibit 2—12   Elements of a Firm's Marketing Program

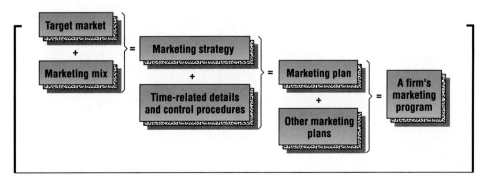

This is practical because it is important to plan each strategy carefully. Too many marketing managers fall into sloppy thinking. They try to develop too many strategies all at once—and don't develop any very carefully. Good plans are the building blocks of marketing management. We'll talk about merging plans into a marketing program in Chapter 20.

Control is analyzing and correcting what you've done

The control job provides the feedback that leads managers to modify their marketing strategies. To maintain control, a marketing manager uses a number of tools—like computer sales analysis, marketing research surveys, and accounting analysis of expenses and profits. Chapter 21 is devoted to the important topic of controlling marketing plans and programs.

In addition, as we talk about each of the marketing decision areas, we will discuss some of the control problems. This will help you understand how control keeps the firm on course—or shows the need to plan a new course.

All marketing jobs require planning and control

At first, it might appear that only high-level management or really large companies need to be concerned with management and control. This is not true. Every organization needs planning—and without control it's impossible to know if the plans are working.

This means that marketing strategy planning may be very important to you soon—maybe in your present job or university activities. In Appendix E on marketing careers, we present some strategy planning ideas for getting a marketing job.

THE IMPORTANCE OF MARKETING STRATEGY PLANNING

We emphasize the planning part of the marketing manager's job for a good reason. The one-time strategy decisions—the decisions that decide what business the company is in and the strategies it will follow—usually determine success—or failure. An extremely good plan might be carried out badly and still be profitable, while a poor but well-implemented plan can lose money. The case history that follows shows the importance of planning—and why we emphasize marketing strategy planning throughout this text.

Time for new strategies in the watch industry

The conventional watch makers—both domestic and foreign—had always aimed at customers who thought of watches as high-priced, high-quality symbols to mark special events—like graduation—or retirement. Advertising was concentrated around Christmas and graduation time and stressed a watch's symbolic appeal. Expensive jewelry stores were the main retail outlets.

This commonly accepted strategy of the major watch companies ignored people in the target market that just wanted to tell the time—and were interested in a reliable, low-priced watch. So the Timex Company developed a successful strategy around its Timex watches—and became the world's largest watch company. Timex completely upset the watch industry—both foreign and domestic—not only by offering a good product (with a one-year repair or replace guarantee) at a lower price, but also by using new, lower-cost channels of distribution. Its watches were widely available in drugstores, discount houses, and just about any other retail store that would carry them.

Marketing managers at Timex soon faced a new challenge. Texas Instruments, a new competitor in the watch market, took the industry by storm with its low-cost but very accurate electronic watches—using the same channels Timex had originally developed. But other firms quickly developed a watch that used a more stylish liquid crystal display for the digital readout. Texas Instruments could not change quickly enough to keep up, and the other companies took away its customers. The competition became so intense that Texas Instruments stopped marketing watches altogether.

While Timex and others were focusing on lower-priced watches, Japan's Seiko captured a commanding share of the high-priced gift market for its stylish and accurate quartz watches by obtaining strong distribution. All of this forced many traditional watch makers—like some of the once-famous Swiss brands—to close their factories.

In 1983, Switzerland's Swatch launched its colorful, affordable plastic watches—and changed what consumers see when they look at their watches. Swatch promoted its watches as fashion accessories and set them apart from those of other firms, whose ads squabbled about whose watches were most accurate and dependable. Swatch was also able to attract new middlemen by focusing its distribution on upscale fashion and department stores. The marketing mix Swatch developed around its fashion watch idea was so successful it didn't just increase Swatch's share of the market. The total size of the watch market increased because many consumers bought several watches to match different fashions.

Swatch's success prompted Timex, Seiko, and others to pay more attention to consumer fashion preferences. For example, Timex developed its fashionable Watercolors line targeted at teens. Timex has also emphasized better styling to compete in the higher-priced market—and broadened its offering to defend its position in the low- to mid-priced segment.

Timex developed a watch with large numbers to meet the needs of older consumers. Tissot developed its Woodwatch to appeal to upscale European consumers interested in distinctive design.

The economic downturn in the early 90s brought more changes. Sales of fashion watches leveled off, so Swatch is now targeting segments with other needs. For example, in 1990 it introduced a $45 scuba watch guaranteed to keep ticking at depths of 600 feet. Consumers have become more cost conscious—and less interested in expensive watches like those made by Rolex that were the "in" status symbol a few years earlier. The reemergence of value-seeking customers prompted Timex to return to its famous advertising tagline of the 1960s: "it takes a licking and keeps on ticking." Its position as the inexpensive-but-durable choice has helped it strengthen its distribution in department stores, sporting goods stores, and other channels.[13]

MARKETING DEMO 2–3
How Amdahl Took on the Big Boys and Won

How do you boost sales and market share when prices for your products are eroding by 20 percent a year, your market is flat, and your main competitor is 40 times your size? "Simple," says Ron Smith, the president of Amdahl Canada Ltd., the Mississauga, Ontario–based vendor of mainframe computers. "You try harder."

Smith is doing something right. In the past four years, sales have jumped by more then 50 percent to $160 million, bumping Amdahl's share of the Canadian high-end market by 4 points, from 22 percent to 26 percent. So far this year, Amdahl has stolen another half point from the competition.

Amdahl's strategy has been to distinguish itself as a specialist in so-called mission-critical systems—the mammoth commerical computer applications such as flight-reservations systems and insurance databases. It's a tough end of the business. Amdahl's market features the most advanced business-oriented mainframes available. Prices range from $2 million to $30 million.

No surprise, then, that buyers are typically more sophisticated and demanding. Smith can live with that—especially since they're also concerned with service and performance and less swayed by IBM's historical brand image. That's given Amdahl an opening, and it's made the most of it by grabbing such customers as Canadian Tire and the University of Manitoba.

Amdahl tries to add value by heaping on services. It offers consulting, for instance, that enables customers to measure the cost effectiveness of Amdahl's computer against the industry average. Amdahl will also show customers how to maximize storage capacity to extend the life of the investment. With those kinds of touches, Amdahl hopes to establish a reputation for customer response.

Although Amdahl's power-hungry market has been relatively unscathed by the rise of personal computers, it has felt the same kind of pressures as other companies in the large mainframe segment. Fierce competition that shaves margins and "outsourcing" companies—independent, fee-based data crunchers—have curbed demand by cramming multiple customers onto one machine. All that has flattened sales in the high-end market in North America to around $13 billion (US) annually since the late 1980s.

But rather than cut down its computer operations, Amdahl took a distinctly practical tack: It asked its 240 employees in Canada to economize voluntarily on such things as travel and to forgo overtime pay. The employees responded, says Smith. And the $3 million the company saved has helped to maintain its competitive pricing. Not incidentally, that means the jobs of some employees as well. Amdahl has also taken on outsourcers by compiling a computing cost-effectiveness test that compares a customer's operations with those of the contractors.

So far, Amdahl's strategy is working especially well in Canada. Its market share is nearly double the 12 percent it enjoys in the United States. "The Canadian market is so small that it's easy to see these issues starkly," says Smith.

Source: Beppi Crosariol, "How Amdahl Took On the Big Boys and Won," *Financial Times of Canada*, August 24–30, 1992, pp. 1, 4.

Creative strategy planning needed for survival

Dramatic shifts in strategy—like those described above—may surprise conventional, production-oriented managers. But such changes are becoming much more common—and should be expected. Industries or firms that have accepted the marketing concept realize that they cannot define their line of business in terms of the products they currently produce or sell. Rather, they have to think about the basic consumer needs they serve—and how those needs may change in the future. If they are too nearsighted, they may fail to see what's coming until too late.

But planning ahead also involves risk taking. Marketing Demo 2–3 examines how Amdahl's strategy has helped it succeed in the Canadian market.

Creative strategy planning is becoming even more important because firms can no longer win profits just by spending more money on plant and equipment. Moreover, domestic and foreign competition threatens those who can't create more satisfying goods and services. New markets, new customers, and new ways of doing things must be found if companies are to operate profitably in the future—and contribute to the macro-marketing system.

STRATEGY PLANNING DOESN'T TAKE PLACE IN A VACUUM

Strategy planning takes place within a framework

Our examples show that a marketing manager's strategy planning cannot take place in a vacuum. Instead, the manager works with controllable variables within a framework involving many variables that must be considered even though the manager can't control them. Exhibit 2–13 illustrates this framework and shows that the typical marketing manager must be concerned about the competitive environment, economic and technological environment, political and legal

Exhibit 2–13 Marketing Manager's Framework

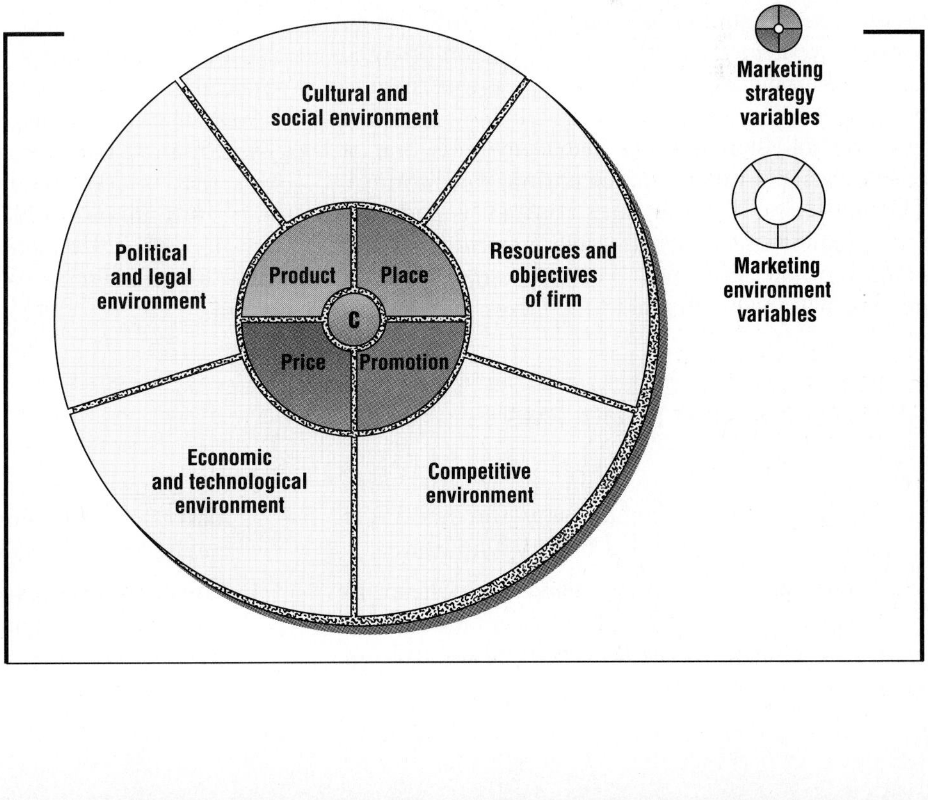

environment, cultural and social environment, and the firm's resources and objectives. We discuss these marketing environment variables in more detail in the next two chapters. But clearly, the environment in which the marketing manager operates affects strategy planning.

MARKET-ORIENTED STRATEGY PLANNING HELPS NONMARKETING PEOPLE TOO

While market-oriented strategy planning is helpful to marketers, it is also needed by accountants, production and personnel people, and all other specialists. A market-oriented plan lets everybody in the firm know what "ballpark" they are playing in—and what they are trying to accomplish. In other words, it gives direction to the whole business effort. An accountant can't set budgets without a plan, except perhaps by mechanically projecting last year's budget. Similarly, a finanical manager can't project cash needs without some idea of expected sales to target customers—and the costs of satisfying them.

We will use the term *marketing manager* for editorial convenience, but really, when we talk about marketing strategy planning, we are talking about the planning that a market-oriented manager should do when developing a firm's strategic plans. This kind of thinking should be done—or at least understood—by everyone in the organization who is responsible for planning. And this means even the entry-level salesperson, production supervisor, retail buyer, or personnel counselor.

CONCLUSION

Marketing's role within a marketing-oriented firm is to provide direction for a firm. The marketing concept stresses that the company's efforts should focus on satisfying some target customers—at a profit. Production-oriented firms tend to forget this. Often, various departments within a production-oriented firm let their natural conflicts of interest lead them to building fences.

The job of marketing management is one of continuous planning, implementing, and control. The marketing manager must constantly study the environment—seeking attractive opportunities and planning new strategies. Possible target markets must be matched with marketing mixes the firm can offer. Then, attractive strategies—really, whole marketing plans—are chosen for implementation. Controls are needed to be sure that the plans are carried out successfully. If anything goes wrong along the way, continual feedback should cause the process to be started over again—with the marketing manager planning more attractive marketing strategies.

A marketing mix has four variables: the four Ps—Product, Place, Promotion, and Price. Most of this text is concerned with developing profitable marketing mixes for clearly defined target markets. So after several chapters on analyzing target markets, we will discuss each of the four Ps in greater detail.

QUESTIONS AND PROBLEMS

1. Define the marketing concept in your own words, and then explain why the notion of profit is usually included in this definition.

2. After having defined the marketing concept in your own words, suggest how acceptance of this concept might affect the organization and operation of your college.

3. Distinguish between production orientation and marketing orientation, illustrating with examples in your local area.

4. Explain why a firm should view its internal activities as part of a total system. Illustrate your answer for (a) a large grocery products producer, (b) a plumbing wholesaler, and (c) a department store chain.

5. Does the acceptance of the marketing concept almost require that a firm view itself as a total system?

6. Distinguish clearly between a marketing strategy and a marketing mix. Use an example.

7. Distinguish clearly between mass marketing and target marketing. Use an example.

8. Why is the customer placed in the center of the four Ps in the diagram of a marketing strategy in Exhibit 2–6? Explain, using a specific example from your own experience.

9. Explain, in your own words, what each of the four Ps involves.

10. Evaluate the text's statement, "A marketing strategy sets the details of implementation."

11. Distinguish between strategy decisions and operational decisions, illustrating for a local retailer.

12. Distinguish between a strategy, a marketing plan, and a marketing program, illustrating for a local retailer.

13. Outline a marketing strategy for each of the following new products: (*a*) a radically new design for a toothbrush, (*b*) a new fishing reel, (*c*) a new wonder drug, and (*d*) a new industrial stapling machine.

14. Provide a specific illustration of why marketing strategy planning is important for all business-people, not just for those in the marketing department.

SUGGESTED CASES

14. Lucas Foods

29. KASTORS, Inc.

Economics Fundamentals

When You Finish This Appendix, You Should

❶

Understand the law of diminishing demand.

❷

Understand demand and supply curves—and how they set the size of a market and its price level.

❸

Know about elasticity of demand and supply.

❹

Know why demand elasticity can be affected by availability of substitutes.

❺

Know the different kinds of competitive situations and understand why they are important to marketing managers.

❻

Recognize the important new terms (shown in blue).

A good marketing manager should be an expert on markets—and the nature of competition in markets. The economist's traditional analysis of demand and supply is a useful tool for analyzing markets. In particular, you should master the concepts of a demand curve and demand elasticity. A firm's demand curve shows how the target customers view the firm's product—really, its whole marketing mix. And the interaction of demand and supply curves helps set the size of a market—and the market price. The interaction of supply and demand also determines the nature of the competitive environment, which has an important effect on strategy planning. These ideas are discussed more fully in the following sections.

PRODUCTS AND MARKETS AS SEEN BY CUSTOMERS AND POTENTIAL CUSTOMERS

Economists provide useful insights

How potential customers (not the firm) see a firm's product (marketing mix) affects how much they are willing to pay for it, where it should be made available, and how eager they are for it—if they want it at all. In other words, their view has a very direct bearing on marketing strategy planning.

Economists have been concerned with market behavior for years. Their analytical tools can be quite helpful in summarizing how customers view products and how markets behave.

Economists see individual customers choosing among alternatives

Economics is sometimes called the dismal science because it says that most customers have a limited income and simply cannot buy everything they want. They must balance their needs and the prices of various products.

Economists usually assume that customers have a fairly definite set of preferences—and that they evaluate alternatives in terms of whether the alternatives will make them feel better (or worse) or in some way improve (or change) their situation.

But what exactly is the nature of a customer's desire for a particular product?

Usually, economists answer this question in terms of the extra utility the customer can obtain by buying more of a particular product—or how much utility would be lost if the customer had less of the product. (Students who wish further discussion of this approach should refer to indifference curve analysis in any standard economics text.)

It is easier to understand the idea of utility if we look at what happens when the price of one of the customer's usual purchases changes.

The law of diminishing demand

Suppose that consumers buy potatoes in 4.5-kilogram (10-pound) bags at the same time they buy other foods such as bread and rice. If the consumers are mainly interested in buying a certain amount of food and the price of the potatoes drops, it seems reasonable to expect that they will switch some of their food money to potatoes and away from some other foods. But if the price of potatoes rises, you expect our consumers to buy fewer potatoes and more of other foods.

The general relationship between price and quantity demanded illustrated by this food example is called the **law of diminishing demand**—which says that if the price of a product is raised, a smaller quantity will be demanded, and if the price of a product is lowered, a greater quantity will be demanded. Experience supports this relationship between prices and total demand in a market, especially for broad product categories or commodities such as potatoes.

Exhibit A–1   Demand Schedule for Potatoes (4.5-kilogram [10-pound] bags)

Point	(1) Price of Potatoes per Bag (P)	(2) Quantity Demanded (bags per month) (Q)	(3) Total Revenue per Month (P × Q = TR)
A	$1.60	8,000,000	$12,800,000
B	1.30	9,000,000	_____
C	1.00	11,000,000	11,000,000
D	0.70	14,000,000	_____
E	0.40	19,000,000	_____

The relationship between price and quantity demanded in a market is what economists call a *demand schedule*. An example is shown in Exhibit A–1. For each row in the table, Column 2 shows the quantity consumers will want (demand) if they have to pay the price given in Column 1. The third column shows that the total revenue (sales) in the potato market is equal to the quantity demanded at a given price times that price. Note that as prices drop, the total *unit* quantity increases, yet the total *revenue* decreases. Fill in the blank lines in the third column and observe the behavior of total revenue—an important number for the marketing manager. We will explain what you should have noticed—and why—a little later.

The demand curve—
usually down-sloping

If your only interest is seeing at which price the company will earn the greatest total revenue, the demand schedule may be adequate. But a demand curve shows more. A **demand curve** is a graph of the relationship between price and quantity demanded in a market—assuming that all other things stay the same. Exhibit A–2 shows the demand curve for potatoes—really, just a plotting of the demand schedule in Exhibit A–1. It shows how many potatoes potential customers will demand at various possible prices. This is a *down-sloping demand curve*.

Most demand curves are down-sloping. This just means that if prices are decreased, the quantity customers demand will increase.

Demand curves always show the price on the vertical axis and the quantity demanded on the horizontal axis. In Exhibit A–2, we have shown the price in dollars. For consistency, we will use dollars in other examples. However, keep in mind that these same ideas hold regardless of what money unit (dollars, yen, francs, pounds, etc.) is used to represent price. Even at this early point, you should keep in mind that markets are not necessarily limited by national boundaries—or by one type of money.

Note that the demand curve only shows how customers will react to various possible prices. In a market, we see only one price at a time—not all of these prices. The curve, however, shows what quantities will be demanded—depending on what price is set.

You probably think that most businesspeople would like to set a price that would result in a large sales revenue. Before discussing this, however, we should consider the demand schedule and curve for another product to get a more complete picture of demand-curve analysis.

Exhibit A–2 Demand Curve for Potatoes (4.5-kilogram [10-pound] bags)

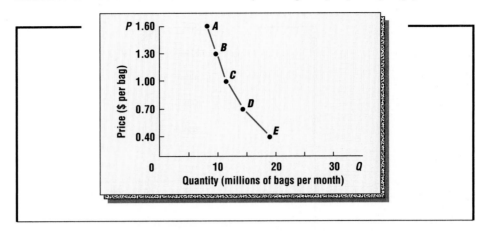

Microwave oven demand curve looks different

A different demand schedule is the one for standard microwave ovens shown in Exhibit A–3. Column (3) shows the total revenue that will be obtained at various possible prices and quantities. Again, as the price goes down, the quantity demanded goes up. But here, unlike the potato example, total revenue increases as prices go down—at least until the price drops to $150.

Every market has a demand curve—for some time period

These general demand relationships are typical for all products. But each product has its own demand schedule and curve in each potential market—no matter how small the market. In other words, a particular demand curve has meaning only for a particular market. We can think of demand curves for individuals, groups of individuals who form a target market, regions, and even countries. And the time period covered really should be specified—although this is often neglected because we usually think of monthly or yearly periods.

The difference between elastic and inelastic

The demand curve for microwave ovens (see Exhibit A–4) is down-sloping—but note that it is flatter than the curve for potatoes. It is important to understand what this flatness means.

Exhibit A–3 Demand Schedule for Microwave Ovens

Point	(1) Price per Microwave Oven (P)	(2) Quantity Demanded per Year (Q)	(3) Total Revenue (TR) per Year (P × Q = TR)
A	$300	20,000	$ 6,000,000
B	250	70,000	15,500,000
C	200	130,000	26,000,000
D	150	210,000	31,500,000
E	100	310,000	31,000,000

Exhibit A–4   Demand Curve for 1-Cubic-Foot Microwave Ovens

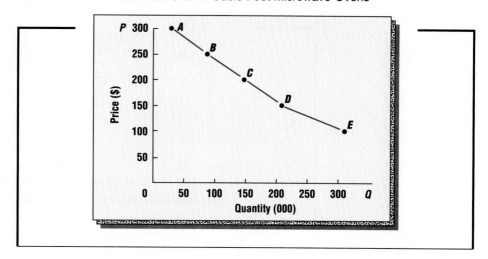

We will consider the flatness in terms of total revenue, since this is what interests business managers.*

When you filled in the total revenue column for potatoes, you should have noticed that total revenue drops continually if the price is reduced. This looks undesirable for sellers—and illustrates inelastic demand. **Inelastic demand** means that although the quantity demanded increases if the price is decreased, the quantity demanded will not "stretch" enough—that is, it is not elastic enough—to avoid a decrease in total revenue.

In contrast, **elastic demand** means that if prices are dropped, the quantity demanded will stretch (increase) enough to increase total revenue. The upper part of the microwave oven demand curve is an example of elastic demand.

But note that if the microwave oven price is dropped from $150 to $100, total revenue will decrease. We can say, therefore, that between $150 and $100, demand is inelastic—that is, total revenue will decrease if price is lowered from $150 to $100.

Thus, elasticity can be defined in terms of changes in total revenue. *If total revenue will increase if price is lowered, then demand is elastic. If total revenue will decrease if price is lowered, then demand is inelastic.* (Note: A special case known as *unitary elasticity of demand* occurs if total revenue stays the same when prices change.)

Total revenue may increase if price is raised

A point often missed in discussions of demand is what happens when prices are raised instead of lowered. With elastic demand, total revenue will *decrease* if the price is *raised*. With inelastic demand, however, total revenue will *increase* if the price is *raised*.

The possibility of raising price and increasing dollar sales (total revenue) at the same time is attractive to managers. This only occurs if the demand curve is

*Strictly speaking, two curves should not be compared for flatness if the graph scales are different, but for our purposes now, we will do so to illustrate the idea of elasticity of demand. Actually, it would be more correct to compare two curves for one product—on the same graph. Then both the shape of the demand curve and its position on the graph would be important.

Exhibit A–5 Changes in Total Revenue as Prices Increase

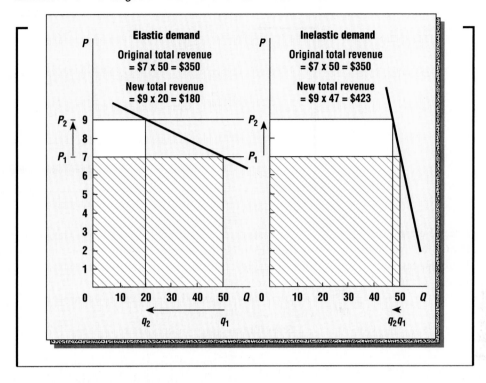

inelastic. Here, total revenue will increase if price is raised, but total costs probably will not increase—and may actually go down—with smaller quantities. Keep in mind that profit is equal to total revenue minus total costs. So—when demand is inelastic, profit will increase as price is increased!

The ways total revenue changes as prices are raised are shown in Exhibit A–5. Here, total revenue is the rectangular area formed by a price and its related quantity. The larger the rectangular area, the greater the total revenue.

P_1 is the original price here, and the total potential revenue with this original price is shown by the area with blue shading. The area with red shading shows the total revenue with the new price, P_2. There is some overlap in the total revenue areas, so the important areas are those with only one color. Note that in the left-hand figure—where demand is elastic—the revenue added (the red-only area) when the price is increased is less than the revenue lost (the blue-only area). Now, let's contrast this to the right-hand figure, when demand is inelastic. Only a small blue revenue area is given up for a much larger (red) one when price is raised.

An entire curve is not elastic or inelastic

It is important to see that it is *wrong to refer to a whole demand curve as elastic or inelastic*. Rather, elasticity for a particular demand curve refers to the change in total revenue between two points on the curve—not along the whole curve. You saw the change from elastic to inelastic in the microwave oven example. Generally, however, nearby points are either elastic or inelastic—so it is common to refer to a whole curve by the degree of elasticity in the price range that normally is of interest—the *relevant range*.

Exhibit A–6   Demand Curve for Hamburger (a product with many substitutes)

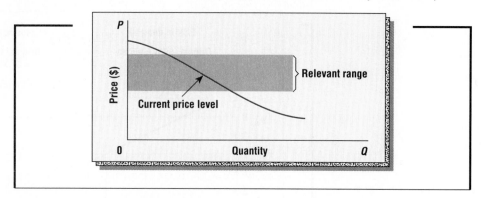

Demand elasticities
affected by availability
of substitutes and
urgency of need

At first, it may be difficult to see why one product has an elastic demand and another an inelastic demand. Many factors affect elasticity—the availability of substitutes, the importance of the item in the customer's budget, and the urgency of the customer's need and its relation to other needs. By looking more closely at one of these factors—the availability of substitutes—you will better understand why demand elasticities vary.

Substitutes are products that offer the buyer a choice. For example, many consumers see grapefruit as a substitute for oranges and hot dogs as a substitute for hamburgers. The greater the number of "good" substitutes available, the greater will be the elasticity of demand. From the consumer's perspective, products are good substitutes if they are very similar (homogeneous). If consumers see products as extremely different—or heterogeneous—then a particular need cannot easily be satisfied by substitutes. And the demand for the most satisfactory product may be quite inelastic.

As an example, if the price of hamburger is lowered (and other prices stay the same), the quantity demanded will increase a lot—as will total revenue. The reason is that not only will regular hamburger users buy more hamburger, but some consumers who formerly bought hot dogs or steaks probably will buy hamburger, too. But if the price of hamburger is raised, the quantity demanded will decrease—perhaps sharply. Still, consumers will buy some hamburger—depending on how much the price has risen, their individual tastes, and what their guests expect (see Exhibit A–6).

In contrast to a product with many substitutes, such as hamburger, consider a product with few or no substitutes. Its demand curve will tend to be inelastic. Motor oil is a good example. Motor oil is needed to keep cars running. Yet no one person or family uses great quantities of motor oil. So it is not likely that the quantity of motor oil purchased will change much as long as price changes are *within a reasonable range*. Of course, if the price is raised to a staggering figure, many people will buy less oil (change their oil less frequently). If the price is dropped to an extremely low level, manufacturers may buy more—say, as a lower-cost substitute for other chemicals typically used in making plastic (Exhibit A–7). But these extremes are outside the relevant range.

Demand curves are introduced here because the degree of elasticity of demand shows how potential customers feel about a product—and especially whether they see substitutes for the product. But to get a better understanding of markets, we must extend this economic analysis.

Exhibit A–7 Demal Curve for Motor Oil (a product with few substitutes)

- *P*
- Consumers buy less often when price goes above this level
- Price ($)
- Relevant range
- Current price level
- Use instead of other chemicals
- 0
- Quantity
- *Q*

MARKETS AS SEEN BY SUPPLIERS

Customers may want some product—but if suppliers are not willing to supply it, then there is no market. So we'll study the economist's analysis of supply. And then we'll bring supply and demand together for a more complete understanding of markets.

Economists often use the kind of analysis we are discussing here to explain pricing in the marketplace. But that is not our intention. Here, we are interested in how and why markets work, and the interaction of customers and potential suppliers. Later in this appendix we will review how competition affects prices, but our full discussion of how individual firms set prices—or should set prices—will come in Chapters 18 and 19.

Supply curves reflect supplier thinking

Generally speaking, suppliers' costs affect the quantity of products they are willing to offer in a market during any period. In other words, their costs affect their supply schedules and supply curves. While a demand curve shows the quantity of products customers will be willing to buy at various prices, a **supply curve** shows the quantity of products that will be supplied at various possible prices. Eventually, only one quantity will be offered and purchased. So a supply curve is really a hypothetical (what-if) description of what will be offered at various prices. It is, however, a very important curve. Together with a demand curve, it summarizes the attitudes and probable behavior of buyers and sellers about a particular product in a particular market—that is, in a product-market.

Some supply curves are vertical

We usually assume that supply curves tend to slope upward—that is, suppliers will be willing to offer greater quantities at higher prices. If a product's market price is very high, it seems only reasonable that producers will be anxious to produce more of the product, even putting workers on overtime or perhaps hiring more workers to increase the quantity they can offer. Going further, it seems likely that producers of other products will switch their resources (farms, factories, labor, or retail facilities) to the product that is in great demand.

On the other hand, if consumers are only willing to pay a very low price for a particular product, it's reasonable to expect that producers will switch to other products—thus reducing supply. A supply schedule (Exhibit A–8) and a supply curve (Exhibit A–9) for potatoes illustrate these ideas. This supply curve shows how many potatoes would be produced and offered for sale at each possible market price in a given month.

Exhibit A–8   Supply Schedule for Potatoes (4.5-kilogram [10-pound] bags)

Point	Possible Market Price per Bag	Number of Bags Sellers Will Supply per Month at Each Possible Market Price
A	$1.60	17,000,000
B	1.30	14,000,000
C	1.00	11,000,000
D	0.70	8,000,000
E	0.40	3,000,000

Note: This supply curve is for a month, to emphasize that farmers might have some control over when they deliver their potatoes. There would be a different curve for each month.

In the very short run (say, over a few hours, a day, or a week), a supplier may not be able to change the supply at all. In this situation, we would see a vertical supply curve. This situation is often relevant in the market for fresh produce. Fresh strawberries, for example, continue to ripen, and a supplier wants to sell them quickly—preferably at a higher price—but in any case, they must be sold.

If the product is a service, it may not be easy to expand the supply in the short run. Additional barbers or medical doctors are not quickly trained and licensed, and they only have so much time to give each day. Further, the prospect of much higher prices in the near future cannot easily expand the supply of many services. For example, a hit play or an "in" restaurant or nightclub is limited in the amount of "product" it can offer at a particular time.

Elasticity of supply

The term *elasticity* also is used to describe supply curves. An extremely steep or almost vertical supply curve, often found in the short run, is called **inelastic supply** because the quantity supplied does not stretch much (if at all) if the price is raised. A flatter curve is called **elastic supply** because the quantity supplied does stretch more if the price is raised. A slightly up-sloping supply curve is typical in

Exhibit A–9   Supply Curve for Potatoes (4.5-kilogram [10-pound] bags)

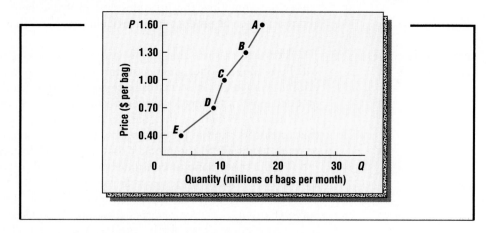

longer-run market situations. Given more time, suppliers have a chance to adjust their offerings, and competitors may enter or leave the market.

DEMAND AND SUPPLY INTERACT TO DETERMINE THE SIZE OF THE MARKET AND PRICE LEVEL

We have treated market demand and supply forces separately. Now we must bring them together to show their interaction. The *intersection* of these two forces determines the size of the market and the market price—at which point (price and quantity) the market is said to be in *equilibrium*.

The intersection of demand and supply is shown for the potato data discussed above. In Exhibit A–10, the demand curve for potatoes is now graphed against the supply curve in Exhibit A–9.

In this potato market, demand is inelastic—the total revenue of all the potato producers would be greater at higher prices. But the market price is at the **equilibrium point**—where the quantity and the price sellers are willing to offer are equal to the quantity and price that buyers are willing to accept. The $1 equilibrium price for potatoes yields a smaller *total revenue* to potato producers than a higher price would. This lower equilibrium price comes about because the many producers are willing to supply enough potatoes at the lower price. *Demand is not the only determiner of price level. Cost also must be considered—via the supply curve.*

Some consumers
get a surplus

Presumably, a sale takes place only if both buyer and seller feel they will be better off after the sale. But sometimes the price a consumer pays in a sales transaction is less than what he or she would be willing to pay.

The reason for this is that demand curves are typically down-sloping, and some of the demand curve is above the equilibrium price. This is simply another way of showing that some customers would have been willing to pay more than the equilibrium price—if they had to. In effect, some of them are getting a bargain

Exhibit A–10   Equilibrium of Supply and Demand for Potatoes
(4.5-kilogram [10-pound] bags)

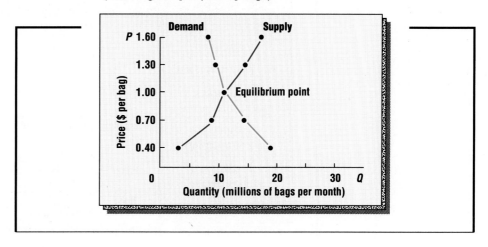

by being able to buy at the equilibrium price. Economists have traditionally called these bargains the **consumer surplus**—that is, the difference to consumers between the value of a purchase and the price they pay.

Some business critics assume that consumers do badly in any business transaction. In fact, sales take place only if consumers feel they are at least getting their money's worth. As we can see here, some are willing to pay much more than the market price.

DEMAND AND SUPPLY HELP US UNDERSTAND THE NATURE OF COMPETITION

The elasticity of demand and supply curves—and their interaction—helps predict the nature of competition a marketing manager is likely to face. For example, an extremely inelastic demand curve means that the manager will have much choice in strategy planning and especially price setting. Apparently, customers like the product and see few substitutes. They are willing to pay higher prices before cutting back much on their purchases.

Clearly, the elasticity of a firm's demand curves makes a big difference in strategy planning, but other factors also affect the nature of competition. Among these are the number and size of competitors and the uniqueness of each firm's marketing mix. Understanding these market situations is important because the freedom of a marketing manager, especially concerning control over price, is greatly reduced in some situations.

A marketing manager operates in one of four kinds of market situations. We'll discuss three kinds: pure competition, oligopoly, and monopolistic competition. The fourth kind, monopoly, isn't found very often and is like monopolistic competition. The important dimensions of these situations are shown in Exhibit A–11.

Exhibit A–11   Some Important Dimensions Regarding Market Situations

Important dimensions	Types of situations			
	Pure competition	Oligopoly	Monopolistic competition	Monopoly
Uniqueness of each firm's product	None	None	Some	Unique
Number of competitors	Many	Few	Few to many	None
Size of competitors (compared to size of market)	Small	Large	Large to small	None
Elasticity of demand facing firm	Completely elastic	Kinked demand curve (elastic and inelastic)	Either	Either
Elasticity of industry demand	Either	Inelastic	Either	Either
Control of price by firm	None	Some (with care)	Some	Complete

When competition
is pure

Many competitors offer about the same thing

Pure competition is a market situation that develops when a market has:

1. Homogeneous (similar) products.
2. Many buyers and sellers who have full knowledge of the market.
3. Ease of entry for buyers and sellers—that is, new firms have little
difficulty starting in business, and new customers can easily come into
the market.

More or less pure competition is found in many agricultural markets. In the
potato market, for example, there are thousands of small producers, and they are
in pure competition. Let's look more closely at these producers.

Although the potato market as a whole has a down-sloping demand curve, each
of the many small producers in the industry is in pure competition, and each of them
faces a flat demand curve at the equilibrium price. This is shown in Exhibit A–12.

As shown at the right of Exhibit A–12, an individual producer can sell as
many bags of potatoes as he or she chooses at $1, the market equilibrium price.
The equilibrium price is determined by the quantity that all producers choose to
sell, given the demand curve they face.

But a small producer has little effect on overall supply (or on the equilibrium
price). If this individual farmer raises 1/10,000th of the quantity offered in the
market, for example, you can see that there will be little effect if the farmer goes
out of business—or doubles production.

The reason an individual producer's demand curve is flat is that the farmer
probably couldn't sell any potatoes above the market price. And there is no point
in selling below the market price! So, in effect, the individual producer has no
control over price.

Markets tend to become
more competitive

Not many markets are *purely* competitive. But many are close enough so we
can talk about "almost" pure competition situations—those in which the
marketing manager has to accept the going price.

Exhibit A–12   Interaction of Demand and Supply in the Potato Industry and the Resulting Demand Curve Facing
Individual Potato Producers

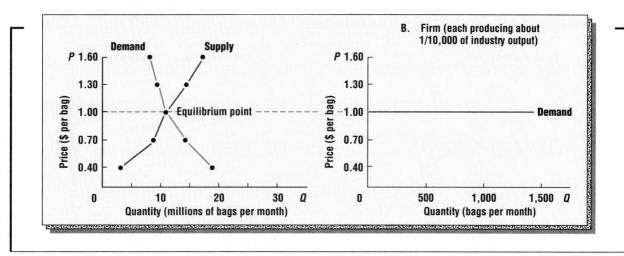

Such highly competitive situations aren't limited to agriculture. Wherever *many* competitors sell *homogeneous* products—such as textiles, lumber, coal, printing, and laundry services—the demand curve seen by *each producer* tends to be flat.

Markets tend to become more competitive, moving toward pure competition (except in oligopolies—see below). On the way to pure competition, prices and profits are pushed down until some competitors are forced out of business. Eventually, in long-run equilibrium, the price level is only high enough to keep the survivors in business. No one makes any profit—they just cover costs. It's tough to be a marketing manager in this situation!

When competition is oligopolistic

A few competitors offer similar things

Not all markets move toward pure competition. Some become oligopolies.

Oligopoly situations are special market situations that develop when a market has:

1. Essentially homogeneous products, such as basic industrial chemicals or gasoline.
2. Relatively few sellers, or a few large firms and many smaller ones who follow the lead of the larger ones.
3. Fairly inelastic industry demand curves.

The demand curve facing each firm is unusual in an oligopoly situation. Although the industry demand curve is inelastic throughout the relevant range, the demand curve facing each competitor looks "kinked." See Exhibit A–13. The current market price is at the kink.

There is a market price because the competing firms watch each other carefully and know it's wise to be at the kink. Each firm must expect that raising its own price above the market price will cause a big loss in sales. Few, if any, competitors will follow the price increase. So the firm's demand curve is relatively flat above the market price. If the firm lowers its price, it must expect competitors to follow. Given inelastic industry demand, the firm's own demand curve is inelastic at lower prices—assuming it keeps "its share" of this market at lower

Exhibit A–13   Oligopoly—Kinked Demand Curve—Situation

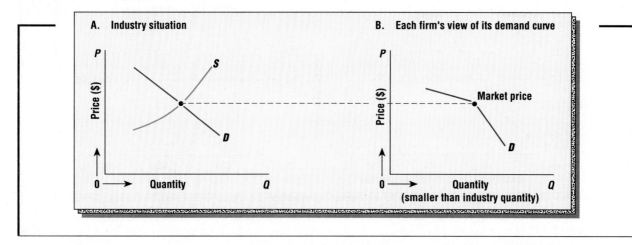

prices. Since lowering prices along such a curve will drop total revenue, the firm should leave its price at the kink, the market price.

Actually, however, there are price fluctuations in oligopolistic markets. Sometimes this is caused by firms that don't understand the market situation and cut their prices to get business. In other cases, big increases in demand or supply change the basic nature of the situation and lead to price-cutting. Price cuts can be drastic, such as Du Pont's price cut of 25 percent for Dacron. This happened when Du Pont decided that industry production capacity already exceeded demand, and more plants were due to start production.

It's important to keep in mind that oligopoly situations don't just apply to whole industries and national markets. Competitors who are focusing on the same local target market often face oligopoly situations. A suburban community might have several gas stations, all of which provide essentially the same product. In this case, the "industry" consists of the gas stations competing with each other in the local product-market.

As in pure competition, oligopolists face a long-run trend toward an equilibrium level, with profits driven toward zero. This may not happen immediately, and a marketing manager may try to delay price competition by relying more on other elements in the marketing mix.

When competition is monopolistic

A price must be set

You can see why marketing managers want to avoid pure competition or oligopoly situations. They prefer a market in which they have more control. **Monopolistic competition** is a market situation that develops when a market has:

1. Different (heterogeneous) products—in the eyes of some customers.
2. Sellers who feel they do have some competition in this market.

The word *monopolistic* means that each firm is trying to get control in its own little market. But the word *competition* means that there are still substitutes. The vigorous competition of a purely competitive market is reduced. Each firm has its own down-sloping demand curve. But the shape of the curve depends on the similarity of competitors' products and marketing mixes. Each monopolistic competitor has freedom—but not complete freedom—in its own market.

Judging elasticity will help set the price

Since a firm in monopolistic competition has its own down-sloping demand curve, it must make a decision about price level as part of its marketing strategy planning. Here, estimating the elasticity of the firm's own demand curve is helpful. If it is highly inelastic, the firm may decide to raise prices to increase total revenue. But if demand is highly elastic, this may mean many competitors with acceptable substitutes. Then the price may have to be set near that of the competition. And the marketing manager probably should try to develop a better marketing mix.

CONCLUSION

The economist's traditional demand and supply analysis provides a useful tool for analyzing the nature of demand and competition. It is especially important that you master the concepts of a demand curve and demand elasticity. How demand and supply interact helps determine the size of a market—

and its price level. The interaction of supply and demand also helps explain the nature of competition in different market situations. We discuss three competitive situations: pure competition, oligopoly, and monopolistic competition. The fourth kind, monopoly, isn't found very often and is like monopolistic competition.

The nature of supply and demand—and competition—is very important in marketing strategy planning. We will return to these topics in Chapters 3 and 4, and then build on them throughout the text. So careful study of this appendix will build a good foundation for later work.

QUESTIONS AND PROBLEMS

1. Explain in your own words how economists look at markets and arrive at the law of diminishing demand.

2. Explain what a demand curve is and why it is usually down-sloping. Then, give an example of a product for which the demand curve might not be down-sloping over some possible price ranges. Explain the reason for your choice.

3. What is the length of life of the typical demand curve? Illustrate your answer.

4. If the general market demand for men's shoes is fairly elastic, how does the demand for men's dress shoes compare to it? How does the demand curve for women's shoes compare to the demand curve for men's shoes?

5. If the demand for perfume is inelastic above and below the present price, should the price be raised? Why or why not?

6. If the demand for shrimp is highly elastic below the present price, should the price be lowered?

7. Discuss what factors lead to inelastic demand and supply curves. Are they likely to be found together in the same situation?

8. Why would a marketing manager prefer to sell a product that has no close substitutes? Are high profits almost guaranteed?

9. If a manufacturer's well-known product is sold at the same price by many retailers in the same community, is this an example of pure competition? When a community has many small grocery stores, are they in pure competition? What characteristics are needed to have a purely competitive market?

10. List three products that are sold in purely competitive markets and three that are sold in monopolistically competitive markets. Do any of these products have anything in common? Can any generalizations be made about competitive situations and marketing mix planning?

11. Cite a local example of an oligopoly, explaining why it is an oligopoly.

Finding Target Market Opportunities with Market Segmentation

When You Finish This Chapter, You Should

❶

Understand how to find marketing opportunities.

❷

Know about the different kinds of marketing opportunities.

❸

Understand why opportunities in international markets should be considered.

❹

Know about defining generic markets and product-markets.

❺

Know what market segmentation is and how to segment product-markets into submarkets.

❻

Know three approaches to market-oriented strategy planning.

❼

Know dimensions that may be useful for segmenting markets.

❽

Know what perceptual mapping is—and why it is useful.

❾

Understand the important new terms (shown in blue).

B C Transit has identified two ways to increase ridership in its target market—maintain a highly satisfied customer base with few customer dropouts or develop new ridership among the nonuser segment. In order to accomplish this, it is important to know who your customers are.

B C Transit set out to identify its target market by using the nature and purpose of the trip and demographic data to segment the market into identifiable groups. They were able to identify nine segments.

1. *Educational/school-based trips*—this applies to three groups: ages 5–17, who require transit service to public schools; ages 14–18, who require service to school and who will use transit for other purposes; and those requiring transit to postsecondary institutions.

2. *Commuter/work-based trips*—this segment consists of the urban- and suburban-based commuters who require service from 6:30 AM to 9:00 AM and from 4:00 PM to 6:00 PM.

3. *Seniors*—ages 65+. This segment is considered to be the fastest growing segment, with a large demand for convenient service.

4. *Accessible*—this encompasses the disabled community, who need specialized service.

5. *Tourist*—the Lower Mainland is a growing tourist destination. As a result, there is considerable demand for transit service to tourist attractions and destinations. This demand is fairly constant, but fluctuates on a seasonal basis.

6. *Sport/special event*—transit needs for the large crowds that occur throughout the year.

7. *Shoppers*—this segment requires service generally during midday to and from the major shopping/urban centers.

8. *Leisure/recreation*—this is the largest of the segments, and it generates the greatest number of trips on any identified day. Routing and frequency demands vary considerably, but service is generally required during the midday and afternoon and evening periods.

9. *Medical/dental/banking*—demand for service is generally heaviest during midday for this segment, and service is usually to the urban centres.

WHAT ARE ATTRACTIVE OPPORTUNITIES?

This book focuses primarily on marketing strategy planning—an important part of which is finding attractive target markets. But how do you identify a target market and decide if it offers good opportunities? Why would a company like B.C. Transit need to identify exactly who takes transit and group these people together into clearly identified groups?

In this chapter and the next, you will learn how to find possible market opportunities and choose the ones to turn into strategies and plans. We will look first at how to identify attractive target markets. Exhibit 3–1 overviews the key topics we will be considering.

We will evaluate possible opportunities against various screening criteria. We will be covering screening criteria in more detail in the next chapter. For now, however, you should see in Exhibit 3–1 that these criteria grow out of analysis of the company's resources, trends in the external environments the firm faces, and the objectives of top management.

Attractive opportunities for a particular firm are those that the firm has some chance of doing something about—given its resources and objectives. Marketing strategy planning tries to match opportunities to the firm's resources (what it can do) and its objectives (what it wants to do).

Exhibit 3–1   Finding and Evaluating Marketing Opportunities

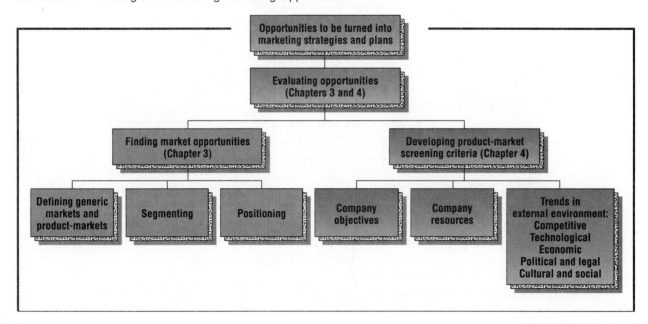

How many opportunities a firm "sees" depends on the thinking of top management and the objectives of the firm. Some want to be innovators and eagerly search out new opportunities. Others are willing to be creative imitators or risk-avoiding "me too" marketers.

Breakthrough opportunities are best

Throughout this book, we will emphasize finding **breakthrough opportunities**—opportunities that help innovators develop hard-to-copy marketing strategies that will be very profitable for a long time. Finding breakthrough opportunities is important because imitators are always waiting to "share" the profits—if they can.

Competitive advantage is needed—at least

Even if a firm can't find a breakthrough opportunity, it should try to obtain a competitive advantage to increase its chances for profit or survival. **Competitive advantage** means that a firm has a marketing mix that the target market sees as better than a competitor's mix. A competitive advantage may result from efforts in different areas of the firm—cost-cutting in production, innovative R&D, more effective purchasing of needed components, or financing for a new distribution facility. Whatever the source, an advantage only succeeds if it allows the firm to satisfy customers better than some competitor.

Sometimes a firm can achieve breakthrough opportunities and competitive advantage by simply fine-tuning its marketing mix(es). Sometimes it may need

Attractive opportunities are often fairly close to markets the firm already knows.

new facilities, new people in new parts of the world, and totally new ways of solving problems. But every firm needs some competitive advantage—so the promotion people have something unique to sell and success doesn't hinge on offering lower and lower prices.[1]

TYPES OF OPPORTUNITIES TO PURSUE

Most people have unsatisfied needs—and alert marketers who see these needs find opportunities all around them. Unfortunately, some opportunities seem obvious only after someone else identifies them. Marketers need a framework for thinking about the kinds of opportunities they may find. Exhibit 3–2 shows the four broad possibilities: market penetration, market development, product development, and diversification. We will look at these separately, but some firms may pursue more than one type of opportunity at the same time.

Market penetration

Market penetration means trying to increase sales of a firm's present products in its present markets, probably through a more aggressive marketing mix. The firm may try to increase customers' rate of use or attract competitors' customers or current nonusers. For example, Visa increased advertising to encourage customers to use its credit card when they travel and to switch from using American Express.

New promotion appeals alone may not be effective. A firm may need to add more stores in present areas for greater convenience. Short-term price cuts or coupon offers may help. But remember, any firm that cuts prices can expect immediate response from its competitors.

Obviously, to do effective analysis and planning, marketers need to understand why some people are buying now and what will motivate them to change brands, buy more, or begin or resume buying.

Market development

Market development means trying to increase sales by selling present products in new markets. Firms may try advertising in different media to reach new target customers. Or they may add channels of distribution or new stores in new areas, including overseas. For example, to reach new customers, McDonald's opens outlets in airports, office buildings, zoos, casinos, hospitals, and military bases. And it's rapidly expanding into international markets with outlets in places like Russia, Brazil, Hong Kong, Mexico, and Australia. Marketing Demo 3–1 describes how one Canadian firm—Moosehead Breweries—is developing markets outside of the Maritimes.

Exhibit 3–2   Four Basic Types of Opportunities

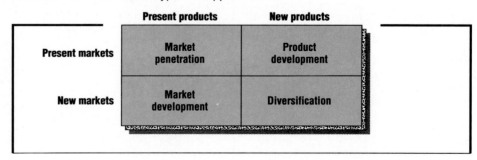

Market development may also involve searching for new uses for a product, as when Lipton provides recipes showing how to use its dry soup mixes for chip dip.

Product development

Product development means offering new or improved products for present markets. By knowing the present market's needs, a firm may see ways to add or modify product features, create several quality levels, or add more types or sizes to better satisfy customers. Computer software firms like Microsoft boost sales by introducing new versions of popular programs. Microsoft also develops other types of new products for its customers. It now sells computer books (some in the new CD-ROM format) and even computer hardware.

Diversification

Diversification means moving into totally different lines of business—perhaps entirely unfamiliar products, markets, or even levels in the production-marketing system. Until recently, Japan's Sony produced electronic equipment. With its purchase of US-based CBS records, Sony expanded into producing music, and in 1989 purchased Columbia Pictures for $5 billion.

MARKETING DEMO 3–1
Family–Run Moosehead Is Successfully Going Global

O ver a lunch of grilled sole and Chablis, Derek Oland is proudly low key as he describes the push of his family's Moosehead Breweries into global markets as "kind of exciting." Earlier, he had to order a glass of Lowenbrau in the dining room of London's Connaught Hotel rather than his favorite Moosehead Canadian Lager. However, the Maritime-brewed beer will be widely available shortly through-out Britain under a marketing and distribution agree-ment with Bass Brewers Ltd. Sales will be aimed at younger, upmarket drinkers, and the first-year target is 200,000 cases. Moosehead also will soon be on sale in Sweden through Systembolaget, the state-owned liquor store system. It will be the first imported Canadian beer listed there.

As trade barriers loosen up, the launch into Europe by Canada's oldest and last major indepen-dent brewery is part of an aggressive program to compete worldwide in the dynamic premium pack-aged lager segment—PPLs, as the imports are known in the trade here. The PPLs are the fastest-growing segment of the deregulated British beer mar-ket. About 300 import brands are now available, and the PPLs take 10 percent of all beer sales.

Moosehead's success is an outstanding example of how Canadian firms with a commitment to quality can make a go of it in global markets. With annual revenue of $130 million, the company now exports about 40 percent of its output. Its "export" push also includes the rest of Canada, which may as well be considered a foreign market because the provinces have long been notorious for interprovincial beer barriers.

Oland believes Moosehead's unique selling point is its provenance. "Where it comes from gives it tremendous credibility and the fact that as a family we have been brewing for so many years." Susannah Oland, Derek's great-great-grandmother, started it all in 1867 by brewing beer in her backyard from family recipes. While Oland admits succession for family firms can be difficult, he clearly wants to take Moose-head into the next century still in the family.

Source: Neville Nankivell, "Family-Run Moosehead Is Successfully Going Global," *The Financial Post*, March 17, 1993, p. 13.

Diversification presents the most challenging opportunities. Diversification involves both new products and new markets. The further the opportunity is from what the firm is already doing, the more attractive it may look to the optimists—and the harder it will be to evaluate. Opportunities very different from a firm's current experiences involve higher risks.

Which opportunities come first?

Usually, firms find attractive opportunities fairly close to markets they already know. This may allow them to capitalize on changes in their present markets or more basic changes in the external environment.

Most firms think first of greater market penetration. They want to increase profits where they already have experience and strengths. Marketers who understand their present markets well may also see opportunities in product development, especially because they already have a way to reach their present customers. But a firm that already has as big a share as it can get in its present markets should consider market development—finding new markets for its present products—including expanding regionally, nationally, or internationally.[2]

INTERNATIONAL OPPORTUNITIES SHOULD BE CONSIDERED

It's easy for a marketing manager to fall into the trap of forgetting about international markets, especially when the firm's domestic market is prosperous. Why go to the trouble of looking elsewhere for opportunities?

The world is getting smaller

Advances in communications and transportation are making it easier and cheaper for even small firms to reach international customers. And national boundaries no longer limit market opportunities. Around the world, potential customers have needs and money to spend. Ignoring these customers doesn't make any more sense than ignoring potential customers in the same town. The real question is whether a firm can effectively use its resources to meet these customers' needs at a profit.

Many firms find attractive opportunities in foreign markets.

Develop a competitive advantage at home and abroad

If customers in other countries are interested in the products a firm offers—or could offer—serving them may result in even more economies of scale. Lower costs (and prices) may give a firm a competitive advantage both in its home markets *and* abroad. This sort of competitive pressure may actually *force* a marketing manager to expand into international markets. Marketing managers who are only interested in the "convenient" customers in their own backyards may be rudely surprised to find that an aggressive, low-cost foreign producer is willing to pursue those customers—even if doing so is not convenient. Many companies that thought they could avoid the struggles of international competition have learned this lesson the hard way.

Get an early start in a new market

A marketing manager looking for development opportunities in international markets often finds them. Different countries are at different stages of economic and technological development, and their consumers have different needs at different times. For example, prior to the unification of Germany, appliance producers in East Germany found their best market opportunities in other countries, where consumers had more money.

A company facing tough competition, thin profit margins, and slow sales growth at home may get a fresh start in another country where demand for its product is just beginning to grow. A marketing manager may be able to "transfer" marketing know-how—or some other competitive advantage—the firm has already developed. Marketing Demo 3–2 shows that Ganong Brothers, a candy maker in New Brunswick, was able to do just that.

MARKETING DEMO 3–2
Ganong Tastes Oriental Success

Ganong Brothers, the 118-year-old candy maker based in St. Stephen, New Brunswick, discovered how profitable foreign markets could be when it began to develop markets in Japan for its chocolates. Candy has not always been a popular item in Japan, but the Japanese do believe in giving gifts. Ganong has been able to tap into that tradition. Japanese custom dictates that while on holiday, a traveler should give a small gift to a very long list of people. Ganong takes the orders from tourists and then ships the candy to Japan so that the travelers do not have to worry about lugging the chocolates themselves. By capitalizing on this Japanese tourist trade, Ganong is entering the Pacific Rim in a big way.

In identifying this market segment, Ganong has been able to sell its premium boxed chocolates successfully in Japan. Export sales in 1990 were 300 percent of what they were in 1989, and that was double the export sales in 1988. In 1990, Ganong shipped nearly half a million boxes of chocolates to Japan. These exports accounted for 8 percent of its sales.

The development of a market in Japan was a positive experience for Ganong, allowing it to gradually learn about the Japanese market and some of the more complex tastes that Japanese people have. The biggest surprise for the company was that the slow, traditional way of doing business on the east coast of Canada was not all that different from doing business in Japan. Ganong admits that many Canadian companies are afraid to move into the Pacific Rim but advises them to consider it. Companies are often afraid of Asian or other distant markets because they have no experience in those markets. By being patient and honest, and taking time to learn and build relationships, Ganong found that opportunities may even be somewhat easier to take advantage of in Japan than in the United States.

Source: Sandra Porteus, "Ganong's Success," *Marketing*, September 9, 1991, p. 15.

Unfavorable trends in the marketing environment at home or favorable trends in other countries may make international marketing particularly attractive. For example, population growth in Canada has slowed and income is leveling off. In other places in the world, population and income are increasing rapidly. Marketing managers for Canadian firms can no longer rely on the constant market growth that drove increased domestic sales during the last 30 years. For many firms, growth—and perhaps even survival—will come only by aiming at more distant customers.

Our point is basic. In today's world, it doesn't make sense for Canadian managers to ignore international markets and casually assume that all of the best opportunities exist at home.

SEARCH FOR OPPORTUNITIES CAN BEGIN BY UNDERSTANDING MARKETS

Breakthrough opportunities from understanding target markets

When marketing managers really understand their target markets, they may see breakthrough opportunities. But a target market's real needs, and the breakthrough opportunities that can come from identifying and serving those needs, are not always obvious. So let's look at some ways to better understand a company's target markets.

What is a company's market?

Identifying a company's market is an important but sticky issue. In general, a **market** is a group of potential customers with similar needs who are willing to exchange something of value with sellers offering various goods and/or services— that is, ways of satisfying those needs.

Market-oriented managers develop marketing mixes for *specific* target markets. Getting the firm to focus on specific target markets is vital. As shown in Exhibit 3–3, target marketing requires a narrowing-down process to get beyond production-oriented mass market thinking. But firms often misunderstand this narrowing-down process.

Don't just focus on the product

Some production-oriented managers ignore the tough part of defining markets. To make the narrowing-down process easier, they just describe their markets in terms of *products* they sell. For example, producers and retailers of greeting cards might define their market as the "greeting card" market. But this production-oriented approach ignores customers—and customers make a market! This also leads to missed opportunities. Hallmark isn't missing these opportunities. Instead, Hallmark aims at the "personal expression" market. It offers all kinds of products that can be sent as "memory makers"—to express one person's feelings toward another. Hallmark has expanded far beyond holiday and birthday cards, the major greeting card days, to jewelry, gift wrap, plaques, candles, and puzzles, as well as to all-occasion and humorous cards.[3]

From generic markets to product-markets

It's useful to think of two basic types of markets. A **generic market** is a market with *broadly* similar needs and sellers offering various—*often diverse*—ways of satisfying those needs. In contrast, a **product-market** is a market with *very* similar needs and sellers offering various *close substitute* ways of satisfying those needs.[4]

A generic market description looks at markets broadly and from a customer's viewpoint. Status seekers, for example, have several very different ways to satisfy status needs. A status seeker might buy a new Mercedes, a deluxe tour, or fashions from a French designer. Any one of these *very different* products may satisfy this status need. Sellers in this generic status-seeker market have to focus on the

Exhibit 3–3   Narrowing Down to Target Markets

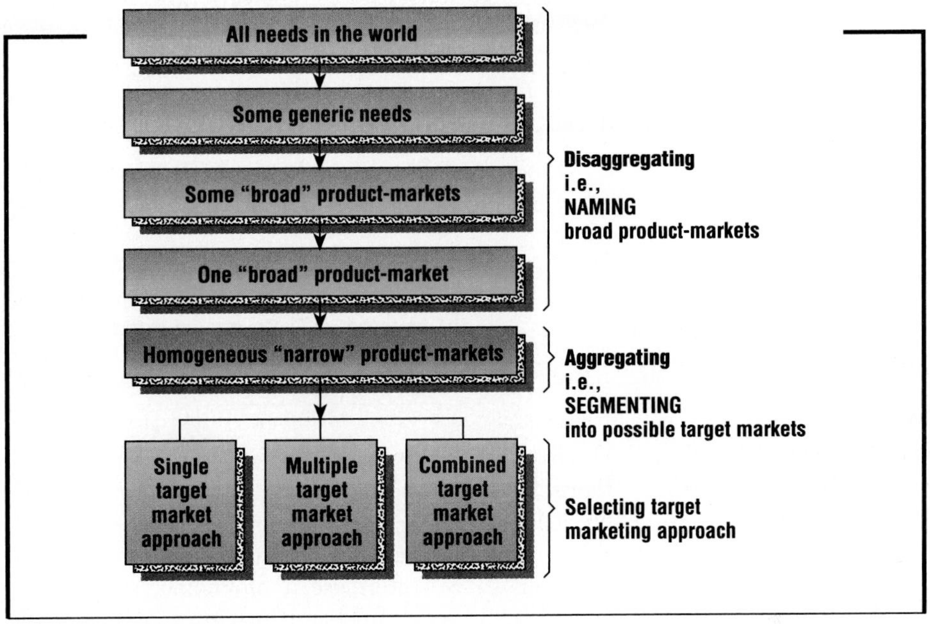

need(s) the customers want satisfied—not on how one seller's product (car, vacation, or designer label) is better than that of another producer.

It is sometimes hard to understand and define generic markets because *quite different product types may compete with each other*. But if customers see all these products as substitutes—as competitors in the same generic market—then marketers must deal with this complication.

Suppose, however, that one of our status seekers decides to satisfy this status need with a new, expensive car. Then, in this product-market, Mercedes, Cadillac, and Lexus may compete with each other for the status-seeker's dollars. In this *product*-market concerned with cars *and* status (not just transportation!), consumers compare similar products to satisfy their status need.

Most companies quickly narrow their focus to product-markets because of the firm's past experience, resources, or management preferences. And we will usually be thinking of product-markets when we refer to markets. But when looking for opportunities, a marketing manager should consider a broader generic market view.

Broaden market definitions to find opportunities

Broader market definitions, including both generic market definitions and product-market definitions, can help firms find opportunities. But deciding *how* broad to go isn't easy. Too narrow a definition will limit a firm's opportunities, but too broad a definition makes the company's efforts and resources seem insignificant.

Our strategy planning process helps define relevant markets. Here, we try to match opportunities to a firm's resources and objectives. So the *relevant market for finding opportunities* should be bigger than the firm's present product-market—but not so big that the firm couldn't expand and be an important competitor. A small manufacturer of screwdrivers in Canada, for example, shouldn't define its market as broadly as "the worldwide tool users market" or as narrowly as "our present screwdriver customers." But it may have the production and/or marketing potential to consider "the handyman's hand-tool market in North America." Carefully naming your product-market can help you see possible opportunities.

NAMING PRODUCT–MARKETS AND GENERIC MARKETS

Product-related terms do not, by themselves, adequately describe a market. A complete product-market definition includes a four-part description.

What:	1. Product type (type of product and type of service).
To meet what:	2. Customer (user) needs.
For whom:	3. Customer types.
Where:	4. Geographic area.

In other words, a product-market description must include customer-related terms, not just product-related terms. We refer to these four-part descriptions as product-market "names" because most managers label their markets when they think, write, or talk about them. Such a four-part definition can be clumsy, however, so we often use a nickname, such as "golden oldies" for well-to-do Canadian retirees interested in winter cruises—as long as everyone understands the underlying four-part terms. And the nickname should refer to people—not products—because, as we emphasize, people make markets!

Product type should meet customer needs

Product type describes the goods and/or services that customers want. Sometimes, the product type is strictly a physical good or strictly a service. But marketing managers who ignore the possibility that *both* are important can miss opportunities. For example, a marketing manager at a videocassette firm may think carefully about all of the benefits customers want from a VCR—but fail to

Sony's new filmless camera may compete in the same broad product-market as Yashica's 35-mm autofocus camera but appeal to a different submarket with different needs.

see that many customers would also like a convenient way to ask *a person* a question about how to use it. A toll-free information service might make a big difference in whether customers are satisfied or even buy the product in the first place.

Customer (user) needs refer to the needs the product type satisfies for the customer. At a very basic level, product types usually provide functional benefits such as nourishing, protecting, warming, cooling, transporting, cleaning, holding, saving time, and so forth. Although we need to identify such basic needs first, in advanced economies, we must go beyond basic needs to emotional needs—such as needs for fun, excitement, pleasing appearance, or status. Correctly defining the need(s) relevant to a market is crucial and requires a good understanding of customers. We discuss these topics more fully in Chapters 7 and 8.

Customer type refers to the final consumer or user of a product type. Here, we want to choose a name that describes all present (possible) types of customers.

To define customer type, marketers should identify the final consumer or user of the product type, rather than the buyer—if they are different. For instance, marketers should avoid treating middlemen as a customer type—unless middlemen actually use the product in their own business.

The *geographic area* is where a firm competes, or plans to compete, for customers. Naming the geographic area may seem trivial, but understanding geographic boundaries of a market can suggest new opportunities. Supermarkets in London, or Los Angeles, or Toronto don't cater to all consumers in these areas—there may be opportunities to serve unsatisfied customers in the same areas. Similarly, a firm aiming only at the Canadian market may want to expand into world markets.

No product type in generic market names

A generic market description *doesn't include any product-type terms*. It consists of only three parts of a product-market definition—without the product type. This emphasizes that any product type that satisfies the customer's needs can compete in this generic market. Recall that in our status-seeker market example, very different product types were competitors. Exhibit 3–4 shows the relationship between generic market and product-market definitions.

Exhibit 3–4   Relationship between Generic and Product-Market Definitions

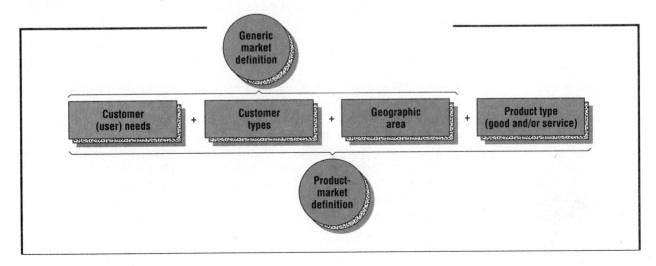

Creativity is needed
in naming markets

By creatively analyzing the needs and attitudes of present and potential target markets—in relation to the benefits offered by a firm and its competitors—you can see new opportunities. Later, we'll study the many possible dimensions of markets. But for now you should see that defining markets only in terms of current products is not the best way to find new opportunities—or plan marketing strategies.

MARKET SEGMENTATION DEFINES POSSIBLE TARGET MARKETS

Market segmentation
is a two-step process

Market segmentation is a two-step process of (1) *naming* broad product-markets and (2) *segmenting* these broad product-markets in order to select target markets and develop suitable marketing mixes.

This two-step process isn't well understood. First-time market segmentation efforts often fail because beginners start with the whole mass market and try to find one or two demographic characteristics to segment this market. Customer behavior is usually too complex to be explained in terms of just one or two demographic characteristics. For example, not all older men—or all young women—buy the same products or brands. Other dimensions usually must be considered, starting with customer needs. Sometimes, many different dimensions are needed to describe the submarkets within a broad product-market.

Naming broad
product-markets
is disaggregating

The first step in effective market segmentation involves naming a broad product-market of interest to the firm. Marketers must break apart—disaggregate—all possible needs into some generic markets and broad product-markets in which the firm may be able to operate profitably. See Exhibit 3–3. No one firm can satisfy everyone's needs. So the naming—disaggregating—step involves brainstorming about very different solutions to various generic needs and selecting some broad areas—broad product-markets—where the firm has some resources and experience. This means that a car manufacturer would probably ignore all the possible opportunities in food and clothing markets and focus on the generic market it might call "transporting people in the world" and probably on the broad product-market "cars and trucks for transporting people in the world."

Disaggregating, a practical, rough-and-ready approach, tries to narrow down the marketing focus to product-market areas where the firm is more likely to have a competitive advantage—or even to find breakthrough opportunities. It looks easy, but disaggregating actually requires a lot of thought and judgment about what the firm may be able to do for some consumers and do better than some or all competitors so it will have a competitive advantage.

Market grid is
a visual aid to
market segmentation

Assuming that any broad product-market (or generic market) may consist of submarkets, picture a market as a rectangle with boxes representing the smaller, more homogeneous product-markets.

Exhibit 3–5, for example, represents the broad product-market of bicycle riders. The boxes show different submarkets. One submarket might focus on people who want basic transportation, another on people who want exercise, and so on. Alternatively, in the generic "transporting market" discussed above, we might see different product-markets of customers for bicycles, motorcycles, cars, airplanes, ships, buses, and others.

Exhibit 3–5   A Market Grid Diagram with Submarkets

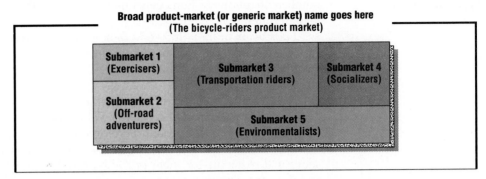

Broad product-market (or generic market) name goes here **(The bicycle-riders product market)**

Submarket 1 (Exercisers)   **Submarket 3 (Transportation riders)**   **Submarket 4 (Socializers)**

Submarket 2 (Off-road adventurers)   **Submarket 5 (Environmentalists)**

Segmenting is an aggregating process

Marketing-oriented managers think of **segmenting** as an aggregating process—clustering people with similar needs into a market segment. A **market segment** is a (relatively) homogeneous group of customers who will respond to a marketing mix in a similar way.

This part of the market segmentation process (see Exhibit 3–3) takes a different approach than the naming part. Here, we look for similarities rather than basic differences in needs. Segmenters start with the idea that each person is one of a kind but that it may be possible to aggregate some similar people into a product-market.

Segmenters see each of these one-of-a-kind people as having a unique set of dimensions. Consider a product-market in which customers' needs differ on two important segmenting dimensions: need for status and need for dependability. In Exhibit 3–6A, each dot shows a person's position on the two dimensions. While each person's position is unique, many people are similar in terms of how much status and dependability they want. So a segmenter may aggregate these people into three (an arbitrary number) relatively homogeneous submarkets—A, B, and C. Group A might be called "status oriented" and Group C "dependability oriented." Members of Group B want both and might be called the "demanders."

Exhibit 3–6   Every Individual Has His or Her Own Unique Position In a Market—Those with Similar Positions Can Be Aggregated into Potential Target Markets

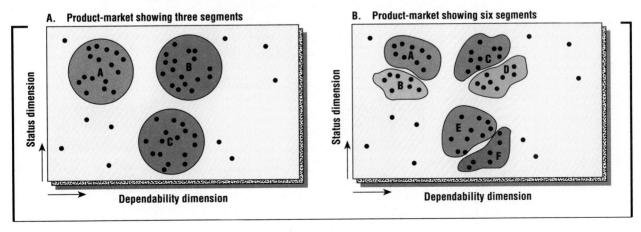

A.   Product-market showing three segments

B.   Product-market showing six segments

How far should the
aggregating go?

The segmenter wants to aggregate individual customers into some workable number of relatively homogeneous target markets—and then treat each target market differently.

Look again at Exhibit 3–6A. Remember, we talked about three segments. But this was an arbitrary number. As Exhibit 3–6B shows, there may really be six segments. What do you think—does this broad product-market consist of three segments or six?

Another difficulty with segmenting is that some potential customers just don't fit neatly into market segments. For example, not everyone in Exhibit 3–6B was put into one of the groups. Forcing them into one of the groups would have made these segments more heterogeneous—and harder to please. Further, forming additional segments for them probably wouldn't be profitable. They are too few and not very similar in terms of the two dimensions. These people are simply too unique to be catered to and may have to be ignored—unless they are willing to pay a high price for special treatment.

The number of segments that should be formed depends more on judgment than on some scientific rule. But the following guidelines can help.

Criteria for segmenting
a broad product-market

Ideally, "good" market segments meet the following criteria (see Exhibit 3–7):

1. *Homogeneous (similar) within*—the customers in a market segment should be as similar as possible with respect to their likely responses to marketing mix variables *and* their segmenting dimensions.

Exhibit 3–7   Criteria for Segmenting

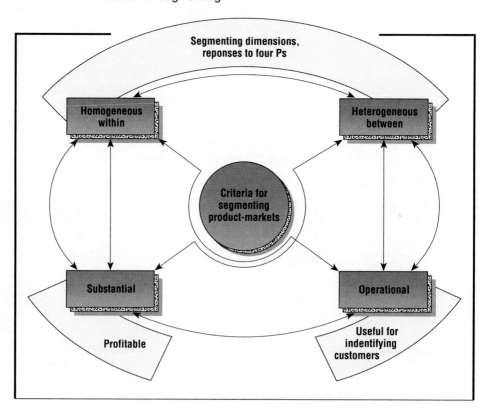

2. *Heterogeneous (different) between*—the customers in different segments should be as different as possible with respect to their likely responses to marketing mix variables *and* their segmenting dimensions.
3. *Substantial*—the segment should be big enough to be profitable.
4. *Operational*—the segmenting dimensions should be useful for identifying customers and deciding on marketing mix variables.

It is especially important that segments be *operational*. This leads marketers to include demographic dimensions such as age, income, location, and family size. Information on these dimensions, usually readily available, can be very useful in determining the size of markets and planning marketing mixes. In fact, it is difficult to make some Place and Promotion decisions without such information.

Avoid segmenting dimensions that have no practical operational use. For example, you may find a personality trait such as moodiness among the traits of heavy buyers of a product, but how could you use this fact? Salespeople can't give a personality test to each buyer. Similarly, advertising media buyers or copywriters couldn't make much use of this information. So although moodiness might be related in some way to previous purchases, it would not be a useful dimension for segmenting.

Target marketers aim at specific targets

Once you accept the idea that broad product-markets may have submarkets, you can see that target marketers usually have a choice among many possible target markets.

There are three basic ways of developing market-oriented strategies in a broad product-market.

1. The **single target market approach**—segmenting the market and picking one of the homogeneous segments as the firm's target market.
2. The **multiple target market approach**—segmenting the market and choosing two or more segments, then treating each as a separate target market needing a different marketing mix.
3. The **combined target market approach**—combining two or more submarkets into one larger target market as a basis for one strategy.

Note that all three approaches involve target marketing. They all aim at specific, clearly defined target markets. See Exhibit 3–8. For convenience, we call people who follow the first two approaches the *segmenters* and the people who use the third approach *combiners*.

Combiners try to satisfy "pretty well"

Combiners try to increase the size of their target markets by combining two or more segments. Combiners look at various submarkets for similarities rather than differences. Then they try to extend or modify their basic offering to appeal to these "combined" customers with just one marketing mix. For example, combiners may try a new package, more service, a new brand, or new flavors. But even if they make product or other marketing mix changes, they don't try to satisfy unique smaller submarkets. Instead, combiners try to improve the general appeal of their marketing mix to appeal to a bigger combined target market.

A combined target market approach may help achieve some economies of scale. It may also require less investment than developing different marketing mixes for different segments, making it especially attractive for firms with limited resources. These potential benefits may be very appealing and make combining seem less risky.

Exhibit 3–8   Target Marketers Have Specific Aims

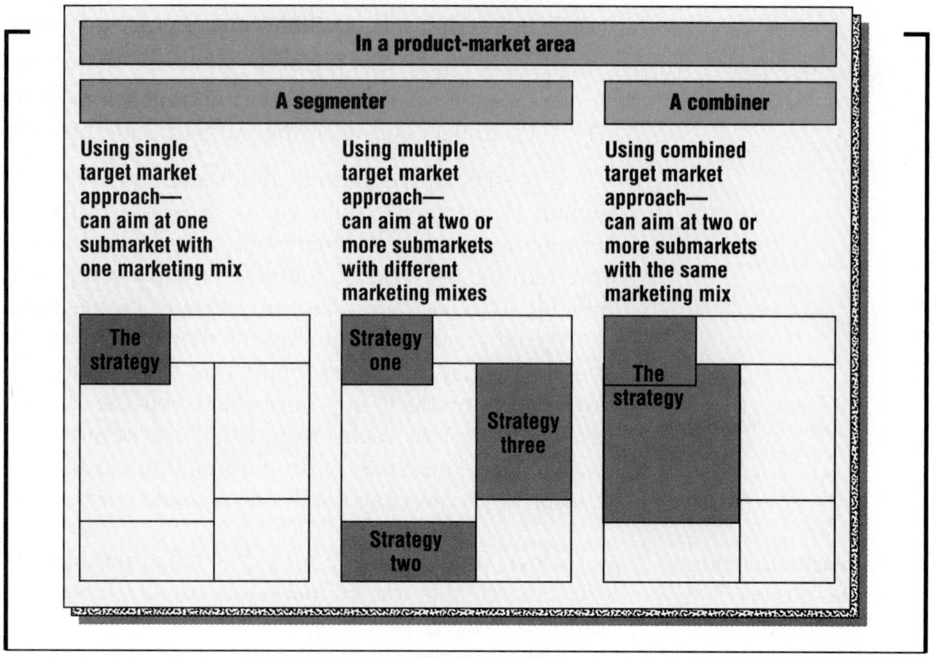

In a product-market area		
A segmenter		**A combiner**
Using single target market approach—can aim at one submarket with one marketing mix	Using multiple target market approach—can aim at two or more submarkets with different marketing mixes	Using combined target market approach—can aim at two or more submarkets with the same marketing mix
The strategy	Strategy one / Strategy three / Strategy two	The strategy

Too much combining is risky

It is tempting to aim at larger combined markets instead of using different marketing mixes for smaller segmented markets. But combiners must be careful not to aggregate too far. As they enlarge the target market, it becomes less homogeneous—and individual differences within each submarket may begin to outweigh the similarities. This makes it harder to develop marketing mixes that can effectively reach and satisfy potential customers within each of the submarkets.

A combiner faces the continual risk of innovative segmenters chipping away at the various segments of the combined target market by offering more attractive marketing mixes to more homogeneous submarkets.

Segmenters try to satisfy "very well"

Segmenters aim at one or more homogeneous segments and try to develop a different marketing mix for each segment. Segmenters usually adjust their marketing mixes for each target market, perhaps making basic changes in the product itself, because they want to satisfy each segment very well.

Instead of assuming that the whole market consists of a fairly similar set of customers (like the mass marketer does) or merging various submarkets together (like the combiner), a segmenter sees submarkets with their own demand curves, as shown in Exhibit 3–9. Segmenters believe that aiming at one—or some—of these smaller markets will satisfy the target customers better and provide greater profit potential for the firm.

Segmenting may produce bigger sales

Note that segmenters are not settling for a smaller sales potential. Instead, they hope to increase sales by getting a much larger share of the business in the market(s) they target. A segmenter who satisfies the target market well enough may have no real competition.

Heinz's multiple target market approach treats consumers and hotels as separate segments needing different marketing mixes.

AFG Industries, a company that manufactures glass, had a small market share when it was trying to sell glass in the construction market. Then AFG's marketing managers focused on the special needs of firms that used tempered and colored glass in their own production. AFG used a multiple target market approach and planned marketing mixes for "niche" segments that didn't get attention from the bigger producers. Because of careful segmenting, AFG now sells 70 percent of the glass for microwave oven doors and 75 percent of the glass for shower enclosures and patio tabletops. AFG also earns the best profit margins in its industry.[5]

Should you segment or combine?

Which approach should a firm use? This depends on the firm's resources, the nature of competition, and—most important—the similarity of customer needs, attitudes, and buying behavior.

Exhibit 3–9   There May Be Different Demand Curves in Different Market Segments

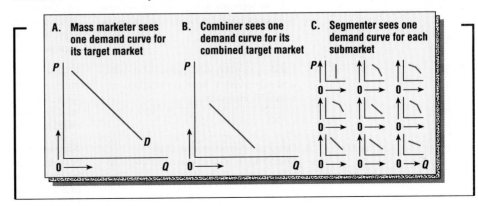

In general, it's usually safer to be a segmenter—that is, to try to satisfy some customers *very* well instead of many just *fairly* well. That's why many firms use the single or multiple target market approach instead of the combined target market approach. Procter & Gamble, for example, offers many products that seem to compete directly with each other (e.g., Tide versus Cheer or Crest versus Gleem). However, P&G offers "tailor-made" marketing mixes to each submarket large— and profitable—enough to deserve a separate marketing mix. Though extremely effective, this approach may not be possible for a smaller firm with more limited resources. A smaller firm may have to use the single target market approach, aiming all its efforts at the one submarket niche where it sees the best opportunity.[6]

Profit is the balancing point

Target marketers develop and implement whole strategies—they don't just segment markets. In practice, cost considerations probably encourage more aggregating, to obtain economies of scale, while demand considerations suggest less aggregating, to satisfy needs more exactly.

Profit is the balancing point. It determines how unique a marketing mix the firm can afford to offer to a particular group.

WHAT DIMENSIONS ARE USED TO SEGMENT MARKETS?

Segmenting dimensions guide marketing mix planning

Market segmentation forces a marketing manager to decide which product-market dimensions might be useful for planning marketing strategies. The dimensions should help guide marketing mix planning. Exhibit 3–10 shows the basic kinds of dimensions we'll be talking about in Chapters 6 through 8—and their probable effect on the four Ps. Ideally, we want to describe any potential product-market in terms of all three types of customer-related dimensions plus a product type description because these dimensions will help us develop better marketing mixes.

Exhibit 3–10   Relation of Potential Target Market Dimensions to Marketing Strategy Decision Areas

Potential Target Market Dimensions	Effects on Strategy Decision Areas
1. Behavioral needs, attitudes, and how present and potential goods and services fit into customers' consumption patterns.	Affects *Product* (features, packaging, product line assortment, branding) and *Promotion* (what potential customers need and want to know about the firm's offering, and what appeals should be used).
2. Urgency to get need satisfied and desire and willingness to seek information, compare, and shop.	Affects *Place* (how directly products are distributed from producer to customer, how extensively they are made available, and the level of service needed) and *Price* (how much potential customers are willing to pay).
3. Geographic location and other demographic characteristics of potential customers.	Affects size of *Target Markets* (economic potential) and *Place* (where products should be made available) and *Promotion* (where and to whom to target advertising and personal selling).

Many segmenting dimensions may be considered

Customers can be described by many specific dimensions. Exhibit 3–11 shows some dimensions useful for segmenting consumer markets. A few are behavioral dimensions, others are geographic and demographic. Exhibit 3–12 shows some additional dimensions for segmenting markets when the customers are businesses, government agencies, or other types of organizations. Regardless of whether customers are final consumers or organizations, segmenting a broad product-market may require using several different dimensions at the same time. Which ones are most important depends on the specific product-market.[7]

With so many possible segmenting dimensions, and knowing that several dimensions may be needed to show what is really important in specific product-markets, how should we proceed?

What are the qualifying and determining dimensions?

To select the important segmenting dimensions, think about two different types of dimensions. **Qualifying dimensions** are those relevant to including a customer type in a product-market. **Determining dimensions** are those that actually affect the customer's purchase of a specific product or brand in a product-market.

A prospective car buyer, for example, has to have enough money—or credit—to buy a car and insure it. Our buyer also needs a driver's license. This still doesn't guarantee a purchase. He or she must have a real need—like a job that requires "wheels" or kids that have to be carpooled. This need may motivate the purchase of *some* car. But these qualifying dimensions don't determine what specific brand or model car the person might buy. That depends on more specific interests—such as the kind of safety, performance, or appearance the customer wants. Determining dimensions related to these needs affects the specific car the customer purchases.

Determining dimensions may be very specific

How specific the determining dimensions are depends on whether you are concerned with a general product type or a specific brand. See Exhibit 3–13. The more specific you want to be, the more particular the determining dimensions may be. In a particular case, the determining dimensions may seem minor. But they are important because they *are* the determining dimensions. In the car status-seekers market, for example, paint colors or brand name may determine which cars people buy.

Qualifying dimensions are important, too

The qualifying dimensions help identify the core features that must be offered to everyone in a product-market. Qualifying and determining dimensions work together in marketing strategy planning.

Different dimensions needed for different submarkets

Note that each different submarket within a broad product-market may be motivated by a different set of dimensions. In the snack food market, for example, health food enthusiasts are interested in nutrition, dieters worry about calories, and economical shoppers with lots of kids may want volume to "fill them up." The related submarkets might be called health-conscious snack food market, dieters' snack food market, and kids' snack food market. They would be in different boxes in a market grid diagram for snack food customers.

? Ethical issues in selecting segmenting dimensions

Marketing managers sometimes face ethical decisions when selecting segmenting dimensions. Problems may arise if a firm targets customers who are somehow at a disadvantage in dealing with the firm or who are unlikely to see the negative effects of their own choices. For example, some people criticize makers of

Exhibit 3–11   Possible Segmenting Dimensions and Typical Breakdowns for Consumer Markets

Dimensions	Typical Breakdowns
Customer-Related	
Geographic	
Region	Atlantic provinces, Quebec, Ontario, Prairie provinces, and British Columbia
City, province, CMA size	Under 5,000; 5,000–19,999; 20,000–49,999; 50,000–99,999; 100,000–249,999; 250,000–499,999; 500,000–999,999; 1,000,000–3,999,999; 4,000,000 or over
Demographic	
Age	Infant; under 6; 6–11; 12–17; 18–24; 25–34; 35–49; 50–64; 65 and over
Sex	Male, female
Family size	1–2, 3–4, 5 +
Family life cycle	Young, single; young, married, no children; young, married, youngest child under 6; young, married, youngest child 6 or over; older, married, with children; older, married, no children under 18; older, single; other
Income	Under $5,000; $5,000–$7,999; $8,000–$9,999; $10,000–$14,999; $15,000–$24,999; $25,000 or over
Occupation	Professional and technical; managers, officials, and proprietors; clerical, sales; craftspeople, foremen; operatives; farmers; retired; students; housewives and househusbands; unemployed
Education	Grade school or less, some high school, high school graduate, some college, college graduate
Religion	Catholic, Protestant, Jewish, other
Race	White, Black, Oriental, other
Nationality	Canadian, British, French, German, etc.
Social class	Lower-lower, upper-lower, lower-middle, upper-middle, lower-upper, upper-upper
Situation-Related	
Benefits Offered	
Need satisfiers	PSSP, economic, and more detailed needs
Product features	Situation-specific, but to satisfy specific or general needs
Consumption or Use Patterns	
Rate of use	Heavy, medium, light, nonusers
Use with other products	Situation-specific (e.g., gas with a traveling vacation)
Brand Familiarity	Insistence, preference, recognition, nonrecognition, rejection
Buying Situation	
Kind of store	Convenience, shopping, specialty
Kind of shopping	Serious versus browsing, rushed versus leisurely
Depth of assortment	Out of stock, shallow, deep
Type of good	Convenience, shopping, specialty, unsought

malt liquor for marketing mixes that appeal to inner-city youths, especially those below the drinking age. Others pinpoint shoe companies for targeting poor, inner-city kids who see expensive athletic shoes as an important status symbol. Many firms, including producers of infant formula, have been criticized for targeting consumers in less-develped nations. Encyclopedia publishers have been

Exhibit 3–12 Possible Segmenting Dimensions for Business/Organizational Markets

Type of Customer	Manufacturer, service producer, government agency, military, nonprofit, wholesaler or retailer (when end user), etc.
Demographics	Geographic location (region of world, country, region within country, urban → rural) Size (number of employees, sales volume) Primary business or industry (Standard Industrial Classification) Number of facilities
How Customer Will Use Product	Installations, components, accessories, raw materials, supplies, professional services
Type of Buying Situation	Decentralized → centralized Buyer → multiple buying influence Straight rebuy → modified rebuy → new-task buying
Kind of Relationship	Weak loyalty → strong loyalty to vendor Single source → multiple vendors "Arm's length" dealings → close partnership No reciprocity → complete reciprocity
Purchasing Methods	Vendor analysis, inspection buying, sampling buying, specification buying, competitive bids, negociated contracts, long-term contracts

Note: Terms used in this table are explained in detail later in the text.

criticized for aggressive selling to less-educated parents who want their children to have better opportunities but who don't seem to understand that the "pennies a day" credit terms add up to more than they can really afford. Some nutritionists criticize firms that market soft drinks, candy, and snack foods to children.

Sometimes a marketing manager must decide whether a firm should serve customers it really doesn't want to serve. For example, banks sometimes offer

Exhibit 3–13 Finding the Relevant Segmenting Dimensions

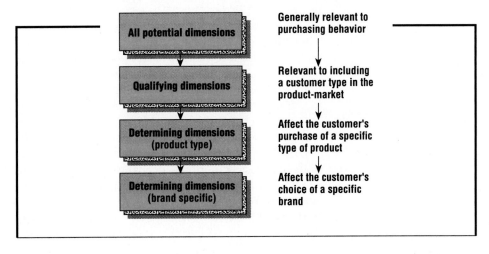

marketing mixes that are attractive to wealthy customers, but which basically drive off low-income consumers.

People often differ about what segmenting dimensions are ethical in a given situation. A marketing manager needs to consider not only his or her own views, but also the views of other groups in society. Even when there is no clear "right" answer, negative publicity may be very damaging.[8]

THE ABOVE APPROACH APPLIES IN BUSINESS MARKETS, TOO

We can apply the above approach to segmenting markets when the customers (or final users) are business organizations rather than individual consumers. There are two main differences. The first difference is in selecting the broad product-market. Business markets, especially in industrial settings, often have different needs.

Business organizations usually make purchases to meet basic functional needs. Their demands derive from final consumer demands—so the business (or non-profit organization) market makes purchases that help it produce finished goods or services. The functions these customers are concerned about include but are not limited to: forming, bending, grading, digging, cutting, heating, cooling, conducting, transmitting, containing, filling, cleaning, analyzing, sorting, training, and insuring. Such firms may buy physical goods and do the work themselves, or they may pay someone else to provide the service as well.

By defining the relevant broad product-market using both geographic dimensions and basic functional needs, we can usually ensure that our focus is broad enough—that is, not exclusively on the product now being supplied to present customers. But it also keeps us from expanding our focus to "all the business needs in the world."

Businesses also should focus on needs

As with consumer markets, it is better to focus on needs satisfied by products, not product characterisitics themselves. We may find new ways of satisfying a need—and completely surprise and upset current producers—if we don't define the product-market too narrowly. For example, desktop computers and printers now compete in what some producers thought was the "typewriter market." And telephone calls and fax machines replaced letters, further reducing the need for typing. Perhaps this broad product-market is concerned with "thought processing and transmitting." Certainly, the typewriter view is too narrow. Market-oriented strategy planners try to avoid surprises that result from such tunnel vision.

The other main difference in segmenting industrial markets is that we use segmenting dimensions like those discussed in Chapter 8.

INTERNATIONAL MARKETING REQUIRES EVEN MORE SEGMENTING

Success in international marketing requries even more attention to segmenting. There are over 140 nations with their own unique cultures! And they differ greatly in language, customs (including business ethics), beliefs, religions, race, and income distribution patterns. (We'll discuss some of these differences in Chapters 6 and 7.) These additional differences can complicate the segmenting process. Even worse, critical data is often less available—and less dependable—as firms move into international markets. The number of variables increases, but the quantity and quality of data decrease. This is one reason why some firms insist that local operations and decisions be handled by natives. They, at least, have a "feel" for their markets.

Segmenting international markets may require more dimensions, but the basic process is the same. The only addition is that marketers should segment by country or region, looking at demographic, cultural, and other characteristics, including stage of economic development, to help them find reasonably similar submarkets. Then depending on whether the firm is aiming at final consumers or business markets, marketers should continue to segment the markets as discussed earlier.

MORE SOPHISTICATED TECHNIQUES MAY HELP IN SEGMENTING

VALS is widely used

Segmenting is not an easy process, and many sophisticated techiniques have been developed to help managers with this task. One method that assists marketing managers for consumer products firms is known as VALS (values, attitudes, and lifestyles). SRI International, a research firm, developed this approach to describe a firm's target market in terms of a set of typical VALS lifestyle groups (segments). An advantage of this approach is that SRI has developed very detailed information about the various VALS groups. The VALS approach has been used to profile consumers in the United Kingdom, Germany, Japan, Canada, and the United States. However, the disadvantage of VALS and other similar approaches is that they may not be very specific to the marketing manager's target market. Marketing Demo 3–3 discusses the 10 segments identified by VALS in a recent international study.

VALS is based on a segmentation approach known as psychographics or lifestyle analysis. It is an analysis of a person's activities, interests, and opinions— sometimes referred to as AIOs. Exhibit 3–14 shows a number of variables for each

MARKETING DEMO 3–3
VALS in a Global Marketplace

Values and lifestyles segmentation of consumers allows marketers to view a population as individuals with feelings and tendencies who can be addressed in compatible groups (segments).

Such segmentation models are not static, however, but alter with changes in society.

The original Values and Lifestyles segmentation (VALS) was launched in 1978 by Stanford Research Institute International. More recently, value segments have been found to be useful in defining international markets. In 1987, several affiliates of Gallup International participated in an international values segmentation survey in the United Kingdom, Germany, Japan, Canada, and the United States using 10 segments:

1. *Basic needs*—this segment includes people who hold traditional views of life, enjoy passive activities, and are fairly satisfied with life. They generally seek security and control in their lives. The segment includes older people who are retired workers and widows.

2. *Fairer deal*—this group is composed of people who are relatively dissatisfied with their lives. What they earn at work is more important than what they do. Compared to the other nine groups, it includes the highest proportion of unskilled and semiskilled workers, and has the greatest confidence in unions. The majority are under 40 years old.

3. *Traditional family life*—the people in this segment, in particular those over 50, consider themselves conservative and retain a strong commitment to traditional family roles and values.

4. *Conventional family life*—these people place a high priority on family and friends. While tending to be less ambitious, they are, however, struggling to improve their basic living standards and to give their families better opportunities than they themselves had. Members are generally younger than 30.

5. *Look-at-mes*—this group includes young people who seek an exciting and prosperous life. Money is vey important to them, but not if it requires financial planning. Unsophisticated, demanding, and active, this segment is mainly less than 30 years of age, and unmarried or with no children to worry about.

6. *Something betters*—people in this group are likely to be well-educated, have a responsible job, and earn an above-average income. They feel confident, ambitious, and tend to have secure, full-time employment.

7. *Real conservatives*—this group is cautious about new things and ideas. They hold traditional religious beliefs and are observers of society rather than participants.

8. *Young optimists*—the people in this segment are generally optimistic about the future and seek to improve their prospects in life and gain a respected place in society. They are interested in style, new technology, and career opportunities. They see themselves as middle to upper-middle class.

9. *Visible achievers*—these people feel in control of their lives and work for both financial rewards and job stimuation. They seek good living, travel, recreation, and other evidence of success. They are over 30 years old and enjoy above-average incomes while retaining traditional values about home, work, and society.

10. *Socially awares*—this segment consists of people who see themselves as middle-class and progressive. They enjoy converting others to their opinions and are likely to be involved in environmental and conservation movements. They are most likely to be employed full time and in middle-management positions.

Canada, Japan, and the United States were found to have the highest proportion of Visible achievers; the United Kingdom, a higher-than-usual proportion of people in the Fairer deal category; Germany, a high proportion of people in the Look-at-me segment; and Australia, fewer people in the Visible achievers segment than any of the other countries surveyed. Australians are seeking something better, but the focus is still on family life.

As global marketing becomes more important for Canadians, marketing research of this nature increases in importance. While elements in each segment's profile remain basically the same, marketers must be sensitive to cultural differences.

Source: "New VALS 2 Takes Psychological Route," *Advertising Age*, February 13, 1989, p. 24; Lynn R. Kahle, Sharon E. Beatty, and Pamela Homer, "Alternative Measurement Approaches to Consumer Values: The List of Values (LOV) and Values and Life Styles (VALS)," *Journal of Consumer Research*, December 1986, pp. 405–10.

Exhibit 3–14 Lifestyle Dimensions (and some related demographic dimensions)

Dimension	Examples		
Activities	Work Hobbies Social events	Vacation Entertainment Club membership	Community Shopping Sports
Interests	Family Home Job	Community Recreation Fashion	Food Media Achievements
Opinions	Themselves Social issues Politics	Business Economics Education	Products Future Culture
Demographics	Income Age Family life cycle	Geographic area City size Dwelling	Occupation Family size Education

of the AIO dimensions, along with some demographics used to add detail to the lifestyle profile of a target market.

Lifestyle analysis assumes that marketers can plan more effective strategies if they know more about their target markets. Understanding the lifestyle of target customers has been especially helpful in providing ideas for advertising themes. Let's see how it adds to a typical demographic description. Will it help Mercury marketing managers to know that an average member of the target market for a Sable station wagon is 34.8 years old and married, lives in a three-bedroom home, and has 2.3 children?

Lifestyles help markets paint a more human portrait of the target market. For example, lifestyle analysis might show that the 34.8-year-old is also a community-oriented consumer with traditional values who especially enjoys spectator sports and spends much time in other family activities. An ad might show the Sable being used by a happy family at a ball game so the target market could really identify with the ad. And the ad might be placed in a magazine like *Sports Illustrated* whose readers match the target lifestyle profile.

B.C. Transit also used psychographics

Markets can be segmented in many different ways. At the beginning of the chapter we identified how B.C. Transit segmented its market in terms of demographics and the purpose of the trip. It also used psychographics to segment that same market. The following are the six segments it identified:

1. *Captive enthusiasts*—this group tends to be female, younger, and single, and have the lowest household income of any of the segments. This segment, environmentally concerned and socially conscious, also finds transit convenient. The primary motivator for this group is fast service.
2. *Timid drivers*—this segment is comprised of a greater proportion of older people, women, retirees, widowed persons, and those who are less well off. They are apprehensive about driving, are not a mobile group, and are not very demanding of the transit system. They have concerns about their personal safety.
3. *Cost conscious driver*—this group is mainly comprised of males. They are busy and like to drive but give moderately positive ratings to B.C.

Transit. Higher driving costs would encourage them to use transit, but they are less swayed by other improvements to the transit system. If they can be convinced that transit is as convenient as their cars, and if the relative cost of operating their cars increases, there is opportunity to achieve increased transit usage.

4. *Demanding commuters*—this segment is generally from the suburbs, members are full-time workers, married, 25–44 years old, and busy, mobile, and affluent. They want the perfect transit system (including rapid transit) and will not use it until it is. They feel transit is complicated to use, and feel they do not have enough information to use it.

5. *Autocentrics*—this group is generally male. They like to drive, work full time, and are affluent. They are similar to demanding commuters but are less demanding of transit and have lower expectations of an ideal transit system. They will drive a car at any cost, are relatively unconcerned about air pollution, and have negative attitudes about public transit.

6. *Elitist drivers*—this segment is a middle-income group comprised equally of males and females. These residents differ from other groups in that they do not see transit as a solution to the stress of driving. They see transit as fine for others but not for themselves. They love the privacy of their cars. They have concerns about the personal safety of the system and tend to see the system as more complicated than do other residents. This group is relatively unconcerned about the environment. They are the least likely of all groups to see transit as a solution to the air pollution problem.

Clustering techniques are also often used to identify market segments. Cluster analysis tries to find similar patterns within sets of data. Clustering groups customers who are similar on their segmenting dimensions into homogeneous segments. Clustering approaches use computers to do what previously was done with much intuition and judgment.

The data to be clustered might include such dimensions as demographic characterisitics, the importance of different needs, attitudes toward the product, and past buying behavior. Computerized statistical programs are used to search all the data for homogeneous groups of people. When such groups are found, marketers study the dimensions of the people in the groups to see why the computer clustered them together. The results sometimes suggest new, or at least better, marketing strategies.[9]

A cluster analysis of the toothpaste market, for example, might show that some people buy toothpaste because it tastes good (the sensory segment), while others are concerned with the effect of clean teeth and fresh breath on their social image (the sociables). Still others worry about decay or tartar (the worriers), and some are just interested in the best value for their money (the value seekers). Each of these market segments calls for a different marketing mix—although some of the four Ps may be similar.

Finally, a marketing manager has to decide which one (or more) of these segments will be the firm's target market(s).

You can see that clustering techinques only *aid* managers. Managers still need judgment to develop an original list of possible dimensions and to name the resulting clusters.

Trade-off analysis
helps develop the
marketing mix

Another computer-based approach often used in segmenting markets is **trade-off analysis** (sometimes called **conjoint analysis**). This technique helps marketing managers determine how important certain elements of the firm's marketing mix are to target customers. It shows how much money (in terms of a higher price) a customer would trade off for a particular product feature.

Marketing managers for Marriott Courtyard motels used trade-off analysis to evaluate customers' reactions to various features Marriott considered offering. For example, the analysis revealed that customers viewed elaborate landscaping as worth about 50 cents a night more than they were willing to pay for a motel with minimal landscaping. Rooms with an enclosed central hall were worth about 65 cents a night more than rooms with outside stairs and walkways. Customers saw a motel with an indoor pool as worth about 85 cents a night more than one with no pool.[10]

PERCEPTUAL MAPS HELP IDENTIFY PRODUCT–MARKET OPPORTUNITIES

After managers have segmented the market, they may want to see how the segment views the company's product in relation to its competitor's offerings. Information of this type will help managers identify product-market opportunities.

Consumer insights
are provided

Perceptual maps show how consumers perceive proposed and/or present brands in a market. Like cluster analysis and trade-off analysis, perceptual maps require some formal marketing research, but they may be helpful when competitive offerings are quite similar. The results are usually plotted on graphs to help show where the products are positioned in relation to competing products. Usually, the products' positions are related to two or three product features that are important to the target market.

Assuming the picture is reasonably accurate, managers then decide whether they want to leave their product (and marketing mix) alone or reposition it. This may mean *physical changes* in the product or *image changes* based on promotion. For example, most beer drinkers can't pick out their favorite brand in a blind test, so physical changes might not be necessary (and might not even work) to reposition a beer brand. Managers develop the perceptual maps for positioning decisions by asking product users to make judgments about different brands—including their ideal brand—and then using computer programs to summarize the ratings and plot the results. The details of perceptual mapping are beyond the scope of this text, but Exhibit 3–15 shows the possibilities.

Exhibit 3–15 shows the perceptual map for different brands of pain relievers using two features (or dimensions)—effectiveness and gentleness. Effectiveness is related to strength and speed of relief, while gentleness is related to the extent to which a brand does not upset one's stomach. For example, consumers see Tylenol as the most gentle and Excedrin as most effective. Bayer and Anacin are close together, implying that consumers think of them as similar on these characteristics. Remember that perceptual maps are based on consumers' perception—the actual characteristics of the brands (as determined by a chemical test) might be very different!

Exhibit 3–15 also includes an ideal point—the combination of the two dimensions that consumers would prefer. In this case, consumers would like a product that is high on gentleness and high on effectiveness.

Exhibit 3–15   Perceptual Map of Pain Relievers

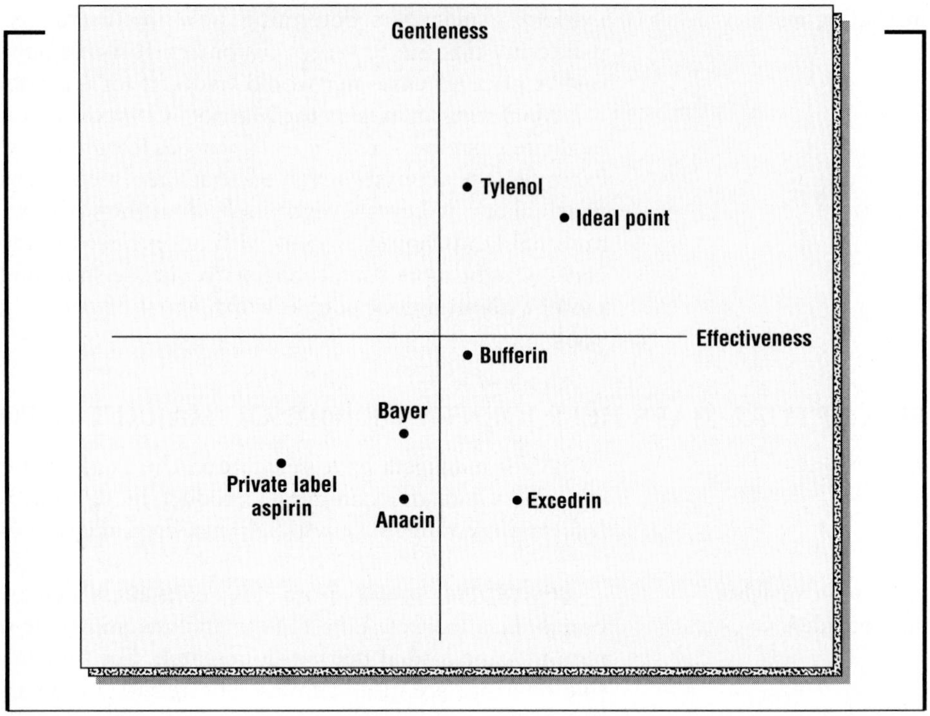

Adapted from Glen L. Urban and Jack R. Hauser, *Design and Marketing of New Products* (Englewood Cliffs, NJ: Prentice Hall, 1980), p. 187.

Maps guide marketing
mix divisions

  The combination of product positions and ideal points provides the manager with information that will guide the development of a marketing mix to maximize potential market opportunities. For example, the brand manager for Tylenol may want to consider repositioning Tylenol closer to the ideal point by changing consumers' perception of its effectiveness. The marketing mix decisions facing Tylenol's brand manager include whether the product's physical properties should be changed to improve effectiveness, whether promotion should emphasize Tylenol's effectiveness, or whether no changes should be made, since its position is already closer to the ideal point compared to competitors.

  Private label aspirin is the furthest from the ideal point. Therefore, some attempt should be made to reposition the product, either through physical or image changes. Alternatively, if private label aspirin is priced lower than competitors, promotion might be used to encourage consumers to think more about this feature so that the brand will be viewed more favorably by some consumers.

  The technique of perceptual mapping provides managers with information on how consumers perceive in relation to one another in the market. It is a procedure that usually focuses on specific product features—that is, it is product-oriented. Important customer-related dimensions, including needs and attitudes, may be overlooked. But as part of a broader analysis of how to position your product against the competition in the target market, perceptual mapping can be very useful. When such an analysis is first done, managers may be shocked to see how much customers' perceptions of a market differ from their own. For this reason, perceptual mapping is useful.

Firms often use promotion to help "position" how a product meets a target market's specific needs.

Premature emphasis on product features is dangerous, however. And it's easy to do if you start with a product-oriented definition of a market. If Coke and Pepsi look only at the market for soft drinks, they may miss more basic shifts in the beverage markets. For example, soft drinks may be losing popularity to fruit drinks with mineral water such as Clearly Canadian or Koala Springs. Or other products, like milkshakes and ice tea, may be part of the relevant competition. Managers wouldn't see these shifts if they looked only at alternative soft drink brands—the focus is just too narrow.

As we emphasize throughout the text, you must understand potential needs and attitudes when planning marketing strategies. If customers treat different products as substitutes, then a firm has to position itself against those products, too. It can't focus on physical product characteristics that aren't determining dimensions of the target market.

CONCLUSION

Firms need creative strategy planning to survive in our increasingly competitive markets. In this chapter, we discussed how to find attractive target market opportunities. We started by considering four basic types of opportunities—market penetration, market development, and diversification—with special emphasis on opportunities in international markets. We also saw that carefully defining generic markets and product-markets can help find new opportunities. We stressed the shortcomings of a too narrow product-oriented view of markets.

We also discussed market segmentation—the process of naming and then segmenting broad product-markets to find potentially attractive target markets. Some people try to segment markets by starting with the mass market and then dividing it into smaller submarkets based on a few dimensions. But this can lead to poor results. Instead, market segmentation should first focus on a broad product-market and then group similar customers into homogeneous submarkets. The more similar the potential customers are, the larger the submarkets can be.

Four criteria for evaluating possible product-market segments were presented.

Once a broad product-market is segmented, marketing managers can use one of three approaches to market-oriented strategy planning: (1) the single target market approach, (2) the multiple target market approach, and (3) the combined target market approach. In general, we encouraged marketers to be segmenters rather than combiners.

We discussed a practical—rough-and-ready—approach to market segmentation that works for both consumer and business markets and, with minor additions, for international markets as well.

We also discussed some computer-aided segmenting approaches—clustering techniques, trade-off analysis, and positioning.

In summary, good marketers should be experts on markets and likely segmenting dimensions. By creatively segmenting markets, they may spot opportunities—even breakthrough opportunities—and help their firms succeed against aggressive competitors offering similar products. Segmenting is basic to target marketing. And the more you practice segmenting, the more meaningful market segments you will see.

QUESTIONS AND PROBLEMS

1. Distinguish between an attractive opportunity and a breakthrough opportunity. Give an example.

2. Explain how new opportunities may be seen by defining a firm's markets more precisely. Illustrate for a situation where you feel there is an opportunity—namely, an unsatisfied market segment—even if it is not very large.

3. Distinguish between a generic market and a product-market. Illustrate your answer.

4. Explain the major differences among the four basic types of opportunities discussed in the text, and cite examples for two of these types of opportunities.

5. Explain why a firm may want to pursue a market penetration opportunity before pursuing one involving product development or diversification.

6. In your own words, explain several reasons why marketing managers should consider international markets when evaluating possible opportunities.

7. Give an example of a foreign-made product (other than an automobile) that you personally have purchased. Give some reasons why you purchased that product. Do you think that there was a good opportunity for a domestic firm to get your business? Explain why or why not.

8. Explain what market segmentation is.

9. List the types of potential segmenting dimensions, and explain which you would try to apply first, second, and third in a particular situation. If the nature of the situation would affect your answer, explain how.

10. Explain why segmentation efforts based on attempts to divide the mass market using a few demographic dimensions may be very disappointing.

11. Illustrate the concept that segmenting is an aggregating process by referring to the admissions policies of your own college and a nearby college or university.

12. Review the types of segmenting dimensions listed in Exhibit 3–11, and select the ones you think should be combined to fully explain the market segment you personally would be in if you were planning to buy a new watch today. List several dimensions and try to develop a shorthand name, like "fashion oriented," to describe your own personal market segment. Then try to estimate what proportion of the total watch market would be accounted for by your market segment. Next, explain if there are any offerings that come close to meeting the needs of your market. If not, what sort of a marketing mix is needed? Would it be economically attractive for anyone to try to satisfy your market segment? Why or why not?

13. Identify the determining dimension or dimensions that explain why you bought the specific brand you did in your most recent purchase of a (a) soft drink, (b) shampoo, (c) shirt or blouse,

and (*d*) larger, more expensive item, such as a bicycle, camera, boat, and so on. Try to express the determining dimension(s) in terms of your own personal characteristics rather than the product's characteristics. Estimate what share of the market would probably be motivated by the same determining dimension(s).

14. Explain how "perceptual mapping" can help a marketing manager identify target market opportunities.

SUGGESTED CASES

3. Gerber Products Company

19. CBUR-AM

Evaluating Opportunities in the Changing Marketing Environment

Chapter **4**

When You Finish This Chapter, You Should

❶
Know the variables that shape the environment of marketing strategy planning.

❷
Understand why company objectives are important in guiding marketing strategy planning.

❸
See how the resources of a firm affect the search for opportunities.

❹
Know how the different kinds of competitive situations affect strategy planning.

❺
Understand how the economic and technological environment can affect strategy planning.

❻
Know why you can go to prison by ignoring the political and legal environment.

❼
Understand how to screen and evaluate marketing strategy opportunities.

❽
Understand the important new terms (shown in blue).

Marketing managers do not plan strategies in a vacuum. When choosing target markets and developing the four Ps, they must work with many variables in the broader marketing environment. Marketing planning at Rubbermaid shows why this is important.

Top executives at Rubbermaid set ambitious objectives for the firm. They wanted to continue the growth in sales and profits the company had achieved every year for a decade—since the early 1980s.

Rubbermaid's marketing managers had built a respected brand name in plastic kitchenware, but they knew that just working harder at their current strategy for kitchenware would not be enough to achieve the firm's objectives. Rubbermaid's marketing environment was changing. The North American target for kitchenware wasn't getting any larger, so the firm's sales growth was slipping. A sluggish economy in 1992 made the problem worse. Rubbermaid had to cut prices to retailers to stimulate in-store promotions and sales, but the lower prices reduced Rubbermaid's profit margin. Competition was also becoming more intense. Tupperware, for example, had introduced new products and was supplementing its Tupperware parties with aggressive advertising.

These changes did not take Rubbermaid's marketing managers by surprise. For a number of years, they had been studying the changing environment and looking for new opportunities. Five years earlier, they saw an opportunity to develop a new marketing mix for consumers interested in plastic toys. Rubbermaid had the money to move quickly. It acquired Little Tikes Co., a small firm that was already producing sturdy plastic toys, and immediately expanded its product assortment. Marketing managers also took advantage of Rubbermaid's strong relationships with retailers to get scarce shelf space for the new toys—and they developed new ads to stimulate consumer interest. Unlike many toy companies, Rubbermaid was sensitive to parents' concerns about TV ads targeted at children. It aimed its cost-effective print ads at parents. This approach helped to speed Rubbermaid's

To achieve its objectives in a changing environment, Rubbermaid is developing new marketing strategies.

entry in the market, and Little Tikes toys proved to be very profitable. However, production capacity limited additional short-term growth from that line, so marketing managers looked for other opportunities as well.

For example, responding to increased environmental concerns in Canadian and US markets, Rubbermaid developed a very successful "litterless" school lunch box. Designed to eliminate disposable drink boxes, aluminum foil, and plastic wrap, the box had reusable sandwich holders and drink bottles. In addition, after extensive research, Rubbermaid introduced a line of household cleaning brushes, ranging from brooms to sink brushes, all with specially designed handles. Rubbermaid also acquired Eldon Industries, a producer of office furnishings, to help accelerate Rubbermaid's growth in the business market for office accessories and products.

Marketing managers also saw opportunities for sales growth with all their products in the newly unified European markets. Pursuing growth in Europe posed new challenges. Rubbermaid was less well known there, it did not have strong relationships with retailers, and the political, legal, and cultural environments were very different. So Rubbermaid formed a partnership with a Dutch firm that already knew the European market, and it worked with wholesalers who could help build strong new distribution channels. By adapting its strategies to these environments, Rubbermaid already earns more than 10 percent of its total profits from European sales—and more growth is expected in the years ahead.[1]

THE MARKETING ENVIRONMENT

You saw in the last chapter that finding target market opportunities takes a real understanding of what makes customers tick. The Rubbermaid case shows that understanding the marketing environment is also important in planning marketing strategy and evaluating opportunities.

The marketing environment falls into five basic areas:

1. Objectives and resources of the firm.
2. Competitive environment.
3. Economic and technological environment.
4. Political and legal environment.
5. Cultural and social environment.

A marketing manager controls the choice of marketing strategy variables within the framework of the broader marketing environment and how it is changing (see Exhibit 2–13). In the short run, the marketing manager doesn't control environmental variables. That's why it's sometimes useful to think of them as uncontrollable variables. Although the marketing manager may not be able to control these environmental variables directly, they must be considered carefully when evaluating opportunities and selecting marketing strategies. In this chapter, we'll see how these variables shape opportunities—limiting some possibilities and making others more attractive. Exhibit 3–1 shows how Chapters 3 and 4 fit together.

OBJECTIVES SHOULD SET FIRM'S COURSE

A company must decide where it's going, or it may fall into the trap expressed so well by the quotation: "Having lost sight of our objective, we redoubled our efforts." **Company objectives** should shape the direction and operation of the whole business. So we will treat this matter in some depth, discussing its effect on both finding attractive opportunities and developing marketing strategies.

It is difficult to set objectives that really guide the present and future development of the company. The process forces top management to look at the whole business, relate its present objectives and resources to the external environment, and then decide what the firm wants to accomplish in the future.

It would be convenient if a company could set one objective—such as making a profit—and let that serve as the guide. Actually, however, setting objectives is much more complicated, which helps explain why it's often done poorly—or not done at all.

Three basic objectives provide guidelines

The following three objectives provide a useful starting point for setting a firm's objectives. They should be sought *together* because, in the long run, a failure in even one of the three areas can lead to total failure of the business. A business should:

1. Engage in specific activities that will perform a socially and economically useful function.
2. Develop an organization to carry on the business and implement its strategies.
3. Earn enough profit to survive.[2]

Should be socially useful

The first objective says that the company should do something useful for society. This isn't just a "do-gooder" objective. Businesses can't exist without the approval of consumers. If a firm's activities appear to be contrary to the consumer "good," it can be wiped out almost overnight by political or legal action—or by consumers' own negative responses.

The first objective also implies that a firm should try to satisfy customer needs. This is why the marketing manager should be heard when the company is setting objectives. But setting whole company objectives within resource limits is ultimately the responsibility of top management. In this sense, whole company objectives are usually outside the marketing manager's "control."

A firm should define its objectives broadly, setting need-satisfying objectives rather than production-oriented objectives. Because customer needs change, too narrow a view may lead the company into a product-market in which the product itself will soon be obsolete.[3]

Should organize to innovate

In a macro-marketing sense, consumers in market-directed economies have granted businesses the right to operate—and to make a profit, if they can. With this right comes the responsibility for businesses to be dynamic agents of change, adjusting their offerings to meet new needs. Competition is supposed to encourage innovation and efficiency. A business firm should develop an organization that ensures that these consumer-assigned tasks are carried out effectively and that the firm itself continues to prosper.

Should earn some profit

In the long run, a firm must make a profit to survive. But just saying that a firm should try to make a profit isn't enough. Management must specify the time period involved, since many plans that maximize profit in the long run lose money during the first few years. On the other hand, seeking only short-term profits may steer the firm from opportunities that would offer larger long-run profits.

Further, trying to maximize profit won't necessarily lead to big profits. Competition in a particular industry may be so fierce as to almost guarantee failure. For example, Greyhound Corp. struggled to maximize profits selling long-distance bus travel, but low airfares attracted much of the business. Even the maximum possible profit was disappointing. In a situation like this, it might be better to set a *target* rate of profit return that will lead the firm into areas with more promising possibilities.

Further complicating the process, management must specify the degree of risk it is willing to assume for larger returns. Very large profits are possible in the oil exploration business, for example, but the probability of success on each hole is quite low.

Objectives should be explicit

Our three general objectives provide guidelines, but a firm has to develop its own *specific* objectives. In spite of their importance, a firm seldom states its objectives explicitly. Too often, it does so after the fact! If objectives aren't clear and specific from the start, different managers may hold unspoken and conflicting objectives, a common problem in large companies and in nonprofit organizations.

The whole firm must work toward the same objectives

Objectives chosen by top management should be compatible, or frustrations and even failure may result. For example, top management may set a 25 percent annual return on investment as one objective, while at the same time specifying that the current plant and equipment be used as fully as possible. In such a case, competition may make it impossible to use resources fully *and* achieve the target return. Efficient papermakers like Canadian Pacific set the objective of operating at nearly full capacity so that they can keep their costs low—and keep foreign competitors out of the market. This does not mean, however, that executives can expect marketing managers to find a way to earn a 25 percent return on investment. To earn that high a profit in the short term, Canadian Pacific would have to set prices too high—so high that they would attract competitors into the market. Soon, sales lost to competitors would prevent Canadian Pacific from running its plant and equipment at full capacity. In a situation like this, conflicting objectives can lead to disaster. Managers may try to achieve the return on investment objective during the year and then, at year end, find it impossible to keep running at full capacity. The two objectives are impossible to achieve together![4]

Top-management myopia may straitjacket marketing

We are assuming that it is the marketing manager's job to work within the framework of objectives provided by top management. But some of these objectives may limit marketing strategies and perhaps damage the whole business. This is another reason why it is desirable for the marketing manager to help shape the company's objectives.

Some top managements want a large sales volume or a large market share because they feel this ensures greater profitability. But many large firms with big market shares have gone bankrupt. Eastern Airlines went under, and so did International Harvester. These firms sought large market shares—but earned little profit. Increasingly, companies are shifting their objectives toward *profitable* sales growth rather than just larger market share, as they realize that the two don't necessarily go together.[5]

Company objectives should lead to marketing objectives

You can see why the marketing manager should be involved in setting company objectives. Company objectives guide managers as they search for and evaluate opportunities—and later plan marketing strategies. Particular *marketing* objectives should be set within the framework of larger, company objectives. As shown in Exhibit 4–1, firms need a hierarchy of objectives—moving from

Exhibit 4–1   A Hierarchy of Objectives

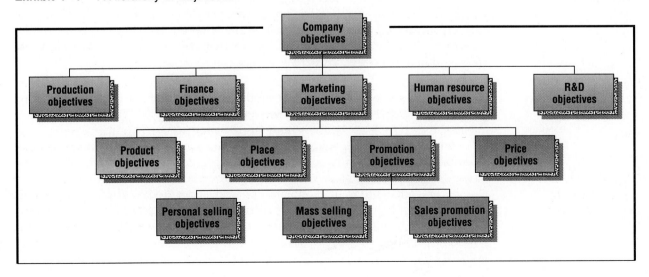

company objectives to marketing department objectives. For each marketing strategy, firms also need objectives for each of the four Ps, as well as more detailed objectives. For example, in the Promotion area, we need objectives for advertising, sales promotion, *and* personal selling.

Both company objectives and marketing objectives should be realistic and achievable. Overly ambitious objectives are useless if the firm lacks resources to achieve them.

COMPANY RESOURCES MAY LIMIT SEARCH FOR OPPORTUNITIES

Every firm has some **resources**—hopefully some unique ones—that set it apart from other firms. Breakthrough opportunities, or at least some competitive advantage, come from making use of these strengths while avoiding direct competition with firms having similar strengths.

To find its strengths, the firm must evaluate its functional areas (production, research and engineering, marketing, general management, and finance) as well as present products and markets. By analyzing successes or failures in relation to the firm's resources, management can discover why the firm was successful, or why it failed, in the past.

Harley-Davidson's motorcycle business was on the ropes, and it was losing customers to Japanese competitors. Competitors' prices were so low that Harley initially thought the Japanese were "dumping"—selling in North America at prices below cost. However, careful analysis revealed that superior manufacturing techniques kept Japanese companies' operating costs 30 percent lower than Harley's. Studying the Japanese firms helped Harley identify ways to use its resources more efficiently and improve the quality of its products. With these resource-use problems resolved, new opportunities opened up—and Harley was again on the road to achieving its objectives.[6]

The pressure of competition focused Harley's attention on manufacturing resources. Other resources that should be considered as part of an evaluation of strengths and weaknesses are discussed in the following sections.

Financial strength

Some opportunities require large amounts of capital just to get started. Money may be required for R&D, production facilities, marketing research, or advertising—before a firm makes its first sale. And even a really good opportunity may not be profitable for years. So lack of financial strength is often a barrier to entry into an otherwise attractive market.

Producing capability and flexibility

In many businesses, the cost of production per unit decreases as the quantity produced increases. Therefore, smaller producers can be at a great cost disadvantage if they try to win business from larger competitors.

On the other hand, new—or smaller—firms sometimes have the advantage of flexibility. They are not handicapped with large, special-purpose facilities that are obsolete or poorly located. U.S. Steel (USX), Bethlehem, and other large steel producers once enjoyed economies of scale. But today, they have trouble competing with producers using smaller, more flexible plants. Similarly, poorly located or obsolete retail or wholesale facilities can severely limit marketing strategy planning.

A familiar brand—and other marketing strengths—can be an advantage in seeking new opportunities.

Firms that own or have assured sources of supply have an important advantage, especially in times of short supply. Big firms often control their own sources of supply. Companies that don't have guaranteed supply sources may have difficulty meeting demand—or even staying in business.

Marketing managers for the Lincoln Continental recently had to deal with this problem. They had developed a new model and a strategy that focused on special safety features, including antilock brakes and dual air bags. Advertising touted these advantages—and safety-oriented luxury car buyers were buying every Continental produced. However sales suffered and the whole strategy had to be changed after a fire at the air bag supplier's factory. Lincoln could no longer equip every car with dual air bags as standard equipment. By the time Lincoln finally got an adequate supply of air bags, several competitors had similar offerings—and Continental had lost its competitive advantage.[7]

Marketing strengths

Our marketing strategy framework helps in analyzing current marketing resources. In the product area, for example, a familiar brand can be a big strength or a new idea or process may be protected by a *patent*. A patent owner has a 17-year monopoly to develop and use its new product, process, or material. If one firm has a strong patent, competitors may be limited to second-rate offerings, and their efforts may be doomed to failure.

Good relations with established middlemen or control of good locations can be important resources in reaching some target markets. When Bic decided to compete with Gillette by selling disposable razors, Bic's other products had already proved profitable to drugstores, grocery stores, and other retailers that could reach the target market. So these retailers were willing to give Bic scarce shelf space.

Promotion and Price resources must be considered, too. Westinghouse already has a skilled sales force. Marketing managers know these sales reps can handle new products and customers. And low-cost facilities may enable a firm to undercut competitors' prices.

Finally, thorough understanding of a target market can give a company an edge. Many companies fail in new product-markets because they don't really understand the needs of the new customers—or the new competitive environment.

THE COMPETITIVE ENVIRONMENT

Choose opportunities that avoid head-on competition

The **competitive environment** affects the number and types of competitors the marketing manager must face—and how they may behave. Although marketing managers usually can't control these factors, they can choose strategies that avoid head-on competition. And, where competition is inevitable, they can plan for it.

Economists describe four basic kinds of market (competitive) situations: pure competition, oligopoly, monopolistic competition, and monopoly. Understanding the differences among these market situations is helpful in analyzing the competitive environment, and our discussion assumes some familiarity with these concepts. (For a review, see Exhibit A–11 and the related discussion in Appendix A, which follows Chapter 2).

The economist's traditional view is that most product-markets head toward pure competition or oligopoly over the long-run. In these situations, a marketing manager competes for customers against competitors who are offering very similar products. Because customers see the different available products (marketing mixes) as close substitutes, competing firms must compete with lower and lower prices, especially in pure competition where there are likely to be large numbers of competitors. Profit margins shrink until they are just high enough to keep the most efficient firms in business. Avoiding pure competition is sensible—and certainly fits with our emphasis on target marketing.

Effective target marketing is fundamentally different than effective decision making in other areas of business. Accounting, production, and financial managers for competing firms can learn about and use the same standardized approaches, and they will work well in each case. By contrast, marketing managers can't just learn about and adopt the same "good" marketing strategy being used by other firms. That just leads to head-on competition—and a downward spiral in prices and profits. So target marketers try to offer customers a marketing mix better suited to their needs than competitors' offerings.

Competition-free environments are rare

Most marketing managers would like to have such a strong marketing mix that customers see it as uniquely able to meet their needs. This competition-free ideal guides the search for breakthrough opportunities. Yet monopoly situations, in which one firm completely controls a broad product-market, are rare in market-directed economies. Further, governments commonly regulate monopolies. For example, in most parts of the world, prices set by utility companies must be approved by a government agency. Although most marketing managers can't expect to operate with complete control in an unregulated monopoly, they can move away from head-on competition.

Monopolistic competition is typical—and a challenge

In monopolistic competition, a number of different firms offer marketing mixes that at least some customers see as different. Each competitor tries to get control (a monopoly) in its "own" target market. But competition still exists because some customers see the various alternatives as substitutes. A subset of these firms may even compete head-on for the same customers with similar marketing mixes. With monopolistic competition, each firm has its own down-

Unitel would like to avoid head-on competition from other communication service providers, but that is difficult if potential customers view the products as extremely similar.

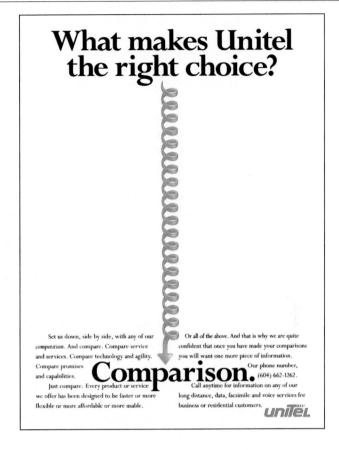

What makes Unitel the right choice?

Set us down, side by side, with any of our *competition*. And compare. Compare service and services. Compare technology and agility. Compare promises and capabilities. Just compare. Every product or service we offer has been designed to be faster or more flexible or more affordable or more usable.

Or all of the above. And that is why we are quite confident that once you have made your comparisons you will want one more piece of information.

Comparison.

Our phone number, (604) 662-1262.

Call anytime for information on any of our long distance, data, facsimile and voice services for business or residential customers.

uniTeL

sloping demand curve. But the shape of the demand curve—and elasticity of demand—depends on how similar competitors' products and marketing mixes are. Most marketing managers in developed economies face monopolistic competition.

In monopolistic competition, marketing managers sometimes try to differentiate very similar products by relying on other elements of the marketing mix. For example, Clorox Bleach uses the same basic chemicals as other bleaches. But marketing managers for Clorox may help to set it apart from other bleaches by offering an improved pouring spout, by producing ads that demonstrate its stain-killing power, or by getting it better shelf positions in supermarkets. Yet such approaches may not work, especially if competitors can easily imitate the new ideas. Efforts to promote real but subtle differences may not do any good, either. If potential customers view the different offerings as essentially similar, the market will become more and more competitive, and firms will have to rely on lower costs to obtain a competitive advantage.

Analyze competitors to find a competitive advantage

The best way for a marketing manager to avoid head-on competition is to find new or better ways to satisfy customers' needs. The search for a breakthrough opportunity—or some sort of competitive advantage—requires an understanding not only of customers but also of competitors. That's why marketing managers turn to **competitor analysis**—an organized approach for evaluating the strengths and weaknesses of current or potential competitors' marketing strategies. A complete discussion of the possible approaches for competitor analysis is beyond the scope of the first marketing course. But we will briefly cover an approach that works well in many different market situations.

The approach we will discuss is a logical extension of the marketing strategy planning framework that is the focus of this book. The basic idea is simple. You compare your current (or planned) target market and marketing mix with what competitors are currently doing or are likely to do in response to your strategy. As Exhibit 4–2 shows, you also consider **competitive barriers**—the conditions that may make it difficult, or even impossible, for a firm to compete in a market. Such barriers may limit your own plans or, alternatively, block competitors' responses to an innovative strategy. For example, NutraSweet's patent on its low-calorie sweetener effectively limited direct competitors from entering a rapidly growing market.

The initial step in competitor analysis is to identify potential competitors. It's useful to start broadly—and from the viewpoint of target customers. Companies may offer quite different products to meet the same needs, but they are competitors if customers see them as offering close substitutes. For example, Dow ZipLock bags, Reynold's aluminum foil, Saran Wrap, and Tupperware containers compete in the same generic market for food storage needs. Identifying a broad set of potential competitors helps marketing managers understand the different ways customers are currently meeting needs—and sometimes points to new opportunities. Usually, however, marketing managers quickly narrow the focus of a competitor analysis to the set of rival firms who will be the closest competitors.

Canadian competitiveness

Canada built much of its current prosperity in a market environment insulated from external and internal rivalry. The bedrock of the economy was Canada's abundant natural resources. Canadian business was content to exploit the profitable home market. The rate of innovation was slow. What emerged was a tendency to administer existing wealth rather than to invest vigorously to create new wealth.

Cross-border shopping, free trade, growing globalization of business, and competition from developing countries in the natural resource sector are putting

Exhibit 4–2   A Framework for Competitor Analysis

	Firm's Current or Planned Strategy	Competitor 1's Strengths and Weaknesses	Competitor 2's Strengths and Weaknesses
Target Market			
Product			
Place			
Promotion			
Price			
Competitive Barriers			
Likely Response(s)			

extreme pressure on Canada's old economic order, forcing Canadian businesses to enter a competitive environment with which they are ill equipped to deal.

Fortunately, there is growing evidence that Canadians will be able to adapt and prosper in this new order. Some of the initiatives being taken by Canadian companies are:

- Total quality management with a focus on the customer.
- Continuous improvement.
- Just-in-time materials management systems.
- Benchmarking on competitors and/or noncompetitors and/or other targets or improvement standards.
- Time-based competition, which focuses on the time it takes to get a new product from the drawing board to the showroom.
- Restructuring or rethinking of labor-management cooperation versus confrontation.

For instance, at Alcan Extrusions in Laval, Quebec, there has been a rethinking of the physical process, the infrastructure process, and the labor-management relationship. All of this has taken that plant from a noncompetitive, eroding market situation into an aggressive posture. It is now ready not only to defend itself against challenges from the northern United States, but also to move into that area.

Marketing Demo 4–1 describes the evolving competitive environment convenience stores must face and how they are dealing with these changes.

MARKETING DEMO 4–1
Corner Stores Battle for Survivial

Survival—not sales and profit—is now the ultimate benchmark of success in the once high-flying convenience store industry. Wide-open Sunday shopping in most provinces may provide the death blow for hundreds of corner stores that are already reeling from overbuilding in the 1980s, aggressive new competitors, and a steep drop in all-important cigarette sales.

The industry leaders—Becker Milk Co. Ltd. and Southland Canada, Inc. (which operates about 500 7-Eleven stores)—are scrambling to reinvent themselves into a format that will prove a hit with consumers. They are trying to build traffic by adding automatic video machines and bank cash dispensers. Convenience stores are also following a US trend—integrating gas bars into their stores.

The big chains' move into gas retailing has an element of justice to it, since traditional gas stations have been squeezing corner stores by selling convenience-type merchandise—cigarettes, pop, and snacks. "That has hurt our business," says Laird Fraser, Becker's vice president of finance. "Without a doubt, we now have many more competitors than before. Every gas station now sells some sort of convenience store products."

Established players such as Becker are waiting for the inevitable industry shakeout and downsizing. "There are too many stores for the number of customers," says Harry O'Grady, Becker marketing vice president. O'Grady predicts that "we'll find a real consolidation over the next year," with larger chains consolidating their hold on the business. The Retail Merchants Association, which represents 2,000 independent store operators, recently released a survey of its members that predicts Sunday shopping alone will force as many as 7 percent of them out of business."

Source: Paul Brent, "Corner Stores Battle for Survival," *The Financial Post*, February 6, 1993, p. 5.

Rivals offering similar products are usually easy to identify. However, with a really new and different product concept, there may not be a current competitor with a similar product. In that case, the closest competitor may be a firm that is currently serving similar needs with a different product. Although such firms may not appear to be close competitors, they are likely to fight back, perhaps with a directly competitive product, if another firm starts to take away customers.

Anticipate competition that will come

Even if no specific competitors can be identified, marketing managers must consider how long it might take for potential competitors to appear and what they might do. It's easy to make the mistake of assuming that there won't be competition in the future, or of discounting how aggressive competition may become. But a successful strategy attracts others who are eager to jump in for a share of the profit—even if profits only hold up for a short time. That is why it is important for firms to find opportunities where they can sustain a competitive advantage over the longer run.

Finding a sustainable competitive advantage requires special attention to competitor strengths and weaknesses. For example, it is very difficult to dislodge a competitor who is already a market leader simply by attacking with a strategy that has similar strengths. An established leader can usually defend its position by quickly copying the best parts of what a new competitor is trying to do. On the other hand, an established competitor may not be able to defend quickly if it is attacked where it is weak. For example, Right Guard deodorant built its strong position with an aerosol spray dispenser. But many consumers don't like the messy aerosol cloud, or have become concerned about the effect of aerosols on the environment. That weakness provided Old Spice with a competitive opportunity for a deodorant in a pump dispenser. Right Guard did not quickly fight back with its own pump. The company thought that promoting a pump could hurt sales of its established product—and might even help the competitor.[8]

Seek information about competitors

A marketing manager should actively seek information about current or potential competitors. Although most firms try to keep the specifics of their plans secret, public information may well be available. For example, many firms routinely monitor competitors' local newspapers. In one such case, an article discussed a change in the competitor's sales organization. An alert marketing manager realized that the change was made to strengthen the competitor's ability to take business from one of her firm's key target markets. This early warning provided time to make adjustments. Other sources of competitor information include trade publications, alert sales reps, middlemen, and other industry experts. In business markets, customers may be quick to explain what competing suppliers are offering.

? Ethical issues may arise

The search for information about competitors sometimes raises ethical issues. For example, it's not unusual for people to change jobs and move to a competing firm in the same industry. Such people may have a great deal of information about a past employer, but is it ethical for them to use it? Similarly, some firms have been criticized for going too far—like waiting at a landfill for competitors' trash to find copies of confidential company reports.

Beyond the moral issues, stepping over the line of ethical behavior can prove to be very costly. Spying on competitors to obtain trade secrets is illegal, and damage awards can be huge. For example, the courts ordered Keebler Co.,

Nabisco Brands, and Frito-Lay to pay Procter & Gamble about $125 million in damages for stealing secrets about its Duncan Hines soft cookies. Nabisco had obtained Duncan Hines' recipe by entering a restricted area. Keebler had gone so far as to hire an airplane to take aerial photographs of a Duncan Hines manufacturing facility that was under construction. A Frito-Lay employee posed as a potential customer to attend a confidential sales presentation.[9]

The competition may vary from country to country

A firm that faces very stiff competition may find that the competitive environment—and the opportunities—are much better in another region or country.

Twenty years ago, when many small US companies were content to build their businesses in the huge North American market, marketing managers at H. B. Fuller Co. saw international markets as an opportunity—and a matter of survival. It was hard for this small firm, a producer of paints, adhesives, and industrial coatings, to compete against giant suppliers like Du Pont and Dow Chemical for a larger share of the North American market. Fuller's marketing managers didn't want to diversify into some other business, so they decided to go where the competition wasn't. They quickly found that developing a competitive advantage with overseas customers required constant sales and service contacts. So instead of exporting from North America, Fuller now produces customized products in plants run by local people in 27 countries across Latin America, Europe, and Asia. That allows the company to be close to its customers and to deliver products quickly. Fuller's move to new competitive environments has been worth the effort. Company sales have grown to over $500 million, and foreign business accounts for half of its profit.[10]

Direct competition cannot always be avoided

Despite the desire to avoid highly competitive situations—especially pure competition—a firm may find that it can't. Some firms are already in an industry before it becomes intensely competitive. Then, as competitors fail, new firms enter the market, possibly because they don't have more attractive alternatives and can at least earn a living. In less-developed economies, this is a common pattern with small retailers and wholesalers. New entrants may not even know how competitive the market is, but they stick it out until they run out of money. Production-oriented firms are more likely to make such a mistake.

THE ECONOMIC ENVIRONMENT

The **economic and technological environment** affects the way firms—and the whole economy—use resources. We'll treat the economic and technological environments separately to emphasize that the technological environment provides a *base* for the economic environment. Technical skills and equipment affect the way an economy's resources are converted into output. The economic environment, on the other hand, is affected by how all the parts of our macro-economic system interact. This, then, affects such things as national income, economic growth, and inflation.

Economic conditions change rapidly

The economic environment can—and does—change quite rapidly. The effects can be far-reaching and require changes in marketing strategy.

Even a well-planned marketing strategy may fail if the country goes through a rapid business decline. As consumers' incomes drop, they must shift their spending patterns. They may simply have to do without some products. Many companies aren't strong enough to survive such bad times.

Inflation and interest rates affect buying

The year 1990 brought on an undeniable economic recession for Canadians. Minister of Finance Michael Wilson and Bank of Canada Governor John Crow stressed the urgent need for strong monetary policies to fight inflation.

To counter high inflation, Canadian interest rates were raised to levels 2 to 5 percent higher than in the United States. This created other problems, however. The Canadian dollar's value rose in relation to the US dollar. This meant that Americans buying Canadian products were forced to pay more, and Canadian industry lost business. The forest industry was particularly hard hit by the high dollar. Noranda, a Quebec-based forest company, lost a reported $23 million with each 1 cent rise in the value of the Canadian dollar.[11]

The interest rate (the charge for borrowing money) affects the total price borrowers must pay for products. So the interest rate affects when—and if—they'll buy. This is an especially important factor in some industrial markets. But it also affects consumer purchases, especially for homes, cars, and other high-ticket items usually bought on credit.

World economies are connected

International trade is affected by changes in and between economies. One such factor is the *exchange rate* (how much our dollar is worth in another country's money). When the dollar is "weak," it's worth less in foreign countries. This sounds bad, but it makes Canadian products less expensive overseas and foreign products more expensive in Canada. In fact, a country's whole economic system can change as the balance of imports and exports shifts, affecting jobs, consumer income, and national productivity.

You can see that the marketing manager must watch the economic environment carefully. Even more than cultural and social environments, economic conditions change all the time. And they can move rapidly—up or down—requiring strategy changes.

National income changes make a difference

Changes in the overall level of economic activity are obviously important. Even the best possible marketing strategy may prove unsuccessful when Canada is in the midst of a depression or suffering from a rapid business decline. As consumers' incomes go down, people have less money to spend and they spend it in different ways. In a mild recession, for example, firms offering luxury goods can be badly hurt while those offering lower-priced goods may continue to prosper.

Resource scarcities may depress economic conditions

The growing shortage of some natural resources—in particular, energy resources—may cause severe upsets. In the petrochemical industry, for example, some plastics manufacturers' costs are so high the manufacturers are priced out of some markets. High gasoline prices have caused some consumers to be less interested in the larger, more profitable (to the auto industry) cars. Further, shifts in auto-buying patterns have a ripple effect throughout the economy because the auto industry is a major buyer of metals, plastics, fabrics, and tires.[12]

High fuel prices may cut economic growth

The continued economic growth we've come to expect may be slowed or stopped by high fuel costs. High fuel prices for imported oil have shifted income to fuel-producing nations outside North America. Furthermore, lower real incomes are possible in the future because of technological factors. Much of our existing plant and equipment is energy-intensive. Some industrial processes that were profitable when energy was cheap are now less profitable or may actually be obsolete. So it's likely that the average job in the future will use less machinery and be less productive. In effect, high energy costs will increase real incomes in the few countries with large energy reserves, but the balance of the world may see lower real incomes. Canada will definitely be hurt both because we're big energy users and, contrary to what people believe, because we're large net importers of crude oil.[13]

Free Trade Agreements: Canada, Mexico, and the United States

New economic conditions that will be watched very closely will be those imposed by free trade with the United States and possibly Mexico. Free trade is the absence of barriers such as tariffs. As the Free Trade Agreement reached in 1988 comes into full effect, it's expected to have a profound impact on Canadian business. Already feeling the effect is the Canadian wine industry. Wine producers in British Columbia, Nova Scotia, and Ontario face a tough battle against higher-quality US wines as they become more available and competitively priced.

These primary grape-growing provinces have responded to free trade by becoming more competitive, with a focus on raising the quality of Canadian wine and aggressively marketing their product. They plan to be in a strong position to compete with American wines by 1995 when Canadian wines will face the same markup as their lower-priced competitors.

Three-way free trade talks between Mexico, Canada, and the United States beginning in 1991 brought a different type of competition to the forefront. Mexico offers North American manufacturers and businesses 81 million employees for whom minimum factory wages are 68 cents an hour or less. Spokespeople for organized labor and others see trilateral free trade as a major threat and predict job losses and plant closures. On the other hand, Canada is expected by many to benefit from this enlarged free trade area. The three nations have a combined yearly output of about $7 trillion. This would eclipse the 12-nation European Community with its annual output of about $6 trillion.[14]

GATT

The General Agreement on Tariffs and Trade (GATT) receives a lot of attention from Canadian businesses, particularly those in the fishing and grain industries. GATT deals with the rates of tariffs applied to imported goods from those countries with which Canada hasn't made separate trade agreements. This affects the price and availability of many products, including Japanese CD players, US videos, and Taiwanese clothing. However, how GATT affects the livelihoods of farmers and fishers is always of major concern.

GATT talks have sometimes faced seemingly unsurmountable obstacles in achieving freer movement of goods and services. GATT trade talks in the early 1990s met with failure when the European communities refused to deal with agricultural issues that could greatly affect the livelihood of their farmers who've enjoyed large farm subsidies. Some Canadian farmers, in the interim, anxiously await the opportunity to gain access to valuable European markets.[15] But other farmers fear that a GATT agreement on agriculture will mean the end of marketing boards.

You can see that the marketing manager must watch the economic environment carefully. In contrast to the cultural and social environment, economic conditions change continuously. And they move rapidly—up or down—requiring tactical and even strategic responses.

THE TECHNOLOGICAL ENVIRONMENT

The technological base affects opportunities

Underlying any economic environment is the **technological base**—the technical skills and equipment that affect the way an economy's resources are converted to output. Technological developments affect marketing in two basic ways: with new products and with new processes (ways of doing things). Many argue, for example, that we are moving from an industrial society to an information society. Advances in electronic communications make it possible for people in different parts of the world to communicate face-to-face with satellite videoconferencing and to transmit faxes, including complex design drawings, by regular telephone, reducing other media's relative importance. Computers allow more sophisticated planning and control of business. And we're in the middle of an explosion of high-tech products from robots in factories to home refrigerators that "talk."

As we move through the text, you should see that some of the big advances in business have come from early recognition of new ways to do things. Marketers should help their firms see such opportunities by trying to understand the why of present markets and what's keeping their firms from being more successful. Then, as new technological developments come along, they'll be alert to possible uses of those technologies and see how opportunities can be turned into profits. Marketing Demo 4–2 shows how one Canadian firm is making inroads with its new TV technology.

Technology also poses challenges

The rapid pace of technological change opens up new opportunities, but it also poses challenges for marketers. For many firms, success hinges on how quickly new ideas can be brought to market. It's easy for a firm to slip into a production orientation in the flush of excitement that follows a new discovery in a research and development lab. That makes it more important than ever for marketing thinking to guide the production process, starting at the beginning with decisions about where basic R&D effort will be focused.

? Technology and ethical issues

Marketers must also help their firms decide what technical developments are ethically acceptable. For example, many firms have now installed a system to identify the telephone number of an incoming telephone call. When linked with a computer, this makes it possible for a firm to know what customer is calling even before the customer says the first word. It also makes instantly available detailed information about what a customer has purchased in the past. This is a very powerful technology, but many people feel that this sort of automatic number identification system is an invasion of privacy.

Similarly, with the growing concern about environmental pollution and the quality of life, some attractive technological developments may be rejected because of their long-run effects on the environment. Aseptic drink boxes, for example, are very convenient but difficult to recycle. In a case like this, what's good for the firm and some customers may not be good for the cultural and social environment—or acceptable in the political and legal environment. Being close to the market should give marketers a better feel for current trends—and help firms avoid serious mistakes.[16]

Canadian R&D means new opportunities

With forestry, mining, fishing, and farming still so much a part of the Canadian psyche, we often forget that we do so much more than provide raw

MARKETING DEMO 4–2
Vidéoway: A New Way of TV

I magine how appealing it would be as an advertiser if an individual TV viewer could indicate which of your products he or she would like to see a commercial for during the next break.

Wouldn't it be convenient if viewers could, simply by pushing a button on their remote control, increase the odds that the commercial they'll be shown is for a brand they're interested in? In other words, wouldn't it be handy if consumers themselves helped make targeting more efficient?

This is not some futuristic possibility but an existing marketing option in Quebec. Yet the Vidéoway system that has made it possible is largely unknown in the rest of Canada—partly because Canadians expect major breakthroughs to originate in the United States or Japan, never at home.

Launched in January 1990, it is now installed in 170,000 households in greater Montreal and Quebec City in areas served by Vidéotron, Montreal, Canada's second-largest cable operator. This is about 20 percent of Vidéotron's subscribers in these areas.

It is not just talk, but an actual, functioning system that has already had a remarkable impact on how subscribers use television.

It has also begun to open up new ways for advertisers to use the medium. A long list of advertisers, including Coca-Cola, Provigo, Petro-Canada, and the National Bank of Canada, are already busy learning how best to take advantage of the system's potential.

But barring a setback not now in sight, interactive TV should spread significantly across Canada in the next few years. It's time advertisers got up to speed in learning about this important new technology.

Viewers can use their remotes for unlimited access to about 160 services, including video games, other videotext services, and interactive TV. In the last of these, by pressing the F1, F2, F3, or F4 buttons on their remotes, viewers can choose among options for enhancing the viewing experience.

For instance, while watching *Le hockey Molson Export à TVA* on Wednesday nights, pushing F1 gives you the regular telecast, F2 and F3 isolation cameras on individual players, and F4 a replay of the last 10 seconds. Unlike some impressive-looking new technologies that have flopped, people actually use Vidéoway—it's *fun*.

A final example of Vidéoway's power is its current use during TVA newscasts. Subscribers can choose the order in which they want to see the local, national, and international news, weather, and sports.

They can also use it to view a four-minute version of a particular item rather than the two-minute version in the standard newscast.

This element of control increases the likelihood viewers will enjoy the telecast and stay with it. If you think this sounds like a whole new way to use television, you'd be right.

Source: Jim McElgunn, "Vidéoway: A New Way of TV," *Marketing*, June 1, 1992, p. 6.

---

products to the rest of the world. Major Canadian exports include automobiles, chemicals, and farm equipment. But because international trade is so important, and because the need, price, and supply of raw products change so frequently, more diversity is always encouraged.

Electronic goods, communication technology, and pharmaceuticals have come on the scene, often with government assistance, to help diversify the Canadian economy. And more research and development efforts are needed to keep corporate Canada competitive. There's a lot of room for Canadian companies to provide specialized products and services and create their own markets.[17] This won't happen to the extent that it should if Canada continues to spend less of its **gross domestic product (GDP)** on research and development than do other industrialized nations.

Rapid changes in information technology are creating many new market opportunities.

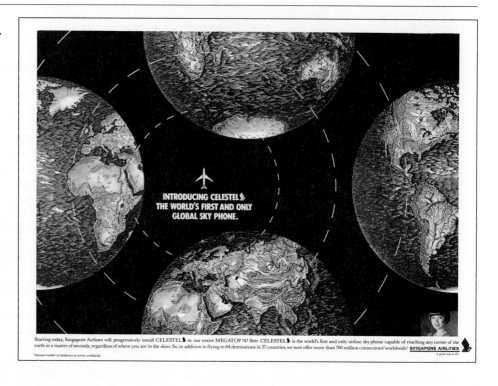

THE POLITICAL ENVIRONMENT

The attitudes and reactions of people, social critics, and governments all affect the **political environment**. Consumers in the same country usually share a common political environment, but the political environment can also have a dramatic effect on opportunities at a local or international level. Some business managers have become very successful by studying the political environment and developing strategies that take advantage of opportunities related to changing political dimensions.

Nationalism
can be limiting in
international markets

Strong sentiments of **nationalism**—an emphasis on a country's interests before everything else—affect how macro-marketing systems work. And they can affect how marketing managers work as well. Nationalistic feelings can reduce sales—or even block all marketing activity—in some international markets. For many years, Japan has made it difficult for outside firms to do business there, in spite of the fact that Japanese producers of cars, color TVs, VCRs, and other products have established profitable markets in North America, Europe, and other parts of the world. Japan is under pressure to change, but the changes are coming slowly.[18]

Nationalistic feelings can determine whether a firm can enter markets because businesses often must get permission to operate. In some political environments, this is only a routine formality. In others, a lot of red tape and personal influence are involved, and bribes are sometimes expected. This raises ethical issues for marketing managers.

**Regional groupings
are becoming
more important**

Important dimensions of the political environment are likely to be similar among nations that have banded together to have common regional economic boundaries. An outstanding example of this sort of regional grouping is the movement toward economic unification of Europe.

The unification effort began when the 12 countries that form the European Community (EC) dared to abandon old political squabbles and nationalistic prejudices in favor of cooperative efforts to reduce taxes and other barriers commonly applied at national boundaries.

In the past, each country had its own trade rules and regulations. These differences made it difficult to move products from one country to the other or to develop economies of scale. Now, the individual countries are reshaping into a unified economic superpower—what some have called the United States of Europe. By the end of 1992, reunification eliminated nearly 300 separate barriers to inter-European trade. Trucks loaded with products spill across the European continent and Britain. The increased efficiency is reducing costs—and the prices European consumers pay—and creating millions of new jobs.

The changes are by no means complete. By the year 2000, the EC may expand to include at least 25 countries and 450 million people (see Exhibit 4–3). Already the EC is forging links with two big trading blocs: the seven countries of the European Free Trade Association and Central Europe's three strongest economies—Hungary, Czechoslovakia, and Poland. Negotiations are also under way with Romania, Bulgaria, and Albania.

Five years ago, few people could have predicted the changes in the political environment—including the fall of communism—that have brought about

Exhibit 4–3 Current and Potential Member Countries of the European Community

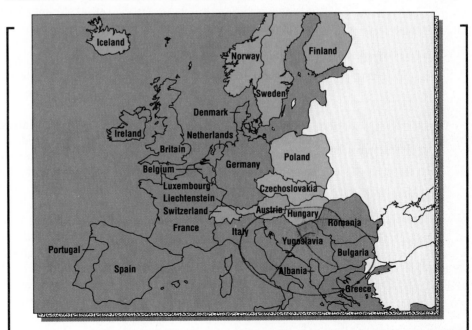

massive changes in these markets. But the changes have dramatically altered opportunities available to marketing managers both in Europe and in other parts of the world. Europe is now the largest unified market in the world.

The unification of European markets

Of course, removal of some economic and political barriers will not eliminate the need to adjust strategies to reach submarkets of European consumers. Centuries of cultural differences will not disappear overnight—they may never disappear. Yet the cooperative arrangement will give firms operating in Europe easier access to larger markets, and the European countries will have a more powerful voice in protecting their own interests.[19]

The political environment usually doesn't change as dramatically or as rapidly as it has in Europe. Some important political changes, both within and across nations, evolve more gradually. The development of consumerism is a good example.

Consumerism is here and basic

Consumerism is a social movement that seeks to increase the rights and powers of consumers and buyers in relation to sellers and the government. It was much more visible in Canada and the United States 25 years ago, in part due to the tireless efforts of consumer activist Ralph Nader. Since then, there have been consumer boycotts, protest marches, and media attention. However, such activities are more commonly undertaken today by those concerned with the environment.

The Canadian consumer scene

Canadian consumerism has been an important movement since the late 1960s. One reason for this increased consumer consciousness was the establishment in 1968 of Consumer and Corporate Affairs Canada (CCAC). This action gave one department the responsibility for administering a number of existing consumer protection laws. It also provided support for a wide variety of new programs designed to further the Canadian consumer's interests.

Consumer and Corporate Affairs Canada (CCAC) has moved aggressively in the area of consumer protection. Additional laws have been passed and existing legislation has been enforced far more vigorously than in the past. (The laws CCAC now administers in whole or in part are discussed in the next section covering the legal environment.)

Great emphasis has also been placed on educating and informing consumers. Complaints received by CCAC have been studied to determine the serious problem areas that remain and the corrective action that seems best. At the provincial level, consumer protection bureaus and agencies have also been greatly strengthened in recent years. Some of these units are becoming at least as active as their federal counterpart.

Consumerists—often but not always working through the Consumers' Association of Canada (CAC)—also try to safeguard the legitimate interest of all consumers. The CAC is an especially influential group at both the provincial and federal level. Since most consumers are unorganized, the CAC is now widely recognized as the voice of the Canadian consumer. And the organization speaks out whenever it believes new consumer protection legislation is needed, defective products must be removed from the market, or some other interest group (business, government, or agriculture) is taking unfair advantage of consumers.[20]

Government efforts at consumer education, as well as the various CAC publications, also increase consumer awareness. Specialized groups with a more limited focus, such as the Automobile Protection Association, are also busy educating and informing consumers. A number of consumer self-help and "rip-off" protection books are now sold across Canada. Many Canadian newspapers publish articles on intelligent purchasing and run columns designed to help complaining consumers obtain a fair deal from local merchants. Also, consumer-oriented programs on network TV and radio talk shows frequently deal with marketplace problems.

Not meeting consumers' expectations could be drastic

Generally, the public seems to like what the consumerists are trying to do. Marketers shouldn't forget that business's role is to satisfy consumers. No firm has a God-given right to operate any way it sees fit. This means the marketing manager as well as top management should give serious consideration to consumer attitudes in marketing planning. The alternative could be drastic from a macro point of view—the rules governing business could change. From a micro point of view, specific businesses might be banned or forced out of business by heavy fines.

Environmentalism

The 1990s brought with them the reemergence of concerns for the environment. Although environmentalism was recognized by some as an important social issue in the 1960s, wide-scale uneasiness over what we buy, how we use products, and how we dispose of them finally surfaced in the late 1980s. Campaigns initiated by environmental organizations, the various levels of government, and business urge Canadians to reduce, recycle, and reuse. Environmental issues are now receiving far more attention than more traditional consumer protection issues.

Environmentalism may not remain at the top of the public agenda forever, but there's little doubt that both consumers and business have begun to look for less environmentally damaging ways to do things. Canadian Pacific Hotels & Resorts is determined to make a difference. Its ambitious environmental program is described in Marketing Demo 4–3. Marketing plays a significant role in this process of identifying consumers' needs and desires, assisting in changing old ways, and communicating an organization's environmental contributions.

Political environment may offer new opportunities

The political environment can be a plus as well as a minus. A government may decide that encouraging business and opening markets are constructive steps for its people. China and Japan recently opened their markets more to foreign investors and competitors. The United States, Canada, and other highly developed countries may give industrial development a boost in Latin America, Africa, and Asia by allowing manufactured goods from those areas to be imported at lower duty rates.

Within Canada, the federal government uses developmental incentives such as accelerated depreciation, commercial loan guarantees, and start-up grants to encourage growth in depressed areas. Provincial and local governments also try to attract and hold businesses, sometimes with tax incentives.

Some business executives have become very successful by studying the political environment and developing strategies that use these political opportunities.

MARKETING DEMO 4–3
Corporate Environment Turns Another Shade of Green

(**A**) nationwide employee survey by Canadian Pacific Hotels and Resorts (CPH&R), the first of its kind in the hospitality industry, the company claims, revealed some interesting findings. Of the 10,000 employees surveyed, more than 92 percent said they strongly support the idea of a companywide green program, and 82 percent said they would work extra hours to make improvements.

"Not only are employees willing to take measures on behalf of the environment, 89 percent said it would make them feel better about their jobs," said CPH&R director of public relations Ann Checkley.

"We interpret this as a mandate to implement the most ambitious environmental program possible."

"Ambitious" is an understatement. The company's 16-point action plan, to be implemented over the next two years, is one of the most comprehensive. Its goals include:

1. A 50 percent reduction in landfill waste and 20 percent reduction in paper use by December 1992.

2. An expanded pilot project of donating surplus soap to Global Ed-Med Supplies.

3. Programs to recycle paper, newspaper, cans, organic waste, motor oils, cardboard, plastics, bottles, coat hangers, and printer cartridges.

4. A policy and procedure for the identification and disposal of hazardous waste.

5. The initiation of "phase out" programs to reduce or eliminate individual sugar packets, individual creamers, individual condiment containers, and disposable cups.

6. Blue boxes in all guest rooms.

7. To retrofit all appropriate lighting from incandescent to compact fluorescent bulbs.

8. Replace all showerheads and taps with low-flow alternatives.

9. Establish standard temperature setting on all hot water tanks.

10. A purchasing policy that imposes, where possible, Environmental Choice standards as the minimum of standards.

11. Convert all necessary paper products to unbleached kraft or recycled materials.

12. Streamline the use of cleaning agents and, where available, replace with nonaerosol products; eliminate hazardous chemicals and synthetic perfumes.

13. Purchase only re-refined motor oil and re-inked printer ribbons.

14. Negotiate with suppliers to eliminate and reduce packaging.

15. Initiate an alliance with Canadian Organic Growers to purchase organically grown foodstuffs.

16. Establish a policy to make toilet dams mandatory in all tanks that flush more than 2 gallons per flush.

Source: Laura Medcalf, "Corporate Environment Turns Another Shade of Green," *Marketing*, June 24, 1991, p. 22.

THE LEGAL ENVIRONMENT

Changes in the political environment often lead to changes in the **legal environment** and in the way existing laws are enforced. It's hard for marketing managers to know all the relevant laws, but it's important that they do because the legal environment sets the basic rules for how a business can operate in society. The legal environment may severely limit some choices, but changes in laws and how they are interpreted also create new opportunities. To illustrate the effects of the legal environment, we will discuss how it has evolved in Canada.

However, keep in mind that laws often vary from one geographic market to another—especially when different countries are involved.

Impact of anticombines legislation

The Combines Investigation Act was established to prevent anticompetitive conduct. It was not very effective legislation because of the difficulty in prosecuting those charged under the Combines Investigation Act. Those offenses had to be treated as violations of criminal law. The government, to win a case, had to prove guilt "beyond any reasonable doubt." Difficulties in establishing this degree of proof discouraged prosecution. They also reduced the likelihood that any firm brought to court would be found guilty.

What, then, did the Combines Investigation Act as amended through 1960 actually accomplish? The legislation prevented two kinds of marketing activity: price-fixing by competitors and misleading price advertising. Even though resale price maintenance was specifically prohibited in 1951, considerable difference of opinion exists as to how often and how effectively manufacturers still controlled retail prices.

Aside from these two or three areas, the Combines Investigation Act had little effect on either prevailing marketing practices or the structure of the Canadian economy. No firm was ever found guilty of price discrimination. In two key cases brought to court under the merger provisions, the government lost and did not appeal.[21]

Bill C-2: The "new" Competition Act— Stage 1

In December 1975, dissatisfaction with the Combines Investigation Act led Parliament to pass Bill C-2, the first part of a proposed two-stage major revision of the existing legislation. The minister who introduced this legislation said the following were its most important features:[22]

1. The bill clarifies and strengthens provisions concerning misleading advertising. It adds new protection in the area of warranties and guarantees. It deals with certain undesirable selling practices such as pyramid selling, referral selling, bait-and-switch selling, selling at a price higher than advertised, the use of promotional contests, and "double ticketing."

2. The bill covers some trade practices that could be acceptable in some circumstances but not in others. The Restrictive Trade Practices Commission is authorized to review these practices (refusal to deal, consignment selling, exclusive dealing, tied sales, and market restriction) and to issue orders prohibiting or modifying them.

3. The commission also has the power to issue orders forbidding the implementation within Canada of foreign judgments, laws, or directives where it finds them contrary to the Canadian public interest.

4. The bill makes bid rigging an indictable offense. It also strengthens existing provisions regarding resale price maintenance.

5. Services are to be covered by the provisions of the Combines Investigation Act. Service activities have become a very important part of the Canadian economy, and there is no logical case for their continued exclusion from our competition legislation.

6. All economic activity in the private sector is covered by federal competition policy. However, activities regulated or authorized by valid

federal or provincial legislation will continue to be exempted from the provisions of the Combines Investigation Act.

7. The bill proposes that, in order to prove that an agreement prevents or lessens competition "unduly," it's not necessary to establish complete or virtual elimination of competition in the relevant market.

8. The courts, for the first time, are able to issue interim injunctions to prevent the commission or continuation of suspected offenses against the act until the main issue is settled.

9. Also for the first time the bill allows for court action by anyone adversely affected by violation of the act to enable such a person to recover his or her damages and full costs.

Other federal legislation exists

Other laws and regulations are designed primarily to strengthen and maintain two very widely recognized consumer rights: to be protected against the marketing of hazardous goods (the right to safety) and to be safeguarded against deceptive promotion (the right to be informed). Here, we'll mention only a few of the many federal laws and regulations designed to protect public well-being.

The Food and Drug Act regulates the sale of foods, drugs, cosmetics, and medical devices. This legislation deals with quality standards, packaging, labelling, and advertising, as well as the manufacturing practices and selling policies of food and drug manufacturers. Certain forms of misrepresentation in food labelling, packaging, selling, and advertising are specifically outlawed by the Food and Drug Act.

The Canadian Radio-Television Commission regulates broadcast advertising. The Standards Branch of Consumer and Corporate Affairs Canada is one of many federal agencies that establish product standards and grades. There are also laws concerning the labelling of wool, furs, precious metals, and flammable fabrics. One form of promotional self-regulation is the voluntary ban on cigarette advertising on Canadian radio and television, which became effective January 1, 1972.

See Exhibit 4–4 for a listing of legislation covered by Consumer and Corporate Affairs Canada.

Provincial and local regulations

Marketers must also be aware of provincial and local laws that affect the four Ps. There are provincial and city laws regulating minimum prices and the setting of prices (to be discussed in Chapter 18); regulations for starting up a business (licenses, examinations, and even tax payments); and, in some communities, regulations prohibiting certain activities, such as door-to-door selling or selling on Sundays or during evenings. Sale and advertising of alcoholic beverages also are provincially controlled.

The provinces have become far more active in protecting consumer rights. All of them have passed laws that regulate the granting of credit and otherwise call for truth in lending. Purchasers are often provided with a cooling-off period within which they may cancel the contract, return any merchandise actually received, and obtain a full refund. The provinces are also more actively exercising their regulatory authority over car dealers, travel agents, and many other types of business that deal with large numbers of consumers spending considerable amounts of money.

Perhaps the most significant development on the provincial scene has been a number of governments passing trade practices legislation. Such legislation

Exhibit 4–4   Legislation Administered by Consumer and Corporate Affairs Canada

1. **Fully administered by CCAC**
   - Bankruptcy Act and Bankruptcy Rules
   - Boards of Trade Act
   - Canada Business Corporations Act
   - Canada Cooperative Associations Act
   - Canada Corporations Act
   - Competition Act
   - Companies' Creditors Arrangement Act
   - Consumer Packaging and Labelling Act
   - Copyright Act
   - Department of Consumer and Corporate Affairs Act
   - Electricity and Gas Inspection Act
   - Government Corporations Operation Act
   - Hazardous Products Act
   - Industrial Design Act
   - National Trade Mark and True Labelling Act
   - Patent Act
   - Pension Fund Societies Act
   - Precious Metals Marking Act
   - Public Servants Invention Act
   - Tax Rebate Discounting Act
   - Textile Labelling Act
   - Timber Marking Act
   - Trade Marks Act
   - Weights and Measures Act

2. **Administered jointly with other departments**
   - Bills of Exchange Act (with Finance)
   - Canada Agricultural Products Standards Act (with Agriculture)
   - Canada Dairy Products Act (with Agriculture)
   - Fish Inspection Act (with Fisheries and Oceans)
   - Food and Drugs Act (with Health and Welfare)
   - Maple Products Industry Act (with Agriculture)
   - Shipping Conferences Exemption Act (with Transport)
   - Winding-Up Act (with Finance)

Source: Montrose S. Sommers, James G. Barnes, and William J. Stanton, *Fundamentals of Marketing* (Toronto: McGraw-Hill Ryerson, 1992), p. 36.

protects the consumer from unconscionable and deceptive practices. Though the laws passed by different provinces aren't identical, they all attempt to deal with the same set of problems.

The legislative environment in Quebec

Like every other major governmental jurisdiction in Canada, Quebec has passed a number of laws to protect its consumers. The most important Quebec legislation, the Consumer Protection Act of 1978, is modeled after, but goes far beyond, trade practices legislation previously passed in British Columbia, Ontario, and Alberta. One unique feature of the Quebec statute is its virtual ban on all advertising directed toward children.

Some laws reflect a growing concern with ensuring the preeminence of the French language in every aspect of Quebec life. Long before the Parti Quebecois came to power, laws required that French be featured either exclusively or as prominently as any other language on the labels of all food products sold in that province. Similar legislation governing billboards, direct mail, and point-of-sale displays was passed in 1974. Bill 101, enacted in August 1977, provides even greater legal support for the primary and sometimes exclusive use of French in all aspects of advertising and promotion.

Although Quebec is too large a part of the total Canadian market to be neglected by most major North American manufacturers, such firms are certain to incur additional costs in complying with language legislation. Smaller Canadian and foreign corporations, on the other hand, may well cease marketing in Quebec. They could decide that the size of this market—as compared with the rest of North America—doesn't justify modifying the firm's promotional efforts to the extent compliance would require.

The Goods
and Services Tax

The Goods and Services Tax (GST) came into effect January 1, 1991. Its purpose is to help reduce a growing federal deficit, and it replaces a less effective federal sales tax. However, the GST was met with dire warnings that it was the wrong time to introduce such a tax. Canada was in a recession, and the business sector saw the tax as taking consumer dollars out of customers' hands. While some consumer goods and services became more expensive with the tax, others dropped in price. Many marketing managers took full advantage of this opportunity to offer a deal. But others confused consumers by advertising "GST Free" sales on items whose prices weren't affected or were reduced by the tax.

The GST presented many interesting challenges to marketing managers and their businesses. While the tax made many consumer items more expensive, those businesses that were prepared for it could inform consumers of potential benefits and win new customers as a result.

Consumerists and the
law say "let the
seller beware"

Traditional thinking about buyer-seller relations has been *let the buyer beware*—but now it seems to be shifting to *let the seller beware*. The number of consumer protection laws has been increasing. These laws and court interpretations suggest the emphasis now is on protecting consumers *directly*—rather than *indirectly* by protecting competition. Production-oriented businesses may find this frustrating, but they'll just have to adapt to this new political and legal environment. As Marketing Demo 4–4 shows, firms that evade the laws are being prosecuted.

Much of the impact of consumer protection legislation tends to fall on manufacturers. They're the producers of the product, and under common law they're supposed to stand behind what they make. Generally, common law warranties have been fairly weak—what was "reasonable" or what the courts would consider "reasonable." But increasingly, the courts are putting greater responsibility on manufacturers and even holding them liable for any injury their product causes, even injury caused by a user's carelessness. In such an environment, businesses clearly must lean over backward. Times have changed—let the seller beware.

Know the laws—
follow the courts

Because the real meaning of a law depends in large part on how it's interpreted, marketers must also be aware of how legislation is being implemented and enforced. Often, good legal assistance is needed to keep up with new rules, regulations, and interpretations.

If marketing managers have a better understanding of the intent of the lawmakers and interpreters, there will be less conflict between business and government—and fewer costly mistakes. Managers should accept the political and

MARKETING DEMO 4–4
Motorcycle Firms Plead Guilty in Price Probe

(F) ive Canadian motorcycle companies and their national industry group have pleaded guilty to collaborating to buoy the price of motorcycles.

The Motorcycle & Moped Industry Council and its five members—Honda Canada, Inc., Yamaha Motor Canada Ltd., Suzuki Canada, Inc., Canadian Kawasaki Motors, Inc., and Fred Deeley Imports Ltd. (which sells Harley-Davidson bikes)—pleaded guilty Friday to 1 count of a 17-count indictment handed down under the federal Competition Act.

Ontario Supreme Court Justice J. R. Ewaschuk dismissed the other 16 counts because Crown prosecutors did not provide evidence as part of a plea-bargain agreement.

In addition to the guilty plea, defendants agreed to the Crown's sentencing recommendation of fines totaling $250,000 and a prohibition on future price maintenance. Ewaschuk reserved sentencing until October 31.

The indictment states that between April 12 and November 12, 1984, the defendants "did, by agreement or threat, attempt to influence upwards or discourage the reduction" of motorcycle prices offered by dealers at the MMIC's spring 1985 trade show in Toronto.

A statement of facts, jointly agreed to by both sides, says the defendants first became concerned about dealers discounting prices during the trade show in 1981.

As a result, exhibitors at the 1983 and 1984 shows were required to display only the manufacturer's suggested list price, and "if an exhibitor failed to follow their rules he would be removed and not allowed to participate in future shows," the statement said.

The defendants believed the policy "would reduce price discounting at the shows and would result in less price competition in the retail market in the long run."

The rule was dropped prior to the 1985 show after "consultation" with officials from the Bureau of Competition Policy of the Department of Consumer and Corporate Affairs, the statement said.

If the recommended fines are accepted by Ewaschuk, they will be the largest total fine for a case under the price-maintenance provisions of the Competition Act, said Wayne Critchley, the bureau's deputy director of investigations and research.

Critchley, in an interview from Ottawa, declined to reveal who filed the complaint that led to the investigation.

The plea bargain calls for fines of $50,000 for the MMIC and $40,000 for the companies.

Crown prosecutors declined to say what fines they first proposed, but a source close to the case said initial proposals called for levies of $750,000 for each of the defendants.

Source: Colin Languedoc, "Motorcycle Firms Plead Guilty in Price Probe," *The Financial Post*, October 16, 1989, p. 3.

legal environment as simply another framework in which business must function. After all, it's the consumers—through their government representatives—who determine the kind of economic system they want.

THE CULTURAL AND SOCIAL ENVIRONMENT

The **cultural and social environment** affects how and why people live and behave as they do—which affects customer buying behavior and eventually the economic, political, and legal environment. Many variables make up the cultural and social environment. Some examples are the languages people speak, the type of education they have, their religious beliefs, what type of food they eat, the style of clothing and housing they have, and how they view marriage and family. Because the cultural and social environment has such broad effects, most people don't stop to think about it, how it may be changing, or how it may differ for other people.

A marketing manager can't afford to take the cultural and social environment for granted. Although changes tend to come slowly, they can have far-reaching effects. A marketing manager who sees the changes early may be able to identify big opportunities. Further, within any broad society, different subgroups of people may be affected by the cultural and social environment in different ways. These differences require special attention when segmenting markets. In fact, dealing with these differences is often one of the greatest challenges managers face when planning strategies for international markets.

Since we will discuss details of how the cultural and social environment relates to buying behavior in Chapters 6 through 8, where we will present only a few examples to emphasize the possible impact on marketing strategy.

Cultural similarities
and differences

Is there a distinct Canadian culture? If so, how do cultural differences and so-called national characteristics help determine the way Canadians live, work, and consume? It's easy to ask such questions but difficult to answer them in a manner helpful to marketers. All we can do now is indicate some of the cultural similarities and differences that must be taken into consideration.

Seymour Lipset has provided important insight into how we differ from our southern neighbor, the United States. He sees distinct differences that find their roots in the American Revolution. From this event the two countries emerged: one victorious and independent of its British ties, the other content to maintain its link to England.

We appear to have more tolerance for "elites," Lipset believes. We also place less importance on equality. Americans are more religious, more patriotic, and more committed to higher education. Americans don't favor large welfare programs or an active role for government in the economy.

National identity is a very important issue for Canadians, and we look endlessly for qualities that make us distinct. Unfortunately, as Lipset says, we often define ourselves by how we differ from Americans. If they're brash risk takers, then we're solid, reliable, and decent. Canadians are more class-aware, law-abiding, and group-oriented.[23]

Whether or not we're really the "kinder, gentler" nation may not be easily established. Lipset argues that the two countries differ on the principles that organize them. Nevertheless, similarities in values, living patterns, work roles, family relationships, and consumer behavior are much more obvious than the differences that might exist between American and Anglo-Canadian families.

Canada is indeed
a mosaic

One of the Canadian market's important characteristics is its distinctive regional differences. The United States is often considered a melting pot. It's best to think of Canada in terms of a mosaic. Incomes, consumption patterns, lifestyles, dialects, and attitudes vary from province to province. For example, average personal disposable income per household is much higher in Ontario than in Prince Edward Island. Unemployment is generally higher in the Atlantic Provinces than in the rest of Canada. Life in the Prairie provinces is usually more relaxed than in other regions—people expect and often experience "western hospitality." Consumption patterns also reflect regional differences. The farther west you go in Canada, the more milk people drink. West Coast dwellers prefer foreign cars; Maritimers opt for compacts. Consumers in the Atlantic region consume more tea per capita than other Canadians.[24] There are fewer golfers, joggers, and gardeners in Quebec. You will find more cyclists, frequent skiers, and theater fans there than in the rest of Canada.

Cultural differences similar to those found between regional areas are also common within large urban areas. Montreal and Toronto, for example, have large Italian, Greek, Jewish, and Chinese communities. Almost 190,000 residents of Metropolitan Toronto report Italian as their mother tongue—an important factor marketers cannot overlook. Food stores, newsstands, travel agencies, credit unions, and restaurants cater specifically to such culturally defined markets. The ethnic market is discussed in greater detail in Chapter 6.

Meech Lake reinforces the trend

With the collapse of the Meech Lake Agreement in 1990, Canadians began the process of reexamining not only the relationship between French- and English-speaking Canadians, but also Native, immigrant, and regional issues. These differences, and the many strengths that Canada's diverse nature offers, can and should be fully recognized by marketing managers. This means treating all Canadians as potential customers, often with unique needs and offering valuable opportunities. Cultural diversity, too, will be explored more fully in Chapter 6.

Bribes or standard operating procedure

Differences between countries in how business is done is both a fact of life and a cause of widespread concern. What some North Americans call a bribe may be accepted as a necessary business expense in other countries. Some cultures even have a special word for financial "favors" and treat them much like Canadians and Americans treat tips. It's just the way things are done. Recently, however, an increasing reluctance at home to sanction bribes and related practices to obtain overseas sales has gotten some firms and even crown corporations into legal hot water. Methods used to sell US aircraft overseas were widely criticized in the United States. In this country, many observers bitterly attacked Atomic Energy of Canada for paying "special commissions" to well-placed foreign sales representatives who helped AEC sell its CANDU reactors. Some felt that such practices violated the spirit, if not the letter, of Canadian law.[25]

In reply, many North American firms say they're merely following the prevailing practices of customer countries. It has also been argued that Canadian firms can't refuse to offer kickbacks or other special inducements as long as companies headquartered elsewhere continue to do business as usual. Unfortunately for the firms concerned, such arguments are no longer accepted by many Canadians as good enough reasons for making illegal or morally questionable payments.

Health and fitness

In the past decade, North American culture has put much more emphasis on health and fitness. There's concern, for example, about the amount of salt, calories, and fiber in diets, so many firms now offer salt-free, low-cal, or high-fiber food products. Responding to such consumer interests can be profitable. A California egg producer who bred a flock of chickens to lay low-cholesterol eggs has a hard-boiled success with eggs that sell at about three times the normal price.

The fitness emphasis has also sparked interest in a wide range of exercise-related products and the growth of companies such as Nike, Nautilus, and Weight Watchers.

Sunday shopping

Imagine a major Canadian department store that modestly covers its windows on Sunday. The T. Eaton's Company did just that as recently as 1960. As Canadian values and ideas about personal choice change, consumer habits and needs change with them. In 1990, Ontario reluctantly allowed retail outlets to open on Sunday. A law against Sunday opening was first struck down as unconstitutional in Ontario's Supreme Court. The law was challenged by retailers who saw Sunday opening as a much needed source of business. It was also opposed by shoppers who felt that the government had no right to tell people when they could shop. Those against Sunday shopping were subsequently pleased to see that Ontario decision overruled by the Supreme Court of Canada.[26] Eventually, however, the Ontario legislature legalized Sunday openings.

Changing women's roles

The shifting roles of women in society illustrate the importance of the cultural and social environment on marketing strategy planning. Forty years ago, most people in Canada felt that a women's role was in the home—first and foremost as a wife and mother. Women had less opportunity for higher education and were completely shut out of many of the most interesting jobs. Obviously, there have been big changes in that stereotyped thinking. With better job opportunities, more women are delaying marriage, and once married they are likely to stay in the work force and have fewer children. We shall see in Chapter 6 how a falling birthrate affects the manufacture and marketing of housing, baby foods, convenience foods, clothing, and cosmetics.

The flood of women into the job market boosted economic growth and changed Canadian society in many other ways. Many in-home jobs that used to be done primarily by women, ranging from family shopping to preparing meals to doing volunteer work, still need to be done by someone. Husbands and children now do some of these jobs, a situation that has changed the target market for many products. Or a working woman may face a crushing "poverty of time" and look for help elsewhere, creating opportunities for producers of frozen meals, child care centers, dry cleaners, financial services, and the like.

Although there is still a big wage gap between men and women, the income working women generate gives them new independence and purchasing power. For example, women now purchase about half of all cars. Not long ago, many car dealers insulted a woman shopper by ignoring her or suggesting that she come back with her husband. Now, car companies have realized that women are important customers. It's interesting that Japanese car dealers, especially Mazda and Toyota, were the first to really pay attention to women customers. In Japan, fewer women have jobs, or buy cars. Japanese society is still very much male oriented. Perhaps it was the extreme contrast with Japanese society that prompted these firms to pay more attention to women buyers in North America.[27]

Women are also becoming employers. Women with university degrees are becoming frustrated with being stuck in middle-management or lower-level positions, and they are starting their own businesses. By 1990, approximately 500,000 women owned businesses in Canada. At the end of 1990, it was estimated that some 33 percent of all businesses belonged to women.

Women's changing role has created opportunities for marketing but also complications. A marketing mix targeted at women, for example, may require a real balancing act. Advertising showing a woman at the office may attract some customers but alienate housewives who feel that their job doesn't command as

Cultural and social trends in North America have prompted increased consumer interest in health and fitness—and new marketing opportunities.

much status as it should. Conversely, an ad that shows a woman doing housework might be criticized for encouraging stereotypes.

Changes come slowly

Most changes in basic cultural values and social attitudes come slowly. An individual firm can't hope to encourage big changes in the short run. Instead, it should identify current attitudes and work within these constraints—as it seeks new and better opportunities.[28]

HOW TO EVALUATE OPPORTUNITIES

A progressive firm constantly looks for new opportunities. Once identified, it must then screen and evaluate. Usually, a firm can't pursue all available opportunities, so it must try to match its opportunities to its resources and objectives. First, management must quickly screen out the obvious mismatches so other opportunities can be analyzed more carefully. Let's look at some approaches for screening and evaluating opportunities.

Developing and applying screening criteria

After you analyze the firm's resources (for strengths and weaknesses), the environmental trends the firm faces, and the objectives of top management, you merge them all into a set of product-market screening criteria. These criteria should include both quantitative and qualitative components. The quantitative components summarize the firm's objectives: sales, profit, and return on investment (ROI) targets. (Note: ROI analysis is discussed briefly in Appendix C, which follows Chapter 18.) The qualitative components summarize what kinds of businesses the firm wants to be in, what businesses it wants to exclude, what weaknesses it should avoid, and what resources (strengths) and trends it should build on.[29]

Developing screening criteria is difficult—but worth the effort. They summarize in quantitative terms in one place what the firm wants to accomplish, as well as roughly how and where it wants to accomplish it. The criteria should be realistic—that is, they should be achievable. Opportunities that pass the screen should be able to be turned into strategies that the firm can implement with the resources it has.

Exhibit 4–5 illustrates the product-market screening criteria for a small retail and wholesale distributor. These criteria help the firm's managers eliminate unsuitable opportunities—and find attractive ones to turn into strategies and plans.

Whole plans should be evaluated

You need to forecast the probable results of implementing a marketing strategy to apply the quantitative part of the screening criteria because only implemented plans generate sales, profits, and return on investment (ROI). For a rough screening, you only need to estimate the likely results of implementing each opportunity over a logical planning period. If a product's life is likely to be three years, for example, then a good strategy may not produce profitable results for 6 to 12 months. But evaluated over the projected three-year life, the product may look like a winner. When evaluating the potential of possible opportunities (product-market strategies), it is important to evaluate similar things—that is, *whole* plans.

Exhibit 4–5   An Example of Product-Market Screening Criteria for a Small Retail and Wholesale Distributor ($5 million annual sales)

1. **Quantitative criteria**
   a. Increase sales by $750,000 per year for the next five years
   b. Earn ROI of at least 25 percent before taxes on new ventures
   c. Break even within one year on new ventures
   d. Opportunity must be large enough to justify interest (to help meet objectives) but small enough so company can handle with the resources available
   e. Several opportunities should be pursued to reach the objectives—to spread the risks

2. **Qualitative criteria**
   a. Nature of business preferred
      (1) Goods and services sold to present customers
      (2) Quality products that can be sold at high prices with full margins
      (3) Competition should be weak and opportunity should be hard to copy for several years
      (4) Should build on our strong sales skills
      (5) There should be strongly felt (even unsatisfied) needs—to reduce promotion costs and permit high prices
   b. Constraints
      (1) Nature of businesses to exclude
         (a) Manufacturing
         (b) Any requiring large fixed capital investments
         (c) Any requiring many people who must be "good" all the time and would require much supervision
      (2) Geographic
         (a) United States, Mexico, and Canada only
      (3) General
         (a) Make use of current strengths
         (b) Attractiveness of market should be reinforced by more than one of the following basic trends: technological, demographic, social, economic, and/or political
         (c) Market should not be bucking any basic trends

Exhibit 4–6   Expected Sales and Cost Curves of Two Strategies over Five-Year Planning Periods

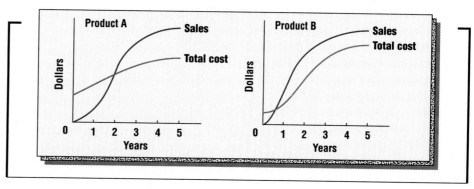

Opportunities that pass the screen—or all opportunities, if you don't use screening criteria—should be evaluated in more detail before being accepted as *the* product-market strategic plans for implementation. Usually, a firm has more opportunities than resources and has to choose among them—to match its opportunities to its resources and objectives. The following approaches help firms select among possible plans.

Total profit approach can help evaluate possible plans

In the total profit approach, management forecasts potential sales and costs during the life of the plan to estimate likely profitability. Managers may evaluate the prospects for each plan over a five-year planning period, using monthly and/or annual sales and cost estimates. This is shown graphically in Exhibit 4–6.

Note that managers can evaluate different marketing plans at the same time. Exhibit 4–6 compares a much improved product and product concept (Product A) with a "me too" product (Product B) for the same target market. In the short run, the me-too product will make a profit sooner and might look like the better choice—if managers consider only one year's results. The improved product, on the other hand, will take a good deal of pioneering—but over its five-year life will be much more profitable.

Return-on-investment (ROI) approach can help evaluate possible plans, too

Besides evaluating the profit potential of possible plans, firms may also calculate the return on investment (ROI) of resources needed to implement plans. One plan may require a heavy investment in advertising and channel development, for example, while another relies primarily on lower price.

ROI analyses can be useful for selecting among possible plans because equally profitable plans may require vastly different resources and offer different rates of return on investment. Some firms are very concerned with ROI, especially those that borrow money for working capital. There is little point in borrowing to implement strategies that won't return enough to meet the cost of borrowing.

PLANNING GRIDS HELP EVALUATE A PORTFOLIO OF OPPORTUNITIES

When a firm has many possibilities to evaluate, it usually has to compare quite different ones. This problem is easier to handle with graphical approaches such as the nine-box strategic planning grid developed by General Electric and used by many other companies. Such grids can help evaluate a firm's whole portfolio of strategic plans or businesses.

General Electric looks for green positions

General Electric's strategic planning grid—see Exhibit 4–7—forces company managers to make three-part judgments (high, medium, and low) about the business strengths and industry attractiveness of all proposed or existing product-market plans. As you can see from Exhibit 4–7, this approach helps a manager organize information about the company's marketing environments (discussed earlier in this chapter) along with information about its strategy.

The industry attractiveness dimension helps managers answer the question: "Does this product-market plan look like a good idea?" The answer, they have to judge such factors as the size of the market and its growth rate, nature of competition, the plan's potential environmental or social impact, and how laws might affect it. Note that an opportunity may be attractive for *some* company— but not well suited to the strengths (and weaknesses) of a particular firm. That is why the GE grid also considers the business strengths dimension.

The business strengths dimension focuses on the ability of the company to pursue a product-market plan effectively. To make judgments along this dimension, a manager evaluates whether the firm has people with the right talents and skills to implement the plan, whether the plan is consistent with the firm's image and profit objectives, and whether the firm could establish a profitable market share given its technical capability, costs, and size.

GE feels opportunities that fall into the green boxes in the upper left-hand corner of the grid are its best growth opportunities. Managers give these opportunities high marks on both industry attractiveness and business strengths. The red boxes in the lower right-hand corner of the grid, on the other hand, suggest a no-growth policy. Existing red businesses may continue to generate earnings, but they no longer deserve much investment. Yellow businesses are borderline cases—they can go either way. GE may continue to support an existing yellow business but will probably reject a proposal for a new one.

Exhibit 4–7   General Electric's Strategic Planning Grid

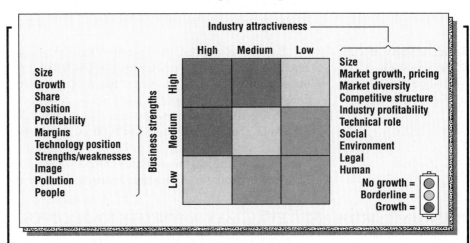

GE's "stop light" evaluation method is a very subjective, multiple-factor approach. It avoids the traps and possible errors of trying to use oversimplified, single-number criteria like ROI or market share. Instead, top managers review detailed written summaries of many factors that help them make summary judgments. Then they make a collective judgment. This approach generally leads to agreement. It also helps everyone understand why the company supports some new opportunities and not others.[30]

Factors can change to reflect objectives

General Electric considers various business strength and industry attractiveness factors that reflect its objectives. Another firm might modify the evaluation to emphasize other factors, depending on its objectives and the type of product-market plans it is considering. For example, a small firm with only one product might consider a similar grid—with different criteria—to evaluate new product or market opportunities. While different firms focus on different factors, using many factors helps ensure that managers consider all the company's concerns when evaluating alternative opportunities.

MULTIPRODUCT FIRMS HAVE A DIFFICULT STRATEGY PLANNING JOB

Multiproduct firms like General Electric obviously have a more difficult strategic planning job than firms with only a few products or product lines aimed at the same or similar target markets. Multiproduct firms have to develop strategic plans for very different businesses. And they have to balance plans and resources so the whole company reaches its objectives. This means they must analyze alternatives using approaches similar to the General Electric strategic planning grid and only approve plans that make sense for the whole company, even if it means getting needed resources by "milking" some businesses and eliminating others.

Details on how to manage a complicated multiproduct firm are beyond our scope. But you should be aware (1) that there are such firms and (2) that the principles in this text are applicable—they just have to be extended. For example, some firms use strategic business units (SBUs), and some use portfolio management.

Strategic business units may help

Some multiproduct firms try to improve their operations by forming strategic business units. A **strategic business unit (SBU)** is an organizational unit (within a larger company) that focuses on some product-markets and is treated as a separate profit center. By forming SBUs, a company formally acknowledges its very different activities. One SBU of Sara Lee, for example, produces baked goods for consumers and restaurants; another produces and markets Hanes brand T-shirts and underwear.

Some SBUs grow rapidly and require a great deal of attention and resources. Others produce only average profits and should be milked—that is, allowed to generate cash for the businesses with more potential. Product lines with poor market position, low profits, and poor growth prospects should be dropped or sold.

Companies that set up strategic business units usually do change their attitudes and methods of operation. They rate managers in terms of achieving strategic plans—rather than short-term profits or sales increases. With SBUs, the emphasis is on developing plans; those accepted are implemented aggressively. Under this concept, companies reward some managers for successfully phasing out product lines, while others are rewarded for expanding sales in other markets.

Each manager carries out a market-oriented strategic plan approved by top management. The manager's job is to help develop effective plans and then implement them—to ensure the company's resources are used effectively and the firm accomplishes its objectives.

Some firms use portfolio management

Some top managements handle strategic planning for a multiproduct firm with an approach called **portfolio management**—which treats alternative products, divisions, or strategic business units (SBUs) as though they were stock investments, to be bought and sold using financial criteria. Such managers make trade-offs among very different opportunities. They treat the various alternatives as investments that should be supported, milked, or sold off, depending on profitability and return on investment (ROI). In effect, they evaluate each alternative just like a stock market trader evaluates a stock.[31]

This approach makes some sense if alternatives are really quite different. Top managers feel they can't become very familiar with the prospects for all of their alternatives, so they fall back on the easy-to-compare quantitative criteria. And because the short run is much clearer than the long run, they place heavy emphasis on *current* profitability and return on investment. This puts great pressure on the operating managers to "deliver" *in the short run*—perhaps even neglecting the long run.

Neglecting the long run is risky, and this is the main weakness of the portfolio approach. This weakness can be overcome by enhancing the portfolio management approach with market-oriented strategic plans. They make it possible for

Large multiproduct firms like Philip Morris evaluate and pursue a portfolio of strategic opportunities all around the world.

managers to more accurately evaluate the alternatives' short-run and long-run prospects.

EVALUATING OPPORTUNITIES IN INTERNATIONAL MARKETS

Evaluate the risks

The approaches we've discussed so far apply to international markets just as they do to domestic ones. But in international markets it is often harder to fully understand the marketing environment variables. This may make it harder to see the risks involved in particular opportunities. Some countries are politically unstable; their governments and constitutions come and go. An investment safe under one government might become a takeover target under another. Further, the possibility of foreign exchange controls—and tax rate changes—can reduce the chance of getting profits and capital back to the home country.

To reduce the risk of missing some basic variable that may help screen out a risky opportunity, marketing managers sometimes need a detailed analysis of the market environment they are considering entering. Such an analysis can reveal facts about an unfamiliar market that a manager in a distant country might otherwise overlook. Further, a local citizen who knows the marketing environment may be able to identify an "obvious" problem ignored even in a careful analysis. Thus, it is very useful for the analysis to include inputs from locals—perhaps cooperative middlemen.[32]

Risks vary with environmental sensitivity

The farther you go from familiar territory, the greater the risk of making big mistakes. But not all products or marketing mixes involve the same risk. Think of the risks as running along a "continuum of environmental sensitivity." See Exhibit 4–8.

Some products are relatively insensitive to the economic and cultural environment they're placed in. These products may be accepted as is, or may require just a little adaptation to make them suitable for local use. Most industrial products are near the insensitive end of this continuum.

At the other end of the continuum, we find highly sensitive products that may be difficult or impossible to adapt to all international situations. Consumer products closely linked to other social or cultural variables are at this end. For example, some of the scanty women's clothing popular in Western countries would be totally inappropriate in Arab countries where women are expected to cover their faces. Similarly, some cultures view dieting as unhealthy, so a diet product that is popular in North America might be a big failure there. "Faddy" type consumer products are also at this end of the continuum. It's sometimes difficult to understand why such products are well accepted in a home market.

Exhibit 4–8   Continuum of Environmental Sensitivity

Insensitive		Sensitive
Industrial products	Basic commodity-type consumer products	Consumer products that are linked to cultural variables

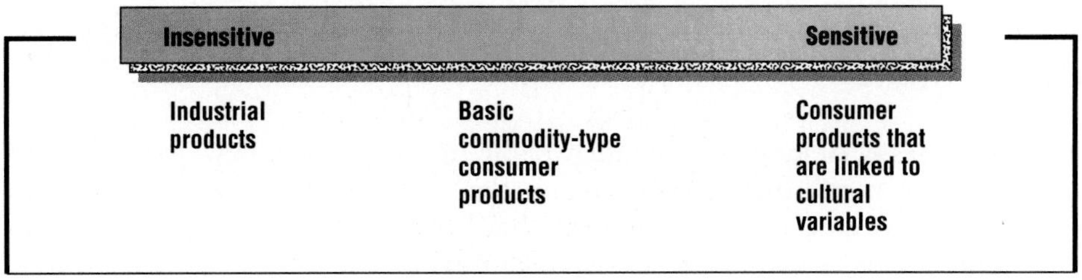

Some products, like Ricoh fax machines, are used the same way all over the world. Other products, like chopsticks and noodle soup, are more sensitive to different cultures.

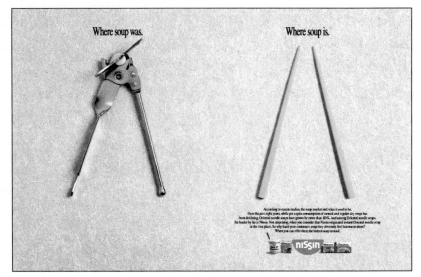

This, in turn, makes it even more difficult to predict how it might be received in a different environment.

This continuum helps explain why many of the early successes in international marketing were basic commodities such as gasoline, soap, transportation vehicles, mining equipment, and agricultural machinery. It also helps explain why some consumer products firms have been successful with basically the same promotion and products in different parts of the globe.

Yet some managers don't understand the reason for these successes. They think they can develop a global marketing mix for just about *any* product. They fail to see that firms producing and/or selling products near the sensitive end of the continuum should carefully analyze how their products will be seen and used in new environments—and plan their strategies accordingly. American-made blue jeans, for example, have been status symbols in Western Europe and Latin America—and producers have been able to sell them at premium prices through the best middlemen.[33]

What if risks are still hard to judge?

If the risks of an international opportunity are hard to judge, it may be wise to look first for opportunities that involve exporting. This gives managers a chance to build experience, know-how, and confidence over time. Then the firm will be in a better position to judge the prospects and risks of taking further steps.

CONCLUSION

Businesses need innovative strategy planning to survive in our increasingly competitive markets. In this chapter, we discussed the variables that shape the environment of marketing strategy planning—

and how they may affect opportunities. First, we looked at how the firm's own resources and objectives may help guide or limit the search for opportunities. Then, we went on to look at the external environments. They are important because changes in these environments present new opportunities—as well as problems—that a marketing manager must deal with in marketing strategy planning.

A manager must study the competitive environment. How well established are competitors? Are there competitive barriers, and what effect will they have? How will competitors respond to a plan?

The economic environment, including chances of recessions or inflation, also affects the choice of strategies. And the marketer must try to anticipate, understand, and deal with these changes—as well as changes in the technological base underlying the economic environment.

The marketing manager must also be aware of legal restrictions and be sensitive to changing political climates. The acceptance of consumerism has already forced many changes.

The social and cultural environment affect how people behave and what marketing strategies will be successful.

Developing good marketing strategies within all these environments isn't easy. You can see that marketing management is a challenging job that requires integration of information from many disciplines.

Eventually, managers need procedures for screening and evaluating opportunities. We explained an approach for developing screening criteria, from an analysis of the strengths and weaknesses of the company's resources, the environmental trends it faces, and top management's objectives. We also considered some quantitative techniques for evaluating opportunities. And we discussed ways for evaluating and managing quite different opportunities, using the GE strategic planning grid, SBUs, and portfolio management.

Now we can go on in the rest of the book to discuss how to turn opportunities into profitable marketing plans and programs.

QUESTIONS AND PROBLEMS

1. Explain how a firm's objectives may affect its search for opportunities.

2. Specifically, how would various company objectives affect the development of a marketing mix for a new type of baby shoe? If this company were just being formed by three former shoemakers with limited financial resources, list the objectives they might have. Then discuss how they would affect the development of their marketing strategy.

3. Explain how a firm's resources may limit its search for opportunities. Cite a specific example for a specific resource.

4. Discuss how a company's financial strength may have a bearing on the kinds of products it produces. Will it have an impact on the other three Ps as well? If so, how? Use an example in your answer.

5. In your own words, explain how a marketing manager might use a competitor analysis to avoid situations that involve head-on competition.

6. The owner of a small grocery store, the only one in a medium-sized town in the mountains, has just learned that a large chain plans to open a new store nearby. How difficult will it be for the owner to plan for this new competitive threat? Explain your answer.

7. Discuss the probable impact on your hometown if a major breakthrough in air transportation allowed foreign producers to ship into any Canadian market for about the same transportation cost that domestic producers incur.

8. Will the elimination of trade barriers between countries in Europe eliminate the need to consider submarkets of European consumers? Why or why not?

9. Which way does the Canadian political and legal environment seem to be moving (with respect to business-related affairs)?

10. Why is it necessary to have so many laws regulating business? Why hasn't Parliament just passed one set of laws to take care of business problems?

11. What and whom is the Canadian government attempting to protect in its effort to preserve and regulate competition?

12. Explain the components of product-market screening criteria that can be used to evaluate opportunities.

13. Explain the differences between the total profit approach and the return-on-investment approach to evaluating alternative plans.

14. Explain General Electric's strategic planning grid approach to evaluating opportunities.

15. Distinguish between the operation of a strategic business unit and a firm that only pays lip service to adopting the marketing concept.

SUGGESTED CASES

10. O & E Farm Supply

17. YTV

5

Getting Information for Marketing Decisions

When You Finish This Chapter, You Should

❶
Know about marketing information systems.

❷
Understand a scientific approach to marketing research.

❸
Know how to define and solve marketing problems.

❹
Know about getting secondary and primary data.

❺
Understand the role of observing, questioning, and using experimental methods in marketing research.

❻
Understand the important new terms (shown in blue).

Marketing managers at Frito-Lay had a problem. They wanted to develop a new snack chip that would appeal to adults. The trick would be to generate new sales, not just take sales away from their other brands, like Cheetos and Fritos, that were already very popular with teens. To develop a strategy, the marketing managers needed good information. And to get that information they turned to marketing research.

A number of focus group interviews provided good ideas. The focus groups liked the concept of a multigrain snack. They also seemed to favor a thin, rectangular chip with ridges and a salty, nutty flavor. The managers then turned to survey research—to see if the opinions of the focus group participants held with larger, more representative samples of target customers. The surveys also provided more details on what consumers liked, and didn't like, about different versions of the chip and about competitors' products.

Next, the Frito-Lay managers tested different variations of the planned marketing mix in specially selected test markets. The test markets provided detailed information from grocery store checkout scanners. The scanner data not only showed how many people tried the new product but how many came back to buy a second or third time. Knowing these repeat purchase rates helped managers estimate the product's real sales potential. Test results also helped managers to choose the Sun Chips brand name and fine-tune other marketing mix decisions. Moreover, the tests confirmed that Sun Chips were attracting the target buyers, especially women in the 25–35 age group.

Now that Sun Chips are distributed nationally, managers need other information to see how well the strategy is working. Much of that information comes from the firm's marketing information system, which is updated daily. In fact, all of Frito-Lay's salespeople are equipped with hand-held computers. Throughout the day they input sales information at the stores they visit. In the evening they send all the data over telephone lines to a central computer, where it is analyzed.

Within 24 hours marketing managers at headquarters and in regional offices get reports and graphs that summarize how sales went the day before, broken down by brands and locations. The information system even allows a manager on a computer terminal to zoom in and take a closer look at a problem in Winnipeg or sales success in Victoria.[1]

MARKETING MANAGERS NEED INFORMATION (why?).

This example shows that successful planning of marketing strategies requires information—information about potential target markets and their likely responses to marketing mixes as well as about competition and other marketing environment variables. Information is also needed for implementation and control. Without good marketing information, managers have to use intuition or guesses—and in today's fast-changing and competitive markets, this invites failure.

Yet managers seldom have all the information they need to make the best decision. Both customers and competitors can be unpredictable. Getting more information may cost too much or take too long. For example, data on international markets are often incomplete, outdated, or difficult to obtain. So managers often must decide if they need more information and—if so—how to get it. In this chapter, we'll talk about how marketing managers can get the information they need to plan successful strategies.

MARKETING INFORMATION SYSTEMS CAN HELP how?.

Marketing managers for some companies make decisions based almost totally on their own judgment, with very little hard data. When it's time to make a decision, they may wish they had more information. But by then it's too late to do anything about it, so they do without.

MIS makes available data accessible

There is a difference between information that is *available* and information that is readily *accessible*. Some information, such as the details of competitors' plans, is just not available. Some information is available but not without time-consuming collection. Such information is not really accessible. For example, a company may have records of customer purchases, what was sold by sales reps last month, or what is in the warehouse. But, if a manager can't get this information when it's needed, it isn't useful.

Some firms like Frito-Lay have realized that it doesn't pay to wait until they have important questions they can't answer. They are working to develop a *continual flow of information*—and to make it more accessible to managers whenever they need it.

A **marketing information system (MIS)** is an organized way of continually gathering and analyzing data to provide marketing managers with information they need to make decisions. In some companies, an MIS is set up by marketing specialists. In other companies, it is set up by a group that provides *all* departments in the firm with information.

The technical details of setting up and running an MIS are beyond the scope of this course. But you should understand what an MIS is so you know some of the possibilities. Exhibit 5–1 shows the elements of a complete MIS.

Exhibit 5–1 Elements of a Complete Marketing Information System

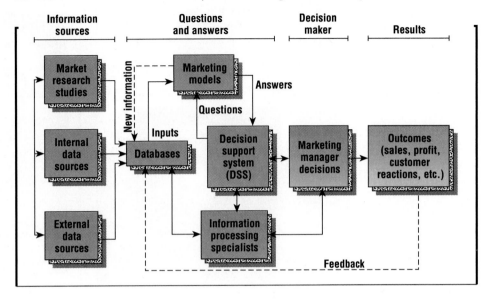

Marketing managers
must help develop
an MIS

Marketing managers often don't know in advance exactly what questions they will have—or when. But they do know what data they've routinely used or needed in the past. They can also foresee what types of data might be useful. They should communicate these needs to the MIS manager so the information will be there when they want it.

Decision support systems
put managers on-line

An MIS system organizes incoming data in a database so that it is available when needed. Most firms with an MIS have information processing specialists who help managers get standard reports and output from the database.

To get better decisions, some MIS systems provide marketing managers with a decision support system. A **decision support system (DSS)** is a computer program that makes it easy for a marketing manager to get and use information *as he or she is making decisions*. Typically, the DSS helps change raw data—for example, product sales for the previous day—into more *useful information*. For example, it may draw graphs to show relationships in data, perhaps comparing yesterday's sales to the sales on the same day in the last four weeks. The Frito-Lay case at the beginning of this chapter illustrates the possibilities.

Some decision support systems go even further. They allow the manager to see how answers to questions might change in various situations. For example, a manager may want to estimate how much sales will increase if the firm expands into a new market area. The DSS will ask the manager for a *personal* judgment about how much business could be won from each competitor in that market. Then, using this input and drawing on data in the database, the system will make an estimate using a marketing model. A **marketing model** is a statement of relationships among marketing variables.

In short, the decision support system puts managers "on-line" so they can study available data and make better marketing decisions—faster.[2]

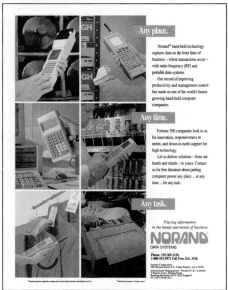

Specialized computer software and hardware help make it easier for companies to gather and analyze marketing information.

Information makes managers greedy for more

Once marketing managers see how a functioning MIS—and perhaps a DSS—can help their decision making, they are eager for more information. They realize that they can improve all aspects of their planning—blending individual Ps, combining the four Ps into mixes, and developing and selecting plans. Further, they can monitor the implementation of current plans, comparing results against plans and making necessary changes more quickly. (Note: The sales and cost analysis techniques discussed in Chapter 21 are often used in an MIS.) Marketing information systems will become more widespread as managers become more sensitive to the possibilities and computer costs continue to drop.

Many firms are not there yet

Of course, not every firm has a complete MIS system. And in some firms that do, managers don't know how to use the system properly. A major problem is that many managers are used to doing it the old way, and they don't think through what information they need.

One sales manager thought he was progressive when he asked his assistant for an MIS report listing each sales rep's sales for the previous month and the current month. The assistant provided the report—but later was surprised to see the sales manager working on the list with a calculator. He was figuring the percentage change in sales for the month and ranking the reps from largest increase in sales to smallest. The computer could have done all of that—quickly—but the sales manager got what he *asked for* not what he really needed. An MIS can provide information—but only the marketing manager knows what problem needs solving. It's the job of the manager—not the computer or the MIS specialist—to ask for the right information in the right form.

MIS use is growing rapidly

Marketing information systems will become even more widespread as marketing people become more sensitive to the possibilities. Some people think that only large firms can develop an effective MIS. Not so! In fact, just the opposite may be true. Low-cost microcomputers make a powerful MIS affordable, even for small firms. Further, big firms with complicated marketing programs often face a challenge trying to develop an MIS from scratch. Small firms can get started with a simple system and then expand it as needs expand. There is a lot of opportunity in this area for students who are able and willing to apply quantitative techniques to solve real marketing problems.[3]

New questions require new answers

MIS systems tend to focus on recurring information needs. Routinely analyzing such information can be valuable to marketing managers. But it shouldn't be their only source of information for decision making. They must try to satisfy ever-changing needs in dynamic markets. So marketing research must be used—to supplement data already available in the MIS.

WHAT IS MARKETING RESEARCH?

Research provides a bridge to customers

The marketing concept says that marketing managers should meet the needs of customers. Yet today, many marketing managers are isolated in company offices, far from potential customers. It is just not possible for managers to keep up with all of the changes taking place in their markets.

This means marketing managers have to rely on help from **marketing research**—procedures to develop and analyze new information to help marketing managers make decisions. One of the important jobs of a marketing researcher is to get the "facts" that are not currently available in the MIS.

Continued improvements in research methods are making marketing research information more dependable. This has encouraged firms to put more money and trust in research. Managers in some consumer product companies don't make any major decisions without the support—and sometimes even the official approval—of the marketing research department. As a result, some marketing research directors rise to high levels in the organization.

Marketing research can provide data to meet the many different informational needs in marketing. It can be useful in estimating market demand, copy testing, and new product development, to name a few areas. Table 5–1 gives a more detailed list of selected marketing research activities conducted by large Canadian companies.[4]

Who does the work?

Most large companies have a separate marketing research department to plan and carry out research projects. These departments often use outside specialists, including interviewing and tabulating services, to handle technical assignments. Further, they may call in specialized marketing consultants and marketing research organizations to take charge of a research project.

Small companies (those with less than $4 to $5 million in sales) usually don't have separate marketing research departments. They often depend on their salespeople or managers to conduct what research they do.

Some nonprofit organizations have begun to use marketing research—usually with the help of outside specialists. For example, many politicians rely on research firms to conduct surveys of voter attitudes.[5]

? Ethical issues in marketing research

The basic reason for doing marketing research is to get information that people can trust in making decisions. But, as you will see in this chapter, research often involves many hidden details. A person who wants to misuse marketing research to pursue a personal agenda can often do so.

Table 5–1   Marketing Research Activities of Larger Canadian Companies

Subject Areas Examined	Percent Doing
Business/Economic and Corporate Research	
Industry/market characteristics and trends	91.5%
Market share analyses	89.7
Corporate image research	72.3
Quality/Satisfaction Research	
Customer satisfaction research	81.6
Customer profiling and segmentation research	74.1
Service quality research	70.9
Product quality research	68.4
Pricing Research	
Profit analysis	80.9
Demand analysis research:	
Market potential	77.0
Sales potential	74.5
Sales forecasts	77.0
Cost analysis	76.2
Product Research	
Concept development/testing	66.3
Competitive product studies	52.5
Testing existing products	50.0
Test marketing	45.4
Distribution Research	
Plant/warehouse location studies	38.7
Channel performance studies	31.6
Advertising and Promotion Research	
Copy testing	52.5
Sales force compensation studies	51.4
Media research	48.9
Public image studies	47.9
Advertising post-testing	42.9
Buyer Behavior Research	
Market segmentation research	56.4
Brand awareness research	48.2
Brand image/attitudes	47.5
Purchase intentions research	46.5

Source: James G. Barnes and Eva Kiess-Moser, *Managing Marketing Information for Strategic Advantage* (Ottawa: The Conference Board of Canada, 1991).

Perhaps the most common ethical issues concern decisions to withhold certain information from the research. For example, a manager might selectively share only those results that support his or her viewpoint. Others involved in a decision might never know that they are getting only partial truths. Or, during a set of interviews, a researcher may discover that consumers are interpreting a poorly worded question many different ways. If the researcher doesn't admit the problem, an unknowing manager may rely on meaningless results.

Another problem involves more blatant abuses. It is unethical for a firm to contact consumers under the pretense of doing research when the real purpose is to sell something. For example, some political organizations have been criticized

MARKETING DEMO 5–1
Ethical Issues in Data Collection

(M) isrepresentation of the data collection process stems from two principal sources. The first is representing as research a marketing activity other than research. The second is the abuse of respondents' rights during the data collection process under the rationale of providing better quality research.

Consumers expect to be sold and to be surveyed and they expect to be able to tell the difference without great difficulty. When a selling or marketing activity uses the forms and language of survey research in order to mask the real nature of the activity being performed, it violates the public trust. Some classic examples of this type of practice are:

- The use of survey techniques for selling purposes. In this case, a person answers a few questions only to find him- or herself suddenly eligible to buy a specific product or service. The misuse of the survey approach as a disguise for sales canvassing is a widespread practice that shows no signs of abating.

- The use of survey techniques to obtain names and addresses of prospects for direct marketing. These efforts are usually conducted by mail. Questionnaires about products or brands are sent to households, and response is encouraged by the offer of free product samples to respondents. The listing firms compile the information by implying to the prospective customer that he or she has been interviewed in a market study.

These practices give legitimate research a bad name in the eyes of consumers. Other practices that abuse the rights of respondents and present ethical dilemmas to the researcher are:

- Disguising the purpose of a particular measurement such as a draw or free product choice question.
- Deceiving the prospective respondent as to the true duration of the interview.
- Misrepresenting the compensation in order to gain cooperation.
- Not mentioning to the respondent that a follow-up interview will be made.
- Using projective tests and unobtrusive measures to circumvent the need for a respondent's consent.
- Using hidden tape recorders to record personal interviews (or recording phone conversations without the permission of the respondent).
- Conducting simulated product tests in which the identical product is tried by the respondent except for variations in characteristics such as color that have no influence on the quality of a product.

Source: ARF position paper, "Phony or Misleading Polls," *Journal of Advertising Research,* Special Issue 26 (January 1987), pp. RC3–RC8; and George S. Day, "The Threats to Marketing Research," *Journal of Marketing Research* 12 (November 1975), pp. 462–67. Taken from David A. Aaker and George S. Day, eds., *Marketing Research,* 4th ed. (New York: John Wiley & Sons), pp. 217, 218.

for surveying consumers to find out their attitudes about various political candidates and issues. Then, armed with that information, someone else calls back to solicit donations. Legitimate marketing researchers are very concerned about such abuses. If the problem were to become widespread, consumers might not be willing to participate in any research. See Marketing Demo 5–1 for other examples of ethical dilemmas in marketing research.

The relationship between the researcher and the manager sometimes creates an ethical conflict, especially when the research is done by an outside firm. Managers must be careful not to send a signal that the only acceptable results from a research project are ones that confirm their existing viewpoints. Researchers are supposed to be objective, but that objectivity may be swayed if future jobs depend on getting the "right" results.

Effective research usually requires cooperation

Good marketing research requires much more than just technical tools. It requires cooperation between researchers and marketing managers. Good marketing researchers must keep both marketing research *and* marketing management in mind to be sure their research focuses on real problems.

Marketing managers must be involved in marketing research, too. Many marketing research details can be handled by company or outside experts. But marketing managers must be able to explain what their problems are—and what kinds of information they need. They should be able to communicate with specialists in the specialists' language. Marketing managers may only be "consumers" of research but they should be informed consumers—able to explain exactly what they want from the research. They should also know about some of the basic decisions made during the research process so they know the limitations of the findings.

For this reason, our discussion of marketing research won't emphasize mechanics—but rather how to plan and evaluate the work of marketing researchers.[6]

THE SCIENTIFIC METHOD AND MARKETING RESEARCH

The scientific method, combined with the strategy planning framework we discussed in Chapter 2, can help marketing managers make better decisions.

The **scientific method** is a decision-making approach that focuses on being objective and orderly in *testing* ideas before accepting them. With the scientific method, managers don't just *assume* that their intuition is correct. Instead, they use their intuition and observations to develop **hypotheses**—educated guesses about the relationships between things or about what will happen in the future. Then they test their hypotheses before making final decisions.

A manager who relies only on intuition might introduce a new product without testing consumer response. But a manager who uses the scientific method might say, "I think (hypothesize) that consumers currently using the most popular brand will prefer our new product. Let's run some consumer tests. If at least 60 percent of the consumers prefer our product, we can introduce it in a regional test market. If it doesn't pass the consumer test there, we can make some changes and try again."

The scientific method forces an orderly research process. Some managers don't carefully specify what information they need. They blindly move ahead, hoping that research will provide "the answer." Other managers may have a clearly defined problem or question but lose their way after that. These hit-or-miss approaches waste both time and money.

FIVE-STEP APPROACH TO MARKETING RESEARCH

The **marketing research process** is a five-step application of the scientific method that includes:

1. Defining the problem.
2. Analyzing the situation.
3. Getting problem-specific data.

Exhibit 5–2 Five-Step Scientific Approach to Marketing Research Process

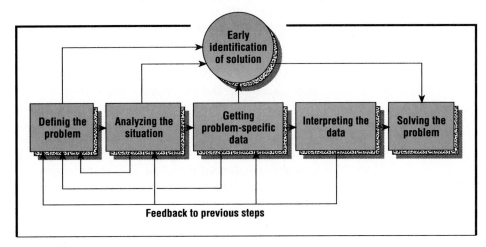

4. Interpreting the data.
5. Solving the problem.

Exhibit 5–2 shows the five steps in the process. Note that the process may lead to a solution before all of the steps are completed. Or, as the feedback arrows show, researchers may return to an earlier step if needed. For example, the interpreting step may point to a new question, or reveal the need for additional information, before a final decision can be made.

DEFINING THE PROBLEM—STEP 1

Defining the problem is the most important—and often the most difficult—step in the marketing research process. Sometimes it takes over half the total time spent on a research project. But it's time well spent if the objectives of the research are clearly defined. The best research job on the wrong problem is wasted effort.

Finding the right problem level almost solves the problem

The strategy planning framework introduced in Chapter 2 can be useful here. It can help the researcher identify the real problem area—and what information is needed. Do we really know enough about our target markets to work out all of the four Ps? Do we know enough to decide what celebrity to use in an ad, or how to handle a price war in Toronto or Tokyo? If not, we may want to do research rather than rely on intuition.

The importance of understanding the problem—and then trying to solve it—can be seen in the introduction of Fab One Shot, a laundry product developed to clean, soften, and reduce static cling all in one step. Marketing managers were sure that Fab One Shot was going to appeal to heavy users—especially working women with large families. As one manager summarized the situation, "our research showed that while over 50 percent of women were going back to work,

70 percent were still responsible for the family wash . . . and 80 percent use three different laundry products. These women are looking for convenience."

When marketing managers found that other firms were testing similar products, they rushed Fab One Shot into distribution. To encourage first-time purchases, they offered introductory price discounts, coupons, and rebates. And they supported the sales promotion with heavy advertising on TV programs that research showed the heavy users watched.

However, research never addressed the problem of how the heavy user target market would react. After the introductory price-off deals were dropped, sales dropped off, too. While the product was convenient, heavy users weren't willing to pay the price—about 25 cents for each washload. For the heavy users, price was a qualifying dimension. And these consumers didn't like Fab's premeasured packets because they had no control over how much detergent they could put in. The competing firms recognized these problems at the research stage—and decided not to introduce their products.

After the fact, it was clear that Fab One Shot was most popular with college students, singles, and people living in small apartments. They didn't use much, so the convenience benefit offset the high price. But the company never targeted those segments. It just assumed that it would be profitable to target the big market of heavy users.[7]

The moral of this story is that our strategy planning framework is useful for guiding the problem definition step—as well as the whole marketing research process. First, a marketing manager should understand the target market and what needs the firm can satisfy. Then the manager can focus on lower-level problems—namely, how sensitive the target market is to a change in one or more of the marketing mix ingredients. Without such a framework, marketing researchers can waste time—and money—working on the wrong problem.

Don't confuse problems with symptoms

The problem definition step sounds simple—and that's the danger. It's easy to confuse symptoms with the problem. Suppose a firm's MIS shows that the company's sales are decreasing in certain territories while expenses are remaining the same, resulting in a decline in profits. Will it help to define the problem by asking: How can we stop the sales decline? Probably not. This would be like fitting a hearing-impaired patient with a hearing aid without first trying to find out *why* the patient was having trouble hearing.

It's easy to fall into the trap of mistaking symptoms for the problem, thus confusing the research objectives. Researchers may ignore relevant questions—while analyzing unimportant questions in expensive detail.

Setting research objectives may require more understanding

Sometimes, the research objectives are very clear. A manager wants to know if the targeted households have tried a new product and what percent of them bought it a second time. But research objectives aren't always so simple. The manager might also want to know *why* some didn't buy—or whether they had even heard of the product. Companies rarely have enough time and money to study everything. Managers must narrow their research objectives. One good way is to develop a "research question" list that includes all the possible problem areas. Then managers can consider the items on the list more completely—in the situation analysis step—before they set final research objectives.

ANALYZING THE SITUATION—STEP 2

What information do we already have?

When the marketing manager thinks the real problem has begun to surface, a situation analysis is useful. A **situation analysis** is an informal study of what information is already available in the problem area. It can help define the problem and specify what additional information—if any—is needed.

Pick the brains around you

The situation analysis usually involves informal talks with informed people. Informed people can be others in the firm, a few good middlemen who have close contact with customers, or others knowledgeable about the industry. In industrial markets, where relationships with customers are close, researchers may even call the customers themselves. Informed customers may have already worked on the same problem or know about a source of helpful information. Their inputs can help to sharpen the problem definition, too.

Situation analysis helps educate a researcher

The situation analysis is especially important if the researcher is a research specialist who doesn't know much about the management decisions to be made—or if the marketing manager is dealing with unfamiliar areas. They both must be sure they understand the problem area, including the nature of the target market, the marketing mix, competition, and other external factors. Otherwise, the researcher may rush ahead and make costly mistakes or simply discover facts that management already knows. The following case illustrates this danger.

A marketing manager at the home office of a large retail chain hired a research firm to do in-store interviews to learn what customers liked most—and least—about some of its stores in other cities. Interviewers diligently filled out their questionnaires. When the results came in, it was apparent that neither the marketing manager nor the researcher had done his or her homework. No one had even talked with the local store managers! Several of the stores were in the middle of some messy remodeling, so all the customers' responses concerned the noise and dust from the construction. The research was a waste of money. You can imagine why this retailer—one of the largest in the country—doesn't want to be named! But the point is: Even big companies make marketing research mistakes if they don't take the situation analysis seriously.

Secondary data may provide the answers— or some background

The situation analysis should also find relevant **secondary data**—information that has been collected or published already. Later, in Step 3, we will cover **primary data**—information specifically collected to solve a current problem. Too often, researchers rush to gather primary data when much relevant secondary information is already available—at little or no cost! See Exhibit 5–3.

Much secondary data is available

Ideally, much secondary data is already available from the firm's MIS. Data that has not been organized in an MIS may be available from the company's files and reports. Secondary data also is available from libraries, trade associations, and government agencies. Appendix B following this chapter gives an excellent list of secondary sources available to the Canadian marketer from both government and private sources.

Syndicated data sources are a blend of primary and secondary data

A third source of information available to researchers is **syndicated data**. This source is a blend of primary and secondary data. Such information is available from private research firms that specialize in supplying data that is regularly

Exhibit 5–3   Sources of Secondary and Primary Data

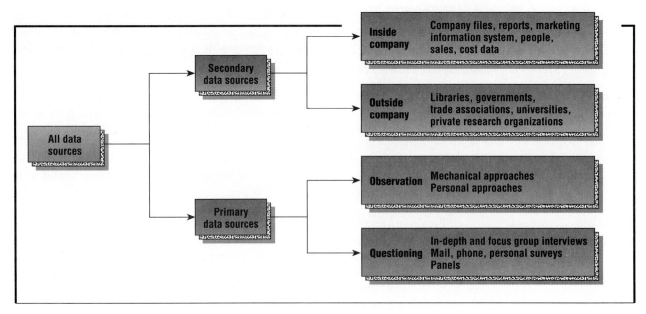

collected to aid marketing managers with specific problems. This data may be collected through surveying, observation, or some combination of the two. The marketing manager subscribes to such a research service and gets regular updates.

Many different marketing managers have to make the same kinds of decisions and have the same type of data needs. So the most economical approach is to have one specialist firm collect and distribute the data to the different users, who share the cost.

By using syndicated data, companies can receive valuable information more quickly and at a lower cost than if the study were conducted for just one subscriber. One problem with using this data source is that no single company can obtain an informational advantage over competitors. Also, the data may not be specifically tailored to address a company's particular problem. Finally, the study may not cover the exact markets or products and services of interest to the user.

Compusearch Market and Social Research Limited is one source of syndicated data in Canada. Compusearch complies data from Statistics Canada and other secondary sources and repackages the information in a form that is useful to the client. The company gathers detailed demographic and other relevant data by neighborhoods, sales territories, trading areas, or any other geographic areas of interest to the companies that purchase the data. Compusearch can provide data by neighborhoods as small as 200 households. This data can be used by clients to identify the characteristics of target markets, to determine where new branches or stores should be located, and to target the most promising consumer groups.

A. C. Nielsen Company of Canada Limited is another source of syndicated data. A. C. Nielsen offers a number of retail indices such as the Food Index, the Drug Index, the Confectionery/Tobacco Index, and the Mass Merchandiser

Index, collectively known as Nielsen's Retail Index Services. For example, the grocery industry is served by the Food Index. This index is based on a sample of 475 grocery stores across Canada, measuring more than 200 product categories. The reports are tailored to clients' needs and contain quantitative results of market size and direction, brand/size sales volume and share, plus a host of "reasons why" data.

The Bureau of Broadcast Measurement (BBM) is a nonprofit organization that provides syndicated data on audience estimates for radio stations and programs in Canada. The BBM has approximately 1,000 members and associates from the broadcasting industry. It conducts surveys of radio audiences up to four times a year, depending on the size and competitive nature of the areas surveyed. Radio audiences for more than 150 markets are developed from this sample. Syndicated reports on listenership are made available to members as part of their membership entitlement.

The Print Measurement Bureau (PMB) is another nonprofit organization that provides syndicated data. It is an industry association that offers standardized readership information on the publications of its member companies. Samples of Canadian residents 12 years of age and older are regularly interviewed. The results of the last two years' worth of data are compiled into an annual report. This report is only available to PMB members. The PMB has also recently expanded its services to include the collection of data on the exposure of consumers to other media, their lifestyles, and their product usage.

Situation analysis yields a lot—for very little

The virtue of a good situation analysis is that it can be very informative but takes little time. And it's inexpensive compared with more formal research efforts like a large-scale survey. Situation analysis can help focus further research or even eliminate the need for it entirely. The situation analyst is really trying to determine the exact nature of the situation—and the problem. Too-hasty researchers may try to skip this step in their rush to get out questionnaires. Often, these researchers find the real problem only when the questionnaires come back—and they must start over. One marketing expert put it this way: "Some people never have time to do research right the first time, but they seem to have time to do it over again."

Determine what else is needed

At the end of the situation analysis, you can see which research questions—from the list developed during the problem definition step—remain unanswered. Then you have to decide exactly what information you need to answer those questions—and how to get it.

This often requires discussion between technical experts and the marketing manager. Often, companies use a written **research proposal**—a plan that specifies what information will be obtained and how—to be sure no misunderstandings occur later. The research plan may include information about costs, what data will be collected, how it will be collected, who will analyze it and how, and how long the process will take. Then the marketing manager must decide if it makes sense to go ahead—if the time and costs involved seem worthwhile. It's foolish to pay $100,000 for information to solve a $50,000 problem! When the decision is not clear-cut, marketing managers should know more about the next steps in the marketing research process.

GETTING PROBLEM–SPECIFIC DATA–STEP 3

Gathering primary data

The next step is to plan a formal research project to gather primary data. There are different methods for collecting primary data. Which approach to use depends on the nature of the problem and how much time and money are available.

In most primary data collection, the researcher tries to learn what customers think about some topic—or how they behave under some conditions. There are two basic methods for obtaining information about customers: *questioning* and *observing*. Questioning can range from qualitative to quantitative research. And many kinds of observing are possible.

Qualitative questioning—open-ended with a hidden purpose

Qualitative research seeks in-depth, open-ended responses, not yes or no answers. The researcher tries to get people to share their thoughts on a topic—without giving them many directions or guidelines about what to say.

A researcher might ask different consumers, "What do you think about when you decide where to shop for food?" One person may talk about convenient location, another about service, and others about the quality of the fresh produce. The real advantage of this approach is *depth*. Each person can be asked follow-up questions so the researcher really understands what *that* respondent is thinking. The depth of the qualitative approach gets at the details, even if the researcher needs a lot of judgment to summarize it all.

Some types of qualitative research don't use specific questions. For example, a cartoon may show a situation such as a woman and a man buying coffee in a supermarket. The respondent may be asked to explain what the woman is saying to the man. Or the consumer might simply be shown a product or an ad and asked to comment.

A skilled leader can learn a lot from a focus group, like this one in which the group is reacting to different brands of toothpaste.

Focus groups stimulate discussion

The most widely used form of qualitative questioning in marketing research is the **focus group interview**, which involves interviewing 6 to 10 people in an informal group setting. The focus group also uses open-ended questions, but here the interviewer wants to get group interaction—to stimulate thinking and get immediate reactions.

A skilled focus group leader can learn a great deal from this approach. A typical session may last an hour, so participants can cover a lot of ground. Sessions are often videotaped, allowing different managers to form their own impressions of what happened.[8] However, a typical problem—and serious limitation—with qualitative research is that it's hard to measure objectively what takes place. The results seem to depend so much on the viewpoint of the researcher. In addition, people willing to participate in a focus group, especially those who talk the most, may not be representative of the broader target market. For an idea of how focus groups work, see Marketing Demo 5–2.

While qualitative research has many supporters, the techniques have limits, even in the hands of a talented researcher. There are also no substitutes for the

---

MARKETING DEMO 5–2
Consumers on the Couch

Here's how focus groups can work: you have been recruited for a focus group because you represent the appropriate segment of the market—the right age, income, and psychological profile for the project at hand. You will be paid an average of $45 for an hour and a half of your time. (If you're a doctor or another sought-after professional, you could make as much as $200 for an evening.)

The session will probably begin with a gimmick—although the industry prefers the terms *innovation* or *technique.* You may be asked to fill in a blank balloon in a cartoon of a woman shopping or a man ordering a beer. You might be handed a pile of products or photographs to sort into groups using any system you choose. (An all-female group recently assigned that task divided packaging of condoms into "bar pickups, romances, and husbands.").

"Let's pretend" is the most popular game with qualitative researchers. After all, most of us would feel rather silly exploring our emotional relationship with a brand of beer. So qualitative researchers routinely ask groups to imagine that the product is something easier to discuss—a person, an animal, a car. ("Everyone uses cars," Graham Denton groans. "They're old

hat.") You may even be told to pretend *you* are a product such as a potato chip. One researcher even asked a group to pretend they were competing brands of dog food, enticing the animals to eat.

Bizarre as they seem, these techniques attract some impressive believers. Major companies—Lever Brothers Ltd., General Foods, Inc., Sanyo Canada, Inc., Procter & Gamble, Inc.—often use qualitative research. So do various federal ministries, airlines, and Bell Canada. Some of Canada's largest financial institutions are steady clients, sending out senior management to role-play in local bank branches. ("Okay, let's pretend you're a consumer trying to buy an RRSP. Which window would you go to?") Royal Trust used qualitative research to pinpoint the anxieties it addressed in a series of five-minute, mini-drama commercials aired on TV last fall. No one knows exactly how much Canadian business spends on qualitative work, but figures compiled by the industry indicate it's at least $30 million a year.

Source: Suanne Kelman, "Consumers on the Couch," *Report on Business Magazine*, February 1991, pp. 50–53.

hard facts and numbers that quantitative studies generate. Qualitative research can provide good ideas—hypotheses. But often we need other approaches, perhaps based on more representative samples and objective measures, to test these hypotheses.

Structured questioning gives more objective results

When researchers use identical questions and response alternatives, they can summarize the information quantitatively. Samples can be larger and more representative, and they can use various statistics to draw conclusions. For these reasons, most survey research is **quantitative research**—which seeks structured responses that can be summarized in numbers, like percentages, averages, or other statistics. For example, a marketing researcher might calculate what percentage of respondents have tried a new product—and then figure an average "score" for how satisfied they were.

Fixed responses speed answering and analysis

Survey questionnaires usually provide fixed responses to questions to simplify analysis of the replies. This multiple-choice approach also makes it easier and faster for respondents to reply. Simple fill-in-a-number questions are also widely used in quantitative research. A questionnaire might ask an industrial buyer, "From approximately how many suppliers do you currently purchase electronic parts?" Fixed responses are also more convenient for computer analysis, which is how most surveys are analyzed.

Quantitative measures of attitudes, too

One common approach to measuring consumers' attitudes and opinions is to have respondents indicate how much they agree or disagree with a questionnaire statement. A researcher interested in what target consumers think about frozen pizzas, for example, might include statements like those at the top of Exhibit 5–4.

Another approach is to have respondents *rate* a product, feature, or store. Exhibit 5–4 shows commonly used rating "scales." Sometimes, rating scales are labeled with adjectives like *excellent, good, fair,* and *poor.*

Surveys by mail, phone, or in person

Decisions about what specific questions to ask, and how to ask them, are usually related to how respondents will be contacted—by mail, on the phone, or in person.

Mail surveys are the most common and convenient

The mail questionnaire is useful when extensive questioning is necessary. With a mail questionnaire, respondents can complete the questions at their convenience. They may be more willing to fill in personal or family characteristics since a mail questionnaire can be returned anonymously. But the questions must be simple and easy to follow since no interviewer is there to help.

A big problem with mail questionnaires is that many people don't complete or return them. The **response rate**—the percent of people contacted who complete the questionnaire—is often around 25 percent in consumer surveys. And it can be even lower. Also, respondents may not be representative. People who are most interested in the questionnaire topic may respond—but answers from this group may be very different from the answers of a typical "don't care" group.[9]

Mail surveys are economical if a large number of people respond. But they may be quite expensive if the response rate is low. Further, it can take a month or more to get the data—too slow for some decisions. Moreover, it is difficult to get respondents to expand on particular points. In markets where illiteracy is a

Exhibit 5–4   Sample Questioning Methods to Measure Attitudes and Opinions

A. Please check your level of agreement with each of the following statements.

	Strongly Agree	Agree	Uncertain	Disagree	Strongly Disagree
1. I add extra toppings when I prepare a frozen pizza.	___	___	___	___	___
2. A frozen pizza dinner is more expensive than eating at a fast-food restaurant.	___	___	___	___	___

B. Please rate how important each of the following is to you in selecting a brand of frozen pizza:

	Not at all Important					Very Important
1. Price per serving	___	___	___	___	___	___
2. Toppings available	___	___	___	___	___	___
3. Amount of cheese	___	___	___	___	___	___
4. Cooking time	___	___	___	___	___	___

C. Please check the rating that best describes your feelings about the last frozen pizza which you prepared.

	Poor	Fair	Good	Excellent
1. Price per serving	___	___	___	___
2. Toppings available	___	___	___	___
3. Amount of cheese	___	___	___	___
4. Cooking time	___	___	___	___

problem, it may not be possible to get any response. In spite of these limitations, the convenience and economy of mail surveys make them popular for collecting primary data.

Telephone surveys—fast and effective

Telephone interviews are growing in popularity. They are effective for getting quick answers to simple questions. Telephone interviews allow the interviewer to probe and really learn what the respondent is thinking. On the other hand, some consumers find calls intrusive—and about a third refuse to answer any questions. Moreover, the telephone is usually not a very good contact method if the interviewer is trying to get confidential personal information such as details of family income. Respondents are not certain who is calling or how such personal information might be used.

Research firms, with up to 50 interviewers calling at the same time on long distance lines, can complete 1,000 or more interviews in one evening. In addition, with computer-aided telephone interviewing, answers are immediately recorded on a computer, resulting in fast data analysis. The popularity of telephone surveys is partly due to their speed and high response rates.[10]

Personal interview surveys—can be in-depth

A personal interview survey is usually much more expensive per interview than a mail or telephone survey. But it's easier to get and keep the respondent's attention when the interviewer is right there. The interviewer can also help explain complicated directions—and perhaps get better responses. For these reasons, personal interviews are commonly used for research on business customers. To reduce the cost of locating consumer respondents, interviews are sometimes done at a store or shopping mall. This is called a mall intercept interview because the interviewer stops a shopper and asks for responses to the survey.

Researchers have to be careful that having an interviewer involved doesn't affect the respondent's answers. Sometimes, people won't give an answer they consider embarrassing. Or they may try to impress or please the interviewer. Further, in some cultures, people don't want to give any information. For example, many people in Africa, Latin America, and Eastern Europe are reluctant to be interviewed. This is also a problem in many low-income, inner-city areas in Canada; even Statistics Canada interviewers have trouble getting cooperation, since questioning has limitations. Then observing may be more accurate or economical.

Observing—what you see is what you get

Observing—as a method of collecting data—focuses on a well-defined problem. Here, we are not talking about the casual observations that may stimulate ideas in the early steps of a research project. With the observation method, researchers try to see or record what the subject does naturally. They don't want the observing to *influence* the subject's behavior.

After extensive research with French consumers, including mall intercept interviews like the one shown here, Colgate-France successfully launched its new Axion 2 detergent.

A museum director wanted to know which of the many exhibits was most popular. A survey didn't help. Visitors seemed to want to please the interviewer and usually said that all of the exhibits were interesting. Putting observers near exhibits—to record how long visitors spent at each one—didn't help either. The curious visitors stood around to see what the observer was recording, and that messed up the measures. Finally, the museum floors were waxed to a glossy shine. Several weeks later, the floors around the exhibits were inspected. It was easy to tell which exhibits were most popular—based on how much wax had worn off the floor!

In some situations, consumers are recorded on videotape. Later, researchers can study the tape by running the film at very slow speed or actually analyzing each frame. Researchers use this technique to study the routes consumers follow through a grocery store—or how they select products in a department store.

Observation data can be plotted on graphs or maps. A shopping center developer wondered if one of its shopping centers was attracting customers from all the surrounding areas. The developer hired a firm to record the license plate numbers of cars in the parking lot. Using registration information, the firm obtained the addresses of all license holders and plotted them on a map. Very few customers were coming from one large area. The developer aimed direct-mail advertising at that area and generated a lot of new business.

Observing is common in advertising research

Observation methods are common in advertising research. For example, A. C. Nielsen Company has developed a device called the *people meter* that adapts the observation method to television audience research. This machine is attached to the TV set in the homes of selected families. It records when the set is on and what station is tuned in. Nielsen uses the results to rate the popularity of TV shows. Some claim that once families get used to the meter, it no longer influences their behavior. Note, however, that the meter only records what channel is on—not whether anyone is watching.

Checkout scanners see a lot

Computerized scanners at retail checkout counters, a major breakthrough in observing, help researchers collect very specific—and useful—information. Often,

---

The producers of Dentax toothbrushes and Pudgies baby wipes did test market experiments in overseas markets, where competitors were less likely to disrupt the results.

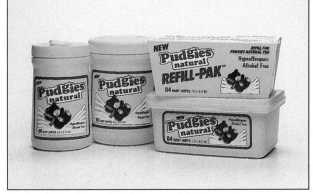

Data from electronic scanning at the supermarket helps retailers to decide what brand they will sell.

this type of data feeds directly into a firm's MIS. Managers of a big department store can see exactly what products have sold each day—and how much money each department earned. But the scanner also has wider applications for marketing research.

Some research firms have set up **consumer panels**—groups of consumers who provide information on a continuing basis. Whenever a panel member shops for groceries, he or she gives an ID number to the clerk, who keys in the number. Then the scanner records every purchase—including brands, sizes, prices, and any coupons used. For a fee, clients can evaluate actual customer purchase patterns—and answer questions about the effectiveness of their discount coupons. Did the coupons draw new customers, or did current customers simply use them to stock up? If consumers switched from another brand, did they go back to their old brand the next time? The answers to such questions are important in planning marketing strategies, and scanners can help marketing managers get the answers.

Some members of the consumer panel are also tied into a special TV cable system. With this system, a company can direct advertisements to some houses and not others. Then researchers can evaluate the effect of the ads by comparing the purchases of consumers who saw the ads with those who didn't.

The use of scanners to "observe" what customers actually do is changing consumer research methods. Companies can turn to firms like Information Resources as a *single source* of complete information about customers' attitudes, shopping behavior, and media habits. The information available is so detailed that the possibilities are limited more by imagination—and money—than by technology.[11]

Experimental method controls conditions

A marketing manager can get a different kind of information—with either questioning or observing—using the experimental method. With the **experimental method**, researchers compare the responses of two or more groups that are similar except on the characteristic being tested. Researchers want to learn if the specific characteristic, which varies among groups, *causes* differences in some response among the groups. For example, a researcher might be interested in comparing responses of consumers who had seen an ad for a new product with consumers who had not seen the ad. The "response" might be an observed behavior, like the purchase of a product, or the answer to a specific question, like "How interested are you in this new product?"

Marketing managers for Mars, the company that makes Snickers candy bars, used the experimental method to help solve a problem. Other candy and snack foods were taking customers. But why? Surveys showed that many consumers thought candy bars were becoming too small. But they also didn't want to pay more for a larger bar. Mars' managers wanted to know if making their candy bar bigger would increase sales enough to offset the higher cost. To decide, they conducted a marketing experiment.

The company carefully varied the size of candy bars sold in *different* markets. Otherwise, the marketing mix stayed the same. Then researchers tracked sales in each market area to see the effect of the different sizes. They saw a difference—a big difference—immediately. It was clear that added sales would more than offset the cost of a bigger candy bar. So marketing managers at Mars made a decision that took them in the opposite direction from other candy companies. And, yes, it proved to be a sweet success.

Test marketing of new products is another type of marketing experiment. In a typical approach, a company tries variations on its planned marketing mix in a few geographic market areas. The results of the tests help to identify problems or refine the marketing mix—before the company decides to go to broader distribution. However, alert competitors may disrupt such tests, perhaps by increasing promotion or offering retailers extra discounts. To avoid these problems, some small firms conduct some of their tests in foreign markets. For example, Carewell, producer of Dentax toothbrushes, tested its new line and various in-store promotions in Singapore and Malta before trying to enter the very competitive North American market. Similarly, the firm that makes Pudgies baby wipes did its test market experiments in the United Kingdom.

Researchers don't use the experimental method as often as surveys and focus groups because it's hard to set up controlled situations where only one marketing variable is different. But there are probably other reasons, too. Many managers don't understand the valuable information they can get from this method. Further, they don't like the idea of some researcher "experimenting" with their business.[12]

INTERPRETING THE DATA—STEP 4

What does it really mean?

After someone collects the data, it has to be analyzed to decide what it all means. In quantitative research, this step usually involves statistics. **Statistical packages**—easy-to-use computer programs that analyze data—have made this step easier. As we noted earlier, some firms provide *decision support systems* so managers can use a statistical package to interpret data themselves. More often, however, technical specialists are involved at the interpretation step.

Cross-tabulation is one of the most frequently used approaches for analyzing and interpreting marketing research data. It shows the relationship of answers to

Exhibit 5–5   Cross-Tabulation Breakdown of Responses to a Phone Company Consumer Survey

	Have You Moved in the Last Year?		
Answers:	*No*	*Yes*	*Total*
Do You Have Touch-Tone *Yes*	10.2%	23.4%	15.5%
Dialing at Your Home? *No*	89.8	76.6	84.5
Total	100 %	100 %	100 %

Interpretation: 15.5 percent of people in the survey said that they had touch-tone dialing in their homes. However, the percentage was much higher (23.4%) among people who had moved in the last year, and lower (10.2%) among people who had not moved.

two different questions. Exhibit 5–5 is an example. In this case, a telephone company was interested in learning more about customers who had adopted its touch-tone dialing service. With a survey, the firm asked customers if they had moved in the last year. The survey also asked if they had adopted the touch-tone service. Then, the answers to the two questions were cross-tabulated. The results of the analysis showed that customers who had moved in the last year were much more likely than nonmovers to have adopted the touch-tone service. So the researchers concluded that people who had just moved were a prime target market for the service.

Cross-tabulation is popular because the results are usually easy to interpret. But there are many other approaches for statistical analysis—the best one depends on the situation. The details of statistical analysis are beyond the scope of this book. But a good manager should know enough to understand what a research project can—and can't—do.[13]

Is your sample really representative?

It's usually impossible for marketing managers to collect all the information they want about everyone in a **population**—the total group they are interested in. Marketing researchers typically study only a **sample**, a part of the relevant population. How well a sample *represents* the total population affects the results. Results from a sample that is not representative may not give a true picture.

The manager of a retail store might want a phone survey to learn what consumers think about the store's hours. If interviewers make all of the calls during the day, the sample will not be representative. Consumers who work outside the home during the day won't have an equal chance of being included. Those interviewed might say the limited store hours are "satisfactory." Yet it would be a mistake to assume that *all* consumers are satisfied. Marketing managers must be aware of how representative a sample really is.

Random samples tend to be representative

You can see that getting a representative sample is very important. One method of doing so is **random sampling**, where each member of the population has the same chance of being included in the sample. Great care must be used to ensure that sampling is really random—not just haphazard.

If a random sample is chosen from a population, it will tend to have the same characteristics and be representative of the population. "Tend to" is important because it is only a tendency—the sample is not exactly the same as the population.

Much marketing research is based on nonrandom sampling because of the high cost and difficulty of obtaining a truly random sample. Sometimes, nonran-

SAS and STATGRAPHICS are statistical packages that make it easy to summarize and graph marketing research data.

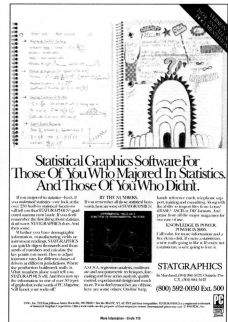

dom samples give very good results—especially in industrial markets where the number of customers may be relatively small and fairly similar. But results from nonrandom samples must be interpreted—and used—with care.

Research results are not exact

An estimate from a sample, even a representative one, usually varies somewhat from the true value for a total population. Managers sometimes forget this. They assume that survey results are exact. Instead, when interpreting sample estimates, managers should think of them as *suggesting* the approximate value.

If random selection is used to develop the sample, researchers can use various methods to help determine the likely accuracy of the sample value. This is done in terms of **confidence intervals**—the range on either side of an estimate that is likely to contain the true value for the whole population. Some managers are surprised to learn how wide that range can be.

Consider a wholesaler who has 1,000 retail customers and wants to learn how many of these retailers carry a product from a competing supplier. If the wholesaler randomly samples 100 retailers and 20 say yes, then the sample estimate is 20 percent. But with that information the wholesaler can only be 95 percent confident that the percentage of all retailers is in the confidence interval between 12 and 28 percent.[14]

The larger the sample size, the greater the accuracy of estimates from a random sample. With a larger sample, a few unusual responses are less likely to make a big difference.

You can see that the nature of the sample—and how it is selected—makes a big difference in how the results of a study can be interpreted. Managers must consider this factor when planning data collection—to make sure that the final results can be interpreted with enough confidence to be useful in marketing strategy planning.

Validity problems can
destroy research

Even if the sampling is carefully planned, it's also important to evaluate the quality of the research data itself.

Managers and researchers should be sure that research data really measures what it is supposed to measure. Many of the variables marketing managers are interested in are difficult to measure accurately. Questionnaires may let us assign numbers to consumer responses, but that still doesn't mean that the result is precise. An interviewer might ask, "How much did you spend on soft drinks last week?" A respondent may be perfectly willing to cooperate—and be part of the representative sample—but just not be able to remember.

Validity concerns the extent to which data measures what it is intended to measure. Validity problems are important in marketing research because most people want to help and will try to answer, even when they don't know what they're talking about. Further, a poorly worded question can mean different things to different people and invalidate the results. Managers must be sure that they only pay for research results that are representative—and valid.

Poor interpretation can
destroy research

Besides sampling and validity problems, a marketing manager must consider whether the analysis of the data supports the *conclusions* drawn in the interpretation step. Sometimes, technical specialists pick the right statistical procedure—their calculations are exact—but they misinterpret the data because they don't understand the management problem. In one survey, car buyers were asked to rank five cars in order from "most preferred" to "least preferred." One car was ranked first by slightly more respondents than any other car, so the researcher reported it as the "most liked car." That interpretation, however, ignored the fact that 70 percent of the respondents ranked the car *last!*

Interpretation problems like this can be subtle but crucial. Some people draw misleading conclusions—on purpose—to get the results they want. Marketing managers must decide whether *all* of the results support the interpretation and are relevant to their problem.

Marketing manager
and researcher should
work together

Marketing research involves some technical details. But you can see that the marketing researcher and the marketing manager must work together to be sure that they really do solve the problem facing the firm. If the whole research process has been a joint effort, then the interpretation step can move quickly to decision making—and solving the problem.

SOLVING THE PROBLEM—STEP 5

The last step is solving
the problem

In the problem solution step, managers use the research results to make marketing decisions.

Some researchers—and some managers—are fascinated by the interesting tidbits of information that come from the research process. They are excited if the research reveals something they didn't know before. But if research doesn't have action implications, it has little value and suggests poor planning by the researcher and the manager.

When the research process is finished, the marketing manager should be able to apply the findings in marketing strategy planning—the choice of a target market or the mix of the four Ps. If the research doesn't provide information to help guide these decisions, the company has wasted research time and money.

We emphasize this step because it is the reason for and logical conclusion to the whole research process. This final step must be anticipated at each of the earlier steps.

HOW MUCH INFORMATION DO YOU NEED?

Information is costly— but reduces risk

We have been talking about the benefits of good marketing information, but dependable information can be expensive. A big company may spend millions developing an information system. A large-scale survey can cost from $20,000 to $100,000—or even more. The continuing research available from companies such as Information Resources can cost a company well over $100,000 a year. And a market test for 6 to 12 months may cost $200,000 to $500,000 per test market!

Companies that are willing and able to pay the cost often find that marketing information pays for itself. They are more likely to select the right target market and marketing mix or see a potential problem before it becomes a costly crisis.

What is the value of information?

The high cost of good information must be balanced against its probable value to management. Managers never get all the information they would like to have. Very detailed surveys or experiments may be "too good" or "too expensive" or "too late" if all the company needs is a rough sampling of retailer attitudes toward a new pricing plan—by tomorrow. Money is wasted if research shows that a manager's guesses are wrong—and the manager ignores the facts. For example, GM faced an expensive disaster with its 1986 Riviera, which was released even after extensive research predicted a flop.[15]

Marketing managers must take risks because of incomplete information. That's part of their job and always will be. But they must weigh the cost of getting more data against its likely value. If the risk is not too great, the cost of getting more information may be greater than the potential loss from a poor decision. A decision to expand into a new territory with the present marketing mix, for example, might be made with more confidence after a $25,000 survey. But just sending a sales rep into the territory for a few weeks to try to sell potential customers would be a lot cheaper. And, if successful, the answer is in and so are some sales.

Faced with many risky decisions, the marketing manager should only seek help from research for problems where the risk can be reduced at a reasonable cost.[16]

CONCLUSION

Marketing managers face difficult decisions in selecting target markets and managing marketing mixes. And managers rarely have all the information they would like to have. But they don't have to rely only on intuition. They can usually obtain good information to improve the quality of their decisions.

Computers are helping marketing managers become full-fledged members of the information age. Both large and small firms are setting up marketing information systems (MIS)—to be certain that routinely needed data is available and accessible quickly.

Marketing managers deal with rapidly changing environments. Available data is not always adequate to answer the detailed questions that arise. A marketing research project may be required to gather new information.

Marketing research should be guided by the scientific method. The scientific approach to solving marketing problems involves five steps: defining the problem, analyzing the situation, obtaining data, interpreting data, and solving the problem. This objective and organized approach helps to keep research on target, reducing the risk of doing costly research that isn't necessary or doesn't solve the problem.

Our strategy planning framework can be helpful in finding the real problem. By finding and focusing on the real problem, the researcher and marketing manager may be able to move quickly to a useful solution—without the cost and risks of gathering primary data in a formal research project. With imagination, they may even be able to find the "answers" in their MIS or in other readily available secondary data.

QUESTIONS AND PROBLEMS

1. Discuss the concept of a marketing information system and why it is important for marketing managers to be involved in planning the system.

2. In your own words, explain why a decision support system (DSS) can add to the value of a marketing information system. Give an example of how a decision support system might help.

3. Discuss how output from an MIS might differ from the output of a typical marketing research department.

4. Discuss some of the likely problems facing the marketer in a small firm that has just purchased an inexpensive personal computer to help develop a marketing information system.

5. Explain the key characteristics of the scientific method and show why these are important to managers concerned with research.

6. How is the situation analysis different from the data collection step? Can both these steps be done at the same time to obtain answers sooner? Is this wise?

7. Distinguish between primary data and secondary data and illustrate your answer.

8. If a firm were interested in estimating the distribution of income in the province of Ontario, how could it proceed? Be specific.

9. Go to the library and find (in some government publication) three marketing-oriented "facts" on international markets that you did not know existed or were available. Record on one page and show sources.

10. Explain why a company might want to do focus group interviews rather than individual interviews with the same people.

11. Distinguish between qualitative and quantitative approaches to research—and give some of the key advantages and limitations of each approach.

12. Define response rate and discuss why a marketing manager might be concerned about the response rate achieved in a particular survey. Give an example.

13. Prepare a table that summarizes some of the key advantages and limitations of mail, telephone, and personal interview approaches for administering questionnaires.

14. Would a firm want to subscribe to a shared cost data service if the same data were going to be available to competitors? Discuss your reasoning.

15. Explain how you might use different types of research (focus groups, observation, survey, and experiment) to forecast market reaction to a new kind of disposable baby diaper, which is to receive no promotion other than what the retailer will give it. Further, assume that the new diaper's name will not be associated with other known products. The product will be offered at competitive prices.

16. Marketing research involves expense—sometimes considerable expense. Why does the text recommend the use of marketing research even though a highly experienced marketing executive is available?

17. Discuss the concept that some information may be too expensive to obtain in relation to its value. Illustrate.

SUGGESTED CASES

4. Diego's

9. Sleepy-Inn Motel

Key Sources of Marketing Information in Canada

Appendix

The Key Sources of Marketing Information for Canada Range from Daily Newspapers to Specific Directories, Including

❶
General sources of information.

❷
Sources of demographic data.

❸
Sources of geographic market and economic data.

❹
Information for advertising, promotion, and media.

❺
Sources for company and product information.

❻
Guides to market research reports.

❼
Directories of trade shows and exhibitions.

❽
Accessing on-line databases.

This appendix was prepared for *Basic Marketing*, Seventh Canadian Edition, by Tania Stastny, Just the Facts Research Inc., Vancouver, British Columbia.

The sources in this appendix are only a partial listing of available business information, and the emphasis is on publications providing the information required to support marketing activities. US sources covering Canadian information are included.

Publishers of many of the major information sources listed here have produced databases that are the electronic equivalent of their printed directories or indexes. Wherever this is the case, the on-line equivalent is noted, giving the database vendor and file name. A list of the major database vendors mentioned here appears at the end of this appendix.

GENERAL SOURCES OF INFORMATION

Guides to
reference sources

These books provide the broadest possible listing of sources in all categories of business and marketing information. They are a starting point for discovering the range of sources available on any subject, company, product, or service.

Access Canada. Micromedia's Directory of Canadian Information Sources

Toronto: Micromedia, 1st ed., 1990
This recent publication supersedes the long-established *Browning Directory of Canadian Business Information*. It covers numerous information sources and is indexed topically by subjects such as marketing as well as by specific products and services.

Encyclopedia of Business Information Sources

Detroit: Gale Research
Frequency: irregular with supplements
A detailed listing of subjects of primary interest to business managers, with a record of sources, periodicals, organizations, directories, handbooks, and on-line databases. Includes Canadian and US sources.

Directories in Print

International Directories in Print

Detroit: Gale Research
Frequency: irregular with supplements
Annotated guides to all types of business, product, service, and industrial directories. Indexes are by title and keywords. Each directory includes ordering and cost information.

Canadian Books in Print

University of Toronto Press
Frequency: annual
On-line: Infoglobe
Subject, author, and title access to all Canadian books in print on any subject. Listings include publisher and price.

Canadiana

National Library of Canada
Frequency: annual with monthly updates
On-line: CAN/OLE File NATCATBN
Lists all books, periodicals, and pamphlets published in Canada on all subjects. This is Canada's national bibliography. Searchable by subject, title, and author.

Guides to associations and government organizations

Associations are a valuable starting-off point for up-to-date information on any subject, industry, or product since they provide personal contact with a person immediately involved with a subject. There are a surprising number of associations for every conceivable activity or industry. For a listing of existing associations, consult the following guides:

Directory of Associations in Canada
University of Toronto Press
Frequency: annual
On-line: CAN/OLE File DAC
The main listing of Canadian associations of all kinds. Covers both national and provincial associations. Each entry includes name, telephone, fax, and contact.

Canadian Almanac and Directory
Canadian Almanac and Directory Publishing
Frequency: annual
Listing of over 5,000 organizations and associations, includes government, financial, broadcasting, and numerous other groups. Entries cover name, address, telephone, fax, and contact person.

Corpus Administrative Index
Corpus Information Services
Frequency: quarterly
This useful guide for identifying sources of government information covers federal and provincial marketing boards, development corporations, commissions, ministries, and crown corporations. Arrangement is geographical. Entries include department name, address, telephone, fax, and contact person.

Encyclopedia of Associations
Detroit: Gale Research
Frequency: annual
On-line: Dialog File 114
International listing of over 75,000 US and international organizations. Includes Canadian branches of US associations.

Newspapers

The leading business newspapers are *The Globe and Mail* (on-line: Infoglobe), *The Financial Post* (on-line: Infomart), and *The Financial Times of Canada* (on-line: Infoglobe). In addition to these, *Canada-Newswire*, providing up-to-date business and new-product news, is available on Infoglobe. Regional Canadian newspapers published by the Southam chain are on-line on the Infomart system.

Journal indexes

Most articles in Canadian and US marketing and advertising journals, as well as newspaper articles, reports from government and private sources, and statistical surveys, are covered by one or more journal indexes. Printed indexes can be searched by subject or keyword, industry, product, personal name, or company name. On-line indexes are far more flexible and can be searched by parts of names or keywords if exact names aren't known.

Canadian News Index

Frequency: monthly
On-line: Infoglobe
Indexes daily Canadian newspapers

Canadian Periodical Index

Frequency: monthly
On-line: Infoglobe
Covers over 350 English- and French-language magazines and newspapers.

Canadian Business Index

Frequency: monthly
On-line: CAN/OLE Canadian Business and Current Affairs
Also available on CD-ROM (compact disc)
Covers over 200 business periodicals and papers.

Business Dateline

On-line only: Dialog File 635
Indexes and provides the full text of regional Canadian and US business magazines such as *B.C. Business* and *Saskatchewan Business*. A useful source for finding hard-to-obtain information on private companies.

Predicasts F & S Index International

Cleveland, Ohio: Predicasts
Frequency: weekly
On-line: Dialog File 16
Covers Canadian magazines, newspapers, trade journals, and reports and studies issued by trade associations and research organizations.

ABI Inform

On-line only: Dialog File 15
Indexes approximately 800 Canadian and US business periodicals. Covers marketing, management, and administration topics.

Periodical directories
These directories list trade and business periodicals on a wide range of subjects, industries, and products.

Ulrich's International Periodicals Directory

New York: Bowker
Frequency: annual
On-line: Dialog File 480
Lists over 68,000 periodicals from around the world. Arranged by topic/subject area. An excellent source for finding periodicals on marketing in general plus trade journals on any industry or product.

Standard Periodicals Directory

New York: Oxbridge Communications
Frequency: annual
A listing similar to *Ulrich's*, but covers more journals, with emphasis on the United States and Canada.

Statistics Sources

Detroit: Gale Research, 1987

Access by subject or product to over 60,000 periodicals containing statistical information from worldwide sources. Arranged by subject and title.

Guide to Special Issues and Indexes of Periodicals

New York: Special Libraries Association

Details periodicals in the United States and Canada that regularly publish special issues on various topics. A useful annual source for collecting statistical and in-depth information from a single source. Arranged by subject.

SOURCES OF DEMOGRAPHIC DATA

The primary source of demographic data is the Census conducted by Statistics Canada in years ending with 6 and 1, which generates information on Canada's population by numbers, geographical distribution, age, sex, mother tongue, language spoken at home, marital status, education, occupation, income level, and housing. Numerous guides to Census publications include the following:

Products and Services of the (latest) Census of Canada

Statistics Canada Publication 99-103

Frequency: annual

On-line: Statistics Canada, Cansim Main Base Series Directory

Index to the latest census. Describes published bulletins and gives expected publication dates for those still being produced.

Current Publications Index

Statistics Canada Catalogue

Statistics Canada

Frequency: annual

On-line: CAN/OLE Database Statcan

This index lists all Statistics Canada publications by industry, topic, or product name. This is the main source for finding Statistics Canada publications on any topic.

Canada Yearbook

Statistics Canada

Frequency: annual

Provides summary statistical and general information on resources, demography, political institutions, and economic conditions. Updates census information. This is also a guide to federal and provincial government programs.

Compusearch

On-line only

A database service providing demographic and consumer spending information, broken down to the six-digit postal code level. Current-year information updates census figures. Database can be searched either via remote access database or on diskette, or, if preferred, printouts can be obtained from the publisher.

Market Research Handbook

Statistics Canada Publication 63-224

Frequency: annual

Contains statistics on such topics as merchandising and media, population characteristics, and personal income and expenditure. Data is broken down by regions, provinces, counties, and metropolitan areas.

Canada, the Provinces and the Territories. A Statistical Profile

Statistics Canada, Small Area Data Program

Frequency: annual

A detailed look at demographic and market information for each province and territory.

Household Income Facilities and Equipment

Statistics Canada Publication 13-218

Frequency: annual

Statistics on income distribution in Canada, intended for the study of types of household facilities with relationship to income. Variables include province, rural/urban size, and number of persons per household.

SOURCES OF GEOGRAPHIC MARKET AND ECONOMIC DATA

The following publications concern the Canadian consumer market broken down by geographic area, with general economic data and projections for various segments of the economy.

Canadian Markets

Toronto: Financial Post Information Service

Frequency: annual

On-line: Diskettes available from Financial Post Publishing.

Marketing information on 345 municipalities, arranged alphabetically. Includes buying power indexes for communities of 10,000 or more, and projections of population, households, retail sales, and income for CMAs.

Handbook of Consumer Markets

Conference Board of Canada

Frequency: annual

Details various segments of the consumer market in Canada.

Department Store Monthly Sales by Province and Metropolitan Area

Ottawa: Statistics Canada

Frequency: monthly

Statistical information on department store sales by region.

Annual Retail Trade

Ottawa: Statistics Canada

Frequency: annual

A compilation of retail sales by type of outlet by geographic area.

Survey of Consumer Buying Intentions
Conference Board of Canada
Frequency: quarterly
Projects consumer expenditures based on monthly surveys, broken down by region.

Survey of Business Attitudes and Investment Spending Intentions
Conference Board of Canada
Frequency: quarterly

Consumer Markets Update
Conference Board of Canada
Frequency: monthly
Statistical data on consumer spending and retail sales. Outlooks for consumer expenditures and inflation.

Canadian Economic Observer
Statistics Canada
Frequency: monthly
On-line: Statistics Canada, Cansim Database
Current coverage of general economic conditions and indicators.

Economic Review (National Bank of Canada)
Montreal: National Bank of Canada, Dept. of Economic Analysis
Frequency: quarterly review of economic developments in Canada

The Canadian Business Review
Conference Board of Canada
Frequency: quarterly
Update on leading business and general economic indicators.

INFORMATION FOR ADVERTISING, PROMOTION, AND MEDIA

National List of Advertisers
Maclean Hunter
Frequency: annual
Lists all firms advertising in Canadian media. Details company size, product range, agency employed, advertising budget, and media used.

Marketing: Advertising Agencies of Canada
Maclean Hunter
Frequency: annual
Lists ranking and statistics on the top 100 advertising agencies across Canada. Arranged by city. Lists name, address, telephone, fax, and senior executives.

Canadian Marketing Gold Book
CMGB Publishing
Frequency: annual
Lists services and suppliers to the advertising, public relations, marketing, and sales promotion sectors.

Canadian Media Directors' Council Media Digest

Maclean Hunter
Frequency: annual
Guide to general media advertising includes market data for television, radio, and newspaper advertising, as well as for other types of advertising such as outdoor, transit, and direct advertising. Details cost of network commercials, page, circulation size, and audience reach.

Standard Directory of Advertising Agencies

National Register
Frequency: three times per year
Directory of advertising agencies in the United States and Canada.

Canadian Advertising Rates and Data

Maclean Hunter
Frequency: annual
Geographical listing of daily and weekly papers plus radio and TV stations. Details advertising rates and how advertisements should be submitted. Lists other advertising media, such as transit and outdoor advertising.

Standard Rate and Data Service

Chicago: Standard Rate and Data Service
Frequency: annual
A directory for buyers of advertising space in the United States and Canada. Includes advertising media and spot radio and television markets. Provides demographic characteristics, spendable income, and retail sales for each region.

Marketing: A Guide to Canadian PR Services

Maclean Hunter
Frequency: annual
Annual issue of *Marketing* covers Canadian public relations services. Arranged geographically, entries include name, address, telephone, fax, contact person/s, and year established.

Marketing: A Guide to Sales Promotion Services

Maclean Hunter
Frequency: annual
Annual issue of journal *Marketing* is devoted to sales promotion services. Lists agencies, consultants, research, database marketing services, and trade associations.

Marketing: A Guide to Direct Marketing Services

Maclean Hunter
Frequency: annual
Annual issue of journal *Marketing* lists agencies and consultants involved in direct mail marketing services.

Television and Cable Fact Book

Washington, D.C.: Television Digest
Frequency: irregular
The most comprehensive guide to Canadian and US television stations. Geographically arranged information includes a map of the market and advertising

rates for each station. Includes directory of lower-power stations, cable systems, and related industries such as production firms and advertising agencies.

Gale Directory of Publications: An Annual Guide to Newspapers, Magazines, Journals and Related Publications.

Detroit: Gale Research
Frequency: annual
Information on over 23,000 newspapers, trade publications, and magazines in the United States and Canada. Contains cost, circulation, and advertising rates for each publication.

PTS Marketing and Advertising Reference Service

On-line only: Dialog File 570
Multi-industry advertising and marketing database covers trade journal articles and reports on advertising campaigns, marketing strategies, new-product introductions, and slogans in Canada and the United States indexed by advertising agency, slogan, and product or service.

SOURCES FOR COMPANY AND PRODUCT INFORMATION

Information on Canadian companies can be obtained from a number of directories, which typically provide name and address, list of officers, number of employees, product or service, and financial data ranging from summary revenue information to several years of financial statements. The following are the major business directories for information on Canadian companies:

Blue Book of Canadian Business

Canadian Newspaper Services International
Frequency: annual
Comprehensive listing of major Canadian corporations offers summary financial information on each company.

Canadian Key Business Directory

Dun & Bradstreet
Frequency: annual
On-line: Dialog File 520
Directory of public and private Canadian companies gives summary sales and directory-type information. Useful for finding information on smaller private companies.

Report on Business: The Top 1000 Companies

The Globe and Mail
Frequency: annual
Special issue of *Report on Business Magazine* ranks top public and private companies in Canada by profits, revenues, earnings per share, and return on equity and capital.

Financial Post 500

Financial Post Publishing
Frequency: annual
Ranks the top 500 public companies by sales, net income, and other factors. Includes information on ownership, number of employees, and major shareholders.

Survey of Industrials

Financial Post Publishing (Directory)
Frequency: annual
On-line: Available on diskette from Financial Post Publishing
Lists over 2,000 Canadian public industrial corporations. Includes detailed stock, management, and financial information.

Corporate Canada Online

On-line only: Infoglobe
Financial and market data on public and private Canadian companies. Includes company profile, past three years' financial information, and current ratios.

Cancorp Canadian Corporations

On-line only: Dialog File 491
Financial and directory information on public and private corporations.

Product Information   Product directories are arranged by name or type of product and are a source of information on products manufactured in Canada.

Fraser's Canadian Trade Directory

Fraser's Trade Directories
Frequency: annual
Four-volume listing of products includes information on manufacturers and suppliers. Gives company name, address, telephone, fax, staff size, and branch locations. Arranged alphabetically by product.

Canadian Trade Index

Canadian Manufacturer's Association
Frequency: annual
On-line: CSG
Lists Canadian manufacturing firms by product. Includes information on branches, plants, and foreign representatives.

Scott's Directories

Scott's Directories Publishing
Frequency: biennial
Published in five editions: Atlantic, Ontario, Quebec, Western, and Metropolitan Toronto and vicinity. Lists directory and product information on each manufacturer. Arranged geographically with indexes of products and product classifications.

GUIDES TO MARKET RESEARCH REPORTS

Market Research Facts and Trends

Toronto, Ontario: Maclean Hunter Research Bureau
Frequency: bimonthly
On-line: CAN/OLE Database NATCATBN
(Search under Corporate Source-Maclean and the name of the industry; for example, food.)
Leaflet describes new Maclean Hunter reports on a wide variety of topics and products in Canadian industry.

Predicasts F & S Index International

Cleveland, Ohio: Predicasts, Inc.
Frequency: annual
On-line: Dialog File 16
Abstracts significant business information appearing in thousands of newspapers, business magazines, and special reports in the United States, Canada, and throughout the world.

Findex

Find/SVP
Frequency: monthly
On-line: Dialog File 196
Directory of market research reports, studies, and surveys. Describes industry and market research reports commercially available from US, Canadian, and international publishers.

Directory of Canadian Marketing Research Organizations

Professional Marketing Research Society
Frequency: irregular
Directory of Canadian organizations that provide market research information on various subjects. Access is by area of expertise.

Arthur D. Little

On-line only: Dialog File 192
On-line database derived from Arthur D. Little, Inc., publications. Includes industry forecasts and product and market overviews.

Industry Data Sources

On-line only: Dialog File 189
Information on sources of financial and marketing data for 65 major industries in Canada, the United States, and abroad. Data sources include market research reports, investment banking studies, special issues of trade journals, and economic forecasts.

DIRECTORIES OF TRADE SHOWS AND EXHIBITIONS

Canadian Industry Shows & Exhibitions: Annual Directory

Toronto, Ontario: Maclean Hunter
Frequency: annual
Canadian trade and consumer shows are arranged by category of product or service. Access is by date, name, and location of the show.

Trade Shows and Professional Exhibits Directory

Detroit: Gale Research
Frequency: annual
Covers over 3,500 exhibitions, trade shows, and conventions in Canada, the United States, and the world.

Eventline
On-line only: Dialog File 165
One-stop source of information on past and future trade shows and meetings of all kinds, worldwide.

ACCESSING ON-LINE DATABASES

On-line databases offer much information on current business news, companies, industries, economic facts and trends, and other subjects of interest to the marketing specialist. The ability to search a remote database containing business information provides the individual or small research center with the same resources as a large corporate library.

For electronic access to databases, you need a terminal or computer, modem, and passwords to a variety of database vendors.

Numerous database vendors provide information from a varying number of databases. The following vendors are only a few among the many supplying marketing-related information. These are some of the most commonly used systems, and the ones whose databases are referred to wherever there's an on-line equivalent mentioned in the sources just listed.

For further information on other available databases, see:

Directory of Online Databases
New York: Cuadra
Frequency: annual with supplements
Comprehensive listing of on-line databases.

Business Online, A Canadian Guide
Toronto: Wiley, 1989
Emphasis on Canadian on-line business information sources.

Encyclopedia of Information Systems and Services
Detroit: Gale Research, 1987
On-line: Dialog File 230
Worldwide directory of databases available by remote access, CD-ROM, or diskette.

For information on the database vendors mentioned in this chapter, contact:

Dialog Information Services
Micromedia Ltd./Dialog
158 Pearl Street
Toronto, Ontario M5H IL3
Tel: (800) 387-2689

Infoglobe
444 Front Street West
Toronto, Ontario M5V 259
Tel: (416) 585-5250

Infomart

1450 Don Mills Road
Don Mills, Ontario M3B 2X7
Tel: (800) 668-9215

Can/Ole

Canadian Institution for Scientific and Technical Information
(National Research Council of Canada)
Client Services
Ottawa, Ontario K1A 0S2
Tel: (613) 993-1210

Compusearch Market and Social Research

1100-330 Front Street West
Toronto, Ontario M5V 3B7
Tel: (416) 348-9180

Demographic Dimensions of the Canadian Consumer Market

6

When You Finish This Chapter, You Should

❶

Know about population and income trends in global markets—and how they affect marketers.

❷

Understand how population growth is shifting in different areas and for different age groups.

❸

Know about the distribution of income in Canada.

❹

Know how consumer spending is related to family life cycle and other demographic dimensions.

❺

Know how to estimate likely consumer purchases for broad classes of products.

❻

Understand the important new terms (shown in blue).

Y ou've probably heard all about the greying of society, and you may even think that senior citizens are about to take over the world. You know about the baby boom. You assume that every developed country had one and that Canada's was typical. And you've seen the rapid growth of Canada's big cities over the last two decades, accompanied by housing shortages and traffic gridlock. You figure things can only get worse because urbanization is unstoppable. But in each case you are wrong, because you haven't paid enough attention to the demographic facts that are staring you in the face.

Demography, the statistical study of human populations, boils down to simple, numerical facts: how many teenagers we've got and how many senior citizens, how many people were born in a given year and how many died, how many immigrants arrived in Canada and how many people left. This knowledge could give us great power if we cared to use it. We could prepare for increases in school enrollments, shortages of young workers, and bursts in demand for housing, all of which are predictable years in advance. But, perversely, hardly anyone pays attention—not government, not business, and not even economists. A rare exception is David Foot, an economist at the University of Toronto, who loves to surprise people with the conclusions he draws from one simple fact: "Every year you get one year older." He maintains that demographics explain about 75 percent of just about everything, including the future.

The following is an example of David Foot's conclusions. "In Japan, the fertility rate started to plunge right after the Second World War, while it didn't start down in North America until the mid-60s. So Japan ran out of young people 25 years before North America ran out of young people. They had to use machines, and their productivity rebounded because they gave each person more machines to work with. It's got nothing to do with Japanese management style. People who say that are completely wrong. It's got to do with demographics.

"Productivity is now rebounding in North America because we are running out of young people and we are turning to machines to produce our output. We are able to do this because the front-end boomers have paid down their mortgages and are accumulating the savings that are going to fuel the investment boom of the 90s." It is, of course, perfectly predictable![1]

Get the facts straight

This chapter focuses on demographic dimensions that provide marketing managers with critical information about the size, location, and characteristics of target markets. Information will be provided on how a marketing manager can work with demographics to strengthen a company's position in the marketplace. A manager who is alert to demographic trends will discover new marketing opportunities or have advanced information on changing trends that require proactive adjustments to existing strategies.

Target marketers believe that the *customer* should be the focus of all business and marketing activity. These marketers hope to develop unique marketing strategies by finding unsatisfied customers and offering them more attractive marketing mixes. They want to work in less competitive markets with more inelastic demand curves. Finding these attractive opportunities takes real knowledge of what makes potential customers tick. This means finding those market dimensions that make a difference in terms of population, income, needs, attitudes, and buying behavior.

Three important questions should be answered about any potential market:

1. What are its relevant segmenting dimensions?
2. How big is it?
3. Where is it?

The first question (relevant dimensions) is basic. Management judgment, perhaps aided by analysis of existing data and new findings from marketing research, is needed to pick the right dimensions.

To help build your judgment regarding buying behavior, this and the following two chapters will discuss what we know about various kinds of customers and their buying behavior. Keep in mind that we aren't trying to make generalizations about "average customers" or how the "mass market" behaves, but rather how *some* people in *some* markets behave. You should expect to find differences.

Fortunately, useful information is available on the demographic dimensions of the Canadian consumer market. Most of it costs very little because it has been collected by government agencies like Statistics Canada. When valid data is available, there's no excuse for decisions based on guesses or rumors. Try to see how the data in the next few chapters can help to estimate the potential in different market segments. Also, check your own assumptions against this data. Now is a good time to get your facts straight!

POPULATION—PEOPLE BUY GOODS AND SERVICES

Present population and its distribution

Exhibit 6–1 shows the population of Canada by province for the years 1982, 1987, 1990, and 1992. The percent change in each area between 1982 and 1992 is also indicated. The consumer market in 1992 consisted of over 27 million people, with the bulk of that group (62.1 percent) living in Quebec and Ontario. Note also that the provinces of British Columbia and Alberta, with 12.0 and 9.4

Exhibit 6–1 Population of Canada by Province, 1977–1992 (estimate), in thousands

	1982		1987		1990		1992		Percent change, 1982–1992
	Total	Percent	Total	Percent	Total	Percent	Total	Percent	
Canada	24,658	100.0%	25,729	100.0%	26,584	100.0%	27,243	100.0%	10.5%
Atlantic provinces	2,245	9.1	2,289	8.9	2,319	8.7	2,336	8.6	4.1
Newfoundland	569	2.3	568	2.2	573	2.1	574	2.1	0.9
Prince Edward Island	123	0.5	128	0.5	130	0.5	129	0.5	5.5
Nova Scotia	853	3.5	881	3.4	892	3.3	906	3.3	6.2
New Brunswick	700	2.8	712	2.8	724	2.7	726	2.7	3.8
Quebec	6,463	26.2	6,609	25.7	6,762	25.4	6,895	25.3	6.7
Ontario	8,736	35.4	9,334	36.3	9,731	36.6	10,018	36.8	14.7
Manitoba/Saskatchewan	2,020	8.2	2,093	8.1	2,090	7.9	2,086	7.7	3.3
Manitoba	1,038	4.2	1,080	4.2	1,090	4.1	1,094	4.0	5.4
Saskatchewan	982	4.0	1,013	3.9	1,000	3.8	992	3.6	1.1
Alberta	2,326	9.4	2,382	9.3	2,470	9.3	2,549	9.4	9.6
British Columbia/Territories	2,870	11.6	3,023	11.8	3,212	12.1	3,356	12.3	16.9
British Columbia	2,798	11.3	2,946	11.5	3,132	11.8	3,273	12.0	17.0
Yukon	24	0.1	25	0.1	26	0.1	27	0.1	14.2
Northwest Territories	48	0.2	52	0.2	54	0.2	55	0.2	15.8

Note: Population numbers in thousands.

Source: Statistics Canada, *Quarterly Estimates of Population for Canada, the Provinces, and the Territories*, July 1, 1971–April 1, 1979, January 1, 1976–July 1, 1986, January 1, 1981–April 1, 1988, January 1, 1980–April 1, 1992, January 1, 1982–January 1, 1992, Cat. 91-001 (Ottawa: Ministry of Supply and Services).

percent of the total population, respectively, are each larger in population than the four Atlantic provinces combined (8.6 percent).

Marketers must never forget the relative sizes of Quebec and Ontario. These two provinces contain more than three-fifths of the country's population. They also account for the majority of consumer income and expenditures and the lion's share of the industrial market. A strong position in these markets is a must for any national marketing strategy. On the other hand, competition is tough since such markets tend to be attractive to everyone. These two provinces also have different linguistic and cultural heritages.

Never overlook the importance of the Atlantic provinces, the Prairies, or the West as regional markets. Some mass marketers pay little attention to these regions because of their relatively small size. Yet they offer opportunities to an alert marketer looking for areas with few competitors or to the company interested in selling a product of particular interest to people in one of these regions.

Where are the people yesterday and today?

Population figures for a single year don't show the dynamic aspects of markets. The population of Canada more than doubled between 1946 and 1990. But—and this is important to marketers—the population did *not* double everywhere. Marketers are always looking for markets that are growing fast. They want to know where the more recent growth has been—and where it's likely to be in the future.

Exhibit 6–1 shows that the national growth rate of 10.5 percent for the years 1982 to 1992 was exceeded in only two provinces: Ontario (14.7 percent) and British Columbia (17.0 percent), plus the Yukon (14.2 percent) and Northwest Territories (15.8 percent). All the other provinces grew at rates below the national average. Quebec, the second most populous province, had an absolute increase of only 432,400.

These different growth rates are especially important to marketers. For example, sudden growth in one area may create demand for many new shopping centers, while new marketing facilities in slow-growing areas can create tough competition for existing retailers. But in rapidly growing areas, demand may increase, so profits in even poorly planned facilities may be good.

Exhibit 6–1 represents big-picture data at the national and provincial levels. However, much more detailed population data is available from Statistics Canada for very small geographical areas. Just as we've considered population changes at the provincial level, a local marketer must divide a city or a big metropolitan area into smaller areas to figure out "where the population's action is."

The shift to urban and suburban areas

Moving from rural to urban areas has been the pattern in Canada for the past 100 years. However, the past 20 years have been marked by a new trend: a decline in the percentage of the population classed as urban residents. More people are moving to the country from the city than the reverse. But this increase in the rural population doesn't mean a return to farms. As a matter of fact, the number of farms continues to decrease. Rather, what seems to be happening is that more Canadians are settling outside the large Census Metropolitan Areas, preferring instead to live in smaller, average-sized cities. And more people within metropolitan areas are choosing to live in the urban and rural fringe areas of those cities rather than in the urban core.

From city to suburbs and then a trickle back

Not only people—but also industries—have left the cities. This continuing decentralization of industry has moved many jobs closer to the suburbs. We may be developing an urban economic system that's not as dependent on central cities. A growing population must go somewhere—and the suburbs can combine pleasant neighborhoods with easy transportation to higher-paying jobs nearby or in the city.

Purchase patterns are different in the suburbs. For example, a big-city resident may not need or own a car. But with no mass transportation, living carless in the suburbs is difficult, and in some areas, it almost seems that a station wagon to carpool kids and haul lawn supplies or pets is required.

Some families, however, have given up on the suburban dream. They found it a nightmare of commuting, yard maintenance, and housework, rising local taxes, and gossiping neighbors. These people are leaving suburbia. The movement back to the city is most evident among older—and sometimes wealthier—families. They feel crowded by suburbia's expansion. Their children have left home or are ready to leave. These older families are creating a market for luxury condominiums and high-rise apartments close to downtown and its shopping, recreation, and office facilities. Some young people are also moving into downtown areas, fixing up old homes that still offer convenience and charm at a reasonable price. They are big buyers in the market for "do-it-yourself" home repair products like paint, insulation, and flooring. They also spend much of their extra money on the city's cultural events and interesting restaurants.

Local political boundaries don't define market areas

Continuing shifts to and from urban and suburban areas suggest that classifying population by arbitrary city and county boundaries has its limitations. Marketers are more interested in the size of homogeneous marketing areas than in the number of people within political boundaries. To meet this need, Statistics Canada developed a separate population classification, the **Census Metropolitan Area (CMA).** The CMA is the "main labor market area" of a continuous built-up area having 100,000 or more population. It's a zone in which a significant number of people are able to commute on a daily basis to their workplaces in the main built-up area.[2]

In other words, CMAs are integrated economic and social units with a large population. They're usually known by the name of their largest city. In 1991, there were 25 CMAs in Canada with a total population of slightly over 16.6 million. This represents almost 61.1 percent of the 1991 Canadian total. Exhibit 6–2 locates Canada's largest urban areas.

These CMAs are major target markets. Toronto, Montreal, and Vancouver are Canada's largest metropolitan areas. Together they comprise approximately 8.1 million people, or 29.8 percent of Canada's 1991 population.

While the CMAs during the past 10 years have grown faster than the overall population, the growth pattern has been uneven across the country. The big winner was Oshawa, with a population growth of 28.7 percent, followed by Vancouver with 26.4 percent, and then by Ottawa-Hull and Kitchener, each with

Exhibit 6–2 Population of Major Canadian Metropolitan Areas, 1981–1991 (in thousands)

	1981	1986	1991	Percent Change 1981–1991
Atlantic provinces				
Halifax	277.7	296.0	320.5	15.4
St. John's, Newfoundland	154.8	161.9	171.9	11.1
Saint John, New Brunswick	121.0	121.3	125.0	3.3
Quebec				
Chicoutimi-Jonquière	158.2	158.5	160.9	1.7
Montreal	2,862.3	2,921.4	3,127.2	9.3
Ottawa-Hull	743.8	819.3	920.9	23.8
Quebec	583.8	603.3	645.6	10.6
Sherbrooke	125.2	130.0	139.2	11.2
Trois-Rivières	125.3	128.9	136.3	8.8
Ontario				
Hamilton	542.1	557.0	599.8	10.6
Kitchener	287.8	311.2	356.4	23.8
London	326.8	342.3	381.5	16.7
Oshawa	186.5	203.5	240.1	28.7
St. Catharines-Niagara	342.7	343.3	364.6	6.4
Sudbury	156.1	148.9	157.6	1.0
Thunder Bay	122.0	122.2	124.4	2.0
Toronto	3,130.4	3,432.0	3,893.0	19.6
Windsor	250.9	254.0	262.1	4.5
Manitoba/Saskatchewan				
Regina	173.2	186.5	191.7	10.7
Saskatoon	175.1	200.7	210.0	19.9
Winnipeg	592.1	625.3	652.4	10.2
Alberta				
Calgary	626.0	681.5	754.0	20.4
Edmonton	740.9	774.0	839.9	13.4
British Columbia				
Vancouver	1,268.2	1,380.7	1,602.5	26.4
Victoria	241.5	225.2	287.9	19.2
Total CMAs	14,314.4	15,155.8	16,665.4	16.4
Total Canada	24,343.2	25,309.3	27,296.9	12.1
Percent CMAs	58.8	59.9	61.1	

Source: Statistics Canada, Cat. 91-210, Vol. 8 (Ottawa, Ministry of Supply and Services, 1991); and Statistics Canada, Cat. 93-303, *Census Metropolitan Areas, Census Agglomerations, Population, Dwelling Counts.*

a 23.8 percent population growth. Note, however, the low growth rates of Chicoutimi-Jonquière in Quebec, of Thunder Bay and Sudbury in Ontario, and of Saint John in New Brunswick.

Big targets are attractive but very competitive

Some marketers sell only in metropolitan areas because of the large, concentrated population. Having so many customers packed into a small area can simplify the marketing effort. Fewer middlemen can be used while still offering products conveniently. One or two local advertising media (city newspaper or TV station) can reach most residents. If a sales force is needed, it will have less wasted travel time and expense because people are closer together.

Metro areas are also attractive markets because they offer greater sales potential than their population alone would indicate. Consumers have more money to spend because wages tend to be higher in these areas. In addition, professional occupations with higher salaries are concentrated in these areas. Densely populated areas offer great opportunities if the competition isn't too strong.

Megalopolis: the continuous city

In 1986, 12 of Canada's 25 CMAs fell within Canada's **megalopolis**. This strip of land runs approximately 750 miles from Quebec City in the east to Windsor in the west, passing through such cities as Trois-Rivières, Sherbrooke, Montreal, Ottawa, Oshawa, Kitchener, Toronto, Hamilton, London, and St. Catharines. This strip, with less than 2 percent of the country's total land mass, contains 39.7 percent of Canada's population.

Another concentration is developing around Vancouver and Victoria. For example, the CMA of Vancouver includes the city of Vancouver with a 1991 population of about 472,000 as well as the municipalities of Surrey and Burnaby with 245,000 and 159,000 persons, respectively. Also, population corridors are building between Calgary and Edmonton and between Regina and Saskatoon.

The mobile ones are an attractive market

People move, stay awhile, and then move again. In fact, the 1986 census classed nearly half of the Canadian population as movers over the previous five years, and about half of that group moved to a new community. Both the long-distance and local mobiles are important market segments.

Often when people move in the same city, it's to trade up to a bigger or better house or neighborhood. Those who move tend to be younger, better educated people on the way up in their careers. Their income is rising and they have money to spend. Buying a new house may spark many other purchases, too. The old draperies may look shabby in the new house; the bigger yard may require a new lawn mower or even a yard service.

Lately, we've been seeing a new development: the moving of older or retired persons. Some are moving from suburbia to downtown areas in their own city. Others are leaving big cities for smaller towns and cities such as Victoria, British Columbia, and Kingston, Ontario.

Many market-oriented decisions have to be made fairly quickly after moves. People must locate new sources of food, clothing, medical and dental care, and household goods. Once these basic buying decisions are made, they may not change for a long time.

Alert marketers should try to locate these mobile people and inform them of their marketing mixes.[3] The mobile market gives special opportunities to retail chains, national brands, and franchised services that are available in different areas. The customer who moves to a new town may find a familiar supermarket sign down the street and never even try the local competitor.

Not only are Canadians frequent movers, but they also like to travel and try new things. Better highways have encouraged more distant vacationing plus ownership of second homes, vacation cabins, travel trailers, and boats. This has led to more retail stores, marinas, and recreation areas. Even the growth of the suburbs was encouraged by a willingness to travel farther to work. And growing suburban areas encouraged the growth of outlying shopping centers.

IMMIGRATION AND THE ETHNIC MARKET

Immigration can also affect growth

Immigration must also be taken into account. Immigration levels fluctuate sharply from year to year, depending on economic and political circumstances both within and outside Canada. International immigration was a major contributor to Canada's population growth in the early and mid-1950s. However, in recent years, immigration's influence has been declining. Statistics Canada is now predicting a net increase from immigration of between 100,000 and 125,000 people each year.

Immigrants can bring growth and diversification to a community. Marketers must keep track of where the immigrants settle, so their unique marketing needs can be satisfied. Marketing Demo 6–1 explores how new Canadians are being acknowledged as important markets in Canada.

Ethnic diversity

Immigration has made Canada rich in many cultures. The country has often been called a **mosaic.** In contrast to the United States, where cultural minorities have usually assimilated as quickly as possible, the Canadian environment has encouraged cultural diversity. Exhibit 6–3 shows some ethnic groups' distribution in each Canadian CMA by their mother tongue.

The wide range of ethnic backgrounds has created a whole host of demands for new products and services. Also, the market for such items as Greek food and bagels isn't confined to the ethnic group where the demand began. As Canadians of all backgrounds are exposed to different cultural influences, their consumption patterns change. This contributes to the growth of markets for a wide variety of ethnic goods and services. Conversely, other markets expand as ethnic groups become more fully assimilated within the Canadian scene.

THE FRENCH CANADIAN MARKET

More than one quarter of Canada's total population comes from a French ethnic background with its own distinct and separate culture and lifestyle. There are some important questions we should ask about the French Canadian market. The demographic issues are discussed next, while social and cultural aspects of the French Canadian market are considered in Chapter 7.

What is a French Canadian consumer?

French Canadians can be defined in many ways. The position most often taken is that a French Canadian consumer is anyone whose mother tongue is French or who tends to speak French rather than English at home.[4] However, marketers must realize that a large number of French Canadians are truly bilingual. They watch English-language television and read English-language publications. For example, most of the people in Montreal who watch English-language television programs such as "The Price is Right" are French-speaking.[5]

Exhibit 6–3   Population by Selected Mother Tongues for Census Metropolitan Areas, 1991

	Total Population	English	Percent	French	Percent	Italian	Percent	German	Percent
Calgary	754,030	611,855	81.14%	10,535	1.40%	5,480	0.73%	14,555	1.93%
Chicoutimi-Jonquière	160,925	1,510	0.94	157,780	98.05	60	0.04	40	0.02
Edmonton	839,925	654,460	77.92	19,630	2.34	5,600	0.67	20,505	2.44
Halifax	320,500	298,500	93.14	8,690	2.71	570	0.18	950	0.30
Hamilton	599,760	476,650	79.47	8,515	1.42	21,460	3.58	8,130	1.36
Kitchener	356,420	283,170	79.45	4,630	1.30	1,755	0.49	15,810	4.44
London	381,520	324,080	84.94	4,310	1.13	3,880	1.02	4,320	1.13
Montreal	3,127,245	445,515	14.25	2,093,395	66.94	117,500	3.76	13,125	0.42
Oshawa	240,105	209,510	87.26	4,950	2.06	2,995	1.25	2,485	1.03
Ottawa-Hull	920,860	492,365	53.47	302,885	32.89	10,575	1.15	6,625	0.72
Quebec	645,550	11,255	1.74	619,370	95.94	580	0.09	400	0.06
Regina	191,690	167,195	87.22	2,505	1.31	465	0.24	5,760	3.00
Saskatoon	210,020	176,390	83.99	3,415	1.63	230	0.11	8,115	3.86
Sherbrooke	139,195	8,495	6.10	125,795	90.37	150	0.11	110	0.08
St. Catherines-Niagara	364,555	293,935	80.63	13,395	3.67	13,485	3.70	8,150	2.24
St. John's	171,860	168,650	98.13	450	0.26	40	0.02	200	0.12
Saint John	124,980	116,565	93.27	5,525	4.42	100	0.08	215	0.17
Sudbury	157,240	94,240	59.93	43,310	27.54	3,770	2.40	1,155	0.73
Thunder Bay	124,430	100,370	80.66	2,880	2.31	4,050	3.25	1,145	0.92
Toronto	3,893,045	2,584,050	66.38	49,800	1.28	189,265	4.86	48,110	1.24
Trois-Rivières	136,305	1,655	1.21	132,620	97.30	60	0.04	80	0.06
Vancouver	1,602,500	1,151,975	71.89	20,585	1.28	17,775	1.11	34,765	2.17
Victoria	287,895	253,740	88.14	4,090	1.42	935	0.32	4,360	1.51
Windsor	262,075	199,190	76.00	12,420	4.74	10,815	4.13	2,895	1.10
Winnipeg	652,355	481,645	73.83	29,465	4.52	4,680	0.72	24,970	3.83
Total	16,664,985	9,606,965		3,680,945		416,275		226,975	

Source: Statistics Canada, *The Nation,* Cat. 93-313.

A significant number of French Canadians who aren't truly bilingual on occasion still prefer to listen to English radio, watch English TV, or read English-language publications. Marketers must carefully study French Canadians' media preferences. They cannot rely exclusively on census discussions of mother tongue or language most often spoken at home.

Where is the French Canadian Market?

Is the French Canadian market essentially Quebec, or should it be defined more broadly? For marketing purposes, Quebec and the French Canadian market are not identical. However, a French Canadian market does not exist in every location where French is a few consumers' mother tongue. Marketers can't afford to develop special programs for very small market segments.

One approach defines the French Canadian market to include Quebec, eight adjacent counties in Ontario, and seven counties in the northern part of New Brunswick. At least 25 percent of the residents in each of these 15 additional counties claim French as their mother tongue. For the 15 counties taken together, the mother tongue of over half the population is French. In addition, flourishing French Canadian institutions are found in these counties. French Canadian assimilation into the English culture is somewhat limited. Also, the same areas

Ukrainian	Percent	Greek	Percent	Arabic	Percent	Punjabi	Percent	Chinese	Percent	Vietnamese	Percent
4,020	0.53%	1,195	0.16%	3,805	0.50%	4,595	0.61%	24,800	3.29%	4,870	0.65%
5	0.00	5	0.00	60	0.04	0	0.00	25	0.02	45	0.03
19,715	2.35	975	0.12	4,025	0.48	4,700	0.56	23,890	2.84	4,825	0.57
100	0.03	735	0.23	1,180	0.37	200	0.06	1,230	0.38	360	0.11
4,305	0.72	2,135	0.36	1,555	0.26	1,785	0.30	4,200	0.70	1,525	0.25
965	0.27	1,485	0.42	750	0.21	1,025	0.29	2,340	0.66	1,525	0.43
1,265	0.33	1,960	0.51	2,480	0.65	400	0.10	2,260	0.59	990	0.26
5,580	0.18	41,000	1.31	37,030	1.18	2,775	0.09	26,770	0.86	14,960	0.48
1,960	0.82	600	0.25	220	0.09	235	0.10	915	0.38	130	0.05
1,760	0.19	1,740	0.19	11,470	1.25	1,285	0.14	11,070	1.20	3,215	0.35
10	0.00	135	0.02	770	0.12	25	0.00	640	0.10	720	0.11
2,285	1.19	450	0.23	95	0.05	165	0.09	2,105	1.10	600	0.31
5,245	2.50	300	0.14	220	0.10	155	0.07	2,210	1.05	455	0.22
15	0.01	60	0.04	310	0.22	10	0.01	170	0.12	275	0.20
3,245	0.89	615	0.17	340	0.09	140	0.04	1,090	0.30	250	0.07
20	0.01	40	0.02	50	0.03	60	0.03	520	0.30	25	0.01
20	0.02	115	0.09	40	0.03	20	0.02	120	0.10	10	0.01
1,205	0.77	165	0.10	155	0.10	40	0.03	345	0.22	55	0.03
2,225	1.79	215	0.17	70	0.06	20	0.02	340	0.27	140	0.11
24,605	0.63	46,875	1.20	19,560	0.50	31,965	0.82	175,035	4.50	18,985	0.49
5	0.00	65	0.05	125	0.09	0	0.00	80	0.06	45	0.03
6,745	0.42	4,885	0.30	2,130	0.13	38,255	2.39	130,680	8.15	7,705	0.48
850	0.30	285	0.10	160	0.06	2,095	0.73	5,280	1.83	455	0.16
1,430	0.55	1,140	0.43	3,140	1.20	440	0.17	2,210	0.84	700	0.27
18,590	2.85	1,335	0.20	475	0.07	2,655	0.41	7,710	1.18	2,040	0.31
106,170		108,510		90,215		93,045		426,035		64,905	

receive a significant amount of overflow advertising from Quebec, and they're frequently served by Quebec-based distributors.[6]

Joe Garreau, author of the best-seller *The Nine Nations of North America*, selected Quebec as one of North America's nine nations. Material provided by Garreau is now being used by advertising agencies and research firms in their efforts to delineate lifestyle segments.[7]

Of all Canadians reporting French as their mother tongue, over 90 percent, or just under 6 million people, live in Quebec or in the 16 adjacent counties. The figure includes immigrants from France, North Africa, Vietnam, Haiti, and other French-speaking nations. A substantial Acadian population in New Brunswick is also unique in some ways. Nevertheless, for marketing planning purposes, Acadians are usually considered to be part of the larger "French" market. Exhibit 6–4 gives more detailed linguistic information for metropolitan Montreal, the rest of Quebec, and the adjacent counties in Ontario and New Brunswick.

How important is the English market in the same area?

Some 601,405 English "mother tongue" individuals (8.7 percent of the total Quebec population) live in that province. The English-speaking community of Quebec is believed to account for an even larger share of the area's total purchasing power. In addition, Quebec has about 605,038 residents who report

MARKETING DEMO 6–1
Get to Know the Chinese Market

Ethnic marketing in Canada is receiving increased attention because of the more culturally diverse population and government policies.

In major urban centres across Canada (excluding Montreal), on average 70 percent of residents are not of British, French, or aboriginal origin.

The Quebec experience in developing specific campaigns for the French market is the ideal role model for ethnic marketing.

The Chinese market has received widespread news coverage with the resettlement of many Hong Kong residents in Canada. Hong Kong is now our number-one source of immigrants.

This segment is expected to grow at an even faster rate during the early 1990s. According to the Commission of Canada in Hong Kong, 26,000 visas for permanent residency will be issued each year between 1991 and 1993 (up from the annual average of 21,000 issued in the late 1980s).

The economic impact of these immigrants is being felt everywhere, but most noticeably in the Toronto, Vancouver, Calgary, and Edmonton markets.

Recent immigrants are better educated as well as more affluent and confident than previous generations from Hong Kong. This new breed of immigrant includes professionals with established careers and most likely with marketing, financial, or entrepreneurial skills.

They are distinctly different from their predecessors, who started restaurants and laundries.

There is a two-year waiting period for immigrants, which means long lead times for resettlement from Hong Kong. The summer, at the end of the Hong Kong school year, is the prime period for visits to Canada.

Major purchases (homes, autos, mortgages) are most likely to be made during the summer months prior to final settlement in Canada. Chinese are more likely to purchase a home than to rent and will pay cash, even for large purchases.

These new immigrants are extremely status conscious and prefer top-of-the-line products.

More than one generation will live in the same household and major decisions will be made with contributions from each.

Many Chinese are superstitious and some customs are built on bringing good luck. The colors red and gold; and the numbers three and eight, are considered lucky. The Chinese "Money God" is an example of the religious overtones that money has in the culture, with many cultural symbols built around success and good fortune.

The effects of this immigration have been felt in the Toronto market. The housing industry saw some condominium projects with more than 60% Chinese ownership. The Chinese population is growing in Scarborough, Markham, and Richmond Hill, particularly.

The impact of the new Chinese market has not yet peaked—the 1990s will see an increase in immigration to as much as 30,000 a year. The needs are unique, and companies that wish to reach them must recognize that.

Source: Martin Seto, "Get to Know the Ethnic Market," *Marketing,* June 17, 1991, p. 32.

some third language as their mother tongue. In the adjacent 15 counties, just under 381,220 claim English as their mother tongue and 23,093 claim a language other than English or French. Also worth noting is the significant number who claim both French and English as mother tongues.

Although some English-speaking consumers have left Quebec, the number of Quebec residents whose mother tongue is not French is still larger than the total population of Manitoba or Saskatchewan. This "other Quebec" market is also less expensive to reach because almost 80 percent of these consumers live in or around Montreal. Obviously, a significant "other" market well worth cultivating still exists in Quebec. In fact, statistics show that "other than French-speaking" Montreal is Canada's fourth largest city after Toronto, French-speaking Montreal, and Vancouver.

Exhibit 6–4   Mother Tongue: The French Canadian Market, 1991

	Population	Percentage
Quebec		
Montreal CMA		
French	2,093,390	66.9%
English	445,515	14.3
English and French	53,140	1.7
Other	535,200	17.1
	3,127,245	
Rest of province		
French	3,504,540	92.9
English	155,890	4.2
English and French	38,450	1.0
Other	69,838	1.9
	3,768,718	
New Brunswick*		
French	221,430	57.8
English	147,420	38.4
English and French	10,805	2.8
Other	3,968	1.0
	383,623	
Ontario†		
French	151,835	36.3
English	233,800	55.7
English and French	14,065	3.4
Other	19,125	4.6
	418,825	
Totals		
French	5,971,195	77.5%
English	982,625	12.8
English and French	116,460	1.5
Other	628,131	8.2
	7,698,411	

*Counties of Gloucester, Kent, Madawaska, Northumberland, Restigouche, Victoria, and Westmorland only.

†Counties of Cochrane, Nipissing, Prescott (including Russell United Counties), Stormont (including Dundas and Glengarry United Counties), Sudbury, Timiskaming.

Source: *Profile of Census Divisions and Subdivisions in Ontario—Part A,* November 1992, Cat 95-337; *Profile of Census Divisions and Subdivisions in New Brunswick—Part A,* November 1992, Cat. 95-319; and *Profile of Census Metropolitan Areas and Agglomerations—Part A,* October 1992, Cat. 93-337.

A LOOK AT THE FUTURE

Population will keep
growing, but . . .

The world's population is growing rapidly—it's expected to double in the next 30 years—but this isn't true of Canada. Our own population growth has slowed dramatically. Canada ranks among the slow-growth population countries in a world where most developing countries are growing quite rapidly. Many Canadian marketers that previously enjoyed rapid and profitable growth at home are turning to international markets—the United States, Europe, and Asia—where future population growth will be much larger than in our own country.

This doesn't mean, however, that our population has stopped increasing. Canada's population will continue to grow at least for another 45 years or even longer. But how much and how fast? Statistics Canada has released an in-depth study of likely population growth in Canada that tries to answer these questions.[8]

Total population projections

Exhibit 6–5 shows expected population increases for Canada to the year 2036 using different projection assumptions. By the turn of the century, Canada's population will be between 28.6 million and 29.7 million, a modest growth of some 1.4 million to 2.5 million from today's 27 million plus. Which projection will turn out to be most accurate? This will depend on Canadians' attitudes toward marriage, family size, and family planning. Marketers must watch such trends carefully because of their impact on future markets.

Birthrate: Boom or bust?

The Canadian **birthrate** (the number of babies born per 1,000 people) has fluctuated greatly in the last 50 years. A post–World War II baby boom began as returning soldiers started families, and it lasted about 15 years into the early 1960s. Then the situation changed. There was a "baby bust" in the 1970s as more women stayed in the work force and couples waited longer to have children. When you see the dip in the birthrate and think about the declining market for baby products, you can understand why Johnson & Johnson started to promote its "baby" shampoo to adults who wanted a gentle product.

While the birthrate is down, the number of births has been rising, but only slightly. That number is expected to drop again in this decade. These shifts are easy to explain. The baby boom generation is now in its childbearing years, so there are simply more women to have babies. But the number of children per family stays low. There may be less need for big "family" homes and large

Exhibit 6–5   Population of Canada, Selected Years, 2001–2036 (in millions)

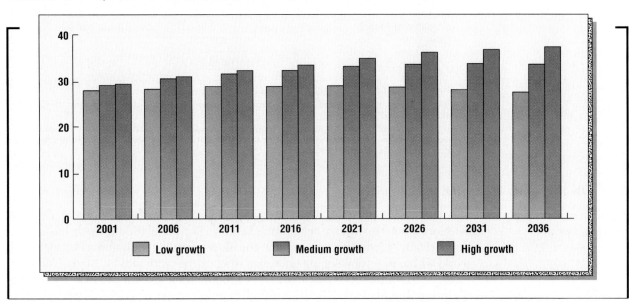

Source: Statistics Canada, *Population Projections for Canada, Provinces and Territories*, 1989–2011, Cat. 91-520 (Ottawa: Minister of Supply and Services, March 1990).

"family-sized" food packages, and more demand for small apartments, out-of-home entertainment, travel, and smaller food packages.

With fewer children, parents can spend more money on each child. For example, expensive bikes, home videogames, and designer clothes for children have all done well in recent years. Parents can indulge one or two children more easily than a house full.

Age distribution is changing

Because population is growing slowly, the median age is rising. In 1991, the median age of the population was 33.5 years, up from 31.6 in 1986 and 26.3 in 1961.

Stated another way, the percentage of the population in different age groups is changing. Exhibit 6–6 shows the number of people in different categories. Note the declines in the younger age groups. The last of the baby boomers have grown up. There are now 600,000 fewer teens in Canada than there were in the early 1980s. That has a great impact on the clothing industry. There are big increases in those age groups classed as senior working age (35–64) and elderly (over 65).

So the focus has changed from teenage fad followers and their throw-away fashions to career women who buy fewer but better-quality garments for the workplace.

Exhibit 6–6 Population Distribution by Age Group, Selected Years, 1971–2031 (in thousands)

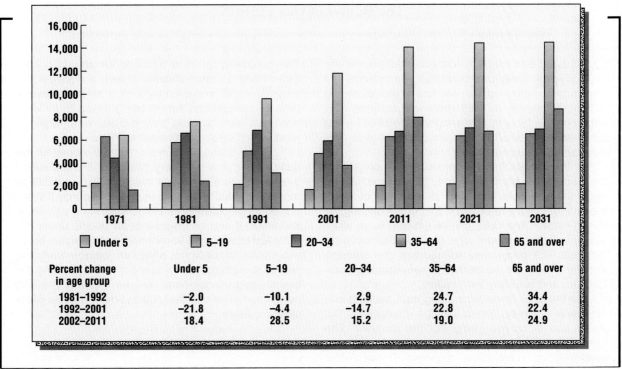

Percent change in age group	Under 5	5–19	20–34	35–64	65 and over
1981–1992	−2.0	−10.1	2.9	24.7	34.4
1992–2001	−21.8	−4.4	−14.7	22.8	22.4
2002–2011	18.4	28.5	15.2	19.0	24.9

Source: Statistics Canada, *Population Projections for Canada, Provinces and Territories*, 1984–2006 and 1990–2011, Cat. 91-520 (Ottawa: Ministry of Supply and Services, May 1985, December 1991).

The shrinking number of teens has also had impacts in other areas. Grocery prices have been going up for three years but grocery spending hasn't—and one reason is a decreasing number of teenagers.

Retail marketing consultant Leonard Kubas said the flat spending is partly a result of the fact that there are over half a million fewer teenagers in the country than there were five to seven years ago—and teens consume more, per capita, than adults or children.

Another interesting finding indicated that 32 percent of shoppers are "very willing to pay more for environmentally safe products, a significant number." Younger people, 18 to 34, are now the most environmentally concerned shoppers of all—a change from having been the least concerned shoppers in recent years.[9] This group of baby busters, also known as "Generation X," sees consumption in a different way than their baby boom predecessors. Some of their purchasing habits are outlined in Marketing Demo 6–2.

The major reason for the changing age distribution is that the post–World War II baby boom produced about one-fourth of our present population. This large group crowded into the schools in the 1950s and 60s and then into the job market in the 1970s. In the 1990s, they're swelling the middle-aged group. And early in the 21st century, they'll reach retirement—still a dominant group in the total population. According to one population expert, "It's like a goat passing through a boa constrictor."

MARKETING DEMO 6–2
The Busters of Generation X

If baby boomers are just now discovering the joys of living on the cheap, for busters it's always been a way of life, not just a way of saving money. Even now as they settle into careers, they choke on the thought of staying in a hotel or buying furniture that doesn't come from a garage sale or a Scandinavian megastore.

If the busters have an answer to Gucci shoes, they are "Doc Martens," an English-made leather boot, indestructible, air-soled, and devoid of ornamentation. The same could be said of the offerings at denim retailer The Gap, one of the few large chain stores to build a solid buster clientele across North America. The colors may change with the seasons and the styles, but the clothes remain durable, comfortable, and relatively inexpensive.

As the book *Generation X* suggests, travel is one area where busters like to indulge themselves. But they'll scrimp on everything but the distance. The buster traveler typically just wants a plane ticket, according to Travel Cuts manager Trynor Tilley.

They're willing to stand by or go on any date, they never book accommodations ahead, and they'd just as soon eat in a marketplace as a sit-down restaurant. It's not just that they're being cheap. They want to experience a place at ground level, not through the windows of an air-conditioned tour bus.

If there is one consumer product designed for the baby buster, it is the Sony Walkman. From a purely practical point of view, it's inexpensive, yet satisfies those who care about the quality of sound. It's designed for people who travel, but not in a car. More important, it acknowledges that for people under 30, recorded music is not so much a social lubricant as an expression of personal style, an escape from the crowd, something to remind the office temp riding the bus at eight o'clock on a Tuesday morning that she has a life that no overdemanding boss or hostile client can take away.

Source: Michael McCullough, "Life from a Window," *BC Business*, July 1992, p. 79.

Some of the effects of this big market are very apparent. For example, record sales exploded to the beat of rock and roll and the Beatles as the baby boom group moved into their record-buying teens. Soon after, universities added facilities and faculty to handle the surge, but then had to cope with excess capacity and loss of revenue when the student-age population dwindled. To relieve financial strain, many universities are now adding special courses and programs for adults to attract the now-aging baby boom students. On the other hand, the "fitness" industry and food producers who offer low-calorie foods are reaping the benefit of a middle-aged "bulge" in the population.

Eventually, Canada's youth culture will give way to a new kind of society. The aging of the population is seriously concerning some planners. Younger people may not be able or willing to support all of the older people in the style they can now expect. Costs will continue to rise as relatively more retired people are supported by fewer young people. The cost of Canada's old age pension plan is already becoming a political issue. In 1985, those over 65 used their political clout to prevent the de-indexing of old age pensions.

Medical advances help people live longer and are also adding to the proportion of the population in the senior citizen group. Note from Exhibit 6–6 that the over-65 age group grew by 34 percent in the last decade and will grow another 22 percent by the turn of the century. As the accompanying Bank of Montreal ad suggests, these dramatic changes are creating new opportunities for such industries as tourism, health care, and financial services.[10] Marketing Demo 6–3 describes how one firm is gearing up to better serve the mature market.

Household composition is changing

The number of families in Canada climbed 9.5 percent from 6.7 million to 7.4 million between 1986 and 1991. Nearly 65 percent of Canada's families have children at home. Statistics Canada says four out of five of these families were traditional husband-wife-children families.

The "typical" Canadian household, however, is not a young, happily married couple with the wife and two children spending all of their time in the suburbs. This was never true, and it's even less true now. Although almost all Canadians marry, they are marrying later, delaying childbearing, having fewer children, and often getting divorced.

Many of those divorced eventually remarry. In 1990, about 20 percent of all marriages were remarriages, resulting in a growing number of "his" and "her" families. So even with delayed marriages and a high divorce rate, the majority of adults are married at any one time.

Redefining the family

Once we get rid of the "couple-with-two-children" image of family life, we should also recognize that many households aren't families in the usual sense. In 1991, single-adult households accounted for 23 percent of all households or 2.3 million people! These households include young adults who leave home when they finish school as well as divorced and widowed people who live alone.

In Canada's urban areas, the percentage of single-person households is even higher. These people need smaller apartments, smaller cars, smaller food packages, and in some cases less expensive household furnishings because they don't have very much money. Other singles have ample discretionary income and are attractive markets for top-of-the-line stereos, clothing, status cars, travel, and nice restaurants and bars.

MARKETING DEMO 6–3
Smashing Age-Old Stereotypes

K en Mader and David Rathbun were babes in the woods of market research three years ago when their employer, Maritime Life, put them in charge of investigating the mature market— consumers 45 years of age and older. The mid-sized, Halifax-based insurer wanted fresh insights and ideas on how to position itself for the anticipated growth in this market.

The mature market presents a rich, and much misunderstood, target, but only a few marketing specialists have as yet looked at it as a distinct phenomenon. According to David Wolfe, author of *Marketing to Baby Boomers and Beyond,* professional researchers are at a disadvantage when they turn to the mature market because a lot of their basic theories and tools just aren't suited to plumbing the needs and desires of older consumers.

The common wisdom is that people become less active, adventurous, and alert as they age. But actually, we grow more individuated and subjective in values and behavior as we get older. Mature consumers don't fit broad stereotypes because they don't identify themselves through affiliation with groups or view products as icons of membership, Wolfe says. And therefore, they confound mass market brand-building practices.

Maritime Life arranged six focus groups with people in the target age group across the country. Next came a written survey of 1,200 Canadians in the mature age bracket, weighted to reflect Maritime Life's primary interest in 45- to 55-year-olds, who are still accumulating wealth. The 23-page question-naire covered everything from attitudes about inflation and government spending to respondents' health concerns, spending, and saving habits and sources of financial information.

The results of the survey backed up Wolfe's basic ideas about the diversity of the mature market. "What we learned," says Rathbun, "is that age is a strong correlate but not a strong determinant of behavior or product preferences. Lifestyles continue to be heterogeneous, not homogeneous." Simply put, some 50-year-olds like to sit in armchairs; others like to heli-ski. Obviously, Maritime Life couldn't hope to conquer the mature market with one product.

On the financial services side, Mader and Rathbun suggested a product that would index pensions to inflation; long-term care insurance for people who live alone; and extra health insurance, for those who think the public system is in decline. Other suggestions included an affinity club for policyholders who like to travel, offering them discounted holiday packages and a national network of home maintenance and repair subcontractors who could help elderly policyholders hold onto their homes longer. Some of these ideas are far from the beaten track for Maritime Life. But, says Rathbun, "We'd like to be a significant player in this market. That may take us into new lines of business or alliances with other organizations in nontraditional areas."

Source: Sandy Fife, "Smashing Age-Old Stereotypes," *Marketing*, February 15, 1993, pp. 1, 3.

There are also well over one million unmarried couples living together in Canada. To reach this market, some banks have changed their policies about loans to unmarried couples for homes, cars, and other major purchases. Some insurance companies are now designing coverage oriented toward unmarried couples.

Single parents — Another sizable nontraditional group, single-parent families, rose 10.6 percent between 1986 and 1991, making it 14 percent of all families. About 82 percent of lone-parent families are headed by women. Sixty-seven percent of female single parents were in the labor force in 1988, 85 percent of whom worked full time.

Exhibit 6–7   Percentage of Women and Men Employed, 1977–1990

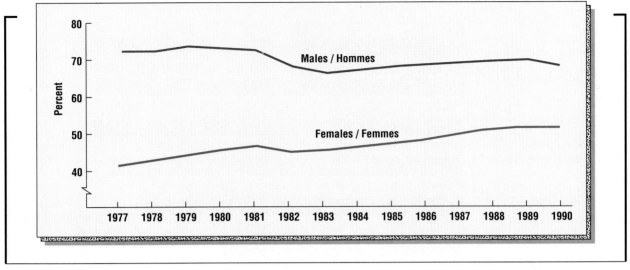

Source: Statistics Canada, Cat. 71-529.

Nontraditional households are still in a minority, but marketers should probably pay special attention to them because they're growing at a much higher rate than traditional family households. This trend will no doubt continue, particularly if the age projections made earlier hold true.

Women in the work force

As shown in Exhibit 6–7, the gap in the percentage of men and women employed is narrowing. In 1977, only about 40 percent of women were employed, compared to over 70 percent of men. In 1990, the percentage of men employed was still about 70 percent, and the percentage of women had jumped to 55 percent.

Exhibit 6–8 shows the breakdown of the female work force into age groups. All age groups have increased their participation in the work force since 1981, with the highest growth being in the over-25 age groups.

Mothers at work

The past decade witnessed an especially sharp increase in labor force participation of women with children. Overall, participation of mothers with children under 16 at home was 69 percent in 1989, up from 49 percent in 1979. This trend includes both mothers with preschool children and those with children in school. In 1989, 62 percent of women with preschool-aged children were in the labor force, compared with 43 percent in 1979.

When the wife earns, the family spends

In families where the wife works, family spending power is increased. This is why median family income is as high as it is. But many families feel they need this income to make ends meet.

Working wives do spend more for food and probably choose more expensive types of food. Families with working wives also spend more on clothing, alcohol and tobacco, home furnishings and equipment, and cars. In short, when a wife works, it affects the family's spending habits. This fact must be considered when analyzing markets and planning marketing strategies.

Exhibit 6–8   Women's Share of the Labor Force, by Selected Age Groups, 1981 and 1990

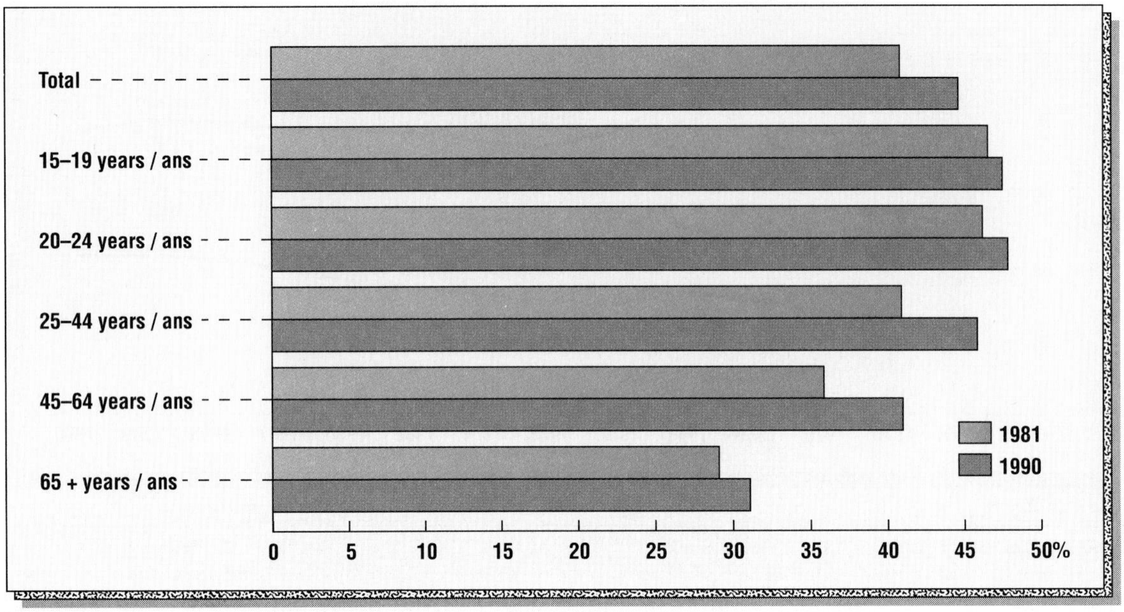

Source: Statistics Canada, Cat. 71-529.

INCOME—MARKETS NEED PEOPLE WITH MONEY

So far, we've been concerned mainly with the *number* of different types of people and *where* they live. But people without money aren't potential customers. And the amount of money people can spend affects the products they're likely to buy. So most marketers study income levels, too.

Changing growth rates

Income comes from producing and selling goods or services in the marketplace. A widely available measure of the output of the whole economy is the gross domestic product (GDP)—the total value of all goods and services produced in a year. As Exhibit 6–9 shows, Canada's gross domestic product in 1973 was $127.3 billion. By 1983, it had risen to $405.7 billion. GDP had grown by $278.4 billion, or almost 219 percent. This means that from 1973 to 1983, Canada's GDP grew at an average rate of slightly over 12 percent annually. Much of the change, however, doesn't represent "real" growth but rather the effects of inflation. In 1986 dollars, the relevant figures were $326.8 billion for 1973 and $439.5 billion for 1983. This represents an increase of 34.5 percent over the 10-year period, or an annual rate of growth of about 3 percent. Since 1983, Canada's growth has been much slower. Indeed, there was no real growth at all between 1988 and 1991.

Family income also climbed very slowly

Family and household incomes in Canada increased between 1980 and 1990 but not as much as you might expect. And the distribution of income has undergone some interesting changes. Let's look more closely at these two developments.

Exhibit 6–10 reveals that in current dollars, the average family income in 1981 was $30,973. This figure grew steadily until it reached $53,131 in 1991, an

Exhibit 6–9   National Accounts in Canada, 1973–1991

Year	Gross Domestic Product in thousands	Gross Domestic Product (1986 prices) in thousands
1973	$127,372	$326,848
1974	152,111	341,235
1975	171,540	350,113
1976	197,924	371,688
1977	217,879	385,122
1978	241,604	402,737
1979	276,096	418,328
1980	309,891	424,537
1981	355,994	440,127
1982	374,442	425,970
1983	405,717	439,448
1984	444,735	467,167
1985	477,988	489,437
1986	505,666	505,666
1987	551,597	526,730
1988	605,906	552,958
1989	649,916	565,779
1990	667,843	563,060
1991	674,388	553,457

Source: Statistics Canada, *Canada Economic Observer,* Cat. 11-210, Annual, July 1992.

Exhibit 6–10   Family Incomes in Canada 1981–1991

Year	Unadjusted Average	Constant 1991 Dollar Average
1981	$30,973	$51,756
1982	33,473	50,481
1983	34,861	49,704
1984	36,384	49,712
1985	38,780	50,944
1986	41,240	52,048
1987	43,604	52,722
1988	46,185	53,669
1989	50,083	55,423
1990	51,633	54,537
1991	53,131	53,131

Source: Statistics Canada, *Income Distribution by Size in Canada,* 1991, Cat. 13-207 (Ottawa: Ministry of Supply and Services, December 1992).

Exhibit 6–11   Percentage Distribution of Families by Income Levels (selected years in 1991 dollars)

Income Class	1980	1985	1988	1991
$75,000 and over	15.0%	14.7%	17.3%	18.2%
$60,000–74,999	14.4	12.7	13.2	14.0
$50,000–59,999	13.3	12.4	12.4	12.1
$40,000–49,999	16.7	15.1	14.3	13.6
$30,000–39,999	14.3	15.1	14.1	14.0
$20,000–29,999	11.8	14.5	13.9	13.7
$10,000–19,999	11.4	12.6	11.3	10.4
under $10,000	3.1	3.0	2.4	2.4

Source: Statistics Canada, *Income Distribution by Size in Canada,* 1991, Cat. 13-207 (Ottawa: Ministry of Supply and Services, December 1992).

increase of some 71.5 percent. However, note what happens when the same data is represented in real terms (constant 1991 dollars). Between 1981 and 1991, real family income increased but by less than 2 percent.

Distribution of families by income level

Exhibit 6–11 shows that the percentage distribution of families by income level has also changed. Since the data is in constant 1991 dollars, the effects of inflation have been taken into account.

The rising income level of the 1970s broadened markets and drastically changed our marketing system. More families became important customers with money to spend. Many products that might previously have been thought of as luxuries could now be sold to mass markets. In this way, the standard of living improved even more because large markets can lead to economies of scale. But as we've just seen, there have been changes. The recession of the early 1990s may well cause this group to lose ground again.

Opinions differ as to what will happen to consumer incomes and income distribution in the future. Some business analysts believe that the lack of income growth is a sign of worse things to come. They think Canada's middle-class standard of living is threatened by a decline in the manufacturing sector of the economy. These analysts argue that industries that traditionally paid high wages are now replacing workers with machines to compete with low-cost foreign producers. At the same time, the lower-paying service industries are growing rapidly. But other analysts aren't so pessimistic. They agree that the percentage of the work force earning middle-income wages has decreased recently, but they think this is a temporary shift, not a long-term trend.

What happens to income levels will be critical to you and to Canadian consumers in general. It's easy for both consumers and marketing managers to be lulled by the promise of a constantly increasing standard of living. Adjustments in consumer thinking and in marketing strategy will be required if growth doesn't resume.

The higher-income groups still receive a big share

Higher-income groups still receive a very large share of total income, as Exhibit 6–12 shows. It divides all households into five equal-sized groups, from lowest income to highest. Although the average income of Canadian families in

Exhibit 6–12   Percentage of Total Family Income Going to Different Income Groups, 1991 (in current dollars)

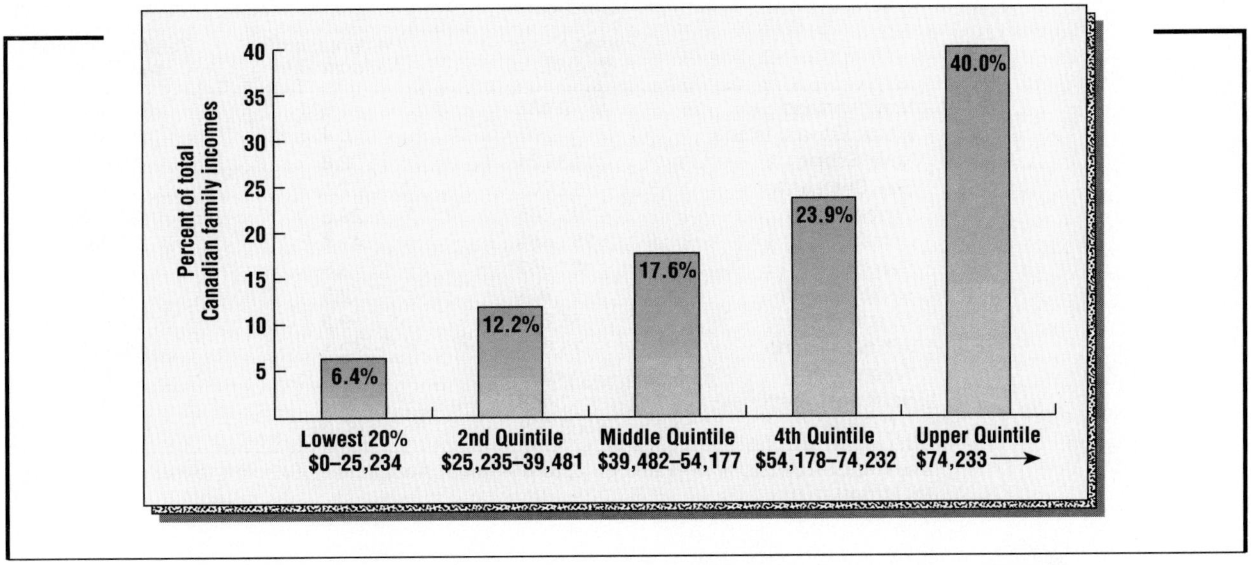

Source: Statistics Canada, *Income Distribution by Size in Canada*, 1991, Cat. 13-207 (Ottawa: Ministry of Supply and Services, December 1992).

1991 was $53,131, the top 20 percent of the households received 40 percent of all total income. This gave them extra buying power, especially for luxury items.

At the lower end of the scale are about 1.7 million families. They also account for 20 percent of the total number of families, but they only receive about 6.4 percent of total income. Even this low-income group—many of whose members are below the poverty level—is an attractive market for some basic commodities, especially food and clothing. Some marketers target this group, usually with a lower-priced marketing mix.

Historically, the distribution of income in Canada has varied very little since 1965. The lowest 20 percent have never received more than 6.4 percent of total family income, and the top 20 percent have always received more than 39 percent. Obviously, the top 2 quintiles are attractive markets for high-ticket luxury items.

How much income is enough?

Income distribution's importance can't be stressed too much. Bad marketing strategy errors have been made by overestimating the amount of income in various target markets. It's all too easy for marketers to fall into such errors because of our natural tendency to associate with people like ourselves and to assume that almost everyone lives the same way.

The 1991 average family income of over $53,000 is a useful reference point. A young working couple together can easily go way over this figure. What's being earned may seem like more than enough in the initial flush of making money, but it's surprising how soon needs and expenses rise and adjust to available income. Before long, it's difficult to see how anyone can live on less.

In fact, many Canadian families must make do on much less. Statistics Canada has for many years used "low-income cutoffs" as a measure of well-being

Exhibit 6–13   Personal Income, Geographic Distribution, 1991

	Personal Income (in millions)	Percentage of National Total	Personal Income per Capita
Newfoundland	$ 9,485	1.6%	$16,553
Prince Edward Island	2,207	0.4	16,847
Nova Scotia	16,734	2.8	18,573
New Brunswick	12,907	2.1	17,778
Quebec	143,685	23.6	20,988
Ontario	251,681	41.4	25,386
Manitoba	21,069	3.5	19,276
Saskatchewan	17,833	2.9	17,941
Alberta	56,687	9.3	22,477
British Columbia	73,870	12.1	22,955
Yukon	697	0.1	25,815
Northwest Territories	1,448	0.2	26,327
Canada	$608,303	100.0%	$22,560

Source: Statistics Canada, *Provincial Economic Accounts Preliminary Estimates*, 1991, Cat. 13-213 (Ottawa: Ministry of Supply and Services).

and a basis for welfare and other transfer payments. Families required to spend more than 62 percent of their income on basic necessities such as food, shelter, and clothing are said to be living below the poverty line. The size of the family unit, as well as the size of the community in which it lives, are also considered. For example, a family of four living in a rural area had a low-income or poverty-line cutoff of $19,117 in 1990. For a similar family in a metropolitan area of 500,000, the low-income cutoff figure was $28,031. So, the fact that many households must make do on much less than the median family income should not be forgotten in marketing strategy planning.

Income isn't equally distributed geographically

Exhibit 6–13 shows how total personal income is distributed throughout Canada and highlights provincial differences in per capita personal income. Companies often map the income of different areas when picking markets. A market area (a city, county, CMA, or province) that has more income will often be more attractive. For example, a chain of retail dress shops might decide to locate in the suburbs around Toronto because a lot of people with high incomes live in this area.

CONSUMER SPENDING PATTERNS ARE RELATED TO POPULATION AND INCOME

We've been using the term *family income* because consumer budget studies show that most consumers spend their incomes as part of family or household units. They usually pool their incomes when planning expenditures. Thus, most of our discussion will be on how households or families spend their income.

Disposable income is what you get to spend

However, families don't get to spend all their income. **Disposable income** is what's left after taxes. Out of this disposable income—together with gifts, pensions, cash savings, or other assets—the family makes its expenditures. Some families don't spend all their disposable income—they save part of it. Therefore, we should distinguish between disposable income and actual expenditures when trying to estimate the size of potential target markets.

Discretionary income is elusive

Most households spend a good portion of their income on necessities: food, rent or house payments, car and home furnishings payments, insurance, and so on. A family's purchase of luxuries comes from **discretionary income** (what's left of disposable income after paying for necessities).

Discretionary income is a difficult concept because the definition of *necessities* varies from family to family and over time. A color TV set might be purchased out of discretionary income by a lower-income family, while a higher-income family could consider it a necessity. But if many people in a lower-income neighborhood start buying color TVs, this might become a necessity for the others and severely reduce their discretionary income available for other purchases.

Measuring discretionary income in a specific situation clearly requires marketing research, but the majority of Canadian families don't have enough discretionary income to afford the leisure-class lifestyles seen on TV and in other mass media. On the other hand, some young adults and older people without family responsibilities may have a large share of the total discretionary income in a given area. They may be especially attractive markets for sellers of CD players, cameras, new cars, foreign travel, and various kinds of recreation (tennis, skiing, plays, concerts, and fine restaurants).

Expenditure data tells how target markets spend

It's common sense that a wealthy family will spend more money than a poor one—and that the money will be spent on different things. But how it's spent and how that varies for different target markets are important to marketers.

The amount spent on major categories such as food, housing, clothing, transportation, and so on does vary by income level. And the relationships are logical when you realize that many of the purchases in these categories are "necessities."

The data in Exhibit 6–14 can help you understand how potential target customers spend their money. Let's make this more concrete with a simple example. You're a marketing manager for a swimming pool manufacturer. You're considering a mail advertisement to consumers in a neighborhood where most families fall in the two upper-income quintiles. Let's assume families in these two quintiles spend an average of $1,800 a year on recreation of all kinds. If you know that it would cost a family at least $1,500 a year for depreciation and maintenance of a pool, it follows that the average family in these two categories would have to make a big shift in its lifestyle in order to purchase a pool.

Data like this won't tell you whether a specific family will buy the pool. But it does supply useful input to help make a sound decision. If more information is needed (perhaps about the strength of the target market's attitudes toward recreation products), then some additional research may be needed. Perhaps you might want to see a budget study on consumers who already have swimming pools to see how they adjusted their spending patterns and how they felt before and after the purchase.

Exhibit 6–14   Distribution of Average Expenditures by Family Income Group, 17 Metropolitan Areas, Canada, 1990

	All Classes	Lowest Quintile	Second Quintile	Third Quintile	Fourth Quintile	Highest Quintile
Food	12.6%	18.4%	15.3%	13.3%	12.3%	10.3%
Shelter	17.3	30.5	21.1	17.6	16.6	13.9
Principle accommodation	16.3	29.8	20.2	16.7	15.6	12.6
Rented living quarters	5.5	20.0	11.5	6.1	3.7	1.5
Owned living quarters	8.3	5.2	5.9	8.0	9.5	8.1
Water, fuel, and electricity	2.5	3.9	2.8	2.7	2.4	2.0
Other accommodation	1.0	0.8	0.9	0.9	0.9	1.3
Household operation	4.0	5.9	4.5	4.1	3.9	3.6
Household furnishings and equipment	3.0	3.1	3.0	2.7	3.0	3.1
Household furnishings	1.7	1.5	1.6	1.4	1.7	1.9
Household equipment	1.1	1.4	1.3	1.2	1.1	1.1
Services	0.2	0.2	0.2	0.1	0.2	0.2
Clothing	5.5	5.5	5.3	5.2	5.5	5.6
Transportation	11.8	9.3	12.7	13.0	12.3	10.9
Private transportation	10.4	7.0	10.9	11.9	11.0	9.8
Public transportation	1.4	2.3	1.8	1.1	1.3	1.2
Health care	1.8	2.6	2.2	1.9	1.7	1.5
Personal care	1.9	2.8	2.2	1.9	1.9	1.5
Recreation	5.0	4.0	4.5	5.3	4.9	5.2
Reading materials	0.6	0.8	0.7	0.6	0.5	0.5
Education	0.9	1.0	0.8	0.7	0.9	1.0
Tobacco products and alcoholic beverages	2.7	3.7	3.3	3.2	2.7	2.0
Miscellaneous	2.7	1.9	2.6	3.3	3.0	2.4
Total current consumption	69.6%	89.5%	78.1%	72.3%	69.2%	61.6%
Personal taxes	22.3	4.9	14.6	18.9	22.6	29.7
Security	4.4	1.1	3.6	4.4	5.0	5.0
Gifts and contributions	3.6	4.5	3.7	3.9	3.3	3.6
Total expenditure	100.0%	100.0%	100.0%	100.0%	100.0%	100.0%

Source: Statistics Canada, *Family Expenditure in Canada*, June 1992, Cat. 62-555.

EXPENDITURE PATTERNS VARY WITH OTHER MEASURABLE FACTORS

Income has a direct bearing on spending patterns—but there are other factors that should not be ignored in any careful analysis of potential markets.

Expenditure patterns in Canada vary by region and with the size and type of family. Differences also exist between renters and home owners. And even among home owners, spending patterns are not the same between those with a mortgage and those without a mortgage.

Spending affected by urban-rural location

Consumer spending data shows that the location of a consumer's household does affect the household's spending habits. We will not present detailed tables here but instead summarize a few important differences. Detailed Statistics Canada data should be analyzed to answer specific questions.

Expenditures on transportation, housing, and food do seem to vary by geographic location. Consumers in urban areas spend a lower percentage of their income on transportation and more on housing than those in rural areas—probably because of higher land and construction costs and greater population density. A rural family spends a larger percentage on food—but lower rural incomes mean that the absolute amount isn't very different.

Exhibit 6–15 Lifestages—An Overview

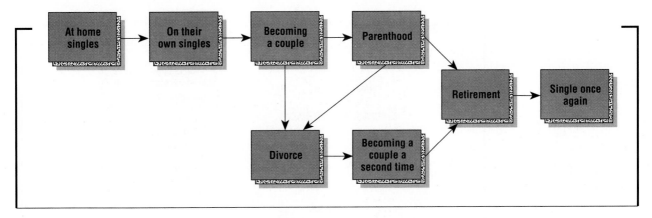

Lifestages affect spending

Two other demographic dimensions affect spending patterns: age of the adults and age of any children. For example, families of adults spent more money for both food and clothing than families of the same size that also include children. However, age alone does not provide much insight into purchasing patterns. We need to know what stage of life a person is in—setting up house, raising a family, divorcing?[11]

Lifestages, a concept used by the ad agency J. Walter Thompson in developing advertising campaigns, is made up of the stages of life that a person passes through from birth to death. These stages are summarized in Exhibit 6–15. The information that follows is based on over 50 group discussions, 300 personal interviews, and 1,500 telephone interviews conducted all over Canada by J. Walter Thompson and Decima Research.

These Lifestage groups can be split into four different segments, as shown in Exhibit 6–16. Each group has different spending patterns and marketers must take this into consideration when developing a marketing mix for one of these segments.

New childless households

Currently, this group represents between a quarter and a third of all households. In the past, this group had a transitory phase of three to five years, but due to delayed marriages and childbirth a person may remain in this stage for 10 to 15 years.

This group likes to live for today, and they like to spend money. They do not automatically buy the brand their parents bought, but they look for products that work and they'll quickly try something else that promises to be better than what they are currently using. This group more than any other is on their guard against being ripped off—so firms must be careful to deliver what is promised. However, when a firm can deliver, they are willing to pay extra for what they recognize as a good product.

New parents

This group represents approximately 16 percent of the adult population, but it has an influence out of proportion to its size. The birth of a child brings this group face-to-face with the inevitability of increasingly scarce resources—both economic and environmental. To this group, the company behind the product is

Exhibit 6–16   Four Distinct Lifestage Segments

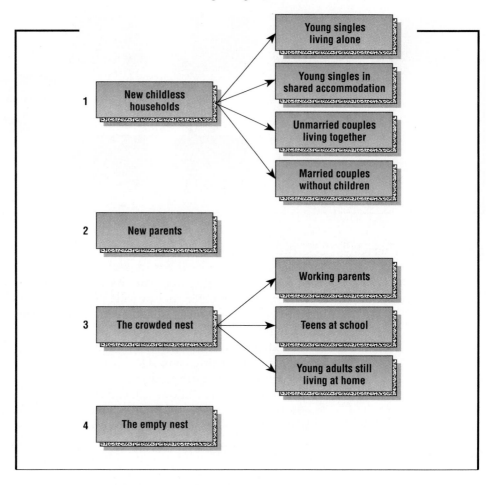

as important as the product itself. These new parents are older, better educated, and more experienced than their predecessors a generation ago. They understand that large corporations have an influence and a role in society beyond the products they make.

The consumption patterns of this group are driven by the needs of their children. These children make a great many financial, emotional, housing, and logistical demands on their parents. These constraints are compounded by the time limitations imposed by an increasingly necessary two paycheque household.

The crowded nest

This group represents one-third of all adults. In this household, 81 percent of teens have an influence on family purchase decisions. Young people often do the grocery shopping, and it is estimated that they control over $4 billion of their parents' expenditures. Parents tend to listen to their children because they believe their children are more up-to-date in their knowledge of things like the environment and electronics.

The empty nester

This group represents a second life, not a fleeting hazy few golden years. The empty nesters are composed of aging baby boomers who fully intend to carry on spending. They spend more time than the average person taking vacations, shopping for pleasure, attending arts and cultural events, and going out to dinner, movies, and bars. They are financially well off, as half of them are still working. Their home is paid for, they are no longer sacrificing for others, and they like to spend much of their money on big-ticket items both for themselves and as gifts for their family. Price ceases to have the importance it used to have because this is the moment they have been saving for.

CONCLUSION

We studied population data, getting rid of various misconceptions about how our more than 27 million people are spread over Canada. We learned that the potential of a given market can't be determined by population figures alone. Income, mother tongue, stage in life cycle, people's geographic location, and other factors are important, too. We talked about some of the ways that these dimensions—and changes in them—affect marketing strategy planning.

We also noted the growth of sprawling metropolitan areas. These urban-suburban systems suggest the shape of future growth in this country. The very high concentration of population and spending power in these markets has already made them attractive and easily reached target markets. Competition in these markets, however, is often tough.

One of Canadians' outstanding characteristics is their mobility. This emphasizes the need for paying attention to changes in markets. The high mobility also reminds us that even relatively new data is not foolproof. Available data can only aid judgment, not replace it.

Canadian consumers are among the most affluent in the world. And this affluence affects purchasing behavior. Beyond buying the necessities of life, they have discretionary income and are able to buy a wide variety of luxuries. Even when buying necessities like food and clothing, they have many choices. And they use them.

The kind of data discussed in this chapter can be very useful for estimating market potential within possible target markets. But, unfortunately, it's not very helpful in explaining specific customer behavior—why people buy *specific* products and *specific* brands. And such detailed forecasts are obviously important to marketing managers. Fortunately, better estimates can come from a fuller understanding of consumer behavior, the subject of the next chapter.

QUESTIONS AND PROBLEMS

1. Discuss how slower population growth (especially the smaller number of young people) will affect businesses in your local community.

2. Discuss the impact of our aging culture on marketing strategy planning.

3. Some demographic characteristics are likely to be more important than others in determining market potential. For each of the following characteristics, identify two products for which this characteristic is *most* important: (*a*) size of geographic area, (*b*) population, (*c*) income, and (*d*) stage of life cycle.

4. Name three specific examples (specific products or brands, not just product categories) illustrating

how demand will differ by geographic location and urban-rural location.

5. Explain how the continuing mobility of consumers as well as the development of big metropolitan areas should affect marketing strategy planning in the future. Be sure to consider the impact on the four Ps.

6. Explain how redistribution of income has affected marketing planning thus far. Then discuss its likely impact in the future.

7. Explain why the concept of the Census Metropolitan Area was developed. Is it the most useful breakdown for retailers?

SUGGESTED CASES

30. Grand Foods, Ltd.

35. Canadian Inland

International Addendum

This addendum assists in introducing the demographic dimensions of both the Canadian and global consumer markets.

International Addendum

Some marketing managers never consider opportunities outside of their own country. That may make sense in some cases, but it may also lead to missed opportunities. For example, crowded cities in North America may seem to offer great potential, but Canada's population makes up less than one-half of 1 percent of the total world population—which is over 5.3 billion.

Exhibit 1 shows population levels in various countries (and regions) around the world. Although the United States is among the largest countries in terms of population, notice the total population of the European countries. You can see why so many firms want to reach consumers in Europe now that trade barriers among the European countries are being removed. India (with a population over 850 million) and China (with a population over a billion) are even larger. Countries in Latin America and Africa have much smaller populations.[1]

Exhibit 1   Population Levels in Different Countries, 1990 (all figures in thousands)

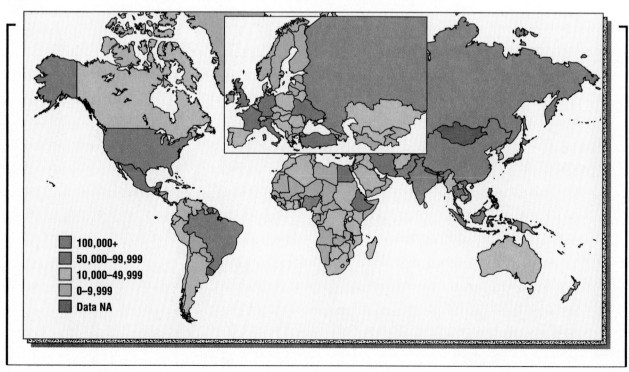

MARKETERS SEARCH FOR GROWING MARKETS

Although a country's current population is important, it provides only a snapshot of the market. The population trend is also important. Generally, population growth is expected in most countries. But how rapidly? And will output increase faster than population? These are important questions for marketers. The answers affect how rapidly a country moves to higher stages of development—and becomes a new market for different kinds of products.

Population, income, and other demographic dimensions help to answer these questions. Exhibit 2 summarizes current data for representative countries from different regions around the world. Note that population growth varies dramatically from country to country. In general, less-developed countries experience the fastest growth. The populations of Kenya, India, and Egypt are expected to double in 35 years or less. It will take more than twice as long for the populations of the United States and Canada to double. Population growth is even slower in Japan and the European countries.[2]

POPULATION IS BECOMING MORE CONCENTRATED

The population in some countries is spread over a very large area. Population density is important to marketers. If the population is very spread out, as it is in many of the African countries, it is difficult and expensive for marketers to adjust time and place discrepancies between producers and consumers. This is especially a problem in countries without efficient highway and rail systems. Similarly, a widely spread population may make promotion more difficult, especially if there are language differences or communication systems are poor. Of course, even in countries with low population density, major cities may be packed with people.

Major cities like Singapore attract many marketers because of their concentration of people and income; by contrast, much of the world's population still lives in poverty in rural villages like this one in China.

Exhibit 2   Demographic Dimensions for Representative Countries

Country	1990 Population (000s)	Percent Annual Growth in Population (1990–2000)	Years for Population to Double	Population Density (people per square mile)	Percent of Population in Urban Areas	1990 GNP (millions of $US)	1990 GNP per Capita	Percent Annual GNP Growth	Literacy Percent
Afghanistan	15,166	4.7%	30	59	17.7%	$3,307	$218	2.4%	12%
Algeria	25,694	2.5	23	27	42.6	60,603	2,382	2.0	45
Argentina	32,297	1.1	58	30	84.7	86,395	2,654	2.0	95
Australia	16,649	1.2	58	6	85.7	211,456	12,638	1.7	100
Bangladesh	117,930	2.6	25	2,063	13.2	17,263	155	-2.9	33
Brazil	153,765	1.7	35	46	73.8	348,210	2,245	2.9	79
Burma	41,261	1.9	35	155	24.0	8,299	201	2.2	79
Cameroon	11,109	2.6	26	59	42.4	11,406	1,048	0.6	55
Canada	26,521	1.0	87	7	76.5	474,079	17,309	4.1	96
Chile	13,019	1.4	47	44	84.1	21,923	1,600	6.8	94
China	1,130,096	1.3	44	300	20.6	439,231	356	11.0	73
Colombia	32,584	1.8	35	73	68.0	41,337	1,228	5.4	69
Cuba	10,544	0.9	77	244	71.6	20,020	1,873	2.3	96
Czechoslovakia	15,689	0.4	347	317	74.7	152,130	9,582	1.4	99
Ecuador	10,508	2.1	29	94	54.2	12,039	1,117	5.0	69
Egypt	56,202	2.3	27	142	45.2	33,583	610	0.5	45
Ethiopia	51,305	3.2	23	105	10.6	6,158	120	3.4	5
Finland	4,979	0.2	231	38	61.8	98,759	19,204	3.6	100
France	56,162	0.4	231	265	73.4	940,485	16,419	2.3	99
Germany	77,546	0.2	n/a	563	90.4	1,415,946	17,659	3.3	99
Ghana	15,215	3.1	24	161	32.0	6,220	399	5.3	53
Greece	10,071	0.1	231	197	58.1	48,040	4,784	0.0	94
Haiti	6,411	2.2	50	590	25.5	2,262	356	0.5	41
Iceland	251	0.9	87	6	89.2	4,723	17,791	6.6	99
India	850,090	1.8	35	657	25.8	277,994	330	1.2	41
Indonesia	191,216	1.6	37	253	26.2	81,843	420	3.8	74
Iran	55,698	3.1	21	85	54.1	81,319	1,540	-2.0	62
Iraq	18,761	3.7	19	108	68.0	40,000	2,213	0.0	46
Israel	4,445	1.5	41	545	88.9	39,213	8,882	1.0	92
Italy	57,673	0.2	347	495	72.0	826,138	13,814	3.9	97
Jamaica	2,512	1.0	63	586	49.4	2,878	1,103	5.0	87
Japan	123,836	0.3	139	845	76.7	2,829,825	21,914	4.8	99
Kenya	25,369	3.6	17	108	19.7	9,127	358	4.8	59
Kuwait	2,080	3.0	20	292	93.7	28,392	13,596	4.0	75

Country	1990 Population (000s)	Percent Annual Growth in Population (1990–2000)	Years for Population to Double	Population Density (people per square mile)	Percent of Population in Urban Areas	1990 GNP (millions of $US)	1990 GNP per Capita	Percent Annual GNP Growth	Literacy Percent
Madagascar	11,796	3.2	22	50	21.8	2,139	185	1.4	68
Malaysia	17,062	2.0	35	131	34.6	36,473	2,030	7.4	73
Mexico	88,266	2.1	32	113	66.3	156,152	1,783	1.4	90
Morocco	26,246	2.0	28	149	42.7	18,369	707	1.5	71
Mozambique	14,532	2.1	39	46	19.4	1,676	113	4.0	17
Nepal	19,149	2.4	29	344	7.4	3,613	180	7.1	21
Netherlands	14,864	0.5	139	923	88.5	231,958	15,080	4.0	99
Nicaragua	3,605	2.7	24	70	56.6	2,267	703	-8.0	74
Nigeria	118,775	3.0	23	323	31.0	30,139	268	-2.6	42
North Korea	23,062	1.5	29	484	63.8	21,407	923	3.0	90
Norway	4,216	0.4	231	34	70.7	86,368	20,285	1.3	100
Pakistan	113,388	2.6	26	356	28.3	40,883	353	4.9	26
Panama	2,423	1.9	33	79	52.2	2,893	1,477	-17.5	88
Peru	21,899	1.9	33	43	68.8	22,579	1,149	-8.4	87
Philippines	66,659	2.2	26	560	41.6	41,575	610	5.0	89
Poland	38,361	0.3	139	316	61.2	284,422	7,298	2.1	99
Romania	23,269	0.5	139	252	54.3	152,459	6,449	2.1	96
Saudi Arabia	16,753	3.8	18	19	73.0	95,760	5,651	5.2	57
Singapore	2,703	1.0	63	10,941	100.0	29,529	9,958	10.9	83
Somalia	8,512	2.1	22	34	32.5	999	119	1.5	55
South Korea	43,911	0.7	54	1,140	69.9	188,499	3,883	12.0	93
South Africa	38,509	2.6	n/a	82	55.9	81,814	2,071	2.6	79
former Soviet Union	291,052	0.7	87	33	65.8	2,557,996	8,728	1.5	99
Spain	39,614	0.3	139	202	91.4	335,943	8,078	5.5	93
Sri Lanka	17,134	1.2	47	666	21.5	7,232	422	1.5	86
Sudan	25,137	3.1	26	25	20.2	9,067	349	6.0	22
Sweden	8,409	0.3	693	48	83.0	170,105	19,639	3.1	99
Switzerland	6,651	0.4	116	415	60.5	187,842	27,693	2.6	99
Syria	12,467	3.8	19	168	49.5	21,790	1,718	5.6	61
Taiwan	20,456	0.9	63	1,456	70.6	94,464	4,355	7.2	91
Tanzania	26,038	3.4	21	69	19.0	4,081	156	3.9	85
Thailand	56,468	1.2	41	280	17.9	67,211	1,091	11.0	89
Turkey	56,518	2.0	33	184	53.0	79,128	1,331	7.4	66
Uganda	17,586	3.3	21	187	9.4	4,744	271	2.9	57
United Kingdom	57,142	0.2	347	603	89.6	646,255	10,917	3.8	99
United States	250,465	0.7	77	69	73.7	4,961,434	19,789	1.0	96
Venezuela	19,745	2.2	28	55	83.2	64,484	3,213	4.2	90
Vietnam	68,492	1.9	28	525	20.1	13,609	199	2.1	94
former Yugoslavia	23,867	0.5	116	240	46.1	153,880	6,480	0.1	90
Zaire	35,273	3.2	24	38	39.6	6,031	172	2.5	61

The extent to which a country's population is clustered around urban areas varies a lot. In Canada, the United States, Venezuela, Australia, Israel, and Singapore, for example, a high percentage of people live in urban areas. See Exhibit 2. By contrast, in China and Afghanistan, less than 20 percent of the people live in major urban areas.

People everywhere are moving off the farm and into industrial and urban areas. Shifts in population—combined with already dense populations—have led to extreme crowding in some parts of the world. And the crowding is likely to get worse.

The worldwide trend toward urbanization has prompted increased interest in international markets. For many firms, the concentration of people in major cities simplifies Place and Promotion strategy decisions—especially for major cities in the wealthiest nations. Affluent, big-city consumers often have similar lifestyles and needs. Thus, many of the products successful in Toronto, New York, or Paris are likely to be successful in Caracas and Toyko.

However, keep in mind that many of the world's consumers, whether crowded in cities or widely spread in rural areas, live in deplorable conditions. These people have little hope of escaping the crush of poverty. They certainly have needs—but they don't have the income to do anything about the needs.

THERE'S NO MARKET WHEN THERE'S NO INCOME

Profitable markets require income—as well as people. The amount of money people can spend affects the products they are likely to buy. When considering international markets, income is often one of the most important demographic dimensions.

The best available measure of total income in most countries is **gross national product (GNP)**—the total market value of goods and services produced in an economy in a year. Unfortunately, GNP measures are not ideal for comparing very different cultures and economies. For instance, do-it-yourself activities, household services, and the growing of produce or meat by family members for their own use are not usually figured as part of GNP. Since the activities of self-sufficient family units are not included, GNP can give a false picture of economic well-being in less-developed countries. At the other extreme, GNP may not do a good job of measuring service-oriented output in highly developed economies.

GNP also has limits when comparing countries with different patterns of international investment. A country's GNP does not include income earned by foreigners who own resources located in that country. For example, the profit earned by Toyota's Canadian operations is not included in the Canadian GNP. On the other hand, that income would be included in Japan's GNP.

But gross national product *is* useful—and sometimes it's the only available measure of market potential. Exhibit 6–2 gives a GNP estimate for each country listed. You can see that the more developed industrial nations—including the United States, Japan, and Germany—have the biggest share of the world's GNP. This is why so much trade takes place between these countries—and why many firms see them as the more important markets.[3]

INCOME GROWTH EXPANDS MARKETS

However, the fastest *growth* in GNP is not, in general, occurring in the nations with the largest GNPs. For example, total US GNP in 1990 was close to $5 trillion dollars; it has increased approximately 3 percent a year since 1880.

This means that GNP doubled—on the average—every 20 years. Recently, this growth slowed—and even declined for a while.

Declines in GNP may not just be due to temporarily bad economic conditions. GNP is related to the output of employees. When the population growth rate slows, there are fewer young workers and more retired people. This may become a serious political problem—everyone expects the economy to deliver more, while fewer young people are available to support the older ones. Many other developed economies face this problem, too.

GNP tells us about the income of a whole nation, but in a country with a large population that income must be spread over more people. GNP per person is a useful figure because it gives some idea of the income level of people in a country. Exhibit 2 shows, for example, that GNP per capita in Canada is quite high—over $17,300. The United States, Japan, Canada, Switzerland, and Germany are among those with the highest GNP per capita. In general, markets like these offer the best potential for products that are targeted at consumers with higher income levels.

A BUSINESS AND A HUMAN OPPORTUNITY

The large number of countries with low GNP per capita is a stark reminder that much of the world's population lives in extreme poverty. Even among countries with the largest overall GNPs, you see some sign of this. In India, for example, GNP per person is only $330 a year. Many countries are in the early stages of economic development. Most of their people work on farms—and live barely within the money economy. At the extreme, in Mozambique GNP per person per year is only about $113 (in US dollars).

These people, however, have needs, and many are eager to improve themselves. But they may not be able to raise their living standards without outside help. This presents a challenge and an opportunity to the developed nations—and to their business firms.

Some companies—including North American firms—are trying to help the people of less-developed countries. Corporations such as Pillsbury, Corn Products, Monsanto, and Coca-Cola have developed nutritious foods that can be sold cheaply—but still profitably—in poorer countries. One firm sells a milk-based drink (Samson)—with 10 grams of protein per serving—to the Middle East and the Caribbean areas. Such a drink can make an important addition to diets. Poor people in less-developed lands usually get only 8 to 12 grams of protein per day in their normal diet (60 to 75 grams per day are considered necessary for an adult.)[4]

(?) **What do Third World consumers really need?**

Marketing managers from developed nations sometimes face an ethical dilemma about whether their products help or hurt consumers in less-developed nations. For example, a United Nations report criticized Coke and Pepsi for expanding their soft-drink sales in the Philippines. The study concluded that consumers have shifted to soft drinks from local beverages—such as a mixture of lime juice and coconut water—that provided needed vitamins.

In another much publicized case, producers of infant formula were criticized for giving free samples to hospitals. Nestle's and American Home Products (AHP) Corp., two of the biggest suppliers in this market, say that they only gave the free samples to children who were in need—and at the request of hospitals. But critics argued that the practice encouraged new mothers to give up breast feeding. Away from the hospital, mothers could not understand the directions for using the formula or would rely on unsanitary water supplies. Improper use of the formula could lead to malnutrition, diarrhea, and other illnesses. In 1991, Nestle's and AHP pledged to stop giving away free samples. Although that step will stop misuse, the formula won't be available to many people who really need it.

In cases like these, a marketing manager may need to weigh the benefits and risks of trying to serve Third World markets. For example, in Canada Quicksilver Enterprises sell its 250-pound aluminum and fiberglass "ultralight" airplanes— that look like go-carts with wings—to wealthy hobbyists. However, Quicksilver found a growing market for ultralights in developing nations, where farmers use them for crop dusting. They help farmers increase production of much needed foods. So what's the problem? In the United States, the government bans ultralights as not being safe enough for crop dusting. Some critics argue that a firm shouldn't sell its products in foreign markets if they are illegal in the United States. But ultimately, the marketing manager often must decide what to do.[5]

READING, WRITING, AND MARKETING PROBLEMS

The ability of a country's people to read and write has a direct influence on the development of its economy—and on marketing strategy planning. The degree of literacy affects the way information is delivered, which in marketing means promotion. Unfortunately, only about two-thirds of the world's population can read and write. Data on literacy rates is inexact because different countries use different measures. Even so, you may be surprised by some of the countries in Exhibit 2 with low literacy rates.

Low literacy sometimes causes difficulties with product labels and instructions, for which we normally use words. This was one issue in the infant formula conflict. In an even more extreme case, some producers of baby food found that consumers misinterpreted a baby's picture on their packages. Illiterate natives believed that the product was just that—a ground-up baby! Many companies meet this lack of literacy with instructions that use pictures instead of words. Singer used this approach with its sewing machines.

Even in Latin America, which has generally higher literacy rates than Africa or Asia, a large number of people cannot read and write. Marketers have to use symbols, colors, and other nonverbal means of communication if they want to reach the masses.[6]

Marketers can learn a great deal about possible opportunities in different countries by studying available demographic data and trends. The examples we considered here give you a feel, but keep in mind that much useful data is available. For example, an easy-to-use computer program called PCGLOBE provides extensive data on every country in the world.

Behavioral Dimensions of the Consumer Market

Chapter 7

When You Finish This Chapter, You Should

①
Understand the economics-orientation model of buyer behavior.

②
Understand how psychological variables affect an individual's buying behavior.

③
Understand how social influences affect an individual's and household's buying behavior.

④
Know how time relates to consumer markets.

⑤
Have some appreciation of how and why the French Canadian market is different.

⑥
Know how consumers use problem-solving processes.

⑦
Have some feel for how a consumer handles all the behavioral variables and incoming stimuli.

⑧
Understand the important new terms (shown in blue).

"Our card is both an emotional and a rational product," says Morris Perlis, who runs Amex Canada from the Toronto suburb of Markham. From here, Perlis presides over Amex's largest and most profitable foreign subsidiary. In some ways, Canadians are its ideal customers. Amex sells security and we are an extremely security-conscious people. That's why, for example, we buy more traveler's cheques per capita than anyone else. Because many of us have close ties to other countries and because Canadian winters are cold, we are three times as likely to take foreign trips as Americans.[1]

The latest brainstorm from Markham is Lifetime Membership, which offers green-card card members of long standing the chance to pay $600 for the privilege of never having to pay an annual fee again. It will be offered later to gold and platinum card members. According to Nick Mancini, the vice president in charge of the program, "We realized that there was a small but significant segment of card members whose lifestyle needs were starting to change." (Translation: The baby boomers are getting older and richer and they want more attention.) "These are people who want to feel special, who have earned the right to be recognized as being special."

To make them feel special, Amex will set up a separate service unit to attend to their needs, publish a newsletter for them, and design travel and other products especially for them. Says Perlis, "They have already demonstrated great loyalty to us, so there is a bond."

The lifetime membership idea is a good example of Amex's acute understanding of the psychology of the middle-aged baby boomer who is its prime customer. It sells a service, but it also sells a sense of exclusivity and self-worth, and that's what aging baby boomers are looking for.

CONSUMER BEHAVIOR—WHY DO THEY BUY WHAT THEY BUY?

In the last chapter, we discussed basic data on population, income, and consumer spending patterns. This information can help marketers predict basic *trends* in consumer spending patterns. Unfortunately, when many firms sell similar products, demographic analysis isn't much help in predicting which specific products and brands consumers will purchase—and why. Our Amex example shows that many other variables can influence consumers and their buying behavior.

To better understand why consumers buy as they do, many marketers turn to the behavioral sciences for help. Marketing Demo 7–1 shows the insights available from this type of research. In this chapter, we'll explore some of the thinking from economics, psychology, sociology, and the other behavioral disciplines.

MARKETING DEMO 7–1
In the Driver's Seat

In the design stages of the 1993 Ford Probe in Detroit, male engineers were asked to don a little extra equipment while on the job—ceramic fingernails. The idea came from the lead designer—Canadian Mimi Vandermolen, one of the highest-ranking female automotive executives in North America.

After all, Ford Motor Co. expects that half of the car's purchasers will be women, so why not keep longer nails, heels, and shorter legs in mind when designing knobs, seat tracks, and accelerator pedals?

There has been a bumper crop of female consumers in the last 10 years, and industry analysts say at this rate, women will hold the balance of purchasing power within five years. Currently, 45 percent of North American car buyers are women, up from 35 percent 10 years ago.

"For a long time, we and most other companies believed you had to sell products differently to men than women," says John Jelinek, Ford Canada's product information manager in Oakville. "You don't need to treat a woman as though she doesn't know which end of the car to put the key in. When you had a salesperson who is condescending and says, 'Come back with the husband,' or 'What color does the little lady like?' what he didn't do was sell cars."

It was then, he says, as the female segment grew, and the salesman's attitude stayed suspended in time, that North American companies lost so much of their market ground to Japanese automakers. Now, Ford is trying to win back that wedge armed with surveys of 40,000 women buyers each year to find out what they are looking for.

Both men and women rate reliability as the main appeal in buying a car. Women pick safety features second compared with men's attraction to handling. The key is to come up with a design that suits both sexes, since women influence the decision made in 75 percent of all sales.

The big-three automakers are responding by working with women's committees. In the past, these committees have lobbied for the installation of power lumbar seats for pregnant women, remote keyless entry, and automatic release mechanisms for heavy tops on convertibles, just to mention a few examples of improved features for the female portion of the population.

Source: Alana Kienz, "In the Driver's Seat," *The Vancouver Sun,* July 14, 1992, p. D1.

Specific consumer behaviors vary a great deal for different products and from one target market to the next. In today's global markets, the variations are countless. That makes it impractical to try to catalogue all the detailed possibilities for every different market situation. For example, how and why a given consumer buys a specific brand of shampoo may be very different from how that same consumer buys motor oil; and different customers in different parts of the world may have very different reactions to either product. But there are *general* behavioral principles—frameworks—that marketing managers can apply to learn more about their specific target markets. Our approach focuses on developing your skill in working with these frameworks.

THE BEHAVIORAL SCIENCES HELP US UNDERSTAND THE BUYING PROCESS

Economic needs affect most buying decisions

Most economists assume that consumers are **economics-oriented**—they know all the facts and logically compare choices in terms of cost and value received to get the greatest satisfaction from spending their time and money. A logical extension of the economics-orientation theory led us to look at consumer spending patterns. This approach is valuable because consumers must at least have income to be in a market. Further, most consumers don't have enough income to buy everything they want. So most consumers want their money to stretch as far as it can.

This view assumes that economic needs guide most consumer behavior. **Economic needs** are concerned with making the best use of a consumer's time and money, as the consumer judges it. Some consumers look for the lowest price. Others will pay extra for convenience. And others may weigh price and quality for the best value. Some economic needs are:

1. Economy of purchase or use.
2. Convenience.
3. Efficiency in operation or use.
4. Dependability in use.
5. Improvement of earnings.

Clearly, marketing managers must be alert to new ways to appeal to economic needs. Most consumers appreciate firms that offer them improved value for the money they spend. But improved value does not just mean offering lower and lower prices. Many consumers face a "poverty of time." Carefully planned Place decisions can make it easier and faster for customers to make a purchase. Products can be designed to work better, require less service, or last longer. Promotion can inform consumers about their choices—or explain product benefits in terms of measurable factors like operating costs or the length of the guarantee.

The economic value that a purchase offers a customer is an important factor in many purchase decisions. But most marketing managers think that buyer behavior is not as simple as the economics-orientation model suggests. A product that one person sees as a good value—and is eager to buy—is of no interest to someone else. So we can't expect to understand buying behavior without taking a broader view.

How we will view consumer behavior

Many behavioral dimensions influence consumers. Let's try to combine these dimensions into a model of how consumers make decisions. Exhibit 7–1 shows

Exhibit 7–1   A Model of Buyer Behavior

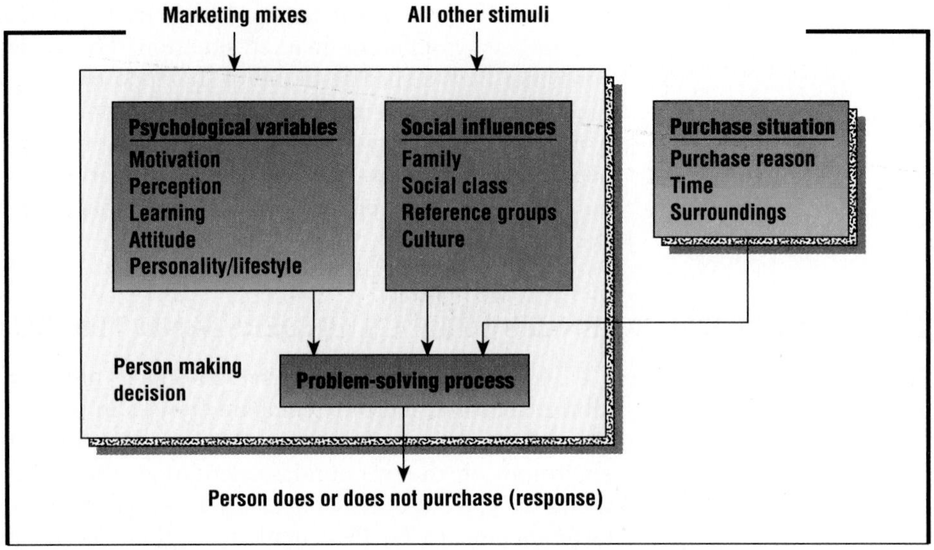

that psychological variables, social influences, and the purchase situation all affect a person's buying behavior. We'll discuss these topics in the next few pages. Then we'll expand the model to include the consumer problem-solving process.

PSYCHOLOGICAL INFLUENCES WITHIN AN INDIVIDUAL

Here, we will discuss some variables of special interest to marketers, including motivation, perception, learning, attitudes, and lifestyle. Much of what we know about these *psychological (intrapersonal) variables* draws from ideas originally developed in the field of psychology.

Needs motivate consumers

Everybody is motivated by needs and wants. **Needs** are the basic forces that motivate a person to do something. Some needs involve a person's physical well-being, others the individual's self-view and relationship with others. Needs are more basic than wants. **Wants** are needs that are learned during a person's life. For example, everyone needs water or some kind of liquid, but some people also have learned to want Perrier with a twist.

When a need is not satisfied, it may lead to a drive. The need for liquid, for example, leads to a thirst drive. A **drive** is a strong stimulus that encourages action to reduce a need. Drives are internal—they are the reasons behind certain behavior patterns. In marketing, a product purchase results from a drive to satisfy some need.

Some critics imply that marketers can somehow manipulate consumers to buy products against their will. But marketing managers can't create internal drives. Most marketing managers realize that trying to get consumers to act against their will is a waste of time. Instead, a good marketing manager studies what consumer drives, needs, and wants already exist and how they can be satisfied better.

Consumers seek benefits to meet needs

We're all a bundle of needs and wants. Exhibit 7–2 lists some important needs that might motivate a person to some action. This list, of course, is not

Exhibit 7–2 Possible Needs Motivating a Person to Some Action

Types of Needs	*Specific Examples*			
Physiological Needs	Hunger Sex Rest	Thirst Body elimination	Activity Self-preservation	Sleep Warmth/coolness
Psychological Needs	Aggression Family preservation Nurturing Playing—relaxing Self-identification	Curiosity Imitation Order Power Tenderness	Being responsible Independence Personal fulfillment Pride	Dominance Love Playing—competition Self-expression
Desire for:	Acceptance Affiliation Comfort Esteem Knowledge Respect Status	Achievement Appreciation Fun Fame Prestige Retaliation Sympathy	Acquisition Beauty Distance—"space" Happiness Pleasure Self-satisfaction Variety	Affection Companionship Distinctiveness Identification Recognition Sociability
Freedom from:	Fear Pain Harm	Depression Imitation Ridicule	Discomfort Loss Sadness	Anxiety Illness Pressure

complete. But thinking about such needs can help you see what *benefits* consumers might seek from a marketing mix.

When a marketing manager defines a product-market, the needs may be quite specific. For example, the food need might be as specific as wanting a thick-crust pepperoni pizza—delivered to your door hot and ready to eat.

Several needs at the same time

Some psychologists argue that a person may have several reasons for buying—at the same time. Maslow is well known for his five-level hierarchy of needs. We will discuss a similar four-level hierarchy that is easier to apply to consumer behavior. Exhibit 7–3 illustrates the four levels, along with an advertising slogan showing how a company has tried to appeal to each need. The lowest-level needs are physiological. Then come safety, social, and personal needs. As a study aid, think of the "PSSP" needs.[2]

Physiological needs are concerned with biological needs—food, drink, rest, and sex. **Safety needs** are concerned with protection and physical well-being (perhaps involving health, food, medicine, and exercise). **Social needs** are concerned with love, friendship, status, and esteem—things that involve a person's interaction with others. **Personal needs**, on the other hand, are concerned with an individual's need for personal satisfaction—unrelated to what others think or do. Examples include self-esteem, accomplishment, fun, freedom, and relaxation.

Motivation theory suggests that we never reach a state of complete satisfaction. As soon as we get our lower-level needs reasonably satisfied, those at higher levels become more dominant. This explains why marketing efforts targeted at affluent consumers in advanced economies often focus on higher-level needs. It

Exhibit 7–3   The PSSP Hierarchy of Needs

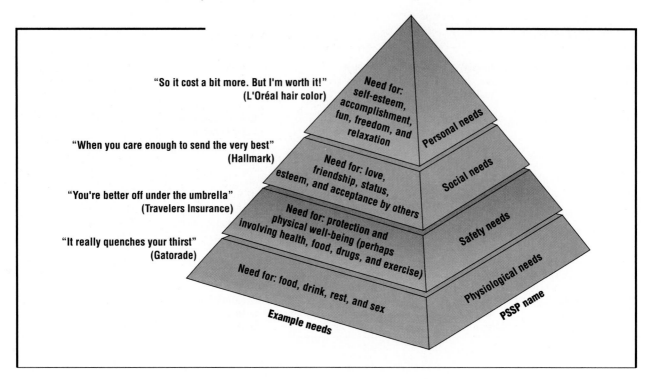

also explains why these approaches may be useless in parts of the world where consumers' basic needs are not being met.

It is important to see, however, that a particular product may satisfy more than one need at the same time. In fact, most consumers try to fill a *set* of needs rather than just one need or another in sequence.

Obviously, marketers should try to satisfy different needs. Yet discovering these specific consumer needs may require careful analysis. Consider, for example, the lowly vegetable peeler. Marketing managers for OXO International realized that many people, especially young children and senior citizens, have trouble gripping the handle of a typical peeler. OXO redesigned the peeler with a bigger handle that addressed this physical need. OXO also coated the handle with dishwasher-safe rubber. This makes cleanup more convenient—and the sharp peeler is safer to use when the grip is wet. The attractively designed grip also appeals to consumers who get personal satisfaction from cooking—and who want to impress their guests. Even though OXO priced the peeler much higher than most kitchen utensils, it has sold very well because it appeals to people with a variety of needs.[3]

Perception determines what consumers see and feel

Consumers select varying ways to meet their needs some times because of differences in **perception**—how we gather and interpret information from the world around us.

We are constantly bombarded by stimuli—ads, products, stores—yet we may not hear or see anything. This is because we apply the following selective processes:

1. **Selective exposure**—our eyes and minds seek out and notice only information that interests us.
2. **Selective perception**—we screen out or modify ideas, messages, and information that conflict with previously learned attitudes and beliefs.
3. **Selective retention**—we remember only what we want to remember.

These selective processes help explain why some people are not affected by some advertising—even offensive advertising. They just don't see or remember it! Even if they do, they may dismiss it immediately. Some consumers are skeptical about any advertising message.

Our needs affect these selective processes. And current needs receive more attention. For example, Michelin tire retailers advertise some sale in the newspaper almost weekly. Most of the time we don't even notice these ads—until we need new tires. Only then do we tune in to Michelin's ads.

Marketers are interested in these selective processes because they affect how target consumers get and retain information. This is also why marketers are interested in how consumers *learn*.

Learning determines what response is likely

Learning is a change in a person's thought processes caused by prior experience. Learning is often based on direct experience: A little girl tastes her first Häagen-Dazs ice cream cone, and learning occurs! Learning may also be based on indirect experience or associations. If you watch a Häagen-Dazs ad that shows other people enjoying a new flavor, you might conclude that you'd like it, too. Consumer learning may result from things that marketers do, or it may result from stimuli that have nothing to do with marketing. Either way, almost all consumer behavior is learned.[4]

Experts describe a number of steps in the learning process. We've already discussed the idea of a drive as a strong stimulus that encourages action.

Depending on the **cues**—products, signs, ads, and other stimuli in the environment—an individual chooses some specific response. A **response** is an effort to satisfy a drive. The specific response chosen depends on the cues and the person's past experience.

Reinforcement of the learning process occurs when the response is followed by satisfaction—that is, reduction in the drive. Reinforcement strengthens the relationship between the cue and the response. And it may lead to a similar response the next time the drive occurs. Repeated reinforcement leads to development of a habit—making the individual's decision process routine. Exhibit 7–4 shows the relationships of the important variables in the learning process.

Exhibit 7–4
The Learning Process

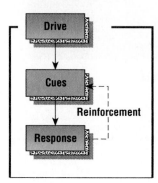

The learning process can be illustrated by a thirsty person. The thirst *drive* could be satisfied in a variety of ways. But if the person happened to walk past a vending machine and saw a 7UP sign—a *cue*—then he or she might satisfy the drive with a *response*—buying a 7UP. If the experience is satisfactory, positive *reinforcement* will occur, and our friend may be quicker to satisfy this drive in the same way in the future. This emphasizes the importance of developing good products that live up to the promises of the firm's advertising. People can learn to like or dislike 7UP—reinforcement and learning work both ways. Unless marketers satisfy their customers, they must constantly try to attract new ones to replace the dissatisfied ones who don't come back.

Good experiences can lead to positive attitudes about a firm's product. Bad experiences can lead to negative attitudes that even good promotion won't be able to change. In fact, the subject of attitudes, an extremely important one to marketers, is discussed shortly.

Positive cues help a marketing mix

Sometimes marketers try to identify cues or images that have positive associations from some other situation and relate them to their marketing mix. Many people associate the smell of lemons with a fresh, natural cleanliness. So companies often add lemon scent to household cleaning products—Joy dishwashing detergent and Pledge furniture polish, for example—because it has these associations. Similarly, many firms use ads suggesting that people who use their products have more appeal to the opposite sex.

Many needs are culturally learned

Many needs are culturally (or socially) learned. The need for food, for instance, may lead to many specific food wants. Many Japanese enjoy raw fish, and their children learn to like it. Few Canadians, however, have learned to like raw fish.

Some critics argue that marketing efforts encourage people to spend money on learned wants totally unrelated to any basic need. For example, Europeans are less concerned about body odor, and few buy or use a deodorant. Yet North Americans spend millions of dollars on such products. Advertising says that using Ban deodorant "takes the worry out of being close." But is marketing activity the cause of the difference in the two cultures? Most research says that advertising can't convince buyers of something contrary to their basic attitudes.

Attitudes relate to buying

An **attitude** is a person's point of view toward something. The "something" may be a product, an advertisement, a salesperson, a firm, or an idea. Attitudes are an important topic for marketers because attitudes affect the selective processes, learning, and eventually the buying decisions people make.

Consumer perceptions of an ad for Scotchgard Fabric Protector might depend on whether they see fabric stains as a big problem.

Because attitudes are usually thought of as involving liking or disliking, they have some action implications. Beliefs are not so action-oriented. A **belief** is a person's opinion about something. Beliefs may help shape a consumer's attitudes but don't necessarily involve any liking or disliking. It is possible to have a belief—say, that Listerine has a medicinal taste—without really caring what it tastes like. On the other hand, beliefs about a product may have a positive or negative effect in shaping consumers' attitudes. For example, people with headaches are unlikely to switch to a new pain medicine unless they believe it will be more effective than what they used in the past.

In an attempt to relate attitude more closely to purchase behavior, some marketers stretched the attitude concept to include consumer "preferences" or "intention to buy." Managers who must forecast how much of their brand customers will buy are particularly interested in the intention to buy. Forecasts would be easier if attitudes were good predictors of intentions to buy. Unfortunately, the relationships usually are not that simple. A person may have positive attitudes toward a Jacuzzi hot tub but no intention of buying one.

Try to understand attitudes and beliefs

Research on consumer attitudes and beliefs can sometimes help a marketing manager get a better picture of markets. For example, consumers with very positive attitudes toward a new product idea might prove a good opportunity—especially if they have negative attitudes about competitors' offerings. Or they may have beliefs that would discourage them from buying a product.

Marketing managers at Levi Strauss & Co. (Canada), Inc., faced this challenge. Its GWG jeans were a once-renowned product that had hit hard times. Their image had become down-market and passé. Based on extensive marketing research, the marketing managers chose to emphasize the company's history and remind the public that GWG stood for the Great Western Garment Company—a Canadian original. A new product was introduced, called 1911, the year the company was founded. Nostalgia for traditional values and workmanship was

Exhibit 7–5   Lifestyle Dimensions (and some related demographic dimensions)

Dimension	Examples		
Activities	Work Hobbies Social events	Vacation Entertainment Club membership	Community Shopping Sports
Interests	Family Home Job	Community Recreation Fashion	Food Media Achievements
Opinions	Themselves Social issues Politics	Business Economics Education	Products Future Culture
Demographics	Income Age Family life cycle	Geographic area City size Dwelling	Occupation Family size Education

something Levi Strauss could capitalize on with the GWG brand. Furthermore, it is a unique position—no other company can claim to have been making jeans in Canada since 1911. Since the change in strategy, GWG has been experiencing the best sales growth in years.[5]

Personality affects how people see things

Many researchers study how personality affects people's behavior, but the results have generally been disappointing to marketers. A trait like neatness can be associated with users of certain types of products—like cleaning materials. But marketing managers have not found a way to use personality in marketing strategy planning.[6] As a result, they've stopped focusing on personality measures borrowed from psychologists and instead developed lifestyle analysis.

Psychographics focus on activities, interests, and opinions

Psychographics or **lifestyle analysis** is the analysis of a person's day-to-day pattern of living as expressed in that person's activities, interests, and opinions— sometimes referred to as AIOs. Exhibit 7–5 shows a number of variables for each of the AIO dimensions—along with some demographics used to add detail to the lifestyle profile of a target market. Psychographics as used by B. C. Transit and the VALS approach to lifestyles were both discussed in Chapter 3. Another illustration of psychographics is provided in this chapter's discussion of the French Canadian consumer.

Most marketers work with existing attitudes

Marketers generally try to understand the attitudes of their potential customers and work with them. We'll discuss this idea again when we review the way consumers evaluate product alternatives. For now, we want to emphasize that it's more economical to work with consumer attitudes than to try to change them. Attitudes tend to be enduring. Changing present attitudes—especially negative ones—is sometimes necessary. But it's probably the most difficult job marketers face.[7]

This ad's copy states, "51% of Swedes are prejudiced against fish-balls. You too?" In Sweden, fish-balls are a traditional dish, but most consumers think the canned variety are tasteless and boring. This ad attempts to change these attitudes by showing an attractive way to serve the products. But overcoming negative attitudes is a difficult job.

Ethical issues may arise

Part of the marketing job is to inform and persuade consumers about a firm's offering. An ethical issue sometimes arises, however, if consumers have *inaccurate* beliefs. For example, many consumers are confused about what foods are really healthy. Marketers for a number of food companies have been criticized for packaging and promotion that take advantage of inaccurate consumer perceptions about the meaning of the words *lite* or *low-fat*. A firm's lite donuts may have less fat or fewer calories than its other donuts—but that doesn't mean that the donut is *low* in fat or calories. Similarly, promotion of a "children's cold formula" may play off of parents' fears that adult medicines are too strong—even though the basic ingredients in the children's formula are the same and only the dosage is different.

Marketers must also be careful about promotion that might encourage false beliefs, even if the advertising is not explicitly misleading. For example, Nike doesn't claim that a kid who buys its fancy shoes will be able to fly through the air like Michael Jordan, but some critics argue that the advertising gives that impression.[8]

SOCIAL INFLUENCES AFFECT CONSUMER BEHAVIOR

We've been discussing some of the ways needs, attitudes, and other psychological variables influence the buying process. Now we'll see that these variables—and the buying process—are usually affected by relations with other people, too. We'll look at how the individual interacts with family, social class, and other groups who may have influence.

Who is the real decision maker in family purchases?

Relationships with other family members influence many aspects of consumer behavior. We saw specific examples of this in Chapter 6 when we considered the effects of the family life cycle on family spending patterns. Family members may also share many attitudes and values, consider each other's opinions, and divide various buying tasks. Historically, most marketers in North America targeted the wife as the family purchasing agent. Now, with more women in the work force and with night and weekend shopping becoming more popular, men and older children do more shopping and decision making. In other countries, family roles vary. For example, in Norway, women still do most of the family shopping.

Although only one family member may go to the store and make a specific purchase, when planning marketing strategy it's important to know who else may be involved. Other family members may have influenced the decision or really decided what to buy. Still others may use the product.

You don't have to watch much Saturday morning TV to see that Kellogg's and General Mills know this. Cartoon characters like Cap'n Crunch and Tony the Tiger tell kids about the goodies found in certain cereal packages—and urge them to remind Dad or Mom to pick up that brand on their next trip to the store. But kids also influence grown-up purchases—to the tune of $130 billion a year. Surveys show that kids often have a big say in a family's choice of products such as apparel, cars, electronics, and health and beauty aids.

Family considerations may overwhelm personal ones

A husband and wife may jointly agree on many important purchases, but sometimes they may have strong personal preferences. However, such individual preferences may change if the other spouse has different priorities. One might want to take a family vacation to Disneyland—when the other wants a new RCA video recorder and Sony large-screen TV. The actual outcome in such a situation is unpredictable. The preferences of one spouse might change because of affection for the other—or because of the other's power and influence.

Buying responsibility and influence vary greatly depending on the product and the family. A marketer trying to plan a strategy will find it helpful to research the specific target market. Remember, many buying decisions are made jointly, and thinking only about who actually buys the product can misdirect the marketing strategy.[9]

Social class affects attitudes, values, and buying

Up to now we have been concerned with the individual and the way individuals relate to their families. Now let's consider how society looks at an individual and perhaps the family—in terms of social class. A **social class** is a group of people who have approximately equal social position as viewed by others in the society.

Almost every society has some social class structure. The Canadian class system is far less rigid than in most countries. Children start out in the same social class as their parents—but they can move to a different social class depending on their educational levels or the jobs they hold.

Marketers want to know what buyers in various social classes are like. Simple approaches for measuring social class groupings are based on a person's *occupation*, *education*, and *type and location of housing*. By using marketing research surveys or available census data, marketers can get a feel for the social class of a target market.

Note that income level is not included in this list. There is *some* general relationship between income level and social class. But the income level of people within the same social class can vary greatly, and people with the same income level may be in different social classes.

To develop better marketing strategies, marketing managers need to understand the differences among social classes. Although we use traditional technical terms like *upper*, *middle*, and *lower*, a word of warning is in order. The terms may seem to imply "superior" and "inferior." But, in sociological and marketing usage, no value judgment is intended. We can't say that any one class is "better" or "happier" than another.

The size of Canadian social classes

Dividing a nation's population into distinctly labeled social classes is no easy task. Would-be marketers needn't concern themselves with the specifics of the various ways this has been done in Canada or the United States. One recent Canadian effort places primary reliance on occupation and education. This data, from the early 1980s, divides the Canadian consumer public into four major but further divisible social strata: the upper classes (11 percent of the total and divisible in turn into very small upper-upper and lower-upper classes and a considerably larger upper-middle class); the middle class (28 percent of the total); the working class (41 percent); and a lower class (20 percent of the total and divided in turn into upper-lower and lower-lower classes of approximately equal size).[10]

Differences in attitudes and behavior

The seven Canadian social classes differ in terms of typical occupational and educational profiles, social and geographic horizons, consumption patterns, and personal values. Detailed comparisons reveal that the old saying "A rich man is simply a poor man with money" isn't true. Given the same income as middle-class people, persons belonging to the lower classes handle themselves and their money very differently. The various classes shop at different stores. They prefer different treatment from salespeople. They buy different brands of products—even when prices are about the same. And they have different spending-saving attitudes. Some of these differences are shown in Exhibit 7–6.

The upper-middle class as a case study

The upper-middle class (about 9 percent of the Canadian population) consists of successful professionals, owners of small businesses, and managers of large corporations. These people are concerned about their quality of life. They view their purchases as symbols of success, so they want quality products. They also want to be seen as socially acceptable. They support the arts and are community-minded. They are ambitious for their children and, in general, are more future-oriented than lower-class groups. Exhibit 7–7 provides additional information on upper-middle class's consumption behavior. The information from

Exhibit 7–6   Characteristics and Attitudes of Middle and Lower Classes

Middle Classes	*Lower Classes*
Plan and save for the future	Live for the present
Analyze alternatives	"Feel" what is "best"
Understand how the world works	Have simplistic ideas about how things work
Feel they have opportunities	Feel controlled by the world
Willing to take risks	Play it safe
Confident about decision making	Want help with decision making
Want long-run quality or value	Want short-run satisfaction

Exhibit 7–7   Consumption Behavior of Canada's Upper-Middle Class

1. Seek out genuine educational experiences for self and children (drama, piano, ballet, Suzuki violin lessons, museums, international student exchanges).
2. Admire those who can speak many languages and often try to learn languages themselves.
3. Believe in high culture (ballet, theater, opera, art galleries, museums).
4. Participate in sports often associated with prestige and serenity, and those that deliver vigorous exercise (sailing, gliding, horseback riding, golf, tennis, squash, cycling).
5. In clothing, prefer organic materials (cotton, wool, silk, leather) and resist wearing synthetic, such as polyester.
6. Preferred colors tend to be navy blue and pastels. Like preppy Ralph Lauren fashions.
7. More willing to experiment with new dishes (foreign and exotic foods, haute cuisine, ethnic restaurants, and the foreign food and ingredients counters at specialty stores).
8. Generally, are more confident shoppers and decision makers than other classes and more skillful at evaluating products.

Source: Gurprit S. Kindra, Michael LaRoche, and Thomas C. Muller, *Consumer Behaviour in Canada* (Scarbourough, Ont.: Nelson Canada, 1989), pp. 311–12.

this and similar descriptions of the other Canadian social classes can be of great value to marketers.

Reference groups are relevant, too

A **reference group** is the people to whom an individual looks when forming attitudes about a particular topic. People normally have several reference groups for different topics. Some they meet face-to-face. Others they may just wish to imitate. In either case, they may take values from these reference groups and make buying decisions based on what the group might accept.

We're always making comparisons between ourselves and others. So reference groups are more important when others will be able to "see" which product or brand we're using. Influence is stronger for products that relate to status in the group. For one group, owning an expensive fur coat may be a sign of "having arrived." A group of animal lovers might view it as a sign of bad judgment. In either case, a consumer's decision to buy or not to buy a fur coat might depend on the opinions of others in that consumer's reference group.[11]

Reaching the opinion leaders who are buyers

An **opinion leader** is a person who influences others. Opinion leaders aren't necessarily wealthier or better educated. And opinion leaders on one subject aren't necessarily opinion leaders on another. Capable homemakers with large families may be consulted for advice on family budgeting. Young women may be opinion leaders for new clothing styles and cosmetics. Each social class tends to have its own opinion leaders. Some marketing mixes aim especially at these people since their opinions affect others and research shows that they are involved in many product-related discussions with "followers." Favorable word-of-mouth publicity from opinion leaders can really help a marketing mix. But the opposite is also true. If opinion leaders aren't satisfied, they're likely to talk about it and influence others.[12]

Culture surrounds the other influences

Culture is the whole set of beliefs, attitudes, and ways of doing things of a reasonably homogeneous set of people. In Chapters 4 and 6, we looked at the broad impact of culture.

We can think of the North American culture, the French culture, or the Latin American culture. People within these cultural groupings tend to be more similar in outlook and behavior. But sometimes it is useful to think of subcultures within such groupings. For example, within the North American culture, there are various religious and ethnic subcultures; also different cultural forces tend to prevail in different regions of the continent.

From a target marketing point of view, a marketing manager will probably want to aim at people within one culture or subculture. If a firm is developing strategies for two cultures, it often needs two different marketing plans.[13]

The attitudes and beliefs that we usually associate with culture tend to change slowly. So once marketers develop a good understanding of the culture they are planning for, they should concentrate on the more dynamic variables discussed previously.

Culture and Canadian marketers

Cultural differences are of obvious importance to Canadian marketers. Canada's various ethnic communities, especially those consisting of post–World War II immigrants and their children, make up important cultural groupings. Such groups haven't yet assimilated into one of Canada's two founding cultures. Most have very distinct product preferences and purchasing habits. Many members of the Italian, Chinese, Greek, Portuguese, and Indo-Pakistani communities prefer to do business in their mother tongue rather than in either English or French. Ethnic communities are often geographically clustered into two or three urban markets. Major Canadian advertisers are now using ethnic media to reach these groups, as indicated in Marketing Demo 7–2.

Culture varies in international markets

Planning strategies that consider cultural differences in international markets can be even harder—and such cultures usually vary more. Each foreign market may need to be treated as a separate market with its own submarkets. Ignoring

MARKETING DEMO 7–2
Cultural Cross Talk: More Companies Cater to Immigrant Taste

The more than 100,000 immigrants who have arrived in Canada from Hong Kong in the past decade are a strong market for many companies. Compared with previous generations of new Canadians, they are generally better educated and wealthier. To reach out to the Hong Kong–born consumers and other ethnic buyers, some companies are using foreign-language advertising on billboards and in newspapers. Despite the added costs of devising special ad campaigns or translating an existing advertisement, advertising executives say that the measures often are cost-effective strategies. "Even those people who do understand English appreciate being spoken to in their own language," says Cleve Lu, president of Toronto-based Era Advertising Ltd.

At first glance, the bed on display in the furniture department at Eaton's downtown Toronto store looks like any other standard-sized double. The $799 price of the model, with rosy-beige damask fabric covering the mattress and box spring, is even in the same range as the others. But the brand name, Dr. Hard, and its extreme firmness, the result of its uniquely constructed layers of padding, make this a bed unlike the others in the department. Toronto-based Simmons Canada Ltd. introduced Dr. Hard mattresses recently after salesclerks passed on requests from Asian Canadians for mattresses that were closer to what they were used to back home. The firmer beds, says Patrick Thody, president of Simmons Canada, are made from specifications that the company's affiliate uses for manufacturing beds on sale in the Far East. Adds Thody: "With the number of Asians coming to Canada, we expect this bed will account for 20 percent of our sales."

Simmons Canada is one of a small but growing number of Canadian companies that are starting to develop new products and advertising strategies specifically for consumers from different cultures and backgrounds. Executives with those firms say that they have already found new lucrative markets among the 3.2 million Canadians—about 13 percent of the population—whose mother tongue is neither English nor French and whose product preferences are still strongly influenced by the prevailing tastes within their ethnic community.

The service sector also has found that it pays to tailor business to newcomers. The Canadian Imperial Bank of Commerce set up a specialized Asian Banking Group several years ago. Today, nine Commerce branches across Canada have Chinese-speaking staff and separate areas where customers can bank in private. "They are used to receiving very good service in Asia, and they expect a comparable level of service here," says the group's general manager, Simon Kwok.

Due to the lack of good research on ethnic tastes and buying habits, marketers must often experiment or rely on past experience. Larry Pascal, president of Toronto-based Pascal Furniture, started advertising in the Chinese-language daily paper *Sing Tao.* "We know the ads worked because people come in clutching them," Pascal says. He and other executives have discovered firsthand that they can generate new profits in many languages.

Source: Barbara Wickins, "Cultural Cross Talk," *Maclean's,* October 28, 1991 p. 42.

cultural differences, or assuming that they are not important, almost guarantees failure in international markets.

For example, when marketing managers for Procter & Gamble first tried to sell the North American version of Cheer to Japanese consumers, they promoted it as an effective all-temperature laundry detergent. But many Japanese wash clothes in cold tap water or leftover bath water—so they don't care about all-temperature washing. In addition, Cheer didn't make suds when it was used with the fabric softeners popular with Japanese consumers. When P&G's marketing managers discovered these problems, they changed Cheer so it wouldn't be affected by the fabric softeners. They also changed Cheer ads to promise superior cleaning *in cold water*. Now Cheer has become one of P&G's best-selling products in Japan.[14]

TIME AND CONSUMER MARKETS[15]

The clock was ticking away before you were born and will continue to tick away long after we are all gone. The decisions one makes are based in a substantial part by one's perception and use of time and by how time is processed within the mind. The ideas that have been considered in this chapter are all impacted by time.

Time as a driver in the purchase decision

Time is believed to be the source or an influencer in many needs and wants. Turn back to Exhibit 7–2, entitled "Possible Needs Motivating a Person to Some Action." You will find several terms that have time implicit in them, including family preservation, relaxing, playing—competition, anxiety, pressure, and rest. In this section, time will be examined as a concept that can lead to a need or a want and therefore acts as a driver. There are four major aspects of time, and each one could be a driver at any point in the buying process. See Exhibit 7–8.

ASPECTS OF TIME

Orientation

Time orientation is defined as the relative importance of past, present, and future. *Horizon* is defined as a length dimension that considers how long a given period may extend, whether immediate (near at hand), intermediate (bounded), or extended (unbounded).

Orientation is a term of direction. Do you find that you focus on things in the future, the present, or the past? Individuals and cultures seem to have different orientations. This impacts their consumption and their use of time.

Exhibit 7–8   Major Aspects of Time Drive Needs and Wants

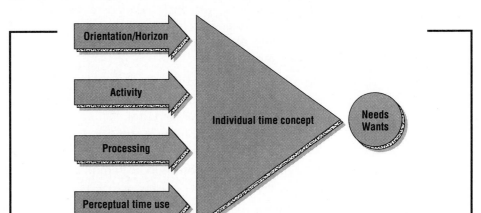

Horizon

In addition to the idea of direction or orientation there is the concept of **horizon.** Horizon represents the degree of futurity that you are considering. Some consumers plan for the future—but only the immediate future. In other situations or with other consumers, the distance out may be much farther.

Examples may be found in many areas. Do you dwell on mistakes of the past? Did your parents always buy clothes too large, expecting you to grow? When you earn money, do you immediately buy something with it or do you save to buy something in the future? Did your family plan many years in advance? Or did your family begin planning only when you were almost ready to enter university?

Look also at how courses are planned throughout your college career. Some students map out each year, even into graduate school. Some plan the next semester during the exam period. And some register a week late for whatever course happens to have room.

Activity

Activity is the need or desire for multiple simultaneous activities. When individuals can choose to combine multiple activities, they are considered to be polychronic time users. The notion of polychronic time use allows clock time to be broadened so that more can be accomplished in a given block of clock time. This is in direct contrast to monochronic time use, where only one thing is done at a time. Students frequently provide excellent examples of polychronic time use. The norm is to attempt some combination of studying, watching TV, visiting with a friend, and eating, all at the same time.

The idea of polychronic time use is a particularly important one in consumer behavior. It helps to explain which selective exposure our eyes and mind are seeking out and why we notice only information that interests us. Just because someone sends a message by mail, TV, radio, or billboard, we cannot assume that people are noticing those advertisements. The target market may be watching TV but not getting the message. They could be running to the kitchen or muting the television to talk with friends every time the advertisement is aired. Stated another way, their minds are fully occupied and have to be jarred to cause them to shift or share additional activities.

Processing

Processing reflects the flow and separability of time. Alternatively, time can be thought of in pieces or units or blocks of events. It can flow smoothly over and through events, with little relation to society's time markers as announced by clocks and calendars. Individuals may view their progression through time using any combination of four major processing variations: cyclical, procedural, linear, and segmented.

1. *Linear*—treats time as a flow of a mutually exclusive chain of events.
2. *Segmented*—time is divided into blocks of clock or calendar time, for measurement and control.
3. *Cyclical*—concentrates attention on the present, which is part of a repetitive cycle.
4. *Procedural*—defined as beginning a task with the idea of working on it until it is done.

Linear time is considered to be the time of most Western cultures. It assumes a past, present, and future with movement generally considered to be in the future direction. In cyclical time, the flow is viewed as recurring. This might be the cycle of the pay period, the cycle of a religion, or the cycle of life. Procedural and segmented are both ways of breaking up the flow of time. In the case of procedural time, things are processed by what needs to be done and not by clock time. In segmented time, time is divided into blocks of clock time that have starting and stopping points but may vary in size.

Segmented time is used in some sports. Basketball and soccer are examples of sports that are played in fixed segments. Procedural time is found in other sports—tennis, golf, and baseball—where the game is played until it is over. Some people make their purchases based on cyclical time. Their decisions are based on how much of their monthly income is available. Buying long-term financial products such as retirement-oriented insurance policies generally requires a linear perspective on time processing.

Perceptual time use

The idea behind perceptual time use is that time use changes depending on the perspective from which observations are made. The focus here is how each individual consumer perceives time use. You and your friend might have the same schedule but perceive the extent of your time obligations and commitments differently. An important distinction here is between **committed time** (something that has to be done but with some flexibility as to just when) and **obligated time** (something that has to be done within a specific time block). For example, students are often committed to meet in group projects but there is some flexibility as to when that meeting will take place. Classes, in contrast, can only be attended when scheduled.

TIME AND PRODUCT CHOICE

Orientation—past or future?

Consider products sold with a past orientation and horizon. These are products that will create the feeling of the good old days—for example, cookies like grandma used to make, music of the 40s or 50s, and so forth. Some high-technology items like the Sony Minicam are sold with a promise of letting you stay in touch with your past. In contrast to this past orientation is the future orientation of some stores and products. The suggestion is that you are buying things ahead of their time.

Activity—alone or together?

Many products permit or encourage polychronic time use. The car phone was basically designed to let you communicate while driving. Many students are experts at using Watchman- or Walkman-type appliances to listen to music or maybe even lectures while walking, working in the library, and so on.

In contrast, there are products such as Nintendo that seem well suited to absorbing all of your attention and encouraging you to do only one thing at a time. If people prefer to do one thing at a time, they may purchase items that create an environment in which monochronic activity is enhanced. Noise filters, for example, let the individual screen out unwanted noises that could distract from the activity at hand. Voice mail allows the individual to work uninterrupted, while calls are stored for future listening.

Processing—the importance of seasons

Many products are sold or used in cycles, depending on the seasons of the year, the day of the week, weather, and so forth. Many of us think annually about the joys of special holidays. Back-to-school sales are anticipated by retailers and consumers alike. We could also consider gardening products as being sold on the basis of planting cycles. Holiday customs and associated products (artifacts) regularly appear in stores to meet the expectations of consumers. However, consumers often complain when products such as Christmas goods appear too early in the year—from their perspective.

Perceptions of
time—how busy?

Perceptual time use may greatly impact the kind of products you will consider. Those who perceive that they are time short or overcommitted may look for products that will allow them in some way to repackage or consolidate time use. Those who are time long or have more than enough time may actually look for products that will use time up.

For example, carpentry or sewing may involve a task that will take several days to complete. But many people do not have several days available to them. They need products that can be finished all at once. Such products have been developed in the form of kits for carpenters and, for sewers, stuffed animals that you just cut out and sew together with simple seams.

A person who is time rich, on the other hand, would look for those projects that are time intensive. Seniors who are time rich consciously choose to purchase a service (craft lessons) that both is time intensive in the lesson taking and offers a time-intensive skill that they can subsequently use.

FRENCH CANADA: A MARKETING PERSPECTIVE[16]

The most often discussed cultural difference in Canada is between English speakers and their French-speaking counterparts. The following is a discussion of differences in purchasing patterns and consumption behaviors between French- and English-speaking Canadians and of possible reasons for those differences.

How does
purchasing differ?

French Canadian housewives seem to like the friendly atmosphere of the boutique and the chance for personal contact with store employees. In the past, such personal contact could be obtained only at small neighborhood food stores offering credit and delivery. In time, these stores expanded, and other, more specialized, food stores appeared on the scene. This may account for Quebec's omnipresent epicierie (grocery store), charcuterie (butcher shop), depanneur (convenience store), and patisserie (bakery). It may also help explain the greater importance of small retail outlets in Quebec as compared to Ontario.

But is there another reason for Quebec's apparent preference both for national brands and for purchasing at relatively small food stores? In Quebec, until 1984, beer and wine were available for home consumption only from corner groceries, depanneurs, and independent supermarkets having three employees or less. This legal restriction generated additional customers for such outlets. It also increased the relative popularity of the national brands these stores carry. Independent outlets are still allowed to have longer operating hours than supermarket chains. These factors may explain, at least in part, the French-English differences in purchasing habits and practices.

Many neighborhood food stores have recently become members either of retailer cooperatives such as Metro or wholesaler-sponsored voluntary chains such as Provigo. Even the ever-present depanneur is now often part of a franchised chain such as Le Maisonnee and Provi-Soir. This trend toward vertical integration and franchising, found not only in the food business but in other sectors of the economy as well (hardware stores, drugs, books, etc.) has had an impact on French Canadian purchasing habits and practices.

The Print Measurement Bureau's psychographic data shows that French Quebecers tend to link price to perceived value, but will pass on a buy rather than pay on credit. They are more willing to pay premium prices for convenience and premium brands. In terms of other attitudes towards purchasing, French Quebecers give greater credence to advertising than the average Canadian, but they are cautious as to the use of new products, often postponing trials until a product has proven itself. They generally show more brand loyalty, but will buy another item if it is on special. Furthermore, Quebec consumers buy few "no name" products but make extensive use of cents-off coupons.

Differences in product use

French Quebecers are less likely to drink tea or diet cola, or eat jam, tuna, cookies, or eggs, on a daily basis than the average Canadian. However, they like presweetened cereals and regular cola and use butter for cooking. They show a strong preference for instant coffee products, giving decaffeinated products a slight edge.

Quebecers feel they give more importance to personal grooming and fashion than most Canadians. This may explain the fact that 64 percent go to specialized clothing boutiques, compared to 52 percent among other Canadians.

In French Quebec there is a lower proportion of regular soap users than in the rest of Canada, but the use of baby soap is twice as high (15 percent versus 8 percent). The use of acne coverups is lower than the national average.

Although French women in Quebec do not use as much lip gloss, pressed powder, foundation makeup, or perfume as the average, they are big users of perfumed body spray, cologne, and toilet water, as well as lipstick. They also buy more panty hose, swimwear, and hair-coloring products (the latter at beauty salons).

Apparently, Quebec women do not like cold feet. Some 14 percent of them buy two or three pairs of boots a year (compared to only 7 percent in the rest of Canada). Only one in four Quebec women (compared to one in two for the rest of Canada) use medicated throat lozenges. They also are less likely to use cold remedies and nasal sprays.

French Quebec has a higher proportion of wine drinkers (51 percent versus 44 percent), beer drinkers (50 percent versus 46 percent), and smokers (38 percent versus 29 percent) than the rest of Canada. On the other hand, Quebecers consume less hard liquor. Although French Quebecers represent 60 percent of Canadian drinkers of Geneva gin and 36 percent of cognac drinkers, they show lower rates of regular consumption of hard liquor (10 ounces and more a week).

In terms of their leisure and sport activities, there are fewer golfers, joggers, and gardeners in Quebec. The proportion of people who go to movies or entertain at home is also lower. However, there are more cyclists, frequent skiers, woodworkers, dressmakers, and live-theater fans.

Quebecers are bigger buyers of lottery tickets than most Canadians and are more likely to subscribe to book clubs—but they make fewer personal long-distance phone calls. French Quebecers also generally travel less, be it for business or pleasure.

The financial and banking habits of Quebecers are subject to great differences, partly because of the widespread popularity of the *caisses populaires* movement. An underdeveloped but growing use of specialty savings tools and trust companies has been recorded.

Purchasing life insurance (65 percent of Quebec adults hold policies compared to 40 percent for the rest of Canada) is still a strong habit. However, the number of credit card holders is falling (holders of two or more cards make up 32 percent of the population in French Quebec versus 39 percent for the rest of Canada).

These are but a few of the many reported differences in product usage and preference. But it's not clear what marketers should do when they discover differences in consumption. Should manufacturers of the underconsumed products pay more attention to the Quebec market? Perhaps there are insurmountable barriers to increasing sales to French Canadians. If so, marketing time and effort could be more profitably spent elsewhere.

THE SEARCH FOR THE REASON WHY

If French-speaking and English-speaking Canadians differ in product usage, brand preference, and shopping habits, what factors account for such differences? With an answer to that question, firms could develop far more effective strategies for these two important segments of the Canadian market. Unfortunately, general agreement is yet to be reached as to why marked variations often exist. What are some of the different explanations that have been advanced?

Is language the reason?

The difference in language is an obvious one, with far-reaching marketing consequences. About half of the French Canadians living in Quebec plus 15 adjoining counties speak only French. Another significant proportion is somewhat bilingual but exposed primarily to French-language advertising media. Such customers should obviously be addressed in their mother tongue. Does this mean, however, that English-language advertising intelligently adapted into French won't be effective? Most marketers believe that the extra costs involved in developing a separate campaign are more than offset by the increased effectiveness of advertising created in an entirely French environment.[17]

Language-related differences in response to advertising do exist. For example, French Canadians are believed to react far more positively when products or services are endorsed by prominent French Canadian athletes or entertainers.[18] French Canadians, one study concluded, pay more attention to the source of advertisements (i.e., spokespersons), while English Canadians are more affected by the message's content.[19] But despite such differences, language isn't generally considered a major cause of existing French-English differences in brand preferences and consumption patterns. We must look beyond language for an explanation.

Is the explanation socioeconomic?

Does the answer lie in the social and economic differences between French Canadian consumers and their English-speaking counterparts? It has been argued that a much larger proportion of French Canadian families belong to the lower socioeconomic classes and that they consume accordingly. As evidence of this fact, some cite the many parallels between the values of French Canadian women and those of American working-class wives. The more commonly mentioned marketing differences between French Canadian and English Canadian consumers, one observer maintained, are similar to those that American researchers have found between the middle and lower classes.[20]

What logically follows from such a socioeconomic explanation? Differences between consumption practices should decline as the relative income and education of French Canadians approaches that of English Canadians. Marketplace behavior of French and English families of equivalent socioeconomic class should be pretty much the same.

Socioeconomic factors, however, aren't universally accepted as either explanations for French-English differences in consumption or predictions of what's likely to happen. Some believe comparable incomes and educations don't necessarily mean similar consumption patterns. They maintain that a different heritage affecting ideas, attitudes, values, and habits could lead to very different French Canadian purchasing patterns.[21] And there's evidence to support this position. Two studies have shown that consumption patterns differed markedly between Quebec (French-language) and Ontario (English-language) households of similar size, income level, and educational background.[22]

What about law and regulation?

Provincial laws and regulations unique to Quebec contribute, at least to some extent, to existing French-English differences in consumption habits and practices. We've already seen that until recently, Quebec's laws aided small stores at the expense of supermarkets. Quebec's best-known piece of marketing legislation is Bill 101, which restricts the use of English in all commercial communications. Consequently, French is the primary language used in advertising, sales slips, catalogues, posters, point-of-purchase displays, direct mail, and even packaging. This legislation makes marketing in Quebec very different from marketing in other parts of Canada. However, it's not clear exactly how Bill 101 affects French-English differences in consumption habits and practices. Two other bills also affect marketing in Quebec. Bill 67 restricts the use of coupons, contests, and lotteries in Quebec, and Bill 34 prohibits advertising directed toward children 13 years of age or younger.

Does culture make the difference?

Many believe culture, broadly defined, underlies many French-English differences in consumption patterns. In addition to language, some important French Canadian culture traits are said to be:

A more homogeneous society with rigid barriers against assimilation forces.

A philosophical and psychological outlook that tends to be more humanistic, more historically oriented, more emotional, and less pragmatic, with lower achievement motivation.

A relatively stronger sense of religious authority.

A greater role for the family unit and the kinship system.

However, the changes associated with Quebec's Quiet Revolution have influenced the prevailing philosophical outlook. In particular, it reduced the importance of both church and family.[23]

A recent study by a Montreal-based market research firm examined Quebecers' values and attitudes. Its results are summarized in Exhibit 7–9. As can be seen in the chart, "enjoyment from life" was at the top of the list of 32 topics respondents rated by importance. Quebecers put great importance on having a family, respecting authority, and being informed of current events, all of which are tied to security. However, the importance of traditional values and earning a lot of money are lower here than in English Canada.

Exhibit 7–9   What Makes the Quebec Consumer Tick

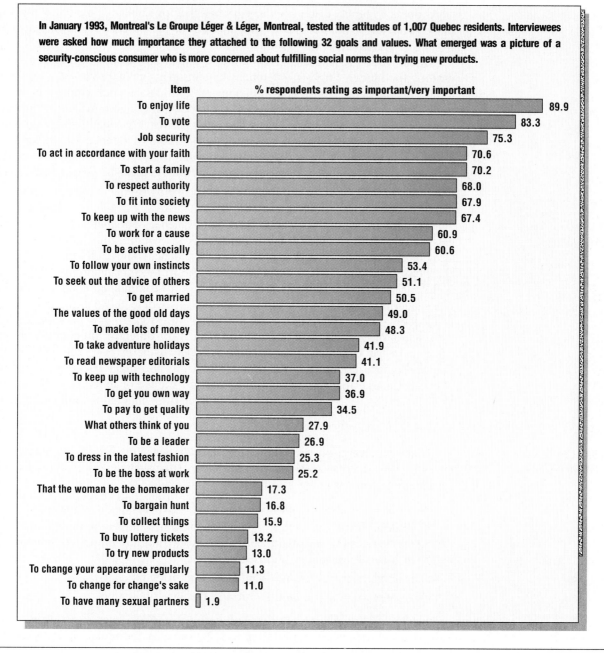

In January 1993, Montreal's Le Groupe Léger & Léger, Montreal, tested the attitudes of 1,007 Quebec residents. Interviewees were asked how much importance they attached to the following 32 goals and values. What emerged was a picture of a security-conscious consumer who is more concerned about fulfilling social norms than trying new products.

Item	% respondents rating as important/very important
To enjoy life	89.9
To vote	83.3
Job security	75.3
To act in accordance with your faith	70.6
To start a family	70.2
To respect authority	68.0
To fit into society	67.9
To keep up with the news	67.4
To work for a cause	60.9
To be active socially	60.6
To follow your own instincts	53.4
To seek out the advice of others	51.1
To get married	50.5
The values of the good old days	49.0
To make lots of money	48.3
To take adventure holidays	41.9
To read newspaper editorials	41.1
To keep up with technology	37.0
To get you own way	36.9
To pay to get quality	34.5
What others think of you	27.9
To be a leader	26.9
To dress in the latest fashion	25.3
To be the boss at work	25.2
That the woman be the homemaker	17.3
To bargain hunt	16.8
To collect things	15.9
To buy lottery tickets	13.2
To try new products	13.0
To change your appearance regularly	11.3
To change for change's sake	11.0
To have many sexual partners	1.9

Source: "Portrait of the Quebec Consumer," *Marketing*, March 22, 1993, p. 14.

A leading French Canadian advertising executive believes that the history of the French Canadian community helps to explain some of the behavioral differences between French and English Canadian consumers. He identifies six determining influences on the French Canadian: moral origin, minority group status within Canada, a North American environment, and Catholic, Latin, and French origins.[24]

Unfortunately, a generalized statement that culture and heritage make the difference doesn't help in developing more appropriate strategies. We need to know how and why social, psychological, cultural, or other market-related factors are reflected in the French Canadian consumer's search for information in exposure to advertising media, and in the selection of the products and brands actually purchased. One consulting firm has attempted to further our understanding of Quebec consumers through the use of psychographics, as discussed in Marketing Demo 7–3.

INDIVIDUALS ARE AFFECTED BY THE PURCHASE SITUATION

Purchase reason can vary

Why a consumer makes a purchase can affect buying behavior. For example, a student buying a pen to take notes might pick up an inexpensive Bic. But the same student might choose a Cross pen as a gift for a friend.

Surroundings affect buying, too

Surroundings can affect buying behavior. The excitement of an auction may stimulate impulse buying. Surroundings may discourage buying, too. For example, some people don't like to stand in a checkout line where others can see what they're buying—even if the other shoppers are complete strangers.

Needs, benefits sought, attitudes, motivation, and even how a consumer selects certain products all vary depending on the purchase situation. So different purchase situations may require different marketing mixes—even when the same target market is involved.[25]

Time affects what happens

We have already seen how time influences a purchase situation. When consumers make a purchase—and the time they have available for shopping—will influence their behavior. A leisurely dinner induces different behavior than grabbing a quick cup of Tim Horton's coffee on the way to work.

CONSUMERS USE PROBLEM-SOLVING PROCESSES

The variables discussed affect *what* products a consumer finally decides to purchase. Marketing managers also need to understand *how* buyers use a problem-solving process to select particular products.

Most consumers seem to use the following five-step problem-solving process:

1. Becoming aware of—or interested in—the problem.
2. Recalling and gathering information about possible solutions.
3. Evaluating alternative solutions—perhaps trying some out.
4. Deciding on the appropriate solution.
5. Evaluating the decision.[26]

Exhibit 7–10 presents an expanded version of the buyer behavior model shown in Exhibit 7–1. Note that this exhibit integrates the problem-solving process with the whole set of variables we've been reviewing.

When consumers evaluate information about purchase alternatives, they may weigh not only a product type in relation to other types of products, but also differences in brands within a product type *and* the stores where the products may be available. This can be a very complicated evaluation procedure, and, depending on their choice of criteria, consumers may make seemingly irrational decisions. If convenient service is crucial, for example, a buyer might pay list price for an unexciting car from a very convenient dealer. Marketers need a way to analyze these decisions.

MARKETING DEMO 7–3   Study of Quebec Consumers Points Out Differences

I n 1981, Goldfarb Consultants, Inc., a Toronto-based marketing and research firm, divided the Canadian population into six psychographic categories. Recently, the psychographics of Quebec consumers were examined in greater detail for the first time. The study concluded that Quebecers are indeed "pas comme les autres."

Old-Fashioned Puritans have a strong resistance to change and are indifferent to the outside world, almost apathetic. About 17 percent of Quebecers and 15 percent of Canadians, including Quebec, fall into this category. People in this group spend more time watching television and less time listening to the radio than other groups, are reluctant to try new products, and shun technological advances.

The Responsible Survivors lack self-confidence but are easy going, sociable, respect the status quo, and follow directives efficiently. People in this group are not particularly materialistic, are avid television news watchers, don't dine out much, exercise little, but support better health care.

Day-to-Day Watchers are basically happy with life in general. They represent the largest group of Canadians, at 24 percent, and Quebecers, at 27 percent. They also represent the average man and woman, tend to be religious, and have solid moral convictions. This segment of the population is open to new products and ideas but is wary of advertising. In terms of media habits, Day-to-Day Watchers reflect those of the average Canadian. In Quebec, they are apt to read upscale magazines. They like to read, skate, bowl, and walk, and are likely to do more charity work than the average Canadian.

People in the Disinterested Self-Indulgent group are self-centered with a live-and-let-live outlook on life. This group cares little about problems of minorities, Third World countries, or drinking and driving. They tend to watch a lot of television sports, dress poorly, buy lottery tickets, eat junk food, and care little about their health.

Aggressive Achievers are not happy with the status quo and follow the latest fashion trends. Psychologically, they tend to be insecure, and their moti- vation is a direct response to their vanity. They are active but superficial, and are like the typical yuppie. Attracted by gadgets, Aggressive Achievers are a marketer's dream, with their purchases of the latest products. But they shun charity work, lack compassion, and waver on their convictions. They also tend to be impulsive shoppers, but shun shopping by phone, catalogues, and shopping clubs.

The final group is Joiner Activists. Socially, this group is the most active and spends the most money. About 26 percent of the Quebec population falls into this category versus only 19 percent for Canada as a whole. Although not terribly religious, this group's support for charitable organizations is the strongest. Joiner Activists go out a lot, spend money on clothes, and are willing to pay for quality. They also buy more imported cars, watch less television, and read more than most Canadians. As well, they are more physically active, twice as likely to own a personal computer than the average Canadian, and likely to travel a lot, especially to Europe.

The psychographic differences between Quebec and the rest of Canada represent significant consequences for manufacturers, marketers, and advertisers, according to Pierre Legendre, president of Legendre Lubawin Goldfarb, Inc. Legendre noted that Quebec is primarily made up of Old-Fashioned Puritans and Day-to-Day Watchers at one extreme, and Joiner Activists at the other. The remaining three segments are only niche segments in Quebec.

"The term *average Canadian* can also be misleading. For example, Quebecers are known to watch a lot of television. But which Quebecers? Old-Fashioned Puritans watch 38 percent more TV than the other groups, but Joiner Activists watch 20 percent less. And Joiner Activists make up a larger part of Quebec than the rest of Canada," points out Legendre. As a result, marketers have to look at the composition of Quebec less from a cultural viewpoint and more through psychographics.

Source: Brian Dunn, "Study of Quebec Consumers Points Out Differences," *The Montreal Gazette*, January 27, 1992, pp. 16–17.

Exhibit 7–10 An Expanded Model of the Consumer Problem-Solving Process

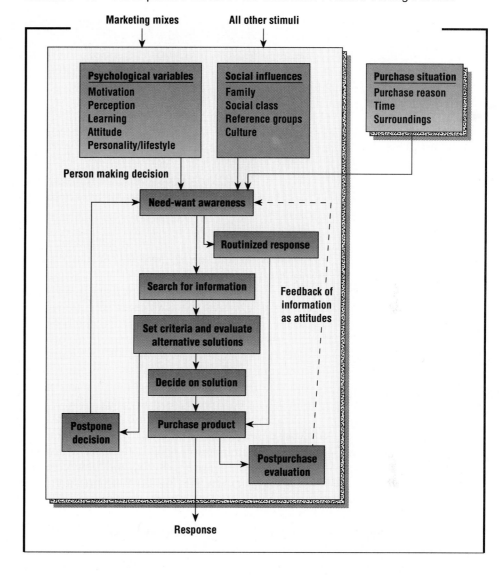

Grid of evaluative
criteria helps

Based on studies of how consumers seek out and evaluate product information, researchers suggest that marketing managers use an evaluative grid showing features common to different products (or marketing mixes). For example, Exhibit 7–11 shows some of the features common to three different cars a consumer might consider.

The grid encourages marketing managers to view each product as a bundle of features or attributes. The pluses and minuses in Exhibit 7–11 indicate one consumer's attitude toward each feature of each car. If members of the target market don't rate a feature of the marketing manager's brand with pluses, it may indicate a problem. The manager might want to change the product to improve that feature—or perhaps use more promotion to emphasize an already acceptable feature. The consumer in Exhibit 7–11 has a minus under gas mileage for the Nissan. If the Nissan really gets better gas mileage than the other cars, promotion

Exhibit 7–11   Grid of Evaluative Criteria for Three Car Brands

Brands	Common features			
	Gas mileage	Ease of service	Comfortable interior	Styling
Nissan	−	+	+	−
Saab	+	−	+	+
Toyota	+	+	+	−

Note: Pluses and minuses indicate a consumer's evaluation of a feature for a brand.

might focus on mileage to improve consumer attitudes toward this feature and toward the whole product.

Some consumers will reject a product if they see *one* feature as substandard—regardless of how favorably they regard the product's other features. The consumer in Exhibit 7–11 might avoid the Saab, which he saw as less than satisfactory on ease of service, even if it were superior in all other aspects. In other instances, a consumer's overall attitude toward the product might be such that a few good features could make up for some shortcomings. The comfortable interior of the Toyota (Exhibit 7–11) might make up for less exciting styling—especially if the consumer viewed comfort as really important.

Of course, consumers don't use a grid like this. However, constructing such a grid helps managers think about what evaluative criteria target consumers consider really important, what consumers' attitudes are toward their product (or marketing mix) on each criteria, and how consumers combine the criteria to reach a final decision. Having a better understanding of the process should help a manager develop a better marketing mix.[27]

Three levels of problem solving are useful

The basic **problem-solving process** shows the steps a consumer may go through trying to find a way to satisfy their needs—but it doesn't show how long this process will take or how much thought a consumer will give to each step. Individuals who have had a lot of experience solving certain problems can move quickly through some of the steps or almost directly to a decision.

It is helpful, therefore, to recognize three levels of problem solving: extensive problem solving, limited problem solving, and routinized response behavior. See Exhibit 7–12. These problem-solving approaches are used for any kind of

Exhibit 7–12   Problem-Solving Continuum

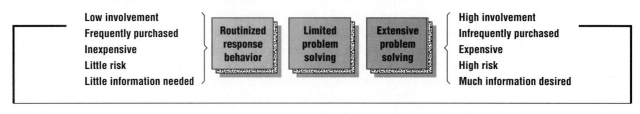

Low involvement
Frequently purchased
Inexpensive
Little risk
Little information needed

Routinized response behavior — Limited problem solving — Extensive problem solving

High involvement
Infrequently purchased
Expensive
High risk
Much information desired

For most consumers, selecting a new stereo system would involve extensive problem solving—but selecting a box of cereal would usually involve routinized response behavior.

product. Consumers use **extensive problem solving** for a completely new or important need—when they put much effort into deciding how to satisfy it. For example, a music lover who wants higher-quality sound might decide to buy a CD player—but not have any idea what to buy. After talking with friends to find out about good places to buy a player, she might visit several stores to find out about different brands and their features. After thinking about her needs some more, she might buy a portable Sony unit—so she could use it in both her apartment and her car.

Consumers use **limited problem solving** when they're willing to put *some* effort into deciding the best way to satisfy a need. Limited problem solving is typical when a consumer has some previous experience in solving a problem but isn't certain which choice is best at the current time. If our music lover wanted some new disks for her player, she would already know what type of music she enjoys. She might go to a familiar store and evaluate what disks they had in stock for her favorite types of music.

Consumers use **routinized response behavior** when they regularly select a particular way of satisfying a need when it occurs. Routinized response behavior is typical when a consumer has considerable experience in how to meet a need and has no need for additional information. For example, our music lover might routinely buy the latest recording by her favorite band as soon as it's available. Most marketing managers would like their target consumers to buy their products in this routinized way.

Routinized response behavior is also typical for **low involvement purchases**—purchases that have little importance or relevance for the customer. Let's face it—buying a box of salt is probably not one of the burning issues in your life.[28]

Problem solving is a learning process

The reason problem solving becomes simpler with time is that people learn from experience—both positive and negative things. As consumers approach the problem-solving process, they bring attitudes formed by previous experiences and social training. Each new problem-solving process may then contribute to or modify this attitude set.

New concepts require an adoption process

When consumers face a really new concept, their previous experience may not be relevant. These situations involve the **adoption process**—the steps individuals go through on the way to accepting or rejecting a new idea. Although the adoption process is similar to the problem-solving process, learning plays a clearer role and promotion's contribution to a marketing mix is more visible.

In the adoption process, an individual moves through some fairly definite steps:

1. *Awareness*—the potential customer comes to know about the product but lacks details. The consumer may not even know how it works or what it will do.
2. *Interest*—if the consumer becomes interested, he or she will gather general information and facts about the product.
3. *Evaluation*—a consumer begins to give the product a mental trial, applying it to his or her personal situation.
4. *Trial*—the consumer may buy the product to experiment with it in use. A product that is either too expensive to try or isn't available for trial may never be adopted.
5. *Decision*—the consumer decides on either adoption or rejection. A satisfactory evaluation and trial may lead to adoption of the product and regular use. According to psychological learning theory, reinforcement leads to adoption.
6. *Confirmation*—the adopter continues to rethink the decision and searches for support for the decision—that is, further reinforcement.[29]

Marketing managers for 3M, the company that makes Scotch tape, worked with the adoption process when they introduced Post-it note pads. Test market ads increased awareness—they explained how Post-it notes could be applied to a surface and then easily removed. But test market sales were slow because most

---

Marketers often want to make it easier for consumers to adopt a product. Pittsburgh Paints' Accuvision video system helps customers see how their paint choices will look. Nabisco offers free samples to encourage consumers to try the product.

consumers were not interested. They didn't see the benefit. To encourage trial, 3M distributed free samples. By using the samples, consumers confirmed the benefit—and when they used the samples up, they started buying Post-its. As Post-it distribution expanded to other market areas, 3M used samples to speed consumers through the trial stage and the rest of the adoption process.[30]

Dissonance may set in after the decision

A buyer may have second thoughts after making a purchase decision. The buyer may have chosen from among several attractive alternatives—weighing the pros and cons and finally making a decision. Later doubts, however, may lead to **dissonance**—tension caused by uncertainty about the rightness of a decision. Dissonance may lead a buyer to search for additional information to confirm the wisdom of the decision and so reduce tension. Without this confirmation, the adopter might buy something else next time—or not comment positively about the product to others.[31]

SEVERAL PROCESSES ARE RELATED AND RELEVANT TO STRATEGY PLANNING

Exhibit 7–13 shows the interrelation of the problem-solving process, the adoption process, and learning. It is important to see this interrelation—and to understand that promotion can modify or accelerate it. Also note that the potential buyers' problem-solving behavior should affect how firms design their physical distribution systems. If customers aren't willing to travel far to shop, a firm may need more outlets to get their business. Similarly, customers' attitudes help determine what price to charge. Knowing how target markets help handle these processes helps companies with their marketing strategy planning.

Exhibit 7–13   Relation of Problem-Solving Process, Adoption Process, and Learning (given a problem)

Problem-solving steps	Adoption process steps	Learning steps
1. Becoming aware of or interested in the problem	Awareness and interest	**Drive**
2. Gathering information about possible solutions	Interest and evaluation	**Cues**
3. Evaluating alternative solutions, perhaps trying some out	Evaluation, maybe trial	**Reinforcement**
4. Deciding on the appropriate solution	Decision	**Response**
5. Evaluating the decision	Confirmation	

CONCLUSION

In this chapter, we analyzed the individual consumer as a problem solver who is influenced by psychological variables, social influences, time, and the purchase situation. All of these variables are related, and our model of buyer behavior helps integrate them into one process. Marketing strategy planning requires a good grasp of this material. However, our discussion of the French Canadian market shows there are no easy answers.

Assuming that everyone behaves the way you do—or even like your family or friends do—can lead to expensive marketing errors.

Consumer buying behavior results from the consumer's efforts to satisfy needs and wants. We discussed some reasons why consumers buy and saw that consumer behavior can't be fully explained by only a list of needs.

We also saw that most societies are divided into social classes, a fact that helps explain some consumer behavior. And we discussed the impact of reference groups and opinion leaders.

We presented a buyer behavior model to help you interpret and integrate the present findings—as well as any new data you might get from marketing research. As of now, the behavioral sciences can only offer insights and theories, which the marketing manager must blend with intuition and judgment in developing marketing strategies.

Companies may have to use marketing research to answer specific questions. But if a firm has neither the money nor the time for research, then marketing managers have to rely on available descriptions of present behavior and guesstimates about future behavior. Popular magazines and leading newspapers often reflect the public's shifting attitudes. And many studies of the changing consumer are published regularly in the business and trade press. This material—coupled with the information in these last two chapters—will help your marketing strategy planning.

Remember that consumers, with all their needs and attitudes, may be elusive, but they aren't invisible. Research has provided more data and understanding of consumer behavior than business managers generally use. Applying this information may help you find your breakthrough opportunity.

QUESTIONS AND PROBLEMS

1. In your own words, explain economic needs and how they relate to the economics orientation model of consumer behavior. Give an example of a purchase you recently made that is consistent with this model. Give another that is not explained by this model. Explain your thinking.

2. Explain what is meant by a hierarchy of needs, and provide examples of one or more products that enable you to satisfy each of the four levels of need.

3. Cut out (or copy) two recent advertisements: one full-page color ad from a magazine and one large display from a newspaper. In each case, indicate which needs the ads are appealing to.

4. Explain how an understanding of consumers' learning processes might affect marketing strategy planning. Give an example.

5. Briefly describe your own *beliefs* about the potential value of a driver-side air bag, your *attitude* toward air bags, and your *intention* about buying a car with an air bag.

6. Explain psychographics and lifestyle analysis. Explain how they might be useful for planning marketing strategies to reach college students as opposed to average consumers.

7. How should the social class structure affect the planning of a new restaurant in a large city? How might the four Ps be adjusted?

8. What social class would you associate with each of the following phrases or items?
   a. A gun rack in a pickup truck.
   b. The *National Enquirer*.
   c. *New Yorker* magazine.

d. People watching soap operas.

e. TV golf tournaments.

f. Men who drink beer after dinner.

g. Families who vacation at a Disney theme park.

h. Families who distrust banks (keep money in socks or mattresses).

i. Owners of pit bulls.

In each case, choose one class, if you can, then provide some justification for your choice. If you can't choose one class, but rather feel that several classes are equally likely, then so indicate. In those cases where you feel that all classes are equally interested or characterized by a particular item, choose all five classes.

9. Illustrate how the reference group concept may apply in practice by explaining how you personally are influenced by some reference group for some product. What are the implications of such behavior for marketing managers?

10. Give two examples of recent purchases where the specific purchase situation influenced your purchase decision. Briefly explain how your decision was affected.

11. Give an example of a recent purchase in which you used extensive problem solving. What sources of information did you use in making the decision?

12. On the basis of the data and analysis presented in Chapters 6 and 7, what kind of buying behavior would you expect to find for the following products: (a) a haircut, (b) a dishwasher detergent, (c) a printer for a personal computer, (d) a tennis racket, (e) a dress belt, (f) a telephone answering machine, (g) life insurance, (h) an ice cream cone, and (i) a new checking account? Set up a chart for your answer with products along the left-hand margin as the row headings and the following factors as headings for the columns: (a) how consumers would shop for these products, (b) how far they would go, (c) whether they would buy by brand, (d) whether they would compare with other products, and (e) any other factors they should consider. Insert short answers—words or phrases are satisfactory—in the various boxes. Be prepared to discuss how the answers you put in the chart would affect each product's marketing mix.

SUGGESTED CASES

5. Time to Buy a New Car?

8. Wilhelm Van Eyck

Business and Organizational Customers and Their Buying Behavior

Chapter

8

When You Finish This Chapter, You Should

❶
Know who the business and organizational customers are.

❷
Understand the problem-solving behavior of organizational buyers.

❸
See why multiple influence is common in business and organizational purchase decisions.

❹
Know the basic methods used in organizational buying.

❺
Know about the number and distribution of manufacturers and why they are an important customer group.

❻
Know how buying by service firms, retailers, wholesalers, and governments is similar to—and different from—buying by manufacturers.

❼
Understand the important new terms (shown in blue).

In 1978, Shahid Kahn used $13,000 in savings and a $50,000 loan to start Bumper Works, a small company that produces lightweight bumpers for pickup trucks. Bumper Works now employs over a hundred people, and its customers include major Japanese automakers like Isuzu and Toyota. But success didn't come overnight.

Kahn started to make sales calls on Toyota's purchasing department in 1980, but it was 1985 before he got his first order. And the first order wasn't a big contract. Toyota had a reputation for quality with North American consumers. Parts buyers at Toyota didn't want to risk tarnishing that reputation by relying too heavily on a new, unproven supplier.

In 1987, Toyota decided to improve the bumpers on its trucks so they would be more durable than the ones on competing pickups. That meant designing a new bumper and rethinking who would provide it. Toyota engineers developed the specifications for the new bumper, and Toyota buyers selected three potential suppliers—including Bumper Works—to compete for the business. This gave Bumper Works a chance to get business that routinely went to other suppliers. Kahn developed an economical design that met the specs and won the contract. The contract involved supplying all of the rear bumpers Toyota needed at some of its U.S. facilities.

Although Kahn won the contract, he still faced challenges. Toyota's quality control people were not satisfied with the number of minor defects in Kahn's bumpers. Further, Bumper Works' deliveries were not as dependable as Toyota's production people required. Kahn knew that he would lose the Toyota account if he couldn't meet the demands of these people—and also keep the price low enough to satisfy the purchasing department.

Toyota's purchasing people concluded that Bumper Works wouldn't be able to resolve these problems unless Kahn could make big improvements in his production process. Kahn was stuck because he didn't know what else he could do. However, rather than shift the business to another supplier, Toyota sent a team of experts to show Bumper Works how to build better bumpers faster and cheaper.

Following the advice of Toyota experts, Kahn reorganized all the equipment in his factory to make it more efficient. He also had to retrain all his employees to do their jobs in new ways. The changes were so complicated that two of Kahn's six production supervisors quit in frustration. But the trouble was worth the effort. Within a year after the changes, productivity at Bumper Works went up 60 percent, and the number of defects dropped by 80 percent. In 1992, the improvements helped Bumper Works get a big new contract with Isuzu.

Of course, Toyota didn't go to all of its effort just to be friendly. It wanted a committed supplier that could meet its standards. In exchange for all its help, Toyota got a big price reduction from Bumper Works.[1]

BUSINESS AND ORGANIZATIONAL CUSTOMERS—A BIG OPPORTUNITY

Most of us think about individual final consumers when we hear the term *customer*. But many marketing managers aim at customers who are not final consumers. In fact, more purchases are made by businesses and other organizations than by final consumers. As the Bumper Works/Toyota case illustrates, the buying behavior of these customers can be very different from the buying behavior of final consumers. Developing marketing strategies for these markets requires a solid understanding of who these customers are and how they buy. That is the focus of this chapter.

What types of customers are involved?

Business and organizational customers are any buyers who buy for resale or to produce other goods and services. Exhibit 8–1 shows the different types of customers in these markets. They include industrial manufacturers, producers of services, middlemen, and various nonprofit organizations, including government agencies. There are great marketing opportunities in serving these customers, and a student heading toward a business career has a good chance of working in this area.

These varied customers do many different jobs. Yet many of the segmenting dimensions a marketing manager needs to describe their buying behavior tend to be common across the different types of organizations. There is a reason for this. Industrial firms originally developed many of the basic approaches for organizational buying. Other types of organizations then adopted the best ideas. So many characteristics of buying behavior are common across different types of organizations. That's why the different kinds of organizational buyers are often loosely referred to as "industrial buyers" or "intermediate buyers." As we discuss organizational buying, we will intermix examples of buying by many different types of organizations. Later in the chapter, however, we will highlight some of the specific characteristics of the different customer groups.

ORGANIZATIONAL CUSTOMERS ARE DIFFERENT

Organizations buy for a basic purpose

Like final consumers, organizations make purchases to satisfy needs. But it's often easier to understand an organization's needs because most organizations make purchases for the same basic reason. They buy goods and services that will

Exhibit 8–1   Examples of Different Types of Business and Organizational Customers

```
All business              Producers of goods        Manufacturers
and organizational        and services
customers                                           Farms, fisheries, forestry,
                                                    mining operations,
                                                    construction firms

                                                    Financial institutions—
                                                    insurance, banks, real estate

                                                    Other service providers—
                                                    transportation firms, utilities,
                                                    hotels, lawyers, doctors

                          Middlemen                 Wholesalers

                                                    Retailers

                          Government units          Federal agencies (U.S. and other
                                                    countries)

                                                    State and local governments

                          Nonprofit                 National organizations (such as Red
                          organizations             Cross, Girl Scouts)

                                                    Local organizations (such as
                                                    churches, colleges, museums)
```

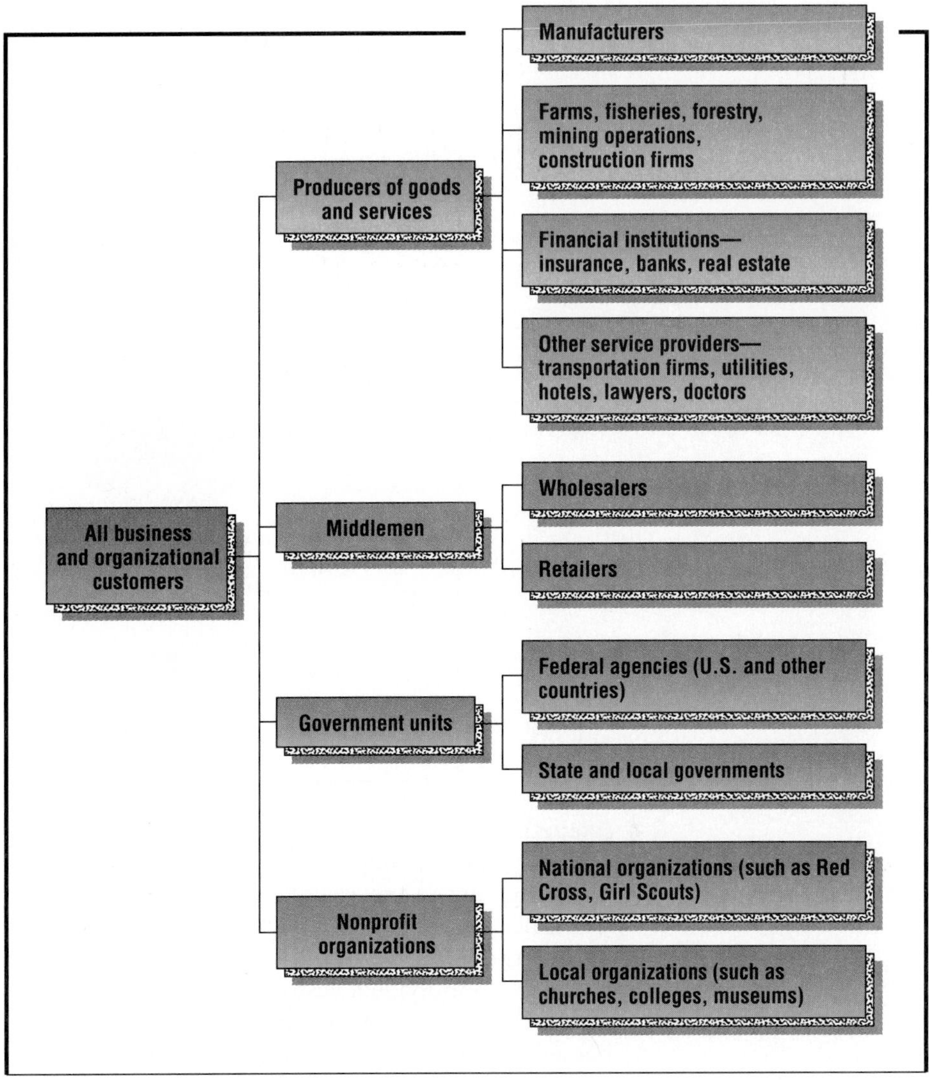

help them meet the demand for the goods and services that they in turn supply to their markets. In other words, their basic need is to satisfy their own customers and clients. A manufacturer buys because it wants to earn a profit by making and selling goods. A wholesaler or retailer buys products it can profitably resell to its customers. A town government wants to meet its legal and social obligations to citizens. Similarly, a country club wants to help its members enjoy their leisure time.

Even small differences are important

Different types of customers may buy for the same basic purpose, but there are many variations in how they buy and why they pick specific suppliers. Understanding how the buying behavior of a particular organization differs from others can be very important. Organizational customers often make large purchases, and

competition for their business is often rugged. Even "trivial" differences in buying behavior may be important because success often hinges on fine-tuning the marketing mix to precisely meet the target customer's needs.

Sellers often approach each organizational customer directly, usually through a sales representative. This gives the seller more chance to adjust the marketing mix for each individual customer. A seller may even develop a unique strategy for each individual customer. This approach carries target marketing to its extreme. But sellers often need unique strategies to compete for large-volume purchases.

In such situations, the individual sales rep takes over responsibility for strategy planning. This is relevant to your career planning since these jobs are very challenging—and they pay well, too.

Serving customers in international markets

Many marketers discover that there are good opportunities to serve business customers in different countries around the world. Specific business customs do vary from one country to another—and the differences can be important. For example, a salesperson working in Japan must know how to handle a customer's business card with respect. Japanese think of a business card as a symbolic extension of the person who presents it. Thus, they consider it rude to write notes on the back of a card or put it in a wallet while the person who presented it is still in the room. While such cultural differences can be very important, the basic approaches marketers use to deal with business customers in different parts of the world are much less varied than those required to reach individual consumers.

Hercules, an international supplier of ingredients to food producers, offers its customers expert help in dealing with the differences in tastes in different parts of the world.

This is probably why the shift to a global economy has been so rapid for many firms. Their business customers in different countries buy in similar ways and can be reached with similar marketing mixes. Moreover, business customers, more so than final consumers, are often willing to work with a distant supplier who has developed a superior marketing mix.

To keep the discussion specific, we will focus on organizational customers in Canada. But most of the ideas apply to international markets in general. Marketing Demo 8–1 describes how MacMillan Bloedel has succeeded in selling lumber from within the Japanese system.

ORGANIZATIONAL BUYERS ARE PROBLEM SOLVERS

Some people think of organizational buying as entirely different from consumer buying—but there are many similarities. In fact, the problem-solving framework introduced in Chapter 7 can be applied here.

Three kinds of buying processes are useful

In Chapter 7, we discussed problem solving by consumers and how it might vary from extensive problem solving to routine buying. In organizational markets, we can adapt these concepts slightly and work with three similar buying processes: a new-task buying process, a modified rebuy process, or a straight rebuy.[2] See Exhibit 8–2.

New-task buying occurs when an organization has a new need and the buyer wants a great deal of information. New-task buying can involve setting product specifications, evaluating sources of supply, and establishing an order routine that can be followed in the future if results are satisfactory.

A **straight rebuy** is a routine repurchase that may have been made many times before. Buyers probably don't bother looking for new information or new

---

MARKETING DEMO 8–1
A Canadian Lumber Company on Japanese Turf

MacMillan Bloedel Ltd., the British Columbia lumber giant, has taken its battle for global markets into the heart of the toughest market of all: Japan.

From the offices of MacMillan Bloedel Building Materials (MBBM) in the Toranomon district of Tokyo, President Joe Chernoff and his Japanese team have been building a lumber distribution business from within the Japanese system for the past five years. Today, the Tokyo-based subsidiary ranks as the second largest importer of North American lumber after Japan's own Mitsubishi Corporation.

The Japanese market, of course, is one of the most protective in the world, and its major trading houses do not easily give up business to foreign competitors. But MacMillan Bloedel has served the Japanese market for some time—beginning as long ago as the Great Kanto Earthquake of 1923, when MacMillan Bloedel salesmen were on hand to supply much-needed lumber and win contracts. But the subsidiary's current success is based on more than just tradition. With muscle and sweat, MBBM has beaten the aggressive Japanese traders at their own game by infiltrating the upper reaches of the all-important domestic wholesale business.

Until 1985, MacMillan Bloedel sold lumber products from Vancouver through an agency system, which in turn sold wood to the major trading companies in Japan. Now, through its own on-site wholesale lumber operation, the company is getting to know its end users face-to-face.

"You just can't ignore the middlemen," says Chernoff. "But our current system allows us to get further downstream with our product." By going downstream on the distribution side, MBBM hopes to get a more accurate fix on the true value of the product to its Japanese customers. By doing so, the company is able to ensure that its big distributors are honest when it comes to pricing.

With offices in Tokyo and Osaka, the company now accounts for more than 25 percent of the total value of lumber sold worldwide by MacMillan Bloedel, and the Japanese market is growing between 10 percent and 15 percent a year. To be sure, this is no noisy invasion. MBBM's "infiltration" of the Japanese market is conducted with good grace and sensitivity.

In Japan, you can't just reach for the phone or send a fax to initiate contact with new customers, Chernoff says. There is an elaborate ritual of introductions to a new client, usually through a third party. At the first meeting, there is little business discussed, as Japanese businessmen see the client-salesman relationship as more important than the actual deal. "We strive to fit into the system," says Chernoff. "It's not as if we are trying to bring in a North American way of doing things. You have to deal with the problems of working with a different culture. I act as a bridge by trying to explain North American philosophies to the Japanese and the ideas of our Japanese managers to North America."

Source: David Lake, "International Business: Tokyo," *Canadian Business,* January 1990, p. 27.

---

sources of supply. Most of a company's small or recurring purchases are of this type—but they take only a small part of an organized buyer's time.

The **modified rebuy** is the in-between process where some review of the buying situation is done, though not as much as in new-task buying. Sometimes a competitor will get lazy, enjoying a straight rebuy situation. An alert marketer can turn these situations into opportunities by providing more information or a better marketing mix.

Customers in a new-task buying situation are likely to seek information from a variety of sources. See Exhibit 8–3. How much information a customer collects also depends on the importance of the purchase and the level of uncertainty about what choice might be best. The time and expense of searching for and analyzing

Exhibit 8–2 Organization Buying Processes

Characteristics	Type of process		
	New-task buying	Modified rebuy	Straight rebuy
Time required	Much	Medium	Little
Multiple influence	Much	Some	Little
Review of suppliers	Much	Some	None
Information needed	Much	Some	Little

a lot of information may not be justified for a minor purchase. But a major purchase often involves real detective work. After all, the consequences of a mistake can be very important.

Note that a particular product may be bought in any of the three ways. The marketing job may be quite different, depending on the buying process. A new-task buy takes much longer than a straight rebuy—and the seller's promotion has much more chance to have an impact.[3]

Purchasing agents are buying specialists

Many organizations, especially large ones, need buying specialists. **Purchasing agents** are buying specialists for their employers. Most purchasing agents and purchasing managers are serious and well educated. In large organizations, they usually specialize by product area and are real experts. Salespeople usually have to see the purchasing agent first—before they contact any other employee. These buyers hold important positions and take a dim view of sales reps who try to go around them.

Rather than being "sold," these buyers want salespeople to provide accurate information that will help them buy wisely. They like information on new goods and services, and tips on potential price changes, supply shortages, and other changes in market conditions.

Exhibit 8–3 Major Sources of Information Used by Organizational Buyers

	Marketing sources	Nonmarketing sources
Personal sources	• Salespeople • Others from supplier firms • Trade shows	• Buying center members • Outside business associates • Consultants and outside experts
Impersonal sources	• Advertising in trade publications • Sales literature • Sales catalogs	• Rating services • Trade associations • News publications • Product directories

Purchasing may be centralized

If a large organization has facilities at many locations, much of the purchasing work may be done at a central location. For example, Canadian Tire handles most of the purchase decisions for stores in its retail chain from its head offices in Ontario. Many of the purchasing decisions for the federal government are handled by Supply and Services Canada.

With centralized buying, a sales rep may be able to sell to facilities all over a country—or even across several countries—without leaving a base city. This makes selling easier for competitors, too, so the market may be extremely competitive. The importance of such big buyers has led some companies to set up "national account" sales forces specially trained to cater to these needs. A geographically bound salesperson can be at a real disadvantage against such competitors.

Basic purchasing needs are economic

Organizational buyers typically focus on economic factors when they make purchase decisions. They are usually less emotional in their buying than final consumers.

Buyers try to consider the total cost of selecting a supplier and a particular product, not just the initial price of the product. For example, a hospital that needs a new type of X-ray equipment might look at both the original cost and ongoing costs, how it would affect doctor productivity, and of course the quality of the images it produces. The hospital might also consider the seller's reliability and general cooperativeness; the ability to provide speedy maintenance and repair, steady supply under all conditions, and reliable and fast delivery; and any past and present relationships (including previous favors).

The matter of dependability deserves further emphasis. An organization may not be able to function if purchases don't arrive when they're expected. For example, there's nothing worse to a purchasing agent and a production manager than shutting down a production line because sellers haven't delivered the goods.

Business customers usually focus on economic needs when they make purchase decisions.

Dependable product quality is important, too. The cost of a small item may have little to do with its importance. For example, a short piece of wire with faulty insulation might cause a large piece of equipment to break down, and the costs of finding and correcting the problem could be completely out of proportion to the cost of the wire.

Considering all of the economic factors relevant to a purchase decision is sometimes complex. A supplier or product that is best in one way may not be best in others. To try to deal with these situations, many buyers use **vendor analysis**—a formal rating of suppliers on all relevant areas of performance. By evaluating suppliers and how they are working out, buyers can make better decisions.[4]

Behavioral needs are relevant, too

Vendor analysis tries to focus on economic factors, but purchasing in organizations may also involve many of the same behavioral dimensions we discussed in Chapter 7. Modern buyers are human—and they want friendly relationships with suppliers. Some buyers seem eager to imitate progressive competitors or even to be the first to try new products. Such "innovators" deserve special attention when new products are being introduced.

Buyers are also human with respect to protecting their own interests—and their own position in the company. That's why many buyers want to avoid taking risks that might reflect badly on their decisions. They have to buy a wide variety of products from many sources and make decisions involving many factors beyond their control. If a new source delivers late or product quality is poor, you can guess who will be blamed. Marketers who can help the buyer avoid taking risks have a definite appeal. In fact, this may make the difference between a successful and unsuccessful marketing mix.

A seller's marketing mix should satisfy *both* the needs of the buyer's company as well as the buyer's individual needs. Therefore, sellers need to find an overlapping area where both can be satisfied. See Exhibit 8–4 for a summary of this idea.

Exhibit 8–4   Overlapping Needs of an Individual Buyer and the Buyer's Organization

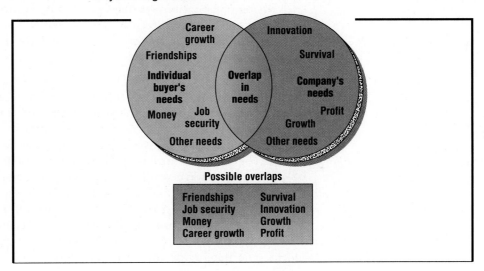

Ethical conflicts may arise

Although organizational buyers are influenced by their own needs, most are real professionals who are careful to avoid a conflict between their own self-interest and company outcomes. Marketers must be careful here. A salesperson who offers one of his company pens to a buyer may view the giveaway as part of the promotion effort—but the customer's firm may have a policy against a buyer accepting *any* gift.

Most organizational buyers do their work ethically—and expect marketers to work the same way. However, some buyers may give contracts to suppliers who offer them vacation trips and other personal favors. Abuses of this sort have prompted many organizations to set up policies that prohibit a buyer from accepting anything from a potential supplier.[5]

Marketers need to take concerns about conflict of interest very seriously. Part of the promotion job in marketing is to identify and persuade different individuals who may influence an organization's purchase decision. Yet the whole marketing effort may be tainted if it even *appears* that a marketer has encouraged a buyer to put personal gain ahead of company interest.

Multiple buying influences in a buying centre

Much of the work of the typical purchasing agent consists of straight rebuys. When a purchase requisition comes in, the purchasing agent places an order without consulting anyone else. But in many cases—especially new-task buying—multiple buying influence is important. **Multiple buying influence** means that several people, perhaps even top management, share in making a purchase decision. Possible buying influences include:

1. *Users*—perhaps production line workers or their supervisors.
2. *Influencers*—perhaps engineering or R&D people who help write specifications or supply information for evaluating alternatives.
3. *Buyers*—the purchasing agents who have the responsibility for working with suppliers and arranging the terms of the sale.
4. *Deciders*—the people in the organization who have the power to select or approve the supplier—usually the purchasing agent for small items but perhaps top management for larger purchases.
5. *Gatekeepers*—people who control the flow of information within the buying organization—perhaps purchasing agents who shield users or other deciders. Gatekeepers can also include receptionists, secretaries, research assistants, and others who influence the flow of information about potential purchases.

An example shows how the different buying influences work.

Suppose Electrolux, the Swedish firm that produces vacuum cleaners, wants to buy a machine to stamp out the various metal parts it needs. Different vendors are eager for the business. Several people (influencers) help to evaluate the choices. A finance manager worries about the high cost and suggests leasing the machine. The quality control people want a machine that will do a more accurate job—although it's more expensive. The production manager is interested in speed of operation. The production line workers and their supervisors want the machine that is easiest to use so workers can continue to rotate jobs.

The company president asks the purchasing department to assemble all the information but retains the power to select and approve the supplier (the decider). The purchasing manager's administrative assistant (a gatekeeper) has

Texaco Chemical Company supplies Owens-Corning with chemicals needed to make insulation, so Texaco's sales reps are in close contact with the different people at Owens-Corning who influence purchase decisions.

been deciding what information to pass on to higher-ups as well as scheduling visits for salespeople. After all these buying influences are considered, one of the purchasing agents for the firm will be responsible for making recommendations and arranging the terms of the sale (the buyer).

It is helpful to think of a **buying centre** as all the people who participate in or influence a purchase. Different people may make up a buying centre from one decision to the next. This makes the marketing job difficult.

The salesperson must study each case carefully. Just learning who to talk with may be hard, but thinking about the various roles in the buying centre can help. See Exhibit 8–5.

Exhibit 8–5   Multiple Influence and Roles in the Buying Centre

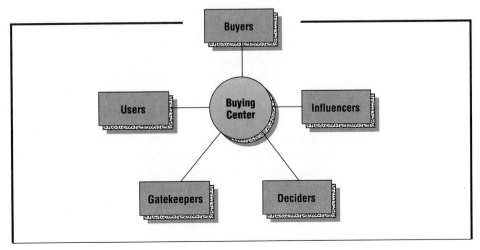

The salesperson may have to talk to every member of the buying centre, stressing different topics for each. This not only complicates the promotion job but also lengthens it. Approval of a routine order may take anywhere from a day to several months. On very important purchases—a new computer system, a new building, or major equipment—the selling period may stretch out to a year or more.[6]

BASIC METHODS AND PRACTICES IN ORGANIZATIONAL BUYING

Should you inspect, sample, describe, or negotiate?

Organizational buyers (really, buyers of all types, including final consumers) use four basic approaches to evaluating and buying products: (1) inspection, (2) sampling, (3) description, and (4) negotiated contracts. Understanding the differences in these buying methods is important in strategy planning, so let's look at each approach.

Inspection looks at everything

Inspection buying means looking at every item. It's used for products that are not standardized and require examination. Here, each product is different—as in the case of livestock or used equipment. Such products are often sold in open markets—or at auction, if there are several potential buyers. Buyers inspect the goods and either haggle with the seller or bid against competing buyers.

Sampling looks at some

Sampling buying means looking at only part of a potential purchase. As products become more standardized, perhaps because of careful grading or quality control, buying by sample becomes possible. For example, a power company might buy miles of heavy electric cable. A sample section might be heated to the melting point to be certain the cable is safe.

Prices may be based on a sample. Although demand and supply forces may set the general price level, actual price may vary depending on the quality of a specific sample. For example, grain markets use this kind of buying. The actual price is based on a sample withdrawn from a carload of grain and analyzed.

People in less-developed economies do a lot of buying by inspection or sampling—regardless of the product. The reason is skepticism about quality—or lack of faith in the seller.

Specifications describe the need

Description (specification) buying means buying from a written (or verbal) description of the product. Most manufactured items and many agricultural commodities are bought this way—often without inspection. When quality can almost be guaranteed, buying by description—grade, brand, or specification—may be satisfactory, especially when there is mutual trust between buyers and sellers. Because this method reduces the cost of buying, buyers use it whenever practical.

Services are usually purchased by description. Since a service is usually not performed until after it's purchased, buyers have nothing to inspect ahead of time.

Once the purchase needs are specified, it's the buyer's job to get the best deal possible. If several suppliers want the business, the buyer will often request competitive bids. **Competitive bids** are the terms of sale offered by different suppliers in response to the buyer's purchase specifications. If different suppliers' quality, dependability, and delivery schedules all meet the specs, the buyer will select the low-price bid. But a creative marketer needs to look carefully at the purchaser's specs—and the need—to see if other elements of the marketing mix could provide a competitive advantage.

Buyers may only inspect a portion of a potential fruit purchase, but the quality of the sample may affect the price or acceptability of the whole order. Most manufactured items, including rolls of aluminum, are bought based on written specifications.

Negotiated contracts handle relationships

Negotiated contract buying means agreeing to a contract that allows for changes in the purchase arrangements.

Sometimes, the buyer knows roughly what the company needs but can't fix all the details in advance. Specifications or total requirements may change over time. This situation is common, for example, in research and development work and in the building of special-purpose machinery or buildings. In such cases, the general project is described, and a basic price may be agreed on—perhaps even based on competitive bids—but with provision for changes and price adjustments up or down. Or a supplier may be willing to accept a contract that provides some type of incentive—such as full coverage of costs plus a fixed fee or full costs plus a profit percentage tied to costs. The whole contract may even be subject to renegotiation as the work proceeds.

Buyers and suppliers form partnerships

To be sure of dependable quality, a buyer may develop loyalty to certain suppliers. This is especially important when buying nonstandardized products. When a supplier and buyer develop a working partnership over the years, the supplier practically becomes a part of the buyer's organization. (Sometimes, the buyer will design a product and simply ask the supplier to build and deliver it at a fair price.)

When a seller proposes a new idea that saves the buyer's company money, the buyer usually rewards the seller with a long-term contract, and this encourages future suggestions. In contrast, buyers who use a bid system exclusively—either by choice or necessity, as in some government and institutional purchasing—may not be offered much beyond basic goods and services. They are interested primarily in price.

A recent purchase by Boeing, the giant airplane manufacturer, illustrates the trend toward closer working partnerships between business customers and their suppliers. Boeing is a big customer for machine tools, the equipment it uses to make airplane parts. Like other manufacturers, Boeing usually designed parts for its planes first and then got competitive bids from machine suppliers. The supplier whose machines met Boeing's specs at the lowest price got the order. Japanese machine tool suppliers, like Toshiba, were beating American suppliers in this price-oriented competition.

Recently, Boeing needed to buy machines to produce landing-gear parts, and it tried a different approach. Boeing invited potential suppliers to study its operations and recommend how the landing-gear parts could be designed so that the machines to produce them would be more efficient. Ingersol, an American machine-tool company, seized the opportunity. It helped Boeing design the landing-gear parts so that the total cost of both the machines and the parts they produced would be lower. The design also helped Boeing speed up its production process. Instead of just trying to sell machines at the lowest price, Ingersol helped Boeing develop a better way to make its airplane—and Ingersol won the $8 million contract.[7]

Business-to-business marketing efforts, whether targeted at middlemen or other types of firms, can be even more demanding than working with final consumers. Building and keeping business partnerships takes constant attention to service quality, not just quality goods. But organizational buyers know that the success of their own firms' marketing strategies depends on such service—so they reward reliable suppliers with their orders.[8] How the need to protect established relationships can even affect plant location decisions is shown in Marketing Demo 8–2.

Powerful customer may control the relationship

A supplier who wants to form a cooperative partnership may find it impossible with large, powerful customers who can dictate how the relationship will work. For example, Duall/Wind, a plastics producer, was a supplier of small parts for Polaroid instant cameras. But when Duall/Wind wanted to raise its prices to cover increasing costs, Polaroid balked. Polaroid's purchasing manager demanded that Duall/Wind show a breakdown of all its costs, from materials to labor to profit. As Duall/Wind's president said, "I had a tough time getting through my head that Polaroid wanted to come right in here and have us divulge all that." But Polaroid is a big account—and it got the information it wanted. Polaroid buyers agreed to a price increase only after they were confident that Duall/Wind was doing everything possible to control costs.[9]

Buyers may use several sources to spread their risk

Even if a firm develops the best marketing mix possible, it may not get all of a business customer's business. Buyers often look for several dependable sources of supply to protect themselves from unpredictable events such as strikes, fires, or floods in one of their suppliers' plants. Still, a good marketing mix is likely to win a larger share of the total business—which can prove to be very important. Moving from a 20 percent to a 30 percent share may not seem like much from a buyer's point of view, but for the seller it's a 50 percent increase in sales![10]

Most buyers try to routinize buying

To save effort and expense, most firms try to routinize the purchase process whenever they can. When some person or unit wants to buy something, a **requisition**—a request to buy something—is filled out. After approval by some

MARKETING DEMO 8–2
Fleck Manufacturing Inc.'s Return to Canada

(A) round midnight, the residents of Huron Park, Ontario, awoke to the sound of their largest employer, Fleck Manufacturing, Inc., decamping for Nogales, Mexico. Fleck workers in the subdivision, a dowdy pocket of converted wartime housing about 45 kilometers north of London, Ontario, had only hours earlier rejected the latest contract offer from the wire-harness manufacturer and voted to strike. Fleck had warned for some time that if the workers struck, it would move the auto parts business south to hang onto its customers. The dead-of-night departure was a high-profile symbol of the growing exodus by Canadian companies to the United States and Mexico.

Although the auto parts unit is probably in Nogales for good, residents of Huron Park might be surprised to learn that Fleck quietly repatriated another business to Canada from one of its three Mexican plants just a few months later under pressure from its largest customer. The customer, a giant US electronics company, was so annoyed with the Mexican plant's defect rate and the two weeks lost in shipping time that it was prepared to buy instead from a US or Canadian plant, even if it meant paying more for the product. Obligingly, Fleck moved the business to its main Tilsonburg, Ontario, facility, upped the product price, and restored the 75 jobs it had eliminated there when it moved the business south. The plant succeeded in cutting shipping time to as little as one day. "In this case, the competitive battle ground has shifted to time," explains Harrison Hawden, Fleck's sales and marketing manager.

Source: Ann Walmsley, "Turning the Tide," *Report on Business Magazine*, June 1992, pp. 20–32.

supervisor, the requisition is forwarded to the buyer for placement with the "best" seller.

Approved requisitions are converted to purchase orders as quickly as possible. Buyers usually make straight rebuys the day they receive the requisition; new-task and modified rebuys take longer. If time is important, the buyer may place the order by telephone, fax, or computer.

Computer buying is becoming common

Many buyers now delegate a large portion of their routine order placing to computer-based systems. They program decision rules that tell the computer how to order and leave the details of following through to the system. When economic conditions change, buyers modify the computer instructions. When nothing unusual happens, however, the computer system continues to routinely rebuy as needs develop—printing out new purchase orders to the regular suppliers.

Obviously, it's a big sale to be selected as a major supplier and routinely called up in the buyer's computer program. It's also obvious that such a buyer will be more impressed by an attractive marketing mix for a whole *line* of products than just a lower price for a particular order. It may be too expensive and too much trouble to change the whole buying system just because somebody is offering a low price on a particular day.[11]

It pays to know the buyer

In routine order situations, it's very important to be one of the regular sources of supply. For straight rebuys, the buyer (or computer) may place an order without even considering other potential sources. Sellers' sales reps regularly call on these buyers—but *not* to sell a particular item. Rather, they want to maintain relations, become a source, and/or point out new developments that might cause the buyer to reevaluate his or her present straight rebuy procedure and give more business to the sales rep's company.

Inventory policy may determine purchases

Business customers generally try to maintain an adequate inventory—certainly enough to prevent stockouts or keep production lines moving. There's no greater disaster in a factory than to have a production line close down. And a retailer or wholesaler can lose sales quickly if popular products are not on the shelf.

On the other hand, keeping too much inventory is expensive. Firms now pay more attention to inventory costs—and look to their suppliers for help in controlling them. This often means that a supplier must be able to provide **just-in-time delivery**—reliably getting products there *just* before the customer needs them.

Just-in-time relationships between buyers and sellers require a lot of coordination. For example, an automobile producer may ask a supplier of automobile seats to load the delivery truck so seats are arranged in the color and style of the cars on the assembly line. This reduces the buyer's costs because the seats only need to be handled one time. However, it may increase the supplier's costs. Most buyers realize they can't just push costs back onto their suppliers without giving them something in return. Often, what they give is a longer-term contract that shares both the costs and benefits of the working partnership. We'll discuss just-in-time delivery arrangements in more detail in Chapter 12.

Reciprocity may influence buying

Reciprocity means trading sales for sales—that is, "if you buy from me, I'll buy from you." If a company's customers also can supply products that the firm buys, then the sales departments of both buyer and seller may try to trade sales for sales. Purchasing agents generally resist reciprocity but often face pressure from their sales departments.

When prices and quality are otherwise competitive, an outside supplier seldom can break a reciprocity relationship. The supplier can only hope to become an alternate source of supply—and wait for the competitor to let its quality slip or prices rise.

Variations in buying by customer type

We've been discussing dimensions and frameworks that marketing managers often use to analyze buying behavior in many different types of customer organizations—both in Canada and internationally. However, it's also useful to have more detail about specific types of customers.

MANUFACTURERS ARE IMPORTANT CUSTOMERS

There aren't many big ones

One of the most striking facts about manufacturers is how few there are compared to final consumers. In the industrial market, Exhibit 8–6 shows there were under 41,000 factories in 1988, the latest date for which information is available, and the majority of these were quite small. The owners may also be the buyers in small plants. And they buy less formally than in the relatively few large manufacturing plants that employ the majority of workers and do most of the manufacturing. In 1988, plants with 200 or more employees numbered only 1,747, approximately 4.33 percent of the total—yet they employed just over 44 percent of all production employees and produced 58.6 percent of all manufacturing

Exhibit 8–6 Canadian Manufacturing Establishments by Number of Employees

	Under 5	*5–9*	*10–19*	*20–49*	*50–99*	*100–199*	*200–499*	*500–999*	*1,000 +*	*Total*
Number of establishments	11,166	7,086	6,522	7,572	3,920	2,254	1,302	318	122	40,262
Percentage of total establishments	27.73%	17.60%	16.20%	18.81%	9.74%	5.60%	3.23%	0.79%	0.30%	100%
Number of employees	23,500	44,007	82,758	207,315	218,668	245,097	293,881	159,289	198,817	1,473,332
Percentage of employees	1.60%	2.99%	5.62%	14.07%	14.84%	16.64%	19.95%	10.81%	13.49%	100%
Percentage of manufacturing shipments	1.0%	1.45%	3.13%	8.80%	11.45%	15.57%	22.49%	13.33%	22.78%	100%

Source: Statistics Canada, *Manufacturing Industries of Canada: National and Provincial Areas,* October 1991, Cat. 31-203 (Ottawa: Ministry of Supply and Services).

shipments. These large plants are important, and it may be desirable to segment industrial markets on the basis of size.

In other countries, the size distribution of manufacturers varies. But across different countries, the same general conclusion holds: it is often desirable to segment industrial markets on the basis of customer size because large plants do so much of the buying.

Customer cluster in geographic areas

In addition to concentration by company size, industrial markets are concentrated in certain geographic areas. Internationally, industrial customers are concentrated in countries that are at the more advanced stages of economic development. Within a country, there is often further concentration in specific areas. In Canada, for example, many factories are concentrated in big metropolitan areas, especially near Montreal and in Southern Ontario. Exhibits 8–7 and 8–8 show how Canadian manufacturing is distributed by province and by industry group.

Exhibit 8–7 Number of Manufacturing Establishments and Value of Shipments by Province

Province	*Number of Establishments*	*Percentage of Establishments*	*Value of Shipments ($000,000)*	*Percentage Value of Shipments*
Newfoundland	347	0.86%	$ 1,726.0	0.58 %
Prince Edward Island	146	0.36	391.7	0.13
Nova Scotia	816	2.02	5,455.7	1.83
New Brunswick	765	1.9	5,627.7	1.89
Quebec	12,073	29.98	73,750.6	24.73
Ontario	16,477	40.92	157,540.2	52.82
Manitoba	1,299	3.23	6,671.0	2.24
Saskatchewan	866	2.15	3,380.1	1.13
Alberta	2,966	7.36	18,100.5	6.07
British Columbia	4,471	11.10	25,510.1	8.55
Yukon	18	0.05	14.2	0.004
Northwest Territories	18	0.05	42.7	0.001
Canada	40,262	100.00%	$298,210.5	100.00 %

Source: Statistics Canada, *Manufacturing Industries of Canada: National and Provincial Areas,* October 1991, Cat. 31-203 (Ottawa: Ministry of Supply and Services).

Exhibit 8–8   Value of Manufacturing Shipments by Industry Group

Industry Group	Value (000,000)	Percentage of Total Value
Foods industries	$ 37,733	13.6 %
Beverage industries	5,900	2.1
Tobacco products industries	2,077	0.7
Rubber products industries	2,439	0.9
Plastic products industries	5,547	2.0
Leather and allied products industries	996	0.36
Primary textile industries	2,610	0.9
Textile products industries	2,899	1.0
Clothing industries	5,945	2.1
Wood industries	12,964	4.7
Furniture and fixture industries	3,808	1.4
Paper and allied products industries	21,466	7.7
Printing, publishing, and allied industries	12,411	4.5
Primary metal industries	17,794	6.4
Fabricated metal products industries	16,060	5.8
Machinery industries	8,853	3.2
Transportation equipment industries	49,355	17.8
Electrical and electronic products industries	17,820	6.4
Nonmetallic mineral products industries	6,231	2.2
Refined petroleum and coal products industries	16,857	6.1
Chemical and chemical products industries	22,186	8.0
Other manufacturing industries	5,872	2.1
Total	$227,824	

Source: Statistics Canada, *Monthly Survey of Manufacturing,* March 1992, Cat. 31-001 (Ottawa: Ministry of Supply and Services).

Concentration by industry

We see concentrations not only by size of firm and geographic location but also by industry. Iron and steel mills cluster in Ontario, while flour mills are in Saskatchewan. Paper and allied industries tend to group in Quebec and British Columbia. Other industries have concentration patterns based on the availability of natural or human resources.

Much data is available on industrial markets by SIC codes

The products an industrial customer needs to buy depend on the business it is in. Because of this, sales of a product are often concentrated among customers in similar businesses. For example, apparel manufacturers are the main customers for buttons. Marketing managers who can relate their own sales to their customers' type of business can focus their efforts.

Detailed information is often available to help a marketing manager learn more about customers in different lines of business. The federal government regularly collects and publishes data by **Standard Industrial Classification (SIC) codes**—groups of firms in similar lines of business. The number of establishments, sales volumes, and number of employees, broken down by geographic areas, are given for each SIC code. A number of other countries collect similar data, and some of them try to coordinate their efforts with an international variation of the SIC system. However, in many countries data on business customers is incomplete or inaccurate.

In Canada, SIC code breakdowns start with broad industry categories such as food and related products (code 20), tobacco products (code 21), textile mill

Exhibit 8–9   SIC Analysis of the Sawmill and Planing Mill Products Industry

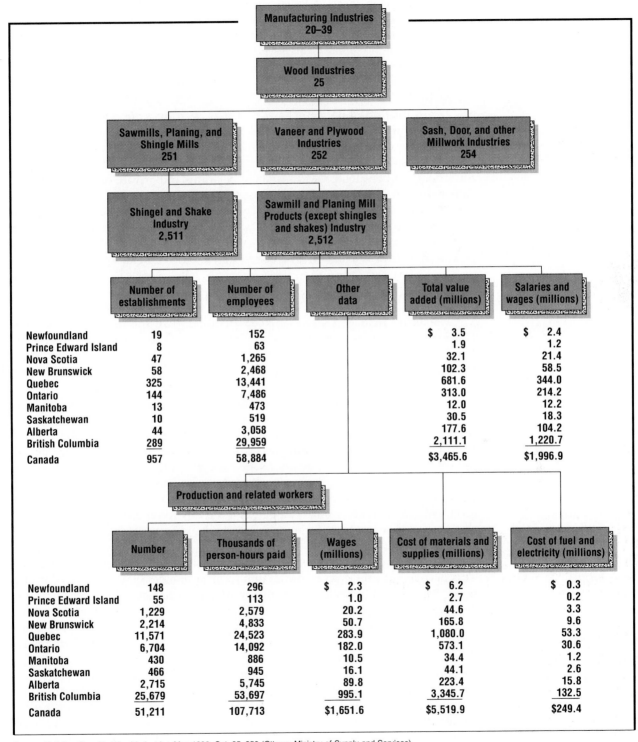

	Number of establishments	Number of employees	Other data	Total value added (millions)	Salaries and wages (millions)
Newfoundland	19	152		$ 3.5	$ 2.4
Prince Edward Island	8	63		1.9	1.2
Nova Scotia	47	1,265		32.1	21.4
New Brunswick	58	2,468		102.3	58.5
Quebec	325	13,441		681.6	344.0
Ontario	144	7,486		313.0	214.2
Manitoba	13	473		12.0	12.2
Saskatchewan	10	519		30.5	18.3
Alberta	44	3,058		177.6	104.2
British Columbia	289	29,959		2,111.1	1,220.7
Canada	957	58,884		$3,465.6	$1,996.9

	Number	Thousands of person-hours paid	Wages (millions)	Cost of materials and supplies (millions)	Cost of fuel and electricity (millions)
Newfoundland	148	296	$ 2.3	$ 6.2	$ 0.3
Prince Edward Island	55	113	1.0	2.7	0.2
Nova Scotia	1,229	2,579	20.2	44.6	3.3
New Brunswick	2,214	4,833	50.7	165.8	9.6
Quebec	11,571	24,523	283.9	1,080.0	53.3
Ontario	6,704	14,092	182.0	573.1	30.6
Manitoba	430	886	10.5	34.4	1.2
Saskatchewan	466	945	16.1	44.1	2.6
Alberta	2,715	5,745	89.8	223.4	15.8
British Columbia	25,679	53,697	995.1	3,345.7	132.5
Canada	51,211	107,713	$1,651.6	$5,519.9	$249.4

Source: Statistics Canada, *Wood Industries,* May 1992, Cat. 35-250 (Ottawa: Ministry of Supply and Services).

products (code 22), apparel (code 23), and so on. Within each two-digit industry breakdown, much more detailed data may be available for three-digit and four-digit industries (that is, subindustries of the two- or three-digit industries). Exhibit 8–9 gives an example of more detailed breakdowns within the sawmill and planing mill products industry. Four-digit detail isn't available for all industries in every geographic area because the government does not provide data when only one or two plants are located in that area.

Many firms find their *current* customers' SIC codes and then look at SIC-coded lists for similar companies that may need the same goods and services. Other companies look at which SIC categories are growing or declining to discover new opportunities. If companies aiming at business target markets in Canada know exactly who they are aiming at, readily available data organized by SIC codes can be valuable. Most trade associations and private organizations that gather data on business markets also use SIC codes.

SIC codes are not perfect. Some companies have sales in several categories but are listed in only one—the code with the largest sales. In addition, some newer businesses don't fit any of the categories very well. So although a lot of good information is available, the codes must be used carefully.[12]

PRODUCERS OF SERVICES—SMALLER AND MORE SPREAD OUT

Marketing managers need to keep in mind that the service side of the Canadian economy is large and has been growing fast. Service operations are also growing in some other countries. There may be good opportunities in providing these companies with the products they need to support their operations. But there are also challenges.

There are about 2 million service firms in North America—about six times as many as there are manufacturers. Some of these are big companies with international operations. Examples include The Royal Bank, Four Seasons Hotels, and Canada Post. These firms have purchasing departments that are like those in large manufacturing organizations. But, as you might guess given the large number of service firms, most of them are small. They're also more spread out around the country than manufacturing concerns. Factories often locate where transportation facilities are good, raw materials are available, and it is less costly to produce goods in quantity. Service operations, in contrast, usually have to be close to their customers.

Buying may not be as formal

Purchases by small service firms are often handled by whoever is in charge. This may be a doctor, lawyer, owner of a local insurance agency, or manager of a hotel. Suppliers who usually deal with purchasing specialists in large organizations may have trouble adjusting to this market. Personal selling is still an important part of promotion, but reading these customers in the first place often requires more advertising. And small service firms may need much more help in buying than a large corporation.

One Japanese company, Canon, capitalized on such needs. Canon knew that Xerox, the familiar name in office copiers, was very successful selling to larger accounts. But Xerox's sales force was not as good at serving the needs of smaller service firms like law offices. Canon seized this opportunity. It developed promotion materials to help first-time buyers understand differences in copiers. It emphasized that its machines were easy to use and maintain. And Canon also used retail channels to make the copiers available in smaller areas where there wasn't enough business to justify using a sales rep. As a result, Canon has been very successful in this market.[13]

SIC data on services is coming

The basic SIC system was set up when Canada was primarily a manufacturing and raw materials economy with less emphasis on services. While the SIC codes have been updated over time, they don't give much detail on service firms. Efforts are now underway to update the SIC system to provide better information on service markets, but it may be some time before detailed data is available.

RETAILERS AND WHOLESALERS BUY FOR THEIR CUSTOMERS

Most retail and wholesale buyers see themselves as purchasing agents for their target customers—remembering the old saying that "Goods well bought are half sold." Typically, retailers do *not* see themselves as sales agents for particular manufacturers. They buy what they think they can sell. And wholesalers buy what they think their retailers can sell. They don't try to make value judgments about the desirability or worth of what they're selling. Rather, they focus on the needs and attitudes of *their* target customers. For example, Super Valu—an $11 billion a year food wholesaler—calls itself "the retail support company." As a top manager at Super Valu put it, "Our mandate is to try to satisfy our retailer customers with *whatever it takes.*"[14]

Reorders are straight rebuys

Retailers and wholesalers usually carry a large number of products. A drug wholesaler, for example, may carry up to 125,000 products. Because they deal with so many products, most middlemen buy their products on a routine, automatic reorder basis—straight rebuys—once they make the initial decision to stock specific items. Sellers to these markets must understand the size of the buyer's job and have something useful to say and do when they call. For example, they might try to save the middleman time by taking inventory, setting up displays, or arranging shelves—while trying to get a chance to talk about specific products and maintain the relationship.

Buyers watch computer output closely

Most larger firms now use sophisticated computerized inventory control systems. Scanners at retail checkout counters keep track of what goes out the door—and computers use this data to update the records. Even small retailers and wholesalers use automated control systems that can print daily unit control reports showing sales of every product on their shelves. This is important to marketing managers selling to such firms because buyers with this kind of information know, in detail, the profitability of the different competing products. If a manufacturer's product isn't moving, the retailer isn't likely to be impressed by a salesperson's request for more in-store attention or added shelf space.

Automatic computer ordering is a natural outgrowth of computerized checkout systems. Canadian Tire dealers, for example, are able to monitor inventory levels and place orders through the company's computer system.[15]

Some are not "open to buy"

Retail buyers are sometimes controlled by a miniature profit and loss statement for each department or merchandise line. In an effort to make a profit, the buyer tries to forecast sales, merchandise costs, and expenses. The figure for "cost of merchandise" is the amount buyers have budgeted to spend over the budget period. If the money has not yet been spent, buyers are **open to buy**—that is, the buyers have budgeted funds that can be spent during the current period. However, if the budget has been spent, they are no longer in the market and no amount of special promotion or price-cutting is likely to induce them to buy.[16]

Buying and selling are closely related

In wholesale and retail firms, there is usually a very close relationship between buying and selling. Buyers are often in close contact with their firm's salespeople and with customers. The housewares buyer for a department store, for example, may even supervise the salespeople who sell housewares. Salespeople are quick to tell the buyer if a customer wants a product that is not available—especially if the salespeople work on commission. A buyer may even buy some items to satisfy the preferences of salespeople. Therefore, salespeople should not be neglected in the promotion effort.

Committee buying is impersonal

Some buyers—especially those who work for big retail chains—are annoyed by the number of wholesalers' and manufacturers' representatives who call on them. Space in their stores is limited and they simply are not interested in carrying every product that some salesperson wants them to sell. Consider the problem facing grocery chains. In an average week, 150 to 250 new items are offered to the buying offices of a large chain like Safeway. If the chain accepted all of them, it would add 10,000 new items during a single year! Obviously, these firms need a way to deal with this overload.[17]

Because of situations like this, in some firms the major decisions to add or drop lines or change buying policies may be handled by a *buying committee*. The seller still calls on and gives a pitch to a buyer—but the buyer does not have final responsibility. Instead, the buyer prepares forms summarizing proposals for new products and passes them on to the committee for evaluation. The seller may not get to present his or her story to the buying committee in person. This rational, almost cold-blooded, approach reduces the impact of a persuasive salesperson.

Wholesalers' and manufacturers' marketing managers must develop good marketing mixes when buying becomes this sophisticated and competitive. And such situations are more common now that so many retailers use computers to improve sales analysis and inventory control.

Resident buyers may help a firm's buyers

Resident buyers are independent buying agents who work in central markets (Toronto, Paris, Rome, Hong Kong, Montreal, etc.) for several retailer or wholesaler customers based in outlying areas or other countries. They buy new styles and fashions and fill-in items as their customers run out of stock during the year. Some resident buyers have hundreds of employees—and buy more than $1 billion worth of goods a year.

Resident buying organizations fill a need. They help small channel members (products and middlemen) reach each other inexpensively. Resident buyers usually are paid an annual fee based on their purchases.

THE FARM MARKET

Agriculture still plays an important role in the Canadian economy. Agricultural production continues to climb from year to year, and agricultural exports account for about one-fifth of all foreign exchange earned.[18] However, farm incomes are greatly influenced by prices received for crops, cost of supplies purchased, and interest rates.

The number of farms has slowly and steadily declined for many years. Average farm size, on the other hand, continues to increase. Although there are still many small units, large farms produce most of the output. The modern commercial farm is highly mechanized, highly specialized, and capital-intensive.[19] Owners of large farms tend to run them as a business rather than a way of life. They respond to sales presentations stressing savings and increases in productivity. Further, they're more knowledgeable and receptive to change than those running smaller operations—and they may have the money to buy what they need.

For some products, however, farmer buying motivations aren't much different from those for consumer goods. This is understandable, since a farmer's home and place of business are the same. Some manufacturers take pride in their office facilities and factories, and the same sort of motive may affect farmer purchasing behavior. And among owners of smaller farms, a new tractor may offer just as much status as a new car would to an urban resident. Also, the farmer's roles in business and as a final consumer sometimes overlap. For example, a station wagon might be used for carrying both feed and the family's groceries. Thus, motives of final consumers and business managers may coincide.

Farmers tend to specialize in one or a few products such as wheat and other grains, dairy, and poultry. These specializations have developed in response to geographic and climatic regions. A farmer in the Prairies growing wheat has different needs from a farmer in Ontario or Quebec engaged in the dairy business. Or a fruit farmer in the Niagara Peninsula would have different needs from a fruit farmer in British Columbia, where fruit is grown on irrigated terraces.

Marketing mixes may have to be developed for each type of farm and, occasionally, even for individual farmers. Fertilizer producers, for example, have moved far beyond selling an all-purpose bag of fertilizer. Now they're able to blend the exact type needed for each farm. Then they load directly onto fertilizer spreaders that do the job more economically than manual methods. Some producers, in fact, are working directly with farmers, providing a complete service, including fertilizing, weeding, and debugging—all tailored to each individual farmer's needs.[20]

Agriculture is becoming agribusiness

Another important factor is the increasing tendency for farmers to engage in **contract farming.** Here, the farmer obtains supplies and perhaps working capital from local dealers or manufacturers that agree to purchase that farm's output, sometimes at guaranteed prices. This limits farmers' buying freedom, since they become, in effect, employees. Such arrangements are becoming more frequent, especially in raising chickens and turkeys and in growing fresh vegetables for commercial canning. A farmer, for example, may contract with Maple Leaf Foods, which will supply chicks and feed. The company, in turn, will receive all the chickens that farmer produces. Such arrangements offer security, but they also limit the markets for sellers. It's all part of the move toward bigger and more businesslike agricultural enterprises—what's called **agribusiness.**

Where such contractual arrangements (or actual ownership) are common, marketing managers will have to adjust their marketing mixes. They may have to sell directly to the large manufacturers or dealers handling the arrangements rather than to each farmer.

Farmers are a market, of course, because farm products are themselves marketed. This is done through a mix of private trading, public sales and auctions, sales under contract, sales through cooperatives, and sales by marketing boards.

Methods vary with the type of product, the region, and the preference of producers. Most products, except western grains and a few special crops, are marketed in more than one way.

For many years, large central markets served as price-making centres for agricultural products. These were places where supply and demand forces came together. It's no longer economically feasible, however, for all commodities of a given type to be brought together when buying and selling occurs. With the introduction of standardized grading procedures, it's no longer necessary to do so.

Canada's principal livestock markets are at Montreal, Toronto, Winnipeg, Calgary, and Edmonton, but there are many other outlets ranging from large stockyards to country collection points. Egg sales are regulated by the Canadian Egg Marketing Agency, and the Canadian Turkey Marketing Agency performs similar services for turkey producers. Marketing fluid milk is a provincial responsibility, with quality, prices, and deliveries regulated by provincial marketing agencies. Fruits and vegetables are distributed through fresh and frozen food markets, canneries, and other processors. Most products are grown under a contract or a prearranged marketing scheme.[21]

Marketing boards

Marketing boards are an important type of marketing institution for agricultural products. For example, the Canadian Wheat Board is responsible for marketing wheat and barley grown in western Canada. In Ontario, all wheat is sold through the Ontario Wheat Producers' Marketing Board.

Other products sold under marketing boards include hogs, milk, fruit, potatoes and other vegetables, tobacco, poultry, eggs, wood, soybeans, honey, maple products, and pulpwood. There are 2 federally authorized marketing boards operating in Canada and over 100 provincial ones. Although these boards differ in the powers they can exercise, their mandate generally includes pricing, quotas for production and/or marketing, licensing, promotion, and the control of interprovincial and export trade.[22]

However, the future of marketing boards is uncertain. The General Agreement on Tariffs and Trade (GATT) is opposed to making exceptions for supply-management schemes in the agricultural sector. If a trade deal is struck, marketing boards may be permitted to exist temporarily, but later may be replaced with tariffs, which also would eventually be eliminated.

It is unclear what this will mean for the Canadian agricultural sector. Some say that increased competition from other countries will destroy Canadian farming. Others believe that farmers' income will actually increase. Most farmers, however, are against the abolition of marketing boards and the protection they offer in the domestic market.[23]

THE GOVERNMENT MARKET

Size and diversity

Governments in Canada are a very large and concentrated market. On the federal level, for example, much of the buying is done through Supply and Services Canada, a department that purchases billions of dollars' worth of goods and services a year for other federal departments and agencies. The Department of National Defense is generally Canada's largest single customer. Other major purchasers include the Canadian Commercial Corporation (a Crown corporation that helps foreign governments purchase goods made in Canada), Transport Canada, and Public Works Canada. Collectively, provincial and local govern-

Exhibit 8–10
Gross Expenditure, All
Levels of Government
(millions of dollars)

1965–66	$ 9,840
1975–76	42,661
1985–86	129,626
1990–91	177,378

Source: Statistics Canada,
Public Finance Historical Data,
1965/66–1991/92, Cat. 68-512
(Ottawa: Minister of Supply and
Services Canada, 1991).

ments are even more important markets than the federal government. Marketing Demo 8–3 describes some of the new, environmentally sound purchasing policies of the Toronto City and Metropolitan Toronto Councils.

Government expenditures for goods and services in select years are shown in Exhibit 8–10. Expenditures at all levels of government have grown by 1,700 percent since the mid 60s. They have started to slow down in the last decade but the growth rate is still very high. While this poses problems for Canada's deficit, it presents opportunities for Canada's marketers.

The range of goods and services purchased by government is vast, including everything from advertising services to appliances. Governments not only run schools, police departments, and military organizations, but also supermarkets, public utilities, research laboratories, offices, hospitals, and liquor stores. And it's

---

MARKETING DEMO 8–3
Environmentally Sound Purchasing

T oronto is big on the environmental three Rs: reduce, reuse, and recycle. While the municipality has been promoting recycling and the management of household waste among its ratepayers, the department of purchasing and supply has been driving a variety of environmental initiatives at City Hall.

"The environment should be moving up towards the top of anyone's list of sourcing criteria," says J. Darcy Duncan, commissioner for the department of purchasing and supply for the City of Toronto and the Municipality of Metropolitan Toronto. "In my opinion, the public is light-years ahead of private industry . . . and the public is going to demand from suppliers and retailers more environmentally sound action."

The City of Toronto and Metro councils' "Statement of Principle on Environmentally Sound Purchasing" declares that wherever possible and economical, all departments amend specifications to include goods and services that make use of a "maximum level" of postconsumer recyclable waste and/or recyclable content.

Procurement specifications have been revised to ensure, when technically possible, that products purchased by the city do not contain, or are not manufactured using, CFCs and halons. To reduce the possibility of CFCs escaping into the atmosphere, service contracts for air conditioners, freezers, and refrigerators have been changed, requiring contractors to use a refrigerant recovery system.

The purchasing department has been doing what it can to increase the demand for paper containing recycled materials. And the standards and specifications section is continually evaluating all kinds of recycled paper products in association with the clients.

Purchasing accounts for about $365 million a year in goods and services, covering items from police cars to live fish. "The fact we are spending $1 million a day of public money is a huge responsibility," says Duncan. "We are very sensitive to the integrity issue, sensitive to long-term supplier relationships, and very sensitive to our client requirements."

Purchasing has a rather extensive outreach in the selection of suppliers. Advertisements are placed in the Toronto newspapers, all ethnic papers, and all regional papers within the greater Toronto area. There are numerous trade shows throughout the year, and a brochure is sent out, printed in several languages, advising the community that the city wants to do business.

Public sector purchasing is an extremely open process, explains Duncan. There is scrutiny from almost every source imaginable, be it the public, the press, politicians, or the suppliers themselves. "The major difference is the private sector is very interested in who is getting the business. In the public sector, there's more interest in who isn't getting the business. It's important the process is right," he says.

Source: Joe Terrett, "Environmentally Sound Purchasing," *Modern Purchasing,* December 1990, pp. 12–14.

expected that government expenditures for these operations will continue to grow. Such opportunities can't be ignored by an aggressive marketing manager.

Government buying methods

Most goods and services are purchased through contracts awarded after a requisition is received from the department that needs these items. Any Canadian business supplying such goods and services is eligible to bid. The only requirements are a desire to sell and evidence of the ability to supply under the terms and conditions of the contract. Any size firm can bid—the overall size of government expenditures is no indication of the size of individual contracts. Despite the overall amount spent by government, firms of all sizes can and do bid for such business, since many thousands of contracts are for less than $10,000.

Bidding is common

Although bidding procedures vary slightly between departments and levels of government, similar practices are followed. Potential suppliers are invited to tender on a particular contract. The government department in question has drawn up its list of specifications carefully in order to clarify what any supplier must bid on and to simplify the selection procedure. The contract is then awarded to the firm submitting the lowest bid that also meets the specifications of the tender call.

Writing specifications isn't easy, and buyers usually appreciate knowledgeable salespeople's help. Salespeople *want* to have input on the specifications so their product can be considered or even have an advantage. One company may get the

Governments help seek out suppliers.

business—even with a bid that is not the lowest—because the lower bids don't meet minimum specifications.

Not all government purchases are made this way. Many branded or standardized items are routinely purchased through standing offer arrangements. These offers are issued to suppliers for specific time periods. They, in turn, agree to supply the goods or services at prearranged prices and delivery conditions. Pharmaceutical supplies, tires and tubes, and petroleum and oil are often bought this way. Invitations to tender on major construction contracts are both advertised and mailed to likely bidders.

Rigged specs are an ethical concern

At the extreme, a government customer who wants a specific brand or supplier may try to write the description so that no other supplier can meet all the specs. The buyer may have good reasons for such preferences—a more reliable product, prompt delivery, or better service after the sale. This kind of loyalty sounds great, but marketers must be sensitive to the ethical issues involved. Laws that require government customers to get bids are intended to increase competition among suppliers, not reduce it. Specs that are written primarily to defeat the purpose of these laws may be viewed as illegal bid rigging.

Negotiated contracts are common, too

Contracts may be negotiated for items that are not branded or easily described, for products that require research and development, or in cases where there is no effective competition. Depending on the government unit involved, the contract may be subject to audit and renegotiation, especially if the contractor makes a larger profit than expected.

Negotiation is often necessary when there are many intangible factors. Unfortunately, this is exactly where favoritism and influence can slip in. Nevertheless, negotiation is an important buying method in government sales—so a marketing mix should emphasize more than just low price.[24]

Learning what government wants

Since most government contracts are advertised, a prospective supplier can focus on particular government agencies or departments. Marketers can learn about potential government target markets using the assistance available from government publications. For example, Supply and Services Canada offers a purchasing and sales directory that explains its procedures.[25] Information on successful bidders for contracts of $10,000 and over is found in a *Weekly Bulletin of Business Opportunities*. Research and development contract awards information appears in a monthly *Research and Development Bulletin*. Invitations to tender (or submit bids) on projects are advertised by Public Works Canada.

Various provincial and local governments also offer assistance. Trade magazines and trade associations provide information on how to reach schools, hospitals, highway departments, park departments, and so on. These are unique target markets and must be treated as such when developing marketing strategies.

Of course, marketers interested in selling to provincial and local governments must be aware of any "province-first" procurement policies. Most of the provinces tend to favor local suppliers at the expense of firms manufacturing elsewhere. Although provincial preference in purchasing may make political sense, it poses real problems for firms trying to sell nationally in what's already a very small "Internal Common Market."[26] Marketing Demo 8–4 presents the Canadian Manufacturers' Association case against interprovincial trade barriers.

MARKETING DEMO 8–4   The Case for a Canadian Common Market

Canada's productivity is being undermined by hundreds of interprovincial barriers to trade in goods and services affecting an estimated 10 to 15 percent of gross domestic product. The provincial and federal governments are fully aware of the problem but are moving far too slowly to address it. To accelerate this process, the Canadian Manufacturers' Association (CMA) is calling on provincial premiers and the federal government to adopt a three-year plan to eliminate all interprovincial barriers to trade.

Interprovincial trade barriers have been around since Confederation and have been used to support the development of local and regional firms in industry, services, and agriculture. Their growth has been spurred over the last 30 years by the belief that regional economies and specific sectors need protection to grow and to safeguard employment. The number of interprovincial trade barriers is now estimated to approach 500. If nothing is done to arrest this trend, barriers will likely continue to increase and adversely influence Canada's ability to grow and compete internationally.

A single market would strengthen Canada. Creating a single economic market in Canada would help counter the current regional drift. It would thereby strengthen Canada both economically and politically.

A single market would promote competitiveness. Interprovincial trade barriers have divided Canada's relatively small domestic market, particularly for the types of goods and services used by the public sector. Discriminatory procurement policies have resulted in the duplication of manufacturing, construction, and services activities across the country. Eliminating interprovincial trade barriers affecting government procurement, alcoholic beverages, and agricultural products would promote the growth of more specialized and productive firms. This would encourage firms to compete more aggressively at home and abroad, thereby enhancing Canada's competitiveness and exports.

A single market could save billions of tax dollars. The total estimated savings from the creation of a single market exceed $6 billion annually. These savings come from many areas. First, a single market for government goods and services procurement could lead to savings estimated at 5 percent of this $100 billion market. Second, the removal of interprovincial trade barriers to agricultural and alcoholic products would allow a rationalization of these sectors, with significant savings accruing to consumers. Third, removing barriers to labor mobility would increase Canadians' freedom to move and work where they choose. Fourth, these economic measures would create a more flexible economy—and flexibility is the best guaranty of success in an era of rapid economic change. Lastly, the combination of these measures would strengthen the political union by increasing the economic interdependence of the provinces.

Canada must learn from the European experience. The creation of a single European market is driven by the knowledge that this is essential to maintaining its competitive position. The "single market" initiative is forecast to increase Europe's total GDP by more than 5 percent. This will make Europeans both richer and more productive. Canada must learn from the "EC 1992" experience, put aside its parochialism, and embark on its own process to create a single market.

Source: Todd Rutley, " 'Canada 1993,' A Plan for the Creation of a Single Economic Market in Canada," The Canadian Manufacturers' Association, April 1991.

Dealing with foreign governments

Government agencies around the world spend a great deal of money, and they are important target customers for some firms. But selling to government units in foreign countries can be a real challenge. In many cases, a firm must get permission from the government in its own country to sell to a foreign government. Moreover, most government contracts favor domestic suppliers if they are available. Even if such favoritism is not explicit, public sentiment may make it very difficult for a foreign competitor to get a contract. Or the government bureaucracy may simply bury a foreign supplier in so much red tape that there's no way to win.

CONCLUSION

In this chapter, we considered the number, size, location, and buying habits of various types of organizational customers—to try to identify logical dimensions for segmenting markets. We saw that the nature of the buyer and the buying situation are relevant. We also saw that the problem-solving models of buyer behavior introduced in Chapter 7 apply here—with modifications.

The chapter focuses on aspects of buying behavior that often apply to different types of organizational customers. However, we discussed some key differences in the manufacturer, middleman, and government markets.

A clear understanding of organizational buying habits, needs, and attitudes can aid marketing strat-

egy planning. And since there are fewer organizational customers than final consumers, it may even be possible for some marketing managers (and their salespeople) to develop a unique strategy for each potential customer.

This chapter offers some general principles that are useful in strategy planning, but the nature of the products being offered may require adjustments in the plans. Different product classes are discussed in Chapter 9. Variations by product may provide additional segmenting dimensions to help a marketing manager fine-tune a marketing strategy.

QUESTIONS AND PROBLEMS

1. Compare and contrast the problem-solving approaches used by final consumers and organizational buyers.

2. Describe the situations that would lead to the use of the three different buying processes for a particular product—lightweight bumpers for a pickup truck.

3. Compare and contrast the buying processes of final consumers and organizational buyers.

4. Briefly discuss why a marketing manager should think about who is likely to be involved in the buying centre for a particular purchase. Is the buying centre idea useful in consumer buying? Explain your answer.

5. If a nonprofit hospital were planning to buy expensive MRI scanning equipment (to detect tumors), who might be involved in the buying centre? Explain your answer and describe the types of influence that different people might have.

6. Why would an organizational buyer want to get competitive bids? What are some of the situations when competitive bidding can't be used?

7. How likely would each of the following be to use competitive bids: (a) a small town that

needed a road resurfaced, (b) a scouting organization that needed a printer to print its scouting handbook, (c) a hardware retailer that wants to add a new lawn mower line, (d) a grocery store that wants to install a new checkout scanner, and (e) a sorority that wants to buy a computer to keep track of member dues? Explain your answers.

8. Discuss the advantages and disadvantages of just-in-time supply relationships from an organizational buyer's point of view. Are the advantages and disadvantages merely reversed from the seller's point of view?

9. IBM has a long-term negotiated contract with Microsoft, a supplier that provides the software operating system for IBM computers. Discuss several of the issues that IBM might want the contract to cover.

10. Would a toy manufacturer need a different marketing strategy for a big retail chain like Toys "R" Us than for a single toy store run by its owner? Discuss your answer.

11. How do you think a furniture manufacturer's buying habits and practices would be affected by the specific type of product to be purchased?

Consider fabric for upholstered furniture, a lathe for the production line, cardboard for shipping cartons, and lubricants for production machinery.

12. Discuss the importance of target marketing when analyzing organizational markets. How easy is it to isolate homogeneous market segments in these markets?

13. Explain how SIC codes might be helpful in evaluating and understanding business markets. Give an example.

14. Considering the nature of retail buying, outline the basic ingredients of promotion to retail buyers. Does it make any difference what kinds of products are involved? Are any other factors relevant?

15. The government market is obviously an extremely large one, yet it is often slighted or even ignored by many firms. Red tape is certainly one reason, but there are others. Discuss the situation and be sure to include the possibility of segmenting in your analysis.

SUGGESTED CASES

20. Mobay Chemicals, Inc.

34. E. D. Smith & Sons Limited

Elements of Product Planning for Goods and Services

When You Finish This Chapter, You Should

❶

Understand what "Product" really means.

❷

Know the key differences between goods and services.

❸

Know the differences among the various consumer and business product classes.

❹

Understand how the product classes can help a marketing manager plan marketing strategies.

❺

Understand what branding is and how to use it in strategy planning.

❻

Understand the importance of packaging in strategy planning.

❼

Understand the important new terms (shown in blue).

Go easy on the environment.

Oxygen-enriched Supremes reduce pollution.

Chevron Supreme and Chevron Supreme Plus are unsurpassed in B.C. at reducing tailpipe and evaporative emissions that contribute to pollution.

By increasing the oxygen content of our Supremes, we cut down the amount of carbon monoxide and hydrocarbon emissions, while delivering improved engine performance.

We also lowered the vapour pressure to reduce the tendency of the gasoline to evaporate during fill-ups.

Our reformulated Supremes are available year-round throughout the Lower Mainland and on Vancouver Island.

Start using them today. And go easy on the environment.

If you want to know more about Chevron gasolines call our toll-free Hotline at 1-800-663-1914.

Chevron. Your Town Pump.

Thanks to gasoline made with grain, cleaner air is on the horizon.

Cleaner gas from a wheat field? There's more than a grain of truth to it. It's from here that Mohawk takes surplus prairie grain and turns it into ethanol, the only truly natural gasoline additive.

Once we blend ethanol with our Regular and Premium gasolines, we've produced the cleanest burning gas in Western Canada.

In fact, it can reduce harmful exhaust emissions by up to 40%.

Cleaner gas. Cleaner air. And a cleaner environment for everyone, including the farmers who grow the wheat that makes the ethanol.

What's more, not only are Mohawk gasolines better for the environment, they're also good for your car. Our Regular Plus and Premium Plus have the highest octane ratings of any regular or premium gasolines in the west.

So next time you're thinking of a fill-up, think of wheat. And look towards a cleaner tomorrow.

For more information, please call toll-free, 1-800-667-4AIR

MOHAWK *Mother Nature's Gas Station.*

The words "Environmental Choice" and EcoLogo are official marks of Environment Canada. *40% for 10% ethanol-blends in Saskatchewan, Manitoba and Ontario. 20% for 5% ethanol-blends in B.C. and Alberta.

S ome people would say that gasoline is a commodity, that it doesn't matter whether you fill up at Petro-Canada or Esso except for possible price differences. Well, two Canadian oil companies are attempting to change that perception. Mohawk Oil of Burnaby, B.C., has built its entire marketing strategy around the environment, to the extent that is has dubbed itself "Mother Nature's Gas Station." Vancouver-based Chevron has also attempted to position itself as a green alternative through its advertising campaign. Says Jeff Campbell, Mohawk's advertising and promotions manager, "It's a marketing war out there and the environment is a major issue."

Both companies have changed the composition of their gasoline—Mohawk by blending it with ethanol and Chevron by mixing in oxygenate methyl tertiary butyl ether—in order to reduce emissions, as part of their long-term strategies. According to Roger Kestell, Chevron's vice president of marketing, "We don't believe we're green marketing as much as positioning ourselves correctly for the 1990s."[1]

THE PRODUCT AREA INVOLVES MANY STRATEGY DECISIONS

The gasoline example highlights some important topics we'll discuss in this chapter and the next. In this chapter, we'll cover the many different elements of product planning. In Chapter 10, we'll focus on the important role of new products and how to develop them.

Exhibit 9–1   Strategy Planning for Product

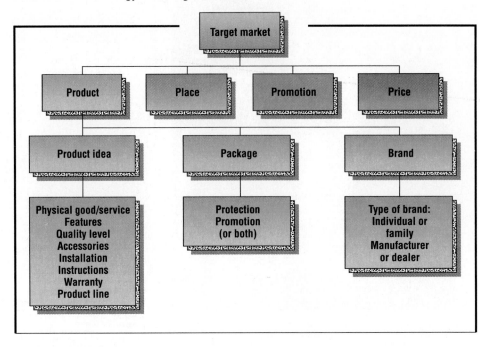

Here, we'll start by looking at how customers see a firm's product. Then we'll talk about product classes to help you better understand marketing strategy planning. We'll also talk about branding and packaging. Most goods need some packaging, and both goods and services should be branded. A successful marketer wants to be sure that satisfied customers know what to ask for the next time.

In summary, we'll cover the strategy planning of producers—and middlemen—who make these Product decisions. Keep in mind that there are many decisions related to the Product area, as shown in Exhibit 9–1.

WHAT IS A PRODUCT?

Customers buy
satisfaction, not parts

First, we have to define what we mean by a *product*.

When Honda sells an Acura, is it just selling a certain number of nuts and bolts, some sheet metal, an engine, and four wheels?

When Sico sells a can of exterior paint, is it just selling a can of chemicals?

When Air Jamaica sells a ticket for a flight to the Caribbean, is it just selling so much wear and tear on an airplane and so much pilot fatigue?

The answer to all these questions is *no*. Instead, what these companies are really selling is the satisfaction, use, or benefit the customer wants.

All most customers care about is that their cars look good and keep running. They want to protect their homes with paint—not analyze it. And when they take a trip on Air Jamaica, they really don't care how hard it is on the plane or the crew. They just want a safe, comfortable trip.

Because customers buy satisfaction, not just parts, marketing managers must be constantly concerned with the product quality of their goods and services.

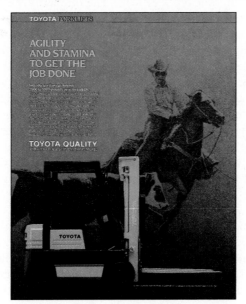

In the same way, when producers and middlemen buy a product, they're mainly interested in the profit they can make from its purchase—through use or resale—not how the product was made.

Product means the need-satisfying offering of a firm. The idea of Product as potential customer satisfaction or benefits is very important. Many business managers—trained in the production side of business—get wrapped up in the technical details. They think of Product in terms of physical components like transistors and screws. These are important to *them,* but components have little effect on the way most customers view the product. Most customers just want a product that satisfies their needs.

Product quality and customer needs

Because consumers buy satisfaction, not just parts, marketing managers must be constantly concerned with product quality. This may seem obvious, but the obvious is sometimes easy to overlook. In the 1980s, many North American firms learned this lesson the hard way when Japanese and European competitors stole market share by offering customers higher quality products. But what does "high quality" mean? Companies focus on better quality control in production—so that products work as they should and consumers really get what they think they're buying. But quality means more than that.

From a marketing perspective, **quality** means a product's ability to satisfy a customer's needs or requirements. This definition focuses on the customer—and how the customer thinks a product will fit some purpose. For example, the "best" credit card may not be the one with the highest credit limit but the one that's accepted where a consumer wants to use it. Similarly, the best quality clothing for casual wear on campus may be a pair of jeans—not a pair of dress slacks made of a higher grade fabric.

Among different types of jeans, the one with the strongest stitching and the most comfortable or durable fabric might be thought of as having the highest grade or *relative quality* for its product type. Marketing managers often focus on relative quality when comparing their products to competitors' offerings. However, a product with more features—or even better features—is not a high-quality product if the features aren't what the target market wants or needs.

Quality and satisfaction depend on the total product offering. If potato chips get stale on the shelf because of poor packaging, the consumer will be dissatisfied. A broken button on a shirt will disappoint the customer—even if the laundry did a nice job cleaning and pressing the collar. A powerful computer is a poor-quality product if it won't work with the software the customer wants to use—or if the seller doesn't answer the phone to respond to a customer's question about how to turn it on.[2]

Goods and/or services are the product

You already know that a product may be a physical *good* or a *service* or a *blend* of both. You need to understand this view thoroughly. It's too easy to slip into a limited, physical-product point of view. We want to think of a product in terms of the needs it satisfies. If a firm's objective is to satisfy customer needs, service can be part of its product—or service alone may *be* the product—and must be provided as part of a total marketing mix.

Exhibit 9–2 shows this bigger view of Product. It shows that a product can range from a 100 percent emphasis on physical goods—for commodities like common nails—to a 100 percent emphasis on service, like advice from a lawyer. Regardless of the emphasis involved, the marketing manager must consider most of the same elements in planning products and marketing mixes. Given this, we usually won't make a distinction between goods and services but will call all of them *Products*. Sometimes, however, understanding the differences in goods and services can help fine-tune marketing strategy planning. So let's look at some of these differences next.

Exhibit 9–2   Examples of Possible Blends of Physical Goods and Services in a Product

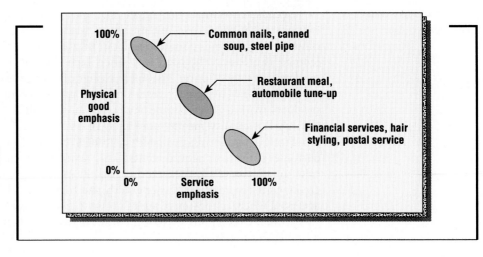

DIFFERENCES IN GOODS AND SERVICES

**How tangible
is the product?**

Because a good is a physical thing, it can be seen and touched. You can try on a Benetton shirt, thumb through the latest *Chatelaine* magazine, smell Colombian coffee as it brews. A good is a *tangible* item. When you buy it, you own it. And it's usually pretty easy to see exactly what you'll get.

On the other hand, a **service** is a deed performed by one party for another. When you provide a customer with a service, the customer can't keep it. Rather, a service is experienced, used, or consumed. You go see a Touchstone Studios movie, but afterwards all you have is a memory. You ride on a ski lift at Whistler, but you don't own the equipment. Services are not physical—they are *intangible*. You can't "hold" a service. And it may be hard to know exactly what you'll get when you buy it.

Most products are a combination of tangible and intangible elements. Petro-Canada gas and the credit card to buy it are tangible—the credit the card grants is not. A McDonald's hamburger is tangible—but the fast service is not.

**Is the product produced
before it's sold?**

Goods are usually produced in a factory and then sold. A Sony TV may be stored in a warehouse or store waiting for a buyer. By contrast, services are often sold first, then produced. And they're produced and consumed in the same time frame. You can't perform a deed and then put it on the shelf. Thus, goods producers may be far away from the customer, but service providers often work in the customer's presence.

A worker in a Sony TV factory can be in a bad mood—and customers will never know. And a faulty TV can be caught by a quality control inspector. But a rude bank teller can drive customers away. The growing use of computers and machines in service businesses is partly an attempt to avoid this problem. An automatic teller machine can't do everything, but it's never rude.

*A good is a physical thing;
a service is a deed performed
by one party for another.*

Services can't be stored
or transported

Services are perishable—they can't be stored. This makes it harder to balance supply and demand.

For example, Bell Canada is a major supplier of long-distance telephone services. Even when demand is high—during peak business hours or on Mother's Day—customers expect the service to be available. They don't want to hear "Sorry, all lines are busy." So Bell Canada must have enough equipment and employees to deal with peak demand times. But when customers aren't making many calls, Bell Canada's facilities are idle. Bell Canada might be able to save money with less capacity (equipment and people), but then it will sometimes have to face dissatisfied customers.

It's often difficult to have economies of scale when the product emphasis is on service. If a firm is serving a large group of customers, it may be able to justify adding more or better equipment, facilities, or people to do a better job. But services can't be produced in large, economical quantities and then transported to customers. In addition, *services often have to be produced in the presence of the customer.* So service suppliers often need duplicate equipment and staff at places where the service is actually provided. Merrill Lynch sells investment advice along with financial products worldwide. That advice could, perhaps, be produced more economically in a single building in Toronto. But Merrill Lynch uses small facilities all over Canada and other countries—to be conveniently available. Customers want a personal touch from the stockbroker telling them how to invest their money.[3]

Think about the
whole product

Providing the right product—when and where and how the customer wants it—is a challenge. This is true whether the product is primarily a service, primarily a good, or, as is usually the case, a blend of both. Marketing managers must think about the "whole" product they provide, and then make sure that all of the elements fit together—and work with the rest of the marketing strategy. Sometimes a single product isn't enough to meet the needs of target customers. Then, assortments of different products may be required.

WHOLE PRODUCT LINES MUST BE DEVELOPED, TOO

A **product assortment** is the set of all product lines and individual products that a firm sells. A **product line** is a set of individual products that are closely related. The seller may see them as related because they're produced and/or operate in a similar way, sold to the same target market, sold through the same types of outlets, or priced at about the same level. For example, Loblaw's, under its President's Choice brand and other labels, has many product lines in its product assortment, including tea, snacks, diapers, hosiery, and shampoo. But Tilden has one product line—different types of cars to rent. An **individual product** is a particular product within a product line. It usually is differentiated by brand, level of service offered, price, or some other characteristic. For example, each size of a brand of soap is an individual product.

Each individual product and target market may require a separate strategy. For example, Imasco's strategy for selling tobacco in Canada is different from its strategy for selling hamburgers in the United States. We'll focus mainly on developing one marketing strategy at a time. But remember that a marketing

Exhibit 9–3 Product Classes

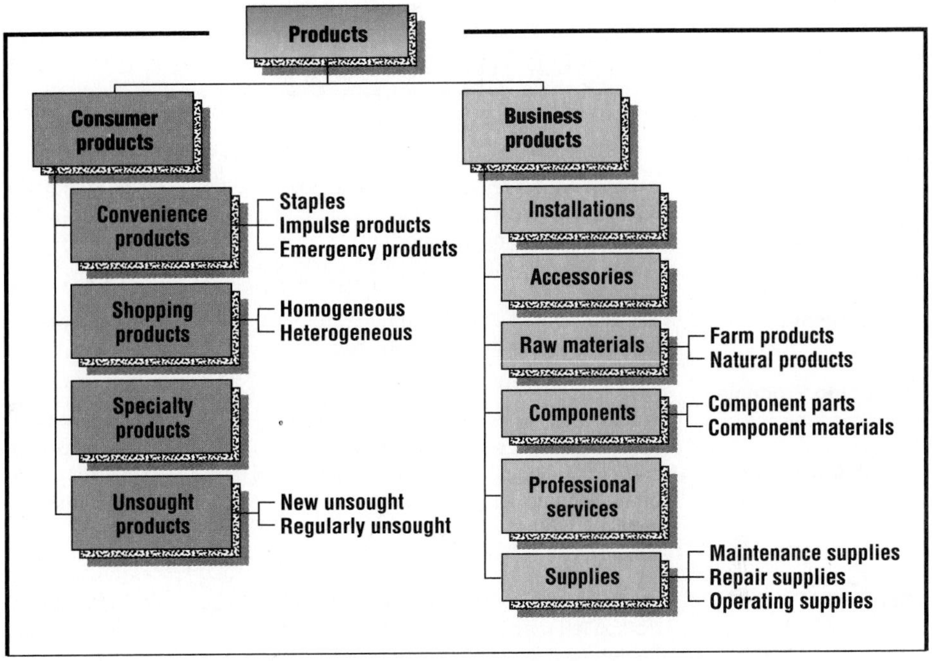

manager may have to plan *several* strategies to develop an effective marketing program for a whole company.

PRODUCT CLASSES HELP PLAN MARKETING STRATEGIES

You don't have to treat *every* product as unique when planning strategies. Some product classes require similar marketing mixes. These product classes are a useful starting point for developing marketing mixes for new products—and evaluating present mixes. Exhibit 9–3 summarizes the product classes.

Product classes start with type of customer

All products fit into one of two broad groups—based on the type of customer that will use them. **Consumer products** are products meant for the final consumer. **Business products** are products meant for use in producing other products. The same product—like Gatorade—*might* be in both groups. But selling the same product to both final consumers and business customers requires (at least) two different strategies.

There are product classes within each group. Consumer product classes are based on *how consumers think about and shop for products*. Business product classes are based on *how buyers think about products and how they'll be used*.

We'll talk about consumer product classes first.

CONSUMER PRODUCT CLASSES

Consumer product classes divide into four groups: (1) convenience, (2) shopping, (3) specialty, and (4) unsought. Each class is based on the way people buy

Exhibit 9–4   Consumer Product Classes and Marketing Mix Planning

Consumer Product Class	Marketing Mix Considerations	Consumer Behavior
Convenience Products		
Staples	Maximum exposure with widespread, low-cost distribution; mass selling by producer; usually low price; branding is important.	Routinized (habitual), low-effort, frequent purchases; low involvement.
Impulse	Widespread distribution with display at point of purchase.	Unplanned purchases bought quickly.
Emergency	Need widespread distribution near probable point of need; price sensitivity low.	Purchase made with time pressure when a need is great.
Shopping Products		
Homogeneous	Need enough exposure to facilitate price comparison; price sensitivity high.	Customers see little difference among alternatives; seek lowest price.
Heterogeneous	Need distribution near similar products; promotion (including personal selling) to highlight product advantages; less price sensitivity.	Extensive problem solving; consumer may need help in making a decision.
Speciality Products	Price sensitivity is likely to be low; limited distribution may be acceptable, but should be treated as a convenience or shopping product (in whichever category product would typically be included) to reach persons not yet sold on its specialty product status.	Willing to expend effort to get specific product, even if not necessary; strong preferences make it an important purchase.
Unsought Products		
New unsought	Must be available in places where similar (or related) products are sought; needs attention getting promotion.	Need for product not strongly felt; unaware of benefits or not yet gone through adoption process.
Regularly unsought	Requires very aggressive promotion, usually personal selling.	Aware of product but not interested; attitude toward product may even be negative.

products. See Exhibit 9–4 for a summary of how these product classes relate to marketing mixes.[4]

CONVENIENCE PRODUCTS—PURCHASED QUICKLY WITH LITTLE EFFORT

Convenience products are products a consumer needs but isn't willing to spend much time or effort shopping for. These products are bought often, require little service or selling, don't cost much, and may even be bought by habit.

The three types of convenience products—staples, impulse products, and emergency products—are again based on *how customers think about products*, not the features of the products themselves.

Staples—purchased regularly by habit

Staples are products that are bought often, routinely, and without much thought—like a favorite breakfast cereal, canned soup, and most other packaged foods used about every day in almost every household. Staples are usually sold in convenient places like food stores, discount stores, or vending machines. Branding is important with staples. It helps customers cut shopping effort and encourages repeat buying of satisfying brands.

Impulse products—
bought immediately
on sight

Impulse products are products that are bought quickly—as *unplanned* purchases—because of a strongly felt need. True impulse products are items that the customer hadn't planned to buy, decides to buy on sight, may have bought the same way many times before, and wants right now. An ice cream seller at a beach sells impulse products. If sun bathers don't buy an ice cream bar when the ice cream seller's bell is rung, the need goes away and the purchase probably won't be made later.

This buying behavior is important because it affects Place—and the whole marketing mix—for impulse products. If the buyer doesn't see an impulse product at the right time, the sale may be lost. That's why retailers put impulse products where they'll be seen and bought—near checkout counters or in other heavy traffic areas of the store. Grocery stores sell gum, candy bars, and magazines this way. And life insurance is sold in airports at convenient booths or vending machines.[5]

Emergency products—
purchased only when
urgently needed

Emergency products are products that are purchased immediately when the need is great. The customer doesn't have time to shop around when a traffic accident occurs, a thunderstorm begins, or an impromptu party starts. The price of the ambulance service, raincoat, or ice cubes won't be important.

Meeting customers' emergency needs may require a different marketing mix—especially regarding Place. Some small neighborhood stores carry "emergency" products to meet these needs—staying open 7 til 11 and stocking fill-in items like milk or bread. A towing service for cars is available 24 hours a day. Customers don't mind the higher prices charged for these purchases because they think of them as emergencies.

SHOPPING PRODUCTS—ARE COMPARED

Shopping products are products that a customer feels are worth the time and effort to compare with competing products.

Shopping products can be divided into two types, depending on what customers are comparing: (1) homogeneous and (2) heterogeneous shopping products.

Homogeneous shopping
products—the price
must be right

Homogeneous shopping products are shopping products the customer sees as basically the same—and wants at the lowest price. Some consumers feel that certain sizes and types of refrigerators, television sets, washing machines, and even cars are very similar. So they shop for the best price.

Firms may try to emphasize and promote their product differences to avoid head-to-head price competition. For example, Royal Trust offices in major Canadian cities offer customers a personal banker who provides information and advice. But if consumers don't think the differences are real or important, they'll just look at price.

Even some inexpensive products like butter or coffee may be considered homogeneous shopping products. *Some* people carefully read food store ads for the lowest prices—and then go from store to store for bargains. They don't do this for staples.

Heterogeneous shopping products—the product must be right

Heterogeneous shopping products are shopping products the customer sees as different—and wants to inspect for quality and suitability. Furniture, clothing, dishes, and some cameras are good examples. Quality and style matter more than price.

It's harder—but less important—to compare prices of nonstandardized items. Once the customer has found the right product, price may not matter—as long as it's reasonable. This is also true when service is a major part of the product, as in a visit to a doctor or car repair service.

Branding may be less important for heterogeneous shopping products. The more consumers compare price and quality, the less they rely on brand names or labels. Some retailers carry competing brands so consumers won't go to a competitor to compare items.

Often, the buyer of heterogeneous shopping products not only wants—but expects—some kind of help in buying. And if the product is expensive, the buyer may want *personalized* services—such as alteration of clothing or installation of appliances.

SPECIALTY PRODUCTS—NO SUBSTITUTES, PLEASE!

Specialty products are consumer products that the customer really wants—and makes a special effort to find. Shopping for a specialty product doesn't mean comparing—the buyer wants that special product and is willing to search for it. It's the customer's *willingness to search*—not the extent of searching—that makes it a specialty product.

Specialty products don't have to be expensive, once-in-a-lifetime purchases. Think of your last perfect haircut—and how long you waited for the barber or hairdresser you wanted. *Any* branded product that consumers insist on by name is a specialty product. People have been observed asking for a drug product by its brand name and—when offered a chemically identical substitute—actually leaving the store in anger.

UNSOUGHT PRODUCTS—NEED PROMOTION

Unsought products are products that potential customers don't yet want or know they can buy. So they don't search for them at all. In fact, consumers probably won't buy these products if they see them—unless Promotion can show their value.

There are two types of unsought products. **New unsought products** are products offering really new ideas that potential customers don't know about yet. Informative promotion can help convince customers to accept or even seek out the product—ending their unsought status. Yoplait Yogurt, Litton's microwave ovens, Sony's videotape recorders, and California Wine Coolers are all popular items now, but initially they were new unsought products because they were innovations—consumers didn't know what benefits they offered.

Regularly unsought products are products—like gravestones, life insurance, and encyclopedias—that stay unsought but not unbought forever. There may be a need, but potential customers aren't motivated to satisfy it. And there's little hope that gravestones will move out of the unsought class. For this kind of product, personal selling is *very* important.

Many nonprofit organizations try to "sell" their unsought products. For example, the Red Cross supplies blood to disaster victims. Few of us see donating blood as a big need. So the Red Cross regularly holds blood drives to remind prospective donors of how important it is to give blood.

ONE PRODUCT MAY BE SEEN AS SEVERAL CONSUMER PRODUCTS

We've been looking at product classes one at a time. But the same product might be seen in different ways by different target markets—at the same time. Each of these markets might need a different marketing mix.

A tale of four motels

Motels are a good example of a service that can be seen as four different kinds of consumer products. Some tired motorists are satisfied with the first motel they come to—a convenience product. Others shop for basic facilities at the lowest price—a homogeneous shopping product. Some shop for the kind of place they want at a fair price—a heterogeneous shopping product. And others study tourist guides, talk with traveling friends, and phone ahead to reserve a place in a recommended motel—a specialty product.

Perhaps one motel could satisfy *all* potential customers. But it would be hard to produce a marketing mix attractive to everyone—easy access for convenience, good facilities at the right price for shopping product buyers, and qualities special enough to attract specialty product travelers. That's why very different kinds of motels may at first seem to be competing with each other. But they're really aiming at different markets.

How consumers shop for a product often varies in different countries. In Japan, for example, motorists buy oil at an auto supply retailer and then take the 4-liter can to be installed. In North America, the oil and service are usually purchased at the same place.

| Product class is likely to vary by country | The consumer product classes are based on how consumers see products—and how they shop for them. It's important to keep in mind that consumers in different countries are likely to vary significantly on these dimensions. |

For example, a product viewed as a staple by most consumers in the United States, Canada, or some similar affluent country might be seen as a heterogeneous shopping product by consumers in another country. The price might be much higher when considered as a proportion of the consumer's budget, and the available choices might be very different. Similarly, a convenient place to shop often means very different things in different countries. In Japan, for example, retail stores tend to be much smaller and carry smaller selections of products.

The product class idea works in different countries, but marketers must look at the products from the viewpoint of the target customers, not from the marketer's.

Of course, marketing strategy planners need to know more about potential customers than how they buy specific products. But these classes are a good place to start strategy planning.

BUSINESS PRODUCTS ARE DIFFERENT

Business product classes are useful for developing marketing mixes, too—since business firms use a system of buying related to these product classes.

Before looking at business product differences, however, we'll note some important similarities that affect marketing strategy planning.

| One demand derived from another | The big difference in the business products market is **derived demand**—the demand for business products is derived from the demand for final consumer products. For example, car manufacturers buy about one-fifth of all steel products. Even a steel company with a good marketing mix will lose sales to car manufacturers if demand for cars drops.[6] |

| Price increases might not reduce quantity purchased | The fact that demand for most business products is derived means that total *industry* demand for such products is fairly inelastic. To satisfy their customers' needs, business firms buy what they need to produce their own products—almost regardless of price. Even if the cost of buttons doubles, for example, the shirt producer needs them. And the increased cost of the buttons won't have much effect on the price of the shirt—or on the number of shirts consumers demand. |

| But suppliers may face almost pure competition | Although the total industry demand for business products may be inelastic, the demand facing *individual sellers* may be extremely elastic—if competitive products are similar and there are many sellers. And to buy as economically as possible, sharp business buyers quickly tell suppliers that competitors are offering lower prices. |

| Tax treatment affects buying, too | How a firm's accountants—and the tax laws—treat a purchase is also important to business customers. A **capital item** is a long-lasting product that can be used and depreciated for many years. Often, it's very expensive. Customers pay for the capital item when they buy it, but for tax purposes the cost is spread over a number of years. This may increase current profits—and taxes—as well as reducing the cash available for other purchases. |

An **expense item** is a product whose total cost is treated as a business expense in the year it's purchased. This reduces current profits and taxes. It doesn't affect long-run profits. Business managers think about a decision's impact on taxes and profits, and this affects the way they look at the products they buy.

BUSINESS PRODUCT CLASSES—HOW THEY ARE DEFINED

Business product classes are based on how buyers see products—and how the products will be used. Firms treat capital items and expense items differently. Products that become part of a firm's own product are seen differently from those that only aid production. And the relative size of a particular purchase can make a difference. A band saw might be a major purchase for a small cabinet shop—but not for a large furniture manufacturer like Broyhill.

The classes of business products are (1) installations, (2) accessories, (3) raw materials, (4) components, (5) supplies, and (6) professional services. Exhibit 9–5 relates these product classes to marketing mix planning.

Exhibit 9–5 Business Product Classes and Marketing Mix Planning

Business Product Classes	Marketing Mix Considerations	Buying Behavior
Installations	Usually requires skilled personal selling by producer, including technical contacts, and/or understanding of applications; leasing and specialized support services may be required.	Multiple buying influence (including top management) and new-task buying are common; infrequent purchase, long decision period, and boom-or-bust demand are typical.
Accessory Equipment	Need fairly widespread distribution and numerous contacts by experienced and sometimes technically trained personnel; price competition is often intense, but quality is important.	Purchasing and operating personnel typically make decisions; shorter decision period than for installations.
Raw Materials	Grading is important, and transportation and storing can be crucial because of seasonal production and/or perishable products; markets tend to be very competitive.	Long-term contracts may be required to ensure supply.
Component Parts and Materials	Product quality and delivery reliability are usually extremely important; negotiation and technical selling typical on less-standardized items; replacement aftermarket may require different strategies.	Multiple buying influence is common; competitive bids used to encourage competitive pricing.
Maintenance, Repair, and Operating (MRO) Supplies	Typically require widespread distribution or fast delivery (repair items); arrangements with appropriate middlemen may be crucial.	Often handled as straight rebuys, except important operating supplies may be treated much more seriously and involve multiple buying influence.
Professional Services	Services customized to buyer's need; personal selling very important; inelastic demand often supports high prices.	Customer may compare outside service with what internal people could provide; needs may be very specialized.

INSTALLATIONS—MAJOR CAPITAL ITEMS

Installations—buildings, land rights, and major equipment—are important capital items. One-of-a-kind installations—office buildings and custom-made equipment—generally require special negotiations for each sale. Standard major equipment is more homogeneous and is treated more routinely. Even so, negotiations for installations involve top management and can stretch over months or even years.

Small number of customers at any one time

Installations are long-lasting products—so they aren't bought very often. The number of potential buyers *at any particular time* is usually small. Custom-made machines may have only a half-dozen potential customers—compared to a thousand or more for standard machines.

Installations, a boom-or-bust business

Installations are a boom-or-bust business. When sales are high, businesses want to expand capacity rapidly. And if the potential return on a new investment is very attractive, firms may accept any reasonable price. But during a downswing, buyers have little or no need for new installations and sales fall off sharply. Even during good times, buyers of installations may be able to request bids and buy in a very competitive market.

May have to be leased or rented

Since installations are relatively expensive, some target markets prefer to lease or rent. Leasing makes it easier for a firm to keep up with advancing technologies. Many firms lease computers so they can expand to bigger systems or incorporate new capabilities as they grow. Leasing also shifts a capital item to an expense item.[7]

Business customers often prefer to lease installations.

Owning your own trucks can cost you a lot of dough.

You own your trucks because you want control of your trucks. But what price are you paying for that control? If your truck breaks down, it can mean missed deliveries, unhappy customers and lost money.

With a Ryder Full Service Lease, you'll get more than custom-specified vehicles and a preventive maintenance program that keeps them running in top condition.

You'll get the competitive edge, because you'll have better control over getting your products into your customers' hands on time.

Ryder can also offer you advice on complex issues like unstable fuel supplies, EPA regulations, new technology, and finding qualified drivers, further decreasing your exposure to unnecessary surprises.

For a free "Lease Versus Own Analysis,"

call Ryder at 1-800-952-9515 and ask for extension 107.

You'll find out that switching to a Ryder Full Service Lease could win you customers and save you money. Or, as they say in the bakery business, bread. **RYDER.**

1-800-952-9515

Specialized services
are needed as part
of the product

To increase an installation's efficiency and the expected return on the buyer's investment, suppliers sometimes include special services at no extra cost. Installing the machine in the buyer's plant, training employees in its use, and supplying repair services are good examples of services that can become part of the final product. Firms selling equipment to dentists, for example, may help the dentist learn to use new equipment—and even provide plans for an office building to hold the equipment.

ACCESSORIES—IMPORTANT BUT SHORT-LIVED CAPITAL ITEMS

Accessories are short-lived capital items—tools and equipment used in production or office activities—like Canon's small copy machines, Sharp's fax machines, Rockwell's portable drills, Clark's electric lift trucks, Olivetti's electronic typewriters, and Steelcase's filing cabinets.

Since these products cost less and last a shorter time than installations, multiple buying influence is less important. Operating people and purchasing agents—rather than top managers—may make the purchase decision. As with installations, some customers may wish to lease or rent—to expense the cost.

More target markets
requiring different
marketing mixes

Accessories are more standardized than installations. And they're usually needed by more customers. For example, IBM sells its robotics systems, which can cost over $1 million, as custom installations to large manufacturers. But IBM's PS/2 desktop computers are accessory equipment for just about every type of modern business all around the world. And these different kinds of customers are spread out geographically. The larger number of different kinds of customers—and increased competition—means that accessories need different marketing mixes than installations.

Special services
may be attractive

Ordinarily, engineering services or special advice is less important for simpler accessory equipment. Yet some companies manage to add attractive services to their accessories—such as office furniture suppliers who offer decorating services and advice on office layout.

RAW MATERIALS—FARM AND NATURAL PRODUCTS ARE EXPENSE ITEMS

They become part
of a physical good

Raw materials are unprocessed expense items—such as logs, iron ore, wheat, and cotton—that are moved to the next production process with little handling. Unlike installations and accessories, *raw materials become part of a physical good—and are expense items*.

We can break raw materials into two types: (1) farm products and (2) natural products. **Farm products** are grown by farmers—examples are oranges, wheat, sugar cane, cattle, poultry, eggs, and milk. **Natural products** are products that occur in nature—such as fish and game, timber and maple syrup, and copper, zinc, iron ore, oil, and coal.

Raw materials involve
grading, storing, and
transporting

The need for grading is one of the important differences between raw materials and other business products. Nature produces what it will—and someone must sort and grade raw materials to satisfy various market segments. Top-graded fruits and vegetables may find their way into the consumer products

Raw cucumbers are sorted, graded, and inspected at the Dean Food Company pickle plant in Green Bay, Wisconsin.

market. Lower grades—which are treated as business products—are used in juices, sauces, and soups.

Raw materials are usually produced in specific geographic areas. In Canada, wheat is produced in Saskatchewan, coal in Nova Scotia, and timber in British Columbia. And many raw materials—like oranges and shrimp—are produced seasonally. Yet the demand for raw materials is geographically spread out and fairly constant all year. As a result, storing and transporting are important.

Large buyers may want long-term contracts

Most buyers of raw materials want ample supplies in the right grades for specific use—fresh vegetables for Birds Eye's production lines or logs for International Paper's paper mills. To ensure steady quantities, raw materials customers often sign long-term contracts, sometimes at guaranteed prices, for a supplier's output. Another way to ensure supply is to buy producers of raw materials. This makes it difficult or impossible for independent producers like family farmers or small coal mines to compete.

Farm products markets are more competitive

Individual producers of farm products usually face tougher competition than suppliers of natural products. There are many farmers—and nearly pure competition may exist. Farmers have to take the market price.

Natural products are usually produced by fewer and larger companies who can adjust supply to maintain stable prices. For example, the amount of iron ore mined in any one year can be adjusted up or down—at least within limits. And most natural products aren't perishable, so they can be easily stored to wait for better market conditions.

COMPONENT PARTS AND MATERIALS—IMPORTANT EXPENSE ITEMS

The whole is no better than . . .

Components are processed expense items that become part of a finished product. They need more processing than raw materials and require different marketing mixes than raw materials—even though they both become part of a finished product.

Component *parts* include items that are (1) finished and ready for assembly or (2) nearly finished—requiring only minor processing (such as grinding or polishing) before being assembled into the final product. Disk drives included in personal computers, batteries in cars, and motors for appliances are examples.

Component *materials* are items such as wire, paper, textiles, or cement. They have already been processed—but must be processed further before becoming part of the final product.

Components must meet specifications

Some components are custom-made. Much negotiation may be necessary between the engineering staffs of both buyer and seller to arrive at the right specifications. If the price of the item is high—or it is extremely important to the final product—top managers may be involved.

Other components are produced in quantity to accepted standards or specifications. Production people in the buying firm may specify quality—but the purchasing agent who does the buying often wants several dependable sources of supply.

Since components become part of the firm's own product, quality is extremely important. The buyer's own name and whole marketing mix are at stake—so a buyer tries to buy from sources that help ensure a good product.

Profitable replacement markets may develop

Since component parts go into finished products, a replacement market often develops. This *aftermarket* can be both large and very profitable. Car tires and batteries are two examples of components originally sold in the OEM (*original equipment market*) that become consumer products in the aftermarket. The target markets are different—and different marketing mixes are usually necessary.[8]

SUPPLIES—SUPPORT MAINTENANCE, REPAIR, AND OPERATIONS

Supplies are expense items that do not become part of a finished product. Buyers may treat these items less seriously. When a firm cuts its budget, orders for supplies may be the first to go.

They are called MRO supplies

Supplies can be divided into three types: (1) maintenance, (2) repair, and (3) operating supplies—giving them their common name: MRO supplies.

Maintenance supplies include products such as paint, light bulbs, and sweeping compounds. *Repair supplies* are parts—like filters, bearings, and gears—needed to fix worn or broken equipment. *Operating supplies* include lubricating oils and greases, grinding compounds, typing paper, paper clips, coal or electricity, and insurance.[9]

Important operating supplies

If operating supplies are needed regularly—and in large amounts—they receive special treatment from buyers. Many companies buy coal and fuel oil in railroad-car quantities. Usually, there are several sources for such homogeneous products—and large volumes may be purchased in highly competitive international markets. Or contracts may be negotiated, perhaps by top-level executives, to ensure lower prices and a continuing supply.

Maintenance and small operating supplies

These products are like convenience products. They're so numerous that a purchasing agent can't possibly be an expert in buying all of them.

Each requisition for maintenance and small operating supplies may be for relatively few items. Although a purchase order may amount to only $1 or $2, handling it may cost $5 to $10. The item will be ordered because it is needed—but buyers won't spend much time on it.

Branding may become important for such products because it makes product identification and buying easier for such "nuisance" purchases. Breadth of assortment and the seller's dependability are also important when buying supplies. Middlemen usually handle the many supply items.

Repair supplies

The original supplier of installations or accessory equipment may be the only source for repair needs. But compared to the cost of a production breakdown, the costs of repairs may be so small that buyers are willing to pay whatever the supplier charges.

PROFESSIONAL SERVICES—PAY TO GET IT DONE

Professional services are specialized services that support a firm's operations. They are usually expense items. Engineering or management consulting services can improve the plant layout—or the company's efficiency. Computer services can process data. Design services can supply designs for a physical plant, products, and promotion materials. Advertising agencies can help promote the firm's products—and food services can improve morale.

Here, the *service* part of the product is emphasized. Goods may be supplied—as coffee and donuts are with food service—but the customer is primarily interested in the service.

Managers compare the cost of buying professional services outside the firm to the cost of having company people do them. For special skills needed only occasionally, an outsider can be the best source. And the number of service specialists is growing in our complex economy.

BRANDING NEEDS A STRATEGY DECISION, TOO

There are so many brands, and we're so used to seeing them, that we take them for granted. In the grocery products area alone, there are more than 70,000 brands. Brands are of great importance to their owners. They help identify the company's marketing mix—and help customers recognize the firm's products and advertising. Marketing Demo 9–1 names some popular brands in Canada. Branding is an important decision area that many businesspeople ignore, so we will treat it in some detail.

What is branding?

Branding means the use of a name, term, symbol, or design—or a combination of these—to identify a product. It includes the use of brand names, trademarks, and practically all other means of product identification.

Brand name has a narrower meaning. A **brand name** is a word, letter, or a group of words or letters. Examples include WD-40, 3M Post-its, and IBM PS/2 computers.

Trademark is a legal term. A **trademark** includes only those words, symbols, or marks that are legally registered for use by a single company. A **service mark** is the same as a trademark except that it refers to a service offering.

MARKETING DEMO 9–1
Market Share: Slicing Up the Pie in Canada

(M) aybe you're wondering where your favorite brands rank in market share in Canada. One place to find out is *The Financial Times' Market Share* issue, which ranks brands in a variety of categories, from fragrances to fast food. A sampling of the rankings follows:

	Rank	Brand or Company	Percent
Best-Selling Ground Coffee, 1992	1	Nabob	26.8%
	2	Maxwell House	24.8
	3	Chase & Sanborn	3.5
	4	MJB	3.5
		Others	41.4
Best-Selling Beer, 1992	1	Blue and Blue Light (Labatt)	16
	2	Canadian and Canadian Light (Molson)	12
	3	Export (Molson)	7
	4	Budweiser (Labatt)	5
	4	Coors and Coors Light (Molson)	5
	4	Labatt Genuine Draft (Labatt)	5
	4	Molson Special Dry (Molson)	5
	5	O'Keefe Ale (Molson)	4
Fast-Food Chains, 1991	1	McDonald's	35.7
	2	KFC	15.4
	3	Swiss Chalet	8.1
	4	A&W	6.3
	5	Harvey's	6.0
	6	Dairy Queen	5.5
	7	Pizza Hut	5.4
	8	Burger King	5.3
	8	St. Hubert BBQ	5.3
	9	Wendy's	3.7
	10	Pizza Pizza	3.3
In-Line Skates, 1992	1	Bauer	44.1
	2	Rollerblade	29.2
	3	Ultrawheels	10.0

Source: "Market Share," *The Financial Times of Canada*, December 5–11, 1992.

The word *Buick* can be used to explain these differences. The Buick car is branded under the brand name Buick (whether it's spoken or printed in any manner). When "Buick" is printed in a certain kind of script, however, it becomes a trademark. A trademark need not be attached to the product. It need not even be a word—it can be a symbol.

These differences may seem technical. But they are very important to business firms that spend a lot of money to protect and promote their brands.

BRANDING—WHY IT DEVELOPED

Brands provide
identification

Branding started during the Middle Ages, when craft guilds (similar to labor unions) and merchant guilds formed to control the quantity and quality of production. Each producer had to mark his goods so output could be cut back when necessary. This also meant that poor quality—which might reflect unfavorably on other guild products and discourage future trade—could be traced back to the guilty producer. Early trademarks also protected the buyer, who could then know the source of the product.

More recently, brands have been used mainly for identification. The earliest and most aggressive brand promoters were the patent medicine companies. They were joined by the food manufacturers, who grew in size during the latter half of the 19th century. Some of the brands started in the 1860s and 1870s (and still going strong) are Borden's Condensed Milk, Quaker Oats, Pillsbury's Best Flour, and Ivory Soap. Today, familiar brands exist for most product categories, ranging from crayons (Crayola) to real estate services (Century 21). However, what is familiar often varies from one country to another.

Brands make consumers'
shopping easier

Well-recognized brands make shopping easier. Think of trying to buy groceries, for example, if you had to evaluate the advantages and disadvantages of each of 20,000 items every time you went to a supermarket.

Many customers are willing to buy new things—but having gambled and won, they like to buy a sure thing the next time. Even on infrequent purchases, consumers often rely on well-known brands as an indication of quality. And if consumers try a brand and don't like it, they know what to avoid in future purchases.

Branding helps
branders, too

Brand promotion has advantages for branders as well as customers. A good brand speeds up shopping for the customer—and thus reduces the marketer's selling time and effort. And, when customers repeatedly purchase by brand, the brander is protected against competition from other firms. Sometimes, a firm's brand name is the only element in its marketing mix that a competitor can't copy.

Good brands can improve the company's image, speeding acceptance of new products marketed under the same name. For example, many consumers quickly tried Snickers Ice Cream Bars when they were introduced because they already knew they liked Snickers candy bars. From a financial perspective, the money that Snickers spent over the years to promote the candy bar paid off again when consumers tried the ice cream bar. The majority of new products introduced in recent years have followed the approach of extending a successful brand name.[10]

CONDITIONS FAVORABLE TO BRANDING

Most firms, especially firms that sell consumer products, work hard to establish respected brands. On the other hand, some product categories have fewer well-known brands. For example, can you recall a brand name for file folders, bed frames, electric extension cords, or nails? As these examples suggest, it's not always easy to establish a respected brand.

The following conditions are favorable to successful branding:

1. The product is easy to identify by brand or trademark.
2. The product quality is the best value for the price. And the quality is easy to maintain.

3. Dependable and widespread availability is possible. When customers start using a brand, they want to be able to continue using it.
4. The demand for the general product class is large.
5. The demand is strong enough so that the market price can be high enough to make the branding effort profitable.
6. There are economies of scale. If the branding is really successful, costs should drop and profits should increase.
7. Favorable shelf locations or display space in stores will help. This is something retailers can control when they brand their own products. Producers must use aggressive salespeople to get favorable positions.

In general, these conditions are less common in less-developed economies, and that may explain why efforts to build brands in less-developed nations often fail.

ACHIEVING BRAND FAMILIARITY IS NOT EASY

Brand acceptance must be earned with a good product and regular promotion. **Brand familiarity** means how well customers recognize and accept a company's brand. The degree of brand familiarity affects the planning for the rest of the marketing mix, especially where the product should be offered and what promotion is needed.

Five levels of brand familiarity

Five levels of brand familiarity are useful for strategy planning: (1) rejection, (2) nonrecognition, (3) recognition, (4) preference, and (5) insistence.

Some brands have been tried and found wanting. **Brand rejection** means that potential customers won't buy a brand unless its image is changed. Rejection may

Hellmann's would like Chilean consumers to insist on the Hellmann's brand when they want mayonnaise to go with avocado and other vegetables. This headline asks "Avocado Mayo?"—and then describes Hellmann's as the "real one."

suggest a change in the product—or perhaps only a shift to target customers who have a better image of the brand. Overcoming a negative image is difficult—and can be very expensive.

Brand rejection is a big concern for service-oriented businesses because it's hard to control the quality of service. A business traveler who gets a dirty room in a Hilton Hotel in Caracas, Venezuela, might not return to any Hilton anywhere. Yet it's difficult for Hilton to ensure that every maid does a good job every time.

Some products are seen as basically the same. **Brand nonrecognition** means final consumers don't recognize a brand at all—even though middlemen may use the brand name for identification and inventory control. Examples include school supplies, pencils, and inexpensive dinnerware.

Brand recognition means that customers remember the brand. This can be a big advantage if there are many "nothing" brands on the market. Even if consumers can't recall the brand without help, they may be reminded when they see it in a store among other less familiar brands.

Most branders would like to win **brand preference**—which means that target customers usually choose the brand over other brands, perhaps because of habit or favorable past experience.

Brand insistence means customers insist on a firm's branded product and are willing to search for it. This is an objective of many target marketers. Here, the firm may enjoy a very inelastic demand curve.

The right brand name can help

A good brand name can help brand familiarity. It can help tell something important about the company or its product. Exhibit 9–6 lists some characteristics of a good brand name. Some successful brand names seem to break all these rules, but many of them got started when there was less competition.

Companies that compete in international markets face a special problem in selecting brand names. A name that conveys a positive image in one language may be meaningless in another. Or, worse, it may have unintended meanings. This can happen even in the same language. For example, the brand name for Snickers candy bars was changed to Marathon when they were introduced in England. Marketing managers were concerned that Snickers sounded too much like knickers, a British term for women's underwear. (Now, however, the name has been changed back to Snickers, so that the product can be sold with the same name throughout Europe.)[11]

A respected name builds brand equity

Because it's difficult and expensive to build brand recognition, some firms prefer to buy established brands rather than try to build their own. The value of a brand to its current owner or to a firm that wants to buy it is sometimes called

Exhibit 9–6   Characteristics of a Good Brand Name

- Short and simple
- Easy to spell and read
- Easy to recognize and remember
- Easy to pronounce
- Can be pronounced in only one way
- Can be pronounced in all languages (for international markets)
- Suggestive of product benefits
- Adaptable to packaging/labelling needs
- Not offensive, obscene, or negative
- Always timely (does not get out-of-date)
- Adaptable to any advertising medium
- Legally available for use (not in use by another firm)

brand equity—the value of a brand's overall strength in the market. For example, brand equity is likely to be higher if many satisfied customers insist on buying the brand and if retailers are eager to stock it. That almost guarantees ongoing profits from the brand and increases the brand's value.

PROTECTING CANADIAN TRADEMARKS AND BRAND NAMES

Benefits of trademark registration

Common law protects the owners of trademarks and brand names. Ownership of brand names and trademarks is established by continued usage.

Since the basic right is found in "use," a Canadian firm need not register its trademark under the **Trademarks Act**. But when a trademark is so registered, the registering firm is legally protected against any other company using a trademark that might be confused with its own. In contrast, the holder of an unregistered trademark couldn't sue a firm merely for using a similar trademark. The owner of an unregistered trademark would have to prove some other firm was deliberately trying to confuse consumers.

Canadian and US laws differ in the types of trademark protection they provide. In Canada, a firm producing a substantially different product may use the same trade name as another product used for some other purpose. This isn't so in the United States. On the other hand, there's less chance of a Canadian trade name being ruled "generic" or a common descriptive term—and therefore no longer protectable by its original owner. For example, Bayer Aspirin is still a protected trademark in Canada, even though *aspirin* has become a generic term in the United States.[12]

You must protect your own

A brand can be a real asset to a company. Each firm should try to see that its brand doesn't become the generic term for its kind of product. When this happens, the brand name or trademark becomes public property—and the owner loses all rights to it. This happened in the United States with the names cellophane, aspirin, shredded wheat, and kerosene. Teflon, Scotch Tape, and Xerox also came close to becoming common descriptive terms there. And Miller Brewing Company tried—unsuccessfully—in the US courts to protect its Lite beer by suing other brewers who wanted to use the word *light*.[13]

(?) Counterfeiting is accepted in some cultures

Even when products are properly registered, counterfeiters may make unauthorized copies. Many well-known brands, ranging from Levi jeans to Rolex watches to Zantax ulcer medicine to Mickey Mouse T-shirts, face this problem. Counterfeiting is especially common in developing nations. For example, counterfeit copies of software programs like WordPerfect are available in hundreds of outlets in Taiwan, often selling for a dollar or two each. Multinational efforts are underway to stop such counterfeiting, but they may meet with limited success. Counterfeiting is big business in some countries, and their government agencies don't want to deal with the problem. There are also differences in cultural values. In South Korea, for example, many people don't see counterfeiting as unethical.[14]

WHAT KIND OF BRAND TO USE?

Keep it in the family

Branders of more than one product must decide whether they are going to use a **family brand**—the same brand name for several products—or individual brands for each product. Examples of family brands are Hostess snack food products and Sears' Craftsman tools and Kenmore appliances.

The use of the same brand for many products makes sense if all are similar in type and quality. The main benefit is that the goodwill attached to one or two products may help the others. Money spent to promote the brand name benefits more than one product, which cuts promotion costs for each product. Using a family brand makes it easier, faster, and less expensive to introduce new products. This can be an important competitive advantage, and it explains why many firms are expanding the number of products sold under family brand names.

A special kind of family brand is a **licensed brand**—a well-known brand that sellers pay a fee to use. For example, the familiar Sunkist brand name is owned by Sunkist Growers, a farmers' cooperative. But the Sunkist brand name has been licensed to many companies for use on more than 400 products in 30 countries. Licensees usually pay royalties ranging from 4 to 8.5 percent of the wholesale sales. In this case, many different companies are in the "family."[15]

Individual brands for outside and inside competition

A company uses **individual brands**—separate brand names for each product—when it's important for the products to each have a separate identity, as when products vary in quality or type.

If the products are really different, such as Elmer's glue and Borden's ice cream, individual brands can avoid confusion. Some firms use individual brands with similar products to make segmentation and positioning efforts easier. Unilever, for example, markets Aim, Close-Up, and Pepsodent toothpastes, but each involves different positioning efforts.

Sometimes firms use individual brands to encourage competition within the company. Each brand is managed by a different group within the firm. Some managers think that internal competition keeps everyone alert. The theory is that if anyone is going to take business away from their firm, it ought to be their own brand.

Many firms that once used this approach have reorganized. Faced with slower market growth, they found they had plenty of competitive pressure from other firms. The internal competition just made it more difficult to coordinate different marketing strategies. For example, Procter & Gamble has a number of different brands of bar soap. Some years ago, the managers for the individual brands were fighting it out, often going after the same target market with similar marketing mixes. Now, one manager has responsibility for developing a coordinated marketing plan for all products in the bar soap category. The result is a better-integrated effort.[16]

Generic "brands"

Products that some consumers see as commodities may be difficult or expensive to brand. Some manufacturers and middlemen have responded to this problem with **generic products**—products that have no brand at all other than identification of their contents and the manufacturer or middleman. Generic products are usually offered in plain packages at lower prices. They are quite common in less-developed nations.

A decade ago, some target markets were interested in buying generic products. But price cuts by branded competitors narrowed the price gap and won back many customers. Now, generics account for only about 1.5 percent of grocery store sales, and in many product categories they've disappeared altogether. However, generics still capture significant market share in a few product categories—especially prescription drugs.[17]

WHO SHOULD DO THE BRANDING?

Manufacturer brands versus dealer brands

Manufacturer brands are brands created by manufacturers. These are sometimes called *national brands* because the brand is promoted all across the country or in large regions. Note, however, that this term became popular before international markets became so important; many manufacturer brands are now distributed globally. Such brands include Kellogg's, Whirlpool, Ford, and IBM. Many creators of service-oriented firms—like McDonald's, Molly Maid, and Midas Muffler—spend a lot of money promoting their brands in the same way other producers do.

Dealer brands, also called **private brands,** are brands created by middlemen. Examples of dealer brands include the brands of Safeway, Home Hardware, and the Bay. Some of these are advertised and distributed more widely than many national brands.

From the middleman's perspective, the major advantage of selling a popular manufacturer brand is that the product is already presold to some target customers. Such products may bring in new customers and can encourage higher turnover with reduced selling cost. The major disadvantage is that manufacturers normally offer lower gross margins than the middleman might be able to earn with a dealer brand. In addition, the manufacturer maintains control of the brand and may withdraw it from a middleman at any time. Customers, loyal to the brand rather than to the retailer or wholesaler, may go elsewhere if the brand is not available.

Dealer branders take on more responsibility. They must promote their own product. They must be able to arrange a dependable source of supply and usually have to buy in fairly large quantities. This increases their risk and cost of carrying inventory. However, these problems are easier to overcome if the middleman deals in a large sales volume, as is the case with many large retail chains.

Who's winning the battle of the brands?

The **battle of the brands,** the competition between dealer brands and manufacturer brands, is just a question of whose brand will be more popular—and who will be in control.

At one time, manufacturer brands were much more popular than dealer brands. But manufacturer brands may be losing the battle. Now, sales of both kinds of brands are about equal—but sales of dealer brands are expected to continue growing. Middlemen have some advantages in this battle. The number of large wholesalers and retail chains is growing. They are better able to arrange reliable sources of supply at low cost. They can also control the point of sale and give the dealer brand special shelf position or promotion. Further, the lower prices possible with dealer brands attract price-sensitive consumers.

Consumers benefit from the battle. Competition has already narrowed price differences between manufacturer brands and well-known dealer brands.[18]

THE STRATEGIC IMPORTANCE OF PACKAGING

Packaging involves promoting and protecting the product. Packaging can be important to both sellers and customers. Packaging can make a product more convenient to use or store. It can prevent spoiling or damage. Good packaging makes products easier to identify and promotes the brand at the point of purchase and even in use. As shown in Marketing Demo 9–2, a great deal of planning goes into designing a successful package.

Packaging can make the difference

A new package can make *the* important difference in a new marketing strategy—by meeting customers' needs better. A better box, wrapper, can, or bottle may help create a "new" product—or a new market. For example, Crest toothpaste is now available in a neat squeeze-pump dispenser that makes less mess and leaves less waste. Quaker State oil comes with a twist-off top and pouring spout to make it more convenient for customers of self-service gas stations, and popcorn for microwave ovens is sold in easy-open bags.

Sometimes a new package improves a product by making it easier or safer to use. Kodak increased sales of its light-sensitive X-ray film by packing each sheet in a separate foil pack—making the film easier to handle. Many drug and food products now have special seals to prevent product tampering. Tylenol caplets, for example, come in a tamper-resistant package.

Packaging sends a message—even for services

Packaging can tie the product to the rest of the marketing strategy. Packaging for Eveready batteries features the pink bunny seen in attention-getting TV ads—and reminds consumers that the batteries are durable. Expensive perfume may come in a crystal bottle, adding to the prestige image.

In a way, the appearance of service providers or the area where a service is provided is a form of packaging. Disney sends the message that its parks are a good

---

MARKETING DEMO 9–2
Shelf Impact

Joseph E. Seagram & Sons Ltd.'s latest foray into the fiercely competitive Canadian vodka market has been purely by design. "To be successful, we recognized that we needed a unique and distinctive bottle to be seen amongst the competition," explains Claus Heinecke from his Montreal office. He's referring to *Platinum,* which was recently launched nationally. "We had to be seen, or else we would have lost the battle before it began."

Heinecke is Seagram's design director and the chief architect of the *Platinum* glass package. He stresses that clarity and purity are the main criteria of a high-quality vodka, and it's an image the bottle successfully conveys.

Vodka remains one of the few growth categories left in the spirits business. There are 82 brands available—56 of them domestic. While European imports are making significant gains, Smirnoff remains the undisputed leader, boasting a market share that exceeds 40 percent. Going head-to-head with Smirnoff didn't make sense, Heinecke observes.

"You can't out-Smirnoff Smirnoff," he points out. So Seagram set out two years ago to become the contemporary alternative to vodka's leading brand, with the bottle designated as an integral part of the endeavor. Heinecke has been told that the bottle resembles a block of ice, a prism, and even a sail. But perhaps the best comments came from organizers of two recent US packaging competitions, where Seagram garnered two prestigious awards for package design.

Seagram is hoping that *Platinum* will earn a spot in the top-10 brand category within five years. At this juncture, company officials will only say that sales are "exceeding all expectations." Company officials say there are no immediate plans to market the product in the United States, although they are monitoring and reviewing its performance on a regular basis.

Source: Douglas Faulkner, "Shelf Impact," *Canadian Packaging*, March 1991, pp. 19–20.

place for family vacations by keeping them spotless. Lawyers put their awards and diplomas on the wall so that clients know they provide a high-quality product. In addition, some firms try to "package" their services so that there is a tangible reminder of the product. For example, the American Express Gold Card sends a signal that is understood worldwide.

Packaging may lower distribution and promotion costs

Better protective packaging is very important to manufacturers and wholesalers. They often have to pay the cost of goods damaged in shipment, and goods damaged in shipment also may delay production—or cause lost sales.

Retailers need good packaging, too. Protective packaging can reduce storing costs by cutting breakage, spoilage, and theft. Packages that are easier to handle can cut costs by speeding price marking, improving handling and display, and saving space.

A good package sometimes gives a firm more promotion effect than it could possibly afford with advertising. Customers see the package in stores—when they're actually buying. For example, a recent study found that 81 percent of customers' purchase decisions on groceries are made at the store. The package may be seen by many more potential customers than the company's advertising. An attractive package may speed turnover enough to reduce total costs as a percentage of sales.

Or it may raise total costs

In other cases, costs (and prices) may rise because of packaging. But customers may be more satisfied because the packaging improves the product by offering much greater convenience or reducing waste.

Packaging costs as a percentage of a manufacturer's selling price vary widely, ranging from 1 to 70 percent. When sugar producers like Lantic sell sugar in 100-pound bags, the cost of packaging is only 1 percent of the selling price. In 2- and 5-pound cartons, it's 25 to 30 percent. And for individual serving packages, it's 50 percent. But consumers don't want to haul a 100-pound bag home. They're quite willing to pay more for convenient sizes. Restaurants use one-serving envelopes of sugar to eliminate the cost of filling and washing sugar bowls—and because customers prefer the sanitary little packages.[19]

WHAT IS SOCIALLY RESPONSIBLE PACKAGING?

Some consumers say that some package designs are misleading—perhaps on purpose. Who hasn't been surprised by a candy bar half the size of the package? Others feel that the great variety of packages makes it hard to compare values. And some are concerned about whether the packages are degradable or can be recycled.

The task of adopting "greener packaging" isn't simple. In addition to establishing costs and benefits, simply coordinating solutions between producers of products, governments, and citizen organizations is an enormous task. In order to help Canadians identify better packaging and products, the "Ecologo" appearing on this page has been adopted.

Federal law tries to help

The **Hazardous Products Act** gives Consumer and Corporate Affairs Canada the authority either to ban or to regulate the sale, distribution, and labelling of hazardous products.

Since 1971, all products considered potentially hazardous (such as cleaning substances, chemicals, and aerosol products) have had to carry on their labels an appropriate symbol that reveals both the possible danger and the necessary precautions. The symbols chosen are used to indicate whether the product is poisonous, flammable, explosive, or corrosive.

The **Consumer Packaging and Labelling Act** calls for bilingual labels as well as the standardization of package sizes and shapes. It also requires that all food products be labelled in metric terms as well as in traditional Canadian measures as of March 1976. When reference is made on a label or package to the number of servings being provided, the average size of these servings must also be indicated. The term *best before* must appear in both official languages along with a date reflecting the product's durability.

Labelling requirements for certain specified products are also set forth in the National Trademark and True Labelling Act, the Textile Labelling Act, and the Precious Metals Marking Act. The Textile Care Labelling Program provides for all garments and other textiles being labelled with washing or dry cleaning instructions. Similarly, the CANTAG program now being widely used provides customers with performance, capacity, and energy consumption data on major appliances.

? Ethical decisions remain

Although various laws provide guidance on many packaging issues, many areas still require marketing managers to make ethical choices.

For example, some firms have been criticized for designing packages that conceal a "downsized" product, giving consumers less for the money. Similarly, some retailers have been criticized for designing packages and labels for their private-label products that look just like—and are easily confused with—manufacturer brands. Furthermore, some producers quickly put their lawyers and

A firm's commitment to recycling has become an important packaging issue.

engineers to work so they can copy a competitor's popular packaging innovation without violating the patent. Are efforts such as these unethical, or are they simply an attempt to make packaging a more effective part of a marketing mix? Different people will answer differently.

Some marketing managers have been criticized for promoting environmentally friendly packaging on some products while simultaneously increasing the use of problematic packages on others. Empty packages now litter our streets, and some plastic packages will lie in a city dump for decades. Empty aerosol cans may explode, and empty bottles often become broken glass. But some consumers like the convenience that accompanies these problems. Is it unethical for a marketing manager to give consumers with different preferences a choice, and to develop different marketing mixes to reach different target markets? Some critics argue that it is. But others praise firms that are taking steps to give consumers a choice.

Many critics feel that labelling information is too often incomplete or misleading. Do consumers really understand the nutritional information required by law? Further, some consumers want information that is difficult—perhaps even impossible—to provide. For example, how can a label accurately describe a product's taste or texture? But the ethical issues focus on how far a marketing manager should go in putting potentially negative information on a package. For example, should Häagen-Dazs affix a label that says "this product will clog your arteries"? That sounds extreme, but what type of information *is* appropriate?[20]

Unit-pricing is a possible help

Some retailers—especially large supermarket chains—make it easier for consumers to compare packages with different weights or volumes. They use **unit-pricing**—which involves placing the price per ounce (or some other standard measure) on or near the product. This makes price comparison easier.[21]

Universal product codes allow more information

To speed handling of fast-selling products, government and industry representatives have developed a **universal product code (UPC)** that identifies each product with marks readable by electronic scanners. A computer then matches each code to the product and its price. Supermarkets and other high-volume retailers have been eager to use these codes. They reduce the need to mark the price on every item. They also reduce errors by cashiers—and make it easy to control inventory and track sales of specific products. Exhibit 9–7 shows a universal product code mark.

Exhibit 9–7   An illustration of a Universal Product Code

The codes help consumers too because they speed the checkout process. Also, most systems now include a printed receipt showing the name, size, and price of each product bought. These codes will become even more widely used in the future because they do lower operating costs.[22]

WARRANTIES ARE IMPORTANT, TOO

Warranty should mean something

Common law says producers should stand behind (i.e., provide a **warranty** for) their products. And both present and proposed warranty legislation tries to see that such warranties or guaranties are neither deceptive nor unfair. Warranties are a major source of consumer complaint and dissatisfaction.

Both provincial and federal legislation attempts to see that any warranty offered is fair to the consumer, easy to understand, and precise as to what is and what isn't covered. Before this increased government concern, some firms simply

In a competitive market, a product warranty is often a very important part of the marketing mix.

said their products were "fully warranted" or "absolutely guaranteed" without either specifying a time period or spelling out the meaning of the guarantee.

On the federal level, protection against misleading warranties is provided by one of the Stage 1 amendments to the Combines Investigation Act. Specifically prohibited are warranties that seem unlikely to be carried out, warranties where excessive labor or handling charges are used to cover the manufacturer's cost of allegedly replacing defective parts "free of charge," and warranties that reduce a purchaser's usual rights under common law.[23]

Provincial legislation designed to make warranties more meaningful was supposed to be greatly affected by the recommendations of a 1972 study of warranties and guaranties made by the Ontario Law Reform Commission.[24] However, changes have not occurred all that quickly. More than 20 years after the Law Reform study, only Saskatchewan had its new legislation in force! Customers might like a strong warranty, but it can be very expensive—even economically impossible—for small firms. Backing up warranties can be a problem, too. Some customers abuse products and then demand a lot of service on warranties. Although manufacturers may be responsible, they may have to depend on reluctant or poorly trained middlemen to do the job. This can make it hard for a small firm to compete with larger firms that have many service centres. Foreign auto producers marketing their cars in Canada, for example, can't match the number of Chevrolet or Ford service locations.

Deciding on the warranty is a strategic matter. Specific decisions should be made about what the warranty will cover. Then the warranty should be communicated clearly to the target customers, as is done, for example, in Marketing Demo 9–3. A warranty can make the difference between success and failure for a whole marketing strategy.[25]

MARKETING DEMO 9–3
Limited Warranty AT&T Products

Warrantor: The Warranty on this AT&T product is provided by Lenbrook Industries Limited through its Service Centre at

Lenbrook Industries Limited
633 Granite Court
Pickering, Ontario
L1W 3K1
1 800 263-4641

What is covered:
Any defect in material and workmanship

For how long:
One year

What Lenbrook will do:
If your AT&T product is defective within one year of the date of purchase, we will repair it or, at our option, replace it at no charge to you. The repair or replacement will be warranted for either (a) 90 days or (b) the remainder of the original one year warranty period, whichever is longer.

Limitations:
Implied warranties, including those of fitness for a particular purpose and merchantability (an unwritten warranty that the product is fit for ordinary use), are limited to one year from date of purchase. We will not pay for loss of time, inconvenience, loss of use of your AT&T product, or property damage caused by your AT&T product or its failure to work, or any other incidental or consequential damages.

Some provinces do not allow limitations on how long an implied warranty lasts or the exclusion or limitation of incidental or consequential damages, so the above exclusions or limitations may not apply to you.

What we ask you to do:
To facilitate the servicing of your AT&T product we suggest that you complete and return the warranty registration card supplied as soon as possible after purchase.

Before returning your set, we recommend that you call us toll-free at 1 800 263-4641 to review the operation of your set.
To obtain warranty service for your AT&T product, you must provide proof of the date of purchase and you should complete the Service Return Form included in this manual when returning your set. You can either return the product to your place of purchase or forward the product directly to Lenbrook Industries Limited at the above address. If you ship your AT&T product to Lenbrook, you must prepay all shipping costs. We suggest that you retain your original packing material in the event you need to ship your AT&T product. When returning your AT&T product, include your name, address, phone number, proof of date of purchase, and a description of the operating problem. After repairing or replacing your AT&T product, we will ship it to your place of purchase or directly to you at no cost to you.

Repair or replacement of your AT&T product at our service location is your exclusive remedy.

What this warranty does not cover:
This warranty does not cover defects resulting from accidents, damage while in-transit to our service location, alterations, unauthorized repair, failure to follow instructions, misuse (including broken antenna), fire, flood, and acts of God. Nor do we warrant your AT&T product to be compatible with any particular telephone equipment or party line, key telephone systems or more sophisticated customer premises switching systems. If your AT&T product is out of warranty, it can still be returned for repair through your place of purchase or directly to our Service Centre. We, at our option, may replace rather than repair your AT&T product with a new or reconditioned one of the same or similar design and we will advise you of the charges. The repair or replacement will be warranted for 90 days.

This warranty is the only one we give on your AT&T product, and it sets forth all our responsibilities regarding your AT&T product. There are no other express warranties.

This warranty gives you specific legal rights and you may also have other rights which vary from province to province.

Source: Courtesy of Lenbrook Industries Ltd.

CONCLUSION

In this chapter, we looked at Product very broadly. A product may not be a physical good at all. It may be a service, or it may be some combination of goods and services—like a meal at a restaurant. Most important, we saw that a firm's Product is *what satisfies the needs of its target market.*

We introduced consumer product and business product classes and showed their effect on planning marketing mixes. Consumer product classes are based on consumers' buying behavior. Business product classes are based on how buyers see the products and how they are used. Knowing these product classes—and learning how marketers handle specific products within these classes—will help you develop your marketing sense.

The fact that different people may see the same product in different product classes helps explain why apparent competitors may succeed with very different marketing mixes.

Branding and packaging can create new and more satisfying products. Packaging offers special opportunities to promote the product and inform customers. Variations in packaging can make a product attractive to different target markets. A specific package may have to be developed for each strategy.

Customers see brands as a guarantee of quality, and this leads to repeat purchasing. For marketers, such routine buying means lower promotion costs and higher sales.

Should companies stress branding? The decision depends on whether the costs of brand promotion and honoring the brand guarantee can be more than covered by a higher price or more rapid turnover—or both. The cost of branding may reduce pressure on the other three Ps.

Branding gives marketing managers a choice. They can add brands and use individual or family brands. In the end, however, customers express their approval or disapproval of the whole Product (including the brand). The degree of brand familiarity is a measure of the marketing manager's ability to carve out a separate market. And brand familiarity affects Place, Price, and Promotion decisions.

Warranties are also important in strategy planning. A warranty need not be strong—it just has to be clearly stated. But some customers find strong warranties attractive.

Product is concerned with much more than physical goods and service. To succeed in our increasingly competitive markets, the marketing manager must also be concerned about packaging, branding, and warranties.

QUESTIONS AND PROBLEMS

1. Define, in your own words, what a Product is.

2. Discuss several ways in which physical goods are different from pure services. Give an example of a good and then an example of a service that illustrates each of the differences.

3. What products are being offered by a shop that specializes in bicycles? By a travel agent? By a supermarket? By a new car dealer?

4. What kinds of consumer products are the following: (*a*) watches, (*b*) automobiles, (*c*) toothpastes? Explain your reasoning.

5. Consumer services tend to be intangible, and goods tend to be tangible. Use an example to explain how the lack of a physical good in a pure service might affect efforts to promote the service.

6. How would the marketing mix for a staple convenience product differ from the one for a homogeneous shopping product? How would the mix for a specialty product differ from the mix for a heterogeneous shopping product? Use examples.

7. Give an example of a product that is a *new* unsought product for most people. Briefly explain why it is an unsought product.

8. In what types of stores would you expect to find (*a*) convenience products, (*b*) shopping prod-

ucts, (c) specialty products, and (d) unsought products?

9. Cite two examples of business products that require a substantial amount of service in order to be useful.

10. Explain why a new law office might want to lease furniture rather than buy it.

11. Would you expect to find any wholesalers selling the various types of business products? Are retail stores required (or something like retail stores)?

12. What kinds of business products are the following: (a) lubricating oil, (b) electric motors, (c) a firm that provides landscaping and grass mowing for an apartment complex? Explain your reasoning.

13. How do raw materials differ from other business products? Do the differences have any impact on their marketing mixes? If so, what specifically?

14. For the kinds of business products described in this chapter, complete the following table (use one or a few well-chosen words).

Products	1	2	3
Installations			
Buildings and land rights			
Major equipment			
Standard			
Custom-made			
Accessories			
Raw materials			
Farm products			
Natural products			
Components			
Supplies			
Maintenance and small operating supplies			
Operating supplies			
Professional services			

1. *Kind of distribution facility(ies) needed and functions they will provide.*
2. *Caliber of salespeople required.*
3. *Kind of advertising required.*

15. Is there any difference between a brand name and a trademark? If so, why is this difference important?

16. Is a well-known brand valuable only to the owner of the brand?

17. Suggest an example of a product and a competitive situation where it would *not* be profitable for a firm to spend large sums of money to establish a brand.

18. List five brand names and indicate what product is associated with the brand name. Evaluate the strengths and weaknesses of the brand name.

19. Explain family brands. Should Toys "R" Us develop its own dealer brands to compete with some of the popular manufacturer brands it carries? Explain your reasons.

20. In the past Sears emphasized its own dealer brands. Now it is carrying more well-known manufacturer brands. What are the benefits to Sears of carrying more manufacturer brands?

21. What does the degree of brand familiarity imply about previous and future promotion efforts? How does the degree of brand familiarity affect the Place and Price variables?

22. You operate a small hardware store with emphasis on manufacturer brands and have barely been breaking even. Evaluate the proposal of a large wholesaler who offers a full line of dealer-branded hardware items at substantially lower prices. Specify any assumptions necessary to obtain a definite answer.

23. Give examples where packaging costs probably (a) lower total distribution costs and (b) raise total distribution costs.

24. Is it more difficult to support a warranty for a service than for a physical good? Explain your reasons.

SUGGESTED CASES

12. A Chance to Be Self-Employed

14. Lucas Foods

Product Management and New-Product Development

Chapter **10**

When You Finish This Chapter, You Should

❶

Understand how product life cycles affect strategy planning.

❷

Know what is involved in designing new products and what "new products" really are.

❸

Understand the new-product development process.

❹

See why product liability must be considered in screening new products.

❺

Understand the need for product brand managers.

❻

Understand the important new terms (shown in blue).

It's lunchtime in downtown Toronto, and the hungry hordes at the crowded McDonald's at Bloor Street and Avenue Road have pizza on their minds. In fact, it's hard to think burger at this McDonald's. Photos of gooey pepperoni pizza explode with cheese; an inflatable pizza blimp hovers above the counter; ceiling streamers tout a new ham and pineapple pizza; and a monstrous banner above Bloor commands: "Try our pizza."

Four stores away, a dark, cool Pizza Hut is half empty. Welcome to the fast-food wars of the 90s—a battle over the juicy pizza market, a market sector worth $27 billion in North America alone.

Burger giant McDonald's of Canada is on the offensive, spending $25 million on product development and a lavish marketing blitz trying to drive a wedge into the pizza business. It's no wonder McDonald's wants in—North Americans are gobbling more pizzas every year, and pizza may soon be the number one selling fast-food item in North America, according to the National Restaurant Association in Washington, DC.

"Overnight we became the pizza leader in Canada. We opened a new business in one day—640 pizzerias in McDonald's," boasts Rem Langan, assistant vice president and director of national marketing and communications, McDonald's Restaurants of Canada Ltd. Langen helped coordinate the launch, but he's quick to give credit to the whole team: "I'm not important in this—some 65,000 employees are working hard selling pizza every day." That's the employee count just in Canada. By the end of the decade, more than 700,000 workers in the 59-country McDonald's empire could be dishing pizza.

McDonald's insists that customer demand—not dropping burger sales—is behind the pizza blitz. "We're consumer driven," says Langan. "Pizza is a very popular product. It's a $2 billion business [in Canada]. We want to get a slice of that segment."

McDonald's mozzarella mindset began almost nine years ago when its product development group began working on a "pizza pocket," a product that ultimately never even made it to the franchises because research found consumers were wary of a quirky takeoff on pizza. That early failure didn't faze anyone. By 1989, the company had tested dozens of pizzas, running through some 75 cheeses and 145 kinds of pepperoni. Taste aside, McDonald's soon realized the key was in the oven. Fast-food customers didn't want to wait 20 minutes for a pizza. Until the oven problem could be solved, McDonald's and other classic fast-food companies were literally left out in the cold.

Plowing money into the problem, McDonald's turned to a team of engineers at Welbilt Corporation, a Connecticut-based company that distributes kitchen appliances. Seven years and half a dozen ovens later, Welbilt came up with a "heat impingement" oven able to bake a pizza in three and a half minutes. Such technology isn't cheap. Although McDonald's won't discuss cost, competitor Pizza Hut estimates each oven costs $75,000.

The campaign began with a toe in the water, a test in the Ottawa-Hull region. "We had to overcome the big hurdle in people's minds that 'Yeah, that's a hamburger company,'" says Paul Lavoie, former creative director at Cossette Communications-Marketing of Montreal.

After the test phase, McDonald's swung into the considerable task of training its over 65,000 employees nationwide. Consistency of product is a key to the McDonald's success story, so a deluxe pizza in Victoria has to taste the same as one in Charlottetown.

Home delivery hasn't been ruled out, either. McDonald's is trying a delivery service at two restaurants. "Probably half of the $2 billion pizza business is takeout and home delivery. So it's certainly a big part of the market and we'll look at it, we'll certainly look at it," Langan says.[1]

McDonald's innovations show that products, markets, and competition change over time. This makes marketing management an exciting challenge. Developing new products and managing existing products to meet changing conditions are important to the success of every firm. In this chapter, we will look at some important ideas in these areas.

MANAGING PRODUCTS OVER THEIR LIFE CYCLES

Products—like consumers—go through life cycles. So product planning and marketing mix planning are important. Competitors are always developing and copying new ideas and products, making existing products out-of-date more quickly than ever.

Product life cycle has four major stages

The **product life cycle** describes the stages a new product idea goes through from beginning to end. The product life cycle is divided into four major stages: (1) market introduction, (2) market growth, (3) market maturity, and (4) sales decline.

A particular firm's marketing mix usually must change during the product life cycle. There are several reasons why. Customers' attitudes and needs may change over the product life cycle. The product may be aimed at entirely different target markets at different stages. And the nature of competition is that it moves toward pure competition or oligopoly.

Further, total sales of the product—by all competitors in the industry—vary in each of its four stages. They move from very low in the market introduction stage, to high at market maturity, and then back to low in the sales decline stage. More important, the profit picture changes, too. These general relationships can be seen in Exhibit 10–1. Note that sales and profits do not move together over time. *Industry profits decline while industry sales are still rising.*[2]

Exhibit 10–1   Life Cycle of a Typical Product

In the **market introduction** stage, sales are low as a new idea is first introduced to a market. Customers aren't looking for the product. They don't even know about it. Informative promotion is needed to tell potential customers about the advantages and uses of the new product concept.

Even though a firm promotes its new product, it takes time for customers to learn that the product is available. Most companies experience losses during the introduction stage because they spend so much money for Promotion, Product, and Place development. Of course, they invest the money in the hope of future profits.

In the **market growth** stage, industry sales grow fast—but industry profits rise and then start falling. The innovator begins to make big profits as more and more customers buy. But competitors see the opportunity and enter the market. Some just copy the most successful product or try to improve it to compete better. Others try to refine their offerings to do a better job of appealing to some target markets. The new entries result in much product variety. So monopolistic competition—with down-sloping demand curves—is typical of the market growth stage.

This is the time of biggest profits *for the industry. But it is also when industry profits begin to decline* as competition increases. See Exhibit 10–1.

Some firms make big strategy planning mistakes at this stage by not understanding the product life cycle. They see the big sales and profit opportunities of the early market growth stage but ignore the competition that will soon follow. When they realize their mistake, it may be too late. Marketing managers who pay attention to competitor analysis are less likely to encounter this problem.

The **market maturity** stage occurs when industry sales level off—and competition gets tougher. Many aggressive competitors have entered the race for profits—except in oligopoly situations. Industry profits go down throughout the market maturity stage because promotion costs rise and some competitors cut prices to attract business. Less efficient firms can't compete with this pressure, and they drop out of the market. Even in oligopoly situations, there is a long-run downward pressure on prices.

New firms may still enter the market at this stage, increasing competition even more. Note that late entries skip the early life-cycle stages, including the

Margin notes:

Market introduction— investing in the future

Market growth—profits go up and down

Market maturity— sales level off, profits continue down

Sony's portable CD-ROM and Grid's pen computer will need informative promotion during the market introduction stage of the product life cycle—so customers will know about their benefits and uses.

profitable market growth stage. And they must try to take a share of the saturated market from established firms, which is difficult and expensive. The market leaders have a lot at stake, so they usually will fight hard to defend their market share and revenue stream.

Persuasive promotion becomes more important during the market maturity stage. Products may differ only slightly if at all. Most competitors have discovered the most effective appeals—or copied the leaders. Although each firm may still have its own demand curve, the curves become increasingly elastic as the various products become almost the same in the minds of potential consumers.

In Canada, the markets for most cars, boats, television sets, and many household appliances are in market maturity.[3] This stage may continue for many years, until a basically new product idea comes along, even though individual brands or models come and go.

Sales decline—a time of replacement

During the **sales decline** stage, new products replace the old. Price competition from dying products becomes more vigorous, but firms with strong brands may make profits until the end. These firms have down-sloping demand curves because they successfully differentiated their products.

As the new products go through their introduction stage, the old ones may keep some sales by appealing to the most loyal customers or those who are slow to try new ideas. These conservative buyers might switch later, smoothing the sales decline.

PRODUCT LIFE CYCLES SHOULD BE RELATED TO SPECIFIC MARKETS

Remember that product life cycles describe industry sales and profits for a *product idea* within a particular product-market. The sales and profits of an individual product or brand may not—and often do not—follow the life-cycle pattern. They may vary up and down throughout the life cycle, sometimes moving in the opposite direction of industry sales and profits. Further, a product idea may be in a different life-cycle stage in different markets.

Individual brands may not follow the pattern

A given firm may introduce or withdraw a specific product during any stage of the product life cycle. A "me too" brand introduced during the market growth stage, for example, may never get any sales at all and suffer a quick death. Or it may reach its peak and start to decline even before the market maturity stage begins. Market leaders may enjoy high profits during the market maturity stage, even though industry profits are declining. Weaker products, on the other hand, may not earn a profit during any stage of the product life cycle. Sometimes the innovator brand loses so much in the introduction stage that it has to drop out just as others are reaping big profits in the growth stage.

Strategy planners who naively expect sales of an individual product to follow the general product life-cycle pattern are likely to be rudely surprised. In fact, it might be more sensible to think in terms of "product-market life cycles" rather than product life cycles—but we will use the term *product life cycle* because it is commonly accepted and widely used.

Each market should be carefully defined

How we see product life cycles depends on how broadly we define a product-market. For example, the majority of North American households own microwave ovens.[4] Although microwave ovens appear to be at the market maturity stage here, in many other countries they're still early in the growth stage. Even in European countries life Belgium, Denmark, Italy, and Spain, fewer than 10 percent of all households own microwave ovens. As this example suggests, a firm with a mature product can sometimes turn back the clock by focusing on new growth opportunities in international markets.

How broadly we define the needs of customers in a product-market also affects how we view product life cycles—and who the competitors are. For example, consider the set of consumer needs related to storing and preparing foods. Wax paper sales in North America started to decline when Dow introduced Saran Wrap. Then, in the early 1970s, sales of Saran Wrap (and other similar products) fell sharply when small plastic storage bags became popular. However, sales picked up again by the end of the decade. The product didn't change, but customers' needs did. Saran Wrap filled a new need—a wrap that would work well in microwave cooking.

If a market is defined broadly, there may be many competitors, and the market may appear to be in market maturity. On the other hand, if we focus on a narrow submarket—and a particular way of satisfying specific needs—then we may see much shorter product life cycles as improved product ideas come along to replace the old.

PRODUCT LIFE CYCLES VARY IN LENGTH

How long a whole product life cycle takes and the length of each stage vary a lot across products. The cycle may vary from 90 days—in the case of toys like Super Soaker water guns—to possibly 100 years for gas-powered cars.

The product life cycle concept does not tell a manager precisely *how long* the cycle will last. But a manager can often make a good guess based on the life cycle for similar products. Sometimes marketing research can help, too. However, it is more important to expect and plan for the different stages than to know the precise length of each cycle.

Some products move fast

A new product idea will move through the early stages of the life cycle more quickly when it has certain characteristics. For example, the greater the *comparative advantage* of a new product over those already on the market, the more rapidly its sales will grow. Sales growth is also faster when the product is *easy to use* and if its advantages are *easy to communicate*. If the product *can be tried* on a limited basis—without a lot of risk to the customer—it can usually be introduced more quickly. Finally, if the product is *compatible* with the values and experiences of target customers, they are likely to buy it more quickly.

The fast adoption of NutraSweet low-calorie sweetener in the North American market is a good example. NutraSweet offered real benefits—fewer calories compared to sugar without the bitter aftertaste of existing diet sweeteners. Free samples of NutraSweet chewing gum made it easy for consumers to try the product. And NutraSweet worked well in many products—like diet soft drinks—that were already a part of consumers' lifestyles. However, in less-developed countries—where malnutrition, not dieting, is the problem—NutraSweet does not have the same comparative advantages.[5]

Product life cycles are getting shorter

Although the life of different products varies, in general product life cycles are getting shorter. This is partly due to rapidly changing technology. One new invention may make possible many new products that replace old ones. Tiny electronic microchips led to hundreds of new products—from Texas Instruments' calculators and Pulsar digital watches in the early days to microchip-controlled heart valves and fax machines now. Fax machines can transmit a letter or illustration anywhere in the world over standard phone lines—in just minutes. They're not only changing how companies communicate; they're also taking business and profits away from overnight delivery services like Federal Express and Priority Post.

Some markets move quickly to market maturity—if there are fast copiers. In the highly competitive grocery products industry, cycles are down to 12 to 18 months for really new ideas. Simple variations of a new idea may have even shorter life cycles. Competitors sometimes copy flavor or packaging changes in a matter of weeks or months.

Patents for a new product may not be much protection in slowing down competitors. Competitors can often find ways to copy the product idea without violating a specific patent. Worse, some firms find out that an unethical competitor simply disregarded the patent protection. Patent violations by foreign competitors are very common. A product's life may be over before a case can get through patent-court bottlenecks. By then, the copycat competitor may even be out of business. These problems are even more severe in international cases because different governments, rules, and court systems are involved. The patent system, in Canada and internationally, needs significant improvement if it is to really protect firms that develop innovative ideas.[6]

Although life cycles are moving faster in the advanced economies, keep in mind that many advances bypass most consumers in less-developed economies. They struggle at the subsistence level, without an effective macro-marketing system to stimulate innovation. However, some of the innovations and economies of scale made possible in the advanced societies do trickle down to benefit these consumers. Inexpensive antibiotics and drought-resistant plants, for example, are making a life-or-death difference.

The early bird usually makes the profits

The increasing speed of the product life cycle means that firms must be developing new products all the time. Further, they must try to have marketing mixes that will make the most of the market growth stage—when profits are highest.

During the growth stage, competitors are likely to introduce product improvements. Fast changes in marketing strategy may be required here because profits don't necessarily go to the innovator. Sometimes, fast copiers of the basic idea will share in the market growth stage. Sony, a pioneer in developing videocassette recorders, was one of the first firms to put VCRs on the market. Other firms quickly followed—and the competition drove down prices and increased demand. As sales of VCRs continued to grow, Sony doggedly stuck to its Beta format VCRs in spite of the fact that most consumers were buying VHS-format machines offered by competitors. Not until a decade later did Sony finally "surrender" and offer a VHS-format machine. However, by then the booming growth in VCR sales had ebbed, and competitors controlled 90 percent of the market. Although Sony was slow to see its mistake, its lost opportunities were minor compared to North American producers who sat on the sidelines and watched as foreign producers captured the whole VCR market. Copiers can be even faster than the innovator in adapting to the market's needs. Marketers must be flexible, *but also* they must fully understand the needs and attitudes of their target markets.[7]

The short happy life of fashions and fads

The sales of some products are influenced by **fashion**—the currently accepted or popular style. Fashion-related products tend to have short life cycles. What is currently popular can shift rapidly. A certain color or style of clothing—bell-bottom jeans, miniskirts, or four-inch-wide ties—may be in fashion one season,

---

A certain color or style may be in fashion one season and outdated the next.

Catimini   Si c'était les enfants qui fai saient les vêtements, ils ne les feraient pas autrement.

outdated the next, but then is rediscovered a generation later. Marketing managers who work with fashions often have to make really fast product changes.

It's not really clear why a particular fashion becomes popular. Most present fashions are adaptations or revivals of previously popular styles. Designers are always looking for styles that will satisfy fashion innovators who crave distinctiveness. And lower cost copies of the popular items may catch on with other groups and survive for a while. Yet the speed of change increases the cost of producing and marketing products. Companies sustain losses due to trial and error in finding acceptable styles, then producing them on a limited basis because of uncertainty about the length of the cycle. These increased costs are not always charged directly to the consumer since some firms lose their investment and go out of business. But in total, fashion changes cost consumers money. Fashion changes are a luxury that most people in less-developed countries simply can't afford.

A **fad** is an idea that is fashionable only to certain groups who are enthusiastic about it. But these groups are so fickle that a fad is even more short lived than a regular fashion. Many toys, like the velcro-covered Super Grip Ball and Hasbro's Transformers, do well during a short-lived cycle. Some teenagers' music tastes are fads. Exhibit 10–2 summarizes the shape of typical life cycles for fashions, fads, and styles. Note that the pattern for a style may go up and down as it comes back into fashion over time.[8] Marketing Demo 10–1 illustrates Rollerblade's attempts to prevent in-line skating from being simply a fad through the development of a long-term strategy.

Exhibit 10–2   Patterns of Fashion, Fad, and Style Cycles for Fashion Products

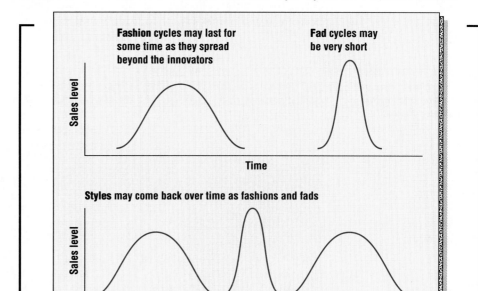

MARKETING DEMO 10–1 Rolling in Dough

L ike psychedelic, space-aged comic book he-roes propelled by jet boots, they zip past at speeds reaching 30 miles per hour, becoming only a flash of neon or pink reef or electric lime or maybe endless wave. In-line skaters have become the hot-test things on eight wheels—for now. The challenge facing marketers today is turning a hip happening into a sport with staying power.

The skates, which come in a bevy of styles and colors, feature a single row of four polyurethane wheels attached to a metal "blade" that is connected to a molded or stitched boot. A rubber stopper on the back of one skate serves as a brake.

Rollerblade, the original manufacturer, knew if the product caught fire in trend-setting California it would spark interest across North America. The com-pany gave away hundreds of skates to rental shops along the beach boardwalk, already considered Nir-vana by rollerskaters, cyclists, and skateboarders.

The marketing scheme paid off, and Rollerblade, a $3 million operation in 1987, now commands more than 50 percent of both the $150 million US market ($US) and its $15 million Canadian counterpart. Paolina Fa-sula, Rollerblade's Canadian marketing manager,

credits the sport's popularity to "the underlying motiva-tion of fun." Now comes the hard part for marketers—keeping the popularity of in-line skating rolling steadily into the future.

Fasula says Rollerblade's long-term marketing program is specifically designed to develop in-line skating into a whole new sport. That includes spon-sored in-line races. There are also several other in-line skating opportunities, including rollerhockey leagues and tournaments; in-line stunt competitions; Club Rollerblade, in which members get discounts and a newsletter; Team Rollerblade, a touring group of professional skaters who combine skating, chore-ography, and music; and demo vans that tour North America, providing free skate test-rides.

In addition, in-line skate manufacturers are cur-rently working together to develop a Skate Smart campaign, which should also contribute to the legiti-macy of the sport, further enhancing its chances of staying out of the fad graveyard. If they are able to establish a base of loyal devotees to in-line skating, they should succeed.

Source: Laura Medcalf, "Rolling in Dough," *Marketing*, July 1, 1991, pp. 1, 3.

PLANNING FOR DIFFERENT STAGES OF THE PRODUCT LIFE CYCLE

Length of cycle affects strategy planning

Where a product is in its life cycle—and how fast it's moving to the next stage—should affect marketing strategy planning. Marketing managers must make realistic plans for the later stages. Exhibit 10–3 shows the relationship of the product life cycle to the marketing mix variables. The technical terms in this figure are discussed elsewhere in this book.

Introducing new products

Exhibit 10–3 shows that a marketing manager has to do a lot of work to introduce a really new product, and this should be reflected in the strategy plan-ning. Money must be spent designing and developing the new product. Even if the product is unique, this doesn't mean that everyone will immediately come running to the producer's door. The firm will have to build channels of distribution—perhaps offering special incentives to win cooperation. Promotion is needed to build demand *for the whole idea*—not just to sell a specific brand. Because all this is expensive, it may lead the marketing manager to try to "skim" the market—charging a relatively high price to help pay for the introductory costs.

The correct strategy, however, depends on how fast the product life cycle is likely to move—that is, how quickly the new idea will be accepted by

Exhibit 10–3   Typical Changes in Marketing Variables over the Product Life Cycle

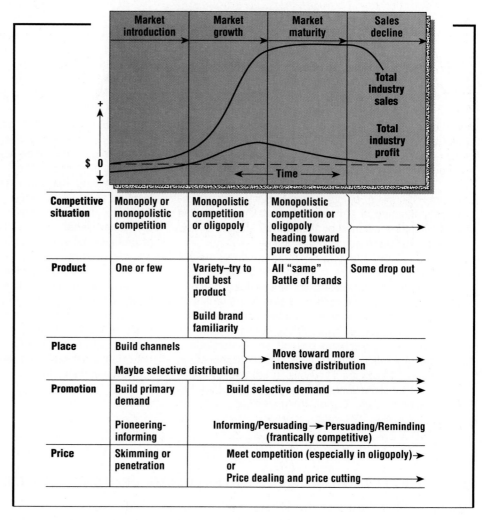

	Market introduction	Market growth	Market maturity	Sales decline
Competitive situation	Monopoly or monopolistic competition	Monopolistic competition or oligopoly	Monopolistic competition or oligopoly heading toward pure competition →	
Product	One or few	Variety–try to find best product Build brand familiarity	All "same" Battle of brands	Some drop out
Place	Build channels Maybe selective distribution	→ Move toward more intensive distribution →		
Promotion	Build primary demand Pioneering-informing	Build selective demand ————————→ Informing/Persuading → Persuading/Reminding (frantically competitive)		
Price	Skimming or penetration	Meet competition (especially in oligopoly) → or Price dealing and price cutting ————→		

customers—and how quickly competitors will follow with their own versions of the product. When the early stages of the cycle will be fast, a low initial (penetration) price may make sense to help develop loyal customers early and keep competitors out.

Of course, not all new product ideas catch on. Customers may conclude that the marketing mix doesn't satisfy their needs, or other new products may meet the same need better. But the success that eludes a firm with its initial strategy can sometimes be achieved by modifying the strategy. Videodisc players illustrate this point. They were a flop during their initial introduction in the home-entertainment market. Consumers didn't see any advantage over cheaper video-tape players. But now new opportunities are developing. For example, a new generation of video games uses laser videodiscs to store sounds and images. These games are really just a special application of multimedia computer systems that link videodisc players with a personal computer. The business market for these systems is also growing. Many firms are buying these systems as a selling aid.

Faced with mature markets in North America, Nabisco varied its products to make them more appealing to some customers—and also looked for new growth opportunities in the Russian market.

Salespeople use them to make presentations, and they are also used for in-store selling. Customers can shop for products by viewing pictures on a computer video screen.[9]

Also relevant is how quickly the firm can change its strategy as the life cycle moves on. Some firms are very flexible. They can compete effectively with larger, less adaptable competitors by adjusting their strategies more frequently.

Managing maturing products

It's important for a firm to have some competitive advantage as it moves into market maturity. Even a small advantage can make a big difference—and some firms do very well by carefully managing their maturing products. They are able to capitalize on a slightly better product or perhaps lower production and/or marketing costs. Or they are simply more successful at promotion, allowing them to differentiate their more or less homogeneous product from competitors. For example, graham crackers were competing in a mature market and sales were flat. Nabisco used the same ingredients to create bite-sized Teddy Grahams and then promoted them heavily. These changes captured new sales and profits for Nabisco. However, competing firms quickly copied this idea with their own brands.[10]

The important point here is that industry profits are declining in market maturity. Top management must see this, or it will continue to expect the attractive profits of the market growth stage—profits that are no longer possible. If top managers don't understand the situation, they may place impossible burdens on the marketing department—causing marketing managers to think about collusion with competitors, deceptive advertising, or some other desperate attempt to reach impossible objectives.

Product life cycles keep moving. But that doesn't mean a firm should just sit by as its sales decline. There are other choices. A firm can improve its product or develop an innovative product for the same market. Or it can develop a strategy for its product (perhaps with modifications) targeted at a new market. For example, it might target a market in another part of the world, as Procter & Gamble did with Camay in Marketing Demo 10–2, or it might try to serve a new

MARKETING DEMO 10–2   A Brand New World

When Procter & Gamble launched Camay soap in Japan several years ago, the company went with a local version of a global advertising execution that showed a Japanese woman lathering herself in the bath. "The execution failed miserably and almost killed the brand," says Alan Middleton, former president of J. Walter Thompson Japan and Enterprise Advertising Associates, Toronto. Middleton says the brand survived, but the incident illustrates that implementing a global advertising program for a relatively simple packaged good can leave it dead in the water. "There were two problems," he says. "First, in Japan, you lather yourself before you get in the bath. Secondly, the Japanese would regard it as very rude if you showed ladies bathing themselves."

Middleton says the brand's marketers' failure to check for cultural appropriateness was enough to sink it in the minds of many Japanese consumers. But Procter & Gamble isn't the only world leader in the packaged goods industry to be forced to navigate the global marketing waters cautiously.

The most recent list of the world's top 50 brands, compiled by Landor Associates, San Francisco, includes the brand names of more than 20 packaged goods. An increasing number of those brands are being marketed globally with the same strategy and, in some cases, the same execution.

Moving to a single worldwide strategy and brand image helps companies drive costs down, but there can be a trade-off, says Rolf Bolhuis, vice president of marketing for Monarch Fine Foods and chair of the marketing committee for Unilever, Toronto. "If you say to the world you've got this terrific soap, people can get it in any color as long as it's black, it certainly limits the freedom to establish exact positioning," he says.

But applying strategic and even tactical ideas from around the world to a given market can also help to fine-tune a brand's position, says Tony Miller, chief executive officer and chairman of Lintas: New York, which represents a number of Unilever and Johnson & Johnson brands.

"When a large and successful company like Lever or Procter & Gamble has success with a product anywhere in the world, that success is carefully dissected by international competitors," Miller says. "The lessons of those successes are translated very specifically around the world."

Source: Hugh Filman, "A Brand New World," *Marketing,* April 6, 1992, pp. 1, 3.

need. Or the firm can withdraw the product before it completes the cycle—and refocus on better opportunities. See Exhibit 10–4.

Improve the product or develop a new one

When a firm's product has won loyal customers, it can be successful for a long time, even in a mature or declining market. However, continued improvements may be needed to keep customers satisfied, especially if their needs shift. An outstanding example is Procter & Gamble's Tide. Introduced in 1947, this powdered detergent gave consumers a much cleaner wash than they were able to get before because it did away with soap film. Tide led to a whole new generation of powdered laundry products that cleaned better with fewer suds. The demands on Tide continued to change because of new washing machines and fabrics—so the powdered Tide sold today is much different than the one sold in 1947. In fact, powdered Tide has had a least 55 (sometimes subtle) modifications.

Do product modifications—like those made with powdered Tide—create a wholly new product that should have its own product life cycle? Or are they technical adjustments of the original product idea? We will take the latter position, focusing on the product idea rather than changes in features. This means that some of these Tide changes were made in the market maturity stage. But this type of product improvement can help to extend the product life cycle.

Exhibit 10–4   Examples of Three Marketing Strategy Choices for a Firm in a Mature Product-Market

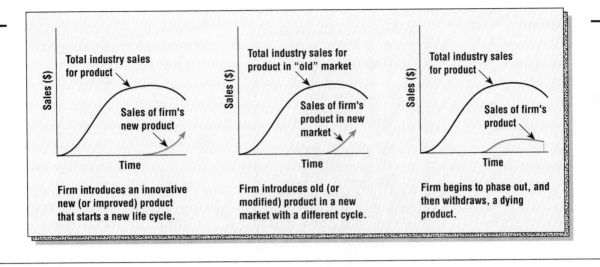

On the other hand, a firm that develops an innovative new product may move to a new product life cycle. For example, by 1985, new liquid detergents like Wisk were moving into the growth stage, and sales of powdered detergents were declining. To share in the growth-stage profits for liquid detergents and to offset the loss of customers from powdered Tide, Procter & Gamble introduced Liquid Tide. Although P&G used the familiar Tide brand name, Liquid Tide appears to be a different product concept that competes in a different product-market.

Even though powdered detergents in general appear to be in the decline stage, powdered Tide continues to sell well because it still does the job for some consumers. But sales growth is likely to come from liquid detergents.[11]

Develop new strategies for different markets

We already highlighted the fact that the same product may be in different life-cycle stages in different markets. That means that a firm may have to pursue very different strategies for a product, at the same time, in different markets.

In a mature market, a firm may be fighting to keep or increase its market share. But if the firm finds a new use for the product, it may need to try to stimulate overall demand. Du Pont's Teflon fluorocarbon resin is a good example. It was developed more than 50 years ago and has enjoyed sales growth as a nonstick coating for cookware, as an insulation for aircraft wiring, and as a lining for chemically resistant equipment. But marketing managers for Teflon are not waiting to be stuck with declining profits in those mature markets. They are constantly developing strategies for new markets where Teflon will meet needs. For example, Teflon is now selling well as a special coating for the wires used in high-speed communications between computers.[12]

Phasing out dying products

Not all strategies have to be exciting growth strategies. If prospects are poor in some product-market, a phase-out strategy may be needed. The need for phasing out becomes more obvious as the sales decline stage arrives. But even in market maturity, it may be clear that a particular product is not going to be profitable enough to reach the company's objectives using the current strategy.

Du Pont has developed new opportunities by finding new markets for Teflon.

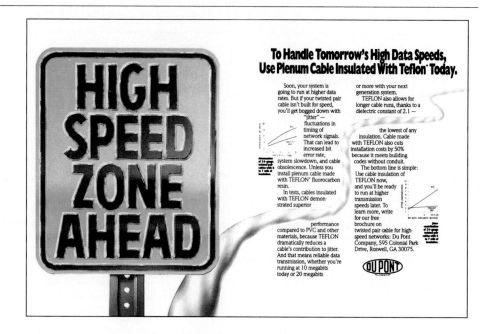

Then, the wisest move may be to develop a strategy that helps the firm phase out of the product-market, perhaps over several years.

Marketing plans are implemented as ongoing strategies. Salespeople make calls, inventory moves in the channel, advertising is scheduled for several months into the future, and so on. So the firm usually experiences losses if managers end a plan too abruptly. Because of this, it's sometimes better to phase out the product gradually. Managers order materials more selectively so production can end with a minimum of unused inventory, and they shift salespeople to other jobs. They may cancel advertising and other promotion efforts more quickly since there's no point in promoting for the long run. These various actions obviously affect morale within the company—and they may cause middlemen to pull back, too. So the company may have to offer price inducements in the channels. Employees should be told that a phase-out strategy is being implemented—and be reassured that they will be shifted to other jobs as the plan is completed.

Obviously, there are some difficult implementation problems here. But phase-out is also a *strategy*—and it must be market-oriented to cut losses. In fact, it is possible to milk a dying product for some time if competitors move out more quickly. This situation occurs when there is still ongoing (though declining) demand—and some customers are willing to pay attractive prices to get their old favorite.

NEW-PRODUCT PLANNING

Competition is strong and dynamic in most markets. So it is essential for a firm to keep developing new products—as well as modifying its current products—to meet changing customer needs and competitors' actions. Not having an active new-product development process means that consciously—or subconsciously—the firm has decided to milk its current products and go out of business. New-product planning is not an optional matter. It has to be done just to survive in today's dynamic markets.

What is a new product?

In discussing the introductory stage of product life cycles, we focused on the type of product innovations that tend to disrupt old ways of doing things. However, each year firms introduce many products that are basically refinements of existing products. So a **new product** is one that is new *in any way* for the company concerned.

A product can become "new" in many ways. A fresh idea can be turned into a new product—and start a new product life cycle. For example, Alza Corporation's time-release skin patches are replacing pills and injections for some medications.

Variations on an existing product idea can also make a product new. Oral B changed its conventional toothbrush to include a strip of colored bristles that fade as you brush; that way you know when it's time for a new brush. Even small changes in an existing product can make it new.[13]

CCAC says product is "new" only 12 months

A firm can call its product new for only a limited time. Twelve months is the limit according to Consumer and Corporate Affairs Canada. To be called new, a product must be entirely new or changed in a "functionally significant or substantial respect." While 12 months may seem a very short time for production-oriented managers, it may be reasonable, given the fast pace of change for many products.

Ethical issues in new-product planning

New product decisions—and decisions to abandon old products—often involve ethical considerations. For example, some firms (including the firm that develops drugs used in treating AIDS) have been criticized for holding back important new-product innovations until patents run out—or sales slow down—on their existing products. At the same time, others have been criticized for "planned obsolescence"—releasing new products that the company plans to soon replace with improved new versions. Similarly, wholesalers and middlemen complain that producers too often keep their new-product introduction plan a secret and leave middlemen with dated inventory that they can only sell at a loss.

Companies also face ethical dilemmas when they decide to stop supplying a product or the service and replacement parts to keep it useful. An old model of a Cuisinart food processor, for example, might be in perfect shape except for a crack in the plastic mixing bowl. It's sensible for the company to improve the design if the crack is a frequent problem, but if consumers can't get a replacement part for the model they already own, they're left holding the bag.

Criticisms are also leveled at firms that constantly release minor variations of products that already saturate markets. Consider what's happening with disposable diapers. Marketing managers may feel that they're serving some customers' needs better when they offer diapers in boys' and girls' versions and in a variety of sizes, shapes, and colors. But many retailers feel that the new products are simply a ploy to get more shelf space. Further, some consumers complain that the bewildering array of choices make it impossible to make an informed choice.

Different marketing managers might have very different reactions to such criticisms. However, the fact remains that product management decisions often have a significant effect, one way or another, on customers and middlemen. A marketing manager who is not sensitive to this may find that a too casual decision leads to a negative backlash that affects the firm's strategy or reputation.[14]

AN ORGANIZED NEW-PRODUCT DEVELOPMENT PROCESS IS CRITICAL

Identifying and developing new-product ideas—and effective strategies to go with them—is often the key to a firm's success and survival. But this isn't easy. New-product development demands effort, time, and talent—and still the risks and costs of failure are high. Experts estimate that consumer packaged-goods companies spend at least $20 million to introduce a new brand—and 70 to 80 percent of these new brands flop. In the service sector, the front-end cost of a failed effort may not be as high, but it can have a devastating long-term effect if dissatisfied consumers turn elsewhere for help.[15]

A new product may fail for many reasons. Most often, companies fail to offer a unique benefit or underestimate the competition. Sometimes, the idea is good but the company has design problems—or the product costs much more to produce than was expected. Some companies rush to get a product on the market without developing a complete marketing plan.[16]

But moving too slowly can be a problem, too. With the fast pace of change for many products, speedy entry into the market can be a key to competitive advantage. A few years ago, marketing managers at Xerox were alarmed that Japanese competitors were taking market share with innovative new models of copiers. It turned out that the competitors were developing new models twice as fast as Xerox and at half the cost. For Xerox to compete, it had to slash its five-year product development cycle. Many other companies, ranging from Chrysler Corporation to Hewlett-Packard to Motorola, are working to speed up the new-product development process.[17]

To move quickly and also avoid expensive new-product failures, many companies follow an organized new-product development process. The following pages describe such a process, which moves logically through five steps: (1) idea generation, (2) screening, (3) idea evaluation, (4) development (of product and marketing mix), and (5) commercialization.[18] See Exhibit 10–5.

Exhibit 10–5   New-Product Development Process

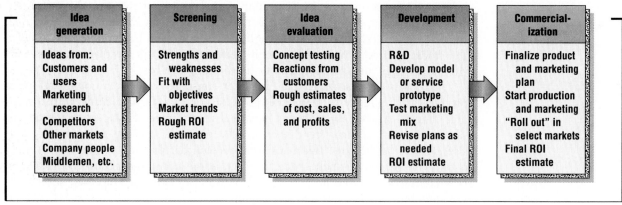

Idea generation	Screening	Idea evaluation	Development	Commercial-ization
Ideas from: Customers and users Marketing research Competitors Other markets Company people Middlemen, etc.	Strengths and weaknesses Fit with objectives Market trends Rough ROI estimate	Concept testing Reactions from customers Rough estimates of cost, sales, and profits	R&D Develop model or service prototype Test marketing mix Revise plans as needed ROI estimate	Finalize product and marketing plan Start production and marketing "Roll out" in select markets Final ROI estimate

The general process is similar for both cons[...] both goods and services. There are some significa[...] emphasize the similarities in the following discussion.

Process tries to kill new ideas—economically

An important element in this new-product development process is [...] evaluation of a new idea's likely profitability and return on investment. In [...] the hypothesis-testing approach discussed in Chapter 5 works well for new-product development. The hypothesis tested is that the new idea will *not* be profitable. This puts the burden on the new idea—to prove itself or be rejected. Such a process may seem harsh, but experience shows that most new ideas have some flaw that can lead to problems—and even substantial losses. Marketers try to discover those flaws early, and either find a remedy or reject the idea completely. Applying this process requires much analysis of the idea, both within and outside the firm, *before* the company spends money to develop and market a product. This is a major departure from the usual production-oriented approach, in which a company develops a product first and then asks sales to "get rid of it."

Of course, the actual new-product success rate varies among industries and companies. But many companies *are* improving the way they develop new products. It's important to see that if a firm doesn't use an organized process like this, it may bring many bad or weak ideas to market—at a big loss.

Step 1: Idea generation

New ideas can come from a company's own sales or production staff, middlemen, competitors, consumer surveys, or other sources such as trade associations, advertising agencies, or government agencies. By analyzing new and different views of the company's markets and studying present consumer behavior,

Speed in the new-product development process can be an important competitive advantage, especially with high-tech products like this cellular Visorphone.

...an spot opportunities that have not yet occurred to ...to potential customers. For example, ideas for new service ...directly from analysis of consumer complaints. Marketing ...ibes how one firm brings inventors, retailers, and distributors

...rm can always be first with the best new ideas. So in their search for ...panies should pay attention to what current or potential competitors ...g. For example, new-product specialists at Ford Motor Company buy ...rms' cars as soon as they're available. Then they take the cars apart to see ...the other firms are doing in the way of new ideas or improvements. British ...rways talks to travel agents to learn about new services offered by competitors. ...Many other companies use similar approaches.[19]

MARKET DEMO 10–3
New Product Store Offers Gadgets Galore

R emember the gadget craze of the 70s, perhaps best epitomized by K-Tel, the Canadian marketing company that tried to convince us we couldn't find our way around a kitchen without the Patty Stacker hamburger maker or the slicing machine that "slices, dices, and juliennes: just about anything edible"? By the time the 80s rolled around, we had tucked most of these cumbersome devices into the far recesses of our cupboards and turned our attention to more substantial gadgets like the VCR and personal computer.

Brian Gray expects the 90s may witness the rebirth of the gadget, and he and two partners have opened The New Product Store on Toronto's Bay Street to prove it. The outlet rents shelf space to inventors who believe they have a sure-fire hit on their hands but who have been unable to access markets. So far, the store has caught the interest of full-time inventors as well as people anxious to turn their leisure-time tinkering into a bona fide marketable product. "We are a sort of minilandlord," Gray explains. "We sublet space on our shelves to people who couldn't get into retail or those who need expert guidance."

The store's bare-bones decor is proof that the concept is not designed to attract customers off the street. It is intended to provide a forum for retailers and distributors interested in viewing hot new products. An inventor or product designer hawking a new item is not likely to meet with anything but closed doors when attempting to interest buyers, but because The New Product Store houses 150-plus items, it carries more clout with potential purchasers.

Although it's located in Toronto, more than 70 percent of business comes from the United States. In addition to carrying products invented by Americans, Gray also sells product lines to American catalogue operations and is negotiating deals with US distributors. New Product Store client Dan Jagdat has just signed a contract with American Airlines to supply the firm with his Snoozer commuter pillow, a device that is attached to airplane windows with a suction cup. Therese Salisbury, who has her Perfect Gentleman automatic toilet seat lifter displayed in the store, has received more interest from buyers in the United States and Hong Kong than in Canada. She expects Canadian consumers don't want to risk being the first one on the block with a pedal on the side of their toilet.

Few of the store's products may save lives (with the exception of the portable smoke detector), but some save time and effort and others are simply amusing. If the aim is to entertain, the store and its clients have every chance for success in Canada. After all, this is the country that provided a market for millions of Taiwanese Rockin' Flowers and pieces of the Berlin Wall.

Source: Pam Bristol, "New Product Store Offers Gadgets Galore," *Retail Directions,* November–December 1990, p. 6.

Many firms now "shop" in international markets for new ideas. Jamaica Broilers, a poultry producer in the Caribbean, moved into fish farming; it learned that many of the techniques it was using to breed chickens were also successful on fish farms in Israel. In the same vein, food companies in the United States and Europe are now experimenting with an innovation recently introduced in Japan—a clear, odorless, natural film for wrapping food. Consumers don't have to unwrap it; when they toss a product in boiling water or a microwave, the wrapper vanishes.[20]

Research shows that many new ideas in business markets come from customers who identify a need they have. Then they approach a supplier with the idea—and perhaps even with a particular design or specification. These customers become the lead-users of the product, but the supplier can pursue the opportunity in other markets.[21]

But finding new product ideas can't be left to chance. Companies need a formal procedure for seeking new ideas. The checkpoints discussed below, as well as the hierarchy of needs and other behavioral elements discussed earlier, should be reviewed regularly to ensure a continual flow of new—and sound—ideas. And companies do need a continual flow so they can spot an opportunity early, while there's still time to do something about it. Although later steps eliminate many ideas, a company must have some that succeed.

Step 2: Screening

Screening involves evaluating the new ideas with the product-market screening criteria described in Chapter 4. Recall that these criteria include the combined output of a resource (strengths and weaknesses) analysis, a long-run trends analysis, and a thorough understanding of the company's objectives. See Exhibit 3–1. Further, a "good" new idea should eventually lead to a product (and marketing mix) that will give the firm a competitive advantage—hopefully, a lasting one.

Opportunities with better growth potential are likely to be more attractive. We discussed this idea earlier when we introduced the GE planning grid (see Exhibit 4–7). Now, however, you know that the life-cycle stage at which a firm's new product enters the market has a direct bearing on its prospects for growth. Clearly, screening should consider how the strategy for a new product will hold up over the whole product life cycle. In other words, screening should consider how attractive the new product will be both in the short and long term.

Some companies screen based on consumer welfare

The firm's final choice in product design should fit with the company's overall objectives and make good use of the firm's resources. But it's also desirable to create a need-satisfying product that will appeal to consumers in the long run as well as the short run. Ideally, the product will increase consumer welfare, too, and not just satisfy a whim. Different kinds of new-product opportunities are shown in Exhibit 10–6. Obviously, a socially responsible firm tries to find desirable opportunities rather than deficient ones. This may not be as easy as it sounds, however. Some consumers want "pleasing products" instead of "desirable products." They emphasize immediate satisfaction and give little thought to their own long-term welfare. And some competitors are quite willing to offer what consumers want in the short run. Generating "socially responsible" new-product ideas is a challenge for new-product planners. Consumer groups are helping to force this awareness on more firms.

Exhibit 10–6
Types of New-Product Opportunities

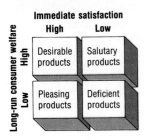

| | Immediate satisfaction | |
	High	Low
Long-run consumer welfare — High	Desirable products	Salutary products
Long-run consumer welfare — Low	Pleasing products	Deficient products

Safety must be considered

Real acceptance of the marketing concept certainly leads to the design of safe products. But some risky products are purchased because they provide thrills and excitement—for example, bicycles, skis, hang gliders, and bungee jumps. Even so, safety features usually can be added—and they're desired by some potential customers.

The **Hazardous Products Act** passed by the Canadian Parliament in June 1969 gives Consumer and Corporate Affairs Canada the authority either to ban outright or to regulate the sale, distribution, labelling, and advertising of potentially dangerous products. This act reemphasizes the need for businesspersons to become more safety-oriented.

Product safety complicates strategy planning because not all customers—even those who want better safety features—are willing to pay more for safer products. Some features cost a lot to add and increase prices considerably. These safety concerns must be considered at the screening step because a firm can later be held liable for unsafe products.

Products can turn to liabilities

Product liability means the legal obligation of sellers to pay damages to individuals who are injured by defective or unsafe products. Product liability is a serious matter. Liability settlements may exceed not only a company's insurance coverage but its total assets! Some experts predict that this could happen to Dow-Corning because of its liability for faulty silicone breast implants.

The courts have been enforcing a very strict product liability standard. Producers may be held responsible for injuries related to their products, no matter how the items are used or how well they are designed. Riddell (whose football helmets protect the pros) recently was hit with a $12 million judgment for a high school football player who broke his neck. The jury concluded that Riddell should have put a sticker on the helmet to warn players of the danger of butting into opponents! Cases and settlements like this are common.

Adopting the marketing concept should lead to the development of safe products.

Product liability is a serious ethical and legal matter. Many countries are attempting to change their laws so that they will be fair to both firms and consumers. But until product liability questions are resolved, marketing managers must be even more sensitive when screening new-product ideas.[22]

ROI is a crucial screening criterion

Getting by the initial screening criteria doesn't guarantee success for the new idea. But it does show that at least the new idea is in the right ballpark *for this firm*. If many ideas pass the screening criteria, a firm must set priorities to determine which ones go on to the next step in the process. This can be done by comparing the ROI (return on investment) for each idea—assuming the firm is ROI-oriented. The most attractive alternatives are pursued first.

Step 3: Idea evaluation

When an idea moves past the screening step, it is evaluated more carefully. Note that an actual product has not yet been developed—and this can handicap the firm in getting feedback from customers. For help in idea evaluation, firms use **concept testing**—getting reactions from customers about how well a new product idea fits their needs. Concept testing uses market research, ranging from informal focus groups to formal surveys of potential customers.

Companies can often estimate likely costs, revenue, and profitability at this stage. And market research can help identify the size of potential markets. Even informal focus groups are useful—especially if they show that potential users are not excited about the new idea. If results are discouraging, it may be best to kill the idea at this stage. Remember, in this hypothesis-testing process, we're looking for any evidence that an idea is *not* a good opportunity for this firm—and should be rejected.

Product planners must think about wholesaler and retailer customers as well as final consumers. Middlemen may have special concerns about handling a proposed product. An ice-cream maker was considering a new line of ice-cream novelty products, and he had visions of a hot market in California. But he had to drop his idea when he learned that grocery store chains wanted payments of $20,000 each just to stock his frozen novelties in their freezers. Without the payment, they didn't want to risk using profitable freezer space on an unproven product. This is not an unusual case. At the idea evaluation stage, companies often find that other members of the distribution channel won't cooperate.[23]

Idea evaluation is more precise in business markets. Potential customers are more informed—and their needs focus on the economic reasons for buying rather than emotional factors. Further, given the derived nature of demand in business markets, most needs are already being satisfied in some way. So new products just substitute for existing ones. This means that product planners can compare the cost advantages and limitations of a new product with those currently being used. And by interviewing well-informed people, they can determine the range of product requirements—and decide whether there is an opportunity.

For example, in 1990 GE was developing a special light bulb for automobile headlights. GE's marketing managers knew that auto designers would like the smaller, low-heat bulb because it would allow sleeker styling and thus better gas mileage, as well as better night visibility. By working with engineers at Ford, GE was able to determine that the switch to the new bulb and headlight assembly would add about $200 to the price of a car. That meant that the bulb would initially be limited to luxury cars—until economies of scale brought down the costs.[24]

Whatever research methods are used, the idea evaluation step should gather enough information to help decide whether there is an opportunity, whether it fits with the firm's resources, *and* whether there is a basis for developing a competitive advantage. With such information, the firm can estimate likely ROI in the various market segments and decide whether to continue the new-product development process.[25]

Step 4: Development

Product ideas that survive the screening and idea evaluation steps must now be analyzed further. Usually, this involves some research and development (R&D) and engineering to design and develop the physical part of the product. In the case of a new service offering, the firm will work out the details of what training, equipment, staff, and so on will be needed to deliver on the idea. Input from the earlier efforts helps guide this technical work.

The most recent computer-aided design (CAD) systems are sparking a revolution in design work. Designers can develop lifelike 3-D color drawings of packages and products. Then the computer allows the manager to look at the product from different angles and views, just as with a real product. Changes can be made almost instantly. And once the designs are finalized, they feed directly into computer-controlled manufacturing systems. Companies like Motorola and Timex have found that these systems cut their new-product development time in half, giving them a leg up on foreign competitors.

Even so, it is still good to test models and early versions of the product in the market. This process may have several cycles. A manufacturer may build a model of a physical product or produce limited quantities; a service firm may try to train a small group of service providers. Product tests with customers may lead to revisions—*before* the firm commits to full-scale efforts to produce the good or service.

With actual goods or services, potential customers can react to how well the product meets their needs. Using small focus groups, panels, and larger surveys, marketers can get reactions to specific features and to the whole product idea.

Computer-aided design is helping to speed up the new-product development process, as in this system that Ford uses in Germany, England, and the United States.

[handwritten marginal notes: Idea generation / Screening / Idea evaluation / Development / (Commercialization]

Sometimes that reaction kills the idea. For example, Coca-Cola Foods believed it had a great idea with Minute Maid Squeeze-Fresh, frozen orange juice concentrate in a squeeze bottle. Coca-Cola thought consumers would prefer to mix one glass at a time rather than find space for another half-gallon jug in the refrigerator. When actually tested, however, Squeeze-Fresh bombed. Consumers loved the idea but hated the product. It was messy to use, and no one knew how much concentrate to squeeze in the glass.[26]

In other cases, testing can lead to revision of product specifications for different markets. For example, AMR Corporation had plans for a new reservation system to help travel agents, hotels, and airlines provide better customer service. But tests revealed too many problems, and plans for the service had to be revised. Sometimes a complex series of revisions may be required. Months or even years of research may be necessary to focus on precisely what different market segments will find acceptable. For example, Gillette's Sensor razor took 13 years and over $300 million to develop.[27]

Firms often use full-scale market testing to get reactions in real market conditions or to test product variations and variations in the marketing mix. For example, a firm may test alternative brands, prices, or advertising copy in different test cities. Note that the firm is testing the whole marketing mix, not just the product. For example, a hotel chain might test a new service offering at one location to see how it goes over.

Test marketing can be risky because it may give information to competitors. In fact, a company in Chicago—Marketing Intelligence Services—monitors products in test markets and then sells the information to competing firms. Similar firms monitor markets in other countries.

But *not* testing is dangerous, too. In 1986, Frito-Lay was so sure it understood consumers' snack preferences that it introduced a three-item cracker line without market testing. Even with network TV ad support, MaxSnax met with overwhelming consumer indifference. By the time Frito-Lay pulled the product from store shelves, it had lost $52 million. Market tests can be very expensive. Yet they can uncover problems that otherwise might go undetected—and destroy the whole strategy.[28]

If a company follows the new-product development process carefully, the market test will provide a lot more information to the firm than to its competitors. Of course, the company must test specific variables—rather than just vaguely testing whether a new idea will "sell." After the market test, the firm can estimate likely ROI for various strategies to determine whether the idea moves on to commercialization.

Some companies don't do market tests because they just aren't practical. In fashion markets, for example, speed is extremely important, and products are usually just tried in market. And durable products—which have high fixed production costs and long production lead times, may have to go directly to market. In these cases, it is especially important that the early steps be done carefully to reduce the chances for failure.[29]

Step 5: Commercialization

A product idea that survives this far can finally be placed on the market. First, the new-product people decide exactly which product form or line to sell. Then they complete the marketing mix—really a whole strategic plan. And top management has to approve an ROI estimate for the plan before it is implemented. Finally, the product idea emerges from the new-product development process—but success requires the cooperation of the whole company.

Putting a product on the market is expensive. Manufacturing or service facilities have to be set up. Goods have to be produced to fill the channels of distribution, or people must be hired and trained to provide services. Further, introductory promotion is costly, especially if the company is entering a very competitive market.

Because of the size of the job, some firms introduce their products city by city or region by region—in a gradual "rollout"—until they have complete market coverage. Rollouts also permit more market testing, although that is not their purpose. Rather, the purpose is to do a good job implementing the marketing plan. But marketing managers also need to pay close attention to control—to ensure that the implementation effort is working and that the strategy is on target.

NEW-PRODUCT DEVELOPMENT—A TOTAL COMPANY EFFORT

Top-level support is vital

Companies that are particularly successful at developing new goods and services seem to have one trait in common: enthusiastic top-management support for new-product development. New products tend to upset old routines that managers of established products often try in subtle but effective ways to maintain. So someone with top-level support—and authority to get things done—needs to be responsible for new-product development.[30]

Put someone in charge

In addition, rather than leaving new-product development to anyone who happens to be interested (perhaps in engineering, R&D, or sales), successful companies put someone in charge—a person, department, or committee.

A new-product development department or committee may help ensure that new ideas are carefully evaluated and profitable ones quickly brought to market. It's important to choose the right people for the job. Overly conservative managers may kill too many—or even all—new ideas. Or committees may create bureaucratic delays leading to late introduction and giving competitors a head start. A delay of even a few months can make the difference between a product's success or failure.

Market needs guide R&D effort

Many new-product ideas come from scientific discoveries and new technologies. That is why firms often assign specialists to study the technological environment in search of new ways to meet customers' needs. Many firms have their own R&D group that works on developing new products and new-product ideas. Even service firms have technical specialists who help in development work. For example, a bank thinking about offering customers a new set of investment alternatives must be certain that it can deliver on its promises. We've touched on this earlier, but the relationship between marketing and R&D warrants special emphasis.

The R&D effort is usually handled by scientists, engineers, and other specialists who have technical training and skills. Their work can make an important contribution to a firm's competitive advantage—especially if it competes in high-tech markets. However, technical creativity by itself is not enough. The R&D effort must be guided by the type of new-product development process we've been discussing.

From the idea-generation stage to the commercialization stage, the R&D specialists, the operations people, and the marketing people must work together to evaluate the feasibility of new ideas. It isn't sensible for a marketing manager to develop elaborate marketing plans for goods or services that the firm simply can't produce—or produce profitably. It also doesn't make sense for R&D people to develop a technology or product that does not have potential for the firm and its markets. Clearly, a balancing act is involved here. But the critical point is the basic one we've been emphasizing throughout the whole book: marketing-oriented firms seek to satisfy customer needs at a profit with an integrated, whole company effort.

A complicated, integrated effort is needed

Developing new products should be a total company effort. The whole process—involving people in management, research, production, promotion, packaging, and branding—must move in steps from early exploration of ideas to development of the product and marketing mix. Even with a careful development process, many new products do fail—usually because a company skips some steps in the process. Because speed can be important, it's always tempting to skip needed steps when some part of the process seems to indicate that the company has a "really good idea." But the process moves in steps, gathering different kinds of information along the way. By skipping steps, a firm may miss an important aspect that could make a whole strategy less profitable—or actually cause it to fail.

Eventually, the new product is no longer new, and it becomes just another product. About this time, the new-product people turn the product over to the regular operating people—and go on to developing other new ideas.

NEED FOR PRODUCT MANAGERS

Product variety leads to product managers

When a firm has only one or a few related products, everyone is interested in them. But when many new products are being developed, someone should be put in charge of new-product planning to be sure it is not neglected. Similarly, when a firm has several different kinds of products, management may decide to put someone in charge of each kind—or even each brand—to be sure they are not lost in the rush of everyday business. **Product managers** or **brand managers** manage specific products—often taking over the jobs formerly handled by an advertising manager. That gives a clue to what is often their major responsibility— Promotion—since the products have already been developed by the new-product people. However, some brand managers start at the new-product development stage and carry on from there.

Product managers are especially common in large companies that produce many kinds of products. Several product managers may serve under a marketing manager. Sometimes, these product managers are responsible for the profitable operation of a particular product's whole marketing effort. Then they have to coordinate their efforts with others, including the sales manager, advertising agencies, production and research people, and even channel members. This is likely to lead to difficulties if product managers have no control over the marketing strategy for other related brands—or authority over other functional areas whose efforts they are expected to direct and coordinate!

To avoid these problems, in some companies the product manager serves mainly as a "product champion"—concerned with planning and getting the promotion effort implemented. A higher-level marketing manager with more authority coordinates the efforts and integrates the marketing strategies for different products into an overall plan. Exhibit 10–7 gives the job description of a product manager for Nabob Coffee.

The activities of product managers vary a lot depending on their experience and aggressiveness—and the company's organizational philosophy. Today, compa-

Exhibit 10–7   Job Description: Product Manager—Nabob

Basic Purpose
Assemble and analyze product, market, financial, competitive, and consumer data to plan and execute strategic marketing direction/specific activities in order to contribute to the achievements of short- and long-term brand goals.

Accountabilities
1. Develop and recommend brand marketing strategies to achieve share, volume, and profit objectives.
2. Prepare and implement brand marketing plans to fulfill these share, volume, and profit objectives.
3. Recommend and direct all activities related to product positioning, market research, pricing, package design, advertising, and promotion in order to execute the brand marketing plan in an effective and efficient manner.
4. Coordinate and communicate effectively with the other departments in order to maximize efficiency of operation and flexibility in capitalizing on the brand's business opportunities.
5. Accurate and timely data input (financial, trade, consumer, and competitive) for analysis, recommendation, and implementation.
6. Monitor brand spending to maximize opportunities and meet agreed spending levels.
7. Ongoing direct liaising with sales department to develop new opportunities and ensure maximum impact of marketing programs.

Unique Critical Attributes (key features, most difficult challenges, uniqueness)

Ability to learn	Fast comprehension and application of new ideas, methods, etc.
Analytical ability	Disciplined thought process, perspective, judgment.
Dedication, motivation to excel	Attention to excellence and high standards.
Energy, drive	High and sustained even when under pressure.
Innovation, initiation	Develops new, practical ideas; seeks to expand self and business.
Relation with others	Takes interest in others, effective delegation, good listening, self-assurance, motivating other departments and outside agencies and suppliers.
Competitive analysis	Monitors and analyzes competition to be proactive and reactive to ensure franchise strength.

Further Documents
(policies, procedures, manuals, signature power)
Marketing plans
Performance report
Market sales and production report

Source: Courtesy of Nabob Foods Ltd.

nies are emphasizing marketing *experience*—because this important job takes more than academic training and enthusiasm. But it is clear that someone must be responsible for developing and implementing product-related plans—especially when a company has many products.[31]

CONCLUSION

New-product planning is an increasingly important activity in a modern economy because it is no longer very profitable to just sell me-too products in highly competitive markets. Markets, competition, and product life cycles are changing at a fast pace.

The product life-cycle concept is especially important to marketing strategy planning. It shows that a firm needs different marketing mixes—and even strategies—as a product moves through its cycle. This is an important point because profits change during the life cycle, with most of the profits going to the innovators or fast copiers.

We pointed out that a product is new to a firm if it is new in any way—or to any target market. But CCAC takes a narrower view of what you can call "new."

New products are so important to business survival that firms need some organized process for developing them. We discuss such a process and emphasize that it requires a total company effort to be successful.

The failure rate of new products is high—but it is lower for better-managed firms that recognize product development and management as vital processes. Some firms appoint product managers to manage individual products and new-product committees to ensure that the process is carried out successfully.

QUESTIONS AND PROBLEMS

1. Explain how industry sales and industry profits behave over the product life cycle.

2. Cite two examples of products that you feel are currently in each of the product life-cycle stages. Consider services as well as physical goods.

3. Explain how you might reach different conclusions about the correct product life-cycle stage(s) in the worldwide automobile market.

4. Explain why individual brands may not follow the product life-cycle pattern. Give an example of a new brand that is not entering the life cycle at the market introduction stage.

5. Discuss the life cycle of a product in terms of its probable impact on a manufacturer's marketing mix. Illustrate using personal computers.

6. What characteristics of a new product will help it to move through the early stages of the product life cycle quickly? Briefly discuss each characteristic—illustrating with a product of your choice. Indicate how each characteristic might be viewed in some other country.

7. What is a new product? Illustrate your answer.

8. Explain the importance of an organized new-product development process and illustrate how it might be used for (a) a new hair care product, (b) a new children's toy, and (c) a new subscribers-only cable television channel.

9. Discuss how you might use the new-product development process if you were thinking about offering some kind of summer service to residents in a beach resort town.

10. Explain the role of product or brand managers. When would it make sense for one of a company's current brand managers to be in charge of the new-product development process? Explain your thinking.

11. If a firm offers one of its brands in a number of different countries, would it make sense for one brand manager to be in charge, or would each country require its own brand manager? Explain your thinking.

12. Discuss the social value of new-product development activities that seem to encourage people to discard products that are not all worn out. Is this an economic waste? How worn out is all worn out? Must a shirt have holes in it? How big?

SUGGESTED CASES

7. Pillsbury's Häagen Dazs

11. Different Strokes

Place and Development of Channel Systems

I n the spring of 1992, Richard Stewert, the owner of a Goodyear tire store, was frustrated as he looked out at the Sears across the street. Along with 2,500 other independent Goodyear tire distributors in North America, Stewert had just learned that Goodyear planned to sell tires to Sears, which in turn would market them at its 850 autocentres. For the first time, Stewert would have to compete with a big chain in selling Goodyear-brand tires. You can see why he might be wondering if he should seek some other brand to carry.

Although Stewert focused on the changes in his local market, they were a part of a chain reaction that started with big changes in international competition among tire producers. Goodyear's sales and profits plummeted after France's Michelin and Japan's Bridgestone aggressively expanded distribution in the North American market. Michelin moved quickly by buying Uniroyal; similarly, Bridgestone took over Firestone and its outlets. Goodyear's direct sales to Detroit automakers held up, but the company was having trouble competing in the market for replacement tires.

One reason for the trouble was that Goodyear simply wasn't putting its tires where shoppers would buy them. Goodyear sold its brands almost exclusively through its own stores and independent dealers loyal to Goodyear. These stores attracted customers who came in for specific high-performance tires, like Goodyear Eagles, and quality service. But many consumers didn't see a difference in the tires or the service—they just wanted the best price. Moreover, an increasing number were buying tires at discount outlets and warehouse clubs that carried several brands.

Goodyear's marketing managers realized they needed to add new distribution channels and change their strategies to reach different target markets. To reach the price-oriented discount shoppers, Goodyear produced private-label tires sold at Wal-Mart and other big chains. Goodyear also converted some of its own company-owned stores to no-frills, quick-serve stores operated under the Just Tires name.

Goodyear's marketing managers knew that selling Goodyear tires through retail discounters was risky. It would put even more pressure on Goodyear dealers' profit margins and encourage dealers to push other brands. However, Goodyear felt that many consumers went to Sears for tires without even considering a Goodyear dealer—and Sears sold 10 percent of all replacement tires in the US market. Further, Sears agreed to devote about 20 percent of the tire inventory at each autocentre to Goodyear tires. Based on that, Goodyear's managers estimated that working with Sears might increase sales by more than 2 million tires a year. For that kind of a boost, they were willing to risk conflict with Richard Stewert and other dealers.

However, to give these dealers a top-quality product that only they could sell, Goodyear introduced a new Aquatred tire designed to be safer on wet roads. Goodyear also put 30 percent more promotion support behind the dealers. Although the heavily advertised Aquatred line increased store traffic, many Goodyear dealers still felt betrayed. They lost sales because they couldn't get inventory on some of the popular sizes.[1]

PLACE DECISIONS ARE AN IMPORTANT PART OF MARKETING STRATEGY

Offering customers a good product at a reasonable price is important to a successful marketing strategy. But it's not the whole story. Managers must also think about **Place**—making goods and services available in the right quantities and locations—when customers want them. And when different target markets have different needs, a number of Place variations may be required.

In this and the next three chapters, we'll deal with the many important strategy decisions that a marketing manager must make concerning Place. Exhibit 11–1 gives an overview. We'll start in this chapter with a discussion of the type of channel that's needed to meet customers' needs. We'll show why specialists are often involved and how they come together to form a **channel of distribution**—any series of firms or individuals who participate in the flow of products from producer to final user or consumer. We'll also consider how to manage relations among channel members to reduce conflict and improve cooperation.

In Chapter 12, we'll expand our coverage of Place to include decisions that marketing managers make to decide what level of distribution service to offer—and why they must coordinate storing and transporting activities to provide the desired service at a reasonable cost. Then, in Chapters 13 and 14, we'll take a closer look at the many different types of retailing and wholesaling firms. We'll consider their role in channels as well as the strategy decisions they make to satisfy their own customers.

PLACE DECISIONS ARE GUIDED BY IDEAL PLACE OBJECTIVES

All marketing managers want to be sure that their goods and services are available in the right quantities and locations—when customers want them. But customers may have different needs with respect to time, place, and possession utility as they make different purchases.

Product classes suggest place objectives

You've already seen this with the product classes—which summarize consumers' urgency to have needs satisfied and willingness to seek information, shop, and

Exhibit 11–1   Strategy Decision Areas in Place

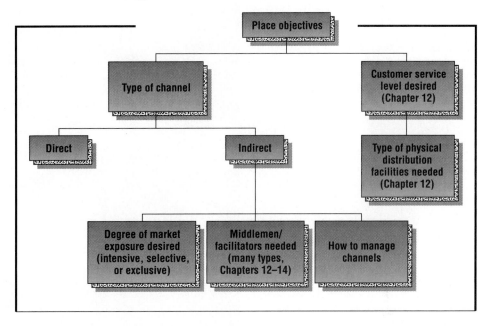

compare. Now you should be able to use the product classes to handle Place decisions.

Exhibit 9–4 shows the relationship between consumer product classes and ideal Place objectives. Similarly, Exhibit 9–5 shows the business product classes and how they relate to customer needs. Study these exhibits carefully. They set the framework for making Place decisions. In particular, the product classes help us decide how much market exposure we'll need in each geographic area.

Place system is not automatic

As the Goodyear case shows, a product may be sold both to final consumers and business customers, and each type of customer may want to purchase in different ways. Further, several different product classes may be involved if different market segments view a product in different ways. Thus, just as there is no automatic classification for a specific product, we can't automatically decide the one best Place arrangement.

However, people in a particular target market should have similar attitudes and therefore should be satisfied with the same Place system. If different target segments view a product in different ways, marketing managers may need to develop several strategies, each with its own Place arrangements.

Place decisions have long-run effects

The marketing manager must also consider Place objectives in relation to the product life cycle; see Exhibit 10–3. Place decisions have long-run effects. They're usually harder to change than Product, Price, and Promotion decisions. It can take years and a great deal of money to develop effective working arrangements with others in the channel. Legal contracts with channel partners may also limit changes. And it's hard to move retail stores and wholesale facilities once leases are signed and customer movement patterns are settled. Yet as products mature, they typically need broader distribution to reach different target customers.

The producer of Vege Burgers is trying to establish widespread, low-cost distribution throughout Great Britain—because British consumers think of Vege Burgers as a staple product.

CHANNEL SYSTEM MAY BE DIRECT OR INDIRECT

One of the most basic Place decisions producers must make is whether to handle the whole distribution themselves—or use wholesalers, retailers, and other specialists (see Exhibit 11–1). Middlemen, in turn, must select the producers they'll work with.

Why a firm might want to use direct distribution

Many firms prefer to distribute direct to the final customer or consumer. One reason is that they want complete control over the marketing job. They may think that they can serve target customers at a lower cost or do the work more effectively than middlemen. Further, working with independent middlemen with different objectives can be troublesome.

Some managers don't have a sensible reason to go direct—they just want to be in charge of a large organization. In any case, there often *are* great advantages in selling direct to the final user or consumer.

Direct contact with customers

If a firm is in direct contact with its customers, it is more aware of changes in customer attitudes. It is in a better position to adjust its marketing mix quickly because there is no need to convince other channel members to help. If a product needs an aggressive selling effort or special technical service, the marketing manager can ensure that the sales force receives the necessary training and motivation. In contrast, middlemen often carry products of several competing producers. So they aren't willing to give any one item the special emphasis its producer wants.

Suitable middlemen are not available

A firm may have to go direct if suitable middlemen are not available—or will not cooperate. This sometimes occurs with new products. Middlemen who have the best contacts with the target market may be hesitant to add unproven products, especially really new products that don't fit well with their current business. Many new products die because the producer can't find willing middlemen and doesn't have the financial resources to handle direct distribution.

Common with business customers and services

Many business products are sold direct-to-customer. Rolm, for example, sells its computerized voice mail systems direct. And Honda sells its motors direct to lawn mower producers. This is understandable since in business markets there are fewer transactions and orders are larger. In addition, customers may be concentrated in a small geographic area, making distribution easier.

Many service firms also use direct channels. If the service must be produced in the presence of customers, there may be little need for middlemen. An accounting firm like Arthur Andersen, for example, must deal directly with its customers. (However, many firms that produce physical goods turn to middlemen specialists to help provide the services customers expect as part of the product. Maytag may hope that its authorized dealers don't get many repair calls, but the service is available when customers need it. Here, the middleman produces the service.)[2]

Some consumer products are sold direct

Of course, some consumer products are sold direct, too. Tupperware, Avon cosmetics, Electrolux vacuum cleaners, Amway household products, and Fuller Brush products are examples. Most of these firms rely on direct selling, which involves personal sales contact between a representative of the company and an individual consumer. However, most of these "salespeople" are *not* company employees. Rather, they usually work as independent middlemen, and the companies that they sell for refer to them as dealers, distributors, agents, or some similar term. So, in a strict technical sense, this is not really direct producer-to-consumer distribution.[3]

Don't be confused by the term *direct marketing*

An increasing number of firms now rely on **direct marketing**—direct communication between a seller and an individual customer using a promotion method other than face-to-face personal selling. Sometimes direct marketing promotion is coupled with direct distribution from a producer to consumers. Park Seed Company, for example, sells the seeds it grows direct to consumers with a mail catalogue. However, many firms that use direct marketing promotion distribute their products through middlemen. So the term *direct marketing* is primarily concerned with the Promotion area, not Place decisions. We'll talk about direct marketing promotion in more detail in Chapter 17.[4]

When indirect channels are best

Even if a producer wants to handle the whole distribution job, sometimes it's simply not possible. Customers often have established buying patterns. For example, Square D, a producer of electrical supplies, might want to sell directly to big electrical contractors. But if contractors like to make all of their purchases in one convenient stop—at a local electrical wholesaler—the only practical way to reach them is through a wholesaler.

Similarly, consumers are spread throughout many geographic areas and often prefer to shop for certain products at specific places. For example, a consumer may

Dell sells computers using a direct-to-customer channel; IBM sells its PS/1 computers in department stores, computer superstores, and electronic chains.

see Shoppers Drug Mart as *the* place to shop for emergency items—because it's conveniently located in the neighborhood. If retailers who serve target customers make most of their purchases from specific wholesalers, the producer may have to work with these wholesalers. This is one reason why most firms that produce consumer products use indirect channels. See Exhibit 2–8.[5]

Direct distribution usually requires a significant investment in facilities and people. A new company or one that has limited financial resources may want to avoid that investment by working with established middlemen. Further, some middlemen play a critical role by providing credit to customers at the end of the channel. Even if the producer could afford to provide credit, a middleman who knows local customers can help reduce credit risks.

As these examples suggest, there may be a number of very specific reasons why a producer might want to work with a specific middleman. However, the most important reason for using indirect channels of distribution is that middlemen can often help producers serve customer needs better and at lower cost. Remember that we discussed this briefly in Chapter 1 (see Exhibit 1–2). Now we'll go into more detail so you'll be able to plan different kinds of distribution channels.

DISCREPANCIES AND SEPARATIONS REQUIRE CHANNEL SPECIALISTS

The assortment and quantity of products customers want may be different from the assortment and quantity of products companies produce. Producers are often located far from their customers and may not know how best to reach them. Customers in turn may not know about their choices. Specialists develop to adjust these discrepancies and separations.[6]

Middlemen supply needed information

Economists often assume that customers have "perfect information" about all producers—and that producers know which customers need what product, where, when, and at what price. But this assumption is rarely true. Specialists develop to help provide information to bring buyers and sellers together.

MARKETING DEMO 11–1
Riding the Wave

To help the uninitiated understand the popularity of his company's natural spring water, Maurice Yammine, vice president of exports and international sales at Nora Beverages, Inc., in Mirabel, Quebec, challenges them to a taste test. Pour a glass of tap water. Then fill a glass with Nora's NAYA water. Let the waters reach room temperature—only then is the true taste fully apparent—and drink. "The difference is amazing," Yammine says. "You can really taste the chemicals used to make tap water potable. Once you get used to bottled water, drinking tap water is like drinking from a swimming pool."

Whether consumers are switching because of the taste, for health reasons, or both, the fact is that the market for bottled water is expanding 12 to 20 percent per year, making it the fastest growing segment of North America's beverage industry. Although the water market is buoyant, it still isn't an easy sell, particularly for exporters like Nora. With a commodity like water that's heavy, bulky, and expensive to ship, local producers will always have a huge cost advantage. Smart marketing is critical but doesn't necessarily give exporters much of an edge, either. Everyone promotes the purity and great taste of their water. Moreover, the export market is already dominated by global giants such as France's Perrier and Evian.

Despite the difficulties facing new brands like NAYA, the company has achieved a remarkable record in a short time. What makes NAYA water a hit is Nora's studied pursuit of export markets and its careful attention to creating a low-cost, top-notch distribution network. While Nora is eager for growth, one of its cardinal rules is to find the best distributor—at the right price—for each market, even if it takes some time. "Distribution is the fundamental basis for success in the beverage industry," says Georges Gaucher, Nora's vice president of Canadian sales and marketing.

In the United States, Nora relies heavily on "direct store" distributors, who take the product directly into a store, price it, and stock the shelves. "We avoid grocery brokers and grocery warehouses, who in turn sell to supermarket chains, because the fees they charge are too high, and they don't give your brand the same attention that direct-store distributors do," says Stewart Levitan, Nora's vice president of US sales.

For better or worse, Nora's executives have no worries about finding consumers who will want their water. "Clean water is a commodity that's becoming rarer all over the world," Yammine explains. "The quality of tap water is deteriorating." Just try the taste test, and see if you agree.

Source: Michael Salter, "Riding the Wave," *Report on Business Magazine*, April 1993, p. 67.

For example, most consumers don't know much about the wide variety of home and auto insurance policies available from many different insurance companies. A local independent insurance agent may help them decide which policy—and which insurance company—best fits their needs. In the same vein, a furniture retailer can help a customer find a producer who has a certain style chair with just the right combination of fabric and finish.

Most producers seek help from specialists when they first enter international markets. Nora Beverages, described in Marketing Demo 11–1, is one such company. Specialists can provide crucial information about customer needs and insights into differences in the marketing environment.

Discrepancies of quantity and assortment

Discrepancy of quantity means the difference between the quantity of products it is economical for a producer to make and the quantity final users or consumers normally want. For example, most manufacturers of golf balls produce large quantities—perhaps 200,000 to 500,000 in a given time period. The average

Wholesalers often accumulate products from many producers and then break bulk to provide the smaller quantities needed by retailers.

golfer, however, wants only a few balls at a time. Adjusting for this discrepancy usually requires middlemen—wholesalers and retailers.

Producers typically specialize by product—and therefore another discrepancy develops. **Discrepancy of assortment** means the difference between the lines a typical producer makes and the assortment final consumers or users want. Most golfers, for example, need more than golf balls. They want golf shoes, gloves, clubs, a bag, and—of course—a golf course to play on. And they usually don't want to shop for each item separately. So, again, there is a need for wholesalers and retailers to adjust these discrepancies.

In actual practice, bringing products to customers isn't as simple as the golf example. Specializing only in golfing products may not achieve all the economies possible in a channel of distribution. Retailers who specialize in sports products usually carry even wider assortments. And they buy from a variety of wholesalers who specialize by product line. Some of these wholesalers supply other wholesalers. These complications will be discussed later. The important thing to remember is that discrepancies in quantity and assortment cause distribution problems for producers—and explain why many specialists develop.

Channel specialists adjust discrepancies with regrouping activities

Regrouping activities adjust the quantities and/or assortments of products handled at each level in a channel of distribution.

There are four regrouping activities: accumulating, bulk-breaking, sorting, and assorting. When one or more of these activities are needed, a marketing specialist may develop to fill this need.

Adjusting quantity discrepancies by accumulating and bulk-breaking

Accumulating involves collecting products from many small producers. Much of the coffee that comes from Columbia is grown on small farms in the mountains. Accumulating the small crops into larger quantities is a way of getting the lowest transporting rate—and making it more convenient for distant food processing companies to buy and handle it. Accumulating is especially important in less-developed countries and in other situations, like agricultural markets, where there are many small producers.

Accumulating is also important with professional services because they often involve the combined work of a number of individuals, each of whom is a specialized producer. A hospital makes it easier for patients by accumulating the services of a number of health care specialists, for example.

Bulk-breaking involves dividing larger quantities into smaller quantities as products get closer to the final market. Sometimes, this even starts at the producer's level. A golf ball producer may need 25 wholesalers to help sell its output. And the bulk-breaking may involve several levels of middlemen. Wholesalers may sell smaller quantities to other wholesalers—or directly to retailers. Retailers continue breaking bulk as they sell individual items to their customers.

Adjusting assortment discrepancies by sorting and assorting

Different types of specialists adjust assortment discrepancies. They perform two types of regrouping activities: sorting and assorting.

Sorting means separating products into grades and qualities desired by different target markets. For example, an investment firm might offer its customers a chance to buy shares in a mutual fund made up only of stocks for certain types of companies—high-growth firms, ones that pay regular dividends, or ones that have good environmental track records.

Similarly, a wholesaler that specializes in serving convenience stores may focus on smaller packages of frequently used products, whereas a wholesaler working with restaurants and hotels might handle only very large institutional sizes.

Sorting is also a very important process for raw materials. Nature produces what it will—and then the products must be sorted to meet the needs of different target markets.

Assorting means putting together a variety of products to give a target market what it wants. This usually is done by those closest to the final consumer or user—retailers or wholesalers who try to supply a wide assortment of products for the convenience of their customers. A grocery store is a good example. But some assortments involve very different products. A wholesaler selling Yazoo tractors and mowers to golf courses might also carry Pennington grass seed, Scott fertilizer, and even golf ball washers or irrigation systems—for its customers' convenience.

Watch for changes

Sometimes these discrepancies are adjusted badly—especially when consumer wants and attitudes shift rapidly. When videotapes became popular, an opportunity developed for a new specialist. Large numbers of consumers were suddenly interested in having an assortment of movies and other tapes available—in one convenient place. Electronics stores focused only on selling the tape players and blank tapes. Videotape rental stores, like Blockbuster, emerged to meet the new need. However, movie studios lowered the prices for tapes—so more customers are buying rather than renting them. Because of that change, many types of retail stores now sell videos.[7] Marketing Demo 11–2 describes some of the problems that exist within Russia's distribution channels.

Specialists should develop to adjust discrepancies *if they must be adjusted*. But there is no point in having middlemen just because that's the way it's always been done. Sometimes, a breakthrough opportunity can come from finding a better way to reduce discrepancies—perhaps eliminating some steps in the channel. For example, Dell Computer found that it could sell computers direct to customers, at

---

MARKETING DEMO 11–2
Russian Pumps Empty as Gasoline Prices Soar

R ussia's unhappy car drivers were repeatedly hit by increases in gasoline prices as the government pursued its desperate effort to cure the ills of what were once the world's richest oil fields. But, as with everything else touched by the government's economic-reform program, the gasoline situation seems destined to get far worse before it gets better.

Along Frunzenskaya Street, cars were lined up three abreast from the embankment of the Moscow River right up to the gasoline pumps. There was no fuel, but maybe, they said, the truck would come.

The absence of gasoline was no surprise. The shortages are chronic throughout Russia and all the other republics of the former Soviet Union, despite the largest petroleum reserves in the world. For Russian drivers, who already put up with roads that are chronically dangerous and cars that constantly break down, the recent doubling of gas prices is just the latest headache.

As a result of the latest boost, gasoline prices are now at least 25 times higher than those that drivers were paying when the economic reform program began in January 1992. As industry managers negotiate their way around the government and its pricing policies, individual entrepreneurs find ways of skirting the industry to make a few rubles. As a result, one of the common sights on Moscow streets is people standing with jerry cans of gasoline, eager to save you a three- or four-hour wait in line at the pumps—for three or four times the pump asking price.

Their investment in full jerry cans is the time they spent lining up for the 40 liters permitted under government regulations or the cost of a bribe for a service-station manager to let them skip the lineup or get more than the permitted 40 liters.

The jerry can sales are an apt image of both the misery of the oil industry and the various kinds of new hustle you find these days in the streets of Moscow and other Russian cities.

Source: John Gray, "Russian Pumps Empty as Gasoline Prices Soar," *The Globe and Mail,* September 19, 1992, p. A11.

---

very low prices, by advertising in computer magazines and taking orders by mail or phone. With such an approach, Dell not only bypassed retail stores and the wholesalers who served them, it also avoided the expense of a large field sales force. This cost advantage let Dell offer low prices and a marketing mix that appealed to some target segments.[8]

CHANNELS MUST BE MANAGED

Marketing manager must choose type of channel

Middlemen specialists can help make a channel more efficient. But there may be problems getting the different firms in a channel to work together well. How well they work together depends on the type of relationship they have. This should be carefully considered, since marketing managers usually have choices about what type of channel system to join—or develop.

The whole channel should have a product-market commitment

Ideally, all of the members of a channel system should have a shared *product-market commitment*—with all members focusing on the same target market at the end of the channel and sharing the various marketing functions in appropriate ways. When members of a channel do this, they are better able to compete effectively for the customer's business.

This simple idea is very important. Unfortunately, many marketing managers overlook it because it's not the way their firms have traditionally handled relationships with others in the channel.

Glen Raven Mills, the
company that produces
Sunbrella brand fabrics, gets
cooperation from many
independent wholesale
distributors because it
develops marketing strategies
that help the whole channel
compete more effectively.

Traditional channel systems are common

In **traditional channel systems,** the various channel members make little or no effort to cooperate with each other. They buy and sell from each other—and that's all. Each channel member does only what it considers to be in its own best interest; it doesn't worry much about the effect of its policies on other members of the channel. This is shortsighted, but it's easy to see how it can happen. The objectives of the various channel members may be different. For example, General Electric wants a wholesaler of electrical building supplies to sell GE products. But a wholesaler who carries an assortment of products from different producers may not care whose products get sold. The wholesaler just wants happy customers and a good profit margin.

Traditional channel systems are still typical—and very important—in some industries. The members of these channels have their independence, but they may pay for it, too. As we will see, such channels are declining in importance—with good reason.

Conflict gets in the way of cooperation

Because members of traditional channel systems often have different objectives—and different ideas about how things should be done—conflict is common.

There are two basic types of conflict in channels of distribution. Vertical conflicts occur between firms at different levels of the channel of distribution. For example, a producer and a retailer may disagree about how much shelf space or promotion effort the retailer should give the producer's product. Or conflict may arise if a producer that wants to reduce its excess inventory pushes a wholesaler to carry more inventory than the wholesaler really needs.

Horizontal conflicts occur between firms at the same level in the channel of distribution. For example, a furniture store that keeps a complete line of furniture on display isn't happy to find out that a store down the street is offering customers lower prices on special orders of the same items. The discounter is getting a free ride from the competing store's investment in inventory. And nothing gets an independent retailer more charged up than finding out that a chain store is selling some product for less than the wholesale price the independent pays.

Specialization has the potential to make a channel more efficient—but not if the specialists are so independent that the channel doesn't work smoothly. Potential conflicts should be anticipated and, if possible, managed. Usually, the best way to do that is to get everyone focused on the same basic objective—satisfying the customer at the end of the channel. This leads us away from traditional channels and to the channel captain concept.

Channel captain can guide channel planning

Each channel system should act as a unit, perhaps directed by a **channel captain**—a manager who helps direct the activities of a whole channel and tries to avoid, or solve, channel conflicts.

The concept of a single channel captain is logical. But some channels, including most traditional ones, don't have a recognized captain. The various firms don't act as a system. The reason may be lack of leadership or the fact that members of the system don't understand their interrelationship. Many managers, more concerned with individual firms immediately above and below them, seem unaware that they are part of a channel.

But, like it or not, firms are interrelated, even if poorly, by their policies. So it makes sense to try to avoid channel conflicts by planning for channel relations. The channel captain arranges for the necessary functions to be performed in the most effective way.

Some producers dominate their channels

In North America, producers frequently take the lead in channel relations. Middlemen often wait to see what the producer intends to do—and wants them to do. After marketing managers for L'eggs set Price, Promotion, and Place policies, wholesalers and retailers decide whether their roles will be profitable—and whether they want to join in the channel effort.

Exhibit 11–2A shows this type of producer-dominated channel system. Here, the producer has selected the target market and developed the Product, set the Price structure, done some consumer and channel Promotion, and developed the Place setup. Middlemen are then expected to finish the Promotion job in their respective places. Of course, in a retailer-dominated channel system, the marketing jobs would be handled in a different way.

Some middlemen are channel captains

Some large or well-located wholesalers or retailers do take the lead. These middlemen analyze the types of products their customers want and then seek out producers—perhaps small ones—who can provide these products at reasonable prices. This is becoming more common in Canada, and it is already typical in many foreign markets. In Japan, for example, very large wholesalers (trading companies) are often the channel captains.

Channel captains who are middlemen often develop their own dealer brands. Retailers like Sears or Loblaw's and wholesalers like Home Hardware in effect act like producers. They specify the whole marketing mix for a product and merely delegate production to a factory. Exhibit 11–2B shows how marketing strategy might be handled in this sort of retailer-dominated channel system.

Middlemen are closer to the final user or consumer and are in an ideal position to assume the channel captain role. Middlemen, especially large retailers, may even dominate the marketing systems of the future.[9]

Exhibit 11–2 How Channel Functions May Be Shifted and Shared in Different Channel Systems

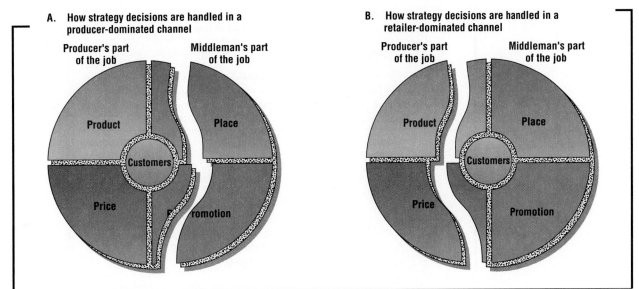

A. How strategy decisions are handled in a producer-dominated channel

Producer's part of the job

Middleman's part of the job

Product

Place

Customers

Price

Promotion

B. How strategy decisions are handled in a retailer-dominated channel

Producer's part of the job

Middleman's part of the job

Product

Place

Customers

Price

Promotion

Many marketing managers accept the view that a coordinated channel system can help everyone in the channel. These managers are moving their firms away from traditional channel systems and instead are developing or joining vertical marketing systems.

VERTICAL MARKETING SYSTEMS FOCUS ON FINAL CUSTOMERS

In contrast to traditional channel systems are **vertical marketing systems**—channel systems in which the whole channel focuses on the same target market at the end of the channel. Such systems make sense—and are growing—because if the final customer doesn't buy the product, the whole channel suffers. There are three types of vertical marketing systems—corporate, administered, and contractual. Exhibit 11–3 summarizes some characteristics of these systems and compares them with traditional systems.

Corporate channel systems shorten channels

Some corporations develop their own vertical marketing systems by internal expansion and/or by buying other firms. With **corporate channel systems**—corporate ownership all along the channel—we might say the firm is going "direct." But actually the firm may be handling manufacturing, wholesaling, *and* retailing—so it's more accurate to think of the firm as a vertical marketing system.

Corporate channel systems develop by vertical integration

Corporate channel systems often develop by **vertical integration**—acquiring firms at different levels of channel activity. Bridgestone, for example, has rubber plantations in Liberia, tire plants in Ohio, and wholesale and retail outlets all over the world. Sherwin Williams produces paint, but it also operates 2,000 retail outlets.

Corporate channel systems are not always started by producers. A retailer might integrate into wholesaling—and perhaps even manufacturing. For example,

Exhibit 11–3   Characteristics of Traditional and Vertical Marketing Systems

Characteristics	Type of channel			
	Traditional	Vertical marketing systems		
		Administered	Contractual	Corporate
Amount of cooperation	Little or none	Some to good	Fairly good to good	Complete
Control maintained by	None	Economic power and leadership	Contracts	Ownership by one company
Examples	Typical channel of "independents"	General Electric, Miller's Beer, O.M. Scott & Sons (lawn products)	McDonald's, Holiday Inn, IGA, Ace Hardware, Super Valu, Coca-Cola, Chevrolet	Florsheim Shoes, Sherwin Williams

A&P owns fish canning plants, Bata and Florsheim make their own shoes, and J. C. Penney controls textile plants.

Vertical integration has many possible advantages—stability of operations, assurance of materials and supplies, better control of distribution, better quality control, larger research facilities, greater buying power, and lower executive overhead. The economies of vertical integration benefit consumers through lower prices and better products.

Provided that the discrepancies of quantity and assortment are not too great at each level in a channel—that is, that the firms fit together well—vertical integration can be extremely efficient and profitable.

Administered and contractual systems may work well

Firms can often gain the advantages of vertical integration without building an expensive corporate channel. A firm can develop administered or contractual channel systems instead. In **administered channel systems,** the channel members informally agree to cooperate with each other. They can agree to routinize ordering, standardize accounting, and coordinate promotion efforts. In **contractual channel systems,** the channel members agree by contract to cooperate with each other. With both of these systems, the members achieve some of the advantages of corporate integration while retaining some of the flexibility of a traditional channel system.

An appliance producer, for example, developed an informal arrangement with the independent wholesalers in its administered channel system. It agrees to keep production and inventory levels in the system balanced—using sales data from the wholesalers. Every week, its managers do a thorough analysis of up to 130,000 major appliances located in the many warehouses operated by its 87 wholesalers. Because of this analysis, both the producer and the wholesalers can be sure that they have enough inventory but not the expense of too much. And the producer has better information to plan its manufacturing and marketing efforts.

Pet food companies typically focus on distribution through grocery stores, but Hill's has been successful reaching consumers in Canada and Japan with a different channel—pet stores and veterinary offices.

Middlemen in the grocery, hardware, and drug industries develop and coordinate similar systems. Computerized checkout systems track sales. The information is sent to the wholesaler's computer, which enters orders automatically when needed. This reduces buying and selling costs, inventory investment, and customer frustration with out-of-stock items throughout the channel.

Vertical marketing systems—new wave in the marketplace

Smoothly operating channel systems are more efficient and successful. In the consumer products field, corporate chains that are at least partially vertically integrated account for about 25 percent of total retail sales. Other vertical systems account for an additional 37.5 percent. Thus, vertical systems in the consumer products area have a healthy majority of retail sales and should continue to increase their share in the future. Vertical marketing systems are becoming the major competitive units in North American distribution systems—and they are growing rapidly in other parts of the world as well.[10]

THE BEST CHANNEL SYSTEM SHOULD ACHIEVE IDEAL MARKET EXPOSURE

You may think that all marketing managers want their products to have maximum exposure to potential customers. This isn't true. Some product classes require much less market exposure than others. **Ideal market exposure** makes a product available widely enough to satisfy target customers' needs but not exceed them. Too much exposure only increases the total cost of marketing.

Ideal exposure may be intensive, selective, or exclusive

Intensive distribution is selling a product through all responsible and suitable wholesalers or retailers who will stock and/or sell the product. **Selective distribution** is selling through only those middlemen who will give the product special attention. **Exclusive distribution** is selling through only one middleman in a particular geographic area. As we move from intensive to exclusive distribution,

we give up exposure in return for some other advantage—including, but not limited to, lower cost.

In practice, this means that Wrigley's chewing gum is handled—through intensive distribution—by about 90,000 Canadian outlets. Rolls Royces are handled—through exclusive distribution—by only a limited number of middlemen across the country.

Intensive distribution— sell it where they buy it

Intensive distribution is commonly needed for convenience products and business supplies—pencils, paper clips, and typing paper—used by all plants and offices. Customers want such products nearby.

The seller's intent is important here. Intensive distribution refers to the *desire* to sell through *all* responsible and suitable outlets. What this means depends on customer habits and preferences. If target customers normally buy a certain product at a certain type of outlet, ideally, you would specify this type of outlet in your Place policies. If customers prefer to buy Sharp portable TVs only at TV stores, you would try to sell all TV stores to achieve intensive distribution. Today, however, many customers buy small portable TVs at a variety of convenient outlets—including London Drugs, a local Zellers, or over the phone from the Sharper Image catalogue. This means that an intensive distribution policy requires use of all these outlets—and more than one channel—to reach one target market.

Selective distribution—
sell it where it sells best

Selective distribution covers the broad area of market exposure between intensive and exclusive distribution. It may be suitable for all categories of products. Only the better middlemen are used here. Companies usually use selective distribution to gain some of the advantages of exclusive distribution—while still achieving fairly widespread market coverage.

A selective policy might be used to avoid selling to wholesalers or retailers who (1) have a poor credit rating, (2) have a reputation for making too many returns or requesting too much service, (3) place orders that are too small to justify making calls or providing service, or (4) are not in a position to do a satisfactory job.

Selective distribution is becoming more popular than intensive distribution as firms see that they don't need 100 percent coverage of a market to justify or support national advertising. Often the majority of sales come from relatively few customers—and the others buy too little compared to the cost of working with them. That is, they are unprofitable to serve. This is called the 80/20 rule—80 percent of a company's sales often come from only 20 percent of its customers *until it becomes more selective in choosing customers*.

Esprit—a producer of colorful, trendy clothing—was selling through about 4,000 department stores and specialty shops nationwide. But Esprit found that about half of the stores generated most of the sales. Sales analysis also showed that sales in Esprit's own stores were about 400 percent better than sales in other sales outlets. As a result, Esprit cut back to about 2,000 outlets and opened more of its own stores—and profits increased.[11]

Selective distribution can produce greater profits not only for the producer but for all channel members—because of the closer cooperation among them. Transactions become more routine, requiring less negotiation in the buying and selling process. Wholesalers and retailers are more willing to promote products aggressively if they know they're going to obtain the majority of sales through their own efforts. They may carry more stock and wider lines, do more promotion, and provide more service—all of which lead to more sales.

Selective distribution makes sense for shopping and specialty products and for those business products that need special efforts from channel members. It reduces competition between different channels and gives each middleman a greater opportunity for profit.

When producers use selective distribution, fewer sales contacts have to be made—and fewer wholesalers are needed. A producer may be able to contact selected retailers directly. Hanes sells men's underwear this way.

In the early part of the life cycle of a new unsought good, a producer's marketing manager may have to use selective distribution to encourage enough middlemen to handle the product. The manager wants to get the product out of the unsought category as soon as possible—but can't if it lacks distribution. Well-known middlemen may have the power to get such a product introduced but sometimes on their own terms—which often include limiting the number of competing wholesalers and retailers. The producer may be happy with such an arrangement at first but dislike it later when more retailers want to carry the product.

Exclusive distribution
sometimes makes sense

Exclusive distribution is just an extreme case of selective distribution—the firm selects only one middleman in each geographic area. Besides the various advantages of selective distribution, producers may want to use exclusive distribution to help control prices and the service offered in a channel.

Retailers of shopping products and specialty products often try to get exclusive distribution rights in their territories. Fast-food franchises often have exclusive distribution—and that's one reason they're popular. Owners of McDonald's franchises willingly pay a share of sales and follow McDonald's strategy to keep the exclusive right to a market.

Unlike selective distribution, exclusive distribution usually involves a verbal or written agreement stating that channel members will buy all or most of a given product from the seller. In return, these middlemen are granted the exclusive rights to that product in their territories. Some middlemen are so anxious to get a producer's exclusive franchise that they will do practically anything to satisfy the producer's demands.

Marketing managers from Acura, the luxury car division of Honda Motor Co., decided to set up new channels of distribution to introduce the car to Canadian consumers. In return for the right to sell the car, each new dealer agreed to focus exclusively on Acura and its target market. Acura also required its dealers to build expensive new showrooms. At first, the strategy seemed to be a big success. Acura lured buyers away from competitors like BMW, Mercedes, and Cadillac. Surveys also showed that Acura owners were more satisfied than buyers of other cars. However, after three years, nearly half of Acura's dealers were still losing money or making only a small profit. Although sales were steady, they often didn't offset the big investment in new facilities. Most other car dealers were earning profits from more than one line of cars. Further, the new and reliable Acuras simply didn't keep the service department busy—and service usually produces a large share of a car dealer's profit.

Acura realized that long-run success would depend on having strong channel partners. To help its troubled dealers pull in more customers, Acura increased its advertising and developed a new sports model. And Acura worked with dealers to identify ways to earn more profit from service and used cars.[12]

But is limiting market exposure legal?

Marketing managers must operate within the law, and any consideration of Place must raise the question of the legality of limiting market exposure.

Exclusive distribution as such isn't illegal in Canada. Indeed "vertical" exclusive distribution contracts between a manufacturer and middleman have never been successfully challenged in the courts. "Horizontal" arrangements among competing retailers, wholesalers, and/or manufacturers operating at the same level would almost certainly be judged a violation of Section 32 of the Competition Act, which deals with monopolies. However, it would have to be proven that such agreements had "unduly lessened competition."

Stage 1 Amendments to the Combines Act (now called the Competition Act) gave the Restrictive Trade Practices Commission the authority to review vertical agreements and to act against those judged as having an adverse effect on competition. This legislation (Bill C-2) also specified that "unduly lessening competition" meant lessening it to any extent judged detrimental to the public interest. (Previously it had to be shown that competition would be completely or virtually eliminated.) However, the same amendments allow temporary exclusive dealing arrangements in order to permit the introduction of a new product or where there's some technological justification for such a policy.

New provisions:
consignment selling
and refusal to supply

Bill C-2 lets the Restrictive Trade Practices Commission bar **consignment selling** when such a policy is being used (1) to fix the price at which a dealer sells the products so supplied or (2) to discriminate between those receiving the product for resale. Until this change was made, a supplier could control the selling price by dealing only on consignment and by specifying the commission level built into the ultimate price. Alternatively, a supplier could allow a favored customer on consignment a larger commission than other customers. Bill C-2's consignment-selling provision made both such practices illegal.

Another Stage 1 provision allows the commission to help someone injured by a **refusal to supply**. It applies when a firm or individual is unable to obtain, on the usual terms, adequate supplies of an article or service not generally in short supply. This amendment doesn't make refusal to supply an offense in itself. However, a complaint concerning such practices can be brought to the Competition Tribunal. If the complaint is upheld, the tribunal can order that one or more suppliers accept that customer on usual trade terms. Marketing Demo 11-3 provides an example of such an order.

Caution is suggested

Obviously, considerable caution must be exercised before firms enter into any exclusive dealing arrangement. The same probably holds true for selective distribution. Here, however, less formal and binding arrangements are typical—and the chance of a harmful impact on competition being proven is more remote.

MARKETING DEMO 11-3   Xerox Must Sell Its Parts to Rival

Ottawa's Competition Tribunal has slammed Xerox Canada for refusing to supply spare parts for its copiers to a smaller competitor. The quasi-judicial tribunal ordered Xerox to resume supplying Toronto's Exdos Corp., which sells and services rebuilt copiers.

"It's a very important precedent," said Howard Wetston, director of the Bureau of Competition Policy, which took the case to the tribunal. The decision sends a message to companies dominant in their industries that they cannot refuse to supply smaller outfits. "It strengthens competition in the Canadian marketplace."

The tribunal said Xerox Canada's refusal to supply the parts to Exdos and to others (except end users) was specifically designed to eliminate competition in the service market.

Exdos was founded by former Xerox employee Terry Reid, who struck a deal with his former employer for spare parts for his business of refurbishing old copiers. However, Reid soon expanded into servicing the machines, as others had done in the United States. The parent company decided it was losing too much of its profitable service revenue and so cracked down on service companies.

The companies offered a welcome alternative to the high-pressure Xerox sales pitch. "Some customers indicated that they preferred to be free of the rather oppressive overselling of Xerox sales representatives," the tribunal said. It cited "continual pressure from Xerox sales personnel to upgrade even though such might not be in the customer's best interest." Some customers told the tribunal they were forced to go to independent service companies because Xerox service was not adequate.

Xerox chief counsel Howard Kaufman said his company will abide by the decision but is considering its options, including an appeal. "We are disappointed," he told Canadian press. "We still believe we were doing what is in the best interests of ourselves and our customers."

Source: Shawn McCarthy, "Xerox Must Sell Its Parts to Rival," *Toronto Star*, November 3, 1990, p. C1.

CHANNEL SYSTEMS CAN BE COMPLEX

Trying to achieve the desired degree of market exposure can lead to complex channels of distribution. Firms may need different channels to reach different segments of a broad product-market—or to be sure they reach each segment. Sometimes, this results in competition between different channels.

Exhibit 11–4 shows the many channels used by a company that produces roofing shingles. It also shows (roughly) what percent of the sales go to different channel members. Shingles are both consumer products (sold to do-it-yourselfers) and business products (sold to building contractors and roofing contractors). This helps explain why some channels develop. But note that the shingles go through different wholesalers and retailers—independent and chain lumberyards, hardware stores, and mass-merchandisers. This can cause problems because different wholesalers and retailers want different markups. It also increases competition—including price competition. And the competition among different middlemen may result in conflicts between the middlemen and the producer.

Dual distribution systems may be needed

Dual distribution occurs when a producer uses several competing channels to reach the same target market—perhaps using several middlemen in addition to selling directly. Dual distribution is becoming more common. Big retail chains

Exhibit 11–4   Roofing Shingles Are Sold through Many Kinds of Wholesalers and Retailers

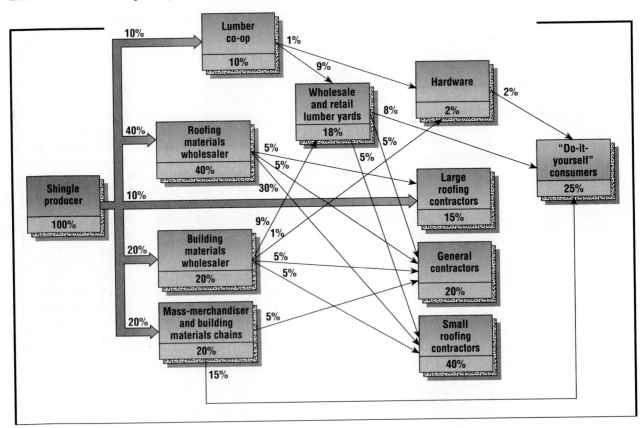

Pepperidge Farm penetrated the Japanese market quickly after Japan's 7-Eleven convenience store chain agreed to carry its cookies; Häagen-Dazs is moving into the Japanese market with its own stores.

want to deal directly with producers. They want large quantities—and low prices. The producer sells directly to retail chains, while relying on wholesalers to sell to smaller accounts. Some established middlemen resent this because they don't appreciate *any* competition—especially price competition set up by their own suppliers.

Other times, producers are forced to use dual distribution because their present channels are doing a poor job or aren't reaching some potential customers. For example, Reebok International had been relying on local sporting goods stores to sell its shoes to high school and college athletic teams. But Reebok wasn't getting much of the business. When it set up its own team-sales department to sell direct to the schools, it got a 30,000-unit increase in sales. Of course, some of the stores weren't happy about their supplier also selling to their potential customers. However, they did get the message that Reebok wanted *someone* to reach that target market.[13]

(?) Ethical decisions may be required

A shared product-market commitment guides cooperation among channel members as long as the channel system is competitive. However, if customers' Place requirements change, the current channel system may not be effective. The changes required to serve customer needs may hurt one or more members of the channel. The most difficult ethical dilemmas in the channels area arise in situations like this—because not everyone can win.

For example, wholesalers and the independent retailers that they serve in a channel of distribution may trust a producer channel captain to develop marketing strategies that will work for the whole channel. However, the producer may conclude that everyone in the channel will ultimately fail if it continues exclusive distribution. It might decide that consumers—and its own business—are best served by an immediate change (say, dropping current middlemen and selling direct to big retail chains). A move of this sort may not give current middlemen-partners a chance to make adjustments of their own. The more dependent they are on the producer, the more severe the impact is likely to be. It's not easy to determine the best or most ethical solutions in these situations. However, marketing managers must think carefully about the implications of strategy changes in the Place area—because they can have very severe consequences for other channel members. In channels, as in any business dealings, relationships of trust must be treated with care.[14]

Reverse channels should be planned

Most firms focus on getting products to their customers. But some marketing managers must also plan for **reverse channels**—channels used to retrieve products that customers no longer want. The need for reverse channels may arise in a variety of different situations. Toy companies, automobile firms, drug companies, and others sometimes have to recall products because of safety problems. A producer that makes an error in completing an order may have to take returns from middlemen or other business customers. If a Panasonic computer monitor breaks while it's still under warranty, someone needs to get it to the authorized repair center. Soft-drink companies may need to recycle empty bottles. And, of course, at some point or other, most consumers buy something in error and want to return it.

When marketing managers don't plan for reverse channels, the firm's customers may be left to solve "their" problem. That usually doesn't make sense. So a complete plan for Place may need to consider an efficient way to return products—with policies that different channel members agree on. It may also require specialists who were not involved in getting the product to the consumer. But if that's what it takes to satisfy customers, it should be part of marketing strategy planning.[15]

CONCLUSION

In this chapter, we discussed the role of Place and noted that Place decisions are especially important because they may be difficult and expensive to change.

Marketing specialists—and channel systems—develop to adjust discrepancies of quantity and assortment. Their regrouping activities are basic in any economic system. And adjusting discrepancies provides opportunities for creative marketers.

Channel planning requires firms to decide on the degree of market exposure they want. The ideal level of exposure may be intensive, selective, or exclusive. They also need to consider the legality of limiting market exposure to avoid having to undo an expensively developed channel system or face steep fines.

The importance of planning channel systems was discussed—along with the role of a channel captain. We stressed that channel systems compete with each other—and that vertical marketing systems seem to be winning.

In this broader context, the "battle of the brands" is only a skirmish in the battle between various channel systems. And we emphasized that producers aren't necessarily the channel captains. Often, middlemen control or even dominate channels of distribution.

QUESTIONS AND PROBLEMS

1. Review the Goodyear case at the beginning of the chapter and discuss how Goodyear's Place decisions relate to the product class concept. Explain your thinking.

2. Give two examples of service firms that work with other channel specialists to sell their products to final consumers. What marketing functions is the specialist providing in each case?

3. Discuss some reasons why a firm that produces installations might use direct distribution in its domestic market but use middlemen to reach overseas customers.

4. Explain discrepancies of quantity and assortment using the clothing business as an example. How does the application of these concepts change when selling steel to the automobile industry? What impact does this have on the number and kinds of marketing specialists required?

5. Explain the four regrouping activities with an example from the building supply industry (nails, paint, flooring, plumbing fixtures, etc.). Do you think that many specialists develop in this industry, or do producers handle the job themselves? What kinds of marketing channels would you expect to find in this industry, and what functions would various channel members provide?

6. Insurance agents are middlemen who help other members of the channel by providing information and handling the selling function. Does it make sense for an insurance agent to specialize and work exclusively with one insurance provider? Why or why not?

7. Discuss the Place objectives and distribution arrangements that are appropriate for the following products (indicate any special assumptions you have to make to obtain an answer):

   a. A postal scale for products weighing up to 2 pounds.
   b. Children's toys: (1) radio-controlled model airplanes costing $80 or more, (2) small rubber balls.
   c. Heavy-duty, rechargeable, battery-powered nut tighteners for factory production lines.
   d. Fiberglass fabric used in making roofing shingles.

8. Give an example of a producer that uses two or more different channels of distribution. Briefly discuss what problems this might cause.

9. Explain how a channel captain can help traditional independent firms compete with a corporate (integrated) channel system.

10. Find an example of vertical integration within your city. Are there any particular advantages to this vertical integration? If so, what are they? If there are no such advantages, how do you explain the integration?

11. What would happen if retailer-organized channels (either formally integrated or administered) dominated consumer product marketing?

12. How does the nature of the product relate to the degree of market exposure desired?

13. Why would middlemen want to be exclusive distributors for a product? Why would producers want exclusive distribution? Would middlemen be equally anxious to get exclusive distribution for any type of product? Why or why not? Explain with reference to the following products: candy bars, batteries, golf clubs, golf balls, steak knives, televisions, and industrial woodworking machinery.

14. Explain the present legal status of exclusive distribution. Describe a situation where exclusive distribution is almost sure to be legal. Describe the nature and size of competitors and the industry, as well as the nature of the exclusive arrangement. Would this exclusive arrangement be of any value to the producer or middleman?

15. Discuss the promotion a new grocery products producer would need in order to develop appropriate channels and move products through those channels. Would the nature of this job change for a new producer of dresses? How about for a new, small producer of installations?

SUGGESTED CASES

13. Fileco, Inc.

31. Dalton Olds, Inc.

Logistics and Distribution Customer Service

Chapter **12**

When You Finish This Chapter, You Should

❶

Understand why physical distribution (logistics) is such an important part of Place *and* marketing strategy planning.

❷

Understand why the physical distribution customer service level is a marketing strategy variable.

❸

Understand the physical distribution concept and why it requires coordination of storing, transporting, and related activities.

❹

Know about the advantages and disadvantages of the various transporting methods.

❺

Know how inventory decisions and storing affect marketing strategy.

❻

Understand the distribution centre concept.

❼

See how computers help improve coordination of physical distribution in channel systems.

❽

Understand the important new terms (shown in blue).

(W) alter Hachborn started his career in hardware when he was 17 years old. The "dirty thirties" were ending and old Mr. Hollinger needed a stock boy to keep up with the new business he was beginning to see. Fifty years later, Hachborn has witnessed and initiated enormous changes in the business. Hollinger's hardware store is now a billion dollar operation with nearly 1,000 stores spread coast to coast.

Hachborn is founder and president of Home Hardware Stores Ltd. In his many travels to the United States in search of new products and suppliers for the modest Hollinger wholesale operation, Hachborn observed a new trend. Independent stores were getting together in buying and marketing groups to take advantage of economies of scale. In 1963, he proposed such a relationship to 122 independent hardware store owners in Ontario who were buying from Hollinger's wholesale division. In 1964, 166 of those dealers bought out the Hollinger operation, made Hachborn president, and emerged under the new name of Home Hardware.

These days, a 1-million-square-foot warehouse sits in St. Jacobs, Ontario, next door to old Mr. Hollinger's original store. It houses most of the 30,000 products available through Home Hardware outlets. Human hands won't touch most of those items until they're loaded onto one of Home Hardware's 350 tractor-trailer trucks for delivery to stores across Canada.

Computer-controlled machines fetch the items to fill an order while keeping track of the inventory change. Computers in St. Jacobs are hooked by satellite to distribution centres in Nova Scotia and Alberta, which send a continual flow of stock orders. A manager in Red Deer, Alberta, can now order stock simply by walking down the aisle with a hand-held computer unit, which orders stock from the warehouse directly by satellite.[1]

This case shows how important *physical distribution* is to individual firms and to the whole macro-marketing system. The many challenges and opportunities in this area are the focus of this chapter.

PHYSICAL DISTRIBUTION GETS IT TO CUSTOMERS

Choosing the right channel of distribution is crucial in getting products to the target market's Place. But as the Home Hardware case shows, that alone is usually not enough to ensure that products are available at the right time and in the right quantities. Whenever the product includes a physical good, Place requires physical distribution decisions. **Physical distribution (PD)** is the transporting and storing of goods to match target customers' needs with a firm's marketing mix—both within individual firms and along a channel of distribution. **Logistics** is another common name for physical distribution.

PD provides time and place utility and makes possession utility possible. A marketing manager may have to make many decisions to ensure that the physical distribution system provides utility—and meets customers' needs with an acceptable service level and cost.

PD costs are very important to both firms and consumers. PD costs vary from firm to firm and, from a macro-marketing perspective, from country to country. However, for many physical goods, firms spend half or more of their total marketing dollars on physical distribution activities. The total amount of money involved is so large that even small improvements in this area can have a big effect on a whole macro-marketing system—and consumers' quality of life.

From the beginning, we've emphasized that marketing strategy planning is based on meeting customers' needs. Planning for physical distribution and Place is no exception. So let's start by looking at PD through a customer's eyes.

PHYSICAL DISTRIBUTION CUSTOMER SERVICE

Customers want products—not excuses

Customers don't care how a product was moved or stored—or what some channel member had to do to provide it. Rather, customers think in terms of the physical distribution **customer service level**—how rapidly and dependably a firm can deliver what they, the customers, want. Marketing managers need to understand the customer's point of view.

What does this really mean? It means that Toyota wants to have enough windshields delivered to make cars *that* day—not late so production stops *or* early so there are a lot of extras to move around or store. It means that a business executive who rents a car from Tilden wants it to be ready when she gets off the plane. It means you want your Old Dutch potato chips to be whole when you buy a bag at the snack bar—not crushed into crumbs from rough handling in a warehouse.

Physical distribution is invisible to most consumers

PD is—and should be—a part of marketing that is "invisible" to most consumers. It only gets their attention when something goes wrong. At that point, it may be too late to do anything that will keep them happy.

In countries where physical distribution systems are inefficient, consumers face shortages and inconvenient waits for the products they need. By contrast, most consumers in Canada and the United States don't think much about physical distribution. This probably means that these market-directed macro-marketing systems work pretty well—that a lot of individual marketing managers have made good decisions in this area. But it doesn't mean that the decisions are always clear-cut or simple. In fact, many trade-offs may be required.

Trade-offs of costs, service, and sales

Most customers would prefer very good service at a very low price. But that combination is hard to provide because it usually costs more to provide higher levels of service. So most physical distribution decisions involve trade-offs between costs, the customer service level, and sales.

Exhibit 12–1   Trade-Offs among Physical Distribution Costs, Customer Service Level, and Sales

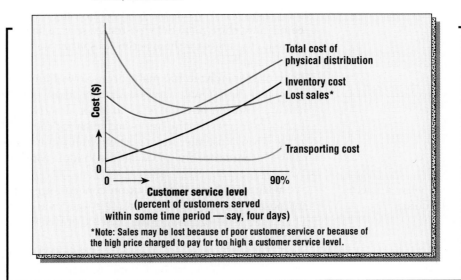

If you want the current top-selling CD and the store where you usually go doesn't have it, you're likely to buy it elsewhere. Perhaps the first store could keep your business by guaranteeing one-day delivery of your CD—using special delivery from the supplier. In this case, the manager is trading the cost of storing a large inventory for the extra cost of speedy delivery.

Exhibit 12–1 illustrates trade-off relationships like those highlighted in the CD example. For example, faster but more expensive transportation may reduce the need for costly storing. There is also a trade-off between the service level and sales. If the service level is too low—if products are not available on a timely and dependable basis—customers will buy elsewhere and sales will be lost. Alternatively, the supplier may hope that a higher service level will attract more customers or motivate them to pay a higher price. But if the service level is higher than customers want or are willing to pay for, sales will be lost.

The important point is that many trade-offs must be made in the PD area. The lowest-cost approach may not be best—if customers aren't satisfied. A higher service level may make a better strategy. Further, if different channel members or target markets want different customer service levels, several different strategies may be needed.[2]

PHYSICAL DISTRIBUTION CONCEPT FOCUSES ON THE WHOLE DISTRIBUTION SYSTEM

The physical distribution concept

The **physical distribution (PD) concept** says that all transporting and storing activities of a business and a channel system should be coordinated as one system, which should seek to minimize the cost of distribution for a given customer service level. It may be hard to see this as a startling development. But until just a few years ago, even the most progressive companies treated PD functions as separate and unrelated activities.

Firms spread the responsibility for different distribution activities among various departments—production, shipping, sales, warehousing, and others. No one person was responsible for coordinating storing and shipping decisions—or seeing how they related to customer service levels. Some firms even failed to calculate the costs for these activities so they never knew the *total* cost of physical distribution.[3]

Unfortunately, in too many firms old-fashioned ways persist—with a focus on individual functional activities rather than the whole physical distribution system. Focusing on individual functional activities may actually increase total distribution costs for the firm—and even for the whole channel. It may also lead to the wrong customer service level. Well-run firms now avoid these problems by paying attention to the physical distribution concept.

Decide what service level to offer

With the physical distribution concept, firms decide what aspects of service are most important to their customers—and what specific service level to provide. Then they focus on finding the least expensive way to achieve the target level of service.

Exhibit 12–2 shows a variety of factors that may influence the customer service level. The most important aspects of customer service depend on target market needs. Canon might focus on how long it takes to deliver copy machine repair parts once it receives an order. When a copier breaks down, customers want the repair "yesterday." The service level might be stated as "we will deliver emergency repair parts within 24 hours." Such a service level might require that almost all such parts be kept in inventory, that order processing be very fast and accurate, and that the parts be sent by airfreight. Obviously, supplying this service level will affect the total cost of the PD system. But it may also beat competitors who don't provide this service level.

Increasing service levels may be very profitable in highly competitive situations where the firm has little else to differentiate its marketing mix. Dow Chemical sells homogeneous basic chemicals that are also sold by many other suppliers. Increasing the service level—perhaps through faster delivery or wider stocks—might allow Dow to make headway in a market without changing Product, Price, or Promotion. Competitors might not realize what has happened—or that Dow's improved customer service level makes its marketing mix better.[4]

Find the lowest total cost for the right service level

In selecting a PD system, the **total cost approach** involves evaluating each possible PD system—and identifying *all* of the costs of each alternative. This

Exhibit 12–2　Examples of Factors that Affect PD Service Level

• Advance information on product availability	• Advance information on delays
• Time to enter and process orders	• Time needed to deliver an order
• Backorder procedures	• Reliability in meeting delivery date
• Where inventory is stored	• Complying with customer's instructions
• Accuracy in filling orders	• Defect-free deliveries
• Damage in shipping, storing, and handling	• How needed adjustments are handled
• Order status information	• Procedures for handling returns

approach uses the tools of cost accounting and economics. Costs that otherwise might be ignored—like inventory carrying costs—are considered. The possible costs of lost sales due to a lower customer service level may also be considered. The following example shows why the total cost approach is useful.

A cost comparison of alternative systems

The Good Earth Vegetable Company was shipping produce to distant markets by train. The cost of shipping a ton of vegetables by train averaged less than half the cost of airfreight, so the company assumed that rail was the best method. But then Good Earth managers did a more complete analysis. To their surprise, they found the airfreight system was faster and cheaper.

Exhibit 12–3 compares the costs for the two distribution systems—airplane and railroad. Because shipping by train was slow, Good Earth had to keep a large inventory in a warehouse to fill orders on time. And the company was also surprised at the extra cost of carrying the inventory in transit. Good Earth's managers also found that the cost of spoiled vegetables during shipment and storage in the warehouse was much higher when they used rail shipping.

In this case, total cost analyses showed that unconventional physical distribution methods provided service as good as or better than conventional means—and at a lower cost. The case also illustrates why it is important to get beyond a focus on individual functional elements of PD and instead consider the costs and service level of a whole physical distribution system. This broader focus should consider how the whole channel operates, not just individual firms.

Functions can be shifted and shared in the channel

As a marketing manager develops the Place part of a strategy, it is important to decide how physical distribution functions can and should be divided within the channel. Who will store and transport the goods—and who will pay for these services? Who will coordinate all of the PD activities?

Exhibit 12–3   Comparative Costs of Airplane versus Rail and Warehouse

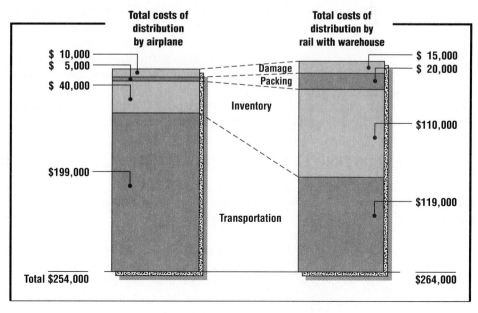

Just deciding to use certain types of wholesalers or retailers doesn't automatically—or completely—answer these questions. A wholesaler may use its own trucks to haul goods from a producer to its warehouse and from there to retailers—but only because the manufacturer gives a transportation allowance. Another wholesaler may want the goods delivered.

There is no right sharing arrangement. Physical distribution can be varied endlessly in a marketing mix and in a channel system. And competitors may share these functions in different ways—with different costs and results.

How PD is shared affects the rest of a strategy

How the PD functions are shared affects the other three Ps—especially Price. The sharing arrangement can also make (or break) a strategy. Consider Channel Master, a firm that wanted to take advantage of the growing market for the large dishlike antennas used by motels to receive Super Channel and other TV signals from satellites. The product looked like it could be a big success, but the small company didn't have the money to invest in a large inventory. So Channel Master decided to work only with wholesalers who were willing to buy (and pay for) several units—to be used for demonstrations and to ensure that buyers got immediate delivery.

In the first few months Channel Master earned $2 million in revenues—just by providing inventory for the channel. And the wholesalers paid the interest cost of carrying inventory—over $300,000 the first year. Here, the wholesalers helped share the risk of the new venture—but it was a good decision for them, too. They won many sales from a competing channel whose customers had to wait several months for delivery. And by getting off to a strong start, Channel Master became a market leader.

Identifying all the alternatives is sometimes difficult

It's important for firms to compare the costs and benefits of all practical PD alternatives, including how functions can be shared in the channel. Sometimes, however, there are so many possible combinations that it is difficult to study each one completely. For example, there may be hundreds of possible locations for a warehouse. And each location might require different combinations of transporting and storing costs.

Some companies use computer simulation to compare the many possible alternatives.[5] But typically, the straightforward total cost analysis discussed above is practical—and will show whether there is need for a more sophisticated analytical approach.

Now that you see why the physical distribution concept is important, let's take a closer look at some of the PD decision areas.

THE TRANSPORTING FUNCTION ADDS VALUE TO A MARKETING STRATEGY

Transporting aids economic development and exchange

Transporting is the marketing function of moving goods. Transportation provides time and place utilities—at a cost. But the cost is less than the value added to products by moving them—or there is little reason to ship in the first place.

Transporting can help achieve economies of scale in production. If production costs can be reduced by producing larger quantities in one location, these savings may more than offset the added cost of transporting the finished products to customers. Without low-cost transportation, both within countries and internationally, there would be no mass distribution as we know it today.

Early Canadian society settled on or near the water's edge, particularly along the St. Lawrence. Although roads existed, transport by water was easier, except for two drawbacks: the winter ice, which was unavoidable, and the many falls and rapids along the waterways. Canoes provided the best means of transport. However, with the introduction of the steamship in the early 1800s, and the construction of canals and locks as ways around the natural obstacles, large vessels became part of the Canadian transportation system, increasing the amounts and types of cargo carried.

Compared with the United States, Canada was slow to build railroads. For example, in 1850 Canada had only 66 miles of railway, whereas the United States had 10,000. Not until 1885 was all of Canada connected by rail. Only after the distant regions were linked with commercial centres both at home and abroad did the economic development of the West become possible. Water and rail transport dominated for generations. However, the increased use of the automobile after 1920 led to building better highways between large cities and roads connecting outlying areas with major markets.

Transporting can be costly

Transporting costs may limit the target markets a marketing manager can consider. Shipping costs increase delivered cost—and that's what really interests customers. Transport costs add little to the cost of products that are already valuable relative to their size and weight. But transporting costs can be a large part of the total cost for heavy products of low value—like many minerals and raw materials. This is illustrated in Exhibit 12–4, which shows transporting costs as a percent of total sales dollars for several products.[6]

Now you have more transporting choices

Today, most of the rules in Canada and in many other countries have been relaxed. For example, as part of their move toward unification, most European countries are dropping their transporting regulations. The construction of the

Exhibit 12–4   Transporting Costs as a Percent of Selling Price for Different Products

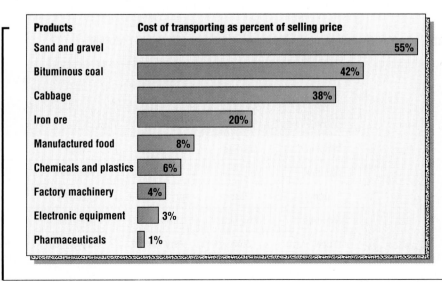

Products	Cost of transporting as percent of selling price
Sand and gravel	55%
Bituminous coal	42%
Cabbage	38%
Iron ore	20%
Manufactured food	8%
Chemicals and plastics	6%
Factory machinery	4%
Electronic equipment	3%
Pharmaceuticals	1%

tunnel under the English Channel is a dramatic example of the changes taking place. The "chunnel" will allow trains to speed between England and the rest of Europe.

As regulations decreased, competition in the transportation industry increased. As a result, a marketing manager generally has many carriers in one or more modes competing for the firm's transporting business. Or a firm can do its own transporting. So knowing about the different modes is important.[7]

WHICH TRANSPORTING ALTERNATIVE IS BEST?

Transporting function must fit the whole strategy

The transporting function should fit into the whole marketing strategy. But picking the best transporting alternative can be difficult. The "best" alternative depends on the product, other physical distribution decisions, and what service level the company wants to offer. The best alternative should not only be as low cost as possible but also provide the level of service (for example, speed and dependability) required. Exhibit 12–5 shows that different modes of transportation have different strengths and weaknesses.[8] Low transporting cost is *not* the only criterion for selecting the best mode.

Railroads—large loads moved at low cost

Railroads are the workhorse of the Canadian transportation system. They carry more freight over more miles than any other mode. In Canada, as in other countries, they carry heavy and bulky goods—such as raw materials, steel, chemicals, cars, canned goods, and machines—over long distances. By handling large quantities, the railroads are able to transport at relatively low cost.

Because railroad freight moves more slowly than truck shipments, it is not as well suited for perishable items or those in urgent demand. Railroads are most efficient at handling full carloads of goods. Less-than-carload (LCL) shipments take a lot of handling and rehandling, which means they usually move more slowly and at a higher price per pound than carload shipments.

Competition has forced railroads to innovate

Railroads earned low profits for many years—in part because trucks took a large share of the most profitable business. Now railroads are cutting costs and improving services—to improve profits. Reduced government regulation helped.

Exhibit 12–5   Benefits and Limitations of Different Transport Modes

Mode	Transporting Features					
	Cost	Delivery speed	Number of locations served	Ability to handle a variety of goods	Frequency of scheduled shipments	Dependability in meeting schedules
Rail	Medium	Average	Extensive	High	Low	Medium
Water	Very low	Very slow	Limited	Very high	Very low	Medium
Truck	High	Fast	Very extensive	High	High	High
Air	Very high	Very fast	Extensive	Limited	High	High
Pipeline	Low	Slow	Very limited	Very limited	Medium	High

Many railroads merged to reduce overlap in equipment and routes. Others increased prices where competition from truck and water transport was weak.

Railroads now cater to the needs of new target customers with a variety of specially designed railcars and services—ranging from double-decker railcars to computerized freight-tracking systems.[9] Intermodal transport is also becoming more common. This method is described in more detail in Marketing Demo 12–1 and the accompanying CN advertisement.

To offset the shortcomings of low speed and high cost—and still get business from small shippers—some railroads encourage **pool car service,** which allows groups of shippers to pool their shipments of like goods into a full car. Sometimes, local retailers buying from a single area like Vancouver combine their shipments in single cars. Local truckers then deliver the goods when they arrive.

Another example of a special railroad service is **diversion in transit,** which allows redirection of carloads already in transit. A Florida grower can ship a carload of oranges toward Canada as soon as they're ripe. While they head north, the grower can find a buyer or identify the market with the best price. Then—for a small fee—the railroad will reroute the car to this destination.

Trucks are more expensive, but flexible and essential

The flexibility of trucks makes them better at moving small quantities of goods for shorter distances. They can travel on almost any road. They go where the rails can't. That's why at least 75 percent of consumer products travel at least

Canada's railroads have become aggressive marketers.

Double-stack container trains offer economic and environmental advantages to shippers and the general public, alike.

CN North America. Bursting through with a more efficient way to move goods.

Double-stacked containers represent the wave of the future in transportation for domestic and overseas shipments.

As Canada's number-one carrier of double-stacks, CN North America is investing heavily to improve our service here, and to extend double-stacking to the entire continent.

We've innovated with new generation railcars to carry a wider variety of container sizes and heavier weight loads. We're expanding our inter-modal terminals on both sides of the border to handle more traffic, more efficiently.

An investment of $155 million in a new tunnel for our Sarnia/Port Huron gateway will speed the flow of containers and tri-level auto carriers to and from Chicago's rail crossroad. A new electronic customs clearance system that we developed will save shippers critical hours at border crossings.

CN North America enters this new era with 40 years of solid intermodal experience behind us. And the things we're doing promise a quality of service second to none.

CN NORTH AMERICA

Heading in all the right directions.

MARKETING DEMO 12-1
Rail Intermodal Traffic Is Picking Up Speed

(N) orth American railways' intermodal traffic—the movement of highway trailers and containers on rail flatcars—rose significantly during the first quarter of 1992. And it will continue to rise as railways increasingly penetrate motor-carrier markets for long-haul truckload traffic, analysts say.

The phenomenon has important implications for the rail industry. Intermodal traffic is high-margin business, and its growth should improve rail profits and the ability to draw new investment.

A variety of factors is fueling higher rail intermodal traffic: new technologies and labor efficiencies, a sharp rise in Asian container volumes, and growing cost pressures on truckers, which, if bulk commodities are excluded, control 80 percent of freight traffic in eastern North America.

CN's new double-stack train service for domestic containers, and plans for a $155 million tunnel between Sarnia, Ontario, and Port Huron, Michigan, should substantially increase transborder intermodal traffic.

Double-stack trains consist of flatcars attached in units of five platforms, each carrying containers one on top of another. The technology's economies of scale and fuel savings have cut rail rates and made it more competitive with long-haul truckload carriers.

Source: Mark Hallman, "Rail Intermodal Traffic Is Picking Up Speed," *The Financial Post*, June 10, 1992, p. 12.

---

part of the way from producer to consumer by truck. And in countries with good highway systems, trucks can give extremely fast service. Truckers also compete with railroads for high-value items.

Critics complain that trucks congest traffic and damage highways. But trucks are essential to our present macro-marketing system.[10]

Ship it overseas— but slowly

Water transportation is the slowest shipping mode—but usually the lowest-cost way of shipping heavy freight. Water transportation is very important for international shipments and often the only practical approach. This explains why port cities like Halifax, Vancouver, Rotterdam, Osaka, and Singapore are important centres for international trade.

Inland waterways are important, too

Inland waterways (such as the St. Lawrence Seaway in Canada and the Rhine and Danube in Europe) are also important, especially for bulky, nonperishable products such as iron ore, grain, steel, petroleum products, cement, gravel, sand, and coal. However, when winter ice closes freshwater harbors, alternate transportation must be used. Some shippers—such as those moving iron ore—ship their total annual supply during the summer months and store it near their production facilities for winter use. Here, low-cost transporting combined with storing reduces *total* cost.

Pipelines are used primarily by the petroleum industry

In Canada, pipelines carry all of the natural gas, most of the crude oil, and more than half of all the liquefied natural gas moving between processing plants and markets. The majority of this pipeline distance runs from Alberta and Saskatchewan to eastern Canada and the United States. Oil pipeline companies are common carriers. They carry oil for a fixed charge, while in most cases gas pipeline companies own the gas being transported.[11]

Water transportation is slow—but it's very important for international shipments.

Airfreight is expensive but fast and growing

The most expensive cargo transporting mode is airplane—but it is fast! Airfreight rates normally are at least twice as high as trucking rates—but the greater speed may offset the added cost. Trucks took the cream of the railroads' traffic. Now airplanes are taking the cream of the cream.

High-value, low-weight goods—like high-fashion clothing and parts for the electronics and metal-working industries—are often shipped by air. Airfreight is also creating new transporting business. Perishable products that previously could not be shipped are now being flown across continents and oceans. Flowers and bulbs from Holland, for example, now are jet-flown to points all over the world. And airfreight is also becoming very important for small emergency deliveries— like repair parts, special orders, and business documents that must be somewhere the next day.

But airplanes may cut the total cost of distribution

An important advantage of using planes is that the cost of packing, unpacking, and preparing the goods for sale may be reduced or eliminated. Planes may help a firm reduce inventory costs by eliminating outlying warehouses. Valuable by-products of airfreight's speed are less spoilage, theft, and damage. Although the *transporting* cost of air shipments may be higher, the *total* cost of distribution may be lower. As more firms realize this, airfreight firms—like DHL Worldwide Express, Federal Express, Purolator, and Priority Post—are enjoying rapid growth.

These firms play an especially important role in the growth of international business. While the bulk of international cargo moves on ships, the speed of airfreight opens up global markets for many businesses that previously had only domestic opportunities. For example, DHL Worldwide Express offers 24-hour delivery service from Tokyo to Los Angeles, New York to Rome, and London to Chicago. For a firm whose products are valuable relative to their weight and size, the cost of air deliveries may seem trivial when compared to the sales potential of competing in new markets.[12]

The growth of airfreight has made it easier and faster for firms to serve customers in foreign markets.

Put it in a container—
and move between
modes easily

We've described the modes separately, but products often move by several different modes and carriers during their journey. This is especially common for international shipments. Japanese firms—like Sony—ship stereos to the United States, Canada, and Europe by boat. When they arrive at the dock, they are loaded on trains and sent across the country. Then, the units are delivered to a wholesaler by truck or rail.

Loading and unloading goods several times used to be a real problem. Parts of a shipment would become separated, damaged, or even stolen. And handling the goods, perhaps many times, raised costs and slowed delivery. Many of these problems are reduced with **containerization**—grouping individual items into an economical shipping quantity and sealing them in protective containers for transit to the final destination. This protects the products and simplifies handling during shipping. Some containers are as large as truck bodies.

Piggyback—a ride on
two or more modes

Piggyback service means loading truck trailers—or flat-bed trailers carrying containers—on railcars to provide both speed and flexibility. Railroads now pick up truck trailers at the producer's location, load them onto specially designed rail flatcars, and haul them as close to the customer as rail lines run. The trailers are then hooked up to a truck tractor and delivered to the buyer's door. Similar services are offered on ocean-going ships—allowing door-to-door service between cities around the world.

To better coordinate the flow of products between modes, transportation companies like CSX now offer customers a complete choice of different transportation modes. Then CSX, not the customer, figures out the best and lowest-cost way to shift and share transporting functions between the modes.[13]

ECONOMIES OF SCALE IN TRANSPORTING

Most transporting rates—the prices charged for transporting—are based on the idea that large quantities of a good can be shipped at a lower transport cost per pound than small quantities. Whether a furniture producer sends a truck to

---

MARKETING DEMO 12-2   A Marketing Niche in Shipping

(W) hat kind of a niche can an international freight forwarder and traffic consultant carve out in a short eight-year period? The answer comes from Montreal-based W. J. Jones Ltd., which shipped close to 7,200 containers out of Montreal last year to both European and Pacific Rim destinations. A good 70 percent of them were loaded with US lumber.

The reason, according to company President Ed Jones, is basically due to freight rates out of Montreal being several hundred dollars below the rates through a US gateway. US-origin lumber is not subject to conference tariff rates by conference carriers serving Canada.

Destinations? Some 800 FEUs (40-foot equivalent units) of logs go to Germany annually, with lesser amounts to the United Kingdom, France, and Italy. A significant amount also moves into the Asia/Pacific region.

In addition to forwarding, the company has a terminal with 20,000 feet of heated space, 30,000 feet outside. It's used for stuffing logs, which are usually trucked in, as well as for a lot of metal stuffing for people such as Alcan. "You could say we're operating a conventional terminal in addition to filling an export market niche," chuckles Jones.

Source: C. M. Seifert, "Quebec Firms Go Global," *Materials Management and Distribution*, April 1990, pp. 33–36.

---

deliver one sofa or a full carload, the company still has to pay for the driver, the truck, the gas, and other expenses like insurance.

Transporters often give much lower rates for quantities that make efficient use of their transport facilities. Thus, transport costs per pound for less-than-full carloads or truckloads are often twice as high as for full loads. These quantity rate differences are one important reason for the development of some wholesalers. They buy in large quantities to get the advantage of economies of scale in transporting. Then they sell in the smaller quantities their customers need.

Freight forwarders accumulate economical shipping quantities

Freight forwarders combine the small shipments of many shippers into more economical shipping quantities. Freight forwarders do not own their own transporting facilities—except perhaps for delivery trucks. Rather, they wholesale air, ship, rail, and truck space. They accumulate small shipments from many shippers and reship in larger quantities to obtain lower transporting rates.

Freight forwarders are especially useful in arranging international shipping. They handle a large percentage of the general cargo shipped from Canadian ports to foreign countries. They are also very helpful for handling international airfreight. For example, Air Express International specializes in helping marketing managers find the most efficient air cargo firm to speed deliveries around the world.[14] Marketing Demo 12–2 shows what one Montreal-based freight forwarder has accomplished in less than a decade.

Should you do it yourself?

To cut transporting costs, some marketing managers do their own transporting rather than buy from specialists. Large producers, like Levi Strauss, often buy or lease their own truck fleets. Shell Oil and other large petroleum, iron ore, and gypsum rock producers have their own ships. Some firms now buy their own planes for airfreight.[15]

*Many firms have their
own truck fleets.*

THE STORING FUNCTION AND MARKETING STRATEGY

Store it and smooth out
sales, increase profits and
consumer satisfaction

Storing is the marketing function of holding goods. It provides time utility.
Inventory is the amount of goods being stored.

Storing is necessary when production of goods doesn't match consumption.
This is common with mass production. Nippon Steel, for example, might produce
thousands of steel bars of one size before changing the machines to produce
another size. Changing the production line can be costly and time-consuming. It's
often cheaper to produce large quantities of one size—and store the unsold
quantity—than to have shorter production runs. Thus, storing goods allows the
producer to achieve economies of scale in production.

Storing helps keep
prices steady

Some products—such as agricultural commodities—can only be produced
seasonally, although they are in demand year-round. If crops could not be stored
when they mature, all of the crop would be thrown onto the market—and prices
might drop sharply. Consumers might benefit temporarily from this surplus. But
later in the year, when supplies were scarce and prices high, they would suffer.
Storing thus helps stabilize prices during the consumption period—although
prices usually do rise slightly over time to cover storing costs.

Withholding products from the market to get better prices is what motivates
the Canadian Wheat Board's storage operations. The same reasoning explains the
policies of some farm marketing boards as well as the occasional stockpiling of
commodities such as rubber, coffee, and cocoa beans in other countries. Storing
may be closely related to Price as well as to Place.

Some buyers purchase in large quantities to get quantity discounts from the
producer or transporter. Then the extra goods must be stored until there is
demand. And goods are sometimes stored as a hedge against future price rises,
strikes, shipping interruptions, and other disruptions.

Storing varies the channel system

Storing allows producers and middlemen to keep stocks at convenient locations—ready to meet customers' needs. In fact, storing is one of the major activities of some middlemen.

Most channel members provide the storing function for some length of time. Even final consumers store some things for their future needs. Since storing can be provided anywhere along the channel, the storing function offers several ways to vary a firm's marketing mix—and its channel system—by (1) adjusting the time goods are held, (2) sharing the storing costs, and (3) delegating the job to a specialized storing facility. This latter variation would mean adding another member to the distribution channel.

Which channel members store the product—and for how long—affects the behavior of all channel members. For example, the producer of Snapper lawn mowers tries to get wholesalers to inventory a wide selection of its machines. That way, retailers can carry smaller inventories since they can be sure of dependable local supplies. And they might decide to sell Snapper—rather than Toro or some other brand that they would have to store at their own expense.

If final customers "store" the product, more of it may be used or consumed. For example, Coke wants customers to buy six packs and 2-liter bottles. Then consumers have an "inventory" in the refrigerator when thirst hits.

Goods are stored at a cost

Storing can increase the value of goods—and make them more available when customers want them. But a manager must remember that *storing always involves costs,* too. Car dealers, for example, must store cars on their lots—waiting for the right customer. The interest expense of money tied up in the inventory is a major cost. In addition, if a new car on the lot is dented or scratched, there is a repair cost. If a car isn't sold before the new models come out, its value drops. There is also a risk of fire or theft—so the retailer must carry insurance. And, of course, dealers incur the cost of leasing or owning the display lot where they store the cars.

In today's competitive markets, most firms watch their inventories closely. Taken in total, the direct and indirect costs of unnecessary inventory can make the difference between a profitable strategy and a loser. On the other hand, a marketing manager must be very careful in making the distinction between unnecessary inventory and inventory that may be needed to provide the kind of service customers expect.[16]

SPECIALIZED STORING FACILITIES CAN BE VERY HELPFUL

New cars can be stored outside on the dealer's lot. Fuel oil can be stored in a specially designed tank. Coal and other raw materials can be stored in open pits. But most products must be stored inside protective buildings. Often, firms can choose among different types of specialized storing facilities. The right choice may reduce costs—and serve customers better.

Private warehouses are common

Private warehouses are storing facilities owned or leased by companies for their own use. Most manufacturers, wholesalers, and retailers have some storing facilities either in their main buildings or in a warehouse district. A sales manager often is responsible for managing a manufacturer's finished-goods warehouse—especially if sales branches aren't near the factory. In retailing, storing is so closely tied to selling that the buyers may control this function.

Firms use private warehouses when a large volume of goods must be stored regularly. Private warehouses can be expensive, however. If the need changes, the extra space may be hard—or impossible—to rent to others.

Public warehouses fill special needs

Public warehouses are independent storing facilities. They can provide all the services that a company's own warehouse can provide. A company might choose a public warehouse if it doesn't have a regular need for space. For example, Tonka Toys uses public warehouses because its business is seasonal. Tonka pays for the space only when it is used. Public warehouses are also useful for manufacturers who must maintain stocks in many locations—including foreign countries.

In most countries, public warehouses are located in all major metropolitan areas and many smaller cities. Many rural towns also have public warehouses for locally produced agricultural commodities. See Exhibit 12–6 for a comparison of private and public warehouses.[17]

Warehousing facilities have modernized

The cost of physical handling is a major storing cost. Goods must be handled once when put into storage—and again when removed to be sold. Further, especially in the typical old downtown warehouse districts, traffic congestion, crowded storage areas, and slow elevators delay the process—and increase the costs.

Today, modern one-story buildings away from downtown traffic are replacing the old multistory warehouses. They eliminate the need for elevators—and permit the use of power-operated lift trucks, battery-operated motor scooters, roller-skating order pickers, electric hoists for heavy items, and hydraulic ramps to speed loading and unloading. Most of these new warehouses use lift trucks and pallets (wooden trays that carry many cases) for vertical storage and better use of space. Computers monitor inventory, order needed stock, and track storing and shipping costs. Some warehouses even have computer-controlled order picking systems that speed the process of locating and assembling the assortment required to fill an order.[18]

Exhibit 12–6   A Comparison of Private Warehouses and Public Warehouses

Characteristics	Type of warehouse	
	Private	**Public**
Fixed investment	Very high	No fixed investment
Unit cost	High if volume is low Very low if volume is very high	Low: charges are made only for space needed
Control	High	Low managerial control
Adequacy for product line	Highly adequate	May not be convenient
Flexibility	Low: fixed costs have already been committed	High: easy to end arrangement

MARKETING DEMO 12–3
Canadian Tire's Computer-Controlled Distribution Centre

Canadian Tire Corp. recently opened its new 1.2 million-square-foot automated distribution centre, the A. J. Billes Distribution Centre, named after one of two brothers who founded the firm. Intended to carry Canada's largest automotive and hard lines chain through 1998, the Billes Distribution Centre is the most automated, computer-controlled facility in North America, the company claims.

What makes the Billes Distribution Centre unique is that it integrates for the first time four major automated handling systems, said general manager Larry Kidd. One of the four, an Automatic Storage and Retrieval System (AS/RS), soars 110 feet high, stretches 600 feet long, and can store 78,000 pallet loads.

Shrink-wrapped pallet loads of goods are carried directly from loading docks to the AS/RS racks on another of the four automated systems, computer-controlled tugs. A towline system pulls the tugs, and a bar code on each tug allows a computer to guide it to the correct one of those 78,000 pallet positions.

When the tug arrives at one of four entrances to the AS/RS, a computer-controlled lift picks up the pallet and delivers it to the designated rack. The other two systems come into play when filling orders. The first is a conveyor system with 11 miles of conveyors and 70 shipping lanes. Bar codes on each case automatically sort each case on its journey to the loading docks.

Then for picking less-than-case quantities, the distribution centre employs a carousel system with 10,000 pick slots on 4 miles of rotating shelves. Synthesized voice commands originating from a personal computer direct the picking, while LED light trees show the operator what's happening.

Even the forklifts feature a computer terminal, with commands delivered over radio frequencies and a handheld scanner. To learn where to deliver a given load, the forklift driver scans the case bar code and the computer terminal spits out a command.

The distribution centre uses 350 computer terminals, 250 scanners, and 50 software systems to keep goods flowing in the proper directions. In a separate control room, dual computer systems keep everything sorted out.

Kidd predicts the automated feature will cut labor costs in the Billes Distribution Centre by 30 percent compared to its present distribution centre, and will employ about 400 people.

Source: "Canadian Tire Unveils Computer-Controlled DC," *Discount Store News*, August 19, 1991, pp. 3, 10.

THE DISTRIBUTION CENTRE—A DIFFERENT KIND OF WAREHOUSE

Is storing really needed?

Discrepancies of assortment or quantity between one channel level and another are often adjusted at the place where goods are stored. It reduces handling costs to regroup and store at the same place—*if both functions are required*. But sometimes regrouping is required when storing isn't.

Don't store it, distribute it

A **distribution centre** is a special kind of warehouse designed to speed the flow of goods and avoid unnecessary storing costs. Anchor Hocking moves over a million pounds of its housewares products through its distribution centre each day. Faster inventory turnover and easer bulk-breaking reduce the cost of carrying inventory. This is important. These costs may run as high as 35 percent of the value of the average inventory a year. The lower costs and faster turnover lead to bigger profits. Marketing Demo 12–3 describes Canadian Tire's new high-tech distribution centre.

Today, the distribution centre concept is widely used by firms at all channel levels. But the basic benefits of this approach are still the same as they were over

Mattel's new, computerized distribution centre in Germany makes it possible to efficiently consolidate, route, and deliver orders to retailers throughout Europe.

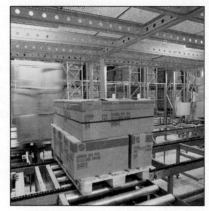

20 years ago when the idea was pioneered. In fact, a good way to see how the distribution centre works is to consider an early application.

PHYSICAL DISTRIBUTION CHALLENGES AND OPPORTUNITIES

Coordinating PD activities among firms

PD decisions interact with other Place decisions, the rest of the marketing mix, and the whole marketing strategy. As a result, if firms in the channel do not plan and coordinate how they will share PD activities, PD is likely to be a source of conflict rather than a basis for competitive advantage. Holly Farms' problems in introducing a new product illustrate this point.

Marketers at Holly Farms were encouraged when preroasted chicken performed well in a market test. But channel conflict surfaced when they moved to broader distribution. As with other perishable food products, the Holly Farm label indicated a date by which the chicken should be sold. Many grocers refused to buy the roast chicken because they worried that they had only a few days after it was delivered to sell it. They didn't want it to spoil—at their expense—on the shelf. Shelf life had not been a problem with Holly Farms's raw chicken. It sold in higher volume and moved off shelves more quickly.

The source of the problem was that it took nine days to ship the roast chicken from the plant to distant stores. Coupled with slow turnover, that didn't leave grocers enough selling time. To address the problem, Holly Farms changed its transportation arrangements. It also developed new packaging that allowed grocers to store the chicken longer. Holly Farms also shifted its promotion budget to put more emphasis on in-store promotions to speed up sales once the chicken arrived. With these changes, Holly Farms was able to win cooperation in the channel and establish its product in the market.[19]

JIT requires even more cooperation

We introduced the concept of just-in-time (JIT) delivery in Chapter 8. Now that you know more about PD alternatives, it's useful to consider some of the marketing strategy implications of this approach.

A key advantage of JIT for business customers is that it reduces their PD costs—especially storing and handling costs. However, if the customer doesn't

Contoured to fit your global shipping needs.

have any backup inventory, there's no "security blanket" if something goes wrong. If a supplier's delivery truck gets stuck in traffic, if there's an error in what's shipped, or if there are any quality problems when the products arrive, the customer's business stops. Thus, a JIT system requires that a supplier have extremely high quality control in production and in every PD activity, including its PD service.

For example, to control the risk of transportation problems, JIT suppliers often locate their facilities close to important customers. Trucks may make smaller and more frequent deliveries—perhaps even several times a day. As this suggests, a JIT system usually requires a supplier to be able to respond to very short order leadtimes. In fact, a supplier's production often needs to be based on the customer's production schedule. However, if that isn't possible, the supplier must have adequate inventory to meet the customer's needs.

You can see that the JIT system shifts greater responsibility for PD activities backward in the channel—to suppliers. If the supplier can be more efficient than the customer could be in controlling PD costs—and still provide the customer with the service level required—this approach can work well for everyone in the channel. However, it should be clear that JIT is not always the lowest cost—or best—approach. It may be better for a supplier to produce and ship in larger, more economical quantities—if the savings offset the distribution system's total inventory and handling costs.

While not every firm can—or should—use a just-in-time approach, it is an important idea. It focuses attention on the need to coordinate the PD system throughout the channel. It also highlights the value of close working relationships—and effective communication—between marketers and their customers. Whether or not a firm uses the JIT approach, good information is often the key to coordinating PD activities.[20]

Better information helps coordinate PD

Coordinating all of the elements of PD has always been a challenge—even in a single firm. Trying to coordinate PD in the whole channel is even tougher.

Keeping track of inventory levels, when to order, and where goods are when they move is difficult. Even so, marketing managers for some firms are finding solutions to these challenges—with help from computers.

Many firms now continuously update their marketing information systems—so they can immediately find out what products have sold, the level of the current inventory, and when goods being transported will arrive. And coordination of physical distribution decisions throughout channels of distribution will continue to improve as more firms are able to have their computers "talk to each other" directly.

Electronic data interchange sets a standard

Until recently, differences in computer systems from one firm to another hampered the flow of information. Many firms now attack this problem by adopting **electronic data interchange (EDI)**—an approach that puts information in a standardized format easily shared between different computer systems. Purchase orders, shipping reports, and other paper documents are now being replaced with computerized EDI. With EDI, a customer transmits its order information directly to the supplier's computer. The supplier's computer immediately processes the order—and schedules production, order assembly, and transportation. Inventory information is automatically updated, and status reports are available instantly. The supplier might then use EDI to send the updated information to the transportation provider's computer. This type of system is becoming very common. In fact, almost all international transportation firms rely on EDI links with their customers.[21]

This improved information flow and coordination affects other PD activities, too. Instantaneous computer-to-computer order processing, for example, can have the same effect on the customer service level as faster, more expensive transportation. And knowing what a customer has in stock can improve a supplier's own inventory planning.

Better coordination of PD activities is a key reason for the success of Pepperidge Farm's line of premium cookies. Less than a decade ago, the company was spending a lot of money making the wrong products and delivering them—too slowly—to the wrong market. Poor information was the problem. Delivery truck drivers took orders from retailers, assembled them manually at regional offices, and then mailed them to Pepperidge's bakeries. Now the company has an almost instantaneous EDI link between sales, delivery, inventory, and production. Hundreds of the company's 2,200 drivers use handheld computers to record the inventory at each stop along their routes. They phone the information into a computer at the bakeries—so that cookies in short supply will be produced. The right assortment of fresh cookies is quickly shipped to local markets, and delivery trucks are loaded with what retailers need that day. Pepperidge Farm now moves cookies from its bakeries to store shelves in about three days; most cookie producers take about 10 days. That means fresher cookies for consumers—and helps to support Pepperidge Farm's high-quality strategy and premium price.[22]

In summary, using computers to coordinate information is helping some firms and channels compete successfully for customers—and increase their own profits.

? Ethical issues may arise

Most of the ethical issues that arise in the PD area concern communications about product availability. For example, some critics say that marketers too often take orders for products that are not available or that they cannot deliver as quickly as customers expect. Yet a marketing manager can't always know precisely how long it will take before a product will be available. It doesn't make sense for the marketer to lose a customer if it appears that he or she can satisfy the customer's needs. But the customer may be inconvenienced or face added cost if the marketer's best guess isn't accurate. Similarly, some critics say that stores too often run out of products that they promote to attract consumers to the store. Yet it may not be possible for the marketer to predict demand or to know when placing an ad that deliveries won't arrive. Different people have different views about how a firm should handle such situations.

Some suppliers criticize customers for abusing efforts to coordinate PD activities in the channel. For example, some retailers hedge against uncertain demand by telling suppliers that they plan to place an order, but then they don't *confirm* the order until the last minute. They want to be able to say that it wasn't an order in the first place—if sales in the store are slow. This shifts the uncertainty to the supplier and reduces the retailer's inventory costs. Is this unethical? Some think it is. However, a marketing manager should realize that the firm's order policies can reduce such problems—if the cost of providing the service customers want is higher than what they will pay. In other words, this may simply be another trade-off that the marketer must consider in setting up the PD system.[23]

Transportation choices affect the environment

Marketing managers must be sensitive to the environmental effects of transportation decisions. Some say trucks cause air pollution in already crowded cities. People who live near airports suffer the consequences of noise pollution. A damaged pipeline can spew thousands of gallons of oil before it can be repaired. The *Exxon Valdez* oil spill in Alaska is a dramatic example of the kind of environmental disaster that can happen when a transportation accident occurs.

Many firms are taking steps to reduce these problems. For example, Conoco, a subsidiary of Du Pont, is building ships with double hulls to reduce the risk of

A marketing manager must be sensitive to the environmental effects of transportation decisions.

leaks. Some trucking and railroad firms establish elaborate safety procedures for dealing with toxic cargo. Today, the public *expects* companies to manufacture, transport, sell, and dispose of products in an environmentally sound manner. If companies are environmentally unsafe, consumers will show their dissatisfaction through their market choices. However, these environmental efforts increase the cost of distribution. Improved technology may help to make trade-offs between cost and environment less difficult. But ultimately, the people in a society must decide whether to bear the consequences of pollution or pay for higher distribution costs.

The transportation choices a firm makes also affect how much fuel is used. Many critics argue that we are carelessly depleting our nonrenewable energy resources. In addition, the cost of fuel has fluctuated drastically in the last 25 years. Fuel costs directly affect transporting costs. Lower fuel costs might lead to new market opportunities. And if fuel costs increase, truck and air transport will be less attractive, and rails will be more appealing. Lower speed limits for trucks may make railroads look even better. Another energy crisis might force even more radical changes—such as limiting the use of private cars and stimulating mass transportation.

Such shifts could affect where people live and work, what they produce and consume, and where and how they buy. In other words, these changes could affect our future macro-marketing system. An alert marketing manager should try to anticipate and plan for this future.[24]

Look for more changes

Deregulation caused drastic changes in transporting. Many transporting firms, including some big ones, went out of business. But deregulation has given market-oriented managers new opportunities. Some firms are meeting the challenge of change and earning bigger profits while serving their customers better. Similarly, changes in technology—such as EDI and computer-controlled warehouses—are creating new opportunities to simultaneously reduce distribution costs and improve service. These changes are part of the marketing environment that marketing managers need to watch carefully.[25]

CONCLUSION

This chapter deals with physical distribution activities—and how they provide *time* and *place* utility. We looked at the PD customer service level and why it is important.

We emphasized the relation between customer service level, transporting, and storing. The physical distribution concept focuses on coordinating all the storing and transporting activities into a smoothly working system—to deliver the desired service level at the lowest cost.

Marketing managers often want to improve service and may select a higher-cost alternative to improve their marketing mix. The total cost approach might reveal that it is possible *both* to reduce

costs and to improve service, perhaps by identifying creative new distribution alternatives.

We discussed various modes of transporting and their advantages and disadvantages. We also discussed the ways to manage inventory needs and costs. We explained why distribution centres have become an important way to cut storing and handling costs, and we explained how computerized information links—within firms and among firms in the channel—are increasingly important in blending all of the activities into a smooth-running system.

Effective marketing managers make important strategy decisions about physical distribution. But many firms have not really accepted the physical distribution concept. Creative marketing managers may be able to cut their PD costs while maintaining or improving their customer service levels. And production-oriented competitors may not even understand what is happening.

QUESTIONS AND PROBLEMS

1. Explain how adjusting the customer service level could improve a marketing mix. Illustrate.

2. Briefly explain which aspects of customer service you think would be most important for a producer that sells fabric to a firm that manufactures furniture.

3. Briefly describe a purchase you made where the customer service level had an effect on the product you selected or where you purchased it.

4. Discuss the types of trade-offs involved in PD costs, service levels, and sales.

5. Discuss the relative advantages and disadvantages of railroads, trucks, and airlines as transporting methods.

6. Discuss why economies of scale in transportation might encourage a producer to include a regional merchant wholesaler in the channel of distribution for its consumer product.

7. Discuss some of the ways that air transportation can change other aspects of a Place system.

8. Explain which transportation mode would probably be most suitable for shipping the following goods to a large Toronto department store:

   a. 300 pounds of Alaskan crab.
   b. 15 pounds of screwdrivers from Quebec.
   c. Three dining room tables from High Point, North Carolina.
   d. 500 high-fashion dresses from the garment district in New York City.
   e. A 10,000-pound shipment of machines from England.
   f. 600,000 pounds of various appliances from Montreal.

   How would your answers change if this department store were the only one in a large factory town in Southern Ontario?

9. Indicate the nearest location where you would expect to find large storage facilities. What kinds of products would be stored there? Why are they stored there instead of some other place?

10. When would a producer or middleman find it desirable to use a public warehouse rather than a private warehouse? Illustrate, using a specific product or situation.

11. Discuss the distribution centre concept. Is this likely to eliminate the storing function of conventional wholesalers? Is it applicable to all products? If not, cite several examples.

12. Clearly differentiate between a warehouse and a distribution centre. Explain how a specific product would be handled differently by each.

13. Discuss some of the ways computers are being used to improve PD decisions.

14. Explain the total cost approach and why it may be controversial in some firms. Give examples of how conflicts might occur between different departments.

15. Would a just-in-time delivery system require a supplier to pay attention to quality control? Give an example to illustrate your points.

SUGGESTED CASES

23. Saskatoon Mobile Homes

35. Canadian Inland

Retailers and Their Strategy Planning

When You Finish This Chapter, You Should

❶
Understand how retailers plan their marketing strategies.

❷
Know about the many kinds of retailers that work with producers and wholesalers as members of channel systems.

❸
Understand the differences among the conventional and nonconventional retailers—including those who accept the mass-merchandising concept.

❹
Understand scrambled merchandising and the "wheel of retailing."

❺
See why size or belonging to a chain can be important to a retailer.

❻
Understand why retailing has developed in different ways in different countries.

❼
Understand the important new terms (shown in blue).

Consumer needs are changing—and many retailers have gone out of business because they didn't adapt to the changes. Other retailers—like Price Club and Costco—are growing fast because they have identified good ways to meet the needs of their target markets.

Aggressive expansion plans of huge, high-volume warehouse retailers could radically alter Canadian retailing, according to industry analysts. The so-called warehouse clubs—already well established in the United States—threaten to steal customers from traditional Canadian retailers already reeling from the recession and cross-border shopping, says consultant John Winter, president of John Winter Associates Ltd.

Price Club Canada, Inc., operates 10 stores, mostly in Eastern Canada, and is continuing to expand. Costco, which has opened nine outlets in Western Canada since coming to Canada in 1985, has several more stores planned for B.C. and Saskatchewan this year. "They will shake up the market," says Winter. "It's just what we need because people are desperate for low prices. It will be a phenomenal success." The merger of these two firms, which took place just as this book was going to press, will make them even more of a force on the Canadian scene.

Price Club and Costco feature merchandise displayed on pallets, concrete floors, with limited service and—most important—low prices. Unlike general merchandisers, these retailers limit access to company owners and their employees. These clubs are not open to the general public because they are geared to small- and medium-sized businesses that have become the victims of high-margin middlemen. But to generate the volume needed to get price rebates from suppliers, they invite participation from employees of utilities, media, government, and health and education institutions.

At the time of the merger, Price Club had 850,000 members and Costco had 350,000. Both sold yearly memberships—$25 at Price Club and $35 at Costco. Their stores offered about 3,500 products—60 percent food items, particularly bulk, nonperishable goods, and 40 percent general merchandise such as detergents, automotive supplies, and household goods. But unlike the traditional competition, which may offer 10 different brands of televisions, for example, the warehouses stock only two or three brands.

Those feeling the pinch from warehouse clubs' growing popularity include cash-and-carry operations, supermarkets, mass-merchandisers, and department stores. Loblaw Cos. Ltd. has not taken the threat lightly. It has counterattacked by offering bulk merchandise and promoting the fact that no membership fees are required.

Winter says warehouse clubs may be the antidote Canadian retailing needs to stop shoppers from crossing the border to quench their need for bargains. "They are at the forefront as a weapon in cross-border shopping," he says. "Why go to Detroit when the prices here are the same?"[1]

THE NATURE OF RETAILING

Retailing covers all of the activities involved in the sale of products to final consumers. Retailers range from large, sophisticated chains of specialized stores to individual merchants like the woman who sells baskets from an open stall in the central market in Ibaden, Nigeria. Each retailer's offering represents some *mix* of many different characteristics—the products it carries, the services it offers, the facilities it uses, where it is located, and so forth. The variations are almost unlimited. Further, as the Price Club/Costco case shows, retailing is very competitive—and constantly changing.

Retailing is crucial to consumers in every macro-marketing system. For example, Canadian consumers spent over $179 billion buying goods and services from retailers in 1991. If the retailing effort isn't effective, everyone in the channel suffers—and some products aren't sold at all. So retailing is important to marketing managers of consumer products at *all* channel levels.

What are the different kinds of retailers, and why did they develop? How do their strategies vary? Why are there differences in retailing from one country to another? How is retailing changing? What trends are likely in the future? In this chapter, we'll answer these questions. And we'll talk about the major decision areas shown in Exhibit 13–1.

Exhibit 13–1   Strategy Decision Areas for a Retailer

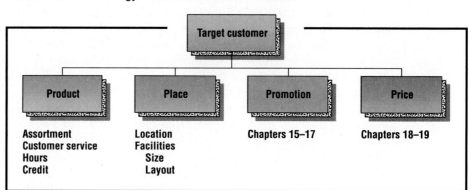

We will emphasize the different types of retailers and how they are evolving. It's important to understand this evolution because the pace of change in retailing has been accelerating. Further, understanding how and why retailing changes will help you understand how retailing differs in other countries.

The nature of retailing—and its rate of change—are generally related to the stage and speed of a country's economic development. In Canada, retailing tends to be more diversified—and more mature—than in most other countries. By studying the Canadian system and how it evolved, you will better understand how retailing is evolving in other parts of the world. After we discuss retailing in Canada, we will explain how and why retailing differs in some other countries—and what to expect in the future.

PLANNING A RETAILER'S STRATEGY

Retailers interact directly with final consumers—so strategy planning is critical to their survival. If a retailer loses a customer to a competitor, the retailer is the one who suffers. Producers and wholesalers still make *their* sale regardless of which retailer sells the product. Retailers must be guided by the old maxim: "Goods well bought are half sold."

Most retailers in developed nations sell more than one kind of product. Think of the retailer's *whole offering*—assortment of goods and services, advice from salesclerks, convenience, and the like—as its "Product." In the case of service retailing—dry cleaning, fast food, or one-hour photo processing, for example—the retailer is also the producer. Now let's look at why customers choose particular retailers.

Consumers have reasons for buying from particular retailers

Different consumers prefer different kinds of retailers. But many retailers either don't know or don't care why. All too often, beginning retailers just rent a store and assume customers will show up. As a result, more than three-fourths of new retailing ventures fail during the first year. To avoid this fate, a new retailer,

Some retailers, including Pizza Hut and the Canadian Home Shopping Network, reach consumers where it's convenient for them to buy—without going to a store.

or one trying to adjust to changing conditions, should carefully identify possible target markets and try to understand why these people buy where they do.[2]

Economic needs—who has the best value?

Consumers consider many factors when choosing a particular retailer. Some of the most important ones relate to their economic needs. Obviously, price is relevant, and so are:

1. Convenience.
2. Variety of selection.
3. Quality of products.
4. Help from salespeople.
5. Reputation for integrity and fairness in dealings.
6. Special services offered—delivery, credit, returned-goods privileges.
7. Value offered.

Emotional needs also affect the choice

Consumers may also have important emotional reasons for preferring particular retailers. Some people get an ego boost from shopping in a prestige store. Some think of shopping as a social outing—and want the experience to be fun. Others just want to shop in a store where they won't feel out of place.

Different stores seem to attract customers from different social classes. People like to shop where salespeople and other customers are similar to themselves. So a store fills the emotional needs of its target market(s). Zellers—a chain of 214 stores with 13,400,000 square feet of retail space—succeeds with a "budget" image that appeals to lower-class customers. Holt Renfrew, on the other hand, works at its upper-class image.

There is no one "right" answer as to whom a store should appeal. But ignorance about emotional dimensions—including social class appeal—could lead to serious errors in marketing strategy planning.[3]

Product classes help explain store types

We can simplify retail strategy planning by extending our earlier discussion of consumer product classes—convenience, shopping, and specialty products—to define three types of stores.

A **convenience store** is a convenient place to shop—either because it is centrally located near other shopping or because it's "in the neighborhood." Because they're so handy, convenience stores attract many customers. Easy parking, fast checkout, and easy-to-find merchandise add to the convenience. **Shopping stores** attract customers from greater distances because of the width and depth of their assortments—and because of their displays, demonstrations, information, and knowledgeable salesclerks. **Speciality stores** are those for which customers have developed a strong attraction. For whatever reasons—service, selection, or reputation—some customers consistently buy at these stores. They insist on shopping there just as some customers insist on a certain brand of a product.

Store types based on how customers see the store

Store types refer to *the way customers think about the store*—not just the kind of products the store carries. Different market segments might see or use a particular store differently. Remember that this was true with the product classes, too. So a retailer's strategy planning must consider potential customers' attitudes toward *both* the product and the store. Exhibit 13–2 classifies market segments by how they see both the store type and the product class.

When planning strategy, a retailer can better understand a market by estimating the relative size of each of the boxes shown in Exhibit 13–2. By identifying which competitors are satisfying which market segments, the retailer may see that some boxes are already "filled." Or a retailer may discover that competitors are all charging head-on after the same customers and completely ignoring others.

For example, houseplants used to be sold only by florists or greenhouses. This was fine for customers who wanted a "shopping store" variety. But for others, going to such outlets was too much trouble, so they just didn't buy plants. Then some retailers targeted the "convenience store" segment with small houseplant departments or stores in neighborhood shopping centres. They found a big market willing to buy plants—at convenience stores.

Different types of retailers emphasize different strategies

All retailers should carefully define their target markets and understand their target customers' buying behavior and needs. But, as we suggested earlier, there are almost an unlimited number of ways in which retailers can alter their offerings—their marketing mixes—to appeal to a target market.

Because of all the variations, it's difficult to classify retailers and their strategies based on a single characteristic—such as merchandise, services, or facilities. But we can describe basic types of retailers—and some differences in their strategies.

Let's look first at conventional retailers—and then see how others successfully modify conventional offerings to better meet the needs of *some* consumers. Think about *why* the changes take place. That will help you identify opportunities and plan better marketing strategies.

Exhibit 13–2   How Customers View Store-Product Combinations

Product class	Store type		
	Convenience	**Shopping**	**Specialty**
Convenience	Will buy any brand at most accessible store	Shop around to find better service and/or lower prices	Prefer store. Brand may be important
Shopping	Want some selection but will settle for assortment at most accessible store	Want to compare both products and store mixes	Prefer store but insist on adequate assortment
Specialty	Prefer particular product but like place convenience too	Prefer particular product but still seeking best total product and mix	Prefer both store and product

In Japan and Europe, small limited-line stores are still much more common.

CONVENTIONAL RETAILERS—TRY TO AVOID PRICE COMPETITION

Single-line, limited-line
retailers specialize
by product

A hundred and fifty years ago, **general stores**—which carried anything they could sell in reasonable volume—were the main retailers in Canada. But with the growing number of consumer products after Canadian Confederation, general stores couldn't offer enough variety in all their traditional lines. So some stores began specializing in dry goods, apparel, furniture, or groceries.

Now, most conventional retailers are **single-line** or **limited-line stores**—stores that specialize in certain lines of related products rather than a wide assortment. Many stores specialize not only in a single line—such as clothing—but also in a *limited-line* within the broader line. For example, within the clothing line, a store might carry *only* shoes, formal wear, men's casual wear, or even neckties—but offer depth in that limited line.

Single-line, limited-line
stores are being squeezed

The main advantage of such stores is that they can satisfy some target markets better. Some even achieve specialty-store status by adjusting their marketing mixes—including store hours, credit, and product assortment—to suit certain customers. But single-line and limited-line stores face the costly problem of having to stock some slow-moving items in order to satisfy the store's target market. Further, many of these stores have the disadvantage of being small—with high expenses relative to sales. Stores of this type have traditionally applied the retailing philosophy of buy low and sell high. If they face much competition, they may expand assortment to specialize further. By avoiding competition on identical products, they try to keep prices up.

Conventional retailers like this have been around for a long time and are still found in every community. They are a durable lot and clearly satisfy some people's needs. In fact, in most countries conventional retailers still handle the vast majority of all retailing sales.

However, this situation is changing—and nowhere is the change clearer than in North America. Conventional retailers are being squeezed by retailers who

Exhibit 13–3 Types of Retailers and the Nature of Their Offerings

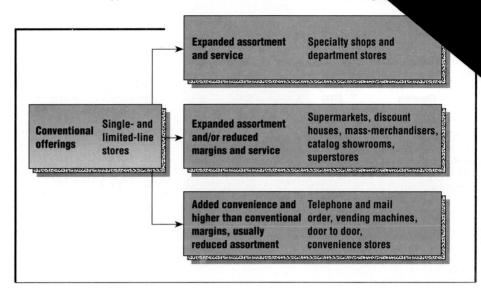

modify their mixes in the various ways suggested in Exhibit 13–3. Let's look closer at some of these other types of retailers.

EXPAND ASSORTMENT AND SERVICE—TO COMPETE AT A HIGH PRICE

Specialty shops usually sell shopping products

A **specialty shop**—a type of conventional limited-line store—is usually small and has a distinct "personality." Specialty shops often sell special types of shopping products—such as high-quality sporting goods, exclusive clothing, cameras, or even microwave ovens. They aim at a carefully defined target market by offering a unique product assortment, knowledgeable salesclerks, and better service. For example, specialty shops developed to satisfy people who want help selecting computer software. Expert clerks know the many different software packages available and can explain and demonstrate the advantages of each. These stores also carry computer books and magazines as well as diskettes and other computer accessories.

The specialty shop's major advantage is that it caters to certain types of customers whom the management and salespeople come to know well. This simplifies buying, speeds turnover, and cuts costs due to obsolescence and style changes. Specialty shops probably will continue to be a part of the retailing scene as long as customers have varied tastes—and the money to satisfy them. But to stay competitive, specialty stores will have to pay special attention to positioning and the shifting demographics and lifestyles of their target customers. Consider, for instance, how the Fairweather chain of stores changed as its target customers grew up. Fairweather now caters to contemporary women with sophisticated clothing in rich-looking stores.[4]

Don't confuse specialty *shops* with specialty *stores*. A specialty store is a store that for some reason (service, quality, etc.) has become *the* store for some customers. For example, some customers see Sears as a specialty store and regularly buy major appliances there—without shopping anywhere else.

...ilers, 1992

	...ue		Profit		Return on Capital		Inventory Turnover		Days Receivable		Operating Revenue per Store
	Percent Change	$000	Percent Change	1-Year Percent	5-Year Percent	Current	Previous	Current	Previous	$000
...3	1%	82,780	−49%	11.18%	9.61%	5.0%	5.2%	67	65	$10,376
Sears ...	...0	−11	−28,800	−235	5.09	11.22	6.0	6.2	105	122	38,577
Zellers Inc.	...56	20	na	nm	na	na	na	na	na	na	10,253
F. W. Woolworth Co.	2,087,526	−10	−18,031	−132	−1.79	16.71	4.1	4.9	11	10	na
Kmart Canada	1,228,144	−5	−4,104	−201	5.10	11.87	4.1	4.4	5	5	8,772
Gendis Inc.	755,561	−3	15,436	−44	12.26	21.98	5.0	4.8	14	13	1,447
Jean Coutu Group (PJC)	644,718	23	30,410	8	29.22	31.09	10.5	10.6	39	36	3,318
Woodward's Ltd.	613,349	−10	−19,477	−1,748	−8.06	−3.46	na	11.6	na	3	10,396
Average		6%		−214%	9.86%	12.13%	7.0%	7.3%	34	33	

Source: "The Top 1000," *Report on Business Magazine*, July 1992, p. 13.

Department stores combine many limited-line stores and specialty shops

Department stores are larger stores that are organized into many separate departments and offer many product lines. Each department is like a separate limited-line store or specialty shop. Department stores usually handle a wide variety of shopping products—such as women's ready-to-wear and accessories, men's and children's wear, textiles, and housewares. Department stores that found their place among *The Globe and Mail's* top retailers in 1992 included Hudson's Bay Company, Sears Canada, and the Jean Coutu Group. See Exhibit 13–4.

Until the 1980s, department stores were often considered the retailing leaders in a community. They usually do lead in size and in customer services—including credit, merchandise return, delivery, fashion shows, and Christmas displays.

Although traditional department stores are still a major force in retailing, they face many challenges. Their share of retail business has been declining since the 1970s. Well-run limited-line stores are competing with good service—and they often carry the same brands. In the United States, Canada, and many other countries, mass-merchandising retailers, who operate at lower cost and sell larger volumes, pose an even bigger threat.[5] We'll discuss them next.

EVOLUTION OF MASS-MERCHANDISING RETAILERS

Supermarkets started the move to mass-merchandising

From a world view, most food stores are relatively small single- or limited-line operations, which make shopping for food inconvenient and expensive. Many Italians, for example, still go to one shop for pasta, another for meat, and yet another for milk. Although this seems outdated, keep in mind that many of the world's consumers don't have access to **supermarkets**—large stores specializing in groceries with self-service and wide assortments.

The basic idea for supermarkets developed in the United States during the early Depression years. Some innovators felt they could increase sales by charging lower prices. They introduced self-service, provided a very broad product assortment in large stores, and offered low prices. Their early experiments in vacant warehouses were an immediate success. Profits came from large-volume sales—not from high traditional markups. Many conventional retailers, both independents and chains, quickly copied the innovators.[6]

Supermarkets sell convenience products—but in quantity. Their target customers don't want to shop for groceries every day like grandma did. To make volume shopping easier, supermarkets typically carry 30,000 product items. Stores are large—newer ones average around 40,000 square feet. In 1991, Canadian supermarkets and grocery stores sold over $43 billion worth of goods.[7]

Modern supermarkets are planned for maximum efficiency. Scanners at checkout counters make it possible to carefully analyze the sales and profit of each item and allocate more shelf space to faster-moving and higher-profit items. This helps sell more products—faster. It also reduces the investment in inventory, makes stocking easier, and minimizes the cost of handling products. *Survival* depends on such efficiency. Grocery competition is keen, and net profits after taxes in grocery supermarkets usually run a thin 1 percent of sales—*or less!*

To increase sales volume, some supermarket operators are opening "super warehouse" stores. These 50,000- to 100,000-square-foot stores carry more items than supermarkets, but they often don't stock perishable items like produce or meat. With lower prices than supermarkets, these super warehouse stores have been very successful. One example is Loblaw's No Frills.[8]

Catalogue showroom retailers preceded discount houses

Catalogue showroom retailers sell several lines out of a catalogue and display showroom—with backup inventories. Before 1940, catalogue sellers were usually wholesalers who also sold at discounted prices to friends and members of groups—such as labor unions or church groups. In the 1970s, however, these operations expanded rapidly by aiming at final consumers and offering attractive catalogues and improved facilities. Catalogue showroom retailers—like Service Merchandise, Consumers Distributing, and Best—offer big price savings and deliver almost all the items in their catalogues from backroom warehouses. They emphasize well-known manufacturer brands of jewelry, gifts, luggage, and small appliances but offer few services.[9]

Early catalogue retailers didn't bother conventional retailers because they weren't well publicized and accounted for only a small portion of total retail sales. If the early catalogue retailers had moved ahead aggressively—as the current catalogue retailers are—the retailing scene might be different. But instead, discount houses developed.

Discount houses upset some conventional retailers

Right after World War II, some retailers moved beyond offering discounts to selected customers. These **discount houses** offered "hard goods" (cameras, TVs, appliances)—at substantial price cuts—to customers who would go to the discounter's low-rent store, pay cash, and take care of any service or repair problems themselves. These retailers sold at 20 to 30 percent off the list price being charged by conventional retailers.

In the early 1950s—with war shortages finally over—manufacturer brands became more available. The discount houses were able to get any brands they wanted—and to offer wider assortments. At this stage, many discounters "turned respectable"—moving to better locations and offering more services and guaranties. They began to act more like regular retailers. But they kept their prices lower than conventional retailers to keep turnover high.

Mass-merchandisers are more than discounters

Mass-merchandisers are larger, self-service stores with many departments that emphasize "soft goods" (housewares, clothing, and fabrics) but still follow the discount house's emphasis on lower margins to get faster turnover.

Mass-merchandisers—like Kmart and Zellers—have checkout counters in the front of the store and little or no sales help on the floor. A conventional retailer tries to reorder sizes and maintain complete stocks in the lines it carries. Originally, mass-merchandisers did less of this. Even today, they emphasize seasonal products because they want to move merchandise fast and are less concerned with continuity of lines and assortment.

The average mass-merchandiser has nearly 60,000 square feet of floor space—twice as much as the average supermarket. Mass-merchandisers have grown rapidly. In fact, they expanded so rapidly in some areas that they were no longer taking customers from conventional retailers but from each other. Recently, profits have declined, and many stores have gone bankrupt. Seeing the declining potential in major metropolitan areas, some mass-merchandisers are concentrating on opening stores in smaller towns. This upsets some small town merchants—who thought they were safe from the competitive rat race.[10]

Superstores meet all routine needs

Some supermarkets and mass-merchandisers have moved toward becoming **superstores (hypermarkets)**—very large stores that try to carry not only foods but all goods and services that the consumer purchases *routinely*. Such a store may look like a mass-merchandiser, but it's different in concept. A superstore is trying to meet *all* the customer's routine needs—at a low price.

Superstores carry about 50,000 items. In addition to foods, a superstore carries personal care products, medicine, some apparel, toys, some lawn and garden products, gasoline—and services such as dry cleaning, travel reservations, bill paying, and banking. Some superstores are very large—over 200,000 square feet is no longer unusual.[11]

New mass-merchandising formats keep coming

The warehouse club is another retailing format gaining in popularity. Recently merged Price Club and Costco were two of the largest. Consumers usually pay an annual membership fee to shop in these large, bare-bones facilities. They are like the super warehouse stores for food, but among the 3,500 items per store, they also carry appliances, yard tools, tires, and other items that many consumers see as homogeneous shopping items—and want at the lowest possible price. While department stores use markups of 40 percent, the warehouses scrape by on markups of 8 to 10 percent.[12]

Single-line mass-merchandisers are coming on strong

Since 1980, some retailers, focusing on single product lines—have adopted the mass-merchandisers' approach with great success. Toys "R" Us pioneered this trend. Similarly, Video Only, Ikea (furniture), and Sports Unlimited also attract large numbers of customers with their convenient assortment and low prices in a specific product category. These stores, called *category killers* because it's so hard for less specialized retailers to compete, don't try just to have the best selection. They earn profits through faster turnover and higher sales volume.[13]

SOME RETAILERS FOCUS ON ADDED CONVENIENCE

Supermarkets, discounters, and mass-merchandisers provide many different products under one roof. Yet they're inconvenient in some ways. Checkout lines may be longer—or stores may be in less convenient locations. The savings may justify these inconveniences when a consumer has a lot to buy. But sometimes, consumers want convenience even if the price is a little higher. Let's look at some retailers who meet this need by focusing on convenience.

Convenience (food) stores must have the right assortment

Convenience (food) stores are a convenience-oriented variation of the conventional limited-line food stores. Instead of expanding their assortment, however, convenience stores limit their stock to pick-up or fill-in items like bread, milk, ice cream, and beer. Stores such as 7-Eleven fill consumers' needs between major shopping trips to a supermarket. They offer convenience—not assortment—and often charge prices 10 to 20 percent higher than nearby supermarkets. They earn approximately 4 percent on sales—rather than the 1 percent earned by supermarkets. This helps explain why the number of such stores has increased rapidly. There has been similar growth in Europe and Japan; in fact, a Japanese firm now owns 7-Eleven. The number of convenience stores will continue to grow in the 1990s but at a slower pace.

In the last decade, many full-service gas stations converted to convenience stores that also sell gas. Many of these stores now sell sandwiches, soup, and other eat-on-the-run snacks. So, convenience stores are competing not only with grocery stores and gas stations but also with fast-food outlets. All of this competition is beginning to put pressure on convenience store profits—but they continue to succeed because they meet the needs of some target markets.[14]

Vending machines are convenient

Automatic vending is selling and delivering products through vending machines. Sales in 1990 totaled $479 million, an increase from $424 million in 1988. The number of firms operating vending machines has risen to 739 from 655 in 1988, indicating that the industry is growing in response to the consumer's increasing preference for convenience.[15]

Vending machines and drive-through windows attract consumers who want to buy convenience products.

MARKETING DEMO 13–1
Canadian Mr. Crispy's Finds Japanese Market

Bruce Lewis looks like the cat that swallowed the canary when he talks about the Japanese market for his state-of-the-art, made-in-Canada product—a french fry vending machine.

"I love french fries. Been eating them all my life. I bought the company, but only after I tasted the fries," said Mr. Lewis, referring to his purchase last year of Mr. Crispy's Ltd. from an operator that could not make the fry fly.

Inventors have been struggling with the idea for years, and competitors have cropped up from time to time. But Mr. Lewis said he has millions of dollars' worth of Japanese and other export orders to prove he has one that works.

The Japanese practically live out of vending machines, happily dropping in their coins for such items as socks, canned coffee, whiskey, bread, noodles, magazines, tissues, and toys. They are a natural market for the fries, along with just about every other country where US-style fast food has taken hold.

Mr. Lewis doesn't mind taking the slow and cautious approach with his product. It has cost about $3 million to get all the bugs out of it. The process of meeting stringent Japanese requirements alone—often held up as an unfair trade barrier by frustrated Western manufacturers—took a year and more than $100,000 in expenses.

Source: Brian Miller, "Canadian Mr. Crispy's Finds Japanese Market," *The Globe and Mail*, January 30, 1990, p. B10.

For some target markets, this retailing method can't be ignored. And it may require other marketing mix changes. For example, granola bars started out as "health food," but now they compete with traditional candy bars. To make granola bars available where other candy is sold, Quaker and other producers make smaller bars that fit in standard vending machines. Different products are also beginning to be offered in vending machines—like french fries, as discussed in Marketing Demo 13–1.

The major disadvantage to automatic vending is high cost. The machines are expensive to buy, stock, and repair relative to the volume they sell. Marketers of similar nonvended products can operate profitably on a margin of about 20 percent. The vending industry requires about 41 percent to break even, so they must charge higher prices. As costs come down—and consumers' desire for convenience rises—we will see more growth in this method of retailing. Automatic bank teller machines—which give a customer cash using a "money card"—show how technology is changing automatic vending.[16]

Shop at home with telephone, TV, and direct-mail retailing

Telephone and mail-order retailing allows consumers to shop at home, usually placing orders by mail or telephone and charging the purchase to a credit card. Typically catalogues let customers "see" the offering, and purchases are delivered by mail. This can be a real convenience to consumers, especially if desired products aren't available at local stores. For some products, the target market is widely scattered. Retail stores don't want to carry an item for which there are few local customers. Telephone and mail-order retailing works well in these situations.

The early mail-order houses in Canada were offshoots of department store operations. They were greatly aided by the spread of the railroads and the

*Avon remains one
of the world's most effective
direct marketers.*

improvement in postal facilities in the late 19th century. They targeted their efforts only to rural areas where consumers had fewer shopping alternatives. They were not only convenient, but also low-priced. They were so successful with their low prices and wide variety of shopping and convenience goods that some conventional retailers sought laws to restrict them.

The mail-order houses have continued to grow. Today, however, mail-order isn't what it used to be. Many companies provide toll-free long-distance telephone numbers for ordering and information—with increasing emphasis on expensive fashion, gift, and luxury items. Computer mailing lists help these retailers target their catalogues and promotions more effectively. Catalogues for narrow lines like car stereos, exotic fruits, and classical records are common.

The big mail-order houses pioneered catalogue selling. But now department stores and limited-line stores see the profit possibilities and sell this way. Not only do they get additional business, but they also lower costs by using warehouse-type buildings and limited sales help. And shoplifting—a big expense for most retailers—isn't a problem. After-tax profits for mail-order retailers average 7 percent of sales—more than twice the profit margins for most other types of retailers. However, increasing competition and slower growth in sales—about 10 percent per year—are beginning to reduce these margins.

Put the "catalogue" on a computer or cable TV

The Canadian Home Shopping Network and others have been successful by devoting cable TV channels to home shopping. Some experts think that as shopping channels become more popular, sales will mushroom to $20 billion a year by the end of the decade in North America.[17]

A number of marketers are trying to offer electronic shopping, which allows consumers to connect their personal computers or a push-button phone to central computer systems. Most of the early efforts in this area fizzled because they proved too complicated for most consumers. Now, however, dial-up systems such as Prodigy—a joint venture between Sears and IBM—seem to be making headway. For example, PC Flowers—a firm that allows consumers to use their computers and the Prodigy system to order flowers for delivery anywhere in the world—is now one of the 10 biggest generators of business in the FTD flower-delivery network.[18]

Door-to-door retailers— give personal attention

As the accompanying ad suggests, **door-to-door selling** means going directly to the consumer's home. It accounts for less than 1 percent of retail sales—but meets some consumers' needs for convenience and personal attention. Door-to-door selling can also be useful with unsought products—like encyclopedias. But with more adults working outside the home, it's getting harder to find someone at home during the day.

While door-to-door retailing declines in Canada, it works well in the newly developing markets of eastern Europe where other retailing alternatives are not well established. In Poland, for example, Sara Lee sells pantyhose this way.

RETAILING TYPES ARE EXPLAINED BY CONSUMER NEEDS FILLED

We've talked about many different types of retailers and how they evolved. Earlier, we noted that no single characteristic provided a good basis for classifying all retailers. Now it helps to see the three-dimensional view of retailing presented in Exhibit 13–5. It positions different types of retailers in terms of three consumer-oriented dimensions: (1) width of assortment desired, (2) depth of assortment desired, and (3) a price/service combination. Price and service are combined because they are often indirectly related. Services are costly to provide. So a retailer that wants to emphasize low prices usually has to cut some services—and stores with a lot of service must charge prices that cover the added costs.

We can position most existing retailers within this three-dimensional market diagram. Exhibit 13–5, for example, suggests the *why* of vending machines. Some people—in the front upper left-hand corner—have a strong need for a specific item and are not interested in width of assortment, depth of assortment, or price.

WHY RETAILERS EVOLVE AND CHANGE

Exhibit 13–5 compares different types of *existing* stores. Now we'll look at some ways that retailing is changing.

Scrambled merchandising—mixing product lines for higher profits

Conventional retailers tend to specialize by product line. But most modern retailers are moving toward **scrambled merchandising**—carrying any product lines they think they can sell profitably. Supermarkets and drugstores sell anything they can move in volume—pantyhose, magazines, one-hour photo processing, antifreeze and motor oil, potted plants, and videotapes. Mass-merchandisers don't

Exhibit 13–5 A Three-Dimensional View of the Market for Retail Facilities and the Probable Position of Some Present Offerings

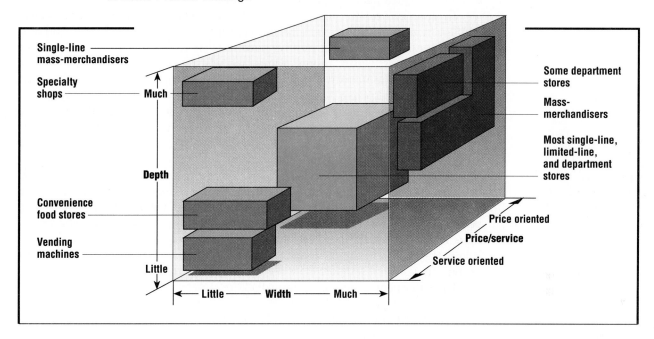

Single-line mass-merchandisers

Specialty shops

Much

Depth

Convenience food stores

Vending machines

Little

Little — Width — Much

Some department stores

Mass-merchandisers

Most single-line, limited-line, and department stores

Price oriented

Price/service

Service oriented

Many retailers scramble their merchandise lines to earn higher profits.

just sell everyday items but also cameras, jewelry, and even home computers. Why is scrambled merchandising becoming so popular?

To survive, a retailer must consistently show at least some profit. But typical retailers' net profit margins on sales are very slim—from 0 to 5 percent. And new types of retailers continually evolve, putting even more pressure on profits. So a firm looking for better profits wants to sell more fast-moving, high-profit items—exactly the items that are scrambling across traditional lines and appearing in unexpected places.

Exhibit 13–6 shows the ranges of gross margins conventional retailers need to stay in business and make *some* profit. We emphasize *some* because net profit—the difference between a seemingly big gross margin and necessary expenses—is usually only 1 or a few percent.

Mass-merchandisers and discounters like to operate on gross margins and markups of 15 to 30 percent. But—as shown in Exhibit 13–6—conventional retailers usually need much higher percentages. This exhibit should give you a better idea of the *why* of scrambled merchandising—and suggest possible directions it will take. Exhibit 13–6 shows, for example, why scramblers want to sell bakery goods, jewelry, appliances, refreshments, and gifts. Try to analyze why some of the conventional retailers have such high gross margins and why other types of retailers can operate more economically.[19]

| The wheel of retailing keeps rolling | The **wheel of retailing theory** says that new types of retailers enter the market as low-status, low-margin, low-price operators and then—if successful—evolve |

Exhibit 13–6   Illustrative Gross Margins in Selected Retail Trades for Recent Years

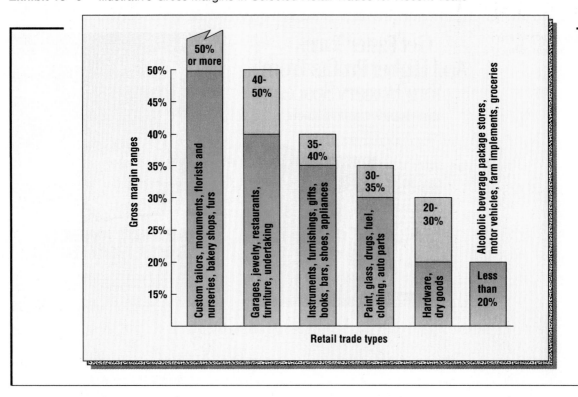

into more conventional retailers offering more services with higher operating costs and higher prices. Then they're threatened by new low-status, low-margin, low-price retailers—and the wheel turns again.

Early department stores began this way. Then they became higher priced—and added bargain basements to serve the more price-conscious customers. Supermarkets started with low prices and little service. Mass-merchandisers went through the same cycle.

Some innovators start with high margins

The wheel of retailing theory, however, doesn't explain all major retailing developments. Vending machines entered as high-cost, high-margin operations. Convenience food stores are high priced. Suburban shopping centres have not had a low-price emphasis.

Product life-cycle concept applies to retailer types, too

We've seen that people's needs help explain why different kinds of retailers developed. But we have to apply the product life-cycle concept to understand this process better. A retailer with a new idea may have big profits—for a while. But if it's a really good idea, he or she can count on speedy imitation—and a squeeze on profits. Other retailers will "scramble" their product mix to sell products that offer them higher margins or faster turnover.

The cycle is illustrated by what happened with video movies. As the popularity of VCRs grew, video stores cropped up across the country. The first ones charged from $5 to $10 a night for a tape. As more competitors entered, however, they drove prices (and profits) down. Competition heated up even more as supermarkets, convenience stores, and drugstores started to carry the most popular tapes—sometimes renting them for as little as 99 cents a night. Many of the original video stores couldn't cover their costs trying to compete at that price—and they went out of business.

Although the cycle for video stores moved very quickly, it can be much slower. But cycles do exist, and some conventional retailers are far along in their life cycles and may be declining. Recent innovators are still in the market growth stage. See Exhibit 13–7. Some of the retailing formats that are mature in North America are only now beginning to see growth in other countries.

The furniture retailing format Ikea developed in Sweden is proving very popular in North America.

Exhibit 13–7   Retailer Life Cycles—Timing and Years to Market Maturity

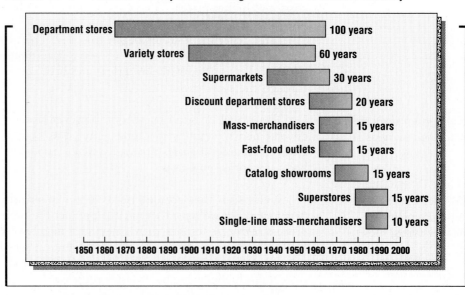

Some retailers are confused by the scrambling going on around them. They don't see this evolutionary process. And they don't understand that some of their more successful competitors are aiming at different target markets—instead of just selling products.

Some modern retailing successes are firms that moved into a new market and started another life cycle—by aiming at needs along the edges of the market shown in Exhibit 13–5. The convenience food stores, for example, don't just sell food. They deliberately sell a particular assortment-service combination to meet a different need. This is also true of specialty shops and some of the mass-merchandisers and department store chains.[20]

Ethical issues may arise

Most retailers face intense competitive pressure. The desperation that comes with such pressure has pushed some retailers toward questionable marketing practices.

Critics argue, for example, that retailers too often advertise special sale items to bring price-sensitive shoppers into the store, but then don't stock enough to meet demand. Other stores have been criticized for pushing consumers to trade up to more expensive items. What is ethical and unethical in situations like these, however, is subject to debate. Retailers can't always anticipate demand perfectly, and deliveries may not arrive on time. Similarly, trading up may be a sensible part of a strategy—if it's done honestly.

Some abuses are more clear-cut. For example, one of the nation's leading retailers of automotive services recently took out nationwide ads to apologize for problems it created with a new system designed to increase sales. On the surface, it seemed simple. Store managers were paid a percentage on sales. However, some of these people abused their customers by suggesting unnecessary repairs.

In retailing, as in other types of business, the marketing concept should guide firms away from unethical treatment of customers. However, a retailer on the edge of going out of business may lose perspective on the need to satisfy customers in both the short and long term.[21]

MARKETING DEMO 13–2
A Small-Business Perspective on the Retail Trade

Not all retail stores are affiliated with chains or part of a franchise system. Some retailers prefer the freedom that comes with owning an independent store. Weymouth Variety Store Limited is such a business. Owner Raymond Hupman worked for Macleod-Stedman's, a mass-merchandiser, for a number of years as a store manager before deciding that the chain store life was not for him.

In 1974, he seized the opportunity to purchase an already-established store located in Weymouth, a village in Southwestern Nova Scotia. Since then, the business has gone through a number of changes, most notably in 1985 when the adjoining building was connected to the original store through a passageway.

With a total of 5,000 square feet, Weymouth Variety offers a wide range of goods, from ladies' wear to candy to greeting cards. One of the most popular areas of the store is the toy department. Customers come from as far away as 75 miles to shop for toys, especially at Christmas.

Due to the wide selection of goods, Weymouth Variety must deal with a large number of suppliers. In fact, the company over the course of a year may purchase goods from over 200 different suppliers. In order to receive volume discounts, orders are sometimes shared with other nearby retailers. The challenge lies in selecting products that give customers the best value for their money—the store's advertising slogan is "Known for Better Values."

Weymouth Variety faces other challenges. Competition, especially from the big chains like Zellers and Kmart in nearby towns, is always a threat to the independent's survival. As well, the economy plays a major role in Weymouth Variety's success. Weymouth is a small town, dependent on primary industries—fishing, forestry, and agriculture—none of which are faring well currently. The advantage to that, of course, is that aspiring retailers are not attracted to Weymouth, keeping local competition to a minimum.

In the future, Ray Hupman doesn't expect high growth, mainly due to the economy in Nova Scotia. One thing is certain, however, and that is when you shop at Weymouth Variety, you'll always have a large selection of goods to choose from, and you'll always get good value for your money.

Source: Roberta Hupman, based on conversations with Raymond Hupman, January 1993.

RETAILER SIZE AND PROFITS

We've talked about different types of retailers and how they evolved. Now let's look at store size and ownership—because these too affect a retailer's strategy planning. They also help explain why some retailers are becoming more powerful members of the distribution channel.

A few big retailers do most of the business

The large number of retailers might suggest that retailing is a field of small businesses. To some extent this is true. On the other hand, the many small retailers can't be ignored. They do reach many consumers—and often are valuable channel members. But their large number—and relatively small sales volume—makes working with them expensive. They often require separate marketing mixes. Marketing Demo 13–2 examines one such small business.

Small size may be hard to overcome

Small retailers often have trouble making enough money to cover expenses. But even an average retail store is too small to gain economies of scale—and that's sometimes necessary to be competitive.

Well-managed larger stores can usually get some economies of scale. They can buy in quantity at lower prices, take advantage of mass advertising, and hire

Exhibit 13–8   Retail Chains (excluding department stores), by Annual Sales Volume, Canada, 1990

Annual Sales Volume	Chains		Stores (maximum)		Sales	
	Number	Percent	Number	Percent	Amount (in thousands)	Percent
Under $2,000,000	117	10.2%	689	1.8%	$ 152,600	0.3%
$ 2,000,000–$ 4,999,999	327	28.4	2,513	6.4	1,083,995	1.9
$ 5,000,000–$24,999,999	440	38.2	7,380	18.8	4,695,173	8.1
$ 25,000,000–$99,999,999	171	14.8	9,518	24.2	8,557,233	14.7
$100,000,000 and over	97	8.4	19,169	48.8	43,737,582	75.1
Total	1,152	100.0%	39,269	100.0%	$ 58,226,583	100.0%

Source: Statistics Canada, *Retail Chain and Department Stores,* 1990, Cat. 63-210.

specialists. But larger size alone doesn't guarantee more efficient operation. For example, individual departments in a department store might not be any larger than independent limited-line stores—and so there may be little possibility for volume buying.[22]

Being in a chain may help

One way for a retailer to achieve economies of scale is with a corporate chain. Statistics Canada defines a corporate chain as "an organization operating four or more retail outlets in the same kind of business, under the same legal ownership." All department stores are considered to be chains, even if they have fewer than four outlets. However, department store statistics are usually not included when figures on corporate chains are quoted. The definition also excludes voluntary chains and franchise operations.

Exhibit 13–8 provides some data on retail chains. It is interesting to note that while only 8.4 percent of retail chains have a sales volume of over $100 million, this group accounts for over 75 percent of sales.

Most chains have at least some central buying for different stores. This allows them to take advantage of quantity discounts or opportunities for vertical integration—including developing their own efficient distribution centres. They can use EDI and other computer links to control inventory costs and stockouts. They may also spread promotion and management costs to many stores. Retail chains have their own dealer brands.

Independents form chains, too

The growth of corporate chains encouraged the development of both cooperative chains and voluntary chains.

Cooperative chains are retailer-sponsored groups—formed by independent retailers—that run their own buying organizations and conduct joint promotion efforts. Sales of cooperative chains have been rising as they learn how to compete with corporate chains. Examples include Associated Grocers, Certified Grocers, and True Value Hardware.

Voluntary chains are wholesaler-sponsored groups that work with "independent" retailers. Some are linked by contracts stating common operating procedures—and requiring the use of common store-front designs, store names, and joint promotion efforts. Examples include IGA and Super Valu in groceries, and Home in hardware.

Exhibit 13–9 Examples of Some Well-Known Franchise Operations

Franchisors form
chains, too

In a **franchise operation**, the franchisor develops a good marketing strategy, and the retail franchise holders carry out the strategy in their own units. The franchisor acts like a voluntary chain operator—or a producer! Each franchise holder benefits from the experience, buying power, and image of the larger company. In return, the franchise holder usually signs a contract to pay fees and commission—and to strictly follow franchise rules designed to continue the successful strategy. Exhibit 13–9 shows examples of well-known franchise operations, and Marketing Demo 13–3 describes a fast-growing Canadian franchise.

Voluntary chains tend to work with existing retailers, while some franchisors like to work with—and train—newcomers. For newcomers, a franchise often reduces the risk of starting a new business. Only about 5 percent of new franchise operations fail in the first few years—compared to about 70 percent for other new retailers.

Franchise holders' sales are growing fast. Franchise holders in the United States now account for over $700 billion in sales, and they will account for half of all retail sales by the year 2000. One important reason for this growth is that franchising is especially popular with service firms, one of the fastest-growing sectors of the economy.[23]

LOCATION OF RETAIL FACILITIES

Location can spell success or failure for a retail facility. But a "good location" depends on target markets, competitors, and costs. Let's review some of the ideas a retailer should consider in selecting a location.

Downtown and shopping
strips—evolve without
a plan

Most cities have a central business district with many retail stores. At first, it may seem that such a district developed according to some plan. Actually, the location of individual stores is more an accident of time—and available spaces.

As cities grow, shopping strips of convenience stores develop along major roads. Generally, they emphasize convenience products. But a variety of single-line and limited-line stores may enter, too, adding shopping products to the mix.

MARKETING DEMO 13–3   Soapberry's "Cottage" Industry Cleans Up

Natasha Rajewski rarely visits her family cottage these days—and the irony of that is not lost on her. It was the pollution of Lake Simcoe, the Ontario Lake on which the cottage is nestled, that inspired her to start Soapberry Shop, a franchised operation that bills itself as "An Environment Conscious Canadian Company." But as president of a burgeoning operation with more than 30 outlets across Canada and the United States, she doesn't have much free time on her hands.

Rajewski opened her first shop in 1983 in Toronto with a small line of shampoos, soap, and shower gels—developed in collaboration with a chemist friend—packaged in plain, recyclable, standard-sized containers. The original idea was to wholesale the products, operating a small retail business initially to support the operation. But the big clients weren't biting. The interest, instead, came from local consumers enticed by the flyer/catalogue that Rajewski sent out into the neighborhood.

Particular attention was paid to educating the consumer about the environmental friendliness of the products and their formulations, which Rajewski says use only plant extracts selected for their therapeutic value.

Susan Whyte, director of marketing, says that almost all product changes stem from customer suggestions, whether it be a request for something completely different or a fragrance change in an existing product. All stores have a log book to record customer suggestions.

Whyte says there is little concern that the essence of Soapberry will be lost through franchising. "The store is an investment for this person, and they will therefore work as hard as we do to make it successful," says Whyte. "But also, when we consider a franchisee, we look for someone who has a lot of heart, someone who believes in the product, who will work in the store and maintain our level of customer service. We are able to pick and choose our franchisees very carefully and can supply them with an extensive operating manual, as well as continued consultation and training."

Soapberry does little advertising, relying instead on media public relations and sponsorships. In-store promotions are often linked with specific causes, such as the David Suzuki Foundation. Limited national magazine advertising has been done, says Whyte, to generate name recognition for new franchises. Whyte says her current marketing goal is "to put Soapberry into every bathroom in Canada." Although this might seem like a rather lofty goal, there is still a huge potential for growth.

Rajewski says "90 percent of the shopping (for skin care products) is still done in drug- and department stores. There's still a lot of market to tap into."

Source: Laura Medcalf, "Soapberry's 'Cottage' Industry Cleans Up," *Marketing*, December 9, 1991, p. 20.

Some retailers dress up the stores in these unplanned strips. The expense of remodeling is small compared to the higher rents at big shopping centres. Even so, strips aren't the planned shopping centres that developed in the last 30 years.

Planned shopping centres—not just a group of stores

A **planned shopping centre** is a set of stores planned as a unit to satisfy some market needs. The stores sometimes act together for promotion purposes—and they usually provide free parking. Many centres are in enclosed malls that make shopping more pleasant, especially in harsh weather.

Do we have too many stores and malls?

Many experts feel that there is just too much retail space—and too many malls. As a result, a great many Canadian retail firms went bankrupt in the early 1990s, and even more retailers are likely to fail in the next few years. However, consumers may ultimately benefit because the oversupply of retail facilities will reduce what retailers pay for space—and the prices they charge consumers. Although there may be too much retail space in total, retailers will continue to

Exhibit 13–10   Number of Shopping Centres, by Type of Centre, by Province, 1973 and 1988

	Neighborhood Type A		Percent Change	Community Type B		Percent Change	Regional Type C		Percent Change
	1973	*1988*		*1973*	*1988*		*1973*	*1988*	
Canada	417	437	4.8%	146	340	132.9%	101	330	226.7%
Newfoundland	2	6	200.0	2	13	550.0	1	3	200.0
Prince Edward Island	2	4	100.0	—	2	...	—	—	...
Nova Scotia	7	24	242.9	4	17	325.0	2	13	550.0
New Brunswick	10	17	70.0	5	10	100.0	1	13	1,200.0
Quebec	89	58	−34.8	32	75	134.4	33	91	175.8
Ontario	161	215	33.5	63	112	77.8	42	116	176.2
Manitoba	20	18	−10.0	4	14	250.0	1	8	700.0
Saskatchewan	14	12	−14.3	6	11	83.3	—	14	...
Alberta	49	35	−28.6	12	33	175.0	11	35	218.2
British Columbia	63	47	−25.4	18	53	194.4	10	37	270.0
Yukon and Northwest Territories	—	1	...	—	—	—	—	—	—

Source: Statistics Canada, *The Market Research Handbook*, Cat. 63-224.

group together in shopping centres, and different types of centres will serve different needs. Exhibit 13–10 summarizes the shopping mall situation in Canada.

Neighborhood shopping centres consist of several convenience stores. These centres usually include a supermarket, drugstore, hardware store, beauty shop, laundry, dry cleaner, gas station, and perhaps others—such as a bakery or appliance shop. They normally serve 7,500 to 40,000 people living within a 6- to 10-minute driving distance.

Community shopping centres are larger and offer some shopping stores as well as the convenience stores found in neighborhood shopping centres. They usually include a small department store that carries shopping products (clothing and home furnishings). But most sales in these centres are convenience products. These centres serve 40,000 to 150,000 people within a radius of five to six miles.

Regional shopping centres are the largest centres and emphasize shopping stores and shopping products. Most of these are enclosed malls, making shopping easier in bad weather. They usually include one or more large department stores and as many as 200 smaller stores. Stores that feature convenience products are often located at the edge of the centre—so they won't get in the way of customers primarily interested in shopping.

Regional centres usually serve 150,000 or more people—like the downtown shopping districts of larger cities. However, regional centres usually are found near populated suburban areas. They draw customers from a radius of 7 to 10 miles—or even farther from rural areas where shopping facilities are poor. Regional shopping centres being built now often cover 2 million square feet—as large as 40 football fields![24]

During the 1980s, many discount malls developed. These shopping centres are often as large as regional shopping centres, and all the stores claim to sell at discounted prices. Some are outlets run by producers who sell seconds or out-of-date lines. Such malls target budget shoppers who are willing to drive long distances for a big assortment of "deals."[25]

The number of new shopping malls expanded rapidly in the 1980s, but some experts believe we now have more retail space in malls than we need.

DIFFERENCES IN RETAILING IN DIFFERENT NATIONS

New ideas spread across countries

New retailing approaches that succeed in one part of the world are often quickly adapted to other countries. Some of these efforts are very successful. For example, self-service approaches that started with supermarkets in North America are now found in many retail operations around the world. Similarly, mass-merchandising approaches are popular in many countries. In 1969, for example, Kmart entered into a joint venture with Australia's largest department store chain to pioneer mass-merchandising there. As a result, Kmart is now the largest discount chain in Australia, but other mass-merchandisers thrive as well.

The superstore concept, on the other hand, initially developed in Europe. ASDA in the United Kingdom and Carrefour in France are still leaders in this approach. Although the superstore format is not yet as successful here, Loblaw's is one of the superstore innovators in Canada with its "Real Canadian Superstore" operations.

Mass-merchandising requires mass markets

While the low prices, selections, and efficient operations offered by mass-merchandisers and other large chains might be attractive to consumers in many countries, the external marketing environment often doesn't support their development. In less-developed nations the most basic problem is economic. Consumers simply don't have the income to support mass distribution. The small shops that survive in these economies sell in very small quantities, often to a small number of consumers.

Some countries block change

The political and legal environment severely limits the evolution of retailing in some nations. Many countries design rules to protect existing retailers, even if they're inefficient. Japan is a prime example. For years its Large Store Law—aimed at protecting the country's politically powerful small shopkeepers—has been a real barrier to retail change. The law restricts development of stores larger than 500 square meters by requiring special permits, which are routinely denied. Under the law, local communities and the Ministry of International Trade and Industry (MITI) managed to stall market entry by big retailers, such as Japanese supermarket operator Daiei, for 10 years or more.

MITI now says that it is taking steps to change the Large Store Law; in fact, that is why Toys "R" Us was able to enter the Japanese market. Even so, Toys "R" Us must limit its hours and close its stores a month out of every year—like other Japanese retailers. Most experts believe that it will be many years before Japan moves away from its system of small, limited-line shops. The inefficiency of that retail distribution system is an important reason why Japanese consumers pay very high prices for consumer products. Many countries in other parts of Asia, Europe, and South America impose similar restrictions—including limits on advertising and when retailers can run nationwide sales.

Whole distribution systems are involved	A number of countries, including many of those in central and eastern Europe, are trying to encourage development of new, more efficient retailers. Because they have little capital to start retail operations, they make it easy for established retailers from other nations to enter the market. But entering the market and making progress are two different issues. Most of these countries have distribution systems similar to the North American system in the 1930s.

Eastern Europe, for example, lacks the technology to support computer systems, which are an important part of many retailers' operations. Even the electrical power is not sufficient. The pace of modernization is also being slowed by questions about how previously state-owned wholesalers and retailers will be privatized.

In eastern Europe, as in other areas of the world, retailing doesn't exist in isolation; rather, it serves a role within overall channel systems. So it is difficult—and in many cases impossible—for retailing to evolve and change faster than other aspects of the marketing environment.

Consumer cooperatives are popular in some countries	Retailing in North America is more diverse than in most other countries. Even so, some retailing formats, notably consumer cooperatives, are more prominent in other countries. Switzerland's Migros is perhaps the most successful example. Migros runs a variety of different types of stores, ranging from supermarkets to appliance and electronics centres.

Migros accounts for about 22 percent of food sales in Switzerland and nearly 16 percent of all retail sales. Consumer cooperatives probably won't become popular in markets where other types of retailers are already established and meeting customers' needs. However, some experts think consumer cooperatives like Migros will become a dominant form of retailing in central and eastern Europe.

Cultural differences can be important	Cultural and social differences across countries have a significant effect on retailing operations. In many countries, religious beliefs prevent retailers from opening on weekends. And many retailers simply don't want to work evenings or weekends. As long as no one else offers convenient hours, consumers don't expect it! However, changes in competition can have fast—and devastating—effects on retailers who are not market-oriented.[26]

WHAT DOES THE FUTURE LOOK LIKE?

Retailing changed rapidly in the last 30 years—and the changes seem to be continuing. Scrambled merchandising may become even more scrambled. Some people predict even larger stores; others predict smaller ones.

More customer-oriented retailing may be coming

Any effort to forecast trends in such a situation is risky, but our three-dimensional picture of the retailing market (Exhibit 13–5) can help. Those who suggest bigger and bigger stores may be primarily concerned with the centre of the diagram. Those who look for more small stores and specialty shops may be anticipating more small—but increasingly wealthy—target markets able to afford higher prices for special goods and services.

To serve small but wealthy markets, convenience stores continue to spread. And sales by "electronic" retailing are expected to grow. For example, Compusave Corporation now has an "electronic catalogue" order system. A videodisc player hooked to a TV-like screen allows the consumer to see pictures and descriptions of thousands of products. The product assortment is similar to that at a catalogue store—and the prices are even lower. The consumer makes a selection and inserts a credit card; the computer places the order and routes it to the consumer's home. These machines, being installed in shopping centres around the country, are popular with hurried, cost-conscious consumers.[27]

Many consumers simply don't have as much time to shop as they once did—and a growing number are willing to pay for convenience. Stores will probably continue to make shopping more convenient by staying open later, carrying assortments that make one-stop shopping possible, and being sure stocks don't run out. This interest in convenience and time savings should also lead to growth of in-home shopping.

In-home shopping will become more popular

More consumers will "let their fingers do the walking"—and telephone shopping will become more popular, too. Mail-order houses and department stores already find phone business attractive. Telephone supermarkets—now a reality—sell only by phone and deliver all orders. Selling to consumers through a home computer has not been very successful so far—but may become more popular in the future. Televised home shopping is also certain to become increasingly popular.

We now have far greater electronic capabilities than we are using. There is no reason why customers can't shop in the home—saving time and gas. Such automated retailing might take over a large share of the convenience products and homogeneous shopping products business.

Goods and Services Tax

Another challenge Canadian retailers are facing is the federal Goods and Services Tax (GST) that replaced the less efficient but less inclusive federal Sales Tax. The GST applies at the rate of 7 percent to practically all goods and services in Canada. Many retailers fear reduced demand due to price increases, especially on products that weren't previously taxed.[28]

Border shopping and free trade

Some Canadians respond to higher Canadian prices by shopping more in the United States. The number of same-day trips to the United States increased sharply during 1990 and 1991. Although these numbers leveled off during 1992

A&P's experiment takes self-service retailing a step further—with a scanner-equipped checkout unit consumers operate themselves.

and fell in 1993 because of a decline in the Canadian dollar, the amount of lost business remained very significant.

In addition to increasing shopping in the United States, free trade will pose another challenge. Most in the industry expect that the free trade deal will lead more US retailers to expand into Canada. Many feel increased competition will be good for business and some Canadian retailers may actually benefit. Others question our retailers' ability to compete.

Retailers must face the challenge

One thing is certain—change in retailing is inevitable. For years, conventional retailers' profits have declined. Even some of the newer discounters and shopping centres have not done well. Department stores and food and drug chains have seen profits decline. Old-style variety stores have done even worse. Some shifted into mass-merchandising operations, which are also becoming less attractive as limited-line stores try to meet competition with lower margins.

A few firms—such as Toys "R" Us and The Gap—have avoided this general profit squeeze so far. But the future doesn't look too bright for retailers who can't—or won't—change. Sad as it is to see fine old retailing names go out of business, many will. And shoppers will be served better because of it.

No easy way for more profit

The "fat" has been squeezed out of retailing—and there isn't an easy route to big profits anymore. To be successful in the future, retailers will need careful strategy planning and implementation. This means more careful market segmenting to find unsatisfied needs that (1) have a long life expectancy and (2) can be satisfied with low levels of investment. This is a big order. But imaginative marketers will find more profitable opportunities than the conventional retailer who doesn't know that the product life cycle is moving along—and just hopes for the best.[29]

CONCLUSION

Modern retailing is scrambled—and we'll probably see more changes in the future. In such a dynamic environment, a producer's marketing manager must choose very carefully among the available kinds of retailers. And retailers must plan their marketing mixes with their target customers' needs in mind—while at the same time becoming part of an effective channel system.

We described many types of retailers—and we saw that each has its advantages and disadvantages. We also saw that modern retailers have discarded conventional practices. The old "buy low and sell high" philosophy is no longer a safe guide. Lower margins with faster turnover is the modern philosophy as more retailers move into mass-merchandising. But even this is no guarantee of success as retailers' product life cycles move on.

Scrambled merchandising will continue as retailing evolves to meet changing consumer demands. But important breakthroughs are still possible because consumers probably will continue to move away from conventional retailers. Convenience products, for example, may be made more easily available by some combination of electronic ordering and home delivery or vending. The big, all-purpose department store may not be able to satisfy anyone's needs exactly. Some combination of mail-order and electronic ordering might make a larger assortment of products available to more people—to better meet their particular needs.

Every society needs a retailing function—but all the present retailers may not be needed. The future retail scene will offer the marketing manager new challenges and opportunities.

QUESTIONS AND PROBLEMS

1. Identify a specialty store selling convenience products in your city. Explain why you think it's that kind of store and why an awareness of this status would be important to a manufacturer. Does it give the retailer any particular advantage? If so, with whom?

2. What sort of a "product" are specialty shops offering? What are the prospects for organizing a chain of specialty shops?

3. Many department stores have a bargain basement. Does the basement represent just another department, like the lingerie department or the luggage department? Or is some whole new concept involved?

4. Distinguish among discount houses, price-cutting by conventional retailers, and mass-merchandising. Forecast the future of low-price selling in food, clothing, and appliances.

5. Discuss a few changes in the marketing environment that you think help to explain why telephone and mail-order retailing has been growing so rapidly.

6. Apply the wheel of retailing theory to your local community. What changes seem likely? Will established retailers see the need for change, or will entirely new firms have to develop?

7. What advantages does a retail chain have over a retailer who operates with a single store? Does a small retailer have any advantages in competing against a chain? Explain your answer.

8. Discuss the kinds of markets served by the three types of shopping centres. Are they directly competitive? Do they contain the same kinds of stores? Is the long-run outlook for all of them similar?

9. Many producers are now seeking new opportunities in international markets. Are the opportunities for international expansion equally good for retailers? Explain your answer.

10. Explain the growth and decline of various retailers and shopping centres in your own community. Use the text's three-dimensional drawing (Exhibit 13–5) and the product life-cycle concept. Also, treat each retailer's whole offering as a "product."

SUGGESTED CASES

6. Boutique Vision

15. West Coast Furniture

Wholesalers and Their Strategy Planning

When You Finish This Chapter, You Should

❶

Understand what wholesalers are and the wholesaling functions they *may* provide for others in channel systems.

❷

Know the various kinds of merchant wholesalers and agent middlemen and the strategies that they use.

❸

Understand when and where the various kinds of merchant wholesalers and agent middlemen are most useful to channel planners.

❹

Know what progressive wholesalers are doing to modernize their operations and marketing strategies.

❺

Understand why wholesalers have lasted.

❻

Understand the important new terms (shown in blue).

①s it possible that a Canadian wholesaler will actually make a successful foray into the US market, the graveyard of so many merchandising dreams? Up to now, at least, the experience of druggist Jean Coutu Group (PJC), Inc., of Montreal has been favorable since it bought the Douglas Drug, Inc., chain of North Providence, Rhode Island, earlier this year. Douglas added 16 stores to the five Jean Coutu already owned in the northeastern United States.

The 21 US stores are all owned and operated by the company, while the 194 Canadian outlets are franchises. They operate mainly in Quebec under the Jean Coutu and Maxi Drug names. A few are also located in New Brunswick and Ontario.

Corporate stores apart, the main business of the company is wholesaling and distribution to its network of franchisees. Jean Coutu also handles marketing, personnel training, advertising, and financial consulting for the chain.

It's a rather complicated formula to any outsider. The stores range in size from 7,000 to 11,000 square feet. Pharmaceutical sections are owned and operated by pharmacists and commercial sections are owned and operated by merchandisers. They are required to buy almost all of their inventory from Jean Coutu, which carries a stock of about 22,000 items in its warehouses and guarantees 24-hour delivery.

In the long run, the company would like to convert the US outlets to franchise operations as well, so that it can concentrate on its real strength of marketing and distribution. In that way, it may also avoid the curse that seems to hang over most Canadian retailers who venture into the US market.[1]

This example shows that wholesalers are often a vital link in a channel system—and in the whole marketing process—helping both their suppliers and customers. It also shows that wholesalers—like other businesses—must select their target markets and marketing mixes carefully. But you can understand

Retailers must be convinced to carry a new line.

wholesalers better if you look at them as members of channels. Wholesalers are middlemen.

In this chapter, you will learn more about wholesalers and their strategy planning. You'll see how they have evolved, how they fit into various channels, why they are used, and what functions they perform.

WHAT IS A WHOLESALER?

It's hard to define what a wholesaler is because there are so many different wholesalers doing different jobs. Some of their activities may even seem like manufacturing. As a result, some wholesalers call themselves "manufacturer and dealer." Some like to identify themselves with such general terms as merchant, jobber, dealer, or distributor. And others just take the name commonly used in their trade—without really thinking about what it means.

To avoid a long, technical discussion on the nature of wholesaling, we'll use the Statistics Canada definition:

Wholesalers are primarily engaged in buying merchandise for resale to retailers; to industrial, commercial, institutional, and professional users; to other wholesalers; for export; to farmers for use in farm production; or acting as agents in such transactions.

Mixed activity businesses (such as firms engaged in both wholesaling and retailing, contracting, service trades, manufacturing, etc.) are considered to be in wholesale trade whenever they derive the largest portion of their gross margin from their wholesaling activity.[2]

POSSIBLE WHOLESALING FUNCTIONS

Wholesalers may perform certain functions for both their suppliers and the wholesalers' own customers—in short, for those above and below them in the channel. *Wholesaling functions* really are variations of the basic marketing functions—buying, selling, grading, storing, transporting, financing, risk taking, and gathering market information. Wholesaling functions are basic to the following discussion because decisions about what combination of functions to perform are a key part of a wholesaler's strategy planning. Keep in mind that *not all* wholesalers provide all of the functions.

What a wholesaler might do for customers

Wholesalers perform a variety of activities that benefit their customers. They:

1. Regroup goods—to provide the quantity and assortment customers want at the lowest possible cost.
2. Anticipate needs—forecast customers' demands and buy accordingly.
3. Carry stocks—carry inventory so customers don't have to store a large inventory.
4. Deliver goods—provide prompt delivery at low cost.
5. Grant credit—give credit to customers, perhaps supplying their working capital. Note: This financing function may be very important to small customers; sometimes it's the main reason they use wholesalers rather than buying directly from producers.

A wholesaler often helps its customers by carrying needed products and providing prompt delivery at low cost.

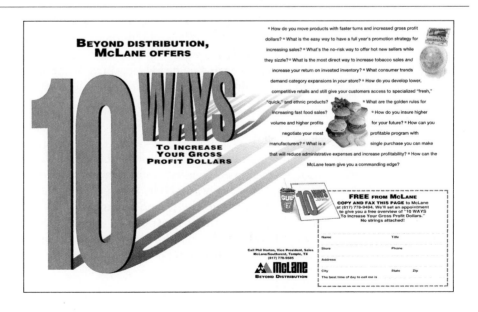

6. Provide information and advisory service—supply price and technical information as well as suggestions on how to install and sell products. Note: The wholesaler's sales reps may be experts in the products they sell.
7. Provide part of the buying function—offer products to potential customers so they don't have to hunt for supply sources.
8. Own and transfer title to products—help complete a sale without the need for other middlemen, speeding the whole buying and selling process.

What a wholesaler might do for producer-suppliers

Wholesalers also benefit producer-suppliers. They:

1. Provide part of a producer's selling function—by going to producer-suppliers instead of waiting for their sales reps to call.
2. Store inventory—reduce a producer's need to carry large stocks, thus cutting the producer's warehousing expenses.
3. Supply capital—reduce a producer's need for working capital by buying the producer's output and carrying it in inventory until it's sold.
4. Reduce credit risk—by selling to customers the wholesaler knows and taking the loss if these customers don't pay.
5. Provide market information—as an informed buyer and seller closer to the market, the wholesaler reduces the producer's need for market research.[3]

Functions are crucial in many channels

You can see the importance of these wholesaling functions by looking at a specific case. George Mariakakas is a heating contractor. His company sells heating systems—and his crew installs them in new buildings. Mariakakas gets a lot of help from Air Control Company, the wholesaler who supplies this equipment. When Mariakakas isn't certain what type of furnace to install, Air Control's experts give him good technical advice. Air Control also stocks an inventory of products from different producers. This means that Mariakakas can order a piece of equipment when he's ready to install it. He doesn't have to tie up capital in a big inventory—or wait for a part to be shipped cross-country from a producer. Air Control even helps finance his business. Mariakakas doesn't have to pay for his purchases until 30 days after he takes delivery. By then, he has finished his work and been paid by his customers. Mariakakas's whole way of doing business would be different without this wholesaler providing wholesaling functions.

KINDS OF AVAILABLE WHOLESALERS

Why do manufacturers use merchant wholesalers costing about 19 percent of sales, as opposed to using their own sales branches? Why use either when agent middlemen cost only about 3 percent? Is the use of wholesalers with higher operating expenses the reason marketing costs so much—if, in fact, it does?

To answer these questions, we must understand what these wholesalers do—and don't do. Exhibit 14–1 gives a big-picture view of the wholesalers described in more detail below. Note that a major difference is whether they *own* the products they sell.

Exhibit 14−1   Type of Wholesalers

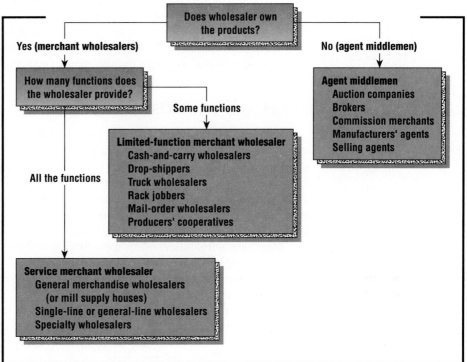

One of a wholesaler's main assets is its customers. A particular wholesaler may be the only one who reaches certain customers. The producer who wants to reach these customers *may have no choice but to use that wholesaler.* "What customers does this wholesaler serve?" should be one of the first questions you ask when planning a channel of distribution.[4]

Wholesaler provides access to a target market

The next important question should be "What functions does this particular wholesaler provide?" Wholesalers typically specialize by product line. But they do provide different functions. And they probably will keep doing what they are doing—no matter what others might like them to do!

Learn the pure to understand the real

To help you understand wholesaling better, we'll discuss "pure" types of wholesalers. In practice, many wholesalers are mixtures of the pure types. Further, the names commonly used in a particular industry may be misleading. Some so-called brokers actually behave as limited-function merchant wholesalers. And some manufacturers' agents operate as full-service wholesalers. Names also vary by country. This casual use of terms makes it all the more important for you to understand the pure types before trying to understand the blends—and the names they're given in the business world.

In Canada, Statistics Canada publishes detailed data concerning wholesalers, including breakdowns by kind of business, product line, and geographic territory. Similar information is available for many other countries, including most of those in the European Community. This kind of data is valuable in strategy planning—

Helpful data is sometimes available

especially to learn whether potential channel members are serving a target market. You can also learn what sales volume current middlemen are achieving.

However, detailed data is not always available. In these cases, it is even more important for a marketing manager to understand the role wholesalers play in a distribution system, what functions they provide, and the strategies they use. In the following pages, we'll discuss the major types of wholesalers.

MERCHANT WHOLESALERS ARE THE MOST NUMEROUS

Merchant wholesalers own (take title to) the products they sell. For example, a wholesale lumber yard that buys plywood from the producer is a merchant wholesaler. It actually owns—takes title to—the plywood for some period of time before selling to its customers. Merchant wholesalers are very common in some countries. Japan is an extreme example. In its unusual multitiered distribution system, products are often bought and sold by a series of merchant wholesalers on their way to the business user or retailer.

Merchant wholesalers often specialize by certain types of products or customers. For example, Fastenal specializes in distributing threaded fasteners used by a variety of manufacturers. Marketing Demo 14–1 discusses McKesson's success as a full-service merchant wholesaler.

Many merchant wholesalers service relatively small geographic areas. And several wholesalers may be competing for the same customers.[5]

Merchant wholesalers also differ in how many of the wholesaling functions they provide. There are two basic kinds of merchant wholesalers: (1) service (sometimes called full-service wholesalers) and (2) limited-function or limited-service wholesalers. Their names explain their difference.

Service wholesalers provide all the functions

Service wholesalers provide all the wholesaling functions. Within this basic group are three types: (1) general merchandise, (2) single-line, and (3) specialty.

General merchandise wholesalers are service wholesalers who carry a wide variety of nonperishable items such as hardware, electrical supplies, plumbing supplies, furniture, drugs, cosmetics, and automobile equipment. These wholesalers originally developed to serve the early retailers—the general stores. Now, with their broad line of convenience and shopping products, they serve hardware stores, drugstores, electric appliance shops, and small department stores. *Mill supply houses* operate in a similar way, but they carry a broad variety of accessories and supplies to serve the needs of manufacturers.

Single-line (or general-line) wholesalers are service wholesalers who carry a narrower line of merchandise than general merchandise wholesalers. For example, they might carry only food, wearing apparel, or certain types of industrial tools or supplies. In consumer products, they serve the single- and limited-line stores. In business products, they cover a wider geographic area and offer more specialized service.

Limited-function wholesalers provide some functions

Limited-function wholesalers provide only *some* wholesaling functions. Exhibit 14–2 shows the functions typically provided—and not provided. In the following paragraphs, we will discuss the main features of these wholesalers. Less numerous in some countries, they are, in fact, not counted separately by Statistics Canada. Nevertheless, these wholesalers are very important for some products.

MARKETING DEMO 14–1
McKesson's Marketing Strategy Is a Wholesale Success

(M)cKesson Drug Co. is a full-service merchant wholesaler—and an innovator when it comes to distributing pharmaceutical and health care products to drugstores. A decade ago, McKesson's drugstore distribution business was doing so poorly that its owners considered selling it. Since then, sales have tripled, even though McKesson's sales force is now only about half as large.

A top executive at the company says that "everything we've been able to do has been driven by getting the customer on computers." When McKesson put its customers on a direct computer-order hookup, it was easier for them to order and less expensive to maintain the right inventory. McKesson's computers don't just dispatch orders to a warehouse. They also print price stickers and add the precise profit margin that the druggist selects. At the end of the month, the druggist even gets a printout that shows the profitability of each department. Other wholesalers now compete with similar systems, but McKesson continues to find new ways to add value in the channel.

In 1991, for example, it modernized its distribution network by installing a state-of-the-art, automated order-picking system in its distribution centre. The new system reduces costs, is more accurate, and fills orders faster—at a rate of nearly 1,200 an hour. Changes like this help McKesson reduce the inventory costs of its manufacturer-suppliers while still achieving the product availability that drugstores need. Such efficiency caused a basic shift in the channel of distribution for drugs. In 1973, only 50 percent of sales were handled by distributors, and the rest were direct sales by manufacturers. Now, 75 percent of sales are handled by distributors.

McKesson also strengthened and expanded Valu-Rite, the voluntary chain it set up for independent drugstores. In addition to providing these retailers with computer services and a reliable supply, McKesson provides private-label brands, promotional circulars, and advertising support. Many independent drugstores credit McKesson with giving them the help—and the technology—they need to compete with the big chains. And their loyalty to McKesson explains why sales to members of the Valu-Rite program have grown at 23 percent a year since 1985.

In Canada, direct sales by manufacturers still account for 57 percent of all pharmaceutical sales. That represents a real opportunity for McKesson's Canadian division. McKesson believes that by expanding the use of its approaches in Canada, it will not only increase its own sales and profits, but also reduce the total cost of distributing drugs and thus the prices that consumers pay.

Source: McKesson, 1990 Annual Report; "Computer Finds a Role in Buying and Selling, Reshaping Businesses," *The Wall Street Journal*, March 18, 1987, p. 1ff.

Cash-and-carry wholesalers want cash

Cash-and-carry wholesalers operate like service wholesalers, except that the customer must pay cash.

Some retailers, such as small auto repair shops, are too small to be served profitably by a service wholesaler. So service wholesalers set a minimum charge—or just refuse to grant credit to a small business that may have trouble paying its bills. Or the wholesaler may set up a cash-and-carry department to supply the small retailer for cash on the counter. The wholesaler can operate at lower cost because the retailers take over many wholesaling functions. And using cash-and-carry outlets may enable the small retailer to stay in business. These cash-and-carry operators are especially common in less-developed nations where very small retailers handle the bulk of retail transactions.

Wholesalers don't always sell goods. Some wholesalers may deal in services. Marketing Demo 14–2 describes a specialty wholesaler of charter tours. Many of the same issues are relevant for both goods and services.

Exhibit 14–2   Functions Provided by Different Types of Limited-Function Merchant Wholesalers

Functions	Cash-and Carry	Drop-Shipper	Truck	Mail-Order	Cooperatives	Rack Jobbers
For Customers						
Anticipates needs	X		X	X	X	X
"Regroups" products (one or more of four steps)	X		X	X	X	X
Carries stocks	X		X	X	X	X
Delivers products			X		X	X
Grants credit		X	Maybe	Maybe	Maybe	Consignment (in some cases)
Provides information and advisory services		X	Some	Some	X	
Provides buying function		X	X	X	Some	X
Owns and transfers title to products	X	X	X	X	X	X
For Producers						
Provides producers' selling function	X	X	X	X	X	X
Stores inventory	X		X	X	X	X
Helps finance by owning stocks	X		X	X	X	X
Reduces credit risk	X	X	X	X	X	X
Provides market information	X	X	Some	X	X	Some

Specialty wholesalers are service wholesalers who carry a very narrow range of products—and offer more information and service than other service wholesalers. A consumer products specialty wholesaler might carry only health foods or oriental foods instead of a full line of groceries. Or a specialty wholesaler might carry only automotive items and sell exclusively to mass-merchandisers.

Specialty wholesalers often know a great deal about the final target markets in their channel. For example, Advanced Marketing is the leading wholesale supplier of books to membership warehouse clubs. The company offers hardcover best-sellers, popular paperbacks, basic reference books, cookbooks, and travel books. Consumers in different geographic areas are interested in different kinds of books and that affects what books will sell in a particular store. Further, consumer preferences change constantly as new books come out. Advanced Marketing has such information—and advises the busy store manager about what to stock. It also helps plan special displays and arrange the stock—to match the needs of local customers. Because Advanced Marketing tailors its strategy to satisfy the unique merchandising requirements of warehouse clubs, it has a distinct competitive advantage in serving this high-growth channel.

A specialty wholesaler of business products might limit itself to fields requiring special technical knowledge or service. Richardson Electronics is an interesting example. It specializes in distributing replacement components, such as electron tubes and power semiconductors, for technologically obsolete equipment that many manufacturers still use on the factory floor. Richardson describes itself as "on the trailing edge of technology," but its unique products, expertise, and service are valuable to its target customers, many of whom operate in countries where advanced technologies are not yet common.[6]

MARKETING DEMO 14–2 Sunquest Tours Is Flying High

(P) at Brigham defines the term *hands-on management*. When the president of Sunquest Tours isn't running Canada's largest independent charter-tour wholesaler from its lavish downtown Toronto headquarters, he can usually be found at one of Sunquest's holiday destinations—following the maids around to check the quality of the rooms. He's also been known to pop up in travel agencies unannounced, to check the supply of brochures. This kind of dedication has paid off. Sunquest is flying high during its 20th year in the same airspace that has seen more than a dozen major charter operators go down in flames in the last five years alone.

The Sunquest chief says he has succeeded by sticking to the fundamentals in a business that is deceptively simple: A wholesale operator books several thousand plane seats, hotel rooms, and cruise-ship berths up to a year in advance and tries to sell them for a profit. What's key, Brigham says, is that these seats and rooms are perishable—if a destination falls out of favor or sales staff don't do their jobs, the operator eats the loss.

Brigham is legendary for not resting (and not letting anyone else rest) until virtually every seat is sold. He claims an average of 98 percent of all seats go for every tour. To do this, his sales staff—like his

expensive shirts—are pressed to perfection. Using a video screen readout in his office, for instance, Brigham instantly detects a backup on the phone lines, which handle 7,000 calls a day. Then he picks up the phone and barks out "Push 22"—meaning "get those people off hold and sell them some seats."

The roll call of companies that weren't as fanatical is long. Among them are Worldways Canada Ltd., once the charter-airline leader, and Soundair Corp.—the parent of Odyssey International, Air Toronto, and leading wholesaler Thomson Vacations.

The top half of the market is shared by Canadian, Sunquest, Carousel, Regent, and Conquest. The four that don't own their own airplanes coexist by focusing on different areas. Sunquest, for instance, positions itself in the higher end of the market and is the industry leader in Las Vegas. It is also big in Venezuela and other sun destinations. It balances this winter trade with a strong European segment. With aging boomers expected to give leisure travel a big boost, Brigham is confident that Sunquest will keep gaining altitude.

Source: Matthew Ingram, "Sunquest Tours Is Flying High," *The Financial Times of Canada*, September 16, 1991, p. 6.

Drop-shipper does not handle the products

Drop-shippers own (take title to) the products they sell—but they do not actually handle, stock, or deliver them. These wholesalers are mainly involved in selling. They get orders—from wholesalers, retailers, or other business users—and pass these orders on to producers. Then the producer ships the order directly to the customers. Because drop-shippers do not have to handle the products, their operating costs are lower.

Drop-shippers commonly sell products so bulky that additional handling would be expensive and possibly damaging. Also, the quantities they usually sell are so large that there is little need for regrouping—for example, rail-carload shipments of coal, lumber, oil, or chemical products.

Truck wholesalers deliver—at a cost

Truck wholesalers specialize in delivering products that they stock in their own trucks. By handling perishable products in general demand—tobacco, candy, potato chips, and salad dressings—truck wholesalers may provide almost the same functions as full-service wholesalers. Their big advantage is that they deliver perishable products that regular wholesalers prefer not to carry. Some truck wholesalers operate 24 hours a day, every day—and deliver an order within hours.

3M produces 1,600 products used by auto body repair shops in North America, Europe, Japan, and other countries. To reach this target market, 3M works with hundreds of specialty wholesalers.

A 7-Eleven store that runs out of potato chips on a busy Friday night doesn't want to be out of stock all weekend!

Truck wholesalers call on many small service stations and "back alley" garages—providing local delivery of the many small items these customers often forget to pick up from a service wholesaler. Truck wholesalers' operating costs are relatively high because they provide a lot of service.

Mail-order wholesalers reach outlying areas

Mail-order wholesalers sell out of catalogues that may be distributed widely to smaller industrial customers or retailers who might not be called on by other middlemen. These wholesalers operate in the hardware, jewelry, sporting goods, and general merchandise lines.[7]

For example, Inmac uses a catalogue to sell a complete line of 3,000 different computer accessories and supplies. Inmac's catalogues are printed in six languages and distributed to business customers in the United States, Canada, the United Kingdom, Germany, Sweden, the Netherlands, and France. Many of these customers—especially those in smaller towns—don't have a local wholesaler.[8]

Producers' cooperatives do sorting

Producers' cooperatives operate almost as full-service wholesalers—with the "profits" going to the cooperative's customer-members. Cooperatives develop in agricultural markets where there are many small producers. Examples of such organizations are Sunkist (citrus fruits), Sunmaid Raisin Growers Association, and B.C. Hothouse, which serves cucumber, tomato, and pepper growers in British Columbia's lower mainland.

Successful producers' cooperatives emphasize sorting—to improve the quality of farm products offered to the market. Some also brand these improved products—and then promote the brands. For example, the California Almond

Mail-order wholesalers sell out of catalogues—usually to widely dispersed customers.

Growers Exchange has captured most of the retail market with its Blue Diamond brand. Colombian Coffee producers use ads and a trademark featuring "Juan Valdez" and his donkey—to encourage consumers to buy brands of coffee made from their beans.

Farmers' cooperatives in the United States sometimes succeed in restricting output and increasing price by taking advantage of the normally inelastic demand for agricultural commodities. In most businesses, it is not legal for a wholesaler to arrange for producers to band together to "fix" prices and output in this way. However, for more than 50 years, US agricultural cooperatives have been specifically excluded from these regulations.[9] In Canada, marketing boards are sometimes allowed to exercise similar powers.

Rack jobbers sell
hard-to-handle
assortments

Rack jobbers specialize in nonfood products sold through grocery stores and supermarkets—and they often display them on their own wire racks. Most grocers don't want to bother with reordering and maintaining displays of nonfood items (housewares, hardware items, and books and magazines) because they sell small quantities of so many different kinds of products. Rack jobbers are almost service wholesalers—except that they usually are paid cash for what is sold or delivered.

This is a relatively expensive operation—with operating costs of about 18 percent of sales. The large volume of sales from these racks encouraged some large chains to experiment with handling such items themselves. But chains often find that rack jobbers can provide this service as well as—or better than—they can themselves. For example, a rack jobber that wholesales paperback books studies which titles are selling in the local area—and applies that knowledge in many stores. A chain has many stores—but often in different areas where preferences vary. It may not be worth the extra effort for the chain to study the market in each area.

This video rental store also sells magazines, but the store manager lets a rack jobber decide what magazines to sell.

AGENT MIDDLEMEN ARE STRONG ON SELLING

They don't own
the products

Agent middlemen are wholesalers who do not own the products they sell. Their main purpose is to help in buying and selling. They usually provide even fewer functions than the limited-function wholesalers. In certain trades, however, they are extremely valuable. They may operate at relatively low cost, too—sometimes 2 to 6 percent of their selling price.

They are important in
international trade

Agent middlemen are common in international trade because financing is often critical. Many markets have only a few well-financed merchant wholesalers. The best many producers can do is get local representation through agents—and then arrange financing through banks that specialize in international trade.

Agent middlemen are usually experts on local business customs and rules concerning imported products in their respective countries. Sometimes, a marketing manager can't work through a foreign government's red tape without the help of a local agent. Because of the work this may require, commissions are sometimes quite high compared with those of similar agents who deal only with domestic suppliers and customers.

They are
usually specialists

Agent middlemen—like merchant wholesalers—normally specialize by customer type and by product or product line. So it's important to determine exactly what each one does.

In the following paragraphs, we'll mention only the most important points about each type. Study Exhibit 14–3 for details on the functions provided by each. It's obvious from the number of empty spaces in Exhibit 14–3 that agent middlemen provide fewer functions than merchant wholesalers.

Exhibit 14–3   Functions Provided by Different Types of Agent Middlemen

Functions	Manufacturers' Agents	Brokers	Commission Merchants	Selling Agents	Auction Companies
For Customers					
Anticipate needs	Sometimes	Some			
"Regroups" products (one or more of four steps)	Some		X		X
Carries stocks	Sometimes		X		Sometimes
Delivers products	Sometimes		X		
Grants credit			Sometimes	X	Some
Provides information and advisory services	X	X	X	X	
Provides buying function	X	Some	X	X	X
Owns and transfers title to products		Transfers only	Transfers only		
For Producer					
Provides selling function	X	Some	X	X	X
Stores inventory	Sometimes		X		X
Helps finance by owning stocks					
Reduces credit risk				X	Some
Provides market information	X	X	X	X	

Manufacturers' agents— free-wheeling sales reps

A **manufacturers' agent** sells similar products for several noncompeting producers—for a commission on what is actually sold. Such agents work almost as members of each company's sales force—but they're really independent middlemen. More than half of all agent middlemen are manufacturers' agents.

Their big plus is that they already call on some customers and can add another product line at relatively low cost—and at no cost to the producer until something sells! If an area's sales potential is low, a company may use a manufacturers' agent instead of its own sales rep because the agent can do the job at lower cost. A small producer often has to use agents everywhere because its sales volume is too small or too spread out to justify paying its own sales force.

The agent's main job is selling. The agent—or the agent's customer—sends the orders to the producer. The agent, of course, gets credit for the sale. Agents seldom have any part in setting prices or deciding on the producer's other policies. Basically, they are independent, aggressive salespeople.

Agents can be especially useful for introducing new products. For this service, they may earn 10 to 15 percent commission. (In contrast, their commission on large-volume established products may be quite low—perhaps only 2 percent.) The higher rates for new products often become the agent's major disadvantage for the producer. A 10 to 15 percent commission rate may seem small when a product is new and sales volume is low. Once the product sells well, the rate seems high. About this time, the producer often begins using its own sales reps—and the manufacturers' agents must look for other new products to sell. Agents are well aware of this possibility. Most try to work for many producers so they aren't dependent on only one or a few lines.

Manufacturers' agents are very useful in fields where there are many small manufacturers who need to contact customers. These agents are often used in the sale of machinery and equipment, electronic items, automobile products, clothing and apparel accessories, and some food products. They may cover a very narrow geographic area, such as a city or state. However, they are also important in international marketing, and an agent may take on responsibility for a whole country or region.

Import and export agents specialize in international trade

While manufacturers' agents operate in every country, **export or import agents** are basically manufacturers' agents who specialize in international trade.

These agent middlemen help international firms adjust to unfamiliar market conditions in foreign markets. A decade ago, Brazilian shoe producers had only a small share of footwear sales in North America. This was true even though their low labor costs—about 70 cents an hour compared to $6 an hour for American workers—gave them a big cost advantage. And they could produce a quality product. But the Brazilian producers had trouble anticipating rapidly changing American styles. So a number of export agents developed. These specialists traveled in North America, keeping Brazilian producers informed about style changes. They also helped identify retailers looking for lower prices for fashionable shoes. With this information, Brazilian firms were able to export $850 million worth of shoes to North America.[10]

Brokers provide information

Brokers bring buyers and sellers together. Brokers usually have a *temporary* relationship with the buyer and seller while a particular deal is negotiated. Their "product" is information about what buyers need—and what supplies are available. They may also aid in buyer-seller negotiation. If the transaction is completed, they earn a commission from whichever party hired them. **Export and import brokers** operate like other brokers, but they specialize in bringing together buyers and sellers from different countries.

Usually, some kind of broker develops whenever and wherever market information is inadequate. Brokers are especially useful for selling seasonal products. For example, brokers may represent a small food canner during canning season—then go on to other activities.

Brokers are also active in sales of used machinery, real estate, and even ships. These products are not similar, but the needed marketing functions are. In each case, buyers don't come into the market often. Someone with knowledge of available products is needed to help both buyers and sellers complete the transaction quickly and inexpensively. In a number of fields, brokers develop computerized databases that make it even cheaper and faster to match sellers with customers.

Selling agents—almost marketing managers

Selling agents take over the whole marketing job of producers—not just the selling function. A selling agent may handle the entire output of one or more producers—even competing producers—with almost complete control of pricing, selling, and advertising. In effect, the agent becomes each producer's marketing manager.

Financial trouble is one of the main reasons a producer calls in a selling agent. The selling agent may provide working capital but may also take over the affairs of the business.

Selling agents are especially common in highly competitive fields—like textiles and coal. They are also used for marketing lumber, certain food products, clothing items, and some metal products. In all these industries, marketing is

AT&T sometimes relies on wholesalers who specialize in international trade to reach customers in foreign markets.

much more important than production for the survival of firms. The selling agent provides the necessary financial assistance and marketing know-how.

A **combination export manager** is a blend of manufacturers' agent and selling agent—handling the entire export function for several producers of similar but noncompeting lines.

Commission merchants handle and sell products in distant markets

Commission merchants and **export or import commission houses** handle products shipped to them by sellers, complete the sale, and send the money—minus their commission—to each seller.

Commission agents are common in agricultural markets where farmers must ship to big-city central markets. They need someone to handle the products there—as well as sell them—since the farmer can't go with each shipment. Although commission merchants don't own the products, they generally are allowed to sell them at the market price—or the best price above some stated minimum. Newspapers usually print the prices in these markets, so the producer-seller has a check on the commission merchant. Costs are usually low because commission merchants handle large volumes of products—and buyers usually come to them.

Commission agents are sometimes used in other trades—such as textiles. Here, many small producers want to reach buyers in a central market, perhaps one in a distant country, without having to maintain their own sales force.

Auction companies— speed up the sale

Auction companies provide a place where buyers and sellers can come together and complete a transaction. There aren't many auction companies, but they are important in certain lines—such as livestock, fur, tobacco, and used cars. For these products, demand and supply conditions change rapidly—and the product must be seen to be evaluated. The auction company brings buyers and sellers together. Buyers inspect the products, then demand and supply interact to determine the price.

Facilities can be plain to keep overhead costs low. Frequently, auction sheds are close to transportation sources so that the commodities can be reshipped quickly. The auction company charges a set fee or commission for the use of its facilities and services.

MANUFACTURERS' SALES BRANCHES PROVIDE WHOLESALING FUNCTIONS, TOO

Manufacturers' sales branches are separate businesses that producers set up away from their factories. For example, computer producers such as IBM set up local branches in markets around the world to provide service, display equipment, and handle sales.

About 9 percent of wholesalers are owned by manufacturers—but they handle 31 percent of total wholesale sales. One reason sales per branch are so high is that the branches are usually placed in the best market areas. This also helps explain why their operating costs are often lower. But cost comparisons between various channels can be misleading, since sometimes the cost of selling is not charged to the branch. If all expenses of the manufacturers' sales branches were charged to them, they probably would be more costly than they seem.

Statistics Canada collects much data showing the number, kind, location, and operating expenses of manufacturers' sales branches. Similar data is available for many other countries. This type of information helps marketers analyze competitors' distribution systems and probable costs. If competitors are using branches, it may mean that no good specialists are available—or at least none who can provide the functions needed.[11]

OTHER SPECIALIZED MIDDLEMEN—FACILITATORS—FILL UNIQUE ROLES

Factors—like a credit department

In competitive markets, producers are often short of cash—working capital— and can't borrow at a bank. So some producers sell their accounts receivable—for less than the amount due—to get cash quicker and be able to pay their bills on time. To sell its accounts receivable, such a producer might turn to a factor.

Factors are wholesalers of credit. In buying accounts receivable, factors provide their clients with working capital—the financing function. A factor may provide advice on customer selection and collection, too. In effect, the factor may assume the function of a credit department—relieving its clients of this expense.

Field warehousing—cash for products on hand

If a firm has accounts receivable, it can use a factor or even borrow at a bank. But if it has financial problems and its products are not yet sold, borrowing may be more difficult. Then the company may wish to use a **field warehouser**—a firm that segregates some of a company's finished products on the company's own property and issues warehouse receipts that can be used to borrow money.

In field warehousing, the producer's own warehouse is used to save the expense of moving the goods to another location. But an area is formally segregated by the field warehouser. The producer retains title to the goods, but control of them passes to the field warehouser. The field warehouser issues a receipt, which can be used as collateral for borrowing. Field warehousing organizations usually know capital sources—and may be able to arrange loans at lower cost than is possible locally.

Sales finance companies—do floor planning

Some **sales finance companies** finance inventories. **Floor planning** is the financing of display stocks for auto, appliance, and electronics retailers. Many auto dealers don't own any of the cars on their display floors. They may have only a 10 percent interest in each of them—the other 90 percent belongs to a sales finance company. When they sell a car, the sales finance company gets its share, and the dealer keeps the rest.

In effect, these companies provide part of the retailer's financing function. But because the products are usually well branded—and therefore easily resold— there is relatively little risk.

WHOLESALERS TEND TO CONCENTRATE TOGETHER

Wholesalers concentrate in large cities

Some wholesalers—such as grain elevator operators—are located close to producers. But most wholesalers are concentrated near transporting, storing, and financing facilities as well as near large populations. In general, that means that they tend to locate in or near large cities. A majority of Canada's wholesale sales are made in Toronto, Montreal, Vancouver, and Winnipeg.

This heavy concentration of wholesale sales in large cities is caused, in part, by the concentration of manufacturers' sales offices and branches in these attractive markets. Further, many businesses do much of their buying for many facilities through one central purchasing department located in a major city. Agent and merchant middlemen tend to locate near these important customers. In addition, large general merchandise wholesalers often are located in these transportation and commerce centres.

Concentration increases competitive pressure

When a number of competing wholesalers are located together, competition can be tough. And channel relations are usually dynamic as producers and middlemen seek lower costs and higher profits. Many wholesalers try to protect themselves from such losses by handling competing lines—or demanding long-term arrangements and exclusive territories.[12] Marketing Demo 14–3 describes the competitive challenges faced by wholesalers in the auto parts industry.

COMEBACK AND FUTURE OF WHOLESALERS

In earlier days, wholesalers dominated distribution channels in Canada and most other countries. The many small producers and small retailers needed their services. This situation still exists in many countries, especially those with less-developed economies.

However, in the developed nations, as producers became larger, some bypassed the wholesalers. Similarly, as retail chains began to spread rapidly, many took control of functions that had previously been handled by wholesalers. In light of these changes, many people predicted a gloomy future for wholesalers.

Not fat and lazy but enduring

Some analysts and critics feel that the decline of wholesalers might be desirable from a macro point of view. They think wholesalers have grown fat and lazy—contributing little more than bulk-breaking—and that their salespeople are often just order takers. They argue that too many wholesalers neglect the selling function, in part because wholesaling has not attracted high-caliber managers.

MARKETING DEMO 14–3   Getting a Part of a $12 Billion Industry

Looking deeply concerned, the General Motors dealership mechanic in the TV ad urges you to buy nothing but "genuine GM parts" for your own good. Another pitchman warns you—you'll have only yourself to blame if you don't follow his instructions—that you can pay him a few bucks now for this oil filter and no other, or pay him later for untold repair bills. It's your call. You can also see the same pitch, with slight variations, in magazines and newspapers. All of which makes Jean Douville laugh. "We buy some of these parts from GM ourselves," says the president of UAP, Inc., of Montreal, Canada's biggest auto parts distributor. They are some of the same parts UAP buys from manufacturers and sells to Sears' repair departments and to some wholesalers, who then resell them to independent garages.

Now that car sales are taking a serious beating and sales of replacement parts aren't growing as before, the gloves are off. The battle for the $12 billion-a-year car aftermarket is revving up, and at the forefront of the fighting are UAP and its closest Quebec rival, Uni-Select, Inc., of Boucherville.

UAP and Uni-Select have similarities: Both distributors are active across Canada, they both serve a network of jobbers who sell to garages and other retail outlets, and both have exclusive supply contracts with some retailers. However, their core business and corporate strategies vary widely.

UAP's acquisition of Auto Marine Electric Ltd. of Vancouver, for example, follows the UAP pattern of buying all the stock of a company, which then becomes a captive corporate member. Uni-Select, on the other hand, owns outright only its six wholesale distribution warehouses, from Moncton to Calgary.

Douville says some of their business acquaintances at times express envy at the car-part business being "recession-proof." That is, counter sales hum along in good times, and when car sales hit the skids, as they have currently, parts must sell because people keep their cars longer and must repair them more often.

That's partly true, concedes Douville. "A recession affects just about everyone. Those of our customers who are entrepreneurs themselves, like fleet operators and transport companies, also have a slowdown in their activities, which translates into a lot less mileage (and hence fewer repairs)."

Most do-it-yourselfers buy from stores like Canadian Tire, which has cornered almost 50 percent of the DIY auto parts market. Canadian Tire sells parts and accessories that it buys directly from the manufacturer under its own label.

But when you buy from a counter affiliated with a distributor or get your car fixed at a garage, the part you are sold goes through several hands, all of which must make their profit margin: the manufacturer, the distributor, the wholesaler, and the garage owner. Cutthroat competition largely dictates the price markups at any one of the four levels and makes the industry less attractive than it seemed at first glance.

Source: François Shalom, "Getting a Part of a $12 Billion Industry," *This Week in Business*, January 7, 1991, pp. 8–9, 11.

Our review here, however, shows that wholesaling functions *are* necessary—and wholesalers have not been eliminated. To the contrary, they continue to hold their own, and many are enjoying significant growth.

Producing profits, not chasing orders

Wholesalers have held their own, in part, because of new management and new strategies. To be sure, many still operate in the old ways—and wholesaling changes less rapidly than retailing. Yet progressive wholesalers are more concerned with their customers—and with channel systems. Some offer more services. Others develop voluntary chains that bind them more closely to their customers. Now their customers can order routinely by telephone and fax—or directly by computer-to-computer EDI hookups.

Modern wholesalers no longer require all customers to pay for all the services they offer simply because certain customers use them. This traditional practice encouraged limited-function wholesalers and direct channels. Now some wholesalers offer basic service at minimum cost—then charge additional fees for any special services required. In the grocery field, for instance, basic servicing might cost a store 3 to 4 percent of wholesale sales. The store can get promotion assistance and other aids at extra cost.

Most modern wholesalers streamlined their operations to cut unnecessary costs and improve profits. Actually, they had no choice. As the head of one leading wholesale firm expressed it, "You'll either be a low-cost supplier in this business, or you won't be in this business." To cut costs, modern wholesalers use computers to keep track of inventory—and to order new stock only when it is really needed. Computerized sales analysis helps them identify and drop unprofitable products. Wholesalers are also more selective in picking customers. They use a selective distribution policy—when cost analysis shows that many of their smaller customers are unprofitable. With these less-desirable customers gone, wholesalers give more attention to more profitable customers. In this way, they help promote healthy retailers and producers who are able to compete in any market.

Some wholesalers rename their salespeople "store advisers" or "supervisors" to reflect their new roles. These representatives provide many management advisory services including location analysis, store design and modernization, legal assistance on new leases or adjustments in old leases, store-opening services, sales training and merchandising assistance, and advertising help. Such salespeople—who really act as management consultants—must be more competent than the order takers of the past.

Progress—or fail

Training a modern wholesaler's sales force isn't easy. It's sometimes beyond the management skills of small wholesale firms. In some fields—such as the plumbing industry—wholesaler trade associations or large suppliers took over the job. They organize training programs designed to show the wholesaler's salespeople how they, in turn, can help their customers manage their businesses and promote sales. These programs give instruction in bookkeeping, figuring markups, collecting accounts receivable, advertising, and selling, all in an effort to train the wholesalers' salespeople to improve the effectiveness of other channel members.

Many wholesalers are also modernizing their warehouses and physical handling facilities. They mark products with bar codes that can be read with handheld scanners—so inventory, shipping, and sales records can be easily and instantly updated. Computerized order-picking systems speed the job of assembling orders. New storing facilities are carefully located to minimize the costs of both incoming freight and deliveries. Delivery vehicles travel to customers in a computer-selected sequence that reduces the number of miles traveled.

Realizing that their own survival is linked to their customers' survival, some wholesalers offer central computing facilities, including accounting services, for their retailers. Such wholesalers are becoming more mindful of the channel system—they no longer try to overload retailers' shelves. Now they try to clear the merchandise *off* retailers' shelves. They follow the old adage, "Nothing is really sold until it is sold retail."

Wholesalers are helping retailers reduce costs, too. Retailers can wait until they really need a product to order it—and the order can be instantly placed with a fax machine, toll-free telephone line, or computer hookup.

Some progressive wholesalers modernize their warehouses and use handheld computers to reduce costs and improve customer service.

Wholesalers who serve manufacturers are rising to the challenge of their customers' demand for just-in-time delivery systems and making renewed efforts to add value in the distribution channel. For example, metal distributors steadily expanded the preprocessing services they offer manufacturers. They charge for the service, but it frees the manufacturer to focus on the products they produce—and reduces their total cost of buying and processing the metal.

Perhaps good-bye to some

Not all wholesalers are progressive, and some of the smaller, less efficient ones may fail. Efficiency and low cost, however, are not all that's needed for success. Some wholesalers will disappear as the functions they provided in the past are shifted and shared in different ways in the channel. Cost-conscious buyers for retail chains are refusing to deal with some of the middlemen who represent small producers. They want to negotiate directly with the producer—not just accept the price traditionally available from a wholesaler. Similarly, more producers see advantages in having closer working relationships with fewer suppliers, and they're paring the vendor roles to exclude wholesalers who do a poor job meeting their needs. Efficient delivery service from UPS and Priority Post are also making it easy and inexpensive for many producers to ship directly to their customers—even ones in foreign markets. The customer knows that having a wholesaler down the street is not the only way to be sure of getting needed orders the next morning.[13]

Is it an ethical issue?

There's no doubt that some wholesalers are being squeezed out of business. Some critics, including many of the wholesalers affected by these changes, argue that it's unethical for powerful suppliers or customers to simply cut out wholesalers who have spent money and time—perhaps decades—developing markets. Contracts between channel members and laws sometimes define what changes are or are not legal. But in some cases, the ethical issues are more ambiguous.

For example, as part of a broader effort to improve profits, Amana recently notified Cooper Distributing Co. that it intended to cancel its distribution agreement—in 10 days. Cooper had been handling Amana appliances for 30 years, and Amana products represented 85 percent of Cooper's sales. Amana's explanation to Cooper? "It's not because you're doing a bad job: We just think we can do it better."

Situations like this arise often. They may be cold-hearted, but are they unethical? Many would argue that it wasn't fair for Amana to try to cut off the relationship with such short notice. But most wholesalers realize that their business is always at risk—if they don't perform channel functions better or cheaper than what their suppliers or customers can do themselves.[14]

Survivors will need effective strategies

The wholesalers who do survive will need to be efficient, but that doesn't mean they'll all have low costs. Some wholesalers' higher operating expenses result from the strategies they select, including the special services they offer to *some* customers. Truck wholesalers are usually small and have high operating costs. Yet some customers willingly pay the higher cost of this service. Although full-service wholesalers may seem expensive, some will continue operating because they offer the wholesaling functions and sales contacts some small producers need.

To survive, each wholesaler must develop a good marketing strategy. Profit margins are not large in wholesaling, typically ranging from less than 1 percent to 2 percent. And they've declined in recent years as the competitive squeeze tightened. Marketing Demo 14–4 describes how Davis Distributing has adapted to the changing environment.

Wholesaling will last—but weaker, less progressive wholesalers may not.[15]

MARKETING DEMO 14–4
How Davis Distributing Became a Sweet Wholesale Success Story

Davis Distributing is a business on the move. The 70-year-old company, once a tiny wholesaler of tobacco and candies, has turned itself into one of Canada's largest independent wholesalers and is thriving in the recession, riding its good reputation for competitive pricing as well as attentive service. Based in Concord, near Toronto, Davis's fleet of blue-and-white 18-wheelers hauls groceries, candy, and health and beauty aid products from its distribution centre to retail clients throughout Southern Ontario. Tobacco still represents about half of the company's business, but sales have declined significantly year by year as the health-awareness movement deglamorized smoking.

"We didn't anticipate tobacco would go quite as crazy as it has," says company president Bernard Davis. "But about a decade ago we did anticipate a gradual downward trend, and that got us into a wider range of products and services, including groceries." The company's prospects widened considerably recently with the addition of 250 stores in the Becker's convenience store chain to its customer base of independent retailers, department stores, and other chains. In addition, the company has purchased a 50 percent interest in a chain of 14 shops in the Toronto area. The shops, already Davis customers, are now a captive market for the innovative wholesaler.

Source: Wendy Smith, "How Davis Distributing Became a Sweet Wholesale Success Story," *The Financial Times of Canada*, October 12, 1992, p. 12.

A STATISTICAL OVERVIEW OF CANADIAN WHOLESALING

Statistics Canada recognizes five different types of wholesale operations. These include wholesale merchants (buying and selling goods on their own account), agents and brokers (buying and selling goods for others on a commission basis), manufacturers' sales branches (wholesale businesses owned by manufacturing firms for marketing their own products), primary product dealers (including cooperative marketing associations), and petroleum bulk tank plants and truck distributors (wholesale distributors of petroleum products).

Wholesalers and distributors are highly concentrated in Ontario and Quebec, as shown in Exhibit 14–4. Except for Manitoba, sales increased for each province between 1981 and 1990, especially in the top two provinces.

Producers who take over wholesaling activities are not considered wholesalers. However, if separate establishments—such as branch warehouses—are set up, some of these facilities are counted as wholesalers by Statistics Canada. Wholesaling is a middleman activity. When a manufacturer goes direct, it still must assume the marketing functions that an independent wholesaler might provide. This is important from a channel standpoint. Wholesaling functions usually must be performed by some channel member—whether a wholesaler, the manufacturer, or a retailer.

Exhibit 14–4   Canadian Wholesaler and Distributor Sales

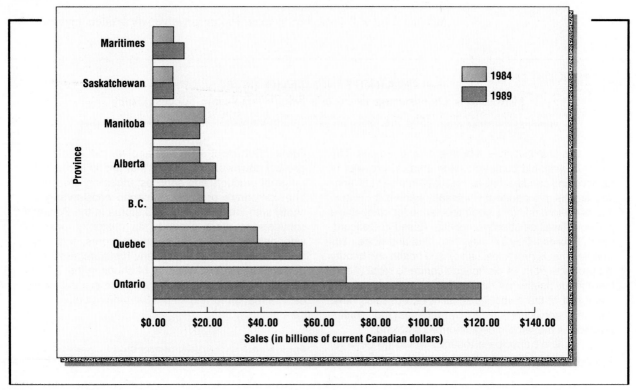

Source: Deborah Zizzo, James M. Kenderdine, and Robert F. Lusch, *The Changing Economics of Wholesaling: A North American Chart Book* (Norman, OK: University of Oklahoma, 1993).

Wholesale merchants

Wholesaling statistics indicate that in 1990 some 70,191 wholesale merchants were in business in Canada. These organizations operated at more than 75,000 different locations and did over $261 billion worth of business.

Wholesale merchant activity is concentrated in Quebec and Ontario. These two provinces accounted for about 65 percent of all establishments and merchant trade. This isn't surprising, given the relative importance of these provinces as measured by population, manufacturing activity, retail trade, and so forth.

Exhibit 14–5 reports on wholesale merchants by kind of business. Are you surprised to find food accounting for only 16 percent of the total volume of wholesale merchant trade? This is due to the way the data is collected. These figures don't include sales made at wholesale merchant locations operated by large supermarkets such as Safeway, A&P, and Loblaw's.

Costs and profits vary with product sold

Is the cost of doing business the same for all classes of wholesale merchants? Gross margins, as a percentage of net sales, average 21.4 percent for all wholesale merchants. However, specific margins range from 11.3 percent in the food business to 33 percent for machinery and equipment wholesalers.[16] Why do such differences exist? It depends on the type of product. It obviously costs more to assemble some products than it does others. The services demanded by the

Exhibit 14–5   Wholesaler and Distributor Sales by Kind of Business

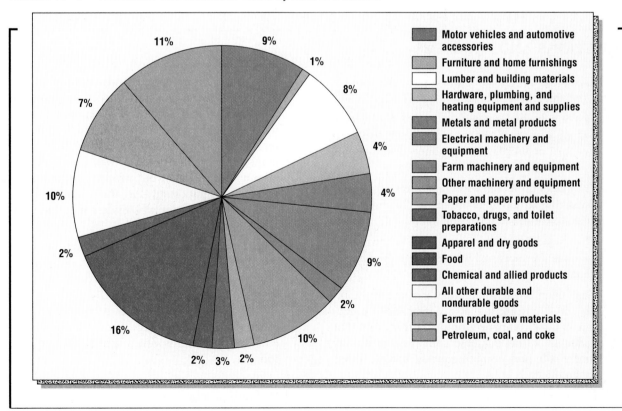

Source: Deborah Zizzo, James M. Kenderdine, and Robert F. Lusch, *The Changing Economics of Wholesaling: A North American Chart Book* (Norman, OK: University of Oklahoma, 1993).

customers for one product category may cost more to provide than those demanded by those purchasing other items. Also, one wholesale business may be much more labor intensive than another. In short, wholesale merchants with high gross margins aren't necessarily the most profitable. Many of these firms also have high operating expenses.

CONCLUSION

Wholesalers can provide functions for those both above and below them in a channel of distribution. These services are closely related to the basic marketing functions. There are many types of wholesalers. Some provide all the wholesaling functions, while others specialize in only a few. Eliminating wholesalers wouldn't eliminate the need for the functions they provide. And we can't assume that direct channels will be more efficient.

Merchant wholesalers are the most numerous and account for most wholesale sales. Their distinguishing characteristic is that they take title to

(own) products. Agent middlemen, on the other hand, act more like sales representatives for sellers or buyers—and they don't take title.

Despite various predictions of the end of wholesalers, they continue to exist. And the more progressive ones have adapted to a changing environment. Wholesaling hasn't experienced the revolutions we saw in retailing, and none seem likely. But some smaller and less progressive wholesalers will probably fail, while larger and more market-oriented wholesalers will continue to provide these necessary functions.

QUESTIONS AND PROBLEMS

1. Discuss the evolution of wholesaling in relation to the evolution of retailing.

2. Does a wholesaler need to worry about new product planning just as a producer needs to have an organized new-product development process? Explain your answer.

3. What risks do merchant wholesalers assume by taking title to goods? Is the size of this risk about constant for all merchant wholesalers?

4. Why would a manufacturer set up its own sales branches if established wholesalers were already available?

5. What is an agent middleman's marketing mix? Why do you think that many merchant middlemen handle competing products from different producers, while manufacturers' agents usually handle only noncompeting products from different producers?

6. Why would a firm use a manufacturer's representative in a foreign market if it could hire a salesperson for a lower commission rate?

7. Discuss the future growth and nature of wholesaling if low-margin retailing and scrambled merchandising become more important. How will wholesalers have to adjust their mixes if retail establishments become larger and retail managers more professional? Will wholesalers be eliminated? If not, what wholesaling functions will be most important? Are there any particular lines of trade where wholesalers may have increasing difficulty?

8. Which types of wholesalers would be most appropriate for the following products? If more than one type of wholesaler could be used, describe each situation carefully. For example, if size or financial strength of a company has a bearing, then so indicate. If several wholesalers could be used in this same channel, explain this, too.

    a. Women's shoes.
    b. Fresh peaches.
    c. Machines to glue packing boxes.
    d. Auto mechanics' tools.

e. A business accessory machine.

f. Used construction equipment.

g. Shoelaces.

9. Would a drop-shipper be desirable for the following products: coal, lumber, iron ore, sand and gravel, steel, furniture, or tractors? Why or why not? What channels might be used for each of these products if drop-shippers were not used?

10. Explain how field warehousing could help a marketing manager.

11. Discuss how computer systems affect wholesalers' operations.

12. Which types of wholesalers are likely to become more important in the next 25 years? Why?

13. What alternatives does a producer have if it is trying to expand distribution in a foreign market and finds that the best existing merchant middlemen won't handle imported products?

SUGGESTED CASES

10. O & E Farm Supply

16. Jenson Company

Promotion—Introduction

Chapter 15

When You Finish This Chapter, You Should

❶

Know the advantages and disadvantages of the promotion methods a marketing manager can use in strategy planning.

❷

Understand the importance of promotion objectives.

❸

Know how the communication process should affect promotion planning.

❹

Know how the adoption processes can guide promotion planning.

❺

Know how typical promotion plans are blended.

❻

Know who plans and manages promotion blends.

❼

Understand the importance and nature of sales promotion.

❽

Understand the important new terms (shown in blue).

The growing popularity of cross promotions is sparking interest in strange quarters. Even companies in dissimilar businesses are discovering there can be a strong crossover appeal by joining forces.

Toronto-based Moneysworth & Best Quality Shoe Repair and Molly Maid International, Inc., of Oakville, Ontario, are typical of the back-scratching trend. A shoe repair chain and a housecleaning service seem odd bedfellows, but the companies say pooling their resources has produced outstanding results.

Their "From our home to your home" promotion, which closed with a draw for a year's free Molly Maid service, cost each firm about $50,000. The centerpiece was a house-shaped box of Moneysworth & Best samples and coupons that Molly Maid cleaners gave their clients as a show of thanks. Flyers and posters in Moneysworth & Best stores advertised the cleaning contest. The entries, forwarded to Molly Maid franchisers, were used as sales leads.

"Not only did we receive phenomenal feedback from our customers, we received tremendous feedback from Molly Maid and their customers," said Stephen Dodds, vice president of Moneysworth & Best. "We were able to get into about 12,000 Molly Maid homes with a very high profile incentive. It would have been extraordinarily expensive for us to try and do that directly."[1]

SEVERAL PROMOTION METHODS ARE AVAILABLE

Promotion is communicating information between seller and potential buyer or others in the channel to influence attitudes and behavior. The marketing manager's main promotion job is to tell target customers that the right Product is available at the right Place at the right Price.

What the marketing manager communicates is determined by target customers' needs and attitudes. *How* the messages are delivered depends on what blend of the various promotion methods the marketing manager chooses.

As the cross promotion example shows, a marketing manager can choose from several promotion methods—personal selling, mass selling, and sales promotion (see Exhibit 15–1).

Personal selling— flexibility is its strength

Personal selling involves direct spoken communication between sellers and potential customers. Face-to-face selling provides immediate feedback—which helps salespeople to adapt. Although salespeople are included in most marketing mixes, personal selling can be very expensive. So it's often desirable to combine personal selling with mass selling and sales promotion.

Mass selling involves advertising and publicity

Mass selling is communicating with large numbers of potential customers at the same time. It's less flexible than personal selling, but when the target market is large and scattered, mass selling can be less expensive.

Advertising is the main form of mass selling. **Advertising** is any *paid* form of nonpersonal presentation of ideas, goods, or services by an identified sponsor. It includes the use of such media as magazines, newspapers, radio and TV, signs, and direct mail. While advertising must be paid for, another form of mass selling— publicity—is "free."

Publicity avoids media costs

Publicity is any *unpaid* form of nonpersonal presentation of ideas, goods, or services. Of course, publicity people are paid. But they try to attract attention to the firm and its offerings *without having to pay media costs*. For example, book publishers try to get authors on TV talk shows because this generates a lot of interest—and book sales—without the publisher paying for TV time.

Exhibit 15–1   Basic Promotion Methods and Strategy Planning

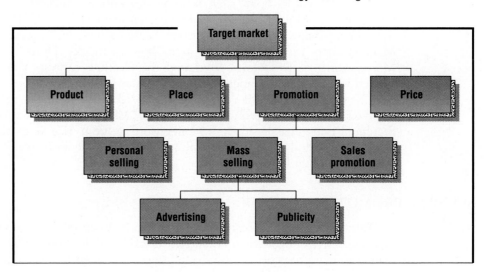

When Coleco introduced its Cabbage Patch dolls, it held parties for reporters and their children. A number of reporters wrote human interest stories about their kids "adopting" the cute dolls. Those stories prompted more media attention—and a very successful product introduction—without Coleco doing any introductory advertising.[2]

If a firm has a really new message, publicity may be more effective than advertising. Trade magazines, for example, may carry articles featuring the newsworthy products of regular advertisers—in part because they *are* regular advertisers. The firm's publicity people write the basic copy and then try to convince magazine editors to print it. Each year, magazines print photos and stories about new cars—and often the source of the information is the auto producers. A consumer might not pay any attention to an ad but carefully read a long magazine story with the same information.

Some companies prepare videotapes designed to get free publicity for their products on TV news shows. For example, one video—distributed to TV stations at Halloween—discussed a government recommendation that parents use makeup rather than masks for young children. The story was effectively tied to a new makeup product for children made by PAAS Products.[3]

Publicity can be negative as well as positive. Companies often enlist the help of public relations (PR) specialists in order to improve the firm's image. As Marketing Demo 15–1 illustrates, there are a number of pitfalls commonly encountered by firms attempting to practice PR.

Sales promotion tries to spark immediate interest

Sales promotion refers to promotion activities—other than advertising, publicity, and personal selling—that stimulate interest, trial, or purchase by final customers or others in the channel. Sales promotion may be aimed at consumers, at middlemen, or even at a firm's own employees. Examples are listed in Exhibit 15–2.

We'll talk more about sales promotion later in this chapter. First, however, you need to understand the role of the whole promotion blend–personal selling, mass selling, and sales promotion combined—so you can see how promotion fits into the rest of the marketing mix.

Exhibit 15–2 Example of Sales Promotion Activities

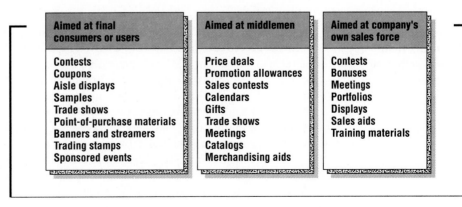

Aimed at final consumers or users	Aimed at middlemen	Aimed at company's own sales force
Contests	Price deals	Contests
Coupons	Promotion allowances	Bonuses
Aisle displays	Sales contests	Meetings
Samples	Calendars	Portfolios
Trade shows	Gifts	Displays
Point-of-purchase materials	Trade shows	Sales aids
Banners and streamers	Meetings	Training materials
Trading stamps	Catalogs	
Sponsored events	Merchandising aids	

MARKETING DEMO 15-1 Practice of PR Is Full of Perils

According to James Hoggan, president of James Hoggan and Associates, a Vancouver public relations firm, Canadian business is giving public relations a bad name. He says that often PR specialists are expected to fix a company's image through corporate double-talk and glitzy ad campaigning rather than developing public understanding and support through honest communications. He names a few of the most common PR blunders and tips on how to avoid them:

Using technical or legal jargon—public statements such as news releases should use everyday English. Although technical or legal advice must always be considered in the preparation of a news release, compromising the effectiveness of a simple, clear message with technological or legal mumbo jumbo is always a mistake.

Waiting until a crisis hits the fan before firing up the PR program—a proactive approach that anticipates potential PR problems and emphasizes taking the initiative on PR issues is always more effective.

Aiming PR efforts at the boss—trying to cover up bad company news with an overly positive press release may please the boss but it won't impress an experienced reporter. Successful PR requires candid discussion of both positive and negative company news. Corporations that endeavor to "tell it like it is" develop credibility.

Believing that, by solving the operational problem, the PR will take care of itself—the view that PR problems magically disappear once operational problems are solved is held by many senior executives but is not necessarily correct.

Underestimating the power of cooperation—a genuinely cooperative attitude toward public concerns, if it permeates the company, will be reflected in more positive news coverage and greater public support.

Being unprepared for a media interview—a "bad" interview can have dire consequences for any company. Executives who are unprepared for the bright lights and harsh questions of the news media often end up watching their worst nightmares unfold on the news.

Using the "no comment" approach—reporters love a good mystery, and so do their readers. "No comment" invites suspicion and distrust because it suggests that you are trying to hide something, even if you are not.

Making off-base public statements—media statements should always answer the question: "What's in it for my target audience?" Corporate messages should always be focused on the opinions that you want to modify, change, or influence.

If a company lacks credibility with its target audience, it is usually a good idea to arrange supporting comments from independent experts or government officials when possible.

Source: James Hoggan, "Practice of PR Is Full of Perils," *Marketing,* April 27, 1992, p. 23.

Less is spent on advertising than personal selling or sales promotion

Many people think that most promotion money gets spent on advertising—because advertising is all around them. The many ads you see in magazines and newspapers and on TV are impressive—and costly. But all the special sales promotions—coupons, sweepstakes, trade shows, sporting events sponsored by firms, and the like—add up to even more money. Similarly, salesclerks complete most retail sales. And behind the scenes, much personal selling goes on in the channels and in other business markets. In total, firms spend less money on advertising than on personal selling or sales promotion.

However, the amount of emphasis on each promotion method usually varies with each specific marketing strategy, depending on the target market and other elements of the marketing mix. When planning the overall strategy, it's important to plan a combination of promotion methods that will work together to achieve specific promotion objectives.

Kellogg's marketing managers plan mass selling to communicate with final consumers, but most of their communication with retailers is handled by salespeople.

WHICH METHODS TO USE DEPENDS ON PROMOTION OBJECTIVES

Overall objective is to affect behavior

The different promotion methods can all be viewed as different forms of communication. But good marketers aren't interested in just communicating. They want to communicate information that will encourage customers to choose *their* product. They know that if they have a better offering, informed customers are more likely to buy. Therefore, they're interested in (1) reinforcing present attitudes that might lead to favorable behavior or (2) actually changing the attitudes and behavior of the firm's target market.

In terms of demand curves, promotion may help the firm make its present demand curve more inelastic, or shift the demand curve to the right, or both. These possibilities are shown in Exhibit 15–3.

The buyer behavior model introduced in Chapter 7 showed the many influences on buying behavior. You saw there that affecting buyer behavior is a tough job—but that is exactly the objective of Promotion.

Informing, persuading, and reminding are basic promotion objectives

For a firm's promotion to be effective, its promotion objectives must be clearly defined—because the right promotion blend depends on what the firm wants to accomplish. It's helpful to think of three basic promotion objectives: *informing,*

Exhibit 15–3 Promotion Seeks to Shift the Demand Curve

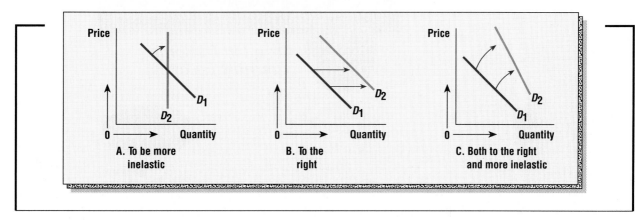

persuading, and *reminding* target customers about the company and its marketing mix. All try to affect buyer behavior by providing more information.

Even more useful is a more specific set of promotion objectives that state *exactly who* you want to inform, persuade, or remind, and *why*. But this is unique to each company's strategy—and too detailed to discuss here. Instead, we'll limit ourselves to the three basic promotion objectives and how you can reach them.

Informing is educating

Potential customers must know something about a product if they are to buy at all. A firm with a really new product may not have to do anything but inform consumers about it—and show that it meets consumer needs better than other products. When Mazda introduced its stylish and affordable Miata roadster, the uniqueness of the car simplified the promotion job. Excitement about the product also generated a lot of free publicity in car magazines.

Persuading usually becomes necessary

When competitors offer similar products, the firm must not only inform customers that its product is available but also persuade them to buy it. A *persuading* objective means the firm will try to develop a favorable set of attitudes so customers will buy—and keep buying—its product. Promotion with a persuading objective often focuses on reasons why one brand is better than competing brands. To help convince consumers to buy Tylenol rather than some other firm's brand, Johnson & Johnson's ads tout Tylenol as the pain relief medicine most

Tourism advertising attempts to be especially persuasive.

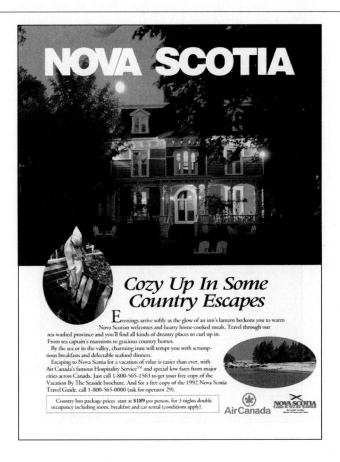

often used in hospitals. The accompanying ad for Nova Scotia tourism is attempting to persuade people to visit Nova Scotia rather than other tourist destinations.

Reminding may be enough, sometimes

If target customers already have positive attitudes about a firm's marketing mix, a *reminding* objective might be suitable. This objective can be extremely important in some cases. Even though customers have been attracted and sold once, they are still targets for competitors' appeals. Reminding them of their past satisfaction may keep them from shifting to a competitor. Campbell realizes that most people know about its soup—so much of its advertising is intended to remind.

PROMOTION REQUIRES EFFECTIVE COMMUNICATION

Communication can break down

Promotion is wasted if it doesn't communicate effectively. But there are many reasons why a promotion message can be misunderstood—or not heard at all. To understand this, it's useful to think about a whole **communication process**—which means a source trying to reach a receiver with a message. Exhibit 15–4 shows the elements of the communication process. Here, we see that a **source**—the sender of a message—is trying to deliver a message to a **receiver**—a potential customer. Research shows that customers evaluate not only the message but also the source of the message in terms of trustworthiness and credibility. For example, American Dental Association (ADA) studies show that Listerine mouthwash helps reduce plaque buildup on teeth. Listerine mentions the ADA endorsement in its promotion to help make the promotion message credible.

A source can use many message channels to deliver a message. The salesperson does it in person with voice and action. Advertising must do it with magazines, newspapers, radio, TV, and other media.

A major advantage of personal selling is that the source—the seller—can get immediate feedback from the receiver. It's easier to judge how the message is being received—and change it if necessary. Mass sellers must depend on marketing research or total sales figures for feedback—and that can take too long.

The **noise**, shown in Exhibit 15–4, is any distraction that reduces the effectiveness of the communication process. Conversations during TV ads are noise. Advertisers planning messages must recognize that many possible distractions—noise—can interfere with communications.

Exhibit 15–4 The Communication Process

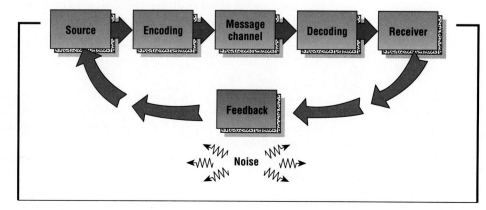

Encoding and decoding depend on a common frame of reference

The basic difficulty in the communication process occurs during encoding and decoding. **Encoding** is the source deciding what it wants to say and translating it into words or symbols that will have the same meaning to the receiver. **Decoding** is the receiver translating the message. This process can be very tricky. The meanings of various words and symbols may differ depending on the attitudes and experiences of the two groups. People need a common frame of reference to communicate effectively. See Exhibit 15–5.

Maidenform encountered this problem with its promotion aimed at working women. The company ran a series of ads depicting women stockbrokers and doctors wearing Maidenform lingerie. The men in the ads were fully dressed. Maidenform was trying to show women in positions of authority, but some women felt the ad presented them as sex objects. In this case, the promotion people who encoded the message didn't understand the attitudes of the target market—and how they would decode the message.[4]

The same message may be interpreted differently

Exhibit 15–5
Encoding and Decoding a Message

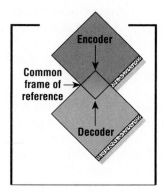

Different audiences may see the same message in different ways—or interpret the same words differently. Such differences are common in international marketing when translation is a problem. General Motors, for example, had trouble in Puerto Rico with its Nova car. It discovered that, while *Nova* means "star" in Spanish—when spoken it sounds like "no va," meaning "it doesn't go." When the company changed the car's name to "Caribe," it sold well. Many other firms make similar mistakes. Coors encouraged its English-speaking customers to "turn it loose," but in Spanish the phrase meant "to suffer from diarrhea." When Frank Perdue said, "It takes a Tough Man to Make a Tender Chicken," Spanish speakers heard "It Takes a Sexually Stimulated Man to Make a Chicken Affectionate."[5]

Problems occur even without translation problems. For example, a new children's cough syrup was advertised as extra strength. The advertising people thought they were assuring parents that the product worked well. But cautious mothers avoided the product because they feared that it might be too strong for their children.

Message channel is important, too

The communication process is complicated even more because the receiver knows the message is not only coming from a source but also through some **message channel**—the carrier of the message. The receiver may attach more value to a product if the message comes in a well-respected newspaper or magazine rather than over the radio. Some consumers buy brands that are tested for quality against other brands and the results reported in *Canadian Consumer*. They have faith in that magazine's objective testing methods and in its role as an advocate for the consumer.

? Ethical issues in marketing communications

Promotion is one of the most often criticized areas of marketing, and many of the criticisms focus on whether communications are honest and fair. Marketers must sometimes make ethical judgments in considering these charges and in planning their promotion.

Video publicity releases provide an interesting example. When a TV news program broadcasts a video publicity release, consumers don't know it was

Effective promotion planning must take into consideration the whole communication process.

prepared to achieve marketing objectives; they think the news staff is the source. That may make the message more credible, but is it fair? Many say yes—as long as the publicity information is truthful. But gray areas still remain. Consider, for example, SmithKline Beecham's video about its new prescription heart attack drug. An estimated 27 million consumers saw the video on various TV news programs. The video included a laundry list of possible side effects and other warnings, just as is required for normal drug advertising. But there's never any guaranty that the warnings won't be edited out by local TV stations.

Critics raise similar concerns about the use of celebrities in advertisements. A person who plays the role of an honest and trustworthy person on a popular TV series may be a credible message source in an ad, but is that misleading to consumers? Some critics believe it is. Others argue that consumers recognize advertising when they see it and know celebrities are paid for their endorsements.

The most common criticisms of promotion relate to promotional messages that make exaggerated claims. What does it mean for an ad or a salesperson to claim that a product is the "best available"? Is that the personal opinion of people in the firm, or should every statement—even very general ones—be backed up by objective proof? What type of proof should be required? Some promotional messages do misrepresent the benefits of a product. However, most marketing managers realize that customers won't come back if the marketing mix doesn't deliver what the promotion promises. Further, consumers are becoming more skeptical about all the claims they hear and see. As a result, most firms work to make their promotion claims more specific and believable.[6]

With over 59,000 florists in 140 countries, Interflora promotes the idea that "Flowers speak louder than words—in any language."

ADOPTION PROCESSES CAN GUIDE PROMOTION PLANNING

The adoption process discussed in Chapter 7 is related to effective communication and promotion planning. You learned the six steps in that adoption process: awareness, interest, evaluation, trial, decision, and confirmation. We saw consumer buying as a problem-solving process in which buyers go through these six steps on the way to adopting (or rejecting) an idea or product.

Now we see that the three basic promotion objectives relate to these six steps. See Exhibit 15–6. *Informing* and *persuading* may be needed to affect the potential customer's knowledge and attitudes about a product—and then bring about its adoption. Later promotion can simply *remind* the customer about that favorable experience—and confirm the adoption decision.

The AIDA model is a practical approach

The basic adoption process fits very neatly with another action-oriented model—called AIDA—that we will use in this and the next two chapters to guide some of our discussion.

The **AIDA model** consists of four promotion jobs—(1) to get *Attention,* (2) to hold *Interest,* (3) to arouse *Desire,* and (4) to obtain *Action.* (As a memory aid, note that the first letters of the four key words spell AIDA—the well-known opera.)

Exhibit 15–6 shows the relationship of the adoption process to the AIDA jobs. Getting attention is necessary to make consumers aware of the company's offering. Holding interest gives the communication a chance to build the consumer's interest in the product. Arousing desire affects the evaluation process, perhaps building preference. And obtaining action includes gaining trial, which may lead to a purchase decision. Continuing promotion is needed to confirm the decision—and encourage additional purchases.

Exhibit 15–6   Relation of Promotion Objectives, Adoption Process, and AIDA Model

Promotion Objectives	Adoption Process (Chapter 7)	AIDA Model
Informing	Awareness Interest Evaluation	Attention Interest Desire
Persuading	Trial	
Reminding	Decision Confirmation	Action

The AIDA and adoption processes look at individuals. This emphasis on individuals helps us understand how people behave. But it's also useful to look at markets as a whole. Different customers within a market may behave differently—with some taking the lead in trying new products and, in turn, influencing others.

Promotion must vary for different adopter groups

Research on how markets accept new ideas has led to the adoption curve model. The **adoption curve** shows when different groups accept ideas. It shows the need to change the promotion effort as time passes. It also emphasizes the relations among groups—and shows that some groups act as leaders in accepting a new idea.

Exhibit 15–7 shows the adoption curve for a typical successful product. Some of the important characteristics of each of these customer groups are discussed below. Which one are you?

Exhibit 15–7   The Adoption Curve

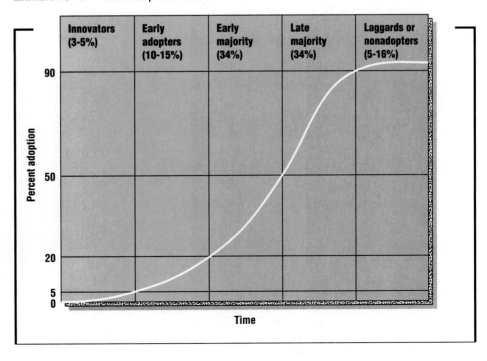

Innovators don't mind taking some risk

The **innovators** are the first to adopt. They are eager to try a new idea—and willing to take risks. Innovators tend to be young and well educated. They are likely to be mobile and have many contacts outside their local social group and community. Business firms in the innovator group usually are large and rather specialized.

An important characteristic of innovators is that they rely on impersonal and scientific information sources—or other innovators—rather than personal sales-people. They often read articles in technical publications or informative ads in special-interest magazines or newspapers.

Early adopters are often opinion leaders

Early adopters are well respected by their peers—and often are opinion leaders. They tend to be younger, more mobile, and more creative than later adopters. But unlike innovators, they have fewer contacts outside their own social group or community. Business firms in this category also tend to be specialized.

Of all the groups, this one tends to have the greatest contact with salespeople. Mass media are important information sources, too. Marketers should be very concerned with attracting and selling the early adopter group. Their acceptance is really important in reaching the next group because the early majority look to the early adopters for guidance. The early adopters can help the promotion effort by spreading *word-of-mouth* information and advice among other consumers.

Opinion leaders help spread the word

Marketers know the importance of personal conversations and recommendations by opinion leaders. If early groups reject the product, it may never get off the ground. For example, some moviegoers are the first to see new movies. If they think a movie is dull, they quickly tell their friends not to waste their time and money.

This UPS ad quickly communicates its message—that UPS is as fast as it is reliable—with an attention-getting photo and simple headline.

But if opinion leaders accept a product, what they say about it can be very important. Such word-of-mouth publicity may do the real selling job—long before the customer ever walks into the retail store. Some companies try to target promotion to encourage opinion leadership. When Canon introduced a high-quality new automatic 35 mm camera, it prepared special ads designed to help opinion leaders explain to others how the camera worked. Other firms take a simpler approach. Their ads just say "tell your friends."[7]

Early majority group is deliberate

The **early majority** avoid risk and wait to consider a new idea after many early adopters have tried it—and liked it. Average-sized business firms that are less specialized often fit in this category. If successful companies in their industry adopt the new idea, they will, too.

The early majority have a great deal of contact with mass media, salespeople, and early adopter opinion leaders. Members usually aren't opinion leaders themselves.

Late majority group is cautious

The **late majority** are cautious about new ideas. Often, they are older than the early majority group—and more set in their ways. So they are less likely to follow opinion leaders and early adopters. In fact, strong social pressure from their own peer group may be needed before they adopt a new product. Business firms in this group tend to be conservative, smaller-sized firms with little specialization.

The late majority make little use of marketing sources of information—mass media and salespeople. They tend to be oriented more toward other late adopters rather than outside sources they don't trust.

Laggards or nonadopters hang on to tradition

Laggards or **nonadopters** prefer to do things the way they've been done in the past and are very suspicious of new ideas. They tend to be older and less well educated. They may also be low in social status and income. The smallest businesses with the least specialization often fit this category. They cling to the status quo and think it's the safe way.

The main source of information for laggards is other laggards. This certainly is bad news for marketers who are trying to reach a whole market quickly—or who want to use only one promotion method. In fact, it may not pay to bother with this group.[8]

HOW TYPICAL PROMOTION PLANS ARE BLENDED

There is no one right blend

Most business firms develop a *promotion blend* of some kind because the three promotion methods complement each other. And some promotion jobs can be done more economically one way than another. But what blend is right in a particular situation?

There is no one *right* promotion blend for all situations. Each one must be developed as part of a marketing mix—and should be designed to achieve the firm's promotion objectives in each marketing strategy. For example, if the channel of distribution for a firm's product involves middlemen, the marketing manager must consider the promotion blend that is appropriate in the channel as well as what type of promotion should be targeted at customers at the end of the channel. Similarly, the emphasis among the three types of promotion typically varies depending on whether the customers at the end of the channel are business users or final consumers. Let's take a closer look at typical promotion blends in these different situations.

Get a push in the channel with promotion to middlemen

When a channel of distribution involves middlemen, their cooperation can be crucial to the success of the overall marketing strategy. **Pushing** (a product through a channel) means using normal promotion effort—personal selling, advertising, and sales promotion—to help sell the whole marketing mix to possible channel members. This approach emphasizes the importance of building a channel and securing the wholehearted cooperation of channel members to push the product down the channel to the final user. Producers usually take on much of the responsibility for the pushing effort in the channel. However, most wholesalers also handle at least some of the promotion to retailers or other wholesalers further down the channel.

Promotion to middlemen emphasizes personal selling

Salespeople handle most of the important communication with middlemen. Middlemen don't want empty promises. They want to know what they can expect in return for their cooperation and help. A salesperson can answer questions about what promotion will be directed toward the final consumer, each channel member's part in marketing the product, and important details on pricing, markups, promotion assistance, and allowances.

A salesperson can help the firm determine when it should adjust its marketing mix from one middleman to another. In highly competitive urban areas, for example, mixes may emphasize price.

When a number of suppliers offer similar products and compete for attention and shelf space, the wholesaler or retailer usually pays attention to the one with the best profit potential. In these situations, the sales rep must convince the middleman that demand for the product exists—and that making a profit will be

Promotion planning must consider the whole channel.

easy. A firm can make the sales rep's job easier by targeting special sales promotion at middlemen, too.

Sales promotions targeted at middlemen usually focus on short-term arrangements that will improve the middleman's profits. For example, a soft-drink bottler might offer a convenience store a free case of drinks with each two cases it buys. The free case improves the store's profit margin on the whole purchase. Or a supplier might offer a price discount if the retailer uses a special point-of-purchase display. Other types of sales promotions—such as contests that offer vacation trips for high-volume middlemen—are also common.

Firms run ads in trade magazines to recruit new middlemen or to inform channel members about a new offering. Trade ads usually encourage middlemen to contact the supplier for more information, and then a salesperson takes over.

Push within a firm— with promotion to employees

Some firms emphasize promotion to their own employees—especially salespeople or others in contact with customers. This type of *internal marketing* effort is basically a variation on the pushing approach. One objective is to inform employees about important elements of the marketing strategy—so they'll work together as a team to implement it. Some firms use promotion to motivate employees to work harder at specific jobs—such as providing customer service or achieving higher sales. For example, many firms use sales contests and award free trips to big sellers.

Some companies design the ads they target at customers so the ads also communicate to employees—and boost the employees' image. This is typical in service-oriented industries where the quality of the employee's efforts is a big part of the product. Some Delta Airlines' ads, for example, use the theme "we like to fly, and it shows." Although the ads communicate primarily to customers, they remind Delta's employees that the service they provide is crucial to the marketing strategy—and to customer satisfaction.

Pulling policy—customer demand pulls the product through the channel

Regardless of what promotion a firm uses to get help from channel members or employees in pushing a product, most producers focus a significant amount of promotion on customers at the end of the channel. This helps to stimulate demand for the firm's offering and can help pull the product through the channel of distribution. **Pulling** means getting customers to ask middlemen for the product.

Pulling and pushing are usually used in combination. However, if middlemen won't work with a producer—perhaps because they're already carrying a competing brand—a producer may try to use a pulling approach by itself. This involves highly aggressive and expensive promotion to final consumers or users—perhaps using coupons or samples—temporarily bypassing middlemen. If the promotion works, the middlemen are forced to carry the product to satisfy customer requests. However, this approach is risky. Companies can waste an expensive promotion effort if customers lose interest before reluctant middlemen make the product available. At minimum, middlemen should be told about the planned pulling effort—so they can be ready if the promotion succeeds.

Who handles promotion to final customers at the end of the channel varies in different channel systems, depending on the mix of pushing and pulling. Further, the promotion blend typically varies depending on whether customers are final consumers or business users.[9]

Merrell Dow's consumer advertising informs consumers about Nicorette and helps to pull it through the channel.

Promotion to final consumers

The large number of consumers almost forces producers of consumer products and retailers to emphasize mass selling and sales promotion. Sales promotion— such as contests or free samples—may build consumer interest and short-term sales of a product. Effective mass selling may build enough brand familiarity so that little personal selling is needed—as in self-service and discount operations.

If a product has already won brand preference or insistence, perhaps after years of satisfactory service, aggressive personal selling may not be needed. Reminder-type advertising may be all that's necessary. Hershey Chocolate long prided itself on not having to do any advertising in the United States! However, Hershey had to start advertising when competitors entered the market and took away customers. In Canada—where Hershey is not well established—the company always advertised aggressively.[10]

Personal selling can be effective, too. Some retailers—specialty shops in particular—rely heavily on well-informed salespeople. Technical products (like VCRs or camcorders) and personal services (like health care and estate planning) may also require personal selling. But aggressive personal selling to final consumers usually is found only in relatively expensive channel systems, such as those for fashionable clothing, furniture, consumer electronics, and automobiles.

Promotion to business customers

Producers and wholesalers who target business customers usually emphasize personal selling. This is practical because these customers are much less numerous than final consumers and their purchases are typically larger.

Moreover, business customers may have technical questions or need adjustments in the marketing mix. An extremely technical business product may require a heavy emphasis on personal selling—using technically trained salespeople. This is the only sure way to make the product understood and get feedback on how customers use it. The technical sales rep meets with engineers, production managers, purchasing agents, and top managers, and can adjust the sales message to the needs of these various influences.

This French ad for Tissaia fashions tries to get the consumer more involved in the message. The copy says, "Let's be objective. Your daughter is really ravishing." The insert says, "Stick a photograph of your daughter here." The punchline at the bottom says, "You are our most beautiful model."

Sales reps can be more flexible in adjusting their companies' appeals to suit each customer—and personal contact is usually required to close a sale. A salesperson is also able to call back later to follow up with additional information or to resolve any problems.

While personal selling dominates in business markets, mass selling is necessary, too. A typical sales call on a business customer costs over $250.[11] That's because salespeople spend less than half their time actually selling. The rest is consumed by such tasks as traveling, paperwork, sales meetings, and strictly service calls. So it's seldom practical for salespeople to carry the whole promotion load. A firm invests too much in its salespeople to use their time and skill for jobs that could be handled in less costly ways.

Ads in trade magazines, for instance, can inform potential customers that a product is available and stimulate inquiries. Domestic and international trade shows also help identify prospects. Even so, in business markets, firms spend only a small percentage of their promotion budget on mass selling and sales promotion.

Each market segment may need a unique blend

Knowing what type of promotion is typically emphasized with different targets is useful in planning the promotion blend. But each unique market segment may need a separate marketing mix—and a different promotion blend. Some mass selling specialists miss this point. They think mainly in mass marketing—rather than target marketing—terms. Aiming at large markets may be desirable in some situations, but promotion aimed at everyone can end up hitting no one. In developing the promotion blend, you should be careful not to slip into a shotgun approach when what you really need is a rifle approach—with a more careful aim.

PROMOTION BLENDS VARY IN DIFFERENT SITUATIONS

The particular promotion blend a firm selects depends on the target of the promotion, but it may be influenced by many other factors, including (1) the promotion budget available, (2) the nature of the product and its stage in the product life cycle, and (3) the nature of competition. Although promotion can be blended in many ways, to round out our discussion let's take a closer look at some typical ways firms spread their promotion budgets across the three promotion methods in these different situations.

Size of promotion budget affects promotion efficiency

There are some economies of scale in promotion. An ad on national TV might cost less *per person* reached than an ad on local TV. Similarly, citywide radio, TV, and newspapers may be cheaper than neighborhood newspapers or direct personal contact. But the *total cost* for some mass media may force small firms—or those with small promotion budgets—to use promotion alternatives that are more expensive per contact. For example, a small retailer might want to use local television but find that he has only enough money for an ad in the Yellow Pages—and an occasional newspaper ad.

Smaller producers and firms that offer relatively undifferentiated consumer products emphasize personal selling first and rely mainly on sales promotion for the balance. The objective is to build good channel relations and encourage channel members to recommend the product. Note that here we are referring to percentages in the promotion blend—not the level of expenditures.

Objectives help set budget priorities

How much to spend on each type of promotion is an important but difficult decision. Some firms just do what they did in the past—perhaps budgeting promotion as a certain percentage of sales or as a fixed dollar amount. Others try to watch competitors and match their promotion if there's enough money. While these approaches are common, they may or may not lead to a sensible level of promotion spending. For example, a firm that routinely bases promotion spending on some percentage of its sales will decrease its promotion whenever sales go down. This approach may just make the problem worse—if weak promotion is the reason for declining sales.

A more practical approach is to determine which promotion objectives are most important and which methods are most economical in achieving them. There's never enough money to do all of the promotion that you might want to do. However, this approach helps you to set priorities so that the money you spend produces specific results. We'll talk more about budgeting to accomplish specific tasks in Chapter 20. For now, you should see that priorities for your promotion dollars—and how to spend them—should be guided by what you need to achieve, as discussed in Marketing Demo 15–2.

Stage of product in its life cycle

A new product seldom becomes a spectacular success overnight. The adoption curve helps explain why. Further, the product must go through the product life-cycle stages described in Chapter 10—market introduction, market growth, market maturity, and sales decline. During these stages, promotion blends may have to change to achieve different promotion objectives.

Market introduction stage—"this new idea is good"

During market introduction, the basic promotion objective is informing. If the product is a really new idea, the promotion must build **primary demand**— demand for the general product idea—not just for the company's own brand.

MARKETING DEMO 15-2   Sponsorship Now a Common Marketing Tool

Sponsoring events has lost its novelty for many backers—a sign that this form of promotion is being entrenched in the marketing mainstream, one industry watcher says.

"It used to be that a lot of the advertisers who were restricted in the media they could use—tobacco and alcohol-beverage companies, for example—went into events almost of necessity," says Mark Smyka, editor of the trade journal *Strategy*. That is no longer the case. "Today, [many more] people are getting involved because they recognize it as an increasingly important marketing tool."

While a number of marketers have long used events to further their promotional goals, wider industry acceptance of sponsorship is a comparatively recent phenomenon. It is part of the trend in marketing circles that began in the 1980s to look beyond the traditional advertising in mass media.

Marketers began to explore how other forms of promotion—contests, direct marketing, and event marketing among them—could be used to sell products. Corporate Canada is becoming increasingly adept at exploiting these promotional activities, learning that they are most effective when integrated into overall marketing schemes, Smyka says.

He points to a recent contest his paper ran that recognizes Canada's best event-marketing programs as proof of sponsorship's popularity. P&G was cited for its 1991 Always Changing Program, which tied its leading feminine-protection brand to an educational effort aimed at teachers, parents, and young girls. In addition to teachers' kits, booklets, and samples, P&G ran an exhibit and workshop at an educators' conference. The program was endorsed by the Ontario Physical and Health Education Association, which P&G credits with boosting its marketing success. Responses increased 600 percent over the previous year's program.

Air Canada and Carlsberg Light—brewed by John Labatt Ltd.—were cited for their sponsorship of Toronto's Festival of Festivals international film program. Air Canada ran a contest in conjunction with the festival, and Carlsberg Light concentrated on a "Midnight Madness" promotion. Box office receipts were up $80,000 over the previous year, and international media coverage was estimated to be worth more than $750,000.

Effective postprogram evaluation and integration of the sponsorship with other promotional efforts are crucial to successful event marketing, says Terri Perras, sales promotion manager of specialty channel YTV Canada, Inc.

Marketers must have clear advance objectives for the events they back, she says. "The key is to really outline what you're trying to achieve." There must also be a logical fit with other components in the promotional mix, and a bottom-line marketing advantage. "Warm and fuzzy just doesn't seem to cut it anymore," she says. "If there's no built-in measurability, how can you justify doing it?"

Source: Randall Scotland, "Sponsorship Now a Common Marketing Tool," *The Financial Post*, June 8, 1992, p. 521.

Cellular phones and laser printers are good examples. There may be few potential innovators during the introduction stage, and personal selling can help find them. Firms also need salespeople to find good channel members and persuade them to carry the new product. Sales promotion may be targeted at salespeople or channel members to get them interested in selling the new product. And sales promotion may also encourage customers to try it.

Market growth stage— "our brand is best"

In the market growth stage, more competitors enter the market, and promotion emphasis shifts from building primary demand to stimulating **selective demand**—demand for a company's own brand. The main job is to persuade customers to buy—and keep buying—the company's product.

Now that more potential customers are trying and adopting the product, mass selling may become more economical. But personal salespeople must still work in the channels—expanding the number of outlets.

Market maturity stage—"our brand is better, really"

In the market maturity stage, even more competitors have entered the market. Promotion becomes more persuasive. At this stage, mass selling and sales promotion may dominate the promotion blends of consumer products firms. Business products may require more aggressive personal selling—perhaps supplemented by more advertising. The total dollars allocated to promotion may rise as competition increases.

If a firm already has high sales—relative to competitors—it may have a real advantage in promotion at this stage. If, for example, Nabisco has twice the sales for a certain type of cookie as Keebler, its smaller competitor, and they both spend the same *percentage* of total sales on promotion—Nabisco will be spending twice as much and will probably communicate to more people. Nabisco may get even more than twice as much promotion because of economies of scale.

Firms that have strong brands can use reminder-type advertising at this stage to be sure customers remember the product name. This may be much less expensive than persuasive efforts.

Sales decline stage— "let's tell those who still want our product"

During the sales decline stage, the total amount spent on promotion usually decreases as firms try to cut costs to remain profitable. Since some people may still want the product, firms need more targeted promotion to reach these customers.

On the other hand, some firms may increase promotion to try to slow the cycle—at least temporarily. Crayola had almost all of the market for children's crayons, but sales were slowly declining as new kinds of markers came along. Crayola slowed the cycle with more promotion spending—and a message to parents to buy their kids a "fresh box."

Nature of competition requires different promotion

Firms in monopolistic competition may favor mass selling because they have differentiated their marketing mixes and have something to talk about. As a market tends toward pure competition—or oligopoly—it is difficult to predict what will happen. Competitors in some markets try to outpromote each other. The only way for a competitor to stay in this kind of market is to match rivals' promotion efforts—unless the whole marketing mix can be improved in some other way. We see a lot of such competitive advertising in our daily newspapers—and in cents-off coupons at grocery store checkout counters.

In markets that are drifting toward pure competition, some companies resort to price-cutting. Lower prices may be offered to middlemen, customers, or both. This *may* increase the number of units sold—temporarily—but it may also reduce total revenue and the amount available for promotion *per unit*. And competitive retaliation may reduce the temporary sales gains and drag price levels down faster. The cash flowing into the business may decline, and promotion may have to be cut back.

SOMEONE MUST PLAN AND MANAGE THE PROMOTION BLEND

Selecting a promotion blend is a strategy decision that should fit with the rest of a company's marketing strategy. Once a firm sets the outlines of its promotion blend, it must develop and implement more detailed plans for the parts of the blend. This is the job of specialists—such as sales managers, advertising managers, and promotion managers.

Sales managers manage salespeople

Sales managers are concerned with managing personal selling. Often, the sales manager is responsible for building good distribution channels and implementing Place policies. In smaller companies, the sales manager may also act as the marketing manager—and be responsible for advertising and sales promotion.

Advertising managers work with ads and agencies

Advertising managers manage their company's mass selling effort—in television, newspapers, magazines, and other media. Their job is choosing the right media and developing the ads. Advertising departments within their own firms may help in these efforts, or they may use outside advertising agencies. The advertising manager may handle publicity, too. Or it may be handled by an outside agency or by whoever handles **public relations**—communication with noncustomers, including labor, public interest groups, stockholders, and the government.

Sales promotion managers need many talents

Sales promotion managers manage their company's sales promotion effort. They fill the gaps between the sales and advertising managers—increasing their effectiveness. In some companies, sales promotion managers have independent status, reporting to the marketing manager. Sometimes, sales or advertising departments handle a firm's sales promotion effort. But sales promotion activities vary so much that many firms use both inside and outside specialists. If a firm's sales promotion expenses exceed those for advertising, it probably needs a separate sales promotion manager.

Marketing manager talks to all, blends all

Because of differences in outlook and experience, the advertising, sales, and sales promotion managers may have trouble working with each other as partners or equals. So the marketing manager must weigh the pros and cons of the various methods, then devise an effective promotion blend, fitting in the various departments and personalities and coordinating their efforts.

To evaluate a company's promotion blend, you must first know more about the individual areas of promotion decisions. We start in that direction in the next section—with more discussion of sales promotion. Then, in the following chapters, we'll take up personal selling and advertising.

SALES PROMOTION—DO SOMETHING DIFFERENT TO STIMULATE CHANGE

Firms generally use sales promotion to complement the other promotion methods. If properly done, it can be very effective. But there are problems in the sales promotion area.

Sales promotion is a weak spot in marketing

Sales promotion is often a weak spot in marketing. Exhibit 15–2 shows that sales promotion includes a wide variety of activities—each of which may be custom-designed and used only once. Thus, the typical company develops little skill in sales promotion, and the mistakes caused by lack of experience can be very costly. You can see how in the following example. A promotion jointly sponsored by Polaroid and Trans World Airlines offered a coupon worth 25 percent off the price of any TWA ticket with the purchase of a $20 Polaroid camera. The companies intended to appeal to vacationers who take pictures when they travel.

Instead, travel agents bought many of the cameras. For the price of the $20 camera, they made an extra 25 percent on every TWA ticket they sold. And big companies bought thousands of the cameras to save on overseas travel expenses.[12]

Sales promotion problems are likely to be worse when a company has no sales promotion manager. If the personal selling or advertising managers are responsible for sales promotion, they often treat it as a stepchild. They allocate money to sales promotion if there is any left over—or if a crisis develops. Many companies, even some large ones, don't have a separate budget for sales promotion or even know what it costs in total.

Making sales promotion work is a learned skill—not a sideline for amateurs. In fact, specialists in sales promotion have developed—both inside larger firms and as outside consultants. Some are extremely creative and might be willing to take over the whole promotion job. But it's the marketing manager's responsibility to set promotion objectives and policies that will fit with the rest of the company's marketing strategy.[13]

Sales promotion spending is big—and getting bigger

Sales promotion expenditures in North America now total over $100 billion.[14] You can see why companies need sales promotion experts—and perhaps separate status for sales promotion within their marketing departments.

Spending on sales promotion is growing—sometimes at the expense of other promotion methods—for several reasons. Sales promotion has proved effective in increasingly competitive markets. Sales promotion can usually be implemented quickly and gets results sooner than advertising.[15]

It is often designed to get *action*. For example, giving out books of coupons in supermarkets for a variety of products has resulted in as many as 12 percent of the coupons being quickly redeemed, nearly half for products the shopper didn't ordinarily buy![16]

Sales promotion for final consumers or users

Firms use sales promotion aimed at final consumers or users to increase demand or speed up the time of purchase. Sales promotion people may develop displays for retailers' stores—including banners, sample packages, calendars, and various point-of-purchase items—or aisle displays for supermarkets. They might

Employees of the typical company develop little skill in sales promotion because promotion includes a wide variety of activities, each of which may be used only once.

be responsible for sweepstakes contests as well as for coupons designed to get customers to buy a product by a certain date. Total coupon distribution in the United States almost tripled in the last 10 years. Now firms distribute more than 275 billion coupons a year—over 1,100 for every man, woman, and child in America! Coupons and other types of sales promotion targeted at consumers are not yet as common in most other countries, but their use is increasing worldwide.[17]

All these sales promotion efforts aim at specific objectives. For example, if customers already have a favorite brand, it may be hard to get them to try anything new. A free trial-size bottle of mouthwash might be just what it takes to get cautious consumers to try—and like—the new product. Such samples might be distributed house to house, at stores, or attached to other products sold by the firm.

Sales promotion directed at business customers uses the same kinds of ideas. In addition, sales promotion people might set up and staff trade show exhibits. They often use attractive models to encourage buyers to look at a firm's product—especially when it's displayed near other similar products in a circuslike atmosphere.

Some industrial sellers give promotion items—pen sets, cigarette lighters, watches, or more expensive items (perhaps with the firm's brand name on them)—to remind business customers of their products. This is common practice in many industries, but it can be a sensitive area. Some companies don't allow buyers to take any kind of gift from a supplier. They don't want the buyer's judgment to be influenced by which supplier gives the best promotion items![18]

Sales promotion for middlemen

Sales promotion aimed at middlemen—sometimes called *trade promotion*—stresses price-related matters. The objective may be to encourage middlemen to stock new items, buy in larger quantity, buy early, or put more push behind certain products. The tools used include price and/or merchandise allowances, promotion allowances, and perhaps sales contests to encourage retailers or wholesalers to sell specific items—or the company's whole line. Trade promotion is one of the fastest growing elements in the promotion blend for producers of consumer products—especially staples. In fact, one recent study suggests that consumer package goods firms now spend about twice as much on trade promotion as they do on advertising to final consumers. Marketing Demo 15–3 describes how Converse celebrated the 75th birthday of one of its shoe styles with a campaign that combined sales promotion for final consumers and middlemen.

Sales promotion activities also help a product manager win support from an already overworked sales force. The sales force may be especially receptive to sales promotion in the channels—because competition is growing and middlemen respond to sales promotion. The sales reps can see that their company is willing to help them win more business.[19]

Sales promotion for employees

Sales promotion aimed at the company's own sales force might try to encourage getting new customers, selling a new product, or selling the company's whole line. Depending on the objectives, the tools might be contests, bonuses on sales or number of new accounts, and fancy resorts for sales meetings to raise everyone's spirits.

Ongoing sales promotion work might also be aimed at the sales force—to help sales management. Sales promotion specialists might be responsible for preparing

MARKETING DEMO 15–3
All Star Promo: A Birthday with Heart and Sole

The Converse "Chuck Taylor" All Star, the original canvas high-top sneaker that generations of kids have worn into the ground while growing up, recently turned an amazing 75 years old. Converse marked the occasion with a special birthday promotion aimed at its best customers—teens and retailers.

The "Happy Birthday Chuck!" program developed by Converse, Mississauga, Ontario, and its Toronto agency, the Tribco Communications Group, featured a "Spot Chuck" contest. It was backed by transit ads in nine major markets and a national TV campaign airing mainly on MuchMusic and Musique-Plus. Its prime goal, says Tribco President Howard Pearl, was to drive kids into shoe stores and thus give retailers the chance to make a sale.

A razzle-dazzle anniversary promotion was apt, as the Chuck Taylor All Star is quite possibly the first product endorsed by a celebrity athlete. The "Chuck" nickname comes from Chuck Taylor, a star basketball player first hired as a spokesman by Massachusetts-based Converse in 1921.

The humble Converse sneaker—which is made in two styles—has gone in and out of fashion over the years. But it has always been a consistent seller, says Martin Sharp, Converse senior director of marketing. The "Birthday" campaign is clearly aimed at teens, although the product also has a residual nostalgic appeal to adults.

Despite nuances for each market, the TV spots all boasted a fast-paced, wild-style feel that mixed animation and live-action footage. They were aired heavily on MuchMusic and MusiquePlus, and on the weekend dance show Electric Circus.

The brand-awareness-building element of the program was important, but the promotion's real heart and soul was its appeal to the shoe retailer. With the changes in the shoe business over the past decade, retailers often carry only three or four of the more than 30 athletic footwear brands, according to Sharp.

All Stars can't hope to compete with the often multimillion-dollar ad weights used by players like Nike, Reebok, and even Converse on some of its higher-end products. As a result, the shoe needs something imaginative to get retailers to pay attention. "[The dealers] constantly tell us 'give me a reason not to buy the big guys,' " Sharp says. "So, we went and did all this work. We bought the advertising. We set up the print. We said, 'Here's the package. All you have to do is make the purchase of 200 pairs.' "

A high-profile media/promotional campaign helps allay dealer fears that they'll be stuck with a storeroom full of unwanted shoes. To make things even easier, with the "Birthday" promotion Converse is assuring retailers that, while it won't take shoes back, it will allow them to exchange sizes and colors.

In addition, participating retailers get mentioned in the supporting media. Sporting goods giant Foot Locker, for instance, is mentioned in the national TV spots, and regional retailer logos appear on the appropriate local transit signs. Retailers were also invited to a 75th birthday party at a Toronto night club, to party, play a little basketball, and watch a preview performance by the All Star hip-hop dancers.

The entire effort, says Sharp, was aimed at making it "real easy for retailers, so they ask: 'How can I lose?' "

Source: Stan Sutter, "All Star Promo: A Birthday with Heart and Sole," *Marketing*, April 6, 1992, pp. 21, 28.

---

sales portfolios, videotapes on new products, displays, and other sales aids. Sales promotion people may develop the sales training material the sales force uses in working with customers and other channel members or special display racks the reps sell or give to retailers. In other words, rather than expecting each salesperson—or the sales manager—to develop sales aids, sales promotion might assume this responsibility.

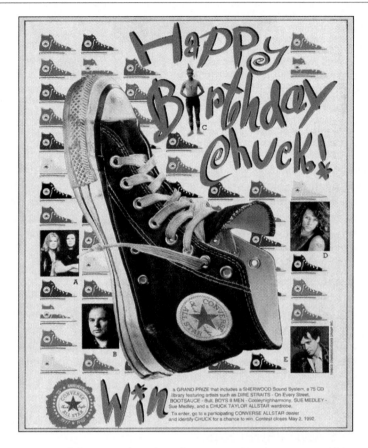

Converse advertising calls attention to its sneaker's 75th birthday.

Service-oriented firms, such as hotels or restaurants, now use sales promotions targeted at their employees. Some, for example, give a monthly cash prize for the employee who provides the best service and display the employee's picture to give recognition.[20]

Sales promotion in mature markets

Some experts think marketing managers, especially those who deal with consumer package goods, emphasize sales promotions too much. They argue that the effect of most sales promotion is temporary and that money spent on advertising and personal selling helps the firm more over the long term. Let's take a closer look at these concerns.

There *is* heavy use of sales promotion in mature markets where competition for customers and attention from middlemen is fierce. Moreover, if the total market is not growing, sales promotions may just encourage deal-prone customers (and middlemen) to switch back and forth among brands. Then the expense of sales promotions and customer swapping simply contributes to lower profits for everyone. However, once a marketing manager is in this situation, there may not be any choice. At this stage of the product life cycle, frequent sales promotions may be needed just to offset the effects of competitors' promotions. To escape from this competitive rat race, the marketing manager must seek new opportunities—with a strategy that doesn't rely solely on short-term sales promotions for competitive advantage.[21]

CONCLUSION

Promotion is an important part of any marketing mix. Most consumers and intermediate customers can choose from among many products. To be successful, a producer must not only afford a good product at a reasonable price but also inform potential customers about the product and where they can buy it. Further, producers must tell wholesalers and retailers in the channel about their product and their marketing mix. These middlemen, in turn, must use promotion to reach their customers.

The promotion blend should fit logically into the strategy being developed to satisfy a particular target market. Strategy planning needs to state *what* should be communicated to them—and *how*.

The overall promotion objective is to affect buying behavior, but the basic promotion objectives are informing, persuading, and reminding.

Three basic promotion methods can be used to reach these objectives. Behavioral science findings can help firms combine various promotion methods for effective communication. In particular, what we know about the communication process and how individuals and groups adopt new products is important in planning promotion blends.

An action-oriented framework called AIDA can help marketing managers plan promotion blends. But the marketing manager has the final responsibility for combining the promotion methods into one promotion blend for each marketing mix.

In this chapter, we considered some promotion basics and went into some detail on sales promotion. Sales promotion spending is big and growing, and it is especially important in prompting action—by customers, middlemen, or salespeople. Many types of sales promotion cause problems for some firms because it's difficult for managers to develop expertise with all of them. However, sales promotion must be managed carefully as part of the overall promotion blend. In the next two chapters, we'll discuss personal selling and mass selling in more detail.

QUESTIONS AND PROBLEMS

1. Briefly explain the nature of the three basic promotion methods available to a marketing manager. What are the main strengths and limitations of each?

2. Relate the three basic promotion objectives to the four jobs (AIDA) of promotion, using a specific example.

3. Discuss the communication process in relation to a producer's promotion of an accessory product—say, a new electronic security system businesses use to limit access to areas where they store confidential records.

4. If a company wants its promotion to appeal to a new group of target customers in a foreign country, how can it protect against its communications being misinterpreted?

5. Explain how an understanding of the adoption process would help you develop a promotion blend for digital tape recorders, a new consumer electronics product that produces high-quality recordings. Explain why you might change the promotion blend during the course of the adoption process.

6. Explain how opinion leaders affect a firm's promotion planning.

7. Discuss how the adoption curve should be used to plan the promotion blend(s) for a new, wireless portable telephone that can be used in cars while traveling.

8. Promotion has been the target of considerable criticism. What specific types of promotion are probably the object of this criticism? Give a specific example that illustrates your thinking.

9. Would promotion be successful in expanding the general demand for (a) raisins, (b) air travel, (c) tennis rackets, (d) cashmere sweaters, (e) high-octane unleaded gasoline, (f) single-serving, frozen gourmet dinners, and (g) cement? Explain why or why not in each case.

10. What promotion blend would be most appropriate for producers of the following established products? Assume average- to large-sized firms in each case and support your answer.

    a. Candy bars.
    b. Pantyhose.
    c. Castings for car engines.
    d. Car tires.
    e. A special computer used by manufacturers for computer-aided design of new products.
    f. Inexpensive plastic raincoats.
    g. A camcorder that has achieved specialty-product status.

11. Discuss the potential conflict among the various promotion managers. How could this be reduced?

12. Explain why sales promotion is currently a weak spot in marketing and suggest what might be done.

13. If sales promotion spending continues to grow—often at the expense of media advertising—how will this affect the rates charged by mass media for advertising time or space? How will it affect advertising agencies?

SUGGESTED CASES

1. The Yaka-Boochee

19. CBUR-AM

Personal Selling

When You Finish This Chapter, You Should

❶

Understand the importance and nature of personal selling.

❷

Know the three basic sales tasks and what the various kinds of salespeople can be expected to do.

❸

Know what the sales manager must do—including selecting, training, and organizing salespeople—to carry out the personal selling job.

❹

Understand how the right compensation plan can help motivate and control salespeople.

❺

Understand when and where to use the three types of sales presentations.

❻

Understand the important new terms (shown in blue).

Atlantic

CUSTOMER • CLIENT
PACKAGING PRODUCTS LTD.

WEYMOUTH VARIETY STORE LTD
P.O. BOX 41
WEYMOUTH, N.S.
BOW 370

	CUSTOMER NUMBER	.	DATE
30	76273E		05 31 92

SH# 25

STATEMENT OF ACCOUNT
TERMS: 30 DAYS FROM DATE OF INVOICE

DATE	REFERENCE	CHARGES	CREDIT	AMOUNT
05 11 92	335277	530.52		530.52
530.52		.00	.00	.00	530.52

FORM 30-08-81

As general manager of the polyethylene division of Atlantic Packaging Products Ltd. of Toronto, Roger Keeley sells plastic bags, shrink-wrap, and industrial and commercial packaging to large retailers such as Canadian Tire and Loblaw's. His aim is to be part of his customers' strategic team.

How does a plastic bag or a roll of shrink-wrap fit into retail strategy? Keeley says it's a matter of finding out how Atlantic's resources can give the client an edge. "It's consultative selling," he says. "You've got to prove to them there's an advantage to doing business with you. You sell the relationship, not the product."

As an integrated manufacturer that also makes corrugated boxes, Atlantic provides such services as a creative design team that conjures up logos and colorful graphics for product packaging; a fleet of more than 100 trucks and trailers that guarantees prompt delivery as well as pickup of old boxes for recycling; and training videos to show retailers how to pack groceries so the bags don't break.

The search for a fit with customers arises out of the relentless quest in the 90s for value. "Customers are smarter and busier," says Keeley. "They look for good value in all their purchases." For instance, Atlantic and Kodak, one of its customers, formed a trouble-shooting team with members from both companies that meets regularly. In one case, the team noticed that Kodak was ordering cartons by the thousand. When the pallets of cartons were stored in Kodak's warehouse on delivery from Atlantic, they left a lot of wasted unused space—which was not very cost effective. The team recommended that Kodak order cartons by the skid load, which would fill up each storage space completely. "Kodak got better space utilization [in its warehouse] and, in fact, reduced the total cost of inventory," says Keeley. "It's a win-win situation all the way down."[1]

THE IMPORTANCE AND ROLE OF PERSONAL SELLING

Salespeople are communicators

Promotion is communicating with potential customers. As the Atlantic Packaging case suggests, personal selling is often the best way to do it. Almost every company can benefit from personal selling. While face-to-face with prospects, salespeople can get more attention than an advertisement or a display. They can adjust what they say or do to take into consideration culture and other behavioral influences on the customer. They can ask questions to find out about a customer's specific interests. They can also stay in tune with the prospect's feedback and adjust the presentation as they move along. If—and when—the prospect is ready to buy, the salesperson is there to ask for the order.

Personal selling requires strategy decisions

Marketing managers must decide how much—and what kind of—personal selling effort each marketing mix needs. Specifically, as part of their strategy planning, they must decide (1) how many salespeople they need, (2) what kind of salespeople they need, (3) what kind of sales presentation to use, (4) how to select and train salespeople, and (5) how to supervise and motivate them. The sales manager provides inputs into these strategy decisions. Once made, it's the sales manager's job to implement the personal selling part of a marketing strategy.

In this chapter, we'll discuss the importance and nature of personal selling so you'll understand the strategy decisions sales and marketing managers face. These strategy decisions are shown in Exhibit 16–1.

We'll also discuss a number of frameworks and how-to approaches that guide these strategy decisions. Because these approaches apply equally to domestic and international markets, we won't emphasize that distinction in this chapter. This does not mean, however, that personal selling techniques don't vary from one country to another. To the contrary, in dealing with *any* customer, the salesperson must be very sensitive to cultural influences and other factors that might affect the communication process. For example, a Japanese customer and an Arab customer might respond differently to subtle aspects of a salesperson's behavior. The Arab customer might expect to be very close to a salesperson, perhaps only two feet away, while they talk. The Japanese customer might consider that distance rude. Similarly, what topics of discussion are considered sensitive, how messages are interpreted, and which negotiating styles are used vary from one country to another. A salesperson must know how to communicate effectively with each customer—wherever and whoever that customer is—but those details are beyond the strategy planning focus of this text.[2]

Personal selling is important

We've already seen that personal selling is important in some promotion blends—and absolutely essential in others. Some feel that personal selling is the dynamic element that keeps our economy going. You would better appreciate the

Exhibit 16–1   Strategy Planning for Personal Selling

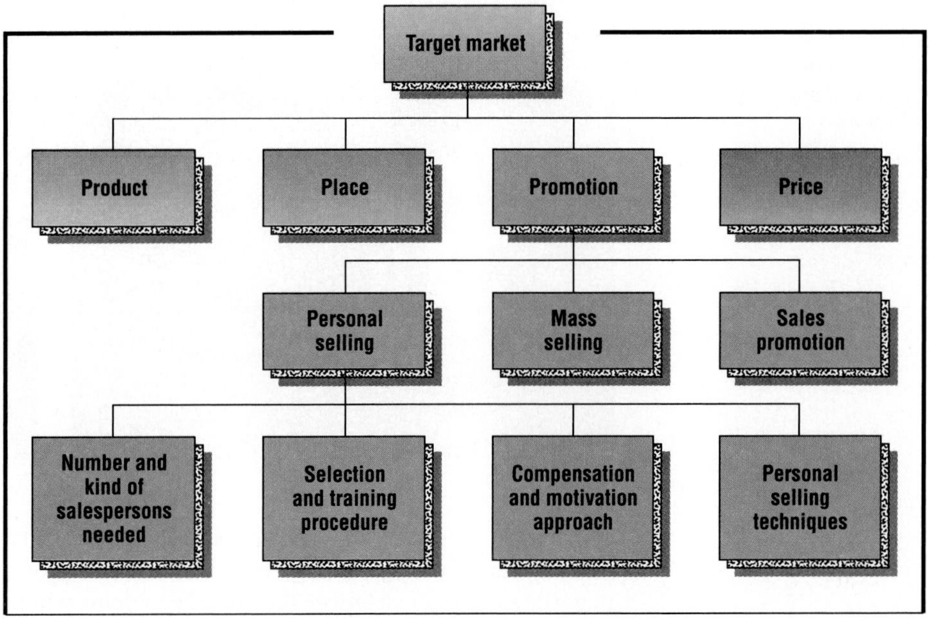

importance of personal selling if you regularly had to meet payrolls and somehow—almost miraculously—your salespeople kept coming in with orders just in time to keep the business from closing.

Personal selling is often a company's largest single operating expense. This is another reason why it is important to understand the decisions in this area. Bad sales management decisions can be costly not only in lost sales but also in actual out-of-pocket expenses.

Every economy needs and uses many salespeople. Government statistics show that about 1 person out of every 10 in the total labor force is involved in sales work. By comparison, that's about 20 times more people than are employed in advertising. Any activity that employs so many people—and is so important to the economy—deserves study. Looking at what salespeople do is a good way to start.

Helping to buy is good selling

Good salespeople don't just try to *sell* the customer. Rather, they try to *help the customer buy*—by understanding the customer's needs and presenting the advantages and disadvantages of their products. Such helpfulness results in satisfied customers—and long-term relationships. And strong relationships often form the basis for a competitive advantage, especially for firms that target business markets.

You may think of personal selling in terms of an old-time stereotype: a bag of wind with no more to offer than a funny story, a big expense account, and an engaging grin. But that isn't true any more. Old-time salespeople are being replaced by real professionals—problem solvers—who have something definite to contribute to their employers *and* their customers.

Salespeople represent the whole company— and customers, too

Increasingly, the salesperson is seen as a representative of the whole company, responsible for explaining its total effort to target customers rather than just pushing products. The sales rep is often the only link between the firm and its

While face-to-face with prospects, salespeople can adjust what they say or do to take into consideration culture and other behavioral influences.

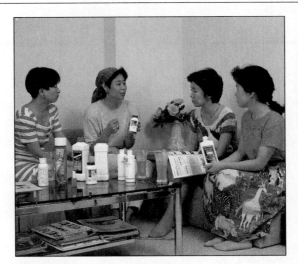

customers, especially if customers are far away. The salesperson may provide information about products, explain and interpret company policies, and even negotiate prices or diagnose technical problems when a product doesn't work well.

In some cases, salespeople represent their *customers* back inside their own firm, too. Recall that feedback is an essential part of both the communication process *and* the basic management process of planning, implementing, and control. For example, the sales rep is the likely one to explain to the production manager why a customer is unhappy with product performance or quality—or to the physical distribution manager why slow shipments are causing problems.

As evidence of these changing responsibilities, some companies give their salespeople such titles as field manager, market specialist, account representative, or sales engineer.

Sales force aids in market information function as well

The sales force can aid in the marketing information function, too. The sales rep may be the first to hear about a new competitor or a competitor's new product or strategy. And, as the following example shows, sales reps who are well attuned to customers' needs can be a key source of ideas for new products.

Ballard Medical Products is a small producer that competes with international giants in the hospital supply business. A key factor in Ballard's success is that its salespeople have the right products to offer when they make a sales call. But that's not just luck. The salespeople all have a lot of say in what products the company produces and how they are designed. Ballard salespeople are trained as information specialists who seek and report on customer feedback. At each hospital, they work closely with the doctor and nurse specialists who use Ballard products. And when one of them says, "we need a product that would solve this problem," the Ballard sales rep is right there to follow up with questions and invite suggestions. The rep quickly relays the customer's needs back to Ballard's new product group.[3]

Salespeople can be strategy planners, too

Some salespeople are expected to be marketing managers in their own territories. And some become marketing managers by default because top management hasn't provided detailed strategy guidelines. Either way, salespeople may take the initiative to fill the gap. They may develop their own marketing mixes or even their own strategies. Some firms fail to give their sales reps a clear idea of who their target customers should be. Although the sales reps are assigned a territory, they may have to start from scratch with strategy planning. The salesperson may have choices about (1) what target customers to aim at, (2) which particular products to emphasize, (3) which middlemen to call on or to work with the hardest, (4) how to use promotion money, and (5) how to adjust prices.

A salesperson who can put together profitable strategies—and implement them well—can rise very rapidly. The opportunity is there for those prepared and willing to work.

Even a starting job may offer great opportunities. Some beginning salespeople, especially those working for producers or wholesalers, are responsible for larger sales volumes than many retail stores achieve. This is a serious responsibility—and the person must be prepared for it.

Further, sales jobs are often viewed as entry-level positions and used to evaluate candidates for promotion. Success in this job can lead to rapid promotion to higher-level sales and marketing jobs—and more money and security.[4]

WHAT KINDS OF PERSONAL SELLING ARE NEEDED?

If a firm has too few salespeople—or the wrong kind—some important personal selling tasks may not be completed. And having too many salespeople—or the wrong kind—wastes money. A sales manager needs to find a good balance—the right number and the right kind of salespeople.

One of the difficulties of determining the right number and kind of salespeople is that every sales job is different. While an engineer or accountant can look forward to fairly specific duties, the salesperson's job changes constantly. However, there are three basic types of sales tasks. This gives us a starting point for understanding what selling tasks need to be done—and how many people are needed to do them.

Personal selling is divided into three tasks

The three **basic sales tasks** are order getting, order taking, and supporting. For convenience, we'll describe salespeople by these terms—referring to their primary task—although one person may do all three tasks in some situations.

As the names imply, order getters and order takers obtain orders for their company. Every marketing mix must have someone or some way to obtain orders. In contrast, supporting salespeople are not directly interested in orders. Their function is to help the order-oriented salespeople. With this variety, you can see that there is a place in personal selling for nearly everyone.

ORDER GETTERS—DEVELOP NEW BUSINESS

Order getters are concerned with getting new business. **Order getting** means seeking possible buyers with a well-organized sales presentation designed to sell a product, service, or idea. The emphasis here is on getting results—orders—not on style, however. A good order getter may appear very low-key if that's what the target customer seems to want.

MARKETING DEMO 16–1
Selling: It's Got to Be a Team Effort

If you want to observe Ian McKay making a sale, set aside a little time. Five years should just about do it—if he's dealing with a customer who's in hurry-up mode. But be patient. Some of McKay's deals simmer for the better part of a generation. And count on building up more frequent-flyer points than you'll ever use. McKay spends four to six months of the year fighting jet lag as he spans the globe in search of business.

Should this sound nightmarish to you, forget about pursuing a sales career. Travel aside, McKay's way will be much closer to the norm than the exception for successful selling in the decade ahead. From the time McKay, manager of international sales of hydraulic turbines for General Electric Canada, Inc., in Montreal, hears about a pending hydro development to the time the contract to supply turbines and generators is awarded, he can spend more than 15 years trying to land the business. To win a contract on these projects, he has to develop teams and networks, build long-term relationships, and know his customers' businesses.

McKay says that hearing promptly about hydro projects depends on developing worldwide networks of multinational sales representatives, consultants, embassy liaisons, World Bank envoys, and officials responsible for developing their countries' energy policies. Because of the massive scale of major projects, bidding means working in teams and consortia and cooperating with other suppliers of many nationalities.

To sell at this level, McKay says, "You have to be an excellent communicator from the time you hear about the project until the postsale follow-through." Negotiations can be complex: How much liability is GE willing to accept? How long will guaranties last? Can it be done more cheaply?

A lot is at stake. McKay is working on a proposal worth $500 million to GE for China's Three Gorges project, one of the world's largest hydroelectric power developments. While still at the preliminary stage—the turbines and generators won't be needed until about 1997—McKay is concentrating on what he calls "strategic positioning," keeping GE's name at the forefront of potential bidders. The role of sales in this field is definitely changing. Future growth is in the export market, which will drive sales and marketing people towards becoming junior diplomats, world travelers and, above all, consummate dealmakers.

Source: John Southerst, "Secrets of Sales Superstars," *Canadian Business*, December 1992, pp. 58–62.

Order getters must know what they're talking about—not just be a personal contact. Order-getting salespeople work for producers, wholesalers, and retailers. They normally are well paid—many earn more than $75,000 a year.

Producers' order getters—find new opportunities

Producers of all kinds of products, especially business products, have a great need for order getters. They use order getters to locate new prospects, open new accounts, see new opportunities, and help establish and build channel relationships.

High-caliber order getters are essential to sell installations and accessory equipment where large sums are involved and where top-level management participates in the buying decision. Marketing Demo 16–1 describes how GE develops relationships in the hydraulic turbine market.

Top-level customers are more interested in ways to save or make more money than in technical details. Good order getters cater to this interest. They help the customer identify ways to solve problems and then sell concepts and ideas—not just physical products. The products are merely the means of achieving the customer's end.

MARKETING DEMO 16–2
Knowing Your Client's Business a Key to Success

L ike many in his industry, insurance broker John Nicola, president of the James E. Rogers Group in Vancouver, specializes in helping business owners and professionals develop financial packages for their companies as well as their families. In addition to selling insurance, he consults on companies' employee benefits, individual retirement investments such as mutual funds, and business and estate planning.

Nicola doesn't rely on the age-old sales formula: make 10 calls, get 3 appointments, close 1 sale. Nor does he pound the pavement or use telemarketing—and he hasn't made a cold call in 15 years. He spends as much time as he can getting to know his customers' financial affairs. By working closely with them and offering them the most sophisticated financial advice available, he becomes indispensable. As a result, he earns his living mainly through referrals. So far this year, 35 percent of unsolicited calls to Nicola's office have been referrals by friends or other financial planners.

Regular customers account for 70 percent of revenue at the Rogers Group. And Nicola doesn't credit it to selling smarts—even though he and four other staffers are members of the top level of the global life insurance industry's Million Dollar Round Table (a status shared each year by only about 50 Canadians and meaning that as agents, they earned at least $265,000 in eligible new commissions last year). "We don't overemphasize the sales ability here," he says. "We think of ourselves much like a specialty law firm. We're successful because of what we know and the service we provide."

Source: John Southerst, "Secrets of Sales Superstars," *Canadian Business*, December 1992, pp. 58–62.

Order getters are also necessary to sell raw materials, components, supplies, and services—but mainly for initial contacts. Since many competitors offer nearly the same product, the order getter's crucial selling job is to get the company's name on the approved suppliers list.

Order getters for professional services—and other products where service is an important element of the marketing mix—face a special challenge. The customer usually can't inspect a service before deciding to buy. The order getter's communication and relationship with the customer may be the only basis on which to evaluate the quality of the supplier. This is demonstrated in Marketing Demo 16–2.

Order getters in business markets need the know-how to help solve their customers' problems. Often, they need to understand both customers' general business concerns and technical details about the product and its applications. This is especially important for salespeople whose customers are producers. To have technically competent order getters, firms often give special training to business-trained college graduates. Such salespeople can then work intelligently with their specialist customers. In fact, they may be more technically competent in their narrow specialty than anyone they encounter—so they provide a unique service. For example, a salesperson for automated manufacturing equipment must understand everything about a prospect's production process as well as the technical details of converting to computer-controlled equipment.

Wholesalers' order getters—almost hand it to the customer

Progressive merchant wholesaler sales reps are developing into counselors and store advisers rather than just order takers. Such order getters may become retailers' partners in the job of moving goods from the wholesale warehouse through the retail store to consumers. These order getters almost become a part of the retailer's staff—helping to check stock, write orders, and conduct demonstrations—and plan advertising, special promotions, and other retailing activities.

Agent middlemen often are order getters—particularly the more aggressive manufacturers' agents and brokers. They face the same tasks as producers' order getters. But, unfortunately for them, once the order getting is done and the customers become established and loyal, producers may try to eliminate the agents and save money with their own order takers.

Retail order getters influence consumer behavior

Convincing consumers about the value of products they haven't seriously considered takes a high level of personal selling ability. Order getters for unsought products must help customers see how a new product can satisfy needs now being filled by something else. Early order getters for microwave ovens, for example, faced a tough job. They had to convince skeptical customers that this new kind of cooking was safe and that it would be more convenient than traditional approaches—once the customer got used to it. Without order getters, many of the products we now rely on—such as refrigerators and air conditioners—might have died in the market introduction stage. The order getter helps bring products out of the introduction stage into the market growth stage. Without sales and profits in the early stages, the product may fail—and never be offered again.

Order getters are helpful for selling *heterogeneous* shopping products. Consumers shop for many of these items on the basis of price and quality. They welcome useful information. Cars, furniture and furnishings, cameras, jewelry, and fashion items can be sold effectively by an aggressive, helpful order getter. Friendly advice, based on thorough knowledge of the product and its alternatives, may really help consumers and bring profits to the salesperson and retailer.

ORDER TAKERS—KEEP THE BUSINESS COMING

Order takers sell the regular or typical customers and complete most sales transactions. After a customer becomes interested in a firm's products through an order getter or supporting salesperson or through advertising or sales promotion, an order taker usually answers any final questions and completes the sale. **Order taking** is the routine completion of sales made regularly to the target customers.

Sometimes, sales managers or customers use the term *order taker* as a put-down when referring to salespeople who don't take any initiative. While a particular salesperson may perform poorly enough to justify criticism, it's a mistake to downgrade the function of order taking. Order taking is extremely important. Many firms lose sales just because no one ever asks for the order—and closes the sale. Moreover, the order taker's job is not just limited to placing orders. Even in business markets where customers place routine orders with computerized order systems and EDI, order takers do a variety of important jobs.

Producers' order takers—train and explain

After order getters open up industrial, wholesale, or retail accounts, regular follow-up is necessary. Order takers work on improving the whole relationship with the customer, not just on completing a single transaction. Even if computers handle routine reorders, someone has to explain details, make adjustments, handle complaints, explain or negotiate new prices and terms, place sales promotion materials, and keep customers informed of new developments. Someone may have to train customers' employees to use machines or products. In sales

A good retail order taker helps to build good relations with customers.

to middlemen, someone may have to train wholesalers' or retailers' salespeople. All these activities are part of the order taker's job.

Producers' order takers often have a regular route with many calls. To handle these calls well, they must have energy, persistence, enthusiasm, and a friendly personality that wears well over time. They sometimes have to take the heat when something goes wrong with some other element of the marketing mix.

Firms sometimes use order-taking jobs to train potential order getters and managers. Such jobs give them an opportunity to meet key customers and to better understand their needs. And frequently, they run into some order-getting opportunities.

Order takers who are alert to order-getting opportunities can make the big difference in generating new sales. Averitt Express, a trucking firm, recognized the opportunities. At most trucking firms, drivers are basically order takers and service providers. When a customer places an order, the driver picks up and delivers the shipment. In contrast, Averitt encourages its drivers to help get new orders. Whenever they deliver a shipment to a firm that is not a regular Averitt customer, they call on the shipping manager at the firm. They give the shipping manager sales literature about Averitt services and ask if Averitt can help handle some of that firm's shipping needs. With 700 drivers all helping out as order getters, it's no wonder that Averitt sales have grown rapidly.[5]

Wholesalers' order takers—not getting orders but keeping them

While producers' order takers usually handle relatively few items—and sometimes even a single item—wholesalers' order takers may sell 125,000 items or more. Most wholesale order takers just sell out of their catalogue. They have so many items that they can't possibly give aggressive sales effort to many—except perhaps newer or more profitable items. There are just too many items to single any out for special attention. The order taker's strength is a wide assortment—rather than detailed knowledge of individual products. However, computers are increasingly being used to the advantage of wholesalers, tracking sales and other data, for example. The use of laptop computers by Shopper's Drug Mart is detailed in Marketing Demo 16–3.

MARKETING DEMO 16–3
"Office-on-the-Roll" Means Sales for *Shopper's*

Sales representatives at Shopper's Drug Mart don't have offices. A 10-hour day is hardly unusual for a rep, and often an entire day is spent on location at a Shopper's store. Laptops, therefore, are essential to their productivity. Shopper's is one of Canada's leading retailers, with over 600 stores across the country, and private label products account for over 30 percent of an average store's revenues. The sales organization is responsible for the management of the inventory, ordering, and business analysis for such goods.

Reps used to be overburdened with the mechanics of a sales call, often getting only 1 hour of real selling time in a 10-hour day. By supplying the sales force with laptop computers, account information, order processing information, and links with the home office and central database, they now perform their duties more efficiently and effectively.

Laptops are used to record inventory status, create and process orders, help store managers track performance to promotions, review sales history, update store information, and record details of telephone calls. With automated ordering, the window of selling time available to each rep is doubled or tripled. The end result is an office-on-the-role—a complete package that can be set up on any available surface and serve as an all-in-one desk.

Reps can request and analyze information normally stored on the central computer that was previously only available as cumbersome paper reports. The Shopper's system, with a remote communications package, allows reps to access information when it's convenient. With access to current sales and stock information, private label reps can make the most of their in-store day, helping the store managers reach target revenue objectives.

Store managers have responded well to reps carrying computers. The reps themselves report that their work is more rewarding; they can spend more time doing what they like best—selling.

Source: Mike Heeney, " 'Office-on-the-Roll' Means Sales for Shopper's," *Computing Canada*, July 6, 1992, p. 48.

The wholesale order taker's main job is to maintain close contact with customers—perhaps once a week—and fill any needs that develop. Sometimes, such order takers get very close to the producer or retailer customers they serve. Some retailers let the salesperson take inventory—and then write up the order. Obviously, this position of trust cannot be abused. After writing up the order, the order taker normally checks to be sure the company fills the order promptly and accurately. The order taker also handles any adjustments or complaints and generally acts as a liaison between the company and its customers.

Such salespeople are usually the low-pressure type—friendly and easygoing. Generally these jobs aren't as high paying as the order-getting variety—but they attract many because they aren't as taxing. They require relatively little traveling, and there is little or no pressure to get new accounts. There can be a social aspect, too. The salesperson sometimes becomes good friends with customers.

Retail order takers— often they are poor salesclerks

Order taking may be almost mechanical at the retail level—for example, at the supermarket checkout counter. Even so, retail order takers play a vital role in a retailer's marketing mix. Customers expect prompt and friendly service. They will find a new place to shop rather than deal with a salesclerk who is rude or acts annoyed by having to complete a sale.

Some retail clerks are poor order takers because they aren't paid much—often only the minimum wage. But they may be paid little because they do little. In any case, order taking at the retail level appears to be declining in quality. And there will probably be far fewer such jobs in the future as more marketers make adjustments in their mixes and turn to self-service selling. Checkout counters now have automated electronic scanning equipment that reads price codes directly from packages. Some supermarkets are even experimenting with systems where customers do their own scanning and the clerk simply accepts the money.

SUPPORTING SALES FORCE—INFORMS AND PROMOTES IN THE CHANNEL

Supporting salespeople help the order-oriented salespeople—but they don't try to get orders themselves. Their activities are aimed at getting sales in the long run. For the short run, however, they are ambassadors of goodwill who may provide specialized services and information. Almost all supporting salespeople work for producers or middlemen who do this supporting work for producers. There are two types of supporting salespeople: missionary salespeople and technical specialists.

Missionary salespeople can increase sales

Missionary salespeople are supporting salespeople who work for producers, calling on their middlemen and their customers. They try to develop goodwill and stimulate demand, help the middlemen train their salespeople, and often take orders for delivery by the middlemen. Missionary salespeople are sometimes called *merchandisers* or *detailers*.

Producers who rely on merchant wholesalers to obtain widespread distribution often use missionary salespeople. The sales rep can give a promotion boost to a product that otherwise wouldn't get much attention from the middlemen because it's just one of many they sell. A missionary salesperson for Vicks's cold remedy products, for example, might visit druggists during the cold season and encourage them to use a special end-of-aisle display for Vicks's cough syrup—and then help set it up. The wholesaler that supplies the drugstore would benefit from any increased sales, but might not take the time to urge use of the special display.

An imaginative missionary salesperson can double or triple sales. Naturally, this doesn't go unnoticed. Missionary sales jobs are often a route to order-oriented jobs. In fact, this position is often used as a training ground for new salespeople—and recent college grads are often recruited for these positions.

Technical specialists are experts who know product applications

Technical specialists are supporting salespeople who provide technical assistance to order-oriented salespeople. Technical specialists usually are science or engineering graduates with the know-how to understand the customer's applications and explain the advantages of the company's product. They are usually more interested in showing the technical details of their product than in helping to persuade customers to buy it. Before the specialist's visit, an order getter probably has stimulated interest. The technical specialist provides the details. The order getter usually completes the sale—but only after the customer's technical people give at least tentative approval.

Today, many of the decision makers who influence organizational purchases have more technical knowledge than they did in the past. As a result, firms need more technical specialists. Many companies train their technical specialists in presentation skills to help them be not only technically accurate but also persuasive. Technical specialists who are also good communicators often become highly paid order getters.

Sales teams at Liz Claiborne join forces to map strategies for introducing each collection they market.

Three tasks may have to be blended

We have described three sales tasks—order getting, order taking, and supporting. However, a particular salesperson might be given two—or all three—of these tasks. Ten percent of a particular job may be order getting, 80 percent order taking, and the additional 10 percent supporting. Another company might have three different people handling the different sales tasks. This can lead to **team selling**—when different sales reps work together on a specific account. Producers of high-ticket items often use team selling. AT&T uses team selling to sell office communications systems for a whole business. Different specialists handle different parts of the job—but the whole team coordinates its efforts to achieve the desired result.[6]

Strategy planners need to specify what types of selling tasks the sales force will handle. Once the tasks are specified, the sales manager needs to assign responsibility for individual sales jobs so that the tasks are completed and the personal selling objectives achieved.

THE RIGHT STRUCTURE HELPS ASSIGN RESPONSIBILITY

A sales manager must organize the sales force so that all the necessary tasks are done well. A large organization might have different salespeople specializing by different selling tasks *and* by the target markets they serve.

Different target markets need different selling tasks

Sales managers often divide sales force responsibilities based on the type of customer involved. For example, Bigelow, a company that makes quality carpet for homes and office buildings, divided its sales force into two groups of specialists. Some Bigelow salespeople call only on architects to help them choose the best type of carpet for new office buildings. These reps know all the technical details, such as how well a certain carpet fiber will wear or its effectiveness in reducing

Telemarketing helps identify prospects and reach small customers, but technical specialists usually must meet with the customer in person.

noise from office equipment. Often no selling is involved because the architect only suggests specifications and doesn't actually buy the carpet.

Other Bigelow salespeople call on retail carpet stores. These reps identify stores that don't carry Bigelow carpets—and work to establish a relationship and get that crucial first order. Once a store is sold, these reps encourage the store manager to keep a variety of Bigelow carpets in stock. They also take orders, help train the store's salespeople, and try to solve any problems that occur.

Big accounts get special treatment

Very large customers often require special selling effort—and are treated differently. Moen, a maker of plumbing fixtures, has a regular sales force to call on building material wholesalers and an elite **major accounts sales force** that sells directly to large accounts—like Sears or other major retail chain stores that carry plumbing fixtures.[7]

Some salespeople specialize in telephone selling

Some firms have a group of salespeople who specialize in **telemarketing**— using the telephone to "call" on customers or prospects. A phone call has many of the benefits of a personal visit, including the ability to modify the message as feedback is received. The big advantage of telemarketing is that it saves time and money. Telemarketing is especially useful when customers are small or in hard-to-reach places. It is also important when many prospects have to be contacted to reach one actually interested in buying. In these situations, telemarketing may be the only economical approach.

Telemarketing is rapidly growing in popularity. Large and small firms alike find that it allows them to extend their personal selling efforts to new target markets. Telemarketing increases the frequency of contact between the firm and its customers. Convenient, toll-free telephone lines make it fast and easy for customers to place orders or get assistance.[8]

Sales tasks are done in sales territories

Often, companies organize selling tasks on the basis of a **sales territory**—a geographic area that is the responsibility of one salesperson or several working together. A territory might be a region of a country, a state, or part of a city, depending on the market potential. Companies like Lockheed Aircraft Corporation often consider a whole country as *part* of a sales territory for one salesperson.

Carefully set territories can reduce travel time and the cost of sales calls. Assigning territories can also help reduce confusion about who has responsibility for a set of selling tasks. But sometimes, simple geographic division isn't easy. A company may have different products that require very different knowledge or selling skills—even if products sell in the same territory or to the same customer. For example, Du Pont makes special films for hospital X-ray departments as well as chemicals used in laboratory blood tests. But a salesperson who can talk to a radiologist about the best film for a complex X ray probably can't be expected to know everything about blood chemistry! See the accompanying ad for the Canadian Professional Sales Association.

Size of sales force depends on workload

Once the important selling tasks are specified and the responsibilities divided, the sales manager must decide how many salespeople are needed. The first step is estimating how much work can be done by one person in some time period. Then

---

This advertisement for the Canadian Professional Sales Association highlights the concern for cutting costs.

the sales manager can make an educated guess about how many people are required in total, as the following example shows.

For many years, the Parker Jewelry Company was very successful selling its silver jewelry to department and jewelry stores in western Canada. But management personnel wanted to expand into the big urban markets of Quebec and Ontario. They realized that most of the work for the first few years would require order getters. They felt that a salesperson would need to call on each account at least once a month to get a share of this competitive business. They estimated that a salesperson could make only five calls a day on prospective buyers and still allow time for travel, waiting, and follow-up on orders that came in. This meant that a sales rep who made calls 20 days a month could handle about 100 stores (5 a day × 20 days).

The managers looked at telephone Yellow Pages for their target cities and estimated the total number of jewelry departments and stores. Then they simply divided the total number of stores by 100 to estimate the number of salespeople needed. This also helped them set up territories—by defining areas that included about 100 stores for each salesperson. Obviously, managers might want to fine-tune this estimate for differences in territories—such as travel time. But the basic approach can be applied to many different situations.[9]

When a company is starting a new sales force, managers are concerned about its size. But many established firms ignore this problem. Some managers forget that over time, the right number of salespeople may change—as selling tasks change. Then, when a problem becomes obvious, they try to change everything in a hurry—a big mistake. Finding and training effective salespeople takes time—and is an ongoing job.

SOUND SELECTION AND TRAINING TO BUILD A SALES FORCE

Selecting good salespeople takes judgment, plus

It is important to hire *good, well-qualified* salespeople. But the selection in many companies is a hit-or-miss affair, done without serious thought about exactly what kind of person the firm needs. Managers may hire friends and relations—or whoever is available—because they feel that the only qualifications for sales jobs are a friendly personality and nice appearance. This approach has led to poor sales—and costly sales force turnover.

Progressive companies try to be more careful. They constantly update a list of possible job candidates. They schedule candidates for multiple interviews with various executives, do thorough background checks, and even use psychological tests. Unfortunately, such techniques can't guarantee success. But a systematic approach based on several different inputs results in a better sales force.

One problem in selecting salespeople is that two different sales jobs with identical titles may involve very different selling tasks—and require different skills. A carefully prepared job description helps avoid this problem.

Job descriptions should be in writing and specific

A **job description** is a written statement of what a salesperson is expected to do. It might list 10 to 20 specific tasks, as well as routine prospecting and sales report writing. Each company must write its own job specifications. And it should provide clear guidelines about what selling tasks the job involves. This is critical to determine the kind of salespeople who should be selected—and later, it provides a basis for seeing how they should be trained, how well they are performing, and how they should be paid. Exhibit 16–2 is an example of a job description for a Nabob salesperson.

Exhibit 16–2   Job Description of a Nabob Salesperson

1.   Position: Sales representative—Nabob
2.   Name:
3.   Reporting to: District sales manager
4.   Reporting to: Sales Representative

5.   Basic task:
5.1 To exceed the territory sales quota in each category.
5.2 To manage the territory within the approved annual expense budget.
5.3 To develop and maintain relationships with customers in the territory for the purpose of building business volume both immediate and future.
5.4 To learn the sales, and administrative relationships required in the territory as a basis for future promotion within the Company, or achieving the fullest potential as a Sales Representative.
5.5 To fulfill the commitments made by the Company, the Region and/or District Manager, in regards to obligations made to the grocery trade and/or the consuming public.

6.   Main accountabilities:
6.1 To exceed tertial quotas in all sales categories, by meeting sales allocations on promotional merchandise, and by selling regular priced stock via creative field activated promotions.
6.2 To operate the sales territory within an operating budget developed by the Sales Representative and approved by the District Manager.
6.3 Maintain a call frequency schedule with all direct and retail calls in the territory as per Regional and District objectives.
6.4 To establish and maintain a program of shelf management for all listed items with all the assigned calls in the territory, as per Nabob shelf management guidelines.
6.5 To fulfill all merchandising and display commitments necessary to successfully promote the Company's products in terms of point-of-sale material, and pricing.
6.6 Maintain accurate customer records in the area of: daily reports, customer call records, key account fact books, co-operative advertising, incremental co-op, and continuous stocking monies, as well as any administration requested of them. All requests are to be reported on time.
6.7 To report all competitive information and activity to the District Manager and, where possible, to obtain copies of such information.
6.8 To conduct oneself in a manner that best communicates professionalism in carrying out the Sales Representative responsibilities and in communicating Nabob as the "Coffee Experts."
6.9 To manage the territory within the policies and procedures adopted for the Sales Department by the Company.
6.10 To work towards improving performance through the implementation of sales training material, training letters, by responding to trade opportunities and by observing sales and trade activities.

7.   Yardsticks for performance:
7.1 Case shipment reports in combination with customer period. Computer reports are used to determine results vs. objectives.
7.2 Expenses vs. budget.
7.3 Following of route lists, completion of yearly advertising schedules with major accounts, quarterly business reviews, and the apportioning of time on the basis of returns are the measurement of effective territory planning.
7.4 Administration should be completed following District, Region and Co. guidelines and should be submitted on or before due dates.
7.5 Co. and policy regs should be adhered to as per the Nabob policy manual. Areas to be considered are care of the Co. car and materials, adherence to co-op spending guidelines, operating efficiently and economically in terms of territory expenses.
7.6 Trade knowledge and application of sales principles as determined by the District Manager.

Source: Courtesy of Nabob Foods Ltd.

Good salespeople are trained, not born

The idea that good salespeople are born may have some truth—but it isn't the whole story. A *born* salesperson—if that term refers to an outgoing, aggressive kind of individual—may not do nearly as well when the going gets rough as a less extroverted co-worker who has had solid, specialized training.

A salesperson needs to be taught—about the company and its products and about giving effective sales presentations. But this isn't always done. Many salespeople fail—or do a poor job—because they haven't had good training. Firms often hire new salespeople and immediately send them out on the road—or the retail selling floor—with no grounding in the basic selling steps and no information about the product or the customer. They just get a price list and a pat on the back. This isn't enough!

All salespeople need some training

It's up to sales and marketing management to be sure that the salespeople know what they're supposed to do—and how to do it. A job description is helpful in telling salespeople what they are expected to do. But showing them how to get the job done is harder—because people may be hired with different backgrounds, skills, and levels of intelligence. Some trainees are hired with no knowledge of the company or its products—and little knowledge of selling. Others may come in with a lot of industry knowledge and much selling experience—but some bad habits developed at another company. Still others may have some selling experience but need to know more about the firm's customers and their needs. Even a firm's own sales veterans may get set in their ways and profit greatly by—and often welcome the chance for—additional training.

The kind of initial sales training should be modified based on the experience and skills of the group involved. But the company's sales training program should cover at least the following areas: (1) company policies and practices, (2) product information, and (3) professional selling skills.

Selling skills can be learned

Many companies spend the bulk of their training time on product information and company policy. They neglect training in selling techniques because they think selling is something anyone can do. More progressive companies know that training on selling skills can pay off. For example, training can help salespeople learn how to be more effective in cold calls on new prospects, in listening carefully to identify a customer's real objections, and in closing the sale. Training can also help a salesperson better analyze why present customers buy from the company, why former customers now buy from competitors, and why some prospects remain only prospects. Later in this chapter, we'll talk about some key ideas in this area, especially those related to different kinds of sales presentations.

Training on selling techniques often starts in the classroom with lectures, case studies, and videotaped trial presentations and demonstrations. But a complete training program adds on-the-job observation of effective salespeople and coaching from sales supervisors.

Training is ongoing

How long the initial training period should last depends on how hard the job is—as shown in the job description. Some training programs go on for many months. For example, some new IBM sales reps don't call on an account by themselves for the first six months or more. Some form of sales training should go on indefinitely. Many companies use weekly sales meetings or work sessions, annual or semiannual conventions or conferences, and regular weekly or biweekly newsletters—as well as normal sales supervision—to keep salespeople up-to-date.[10]

COMPENSATING AND MOTIVATING SALESPEOPLE

To recruit—and keep—good salespeople, a firm has to develop an attractive compensation plan designed to motivate. Ideally, sales reps should be paid in such a way that what they want to do—for personal interest and gain—is in the company's interest, too. Most companies focus on financial motivation—but public recognition, sales contests, and simple personal recognition for a job well done can be highly effective in encouraging greater sales effort.[11] Our main emphasis here, however, will be on financial motivation.[12]

Two basic decisions must be made in developing a compensation plan: (1) the level of compensation and (2) the method of payment.

Compensation varies with job and needed skills

To attract good salespeople, a company must pay at least the going market wage for different kinds of salespeople. Order getters are paid more than order takers, for example.

The job description explains the salesperson's role in marketing mix. It should show whether the salesperson needs any special skills or has any special responsibilities that require higher pay levels. To be sure it can afford a specific type of salesperson, the company should estimate—when the job description is written—how valuable such a salesperson will be. A good order getter may be worth $50,000 to $100,000 to one company but only $15,000 to $25,000 to another—just because the second firm doesn't have enough to sell. In such a case, the second company should rethink its job specifications—or completely change its promotion plans—because the going rate for order getters is much higher than $15,000 a year.

If a job requires extensive travel, aggressive pioneering, or contacts with difficult customers, the pay may have to be higher. But the salesperson's compensation level should compare, at least roughly, with the pay scale of the rest of the firm. Normally, salespeople earn more than the office or production force but less than top management.

Payment methods vary

Once a firm decides on the general level of compensation, it has to set the method of payment. There are three basic methods of payment: (1) *straight salary*, (2) *straight commission*, or (3) a *combination plan*. Straight salary normally supplies the most security for the salesperson—and straight commission the most incentive. These two represent extremes. Most companies want to offer their salespeople some balance between incentive and security, so the most popular method of payment is a combination plan that includes some salary and some commission. Bonuses, profit sharing, pensions, insurance, and other fringe benefits may be included, too. Still, some blend of salary and commission provides the basis for most combination plans.

What determines the choice of the pay plan? Four standards should be applied: control, incentive, flexibility, and simplicity.

Salary gives control—if there is close supervision

The proportion of a salesperson's compensation paid as salary affects how much *control* the sales manager has. It also affects how much supervision is required. A salesperson on straight salary earns the same amount regardless of how he or she spends time. So the salaried salesperson is expected to do what the sales manager asks—whether it is order taking, supporting sales activities, or completing sales call reports. However, the sales manager maintains control *only* by close supervision. As a result, straight salary or a large salary element in the compensation plan increases the amount of sales supervision needed.

If such personal supervision would be difficult, a firm may get better control with a compensation plan that includes some commission—or even a straight commission plan with built-in direction. For example, if a company wants its salespeople to devote more time to developing new accounts, it can pay higher commission for first orders from a new customer. However, a salesperson on a straight commission tends to be his or her own boss. The sales manager is less likely to get help on sales activities that won't increase the salesperson's earnings.

Incentives can be direct or indirect	An *incentive* plan can range anywhere from an indirect incentive (a modest sharing of company profits) to a very direct incentive—where a salesperson's income is strictly commission on sales. The incentive should be large only if there is a direct relationship between the salesperson's effort and results. The relationship is less direct if a number of people are involved in the sale—engineers, top management, or supporting salespeople. In this case, each one's contribution is less obvious, and greater emphasis on salary may make more sense.

When a company wants to expand sales rapidly, it usually offers strong incentives to order-getting salespeople. Strong incentives may also be sensible when the company's objectives are shifting or varied. In this way, the salesperson's activities and efforts can be directed and shifted as needed. One trucking company, for example, has a sales incentive plan that pays higher commissions on business needed to balance freight movements—depending on how heavily traffic has been moving in one direction or another.

Flexibility is desirable— but difficult to achieve	*Flexibility* is probably the most difficult aspect to achieve. One major reason that combination plans have become more popular is that they offer a way to meet varying situations. We'll consider four major kinds of flexibility.

Flexibility in selling costs is especially important for most small companies. With limited working capital and uncertain markets, small companies like straight commission—or combination plans with a large commission element. When sales drop off, costs do, too. Such flexibility is similar to using manufacturers' agents who get paid only if they deliver sales. This advantage often dominates in selecting a sales compensation method. Exhibit 16–3 shows the general relation between personal selling expense and sales volume for each of the basic compensation alternatives.

Sales potential usually differs from one sales territory to another, so it is desirable for a compensation plan to offer *flexibility among territories*. Unless the pay plan allows for territory differences, the salesperson in a growing territory might have rapidly increasing earnings—while the sales rep in a poor area will have little to show for the same amount of work. Such a situation isn't fair, and it can lead to high turnover and much dissatisfaction. A sales manager can take such differences into consideration when setting a salesperson's **sales quota**—the specific sales or profit objective a salesperson is expected to achieve.

Flexibility among people is important because most companies' salespeople vary in their stage of professional development. Trainees and new salespeople

Exhibit 16–3   Relation between Personal Selling Expenses and Sales Volume—for Three Basic Personal Selling Compensation Alternatives

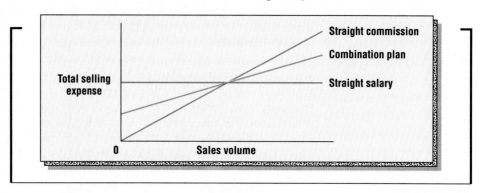

usually require a special pay plan with emphasis on salary. This provides at least some stability of earnings.

Flexibility among products is desirable because most companies sell several different products with different profit potentials. Unless firms recognize this fact, the salespeople may push the products that sell best—ignoring overall company profit. A flexible commission system can more easily adjust to changing profit potentials.

Simplicity

A final consideration is the need for *simplicity*. Complicated plans are hard for salespeople to understand. Salespeople become dissatisfied if they can't see a direct relationship between their effort and their income.

Simplicity is best achieved with straight salary. But in practice, it's usually better to sacrifice some simplicity to gain some incentive, flexibility, and control. The best combination of these factors depends on the job description and the company's objectives.

Sales managers must plan, implement, and control

There are no easy answers to the compensation problem. It is up to the sales manager—together with the marketing manager—to develop a good compensation plan. The sales manager's efforts must be coordinated with the whole marketing mix because personal selling objectives can be accomplished only if enough money is allocated for this job. Further, managers must regularly evaluate each salesperson's performance—and be certain that all the needed tasks are being done well. The compensation plan may have to be changed if the pay and work are out of line. And by evaluating performance, firms can also identify areas that need more attention—by the salesperson or management.[13] In Chapter 21, we'll talk more about controlling marketing activities.

PERSONAL SELLING TECHNIQUES—PROSPECTING AND PRESENTING

When we discussed the need for sales training programs, we stressed the importance of training in selling techniques. Now let's discuss these ideas in more detail so you understand the basic steps each salesperson should follow—including prospecting, planning sales presentations, making sales presentations, and following up after the sale. Exhibit 16–4 shows the steps we'll consider. You can see that

Exhibit 16–4   Key Steps in the Personal Selling Process

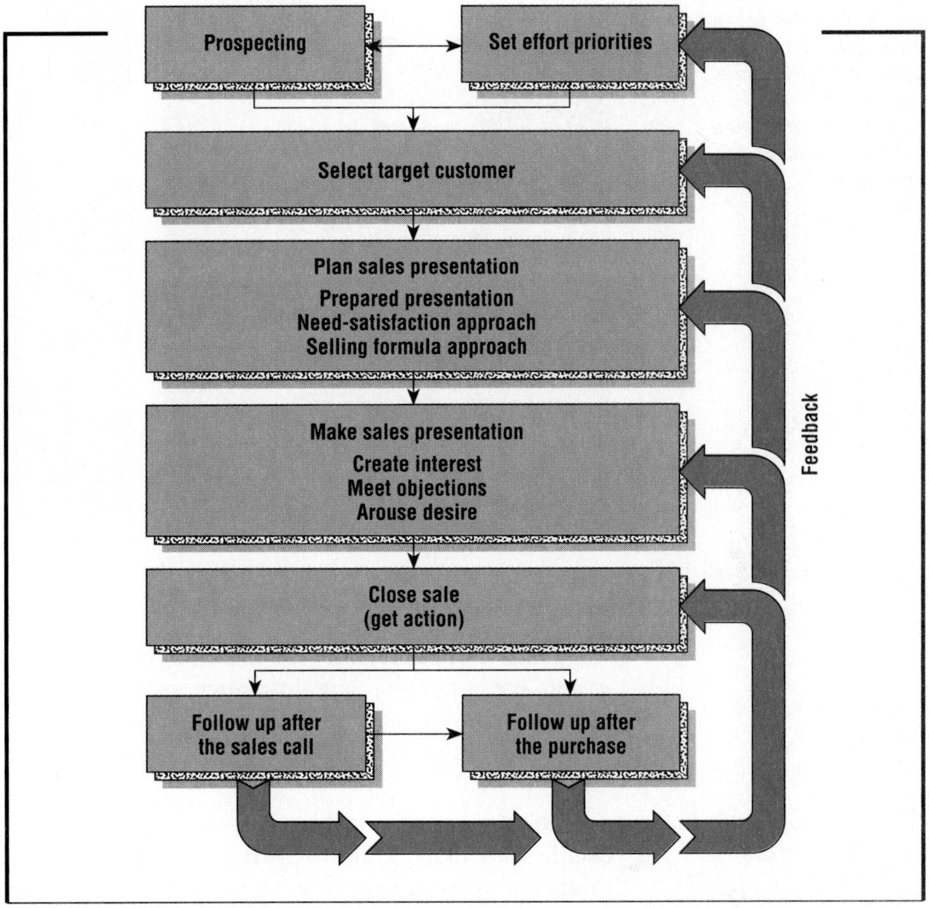

the salesperson is just carrying out a planned communication process—as we discussed in Chapter 15.[14]

Prospecting—narrowing
down to the right target

Although a marketing strategy should specify the segmenting dimensions for a target market, that doesn't mean that each target customer is individually identified! Narrowing the personal selling effort down to the right target requires constant, detailed analysis of markets, and much prospecting. Basically, **prospecting** involves following all the leads in the target market to identify potential customers.

Finding live prospects who will help make the buying decision isn't as easy as it sounds. In business markets, for example, the salesperson may need to do some real detective work to find the real purchase decision makers. Multiple buying influence is common, and companies regularly rearrange their organization structures and buying responsibilities.

Most salespeople use the telephone for much of their detective work. A phone call often saves the wasted expense of personal visits to prospects who are not interested—or it can provide much useful information for planning a follow-up sales visit. Some hot prospects can even be sold on the phone.

Giltspur offers a training program to help salespeople do a better job qualifying prospects; SPC offers software that helps salespeople give more interesting sales presentations.

Some companies provide prospect lists to make this part of the selling job easier. For example, one insurance company checks the local newspaper for marriage announcements—then a salesperson calls to see if the new couple is interested in finding out more about life insurance.

How long to spend with whom?

Once a set of possible prospects has been identified, the salesperson must decide how much time to spend on which prospects. A sales rep must qualify prospects to see if they deserve more effort. The salesperson usually makes these decisions by weighing the potential sales volume as well as the likelihood of a sale. This requires judgment. But well-organized salespeople usually develop some system because they have too many prospects. They can't wine and dine all of them.[15]

Some firms provide their reps with personal computers—and specially developed computer programs—to help with this process. Most of them use some grading scheme. A sales rep might estimate how much each prospect is likely to purchase and the probability of getting the business, given the competition. The computer then combines this information and grades each prospect. Attractive accounts may be labeled A—and the salesperson may plan to call on them weekly until the sale is made or they are placed in a lower category. B customers might offer somewhat lower potential—and be called on monthly. C accounts might be called on only once a year—unless they happen to contact the salesperson. And D accounts might be ignored—unless the customer takes the initiative.[16]

Three kinds of sales presentations may be useful

Once a promising prospect is located, it's necessary to make a **sales presentation**—a salesperson's effort to make a sale. But someone has to plan what kind of sales presentation to make. This is a strategy decision. The kind of presentation should be set before the sales rep goes prospecting. And in situations where the customer comes to the salesperson—in a retail store, for instance—planners have to make sure that prospects are brought together with salespeople.

A marketing manager can choose two basically different approaches to making sales presentations: the prepared approach or the consultative selling approach. Another approach—the selling formula approach—is a combination of the two. Each of these has its place.

The prepared sales presentation

The **prepared sales presentation** approach uses a memorized presentation that is not adapted to each individual customer. A prepared (canned) presentation builds on the stimulus-response ideas discussed in Chapter 7. This model says that a customer faced with a particular stimulus will give the desired response—in this case, a yes answer to the salesperson's prepared statement, which includes a **close**, the salesperson's request for an order.

If one trial close doesn't work, the sales rep tries another prepared presentation—and attempts another closing. This can go on for some time—until the salesperson runs out of material or the customer either buys or decides to leave. Exhibit 16–5 shows the relative participation of the salesperson and customer in the prepared approach. Note that the salesperson does most of the talking.

In modern selling, firms commonly use the canned approach when the prospective sale is low in value and only a short presentation is practical. It's also sensible when salespeople aren't very skilled. The company can control what they say—and in what order. For example, a sales rep for *Time* magazine can call a prospect—perhaps a person whose subscription is about to run out—and basically read the prepared presentation. The caller needs little training or ability.

But a canned approach has a weakness. It treats all potential customers alike. It may work for some and not for others—and the salespeople probably won't know why or learn from experience. A prepared approach may be suitable for simple order taking, but it is no longer considered good selling for complicated situations.

Consultative selling—builds on the marketing concept

The **consultative selling approach** involves developing a good understanding of the individual customer's needs before trying to close the sale. This name is used because the salesperson is almost acting as a consultant to help identify and solve the customer's problem. With this approach, the sales rep makes some general benefit statements to get the customer's attention and interest. Then the salesperson asks questions and *listens carefully* to understand the customer's needs. The customer does most of the talking at this stage. Once they agree on needs, the seller tries to show the customer how the product fills those needs—and to close the sale. This is a problem-solving approach—in which the customer and salesperson work together to satisfy the customer's needs. That's why it's sometimes called the need-satisfaction approach. Exhibit 16–6 shows the participation of the customer and the salesperson during such a sales presentation.

The consultative selling approach is most useful if there are many subtle differences among the customers in one target market. In the extreme, each customer may be thought of as a separate target market—with the salesperson trying to adapt to each one's needs and attitudes. This kind of selling takes more skill—and time. The salesperson must be able to analyze what motivates a

Exhibit 16–5
Prepared Approach to
Sales Presentation

Exhibit 16–6
Consultative Selling Approach
to Sales Presentation

Exhibit 16–7
Selling Formula Approach
to Sales Presentation

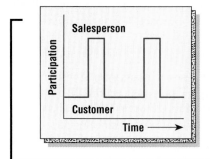

particular customer—and show how the company's offering would help the customer satisfy those needs.

Selling formula approach—some of both

The **selling formula approach** starts with a prepared presentation outline, much like the prepared approach, and leads the customer through some logical steps to a final close. The prepared steps are logical because we assume that we know something about the target customer's needs and attitudes.

Exhibit 16–7 shows the selling formula approach. The salesperson does most of the talking at the beginning of the presentation—to communicate key points early. This part of the presentation may even have been prepared as part of the marketing strategy. As the sales presentation moves along, however, the salesperson brings the customer into the discussion to help clarify just what needs this customer has. The salesperson's job is to discover the needs of a particular customer to know how to proceed. Once it is clear what kind of customer this is, the salesperson comes back to show how the product satisfies this specific customer's needs—and to close the sale.

This approach can be useful for both order-getting and order-taking situations—where potential customers are similar and firms must use relatively untrained salespeople. Some office equipment and computer producers use this approach. They know the kinds of situations their salespeople meet—and roughly what they want them to say. Using this approach speeds training and makes the sales force productive sooner. Exhibit 16–8 shows the sales process as London Life sees it.

AIDA helps plan sales presentations

AIDA—Attention, Interest, Desire, Action—each sales presentation, except for some very simple canned types, follows this AIDA sequence. The how-to-do-it might even be set as part of the marketing strategy. The time a sales rep spends on each of the steps might vary depending on the situation and the selling approach being used. But it is still necessary to begin a presentation by getting the prospect's *attention,* and hopefully, to move the customer to *action* through a close.[17]

Each sales manager—and salesperson—needs to think about this sequence in deciding what sales approach to use and in evaluating a possible presentation. Does the presentation get the prospect's attention quickly? Will the presentation be interesting? Will the benefits be clear so that the prospect is moved to buy the product? Does the presentation consider likely objections—and anticipate problems—so the sales rep can act to close the sale when the time is right? These

Exhibit 16—8   The London Life Sales Process (general sales division)

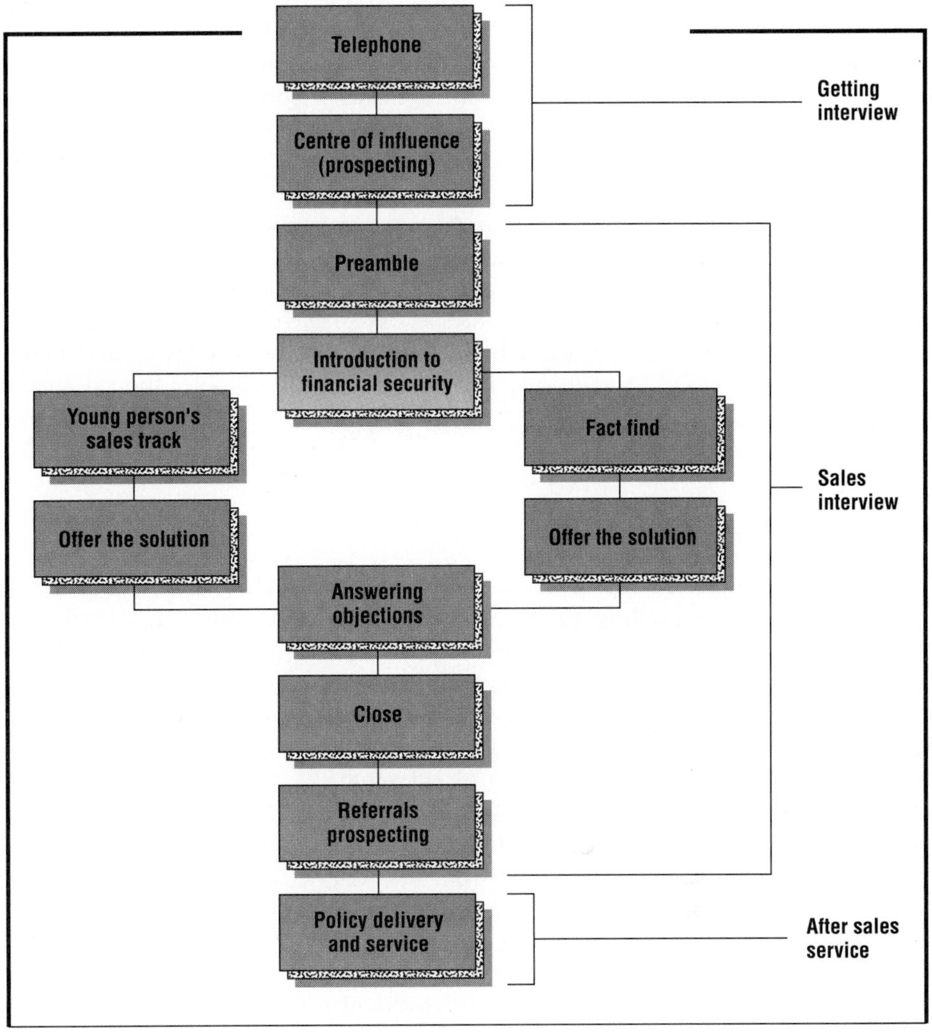

may seem like simple things. But too frequently they aren't done at all—and a sale is lost.

? **Ethical issues may arise**

As in every other area of marketing communications, ethical issues arise in the personal selling area. The most basic issue, plain and simple, is whether a salesperson's presentation is honest and truthful. But addressing that issue is a no-brainer. No company is served well by a salesperson who lies or manipulates customers to get their business.

On the other hand, most sales reps sooner or later face a sales situation in which they must make more difficult ethical decisions about how to balance company interests, customer interests, and personal interests. Conflicts are less likely to arise if the firm's marketing mix really meets the needs of its target market. Then, the salesperson is arranging a happy marriage. Similarly, they are less likely to arise when the firm has a longer-term relationship with the customer.

By contrast, they are more likely when the sales rep's personal outcomes (such as commission income) or the selling firm's profits hinge on making sales to customers whose needs are only partially met by the firm's offering. But how close must the fit be between the firm's products and the customer's needs before it is appropriate for the salesperson to push for a sale?

Ideally, companies can avoid the whole problem by supporting their salespeople with a marketing mix that really offers target customers unique benefits. However, marketing managers and salespeople alike should recognize that the ideal may not exist in every sales call. Top executives, marketing managers, and sales managers set the tone for the ethical climate in which a salesperson operates. If they set impossible goals or project a "do-what-you-need-to-do" attitude, a desperate salesperson may yield to the pressure of the moment. When a firm clearly advocates ethical selling behavior and makes it clear that manipulative selling techniques are not acceptable, the salesperson is not left trying to swim "against the flow."[18]

CONCLUSION

In this chapter, we discussed the importance and nature of personal selling. Selling is much more than just getting rid of the product. In fact, a salesperson who is not given strategy guidelines may have to become the strategy planner for the market he or she serves. Ideally, however, the sales manager and marketing manager work together to set some strategy guidelines: the kind and number of salespersons needed, the kind of sales presentation desired, and selection, training, and motivation approaches.

We discussed the three basic sales tasks: (1) order getting, (2) order taking, and (3) supporting. Most sales jobs combine at least two of these three tasks. Once a firm specifies the important tasks, it can decide on the structure of its sales organization and the number of salespeople it needs. The nature of the job—and the level and method of compensation—also depend on the blend of these tasks. Firms should develop a job description for each sales job. This, in turn, provides guidelines for selecting, training, and compensating salespeople.

Once the marketing manager agrees to the basic plan and sets the budget, the sales manager must implement the plan—including directing and controlling the sales force. This includes assigning sales territories and controlling performance. You can see that the sales manager has more to do than jet around the country sipping martinis and entertaining customers. A sales manager is deeply involved with the basic management tasks of planning and control—as well as ongoing implementation of the personal selling effort.

We also reviewed some basic selling techniques and identified three kinds of sales presentations. Each has its place—but the consultative selling approach seems best for higher-level sales jobs. In these kinds of jobs, personal selling is achieving a new, professional status because of the competence and level of personal responsibility required of the salesperson. The day of the old-time glad-hander is passing in favor of the specialist who is creative, industrious, persuasive, knowledgeable, highly trained—and therefore able to help the buyer. This type of salesperson always has been—and probably always will be—in short supply. And the demand for high-level salespeople is growing.

QUESTIONS AND PROBLEMS

1. What strategy decisions are needed in the personal selling area? Why should the marketing manager make these strategy decisions?

2. What kind of salesperson (or what blend of the basic sales tasks) is required to sell the following products? If there are several selling jobs in the

channel for each product, indicate the kinds of salespeople required. Specify any assumptions necessary to give definite answers.

a. Laundry detergent.
b. Costume jewelry.
c. Office furniture.
d. Men's underwear.
e. Mattresses.
f. Corn.
g. Life insurance.

3. Distinguish among the jobs of producers', wholesalers', and retailers' order-getting salespeople. If one order getter is needed, must all the salespeople in a channel be order getters? Illustrate.

4. Discuss the role of the manufacturers' agent in a marketing manager's promotion plans. What kind of salesperson is a manufacturers' agent? What type of compensation plan is used for a manufacturers' agent?

5. Discuss the future of the specialty shop if producers place greater emphasis on mass selling because of the inadequacy of retail order taking.

6. Compare and contrast missionary salespeople and technical specialists.

7. How would a straight commission plan provide flexibility in the sale of a line of women's clothing products that continually vary in profitability?

8. Explain how a compensation plan could be developed to provide incentives for experienced salespeople and yet make some provision for trainees who have not yet learned the job.

9. Cite an actual local example of each of the three kinds of sales presentations discussed in the chapter. Explain for each situation whether a different type of presentation would have been better.

10. Describe a consultative selling sales presentation that you experienced recently. How could it have been improved by fuller use of the AIDA framework?

11. How would our economy operate if personal salespeople were outlawed? Could the economy work? If so, how? If not, what is the minimum personal selling effort necessary? Could this minimum personal selling effort be controlled by law?

SUGGESTED CASES

21. Bemis Cable, Inc.

28. Cutters, Inc.

Advertising

When You Finish This Chapter, You Should

❶
Understand why a marketing manager sets specific objectives to guide the advertising effort.

❷
Understand when the various kinds of advertising are needed.

❸
Understand how to choose the "best" medium.

❹
Understand how to plan the "best" message—that is, the copy thrust.

❺
Understand what advertising agencies do—and how they are paid.

❻
Understand how to advertise legally.

❼
Understand the important new terms (shown in blue).

When television viewers tuned into CTV recently to watch the romantic tribulations of the baby boomers in *When Harry Met Sally*, they got more than they bargained for. General Motors of Canada Ltd. bought the entire 20 minutes of commercial time for a total-immersion Canadian unveiling of its new Saturn car. "We felt it was the sort of show that would attract the people we're aiming for," says Don Johnston, marketing manager for GM's automobile division. "And the product is so important, we decided to buy it all."

With Saturn, GM is taking a $4 billion gamble that it can win over auto buyers who normally wouldn't even look at a domestic car. These "import intenders," as they're called, are the battleground in the war for market share between the domestic and foreign manufacturers. So far, the foreigners are winning; GM's Canadian market share has skidded to 34 percent from 41 percent in the early 1980s.

To win over hardened import intenders, who view Detroit as the birthplace of poor quality clunkers, GM figured it had to start anew. It created a separate company, Saturn Corp., which built its assembly plant in Spring Hill, Tennessee. The ad campaign emphasizes the theme of newness—"Saturn. A different kind of company. A different kind of car"—and comfortable, home-grown values, from Mary Waldrip, a schoolteacher from Pickle Lake, Ontario, endorsing the car's sensible mileage, to the small boy who moved to Tennessee with his father for the Saturn project.

Before being broadcast, the ads were shown to test groups of people in Montreal, Toronto, and Vancouver. Most people in English Canada had no problem with them, but in Quebec they were considered too American. French Canadians were found to be the most hardened import intenders, so Cossette Communication-Marketing produced ads touting Saturn's world-class features such as dent-resistant thermoplastic body panels in order to appeal to them.[1]

ADVERTISING PLANNING AND MARKETING STRATEGY DECISIONS

Advertising makes widespread distribution possible. Although a marketing manager might prefer to use personal selling, it can be expensive on a per contact or per sale basis. Advertising is a way around this problem. Although not as flexible as personal selling, it can reach large numbers of potential customers at the same time. It can inform and persuade customers—and help position a firm's marketing mix as the one that meets customers' needs. Today, most promotion blends contain advertising and publicity as well as personal selling and sales promotion.

Advertising contacts vary in cost and results. This means marketing managers—and the advertising managers who work with them—have important strategy decisions to make. As the Saturn case illustrates, they must decide (1) who their target audience is, (2) what kind of advertising to use, (3) how to reach customers (via which types of media), (4) what to say to them (the copy thrust), and (5) who will do the work—the firm's own advertising department or outside agencies. See Exhibit 17–1. We'll talk about these decisions in this chapter. We'll also consider how to measure advertising effectiveness—and legal limits on advertising—in an increasingly competitive environment.

The basic strategy planning decisions for advertising are the same regardless of where in the world the target market is located. From the outset, however, remember that the choices available to a marketing manager within each of the decision areas may vary dramatically from one country to another. The target audience may be illiterate—making print ads useless. Commercial television may

Exhibit 17-1   Strategy Planning for Advertising

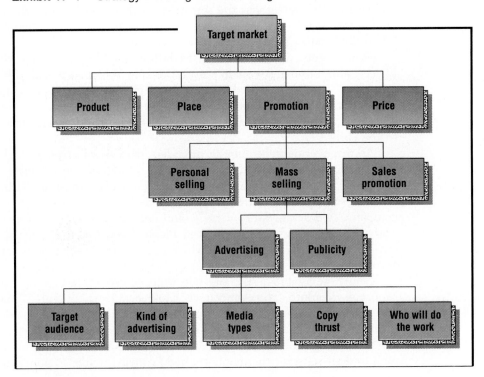

not be available. If it is, governments may place severe limits on the type of advertising permitted or when ads can be shown. Radio broadcasts in a market area may not be in the target market's language. Cultural, social, and behavioral influences may limit what type of advertising messages can be communicated. Advertising agencies ignorant of a nation's unique advertising environment may be less than helpful. Throughout this chapter, we'll consider a number of these issues, but we'll focus on the array of choices available in Canada and other advanced, market-directed economies.[2]

ADVERTISING OBJECTIVES ARE A STRATEGY DECISION

Advertising objectives must be specific

Every ad and every advertising campaign should have clearly defined objectives. These should grow out of the firm's overall marketing strategy—and the jobs assigned to advertising. It isn't enough for the marketing manager to say, "Promote the product." The marketing manager must decide exactly what advertising should do.

Advertising objectives should be more specific than personal selling objectives. One of the advantages of personal selling is that salespeople can shift their presentations to meet customers' needs. Each ad, however, is a specific communication. It must be effective not just for one customer but for thousands—or millions—of them.

The marketing manager sets the overall direction

The marketing manager might give the advertising manager one or more of the following specific objectives—along with the budget to accomplish them:

1. Help introduce new products to specific target markets.
2. Help position the firm's brand or marketing mix by informing and persuading target customers or middlemen about its benefits.

Producers of consumer products often rely on mass selling to inform customers about new products—and to persuade them about the benefits of established products.

3. Help obtain desirable outlets and tell customers where they can buy a product.

4. Provide ongoing contact with target customers—even when a salesperson isn't available.

5. Prepare the way for salespeople by presenting the company's name and the merits of its products.

6. Get immediate buying action.

7. Help buyers confirm their purchase decisions.

If you want half the market, say so!

The objectives listed above are not as specific as they could be. If a marketing manager really wants specific results, they should be clearly stated. A general objective—"To help expand market share"—could be rephrased more specifically—"To increase shelf space in our cooperating retail outlets by 25 percent during the next three months."

Once the marketing manager sets the overall objectives, the advertising manager should set specific objectives for each ad—as well as a whole advertising campaign. Without specific objectives, the creative people who develop individual ads may pursue their own objectives. They might set some vague objective—like promote the product—and then create ads that win advertising industry artistic awards but fail to achieve the desired results.

Objectives guide implementation, too

The specific objectives obviously affect implementation. Advertising that might be right for building a good image among opinion leaders might be all wrong for getting typical customers into the retailers' stores. And, as Exhibit 17–2 shows, the type of advertising that achieves objectives for one stage of the adoption process may be off target for another. For example, most advertising for cameras in North America, Germany, and Japan focuses on foolproof pictures or state-of-the-art design because most consumers in these countries already own *some* camera. In Africa, where less than 20 percent of the population owns a camera, ads must sell the whole concept of picture taking.

With new products, most of the target market may have to be brought through the early stages of the adoption process. The advertising manager may use teaser campaigns designed to attract attention and arouse curiosity, along with informative ads. For more established products, advertising's job might be to build brand preference as well as help purchasers confirm their decisions.

Exhibit 17–2   How Different Types of Advertising Are Used over Adoption Process Stages

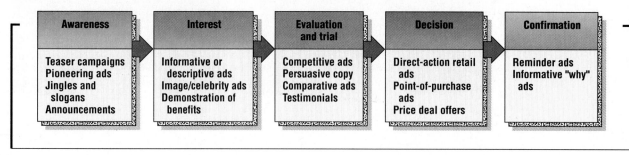

OBJECTIVES DETERMINE THE KINDS OF ADVERTISING NEEDED

The advertising objectives largely determine which of two basic types of advertising to use—product or institutional.

Product advertising tries to sell a product. It may be aimed at final users or channel members.

Institutional advertising tries to promote an organization's image, reputation, or ideas—rather than a specific product. Its basic objective is to develop goodwill or improve an organization's relations with various groups—not only customers but also current and prospective channel members, suppliers, shareholders, employees, and the general public. Dow, for example, appeals to college grads and other potential employees with image-oriented ads that proclaim "Dow lets you do great things." The British government, one of the top 50 advertisers in the world, uses institutional advertising to promote England as a place to do business.

Product advertising—know us, like us, remember us

Product advertising falls into three categories: pioneering, competitive, and reminder advertising.

Pioneering advertising—builds primary demand

Pioneering advertising tries to develop primary demand for a product category rather than demand for a specific brand. Pioneering advertising is usually done in the early stages of the product life cycle; it informs potential customers about the new product and helps turn them into adopters. When Merrell Dow Pharmaceutical introduced a prescription drug to help smokers break the habit, it did pioneering advertising to inform both doctors and smokers about its breakthrough. The ad didn't even mention the name of the drug. Instead, it informed smokers who wanted to quit that doctors could now help them overcome their

---

Real uses pioneering ads to build primary demand for butter. Plugra uses competitive advertising to develop selective demand for the Plugra brand.

nicotine dependence. Later, as other firms put similar drugs on the market, Merrell Dow turned to competitive advertising.

Competitive advertising—emphasizes selective demand

Competitive advertising tries to develop selective demand for a specific brand. A firm is forced into competitive advertising as the product life cycle moves along—to hold its own against competitors. The United Fruit Company gave up a 20-year pioneering effort to promote bananas in favor of promoting its own Chiquita brand. The reason was simple. While United Fruit was single-handedly promoting bananas, it slowly lost market share to competitors. It launched its competitive advertising campaign to avoid further losses.

Competitive advertising may be either direct or indirect. The **direct type** aims for immediate buying action. The **indirect type** points out product advantages to affect future buying decisions.

Most of Air Canada's advertising is of the competitive variety. Much of it tries for immediate sales—so the ads are the direct type, with prices, timetables, and phone numbers to call for reservations. Some of its ads are the indirect type. They focus on the quality of service and number of cities served—and suggest you mention Air Canada the next time you talk to your travel agent.

Comparative advertising is even rougher. **Comparative advertising** means making specific brand comparisons—using actual product names. A recent

---

The copy thrust for Columbia Sportswear Company shows that the rough and durable jeans are patterned after the rough and demanding company chair.

comparative ad shows a large package of Tyco plastic toy blocks next to a smaller package of very similar Lego blocks with the headline "More or Less." The copy for the Tyco ad goes on to say, "We've priced our new 600-piece Giant Storage Bucket to sell for the same as the Lego 359-piece bucket . . . so which would you choose . . . more or less?" In the same vein, a magazine ad for Ford trucks belittles Chevy trucks—by name—as more expensive to buy and worth less later.

Many countries forbid comparative advertising, but that situation is changing. For example, Japan banned comparative advertising until fairly recently, when the restrictions were relaxed. Japan's move followed an earlier change in the United States. The Federal Trade Commission decided to encourage comparative ads, after banning them for years, because it thought they would increase competition and provide consumers with more useful information. But this approach led to legal as well as ethical problems, and some advertisers and their agencies now back away from comparative advertising even in countries where it is allowed. Marketing Demo 17–1 describes the Canadian guidelines for comparative advertising.

In Canada, superiority claims are supposed to be supported by research evidence—but the guidelines aren't clear. Some firms just keep running tests until they get the results they want. Others talk about minor differences that don't reflect a product's overall benefits. Some comparative ads leave consumers confused—or even angry if the product they're using is criticized. And, in at least one case, comparative ads benefitted the competitive product (Tylenol) more than the advertisers' products (Datril, Anacin, and Bayer aspirin).[3]

Tyco's comparative ad makes specific product comparisons with Lego, a competitor that sells a very similar toy.

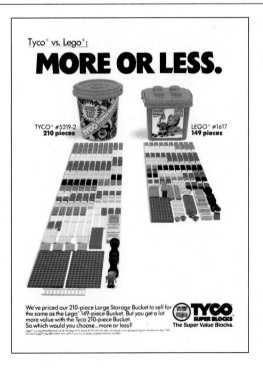

MARKETING DEMO 17–1
Canadian Guidelines for Comparative Advertising

I n 1982, in response to the increasing prevalence of comparative advertising, government, industry, consumer groups, and the Canadian Advertising Foundation developed Guidelines for the Use of Comparative Advertising in Food Commercials. They also developed complementary guidelines for using research and survey data.

"Comparative advertising was becoming a process of denigration rather than promotion," says Bob Oliver, who heads the Advertising Standards Council (ASC).

The guidelines, which are administered by ASC, define comparative advertising as: *A comparison between two or more products or services (for example, concerning product or service characteristics, value, performance, consumer preference, market share, sales origin or availability) where the competitor's name and/or brand are known to the consumer or can be readily identified by cues in the advertisement.*

The guidelines are designed to ensure that comparisons are fair and factual and based on adequate and proper tests. All comparative claims must be supportable.

If CCAC receives a comparative script, it may ask the advertiser for substantiation of claims. When research studies—for example, a taste test—are involved, CCAC evaluates the research to ensure validity of the claims.

Article 2 of the guidelines specifies that competitors *must not be unfairly discredited or unjustly disparaged by the specific or overall impression created by the advertisement.*

If CCAC suspects that a script may be disparaging, it asks the advertiser to take the script to ASC. That is what happened with this summer's "Taste Above All" Diet Pepsi commercial. ASC approved the script and sent it to Ottawa, which gave it final approval.

Siwicky at CCAC says between 10 and 20 cases a year are referred to ASC.

Source: "How to Play the Game by the Rules," *Marketing*, October 27, 1986, pp. 28, 31.

Comparative advertising may be a can of worms that some advertisers wish they hadn't opened. But comparative ads seem to attract attention. So some advertisers will probably continue using this approach—at least in countries that allow it.[4]

Reminder advertising—reinforces early promotion

Reminder advertising tries to keep the product's name before the public. It may be useful when the product has achieved brand preference or insistence—perhaps in the market maturity or sales decline stages. Here, the advertiser may use soft-sell ads that just mention or show the name—as a reminder. For many years, Michelin used competitive ads to emphasize the safety and durability of its tires. Now that the Michelin brand is more familiar in North America, the company uses more reminder ads.

Institutional advertising—remember our name

Institutional advertising usually focuses on the name and prestige of an organization or industry. It may seek to inform, persuade, or remind.

Large companies with several divisions sometimes use a persuading kind of institutional advertising to link the divisions in customers' minds. AT&T, for example, advertises the AT&T name—emphasizing the quality and research behind *all* AT&T products. Similarly, many Japanese firms emphasize institutional advertising, in part because they often use the company name as a brand name.

Michelin uses reminder advertising for its popular performance tires.

Companies sometimes rely on institutional advertising to present the company in a favorable light—perhaps to overcome image problems. Ads for an oil company, for example, might highlight its concern for the environment.

Some organizations use institutional advertising to advocate a specific cause or idea. Insurance companies and organizations like Mothers Against Drunk Driving, for example, use these advocacy ads to encourage people not to drink and drive.[5]

COORDINATING ADVERTISING EFFORTS

Vertical cooperation—advertising allowances, cooperative advertising

Sometimes, a producer knows that a promotion or advertising task must be carried out, but finds it can be done more effectively or more economically by someone farther along in the channel. Alternatively, a large retail chain may approach manufacturers with a catalogue or program—and tell them how much it will cost to participate. In either case, the producer may offer **advertising allowances**—price reductions to firms farther along in the channel to encourage them to advertise or otherwise promote the firm's products locally.

Cooperative advertising involves middlemen and producers sharing in the cost of ads. This helps middlemen compete in their local markets. It also helps the producer get more promotion for the advertising dollar because media usually give local advertisers lower rates than national or international firms. In addition, a retailer or wholesaler who is paying a share of the cost is more likely to follow through.

Coordination in the channel is another reason for cooperative advertising. One big, well-planned advertising effort is often better than many different—perhaps inconsistent—local efforts. Many franchise operations like the idea of communicating with one voice. KFC, for example, encourages its franchises to use a common advertising program. Before, many developed their own local ads—with themes like "Eight clucks for four bucks"—that didn't fit with the company's overall marketing strategy.

Producers often get this coordination—and reduce local middlemen costs—by providing a master of an ad on a videotape, cassette tape, or printed sheets. The middlemen add their identification before turning the advertisement over to local media.

Ethical concerns may arise

Ethical issues sometimes arise concerning advertising allowance programs. For example, a retailer may run one producer's ad to draw customers to the store but then sell them another brand. Is this unethical? Some producers think it is—that the retailer is intentionally misusing the money and switching customers to brands that pay the retailer a higher profit margin. A different view is that retailers are obligated to the producer to run the ad—but obligated to consumers to sell them what they want, no matter whose brand it may be. A producer can often avoid the problem with a strategy decision—by setting the allowance amount as a percent of the retailer's *actual purchases*. That way, a retailer who doesn't produce sales doesn't get the allowance.

Sometimes, a retailer takes advertising allowance money but doesn't run the ads at all. Some producers close their eyes to this problem because they don't know what to do about intense competition from other suppliers for the retailer's attention. But there are also legal and ethical problems with that response. Basically, the allowance may have become a disguised price concession that results in price discrimination. Some firms pull back from cooperative advertising to avoid these problems. Smart producers insist on proof that the advertising was really done.

Horizontal cooperation—promotes different firms

As we saw with Molly Maid and Moneysworth at the beginning of Chapter 15, two or more firms with complementary products may join together in a common advertising effort. Joint ads encourage travelers to stay at a Hyatt Hotel and handle the expenses with an American Express card. Retailers in the same shopping centre often share the costs of promotion efforts. They might buy full-page newspaper ads listing the individual stores or promoting sale days. Generally, the objective is the same as in vertical cooperation—to get more for the advertising dollar.[6]

CHOOSING THE BEST MEDIUM—HOW TO DELIVER THE MESSAGE

What is the best advertising medium? There is no simple answer to this question. Effectiveness depends on how well the medium fits with the rest of a marketing strategy—that is, it depends on (1) your promotion objectives, (2) what target markets you want to reach, (3) the funds available for advertising, and (4) the nature of the media—including whom they *reach*, with what *frequency*, with what *impact*, and at what *cost*. Exhibit 17–3 summarizes the major media in Canada.

Exhibit 17–4 shows some pros and cons of major kinds of media—and some typical costs. However, some of the advantages noted in this table may not apply in all markets. In less-developed nations, for example, newspapers may *not* be timely. Placing an ad may require a long lead time if only a limited number of pages are available for ads. Similarly, direct mail may not be a flexible choice in a country with a weak postal system or high rate of illiteracy.[7]

Exhibit 17–3   A Capsule View of Major Canadian Media

Television	40 television markets covered by 125 commercial television stations, most of which belong to 1 of 13 networks.
Radio	710 radio stations (377 AM and 333 FM).
Daily Newspapers	110 daily newspapers with an average daily paid circulation of 5.2 million. Gross circulation as a percentage of households is approximately 63%.
Consumer Magazines	Over 500 consumer magazines ranging in content from general editorial to special-interest categories (such as photography and music).
Business Publications	Listed in *Canadian Advertising Rates and Data* (CARD) with circulations of 20,000 plus.
Ethnic Press	120 publications covering 35 ethnic groups other than English and French.
Farm Publications	101 farm publications whose circulation ranges from 1,000 copies to large mass-appeal publications with over 200,000 circulation.
Community Newspapers	Approximately 1,139, with an average weekly circulation of 11.6 million.
Weekend Newspapers	Essentially a Quebec phenomenon; 11 such papers are published in French.
Religious Publications	24 publications listed under the religious category in CARD; they range in circulation from 1,300 to over 270,200.
University and School Publications	212 university, community college, alumni, and scholarly publications
Outdoor Advertising	Poster space is available in more than 400 Canadian municipalities.

Source: *The Canadian Media Directors' Council Media Digest*, 1992–93.

Specify promotion objectives

Before you can choose the best medium, you have to decide on your promotion objectives. If the objective is to increase interest and that requires demonstrating product benefits, TV may be the best alternative. If the objective is to inform—telling a long story with precise detail—and if pictures are needed, then print media, including magazines and newspapers—may be better. For example, Jockey switched its advertising to magazines from television when it decided to show the variety of colors, patterns, and styles of its men's briefs. Jockey felt that it was too hard to show this in a 30-second TV spot. Further, Jockey felt that there were problems with modeling men's underwear on television. However, Jockey might have stayed with TV if it had been targeting consumers in France or Brazil—where nudity in TV ads is common.[8]

Match your market with the media

To guarantee good media selection, the advertiser first must *clearly* specify its target market—a necessary step for all marketing strategy planning. Then the advertiser can choose media that are heard, read, or seen by those target customers.

The media available in a country may limit the choices. In less-developed nations, for example, radio is often the only way to reach a broad-based market of poor consumers who can't read or afford television.

In most cases, however, the major problem is to select media that effectively reach the target audience. Most of the major media use marketing research to

Exhibit 17–4   Relative Size, Cost, and Advantages and Disadvantages of Major Kinds of Media

Kinds of Media	Typical Cost	Advantages	Disadvantages
Newspaper	$4,887 for one page in the television tabloid, *Winnipeg Free Press*	Flexible Timely Local market	May be expensive Short life No "pass-along"
Television	$2,500 for a 30-second ad on CBC's western region stations	Offers sight, sound, and motion Good attention Wide reach	Expensive in total "Clutter" Short exposure Less selective audience
Direct Mail and Other Print	$170–$250 for 1,500 screened names in selected categories	Selected audience Flexible Can personalize	Relatively expensive per contact Junk mail—hard to retain attention
Radio	$165 for five 60-second ads on the morning show on CIFX/CHIQ-FM in Winnipeg	Wide reach Segmented audiences Inexpensive	Offers audio only Weak attention Many different rates Short exposure
Periodicals	$39,710 for one page, 4-color in *Chatelaine,* French and English	Very segmented audiences Credible source Good reproduction Long life Good "pass-along"	Inflexible Long lead times
Outdoor	$5,328 for four prime billboards showing four weeks, Regina/Moose Jaw	Flexible Repeat exposure Inexpensive	Mass market Very short exposure

Source: *Canadian Advertising Rates and Data,* December 1992, and the *Canadian Media Directors' Council Media Digest,* 1992–93.

develop profiles of the people who buy their publications—or live in their broadcasting area. Generally, media research focuses on demographic characteristics. But the research seldom includes information on the segmenting dimensions specific to the product-markets that are important to *each* different advertiser. Research also can't be definite about who actually reads each page or sees or hears each show.

In some countries, the problem is even worse because the media don't provide any information, or they provide audience profiles that make the media seem more attractive than it is.

Another problem is that the audience for media that *do* reach your target market may also include people who are *not* in the target group. But *you pay for the whole audience the media delivers*—including those who aren't potential customers. Levi's, for example, advertised on TV broadcasts of the Olympics because many of the viewers were 18- to 24-year-old jeans buyers. But they were only a portion of the total audience, and the size of the total audience determined the cost of the advertising time. Research showed that Levi's spent about twice as much reaching an actual jeans buyer with its Olympics message than it would have by advertising on programs more attractive to its specific target market.[9]

Because it is so difficult to evaluate alternative media, some media analysts focus on objective measures—such as cost per thousand of audience size or circulation. But advertisers preoccupied with keeping these costs down may ignore the relevant segmenting dimensions—and slip into mass marketing. The media buyer may look only at the relatively low cost of mass media when a more specialized medium might be a much better buy. Its audience might have more interest in the product—or more money to spend—or more willingness to buy. Gillette Co. buys advertising time on cable TV—especially MuchMusic—to increase its market penetration with teenagers and young adults, who are more willing to try new products.

Some media help zero in on specific target markets

Today, the major media direct more attention to reaching smaller, more defined target markets.

National print media may offer specialized editions. *Time* magazine, for example, offers not only several regional and metropolitan editions but also special editions for college students, educators, doctors, and business managers. Magazines like *Newsweek*, France's *Paris Match International*, and Germany's *Wirtschaftwoche* provide international editions.

Large metro newspapers often have several editions to cater to city and suburban areas. Where these outlying areas are not adequately covered, however, suburban newspapers are prospering—catering to the desire for local news.

Many magazines serve only special-interest groups—such as fishermen, soap opera fans, new parents, professional groups, and personal computer users. In fact, the most profitable magazines seem to be the ones aimed at clearly defined markets. Many specialty magazines also have international editions that help marketers reach consumers with similar interests in different parts of the world. *PC Magazine*, for example, offers European and Japanese editions.

There are trade magazines in many fields—such as chemical engineering, furniture retailing, electrical wholesaling, farming, and the defense market. *Canadian Advertising Rates and Data* provides a guide to the thousands of magazines now available in Canada. Similar guides exist in most other countries.

In addition to trade magazines bought at newsstands or through subscription, there's an important class of magazine in Canada called *controlled circulation*.[10] These magazines are distributed free to special-interest groups—the publisher gets all its revenue from advertising. The largest of these is *Homemaker's*. With its French counterpart, *Madame au Foyer*, it offers a combined circulation of over 1.9 million delivered to preselected homes in middle- and upper-income areas. In addition, some magazines are sent without charge to narrow, well-defined segments.

In comparing print with broadcast media, remember that circulation isn't directly comparable to, say, TV or radio audience figures. Readership figures should be used for such comparisons. A magazine or newspaper is usually read by more than one person (just as a TV program is often viewed by a family group). Thus, advertising in print media can have a much broader exposure than the circulation figures alone suggest.

Advertising managers always look for cost-effective media that will make their message stand out from the usual advertising clutter in mass media.

Radio has become a more specialized medium. Some stations cater to particular ethnic and racial groups—such as Hispanics, African-Americans, or French Canadians. Others aim at specific target markets with rock, country, or classical music. Stations that play golden oldies have been popping up around Canada to appeal to the baby-boomer crowd.

Cable TV channels—like MuchMusic, CBC Newsworld, TSN, and YTV—also target specific audiences. TSN, for example, has an audience heavily weighted toward affluent, male viewers. MuchMusic appeals most strongly to affluent young viewers. British Sky Broadcasting does a good job of reaching homemakers with young children.

Specialized media are small—but gaining

The *major* advertising media listed in Exhibit 17–4 attract the vast majority of advertising media budgets. But advertising specialists always look for cost-effective new media that will help advertisers reach their target markets. For example, one company successfully sells space for signs on bike racks that it places in front of 7-Eleven stores. In China, where major media are limited, companies like Kodak pay to put ads on bus shelters. "Wearable" advertising is also growing, as indicated in Marketing Demo 17–2. Hotels and auto rental companies buy space on advertising boards placed in the restrooms on airplanes.

In recent years, these specialized media gained in popularity. One reason is that they get the mass selling message to the target market close to the point of purchase. They also offer the advantage of making an advertiser's message stand out from the usual advertising clutter in the mass media. For example, Actmedia sells advertising space on little message boards that hang on shopping carts and

MARKETING DEMO 17–2   Sales Promotions Reach Out to Touch Tone

For decades, marketers had little choice but to use the post office to gather entries to large-scale promotional games, contests, and sweepstakes. Today, most contest entries continue to be made by mail. But for a fast-growing number of them, consumers can instead use a touch tone telephone to dial a number that connects them with an interactive computer system.

This technology is not merely a new way to handle an old task. It is changing the nature of the contests themselves, including their cost to consumers and sponsors, response rates, measurement of results, and public perceptions of them.

The first company to use a 900 line for interactive processing of contest entries in Canada was Ford Motor Co., Oakville, Ontario, which worked with CTV, Young and Rubicam, and Phoneworks to promote Ford's sponsorship of the Canadian Open golf tournament.

Daniel Melymuk, team leader at Phoneworks, the phone marketing and promotional services supplier responsible for the interactive service, says that 900 programs, along with the large number of 800 ones, share several strengths:

Ease of entry—many people are willing to enter a contest by phone but can't be bothered to fill out a form, find a stamp, and mail in an entry.

Instant gratification—entrants can find out immediately whether they have won rather than having to wait several weeks.

Consumer perception of greater fairness—a mail-in contest may attract 1,000 entries from a single professional contest player, but phone systems are harder to cheat.

Ability to offer a fun experience—the technology lets a sponsor make it fun to enter by including sound effects, music, and professional or celebrity voices.

Tracking capability—response rates can be measured daily, and changes made if they prove lower than expected. For instance, a client may learn in the early days of a contest that few entries are coming from a particular area, then discover that this is because point-of-sale materials have not been placed yet in stores in that area.

Higher response rates—Randee Rosenthal, team associate at Phoneworks for consumer packaged goods promotion and sweepstakes, says the rule of thumb is that the response rate will be twice that of a mail-in contest.

Melymuk offers a striking comparison to suggest how much potential for growth exists. Consider, he says, that usage of 800 and 900 lines accounts for 18 percent of all phone traffic in Canada. Then look at AT&T in the United States, where these lines generate half the entire business.

Source: Jim McElgrinn, "Sales Promotions Reach Out to Touch Tone," *Marketing,* November 30, 1992, p. 24.

---

shelves in grocery stores and drugstores. These ads reach target customers in the store, where 80 percent of the purchase decisions are made. Other advertising specialists offer special in-store radio and TV advertising and ads on grocery bags.[11]

There are too many specialized media to discuss in detail here. But all of them require the same type of strategy decisions as the more typical mass media.

"Must buys" may use up available funds

Selecting which media to use is still pretty much an art. The media buyer may start with a budgeted amount and try to buy the best blend to reach the target audience.

Some media are obvious "must buys"—such as *the* local newspaper for a retailer in a small or medium-sized town. Most firms serving local markets view a Yellow Pages listing as a must buy. These ads may even use up the available funds.

Most marketing managers serving local markets view Yellow Pages adverstising as a must buy—because it usually reaches customers when they're ready to buy.

If not, the media buyer must compare the relative advantages and disadvantages of alternatives—and select a media *blend* that helps achieve the promotion objectives, given the available budget.

For many firms, even national advertisers, the high cost of television may eliminate it from the media blend. In the United States, a 30-second commercial on a prime-time show averages about $125,000—the price goes up rapidly for shows that attract a large audience. A spot on the most popular series costs $200,000 or more, and the Super Bowl costs $800,000.[12]

Because TV advertising costs so much, many firms are moving away from television and experimenting with combinations of other media.

Integrated direct marketing is very targeted

The challenge of finding media that reach specific target customers has prompted many firms to turn to direct marketing—direct communication between a seller and an individual customer using a promotion method other than face-to-face personal selling.

Early efforts in the direct-marketing area focused on direct-mail advertising. A carefully selected mailing list—from the many available—allowed advertisers to reach a specific target audience with specific interests. And direct-mail advertising proved to be very effective when the objective was to get direct response by the customer.

Canada Post aggressively promotes direct marketing.

Now it's more than
direct-mail advertising

Achieving a measurable, direct response from specific target customers is still the heart of direct marketing. But the advertising medium is evolving to include not just mail but telephone, print, computer, broadcast, or even interactive video. The customer's response may be a purchase (or donation), a question, or a request for more information. More often than not, the customer responds by calling a toll-free telephone number. A knowledgeable salesperson talks with the customer on the phone and follows up. That might involve filling an order and having it shipped to the customer or putting an interested prospect in touch with a salesperson who makes a personal visit. The term *integrated direct marketing* developed because direct-response advertising is closely integrated with the other elements of the marketing mix. However, what distinguishes this general approach is that the marketer targets the advertising at specific individuals who respond directly. In Marketing Demo 17–2, consumers use a 900 line to enter a contest.

Target customer directly
with a database

Direct advertisers rely on a customer (or prospect) database to target specific individuals. The computerized database includes customers' names and addresses (or telephone numbers) as well as past purchases and other segmenting characteristics. Individuals (or segments) who respond to direct advertising are the target for additional ads. For example, a customer who buys lingerie from a catalogue once is a good candidate for a follow-up. The follow-up might extend to

---

MARKETING DEMO 17–3   Direct Marketers Drive into New Territory

D irect marketers have weathered the recession by carving out a new and lucrative niche for themselves as sellers of just about everything—including luxury cars. Today, direct marketing—like telemarketing—is being used to sell an increasing number of luxury goods and highly specialized services. A recent campaign by Lexus Motor Co. of Canada illustrated how, according to those who champion it, direct marketing has shed its junk-mail image.

Selling luxury cars through the mail would have been unheard of several years ago. But Lexus Canada general manager Wayne Jeffrey said a recent $1 million direct marketing campaign had been a "terrific success" at selling Toyota's top-of-the-line car.

He said direct marketing enabled Lexus to hone in on high-income professionals whose lifestyles seemed made for an upmarket automobile. The company was then able to plot the correlation between the number of respondents and the number of potential sales. "It became a very important part of our marketing campaign," he said. "I would say there's no

question it will form an important part of future campaigns as well."

The junk-mail juggernaut rolled on through the last decade, building up sophisticated data banks that enable advertisers to target highly specialized markets. John Gustavson, president and chief executive of the Canadian Direct Marketing Association, predicts that bigger and better things lie ahead. The secret, Gustavson says, is in the changing demographics of an aging population that finds itself with less time to shop by traditional methods.

"More people are turning to direct marketing because, unlike other advertising methods, you can measure how effective you've been by the number of responses you get. And because companies now use highly sophisticated databases, they reach people who have an interest in what they're selling. There's no point in trying, for example, to sell cars to people who don't drive."

Source: Adrian Bradley, "Direct Marketers Drive into New Territory," *The Financial Post*, October 7, 1991, p. 5.

---

other types of clothing. Greenpeace and the Cousteau Society send mail advertisements to people interested in environmental issues. They ask for donations or other types of support.

BMW and other car companies found that videotapes are a good way to provide consumers with a lot of information about a new model. However, it's too expensive to send tapes to everyone. To target the mailing, BMW first sends likely car buyers (high-income consumers who own a BMW or competing brand) personalized direct-mail ads that offer a free videotape. Interested consumers send back a return card. Then BMW sends the advertising tape and updates its database so a dealer will know to call the consumer. As indicated in Marketing Demo 17–3, Lexus Canada is another firm that has experienced success with direct mail advertising.

Direct advertising has become an important part of many marketing mixes, and many customers find it very convenient. But not everyone is enthusiastic. Some critics argue that thousands of acres of trees are consumed each week just to make the paper for junk mail that consumers don't want. Other critics worry about privacy issues related to how a direct-response database might be used, especially if it includes detailed information about a consumer's purchases. Most firms that use direct-response advertising are very sensitive to these concerns—and take steps to address them.[13]

PLANNING THE BEST MESSAGE—WHAT TO COMMUNICATE

Specifying the copy thrust

Once you decide *how* the messages will reach the target audience, you have to decide on the **copy thrust**—what the words and illustrations should communicate. This decision should flow from the promotion objectives—and the specific jobs assigned to advertising.

Carrying out the copy thrust is the job of advertising specialists. But the advertising manager and the marketing manager need to understand the process to be sure that the job is done well.

There are few tried-and-true rules in message construction, but behavioral research can help. Recall our discussion of the communication process and common frames of reference in Chapter 15. The concepts of needs, learning, and perception discussed in Chapter 7 apply here, too. We know, for example, that consumers have a fantastic ability to tune out messages or ideas that don't interest them. How much of the daily newspaper do you actually see as you page through it? We don't see everything the advertisers want us to see—or learn all they want us to learn. How can an advertiser be more effective?

Let AIDA help guide message planning

Basically, the overall marketing strategy should determine *what* the message should say. Then management judgment—perhaps aided by marketing research—can help decide how to encode this content so it will be decoded as intended.

As a guide to message planning, we can use the AIDA concept: getting Attention, holding Interest, arousing Desire, and obtaining Action.

Getting attention

Getting attention is an ad's first job. If that ad doesn't get attention, it doesn't matter how many people are exposed to it. Many readers leaf through magazines and newspapers without paying attention to any of the ads. Many listeners or viewers do chores or get snacks during radio and TV commercials. When watching a program on videotape, they may zap past the commercial with a flick of the fast-forward button.

Many attention-getting devices are available. A large headline, newsy or shocking statements, attractive models, babies, animals, special effects—anything different or eye-catching—may do the trick. However, the attention-getting device can't detract from—and hopefully should lead to—the next step, holding interest.

Holding interest

Holding interest is more difficult. A humorous ad, an unusual video effect, or a clever photo may get your attention—but once you've seen it, then what? You may pause to appreciate it, but if there is no relation between what got your attention and the marketing mix, you'll move on.

The behavioral sciences give advertisers some insight about how to hold interest. The tone and language of the ad must fit with the experiences and attitudes of the target customers—and their reference groups. As a result, many advertisers develop ads that relate to specific emotions. They hope that the good feeling about the ad (and the whole marketing mix) will stick—even if the specific details of the copy thrust are forgotten.

To hold interest, informative ads need to speak the target customer's language. Persuasive ads must provide evidence that convinces the customer. Celebrity endorsements may help. TV ads often demonstrate a product's benefits. Layouts for print ads should look right to the customer. Print illustrations and

copy should be arranged to encourage the eye to move smoothly through the ad—perhaps from a headline that starts in the upper left-hand corner to the illustration or body copy in the middle and finally to the company or brand name ("signature") at the lower right-hand corner. If all of the elements of the ad work together as a whole, they will help to hold interest and build recall.[14]

Arousing desire

Arousing desire to own or use a particular product is one of an ad's most difficult jobs. The advertiser must communicate with the customer. To do this effectively, the advertiser must understand how target customers think, behave, and make decisions. Then the ad must convince customers that the product can meet their needs. Testimonials may persuade a consumer that other people—with similar needs—have purchased the product and liked it. Product comparisons may highlight the advantages of a particular brand.

Some experts feel that an ad should focus on one *unique selling proposition* that aims at an important unsatisfied need. They discourage the typical approach of trying to tell the whole story in a single ad. Telling the whole story is the job of the whole promotion blend—not one ad.

If consumers see many different competing brands as essentially the same, focusing on a unique selling proposition may be particularly important. This can help set the brand apart—and position it as especially effective in meeting the needs of the target market. For example, Wrigley developed a series of ads targeted at smokers—suggesting that Wrigley's gum is a good substitute when smoking is not permitted. However, focusing on a unique selling proposition makes the most sense when a brand really does have a comparative advantage on an *important* benefit. That reduces the likelihood of competitors imitating the same idea.

An ad may also have the objective—especially during the market growth and market maturity stages—of supplying words customers can use to rationalize their desire to buy. Although products may satisfy certain emotional needs, many consumers find it necessary to justify their purchases on some economic or rational basis. Snickers candy bar ads help ease the guilt of calorie-conscious snackers by assuring them that "Snickers satisfies you when you need an afternoon energy break."

Obtaining action

Getting action is the final requirement—and not an easy one. From communication research, we now know that prospective customers must be lead beyond considering how the product *might* fit into their lives—to actually trying it or letting the company's sales rep come in and demonstrate it.

To communicate more effectively, the ads might emphasize strongly felt customer needs. Careful research on attitudes in the target market may help uncover such strongly felt *unsatisfied* needs.

Appealing to these needs can get more action—and also provide the kind of information buyers need to confirm their decisions. Postpurchase dissonance may set in—and obtaining confirmation may be one of the important advertising objectives. Some customers seem to read more advertising *after* a purchase than before. The ad may reassure them about the correctness of their decision—and also supply the words they use to tell others about the product.

Can global messages work?

During the 1980s, many international consumer products firms tried to use one global advertising message all around the world. Of course, they translated the message or made other minor adjustments—but the focus was one global copy thrust. Some did it because it looked like it would save the cost of developing different ads for different countries. Others did it because they felt their customers' basic needs were the same, even if they lived in different countries. Some just did it because it was fashionable to "go global."

This approach worked for some firms. Coca-Cola and Gillette, for example, feel that the needs their products serve are very similar for all consumers. They focus on the similarities among consumers who make up their target market rather than the differences. However, many firms who used this approach experienced terrible results. They may have saved money by developing fewer ads, but they lost sales because they did not develop advertising messages—and whole marketing mixes—aimed at specific target markets. They just tried to appeal to a global mass market.

Combining smaller market segments into a single, large target market makes sense if the different segments can be served with a single marketing mix. But when that is not the case, the marketing manager should treat them as different target markets—and develop different marketing mixes for each target.[15]

ADVERTISING AGENCIES OFTEN DO THE WORK

An advertising manager manages a company's advertising effort. Many advertising managers—especially those working for large retailers—have their own advertising departments that plan specific advertising campaigns and carry out the details. Others turn over much of the advertising work to specialists—the advertising agencies.

Ad agencies are specialists

Advertising agencies are specialists in planning and handling mass selling details for advertisers. Agencies play a useful role—because they are independent of the advertiser and have an outside viewpoint. They bring experience to an individual client's problems because they work for many other clients. Further, as specialists they can often do the job more economically than a company's own department.

Some full-service agencies handle any activities related to advertising. They may even handle overall marketing strategy planning—as well as marketing research, product and package development, and sales promotion. Some agencies make good marketing partners—and almost assume the role of the firm's marketing department.

Some agencies don't offer a full line of services. *Media buying services* specialize in selecting media to fit a firm's marketing strategy. They are used when a firm wants to schedule a number of ads—perhaps in different media—and needs help finding the blend that will deliver what it needs at the lowest cost. Similarly, creative specialists just create ads. These agencies handle the artistic elements of advertising but leave media planning, research, and related services to others.

The biggest agencies handle much of the advertising

The vast majority of advertising agencies are small—with 10 or fewer employees. But the largest agencies account for most of the billings.

Recently, some big agencies merged—creating mega-agencies with worldwide networks. Exhibit 17–5 shows a list of 10 of the largest Canadian agencies and examples of some of the products they advertise. Almost all of these firms are owned at least in part by the international mega-agencies. The move toward international marketing is a key reason behind such mergers.

Before the mergers, marketers in one country often had difficulty finding a capable, full-service agency in the country where they wanted to advertise. The mergers combined the strengths of the individual agencies. The mega-agency can offer varied services—wherever in the world a marketing manager needs them. This may be especially important for managers in large corporations—like Toyota, Renault, Unilever, NEC, Phillips, Procter & Gamble, Nestlé, and Coca-Cola—that advertise worldwide.[16]

In spite of the growth of these very large agencies, smaller agencies will continue to play an important role. The really big agencies are less interested in smaller accounts. Smaller agencies will continue to appeal to customers who want more personal attention.

It's easy to fire an ad agency

One of the advantages of using an ad agency is that the advertiser is usually free to cancel the arrangement at any time. This gives the advertiser extreme flexibility. Some companies even use their advertising agency as a scapegoat. Whenever anything goes wrong, they blame the agency—and shop around for a new one. While agency-swapping is common, in some countries, like Brazil, it's tougher for a firm to dump its agency.

Are they paid too much?

Traditionally, most advertising agencies are paid a commission of about 15 percent on media and production costs. This arrangement evolved because media usually have two prices: one for national advertisers and a lower rate for local advertisers, such as local retailers. The advertising agency gets a 15 percent commission on national rates—but not on local rates. This makes it worthwhile for producers and national middlemen to use agencies. National advertisers have to pay the full media rate anyway, so it makes sense to let the agency experts do the work—and earn their commission. Local retailers—allowed the lower media rate—seldom use agencies. Even large retail chains may do most of their advertising in local markets where they have stores; Toys "R" Us, for example, uses local newspapers for most of its ads.

There is growing resistance to the idea of paying agencies the same way regardless of the work performed or *the results achieved*. The commission approach also makes it hard for agencies to be completely objective about inexpensive media—or promotion campaigns that use little space or time. Much of the

Exhibit 17–5 Canada's Top 10 Advertising Agencies and Their Clients, 1992

1	McKim Baker Lovick/BBDO (–)*	Apple Canada, B.C. Tel, Bell Canada, Black & Decker, CP Hotels & Resorts, Campbell Soup, Canadian Imperial Bank of Commerce, Chrysler, Church & Dwight, Dairy Queen, Dow Brands, Federal Express, Hostess Foods, Kraft General Foods, Ontario Milk Marketing Board, Polaroid Canada, Tele-Direct (Yellow Pages), Wrigley Canada.	46,000
2	Young & Rubicam, Ltd. (3)	American Express Canada Inc., Bombardier Inc., Cadbury Beverages Canada Inc., Colgate-Palmolive, Ford Motor Company of Canada Ltd., Ford Mercury Dealer Association, Hostess Frito-Lay, Kentucky Fried Chicken, Kodak Canada Inc., Kraft General Foods Canada, Labatt Breweries of Canada, Whitehall-Robins Inc.	39,962
3	Cossette Communication-Marketing (1)	Bell Canada, Bell Mobility, Bank of Bermuda, Culinar, Cosmair, Canada Deposit Insurance, Egg Marketing Board, enRoute, Esso, General Motors, Gilbey's, Hydro-Québec, ICBC, L & F Canada, McDonald's Restaurants, New Zealand Tourism Office, Novotel, Provigo, Royal Canadian Mint, Saturn-SAAB-Isuzu, SEPAQ-Mont Ste-Anne, Schering, Scotia Bank, Sports Experts, Stentor, The Manufacturers, Tourisme Quebéc, Ville de Montréal, Whistler.	37,111
4	MacLaren:Lintas Inc. (2)	Coca-Cola, General Motors, Hershey Foods, Molson Breweries, Nestlé, Royal Bank, Unilever.	30,572
5	Ogilvy & Mather (Canada) Ltd. (6)	AT&T, American Express, Campbell Soup, Canadian Airlines, Chesebrough-Pond's, Duracell, Financial Post, First Calgary Financial, Glaxo, Hoffmann-LaRoche, IKEA, Kimberly-Clark, Kraft General Foods, Laura Secord, Lever Brothers, Mark's Work Wearhouse, Midas, Monarch Fine Foods, Nestlé Confectionery, Norwich Union, Nutrasweet, Quaker Oats, Robin Hood Multifoods, Rothmans, Pepperidge Farm, Seagram, Shell, SmithKline Beecham, Timex, TransAlta Utilities, Unilever, Unitel.	24,406
6	J. Walter Thompson Company Ltd. (8)	Alcan, B.C. Packers, B.C. Rail, Big V, Canadair, Chesebrough-Pond's, De Beers, Hammerson Properties Inc., Kellogg's, Kodak, Kraft, Lever Brothers, Mattel, Northern Telecom, Peerless Carpet, Pepsi, Scott Paper, Speedy Muffler King, T.J. Lipton, Teledyne, United Distillers, Warner-Lambert, Workers' Compensation Board of B.C.	22,395
7	Grey Advertising Ltd. (7)	B.C. Hydro, Canon, Hoechst, Kraft General Foods, Parke Davis, Procter & Gamble, Schering, SmithKline Beecham, Stella Pharmaceuticals, Toronto-Dominion Bank, Valdi Foods, Warner Bros., Wine Institute of California.	22,087
8	McCann-Erickson Advertising of Canada Ltd. (10)	American Express, Coca-Cola Ltd., Coca-Cola Foods, Columbia Tri-Star Films, Gillette, Goodyear Canada, Investors Group, J.M. Schneider, Johnson & Johnson, Mennen, Monarch Fine Foods/Unilever, Nabisco Brands, Nestlé, Robin Hood Multifoods, WD-40.	21,545
9	FCB/Ronalds-Reynolds Ltd. (9)	Air Canada, Air BC, Blue Diamond Growers, Burroughs-Wellcome, California Raisin Advisory Board, Colgate-Palmolive Canada Inc., Corby Distilleries Limited, First Brands (Canada) Corp., Fisher-Price Canada (A.O.R.), General Mills Canada, Inc., Hasbro Canada Inc., Hilton International, Hiram Walker, IBM, Jamaica Tourist Board, S.C. Johnson, Limited, Kimberly-Clark Canada Inc., Mazda Canada Inc., Molson Breweries, Nestlé Canada Limited, Pepsico Food Services (Pizza Hut), Taco Bell Corp., Zenith Electronics Corp.	20,268
10	Leo Burnett Company Ltd. (11)	Allstate, Beatrice, Bell Canada, Canadian Home Products, Carter Products, Cathay Pacific, Genesco, Hallmark Cards, Jenn-Air, Kellogg Canada, Kraft General Foods, Maytag, National Sea, Neilson Cadbury, Nintendo, Pillsbury, Procter & Gamble, Reckitt & Colman, Joseph E. Seagram, Tambrands, Tropicana, VISA, Wrigley.	19,230

Number in brackets denotes agency's ranking in Marketing's 1991 'Canada's Top Agencies' listing

Source: "Canada's Top Ten Advertising Agencies and Their Clients, 1992," *Marketing*, December 1992, p. 29.

opposition to the traditional commission system comes from very large consumer products advertisers. They spend the most on media ads, and they think a 15 percent fee is often too high—especially when an expensive ad campaign doesn't produce the desired results. Not all agencies are satisfied with the present arrangement, either. Some would like to charge additional fees as their costs rise and advertisers demand more services.

Firms that need a lot of service but spend relatively little on media—including most producers of business products—favor a fixed commission system. These are the firms the agencies would like to—and sometimes do—charge additional fees.

Fee-for-service commonly used

Canadian advertising budgets are, on the average, much smaller than US ones. And the rates charged by Canadian media reaching a more limited audience are, on a per page or per minute basis, far lower than US rates. On the other hand, the work Canadian agencies must do when planning campaigns and preparing effective advertisements isn't much different or less demanding, and the salaries they must pay aren't much lower. Because of these factors, the fee-for-service basis of agency compensation is well established and widely used in Canada.

Some firms pay the agency based on results

A number of advertisers now "grade" the work done by their agencies—and the agencies' pay depends on the grade. For example, General Foods lowered its basic commission to about 13 percent. However, the company pays the agency a bonus of about 3 percent on campaigns that earn an A rating. If the agency only earns a B, it loses the bonus. If it earns a C, it must improve fast—or GF removes the account.

Variations on this approach are becoming common. For example, Carnation directly links its agency's compensation with how well its ads score in market research tests. Gillette and Lorillard use a sliding scale, and the percentage

A unique selling proposition can help position a brand as especially effective in meeting the needs of a target market.

compensation declines with increased advertising volume. And some agencies develop their own plans in which they guarantee to achieve the results expected or give the advertiser a partial refund.

An advantage of this approach is that it forces the advertiser and agency to agree on very specific objectives for their ads—and what they expect to achieve. Yet many ad agencies dislike the idea of being so closely scrutinized by clients—or having to negotiate what they're paid. But if the current trends continue, they may have to get used to it.[17]

Conflicts between ad agencies and clients

The creative people in ad agencies and their more business-oriented clients often disagree. Some creative people are production-oriented. They create an ad they like themselves—or that will win artistic approval within their industry—and are less concerned about how well it fits into the rest of the client's marketing mix.

You can see why this creates conflict. The advertiser's product managers or brand managers may be personally responsible for the success of particular products—and feel that they have some right to direct and even veto the work of the creative agency people. Because the advertiser is paying the bills, the agency often loses these confrontations.

Ethical conflicts may arise

Ad agencies usually work closely with their clients, and they often have access to confidential information. This can create ethical conflicts if an agency is working with two or more competing clients. Most agencies are very sensitive to the potential problems and work hard to keep people and information from competing accounts completely separated. But many advertisers don't think that's enough—and they don't want to risk a problem. They refuse to work with an agency that handles any competing accounts, even when they're handled in different offices in different parts of the world. This has been a problem for some of the international mega-agencies. Saatchi & Saatchi, for example, gained over $300 million in billings through its mergers but then quickly lost $462 million in billings when old clients departed because Saatchi's new clients included competitors.[18]

MEASURING ADVERTISING EFFECTIVENESS IS NOT EASY

Success depends on the total marketing mix

It would be convenient if we could measure the results of advertising by looking at sales. Certainly some breakthrough ads do have a very direct effect on a company's sales—and the advertising literature is filled with success stories that "prove" advertising increases sales. Unfortunately, we usually can't measure advertising success just by looking at sales. The total marketing mix—not just promotion generally or advertising specifically—is responsible for the sales result. And sales results are also affected by what competitors do and by other changes in the external marketing environment. Only with direct-response advertising can a company make a direct link between advertising and sales results. If an ad doesn't produce immediate results, it's considered a failure.

Research and testing can improve the odds

Ideally, advertisers should pretest advertising before it runs—rather than relying solely on their own guesses about how good an ad will be. The judgment of creative people or advertising experts may not help much. They often judge only on the basis of originality—or cleverness—of the copy and illustrations.

Some progressive advertisers now demand laboratory or market tests to evaluate an ad's effectiveness. In addition, before ads run generally, attitude research is sometimes used. Researchers often try to evaluate consumers' reaction to particular ads—or parts of ads. For example, American Express used focus group interviews to get reactions to a series of possible TV ads. The company wanted the ads to convey the idea that younger people could qualify for its credit cards—but it still wanted to present a prestige image. The agency prepared picture boards presenting different approaches—as well as specific copy. Four of six possible ads failed to communicate the message to the focus groups. One idea that seemed to be effective became the basis for an ad that was tested again before being launched on TV.[19]

Sometimes laboratory-type devices that measure skin moisture or eye reaction are used to gauge consumer responses. In addition, split runs on cable TV systems in test markets are now proving to be an important approach for testing ads in a normal viewing environment. Scanner sales data from retailers in those test markets can provide an estimate of how an ad is likely to affect sales. This approach provides marketing managers with a powerful new tool—and it will become even more powerful in the future as more cable systems and telephone companies add new technology that allows viewers to provide immediate feedback to an ad as it appears on the TV.

Hindsight may lead to foresight

After ads run, researchers may try to measure how much consumers recall about specific products or ads. Inquiries from customers may be used to measure the effectiveness of particular ads. The response to radio or television commercials—or magazine readership—can be estimated using various survey methods to check the size and composition of audiences (the Nielsen and Starch reports are examples).

Various media audiences are measured by three major services in Canada: the Bureau of Broadcast Measurement (BBM) for radio and TV, Nielsen for TV, and the Print Measurement Bureau (PMB) for major consumer magazines and newspaper weekend supplements. In addition, the Canadian Outdoor Measurement Bureau (COMB) measures the total traffic passing by all outdoor advertising.

While advertising research methods aren't foolproof, they're far better than relying on judgment by advertising "experts." Until more effective advertising research tools are developed, the present methods—carefully defining specific advertising objectives, choosing media and messages to accomplish these objectives, testing plans, and then evaluating the results of actual ads—seem to be most productive.[20]

THE IMPORTANCE OF CANADIAN ADVERTISING

Canadian expenditures

Canadian advertising expenditures are substantial. They reached over $3 billion in 1991. However, both US per capita advertising and aggregate US expenditures on advertising, expressed as a percentage of GNP, are consistently about 50 percent greater than the corresponding Canadian figures.

Exhibit 17-6 shows the changes over time in how Canadian net advertising revenues have been divided among different media. Not surprisingly, television's share of the media dollar has climbed over the years as the percentage of Canadian homes with TV sets steadily increased. But our figures don't always reveal the obvious. Would you have expected in 1956 that radio would almost

Exhibit 17–6 Net Advertising Revenues, Percent Share by Media, 1956–1990

Media	Percent Share							
	1956	*1964*	*1972*	*1980*	*1984*	*1986*	*1988*	*1990*
Radio	9.0%	9.7%	11.1%	11.2%	10.0%	9.7%	8.9%	8.6%
TV	6.3	12.0	12.7	17.6	17.8	17.6	17.0	16.7
Daily newspapers	32.9	29.0	28.7	20.9	19.1	18.0	17.4	17.5
Weekend newspaper supplements	3.4	2.7	2.0	0.9	0.7	0.7	0.3	0.2
Weekly semi-tri	4.5	4.0	4.9	5.8	6.2	6.0	7.3	7.5
General magazines	4.1	2.6	2.4	4.8	4.7	4.6	3.5	2.7
Business papers	4.8	3.9	2.5	3.7	3.0	3.4	2.2	1.6
Farm papers	1.5	0.8	0.6	0.5	0.4	0.4	0.3	0.3
Directories (phone, city)	3.7	5.1	5.5	6.3	6.6	6.6	10.6	12.1
Religious, school, and other publications	0.6	0.3	0.4	0.5	0.4	0.4	0.9	0.6
Catalogues, direct mail	23.4	22.2	20.8	21.6	23.9	25.2	23.2	23.9
Billboards, car cards, signs	5.8	7.7	8.4	6.9	7.2	7.7	8.4	8.3

Source: Statistics Canada and *The Canadian Media Directors' Council Digest,* 1984/85, 1987/88, 1989/90, and 1990/91.

hold its own over the next few decades? Would you have predicted the continuing importance of catalogue selling and direct mail? Aren't you surprised even now to find advertiser expenditures in this category to be greater than those in TV?

Canadian and US advertisers differ in the way they allocate their advertising dollars. Television and general circulation magazines obtain a much larger percentage of the US media dollar than newspapers. Direct mail and radio receive less than their Canadian counterparts. Why such differences exist has never been thoroughly investigated.

Some spend more than others

Canadian firms and industries differ in the percentage of their sales spent on advertising. This reflects advertising's relative importance to the firm's or the industry's marketing mix. The last Canadian study of advertising as a percentage of industry sales showed that soap and related products manufacturers spent 10.9 percent of industry sales on advertising. Drug manufacturers spent 8.65 percent, and toilet article manufacturers 15.2 percent. At the other extreme, artificial ice manufacturers, pulp and paper mills, and sugar refineries all spent less than one quarter of 1 percent of their sales on advertising.[21]

Exhibit 17–7 lists Canada's top 25 advertisers in print, radio, and TV during 1992 and the breakdown of their media expenditures. It shows that advertising expenditures are concentrated in a limited number of consumer product categories: food products, drugs and cosmetics, automotives, brewers and distillers, financial and insurance, and household supplies.[22] The exhibit reveals that the federal, Quebec, and Ontario governments are among Canada's largest advertisers. It also shows that, in most cases, the largest share of advertising spending went toward television and daily newspapers.

Less costly than personal selling

Clearly, advertising is an important factor in certain markets, especially consumer goods markets. Nevertheless, in total, much less is spent on advertising than on personal selling. And although total advertising expenditures are large, the advertising industry itself employs relatively few people. Probably fewer than 30,000 people work directly in Canadian advertising. This figure includes everyone who helps create or sell advertising for the different advertising media as

Exhibit 17–7   Canada's Top 25 Advertisers, 1992 (in thousands)

	Total	Television	Daily Newspapers	Magazines	Out-of-Home	Radio
1 Government of Canada	$113,274.8	$68,081.2	$23,867.3	$7,256.6	$4,831.6	$9,238.1
2 General Motors of Canada	109,002.0	55,634.1	42,730.0	4,984.9	2,999.6	2,653.3
3 Procter & Gamble	99,589.5	90,538.6	70.0	8,510.9	33.7	436.1
4 The Thomson Group	81,635.6	27,758.6	50,261.7	2,041.5	905.9	667.9
5 Sears Canada	58,996.9	19,100.5	32,198.0	3,901.2	18.6	3,778.6
6 The Molson Companies	57,420.2	40,959.2	7,744.9	1,109.5	1,363.0	6,243.7
7 Eaton's of Canada	46,337.4	9,106.2	31,967.1	2,592.9	351.9	2,319.4
8 BCE	44,776.9	20,074.7	14,854.3	5,384.4	1,610.7	2,852.7
9 John Labatt Ltd.	40,920.9	28,423.4	2,897.8	729.6	2,495.6	6,374.6
10 Imasco	38,907.7	15,310.5	18,725.6	1,054.8	962.9	2,853.9
11 Unilever	38,450.7	27,811.3	222.2	8,002.8	1,133.2	1,281.2
12 Kraft General Foods Group	37,875.3	31,637.8	372.6	5,473.8	354.9	36.2
13 Paramount Communications	34,897.1	3,734.0	30,353.9	373.2	30.2	405.8
14 Government of Ontario	34,542.9	16,534.9	10,982.3	2,775.1	438.6	3,812.0
15 Toyota Canada	34,133.8	20,063.5	6,935.6	6,612.8	499.8	22.0
16 McDonald's Restaurants of Canada	33,676.4	29,420.1	716.4	10.5	2,827.6	701.9
17 Cineplex Odeon	33,536.8	325.4	33,108.1	70.6	—	32.7
18 Kellogg Canada	33,459.3	33,168.6	7.1	283.6	—	—
19 Chrysler Canada	33,388.7	22,198.8	7,124.4	2,920.0	991.4	154.1
20 Southam	33,350.1	1,285.0	31,301.8	366.0	384.9	12.4
21 Nestlé Enterprises	28,435.9	24,815.6	703.0	1,831.5	379.9	705.8
22 Canadian Tire	28,190.8	22,380.1	5,291.2	207.0	8.3	304.3
23 Government of Quebec	27,609.5	13,772.3	9,959.6	1,290.6	746.6	1,840.3
24 Mazda Canada	27,133.6	19,526.9	1,271.9	5,877.8	319.2	137.9
25 George Weston Ltd.	27,037.4	12,738.7	13,503.7	462.4	17.3	315.3

Source: "Canada's Top 100 Advertisers," *Marketing*, April 12, 1993, pp. 8–9.

well as those in advertising agencies. It also includes those working for retailers, wholesalers, and manufacturers who either create their own advertising or at least manage that activity.[23]

REGULATION OF ADVERTISING

Government agencies may say what is fair

In most countries, the government takes an active role in deciding what kinds of advertising are allowable, fair, and appropriate. For example, France and Japan limit the use of cartoon characters in advertising to children, while Sweden bans *any* advertising targeted directly at children. In Switzerland, an advertiser cannot use an actor to represent a consumer. New Zealand and Switzerland limit political ads on TV. In the United States, print ads must be identified so they aren't confused with editorial matter; in other countries, ads and editorial copy can be intermixed. Most countries limit the number and length of commercials on broadcast media. In Italy, a TV ad can be shown only 10 times a year (but this restriction may change as broadcast rules in Europe become more unified).

What is seen as positioning in one country may be viewed as unfair or deceptive in another. For example, in many countries Pepsi advertises its cola as "the choice of the new generation." Japan's Fair Trade Committee doesn't allow it—because right now Pepsi is not "the choice."[24]

Radio Marketing Services (RMS), a group of private radio stations in Germany, uses a TV spot to show a man being pressured from all sides by state-owned radio. The RMS ad promises potential advertisers that "Your opinions are your own private business."

Differences in rules mean that a marketing manager may face very specific limits in different countries, and local experts may be required to ensure that a firm doesn't waste money developing advertising programs that will never be shown—or which consumers will think are deceptive.

Advertising abuses have been a favorite target of Canadian consumerists. Their efforts, along with those of Consumer and Corporate Affairs Canada, have led to stricter enforcement of existing laws and to new legislation. A number of Canadian firms have been brought to court for use of misleading advertising. For up-to-date information on enforcement efforts, check the *Misleading Advertising Bulletin* published quarterly by Consumer and Corporate Affairs Canada.

The provinces are also active

The stricter federal controls on advertising have their provincial counterparts. Almost all the provinces now regulate advertising far more aggressively than they once did. Such regulation is an especially prominent feature of the trade practices laws that have been passed by many Canadian provinces.

Conflicting provincial legislation can make it impossible for national advertisers to use the same campaign across Canada. Provincial differences are greatest in the advertising of liquor, beer, and wine. Some provinces ban it outright, others place restrictions on what can be said, and still others limit the advertiser to specific media. Complying with all this legislation is no easy task.

The Canadian Radio-Television and Telecommunications Commission (CRTC) controls the content of all radio and television commercials. The CRTC lets the Health Protection Branch of the Department of National Health and

Welfare regulate advertising of drugs, cosmetics, and birth control devices. Similarly, the CRTC allows other types of advertising to be regulated by Consumer and Corporate Affairs Canada.

These government agencies don't have the same kind of advance veto power over print advertising. However, they can and do insist that print advertisements that violate existing regulations be corrected. Also, both advertisers and their agencies have been brought to court for violating the false advertising provisions of the Combines Act or comparable provincial legislation.[25]

Self-regulation also a factor

Additional forms of regulation are imposed by the media themselves and by industry associations. The CBC and CTV networks also have their own codes of advertising acceptability. The Canadian Advertising Foundation has a self-regulating arm, the Advertising Standards Council. The council (which includes public representatives) administers both a Code of Advertising Standards and more specific codes governing advertisements directed toward children and the advertising of nonprescription drug items, as well as food and nonalcoholic beverages.

Supporting ad claims is a fuzzy area

Companies get no clear guidelines about how much research support they need to back up their ad claims. Unfortunately, there are many ways to lie with statistics, and unethical and/or desperate advertisers of me-too products try many of them. It only takes one such competitor in an industry to cause major shifts in market share—and affect the nature of competition in that market. As an old cliché says: One bad apple can spoil the whole barrel.

Most advertisers have good intentions and aren't trying to compete unfairly or deceive consumers. Clear guidelines on research support might eliminate much unfair or deceptive advertising. Those in favor of self-regulation are well aware of this. This is why they organized and work cooperatively with the government—and probably will continue to do so.[26]

CONCLUSION

Theoretically, it may seem simple to develop an advertising campaign. Just pick the media and develop a message. But it's not that easy. Effectiveness depends on using the "best" available medium and the "best" message considering (1) promotion objectives, (2) the target markets, and (3) the funds available for advertising.

Specific advertising objectives determine what kind of advertising to use—product or institutional. If product advertising is needed, then the particular type must be decided—pioneering, competitive (direct or indirect), or reminder. And advertising allowances and cooperative advertising may be helpful.

Many technical details are involved in mass selling, and specialists—advertising agencies—handle some of these jobs. But specific objectives must be set for them, or their advertising may have little direction and be almost impossible to evaluate.

Effective advertising should affect sales. But the whole marketing mix affects sales—and the results of advertising can't be measured by sales changes alone. Advertising is only a part of promotion—and promotion is only a part of the total marketing mix a marketing manager must develop to satisfy target customers.

QUESTIONS AND PROBLEMS

1. Identify the strategy decisions a marketing manager must make in the advertising area.

2. Discuss the relation of advertising objectives to marketing strategy planning and the kinds of advertising actually needed. Illustrate.

3. List several media that might be effective for reaching consumers in a developing nation with low per capita income and a high level of illiteracy. Briefly discuss the limitations and advantages of each media you suggest.

4. Give three examples where advertising to middlemen might be necessary. What are the objective(s) of such advertising?

5. What does it mean to say that "money is invested in advertising?" Is all advertising an investment? Illustrate.

6. Find advertisements to final consumers that illustrate the following types of advertising: (*a*) institutional, (*b*) pioneering, (*c*) competitive, (*d*) reminder. What objective(s) does each of these ads have? List the needs each ad appeals to.

7. Describe the type of media that might be most suitable for promoting: (*a*) tomato soup, (*b*) greeting cards, (*c*) a business component material, (*d*) playground equipment. Specify any assumptions necessary to obtain a definite answer.

8. Discuss the use of testimonials in advertising. Which of the four AIDA steps might testimonials accomplish? Are they suitable for all types of products? If not, for which types are they most suitable?

9. Find a magazine ad that you think does a particularly good job of communicating to the target audience. Would the ad communicate well to an audience in another country? Explain your thinking.

10. Johnson & Johnson sells its baby shampoo in many different countries. Do you think baby shampoo would be a good product for Johnson & Johnson to advertise with a single global message? Explain your thinking.

11. Discuss the future of smaller advertising agencies now that many of the largest are merging to form mega-agencies.

12. Does advertising cost too much? How can this be measured?

13. How would your local newspaper be affected if local supermarkets switched their weekly advertising and instead used a service that delivered weekly, freestanding ads directly to each home?

14. Is it unfair to advertise to children? Is it unfair to advertise to less-educated or less-experienced people of any age? Is it unfair to advertise for "unnecessary" products? Is it unfair to criticize a competitor's product in an ad?

SUGGESTED CASES

30. Grand Foods, Ltd.

33. Lever, Ltd.

18

Pricing Objectives and Policies

When You Finish This Chapter, You Should

❶

Understand how pricing objectives should guide strategy planning
for pricing decisions.

❷

Understand choices the marketing manager must make about price flexibility and
price levels over the product life cycle.

❸

Understand the legality of price level and price flexibility policies.

❹

Understand the many possible variations of a price structure including discounts,
allowances, and who pays transportation costs.

❺

Understand the important new terms (shown in blue).

D ennis Klein proudly describes himself as the "King of the Dollar Stores." With 50 stores selling thousands of items for $1 to $2, Klein's Toronto-based Buck or Two Stores is the leading player in the deep-discount sector. It also ranks among the country's fastest-growing retailers in terms of sales and expansion.

However, competition for value-conscious consumers has become intense. The market is now being flooded by like-minded entrepreneurs who see a golden opportunity in this thriving segment, now worth about $250 million to $300 million a year. The *Monday Report on Retailers,* a weekly publication listing franchise opportunities, has featured seven dollar store concepts in the past four months.

Dollar stores have become popular as the recession forces consumers to hunt for bargains and more off-price products become available due to the increased bankruptcy rate. Dollar stores are also filling a void left in the marketplace as discount chains such as Bi-Way Stores Ltd. moved upmarket.

Klein, who opened his first store in 1987, said selling low-price merchandise is not easy, despite the sector's impressive sales growth, "It's a very complicated business because you're fixed with a certain retail price point and you better know what you're doing. A lot of competitors are getting into the business because they see potential, but they don't know what they're getting into.[1]

PRICE HAS MANY STRATEGY DIMENSIONS

Price is one of the four major variables a marketing manager controls. Price level decisions are especially important because they affect both the number of sales a firm makes and how much money it earns.

Guided by the company's objectives, marketing managers must develop a set of pricing objectives and policies. They must spell out what price situations the firm will face and how it will handle them. These policies should explain (1) how flexible prices will be, (2) at what level they will be set over the product life cycle,

Exhibit 18–1   Strategy Planning for Price

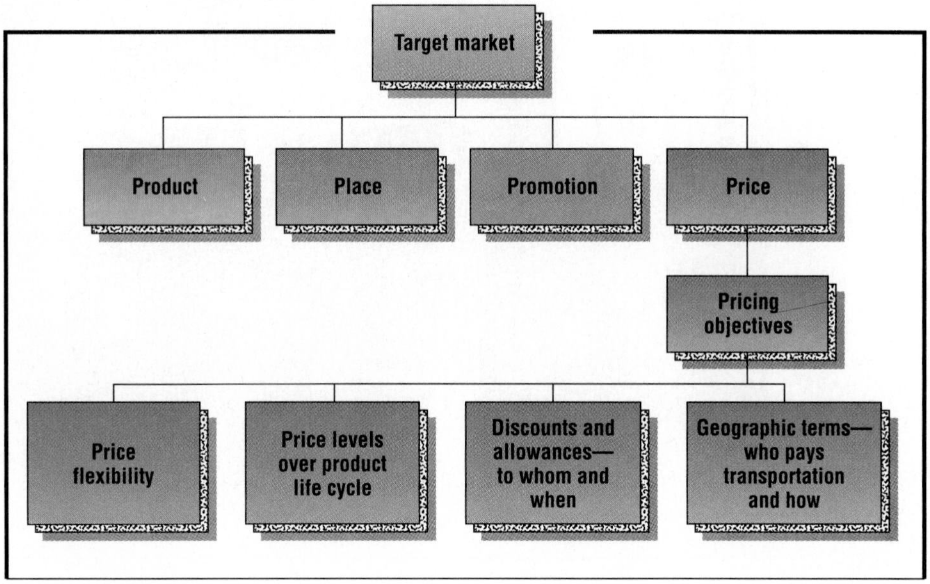

(3) to whom and when discounts and allowances will be given, and (4) how transportation costs will be handled. See Exhibit 18–1. These Price-related strategy decision areas are the focus of this chapter. In the next chapter, we will discuss how specific prices are set—consistent with the firm's pricing objectives and policies and its whole marketing strategy.

It's not easy to define price in real-life situations because prices reflect many dimensions. People who don't realize this can make big mistakes.

Suppose you've been saving to buy a new car and you see in an ad that the base price for the new-year model has been dropped to $9,494—5 percent lower than the previous year. At first, this might seem like a real bargain. However, your view of this deal might change if you found out you also had to pay a $400 transportation charge—and an extra $480 for an extended service warranty. The price might look even less attractive if you discovered the options you wanted— air conditioning, power windows, and an AM-FM radio—cost $1,200 more than the previous year. The sales tax on all of this might come as an unpleasant surprise, too. Further, how would you feel if you bought the car anyway and then learned that a friend who just bought the exact same model had negotiated a much lower price?[2]

The price equation: price equals something

This example emphasizes that when a seller quotes a price, it is related to *some* assortment of goods and services. So **Price** is what is charged for "something." Of course, price may be called different things in different settings. Colleges charge tuition. Landlords collect rent. Motels post a room rate. Banks ask for interest when they loan money. Transportation companies have fares. Doctors, lawyers, and consultants set fees. Employees want a wage. People may call it different things, but *any business transaction in our modern economy can be thought of as an exchange of money—the money being the Price—for something.*

When producers reduce the price of their products by offering retailers special discounts and allowances, retailers often set temporary low prices to pass along some of the savings to consumers.

The something can be a physical product in various stages of completion, with or without supporting services, with or without quality guaranties, and so on. Or it could be a pure service—dry cleaning, a lawyer's advice, or insurance on your car.

The nature and extent of this something determines the amount of money exchanged. Some customers pay list price. Others obtain large discounts or allowances because something is *not* provided. Exhibit 18–2 summarizes some possible variations for consumers or users and Exhibit 18–3, for channel members. These variations are discussed more fully below. But here it should be clear that Price has many dimensions.

Exhibit 18–2   Price as Seen by Consumers or Users

Price		*Something*
List price		**Product:**
Less: **Discounts:**		Physical good
Quantity		Service
Seasonal		Assurance of quality
Cash	equals	Repair facilities
Temporary sales		Packaging
Less: **Allowances:**		Credit
Trade-ins		Trading stamps
Damaged goods		**Place of delivery or when available**
Less: **Rebate and coupon value**		
Plus: **Taxes**		

Exhibit 18-3   Price as Seen by Channel Members

Price		Something
List price		**Product:**
Less: **Discounts:**		Branded—well known
Quantity		Guaranteed
Seasonal		Warranted
Cash		Service—repair facilities
Trade or functional		Convenient packaging for handling
Temporary "deals"	equals	**Place:**
Less: **Allowances:**		Availability—when and where
Damaged goods		**Price:**
Advertising		Price level guarantee
Push money		Sufficient margin to allow chance for profit
Stocking		**Promotion:**
Plus: **Taxes and tariffs**		Promotion aimed at customers

OBJECTIVES SHOULD GUIDE STRATEGY PLANNING FOR PRICE

Pricing objectives should flow from—and fit in with—company-level and marketing objectives. Pricing objectives should be *explicitly stated* because they have a direct effect on pricing policies as well as the methods used to set prices.

Exhibit 18-4 shows the various types of pricing objectives we'll discuss.

Exhibit 18-4   Possible Pricing Objectives

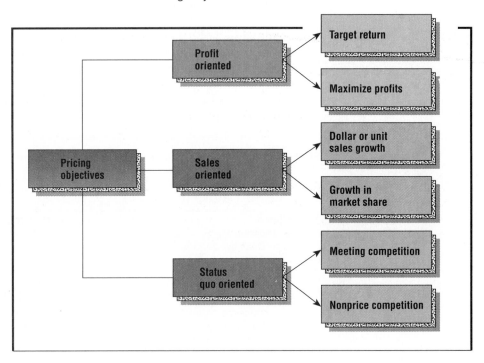

PROFIT–ORIENTED OBJECTIVES

Target returns provide
specific guidelines

A **target return objective** sets a specific level of profit as an objective. Often, this amount is stated as a percentage of sales or of capital investment. A large manufacturer like Motorola might aim for a 15 percent return on investment. The target for Safeway and other grocery chains might be a 1 percent return on sales.

A target return objective has administrative advantages in a large company. Performance can be compared against the target. Some companies eliminate divisions—or drop products—that aren't yielding the target rate of return. For example, General Electric sold its small appliance division to Black & Decker because it felt it could earn higher returns in other product-markets.

Some just want
satisfactory profits

Some managers aim for only satisfactory returns. They just want returns that ensure the firm's survival and convince stockholders they're doing a good job. Similarly, some small family-run businesses aim for a profit that will provide a comfortable lifestyle.[3]

Many private and public nonprofit organizations set a price level that will just recover costs. In other words, their target return figure is zero. For example, a government agency may charge motorists a toll for using a bridge, but then drop the toll when the cost of the bridge is paid.

Companies that are leaders in their industries—like Alcan and Du Pont of Canada—sometimes pursue only satisfactory long-run targets. They are well aware that their activities are in public view. The public—and government officials— expect them to follow policies that are in the public interest when they play the role of price leader or wage setter. Too large a return might invite government action. Similarly, firms that provide critical public services—including many utility and insurance companies, transportation firms, and defense contractors— face public or government agencies that review and approve prices.[4]

But this kind of situation can lead to decisions that are not in the public interest. For example, before imported cars became popular, many GM managers were afraid of making too much profit—so they were not motivated to keep costs and prices low. They thought that lower costs—reflected in lower prices to consumers—might result in an even larger market share—and antitrust action by the government. Then, when low-cost foreign producers entered the Canadian market, GM was not able to quickly reduce costs—or prices.

Profit maximization can
be socially responsible

A **profit maximization objective** seeks to get as much profit as possible. It might be stated as a desire to earn a rapid return on investment. Or, more bluntly, to charge all the traffic will bear.

Some people believe that anyone seeking a profit maximization objective will charge high prices—prices that are not in the public interest. However, this point of view is not correct. Pricing to achieve profit maximization doesn't always lead to high prices. Demand and supply *may* bring extremely high prices if competition can't offer good substitutes. But this happens if and only if demand is highly inelastic. If demand is very elastic, profit maximizers may charge relatively low prices. Low prices may expand the size of the market—and result in greater sales and profits. For example, when prices of VCRs were very high, only innovators and wealthy people bought them. When Sony and its competitors lowered prices,

most Canadian families bought a VCR. In other words, when demand is elastic, profit maximization may occur at a *lower* price.

Profit maximization objectives can also produce desirable results indirectly. Consumers vote with their purchase dollars for firms that do the right thing. The results of this voting guide other firms in deciding what they should do. If a firm is earning a very large profit, other firms will try to copy or improve on what the company offers. Frequently, this leads to lower prices. IBM sold its original personal computer for about $4,500 in 1981. As Compaq, Dell, and other competitors started to copy IBM, it added more power and features and cut prices. Ten years later, customers could buy a significantly better machine for about $600, and prices continued to drop.[5]

We saw this process at work in Chapter 10—in the rise and fall of profits during the product life cycle. Contrary to popular belief, a profit maximization objective is often socially desirable.

SALES–ORIENTED OBJECTIVES

A **sales-oriented objective** seeks some level of unit sales, dollar sales, or share of market—*without referring to profit.*

Sales growth doesn't necessarily mean big profits

Some managers are more concerned about sales growth than profits. They think sales growth always leads to more profits. This kind of thinking causes problems when a firm's costs are growing faster than sales—or when managers don't keep track of their costs. Recently, many major corporations have had declining profits in spite of growth in sales. At the extreme, International Harvester kept cutting prices on its tractors—trying to reach its target sales levels in a weak economy—until it had to sell that part of its business. Generally, however, business managers now pay more attention to profits—not just sales.[6]

Managers of some nonprofit organizations set prices to increase market share—precisely because they are *not* trying to earn a profit. For example, many cities set low fares to fill up their buses. Buses cost the same to run empty or full, and there's more benefit when they're full even if the total revenue is no greater.

Market share objectives are popular

Many firms seek to gain a specified share (percent) of a market. A benefit of a market share objective is that it forces a manager to pay attention to what competitors are doing in the market. In addition, it's usually easier to measure a firm's market share than to determine if profits are being maximized. Large consumer package goods firms—such as Procter & Gamble, Coca-Cola, and General Foods—often use market share objectives.

Aggressive companies often aim to increase market share—or even to control a market. Sometimes, this makes sense. If a company has a large market share, it may have better economies of scale than its competitors. Therefore, if it sells at about the same price as its competitors, it gets more profit from each sale. Or lower costs may allow it to sell at a lower price—and still make a profit.

A company with a longer-run view may decide that increasing market share is a sensible objective when the overall market is growing. The hope is that larger future volume will justify sacrificing some profit in the short run. Companies as diverse as 3M, Coca-Cola, and IBM look at opportunities in eastern Europe this way. Of course, objectives aimed at increasing market share have the same limitations as straight sales growth objectives. A larger market share, if gained at too low a price, may lead to profitless "success."

The key point regarding sales-oriented objectives is: larger sales volume, by itself, doesn't necessarily lead to higher profits.

STATUS QUO PRICING OBJECTIVES

Don't-rock-the-boat objectives

Managers satisfied with their current market share and profits sometime adopt **status quo objectives**—don't-rock-the-*pricing*-boat objectives. Managers may say that they want to stabilize prices, or meet competition, or even avoid competition. This don't-rock-the-boat thinking is most common when the total market is not growing. Maintaining stable prices may discourage price competition and avoid the need for hard decisions.

Or stress nonprice competition instead

A status quo pricing objective may be part of an aggressive overall marketing strategy focusing on **nonprice competition**—aggressive action on one or more of the Ps other than Price. Fast-food chains like McDonald's, Wendy's, and Burger King experienced very profitable growth by sticking to nonprice competition for many years. However, when Taco Bell and others started to take away customers with price-cutting, the other chains also turned to price competition.[7]

MOST FIRMS SET SPECIFIC PRICING POLICIES—TO REACH OBJECTIVES

Specific pricing policies are vital for any firm. Otherwise, the marketing manager has to rethink the marketing strategy every time a customer asks for a price.

Administered prices help achieve objectives

Price policies usually lead to **administered prices**—consciously set prices. In other words, instead of letting daily market forces decide their prices, most firms (including *all* of those in monopolistic competition) set their own prices. They may hold prices steady for long periods of time or change them more frequently if that's what's required to meet objectives.

If a firm doesn't sell directly to final customers, it usually wants to administer both the price it receives from middlemen and the price final customers pay. After all, the price final customers pay will ultimately affect the quantity that firm sells.

Yet it is often difficult to administer prices throughout the channel. Other channel members may also wish to administer prices to achieve their own objectives. This is what happened to Alcoa, one of the largest aluminum producers. To reduce its excess inventory, Alcoa offered its wholesalers a 30 percent discount off its normal price. Alcoa expected the wholesalers to pass most of the discount along to their customers to stimulate sales throughout the channel. Instead, wholesalers bought *their* aluminum at the lower price but passed on only a small part of the discount to customers. As a result, the quantity Alcoa sold didn't increase much, and it still had excess inventories, while the wholesalers made more profit on the aluminum they did sell.[8]

Some firms don't even try to administer prices. They just meet competition—or worse, mark up their costs with little thought to demand. They act as if they have no choice in selecting a price policy.

Remember that Price has many dimensions. Managers *do* have many choices. They *should* administer their prices. And they should do it carefully because, ultimately, customers must be willing to pay these prices before a whole marketing mix succeeds. In the rest of this chapter, we'll talk about policies a marketing manager must set to do an effective job of administering Price.[9]

PRICE FLEXIBILITY POLICIES

One of the first decisions a marketing manager has to make is about price flexibility. Should the firm use a one-price or a flexible-price policy?

One-price policy—the same price for everyone

A **one-price policy** means offering the same price to all customers who purchase products under essentially the same conditions and in the same quantities. The majority of Canadian firms use a one-price policy—mainly for administrative convenience and to maintain goodwill among customers.

A one-price policy makes pricing easier. But a marketing manager must be careful to avoid a rigid one-price policy. This can amount to broadcasting a price that competitors can undercut—especially if the price is somewhat high. One reason for the growth of discount houses is that conventional retailers rigidly applied traditional margins—and stuck to them.

Flexible-price policy—different prices for different customers

A **flexible-price policy** means offering the same product and quantities to different customers at different prices. Flexible-price policies often specify a *range* in which the actual price charged must fall.

Flexible pricing is most common in the channels, in direct sales of business products, and at retail for expensive items and homogeneous shopping products. Retail shopkeepers in less-developed economies typically use flexible pricing. These situations usually involve personal selling—not mass selling. The advantage of flexible pricing is that the salesperson can make price adjustments—considering prices charged by competitors, the relationship with the customer, and the customer's bargaining ability.[10]

Most auto dealers use flexible pricing. The producer suggests a list price, but the dealers bargain for what they can get. Their salespeople negotiate prices every day. Inexperienced consumers—reluctant to bargain—often pay hundreds of dollars more than the dealer is willing to accept. However, Saturn's new dealers have had success attracting haggle-weary consumers with a one-price policy.

Flexible pricing does have disadvantages. A customer who finds that others paid lower prices for the same marketing mix will be unhappy. This can cause real conflict in channels. For example, the Winn-Dixie supermarket chain stopped carrying products of some suppliers who refused to give Winn-Dixie the same prices available to chains in other regions of the United States.[11]

If buyers learn that negotiating can be in their interest, the time needed for bargaining will increase. This can affect selling costs. In addition, some sales reps let price-cutting become a habit. This reduces the role of price as a competitive tool—and leads to a lower price level.

PRICE LEVEL POLICIES—OVER THE PRODUCT LIFE CYCLE

When marketing managers administer prices—as most do—they must consciously set a price level policy. As they enter the market, they have to set introductory prices that may have long-run effects. They must consider where the product life cycle is—and how fast it's moving. And they must decide if their prices should be above, below, or somewhere in between relative to the market.

Let's look for a moment at a new product in the market introduction stage of its product life cycle. The price level decision should focus first on the nature of market demand. There are few (or no) direct substitute marketing mixes. And considering the demand curve for this product, a high price may lead to higher profit from each sale, but also to fewer units sold. A lower price might appeal to more potential customers. With this in mind, should the firm set a high or low price?

Skimming pricing—feeling out demand at a high price

A **skimming price policy** tries to sell the top (skim the cream) of a market—the top of the demand curve—at a high price before aiming at more price-sensitive customers. A skimming policy is more attractive if demand is quite inelastic—at least at the upper price ranges.

Skimming may maximize profits in the market introduction stage for an innovation, especially if there is little competition. Competitor analysis may help clarify whether barriers will prevent or discourage competitors from entering.

(?) Skimming has critics

Some critics argue that firms should not try to maximize profits by using a skimming policy on new products that have important social consequences. A patent-protected life-saving drug or a genetic technique that increases crop yields, for example, is likely to have an inelastic demand curve. Yet many of those who need the product may not have the money to buy it. This is a serious concern. However, it's also a serious problem if firms don't have any incentive to take the risks required to develop breakthroughs in the first place.[12]

Price moves down the demand curve

A skimming policy usually involves a slow reduction in price over time. See Exhibit 18–5. Note that as price is reduced, new target markets are probably being sought. So as the price level steps down the demand curve, new Place, Product, and Promotion policies may be needed, too.

Skimming may maximize profits in the market introduction stage, but as more firms enter, market competition typically pushes prices down.

When Hewlett-Packard (HP) introduced its laser printer for personal computers, it initially set a high price—around $4,000. HP had a good headstart on competitors—and no close substitute was available. HP sold the high-priced printers mainly to computer professionals and business users with serious desktop publishing needs—and distributed them through a select group of authorized HP computer dealers whose salespeople could explain the printer. When other firms entered the market with similar printers, HP added features and lowered its price. It also did more advertising and added mail-order middlemen to reach new target markets. Then, just as competitors were entering the market to go after budget-oriented buyers, HP introduced a new model at a lower price. This is very typical of skimming. It involves changing prices through a series of marketing strategies over the course of the product life cycle.

Skimming is also useful when you don't know very much about the shape of the demand curve. It's safer to start with a high price that customers can refuse—and then reduce it if necessary.[13]

Penetration pricing—get volume at a low price

A **penetration pricing policy** tries to sell the whole market at one low price. Such an approach might be wise when the elite market—those willing to pay a high price—is small. This is the case when the whole demand curve is fairly elastic. See Exhibit 18–5.

A penetration policy is even more attractive if selling larger quantities results in lower costs because of economies of scale. Penetration pricing may be wise if the firm expects strong competition very soon after introduction.

Exhibit 18–5 Alternative Introductory Pricing Policies

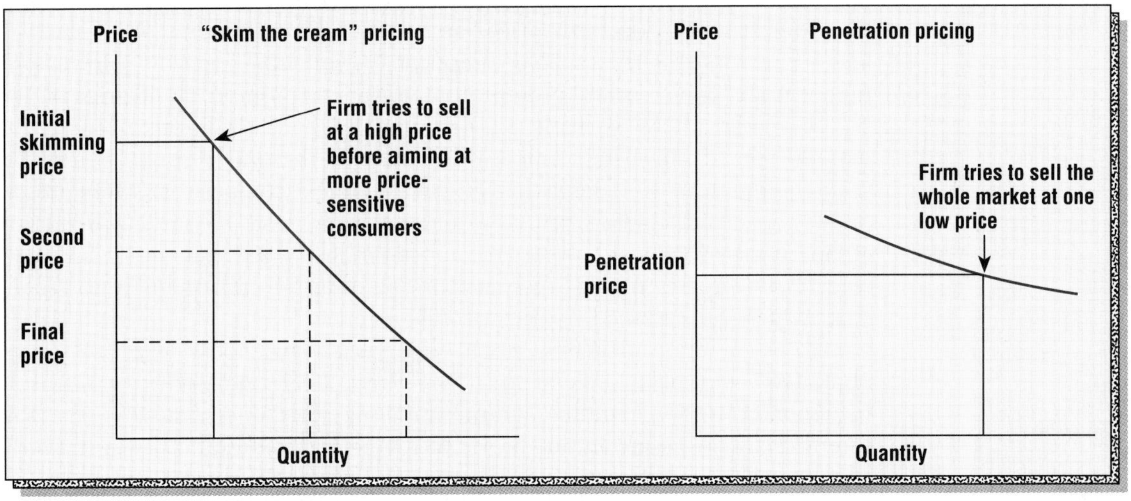

A low penetration price may be called a stay-out price. It discourages competitors from entering the market. When personal computers became popular, Borland International came out with a complete programming language—including a textbook—for under $50. Business customers had paid thousands of dollars for similar systems for mainframe computers. But Borland felt it could sell to hundreds of thousands of customers—and earn large total profits—by offering a really low price that would attract individual users as well as business firms. A low price helped Borland penetrate the market early. For several years, IBM, Microsoft, and other big companies weren't able—or willing—to compete directly with Borland at that price. When they finally did match Borland's price, Borland already had a large base of very loyal customers who weren't interested in switching to something new.

Introductory price dealing—temporary price cuts

Price cuts do attract customers. Therefore, marketers often use **introductory price dealing**—temporary price cuts—to speed new products into a market. However, don't confuse these *temporary* price cuts with low penetration prices. The plan here is to raise prices as soon as the introductory offer is over. Introductory price dealing may be used with a new product concept as part of the pioneering effort—or to attract customers to a new brand entry later in the life cycle.

Established competitors often choose not to meet introductory price dealing—as long as the introductory period is not too long or too successful.

Meeting competition may be necessary

Regardless of their introductory pricing policy, most firms face competition sooner or later in the product life cycle. When that happens, how high or low a price is may be relative not only to the market demand curve but also to the prices charged by competitors.

The nature of competition usually affects whether companies set their prices below, at, or above competition. The clearest case is pure competition. The market really makes the decision. To offer products above or below the market price is foolish.

Meeting competitors' prices may also be the practical choice in mature markets that are moving toward pure competition. Here, firms typically face downward pressure on both prices and profits. Profit margins are already thin—and for many firms they would disappear or turn into losses at a lower price. A higher price would simply prompt competitors to promote their price advantage.

Similarly, there is little choice in oligopoly situations. Pricing at the market—that is, meeting competition—may be the only sensible policy. To raise prices might lead to a large loss in sales—unless competitors adopt the higher price, too. And cutting prices would probably lead to similar reductions by competitors—downward along an inelastic industry demand curve. This can only lead to a decrease in total revenue for the industry and probably for each firm. The major airlines faced these problems recently.

To avoid these problems, each oligopolist may choose a status quo pricing objective—and set its price at the competitive level. Some critics call this pricing behavior conscious parallel action, implying it is unethical and the same as intentional conspiracy among firms. As a practical matter, however, that criticism seems overly harsh. It isn't sensible for firms to ignore their competitors.[14]

There are alternatives in monopolistic competition

In monopolistic competition, there are more pricing options. At one extreme, some firms are clearly above the market—they may even brag about it. Tiffany's is well known as one of the most expensive jewelry stores in the world. Other firms emphasize below-the-market prices in their marketing mixes. Prices offered by discounters and mass-merchandisers, such as Zellers and the Brick, illustrate this approach. They may even promote their pricing policy with catchy slogans like "guaranteed lowest prices" or "we'll beat any advertised price."

Above or below what market?

These examples raise an important question. Do these various strategies promote prices that are above or below the market—or are they really different prices for different target markets or different marketing mixes? In setting price level policies, it is important to clearly define the *relevant target market* and *competitors* when making price comparisons.

Perhaps some target customers do see important differences in the product, or in the convenience of location, or in the whole marketing mix. Then what we're talking about are different marketing strategies—not just different price levels.

Consider Kmart prices again from this view. Kmart may have lower camera prices than conventional camera retailers, but it offers less help in the store, less selection, and it won't take old cameras in trade. Kmart may be appealing to budget-oriented shoppers who compare prices among different mass-merchandisers. A specialty camera store, appealing to different customers, may not be a direct competitor! Thus, it may be better to think of Kmart's price as part of a different marketing mix for a different target market—not as a below-the-market price.

Different price level policies through the channel

When a product is sold to channel members instead of final consumers, the price should be set so that the channel members can cover costs and make a profit. To achieve its objectives, a manufacturer may set different price level policies for different levels in the channel. For example, a producer of a slightly better product might set a price level that is low relative to competitors when selling to retailers, while suggesting an above-the-market retail price. This encourages retailers to carry the product—and to emphasize it in their marketing mix—because it yields higher profits.

The price of money may affect the price level

We've been talking about the price level of a firm's product. But a nation's money also has a price level—what it's worth in some other currency. For example, in the summer of 1992 one US dollar was worth 1.48 German marks. In other words, the exchange rate for the German mark against the US dollar was 1.48. Exhibit 18–6 lists exchange rates from several countries. Exchange rates change over time—and sometimes the changes are significant. For example, at one point in 1989 a German mark was worth $1.95 US; in 1982, it was as high as $2.69.

Exchange rate changes can have a significant effect on whether or not a marketing manager's price level has the expected result. As the following example shows, this can be an important factor even for a small firm that sells only in its own local market.

In 1989, the marketing manager for Colorfast—a small firm that mixes and sells special dyes used by textile producers—set a meeting-competition wholesale price of about $100 for a barrel of dye. The wholesalers who distribute the dyes also carried competing products, including one produced by a German firm. Its wholesale price was also $100, which means that it got about 51.3 German marks ($100 divided by the exchange rate of 1.95 marks per dollar) per barrel. However, when the exchange rate for the mark against the dollar fell from 1.95 to 1.48, the German producer got an extra 16.3 marks for each $100 barrel of dye ($100 ÷ by 1.48 marks per dollar = 67.6 marks; 67.6 marks − 51.3 marks = 16.3 marks).

Because Colorfast's marketing manager was only selling dye to local customers, she didn't pay any attention to the drop in the exchange rate—at first. However, she did pay attention when the German producer decided to lower its wholesale price to $80 a barrel. At the $80 price, the German firm still got about 54 marks per barrel—more than it was getting before the exchange rate change. And its sales increased substantially—at Colorfast's expense—because of the low price. Colorfast's marketing manager concluded that it would take a while for the German firm to raise its price again, even if the exchange rate went up again, so she decided she had no alternative but to lower her price level.[15]

Consumers want value pricing

Sooner or later, there's competition in most product-markets. And in today's competitive markets, more and more customers are demanding real value. **Value pricing** means setting a fair price level for a marketing mix that really gives customers what they need. Value pricing doesn't necessarily mean cheap if cheap means bare bones or low-grade. It doesn't mean high prestige either if the prestige is not accompanied by the right quality goods and services. Rather, the focus is on the customer's requirements—and the whole strategy.

Exhibit 18–6   Exchange Rates for Various Currencies against the Canadian Dollar, Sept. 21, 1993

Base Currency	Number of Units of Base Currency per Canadian Dollar
Germany (mark)	1.24
Japan (yen)	80.72
France (franc)	4.32
Australia (dollar)	1.15
United States (dollar)	0.76
United Kingdom (pound sterling)	0.50

Toyota is a good example of a firm that has been effective with value pricing. It has different marketing mixes for different target markets. But whether it be the Tercel or the Lexus, the Japanese automaker consistently offers better quality and lower prices than its competitors. Among discount retailers, Wal-Mart is a value pricing leader. Its motto, "the low price on the brands you trust," says it all. In the product-market for hosiery, Sara Lee is a value pricer; its L'eggs are priced lower than many dealer brands but it still offers customers the selection, fit, and wear they want.

These companies deliver on their promises. They try to give the consumer pleasant surprises—like an unexpected service or a useful new feature or environmentally sound packaging—because it builds customer loyalty. They guarantee what they offer—and they refund the purchase price if the customer isn't completely satisfied. They avoid unrealistic price levels—prices that are high only because consumers already know the brand name. They build relationships with customers so the customers will be loyal and come back the next time they purchase.[16]

When you stop to think about it, value pricing is simply the best pricing decision for the type of market-oriented strategy planning we've been discussing throughout this whole text. To built profits and customer satisfaction, the whole marketing mix—including the price level—must meet target customers' needs.

MOST PRICE STRUCTURES ARE BUILT AROUND LIST PRICES

Prices start with a list price

Most price structures are built around a base price schedule or price list. **Basic list prices** are the prices final customers or users are normally asked to pay for products. In this book, unless noted otherwise, list price refers to basic list price.

In the next chapter, we discuss how firms set these list prices. For now, however, we'll consider variations from list price—and why they are made.

DISCOUNT POLICIES—REDUCTIONS FROM LIST PRICES

Discounts are reductions from list price given by a seller to buyers who either give up some marketing function or provide the function themselves. Discounts can be useful in marketing strategy planning. In the following discussion, think about what function the buyers are giving up—or providing—when they get each of these discounts.

Quantity discounts encourage volume buying

Quantity discounts are discounts offered to encourage customers to buy in larger amounts. This lets a seller get more of a buyer's business, or shifts some of the storing function to the buyer, or reduces shipping and selling costs—or all of these. Such discounts are of two kinds: cumulative and noncumulative.

Cumulative quantity discounts apply to purchases over a given period—such as a year—and the discount usually increases as the amount purchased increases. Cumulative discounts are intended to encourage *repeat* buying by a single customer by reducing the customer's cost for additional purchases. For example, Beaver Lumber might give a cumulative quantity discount to a building contractor who is not able to buy all of the needed materials at once. Beaver Lumber wants to reward the contractor's patronage—and discourage shopping around. Beaver Lumber knows that its market is very competitive. So the cumulative discount is just part of an effort to build loyalty with the customers it has; the discount is small relative to the cost of constantly trying to attract new customers to replace departures.

Noncumulative quantity discounts apply only to individual orders. Such discounts encourage larger orders—but do not tie a buyer to the seller after that one purchase. These discounts are often used to discourage small orders, which are expensive to handle. But they are mainly used to encourage bigger orders. Beaver Lumber may purchase and resell insulation products made by several competing producers. Owens/Corning might try to encourage Beaver Lumber to stock larger quantities of its insulation by offering a noncumulative quantity discount. The objective would be to encourage Beaver Lumber to push those products to its customers.

Quantity discounts may be based on the dollar value of the entire order, or on the number of units purchased, or on the size of the package purchased. While quantity discounts are usually given as price cuts, sometimes they are given as free or bonus products. Airline frequent flier programs use this approach.

Quantity discounts can be a very useful tool for the marketing manager. Some customers are eager to get them. But marketing managers must use quantity discounts carefully. In business markets, they must offer such discounts to all customers on equal terms—to avoid price discrimination.

Noncumulative discounts sometimes produce unexpected results. If the discount is too big, wholesalers or retailers may buy more than they can possibly sell to their own customers—to get the low price. Then they sell the excess at a low price to whoever will buy it—as long as the buyer doesn't compete in the same market area. These gray market channels often take customers away from regular channel members, perhaps with a retail price even lower than what most channel members pay. To avoid these problems, a marketing manager must consider the effect of discounts on the whole strategy—not just the effect on sales to a given middleman.

Seasonal discounts— buy sooner and store

Seasonal discounts are discounts offered to encourage buyers to buy earlier than present demand requires. If used by producers, this discount tends to shift the storing function further along in the channel. It also tends to even out sales over the year and therefore permit year-round operation. If seasonal discounts are large, they may be passed along to other customers down the channel of distribution. For example, Kyota offers wholesalers a lower price on its garden tillers if they buy in the fall—when sales are slow. The wholesalers can then offer a seasonal discount to retailers—who may try to sell the tillers during a special fall sale.

Payment terms and cash discounts set payment dates

Most sales to businesses are made on credit. The seller sends a bill (invoice), and the buyer's accounting department processes it for payment. Some firms depend on their suppliers for temporary working capital (credit). Therefore, it is very important for both sides to clearly state the terms of payment, including the availability of cash discounts, and to understand the commonly used payment terms.

Net means that payment for the face value of the invoice is due immediately. These terms are sometimes changed to net 10 or net 30—which means payment is due within 10 or 30 days of the date on the invoice.

Cash discounts are reductions in price to encourage buyers to pay their bills quickly. The terms for a cash discount usually modify the net terms.

2/10, net 30 means the buyer can take a 2 percent discount off the face value of the invoice if the invoice is paid within 10 days. Otherwise, the full face value is due within 30 days. And it usually is stated or understood that an interest charge will be added after the 30-day free-credit period.

Why cash discounts are given and should be taken

Smart buyers take advantage of cash discounts. A discount of 2/10, net 30 may not look like much at first. But the buyer earns a 2 percent discount for paying the invoice just 20 days sooner than it should be paid anyway. By not taking the discount, the company—in effect—is borrowing at an annual rate of 36 percent. That is, assuming a 360-day year and dividing by 20 days, there are 18 periods during which the company could earn 2 percent—and 18 times 2 equals 36 percent a year.

While the marketing manager can often use a cash discount as a marketing variable, this isn't always true. Purchasing agents who value cash discounts may insist that the marketing manager offer the same discount offered by competitors. In fact, some buyers automatically deduct the traditional cash discount from their invoices regardless of the seller's invoice terms!

Some sellers find themselves in trouble when they don't state exactly when payment is due—or what the penalty will be for late payment. Customers may wait as long as possible to pay the invoice, especially if they are short of cash or if interest rates are high.

Consumers say "charge it"

Credit sales are also important to retailers. Some stores have their own credit systems. But most retailers use credit card services, such as Visa or MasterCard. The retailers pay a percent of the revenue from each credit sale for this service—from 1 to 7 percent depending on the card company and the store's sales volume. For this reason, some retailers offer discounts to consumers who pay cash.

Many consumers like the convenience of credit card buying. But some critics argue that the cards make it too easy for consumers to buy things they really can't afford. Further, because of high interest charges, credit card buying can increase the total costs to consumers.[17]

Trade discounts often are set by tradition

A **trade (functional) discount** is a list price reduction given to channel members for the job they are going to do.

A manufacturer, for example, might allow retailers a 30 percent trade discount from the suggested retail list price to cover the cost of the retailing function and their profit. Similarly, the manufacturer might allow wholesalers a *chain* discount of 30 percent and 10 percent off the suggested retail price. In this case, the wholesalers would be expected to pass the 30 percent discount on to retailers. But, while such discounts are legal and widely offered in the United States, they violate the price discrimination provisions of Canada's Competition Act. A Canadian wholesaler cannot legally be offered a larger discount than a retailer purchasing the same quantity of merchandise.

Special sales reduce list prices—temporarily

A **sale price** is a temporary discount from the list price. Sale price discounts encourage immediate buying. In other words, to get the sale price, customers give up the convenience of buying when they want to buy—and instead buy when the seller wants to sell.

Special sales provide a marketing manager with a quick way to respond to changing market conditions—without changing the basic marketing strategy. For

example, a retailer might use a sale to help clear extra inventory or to meet a competing store's price. Or a producer might offer a middleman a special deal—in addition to the normal trade discount—that makes it more profitable for the middleman to push the product. Retailers often pass some of the savings along to consumers.

In recent years, sale prices and deals have become much more common. Some retailers who had an occasional sale a few years ago now have weekly sales. And for some consumer convenience products, the majority of purchases by middlemen involve some sort of deal. At first it may seem that consumers benefit from all this. But that may not be the case. Prices that change constantly may confuse customers and increase selling costs.

To avoid these problems, some firms that sell consumer convenience products offer **everyday low pricing**—setting a low list price rather than relying on a high list price that frequently changes with various discounts or allowances. Many grocery stores use this approach. And some producers, including P&G, are now using it with some product lines. Marketing Demo 18–1 describes how Quebec supermarkets are using such a strategy to battle warehouse clubs.

MARKETING DEMO 18–1
Slashed Food Prices a "Strategy"—Not a "War"

Q uebec's three major supermarket chains have slashed prices in order to battle for a bigger share of consumers' grocery dollars. Executives of all three deny it's a price war. In fact, Provigo, Metro-Richelieu, and IGA all claim to have built unique, long-term competitive strategies based on pricing. But in the short term, at least, consumers are unlikely to see it that way.

"Price wars are usually short-term (incentives) where everybody loses money," says Barbara Ann Thompson, director of advertising and promotion for Provigo. "Ours is a long-term move that will see 80 percent of our prices lowered permanently. It involves 8,000 to 10,000 products." The other two chains are planning similar programs. Metro's will see prices on 3,500 brand name products reduced on a rotating basis, in addition to its 1,000 house brands. IGA has lowered prices on milk, eggs, bread, and butter to keep up with Provigo's first round of price cuts. But about 2,000 products are already covered by its two-year-old Duraprix program, prompting its claim that the two competitors are simply playing catch-up.

Metro, Provigo, and IGA hope their permanent low-pricing policies will help draw customers back from warehouse-style discounters like Club Price. A recent survey by research firm CROP showed that 41 percent of consumers are trying to cut expenses, 57 percent are looking for bargains, and 51 percent are ready to drop their favorite brands in favor of cheaper ones. The survey also revealed that consumers prefer the neighborhood supermarket style of customer service to the serviceless warehouse store approach, where shoppers have a narrower selection of products from which to choose and must often buy in bulk.

The grocery chains claim offering competitive prices on a wide variety of items won't hurt their profits because it will crank up their sales volume. All three chains have cut new deals with their suppliers and say their permanent low-price objectives are achievable, thanks to various operating efficiencies and fewer promotions. With lower prices and consumer preference for more service rather than less, Quebec's major supermarkets should be able to battle back from the inroads made by warehouse retailers.

Source: Gail Chiasson, "Slashed Food Prices a 'Strategy'—Not a 'War,' " *Marketing,* January 25, 1993, p. 4.

Sale prices should be used carefully, consistent with well thought out pricing objectives and policies. A marketing manager who constantly uses temporary sales to adjust the price level probably has not done a good job setting the normal price.[18]

ALLOWANCE POLICIES—OFF LIST PRICES

Allowances—like discounts—are given to final consumers, customers, or channel members for doing something or accepting less of something.

Advertising allowances—something for something

Advertising allowances are price reductions given to firms in the channel to encourage them to advertise or otherwise promote the supplier's products locally. For example, General Electric gave an allowance (1.5 percent of sales) to its wholesalers of housewares and radios. They, in turn, were expected to spend the allowance on local advertising.

Stocking allowances—get attention and shelf space

Stocking allowances—sometimes called slotting allowances—are given to a middleman to get shelf space for a product. For example, a producer might offer a retailer cash or free merchandise to stock a new item. Stocking allowances are a recent development. So far, they're used mainly to prompt supermarket chains to handle new products. Supermarkets don't have enough slots on their shelves to handle all of the available new products. They're more willing to give space to a new product if the supplier will offset their handling costs—like making space in the warehouse, adding information on computer systems, and redesigning store shelves, for example.

Some retailers get allowances that cover more than handling costs. With a big stocking allowance, the middleman makes extra profit—even if a new product fails and the producer loses money.

(?) Are stocking allowances ethical?

There is great controversy over stocking allowances. Critics say that retailer demands for big stocking allowances slow new product introductions—and make it hard for small producers to compete. Some producers feel that retailers' demands are unethical—just a different form of extortion. Retailers, on the other hand, point out that the fees protect them from producers that simply want to push more and more me-too products onto their shelves. Perhaps the best way for a producer to cope with the problem is to develop new products that offer consumers a real comparative advantage. Then it will benefit everyone in the channel—including retailers—to get the products to the target market.[19]

PMs—push for cash

Push money (or prize money) allowances—sometimes called PMs or spiffs—are given to retailers by manufacturers or wholesalers to pass on to the retailers' salesclerks for aggressively selling certain items. PM allowances are used for new items, slower-moving items, or higher-margin items. They are often used for pushing furniture, clothing, consumer electronics, and cosmetics. A salesclerk, for example, might earn an additional $5 for each new model Pioneer cassette deck sold.

Bring in the old, ring up the new—with trade-ins

A **trade-in allowance** is a price reduction given for used products when similar new products are bought.

Trade-ins give the marketing manager an easy way to lower the effective price without reducing list price. Proper handling of trade-ins is important when selling durable products. Customers buying machinery, for example, buy long-term satisfaction in terms of more production capacity. If the list price less the trade-in allowance doesn't offer greater satisfaction—as the customer sees it—then no sale will be made.

SOME CUSTOMERS GET EXTRA SOMETHINGS

Clipping coupons— more for less

Many producers and retailers offer discounts (or free items) through coupons distributed in packages, mailings, or print ads, or at the store. By presenting a coupon to a retailer, the consumer is given a discount off list price. This is especially common in the consumer packaged goods business—but the use of price-off coupons is growing in other lines of business, too. Marketing Demo 18–2 discusses the growth of couponing in Canada.

Retailers are willing to redeem producers' coupons because it increases their sales—and they usually are paid for the trouble of handling the coupon. For example, a retailer who redeems a 50 cents off coupon might be repaid 75 cents. In effect, the coupon increases the functional discount and makes it more attractive to sell the couponed product.

Coupons are often distributed in special newspaper supplements.

MARKETING DEMO 18–2
Coupon Distribution: Coupon Usage Increases Again

Canadian consumers redeemed a record 327 million coupons in 1992. This is 12.8 percent more than in 1991 and continues the positive trend in consumer use that began in the fourth quarter of 1990. This increase can be partially explained by an increase in coupon face values to 65 cents per coupon distributed, up from 58 cents in 1991. In addition, a 5 percent growth in coupons distributed directly to consumers positively affected redemption since these coupons tend to achieve higher redemption rates than in-ad offers distributed in retailers' newspaper ads and flyers. The number of retailer in-ad coupons distributed decreased last year to 17.5 billion, for the first time since they became popular as a retail marketing tool in 1985.

The average redemption rates for many distribution methods also grew last year. In particular, rates increased for retailer in-ads and for some in-store and in/on-package distribution methods. The freestanding insert continues to be the most frequently used method to distribute coupons directly to consumers, even though there was no change in the number of freestanding insert coupons distributed.

An above average overall redemption rate was achieved by the in-store shelf vehicle that places coupons at shelf level next to the product either in the form of ad pads or in special coupon dispensers. This media accounted for approximately 5 percent of the direct-to-consumer coupons distributed but represented 20 percent of redemptions. In/on-pack and freestanding insert coupons accounted for more redemptions.

In 1992, some major retailers also began to distribute "coupon savings" electronically via frequent or preferred shopper programs. In some stores, these electronic discounts have at least partly replaced in-ad coupons, which may partially explain why in-ad distributions have decreased. The level of "electronic couponing" activity in the industry, however, is not available to be measured.

In-ad couponing works for most marketers because the full "in-ad plus feature price" discount is limited to the consumers who clip and present the coupon when buying the brand at a participating retailer. This means the cost of the full in-ad coupon discount is intended to be applied to only a part of a retailer's brand sales during the promotion period. If the same scenario applies to electronic coupons, the amount of support and level of discounts funded by markets will be determined by the proportion of the retailer's customers buying a brand that is given the electronic discount.

For 1993, the market continues to evolve. One recent development is the freestanding insert-plus format. This is a freestanding insert booklet format that is distributed to households by Canada Post and is being offered a couple of times a year. For example, this type of format was used for the 1993 Ontario Cash for Kids program. Judging from recent changes in the coupon distribution and redemption industry, there will be many more changes in the years to come.

Source: Wayne Mouland, "in 1992," special release from NCH Promotional Services, February 1993.

Couponing is so common that firms have been set up to help repay retailers for redeeming manufacturers' coupons. The total dollar amounts involved are so large that crime has become a big problem. Some dishonest retailers have gone to jail for collecting on coupons they redeemed without requiring customers to buy the products.

Cash rebates when you buy

Some producers offer **rebates**—refunds paid to consumers after a purchase. Sometimes the rebate may be very large. Some automakers offer rebates of $500 to $2,500 to promote sales of slow-moving models. Rebates are used on lower-priced items, too—ranging from Duracell batteries to Paul Masson wines.

Rebates give the producer a way to be certain that final consumers actually get the price reduction. If the rebate amount were just taken off the price charged

Retailers are willing to redeem coupons because it increases their sales—and they usually are paid for handling the coupons.

middlemen, they might not pass the savings along to consumers. In addition, many consumers buy because the price looks lower with the rebate—but then they don't request the refund.[20]

LIST PRICE MAY DEPEND ON GEOGRAPHIC PRICING POLICIES

Retail list prices sometimes include free delivery. Or free delivery may be offered to some customers as an aid to closing the sale. What the retail list price includes (or does not include) may not be formally stated. That way, the retailer can adjust its marketing mix—depending on the customer's needs or bargaining ability.

Deciding who pays the freight charge is more important on sales to business customers than to final consumers because more money is involved. Usually, purchase orders specify place, time, method of delivery, freight costs, insurance, handling, and other charges. There are many possible variations for an imaginative marketing manager, and some specialized terms have developed.

FOB pricing is easy

A commonly used transportation term is **FOB**—which means free on board some vehicle at some place. Typically, FOB pricing names the place—often the location of the seller's factory or warehouse—as in FOB Taiwan or FOB mill. This means that the seller pays the cost of loading the products onto some vehicle—usually a truck, railcar, or ship. At the point of loading, title to the products passes to the buyer. Then the buyer pays the freight and takes responsibility for damage in transit—except as covered by the transporting company.

The marketing manager can make variations easily by changing the place named in the FOB description. If a firm wants to pay the freight for the convenience of customers, it can use FOB delivered or FOB buyer's factory. In this case, title does not pass until the products are delivered. If the seller wants title to pass immediately but is willing to prepay freight (and then include it in the invoice), FOB seller's factory—freight prepaid can be used.

FOB shipping point pricing simplifies the seller's pricing—but it may narrow the market. Since the delivered cost varies depending on the buyer's location, a customer located farther from the seller must pay more and might buy from closer suppliers.

Zone pricing smooths delivered prices

Zone pricing means making an average freight charge to all buyers within specific geographic areas. The seller pays the actual freight charges and bills each customer for an average charge. For example, a company in Canada might divide the United States into seven zones, then bill all customers in the same zone the same amount for freight even though actual shipping costs might vary.

Zone pricing reduces the wide variation in delivered prices that results from an FOB shipping point pricing policy. It also simplifies transportation charges.

Uniform delivered pricing—one price to all

Uniform delivered pricing means making an average freight charge to all buyers. It is a kind of zone pricing—an entire country may be considered as one zone—that includes the average cost of delivery in the price. Uniform delivered pricing is most often used when (1) transportation costs are relatively low and (2) the seller wishes to sell in all geographic areas at one price—perhaps a nationally advertised price.

German firms will have new opportunities in a unified Europe, but they may need different geographic pricing policies to expand into new territories.

Freight-absorption
pricing—competing
on equal grounds in
another territory

When all firms in an industry use FOB shipping point pricing, a firm usually competes well near its shipping point but not farther away. As sales reps look for business farther away, delivered prices rise and the firm finds itself priced out of the market.

This problem can be reduced with **freight absorption pricing**—which means absorbing freight cost so that a firm's delivered price meets the nearest competitor's. This amounts to cutting list price to appeal to new market segments.

With freight absorption pricing, the only limit on the size of a firm's territory is the amount of freight cost it is willing to absorb. These absorbed costs cut net return on each sale—but the new business may raise total profit. Some small firms look at international markets this way; they just figure that any profit from export sales is a bonus.

LEGALITY OF PRICING POLICIES

Even very high prices
may be OK if they're
not fixed

Generally speaking, the prices firms charge don't need government approval. Businesses can charge what they want—even outrageously high prices—if these prices aren't fixed with competitors.

Price fixing is illegal—
you can go to jail

Difficulties with pricing—and violations of price legislation—usually occur when competing marketing mixes are quite similar. When the success of an entire marketing strategy depends on price, there's pressure (and temptation) to make agreements with competitors (conspire). And **price-fixing** (competitors getting together to raise, lower, or stabilize prices) is common and relatively easy. *But it's also completely illegal.* It's "conspiracy" under Canada's Competition Act. To discourage price-fixing, both companies and individual managers are held responsible. Some executives have already gone to jail! And governments are getting tougher on price-fixing.[21]

The first step to understanding pricing legislation is to know the thinking of legislators and the courts. Ideally, they try to help the economy perform more effectively in consumers' interest. In practice, this doesn't always work out as neatly as planned. But generally, their intentions are good. And if we take this view, we get a better idea of the "why" of legislation. This helps us to anticipate future rulings.

We'll look at Canadian legislation here, but other countries have similar laws on pricing.[22] More specifically we'll discuss the kinds of pricing action the Combines Act made illegal, past difficulties in enforcing that law, and subsequent efforts to make enforcement easier by the passage of Bill C-2 in December 1975.

Price discrimination as
a violation of the
Combines Act

Before its amendment by Bill C-2, section 34a of the Combines Act made it illegal for a supplier to discriminate in price between competitors purchasing like quantities of goods or for a buyer knowingly to benefit from such discrimination. But it wasn't easy to prove that price discrimination had actually occurred. To do so, the government had to establish:

1. There were two or more sales that could be compared.
2. There was a discount, rebate, allowance, price concession, or other advantage granted to one purchaser that wasn't available to another.
3. The persons between whom there was discrimination were purchasers in competition with each other.

4. The discriminatory prices were applied to articles of like quality and like quantity.

5. The discriminatory transaction was part of a practice of discrimination.

One-shot deals or arrangements such as store-opening specials, anniversary specials, and stock clearance sales weren't forbidden since they failed to constitute "a practice." Quantity and volume discounts also weren't prohibited as long as they were available to all competing purchasers of like quantities. However, functional discounts (offering a larger discount to wholesalers than to retailers) were illegal. Such discounts were based on a test other than quality and quantity of the goods purchased.

Section 34a was intended to make price discrimination illegal. But because of difficulties in enforcement, no Canadian manufacturer was ever convicted of price discrimination.[23]

Amendments contained in Bill C-2 dealt with some of these barriers to enforcement. Discrimination in the pricing of services as well as goods is now banned. The provision requiring "a practice" of discrimination has been dropped. But defining what constitutes "competing customers" and "like quality" still poses problems. Also, differences in the amount purchased—even small differences— still justify whatever quantity discount structure a manufacturer chooses to use.[24]

Legal barriers to predatory pricing

Section 34b of the Competition Act outlaws regional price differentials that limit competition. This provision forbids a company making profits in one area from charging unreasonably low prices in another area in order to eliminate local competition. But the government must prove (1) that the company had a policy of selling the articles in one area of Canada at prices lower than those charged elsewhere in Canada and (2) that this policy had the effect, tendency, or intent of substantially lessening competition or eliminating a competitor. Section 34c of the same act contained a more general bar to predatory pricing. Very few Canadian firms have been brought to court under either of these two predatory price-cutting provisions. Bill C-2, which less strictly defines a substantial lessening of competition, may lead to more aggressive enforcement.

Discriminatory promotional allowances and the law

Section 35 of the Competition Act makes it an offense either for a seller to offer or for a customer to seek any form of promotional allowance (including discounts, rebates, and price concessions) not offered on proportionate terms to all other competing customers. A small customer purchasing half as much as a larger competitor must receive a promotional allowance equal to half of what was offered the larger firm. This means promotional allowances must be granted on a per case or per dozen basis.

This section of the Competition Act resembles the Robinson-Patman Act, which requires US manufacturers to offer competing customers "proportionately equal" promotional allowances. However, remember that in Canada, unlike in the United States, functional discounts are illegal. Wholesalers and retailers are considered directly competing customers who must receive proportionately equal promotional allowances.

No Canadian manufacturer has as yet been convicted under this provision. This is true even though discrimination in the offering of promotional allowances is a *per se* offense. (It need not be part of a practice of discrimination or be proven substantially to have lessened competition.) A manufacturer who wanted to

A retail chain may get a special functional discount.

discriminate would use a quantity discount structure favoring large customers, rather than a promotional allowance. Such discount structures are safe from legal challenge in Canada. In the United States, however, quantity discount structures must be cost justified.

Legislation against misleading price advertising

Deceptive price advertising has been actively policed in the courts. More aggressive prosecution may be due to the fact that misleading price advertising is a lesser offense under the Criminal Code and one easier to establish. Although the publicity surrounding a conviction may greatly harm the offender's public image, violations are usually punished by relatively modest fines. In recent years, however, more substantial fines, in one case $1 million, have been levied.[25]

Bill C-2 introduced additional restrictions on misleading price advertising. One such section was directed against "bait and switch" advertising, which lures customers to a store by stressing the low price of an article that the retailer either doesn't stock at all or stocks only in token amounts. Under the new provision, an advertiser must stock reasonable quantities of any advertised product. However, a merchant won't be prosecuted if it offers rain checks in place of an advertised but unavailable item. These rain checks must be redeemable within a reasonable period of time.

Legislation against resale price maintenance

Resale price maintenance occurs when a producer or brander of an article requires subsequent resellers to offer it at a stipulated (or not below a stated minimum) price. But although such a practice has been illegal in Canada since 1951, has that law been enforced? Some argue that efforts at resale price maintenance are few and far between. Others maintain that this restriction has been relatively ignored.[26]

Section 38 of Bill C-2 corrects one apparent weakness in the law against resale price maintenance: the inability to deal with suppliers' orders to "get your price up." Any effort to bring about an increase in price or to discourage a reduction is now illegal. A number of other changes were also designed to tighten up the price discrimination rules.

Provincial pricing legislation

British Columbia, Alberta, and Manitoba have provincial legislation that prevents firms from selling below "landed" invoice cost plus a minimum markup, such as 5 percent. Such legislation outlaws predatory pricing. But the real intent is to protect limited-line retailers from "ruinous" competition were full-line stores to sell milk below cost as a loss leader. However, this type of legislation hasn't been vigorously enforced.

Provincial Trade Practices Legislation has focused on protecting consumers from misleading price advertising and the deceptive pricing practices of door-to-door salespeople. Particular attention has been paid to seeing that any comparison of a sale price with a so-called regular price is valid.

Competition Act versus Charter of Rights and Freedoms

Recently, Provincial Courts have ruled that provisions of the Competition Act violate the Charter of Rights and Freedoms. Since the charter governs, these courts have stayed (that is, put on hold) charges of price-fixing, unfair competition, and the like. Ultimately, the issue will be decided by the Supreme Court of Canada.

CONCLUSION

The Price variable offers an alert marketing manager many possibilities for varying marketing mixes. What pricing policies should be used depends on the pricing objectives. We looked at profit-oriented, sales-oriented, and status quo–oriented objectives.

A marketing manager must set policies about price flexibility, price levels over the product life cycle, who will pay the freight, and who will get discounts and allowances. While doing this, the manager should be aware of legislation that affects pricing policies.

In most cases, a marketing manager must set prices—that is, administer prices. Starting with a list price, a variety of discounts and allowances may be offered to adjust for the something being offered in the marketing mix.

Throughout this chapter, we talk about what may be included (or excluded) in the something—and what objectives a firm might set to guide its pricing policies. Price setting itself is not discussed. It will be covered in the next chapter—where we show ways to carry out the various pricing objectives and policies.

QUESTIONS AND PROBLEMS

1. Identify the strategy decisions a marketing manager must make in the Price area. Illustrate your answer for a local retailer.

2. How should the acceptance of a profit-oriented, a sales-oriented, or a status quo–oriented pricing objective affect the development of a company's marketing strategy? Illustrate for each.

3. Distinguish between one-price and flexible-price policies. Which is most appropriate for a hardware store? Why?

4. How would differences in exchange rates between different countries affect a firm's decisions concerning the use of flexible-price policies in different foreign markets?

5. Cite two examples of continuously selling above the market price. Describe the situations.

6. Explain the types of competitive situations that might lead to a meeting-competition pricing policy.

7. What pricing objective(s) is a skimming pricing policy most likely implementing? Is the same true for a penetration pricing policy? Which policy is probably most appropriate for each of the following products: (*a*) a new type of home lawn-sprinkling system, (*b*) a new skin patch drug to help smokers quit, (*c*) a videotape of a best-selling movie, and (*d*) a new children's toy?

8. Would consumers be better off if all nations dropped their antidumping laws? Explain your thinking.

9. How would our marketing system change if manufacturers were required to set fixed prices on *all* products sold at retail and *all* retailers were required to use these prices? Would a manufacturer's marketing mix be easier to develop? What kind of an operation would retailing be in this situation? Would consumers receive more or less service?

10. Is price discrimination involved if a large oil company sells gasoline to taxicab associations for resale to individual taxicab operators for 2½ cents a gallon less than the price charged to retail service stations? What happens if the cab associations resell gasoline not only to taxicab operators but to the general public as well?

11. Do stocking allowances increase or reduce conflict in a channel of distribution? Explain your thinking.

12. Are seasonal discounts appropriate in agricultural businesses (which are certainly seasonal)?

13. What are the effective annual interest rates for the following cash discount terms: (*a*) 1/10, net 20; (*b*) 1/5, net 10; and (*c*) net 25?

14. Why would a manufacturer offer a rebate instead of lowering the suggested list price?

15. How can marketing managers change their FOB terms to make their otherwise competitive marketing mix more attractive?

16. What type of geographic pricing policy is most appropriate for the following products (specify any assumptions necessary to obtain a definite answer): (*a*) a chemical by-product, (*b*) nationally advertised candy bars, (*c*) rebuilt auto parts, and (*d*) tricycles?

17. How would a ban on freight absorption (that is, requiring FOB factory pricing) affect a producer with substantial economies of scale in production?

SUGGESTED CASES

24. AAA Photo Labs, Inc.

25. Kelman Mfg., Inc.

Marketing Arithmetic

Appendix **C**

When You Finish This Appendix, You Should

❶

Understand the components of an operating statement (profit and loss statement).

❷

Know how to compute the stockturn rate.

❸

Understand how operating ratios can help analyze a business.

❹

Understand how to calculate markups and markdowns.

❺

Understand how to calculate return on investment (ROI) and return on assets (ROA).

❻

Understand the important new terms (shown in blue).

Marketing students must become familiar with the essentials of the language of business. Businesspeople commonly use accounting terms when talking about costs, prices, and profit. And using accounting data is a practical tool in analyzing marketing problems.

THE OPERATING STATEMENT

An **operating statement** is a simple summary of the financial results of a company's operations over a specific period of time. Some beginning students may feel that the operating statement is complex, but as we'll soon see, this really isn't true. *The main purpose of the operating statement is determining the net profit figure—and presenting data to support that figure.* This is why the operating statement is often referred to as the *profit and loss statement.*

Exhibit C–1 shows an operating statement for a wholesale or retail business. The statement is complete and detailed so you will see the framework throughout the discussion, but the amount of detail on an operating statement is *not* standardized. Many companies use financial statements with much less detail than this one. They emphasize clarity and readability rather than detail. To really understand an operating statement, however, you must know about its components.

Only three basic components

The basic components of an operating statement are *sales*—which come from the sale of goods and services; *costs*—which come from the making and selling process; and the balance—called *profit or loss*—which is just the difference between sales and costs. So there are only three basic components in the statement: sales, costs, and profit (or loss). Other items on an operating statement are there only to provide supporting details.

Time period covered may vary

There is no one time period an operating statement covers. Rather, statements are prepared to satisfy the needs of a particular business. This may be at the end of each day or at the end of each week. Usually, however, an operating statement summarizes results for one month, three months, six months, or a full year. Since the time period does vary, this information is included in the heading of the statement as follows:

SMITH COMPANY
Operating Statement
For the (Period) Ended (Date)

Also, see Exhibit C–1.

Management uses of operating statements

Before going on to a more detailed discussion of the components of our operating statement, let's think about some of the uses for such a statement. Exhibit C–1 shows that a lot of information is presented in a clear and concise manner. With this information, a manager can easily find the relation of net sales to the cost of sales, the gross margin, expenses, and net profit. Opening and closing inventory figures are available—as is the amount spent during the period

Exhibit C–1   An Operating Statement (profit and loss statement)

SMITH COMPANY
Operating Statement
For the Year Ended December 31, 199X

Gross sales.....................................			$540,000
Less: Returns and allowances			40,000
Net sales......................................			$500,000
Cost of sales:			
Beginning inventory at cost....................		$ 80,000	
Purchases at billed cost.......................	$310,000		
Less: Purchase discounts	40,000		
Purchases at net cost.........................	$270,000		
Plus freight-in...............................	20,000		
Net cost of delivered purchases.............		$290,000	
Cost of products available for sale..............		$370,000	
Less: Ending inventory at cost................		70,000	
Cost of sales			$300,000
Gross margin (gross profit)			$200,000
Expenses:			
Selling expenses:			
Sales salaries..............................	$ 60,000		
Advertising expense	20,000		
Delivery expense............................	20,000		
Total selling expense		$100,000	
Administrative expense			
Office salaries	$ 30,000		
Office supplies	10,000		
Miscellaneous administrative expense	5,000		
Total administrative expense................		$ 45,000	
General expense:			
Rent expense................................	$ 10,000		
Miscellaneous general expenses..............	5,000		
Total general expense		$ 15,000	
Total expenses...........................			$160,000
Net profit from operation			$ 40,000

for the purchase of goods for resale. Total expenses are listed to make it easier to compare them with previous statements—and to help control these expenses.

All this information is important to a company's managers. Assume that a particular company prepares monthly operating statements. A series of these statements is a valuable tool for directing and controlling the business. By comparing results from one month to the next, managers can uncover unfavorable trends in the sales, costs, or profit areas of the business—and take any needed action.

A skeleton statement gets down to essential details

Let's refer to Exhibit C–1 and begin to analyze this seemingly detailed statement to get first-hand knowledge of the components of the operating statement.

As a first step, suppose we take all the items that have dollar amounts extended to the third, or right-hand, column. Using these items only, the operating statement looks like this:

Gross sales	$540,000
Less: Returns and allowances	40,000
Net sales	$500,000
Less: Cost of sales	$300,000
Gross margin	$200,000
Less: Total expenses	$160,000
Net profits (loss)	$ 40,000

Is this a complete operating statement? This answer is *yes*. This skeleton statement differs from Exhibit C–1 only in supporting detail. All the basic components are included. In fact, the only items we must list to have a complete operating statement are:

Net sales	$500,000
Less: Costs	460,000
Net profit (loss)	$ 40,000

These three items are the essentials of an operating statement. All other subdivisions or details are just useful additions.

Meaning of sales

Now let's define the meaning of the terms in the skeleton statement.

The first item is sales. What do we mean by sales? The term **gross sales** is the total amount charged to all customers during some time period. However, there is always some customer dissatisfaction—or just plain errors in ordering and shipping goods. This results in returns and allowances—which reduce gross sales.

A **return** occurs when a customer sends back purchased products. The company either refunds the purchase price or allows the customer dollar credit on other purchases.

An **allowance** occurs when a customer is not satisfied with a purchase for some reason. The company gives a price reduction on the original invoice (bill), but the customer keeps the goods and services.

These refunds and price reductions must be considered when the firm computes its net sales figure for the period. Really, we're only interested in the revenue the company manages to keep. This is **net sales**—the actual sales dollars the company receives. Therefore, all reductions, refunds, cancellations, and so forth made because of returns and allowances are deducted from the original total (gross sales) to get net sales. This is shown below:

Gross sales	$540,000
Less: Returns and allowances	40,000
Net sales	$500,000

Meaning of cost of sales

The next item in the operating statement—**cost of sales**—is the total value (at cost) of the sales during the period. We'll discuss this computation later. Meanwhile, note that after we obtain the cost of sales figure, we subtract it from the net sales figure to get the gross margin.

Meaning of gross margin and expenses

Gross margin (gross profit) is the money left to cover the expenses of selling the products and operating the business. Firms hope that a profit will be left after subtracting these expenses.

Selling expense is commonly the major expense below the gross margin. Note that in Exhibit C–1, **expenses** are all the remaining costs subtracted from the gross margin to get the net profit. The expenses in this case are the selling, administrative, and general expenses. (Note that the cost of purchases and cost of sales are not included in this total expense figure—they were subtracted from net sales earlier to get the gross margin. Note, also, that some accountants refer to cost of sales as cost of goods sold.)

Net profit—at the bottom of the statement—is what the company earned from its operations during a particular period. It is the amount left after the cost of sales and the expenses are subtracted from net sales. *Net sales and net profit are not the same.* Many firms have large sales and no profits—they may even have losses! That's why understanding costs—and controlling them—is important.

DETAILED ANALYSIS OF SECTIONS OF THE OPERATING STATEMENT

Cost of sales for a wholesale or retail company

The cost of sales section includes details that are used to find the cost of sales ($300,000 in our example).

In Exhibit C–1, you can see that beginning and ending inventory, purchases, purchase discounts, and freight-in are all necessary to calculate cost of sales. If we pull the cost of sales section from the operating statement, it looks like this:

Cost of sales:		
Beginning inventory at cost......................		$ 80,000
Purchases at billed cost........................	$310,000	
Less: Purchase discounts	40,000	
Purchases at net cost...........................	$270,000	
Plus: Freight-in................................	20,000	
Net cost of delivered purchases...................		$290,000
Cost of goods available for sale..................		$370,000
Less: Ending inventory at cost..................		70,000
Cost of sales		$300,000

Cost of sales is the cost value of what is *sold*—not the cost of goods on hand at any given time.

Inventory figures merely show the cost of goods on hand at the beginning and end of the period the statement covers. These figures may be obtained by physically counting goods on hand on these dates—or estimated from perpetual inventory records that show the inventory balance at any given time. The methods used to determine the inventory should be as accurate as possible because these figures affect the cost of sales during the period—and net profit.

The net cost of delivered purchases must include freight charges and purchase discounts received, since these items affect the money actually spent to buy goods and bring them to the place of business. A **purchase discount** is a reduction of the original invoice amount for some business reason. For example, a cash discount may be given for prompt payment of the amount due. We subtract the total of such discounts from the original invoice cost of purchases to get the *net* cost of purchases. To this figure, we add the freight charges for bringing the goods to the place of business. This gives the net cost of *delivered* purchases. When we add the net cost of delivered purchases to the beginning inventory at cost, we have the total cost of goods available for sale during the period. If we now subtract the ending inventory at cost from the cost of the goods available for sale, we get the cost of sales.

One important point should be noted about cost of sales. The way the value of inventory is calculated varies from one company to another—and can cause big differences in the cost of sales and the operating statement. (See any basic accounting textbook for how the various inventory valuation methods work.)

Cost of sales for a manufacturing company

Exhibit C–1 shows the way the manager of a wholesale or retail business arrives at cost of sales. Such a business *purchases* finished products and resells them. In a manufacturing company, the purchases section of this operating statement is replaced by a section called cost of production. This section includes purchases of raw materials and parts, direct and indirect labor costs, and factory overhead charges (such as heat, light, and power) that are necessary to produce finished products. The cost of production is added to the beginning finished products inventory to arrive at the cost of products available for sale. Often, a separate cost of production statement is prepared, and only the total cost of production is shown in the operating statement. See Exhibit C–2 for an illustration of the cost of sales section of an operating statement for a manufacturing company.

Expenses

Expenses go below the gross margin. They usually include the costs of selling and the costs of administering the business. They do not include the cost of sales—either purchased or produced.

There is no right method for classifying the expense accounts or arranging them on the operating statement. They can just as easily be arranged alphabetically or according to amount, with the largest placed at the top and so on down the line. In a business of any size, though, it is clearer to group the expenses in some way and use subtotals by groups for analysis and control purposes. This was done in Exhibit C–1.

Summary on operating statements

The statement presented in Exhibit C–1 contains all the major categories in an operating statement—together with a normal amount of supporting detail. Further detail can be added to the statement under any of the major categories

Exhibit C–2   Cost of Sales Section of an Operating Statement for a Manufacturing Firm

Cost of sales:		
Finished products inventory (beginning)	$ 20,000	
Cost of production (Schedule 1)	100,000	
Total cost of finished products available for sale	$120,000	
Less: Finished products inventory (ending).......	30,000	
Cost of sales		$ 90,000
Schedule 1, Schedule of cost of production		
Beginning work in process inventory		$ 15,000
Raw materials:		
Beginning raw materials inventory	$ 10,000	
Net cost of delivered purchases..................	80,000	
Total cost of materials available for use...........	$ 90,000	
Less: Ending raw materials inventory...........	15,000	
Cost of materials placed in production	$ 75,000	
Direct labor......................................	20,000	
Manufacturing expenses:		
Indirect labor $4,000		
Maintenance and repairs....................... 3,000		
Factory supplies 1,000		
Heat, light, and power 2,000		
Total manufacturing expenses	$ 10,000	
Total manufacturing costs		$105,000
Total work in process during period................		$120,000
Less: Ending work in process inventory...........		20,000
Cost of production......................		$100,000

without changing the nature of the statement. The amount of detail normally is determined by how the statement will be used. A stockholder may be given a sketchy operating statement—while the one prepared for internal company use may have a lot of detail.

COMPUTING THE STOCKTURN RATE

A detailed operating statement can provide the data needed to compute the **stockturn rate**—a measure of the number of times the average inventory is sold during a year. Note that the stockturn rate is related to the *turnover during a year*—not the length of time covered by a particular operating statement.

The stockturn rate is a very important measure because it shows how rapidly the firm's inventory is moving. Some businesses typically have slower turnover than others. But a drop in turnover in a particular business can be very alarming. It may mean that the firm's assortment of products is no longer as attractive as it was. Also, it may mean that the firm will need more working capital to handle the same volume of sales. Most businesses pay a lot of attention to the stockturn rate—trying to get faster turnover (and lower inventory costs).

Three methods—all basically similar—can be used to compute the stockturn rate. Which method is used depends on the data available. These three methods, which usually give approximately the same results, are shown below:*

(1) $$\frac{\text{Cost of sales}}{\text{Average inventory at cost}}$$

(2) $$\frac{\text{Net sales}}{\text{Average inventory at selling price}}$$

(3) $$\frac{\text{Sales in units}}{\text{Average inventory in units}}$$

Computing the stockturn rate will be illustrated only for Formula 1, since all are similar. The only difference is that the cost figures used in Formula 1 are changed to a selling price or numerical count basis in Formulas 2 and 3. Note: regardless of the method used, the numerator and denominator of the formula must both be expressed in the same terms.

If the inventory level varies a lot during the year, you may need detailed information about the inventory level at different times to compute the average inventory. If it stays at about the same level during the year, however, it's easy to get an estimate. For example, using Formula 1, the average inventory at cost is computed by adding the beginning and ending inventories at cost and dividing by 2. This average inventory figure is then divided into the cost of sales (in cost terms) to get the stockturn rate.

For example, suppose that the cost of sales for one year was $1,000,000. Beginning inventory was $250,000 and ending inventory $150,000. Adding the two inventory figures and dividing by 2, we get an average inventory of $200,000. We next divide the cost of sales by the average inventory ($1,000,000 ÷ $200,000) and get a stockturn rate of 5.

The stockturn rate is covered further in Chapter 19.

OPERATING RATIOS ANALYZE THE BUSINESS

Many businesspeople use the operating statement to calculate **operating ratios**—the ratio of items on the operating statement to net sales—and compare these ratios from one time period to another. They can also compare their own operating ratios with those of competitors. Such competitive data is often available through trade associations. Each firm may report its results to a trade association, which then distributes summary results to its members. These ratios help managers control their operations. If some expense ratios are rising, for example, those particular costs are singled out for special attention.

Operating ratios are computed by dividing net sales into the various operating statement items that appear below the net sales level in the operating statement. The net sales is used as the denominator in the operating ratio because it shows the sales the firm actually won.

---

*Differences occur because of varied markups and nonhomogeneous product assortments. In an assortment of tires, for example, those with low markups might have sold much better than those with high markups. But with Formula 3, all tires would be treated equally.

We can see the relation of operating ratios to the operating statement if we think of there being another column to the right of the dollar figures in an operating statement. This column contains percentage figures—using net sales as 100 percent. This approach can be seen below:

Gross sales	$540,000	
Less: Returns and allowances	40,000	
Net sales	$500,000	100%
Cost of sales	300,000	60
Gross margin	$200,000	40
Expenses	160,000	32
Net profit	$40,000	8%

The 40 percent ratio of gross margin to net sales in the above example shows that 40 percent of the net sales dollar is available to cover sales expenses and administering the business—and to provide a profit. Note that the ratio of expenses to sales added to the ratio of profit to sales equals the 40 percent gross margin ratio. The net profit ratio of 8 percent shows that 8 percent of the net sales dollar is left for profit.

The value of percentage ratios should be obvious. The percentages are easily figured—and much easier to compare than large dollar figures.

Note that because these operating statement categories are interrelated, only a few pieces of information are needed to figure the others. In this case, for example, knowing the gross margin percent and net profit percent makes it possible to figure the expenses and cost of sales percentages. Further, knowing just one dollar amount and the percentages lets you figure all the other dollar amounts.

MARKUPS

A **markup** is the dollar amount added to the cost of sales to get the selling price. The markup usually is similar to the firm's gross margin because the markup amount added onto the unit cost of a product by a retailer or wholesaler is expected to cover the selling and administrative expenses—and to provide a profit.

The markup approach to pricing is discussed in Chapter 19, so it will not be discussed at length here. But a simple example illustrates the idea. If retailers buy an article that costs $1 when delivered to their store, they must sell it for more than this cost if they hope to make a profit. So they might add 50 cents onto the cost of the article to cover their selling and other costs and, hopefully, to provide a profit. The 50 cents is the markup.

The 50 cents is also the gross margin or gross profit from that item *if* it is sold. But note that it is *not* the net profit. Selling expenses may amount to 35 cents, 45 cents, or even 55 cents. In other words, there is no guarantee that markup will cover costs. Further, there is no guarantee that customers will buy at the marked-up price. This may require markdowns, which are discussed later in this appendix.

Markup conversions

Often, it is convenient to use markups as percentages rather than focusing on the actual dollar amounts. But markups can be figured as a percent of cost or selling price. To have some agreement, *markup* (*percent*) will mean percentage of selling price unless stated otherwise. So the 50-cent markup on the $1.50 selling price is a markup of 33⅓ percent. On the other hand, the 50-cent markup is a 50 percent markup on cost.

Some retailers and wholesalers use markup conversion tables or spreadsheets to easily convert from cost to selling price—depending on the markup on selling price they want. To see the interrelation, look at the two formulas below. They can be used to convert either type of markup to the other.

$$(4) \quad \frac{\text{Percent markup}}{\text{on selling price}} = \frac{\text{Percent markup on cost}}{100\% + \text{Percent markup on cost}}$$

$$(5) \quad \frac{\text{Percent markup}}{\text{on cost}} = \frac{\text{Percent markup on selling price}}{100\% - \text{Percent markup on selling price}}$$

In the previous example, we had a cost of $1, a markup of 50 cents, and a selling price of $1.50. We saw that the markup on selling price was 33⅓ percent—and on cost, it was 50 percent. Let's substitute these percentage figures—in Formulas 4 and 5—to see how to convert from one basis to the other. Assume first of all that we only know the markup on selling price and want to convert to markup on cost. Using Formula 5, we get:

$$\text{Percent markup on cost} = \frac{33\tfrac{1}{3}\%}{100\% - 33\tfrac{1}{3}\%} = \frac{33\tfrac{1}{3}\%}{66\tfrac{2}{3}\%} = 50\%$$

On the other hand, if we know only the percent markup on cost, we can convert to markup on selling price as follows:

$$\text{Percent markup on selling price} = \frac{50\%}{100\% + 50\%} = \frac{50\%}{150\%} = 33\tfrac{1}{3}\%$$

These results can be proved and summarized as follows:

$$\begin{array}{ll} \text{Markup } \$0.50 = & 50\% \text{ of cost, or } 33\tfrac{1}{3}\% \text{ of selling price} \\ + \quad \text{Cost } \$1.00 = & 100\% \text{ of cost, or } 66\tfrac{2}{3}\% \text{ of selling price} \\ \hline \text{Selling price } \$1.50 = & 150\% \text{ of cost, or } 100\% \text{ of selling price} \end{array}$$

It is important to see that only the percentage figures change while the money amounts of cost, markup, and selling price stay the same. Note, too, that when selling price is the base for the calculation (100 percent), then the cost percentage plus the markup percentage equal 100 percent. But when the cost of the product is used as the base figure (100 percent), the selling price percentage must be greater than 100 percent by the markup on cost.

MARKDOWN RATIOS HELP CONTROL RETAIL OPERATIONS

The ratios we discussed above were concerned with figures on the operating statement. Another important ratio—the **markdown ratio**—is a tool many retailers use to measure the efficiency of various departments and their whole business. But note that it is *not directly related to the operating statement*. It requires special calculations.

A **markdown** is a retail price reduction required because customers won't buy some item at the originally marked-up price. This refusal to buy may be due to a variety of reasons—soiling, style changes, fading, damage caused by handling, or an original price that was too high. To get rid of these products, the retailer offers them at a lower price.

Markdowns are generally considered to be due to business errors—perhaps because of poor buying, original markups that are too high, and other reasons. (Note, however, that some retailers use markdowns as a way of doing business rather than a way to correct errors. For example, a store that buys out overstocked fashions from other retailers may start by marking each item with a high price and then reduce the price each week until it sells.) Regardless of the reason, however, markdowns are reductions in the original price—and they are important to managers who want to measure the effectiveness of their operations.

Markdowns are similar to allowances because price reductions are made. Thus, in computing a markdown ratio, markdowns and allowances are usually added together and then divided by net sales. The markdown ratio is computed as follows:

$$\text{Markdown \%} = \frac{\text{\$ Markdowns} + \text{\$ Allowances}}{\text{\$ Net sales}} \times 100$$

The 100 is multiplied by the fraction to get rid of decimal points.

Returns are *not* included when figuring the markdown ratio. Returns are treated as consumer errors—not business errors—and therefore are not included in this measure of business efficiency.

Retailers who use markdown ratios usually keep a record of the amount of markdowns and allowances in each department and then divide the total by the net sales in each department. Over a period of time, these ratios give management one measure of the efficiency of buyers and salespeople in various departments.

It should be stressed again that the markdown ratio is not calculated directly from data on the operating statement since the markdowns take place before the products are sold. In fact, some products may be marked down and still not sold. Even if the marked-down items are not sold, the markdowns—that is, the reevaluations of their value—are included in the calculations in the time period when they are taken.

The markdown ratio is calculated for a whole department (or profit centre)—*not* individual items. What we are seeking is a measure of the effectiveness of a whole department—not how well the department did on individual items.

RETURN ON INVESTMENT (ROI) REFLECTS ASSET USE

Another off-the-operating-statement ratio is **return on investment (ROI)**—the ratio of net profit (after taxes) to the investment used to make the net profit, multiplied by 100 to get rid of decimals. Investment is not shown on the operating statement. But it is on the **balance sheet** (statement of financial condition)—another accounting statement—that shows a company's assets, liabilities, and net worth. It may take some digging or special analysis, however, to find the right investment number.

Investment means the dollar resources the firm has invested in a project or business. For example, a new product may require $4 million in new money—for inventory, accounts receivable, promotion, and so on—and its attractiveness may be judged by its likely ROI. If the net profit (after taxes) for this new product is expected to be $1 million in the first year, then the ROI is 25 percent—that is, ($1 million ÷ $4 million) × 100.

There are two ways to figure ROI. The *direct* way is:

$$\text{ROI (in \%)} = \frac{\text{Net profit (after taxes)}}{\text{Investment}} \times 100$$

The *indirect* way is:

$$\text{ROI (in \%)} = \frac{\text{Net profit (after taxes)}}{\text{Sales}} \times \frac{\text{Sales}}{\text{Investment}} \times 100$$

This way is concerned with net profit margin and turnover—that is:

$$\text{ROI (in \%)} = \text{Net profit margin} \times \text{Turnover} \times 100$$

This indirect way makes it clearer how to *increase* ROI. There are three ways:

1. Increase profit margin (with lower costs or a higher price).
2. Increase sales.
3. Decrease investment.

Effective marketing strategy planning and implementation can increase profit margins and/or sales. And careful asset management can decrease investment.

ROI is a revealing measure of how well managers are doing. Most companies have alternative uses for their funds. If the returns in a business aren't at least as high as outside uses, then the money probably should be shifted to the more profitable uses.

Some firms borrow more than others to make investments. In other words, they invest less of their own money to acquire assets—what we called *investments*. If ROI calculations use only the firm's own investment, this gives higher ROI figures to those who borrow a lot—which is called *leveraging*. To adjust for different borrowing proportions—to make comparisons among projects, departments, divisions, and companies easier—another ratio has come into use. **Return on assets (ROA)** is the ratio of net profit (after taxes) to the assets used to make the net profit—times 100.

Both ROI and ROA measures are trying to get at the same thing—how effectively the company is using resources. These measures became increasingly popular as profit rates dropped and it became more obvious that increasing sales volume doesn't necessarily lead to higher profits—or ROI or ROA. Inflation and higher costs for borrowed funds also force more concern for ROI and ROA. Marketers must include these measures in their thinking or top managers are likely to ignore their plans—and requests for financial resources.

QUESTIONS AND PROBLEMS

1. Distinguish between the following pairs of items that appear on operating statements: (*a*) gross sales and net sales, and (*b*) purchases at billed cost and purchases at net cost.

2. How does gross margin differ from gross profit? From net profit?

3. Explain the similarity between markups and gross margin. What connection do markdowns have with the operating statement?

4. Compute the net profit for a company with the following data:

Beginning inventory (cost)	$ 150,000
Purchases at billed cost	330,000
Sales returns and allowances	250,000
Rent	60,000
Salaries	400,000
Heat and light	180,000
Ending inventory (cost)	250,000
Freight cost (inbound)	80,000
Gross sales	1,300,000

5. Construct an operating statement from the following data:

Returns and allowances	$ 150,000
Expenses	20%
Closing inventory at cost	600,000
Markdowns	2%
Inward transportation	30,000
Purchases	1,000,000
Net profit (5%)	300,000

6. Compute net sales and percent of markdowns for the data given below:

Markdowns	$ 40,000
Gross sales	400,000
Returns	32,000
Allowances	48,000

7. (*a*) What percentage markups on cost are equivalent to the following percentage markups on selling price: 20, 37½, 50, and 66⅔? (*b*) What percentage markups on selling price are equivalent to the following percentage markups on cost: 33⅓, 20, 40, and 50?

8. What net sales volume is required to obtain a stockturn rate of 20 times a year on an average inventory at cost of $100,000 with a gross margin of 25 percent?

9. Explain how the general manager of a department store might use the markdown ratios computed for various departments. Is this a fair measure? Of what?

10. Compare and contrast return on investment (ROI) and return on assets (ROA) measures. Which would be best for a retailer with no bank borrowing or other outside sources of funds; that is, the retailer has put up all the money that the business needs?

Price Setting in the Business World

When You Finish This Chapter, You Should

❶

Understand how most wholesalers and retailers set their prices—using markups.

❷

Understand why turnover is so important in pricing.

❸

Understand the advantages and disadvantages of average cost pricing.

❹

Know how to use break-even analysis to evaluate possible prices.

❺

Know how to find the most profitable price and quantity—using marginal analysis, total revenue, and total cost.

❻

Know the many ways that price setters use demand estimates in their pricing.

❼

Understand the important new terms (shown in blue).

At Ottawa's Colonial Furniture two years ago, customers thought nothing of plunking down $995 for a plush, three-seat sofa dressed up in a modish floral chintz cover. No more. "Customers come in, look at the same sofa, and won't pay a cent over $775," says Colonial's Sales Vice President Eugene Gorgichuk. To keep the cash registers ringing, the venerable Ottawa furniture retailer has slashed inventory and other costs and ordered lower prices from its suppliers.

The story at the checkout counter is falling prices—disinflation. Electronic goods have probably figured most prominently in the price-cutting wave. One reason: Ottawa lifted duties on a host of foreign-made products recently in an effort to combat cross-border shopping. But the price-cutting wave is visible at Eaton's, The Bay, Sears, Kmart, you name it.

At Eaton's, for example, regular prices have fallen across the board under its "Everyday Low Prices" sales campaign. Take mattresses: With just-in-time delivery from its suppliers, Eaton's has junked its mattress warehouses, sharply cutting fixed costs that used to be added into the price on the sales floor.

Retail Analyst John Winter points out that with the market share of major department store chains falling precipitously, cost-cutting to survive on permanently lower margins is essential. Better inventory controls, lower operating costs, and more focused merchandising strategies are only just beginning to sweep the long-sleepy Canadian industry.

Observes John William, another Toronto-based retail analyst who's tracking the revolution: "Traditional department store chains have typically operated with a 40 percent gross margin on sales. Mass merchants like Zellers and Kmart are in the 33 percent to 36 percent range. Supermarkets are between 20 percent and 25 percent. But warehouse-type stores have gross margins of 20 percent and Price Costco has 12 percent. That's the competition."[1]

PRICE SETTING IS A KEY STRATEGY DECISION

In the last chapter, we discussed the idea that pricing objectives and policies should guide pricing decisions. We accepted the idea of a list price and went on to discuss variations from list. Now, we'll see how the basic list price is set in the first place—based on information about costs, demand, and profit margins. See Exhibit 19–1.

There are many ways to set list prices. But—for simplicity—they can be reduced to two basic approaches: *cost-oriented* and *demand-oriented* price setting. We will discuss cost-oriented approaches first because they are most common. Also, understanding the problems of relying on a cost-oriented approach shows why a marketing manager must also consider demand to make good price decisions. Let's begin by looking at how most retailers and wholesalers set cost-oriented prices.

Exhibit 19–1　Key Factors that Influence Price Setting

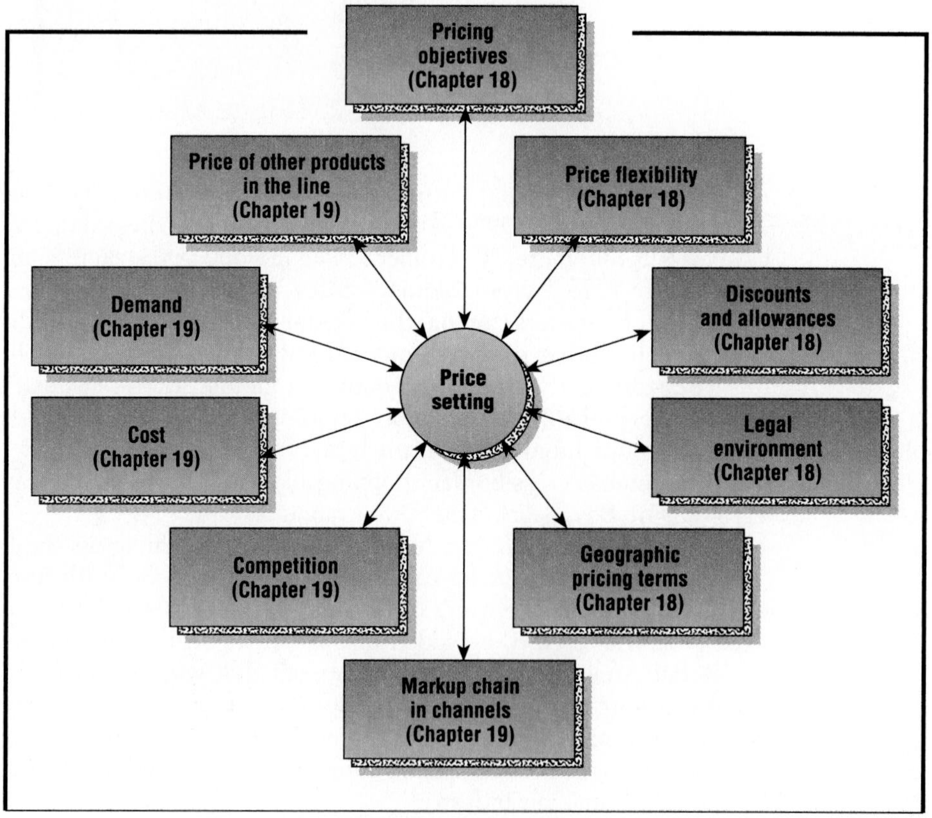

SOME FIRMS JUST USE MARKUPS

Markups guide pricing by middlemen

Some firms, including most retailers and wholesalers, set prices by using a **markup**—a dollar amount added to the cost of products to get the selling price. For example, suppose that a Shopper's Drug buys a bottle of Prell shampoo for $1. To make a profit, the drugstore obviously must sell the shampoo for more than $1. If it adds 50 cents to cover operating expenses and provide a profit, we say that the store is marking up the item 50 cents.

Markups, however, usually are stated as percentages rather than dollar amounts. And this is where confusion sometimes arises. Is a markup of 50 cents on a cost of $1 a markup of 50 percent? Or should the markup be figured as a percentage of the selling price—$1.50—and therefore be 33⅓ percent? A clear definition is necessary.

Markup percent is based on selling price— a convenient rule

Unless otherwise stated, **markup (percent)** means percentage of selling price that is added to the cost to get the selling price. So the 50-cent markup on the $1.50 selling price is a markup of 33⅓ percent. Markups are related to selling price for convenience.

New competition has made the long distance market price competitive.

There's nothing wrong with the idea of markup on cost. However, to avoid confusion, it's important to state clearly which markup percent you're using.

Managers often want to change a markup on cost to one based on selling price—or vice versa. The calculations used to do this are simple (see the section on markup conversion in Appendix C, Marketing Arithmetic, which follows Chapter 18).[2]

Many use a "standard" markup percent

Many middlemen select a standard markup percent and then apply it to all their products. This makes pricing easier. When you think of the large number of items the average retailer and wholesaler carry—and the small sales volume of any one item—this approach may make sense. Spending the time to find the best price to charge on every item in stock (day-to-day or week-to-week) might not pay.

Moreover, different companies in the same line of business often use the same markup percent. There is a reason for this: Their operating expenses are usually similar. So a standard markup is acceptable as long as it's large enough to cover the firm's operating expenses—and provide a reasonable profit.

Markups are related to gross margins

How do managers decide on a standard markup in the first place? A standard markup is usually set close to the firm's *gross margin*. Managers regularly see gross margins on their operating (profit and loss) statements. (See Appendix C, Marketing Arithmetic, if you are unfamiliar with these ideas.) Our Shopper's Drug manager knows that there won't be any profit if the gross margin is not large enough. For this reason, Shopper's Drug might accept a markup percent on Prell shampoo that is close to the store's usual gross margin.

Smart producers pay attention to the gross margins and standard markups of middlemen in their channel. They usually allow trade (functional) discounts similar to the standard markups these middlemen expect.

Products for which consumers do extensive comparisons put pressure on everyone in the channel to be more price competitive.

Markup chain may be used in channel pricing

Different firms in a channel often use different markups. A **markup chain**—the sequence of markups firms use at different levels in a channel—determines the price structure in the whole channel. The markup is figured on the *selling price* at each level of the channel.

For example, Black & Decker's selling price for an electric drill becomes the cost the Home Hardware wholesaler pays. The wholesaler's selling price becomes the hardware retailer's cost. And this cost plus a retail markup becomes the retail selling price. Each markup should cover the costs of running the business—and leave a profit.

Exhibit 19–2 illustrates the markup chain for an electric drill at each level of the channel system. The production (factory) cost of the drill is $21.60. In this case, the producer takes a 10 percent markup and sells the product for $24. The markup is 10 percent of $24 or $2.40. The producer's selling price now becomes the wholesaler's cost—$24. If the wholesaler is used to taking a 20 percent markup on selling price, the markup is $6—and the wholesaler's selling price becomes $30. Now $30 becomes the cost for the hardware retailer. And if retailers are used to a 40 percent markup, they add $20, and the retail selling price becomes $50.

High markups don't always mean big profits

Some people, including many traditional retailers, think high markups mean big profits. Often, this isn't true. A high markup may result in a price that's too high—a price at which few customers will buy. And you can't earn much if you don't sell much, no matter how high your markup. But many retailers and wholesalers seem more concerned with the size of their markup on a single item than with their total profit. And their high markups may lead to low profits—or even losses.

Lower markups can speed turnover—and the stockturn rate

Some retailers and wholesalers, however, try to speed turnover to increase profit, even if this means reducing their markups. They realize that a business runs up costs over time. If they can sell a much greater amount in the same time period, they may be able to take a lower markup—and still earn higher profits at the end of the period.

An important idea here is the **stockturn rate**—the number of times the average inventory is sold in a year. Various methods of figuring stockturn rates can

Exhibit 19–2 Example of a Markup Chain and Channel Pricing

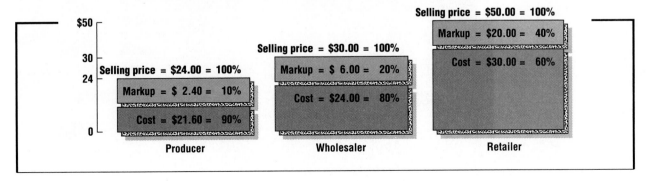

be used (see the section "Computing the Stockturn Rate" in Appendix C). A low stockturn rate may be bad for profits.

At the very least, a low stockturn increases inventory carrying cost and ties up working capital. If a firm with a stockturn of 1 (once per year) sells products that cost it $100,000, it has that much tied up in inventory all the time. But a stockturn of 5 requires only $20,000 worth of inventory ($100,000 cost ÷ 5 turnovers a year).

Whether a stockturn rate is high or low depends on the industry and the product involved. A NAPA auto parts wholesaler may expect an annual rate of 1—while an A&P store might expect 10 to 12 stockturns for soaps and detergents and 50 to 60 stockturns for fresh fruits and vegetables.

Mass-merchandisers run in fast company

Although some middlemen use the same standard markup percent on all their products, this policy ignores the importance of fast turnover. Mass-merchandisers know this. They put low markups on fast-selling items and higher markups on items that sell less frequently. For example, Kmart may put a small markup on fast-selling health and beauty aids (like toothpaste or shampoo) but higher markups on appliances and clothing. Similarly, supermarket operators put low markups on fast-selling items like milk, eggs, and detergents. The markup on these items may be less than half the average markup for all grocery items, but this doesn't mean they're unprofitable. The store earns the small profit per unit more often.

Where does the markup chain start?

Some markups eventually become standard in a trade. Most channel members tend to follow a similar process—adding a certain percentage to the previous price. But who sets price in the first place?

The firm that brands a product is usually the one that sets its basic list price. It may be a large retailer, a large wholesaler, or, most often, the producer.

Items with a high stockturn rate may have a lower markup.

Some producers just start with a cost per unit figure and add a markup—perhaps a standard markup—to obtain their selling price. Or they may use some rule-of-thumb formula such as:

Selling price = Average production cost per unit × 3

A producer who uses this approach might develop rules and markups related to its own costs and objectives. Yet even the first step—selecting the appropriate cost per unit to build on—isn't easy. Let's discuss several approaches to see how cost-oriented price setting really works.

AVERAGE-COST PRICING IS COMMON AND DANGEROUS

Average-cost pricing means adding a reasonable markup to the average cost of a product. A manager usually finds the average cost per unit by studying past records. Dividing the total cost for the last year by all the units produced and sold in that period gives an estimate of the average cost per unit for the next year. If the cost was $32,000 for all labor and materials and $30,000 for fixed overhead expenses—such as selling expenses, rent, and manager salaries—then the total cost is $62,000. If the company produced 40,000 items in that time period, the average cost is $62,000 divided by 40,000 units, or $1.55 per unit. To get the price, the producer decides how much profit per unit to add to the average cost per unit. If the company considers 45 cents a reasonable profit for each unit, it sets the new price at $2. Exhibit 19–3A shows that this approach produces the desired profit—if the company sells 40,000 units.

Exhibit 19–3   Results of Average-Cost Pricing

A. Calculation of Planned Profit if 40,000 Items Are Sold		B. Calculation of Actual Profit if Only 20,000 Items Are Sold	
Calculation of Costs		**Calculation of Costs**	
Fixed overhead expenses	$30,000	Fixed overhead expenses	$30,000
Labor and materials	32,000	Labor and materials	16,000
Total costs	$62,000	Total costs	$46,000
"Planned" profit	18,000		
Total costs and planned profit	$80,000		
Calculation of Profit (or loss)		**Calculation of Profit (or loss)**	
Actual unit sales × price ($2.00*)	$80,000	Annual unit sales × price ($2.00*)	$40,000
Minus: total costs	62,000	Minus: total costs	46,000
Profit (loss)	$18,000	Profit (loss)	($6,000)
Result		**Result**	
Planned profit of $18,000 is earned if 40,000 items are sold at $2 each.		Planned profit of $18,000 is not earned. Instead, $6,000 loss results if 20,000 items are sold at $2 each.	

*Calculation of "reasonable" price: $\frac{\text{Expected total costs and planned profit}}{\text{Planned number of items to be sold}} = \frac{\$80,000}{40,000} = \$2$

MARKETING DEMO 19–1
Are Women Consumers Being Taken to the Cleaners?

Diane Dunlap was annoyed when a local laundry charged more to wash and iron her white blouses than to clean her husband's white shirts. Actually, she was more than just annoyed. She telephoned 61 cleaners and asked each one's price to launder a no-frills white oxford cotton blouse the same style and size as a man's shirt. Twenty-one of them quoted higher prices for blouses. Then she did an experiment. She cut the label out of a blouse, sewed in the label for a man's shirt, and took the blouse to the cleaner along with three of her husband's shirts. The cleaner charged her $1.25. Later she did the same thing, but with a blouse that had the original label. The cleaner charged her $2.25. Dunlap feels that the cleaners' pricing is unethical—that they are discriminating against women and charging arbitrarily higher prices. She wants her local city government to pass an ordinance that prohibits laundry and dry cleaning businesses from discriminatory pricing based on gender.

The president of the Association of Launderers and Cleaners has a different view. "The automated equipment we use fits a certain range of standardized shirts," he said. "A lot of women's blouses have different kinds of trim, different kinds of buttons, and

lots of braid work, and it all has to be hand-finished. If it involves hand-finishing, we charge more." In other words, some cleaners charge more for doing women's blouses because the average cost is higher than the average cost for men's shirts. Of course, the cost of cleaning and ironing any specific shirt may not be higher or lower than the average.

A consumer-protection specialist said that there were no laws to regulate what the cleaners could charge. She said that customers who don't like a particular cleaner's rates are free to visit a competitor who may charge less.

Many firms face the problem of how to set prices when the costs are different to serve different customers. For example, poor, inner-city consumers often pay higher prices for food. But inner-city retailers also face higher average costs for facilities, shoplifting, and insurance. Some firms don't like to charge different consumers different prices, but they also don't want to charge everyone a higher average price to cover the expense of serving high-cost customers.

Source: "Blouse-Cleaning Rates Are Unfair, Woman Charges," *The Raleigh News & Observer,* July 7, 1992, p. 3B.

It does not make allowances for cost variations as output changes

Average-cost pricing is simple. But it can also be dangerous. It's easy to lose money with average-cost pricing. To see why, let's follow this example further.

First, remember that the average cost of $2 per unit was based on output of 40,000 units. But if the firm is only able to produce and sell 20,000 units in the next year, it may be in trouble. Twenty thousand units sold at $2.00 each ($1.55 cost plus 45 cents for expected profit) yield a total revenue of only $40,000. The overhead is still fixed at $30,000, and the variable material and labor cost drops by half to $16,000—for a total cost of $46,000. This means a loss of $6,000, or 30 cents a unit. The method that was supposed to allow a profit of 45 cents a unit actually causes a loss of 30 cents a unit! See Exhibit 19–3B.

The basic problem with the average-cost approach is that it doesn't consider cost variations at different levels of output. In a typical situation, costs are high with low output, and then economies of scale set in—the average cost per unit drops as the quantity produced increases. This is why mass production and mass distribution often make sense. It's also why it's important to develop a better understanding of the different types of costs a marketing manager should consider when setting a price. Marketing Demo 19–1 presents an ethical controversy related to average-cost pricing.

Average fixed costs are lower when a larger quantity is produced.

MARKETING MANAGER MUST CONSIDER VARIOUS KINDS OF COSTS

Average-cost pricing may lead to losses because there are a variety of costs—and each changes in a *different* way as output changes. Any pricing method that uses cost must consider these changes. To understand why, we need to define six types of costs.

There are three kinds of total cost

1. **Total fixed cost** is the sum of those costs that are fixed in total—no matter how much is produced. Among these fixed costs are rent, depreciation, managers' salaries, property taxes, and insurance. Such costs stay the same even if production stops temporarily.
2. **Total variable cost**, on the other hand, is the sum of those changing expenses that are closely related to output—expenses for parts, wages, packaging materials, outgoing freight, and sales commissions.

At zero output, total variable cost is zero. As output increases, so do variable costs. If Wrangler doubles its output of jeans in a year, its total cost for denim cloth also (roughly) doubles.

3. **Total cost** is the sum of total fixed and total variable costs. Changes in total cost depend on variations in total variable cost—since total fixed cost stays the same.

There are three kinds of average cost

The pricing manager usually is more interested in cost per unit than total cost because prices are usually quoted per unit.

1. **Average cost** (per unit) is obtained by dividing total cost by the related quantity (that is, the total quantity that causes the total cost).
2. **Average fixed cost** (per unit) is obtained by dividing total fixed cost by the related quantity.
3. **Average variable cost** (per unit) is obtained by dividing total variable cost by the related quantity.

An example shows
cost relations

A good way to get a feel for these different types of costs is to extend our average-cost pricing example (Exhibit 19–3A). Exhibit 19–4 shows the six types of cost and how they vary at different levels of output. The line for 40,000 units is highlighted because that was the expected level of sales in our average-cost pricing example. For simplicity, we assume that average variable cost is the same for each unit. Notice, however, that total variable cost increases when quantity increases.

Exhibit 19–5 shows the three average-cost curves from Exhibit 19–4. Notice that average fixed cost goes down steadily as the quantity increases. Although the average variable cost remains the same, average cost decreases continually, too. This is because average fixed cost is decreasing. With these relations in mind, let's reconsider the problem with average-cost pricing.

Ignoring demand is the
major weakness of
average-cost pricing

Average-cost pricing works well if the firm actually sells the quantity it used to set the average-cost price. Losses may result, however, if actual sales are much lower than expected. On the other hand, if sales are much higher than expected, then profits may be very good. But this will only happen by luck—because the firm's demand is much larger than expected.

To use average-cost pricing, a marketing manager must make *some* estimate of the quantity to be sold in the coming period. Without a quantity estimate, it isn't possible to compute average cost. But unless this quantity is related to price—that is, unless the firm's demand curve is considered—the marketing manager may set a price that doesn't even cover a firm's total cost! You saw this happen in Exhibit 19–3B, when the firm's price of $2 resulted in demand for only 20,000 units—and a loss of $6,000.

The demand curve is still important even if management doesn't take time to think about it. For example, Exhibit 19–6 shows the demand curve for the firm we're discussing. This demand curve shows *why* the firm lost money when it tried to use average-cost pricing. At the $2 price, quantity demanded is only 20,000.

Exhibit 19–4   Cost Structure of a Firm

Quantity (Q)	Total Fixed Costs (TFC)	Average Fixed Costs (AFC)	Average Variable Costs (AVC)	Total Variable Costs (TVC)	Total Cost (TC)	Average Cost (AC)
0	$30,000	—	—	—	$ 30,000	—
10,000	30,000	$3.00	$0.80	$ 8,000	38,000	$3.80
20,000	30,000	1.50	0.80	16,000	46,000	2.30
30,000	30,000	1.00	0.80	24,000	54,000	1.80
40,000	30,000	0.75	0.80	32,000	62,000	1.55
50,000	30,000	0.60	0.80	40,000	70,000	1.40
60,000	30,000	0.50	0.80	48,000	78,000	1.30
70,000	30,000	0.43	0.80	56,000	86,000	1.23
80,000	30,000	0.38	0.80	64,000	94,000	1.18
90,000	30,000	0.33	0.80	72,000	102,000	1.13
100,000	30,000	0.30	0.80	80,000	110,000	1.10

$$\begin{bmatrix} 110,000 \text{ (TC)} \\ -80,000 \text{ (TVC)} \\ 30,000 \text{ (TFC)} \end{bmatrix} \quad \text{(Q) } 100,000 \begin{bmatrix} 0.30 \text{ (AFC)} \\ 30,000 \text{ (TFC)} \\ 0.80 \text{ (AVC)} \end{bmatrix} \begin{bmatrix} 100,000 \text{ (Q)} \\ \times \quad 0.80 \text{ (AVC)} \\ 80,000 \text{ (TVC)} \end{bmatrix} \begin{bmatrix} 30,000 \text{ (TFC)} \\ +80,000 \text{ (TVC)} \\ 110,000 \text{ (TC)} \end{bmatrix} \quad \text{(Q) } 100,000 \begin{bmatrix} 1.10 \text{(AC)} \\ 110,000 \text{ (TC)} \end{bmatrix}$$

Exhibit 19–5 Typical Shape of Cost (per unit) Curves when AVC Is Assumed Constant per Unit

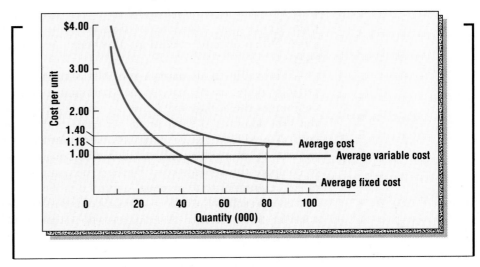

With this demand curve and the costs in Exhibit 19–4, the firm will incur a loss whether management sets the price at a high $3.00 or a low $1.20. At $3, the firm will sell only 10,000 units for a total revenue of $30,000. But total cost will be $38,000—for a loss of $8,000. At the $1.20 price, it will sell 60,000 units—at a loss of $6,000. However, the curve suggests that at a price of $1.65, consumers will demand about 40,000 units, producing a profit of about $4,000.

Exhibit 19–6 Evaluation of Various Prices along a Firm's Demand Curve

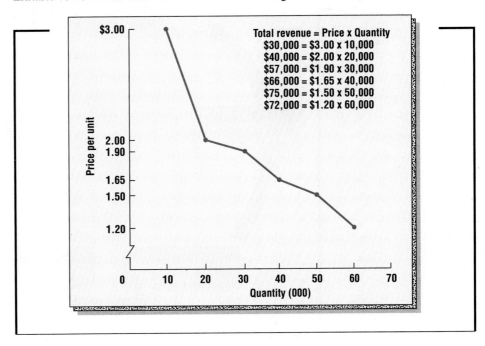

In short, average-cost pricing is simple in theory—but often fails in practice. In stable situations, prices set by this method may yield profits—but not necessarily *maximum* profits. And note that such cost-based prices may be higher than a price that would be more profitable for the firm—as shown in Exhibit 19–6. When demand conditions are changing, average-cost pricing is even more risky.

Exhibit 19–7 summarizes the relationships discussed above. Cost-oriented pricing requires an estimate of the total number of units to be sold. That estimate determines the *average* fixed cost per unit and thus, the average total cost. Then the firm adds the desired profit per unit to the average total cost to get the cost-oriented selling price. How customers react to that price determines the actual quantity the firm will be able to sell. But that quantity may not be the quantity used to compute the average cost! Further, the quantity the firm actually sells (times price) determines total revenue (and total profit or loss). A decision made in one area affects each of the others—directly or indirectly. Average-cost pricing does not consider these effects.[3] A manager who forgets this can make serious pricing mistakes.

Experience curve pricing is even riskier

In recent years, some aggressive firms have used a variation of average-cost pricing called experience curve pricing. **Experience curve pricing** is average-cost pricing using an estimate of *future* average costs. This approach is based on the observation that over time, as an industry gains experience in certain kinds of production, managers learn new ways to reduce costs. The effect of such learning

Exhibit 19–7   Summary of Relationships among Quantity, Cost, and Price Using Cost-Oriented Pricing

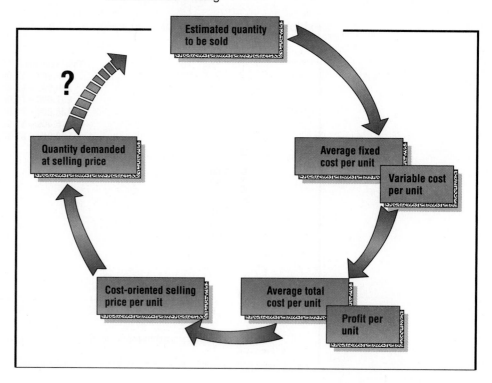

on costs varies in different businesses. Studies suggest that costs decrease about 15 to 20 percent each time cumulative production volume (experience) doubles, at least in some industries. So some firms set average-cost prices where they expect costs to be when products are sold in the future—not where costs actually are when the strategy is set. This approach is more common in rapidly growing markets (such as in the electronics business) because cumulative production volume (experience) grows faster.

If costs drop as expected, this approach can work fairly well. But it has the same risks as regular average-cost pricing—unless demand is included in the price setting. This means the price setter has to estimate what quantity will be sold to be able to read the right price from the experience-based average-cost curve.[4]

SOME FIRMS ADD A TARGET RETURN TO COST

Target return pricing scores sometimes

Target return pricing—adding a target return to the cost of a product—has become popular in recent years. With this approach, the price setter seeks to earn (1) a percentage return (say 10 percent per year) on the investment or (2) a specific total dollar return.

This method is a variation of the average-cost method since the desired target return is added into total cost. As a simple example, if a company had $180,000 invested and wanted to make a 10 percent return on investment, it would add $18,000 to its annual total costs in setting prices.

This approach has the same weakness as other average-cost pricing methods. If the quantity actually sold is less than the quantity used to set the price, then the company doesn't earn its target return—even though the target return seems to be part of the price structure. In fact, we already saw this in Exhibit 19–3. Remember that we added $18,000 as an expected profit—or target return. But the return was much lower when the expected quantity was not sold. (It could be higher, too—but only if the quantity sold is much larger than expected.) Target return pricing clearly does not guarantee that a firm will hit the target.

Hitting the target in the long run

Managers in some larger firms, who want to achieve a long-run target return objective, use another cost-oriented pricing approach—**long-run target return pricing**—adding a long-run average target return to the cost of a product. Instead of estimating the quantity they expect to produce in any one year, they assume that during several years' time their plants will produce at, say, 80 percent of capacity. They use this quantity when setting their prices.

Companies that take this longer-run view assume that there will be recession years when sales drop below 80 percent of capacity. For example, Owens/Corning Fiberglas sells insulation. In years when there is little construction, output is low and the firm does not earn the target return. But the company also has good years when it sells more insulation and exceeds the target return. Over the long run, Owens/Corning managers expect to achieve the target return. And sometimes they're right—depending on how accurately they estimate demand!

BREAK-EVEN ANALYSIS CAN EVALUATE POSSIBLE PRICES

Some price setters use break-even analysis in their pricing. **Break-even analysis** evaluates whether the firm will be able to break even—that is, cover all its costs—with a particular price. This is important because a firm must cover all costs in the long run or there is not much point being in business. This method focuses on the **break-even point (BEP)**—the quantity where the firm's total cost will just equal its total revenue.

Break-even charts help find the BEP

To help understand how break-even analysis works, look at Exhibit 19–8, an example of the typical break-even chart. *The chart is based on a particular selling price*—in this case, $1.20 a unit. The chart has lines that show total costs (total variable plus total fixed costs) and total revenues at different levels of production. The break-even point on the chart is at 75,000 units—where the total cost and total revenue lines intersect. At that production level, total cost and total revenue are the same—$90,000.

This chart also shows some typical assumptions made to simplify break-even analysis. Note that the total revenue curve is assumed to be a straight line. This means that each extra unit sold adds the same amount to total revenue. Stated differently, this assumes that *any quantity can be sold at the same price*. For this chart, we are assuming a selling price of $1.20 a unit. You can see that if the firm sells the break-even quantity of 75,000 at $1.20 each, it will earn a total revenue of $90,000.

In addition, the total cost curve in the chart is assumed to be a straight line. This means that average variable cost (AVC) is the same at different levels of output. For Exhibit 19–8, the AVC is 80 cents per unit.

The difference between the total revenue and total cost at a given quantity is the profit—or loss! The chart shows that below the break-even point, total cost is higher than total revenue, and the firm incurs a loss. The firm would make a profit above the break-even point. However, the firm would only reach the break-even point, or get beyond it into the profit area, *if* it could sell at least 75,000 units at the $1.20 price.

Break-even analysis can be very helpful if used properly, so let's look at this approach more closely.

Exhibit 19–8   Break-Even Chart for a Particular Situation

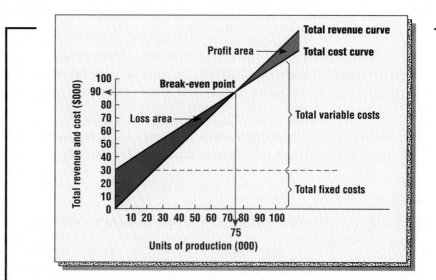

How to compute a break-even point

A break-even chart is an easy-to-understand visual aid, but it's also useful to be able to compute the break-even point.

The BEP, in units, can be found by dividing total fixed costs (TFC) by the **fixed-cost (FC) contribution per unit**—the assumed selling price per unit minus the variable cost per unit. This can be stated as a simple formula:

$$\text{BEP (in units)} = \frac{\text{Total fixed cost}}{\text{Fixed cost contribution per unit}}$$

This formula makes sense when we think about it. To break even, we must cover total fixed costs. Therefore, we must figure the contribution each unit will make to covering the total fixed costs (after paying for the variable costs to produce the item). When we divide this per unit contribution into the total fixed costs that must be covered, we have the BEP (in units).

To illustrate the formula, let's use the cost and price information in Exhibit 19–8. The price per unit is $1.20. The average variable cost per unit is 80 cents. So the FC contribution per unit is 40 cents ($1.20 – 80 cents). The total fixed cost is $30,000 (see Exhibit 19–8). Substituting in the formula:

$$\text{BEP} = \frac{\$30,000}{.40} = 75{,}000 \text{ units}$$

From this you can see that if this firm sells 75,000 units, it will exactly cover all its fixed and variable costs. If it sells even one more unit, it will begin to show a profit—in this case, 40 cents per unit. Note that once the fixed costs are covered, the part of revenue formerly going to cover fixed costs is now *all profit*.

BEP can be stated in dollars, too

The BEP can also be figured in dollars. The easiest way is to compute the BEP in units and then multiply by the assumed per unit price. If you multiply the selling price ($1.20) by the BEP in units (75,000) you get $90,000—the BEP in dollars.

Each possible price has its own break-even point

Often, it's useful to compute the break-even point for each of several possible prices and then compare the BEP for each price to likely demand at that price. The marketing manager can quickly reject some price possibilities when the expected quantity demanded at a given price is way below the break-even point for that price.

A target profit can be included

So far in our discussion of BEP we've focused on the quantity at which total revenue equals total cost—where profit is zero. We can also vary this approach to see what quantity is required to earn a certain level of profit. The analysis is the same as described above for the break-even point in units, but the amount of target profit is added to the total fixed cost. Then, when we divide the total fixed cost plus profit figure by the contribution from each unit, we get the quantity that will earn the target profit.

Break-even analysis is helpful—but not a pricing solution

Break-even analysis is helpful for evaluating alternatives. It is also popular because it's easy to use. Yet break-even analysis is too often misunderstood. Beyond the BEP, profits seem to be growing continually. And the graph—with its straight-line total revenue curve—makes it seem that any quantity can be sold at the assumed price. But this usually isn't true. It is the same as assuming a perfectly horizontal demand curve at that price. In fact, most managers face down-sloping demand situations. And their total revenue curves do *not* keep going up.

The firm and costs we discussed in the average-cost pricing example earlier in this chapter illustrate this point. You can confirm from Exhibit 19–4 that the total fixed cost ($30,000) and average variable cost (80 cents) for that firm are the same ones shown in the break-even chart (Exhibit 19–8). So this break-even chart is the one we would draw for that firm, assuming a price of $1.20 a unit. But the demand curve for that case showed that the firm could only sell 60,000 units at a price of $1.20. So that firm would never reach the 75,000 unit break-even point at a $1.20 price. It would only sell 60,000 units, and it would lose $6,000! A firm with a different demand curve—say, one where the firm could sell 80,000 units at a price of $1.20—would in fact break even at 75,000 units.

Break-even analysis is a useful tool for analyzing costs. But it is a cost-oriented approach and suffers the same limitation as other cost-oriented approaches. Specifically, it does not consider the effect of price on the quantity that consumers will want—that is, the demand curve.

So to really zero in on the most profitable price, marketers are better off estimating the demand curve itself and then using marginal analysis, which we'll discuss next.[5]

MARGINAL ANALYSIS CONSIDERS BOTH COSTS AND DEMAND

Our examples of cost-oriented pricing approaches show that a marketing manager—and anyone else involved in setting a price—must really understand how costs vary at different sales quantities. However, the examples also show that it's not enough just to understand costs. The price setter should also consider demand. The challenge is to consider both demand and costs at the same time because the price decision usually affects both costs and revenue—and they determine profit.

Marginal analysis—helps find the best price

The best pricing tool marketers have for looking at costs and revenue (demand) at the same time is marginal analysis. **Marginal analysis** focuses on the change in total revenue and total cost from selling one more unit to find the most profitable price and quantity. Marginal analysis doesn't just seek a price that will result in *some* profit. It seeks the price that *maximizes* profits. This objective makes sense. If you know how to make the biggest profit, you can always adjust to pursue other objectives—while knowing how much profit you're giving up!

Marginal analysis when demand curves slope down

We'll focus on the many situations in which demand curves are down-sloping, especially monopolistic competition.[6] In these situations, the firm has carved out a market niche for itself—and does have a pricing decision to make. We'll also briefly discuss the special case of oligopoly. We won't deal with pure or nearly pure competition. In that situation, marketing managers have little difficulty with the pricing decision. They simply use the market price.

In monopolistic competition, the firm faces a down-sloping demand curve. The price setter must pick a specific price on that curve—and generally will offer that price to all potential buyers (to avoid charges of price discrimination) for the life of the plan. The marketer can hope to increase sales volume by lowering the price. But all customers—even those who might be willing to pay more—pay this lower price. Even though the quantity has increased, the total revenue may decrease. Therefore, a manager should consider the effect of alternative prices on total revenue (and profit). The way to do this is to look at marginal revenue.

Marginal revenue can be negative

Marginal revenue is the change in total revenue that results from the sale of one more unit of a product. When the demand curve is down-sloping, this extra unit can be sold only by reducing the price of *all* items.

Exhibit 19–9 shows the relationship between price, quantity, total revenue, and marginal revenue in a situation with a straight-line, down-sloping demand curve.

If a firm can sell four units for a total revenue of $420 and five units for $460, then marginal revenue for the fifth unit is $40. Considering only revenue, it would be desirable to sell this extra unit. But will revenue continue to rise if the firm sells more units at lower prices? No! Exhibit 19–9 shows that negative marginal revenues occur at lower price levels. Obviously, this is not good for the firm! (Note: The total revenue obtained if price is cut may still be positive, but the marginal revenue—the extra revenue gained—may be positive or negative.)

Marginal revenue curve and demand curve are different

The marginal revenue curve is always below a down-sloping demand curve because the price of each last unit must be lower to sell more. You can see this in Exhibit 19–10, where we plot the data from Exhibit 19–9. The fact that the demand curve and the marginal revenue curve are different in monopolistic competition is very important. We will use both curves to find the best price and quantity.

Marginal cost—the cost of one more unit

As we've already seen, various kinds of costs behave differently. Further, there is an important kind of cost similar to marginal revenue: marginal cost. This cost is vital to marginal analysis.

Marginal cost is the change in total cost that results from producing one more unit. If it costs $275 to produce 9 units of a product and $280 to produce 10 units, then marginal cost is $5 for the 10th unit. In other words, marginal cost—contrasted to average cost per unit—is the additional cost of producing one more *specific unit;* average cost is the average for *all units.*

Exhibit 19–9 Marginal Revenue and Price

(1) Quantity Q	(2) Price P	(3) Total Revenue (1) × (2) = TR	(4) Marginal Revenue MR
0	$150	$ 0	
1	140	140	$140
2	130	260	120
3	117	351	91
4	105	420	69
5	92	460	40
6	79	474	14
7	66	462	−12
8	53	424	−38
9	42	378	−46
10	31	310	−68

Exhibit 19–10   A Plotting of the Demand and Marginal Revenue Data in Exhibit 19–9

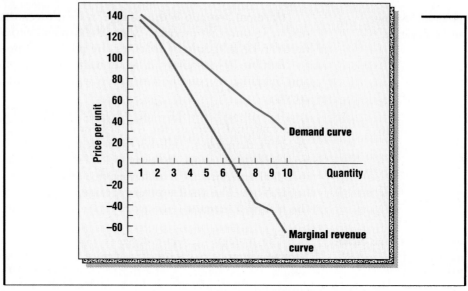

Cost structure example

Exhibit 19–11 shows how these costs can vary for a typical firm. *Fill in the missing numbers in this exhibit.* Notice that variable cost no longer is assumed constant per unit in Exhibit 19–11. Here, we use the more realistic assumption that variable costs will go down for a while and then rise.

Exhibit 19–11 illustrates three important points. *First,* total fixed costs do not change over the entire range of output—but total variable costs increase continually as more and more units are produced. Therefore, total costs—the sum

Exhibit 19–11   Cost Structure for Individual Firm (fill in the missing numbers)

(1) Quantity Q	(2) Total Fixed Cost TFC	(3) Average Fixed Cost AFC	(4) Total Variable Cost TVC	(5) Average Variable Cost AVC	(6) Total Cost (TFC + TVC = TC) TC	(7) Average Cost (AC = TC ÷ Q) AC	(8) Marginal Cost (per unit) MC
0	$200	$ 0	$ 0	$ 0	$200	Infinity	
1	200	200	96	96	296	$ 296	$ 96
2	200	100	116	58	316	_____	20
3	200	_____	_____	_____	331	110.33	_____
4	200	50	_____	_____	344	_____	_____
5	200	40	155	31	_____	71	11
6	200	_____	168	_____	_____	61.33	13
7	_____	_____	183	_____	_____	_____	15
8	_____	_____	223	_____	_____	_____	_____
9	_____	_____	307	_____	507	56.33	_____
10	_____	20	510	51	710	71	203

of total fixed costs and total variable costs—will increase as total quantity increases.

Second, average costs will decrease—for a while—as quantity produced increases. Remember that average costs are the sum of average fixed costs and average variable costs—and here, average fixed costs are going down because total fixed costs are divided by more and more units as output increases. For example, given a total fixed cost of $200, at a production level of four units, the average fixed cost is $50. At a production level of five units, the average fixed cost is $40.

Third, average costs in this table start rising for the last two units because average variable costs are increasing faster than average fixed costs are decreasing. The firm may be forced to use less efficient facilities and workers, go into overtime work, or pay higher prices for the materials it needs. This turn-up of the average cost curve is common after economies of scale run out.

The marginal cost of just one more is important

The marginal cost column in Exhibit 19–11 is the most important cost column for our purposes. It shows what each extra unit costs. This suggests the *minimum* extra revenue we would like to get for that additional unit. Like average cost, marginal cost drops—but it begins to rise again at a lower level of output than average cost does.

Marginal cost starts to increase at five units. This can be seen in Exhibit 19–12, which shows the behavior of the average cost, average variable cost, and marginal cost curves. Note that the marginal cost curve intersects the average variable cost and average cost curves from below *at their low points*, and then rises rapidly. This is how this curve typically behaves.

How to find the most profitable price and the quantity to produce

Since a manager must choose only *one* price level (for a time period), the question is which price to choose. This price determines the quantity that will be sold. To maximize profit, a manager should be willing to sell more units if the marginal revenue from selling them is at least equal to the marginal cost of the

Exhibit 19–12   Per Unit Cost Curves (for data in Exhibit 19–11)

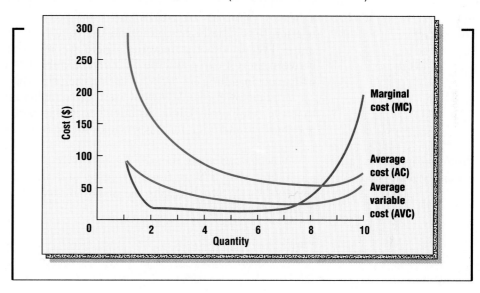

Exhibit 19–13   Revenue, Cost, and Profit for an Individual Firm

(1) Quantity Q	(2) Price P	(3) Total Revenue TR	(4) Total Cost TC	(5) Profit (TR – TC)	(6) Marginal Revenue MR	(7) Marginal Cost MC	(8) Marginal Profit (MR – MC)
0	$150	$ 0	$200	$–200			
1	140	140	296	–156	$140	$ 96	$+ 44
2	130	260	316	– 56	120	20	+100
3	117	351	331	+ 20	91	15	+ 76
4	105	420	344	+ 76	69	13	+ 56
5	92	460	355	+105	40	11	+ 29
6	79	474	368	+106	14	13	+ 1
7	66	462	383	+ 79	–12	15	– 27
8	53	424	423	+ 1	–38	40	– 78
9	42	378	507	–129	–46	84	–130
10	31	310	710	–400	–68	203	–271

extra units. From this we get the following **rule for maximizing profit**: the highest profit is earned at the price where marginal cost is just less than or equal to marginal revenue.*

This optimal price is *not* found on the marginal revenue curve. This profit-maximizing selling price is found by referring to the demand curve—which shows what price customers are willing to pay for the optimum quantity.

To make sure you understand the method for finding this optimal price, study the following example carefully. To make doubly sure that this approach is fully explained, we will calculate the most profitable price and quantity using total revenue and total cost curves first and then show that you will get the same answer with marginal curves. This will give you a check on the method—as well as help you see how the marginal revenue–marginal cost method works.

Profit maximization with total revenue and total cost curves

Exhibit 19–13 provides data on total revenue, total cost, and total profit for a firm. Exhibit 19–14 graphs the total revenue, total cost, and total profit relationships. The highest point on the total profit curve is at a quantity of six units. This is also the quantity where we find the greatest vertical distance between the TR curve and the TC curve. Exhibit 19–13 shows that a price of $79 will result in selling six units, so $79 is the price that leads to the highest profit.

A price lower than $79 would result in a higher sales volume. But you can see that the total profit curve declines beyond a quantity of 6 units. So a profit-maximizing marketing manager would not be interested in setting a lower price.

Profit maximization using marginal curves

Now we can apply the rule for maximizing profit using marginal curves. We again find that $79 is the best price and that 6 is the best quantity. See Exhibit 19–15, which graphs the marginal revenue and marginal cost data from Exhibit 19–13.

---

*This rule applies in the typical situations where the curves are shaped similarly to those discussed here. Technically, however, we should add the following to the rule for maximizing profit: the marginal cost must be increasing, or decreasing at a lesser rate than marginal revenue.

Exhibit 19–14 Graphic Determination of the Output Giving the Greatest Total Profit for a Firm

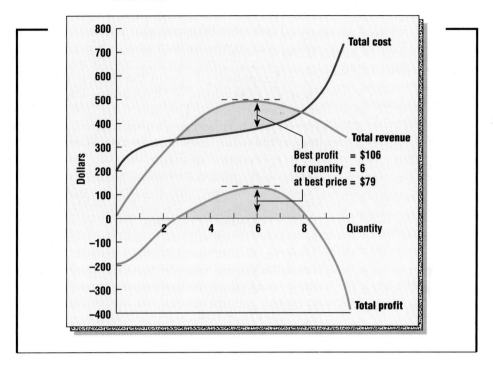

Exhibit 19–15 Alternate Determination of the Most Profitable Output and Price for a Firm

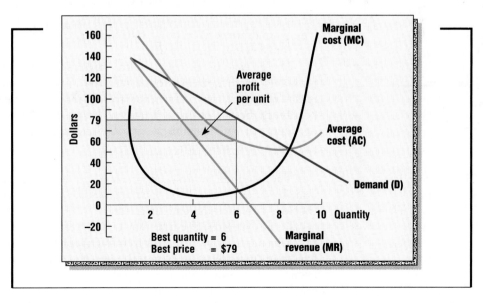

In Exhibit 19–15, the intersection of the marginal cost and marginal revenue curves occurs at a quantity of 6. This is the most profitable quantity. But the best price must be obtained by going up to the demand curve and then over to the vertical axis—*not* by going from the intersection of MR and MC over to the vertical axis. Again, the best price is $79.

The graphic solution is supported by the data in Exhibit 19–13. At a price of $79 and a quantity of 6, marginal revenue equals $14 and marginal cost is $13. There is a profit margin of $1, suggesting that it might be profitable to offer seven rather than six units. This is not the case, however. The marginal cost of the seventh unit is $15, while its marginal revenue is actually negative. Lowering the price to $66 to sell seven units (instead of only six) will reduce total profit by $27.

It is important to realize that *total* profit is *not* near zero when marginal revenue (MR) equals marginal cost (MC). **Marginal profit**—the extra profit on the last unit—is near zero. But that is exactly why the quantity obtained at the MR/MC intersection is the most profitable. Marginal analysis shows that when the firm is finding the best price to charge, it should lower the price—to increase the quantity it will sell—as long as the last unit it sells will yield *extra* profits.

Again, the marketing manager must choose only *one* price. Marginal analysis is useful in helping to set the best price to charge for all that will be sold. It might help to think of the demand curve as an if-then curve—*if* a price is selected, *then* its related quantity will be sold. Before the marketing manager sets the actual price, all these *if-then* combinations can be evaluated for profitability. But once the price level is set, the results will follow—that is, the related quantity will be sold.

A profit range is reassuring

We've been trying to find the most profitable price and quantity. But in a changing world, this is difficult. Fortunately, this best point is surrounded by a profitable range.

Note that in Exhibit 19–14, there are two break-even points rather than a single point, which was the case when we were discussing break-even analysis. The second break-even point falls farther to the right because total costs turn up and total revenue turns down.

These two break-even points are important. They show the range of profitable operations. Although marginal analysis seeks the price that gives the *maximum* profit, we know that this point is an ideal rather than a realistic possibility. So it's essential that you know there is a *range of profit* around the optimum—it isn't just a single point. This means that pursuing the most profitable price is a wise approach.

How to lose less, if you must

The marginal analysis approach to finding the most profitable price will also find the price that will be *least unprofitable* when market conditions are so poor that the firm must operate at a loss.

If sales are slow, the firm may even have to consider closing. But a marketing manager might have something to say about that. A key point here is that most fixed costs will continue even if the firm stops its operations. Some fixed costs may even involve items that are so "sunk" in the business that they cannot be sold for anything near the cost shown on the company's records. An unsuccessful company's special-purpose buildings and machines may be worthless to anyone else. So fixed costs may be irrelevant to a decision about closing the business.

Marginal costs are another matter. If the firm can recover the marginal cost of the last unit (or, more generally, the variable cost of the units being considered), it may want to continue operating. The extra income would help pay the fixed costs and reduce the firm's losses. If it can't meet marginal costs, it should stop operations temporarily or go out of business. The exceptions involve social or humanitarian considerations—or the fact that the marginal costs of closing temporarily are high and stronger demand is expected *soon*. But if marginal costs can be covered in the short run, even though all fixed costs cannot, the firm should stay in operation.

Marginal analysis helps get the most in pure competition

Marketing managers caught in pure competition can also apply marginal methods. They don't have a price decision to make since the demand curve is flat. (Note: This means that the marginal revenue curve is flat at the same level.) But they do have output decisions. They can use the marginal revenue curve, therefore, with their own unique marginal cost curve to determine the most profitable (or least unprofitable) output level. See Exhibit 19–16. And this approach leads to a different (and more profitable) output than the lowest average-cost decision favored by some commonsense managers. Note in Exhibit 19–16 that the quantity associated with the lowest average cost is not the most profitable quantity.

Marginal analysis applies in oligopoly, too

In Chapter 18, we noted that marketing managers who compete in oligopoly situations often just set a price that meets what competitors charge. Marginal analysis helps us understand this situation better.

Exhibit 19–17 shows a demand curve and marginal revenue curve typical of what a marketing manager in an oligopoly situation faces. The demand curve is kinked, and the current market price is at the kink. The dashed part of the

Exhibit 19–16   Finding the Most Profitable (or least unprofitable) Price and Quantity in Pure Competition (in the short run)

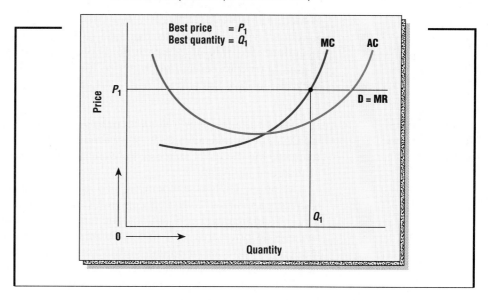

Exhibit 19–17   Marginal Revenue Drops Fast in an Oligopoly

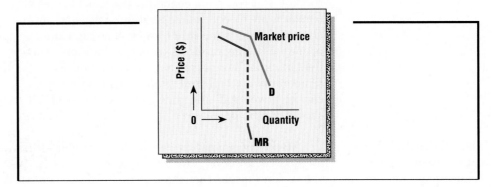

marginal revenue line in Exhibit 19–17 shows that marginal revenue drops sharply at the kinked point. This is a technical but important matter. It helps explain why prices are relatively "sticky" at the kinked point.

Even if costs change (and each firm's supply curve moves up or down), the marginal cost curve is still likely to cross the marginal revenue curve someplace along the drop in the marginal revenue curve. In this case, even though costs are changing—and there may seem to be a reason for changing the price—setting the price at the level of the kink maximizes profit!

A price leader usually sets the price

Most of the firms in an oligopoly are aware of the economics of their situation—at least intuitively. Usually, a **price leader** sets a price for all to follow—perhaps to maximize profits or to get a certain target return on investment—and (without any collusion) other members of the industry follow. The price leader is usually the firm with the lowest costs. That may give it more flexibility than competitors. This price may be maintained for a long time—or at least as long as all members of the industry continue to make a reasonable profit. Sometimes, however, a price leader tries to lower the price, and a competitor lowers it even further. This can lead to price wars—at least temporarily. You sometimes see this in competition between major airlines. But price wars in oligopoly tend to be very unprofitable for each firm and the whole industry—so they usually pass fairly quickly.

A rough demand estimate is better than none

Marginal analysis is a flexible and useful tool for marketing managers. Some managers don't take advantage of it because they think it's just not practical to try to determine the exact shape of the demand curve. But that view misses the point of marginal analysis.

Marginal analysis encourages managers to think very carefully about what they *do know* about costs and demand. Only rarely is either type of information exact. So in practical applications, the focus of marginal analysis is not on finding the precise price that will maximize profit. Rather, the focus is on getting an estimate of how profit might vary across a *range of relevant prices*. Further, a number of practical demand-oriented approaches can help a marketing manager do a better job of understanding the likely shape of the demand curve for a target market. We'll discuss these approaches next.

Value in use pricing considers what a customer will save by buying a product.

DEMAND-ORIENTED APPROACHES FOR SETTING PRICES

Value in use pricing—how much will the customer save?

Organizational buyers think about how a purchase will affect their total costs. Many marketers who aim at business markets keep this in mind when estimating demand and setting prices. They use **value in use pricing**—which means setting prices that will capture some of what customers will save by substituting the firm's product for the one currently being used.

For example, a producer of computer-controlled machines used to assemble cars knows that its machine doesn't just replace a standard machine. It also reduces labor costs, quality control costs, and—after the car is sold—costs of warranty repairs. The potential savings (value in use) might be different for different customers—because they have different operations, costs, and the like. The marketer can estimate what each auto producer will save by using the machine—and then set a price that makes it less expensive for the auto producer to buy the computerized machine than to stick with the old methods. The number of customers who have different levels of potential savings also provides some idea about the shape of the demand curve.[7]

Customers may have reference prices

Some people don't devote much thought to what they pay for the products they buy—including some frequently purchased goods and services. But most consumers have a **reference price**—the price they expect to pay—for many of the products they purchase. And different customers may have different reference prices for the same basic type of purchase. For example, a person who really enjoys reading might have a higher reference price for a popular paperback book than another person who is only an occasional reader. Marketing research can sometimes identify different segments with different reference prices.[8]

Leader pricing—make it low to attract customers

Leader pricing means setting some very low prices—real bargains—to get customers into retail stores. The idea is not to sell large quantities of the leader items but to get customers into the store to buy other products.[9] Certain products are picked for their promotion value and priced low—but above cost. In food stores, the leader prices are the "specials" that are advertised regularly to give an image of low prices. Leader items are usually well-known, widely used items that customers don't stock heavily—milk, butter, eggs, or coffee—but on which they will recognize a real price cut. In other words, leader pricing is normally used with products for which consumers do have a specific reference price.

Leader pricing may try to appeal to customers who normally shop elsewhere. But it can backfire if customers buy only the low-price leaders. To avoid hurting profits, managers often select leader items that aren't directly competitive with major lines—as when bargain-priced recording tape is the leader for a stereo equipment store.

The problem with leader pricing is that it leads to uneven production, stocking, and distribution for the supplier. Some suppliers are beginning to look at an everyday low-pricing policy as a way to solve these problems. See Marketing Demo 19–2 for the obstacles faced by Procter & Gamble as it tries to introduce an everyday low-price policy.

Bait pricing—offer a steal, but sell under protest

Bait pricing is setting some very low prices to attract customers—but trying to sell more expensive models or brands once the customer is in the store. For example, a furniture store may advertise a color TV for $199. But once bargain hunters come to the store, salesclerks point out the disadvantages of the low-price TV and try to convince them to trade-up to a better (and more expensive) set. Bait pricing is something like leader pricing. But here the seller *doesn't* plan to sell many at the low price.

If bait pricing is successful, the demand for higher-quality products expands. This approach may be a sensible part of a strategy to trade-up customers. And customers may be well-served if—once in the store—they find a higher-priced product offers features better suited to their needs. But bait pricing is also criticized as unethical and throughout Canada bait pricing (either specifically or indirectly) is illegal.

Psychological pricing—some prices just seem right

Psychological pricing means setting prices that have special appeal to target customers. Some people think there are whole ranges of prices that potential customers see as the same. So price cuts in these ranges do not increase the quantity sold. But just below this range, customers may buy more. Then, at even lower prices, the quantity demanded stays the same again—and so on. Exhibit 19–18 shows the kind of demand curve that leads to psychological pricing. Vertical drops mark the price ranges that customers see as the same. Pricing research shows that there *are* such demand curves.[10]

Odd-even pricing is setting prices that end in certain numbers. For example, products selling below $50 often end in the number 5 or the number 9—such as 49 cents of $24.95. Prices for higher-priced products are often $1 or $2 below the next even dollar figure—such as $99 rather than $100.

Some marketers use odd-even pricing because they think consumers react better to these prices—perhaps seeing them as "substantially" lower than the next highest even price. Marketers using these prices seem to assume that they have a rather jagged demand curve—that slightly higher prices will substantially reduce the quantity demanded. Long ago, some retailers used odd-even prices to force their clerks to make change. Then the clerks had to record the sale and could not pocket the money. Today, however, it's not always clear why firms use these prices—or whether they really work. Perhaps it's done simply because everyone else does it.[11]

MARKETING DEMO 19–2
Supermarkets Wary of Procter & Gamble Pricing Plan

Consumer products giant Procter & Gamble appears to be trying to rein in supermarkets' growing clout over which suppliers get to stock their goods on the store shelves—and at what price.

For more than a decade, retail chains have charged suppliers such as Toronto-based P&G fees for putting their products on the shelves; the better the placement, the heftier the fee.

The suppliers often sell their goods to retailers at bargain prices, and the discounts are passed on to consumers in special promotions. But the grocers also store some of the excess cheap products and sell them to customers later at regular prices—with the grocers pocketing the difference.

Now, P&G in Canada is considering following the lead of its US parent and implementing an everyday low-pricing policy—thus halting the high-low price cycle.

South of the border, P&G's everyday low prices have prompted sharp criticism from many retailers—and even spurred some to stop stocking some P&G products or to give them poorer exposure in the store.

The worry among retailers, on both sides of the border, is that once a leader such as P&G implements a new policy such as this, other suppliers will quickly follow suit.

Some industry insiders say retailers make up to 70 percent of their profit from the extra allowances they get from manufacturers.

Still, in Canada, P&G wants to move slowly on any new pricing policy and communicate better with the retail trade than the company did in the United States, said Thomas Gove, a spokesman for P&G in Toronto.

High-low pricing drives up overall costs because it leads to uneven production, stocking, and distribution, he said. At peak periods, when demand for the cheap items is high, the company is overworked, while at other times there isn't enough work to go around.

As well, the constant price promotions at the supermarkets can erode the distinction of P&G's heavily advertised brand names such as Tide detergent and Crest toothpaste, observers say.

Still, P&G recognizes the attractiveness for stores of having cut-rate specials periodically to stimulate traffic and sales, especially during slow times, Mr. Gove said.

The shift of power to the supermarket chains and away from suppliers has meant that packaged goods manufacturers have had to shift a lot of their marketing spending to retailers from consumers.

Manufacturers can easily spend up to four times as much on retailer marketing as on consumer marketing, said Chris Walker, a vice president at ISL International Surveys Ltd. in Toronto.

Ten years ago, the spending on retailer and consumer marketing was about equal, he said.

"Retailers are in the business of buying packaged goods, not selling them," Mr. Walker said. "They make their money on the buy function, not the sell function . . . It's just gone crazy now."

Source: Marina Strauss, "Supermarkets Wary of P&G Pricing Plan," *The Globe and Mail*, Report on Business Section, August 11, 1992, p. B5.

Prestige pricing indicates quality

Prestige pricing is setting a rather high price to suggest high quality or high status. Some target customers want the best, so they will buy at a high price. But if the price seems cheap, they worry about quality and don't buy.[12] Prestige pricing is most common for luxury products—such as furs, jewelry, and perfume.

It is also common in service industries—where the customer can't see the product in advance and relies on price to judge its quality. Target customers who respond to prestige pricing give the marketing manager an unusual demand curve. Instead of a normal down-sloping curve, the curve goes down for a while and then bends back to the left again. See Exhibit 19–19.

Exhibit 19–18
Demand Curve when Psychological
Pricing Is Appropriate

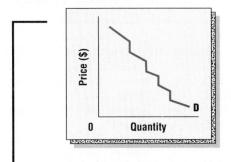

Exhibit 19–19
Demand Curve Showing a Prestige
Pricing Situation

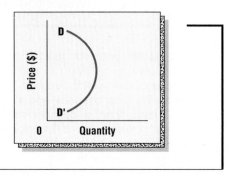

Price lining—a few
prices cover the field

Price lining is setting a few price levels for a product line and then marking all items at these prices. This approach assumes that customers have a certain reference price in mind that they expect to pay for a product. For example, most neckties are priced between $10 and $40. In price lining, there are only a few prices within this range. Ties will not be priced at $10.00, $10.50, $11.00, and so on. They might be priced at four levels—$10, $20, $30, and $40.

Price lining has advantages other than just matching prices to what consumers expect to pay. The main advantage is simplicity—for both clerks and customers. It is less confusing than having many prices. Some customers may consider items in only one price class. Their big decision, then, is which item(s) to choose at that price.

For retailers, price lining has several advantages. Sales may increase because (1) they can offer a bigger variety in each price class and (2) it's easier to get customers to make decisions within one price class. Stock planning is simpler

Prestige pricing is most common for luxury products such as furs, jewelry, and perfume.

The One-Price Clothing Stores chain plans its marketing mix based on the $7 price line it thinks customers want to pay per item.

because demand is larger at the relatively few prices. Price lining can also reduce costs because inventory needs are lower.

Demand-backward pricing

Demand-backward pricing is setting an acceptable final consumer price and working backward to what a producer can charge. It is commonly used by producers of final consumer products, especially shopping products such as women's and children's clothing and shoes. It is also used for toys or gifts for which customers will spend a specific amount—because they are seeking a $5 or a $10 gift. Here, a reverse cost-plus pricing process is used. This method has been called market-minus pricing.

The producer starts with the retail (reference) price for a particular item and then works backward—subtracting the typical margins that channel members expect. This gives the approximate price the producer can charge. Then, the average or planned marketing expenses can be subtracted from this price to find how much can be spent producing the item. Candy companies do this. They alter the size of the candy bar to keep the bar at the expected price.

Demand estimates are needed for demand-backward pricing to be successful. The quantity that will be demanded affects production costs—that is, where the firm will be on its average cost curve. Also, since competitors can be expected to make the best product possible, it is important to know customer needs to set the best amount to spend on manufacturing costs. By increasing costs a little, the product may be so improved in consumers' eyes that the firm will sell many more units. But if consumers only want novelty, additional quality may not increase the quantity demanded—and shouldn't be offered.

Green pricing

Another method being discussed in various circles is "green" pricing. This pricing method takes into consideration the environmental costs of production and waste disposal. Marketing Demo 19–3 highlights this concept.

PRICING A FULL LINE

Our emphasis has been—and will continue to be—on the problem of pricing an individual product mainly because this makes our discussion clearer. But most

---

MARKETING DEMO 19–3   "Green" Pricing Needed

T he price of goods and services must reflect the environmental cost of production and waste disposal if sustainable development is to be achieved, the chairman of Quaker Oats Company of Canada Ltd. said.

"Unless we stop looking at the environment as a free resource and adopt full-cost accounting, the market will not give its normal warning signals that the environment is being abused and overused," Jon Grant told a Toronto business conference.

"If national-income accounts reflect the value of the environment, then society . . . can evaluate the merits of a regulation by comparing its cost against the incremental increase in the value of our environment."

Grant, who is also chairman of the Ontario Round Table on Environment and Economy, said environmental protection and economic growth must be achieved simultaneously.

"Canadian business does not have to wait until all wrinkles are ironed out of our public policy framework. As businesspeople, we have every opportunity to take the initiative and voluntarily move our companies and our industries toward sustainable development."

While the government has an important role to play in protecting the environment, he warned of the duplication of federal and provincial regulations that raise enforcement costs and do little or nothing for the environment.

"Environmental costs are no longer some economist's bloodless externality," said Arthur Campeau, the prime minister's representative at the Earth Summit in Rio de Janeiro.

Source: Erik Heinrich, " 'Green' Pricing Needed, Quaker Oats Chief Says," *The Financial Post*, October 16, 1992, p. 9.

---

marketing managers are responsible for more than one product. In fact, their "product" may be the whole company line! So we'll discuss this matter briefly.

Full-line pricing—market- or firm-oriented?

Full-line pricing is setting prices for a whole line of products. How to do this depends on which of two basic situations a firm is facing.

In one case, all products in the company's line are aimed at the same general target market, which makes it important for all prices to be related. For example, a producer of TV sets can offer several price and quality levels to give its target customers some choice. The different prices should appear reasonable when the target customers are evaluating them.

In the other case, the different products in the line are aimed at entirely different target markets so there doesn't have to be any relation between the various prices. A chemical producer of a wide variety of products with several target markets, for example, probably should price each product separately.

Cost is not much help in full-line pricing

The marketing manager must try to recover all costs on the whole line—perhaps by pricing quite low on competitive items and much higher on less competitive items. Estimating costs for each product is a big problem because there is no single right way to assign a company's fixed costs to each of the products. Further, if any cost-oriented pricing method is carried through without considering demand, it can lead to very unrealistic prices. To avoid mistakes, the marketing manager should judge demand for the whole line as well as demand for each individual product in each target market.

As an aid to full-line pricing, marketing managers can assemble directly variable costs on the many items in the line to calculate a price floor. To this floor they can add a reasonable markup based on the quality of the product, the strength of the demand for the product, and the degree of competition. But finally, the image projected by the full line must be evaluated.

Complementary product pricing

Complementary product pricing is setting prices on several products as a group. This may lead to one product being priced very low so that the profits from another product will increase—and increase the product group's total profits. A new Gillette shaver, for example, may be priced low to sell the blades, which must be replaced regularly.

Complementary product pricing differs from full-line pricing because different production facilities may be involved—so there's no cost allocation problem. Instead, the problem is really understanding the target market and the demand curves for each of the complementary products. Then, various combinations of prices can be tried to see what set will be best for reaching the company's pricing objectives.

Product-bundle pricing—one price for several products

A firm that offers its target market several different products may use **product-bundle pricing**—setting one price for a set of products. Firms that use product-bundle pricing usually set the overall price so that it's cheaper for the customer to buy the products at the same time than separately. Drugstores sometimes bundle the cost of a roll of film and the cost of the processing. A bank may offer a product-bundle price for a safe deposit box, travelers cheques, and a saving account. Bundling encourages customers to spend more and buy products that they might not otherwise buy—because the "added cost" of the extras is not as high as it would normally be.

Most firms that use product-bundle pricing also set individual prices for the unbundled products. This may increase demand by attracting customers who want one item in a product assortment but don't want the extras. Many firms treat services this way. A software company may have a product-bundle price for its software and access to a toll-free telephone assistance service. However, customers who don't need help can pay a lower price and get just the software.[13]

BID PRICING AND NEGOTIATED PRICING DEPEND HEAVILY ON COSTS

A new price for every job

Bid pricing means offering a specific price for each possible job rather than setting a price that applies for all customers. Building contractors, for example, must bid on possible projects. And many companies selling services (like cleaning or data processing) must submit bids for jobs they would like to have.

The big problem in bid pricing is estimating all the costs that will apply to each job. This may sound easy, but a complicated bid may involve thousands of cost components. Further, management must include an overhead charge and a charge for profit.

Sometimes it isn't even possible to figure out costs in advance. This may lead to a contract where the customer agrees to pay the supplier's total cost plus an agreed-on profit figure (say, 10 percent of costs or a dollar amount)—after the job is finished.

Some unethical sellers give bid prices based on cost-plus contracts a bad reputation by faking their records to make costs seem higher than they really are. In other cases, there may be honest debate about what costs should be allowed.

Demand must be considered, too

Competition must be considered when adding in overhead and profit for a bid price. Usually, the customer will get several bids and accept the lowest one. So unthinking addition of typical overhead and profit rates should be avoided. Some bidders use the same overhead and profit rates on all jobs—regardless of competition—and then are surprised when they don't get some jobs.

Because bidding can be expensive, marketing managers may want to be selective about which jobs to bid on and choose those where they feel they have the greatest chance of success. Firms can spend thousands—or even millions—of dollars just developing bids for large business or government customers.[14]

Sometimes bids are negotiated

Some buying situations (including much government buying) require the use of bids—and the purchasing agent must take the lowest bid. In other cases, however, the customer asks for bids and then singles out the company that submits the *most attractive* bid—not necessarily the lowest—for further bargaining.

Negotiated prices— what will a specific customer pay?

The list price or bidding price the seller would like to charge is sometimes only the *starting point* for discussions with individual customers. What a customer will buy—if the customer buys at all—depends on the **negotiated price**, a price set based on bargaining between the buyer and seller.

As with simple bid pricing, negotiated pricing is most common in situations where the marketing mix is adjusted for each customer—so bargaining may involve the whole marketing mix, not just the price level. For example, a firm that produces machine tools used by other manufacturers to make their products might use this approach. Each customer may need custom-designed machines and different types of installation service. Through the bargaining process, the seller tries to determine what aspects of the marketing mix are most important to the customer. For one customer, selling price may be most important. There, the seller might try to find ways to reduce costs of other elements of the marketing mix—consistent with the customer's needs—in order to earn a profit. Another customer might want more of some other element of the marketing mix—like more technical help after the sale—and be less sensitive to price.

Sellers must know their costs to negotiate prices effectively. However, negotiated pricing *is* a demand-oriented approach. Here, the seller is very carefully analyzing a particular customer's position on a demand curve—or on different possible demand curves based on different offerings—rather than the overall demand curve for a group of customers. This is a challenging job, and the details are beyond the scope of this book. However, the techniques for supply and demand analysis we've been discussing apply here as they do with other price setting approaches.

CONCLUSION

In this chapter, we discussed various approaches to price setting. Generally, retailers and wholesalers use traditional markups. Some use the same markups for all their items. Others find that varying the markups increases turnover and profit. In other words, they consider demand and competition!

Many firms use average-cost pricing to help set their prices. But this approach sometimes ignores demand completely. A more realistic approach to average-cost pricing requires a sales forecast— maybe just assuming that sales in the next period will be roughly the same as in the last period. This approach *does* enable the marketing manager to set a price—but the price may or may not cover all costs and earn the desired profit.

Break-even analysis is useful for evaluating possible prices. It provides a rough-and-ready tool for eliminating unworkable prices. But management must estimate demand to evaluate the chance of reaching these possible break-even points.

Marginal analysis is a useful tool for finding the most profitable price—and the quantity to produce. The most profitable quantity is found at the intersection of the marginal revenue and marginal cost curves. To determine the most profitable price, a manager takes the most profitable quantity to the firm's demand curve to find the price target customers will be willing to pay for this quantity.

The major difficulty with demand-oriented pricing is estimating the demand curve. But experienced managers—aided perhaps by marketing research—can estimate the nature of demand for their products. Such estimates are useful—even if they aren't exact. They get you thinking in the right ballpark. Sometimes, when all you need is a decision about raising or lowering price, even rough demand estimates can be very revealing. Further, a firm's demand curve does not cease to exist simply because it's ignored. Some information is better than none at all. And it appears that some marketers do consider demand in their pricing. We see this with value in use pricing, leader pricing, bait pricing, odd-even pricing, psychological pricing, full-line pricing, and even bid pricing.

Throughout the book, we stress that firms must consider the customer before they do anything. This certainly applies to pricing. It means that when managers are setting a price, they have to consider what customers will be willing to pay. This isn't always easy. But it's nice to know that there is a profit range around the best price. Therefore, even rough estimates about what potential customers will buy at various prices will probably lead to a better price than mechanical use of traditional markups or cost-oriented formulas.

While our focus in this chapter is on price setting, it's clear that pricing decisions must consider the cost of offering the whole marketing mix. Smart marketers don't just accept costs as a given. Target marketers always look for ways to be more efficient—to reduce costs while improving what they offer customers. Improved coordination of physical distribution, for example, may improve customer service and reduce costs. Carefully defined target markets may make promotion spending more efficient. Products that really meet customers' needs reduce costly new-product failure. Channel members can shift and share functions—so that the cost of performing needed marketing activities is as low as possible. Marketers should set prices based on demand as well as on costs. But creative marketers look for ways to reduce costs—because costs affect profit.[15]

QUESTIONS AND PROBLEMS

1. Why do many department stores seek a markup of about 40 percent when some discount houses operate on a 20 percent markup?

2. A producer distributed its riding lawn mowers through wholesalers and retailers. The retail selling price was $800, and the manufacturing cost to the company was $312. The retail markup was 35 percent and the wholesale markup 20 percent. (*a*) What was the cost to the wholesaler? To the retailer? (*b*) What percentage markup did the producer take?

3. Relate the concept of stock turnover to the growth of mass-merchandising. Use a simple example in your answer.

4. If total fixed costs are $200,000 and total variable costs are $100,000 at the output of 20,000 units, what are the probable total fixed costs and total variable costs at an output of 10,000 units? What are the average fixed costs, average variable costs, and average costs at these two output levels? Explain what additional information you would want to determine what price should be charged.

5. Explain how experience curve pricing differs from average-cost pricing.

6. Construct an example showing that mechanical use of a very large or a very small markup might

still lead to unprofitable operation while some intermediate price would be profitable. Draw a graph and show the break-even point(s).

7. The Davis Company's fixed costs for the year are estimated at $200,000. Its product sells for $250. The variable cost per unit is $200. Sales for the coming year are expected to reach $1,250,000. What is the break-even point? Expected profit? If sales are forecast at only $875,000, should the Davis Company shut down operations? Why?

8. Distinguish among price, marginal revenue, and average revenue (where average revenue is total revenue divided by the quantity sold).

9. Draw a graph showing a demand and supply situation where marginal analysis correctly indicates that the firm should continue producing even though the profit and loss statement shows a loss.

10. Discuss the idea of drawing separate demand curves for different market segments. It seems logical because each target market should have its own marketing mix. But won't this lead to many demand curves and possible prices? And what will this mean with respect to functional discounts and varying prices in the marketplace? Will it be legal? Will it be practical?

11. Nicor Company is having a profitable year. Its only product sells to wholesalers for 80 cents a can. Its managers feel that a 60 percent gross margin should be maintained. Its manufacturing costs consist of: material, 50 percent of cost; labor, 40 percent of cost; and overhead, 10 percent of cost. Both material and labor costs increased 10 percent since last year. Determine the new price per can based on its present pricing method. Is it wise to stick with a 60 percent margin if a price increase would mean lost customers? Answer using graphs and MC–MR analysis. Show a situation where it would be most profitable to (a) raise price, (b) leave price alone, (c) reduce price.

12. How does a prestige pricing policy fit into a marketing mix? Would exclusive distribution be necessary?

13. Cite a local example of odd-even pricing and evaluate whether it makes sense.

14. Cite a local example of psychological pricing and evaluate whether it makes sense.

15. Distinguish between leader pricing and bait pricing. What do they have in common? How can their use affect a marketing mix?

16. Is a full-line pricing policy available only to producers? Cite local examples of full-line pricing. Why is full-line pricing important?

SUGGESTED CASES

22. Classy Formal Wear

26. Fraser Company

20

Planning and Implementing Quality Marketing Programs

When You Finish This Chapter, You Should

①
Know that strategy planning is much more than assembling the four Ps.

②
Understand the basic forecasting approaches and why they are used.

③
Understand why typical mixes are a good starting point for planning.

④
Understand the different ways a firm can plan to become involved in international marketing.

⑤
Know the content of and differences among strategies, marketing plans, and a marketing program.

⑥
Know about allocating budgets for marketing plans.

⑦
Know how total quality management can improve implementation—including implementation of service quality.

⑧
Understand the important new terms (shown in blue).

As a freshman in college, Michael Dell started buying and reselling computers from his dorm room. When he saw how big the opportunity was, he developed a marketing plan and worked to implement it. Over time, he added innovative new strategies to reach new target markets—and in the process he built Dell Computer Corp. into a profitable business that earns top customer satisfaction ratings.

When Dell started, the typical marketing mix for PCs emphasized distribution through computer stores that sold to both consumers and businesses. The quality of the dealers' machines and service didn't always justify the high prices they charged. Moreover, dealers often couldn't give customers the combination of features they wanted from machines they had in stock, and repairs were a hassle.

Dell decided there was a large target market of price-conscious consumers who would respond to a different marketing mix. He used direct-response advertising in computer magazines—and customers called a toll-free number to order a computer with the exact features they wanted. Dell used UPS to quickly ship orders directly to the customer. Prices were low, too, because the direct channel held down costs. It also kept Dell in constant contact with customers. Equally important, Dell implemented the plan well—with constant improvements—to make good on its promise of reliable machines and superior service. For example, Dell pioneered a system of guaranteed on-site service—within 24 hours. It also offers ongoing training programs so all employees work together to "please, not just satisfy" customers.

Other firms imitated Dell's approach when they saw how customers responded to it, but Dell continually improved its offerings and at the same time developed new strategies to reach new markets. For example, Dell put money into R&D specifically focused on creating the powerful machines that business customers said they wanted. And in 1987, Dell added a direct sales force to call on

Dell continues to find new ways to satisfy customers.

government and corporate buyers—because they expected in-person selling. Now Dell does more than half of its business that way. And the higher-end machines that these customers buy to run their corporate networks offer bigger profit margins.

Dell also realized that there were big opportunities in Europe. Many Japanese, Korean, and US firms moved into that market by exporting, but Dell set up its own operations there—because that was a way to control its direct approach. Dell knew it would be a challenge to win over skeptical European buyers. They had never bought big-ticket items such as PCs through the mail—and many thought low prices meant shoddy machines and service. Yet Dell's marketing mix delighted European customers, and in less than five years annual sales in Europe grew to $240 million—40 percent of Dell's revenue.

In late 1989, Dell broke with its tradition and added indirect distribution but not through traditional computer dealers. Rather, Dell worked with office supply superstores because they were an important new channel for reaching small- and medium-sized businesses.

Dell has made mistakes along the way. For example, an overly optimistic sales forecast—based mainly on past trends of the growth stage in the product life cycle rather than the move to market maturity—resulted in excess inventories and weak profits in 1988. But Dell learned from the mistake and currently has one of the leanest inventories of any computer company. That helps hold down operating expenses in a business now marked by frantic competition and slim profit margins.

By the summer of 1992, big-name companies like IBM and Compaq cut prices deeply—to squeeze Dell and other smaller competitors. Industry experts predicted that the resulting price war might go on for years. Dell's success will depend on careful strategy planning and skillful implementation. But perhaps Dell can continue to find new ways to satisfy customers' PC-related needs—or even identify new, higher-growth opportunities to pursue.[1]

MARKETING PLANNING IS MORE THAN ASSEMBLING THE FOUR Ps

They must be
blended together

The Dell case shows that marketing planning involves much more than assembling the four parts of a marketing mix. The four Ps must be creatively *blended*—so the firm develops the best mix for its target market. The ideas of the product manager, advertising manager, sales manager, and physical distribution manager may have to be adjusted to improve the whole mix.

Throughout the text, we've given the job of integrating the four Ps to the marketing manager. Now you should see the need for this integrating role. It is easy for specialists to focus on their own areas and expect the rest of the company to work for or around them. This is especially true in larger firms—where specialists are needed—just because the size of the whole marketing job is too big for one person.

Need plans and program

Marketing managers must plan strategies, marketing plans, and, finally, a whole marketing program. As we said earlier, a marketing *strategy* is a big picture of what a firm will do in some target market. A marketing *plan* includes the time-related details for that strategy. A marketing *program* combines the firm's marketing plans.

Some time schedule is implicit in any strategy. A marketing plan simply spells out this time period—and the time-related details. Usually, we think in terms of some reasonable length of time, such as six months, a year, or a few years. But it might be only a month or two in some cases, especially when rapid changes in fashion or technology are important. Or a strategy might be implemented over several years—perhaps the length of a product life cycle or at least the early stages of the product's life.

You can see that marketing strategy planning is a creative process. But it is also a logical process. The marketing concept emphasizes that all of a firm's activities should focus on its target markets. Further, a firm should try to meet the needs of some target market (or markets) that is large enough to support its efforts—and yield a profit. Exhibit 20–1 shows three positions within an organization responsible for the marketing planning process.

In this chapter, we'll develop these ideas further. We'll start with a discussion of forecasting target market potential and sales, which is important not only in evaluating opportunities but also in developing the time-related details for a plan. We'll also review and highlight some of the key ways a marketing manager can identify the right blend of the marketing mix for a strategy. Planning strategies for international markets presents some special challenges, but we'll describe the different ways a marketer can address these challenges. Of course, plans must ultimately be implemented, and we'll suggest ways in which the total quality of the implementation effort can be continuously improved—to better meet customer needs.

Exhibit 20–1   Marketing Professionals

MARKETING PROFESSIONALS

Our dynamic environment has generated opportunities for results-oriented Marketing professionals. We have immediate openings on our management team for the following positions:

METHODS ANALYST

The successful candidate will be responsible for:
- providing marketing and sales personnel with effective support of information and decision support systems;
- determining client requirements, analyzing problems and developing solutions, providing instructions and support;
- maintaining and supporting existing systems; assisting in the interpretation of results.

This position will be of interest to individuals who have:
- 2-4 years working experience in MVS/TSO/SAS environment (systems analysis and programming);
- proven ability to work effectively with clients at all levels, proficiency in innovative problem solving with a view to results, good communication skills.

To qualify applicants must have a University Degree or Certificate/Diploma in Commerce or Business Administration with strong emphasis in information systems and marketing.

MARKETING PLANNING ANALYST

The successful candidate will be responsible for:
- managing a dynamic competitive product portfolio including either business terminal or network communications equipment.

This position will be of interest to individuals who have:
- 3-5 years of telecommunications experience, preferably in the data industry;
- professional marketing skills and approach to problems with a view to results.

To qualify applicants must have a University Degree or Certificate/Diploma in Marketing, Commerce or Business Administration.

MARKETING PLANNING SPECIALIST

The successful candidate will be responsible for:
- managing a constantly changing retail product line of single line terminal equipment and related accessories sold through B.C. Tel PhoneMarts.

This position will be of interest to individuals who have:
- 3-5 years retail buying experience, preferably in the consumer electronics industry;
- sound working knowledge of the market planning/product management process;
- demonstrated negotiation skills and ability to make sound decisions in very short time frames;
- proven ability to work effectively as a team member.

To qualify applicants must have a University Degree or Certificate/Diploma in Marketing, Commerce or Business Administration.

B.C. Tel is an equal opportunity employer offering a salary commensurate with experience and an excellent benefit package.

Highly motivated individuals, who are committed to exceeding customer expectations in a competitive industry, should send a resume including salary expectations to:

Jeannine Drewitt
Employment Manager
B.C. Telephone Company
6th Floor – 3777 Kingsway
Burnaby, B.C.
V5H 3Z7

To be considered, resumes must be received by September 5.

B.C.Tel *Quality*
We make it a way of life.

Source: *Province*, August 20, 1989, p. 87.

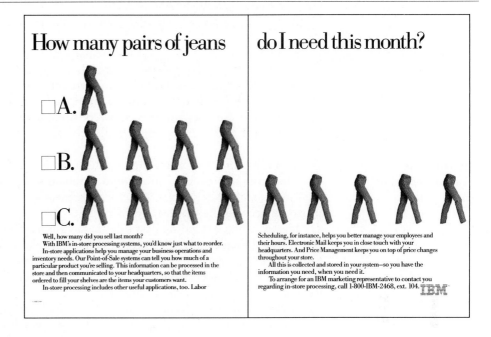

FORECASTING TARGET MARKET POTENTIAL AND SALES

Estimates of target **market potential**—what a whole market segment might buy—and a **sales forecast**—an estimate of how much an industry or firm hopes to sell to a market segment—are necessary for effective strategy planning. Without such information, it's hard to know if a strategy is potentially profitable.

We must first try to judge market potential before we can estimate what share a particular firm may be able to win with its particular marketing mix.

Three levels of forecast are useful

We're interested in forecasting the potential in specific market segments. To do this, it helps to make three levels of forecasts.

Some economic conditions affect the entire global economy. Others may influence only one country or a particular industry. And some may affect only one company or one product's sales potential. For this reason, a common approach to forecasting is to:

1. Develop a *national income forecast* (for each country in which the firm operates) and use this to:
2. Develop an *industry sales forecast*, which then is used to:
3. Develop *specific company* and *product forecasts*.

Generally, a marketing manager doesn't have to make forecasts for a national economy or the broad industry. This kind of forecasting—basically trend projecting—is a specialty in itself. Such forecasts are available in business and government publications, and large companies often have their own technical specialists. Managers can use just one source's forecast or combine several. Unfortunately, however, the more targeted the marketing manager's earlier segmenting efforts have been, the less likely that industry forecasts will match the firm's product-markets. So managers have to move directly to estimating potential for their own companies—and for their specific products.

Two approaches to forecasting

Many methods are used to forecast market potential and sales, but they can all be grouped into two basic approaches: (1) extending past behavior and (2) predicting future behavior. The large number of methods may seem confusing at first, but this variety has an advantage. Forecasts are so important that managers often develop forecasts in two or three different ways and then compare the differences before preparing a final forecast.

Extending past behavior can miss important turning points

When we forecast for existing products, we usually have some past data to go on. The basic approach—called **trend extension**—extends past experience into the future. With existing products, for example, the past trend of actual sales may be extended into the future. See Exhibit 20–2.

Ideally, when extending past sales behavior, we should decide why sales vary. This is the difficult and time-consuming part of sales forecasting. Usually, we can gather a lot of data about the product or market or about changes in the marketing environment. But unless we know the *reason* for past sales variations, it's hard to predict in what direction—and by how much—sales will move. Graphing the data and statistical techniques, including correlation and regression analysis, can be useful here. (These techniques, which are beyond our scope, are discussed in beginning statistics courses.)

Once we know why sales vary, we can usually develop a specific forecast. Sales may be moving directly up as population grows, for example. So we can just estimate how population is expected to grow and project the impact on sales.

The weakness of the trend extension method is that it assumes past conditions will continue unchanged into the future. In fact, the future isn't always like the past. For example, for years the trend in sales of disposable diapers moved closely with the number of new births. However, as the number of women in the work force increased and as more women returned to jobs after their babies were born, use of disposable diapers increased and the trend changed. As in this example, trend extension estimates will be wrong whenever big changes occur. For this reason—although they may extend past behavior for one estimate—most managers look for another way to help them forecast sharp economic changes.

Predicting future behavior takes judgment

When we try to predict what will happen in the future—instead of just extending the past—we have to use other methods and add a bit more judgment.

Exhibit 20–2   Straight-Line Trend Projection—Extends Past Sales into the Future

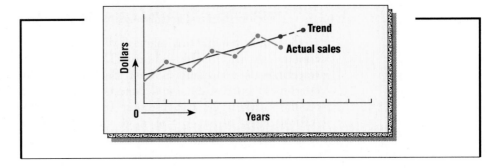

Some of these methods (to be discussed later) include juries of executive opinion, salespeople's estimates, surveys, panels, and market tests.

FORECASTING COMPANY AND PRODUCT SALES BY EXTENDING PAST BEHAVIOR

Past sales
can be extended

At the very least, a marketing manager ought to know what the firm's present markets look like and what it has sold to them in the past. A detailed sales analysis for products and geographic areas helps to project future results.

Just extending past sales into the future may not seem like much of a forecasting method. But it's better than just assuming that next year's total sales will be the same as this year's.

Factor method includes
more than time

A simple extension of past sales gives one forecast. But it's usually desirable to tie future sales to something more than the passage of time.

The factor method tries to do this. The **factor method** tries to forecast sales by finding a relation between the company's sales and some other factor (or factors). The basic formula is: something (past sales, industry sales, etc.) *times* some factor *equals* sales forecast. A **factor** is a variable that shows the relation of some other variable to the item being forecast. For instance, in our example above, both the birthrate and the number of working mothers are factors related to sales of disposable diapers.

A bread producer
example

The following example about a bread producer shows how firms can make forecasts for many geographic market segments using the factor method and available data. This general approach can be useful for any firm: producer, wholesaler, or retailer.

Analysis of past sales relationships showed that the bread manufacturer regularly sold 0.5 percent (0.005) of the total retail food sales in its various target markets. This is a single factor. By using this single factor, estimates of the manufacturer's sales for the coming period could be obtained by multiplying a forecast of expected retail food sales by 0.005.

Let's carry this bread example further, using data for Victoria, British Columbia. Let's assume Victoria's food sales were $400,000,000 for the previous year. Start by simply accepting last year's food sales as an estimate of current year's sales. Then multiply the food sales estimate for Victoria by the 0.005 factor (the firm's usual share in such markets). The manager would now have an estimate of the current year's bread sales in Victoria. That is, last year's food sales estimate ($400,000,000) times 0.005 equals this year's bread sales estimate of $2,000,000.

Going further, let's assume the marketing manager expected that an especially aggressive promotion campaign would increase the firm's share by 10 percent. The single factor could be increased from 0.005 to 0.0055 and then multiplied by the food sales estimate for Victoria to obtain an estimate for the firm's Victoria bread sales.

Factor method can
use several factors

The factor method isn't limited to using just one factor. Several factors can be used together. For example, *Sales and Marketing Management* regularly gives a "buying power index" (BPI) as a measure of the potential in different geographic areas. See Exhibit 20–3. This index takes into consideration (1) the population in a market, (2) the market's effective buying income (EBI), and (3) retail sales in that market. The BPI for Calgary, Alberta, for example, is 3.3921, meaning

Exhibit 20-3   Survey of Buying Power: Population and Retail Sales by Metropolitan Area

Province S&MM Metro Area	Population (000)	Percentage of Canada	Households (000)	Percentage of Canada	Total Retail Sales ($000)
Alberta					
Calgary	763.2	2.8865%	288.6	2.9826%	$ 7,996,717
Edmonton	831.3	3.1441	307.6	3.1790	6,923,933
British Columbia					
Kamloops	98.4	.3722	35.8	.3700	1,121,670
Kelowna	100.1	.3786	39.4	.4072	694,063
Prince George	86.1	.3256	29.2	.3017	737,702
Vancouver	1,474.9	5.5783	583.6	6.0315	10,872,373
Victoria	288.2	1.0900	121.7	1.2578	3,178,308
Manitoba					
Winnipeg	608.5	2.3014	238.1	2.4607	4,205,542
New Brunswick					
Moncton	140.1	.5298	49.3	.5095	970,124
St. John	141.8	.5363	50.4	.5209	1,169,726
Newfoundland					
St. John's	250.1	.9459	76.4	.7896	1,901,722
Nova Scotia					
Halifax-Dartmouth	319.0	1.2065	116.0	1.1988	2,200,174
Sydney-Glace Bay	123.1	.4656	40.2	.4155	410,545
Ontario					
Brantford	111.9	.4232	40.9	.4227	565,639
Guelph	151.8	.5741	53.6	.5540	1,164,577
Hamilton	440.3	1.6653	166.2	1.7176	3,279,149
Kingston	122.9	.4648	46.4	.4796	1,397,310
Kitchener-Cambridge	358.8	1.3570	129.4	1.3373	5,247,757
London	356.9	1.3499	137.6	1.4221	4,816,753
North Bay	82.9	.3135	29.5	.3048	684,520
Oshawa	387.6	1.4660	130.4	1.3477	4,248,617
Ottawa	882.3	3.3370	334.3	3.4550	5,729,909
Peterborough	115.7	.4376	43.1	.4454	1,700,472
St. Catharines-Niagara	384.0	1.4523	141.9	1.4666	1,980,971
Sarnia	128.0	.4842	46.6	.4816	415,893
Sault Ste. Marie	131.4	.4970	46.0	.4754	1,246,314
Sudbury	154.3	.5836	54.9	.5674	978,264
Thunder Bay	157.2	.5945	56.5	.5839	1,242,184
Toronto	3,602.4	13.6247	1,290.5	13.3371	25,753,925
Windsor	323.3	1.2228	118.1	1.2205	2,935,320
Quebec					
Chicoutimi-Jonquière	175.3	.6630	58.5	.6046	976,135
Montreal	3,096.5	11.7113	1,224.4	12.6540	25,629,741
Quebec	614.7	2.3249	231.8	2.3957	5,411,199
Sherbrooke	125.4	.4742	49.2	.5085	1,451,996
Trois Rivières-Shawinigan	233.5	.8831	88.9	.9188	1,830,684
Saskatchewan					
Regina	217.1	.8211	80.6	.8330	1,639,640
Saskatoon	221.1	.8362	83.6	.8640	1,300,575
Total	17,800.1	67.3221%	6,659.2	68.8221%	$144,010,143

Source: *Sales and Marketing Management,* November 1990.

Percentage of Canada	Total EBI ($000)	Percentage of Canada	Per Capita EBI ($)	Average Household EBI ($)	Sales/Advertising Indexes		
					Sales Activity	Buying Power	Quality
3.8456%	$ 12,795,364	3.3223%	$16,765	$44,336	133	3.3921	118
3.3298	12,818,725	3.3284	15,420	41,673	106	3.2919	105
.5394	1,237,481	.3213	12,576	34,567	145	.3970	107
.3338	1,362,131	.3537	13,608	34,572	88	.3526	93
.3547	1,173,431	.3047	13,629	40,186	109	.3239	99
5.2286	22,951,157	5.9593	15,561	39,327	94	5.6639	102
1.5284	4,368,565	1.1343	15,158	35,896	140	1.2437	114
2.0225	8,958,567	2.3261	14,722	37,625	88	2.2301	97
.4666	1,766,120	.4585	12,606	35,824	88	.4751	90
.5625	1,813,624	.4709	12,790	35,985	105	.5114	95
.9146	2,981,221	.7740	11,920	39,021	97	.8507	90
1.0581	4,598,212	1.1939	14,414	39,640	88	1.1556	96
.1974	1,348,183	.3501	10,952	33,537	42	.3274	70
.2721	1,638,497	.4255	14,643	40,061	64	.3789	90
.5600	2,379,328	.6178	15,674	44,390	98	.5917	103
1.5769	6,778,804	1.7601	15,396	40,787	95	1.6861	101
.6720	1,826,471	.4742	14,861	39,364	145	.5317	114
2.5237	5,722,230	1.4858	15,948	44,221	186	1.7714	131
2.3164	5,825,013	1.5125	16,321	42,333	172	1.7212	128
.3292	1,138,219	.2956	13,730	38,584	105	.3091	99
2.0431	6,520,903	1.6932	16,824	50,007	139	1.7528	120
2.7555	14,956,913	3.8835	16,952	44,741	83	3.4359	103
.8178	1,758,106	.4565	15,195	40,791	187	.5610	128
.9526	5,730,958	1.4880	14,924	40,387	66	1.3204	91
.2000	1,937,956	.5032	15,140	41,587	41	.4085	84
.5993	1,772,482	.4602	13,489	38,532	121	.5093	102
.4704	2,191,434	.5690	14,202	39,917	81	.5424	93
.5973	2,426,683	.6301	15,437	42,950	100	.6132	103
12.3852	63,596,269	16.5130	17,654	49,280	91	14.6968	108
1.4116	5,123,267	1.3303	15,847	43,381	115	1.3332	109
.4694	1,970,821	.5117	11,243	33,689	71	.5292	80
12.3256	45,152,611	11.7240	14,582	36,877	105	11.9022	102
2.6023	8,918,107	2.3156	14,508	38,473	112	2.4035	103
.6983	1,674,674	.4348	13,355	34,038	147	.5217	110
.8803	2,793,285	.7253	11,963	31,421	100	.8033	91
.7886	3,035,859	.7883	13,984	37,666	96	.7950	97
.6254	2,961,509	.7690	13,394	35,425	75	.7393	88
69.2550%	$276,003,180	71.6647%	$15,506	$41,447	103	70.0732	104

Calgary accounts for 3.3921 percent of the total Canadian buying power. This means Calgary is a fairly attractive market, because its BPI is much greater than would be expected based on population alone. That is, although Calgary accounts for 2.8865 percent of the Canadian population, it has a much larger share of the buying power because its income and retail sales are above average.

Using several factors rather than only one factor enables us to work with more information. And in the case of the BPI, it gives a measure of a market's potential, which may be quite important if, for example, a company's sales are not limited to one type of retail store. Then, rather than falling back on using population only, or income only, or trying to develop one's own special index, the BPI can be used in the same way that we used the 0.005 factor in the bread example.

When several factors are used, they may be put together—as with the BPI—or used separately. But the basic factor method is the same. This is shown for a retailer who might be interested in estimating the potential for sets of novelty beer mugs in the Winnipeg area. If about 5 percent of its target market could be expected to buy a $10 set within a one-year period, and this target market consisted of just about every household, the appropriate numbers could be multiplied to get the following forecast. The example shows that 11,905 buying households spend $10 each, for a total sales potential of $119,050.

Households in Winnipeg	238,100
× Share of market (5%)	.05
	11,905
× Price of product ($10)	10
Total sales potential	$119,050

Producers of business products can use several factors, too. Exhibit 20–4 shows how one manufacturer estimated the market for fiber boxes for a particular CMA. This approach could be used in each CMA to estimate the potential in many geographic target markets.

In this case, SIC code data is used. This is common in the industrial area because SIC code data is readily available and often very relevant. In this case, the value of box shipments by SIC code was collected by a trade association, but the rest of the data was available from government sources.

Basically, the approach is to calculate the typical consumption per employee for each SIC industry group in the particular CMA to estimate market potential for each group. Then the sum of these estimates becomes the total market potential in that CMA. A firm thinking of going into that market would need to estimate the share it could get with its own marketing mix.

Note that this approach can also aid management's control job. If the firm were already in this industry, it could compare its actual sales (by SIC code) with the potential and see how it's doing. If its typical market share is 10 percent of the market and it's obtaining only 2 to 5 percent of the market in various SIC submarkets, then some marketing mix changes may be in order.

Time series and leading series may help estimate a fluctuating future

Not all past economic or sales behavior can be neatly extended with a straight line or some manipulation. Economic activity has its ups and downs. To cope with such variation, statisticians have developed *time series* analysis tech-

Exhibit 20–4   Estimated Market for Corrugated Boxes and Cartons (by industry groups, Toronto CMA)

Industry	(1) Value of Box Shipments (by end use) ($000)	(2) Production Workers (by industry group)	(3) Consumption per Worker (1) ÷ (2) (dollars)	Toronto (4) Production Workers (by industry group)	(5) Estimated Size of the Market (3) × (4) ($000)
Food and beverage	$316,752	159,703	$1,983	24,343	$ 48,272
Tobacco products	6,100	5,606	1,088	—	—
Rubber and plastics products	35,375	45,681	774	12,546	9,711
Leather	6,450	22,577	286	3,986	1,140
Textile	19,504	53,073	367	7,195	2,641
Knitting mills	3,140	17,851	179	3,288	589
Clothing	10,670	83,418	128	13,467	1,724
Wood	4,694	94,328	48	3,499	168
Furniture and fixtures	30,968	44,328	699	13,780	9,632
Paper	51,785	99,491	520	12,824	6,668
Printing and publishing	9,492	63,964	148	19,020	2,815
Primary metal	2,916	92,337	32	—	—
Metal fabricating	38,895	120,450	323	30,024	9,698
Machinery	9,883	70,784	140	14,238	1,993
Transportation equipment	11,905	136,102	87	25,899	2,253
Electrical products	40,856	84,282	485	26,834	13,014
Nonmetallic mineral products	40,294	40,145	1,004	5,919	5,943
Petroleum and coal products	3,800	8,457	449	—	—
Chemical and chemical products	50,176	46,398	1,081	11,600	12,540
Miscellaneous manufacturing	25,292	48,354	523	19,263	10,075
Total	$718,947				$138,876

Source: Statistics Canada, Cats. 31-209, 31-203, and 31-212.

niques. **Time series** are historical records of the fluctuations in economic variables. We can't go into a detailed discussion of these techniques here, but note that there are techniques to handle daily, weekly, monthly, seasonal, and annual variations.[2]

The dream of all forecasters is to find an accurate **leading series** (a time series that changes in the same direction *but ahead of* the series to be forecasted). For example, if an index of electrical power consumption always went up three months before a company's own sales of products that have some logical relation to electric power consumption (it's important that there be some logical relation!), then the managers might watch this "leading" series very carefully when forecasting monthly sales of its products.

No single series has yet been found that leads GNP or other important quantities. Lacking such a series, forecasters develop **indices** (statistical combinations of several time series) in an effort to find some time series that will lead the series they're attempting to forecast. The Bank of Canada, The Conference Board in Canada, and the chartered banks offer statistical information in their monthly reviews. The Conference Board also provides detailed information on many generally accepted measures of economic activity. And business magazines such as *Canadian Business* publish their own series and predictions.

PREDICTING FUTURE BEHAVIOR CALLS FOR MORE JUDGMENT AND SOME OPINIONS

These past-extending methods use quantitative data, projecting past experience into the future and assuming that the future will be like the past. But this is risky in competitive markets. Usually, it's desirable to add some judgment to other forecasts before making the final forecast yourself.

Jury of executive opinion adds judgment

One of the oldest and simplest methods of forecasting—the **jury of executive opinion**—combines the opinions of experienced executives, perhaps from marketing, production, finance, purchasing, and top management. Each executive estimates market potential and sales for the *coming years*. Then they try to work out a consensus.

The main advantage of the jury approach is that it can be done quickly and easily. On the other hand, the results may not be very good. There may be too much extending of the past. Some of the executives may have little contact with outside market influences. But their estimates could point to major shifts in customer demand or competition.

Estimates from salespeople can help, too

Using salespeople's estimates to forecast is like the jury approach. But salespeople are more likely than home office managers to be familiar with customer reactions—and what competitors are doing. Their estimates are especially useful in some business markets where the few customers may be well known to the salespeople. But this approach may be useful in any type of market. Good retail clerks have a feel for their markets and their opinions shouldn't be ignored.

However, managers who use estimates from salespeople should be aware of the limitations. For example, new salespeople may not know much about their markets. Even experienced salespeople may not be aware of possible changes in the economic climate or the firm's other environments. And if salespeople think the manager is going to use the estimates to set sales quotas, the estimates may be low!

Surveys, panels, and market tests

Special surveys of final buyers, retailers, and/or wholesalers can show what's happening in different market segments. Some firms use panels of stores—or final consumers—to keep track of buying behavior and to decide when just extending past behavior isn't enough.

Surveys are sometimes combined with market tests when the company wants to estimate customers' reactions to possible changes in its marketing mix. A market test might show that a product increased its share of the market by 10 percent when its price was dropped 1 cent below competition. But this extra business might be quickly lost if the price were increased 1 cent above competition. Such market experiments help the marketing manager make good estimates of future sales when one or more of the four Ps are changed.

Accuracy depends on the marketing mix

Forecasting can help a marketing manager estimate the size of possible market opportunities. But the accuracy of any sales forecast depends on whether the firm selects and implements a marketing mix that turns these opportunities into sales and profits.[3]

BLENDING THE FOUR PS TAKES UNDERSTANDING OF A TARGET MARKET

Developing a good marketing mix requires blending many of the ideas discussed in this text. Exhibit 20–5 reviews the marketing strategy decision areas we've been talking about. Now we must integrate them into logical marketing mixes, marketing strategies, marketing plans—and a marketing program.

Marketing mix flows from target market dimensions

Ideally, the ingredients of a good marketing mix flow logically from all the relevant dimensions of a target market. The market definition and segmenting approaches we discussed in Chapter 3 help the marketing manager identify which dimensions are qualifying and which are determining in customers' choices. Product benefits must match needs. If and how customers search for information help to define the promotion blend. Demographic dimensions reveal where customers are located and if they have the income to buy. Where customers shop for or buy products helps define channel alternatives. The value of the whole marketing mix and the urgency of customer needs, combined with an understanding of what customers see as substitute ways of meeting needs, help companies estimate price sensitivity.

If we fully understand the needs and attitudes of a target market, then combining the four Ps should be easy. There are three gaps in this line of reasoning, however: (1) We don't always know as much as we would like to about the needs and attitudes of our target markets. (2) Competitors are also trying to satisfy these or similar needs—and their efforts may force a firm to shift its marketing mix. (3) The other dimensions of the marketing environment may be changing—which may require more changes in marketing mixes.

Product classes suggest typical marketing mixes

Even if you don't or can't know all you would like to about a potential target market, you usually know enough to decide whether the product is a consumer product or a business product—and which product class is most relevant. Exhibit 9–3 summarizes the product classes.

Exhibit 20–5 Strategy Decision Areas Organized by the Four Ps

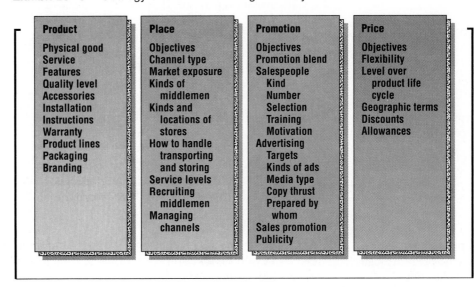

Product	Place	Promotion	Price
Physical good	Objectives	Objectives	Objectives
Service	Channel type	Promotion blend	Flexibility
Features	Market exposure	Salespeople	Level over
Quality level	Kinds of	Kind	product life
Accessories	middlemen	Number	cycle
Installation	Kinds and	Selection	Geographic terms
Instructions	locations of	Training	Discounts
Warranty	stores	Motivation	Allowances
Product lines	How to handle	Advertising	
Packaging	transporting	Targets	
Branding	and storing	Kinds of ads	
	Service levels	Media type	
	Recruiting	Copy thrust	
	middlemen	Prepared by	
	Managing	whom	
	channels	Sales promotion	
		Publicity	

Identifying the proper product class helps because it suggests how a typical product should be distributed and promoted. So if you don't know as much as you'd like about potential customers' needs and attitudes, at least knowing how *they* would view the company's product can give you a head start on developing a marketing mix. A convenience product, for example, usually needs more intensive distribution and the producer usually takes on more responsibility for promotion. A specialty product needs a clear brand identity—which may require a positioning effort. A new unsought product will need a mix that leads customers through the adoption process.

It's reassuring to see that product classes do summarize some of what you would like to know about target markets and what marketing mixes are relevant. After all, what others have done in similar situations must have satisfied someone—and that can serve as a guide. Beyond this, you need judgment or perhaps some marketing research. In this way, you can use past experience—while not relying on it blindly.

Typical is not necessarily right

The typical marketing mix for a given product class is not necessarily right for all situations. Some very profitable marketing mixes depart from the typical—to satisfy some target markets better.

A marketing manager may have to develop a mix that is *not* typical because of various market realities, including special characteristics of the product or target market, the competitive environment, and each firm's capabilities and limitations.

Superior mixes may be breakthrough opportunities

When marketing managers fully understand their target markets, they may be able to develop marketing mixes that are superior to competitors' mixes. Such understanding may provide breakthrough opportunities. Taking advantage of

---

MARKETING DEMO 20–1
Quick Metal Strategy Planning Fastens on Customer Needs—and Profits

L octite Corporation, a producer of industrial supplies, used careful strategy planning to launch Quick Metal—a puttylike adhesive for repairing worn machine parts. Loctite chemists had developed similar products in the past. But managers had paid little attention to developing a *complete marketing strategy*—and sales had been poor.

Before creating Quick Metal, Loctite identified some attractive target customers. Research showed that production people were eager to try any product that helped get broken machines back into production. Quick Metal was developed to meet the needs of this target market. Ads appealed to such needs with copy promising that Quick Metal "keeps machinery running until the new parts arrive." Channel members also received attention. During the introduction stage, sales reps made frequent phone calls and sales visits to the nearly 700 wholesalers who handle Loctite products. Loctite awarded cash prizes to those selling the most Quick Metal.

A tube of Quick Metal was priced at $17.75—about twice the price (and profit margin) of competing products. But Loctite's customers weren't concerned about price. They responded to a quality product that could keep their production lines operating.

Based on past experience, some estimated that a typical product for this market might reach sales of $300,000 a year. But Loctite didn't rely on a typical strategy. Instead, the company offered a carefully targeted marketing mix to meet the needs of a *specific* target market. It sold 100,000 tubes the first week—and within seven months, sales exceeded $2.2 million. Loctite's careful planning paid off in an immediate market success—and high profits.

Source: Loctite, 1990 Annual Report; "Companies to Watch: Loctite Corporation," *Fortune*, June 19, 1989, p. 148; "Loctite: Home Is Where the Customers Are," *Business Week*, April 13, 1987, p. 63; Loctite Corporation, 1987 Annual Report; "Loctite 'Listens' to the Marketplace," in Ronald Alsop and Bill Abrams, *The Wall Street Journal on Marketing* (New York: Dow Jones & Co., 1986), pp. 281–83.

---

these opportunities can lead to large sales—and profitable growth. This is why we stress the importance of looking for breakthrough opportunities rather than just trying to imitate competitors' offerings.

NutraSweet built its original success on an innovative product that met consumers' needs. But the strategy NutraSweet's marketing managers planned involved more than a good product. The typical marketing strategy for firms that supply ingredients to food and soft-drink companies emphasized personal selling to producers. In contrast, NutraSweet's marketing managers used mass selling to promote their brand name and red swirl logo directly to consumers.

They also persuaded producers who used the ingredient to feature the NutraSweet brand name prominently on containers and in ads. In addition, because there was little direct competition, they used a profitable skimming approach to pricing—and charged different producer-customers different prices depending on the value NutraSweet added to their product. Now that NutraSweet's patent has expired, competitors will face a challenge entering the market because it will take a huge marketing effort—and a high promotion budget—to offset consumers' familiarity with the NutraSweet name.[4] Another example of clever strategic planning is presented in Marketing Demo 20–1.

Inferior mixes are easy to reject

Just as some mixes are superior, some mixes are clearly inferior—or unsuitable. For example, a national TV advertising campaign might make sense for a large company, but it might be completely out of the question for a small manufacturer that only has the resources to start offering a new product in a limited geographic area.

Product life cycle
guides planning

Careful consideration of where a firm's offering fits in the product life cycle can also be a big help in evaluating the best marketing mix. Exhibit 20-6 summarizes how marketing mix variables typically change over the product life cycle. This exhibit is a good review of many topics we've discussed throughout the text. Certainly, the pioneering effort required for a really new product concept is different than the job of taking market share away from an established competitor late in the market growth stage.

Further, if you're thinking about the product life cycle, don't forget that markets change continually. This means you must plan strategies that can adjust to changing conditions. The original marketing plan may even include details about what adjustments in the marketing mix will be required as the nature of competition changes.[5]

Exhibit 20-6   Typical Changes in Marketing Variables over the Product Life Cycle

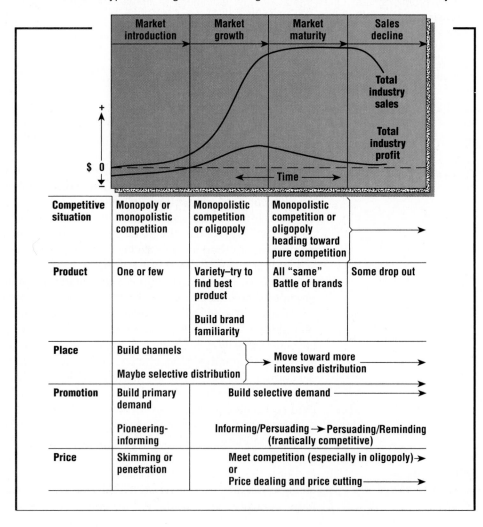

	Market introduction	Market growth	Market maturity	Sales decline
Competitive situation	Monopoly or monopolistic competition	Monopolistic competition or oligopoly	Monopolistic competition or oligopoly heading toward pure competition	
Product	One or few	Variety–try to find best product Build brand familiarity	All "same" Battle of brands	Some drop out
Place	Build channels Maybe selective distribution	Move toward more intensive distribution →		
Promotion	Build primary demand Pioneering-informing	Build selective demand → Informing/Persuading → Persuading/Reminding (frantically competitive)		
Price	Skimming or penetration	Meet competition (especially in oligopoly) → or Price dealing and price cutting →		

ANALYSIS OF COSTS AND SALES CAN GUIDE PLANNING

Once a manager has narrowed down to a few reasonable marketing mixes, comparing the sales, costs, and profitability of the different alternatives helps in selecting the marketing mix the firm will implement. Exhibit 20–7 shows such a comparison for a small appliance currently selling for $15—Mix A in the example. Here, the marketing manager simply estimates the costs and likely results of four reasonable alternatives. And, assuming profit is the objective *and* there are adequate resources to consider each of the alternatives, marketing Mix C is obviously the best alternative.

Spreadsheet analysis speeds through calculations

Comparing the alternatives in Exhibit 20–7 is quite simple. But sometimes marketing managers need much more detail to evaluate a plan. Hundreds of calculations may be required to see how specific marketing resources relate to expected outcomes—like total costs, expected sales, and profit. To make that part of the planning job simpler and faster, marketing managers often use spreadsheet analysis. With **spreadsheet analysis**, costs, sales, and other information related to a problem are organized into a data table—a spreadsheet—to show how changing the value of one or more of the numbers affects the other numbers. This is possible because the relationships among the variables are programmed in the computer software. Lotus 1-2-3, Excel, Supercalc, and Appleworks are examples of well-known spreadsheet programs. You may already be familiar with spreadsheet analysis. Even if you aren't, the basic idea is not complicated.

A spreadsheet helps answer what-if questions

Spreadsheet analysis allows the marketing manager to evaluate what-if type questions. For example, a marketing manager might be interested in the question "What if I charge a higher price and the number of units sold stays the same? What will happen to profit?" To look at how a spreadsheet program might be used to help answer this what-if question, let's take a closer look at Exhibit 20–7.

The manager might set up the data in this table as a computer spreadsheet. The table involves a number of relationships. For example, price times total units equals sales; and total cost equals selling cost plus advertising cost plus overhead cost plus total product costs (7,000 units × $5 per unit). If these relationships are programmed in the spreadsheet, a marketing manager can ask questions like: "What if I raise the price to $20.20 and still sell 7,000 units? What will happen to profit?" To get the answer, all the manager needs to do is type the new price in the spreadsheet and the program computes the new profit—$26,400.

Exhibit 20–7   Comparing the Estimated Sales, Costs, and Profits of Four "Reasonable" Alternative Marketing Mixes*

Marketing Mix	Price	Selling Cost	Advertising Cost	Total Units	Sales	Total Cost	Total Profit
A	$15	$20,000	$ 5,000	5,000	$ 75,000	$ 70,000	$ 5,000
B	15	20,000	20,000	7,000	105,000	95,000	10,000
C	20	30,000	30,000	7,000	140,000	115,000	25,000
D	25	40,000	40,000	5,000	125,000	125,000	0

*For the same target market, assuming product costs per unit are $5 and fixed (overhead) costs are $20,000.

In addition, the manager may also want to do many what-if analyses—for example, to see how sales and profit change over a range of prices. Computerized spreadsheet analysis does this quickly and easily. For example, if the manager wants to see what happens to total revenue as the price varies between some minimum (say, $19.80) and a maximum (say, $20.20), the program can show the total revenue and profit for a number of price levels in the range from $19.80 to $20.20. See Exhibit 20–8.

In a problem like this, the marketing manager might be able to do the same calculations quickly by hand. But with more complicated problems, the spreadsheet program can be a big help, making it very convenient to more carefully analyze different alternatives.

Exhibit 20–8   A Spreadsheet Analysis Showing How a Change in Price Affects Sales and Profit (based on Marketing Mix C from Exhibit 20–7)

Price	Selling Cost	Advertising Cost	Total Units	Sales	Total Cost	Total Profit
$19.80	$30,000	$30,000	7,000	$138,600	$115,000	$23,600
19.90	30,000	30,000	7,000	139,300	115,000	24,300
20.00	30,000	30,000	7,000	140,000	115,000	25,000
20.10	30,000	30,000	7,000	140,700	115,000	25,700
20.20	30,000	30,000	7,000	141,400	115,000	26,400

PLANNING FOR INVOLVEMENT IN INTERNATIONAL MARKETING

When developing a plan for international markets, marketing managers must decide how involved the firm will be. We will discuss six basic kinds of involvement: exporting, licensing, contract manufacturing, management contracting, joint venturing, and wholly owned subsidiaries.

Exporting often
comes first

Some companies get into international marketing just by **exporting**—selling some of what the firm produces to foreign markets. Some firms start exporting just to get rid of surplus output. For others, exporting comes from a real effort to look for new opportunities.

Some firms try exporting without doing much planning. They don't change the product—or even the service or instruction manuals! As a result, some early efforts are not very satisfying, to buyers or sellers. When Toyota first exported cars to the United States, the effort was a failure. Americans just weren't interested in the Toyota model that sold well in Japan. Toyota tried again three years later with a new design and a new marketing mix. Obviously, Toyota's second effort was a real success.[6]

Specialists can help develop the plan

Exporting does require knowledge about the foreign market. But managers who don't have enough knowledge to plan the details of a program can often get expert help from middlemen specialists. As we discussed in Chapter 14, export agents can handle the paperwork as products are shipped outside the country. Then agents or merchant wholesalers can handle the importing details. Even large producers with many foreign operations turn to international middlemen for some products or

*Exporting is often
the first step into
international marketing.*

markets. Such middlemen know how to handle the sometimes confusing formalities and specialized functions. A manager trying to develop a plan alone can make a small mistake that ties products up at national borders for days—or months.[7]

Exporting doesn't have to involve permanent relationships. Of course, channel relationships take time to build and shouldn't be treated lightly—sales reps' contacts in foreign countries are investments. But it's relatively easy to cut back on these relationships, or even drop them, if the plan doesn't work.

Some firms, on the other hand, plan more formal and permanent relationships with nationals in foreign countries. The relationships might involve licensing, contract manufacturing, management contracting, and joint venturing.

Licensing is an easy way

Licensing is a relatively easy way to enter foreign markets. **Licensing** means selling the right to use some process, trademark, patent, or other right for a fee or royalty. The licensee takes most of the risk because it must invest some capital to use the right. Further, the licensee usually does most of the planning for the markets it is licensed to serve. If good partners are available, this can be an effective way to enter a market. Gerber entered the Japanese baby food market this way but still exports to other countries.[8]

Contract manufacturing takes care of the production problems

Contract manufacturing means turning over production to others while retaining the marketing process. Sears used this approach when it opened stores in Latin America and Spain. This approach doesn't make it any easier to plan the marketing program, but it may make it a lot easier to implement.

For example, this approach can be especially desirable where labor relations are difficult or where there are problems obtaining supplies or government cooperation. Growing nationalistic feelings may make this approach more attractive in the future.

Management contracting sells know-how

Management contracting means the seller provides only management skills—others own the production and distribution facilities. Some mines and oil refineries are operated this way—and Hilton operates hotels all over the world for local owners. This is a relatively low-risk approach to international marketing. The company makes no commitment to fixed facilities, which can be taken over or damaged in riots or wars. If conditions get too bad, key management people can fly off on the next plane—and leave the nationals to manage the operation.

Joint venturing is more involved

Joint venturing means a domestic firm entering into a partnership with a foreign firm. As with any partnership, there can be honest disagreements over objectives—for example, how much profit is desired and how fast it should be paid out—as well as operating policies. Where a close working relationship can be developed, perhaps based on one firm's technical and marketing know-how and the foreign partner's knowledge of the market and political connections, this approach can be very attractive to both parties.

In some situations, a joint venture is the only type of involvement possible. For example, IBM wanted to increase its 2 percent share of the $1 billion a year that business customers in Brazil spend on data processing services. But a Brazilian law severely limited expansion by foreign computer companies. To grow, IBM had to develop a joint venture with a Brazilian firm. Because of Brazilian laws, IBM could own only a 30 percent interest in the joint venture. But IBM decided it was better to have a 30 percent share of a business—and be able to pursue new market opportunities—than to stand by and watch competitors take the market.[9]

A joint venture usually requires a big commitment from both parties, and they both must agree on a joint plan. When the relationship doesn't work out well, the ensuing nightmare can make the manager wish that the venture had been planned as a wholly owned operation. But the terms of the joint venture may block this for years.[10]

Wholly owned subsidiaries give more control

When a firm thinks a foreign market looks really promising, it may want to take the final step. A **wholly owned subsidiary** is a separate firm—owned by a parent company. This gives the firm complete control of the marketing plan and operations, and also helps a foreign branch work more easily with the rest of the company. If a firm has too much capacity in a country with low production costs, for example, it can move some production there from other plants and then export to countries with higher production costs.

Multinational corporations evolve to meet the challenge

As firms become more involved in international marketing, some begin to see themselves as worldwide businesses that transcend national boundaries. These **multinational corporations** have a direct investment in several countries and run their businesses depending on the choices available anywhere in the world. Well-known North American–based multinational firms include Coca-Cola, Eastman Kodak, Warner-Lambert, Goodyear, Ford, and IBM. They regularly earn over a third of their total sales or profits abroad. And well-known foreign-based multinationals—such as Nestlé, Shell (Royal Dutch Shell), Unilever, Sony, and Honda—have well-accepted brands all around the world.

These multinational operations no longer just export or import. They hire local workers and build local plants. They have relationships with local businesses and politicians. These powerful organizations learn to plan marketing strategies that deal with nationalistic feelings and typical border barriers, treating them simply as part of the marketing environment. We don't yet have one world politically—but business is moving in that direction. We may have to develop new kinds of corporations and laws to govern multinational operations. In the future, it will make less and less sense for business and politics to be limited by national boundaries.

Planning for international markets

Usually, marketing managers must plan the firm's overall marketing program so it's flexible enough to be adapted for differences in different countries. When the differences are significant, top management should delegate a great deal of responsibility for strategy planning to local managers (or even middlemen). In many cases, it's not possible to develop a detailed plan without a "local feel." In extreme cases, local managers may not even be able to fully explain some parts of their plans because they're based on subtle cultural differences. Then plans must be judged only by their results. The organizational setup should give these managers a great deal of freedom in their planning—but ensure tight control against the plans they develop. Top management can simply insist that managers stick to their budgets and meet the plans that they themselves create. When a firm reaches this stage, it is being managed like a well-organized domestic corporation—which insists that its managers (of divisions and territories) meet their own plans so that the whole company's program works as intended.[11] Marketing Demo 20–2 highlights Northern Telecom's strategy to build long-term

---

MARKETING DEMO 20-2
Northern Telecom Develops Its Foreign Markets

T elecommunications is expected to explode with the breakdown of national barriers after 1992, and Northern Telecom Ltd. is intent on making the digital revolution a reality in a region primed for new innovation. Using a strategic mix of direct sales and licensee and distribution agreements, Northern has become the No. 1 supplier of digital PBXs, the top seller of data packet switching, and a supplier of digital multiplex system (DMS) central office switches to public telephone utilities.

Currently, though, less than 10 percent of Northern's global business is derived from Europe, so the company believes room for expansion is huge. Large parts of Europe's telecommunications systems are still analog (as opposed to digital) and in need of extensive modernization. With telecommunications at the forefront in the EC development of a single market and governments relaxing their monopoly on communications networks, opportunities for Northern are pronounced.

Northern is well positioned to take advantage of the new climate. The company has been marketing in Europe for almost two decades; its first PBX and telephone set manufacturing plant opened in Galway, Ireland, in 1973. Subsequent PBX facilities have been built in France, and Bell-Northern Research Ltd. laboratories have been set up in the United Kingdom. Today, Northern's European arm regards itself as a local firm, while its EC manufacturing plants eliminate local content problems.

As the US market matures, it is only natural that Northern must look to Europe as a new market for its wares. Northern wants to hit $1 billion in annual revenues in Europe in the mid-90s, a major rise from an estimated $300 million in sales for 1989. This will be an important revenue boost if Northern is going to fulfill its stated objective of being the leading telecommunications supplier in the world by the end of the 1990s.

To date, Northern has focused its European sales activities on the United Kingdom, France, and Germany (with some activity in Turkey), while working with third parties to break into other markets—as when Northern's licensee Austria Telecom supplied DMS technology to Hungary. "It is too early to say whether we can make other successful forays in Eastern Europe," says Hogan. "Yet, the market now looks hopeful whereas before it was nonexistent."

Yet, winning market share will not be an easy task. The war for business is being waged with giants such as Siemens AG, Alcatel NV, LM Ericsson, NEC Corp., and AT&T Co., and only time will tell where Northern will end up in the pecking order. In such an environment, Northern is hoping to leverage off its global expertise in digital PBXs and central switching and win market share by supplying state-of-the-art telecommunications equipment.

Source: David Lake, "The New Europe," *Canadian Business,* March 1990, pp. 49–54.

---

relationships in Europe through the use of direct sales and licensee and distribution agreements.

COMPANIES PLAN AND IMPLEMENT MARKETING PROGRAMS

Several plans make a program

Most companies implement more than one marketing plan at the same time. A *marketing program* blends all a firm's marketing plans into one big plan.

When the various plans in the company's program are different, managers may be less concerned with how well the plans fit together—except as they compete for the firm's usually limited financial resources.

When the plans are more similar, however, the same sales force may be expected to carry out several plans. Or the firm's advertising department may develop the publicity and advertising for several plans. In these cases, product

AIG, an international financial services firm, relies on local managers who understand their own markets to develop marketing plans that meet the needs of local clients.

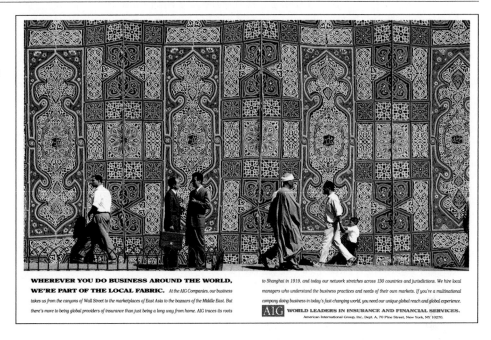

WHEREVER YOU DO BUSINESS AROUND THE WORLD, WE'RE PART OF THE LOCAL FABRIC. *At the AIG Companies, our business takes us from the canyons of Wall Street to the marketplaces of East Asia to the bazaars of the Middle East. But there's more to being global providers of insurance than just being a long way from home. AIG traces its roots to Shanghai in 1919, and today our network stretches across 130 countries and jurisdictions. We hire local managers who understand the business practices and needs of their own markets. If you're a multinational company doing business in today's fast-changing world, you need our unique global reach and global experience.*

AIG **WORLD LEADERS IN INSURANCE AND FINANCIAL SERVICES.** American International Group, Inc. Dept. A, 70 Pine Street, New York, NY 10270.

managers try to get enough of the common resources—say, salespeople's time—for their own plans.

Since a company's resources are usually limited, the marketing manager must make hard choices. You can't launch plans to pursue every promising opportunity. Instead, limited resources force you to choose among alternative plans—while you develop the program.

Outlines can make planning easier

Forms such as the one in Exhibit 20–9 improve the planning process and help communicate its results to others—including top management, who must review the plans. This form spells out everything that should be covered in a marketing plan.

Find the best program by trial and error

How do you find the best program? There is no one best way to compare various plans. Firms have to rely on management judgment and the evaluation tools discussed in Chapter 4. Some calculations are helpful, too. If a five-year planning horizon seems realistic for the firm's markets, managers can compare expected profits over the five-year period for each plan.

Assuming the company has a profit-oriented objective, managers can evaluate the more profitable plans first—in terms of both potential profit and resources required. They also need to evaluate a plan's impact on the entire program. One profitable-looking alternative might be a poor first choice if it eats up all the company's resources—and sidetracks several plans that together would be more profitable and spread the risks.

Some juggling among the various plans—comparing profitability versus resources needed and available—moves the company toward the most profitable program. A computer program can help if managers have to evaluate a large number of alternatives.[12]

Exhibit 20–9   Marketing Plan Format

Executive Summary
Situation Analysis (Where Are We Now?)
  External
    Environment (political, regulatory, economic, social, technical, and other relevant areas)
    Consumers and markets
    Employees
    Suppliers and distributors
    Competition
  Internal
    Objectives
    Strengths and weaknesses
  Problems and opportunities
    Momentum forecast
    Gap identification
Marketing Program Goals (Where Do We Want to Go?)
Marketing Strategies (How Are We Going to Get There?)
  Positioning
    Target segments
    Competitive stance
    Usage incentive
  Marketing mix
    Product
    Price
    Distribution
    Marketing communication: Advertising, personal selling, promotion, etc.
  Contingency strategies
Marketing Budget (How much do we need and where should we allocate it?)
  Resources (money, people, time)
  Amount and allocation
Marketing Action Plan (What do we need to do?)
  Detailed breakdown of activities required
  Responsibility by name
  Activity schedule in milestone format
  Tangible and intangible results expected from each activity
Monitoring System (Are we performing?)

Source: Charles B. Weinberg and Gordon H. G. McDougall, *Canadian Marketing: Cases and Exercises* (McGraw-Hill Ryerson Ltd., 1988), p. 364.

ALLOCATING BUDGETS FOR A MARKETING PROGRAM

Once a company sets its overall marketing program and long-term plans, it has to work out its shorter-term plans. Typically, companies use annual budgets both to plan what they're going to do and to control various functions. Each department may be allowed to spend its budgeted amount, perhaps monthly. As long as departments stay within their budgets, they're allowed considerable (or complete) freedom.

Budgeting for marketing—50 percent, 30 percent, or 10 percent is better than nothing

The most common method of budgeting for marketing expenditures is to compute a percentage of sales—either past or future. The virtue of this method is its simplicity. A similar percentage can be used automatically each year, eliminating the need to keep evaluating the kind and amount of marketing effort needed and its probable cost. It allows executives who aren't too tuned into the marketing concept to write off a certain percentage or number of dollars while

Inexpensive computer programs for personal computers make it easier for marketing managers to plan and implement marketing programs.

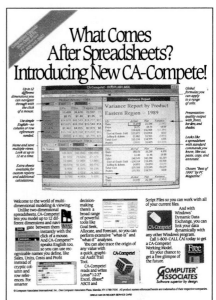

controlling the total amount spent. When a company's top managers have this attitude, they often get what they deserve—something less than the best results.

Find the task, budget for it

Mechanically budgeting a certain percentage of past or forecast sales leads to expanding marketing expenditures when business is good and cutting back when business is poor. It may be desirable to increase marketing expenditures when business is good. But when business is poor, the most sensible approach may be to be *more*, not less, aggressive!

Other methods of budgeting for marketing expenditures are:

1. Match expenditures with competitors.
2. Set the budget as a certain number of cents or dollars per sales unit (by case, by thousand, or by ton) using the past year or estimated year ahead as a base.
3. Set aside all uncommitted revenue—perhaps including budgeted profits. Companies willing to sacrifice some or all their current profits for future sales may use this approach—that is, they *invest* in marketing.
4. Base the budget on the job to be done—perhaps the number of new customers desired or the number required to reach some sales objective. This is called the **task method**—basing the budget on the job to be done.

Task method can lead to budgeting without agony

In the light of our continuing discussion about planning marketing strategies to reach objectives, the most sensible approach to budgeting marketing (and other functional) expenditures is the task method.

The amount budgeted using the task method can be stated as a percentage of sales. But calculating the right amount is much more involved than picking up a past percentage. It requires careful review of the firm's strategic (and marketing) plans and the specific tasks to be accomplished this year as part of each of these

MARKETING DEMO 20–3   Task Method Budgeting in a Recession

D uring slow times, companies spend their money cautiously, and many managers report a significant decrease in their marketing efforts as a result. The question to ask is, "Is this the correct response?" If the answer is no, managers must stop looking at how much money is spent on marketing and start looking at how that money is spent, and this often requires a change in budgeting methods.

Conditions change over time, and if you really believe in strategy, then you should have some customer- or competitive-based behavior underlying your spending decisions. Marketing in hard times means paying attention to both the quality and quantity of marketing efforts. The marketing plan must be designed to:

- Generate an awareness of what the company has to sell.
- Make the right kinds of "promises" to provide incentives for customer trial.
- Deliver on those promises (via product design, quality, and service) in a way that satisfies the customer so much better than competitors that customers adopt ours as their "normal" brand.

When the marketing plan is viewed in this manner, the decision on "how much marketing" is really a derivative of how much opportunity there is to expand awareness. The common methods of budget setting, percent of sales and "as much as you can afford," are processes used when the manager doesn't have the knowledge or time to really think about these issues. When the manager does have the time and knowledge, the most effective method of budget setting is the task method. The manager determines how much money is needed to get the job done. In order for a manager to effectively do this, he or she must understand the customer behaviors that underlie awareness levels and assess the firm's ability to convert that awareness into adoption.

Many managers do not use the task method of budgeting because they think of a marketing plan as little more than "filling in the blanks" on whatever marketing planning form was used by their predecessor or they argue that the type of information needed for detailed, task-based spending allocation isn't available.

Managers that attempt a task-based method of budget setting found that hard times actually improved the quality of marketing in their firm. Sometimes, more money was spent, sometimes less, and sometimes the same amount. What was different was that every expenditure had a purpose. Each expenditure was directed against a specific class of customer and competitive challenge, and the customer behaviors they intended to effect were top-of-mind for everyone involved.

Firms that follow a task-based budgeting process found that it required hard-nosed analysis and thinking about why they do what they do. The issue became how to spend, not how much to spend— quality of effort versus quantity. Task-based budgeting is a more difficult budgeting method but a method that can generate an effective allocation system for a company's marketing plans.

Source: Ken Wong, "Fundamentals Are Key in Any Economy," *Marketing*, February 3, 1992, p. 27.

plans. The costs of these tasks are then added up to determine how much should be budgeted for marketing and the other business functions provided for in the plans. In other words, the firm can assemble its budgets directly from detailed strategic plans—rather than from historical patterns or ratios. Marketing Demo 20–3 discusses the task method of budgeting in more detail.

After the marketing department receives its budget for the coming year, it can, presumably, spend its money any way it sees fit. But if the firm follows the previous planning-budgeting procedure, it makes sense to continue allocating expenditures within the marketing function according to the plans in the program. Again, everyone in the marketing department—and in the business—

should view the company as a total system and plan accordingly. This eliminates some of the traditional planning-budgeting fights—which are often so agonizing because managers and departments are pitted against each other.[13]

PROGRAM IMPLEMENTATION MUST BE PLANNED

Up to now, we've mainly been concerned with planning strategies—that is, the big picture. Plans and a program bring this down to earth by adding the time-related details. Now we want to go a step further—illustrating graphic techniques that help marketing managers carry out their plans and programs. First, we'll discuss techniques that are helpful for introducing new products or controlling special projects. Then we'll consider an approach for ongoing improvements in the implementation effort.

New products or projects can use PERT flowcharts

Some marketing managers draw flowcharts or diagrams of all the tasks that must be accomplished on schedule. In recent years, many firms have successfully applied such flowcharting techniques as CPM (critical path method) or PERT (program evaluation and review technique). These methods were originally developed as part of the US space program (NASA) to ensure that the various contractors and subcontractors stayed on schedule—and reached their goals as planned. PERT and CPM are even more popular now since inexpensive programs for personal computers make them easier and faster to use. Updating is easier, too.

The computer programs develop detailed flowcharts to show which marketing activities must be done in sequence and which can be done concurrently. These charts also show the time needed for various activities. Totaling the time allotments along the various chart paths shows the most critical (the longest) path—as well as the best starting and ending dates for the various activities.

Flowcharting is not really complicated. Basically, it requires that all the activities—which have to be performed anyway—be identified ahead of time and their probable duration and sequence shown on one diagram. (It uses nothing more than addition and subtraction.) Working with such information should already be part of the planning function. Then the chart can be used to guide implementation and control.

Regular plans call for monthly charts

Some marketing managers find that flowcharts help them track all the tasks in their ongoing plans. Each week or month in an ongoing 12-month plan, for example, can be graphed horizontally. Then managers can see how long each activity should take—and when it should be started and completed. If it's impossible to accomplish some of the jobs in the time allotted, the flowcharting process will make this clear—and managers will be able to make adjustments. Adjustments might be necessary, for example, when several product managers plan more work than the salespeople can do during one month.

Planning ahead, including careful scheduling, makes it easier to avoid conflicts that can wreck implementation of the company's plans and program.[14]

BUILDING QUALITY INTO THE IMPLEMENTATION EFFORT

Marketing strategy should define the blend of marketing mix elements that will meet target customers' needs. Once that is done—and the plan puts the time-related details in place—implementing the strategy should be straightforward. The plan lays out what everyone is trying to accomplish in order to satisfy the customer and make a profit. And, in organizations that accept the marketing concept, everyone should work together to achieve these objectives. Unfortunately, that often doesn't happen.

There are many ways things can go wrong with the implementation effort. Even people with the best intentions sometimes lapse into a production orientation. When the pressure's on to get a job done, they forget about satisfying the customer—to say nothing about working together! When the product manager is screaming for a budget report, the accountant may view a customer's concerns about a billing error as something a salesperson can smooth over—alone.

Total quality management meets customer requirements

Even though the marketing concept is a philosophy that should guide the whole organization, most managers need to work at keeping implementation on target. There are many different ways to improve implementation in each of the four Ps decision areas, but here we will focus on total quality management, which you can use to improve *any* implementation effort. With **total quality management (TQM)**, everyone in the organization is concerned about quality, throughout all of the firm's activities, to better serve customer needs.

In Chapter 9, we explained that product quality means the ability of a product to satisfy a customer's needs or requirements. Now we'll expand that idea and think about the quality of the whole marketing mix and how it is implemented—to meet customer requirements.

Total quality management is not just for factories

Most of the early attention in quality management focused on reducing defects in goods produced in factories. Reliable goods are important, but there's usually a lot more to marketing implementation than that. Yet if we start by considering product defects, you'll see how the total quality management idea has evolved and how it applies to implementing a marketing program. At one time, most firms assumed defects were an inevitable part of mass production. They assumed the cost of replacing defective parts or goods was just a cost of doing business—an insignificant one compared to the advantages of mass production. However, many firms were forced to rethink this assumption when Japanese producers of cars, electronics, and cameras showed that defects weren't inevitable. And their success in taking customers away from established competitors made it clear that the cost of defects wasn't just the cost of replacement!

Having dissatisfied customers is costly

From the customer's point of view, getting a defective product and having to complain about it is a big headache. The customer can't use the defective product and suffers the inconvenience of waiting for someone to fix the problem—if *someone* gets around to it. That erodes goodwill and leaves customers dissatisfied. The big cost of poor quality is the cost of lost customers.

Much to the surprise of some production-oriented managers, the Japanese experience showed that it is less expensive to do something right the first time rather than pay to do it poorly and *then* pay again to fix problems. And quality wasn't just a matter of adding more assembly-line inspections. Products had to be designed to meet customer needs from the start. One defective part in 10,000 may not seem like much, but if that part keeps a completed car from starting at the end of the automaker's production line, finding the problem is a costly nightmare.

Firms that adopted TQM methods to reduce manufacturing defects soon used the same approaches to overcome many other implementation problems. Their

Quality is becoming an important marketing tool.

success brought attention to what is possible with TQM—whether the implementation problem concerns unreliable delivery schedules, poor customer service, advertising that appears on the wrong TV show, or salespeople who can't answer customers' questions.

Getting a handle on doing things right— the first time

The idea of doing things right the first time seems obvious, but it's easier said than done. Problems always come up, and it's not always clear what isn't being done as well as it could be. Most people tend to ignore problems that don't pose an immediate crisis. But firms that adopt TQM always look for ways to improve implementation with **continuous improvement**—a commitment to constantly make things better one step at a time. Once you accept the idea that there *may* be a better way to do something and you look for it, you may just find it! The place to start is to clearly define "defects" in the implementation process—from the customers' point of view.

Things gone right and things gone wrong

Managers who use the TQM approach think of quality improvement as a sorting process—a sorting out of things gone right and things gone wrong. The sorting process calls for detailed measurements related to a problem. Then managers use a set of statistical tools to analyze the measurements and identify the problem areas that are the best candidates for fixing. The statistical details are beyond our focus here, but it's useful to get a feel for how managers use the tools.

Starting with customer needs

Let's consider the case of a restaurant that does well during the evening hours but wants to improve its lunch business. The restaurant develops a strategy that targets local businesspeople with an attractive luncheon buffet. The restaurant decides on a buffet because research shows that target customers want a choice of good healthy food and are willing to pay reasonable prices for it—as long as they can eat quickly and get back to work on time.

As the restaurant implements its new strategy, the manager wants a measure of how things are going. So she encourages customers to fill out comment cards that ask, "How did we do today?" After several months of operation, things seem to be going reasonably well—although business is not as brisk as it was at first. The manager reads the comment cards and divides the ones with complaints into categories—to count up different reasons why customers weren't satisfied.

Slay the dragons first

Then the manager creates a graph showing a frequency distribution for the different types of complaints. Quality people call this a **Pareto chart**—a graph that shows the number of times a problem cause occurs, with problem causes ordered from most frequent to least frequent. The manager's Pareto chart, shown in Exhibit 20–10, reveals that customers complain most frequently that they have to wait for a seat. There were other common complaints—the buffet was not well organized, the table was not clean, and so on. However, the first complaint is much more common than the next most frequent.

This type of pattern is typical. The worst problems often occur over and over again. This focuses the manager's attention on which implementation problem to fix first. A rule of quality management is to slay the dragons first—which simply means start with the biggest problem. After removing that problem, the battle moves on to the next most frequent problem. If you do this *continuously,* you solve a lot of problems—and you don't just satisfy customers, you delight them.

Figure out why things go wrong

So far, our manager has only identified the problem. To solve it, she creates a **fishbone diagram**—a visual aid that helps organize cause-and-effect relationships for "things gone wrong."

Our restaurant manager, for example, discovers that customers wait to be seated because tables aren't cleared soon enough. In fact, the Pareto chart (Exhibit 20–10) shows that customers also complain frequently about tables not being clean. So the two implementation problems may be related.

Exhibit 20–10   Pareto Chart Showing Frequency of Different Complaints

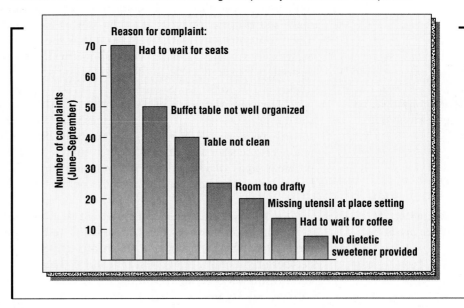

The manager's fishbone diagram (Exhibit 20–11) summarizes the various causes for tables not being cleaned quickly. There are different basic categories of causes—restaurant policy, procedures, people problems, and the physical environment. With this overview of different ways the service operation is going wrong, the manager can decide what to fix. She establishes different formal measures. For example, she counts how frequently different causes delay customers from being seated. She finds that the cashier's faulty credit card machine holds up check processing. The fishbone diagram shows that restaurant policy is to clear the table after the entire party leaves. But customers have to wait at their tables while the staff deals with the jammed credit card machine, and cleaning is delayed. With the credit card machine replaced, the staff can clear the tables sooner—and because they're not so hurried, they do a better cleaning job. Two dragons are on the way to being slayed!

Our case shows that people in different areas of the restaurant affect customer satisfaction. The waitperson couldn't do what was needed to satisfy customers because the cashier had trouble with the credit card machine. The TQM approach helps everyone see—and understand—how each job affects what others do—and the customer's satisfaction.[15]

Building quality into services

The restaurant case illustrates how a firm can improve implementation with TQM approaches. We used a service example because providing customer service is often a difficult area of implementation. Recently, marketers in service businesses have been paying a lot of attention to improving service quality.

Exhibit 20–11   Fishbone Diagram Showing Cause and Effect for "Why Tables Are Not Cleared Quickly"

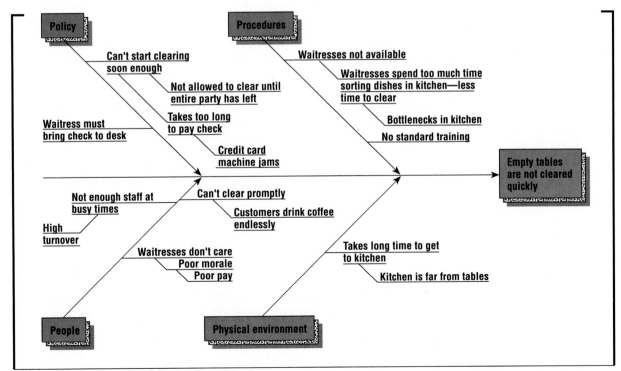

But some people seem to forget that almost every firm must implement service quality as part of its plan—whether its product is primarily a service, primarily a physical good, or a blend of both. For example, a manufacturer of ball bearings isn't just providing wholesalers or producers with round pieces of steel. Customers need information about deliveries, they need orders filled properly, and they may have questions to ask the firm's accountant, receptionist, or engineers. Because almost every firm must manage the service it provides customers, let's focus on some of the special concerns of implementing quality service.

Train people and empower them to serve

Quality gurus like to say that the firm has only one job: to give customers exactly what they want, when they want it, and where they want it. Marketing managers have been saying that for some time, too. But customer service is hard to implement because the server is inseparable from the service. A person doing a specific service job may perform one specific task correctly but still annoy the customer in a host of other ways. Customers will not be satisfied if employees are rude or inattentive—even if they "solve the customer's problem." There are two keys to improving how people implement quality service: (1) training and (2) empowerment.

Firms that commit to customer satisfaction realize that all employees who have any contact with customers need training—many firms see 40 hours a year of training as a minimum. Simply showing customer-contact employees around the rest of the business—so that they learn how their contribution fits in the total effort—can be very effective. Good training usually includes role-playing on handling different types of customer requests and problems. This is not just sales training! A rental car attendant who is rude when a customer is trying to turn in a car may leave the customer dissatisfied—even if the rental car was perfect. How employees treat a customer is as important as whether they perform the task correctly.

Companies can't afford an army of managers to inspect how each employee implements a strategy—and such a system usually doesn't work, anyway. Quality cannot be "inspected in." It must come from the people who do the service jobs. So firms that commit to service quality empower employees to satisfy customers' needs. **Empowerment** means giving employees the authority to correct a problem without first checking with management. At a Guest Quarters hotel, an empowered room-service employee knows it's OK to run across the street to buy the specific mineral water a guest requests. In the new Saturn car manufacturing plant, employees can stop the assembly line to correct a problem rather than passing it down the line. At Upton's clothing stores, a salesclerk can make an immediate price adjustment if there's a flaw in an item the customer wants.

Manage expectations—with good communication

The implementation effort sometimes leaves customers dissatisfied because they expect much more than it is possible for the firm to deliver. Some firms react to this by shrugging their shoulders and faulting customers for being unreasonable. Research in the service quality area, however, suggests that the problems often go away if marketers clearly communicate what they are offering. Customers are satisfied when the service matches their expectations, and careful communication leads to reasonable expectations.

Customers often tolerate a delay and remain satisfied with the service when they are given a full explanation. Most airline passengers seethe at the announcement of a takeoff delay but are much more willing to wait if they know the delay is caused by a thunderstorm high over the airport.

Separate the routine and plan for the special

Implementation usually involves some routine services and some that require special attention. Customer satisfaction increases when the two types of service encounters are separated. For example, banks set up special windows for commercial deposits and supermarkets have cash-only lines. In developing the marketing plan, it's important to analyze the types of service customers will need and plan for both types of situations. In some cases, completely different strategies may be required.

Increasingly, firms try to use computers and other equipment to handle routine services. ATMs are quick and convenient for dispensing cash. American Airlines' Dial a Flight system allows customers to use a touch tone phone to check fares, schedules, and arrival times—without the need for an operator.

Firms that study special service requests can use training so that even unusual customer requests become routine to the staff. Every day, hotel guests lose their keys, bank customers run out of checks, and supermarket shoppers leave their wallets at home. A well-run service operation anticipates these special events so service providers can respond in a way that satisfies customers' needs.

Managers lead the quality effort

Quality implementation, whether in a service activity or in another activity, doesn't just happen by itself. Managers must show that they are committed to doing things right to satisfy customers—and that quality is everyone's job. Without top-level support, some people won't get beyond their business-as-usual attitude—and TQM won't work. The top executive at American Express had his board of directors give him the title Chief Quality Officer so that everyone in the company would know he was personally involved in the TQM effort.

TQM is not the only method for improving marketing implementation, but it is an important approach. Some firms don't yet use TQM; they may be missing an opportunity. Other firms apply some quality methods—but act like they are the private property of a handful of "quality specialists" who want to control things. That's not good either. Everyone must own a TQM effort. As more marketing managers see the benefits of TQM, it will become a more important part of marketing thinking, especially marketing implementation. And when managers really understand implementation, they can do a better job developing strategies and plans in the first place.[16]

CONCLUSION

In this chapter, we stressed the importance of developing whole marketing mixes—not just developing policies for the individual four Ps and hoping they will fit together into some logical whole. The marketing manager is responsible for developing a workable blend—integrating all of a firm's efforts into a coordinated whole that makes effective use of the firm's resources and guides it toward its objectives.

This usually requires that the manager use some approach to forecasting. We talked about two basic

approaches to forecasting market potential and sales: (1) extending past behavior and (2) predicting future behavior. The most common approach is to extend past behavior into the future. This gives reasonably good results if market conditions are fairly stable. Methods here include extension of past sales data and the factor method. We saw that projecting the past into the future is risky when big market changes are likely. To make up for this possible weakness, marketers predict future behavior using their own experience and judgment. They also bring in the judgment of others—using the jury of executive opinion method and salespeople's estimates. And they may use surveys, panels, and market tests.

Of course, any sales forecast depends on the marketing mix the firm actually selects. As a starting place for developing new marketing mixes, a marketing manager can use the product classes that have served as a thread throughout this text. Even if the manager can't fully describe the needs and attitudes of target markets, it is usually possible to select the appropriate product class for a particular product. This, in turn, will help set Place and Promotion policies. Similarly, seeing where a firm's offering fits in the product life cycle helps to clarify how current marketing mixes are likely to change in the future.

Throughout the text, we've emphasized the importance of marketing strategy planning. In this chapter, we went on to show that the marketing manager must develop a marketing plan for carrying out each strategy and then merge a set of plans into a marketing program. If this planning is effective, then budgeting should be relatively simple.

Finally, it's the marketing manager's job to coordinate implementation of the whole marketing program. We discussed two helpful scheduling techniques. Then we went on to show how total quality management can help the firm get the type of implementation it needs—implementation that continuously improves and does a better job of meeting customers' needs.

QUESTIONS AND PROBLEMS

1. Explain the difference between a forecast of market potential and a sales forecast.

2. Suggest a plausible explanation for sales fluctuations for (a) bicycles, (b) ice cream, (c) lawn mowers, (d) tennis rackets, (e) oats, (f) disposable diapers, and (g) latex for rubber-based paint.

3. Explain the factor method of forecasting. Illustrate your answer.

4. Based on data in Exhibit 20–3, discuss the relative market potential of Oshawa and Sudbury, Ontario, for (a) prepared cereals, (b) automobiles, and (c) furniture.

5. Distinguish between competitive marketing mixes and superior mixes that lead to breakthrough opportunities.

6. Why is spreadsheet analysis a popular tool for marketing strategy planning?

7. Distinguish clearly between marketing plans and marketing programs.

8. Consider how the marketing manager's job becomes more complex when it's necessary to develop and plan several strategies as part of a marketing program. Be sure to discuss how the manager might have to handle different strategies at different stages in the product life cycle. To make your discussion more concrete, consider the job of a marketing manager for a sporting product manufacturer.

9. Briefly explain the task method of budgeting.

10. Discuss how a marketing manager could go about choosing among several possible marketing plans, given that choices must be made because of limited resources. Would the job be easier in the consumer product or in the business product area? Why?

11. Explain why the budgeting procedure is typically so agonizing, usually consisting of extending past budgets, perhaps with small modifications from current plans. How would the budgeting procedure be changed if the marketing program planning procedure discussed in the chapter were implemented?

12. How would marketing planning be different for a firm that has entered foreign marketing with a joint venture and a firm that has set up a wholly owned subsidiary?

13. How can a firm set the details of its marketing plan when it has little information about a foreign market it wants to enter?

14. What are the major advantages of total quality management as an approach for improving implementation of marketing plans? What limitations can you think of?

SUGGESTED CASES

34. E. D. Smith & Sons Limited

36. Laskers Foods Limited

Social Marketing*

Appendix **D**

---

*This appendix was written by Brahm Canzer, who at the time of its preparation was associated with John Abbot College and Concordia University. © Copyright 1993.

INTRODUCTION

Social marketing, the idea of using strategic business thinking and techniques to promote positive social behaviour such as non-smoking, non-drug abuse, safe driving, and so forth fully emerged as a specialized area of marketing in the early 1970s.

Social marketing most often concerns the "selling of an idea" rather than a tangible product. Similar in nature to service marketing, social marketing focuses on communication and persuasion. The target audience is moved from one way of thinking about the service or idea to another where the action of adopting the desired behaviour is achieved.

As such, social marketing is about understanding the behaviour of the target audience and finding ways to redirect that behaviour. This simple objective is often more difficult to achieve than in conventional consumer marketing because social marketers are dealing with changing an existing attitude which may have been comfortably established in the target's mind for some time.

In contrast, asking a consumer to try a new candy bar or soft drink involves little behavioural change or perceived risk to the consumer. Small movements are easier to achieve than great ones. Generally however, the social marketing focus requires drastic change in behaviour or complex problem-solving involving personal, social, and cultural issues.

ORGANIZATION MISSION STATEMENT AND GOALS

Planning begins with the establishment of the organization's mission statement. The mission statement may be established by government charter or the board of directors. For example, the mission statement of the Health Promotion Directorate of Health and Welfare Canada includes the goals "to change the perceptions, attitudes and opinions that underlie an individual's health or lifestyle habits . . . to change social attitudes towards activities that are harmful to health."

CREATING THE SOCIAL MARKETING PLAN

As with traditional marketing, the social marketing plan would involve selecting appropriate decisions about the social product design, the distribution of the product, the price to the consumer, and the promotional campaign.

The development of a specific social marketing plan, its implementation, direction, and control originate and are guided by research. For example, a survey of college students may uncover a potential alcohol abuse problem. All of the relevant influences on the target audience would be studied to the degree deemed appropriate and a plan of strategies would be developed to change the behaviour of the students. After implementation of the plan, the impact of the marketing effort would be examined in order to assess the effectiveness of the current strategy and the need for modifications.

SOCIAL PRODUCT DESIGN

In some cases, as with service marketing, the task at hand involves a combination of behavioural change and tangible product purchasing. Such is the case with promoting bicycle helmet use. First the idea of wearing a helmet has to be "sold" and then the actual behavioural change of buying and wearing them must be achieved. In other situations, there is no tangible product purchase linked to the campaign such as encouraging safe driving habits.

DISTRIBUTION

Consideration for distribution of the product or service must be decided. For example, the distribution or availability of condoms on campus or of information booklets about sexually transmitted diseases in the library or health centre may be decided or rejected in favour of other dissemination strategies.

PRICE

The price or cost to the target audience may involve no monetary charge but still an emotional or psychological cost. For example, persuading a smoker to quit will in fact save him money but at the same time may cause great stress and physical or social discomfort. Transferring these pricing concepts to the social marketing environment requires a different perspective and broader definition in the term. The designated driver who will not drink on a night out with his friends is in fact paying a price of "lost fun and enjoyment" as seen from his eyes. The social marketer should address these costs as quite real and significant to the target audience. Substitution for other benefits and enjoyment such as low alcohol beer or knowledge that the individual is doing the right thing which is appreciated by his friends and society as a whole may form the focus of persuasion to adopt this behaviour.

PROMOTION

Promotional or communication strategies may include direct personal counselling, mass communication, publicity, and special promotions.

Direct personal counselling or persuasion is commonly experienced when the target audience receives information, instruction, and advice from a professional trained in the field. Doctors tell patients at risk of heart disease to stop smoking, lose weight, and exercise. The health care professional may put the patient on a program of care or refer the patient to another health professional such as a nutritionist.

In this type of situation where communication is direct, personalized, regimented, monitored, and readily modified to suit the unique requirements of the individual, motivation to change may be quite strong. The strength of the message is also enhanced by the social image of the health professional and the fact that, often, a monetary cost is charged for services.

Mass communication in the form of advertisements in magazines, television, radio, posters, billboards, and so on serve primarily to inform and remind the consumer. Highway signs indicating the location of a fatal accident several years earlier may have dramatic immediate impact on drivers who are speeding by.

Attribution theory suggests most drivers will accept that the cause of the fatal accident can be attributed to speeding and will respond immediately by slowing down. Perhaps more importantly is the psychological reaction of the driver passing by the location where death occurred. The eerie sense of temporal association and connection with the past can have a dramatic impact on present behaviour. Whether longer-term behaviour is changed is debatable, but observation of drivers who slow down in the dangerous road area ahead can be experimentally proven. This is similar to the use of signs that warn of radar police patrol or the parking of a police car at the side of the highway. The reaction is immediate and serves as a reminder for the longer term.

Public service announcements (PSA) for or against some social behaviour must be carefully designed for the intended target audience. A successful message for safe driving targeted to middle aged, married men may be ridiculed and rejected by teenaged drivers. Madonna may be seen as a great spokeswoman for encouraging safe sexual practice among young adults that accept her lifestyle but be rejected by more conservative audiences of older people.

In fact, an opposite effect may be triggered inadvertantly. As commercial marketers have discovered, each target market is different in its perception of the intended message. The social marketer must therefore design and test the effectiveness of message design for each public service announcement. Furthermore, placing the PSA in appropriate media and specific programs attended by the target audience is critical to efficient use of budgetary funds. For example, a message from Madonna to teenagers and young adults designed to take advantage of her familiarity as a music video performer can be best achieved by designing a PSA as a music video and playing it on the music video cable channel. In this way, the target audience gets the best persuasive PSA design without alienating other target groups who might get confused or offended by the Madonna endorsement.

There is general acceptance among social marketers that PSAs are successful at the task of informing the targeted audience. However, the extent to which they are successful at changing behaviour is not so certain. For example, PSAs concerning cigarette smoking use may inform young adults about the health risks and associated diseases but they have not been overwhelmingly successful in triggering a change in actual behaviour.

Publicity is any unpaid communication about the social issue and is perhaps the strongest marketing tool available. The reason for this lies in the perceived credibility and motivation of the message sender. The positive publicity generated by Magic Johnson and the late Arthur Ashe about AIDS transmission, risk, and more importantly the human side of the issue was strongly advanced by their public interviews and news conferences. The audience perception of these men, these heros of our culture, sharing their views and suggesting a change in social behaviour to an audience seeing no attributable personal financial gain by their action can have significantly greater impact than any public service announcement.

Furthermore, peers telling others in their social circle to change will have greater impact than those outside the social environment of the target audience. Therefore, group discussion, radio talk shows, and television forums may act to motivate audiences far more effectively than PSAs or paid endorsements.

Special promotions can be thought of as any special activity promoting the social marketing issue. For example, passing out bookmarks with message reminders to take care of public property, calendars with information on healthy lifestyle facts, and special events like Earth Day can act to increase awareness, inform, remind, and motivate behavioural change.

MOTIVATION THEORY, ATTITUDE FORMATION, AND CHANGE

Social behaviour is generally thought to be motivated. That is to say, a person will behave in a particular manner in order to achieve some goal or satisfy a need. That goal might be pleasure, social approval of their peers, or whatever. To motivate someone, the individual must be convinced of the causal relationship between their behaviour and the outcome. The commercial marketing world has successfully worked this theory by convincing consumers that whiter teeth will increase sexual attraction, that an American Express card holder is socially higher up than a bank card user, that a sports car can help recapture lost youth, and so on.

Experience and socially reinforced behaviour are pivotal in forming beliefs or cognitive models about the object or the behaviour related to the object. If an individual is told in a PSA that drinking low alcohol beer can be as socially acceptable as regular beer but the experience of the consumer does not reinforce this suggestion, then the belief will be discarded.

In concert with the cognitive component is the affective or emotional dimension to the object or the behaviour. How the consumer feels about smoking or people who smoke weighs heavily in forming his attitude. This recognition of the cognitive and affective components constitute the core of Martin Fishbein's model of an individual's attitude. To change an attitude, the social marketer must attempt to change beliefs and/or feelings about the object or the behaviour related to the object.

It is here that PSAs can have their greatest potential impact on attitude and hence motivating behaviour. By attempting to change the consumer's existing beliefs and feelings about smoking by showing smokers in a negative way and providing truthful messages about the dangers of the behaviour, the social marketer may be able to "re-position" the orientation of the target consumer.

POSITIONING AND REPOSITIONING

Positioning refers to the internal mental image or schema a consumer has of the product, competing products, and the behaviour of using these products. For example, the perceived status value of using an American Express card is greater than using MasterCard or Visa, which are higher than using store charge cards such as Eaton's. In this case the criterion is the status value of possessing and using various credit cards. However, other criteria can also be of value in assessing the relative positioning of competing cards—for instance, perceived cost to the user, number of retailers accepting the card, and, perhaps, degree of international recognition of the card.

Multi-dimensional perceptual maps help show areas of congestions where too many cards may be vying for the same perceptual space and areas open to unique positioning with little or no competition.

A common strategy for commercial marketers is to re-position the image of the product or brand in the target market's mind to a more favorable place. Black Label beer was re-positioned several years ago as a swinging singles beer by use of sexually suggestive advertising and exciting lifestyle imagery.

Similarly, fruit juice companies such as EverFresh have re-positioned the image of fruit juice to the younger consumer who is now informed that fruit juices can be bought from vending machines, (positioned) like soft drinks, but are consistent with a healthier lifestyle. This message is reinforced by commercials on television which show attractive young people passing by the soft drink vending machine in favour of the fruit juice machine next to it. The young man, having bought a soft drink and hanging around trying to meet girls is passed repeatedly by attractive women in bathing suits heading for the EverFresh vendor.

The message is clear and successful in persuading the target market that they can in fact "do better" by substituting one behaviour for another. In this case where the behaviour patterns are remarkably similar, the task is easier to accomplish. The social marketer is not telling young people to stop drinking unhealthy soft drinks which cause cavities and are nutritionally worthless. Instead, they are being offered an alternative but similar product and behaviour pattern which is not all that different from what is already well entrenched in their minds. In fact, an improvement in social success, that is, meeting girls, is being associated along with the behavioural change to buying fruit juices.

SELF-IMAGE THEORY

Probably most important of all social psychology theories is self-image or self-concept, that is, how an individual perceives himself and how he thinks others see him. Commercial advertising has always made good use of this approach by presenting products and their usage as short routes to improved self-image. Cosmetics, cigarettes, and alcohol products have always promised improved social looks and feelings of improved stature to their markets. Children wanting to look more adult-like will smoke and drink alcohol in attempts to experiment and explore adult identities remote from their own world.

Social marketers can make use of self-image theory by tying into the existing positive social images now used by commercial marketers to sell their products. For example, the healthy and youthful image popularized in commercial advertising for selling soft drinks and beer can also be positioned with the more socially positive behaviour of drinking water, fruit juices, or milk. The camaraderie and male bonding used in beer commercials can also be used to position the idea of the designated non-drinking driver who cares so much for his friends that he's willing to pass up a night of fun for less fun but living friends who can appreciate this "sacrifice." The popular image of the hero and savior could be used to change existing perceptions of the friend that won't drink or is afraid to risk drinking and driving.

CONCLUSION

Social marketing includes a wide variety of inter-related theories and practices. In the final analysis, each case will demand a unique set of strategies which can change the target audience's attitude and subsequent social behaviour.

The best use of social marketing is in situations where the primary tasks are informing and disseminating information to target audiences which have yet to form strong attitudes towards the desired behaviour. This implies targets who are young and who are more "open" to suggestions to change their self-concept.

Audiences which have small distances to move in their perceptual spaces are more easily moved than those who are far away. For the latter, smaller steps may be the wise choice for campaign planners. For example, trying to get people who never exercise to take up a regimen which is too demanding will likely fail. Instead, starting off with a reasonable goal for their level such as a step exercise for one minute and then moving forward to the ultimate goal of regular exercise three or four times a week is more likely to succeed.

Controlling Marketing Plans and Programs

21

When You Finish This Chapter, You Should

1
Understand how sales analysis can aid marketing strategy planning.

2
Understand the differences in sales analysis, performance analysis, and performance analysis using performance indices.

3
Understand the difference between natural accounts and functional accounts—and their relevance for marketing cost analysis.

4
Know how to do a marketing cost analysis for customers or products.

5
Understand the difference between the full-cost approach and the contribution-margin approach.

6
Understand how planning and control can be combined to improve the marketing management process.

7
Understand what a marketing audit is—and when and where it should be used.

8
Understand the important new terms (shown in blue).

In 1990, the Eaton Centre Mall in Edmonton was in serious financial trouble. The city was overbuilt with shopping centres. Twelve malls totaling more than 400,000 square feet of retail space, Canada's highest per capita count, were battling to survive in a retail slump. Sandy McNair, vice president in charge of investments at Confed Realty Services, the owners of the mall, knew something had to be done. Many of the tenants wanted him to give them rent rebates on their leases but McNair felt that would only be a short-term solution. A longer view had to be taken.

The focus of McNair's new strategy was customer loyalty through the development of a mallwide frequent shopper card, similar to the airlines' frequent flier programs. Customers gain points for purchases that can be used towards various prizes, store owners gain customer loyalty, and McNair gains valuable information that can be used to track customers.

The campaign was launched in late October 1991 with a mailing to 240,000 households in Edmonton and northern Alberta. By June 1992, membership stood at 50,000 and was expected to triple by the end of the year. According to some recent figures, only 3.1 percent of members generated 25 percent of member sales, and 10.7 percent accounted for 50 percent, a textbook demonstration of the importance of customer loyalty. Surprisingly, the top 0.2 percent spent an average of $3,283 in six months, totaling 5 percent of member sales.

Knowing who the stores' best customers are and what they buy counts among the biggest bonuses. The mall's United Cigar Store manager was shocked to discover through purchase data that some customers returned 8 or 10 times a week and sometimes 2 or 3 times a day. UCS now plans to give these preferred customers the same discounts as mall employees.

McNair plans to build future promotions right into the card program. A top priority is to increase weekend traffic to buttress the mall's new status as a family shopping centre, not just a workweek stop-off point. To get families in the door, Confed is offering bonus points for Sunday purchases. In the fall, secretaries and students will get special stickers for their Eaton Centre Cards entitling them to extra purchase points. With the card, McNair can easily analyze how many customers pick up on a promotion and tailor future promotions according to this feedback.[1]

CONTROL PROVIDES FEEDBACK TO IMPROVE PLANS AND IMPLEMENTATION

Our primary emphasis so far has been on planning. Now we'll discuss **control**—the feedback process that helps the marketing manager learn (1) how ongoing plans are working and (2) how to plan for the future.

As the Eaton Centre example shows, marketing control is important. Not long ago, marketing managers planned their strategies and put them into action, but then it took a long time before they got feedback to know if the strategy was working. Sometimes the feedback took so long that there wasn't anything they could do about a problem except start over. That situation has now changed dramatically in many types of business. In Chapter 5, we discussed how firms use marketing information systems to track sales and cost details day by day and week by week. Throughout the book, we gave examples of how marketers get more information faster and use it quickly to improve a strategy or its implementation. Marketing managers who take this approach often develop a competitive advantage. They can spot potential problems early—and keep them from turning into big problems.

Keeping a firmer hand on the controls

A good manager wants to know which products' sales are highest and why, which products are profitable, what is selling where, and how much the marketing process is costing. Managers need to know what's happening—in detail—to improve the bottom line.

But traditional accounting reports are too general to be much help to the marketing manager. A company may be showing a profit, while 80 percent of its business comes from only 20 percent of its products—or customers. The other 80 percent may be unprofitable. But without special analyses, managers won't know it. This 80/20 relationship is fairly common—and it is often referred to as the *80/20 rule*.

It *is* possible for marketing managers to get detailed information about how marketing plans are working—but only if they ask for and help develop the necessary data. In this chapter, we'll discuss the kinds of information that can be available and how to use it. The techniques are not really complicated. They basically require only simple arithmetic and perhaps a computer, if a large volume of sorting, adding, and subtracting is required.[2]

SALES ANALYSIS SHOWS WHAT'S HAPPENING

Sales analysis—a detailed breakdown of a company's sales records—can be very informative, especially the first time it's done. Detailed data can keep marketing executives in touch with what's happening in the market. In addition, routine sales analyses prepared each week, month, or year may show trends—and allow managers to check their hypotheses and assumptions.[3]

Some managers resist sales analysis—or any analysis, for that matter—because they don't appreciate how valuable it can be. One top executive in a large firm made no attempt to analyze company sales—even by geographic area. When asked why, the executive replied: "Why should we? We're making money!"

But today's profit is no guarantee that you'll make money tomorrow. In fact, ignoring sales analysis can lead not only to poor sales forecasting but to poor decisions in general. One manufacturer did a great deal of national advertising on the assumption that the firm was selling all over the country. But a simple sales analysis showed that most present customers were located within a 250-mile radius of the factory! In other words, the firm didn't know who and where its customers were—and it wasted most of the money it spent on national advertising.

But a marketing manager must ask for it

Detailed sales analysis is only possible if a manager asks for the data. Valuable sales information is often buried—perhaps on sales invoices or in billing records on an accountant's computer.

Today, with computers and organized marketing information systems, effective sales analysis can be done easily and at relatively small cost—if marketing

Every customer at this Minit-Lube service centre becomes part of a computerized database, which allows the company to analyze the cost and revenue from different types of customers.

managers decide they want it done. In fact, the desired information can be obtained as a by-product of basic billing and accounts receivable procedures. The manager simply must make sure the company captures identifying information on important dimensions such as territory, sales reps, and so forth. Then, computers can easily run sales analyses and simple trend projections.

What to ask for varies

There is no one best way to analyze sales data. Several breakdowns may be useful—depending on the nature of the company and product and what dimensions are relevant. Typical breakdowns include:

1. Geographic region—province, city, sales rep's territory.
2. Product, package size, grade, or color.
3. Customer size.
4. Customer type or class of trade.
5. Price or discount class.
6. Method of sale—mail, telephone, or direct sales.
7. Financial arrangement—cash or charge.
8. Size of order.
9. Commission class.

Too much data can drown a manager

While some sales analysis is better than none—or better than getting data too late for action—sales breakdowns that are too detailed can drown a manager in reports. Computer printers can print over 1,500 lines per minute—faster than any manager can read. So wise managers only ask for breakdowns that will help them make decisions. Further, they use computer programs that draw graphs and figures to make it easy to see patterns that otherwise might be hidden in a 1-inch thick computer printout. But to avoid coping with mountains of data—much of which may be irrelevant—most managers move on to *performance analysis*.

PERFORMANCE ANALYSIS LOOKS FOR DIFFERENCES

Numbers are compared

Performance analysis looks for exceptions or variations from planned performance. In simple sales analysis, the figures are merely listed or graphed—they aren't compared against standards. In performance analysis, managers make comparisons. They might compare one territory against another, against the same territory's performance last year, or against expected performance.

The purpose of performance analysis is to improve operations. The salesperson, territory, or other factors showing poor performance can be identified—and singled out for detailed analysis and corrective action. Or outstanding performances can be analyzed to see if the successes can be explained and made the general rule.

Performance analysis doesn't have to be limited to sales. Other data can be analyzed, too. This data may include miles traveled, number of calls made, number of orders, or the cost of various tasks.

A performance analysis can be quite revealing, as shown in the following example.

Exhibit 21–1   Comparative Performance of Sales Reps

Sales Area	Total Calls	Total Orders	Order-Call Ratio	Sales by Sales Rep	Average Sales Rep Order	Total Customers
A	1,900	1,140	60.0%	$ 912,000	$800	195
B	1,500	1,000	66.7	720,000	720	160
C	1,400	700	50.0	560,000	800	140
D	1,030	279	27.1	132,000	478	60
E	820	165	20.1	62,000	374	50
Total	6,650	3,284	49.3%	$2,386,000	$634	605

Straight performance analysis—an illustration

A manufacturer of business products sells to wholesalers through five sales reps, each serving a separate territory. Total net sales for the year amount to $2,386,000. Sales force compensation and expenses come to $198,000, yielding a direct-selling expense ratio of 8.3 percent—that is, $198,000 ÷ $2,386,000 × 100.

This information, taken from a profit and loss statement, is interesting, but it doesn't explain what's happening from one territory to another. To get a clearer picture, the manager compares the sales results with other data *from each territory*. See Exhibits 21–1 and 21–2. Keep in mind that exhibits like these and others that follow in this chapter are now very easy to generate. Popular computer programs like Lotus 1-2-3 and dBASE IV make it easy to apply the ideas discussed here, even on inexpensive desktop computers. Marketing Demo 21–1 highlights how Harry Rosen, Inc., has used technology to analyze and improve its sales function.

The reps in sales areas D and E aren't doing well. Sales are low and marketing costs are high. Perhaps more aggressive sales reps could do a better job, but the number of customers suggests that sales potential might be low. Perhaps the whole plan needs revision.

The figures themselves, of course, don't provide the answers. But they do reveal the areas that need improvement. This is the main value of performance analysis. It's up to management to find the remedy—either by revising or changing the marketing plan.

Exhibit 21–2   Comparative Cost of Sales Reps

Sales Area	Annual Compensation	Expense Payments	Total Sales Rep Cost	Sales Produced	Cost-Sales Ratio
A	$ 22,800	$11,200	$ 34,000	$ 912,000	3.7%
B	21,600	14,400	36,000	720,000	5.0
C	20,400	11,600	32,000	560,000	5.7
D	19,200	24,800	44,000	132,000	33.3
E	20,000	32,000	52,000	62,000	83.8
Total	$104,000	$94,000	$198,000	$2,386,000	8.3%

MARKETING DEMO 21–1   Harry Rosen Improves Selling Process

At a time of no-growth sales, Dylex Limited's Harry Rosen, Inc., is investing in information technology to benefit the 600 sales associates in the 25-store chain.

"Ultimately a PC with its own database will be the device that we use to do the work that is being done on the mainframe now," reports Bob Humphrey, president of Harry Rosen. "Much more activity will take place at the store, including processing of the information that will then be sent down to the mainframe. Since each store will have its own database, all the information related to a client, for instance, will be processed on site, in that store. It will allow sales associates to have much more rapid access to client information."

Using technology to track client information is hardly an innovation, but it has traditionally been relevant only to a retailer's accounting department.

With the PC controlling the point-of-sale network, the physical plant of machines will also be reduced. Datapac, a Telecom Canada offering that allows constant and direct telephone line service between Toronto headquarters and stores on both coasts, has been a boon in monitoring daily sales revenues.

The technology being adopted at Harry Rosen offers plenty of practical benefits. For instance, if a sales associate is stuck with a large inventory of J. P. Tilford suits in size 42 and has a list of all the clients who bought this label in size 42 over the past nine months, that's pretty valuable information. "The most efficient use of dollars is to go back and talk to people who are happy with you already—rather than running an ad or trying to attract new clients," says Humphrey.

The use of networked PCs will also allow the company to monitor the success level of buying activity. A size profile of regular customers who shop at a particular store will be on file at each outlet. Buyers can refer to the breakdown to make sure they are beefing up their inventory appropriately. This same customer profile can be used as a test in a new location to interpret the difference in that site's demographics.

For Humphrey, who used to receive reams of paper a day, exception reporting represents one of the most useful applications of information technology. Using PROFS (short for IBM's Professional Office System), he can immediately have staff in locations outside Toronto take action on what he likes to call "sales anomalies." Says Humphrey: "I can sit down with a page of anomalies in front of me and address the problems right away."

Source: Stella Skerlec, "Harry Rosen Improves Selling Process," *Retail Directions*, January–February 1991, p. 22.

PERFORMANCE INDICES SIMPLIFY HUMAN ANALYSIS

Comparing against "what ought to have happened"

With a straight performance analysis, the marketing manager can evaluate the variations among sales reps to try to explain the "why." But this takes time. And poor performances are sometimes due to problems that bare sales figures don't reveal. Some uncontrollable factors in a particular territory—tougher competitors or ineffective middlemen—may lower the sales potential. Or a territory just may not have much potential.

To get a better check on performance effectiveness, the marketing manager compares what did happen with what ought to have happened. This involves the use of performance indices.

A performance index is like a batting average

When a manager sets standards—that is, quantitative measures of what ought to happen—it's relatively simple to compute a **performance index**—a number like a baseball batting average that shows the relation of one value to another.

Baseball batting averages are computed by dividing the actual number of hits by the number of times at bat (the possible number of times the batter could have

Exhibit 21–3   Development of a Measure of Sales Performance by Region

Regions	(1) Population as Percentage of Canada	(2) Expected Distribution of Sales Based on Population	(3) Actual Sales	(4) Performance Index
Atlantic	10%	$ 100,000	$ 60,000	60
Quebec	28	280,000	300,000	107
Ontario	36	360,000	360,000	100
Prairies	16	160,000	180,000	113
British Columbia, Yukon, and N.W.T.	10	100,000	100,000	100
Total	100%	$1,000,000	$1,000,000	

had a hit) and then multiplying the result by 100 to get rid of decimal points. A sales performance index is compared the same way—by dividing actual sales by expected sales for the area (or sales rep, product, etc.) and then multiplying by 100. If a sales rep is batting 82 percent, the index is 82.

A simple example shows where the problem is

Computing a performance index is shown in the following example, which assumes that population is an effective measure of sales potential.

Exhibit 21–3 breaks down Canada's population by regions as a percentage of the total population. The regions are the Atlantic Provinces, Quebec, Ontario the Prairies, and British Columbia, the Yukon, and the Northwest Territories.

Let's assume a firm with $1 million in sales now wants to evaluate performance in each region. Column 2 shows the actual sales of $1 million broken down in proportion to the population in the five regions. This is what sales *should* have been if population were a good measure of future performance. Column 3 in Exhibit 21–3 shows the actual sales for the year for each region. Column 4 shows measures of performance (performance indices): Column 3 ÷ Column 2 × 100.

The Atlantic region isn't doing as well as expected. It has 10 percent of the total population, and expected sales (based on population) are $100,000. Actual sales, however, are only $60,000. This means that the Atlantic region's performance index is only 60, calculated as (120,000 ÷ 200,000) × 100, because actual sales are much lower than expected on the basis of population. If population is a good basis for measuring expected sales (an important *if*), poor sales performance should be analyzed further. Perhaps sales reps in the Atlantic region aren't working as hard as they should. Perhaps promotion there isn't as effective as elsewhere. Or competitive products may have entered the market.

Whatever the cause, it's clear that performance analysis doesn't solve problems. It only points out potential problems, and it does this well.

A SERIES OF PERFORMANCE ANALYSES MAY FIND THE REAL PROBLEM

Performance analysis helps a marketing manager see if the firm's marketing plans are working properly—and, if they aren't, it can lead to solutions to the problems. But this may require a series of performance analyses, as the following example shows.

To get a feel for how performance analysis can be part of a problem-solving process, follow this example carefully, one exhibit at a time. Try to anticipate the marketing manager's decision.

The case of Stereo, Inc.

Stereo's sales manager found that sales for the Ontario region were $130,000 below the quota of $14,500,000 (that is, actual sales were $14,370,000) for the January to June period. The quota was based on forecast sales of the various types of stereo equipment the company sells. Specifically, the quota was based on forecasts for each product type in each store in each sales rep's territory.

Pam Dexter, the sales manager, felt this difference was not too large (1.52 percent) and was inclined to forget the matter, especially since forecasts are usually in error to some extent. But she thought about sending a letter to all sales reps and district supervisors in the region—a letter aimed at stimulating sales effort.

Exhibit 21–4 shows the overall story of what was happening to Stereo's sales in Ontario. What do you think the manager should do?

The Hamilton district had the poorest performance, but it wasn't too bad. Before writing a "let's get with it" letter to Hamilton and then relaxing, the sales manager decided to analyze the performance of the four sales reps in the Hamilton district. Exhibit 21–5 breaks down Hamilton's figures by sales rep. What conclusion or action do you suggest now?

Since Ted Smith previously had been the top sales rep, the sales manager wondered if Smith was having trouble with some of his larger customers. Before making a drastic move, she obtained an analysis of Smith's sales to the five largest customers. See Exhibit 21–6. What action could the sales manager take now? Should Smith be fired?

Smith's sales in all the large stores were down significantly, although his sales in many small stores were holding up well. Smith's problem seemed to be general.

Exhibit 21–4   Sales Performance, Ontario Region, January–June
(in thousands of dollars)

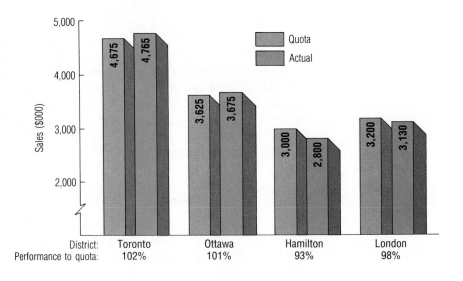

Exhibit 21−5 Sales Performance, Hamilton District, January−June (in thousands of dollars)

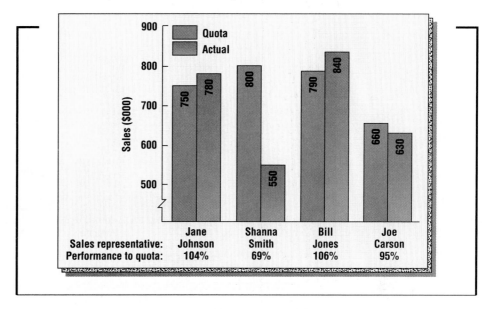

Exhibit 21−6 Sales Performance, Selected Stores of Ted Smith in Hamilton District, January−June (in thousands of dollars)

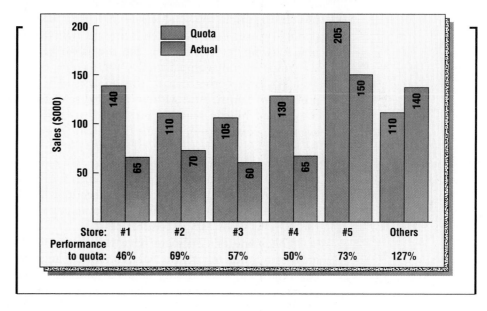

Perhaps he just wasn't working. Before calling him, the sales manager decided to look at Smith's sales of the four major products, as Exhibit 21−7 shows. What action is indicated now?

Smith was having real trouble with portable cassette players. Was the problem Smith or the players?

Exhibit 21–7   Sales Performance by Product for Ted Smith in Hamilton District, January–June (in thousands of dollars)

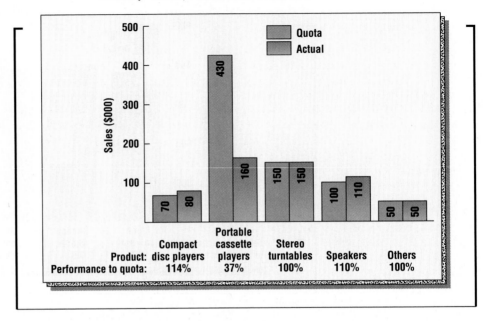

Further analysis by products for the whole region showed that everyone in Ontario was having trouble with portable players because a regional competitor was cutting prices. But higher sales on other products had hidden this fact. Since portable player sales had been doing all right nationally, the problem was only now showing up. You can see that this is the *major* problem.

Since overall company sales were going fairly well, many sales managers wouldn't have bothered with this analysis. They might merely have traced the problem to Smith. And without detailed sales records and performance analysis, the natural human reaction for Smith would be to blame business conditions, aggressive competition, or some other handy excuse.

Stay home and use the computer

This case shows that total figures can be deceiving. Marketing managers should not jump on the first plane or reach for the phone until they have all the facts. Even worse than rushing to the scene would be a rash judgment based on incomplete information. Some students might want to fire Smith after they see the store-by-store data in Exhibit 21–6.

The home office should have the records and facilities to isolate problem areas—and then rely on the field staff for explanations and help with locating the exact problem. Continuing detailed analysis usually gives better insights into problems, as this case shows. With computers, this can be done routinely and in great detail *provided marketing managers ask for it.* Marketing Demo 21–2 shows what careful analysis can achieve.

The iceberg principle—90 percent is below the surface

One of the most interesting conclusions from the Stereo illustration is the **iceberg principle**—much good information is hidden in summary data. Icebergs show only about 10 percent of their mass above the water level. The other 90 percent is below the water level—and not directly below, either. The submerged portion almost seems to search out ships that come too near.

MARKETING DEMO 21–2
Ben and Jerry's Sales Pop in Convenience Stores

Ben Cohen and Jerry Greenfield plunged into the ice cream business in the late 1970s with only a correspondence course under their belts. Now their company, Ben & Jerry's Homemade, Inc., is one of the leading producers of superpremium ice cream and upscale ice milk.

Cohen and Greenfield receive a lot of attention for being caring capitalists who worry as much about social issues as profit. But their company also earns strong profits—because they continue to plan new strategies to satisfy their target market—and modify those strategies when they don't perform as expected. What happened when the company introduced Peace Pops premium ice-cream bars is a good example. The initial plan called for intensive distribution of boxes of Peace Pops in supermarket freezer cases—to compete with competitors like Dove Bar and Häagen-Dazs. But after six months, total sales were 50 percent lower than expected. However, detailed sales analysis by package and channel revealed a bright spot: Individual Peace Pops were selling very well in local delis. After further work to better understand the reasons for this focused success, Ben and Jerry's marketing people realized that most of their target customers saw the premium-priced Peace Pop as an impulse product—rather than as a staple they were willing to heap into a shopping cart. So Ben & Jerry's revised the strategy to better reach impulse buyers—at convenience stores. Within a year, the revised strategy worked. Sales increased 60 percent, and sales analysis showed that 70 percent of the sales were at convenience stores.

Source: "Ben & Jerry's: Surviving the Big Squeeze," *Food Business*, May 6, 1991, pp. 10–12; "The Peace Pop Puzzle," *Inc.*, March 1990, p. 25; Ben & Jerry's, 1990 Annual Report.

The same is true of much business and marketing data. Since total sales may be large and company activities varied, problems in one area may hide below the surface. Everything looks calm and peaceful. But closer analysis may reveal jagged edges that can severely damage or even sink the business. The 90:10 ratio—or the 80/20 rule we mentioned earlier—must not be ignored. Averaging and summarizing data are helpful, but be sure summaries don't hide more than they reveal.

MARKETING COST ANALYSIS—CONTROLLING COSTS, TOO

So far, we've emphasized sales analysis. But sales come at a cost. And costs can and should be analyzed and controlled, too. You can see why in the case of Watanake Packaging, Ltd. (WPL). WPL developed a new strategy to target the packaging needs of producers of high-tech electronic equipment. WPL designed unique styrofoam inserts to protect electronic equipment during shipping. It assigned order getters to develop new accounts and recruited agent middlemen to develop overseas markets. The whole marketing mix was well received—and the firm's skimming price led to good profits. But over time, competing suppliers entered the market. When marketing managers at WPL analyzed costs, they realized their once-successful strategy was slipping. Personal selling expense as a percent of sales had doubled because it took longer to find and sell new accounts. It was costly to design special products for the many customers who purchased only small quantities. Profit margins were falling, too, because of increased price competition. In contrast, the analysis showed that sales of ordinary cardboard shipping boxes for agricultural products were very profitable. So WPL stopped calling on *small* electronics firms—and developed a new plan to build the firm's share of the less glamorous but more profitable cardboard box business.

Detailed cost analysis is very useful in understanding production costs—but much less is done with *marketing cost analysis*.[4] One reason is that many accountants show little interest in their firm's marketing process—or they don't understand the different marketing activities. They just treat marketing as overhead and forget about it.

But careful analysis of most marketing costs shows that the money is spent for a specific purpose—either to develop or promote a particular product or to serve particular customers. So it makes sense to allocate costs to specific market segments—or customers—or to specific products. In some situations, companies allocate costs directly to the various geographical market segments they serve. This may let managers directly analyze the profitability of the firm's target markets. In other cases, companies allocate costs to specific customers or specific products—and then add these costs for market segments depending on how much of which products each customer buys.

In either case, marketing cost analysis usually requires a new way of classifying accounting data. Instead of using the type of accounts typically used for financial analysis, we have to use functional accounts.

Natural accounts are the categories to which various costs are charged in the normal financing accounting cycle. These accounts include salaries, wages, social security, taxes, supplies, raw materials, auto, gas and oil expenses, advertising, and others. These accounts are called natural because they have the names of their expense categories.

However, factories don't use this approach to cost analysis—and it's not the one we will use. In the factory, **functional accounts** show the *purpose* for which expenditures are made. Factory functional accounts include shearing, milling, grinding, floor cleaning, maintenance, and so on. Factory cost accounting records are organized so that managers can determine the cost of particular products or jobs and their likely contribution to profit.

Marketing jobs are done for specific purposes, too. With some planning, the costs of marketing can also be assigned to specific categories—such as customers and products. Then their profitability can be calculated.

The first step in marketing cost analysis is to reclassify all the dollar cost entries in the natural accounts into functional cost accounts. For example, the many cost items in the natural *salary* account may be allocated to functional accounts with the following names: storing, inventory control, order assembly, packing and shipping, transporting, selling, advertising, order entry, billing, credit extension, and accounts receivable. The same is true for rent, depreciation, heat, light, power, and other natural accounts.

The way natural account amounts are shifted to functional accounts depends on the firm's method of operation. It may require time studies, space measurements, actual counts, and managers' estimates.

Then reallocate to
evaluate profitability
of profit centres

The next step is to reallocate the functional costs to those items—or customers or market segments—for which the amounts were spent. The most common reallocation of functional costs is to products and customers. After these

Levi Straus's advertising costs can often be allocated to specific products, just as the cost of labor in the factory can be allocated to specific products.

"Woman Combing Hair"

Levi's 900 Series* New Cut. Styled and Sized for Women.

costs are allocated, the detailed totals can be combined in any way desired—for example, by product or customer class, region, and so on.

The costs allocated to the functional accounts equal, in total, those in the natural accounts. They're just organized differently. But instead of being used only to show *total* company profits, the costs can now be used to calculate the profitability of territories, products, customers, salespeople, price classes, order sizes, distribution methods, sales methods, or any other breakdown desired. Each unit can be treated as a profit centre.

Cost analysis helps track down the loser

The following example illustrates these ideas. This case is simplified—and the numbers are small—so you can follow each step. However, you can use the same basic approach in more complicated situations.

In this case, the usual financial accounting approach—with natural accounts—shows that the company made a profit of $938 last month (Exhibit 21–8). But such a profit and loss statement doesn't show the profitability of the company's three customers. So the managers decide to use marketing cost analysis because they want to know whether a change in the marketing mix will improve profit.

First, we distribute the costs in the five natural accounts to four functional accounts—sales, packaging, advertising, and billing and collection (see Exhibit 21–9)—according to the functional reason for the expenses. Specifically, $1,000 of the total salary cost is for sales reps who seldom even come into the office since their job is to call on customers; $900 of the salary cost is for packaging labor; and

Exhibit 21–8   Profit and Loss Statement, One Month

Sales		$17,000
Cost of sales		11,900
Gross margin		$ 5,100
Expenses:		
Salaries	$2,500	
Rent	500	
Wrapping supplies	1,012	
Stationery and stamps	50	
Office equipment	100	
		$ 4,162
Net profit		$ 938

$600 is for office help. Assume that the office force split its time about evenly between addressing advertising material and billing and collection. So we split the $600 evenly into these two functional accounts.

The $500 for rent is for the entire building. But the company uses 80 percent of its floor space for packaging and 20 percent for the office. Thus, $400 is allocated to the packaging account. We divide the remaining $100 evenly between the advertising and billing accounts because these functions use the office space about equally. Stationery, stamps, and office equipment charges are allocated equally to the latter two accounts for the same reason. Charges for wrapping supplies are allocated to the packaging account because these supplies are used in packaging. In another situation, different allocations and even different accounts may be sensible—but these work here.

Allocating functional cost to customers

Now we can calculate the profitability of the company's three customers. But we need more information before we can allocate these functional accounts to customers or products. It is presented in Exhibit 21–10.

Exhibit 21–10 shows that the company's three products vary in cost, selling price, and sales volume. The products also have different sizes, and the packaging costs aren't related to the selling price. So when packaging costs are allocated to products, size must be considered. We can do this by computing a new

Exhibit 21–9   Spreading Natural Accounts to Functional Accounts

		Functional Accounts			
Natural Accounts		*Sales*	*Packaging*	*Advertising*	*Billing and Collection*
Salaries	$2,500	$1,000	$ 900	$300	$300
Rent	500		400	50	50
Wrapping supplies	1,012		1,012		
Stationery and stamps	50			25	25
Office equipment	100			50	50
Total	$4,162	$1,000	$2,312	$425	$425

Exhibit 21–10 Basic Data for Cost and Profit Analysis Example

Products

Products	Cost per Unit	Selling Price per Unit	Number of Units Sold in Period	Sales Volume in Period	Relative "Bulk" per Unit	Packaging "Units"
A	$ 7	$ 10	1,000	$10,000	1	1,000
B	35	50	100	5,000	3	300
C	140	200	10	2,000	6	60
			1,110	$17,000		1,360

Customers

Customers	Number of Sales Calls in Period	Number of Orders Placed in Period	Number of Each Product Ordered in Period		
			A	B	C
Smith	30	30	900	30	0
Jones	40	3	90	30	3
Brown	30	1	10	40	7
Total	100	34	1,000	100	10

measure—a packaging unit—which is used to allocate the costs in the packaging account. Packaging units adjust for relative size and the number of each type of product sold. For example, Product C is six times larger than A. While the company sells only 10 units of Product C, it is bulky and requires 10 times 6, or 60, packaging units. So we must allocate more of the costs in the packaging account to each unit of Product C.

Exhibit 21–10 also shows that the three customers require different amounts of sales effort, place different numbers of orders, and buy different product combinations.

Jones seems to require more sales calls. Smith places many orders that must be processed in the office—with increased billing expense. Brown placed only one order—for 70 percent of the sales of high-valued Product C.

Exhibit 21–11 shows the computations for allocating the functional amounts to the three customers. There were 100 sales calls in the period. Assuming that all calls took the same amount of time, we can figure the average cost per call by dividing the $1,000 sales cost by 100 calls—giving an average cost of $10. We use similar reasoning to break down the billing and packaging account totals.

Exhibit 21–11 Functional Cost Account Allocations

Sales Calls	$1,000 per 100 calls	= $10 per call
Billing	$425 per 34 orders	= $12.50 per order
Packaging Units Costs	$2.312 per 1,360 packaging units	= $1.70 per packaging unit or
		$1.70 for Product A
		$5.10 for Product B
		$10.20 for Product C
Advertising	$425 per 10 units of C	= $42.50 per unit of C

Advertising during this period was for the benefit of Product C only—so we split this cost among the units of C sold.

Calculating profit and loss for each customer

Now we can compute a profit and loss statement for each customer. Exhibit 21–12 shows how each customer's purchases and costs are combined to prepare a statement for each customer. The sum of each of the four major components (sales, cost of sales, expenses, and profit) is the same as on the original statement (Exhibit 21–8)—all we've done is rearrange and rename the data.

For example, Smith bought 900 units of A at $10 each and 300 units of B at $50 each—for the respective sales totals ($9,000 and $1,500) shown in Exhibit 21–12. We compare cost of sales in the same way. Expenses require various calculations. Thirty sales calls cost $300—30 × $10 each. Smith placed 30 orders at an average cost of $12.50 each for a total ordering cost of $375. Total packaging costs amounted to $1,530 for A (900 units purchased × $1.70 per unit) and $153 for B (30 units purchased × $5.10 per unit). There were no packaging costs for C because Smith didn't buy any of Product C. Neither were any advertising costs charged to Smith—all advertising costs were spent promoting Product C, which Smith didn't buy.

Exhibit 21–12   Profit and Loss Statements for Customers

	Smith		Jones		Brown		Whole Company
Sales							
A	$9,000		$ 900		$ 100		
B	1,500		1,500		2,000		
C			600		1,400		
Total sales		$10,500		$3,000		$3,500	$17,000
Cost of Sales							
A	6,300		630		70		
B	1,050		1,050		1,400		
C			420		980		
Total cost of sales		$ 7,350		$2,100		$2,450	$11,900
Gross margin		$ 3,150		$900		$1,050	$ 5,100
Expenses							
Sales calls ($10 each)	$ 300		$400.00		$300.00		
Order costs ($12.50 each)	375		37.50		12.50		
Packaging costs							
A	1,530		153.00		17.00		
B	153		153.00		204.00		
C			30.60		71.40		
Advertising			127.50		297.50		
		$ 2,358		$901.60		$902.40	$ 4,162
Net profit (or loss)		$ 792		$(1.60)		$147.60	$ 938

Analyzing the results

We now see that Smith was the most profitable customer, yielding over 75 percent of the net profit.

This analysis shows that Brown was profitable, too—but not as profitable as Smith because Smith bought three times as much. Jones was unprofitable. Jones didn't buy very much and received one-third more sales calls.

The iceberg principle is operating again here. Although the company as a whole is profitable, customer Jones is not. But before dropping Jones, the marketing manager should study the figures and the marketing plan very carefully. Perhaps Jones should be called on less frequently. Or maybe Jones will grow into a profitable account. Now the firm is at least covering some fixed costs by selling to Jones. Dropping this customer may only shift those fixed costs to the other two customers—making them look less attractive. (See the discussion on contribution margin later in this chapter.)

The marketing manager may also want to analyze the advertising costs against results—since a heavy advertising expense is charged against each unit of Product C. Perhaps the whole marketing plan should be revised.

Cost analysis is not performance analysis

Such a cost analysis is not a performance analysis, of course. If the marketing manager budgeted costs to various jobs, it would be possible to extend this analysis to a performance analysis. This would be logical—and desirable—but many companies have not yet moved in this direction.

Now that more accounting and marketing information is routinely available on computers—and software to analyze it is easier to use—many managers are seizing the opportunity to do marketing cost and performance analysis, just like factory cost accounting systems develop detailed cost estimates for products. These changes also mean that more managers are able to compare marketing cost and performance figures with "expected" figures to evaluate and control their marketing plans.

SHOULD ALL COSTS BE ALLOCATED?

So far, we've discussed general principles. But allocating costs is tricky. Some costs are likely to be fixed for the near future, regardless of what decision is made. And some costs are likely to be *common* to several products or customers, making allocation difficult.

Two basic approaches to handling this allocating problem are possible—the full-cost approach and the contribution-margin approach.

Full-cost approach— everything costs something

In the **full-cost approach**, all functional costs are allocated to products, customers, or other categories. Even fixed costs and common costs are allocated in some way. Because all costs are allocated, we can subtract costs from sales and find the profitability of various customers, products, and so on. This *is* of interest to some managers.

The full-cost approach requires that difficult-to-allocate costs be split on some basis. Here, the managers assume that the work done for those costs is equally beneficial to customers, to products, or to whatever group they are allocated.

Computer programs that help to control costs are getting ever easier to use.

Sometimes, this allocation is done mechanically. But often, logic can support the allocation—if we accept the idea that marketing costs are incurred for a purpose. For example, advertising costs not directly related to specific customers or products might be allocated to *all* customers based on their purchases—on the theory that advertising helps bring in the sales.

Contribution margin—
ignores some costs
to get results

When we use the **contribution-margin approach**, all functional costs are not allocated in *all* situations. Why?

When we compare various alternatives, it may be more meaningful to consider only the costs directly related to specific alternatives. Variable costs are relevant here.

The contribution-margin approach focuses attention on variable costs—rather than on total costs.* Total costs may include some fixed costs that do not change in the short run and can safely be ignored or some common costs that are more difficult to allocate.[5]

---

*Technically, a distinction should be made between variable and direct costs, but we will use these terms interchangeably. Similarly, not all common costs are fixed costs, and vice versa. But the important point here is to recognize that some costs are fairly easy to allocate and other costs are not.

Exhibit 21–13   Profit and Loss Statement by Department

	Totals	Dept. 1	Dept. 2	Dept. 3
Sales	$100,000	$50,000	$30,000	$20,000
Cost of sales	80,000	45,000	25,000	10,000
Gross margin	$ 20,000	$ 5,000	$ 5,000	$10,000
Other expenses:				
Selling expenses	$ 5,000	$ 2,500	$ 1,500	$ 1,000
Administrative expenses	6,000	3,000	1,800	1,200
Total other expenses	$ 11,000	$ 5,500	$ 3,300	$ 2,200
Net profit or (loss)	$ 9,000	$ (500)	$ 1,700	$ 7,800

The two approaches
can lead to different
decisions

The difference between the full-cost approach and the contribution-margin approach is important. The two approaches may suggest different decisions, as we'll see in the following example.

Full-cost example

Exhibit 21–13 shows a profit and loss statement—using the full-cost approach—for a department store with three operating departments. (These could be market segments or customers or products.)

The administrative expenses, which are the only fixed costs in this case, have been allocated to departments based on the sales volume of each department. This is a typical method of allocation. In this case, some managers argued that Department 1 was clearly unprofitable—and should be eliminated—because it showed a net loss of $500. Were they right?

To find out, see Exhibit 21–14, which shows what would happen if Department 1 were eliminated.

Several facts become clear right away. The overall profit of the store would be reduced if Department 1 were dropped. Fixed costs of $3,000, now being charged to Department 1, would have to be allocated to the other departments. This would reduce net profit by $2,500, since Department 1 previously covered $2,500 of the $3,000 in fixed costs. Such shifting of costs would then make Department 2 unprofitable!

Exhibit 21–14   Profit and Loss Statement by Department if Department 1
Were Eliminated

	Totals	Dept. 2	Dept. 3
Sales	$50,000	$30,000	$20,000
Cost of sales	35,000	25,000	10,000
Gross margin	$15,000	$ 5,000	$10,000
Other expenses:			
Selling expenses	$ 2,500	$ 1,500	$ 1,000
Administrative expenses	6,000	3,600	2,400
Total other expenses	$ 8,500	$ 5,100	$ 3,400
Net profit or (loss)	$ 6,500	$ (100)	$ 6,600

Contribution-margin example

Exhibit 21–15 shows a contribution-margin income statement for the same department store. Note that each department has a positive contribution margin. Here, the Department 1 contribution of $2,500 stands out better. This actually is the amount that would be lost if Department 1 were dropped. (Our example assumes that the fixed administrative expenses are *truly* fixed—that none of them would be eliminated if this department were dropped.)

A contribution-margin income statement shows the contribution of each department more clearly, including its contribution to both fixed costs and profit. As long as a department has some contribution-margin—and as long as there is no better use for the resources it uses—the department should be retained.

Contribution-margin versus full cost— choose your side

Using the full-cost approach often leads to arguments within a company. Any method of allocation can make some products or customers appear less profitable.

For example, it's logical to assign all common advertising costs to customers based on their purchases. But this approach can be criticized on the grounds that it may make large-volume customers appear less profitable than they really are—especially if the marketing mix aimed at the larger customers emphasizes price more than advertising.

Those in the company who want the smaller customers to look more profitable usually argue *for* this allocation method on the grounds that general advertising helps build good customers because it affects the overall image of the company and its products.

Arguments over allocation methods can be deadly serious. The method used may reflect on the performance of various managers—and it may affect their salaries and bonuses. Product managers, for example, are especially interested in how the various fixed and common costs are allocated to their products. Each, in turn, might like to have costs shifted to others' products.

Arbitrary allocation of costs also may have a direct impact on sales reps' morale. If they see their variable costs loaded with additional common or fixed costs over which they have no control, they may ask what's the use?

To avoid these problems, firms often use the contribution-margin approach. It's especially useful for evaluating alternatives—and for showing operating

Exhibit 21–15 Contribution-Margin Statement by Departments

	Totals	Dept. 1	Dept. 2	Dept. 3
Sales	$100,000	$50,000	$30,000	$20,000
Variable costs:				
Cost of sales	$ 80,000	$45,000	$25,000	$10,000
Selling expenses	5,000	2,500	1,500	1,000
Total variable costs	$ 85,000	$47,500	$26,500	$11,000
Contribution margin	15,000	2,500	3,500	9,000
Fixed costs:				
Administrative expenses	6,000			
Net profit	$ 9,000			

managers and salespeople how they're doing. The contribution-margin approach shows what they've actually contributed to covering general overhead and profit.

Top management, on the other hand, often finds full-cost analysis more useful. In the long run, some products, departments, or customers must pay for the fixed costs. Full-cost analysis has its place, too.

PLANNING AND CONTROL COMBINED

We've been treating sales and cost analyses separately up to this point. But management often combines them to keep a running check on its activities—to be sure the plans are working—and to see when and where new strategies are needed.

Sales + Costs + Everybody helps = $163,000

Let's see how this works at Cindy's Fashions, a typical apparel retailer. This firm netted $155,000 last year. Cindy Reve, the owner, expects no basic change in competition and slightly better local business conditions. So she sets this year's profit objective at $163,000—an increase of about 5 percent.

Next, she develops tentative plans to show how she can make this higher profit. She estimates the sales volumes, gross margins, and expenses—broken down by months and by departments in her store—that she would need to net $163,000.

Exhibit 21–16 is a planning and control chart Reve developed to show the contribution each department should make each month. March through October's data is omitted for the sake of brevity. At the bottom of Exhibit 21–16, the plan for the year is summarized. Note that space is provided to insert the actual performance and a measure of variation, so this chart can be used to do both planning and control.

Based on inputs from a retailer about which locks sell the fastest and have the highest margins in its market, Master Lock helps the retailer determine what mix of locks will achieve maximum sales margins and profitability.

Exhibit 21–16   Planning and Control Chart for Cindy's Fashions

	Contribution to Store					Store Expense	Operating Profit	Cumulative Operating Profit
	Dept. A	Dept. B	Dept. C	Dept. D*	Total			
January								
Planned	$ 27,000	$ 9,000	$ 4,000	$–1,000	$ 39,000	$ 24,000	$ 15,000	$ 15,000
Actual								
Variation								
February								
Planned	20,000	6,500	2,500	–1,000	28,000	24,000	4,000	19,000
Actual								
Variation								
.								
.								
.								
November								
Planned	32,000	7,500	2,500	0	42,000	24,000	18,000	106,500
Actual								
Variation								
December								
Planned	63,000	12,500	4,000	9,000	88,500	32,000	56,500	163,000
Actual								
Variation								
Total								
Planned	$316,000	$70,000	$69,000	$–4,000	$453,000	$288,000	$163,000	$163,000
Actual								
Variation								

*The objective of minus $4,000 for this department was established on the same basis as the objectives for the other departments—that is, it represents the same percentage gain over last year, when Department D's loss was $4,200. Plans call for discontinuance of the department unless it shows marked improvement by the end of the year.

Exhibit 21–16 shows that Reve is focusing on the monthly contribution by each department. The purpose of monthly estimates is to get more frequent feedback and allow faster adjustment of plans. Generally, the shorter the planning and control period, the easier it is to correct problems before they become emergencies.

In this example, Reve uses a modified contribution-margin approach—some of the fixed costs can be allocated logically to particular departments. On this chart, the balance left after direct fixed and variable costs are charged to departments is called Contribution to Store. The idea is that each department will contribute to covering *general* store expenses—such as top-management salaries and holiday decorations—and to net profits.

In Exhibit 21–16, we see that the whole operation is brought together when Reve computes the monthly operating profit. She totals the contribution from each of the four departments, then subtracts general store expenses to obtain the operating profit for each month.

Each department must plan and control, too

Exhibit 21–17 shows a similar planning and control chart for a single department—Department B. In this exhibit, actual results are entered for the month of January. The chart shows an unfavorable difference between planned and actual sales performance ($–14,000) and gross profit ($–1,700).

Exhibit 21-17   Planning and Control Chart for Cindy's Fashions—Department B

	Sales	Gross Profit	Direct Expense Total	Fixed	Variable	Contribution to Store	Cumulative Contribution to Store
January							
Planned	$ 60,000	$ 18,000	$ 9,000	$ 6,000	$ 3,000	$ 9,000	$ 9,000
Actual	46,000	16,300	8,300	6,000	1,150	8,000	8,000
Variation	−14,000	−1,700	700	0	700	−1,000	−1,000
February							
Planned	50,000	15,000	8,500	6,000	2,500	6,500	15,500
Actual							
Variation							
.							
.							
.							
November							
Planned	70,000	21,000	13,500	10,000	3,500	7,500	57,500
Actual							
Variation							
December							
Planned	90,000	27,000	14,500	10,000	4,500	12,500	70,000
Actual							
Variation							
Total							
Planned	$600,000	$180,000	$110,000	$80,000	$30,000	$70,000	$70,000
Actual							
Variation							

Now the marketing manager must decide why actual sales were less than projected and begin to make new plans. Possible hypotheses are (1) prices were too high, (2) promotion was ineffective, and (3) the product selection did not appeal to the target customers.

Corrective action could take either of two courses: improving implementation efforts or developing new, more realistic strategies.

SPEED UP THE INFORMATION FOR BETTER CONTROL

The marketing manager must take charge

Computers now take the drudgery out of analyzing data. But this kind of analysis is not possible unless the data is in machine-processable form—so it can be sorted and analyzed quickly. Here, the creative marketing manager plays a crucial role by insisting that the necessary data be collected. If the data he or she wants to analyze is not captured as it comes in, information will be difficult—if not impossible—to get later.

Speed is a key factor

A marketing manager may need many different types of information to improve implementation efforts or develop new strategies. In the past, this has often caused delays even if the information was in a machine-processable form. In a large company, for example, it could take days or even weeks for a marketing manager to find out how to get needed information from another department. Imagine how long it could take for a marketing manager to get needed sales data from sales offices in different countries all over the world.

New approaches for electronic data interchange help solve these problems. For example, many companies are using fiber-optic telephone lines or satellite transmission systems to *immediately* transfer data from a computer at one location to another. A sales manager with a portable computer can use a regular telephone to pull data off his or her firm's mainframe computer. And marketing managers working at different locations on different aspects of a strategy can communicate through networks that link their computers for easy data transfer.

This type of electronic pipeline makes data available instantly. A sales or performance analysis that in the past was done once a month now might be done weekly or even daily.

Of course, many firms don't consider or use these types of approaches. But they are becoming much more common—especially as more marketing managers find that they are losing out to more nimble competitors who get information more quickly and adjust their strategies more often.[6]

THE MARKETING AUDIT

While crises pop, planning and control must go on

The analyses we've discussed so far are designed to help a firm plan and control its operations. They can help a marketing manager do a better job. Often, however, the control process tends to look at only a few critical elements—such as sales variations by product in different territories. It misses such things as the effectiveness of present and possible marketing strategies and mixes.

The marketing manager usually is responsible for day-to-day implementing as well as planning and control—and may not have the time to evaluate the effectiveness of the firm's efforts. Sometimes, crises pop up in several places at the same time. Attention must focus on adjusting marketing mixes—or on shifting strategies in the short run.

To make sure that the whole marketing program is evaluated *regularly*, not just in times of crisis, marketing specialists developed the marketing audit. A marketing audit is similar to an accounting audit or a personnel audit, which businesses have used for some time.

The **marketing audit** is a systematic, critical, and unbiased review and appraisal of the basic objectives and policies of the marketing function—and of the organization, methods, procedures, and people employed to implement the policies.[7] Exhibit 21–18 shows what a marketing audit for a nonprofit group would involve.

A marketing audit requires a detailed look at the company's current marketing plans to see if they are still the best plans the firm can offer. Customers' needs and attitudes change—and competitors continually develop new and better plans. Plans more than a year or two old may be out-of-date—or even obsolete. Sometimes, marketing managers are so close to the trees that they can't see the forest. An outsider can help the firm see whether it really focuses on some unsatisfied needs and offers appropriate marketing mixes. Basically, the auditor uses our strategy planning framework. But instead of developing plans, the auditor works backward—and evaluates the plans being implemented. The auditor also evaluates the quality of the effort, looking at who is doing what and how well. This means interviewing customers, competitors, channel members, and employees. A

Exhibit 21–18 A Marketing Audit for a Nonprofit Group

I. The Marketing Environment Review

A. Markets
1. Who are the organization's major markets (publics) for fund raising?
2. What are the major market segments in each market?
3. What are the characteristics of each market segment? Identify the following:
   a. Demographic.
   b. Psychographic.
   c. Linkage to the organization.
4. How is the organization perceived by each of the market segments identified above?
5. What are the present and expected future sizes of each market and market segment?

B. Donors
1. How does the general public feel toward the organization's mission?
2. How do the market segments (identified above) feel about organization's fund-raising offerings?
3. What are the present and expected future states of the general public's perceptions of fund raising?

C. Competitors
1. Who are the major competitors in fund raising?
2. What are the competitors' strengths and weaknesses?
3. What trends can be foreseen in competition?

D. Macroenvironment
1. What are the main relevant developments in the following areas that will affect fund raising:
   a. Demography.
   b. Economy.
   c. Technology.
   d. Government.
   e. Culture.

II. Marketing System Review

A. Objectives
1. What are the development department's long-term and short-term objectives?
2. Are these objectives stated in a clear hierarchical order and in a form that permits planning and measurement of achievement?
3. Are these objectives consistent with the organization's purpose and mission?
4. Are the fund-raising objectives reasonable for the organization, given its competitive position, resources, and opportunities?
5. Who (volunteer and staff positions) in the organization has general responsibility for these objectives?

B. Program Strategy
1. What is the fund-raising core strategy for achieving its objectives, and is it likely to succeed?
2. Is the organization allocating enough resources (or too many) to accomplish the fund-raising task?
3. Are the fund-raising resources allocated optimally to the various markets and offerings?

Exhibit 21–18   A Marketing Audit for a Nonprofit Group (*concluded*)

C. Implementation
1. Does the organization develop an annual fund-raising plan? Is the planning process effective?
2. Does a standing committee of the board participate with staff in research, development, and revision of fund-raising policy and program plans for full board review and ratification? Does it monitor the implementation of policies and plans?
3. Does the organization implement control procedures (monthly, quarterly, etc.) to ensure that its annual plan objectives are being achieved?
4. Does the organization carry out periodic studies to determine the effectiveness of various fund-raising activities?

III. Detailed Marketing Activity Review

A. Fund-Raising Offerings
1. What are the major fund-raising offerings of the organization?
2. How has the market for each offering been traditionally defined?
3. Should any offerings be phased out?
4. Should any offerings be added?
5. What is the general state of health of each offering and the program mix as a whole?

B. Distribution
1. How does the organization reach the target markets with its fund-raising offerings?

C. Volunteer Structure
1. Is the volunteer force large enough to accomplish the development department's objectives?
2. Is the volunteer force organized along the proper principles of specialization (territory, market, programs)?
3. Does the volunteer force show high morale, ability, and effort? Is it sufficiently trained and motivated?

D. Publicity
1. Does the organization have a carefully formulated program for publicity regarding fund-raising efforts?

E. Fund-Raising Promotion
1. What medium carries the fund-raising message and position to the donors?
2. Which medium is utilized?
3. How effective are these messages and media?

Source: Daniel E. Hansler, *Fund Raising Management*, March 1988, p. 82.

marketing audit can be a big job. But if it helps ensure that the company's strategies are on the right track—and being implemented properly—it can be well worth the effort.

An audit shouldn't be necessary—but often it is

A marketing audit takes a big view of the business, and it evaluates the whole marketing program. It might be done by a separate department within the company, perhaps by a marketing controller. But to avoid bias, it might be better to use an outside organization such as a management consulting firm.

Ideally, a marketing audit should not be necessary. Good managers do their very best in planning, implementing, and control—and should continually evaluate the effectiveness of the operation.

In practice, however, managers often become identified with certain strategies—and pursue them blindly—when other strategies might be more effective. Since an outside view can give needed perspective, marketing audits may be more common in the future.

CONCLUSION

In this chapter, we saw that sales and cost analyses can help a marketing manager control a marketing program—and that control procedures provide feedback that aids future planning.

Simple sales analysis just gives a picture of what happened. But when sales forecasts or other data showing expected results is brought into the analysis, we can evaluate performance—using performance indices.

Cost analysis also can be useful—if natural account costs are moved to functional cost accounts and then allocated to market segments, customers, products, or other categories. There are two basic approaches to cost analysis—full-cost and contribution-margin. Using the full-cost approach, all costs are allocated in some way. Using the contribution-margin approach, only the variable costs are allocated. Both methods have their advantages and special uses.

Ideally, the marketing manager should arrange for a constant flow of data that can be analyzed routinely—preferably by computer—to help control present plans and plan new strategies. A marketing audit can help this ongoing effort. Either a separate department within the company or an outside organization may conduct this audit.

A marketing program must be controlled. Good control helps the marketing manager locate and correct weak spots—and at the same time find strengths that may be applied throughout the marketing program. Control works hand in hand with planning.

QUESTIONS AND PROBLEMS

1. Various breakdowns can be used for sales analysis, depending on the nature of the company and its products. Describe a situation (one for each) where each of the following breakdowns would yield useful information. Explain why.

   a. By geographic region.
   b. By product.
   c. By customer.
   d. By size of order.
   e. By size of sales rep commission on each product or product group.

2. Distinguish between a sales analysis and a performance analysis.

3. Carefully explain what the iceberg principle should mean to the marketing manager.

4. Explain the meaning of the comparative performance and comparative cost data in Exhibits 21–1 and 21–2. Why does it appear that eliminating sales areas D and E would be profitable?

5. Most sales forecasting is subject to some error (perhaps 5 to 10 percent). Should we then expect variations in sales performance of 5 to 10 percent above or below quota? If so, how should we treat such variations in evaluating performance?

6. Why is there controversy between the advocates of the full-cost and the contribution-margin approaches to cost analysis?

7. The June profit and loss statement for the Browning Company is shown. If competitive conditions make price increases impossible—and management has cut costs as much as possible—should the Browning Company stop selling to hospitals and schools? Why?

Browning Company Statement

	Retailers	Hospitals and Schools	Total
Sales:			
80,000 units at $0.70.	$56,000		$56,000
20,000 units at $0.60.		$12,000	12,000
Total	$56,000	$12,000	$68,000
Cost of sales.	40,000	10,000	50,000
Gross margin	$16,000	$ 2,000	$18,000
Sales and administrative expenses:			
Variable	$ 6,000	$ 1,500	$ 7,500
Fixed.	5,600	900	6,500
Total	$11,600	$ 2,400	$14,000
Net profit (loss).	$ 4,400	$ (400)	$ 4,000

8. Explain why it's so important for the marketing manager to be directly involved in planning control procedures.

9. Explain why a marketing audit might be desirable—even in a well-run company. Who or what kind of an organization would be best to conduct a marketing audit? Would a marketing research firm be good? Would the present accounting firm be most suitable? Why?

SUGGESTED CASES

27. London Life Insurance Company

32. Strategic Adventure Park

Ethical Marketing in a Consumer-Oriented World: Appraisal and Challenges

Chapter

When You Finish This Chapter, You Should

❶

Understand why marketing must be evaluated differently at the micro and macro levels.

❷

Understand why the text argues that micro-marketing costs too much.

❸

Understand why the text argues that macro-marketing does not cost too much.

❹

Know some of the challenges marketers face as they work to develop ethical marketing strategies that serve consumers' needs.

M ore than ever, the macro-marketing systems of the world are interconnected. The collapse of communism and the worldwide drive toward market-directed economies is dramatic evidence that consumer-citizens want freedom and choices—not only in politics but in markets. Centrally planned economies simply weren't able to meet needs.

Although there's much talk about the world as a global village, we're not there yet. People in a *real* village on the plains of Niger may be able to crowd around a single TV and get a glimpse of the quality of life that consumers in the advanced western economies enjoy, but for them it doesn't seem real. What is real is their struggle to meet the basic physical needs of life—to survive starvation, malnutrition, and epidemic-carrying water. The plight of consumers doesn't seem quite as severe in the fragile and emerging democracies, like those in Latin America and Eastern Europe. But the vast majority of citizen-consumers in those societies can only wonder if they'll ever have choices among a wide variety of goods and services—and the income to buy them—that most consumers take for granted in Canada, the United States, western Europe, Australia, and a few other advanced economies.[1]

The challenges faced by consumers—and marketing managers—in the advanced economies seem minor by contrast. When we worry about products being available, we're more likely thinking about instant gratification. We expect the corner convenience store to have a nice selection of frozen gourmet dinners that we can prepare in minutes in a microwave oven. Or perhaps that's too much hassle. After all, Domino's will deliver a pizza in less than 30 minutes. And McDonald's has our Egg McMuffins ready when we pull up at the drive-thru at 7 in the morning. We want supermarkets and drugstores handy. And we expect everything from fresh tropical fruits to camera batteries to brand name fashions to be available when—and where—we want them. In a relative sense, few of the world's consumers can expect so much—and get so much of what they expect. All of this has a price, of course—and we, as consumers, pay the bill.[2]

When you think about these contrasts, it's not hard to decide which set of consumers is better off. But are we making a straw man comparison? Is the first situation one extreme, with the system in Canada and similar societies just as extreme—only in a different way? Would we be better off if we didn't put quite so much emphasis on marketing? Do we need so many brands of products? Does all the money spent on advertising really help consumers? Do middlemen just add to the price consumers pay? More generally, does marketing serve society well? In other words, does marketing cost too much? This is a fundamental question. Some people feel strongly that marketing *does* cost too much—that it's a waste of resources we could better use elsewhere.

Now that you have a better understanding of what marketing is all about—and how the marketing manager contributes to the *macro*-marketing process—you should be able to decide whether marketing costs too much. That's what this chapter is about.

Your answer is very important. It will affect your own business career and the economy in which you live.

Do car producers, for example, produce lower-quality cars than they could? Do producers of food and drug products spend too much money advertising trivial differences between their brands? Should they stop trying to brand their products at all—and instead sell generics at lower prices? Does marketing encourage us to want too much of the wrong products? Are there too many retailers and wholesalers, all taking "too big" markups? Some critics of marketing would answer Yes! to *all* these important questions. Such critics believe we should change our political and legal environments—and the world in which you live and work. Do you agree? Or are you fairly satisfied with the way our system works? How will you vote on your consumer ballot?

HOW SHOULD MARKETING BE EVALUATED?

We must evaluate at two levels

As we saw in Chapter 1, it's useful to distinguish between two levels of marketing: the *micro* level (how individual firms run) and the *macro* level (how the whole system works). Some complaints against marketing are aimed at only one of these levels at a time. In other cases, the criticism *seems* to be directed at one level—but actually is aimed at the other. Some critics of specific ads, for example, probably wouldn't be satisfied with *any* advertising. When evaluating marketing, we must treat each of these levels separately.

Nation's objectives affect evaluation

Different nations have different social and economic objectives. Dictatorships, for example, may be mainly concerned with satisfying the needs of society as seen by the political elite. In a socialist state, the objective might be to satisfy society's needs as defined by government planners. In a society that has just broken the chains of communism, the objective may be to make the transition to a market-directed economy as quickly as possible—before there are more revolts.

Consumer satisfaction is the objective in North America

In Canada, *the basic objective of our market-directed economic system has been to satisfy consumer needs as they—the consumers—see them.* This objective implies that political freedom and economic freedom go hand in hand—and that citizens in a free society have the right to live as they choose. The majority of Canadian consumers would be unwilling to give up the freedom of choice they now enjoy. The same can be said for the United States, Great Britain, and most other

The lifestyle of a middle-class, urban family in Russia (on left) is a stark contrast to the lifestyle of a middle-class family in Canada (on right).

countries in the European community. However, for focus we will concentrate on marketing as it exists in North American society.

Therefore, let's try to evaluate the operation of marketing in the North American economy—where the present objective is to satisfy consumer needs *as consumers see them*. This is the essence of our system. The business firm that ignores this fact is asking for trouble.

CAN CONSUMER SATISFACTION BE MEASURED?

Since consumer satisfaction is our objective, marketing's effectiveness must be measured by *how well* it satisfies consumers. Unfortunately, consumer satisfaction is hard to define—and even harder to measure.

Satisfaction depends on individual aspirations

There have been various efforts to measure overall consumer satisfaction not only in Canada but also in other countries. However, measuring consumer satisfaction is difficult because satisfaction depends on your level of aspiration or expectation. Less prosperous consumers begin to expect more out of an economy as they see the higher living standards of others. Also, aspiration levels tend to rise with repeated successes—and fall with failures. Products considered satisfactory one day may not be satisfactory the next day, or vice versa. A few years ago, most of us were more than satisfied with a 19-inch color TV that pulled in three or four channels. But once you've watched one of the newer large-screen models and enjoyed all the options possible with a cable hookup or VCR, that old TV is never the same again. And when high-definition TVs become readily available, today's satisfying units won't seem quite so acceptable. So consumer satisfaction is a highly personal concept—and looking at the satisfaction of a whole society does not provide a reliable standard for evaluating macro-marketing effectiveness.[3]

Measuring macro-marketing must be subjective

If the objective of macro-marketing is maximizing consumer satisfaction, then we must measure total satisfaction—of everyone. But there's no good way to measure aggregate consumer satisfaction. At a minimum, some consumers are more satisfied than others. So our evaluation of macro-marketing effectiveness has to be subjective.

Probably the supreme test is whether the macro-marketing system satisfies enough individual consumer-citizens so that they vote—at the ballot box—to keep it running. So far, we've done so in Canada.

Measuring micro-marketing can be less subjective

Measuring micro-marketing effectiveness is also difficult, but it can be done. Individual business firms can and should try to measure how well their marketing mixes satisfy their customers (or why they fail). In fact, most large firms now have some type of ongoing effort to determine whether they're satisfying their target markets. Many large and small firms measure customer satisfaction with attitude research studies. For example, the J. D. Powers marketing research firm is well known for its studies of consumer satisfaction with different makes of automobiles and computers. Other widely used methods include unsolicited consumer responses (usually complaints), opinions of middlemen and salespeople, market test results, and profits. Of course, customers may be very satisfied about some aspects of what a firm is doing, but dissatisfied about other dimensions of performance.[4]

In our market-directed system, it's up to each customer to decide how effectively individual firms satisfy his or her needs. Usually, customers will buy more of the products that satisfy them—and they'll do it repeatedly. Thus, efficient marketing plans can increase profits, and profits can be used as a rough measure of a firm's efficiency in satisfying customers. Nonprofit organizations have a different bottom line, but they too will fail if they don't satisfy supporters and get the resources they need to continue to operate.

Evaluating marketing effectiveness is difficult—but not impossible

Because it's hard to measure consumer satisfaction—and, therefore, the effectiveness of micro- and macro-marketing—it's easy to see why opinions differ. If the objective of the economy is clearly defined, however—and the argument is stripped of emotion—the big questions about marketing effectiveness probably *can* be answered.

In this chapter, we argue that micro-marketing (how individual firms and channels operate) frequently *does* cost too much but that macro-marketing (how the whole marketing system operates) *does not* cost too much, *given the present objective of the Canadian economy—consumer satisfaction*. Don't accept this position as *the* answer—but rather as a point of view. In the end, you'll have to make your own decision.[5]

MICRO-MARKETING OFTEN *DOES* COST TOO MUCH

Throughout the text, we've explored what marketing managers could or should do to help their firms do a better job of satisfying customers—while achieving company objectives. Many firms implement highly successful marketing programs, but others are still too production-oriented and inefficient. For customers of these latter firms, micro-marketing often does cost too much.

Research shows that many consumers are not satisfied. But you know that already. All of us have had experiences when we weren't satisfied—when some firm didn't deliver on its promises. And the problem is much bigger than some marketers want to believe. Research suggests that the majority of consumer complaints are never reported. Worse, many complaints that are reported never get fully resolved.

The failure rate is high

Further evidence that too many firms are too production-oriented—and not nearly as efficient as they could be—is the fact that so many new products fail. New and old businesses fail regularly, too.

Generally speaking, marketing inefficiencies are due to one or more of three reasons:

1. Lack of interest in—or understanding of—the sometimes fickle customer.
2. Improper blending of the four Ps—caused in part by overemphasis on production and/or internal problems as contrasted with a customer orientation.
3. Lack of understanding of—or adjustment to—the marketing environment, especially what competitors do.

The high cost of poor marketing mixes

Perhaps lack of concern for the customer is most noticeable in the ways the four Ps are sometimes combined—or forced—into a marketing mix. This can happen in many ways.

Too many firms develop a new product to satisfy some manager's pet idea—not to meet the needs of certain target customers. Or they see another company with a successful product and try to jump into the market with another me-too imitation—without even thinking about the competition they'll encounter. Often, they don't worry about quality. In fact, until fairly recently, most North American manufacturers lacked *any* quality control procedures even in the production of goods or services. The idea of using total quality management to implement marketing plans to meet customers' requirements was foreign.

Some marketing managers don't pay attention to getting needed support from middlemen. Too many producers don't even consider the possibility that a big retail chain may see better value for its customers—and greater profit potential—in someone else's product.

Du Pont tries to meet the needs of its target markets—so that retailers will want to carry its products and the success of its strategies doesn't just rely on promotion.

Firms often ignore demand and set prices on a cost-plus basis. While margins are fairly definite, firms can only predict volume. So they choose high margins—which may lead to high prices and reduced volume.

If a product is poorly designed—or if a firm uses inadequate channels or pricing that isn't competitive—it's easy to see why promotion may be costly. Aggressive spending on promotion doesn't make up for the other types of mistakes.

Top-management decisions on company objectives may increase the cost of marketing unnecessarily. Seeking growth for growth's sake, for example, often leads to too much spending for promotion.

Another sign of failure is the inability of firms to identify new target markets and new opportunities. A new marketing mix that isn't offered doesn't fail—but the lost opportunity can be significant for both a firm and society. Too many seize on whatever strategy seems easiest rather than seeking really new ways to satisfy customers.

Micro-marketing does cost too much—but things are changing

For reasons like these, marketing does cost too much in many firms. Despite much publicity, the marketing concept is not really applied in many places.

But not all firms and marketers deserve criticism. More of them *are* becoming customer-oriented. And many are paying more attention to market-oriented planning to carry out the marketing concept more effectively. Throughout the text, we've highlighted firms and strategies that are making a difference. Yes, firms make some mistakes. That's human—and marketing is a human enterprise. But such firms have also showed the results that market-oriented strategy planning can produce.

Another encouraging sign is the end of the idea that anybody can run a business successfully. This never was true. Today, the growing complexity of business draws more and more professionals—not only business managers but computer and communications specialists, psychologists, statisticians, and economists.

Managers who adopt the marketing concept as a way of business life do a better job. They look for target market opportunities and carefully blend the elements of the marketing mix to meet their customers' needs. As more of these managers rise in business, we can look forward to much lower micro-marketing costs—and strategies that do a better job of satisfying customer needs.

MACRO-MARKETING DOES NOT COST TOO MUCH

Many critics of marketing take aim at the macro-marketing system. They think (1) advertising—and promotion in general—is socially undesirable and (2) the macro-marketing system causes poor use of resources, limits income and employment, and leads to an unfair distribution of income. Most of these complaints imply that some micro-marketing activities should not be permitted—and, because they are, our macro-marketing system does a poor job. Let's look at some of these positions to help you form your own opinion.

Micro-efforts help the economy grow

Some critics feel that marketing helps create monopoly or at least monopolistic competition. Further, they think this leads to higher prices, restricted output, and reduction in national income and employment.

Marketing stimulates innovation and the development of new ways to meet customers' needs.

It's true that firms in a market-directed economy try to carve out separate monopolistic markets for themselves with new products. But consumers do have a choice. They don't *have* to buy the new product unless they think it's a better value. The old products are still available. In fact, to meet the new competition, prices of the old products usually drop. And that makes them even more available.

Over several years, the innovator's profits may rise—but rising profits also encourage further innovation by competitors. This leads to new investments—which contribute to economic growth and higher levels of national income and employment. Around the world, many countries failed to achieve their potential for economic growth under centrally planned systems because this type of profit incentive didn't exist.

Increased profits also attract competition. Profits then begin to drop as new competitors enter the market and begin producing somewhat similar products. (Recall the rise and fall of industry profit during the product life cycle.)

Is advertising a waste of resources?

Advertising is the most criticized of all micro-marketing activities. Indeed, many ads *are* annoying, insulting, misleading, and downright ineffective. This is one reason why micro-marketing often does cost too much. However, advertising can also make both the micro- and macro-marketing processes work better.

Advertising is an economical way to inform large numbers of potential customers about a firm's products. Provided that a product satisfies customer needs, advertising can increase demand for the product—resulting in economies of scale in manufacturing, distribution, and sales. Because these economies may more than offset advertising costs, advertising can actually *lower* prices to the consumer.[6]

At the macro level, the increased demand brought about by advertising gives producers a faster return on their investment. This, in turn, stimulates further investment, encourages innovation, creates jobs, raises personal incomes, and generates economic growth.

Does marketing make people buy things they don't need?

From our discussion so far, it seems that micro-marketing activities aimed at satisfying consumer needs do *not* lead to improper use of resources. Giving individuals what they want, after all, is the purpose of our market-directed economic system. However, some critics feel that most firms—especially large corporations—don't really cater to the needs and wants of the consumer. They think such firms use clever ads to persuade consumers to buy whatever the firms want to sell.

Historian Arnold Toynbee, for example, felt that North American firms manipulated consumers into buying products that aren't necessary to satisfy "the minimum material requirements of life." Toynbee saw North American firms as mainly trying to fulfill "unwanted demand"—demand created by advertising—rather than "genuine wants." He defined genuine wants as "wants that we become aware of spontaneously, without having to be told by advertisers that we want something that we should never have thought of wanting if we had been left in peace to find out our wants for ourselves."[7]

What are the minimum requirements of life?

One problem with this line of reasoning is how to determine the minimum material requirements of life. Does this mean that people should go back to living in caves or log cabins? Which products consumed today are unnecessary—and should not be produced?

Obviously, we have to make some value judgments to answer such questions—and few of us share the same values. One critic suggested that North Americans could and should do without such items as pets, newspaper comic strips, second family cars, motorcycles, snowmobiles, campers, recreational boats and planes, aerosol products, pop and beer cans, and hats.[8] You may agree with some of these. But who should determine minimum material requirements of life—consumers or critics?

Consumers are not puppets

The idea that firms can manipulate consumers to buy anything the company chooses to produce simply isn't true. A consumer who buys a soft drink that tastes terrible won't buy another can of that brand, regardless of how much it's advertised. In fact, many new products fail the test of the market. Not even large corporations are assured of success every time they launch a new product. Consider, for example, the dismal fate of products such as Ford's Edsel, Du Pont's Corfam, Campbell's Red Kettle Soups, and RCA's computers. And if powerful corporations know some way to get people to buy products against their will, would General Motors have recently tallied the biggest loss in history?

Needs and wants change

Consumer needs and wants change constantly. Few of us would care to live the way our grandparents lived when they were our age—let alone like the pioneers who traveled to unknown destinations in covered wagons. Marketing's job is not just to satisfy consumer wants as they exist at any particular point in time. Rather, marketing must keep looking for new—and better—ways to serve consumers.[9]

In the 1920s, few consumers saw the need for an electric icebox. Now we all feel a refrigerator is a necessity—but some consumers don't see the need for special features. Who should decide what you need?

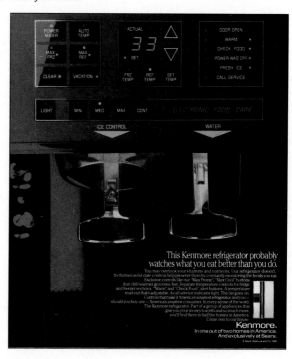

| Does marketing make people materialistic? | There is no doubt that marketing caters to materialistic values. However, people disagree as to whether marketing creates these values—or simply appeals to values already there. |

Even in the most primitive societies, people want to accumulate possessions. In fact, in some tribal villages, social status is measured by how many goats or sheep a person owns. Further, the tendency for ancient pharaohs and kings to surround themselves with wealth and treasures can hardly be attributed to the persuasive powers of advertising agencies!

The idea that marketers create and serve "false tastes"—as defined by individual critics—was answered by a well-known economist who said:

> The marketplace responds to the tastes of consumers with the goods and services that are salable, whether the tastes are elevated or depraved. It is unfair to criticize the marketplace for fulfilling these desires . . . it is like blaming waiters in restaurants for obesity.[10]

Marketing reflects our own values

Experts who study materialism seem to agree that—in the short run—marketing reflects social values, while—in the long run—it enhances and reinforces them. One expert pointed out that consumers vote for what they want in the marketplace and in the polling place. To say that what they choose is wrong, he said, is to criticize the basic idea of free choice and democracy.[11]

Products do improve the quality of life

More is not always better. The quality of life can't be measured just in terms of quantities of material goods. But when we view products as the means to an end—rather than the end itself—they *do* make it possible to satisfy higher-level needs. Microwave ovens, for example, greatly reduced the amount of time and effort people must spend preparing meals—leaving them free to pursue other interests. And more dependable cars expanded people's geographic horizons—affecting where they can live and work and play.

Consumers ask for it, consumers pay for it

The monopolistic competition typical of our economy results from customer preferences—*not* manipulation of markets by business. Monopolistic competition may seem costly at times when we look at micro-level situations. But if the role of the marketing system is to serve consumers, then the cost of whatever services they demand cannot be considered too high. It's just the cost of serving consumers the way they want to be served.

Not all needs are met

Some critics argue that our macro-marketing system is flawed because it does not provide solutions to important problems, such as questions about how to help the homeless, the uneducated, dependent children, minorities who have suffered discrimination, the elderly poor, and the sick. Many of these people do live in dire circumstances. But is that the result of a market-directed system?

There is no doubt that many firms focus their effort on people who can pay for what they have to offer. But as the forces of competition drive down prices, more people are able to afford more of what they need. And the matching of supply and demand stimulates economic growth, creates jobs, and spreads income

Is it the responsibility of business to meet the needs of all people, including the homeless and others who have no money to spend?

among more people. In other words, a market-directed economy makes efficient use of resources. However, it can't guarantee that government aid programs are effective. It doesn't ensure that all voters and politicians agree on which problems should be solved first—or how taxes should be set and allocated. It can't eliminate the possibility of a child being ignored.

These are important societal issues. But they are not the result of a market-directed system. Citizen-consumers in a democratic society assign some responsibilities to business and some to government. Most people in business share the concern that government too often does not do an effective job in addressing these problems. Many firms are working to identify and contribute solutions. But ultimately, consumer-citizens vote in the ballot box for how to deal with these concerns—just as they vote with their dollars for which firms to support. As more managers in the public sector understand and apply marketing concepts, we should be able to do a better job meeting the needs of all people.

CHALLENGES FACING MARKETERS

We've said that our macro-marketing system does *not* cost too much—given the present objective of our economy. But we admit that the performance of many business firms leaves a lot to be desired. This presents a challenge to serious-minded students and marketers. What needs to be done—if anything?

We need better performance at the micro level

Some business executives seem to feel that they should be completely free in a market-directed economy. They don't understand that ours is a market-directed system—and that they must serve the needs of consumer-citizens. Instead, they focus on their own internal problems—and don't satisfy consumers very well. As Marketing Demo 22–1 shows, consumer groups often seek to influence other consumers' behavior.

We need better market-oriented planning

Many firms are still production-oriented. Some hardly plan at all, and others simply extend one year's plans into the next. Progressive firms are beginning to realize that this doesn't work in our fast-changing markets. Market-oriented strategy planning is becoming more important in many companies. Firms are paying more attention to changes in the market—including trends in the marketing environment—and how marketing strategies need to be adapted to consider these changes. Exhibit 22–1 lists some of the trends and changes we've discussed throughout this text.

We need continuous improvement

Good marketing strategy planning needs to focus on a specific target market and a marketing mix to meet its needs. The basic frameworks and ideas about how to do that haven't changed as much as the long list in Exhibit 22–1 seems to suggest. At the same time, thinking about all these changes highlights the fact that marketing is dynamic. Marketing managers must constantly evaluate their strategies to be sure they're not being left in the dust by competitors who see new and better ways of doing things.

It's crazy for a marketing manager to constantly change a strategy that's working well. But too many fail to see or plan for needed changes. They're afraid to do anything different and adhere to the idea that "If it ain't broke, don't fix it."

MARKETING DEMO 22–1
Fur Sales Caught in Slump: Antifur Militants Taking the Credit

---

Linda Ethier, a fur saleswoman at Eaton's, enjoyed rising commissions during the fur boom of the 80s. Things have changed. She's suffering through the "drastic" slide in sales in the past year or so.

"It upsets me as a salesperson," said Ms. Ethier, who has worked at Eaton's fur salon at the Toronto Eaton Centre for seven years. "This is affecting my livelihood. Plus, I love furs."

The $850 million fur industry is in the dumps these days, and the antifur militants—who have been particularly active in the past year—are taking credit for the decline.

The Fur Council of Canada, the official industry group, attributes the slump solely to the recession and a glut of pelts that resulted in plummeting prices and squeezed profit margins. Still, even Ms. Ethier acknowledged that the antifur forces are making inroads. "I'm sure they've killed a lot of it," Ms. Ethier said.

Those forces will be demonstrating in front of fur stores in 17 Canadian cities to mark Valentine's Day in advance, with "Have a Heart" marches, said Susan Hargreaves, an organizer of the Action Volunteers for Animals in Toronto.

Ms. Hargreaves and groups like hers have already celebrated the change at Hudson's Bay Co., the one-time giant in the fur field that announced it was getting out of the fur business on which its retail empire was founded. And she pointed to other furriers closing their doors, too, such as a Makos Furs Ltd. store in Toronto.

"It is wrong to cause suffering for this luxury market," said Ann Doncaster of the International Wildlife Coalition, who predicted the movement's next target will be the leather industry.

Source: Marina Strauss, "Fur Sales Caught in Slump," *The Globe and Mail*, February 9, 1991, pp. B1, 18.

But a firm can't always wait until a problem becomes completely obvious to do something about it. When customers move on and profits disappear, it may be too late to fix the problem. Marketing managers who take the lead in finding innovative new markets and approaches get a competitive advantage.

Most of the changes and trends summarized in Exhibit 22–1 are having a positive effect on how marketers serve society. Whether its because marketers are applying new technologies to solve old marketing problems or applying classic marketing concepts to new kinds of opportunities, consumers are better off. And this ongoing improvement is self-directing. As consumers shift their support to firms that do meet their needs, laggard businesses are forced to either improve or get out of the way.

We need to welcome international competition

Increasingly, marketing managers face global competition. Some managers hate that thought. Worldwide competition creates even more pressure on marketing managers to figure out what it takes to gain a competitive advantage, both at home and in foreign markets. But with the challenge comes opportunities. The forces of competition in and among market-directed economies will help speed the diffusion of marketing advances to consumers everywhere. As macromarketing systems improve worldwide, more consumers will have income to buy products—wherever in the world the products come from. Marketing Demo 22–2 describes one attempt to bring Third World products to consumers in Canada.

Marketers can't afford to bury their heads in the sand and hope that international competition will go away. Rather, they must realize that it is part of

Exhibit 22–1   Some Important Changes and Trends Affecting Marketing Strategy Planning

Communication Technologies
Computer-to-computer data exchange
Satellite communications
Fax machine transmissions
Cable television
Telemarketing
Cellular

Role of Computerization
Personal computers and laptops
Spreadsheet analysis
Computer networks
Checkout scanners
Bar codes for tracking inventory
Computer-to-computer ordering (EDI)

Marketing Research
Growth of marketing information systems
Decision support systems
Single source data
People meters
Use of scanner data
Easy-to-use statistical packages

Demographic Patterns
Aging of baby boomers
Slowdown in North American population growth
Growth of ethnic submarkets
Geographic shifts in population
Slower real income growth

Business and Organizational Customers
Closer buyer/seller relationships
Just-in-time inventory systems
More single-vendor sourcing

Product Area
More attention to innovation/new-product development
Faster new-product development
Computer-aided package/product design
Market-driven focus on research and development
More attention to quality and quality control
More attention to services
Advances in packaging
Extending established family brand names to
  new products

Channels and Logistics
More vertical market systems
Larger, more powerful retail chains
More conflict between producers/chains
More attention to physical distribution service
Better inventory control
Automated warehouses
Integrated distribution centres
More competition among transportation companies
Coordination of logistics in the channel

Channels and Logistics (*continued*)
Growing role of airfreight
Growth of mass-merchandising
Catalogue, TV retailing

Sales Promotion
Increased promotion to middlemen
Event sponsorships
Greater use of coupons
Stocking allowances

Personal Selling
Automated order taking
Use of portable computers
More specialization
  Major accounts
  Telemarketing
  Team selling

Mass Selling
More targeted mass media
  Specialty publications
  Cable, satellite TV
  Specialty media, especially in-store
Shorter TV commercials
Larger advertising agencies
Changing agency compensation
Growth of direct-response advertising
Shrinking percentage of total promotion budgets

Pricing
Value pricing
Less reliance on traditional markups by middlemen
Overuse of sales and deals on consumer products
Bigger differences in functional discounts
More attention to exchange rate effects
Focus on higher stockturn at lower margins

International Marketing
Collapse of communism worldwide
More international market development
New and different competitors—at home and abroad
Need to adjust to unfamiliar markets, cultures
Widely spread markets
Changing trading restrictions (unification of Europe, tariffs,
  quotas, etc.)
More attention to exporting by small firms
Growth of multinational corporations

General
Less regulation of business
More attention to marketing ethics
Shift of emphasis away from diversification
More attention to profitability, not just sales
Greater attention to competitive advantage
Implementation of total quality management
Greater attention to environmental issues

MARKETING DEMO 22–2   Social Justice in a Chocolate Bar

We cannot deny being consumers. All life must consume matter and energy. However, it is now undeniable that current patterns of consumption must change to save the planet and give humans a chance to live within balanced ecological systems. By examining ATOs, or Alternative Trading Organizations, we can consider the question of fair trade, the roles of multinational corporations, and ethical standards that may be applied to the complicated way we exchange resources in the global marketplace.

Canada's best-known ATO is Bridgehead, a wholly owned subsidiary of OXFAM Canada, whose objective is "to build a partnership between Canadian buyers and Third World artisans based on social and economic justice." From Bridgehead, as well as astonishingly beautiful artifacts, you can buy gourmet products including spices, nuts, coffee, wild rice, and now "the best chocolate in the world." Not only do these chocolate bars retail at a reasonable price and give 6,500 people decent work, they are just about the best product on the market. The sugar is grown free of chemicals and made from traditionally evaporated cane juice, retaining its minerals and vitamins. Bridgehead and other ATOs around the world help us to recognize the connection between the products we buy and the state of the world.

A number of characteristics distinguish ATOs from commercial importers. First, their goal is to benefit the poor, not maximize profits. Second, they want to educate consumers as well as sell to them. And third, they often work with producers commercial distributors shun.

ATOs are well aware of the obstacles they face in attempting to initiate a new world trading system. They have no control over world commodity pricing. They are criticized on ecological and health grounds for selling tea and coffee. They face the dilemma of importing food from countries going hungry. And they know their work reinforces dependency on foreign markets. ATOs distributing crafts know that when you put them in catalogues, you are contributing to the standardization of traditional art forms, as well as placing fierce physical demands on producers for a greedy northern market. They know about the use of environmentally threatened materials and that only the rich can afford some of their products.

Total sales of the global ATO movement came to about $75 million in 1987. This is only a tiny fraction of imports from the Third World, but the spin-off is not negligible. They are helping those most in need to better their situations. And when they buy, they force surrounding middlemen to increase their prices. ATO trade where farmers are forced into distant migrant labor gives them the extra income they need to avoid the horrors of the work camps.

Today, as they grow larger, ATOs find that to help more people, they must take on some of the characteristics of the business world they shun. But the mutual support among them is unheard of in traditional business circles. And they can depend on a kind of customer loyalty that brings people across town again and again because "I figure the least I can do is spend my money where it's doing some good."

A 1990 publication cites over 40 ATOs from Finland to New Zealand forming the International Federation for Alternative Trade, based in Holland. Paul Freundlich of Co-Op America, a mail-order organization, sums up the ATO potential in prophetic words, "By building an alternative, we are challenging the basic economic assumptions that presently regulate our economy and world trade. We're creating an alternative that is accountable to workers, to communities, to the environment. And if enough of us support these alternative structures, who knows? Maybe one day we won't have to call ourselves 'alternative' any more."

Source: Marjorie Stewart, "ATOs: A Way to Tackle the Juggernaut of Consumerism," *Teaching Our Common Future*, Spring 1993, pp. 3–5.

---

today's marketing environment—and they must do marketing strategy planning that rises to the challenge it poses.

May need more social responsibility

Good business managers put themselves in the consumer's position. A useful rule to follow might be: Do unto others as you would have others do unto you. In practice, this means developing satisfying marketing mixes for specific target

Socially responsible
marketing managers are
concerned about the
environmental impact
of their products.

markets. It may mean building in more quality or more safety. The consumer's long-run satisfaction should be considered, too. How will the product hold up in use? What about service guarantees? While trying to serve the needs of some target market, does the marketing strategy disregard the rights and needs of other consumers—or create problems that will be left for future generations?

Short-sighted, production-oriented approaches undoubtedly won't work in the future. Tougher competition—from companies at home and abroad—may force old-style production-oriented business managers to change their thinking—just to survive.

The environment is everyone's need

Marketers need to work harder and smarter at finding ways to satisfy consumer needs without sacrificing the current or future environment. All consumers need the environment—whether they realize it yet or not. We are only beginning to understand the consequences of the environmental damage that's already been done. Acid rain, depletion of the ozone layer, and toxic waste in water supplies—to mention but a few current environmental problems—have catastrophic effects. Many top executives now say that preserving and protecting the environment will be one of the major challenges—if not *the* major challenge—of business firms in the next decade.

In the past, most firms didn't pass on the cost of environmental damage to consumers in the prices that they paid. Pollution was a hidden and unmeasured

MARKETING DEMO 22–3
It Isn't Easy Being "Green" under Today's Rules

I n the early 1990s, Consumer and Corporate Affairs Canada issued its *Guiding Principles for Environmental Labeling and Advertising.* These guidelines do not establish environmental standards or definitions, nor do they provide solutions to complex scientific and technological issues relating to the environment. They simply aim to provide consumers with objective, credible, and truthful information. They also seek to help industry comply with existing federal legislation (such as the Competition Act and the Consumer Packaging and Labelling Act), which prohibit false and misleading representations and claims not based on adequate and proper tests, among other things.

The guidelines set out the following guiding principles:

- Industry is responsible for ensuring that any claims and/or representations are accurate and in compliance with the relevant legislation.

- Consumers are responsible, to the extent possible, for appropriately using information made available to them in labelling and advertising, thereby enhancing their role in the marketplace.

- Environmental claims and/or representations that are ambiguous, vague, incomplete, misleading, or irrelevant, or that cannot be substantiated through credible information and/or test methods, should not be used.

- Claims and/or representations should indicate whether they are related to the product or the packaging materials.

The guidelines also issued the following warnings:

- Claims of degradability should not be used for packaging materials.

- Claims of degradability may be used for products disposed of through the sewage system, provided that the by-products of degradation and the product in question do not contain ingredients that are known to be damaging to the environment or the sewage or treatment facility.

- In exceptional circumstances, claims of degradability may be considered for solid products that would not normally be destined for a landfill.

- If a claim of degradability is used, it should be accompanied by a statement indicating the degree of degradation and the conditions under which degradation will occur, or a recognized test method that was used to determine the degree of degradability.

While the guidelines are only voluntary and do not provide for specific penalties outside the context of existing federal legislation, it is the view of the federal government that this is only a first step in addressing the issue.

Clarifications and additions to the guidelines are in the works, and it is expected that revised guidelines will be released. Green marketers would be wise to keep informed of the way the guidelines develop.

Source: Bill Hearn, "It Isn't Easy Being 'Green' under Today's Rules," *Marketing,* June 22, 1992, p. 12.

cost for most companies. That is changing rapidly. Firms are already paying billions of dollar to correct problems, including problems created years ago. The government isn't accepting the excuse that "nobody knew it was a big problem." Consider yourself warned: Businesspeople who fail to anticipate an increasing public backlash on this issue put their careers and businesses at risk! Meeting environmental concerns won't be easy. Marketing Demo 22–3 highlights some of the guidelines a firm wishing to be "green" should meet.

May need attention to consumer privacy

While focusing on consumers' needs, marketers also must be sensitive to other consumer concerns. Today, sophisticated marketing research methods and new technologies make it easier to abuse consumers' rights to privacy. For example, credit card records, which reveal much about consumers' purchases and private lives, are routinely computerized and sold to anybody who pays for the list.

Most consumers don't realize how much data about their personal lives—some of it incorrect but treated as fact—is collected and available. A simple computer billing error may land consumers on a computer bad-credit list—without their knowledge. Marketing managers should use technology responsibly to improve the quality of life—not disrupt it.

Need to rethink some present laws

One of the advantages of a market-directed economic system is that it operates automatically. But in our version of this system, consumer-citizens provide certain constraints (laws), which can be modified at any time. Managers who ignore consumer attitudes must realize that their actions may cause new restraints.

Before piling on too many new rules, however, we should review the ones we have. Some of them may need to be changed—and others may need to be enforced more carefully. Antitrust laws, for example, are often applied to protect competitors from each other—when they were really intended to encourage competition.

On the other hand, Canadian antitrust laws were originally developed with the idea that all firms competing in a market would be on a level playing field. That is no longer always true. For example, in many markets, individual Canadian firms compete with foreign firms whose governments urge them to cooperate with each other. Such foreign firms don't see each other as competitors; rather, they see Canadian firms—as a group—as the competitors.

Laws should affect top managers

Strict enforcement of present laws could have far-reaching results if more price-fixers, fraudulent or deceptive advertisers, and others who violate existing laws—thus affecting the performance of the macro-marketing system—were sent to jail or given heavy fines. A quick change in attitudes might occur if unethical top managers—those who plan strategy—were prosecuted, instead of the salespeople or advertisers expected to deliver on weak or undifferentiated strategies.

In other words, if the government made it clear that it was serious about improving the performance of our economic system, much could be achieved within the present system—*without* adding new constraints.

Laws merely define minimal ethical standards

As we discussed ethical issues in marketing throughout the text, we emphasized that a marketing manager doesn't face an ethical dilemma about complying with laws and regulations. Whether a marketer is operating in his or her own country or in a foreign nation, the legal environment sets the *minimal* standards of ethical behavior as defined by a society. In addition, the American Marketing Association's code of ethics (Exhibit 2–4) provides a checklist of basic guidelines that a marketing manager should observe. But marketing managers constantly face ethical issues where there are no clearly defined answers. Every marketing manager should be aware of this and make a personal commitment to carefully evaluate the ethical consequences of marketing strategy decisions.

On the other hand, our marketing system is designed to encourage firms to compete aggressively as long as they do it in a fair way. New and better ways of serving customers and society give a firm a competitive advantage—at least for some period of time. This is how we move forward as a society. Innovative new marketing strategies *do* sometimes cause problems for those who have a vested interest in the old ways. Some people try to portray anything that disrupts their own personal interest as unethical. But protecting the status quo is not by itself an appropriate ethical standard. To the contrary, our society's most basic ethical charge to marketers is to find new and better ways to serve society's needs.

Need socially responsible consumers

We've stressed that marketers should act responsibly—but consumers have responsibilities too.[12] Some consumers abuse policies about returning goods, change price tags in self-service stores, and expect attractive surroundings and courteous, well-trained sales and service people—*and* want discount prices. Some are downright abusive to salespeople. Others think nothing of ripping off businesses because "they're rich." Shoplifting is a major problem for most retailers—and honest consumers pay for the cost of shoplifting in higher prices.

Canadians tend to perform their dual role of consumer-citizens with a split personality. We often behave one way as consumers—then take the opposite position at the ballot box. For example, we cover our beaches and parks with garbage and litter, while urging our legislators to take stiff action to curb pollution. We protest sex and violence in the media—and then flock to see the latest R- or X-rated movies. Parents complain about advertising aimed at children—then use TV as a Saturday morning babysitter.

Consumers share the responsibility for preserving an effective macro-marketing system. And they should take this responsibility seriously.

Let's face it, there's a wealth of information already available to aid consumer decision making. The consumerism movement has encouraged nutritional labelling, open dating, unit pricing, truth-in-lending, plain-language contracts and warranties, and so on. Yet the majority of consumers continue to ignore most of this information.

HOW FAR SHOULD THE MARKETING CONCEPT GO?

Our macro-marketing system is built on the assumption that we are trying to satisfy consumers. But how far should the marketing concept be allowed to go?

Should marketing managers limit consumers' freedom of choice?

Achieving a better macro-marketing system is certainly a desirable objective. But what part should a marketer play in deciding what products to offer?

This is extremely important, because some marketing managers—especially those in large corporations—can have an impact far larger than they do in their roles as consumer-citizens. For example, should they refuse to produce hazardous products—like skis or motorcycles—even though such products are in strong demand? Should they install safety devices that increase costs and customers don't want?

These are difficult questions to answer. Some things marketing managers do clearly benefit both the firm and consumers because they lower costs and/or improve consumers' options. But other choices may actually reduce consumer choice and conflict with a desire to improve the effectiveness of our macro-marketing system.

Consumer-citizens should vote on the changes

It seems fair to suggest, therefore, that marketing managers should be expected to improve and expand the range of goods and services they make available to consumers—always trying to better satisfy their needs and preferences. This is the job we've assigned to business.

If pursuing this objective makes excessive demands on scarce resources—or has an unacceptable ecological effect—then consumer-citizens have the responsibility to vote for laws restricting individual firms that are trying to satisfy consumers' needs. This is the role that we, as consumers, have assigned to the government—to ensure that the macro-marketing system works effectively.

It is important to recognize that some *seemingly minor* modifications in our present system *might* result in very big, unintended problems. Allowing some government agency to prohibit the sale of products for seemingly good reasons could lead to major changes we never expected. (Bicycles, for example, are a very hazardous consumer product. Should they continue to be sold?) Clearly, such government actions could seriously reduce consumers' present rights to freedom of choice—including "bad" choices.[13]

We, as consumer-citizens, should be careful to distinguish between proposed changes designed simply to modify our system and those designed to change it—perhaps drastically. In either case, we should have the opportunity to make the decision (through elected representatives). This decision should not be left in the hands of a few well-placed managers or government planners.

Marketing people may be even more necessary in the future

Regardless of the changes consumer-citizens may enact, we will need some kind of a marketing system in the future. Further, if satisfying more subtle needs—such as for the good life—becomes our objective, it could be even more important to have market-oriented firms. We may have to define not only an individual's needs, but also society's needs—perhaps for a better neighborhood or more enriching social experiences, and so on. As we go beyond tangible physical goods into more sophisticated need-satisfying blends of goods and services, the trial-and-error approach of the typical production-oriented manager will become even less acceptable.

CONCLUSION

Macro-marketing does *not* cost too much. Consumers have assigned business the role of satisfying their needs. Customers find it satisfactory—and even desirable—to permit businesses to cater to them and even to stimulate wants. As long as consumers are satisfied, macro-marketing will not cost too much—and business firms will be permitted to continue as profit-making entities.

But business exists at the consumer's discretion. It's mainly by satisfying the consumer that a particular firm—and our economic system—can justify its existence and hope to keep operating.

In carrying out this role—granted by consumers—business firms are not always as effective as they could be. Many business managers don't understand the marketing concept or the role that marketing plays in our way of life. They seem to feel that business has a God-given right to operate as it chooses. And they proceed in their typical production-oriented ways. Further, many managers have had little or no training in business management—and are not as competent as they should be. Others fail to adjust to the changes taking place around them. And a few dishonest or unethical managers can do a great deal of damage before consumer-citizens take steps to stop them. As a result, micro-marketing often *does* cost too much. But the situation is improving. More business training is now available, and more competent people are being attracted to marketing and business generally. Clearly, *you* have a role to play in improving marketing activities in the future.

Marketing has new challenges to face in the future. *Our* consumers may have to settle for a lower standard of living. Resource shortages, slower population growth, and a larger number of elderly—with a small proportion of the population in the work force—may all combine to reduce our income growth. This may force consumers to shift their consumption patterns—and politicians to change some of the rules governing business. Even our present market-directed system may be threatened.

To keep our system working effectively, individual firms should implement the marketing concept in a more efficient, ethical, and socially responsible way. At the same time, we—as consumers—should consume goods and services in an intelligent and socially responsible way. Further, we have the responsibility to vote and ensure that we get the kind of macro-marketing system we want. What kind do you want? What should you do to ensure that fellow consumer-citizens will vote for your system? Is your system likely to satisfy you as well as another macro-marketing system? You don't have to answer these questions right now—but your answers will affect the future you'll live in and how satisfied you'll be.

QUESTIONS AND PROBLEMS

1. Explain why marketing must be evaluated at two levels. What criteria should be used to evaluate each level of marketing? Defend your answer. Explain why your criteria are better than alternative criteria.

2. Discuss the merits of various economic system objectives. Is the objective of the North American economic system sensible? Could it achieve more consumer satisfaction if sociologists—or public officials—determined how to satisfy the needs of lower-income or less-educated consumers? If so, what education or income level should be required before an individual is granted free choice?

3. Should the objective of our economy be maximum efficiency? If your answer is yes, efficiency in what? If not, what should the objective be?

4. Discuss the conflict of interests among production, finance, accounting, and marketing executives. How does this conflict affect the operation of an individual firm? The economic system? Why does this conflict exist?

5. Why does adoption of the marketing concept encourage a firm to operate more efficiently? Be specific about the impact of the marketing concept on the various departments of a firm.

6. In the short run, competition sometimes leads to inefficiency in the operation of our economic system. Many people argue for monopoly in order to eliminate this inefficiency. Discuss this solution.

7. How would officially granted monopolies affect the operation of our economic system? Consider the effect on allocation of resources, the level of income and employment, and the distribution of income. Is the effect any different if a firm obtains monopoly by winning out in a competitive market?

8. Comment on the following statement: "Ultimately, the high cost of marketing is due only to consumers."

9. How far should the marketing concept go? How should we decide this issue?

10. Should marketing managers, or business managers in general, refrain from producing profitable products that some target customers want but that may not be in their long-run interest? Should firms be expected to produce "good" but less profitable products? What if such products break even? What if they are unprofitable but the company makes other profitable products—so on balance it still makes some

profit? What criteria are you using for each of your answers?

11. Should a marketing manager or a business refuse to produce an "energy-gobbling" appliance that some consumers are demanding? Should a firm install an expensive safety device that will increase costs but that customers don't want? Are the same principles involved in both these questions? Explain.

12. Discuss how one or more of the trends or changes shown in Exhibit 22–1 is affecting marketing strategy planning for a specific firm that serves the market where you live.

13. Discuss how slower economic growth or no economic growth would affect your university community—in particular, its marketing institutions.

SUGGESTED CASES

6. Boutique Vison
12. A Chance to Be Self-Employed

37. Health and Welfare Canada

Career Planning in Marketing

When You Finish This Appendix, You Should

❶
Know that there is a job—or a career—for you in marketing.

❷
Know that marketing jobs can be rewarding, pay well, and offer opportunities for growth.

❸
Understand the difference between "people-oriented" and "thing-oriented" jobs.

❹
Know about the many marketing jobs you can choose from.

One of the hardest jobs most college students face is the choice of a career. Of course, we can't make this decision for you. You must be the judge of your own objectives, interests, and abilities. Only you can decide what career *you* should pursue. However, you owe it to yourself to at least consider the possibility of a career in marketing.

THERE'S A PLACE IN MARKETING FOR YOU

We're happy to tell you that many opportunities are available in marketing. There's a place in marketing for everyone—from a service provider in a fast-food restaurant to a vice president of marketing in a large consumer products company such as Procter & Gamble or General Foods. The opportunities range widely—so it will help to be more specific. In the following pages, we'll discuss (1) the typical pay for different marketing jobs, (2) setting your own objectives and evaluating your interests and abilities, and (3) the kinds of jobs available in marketing.

MARKETING JOBS CAN PAY WELL

There are many interesting and challenging jobs for those with marketing training. Fortunately, marketing jobs open to college-level students do pay well! At the time this went to press, marketing undergraduates were being offered starting

Exhibit E–1   Main Career Emphasis of Corporate Chief Executive Officers*

	Percent
Marketing, distribution	27.9
Financial	25.3
Production, operations	18.6
Legal	13.6
Engineering, R&D	7.4
General management	5.3
Other	3.8

*Based on a survey of the chief executive officers of the United States' 500 largest industrial corporations and 300 nonindustrial corporations (including commercial banks, life insurance firms, retailers, transportation companies, utilities, and diversified financial enterprises).

salaries ranging from $18,000 to $36,000 a year. Of course, these figures are extremes. Starting salaries can vary considerably—depending on your background, experience, and location. But many jobs are in the $22,000–$26,000 range.

Starting salaries in marketing compare favorably with many other fields. They are lower than those in such fields as computer science and engineering, where college graduates are currently in very high demand. But there is even better opportunity for personal growth, variety, and income in many marketing positions. *The American Almanac of Jobs and Salaries* ranks the median income of marketers number 10 in a list of 125 professions. Marketing also supplies about 50 percent of the people who achieve senior management ranks.

How far and fast your career and income rise above the starting level, however, depends on many factors—including your willingness to work, how well you get along with people, and your individual abilities. But most of all, it depends on *getting results*—individually and through other people. And this is where many marketing jobs offer the newcomer great opportunities. It's possible to show initiative, ability, and judgment in marketing jobs. And some young people move up very rapidly in marketing. Some even end up at the top in large companies—or as owners of their own businesses.

Marketing is often the route to the top

Marketing is where the action is! In the final analysis, a firm's success or failure depends on the effectiveness of its marketing program. This doesn't mean the other functional areas aren't important. It merely reflects the fact that a firm won't have much need for accountants, finance people, production managers, and so on if it can't successfully sell its products.

Because marketing is so vital to a firm's survival, many companies look for people with training and experience in marketing when filling key executive positions. A survey of the largest US corporations shows that the greatest proportion of chief executive officers have backgrounds in marketing and distribution. See Exhibit E–1.

Exhibit E–2   Organizing Your Own Personal Marketing Strategy Planning

Personal analysis	Environment analysis
• Set broad long-run objectives • Evaluate personal strengths and weaknesses • Set preliminary timetables	• Identify current opportunities • Examine trends which may affect opportunities • Evaluate business practices

Develop objectives
• Long-run
• Short-run

Develop your marketing plan
• Identify likely opportunities
• Plan your product
• Plan your promotion

Implement your marketing plan

DEVELOP YOUR OWN PERSONAL MARKETING STRATEGY

Now that you know there are many opportunities in marketing, your problem is matching the opportunities to your own personal objectives and strengths. Basically, the problem is a marketing problem: developing a marketing strategy to sell a product—yourself—to potential employers. Just as in planning strategies for products, developing your own strategy takes careful thought. Exhibit E–2 shows how you can organize your own strategy planning. This exhibit shows that you should evaluate yourself first—a personal analysis—and then analyze the environment for opportunities. This will help you sharpen your own long- and short-run objectives, which will lead to developing a strategy. And, finally, you should start implementing your own personal marketing strategy. These ideas are explained more fully below.

CONDUCT YOUR OWN PERSONAL ANALYSIS

You are the Product you are going to include in your own marketing plan. So first you have to decide what your long-run objectives are—what you want to do, how hard you want to work, and how quickly you want to reach your objectives. Be honest with yourself—or you will eventually face frustration. Evaluate your own personal strengths and weaknesses—and decide what factors may become the key to your success. Finally, as part of your personal analysis, set some preliminary timetables to guide your strategy planning and implementation efforts. Let's spell this out in detail.

Set broad long-run objectives

Strategy planning requires much trial-and-error decision making. But at the very beginning, you should make some tentative decisions about your own objectives—what you want out of a job and out of life. At the very least, you should decide whether you are just looking for a job—or whether you want to build a career. Beyond this, do you want the position to be personally satisfying—or is the financial return enough? And just how much financial return do you need? Some people work only to support themselves and their leisure-time activities. Others work to support themselves and their families. These people seek only financial rewards from a job. They try to find job opportunities that provide adequate financial returns but aren't too demanding of their time or effort.

Other people look first for satisfaction in their job—and they seek opportunities for career advancement. Financial rewards may be important, too, but these are used only as measures of success. In the extreme, the career-oriented individual may be willing to sacrifice a lot—including leisure and social activities—to achieve success in a career.

Once you've tentatively decided these matters, you can get more serious about whether you should seek a job—or a career—in marketing. If you decide to pursue a career, you should set your broad long-run objectives to achieve it. For example, one long-run objective might be to pursue a career in marketing management (or marketing research). This might require more academic training than you planned—as well as a different kind of training. If your objective is to get a job that pays well, on the other hand, this calls for a different kind of training and different kinds of job experiences before completing your academic work.

What kind of a job is right for you?

Because of the great variety of marketing jobs, it's hard to generalize about what aptitudes you should have to pursue a career in marketing. Different jobs

---

Large companies like Kraft and Colgate-Palmolive regularly recruit college graduates in marketing and other fields.

attract people with various interests and abilities. We'll give you some guidelines about what kinds of interests and abilities marketers should have. However, if you're completely lost about your own interest and abilities, see your campus career counselor and take some vocational aptitude and interest tests. These tests will help you to compare yourself with people who are now working in various career positions. They will *not* tell you what you should do, but they can help—especially in eliminating possibilities you're less interested in and/or less able to do well in.

Are you "people-oriented" or "thing-oriented"?

One of the first things you need to decide is whether you are basically "people-oriented" or "thing-oriented." This is a very important decision. A people-oriented person might be very unhappy in an inventory management job, for example, while a thing-oriented person might be miserable in a personal selling or retail management job that involves a lot of customer contact.

Marketing has both people-oriented and thing-oriented jobs. People-oriented jobs are primarily in the promotion area—where company representatives must make contact with potential customers. This may be direct personal selling or customer service activities—for example, in technical service or installation and repair. Thing-oriented jobs focus more on creative activities and analyzing data—as in advertising and marketing research—or on organizing and scheduling work—as in operating warehouses, transportation agencies, or the back-end of retailers.

People-oriented jobs tend to pay more, in part because such jobs are more likely to affect sales—the lifeblood of any business. Thing-oriented jobs, on the other hand, are often seen as cost generators rather than sales generators. Taking a big view of the whole company's operations, the thing-oriented jobs are certainly necessary—but without sales, no one is needed to do them.

Thing-oriented jobs are usually done at a company's facilities. Further, especially in lower-level jobs, the amount of work to be done—and even the nature of the work—may be spelled out quite clearly. The time it takes to design questionnaires and tabulate results, for example, can be estimated with reasonable accuracy. Similarly, running a warehouse, totaling inventories, scheduling outgoing shipments, and so on are more like production operations. It's fairly easy to measure an employee's effectiveness and productivity in a thing-oriented job. At least, time spent can be used to measure an employee's contribution.

A sales rep, on the other hand, might spend all weekend thinking and planning how to make a half-hour sales presentation on Monday. For what should the sales rep be compensated—the half-hour presentation, all of the planning and thinking that went into it, or the results? Typically, sales reps are rewarded for their sales results—and this helps account for the sometimes extremely high salaries paid to effective order getters. At the same time, some people-oriented jobs can be routinized and are lower paid. For example, salesclerks in some retail stores are paid at or near the minimum wage.

Managers needed for both kinds of jobs

Here, we have oversimplified deliberately to emphasize the differences among types of jobs. Actually, of course, there are many variations between the two extremes. Some sales reps must do a great deal of analytical work before they make a presentation. Similarly, some marketing researchers must be extremely people-sensitive to get potential customers to reveal their true feelings. But the division is still useful because it focuses on the primary emphasis in different kinds of jobs.

Career opportunities can be found—at home and abroad.

Managers are needed for the people in both kinds of jobs. Managing others requires a blend of both people and analytical skills—but people skills may be the more important of the two. Therefore, people-oriented persons are often promoted into managerial positions.

What will differentiate your Product?

After deciding whether you're generally people-oriented or thing-oriented, you're ready for the next step—trying to identify your specific strengths (to be built on) and weaknesses (to be avoided or remedied). It is important to be as specific as possible so you can develop a better marketing plan. For example, if you decide you are more people-oriented, are you more skilled in verbal *or* written communication? Or if you are more thing-oriented, what specific analytical or technical skills do you have? Are you good at working with numbers, solving complex problems, or coming to the root of a problem? Other possible strengths include past experience (career-related or otherwise), academic performance, an outgoing personality, enthusiasm, drive, motivation, and so on.

Your plan should build on your strengths. An employer will be hiring you to do something—so promote yourself as someone who is able to do something *well*. In other words, find your competitive advantage in your unique strengths—and then communicate these unique things about *you* and what you can do.

While trying to identify strengths, you also must realize that you may have some important weaknesses—depending on your objectives. If you are seeking a career that requires technical skills, for example, then you need to get these skills.

Or if you are seeking a career that requires independence and self-confidence, then you should try to develop these characteristics in yourself—or change your objectives.

Set some timetables

At this point in your strategy planning process, set some timetables to organize your thinking and the rest of your planning. You need to make some decisions at this point to be sure you see where you're going. You might simply focus on getting your first job, or you might decide to work on two marketing plans: (1) a short-run plan to get your first job and (2) a longer-run plan—perhaps a five-year plan—to show how you're going to accomplish your long-run objectives. People who are basically job-oriented may get away with only a short-run plan—just drifting from one opportunity to another as their own objectives and opportunities change. But those interested in careers need a longer-run plan. Otherwise, they may find themselves pursuing attractive first job opportunities that satisfy short-run objectives—but quickly leave them frustrated when they realize that they can't achieve their long-run objectives without additional training or other experiences.

ENVIRONMENT ANALYSIS

Strategy planning is a matching process. For your own strategy planning, this means matching yourself to career opportunities. So let's look at opportunities available in the marketing environment.

Identifying current
opportunities in
marketing

Because of the wide range of opportunities in marketing, it's helpful to narrow your possibilities. After deciding on your own objectives, strengths, and weaknesses, think about where in the marketing system you might like to work. Would you like to work for manufacturers, or wholesalers, or retailers? Or does it really matter? Do you want to be involved with consumer products or business products? By analyzing your feelings about these possibilities, you can begin to zero in on the kind of job and the functional area that might interest you most.

One simple way to get a better idea of the kinds of jobs available in marketing is to review the chapters of this text—this time with an eye for job opportunities rather than new concepts. The following paragraphs contain brief descriptions of job areas that marketing graduates are often interested in, with references to specific chapters in the text. Some, as noted below, offer good starting opportunities, while others do not. While reading these paragraphs, keep your own objectives, interests, and strengths in mind.

Marketing manager (Chapter 2)

This is usually not an entry-level job, although aggressive students may move quickly into this role in smaller companies.

Marketing research opportunities (Chapter 5)

There are entry-level opportunities at all levels in the channel (but especially in large firms where more formal marketing research is done) and in advertising agencies and marketing research firms. Quantitative and behavioral science skills are extremely important in marketing research, so many firms prefer to hire statistics or psychology graduates rather than business graduates. But there still are many opportunities in marketing research for marketing graduates. A recent graduate might begin in a training program—conducting interviews or summarizing open-ended answers from questionnaires—before being promoted to assistant project manager and subsequent management positions.

Customer or market analyst (Chapters 3 and 5)

Opportunities as consumer analysts and market analysts are commonly found in large companies, marketing research organizations, and advertising agencies. Beginners start in thing-oriented jobs until their judgment and people-oriented skills are tested. The job may involve collecting or analyzing secondary data or preparation of reports and plans. Because knowledge of statistics, computer software, and/or the behavioral sciences is very important, marketing graduates often find themselves competing with majors in fields such as psychology, sociology, statistics, and computer science. Graduates who have courses in marketing *and* one or more of these areas may have the best opportunities.

Purchasing agent/buyer (Chapter 8)

Entry-level opportunities are commonly found in large companies. Beginners start as trainees or assistant buyers under the supervision of experienced buyers. That's good preparation for a promotion to more responsibility.

Product planner (Chapter 10)

This is usually not an entry-level position. Instead, people with experience on the technical side of the business and/or in sales might be moved into new-product development as they demonstrate judgment and analytical skills.

Product/brand manager (Chapters 9 and 10)

Many multiproduct firms have brand or product managers handling individual products—in effect, managing each product as a separate business. Some firms hire marketing graduates as assistant brand or product managers, although typically, only MBAs are considered. Most firms prefer that recent college graduates spend some time in the field doing sales work before moving into brand or product management positions.

Packaging specialists (Chapter 9)

Packaging manufacturers tend to hire and train interested people from various backgrounds—there is little formal academic training in packaging. There are many sales opportunities in this field—and with training, interested people can become specialists fairly quickly in this growing area.

Distribution channel management (Chapter 11)

This work is typically handled or directed by sales managers—and therefore is not an entry-level position.

Physical distribution opportunities (Chapter 12)

There are many sales opportunities with physical distribution specialists—but there are also many thing-oriented jobs involving traffic management, warehousing, and materials handling. Here, training in accounting, finance, and quantitative methods could be very useful. These kinds of jobs are available at all levels in the channels of distribution.

Retailing opportunities (Chapter 13)

Most entry-level marketing positions in retailing involve some kind of sales work. Retailing positions tend to offer lower-than-average starting salaries—but they often provide opportunities for very rapid advancement. Most retailers require new employees to have some selling experience before managing others—or buying. A typical marketing graduate can expect to do some sales work and manage one or several departments before advancing to a store management position—or to a staff position that might involve buying, advertising, marketing research, and so on.

Wholesaling opportunities (Chapter 14)

Entry-level jobs with merchant wholesalers typically fall into one of two categories. The first is in the logistics area—working with transportation management, inventory control, distribution customer service, and related activities. The other category usually involves personal selling and customer support. Agent wholesalers typically focus on selling, and entry-level jobs often start out with order-taking responsibilities that grow into order-getting responsibilities.

Sales promotion opportunities (Chapter 15)

There are not many entry-level positions in this area. Creativity and judgment are required, and it is difficult for an inexperienced person to demonstrate these skills. A beginner would probably move from sales or advertising jobs into sales promotion.

Personal sales opportunities (Chapter 16)

Most of the job opportunities—especially entry-level jobs—are in personal selling. This might be order getting, order taking, or missionary selling. Many students are reluctant to get into personal selling—but this field offers benefits that are hard to match in any other field. These include the opportunity to earn extremely high salaries and commissions quickly, a chance to develop your self-confidence and resourcefulness, an opportunity to work with minimal supervision—almost to the point of being your own boss—and a chance to acquire product and customer knowledge that many firms consider necessary for a successful career in product/brand management, sales management, and marketing management. Many salespeople spend their entire careers in selling—preferring the freedom and earning potential that go with a sales job over the headaches and sometimes lower salaries of sales management positions.

Advertising opportunities (Chapter 17)

Job opportunities are varied in this area—and highly competitive. And because the ability to communicate and knowledge of the behavioral sciences are important, marketing graduates often find themselves competing with majors from fields such as English, journalism, psychology, and sociology. There are thing-oriented jobs such as copywriting, media buying, art, and so on. Competition for these jobs is very competitive—and they go to people with a track record. So the entry-level positions are as assistant to a copywriter, media buyer, or art director. There are also people-oriented positions involving work with clients—which are probably of more interest to marketing graduates. This is a glamorous but small and extremely competitive industry where young people can rise very rapidly—but they can also be as easily displaced by new bright young people. Entry-level salaries in advertising are typically low. There are sometimes good opportunities to get started in advertising with a retail chain that prepares its advertising internally. Another way to get more experience with advertising is to take a sales job with one of the media. Selling advertising space in a newspaper or for a magazine may not seem as glamorous as developing TV ads, but media salespeople help their customers solve promotion problems—and get experience dealing with both the business and creative sides of advertising.

Pricing opportunities (Chapters 18 and 19)

Pricing is generally handled by experienced executives, so there are no entry-level opportunities here. However, in a few large companies there are opportunities for marketing graduates who have quantitative skills as pricing analysts. These people work as assistants to higher-level executives and collect and analyze information about competitors' prices and costs as well as the firm's own costs. The route to these jobs is usually through experience in marketing research or product management.

Credit management opportunities

Specialists in credit have a continuing need for employees who are interested in evaluating customers' credit ratings and ensuring that money gets collected. Both people skills and thing skills can be useful here. Entry positions normally involve a training program—and then working under the supervision of others until your judgment and abilities are tested.

International marketing opportunities

Many marketing students are intrigued with the adventure and foreign travel promised by careers in international marketing. Some firms hire recent college graduates for positions in international marketing, but more often these positions go to MBA graduates. However, that is changing as more and more firms are pursuing international markets. It's an advantage in seeking an international marketing job to know a second language and to know about the culture of the countries where you would like to work. Your college may have courses that would help in these areas. Graduates aiming for a career in international marketing usually must spend time mastering the firm's domestic marketing operations before being sent abroad. So a good way to start is to focus on firms that are already involved in international marketing or planning to move in that direction soon.

Customer relations/consumer affairs opportunities (Chapters 16 and 22)

Most firms are becoming more concerned about their relations with customers and the general public. Employees in this kind of work, however, usually have held various positions with the firm before doing customer relations.

Study trends that may affect your opportunities

A strategy planner should always be evaluating the future because it's easier to go along with trends than to buck them. This means you should watch for political, technical, or economic changes that might open—or close—career opportunities.

If you can spot a trend early, you may be able to prepare yourself to take advantage of it as part of your long-run strategy planning. Other trends might mean you should avoid certain career options. For example, rapid technological changes in computers and communications are likely to lead to major changes in retailing and advertising—as well as in personal selling. Cable television, telephone selling, and direct-mail selling may reduce the need for routine order takers—while increasing the need for higher-level order getters. More targeted and imaginative sales presentations for delivery by mail, phone, or TV screen may be needed. The retailers who survive may need a better understanding of their target markets. And they may need to be supported by wholesalers and manufacturers who can plan targeted promotions that make economic sense. This will require a better understanding of the production and physical distribution side of business—as well as the financial side. And this means better training in accounting, finance, inventory control, and so on. So plan your personal strategy with such trends in mind.

Evaluate business practices

Finally, you need to know how businesses really operate—and the kind of training required for various jobs. We've already seen that there are many opportunities in marketing—but not all jobs are open to everyone, and not all jobs are entry-level jobs. Positions such as marketing manager, brand manager, and sales manager are higher rungs on the marketing career ladder. They become available only when you have a few years of experience and have shown leadership and judgment. Some positions require more education than others. So take a hard look at your long-run objectives—and then see what degree you may need for the kinds of opportunities you might like.

Considerable demand exists for those who can write effective advertising.

The Financial Post

Copywriter

The Financial Post Promotion Department is currently seeking a full-time Copywriter to create promotional material and advertising campaigns for the newspaper and the Company's various divisions.

Day-to-day responsibilities will include writing print, radio and television advertisements, brochures, sales letters, news releases and promotional packages.

The successful candidate will have a strong command of the English language with a demonstrated ability to write creative, clear and convincing copy.

Experience in advertising, proficiency with Macintosh, as well as knowledge of financial markets and business would be definite assets.

All qualified applicants are invited to write in confidence to:

Patty Lou Andrews
Director of Communications
The Financial Post
333 King Street East
Toronto, Ontario
M5A 4N2

DEVELOP OBJECTIVES

Once you've done a personal analysis and environment analysis—identifying your personal interests, your strengths and weaknesses, and the opportunities in the environment—define your short-run and long-run objectives more specifically.

Develop long-run objectives

Your long-run objectives should clearly state what you want to do—and what you will do for potential employers. You might be as specific as indicating the exact career area you want to pursue over the next 5 to 10 years. For example, your long-run objective might be to apply a set of marketing research and marketing management tools to the food manufacturing industry—with the objective of becoming director of marketing research in a small food manufacturing company.

Your long-run objectives should be realistic and attainable. They should be objectives you have thought about and for which you think you have the necessary skills (or the capabilities to develop those skills) as well as the motivation to reach the objectives.

Develop short-run objectives

To achieve your long-run objective(s), you should develop one or more short-run objectives. These should spell out what you need to reach your long-run objective(s). For example, you might need to develop a variety of marketing research skills *and* marketing management skills—because both are needed to

SALES PROMOTION MANAGER

oronto Life has an immediate opening for a Sales Promotion Manager who will be responsible for developing and executing all promotional activities related to advertising sales, including innovative promotional concepts for clients, sales literature, consumer shows and client entertainment events.

You are a master of grace under pressure, able to juggle a million things and keep smiling. You are a creative thinker with strong interpersonal skills. You are detail oriented and able to work to tight deadlines. And you have a proven track record in promotions with copywriting experience (three-plus years).

If you want to make your mark in this challenging, creative and entrepreneurial environment, please forward your résumé to:

Brian Stendel
59 Front Street East
Toronto, Ontario M5E 1B3
Fax: 861-1169

reach the longer-run objective. Or you might need an entry-level position in marketing research for a large food manufacturer—to gain experience and background. An even shorter-run objective might be to take the academic courses necessary to get that desired entry-level job. In this example, you would probably need a minimum of an undergraduate degree in marketing—with an emphasis on marketing research. (Note that, given the longer-run objective of managerial responsibility, a business degree would probably be better than a degree in statistics or psychology.)

DEVELOP YOUR MARKETING PLAN

Now that you've developed your objectives, move on to developing your own personal marketing plan. This means zeroing in on likely opportunities and developing a specific marketing strategy for these opportunities. Let's talk about that now.

Identify likely opportunities

An important step in strategy planning is identifying potentially attractive opportunities. Depending on where you are in your academic training, this can vary all the way from preliminary exploration to making detailed lists of companies offering the kinds of jobs that interest you. If you're just getting started, talk to your school's career counselors and placement officers about the kinds of jobs being offered to your school's graduates. Your marketing instructors can help you be more realistic about ways you can match your training, abilities, and interests to job opportunities. Also, it helps to read business publications such as *The Globe and Mail, Fortune, The Financial Post,* and *Advertising Age.* If you're interested in opportunities in a particular industry, check at your library to see if there are trade publications that can bring you up to speed on the marketing issues in that area. Don't overlook the business sections of your local newspapers to keep in touch with marketing developments in your area. And take advantage of any opportunity to talk with marketers directly. Ask them what they're doing—and what satisfactions they find in their jobs. Also, if your college has a marketing club, join it and participate actively in the club's programs. It will help you meet marketers and students with serious interest in the field. Some may have had interesting job experiences and can provide you with leads on part-time jobs or exciting career opportunities.

If you're far along in your present academic training, list companies that you know something about or are willing to investigate—trying to match your skills and interests with possible opportunities. Narrow your list to a few companies you might like to work for.

If you have trouble narrowing down to specific companies, make a list of your personal interest areas—sports, travel, reading, music, or whatever. Think about the companies that compete in markets related to these interests. Often, your own knowledge about these areas—and interest in them—can give you a competitive advantage in getting a job. This helps you focus on companies that serve needs you think are important or interesting.

Then do some research on these companies. Find out how they're organized, their product lines, and their overall strategies. Try to get clear job descriptions for the kinds of positions you're seeking. Match these job descriptions against your understanding of these jobs and your objectives. Jobs with similar titles may offer very different opportunities. By researching job positions and companies in depth, you should begin to have a feel for where you would be comfortable as an employee. This will help you narrow your target market of possible employers to perhaps five firms. For example, you may decide that your target market for an entry position is large corporations with (1) in-depth training programs, (2) a wide product line, and (3) a wide variety of marketing jobs that will enable you to get a range of experiences and responsibilities within the same company.

Planning your Product

Just like any strategy planner, you must decide what Product features are necessary to appeal to your target market. Identify which credentials are mandatory—and which are optional. For example, is your present academic program enough, or will you need more training? Also identify what technical skills are needed—such as computer programming or accounting. Further, are there any business experiences or extracurricular activities that might help make your Product more attractive to employers? This might involve active participation in college organizations or work experience—either on the job or in internships.

Planning your promotion

Once you identify target companies and develop a Product you hope will be attractive to them, you have to tell these potential customers about your Product. You can write directly to prospective employers—sending a carefully developed résumé that reflects your strategy planning. Or you can visit them in person (with your résumé). Many colleges run well-organized interviewing services. Seek their advice early in your strategy planning effort.

IMPLEMENT YOUR MARKETING PLAN

When you complete your personal marketing plan, you have to implement it—starting with working to accomplish your short-run objectives. If, as part of your plan, you decide that you need specific outside experience, arrange to get it. This may mean taking a low-paying job—or even volunteering to work in political organizations or volunteer organizations where you can get that kind of experience. If you decide that you need skills you can learn in academic courses, plan to take these courses. Similarly, if you don't have a good understanding of your opportunities, then learn as much as you can about possible jobs by talking to professors, taking advanced courses, and talking to businesspeople. And, of course, trends and opportunities can change—so continue to read business publications, talk with professionals in your areas of interest, and be sure that the planning you've done still makes sense.

Strategy planning must adapt to the environment. If the environment changes or your personal objectives change, you have to develop a new plan. This is an ongoing process—and you may never be completely satisfied with your strategy planning. But even trying will make you look much more impressive when you begin your job interviews. Remember, while all employers would like to hire a Superman or a Wonder Woman, they are also impressed with candidates who know what they want to do and are looking for a place where they can fit in—and make a contribution. So planning a personal strategy and implementing it almost guarantee you'll do a better job of career planning, and this will help ensure that you reach your own objectives—whatever they are.

Whether or not you decide to pursue a marketing career, the authors wish you the best of luck in your search for a challenging and rewarding career—wherever your interests and abilities may take you.

Cases

Guide to the Use of These Cases

Cases can be used in many ways. And the same case can be analyzed several times for different purposes.

Suggested cases are listed at the end of most chapters, but these cases can also be used later in the text. The main criterion for the order of these cases is the amount of technical vocabulary or text principles that is needed to read the case meaningfully. The first cases are easiest in this regard. This is why an early case can easily be used two or three times—with different emphasis. Some early cases might require some consideration of Product and Price, for example, and might be used twice, perhaps regarding product planning and later pricing. In contrast, later cases, which focus more on Price, might be treated more effectively *after* the Price chapters are covered.

1 The Yaka-Boochee*

Lorne Davies, Jr., and Bud Keyes, two young entrepreneurs, were in the business of creating and marketing games, toys, and novelties. They had been successful in developing four board games. Two of these games, Cops and Robbers and The Railway Tycoon, were considered marketing successes.

During January 1985, Davies worked on an idea for a game using a plastic tube and two balls on the end of a string. After experimenting with various tube lengths and diameters, string lengths, and ball sizes, he came up with a working model. The plastic tube acted as a handle, and by rolling his wrist, Davies was able to make the balls orbit on the string around the handle. See Figure 1.

Convinced that the concept had merit, Davies and Keyes conducted more trials and made some product adjustments. The partners thought about the new toy in the same way as a yo-yo. It required some dexterity to learn to use the toy, but once the basic action was mastered, it was possible to begin to do a number of tricks.

Just three weeks after invention, Davies and Keyes felt the product was ready to go to market. The toy, by this time, had been dubbed the Yaka-Boochee. The name had no meaning or relevance to the toy; it was simply a phonetic spelling of the name of one of Keyes's neighbors.

Davies and Keyes had had some success in marketing games through Spran Enterprises, so they took their new product to this company on March 1, 1985. At this meeting, Davies introduced the toy to the three principals of the firm, Bill MacCartney, Raymond Lavassere, and Doug Matheson. He demonstrated a number of simple tricks that he and Keyes had invented, stressing the indoor-outdoor nature of the product. The two partners outlined their feeling that the toy should be thought of as a yo-yo–type product.

The executives of Spran were very excited by the Yaka-Boochee. It seemed to be a product that would appeal to children from 6 to 12 years. It might be the sort of product that could be brought out annually and, with demonstrations and other promotions, sell well each year. As well, it was simple and appeared to be cheap to manufacture.

On the spot, MacCartney, Lavassere, and Matheson decided to drop their immediate involvement in the games industry and concentrate on the Yaka-Boochee. They agreed that it was critical to gear up immediately for production in order to have the product available before

*This case was written by Dr. Robert G. Wyckham and Peter Dupuis, who at the time of its preparation were associated with Simon Fraser University.

Figure 1

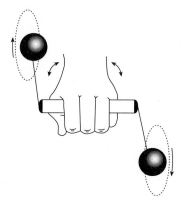

the summer season. Although Spran Enterprises had never marketed a toy product, they were aware of three vital facts:

1. Toy sales are extremely poor in the summer months.
2. During the summer period, many retail buyers are in a "cutoff" position—that is, they have used up all their yearly budget for toy products.
3. Television is the best advertising vehicle for promoting toy sales, and viewing by children in the summer is very low.

The following day, Davies and Keyes met with the principals of Spran and a verbal agreement was hammered out. It was established that, through Spran, Matheson, Lavassere, and MacCartney would each put up $50,000 to provide the capital to manufacture and promote the Yaka-Boochee. Spran would produce, package, and market the product and pay all legal expenses, including patent and trademark applications. Action Games Ltd., Davies and Keyes's company, would receive a royalty of 12 percent of the wholesale price of the product.

At the meeting, Lavassere reported that he had contacted Viceroy Rubber Company in Montreal and determined that Viceroy could ship only 50,000 rubber balls on short notice. The price would be 8 cents per ball. The Spran executives were so impressed with the product and what Davies and Keyes could do with it that they were convinced that no marketing research was needed. They felt that it was just a matter of producing the toy and demonstrating it to the target market.

The first step taken by Spran Enterprises was to hire a product design engineer to design the parts required to mass-produce the toy. On the basis of the analysis by the design engineer, it was clear the only parts that had to be specially manufactured were the end caps for the handle. The handle, the string, the balls, and the buttons to hold the balls on the string were all available off the shelf from various manufacturers. To produce the handle caps, it was necessary to purchase a mold at a cost of $15,000. Various pieces of production equipment needed to make the caps amounted to $10,000. Spran ordered 50,000 balls from Viceroy Rubber and the handles and buttons from Pulse Plastics in Vancouver.

To cut down on production costs, it was decided to sell the product unassembled. A set of instructions would be included to show the consumer how to put the Yaka-Boochee together.

In the weeks that followed, the principals of Spran examined various ways to package and ship the product. It was finally agreed to package the Yaka-Boochee in a clear plastic tube to allow the consumer to see the toy before purchasing. The label and instruction booklet would also be included inside the tube. The heavy cardboard shipping cartons were designed to be turned into retail displays for the Yaka-Boochee.

Keyes and Davies continued to invent tricks that could be done on the Yaka-Boochee. The final instruction booklet described 32 tricks, including the whip, the flip, the flop, through the chute, shooting the moon, and the gyro-spin.

After the orders had been placed for all the production components, the printed materials, and the packages, the following costs were determined:

Production components		
Balls (2)	$.16	
Handle	.07	
End caps	.04	
String	.02	
Buttons	.03	
Total production		$ .32
Overhead (including packing)		.15
Instruction booklet		.05
Packaging		
Plastic tubes	$.21	
Shipping carton	.03	
Display component	.08	
Label	.06	
Total packaging		$ .38
Advertising		.25
Royalty (to Action Games Ltd.)		.18
Profit to Spran		.16
		$1.49

The executives of Spran decided that the retail price should be $3.49. Lavassere, the marketing partner, had

argued for a retail price of $2.99 He felt the $3.49 price might put the Yaka-Boochee out of line with other toys. The breakdown of the retail price was as follows:

Retail price	$3.49
Retailer markup (50%)	1.75
Wholesaler markup (10%)	.17
Commission to salespeople (5%)	.08
Net to Spran	$1.49

During the last week of March 1985, Raymond Lavassere proceeded to organize the promotion campaign for the Yaka-Boochee. Television was to be the major advertising vehicle. The Vrlak Robinson advertising agency prepared a 30-second television commercial that showed Davies and Keyes doing a variety of Yaka-Boochee tricks. The commercial provided a short description of the product and a "tag" indicating where the product would be available. Coast-to-coast presentation of the commercial was planned with heavy frequency— 40 times per week for four weeks during June.

A publicity plan was set out to take advantage of the unique qualities of the new toy. Lavassere made arrangements for Keyes and Davies to appear on a number of radio talk shows as well as on the Alan Hamel television program. Contact was also made with the Vancouver newspapers to obtain write-ups describing the Yaka-Boochee. The publicity was to be carried out during April. The third component in the Spran promotion mix was demonstrations. Teams of school children were to be trained by Davies and Keyes to do the various Yaka-Boochee tricks. These demonstration teams would then put on shows promoting the product in shopping malls, department stores, and schools.

Yaka-Boochee sales were the responsibility of Doug Matheson. Throughout April, Matheson, Keyes, and Davies traveled across the country demonstrating and selling the Yaka-Boochee to wholesalers and department store buyers. By the end of the month, orders for 110,000 Yaka-Boochees had been obtained. The first 30,000 were to be delivered by the last week in May. The remaining 80,000 were to be shipped throughout June.

All Yaka-Boochees were sold on consignment—that is, if the product did not sell at retail, the department store or wholesaler could ship the product back to Spran. According to Bill MacCartney, this showed the trade that Spran had great confidence in the product.

Tri-Lite Plastics, a Vancouver company, was contracted to produce and package the Yaka-Boochee. Two weeks after Tri-Lite had started production, they informed Bill MacCartney that they had run into problems. The first 30,000 units could not be completed until mid-June, with the second run of 80,000 not being

Figure 2

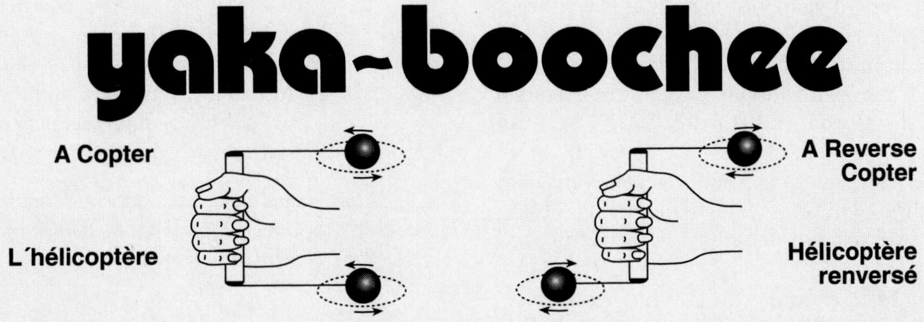

yaka-boochee

A Copter

L´hélicoptère

A Reverse Copter

Hélicoptère renversé

A Copter: Hold the stick up and down in front of your body. Move the stick in a circular motion causing the ball below your wrist and the ball above your wrist to move in a circle, parallel to the ground in a clockwise motion.

L'hélicoptère: Tenez le bâton droit et bas en face du corps. Faites tourner le bâton de façon circulaire pour que la balle sous votre poignet et la balle au-dessus de votre poignet fassent un cercle, parallèle au sol et vers la droite.

A Reverse Copter: Same as a "Copter" but in the reverse or counter-clockwise direction.

Hélicoptère renversé: Comme "Hélicoptère" mais renversé, c'est-à-dire vers la gauche.

Gyro-Copter: While doing a "Copter", hit the top ball with your free hand, so it will go in the reverse direction.

Hélicoptère "gyro": Tout en faisant l' "Hélicoptère", frappez le dessus de la balle avec votre main libre, pour qu'elle aille en direction opposée.

Side Copter: It is a "Copter" done with the stick held at a 45° angle to your body.

Hélicoptère de côté: C'est un "Hélicoptère" fait avec le bâton étant tenu à un angle de 45° de votre corps.

The High Sky: While doing a "Backward Roll", throw the stick up into the air. Catch the stick and continue on with the "Backward Roll" or change into a "Forward Roll".

Jusqu'au ciel: Tout en faisant une "Rotation arrière", lancez le bâton en l'air. Attrapez le bâton au vol et continuez avec la "Rotation arrière" ou changez en une "Rotation avant".

There are many tricks one can do with his or her "YAKA-BOOCHEE". Have fun in practising the tricks we have shown and in the development of your own.

Vous pouvez faire beaucoup de trucs avec "YAKA-BOOCHEE". Amusez-vous à pratiquer les trucs que nous vous avons montrés et à inventer vos propres trucs.

completed until the first week in July. Realizing the implications of the situation, Bill MacCartney called a meeting to discuss the problem.

"Gentlemen, Tri-Lite informs me that our product will not be ready for shipping until the middle of June," MacCartney began. "Apparently, there has been a problem obtaining the materials required to manufacture the product, and to compound this situation, the molds have been causing them problems."

"The bottom line," Matheson added, "is that the Yaka-Boochee won't hit the retail market until late June."

"The end of June! What about our promotional program?" Lavassere asked. "As I explained before, the timing is crucial, and besides, we have a contract with CTV. Those commercials are going to run whether we're ready or not."

"How do you think this will influence sales, Doug?" MacCartney inquired.

"Well . . . they won't be as good as if we had released the product in early June," said Matheson. "However, there should be some lasting effect from the television advertisements in June. I would estimate that the product will still move well."

After much discussion, the three businessmen agreed that as much of the promotional program as possible would be moved up and the Yaka-Boochee program should continue as planned.

Throughout June, the television advertisements ran across Canada during children's viewing hours. No Yaka-Boochees were available in retail stores until the last week in June.

On June 26, 1985, the first 30,000 units were delivered to the retail outlets. Sales were very good and all of the product sold within the next 14 days. Although sales were doing well, a number of problems were encountered with the first 30,000 Yaka-Boochees.

• The end caps were too big, making the product very difficult for consumers to assemble.
• Many of the tubes used for packaging the product were crushed during shipping. As well, many of the lids on the tubes popped off and the product components became mixed up inside the shipping case.
• In some instances, the pieces required to assemble the Yaka-Boochee were either lost while being shipped or were not included when being packaged.
• The instruction booklet did not give an adequate description to help the consumer assemble the product. As well, many of the tricks described in the booklet were difficult and impractical.

Before the second run of 80,000 units was produced, Spran and Tri-Lite eliminated all of the packaging problems.

By the end of the first week of July, the television advertisements had finished and the other promotional activities started to slow down.

Only July 10, 1985, the second batch of 80,000 Yaka-Boochees was delivered to retail outlets across Canada.

Sales at retail during July were steady; not as high as hoped for, but good considering the lack of promotion. In August, sales slowed down considerably and continued at a low ebb during September. At the end of September, some wholesalers and department stores began to return cases of Yaka-Boochees to Spran.

In late October, the executives of Spran and the two inventors met to discuss the situation.

"It doesn't look good, does it? As of today, our warehouse reports that over 40,000 units have been returned. This gives us over 60,000 Yaka-Boochees gath-ering dust. Tri-Lite reports that they have stockpiled about 100,000 balls and enough material to produce about 40,000 Yaka-Boochees."

"I can't figure it out," Doug Matheson said. "Sales started out really well. Where did we go wrong? Surely the product can sell!"

"Well, gentlemen," Lavassere said, "we have finished goods and raw materials equivalent to 100,000 Yaka-Boochees. What are we going to do with them all?"

What should have been done differently when the Yaka-Boochee was launched? What should be done now to make the best of the current situation?

2 Canbank*

Arnie Johannsen, new product development and merchandising manager at Canbank's Toronto corporate office, was annoyed. He had spent five months and $700,000 developing a new retail product to the point of launch, and now something was terribly wrong.

In October 1990, he had been given the go-ahead to launch his latest product—Canshare, a discount stock brokerage service. With no sign-up charges, it would offer qualifying Canbank customers the opportunity to purchase stocks on the Montreal Stock Exchange, the TSE, VSE, NYSE, and NASDAQ at a discount of between 20 to 80 percent of the brokerage fees charged by full-service stockbrokers.

The target market was defined as knowledgeable Canbank account holders who would like to buy stocks and who did not require investment counseling. There were 2,500,000 customers in the Canbank system. Arnie expected that 625,000 of these Canbank account holders would take advantage of the new product.

The discount brokerage product concept was not a new one among Canadian banks. The lead bank in this market was the Toronto-Dominion Bank, with its very successful Green Line Investment Services. Among other bank-affiliated competitors were National Bank's Investel, Bank of Montreal's Investor Line, Royal Bank's Action Direct, and Scotia Securities.

To develop a name for the product, Arnie had hired an agency, which provided 200 computer-generated potential brand names. Arnie asked Canbank's lawyers to search these names and found that 150 of them already had been registered for copyright protection. After screening the 50 remaining names, another 45 were rejected as inappropriate for Canbank. The five finalists

*This case was written by Dr. Peter M. Banting, who at the time of its preparation was associated with McMaster University.

were presented to Canbank executives, who settled on "Canshare" as the best one to identify their new discount brokerage service.

An agreement was signed with a full-service stock brokerage service to process share transactions generated by Canshare. Neither the broker nor Canbank would offer investment advice.

On October 15, Arnie began planning the introduction of the new product. Promotion was an important part of the plan. A top free-lance advertising copywriter was hired to develop promotional copy in English. The French-language copy was created by a Quebec advertising agency, with the content loosely based on the finished English language promotional materials.

On March 18, pamphlets and window posters, together with application forms, were distributed to the Canbank branches nationwide—in plenty of time to be in place for the April 2 advertising campaign launching Canshare. Because of its high cost, television advertising was not used. Instead, media advertising was concentrated on newspaper ads in every major city in Canada. The campaign theme was "Making Your Own Decisions." This was to be followed up with inserts in all account statements mailed during the month of April, and using the same theme. By that time, Canbank had invested $700,000 in the new product.

On April 15, Arnie, feeling like a proud new father, went to Canbank's main branch in Toronto to see first-hand how his "baby" was doing. From the street he felt his first surge of joy. The Canshare poster was displayed in a prominent window position. But his pleasure quickly dissolved when he stepped inside the branch. On checking the literature display he could find no Canshare brochures. Recognizing that the branch's supply of brochures could not possibly be exhausted so soon, even if the product were an instant success, Arnie asked the branch manager where they were.

The branch manager didn't know. Indeed, it took him a full five minutes to find them, still sealed in their shipping package. When Arnie asked him why they weren't on display with the bank's other brochures, the manager said, "I was hoping that no one would ask me about Canshare."

After a few short, sharp words with the manager, Arnie stormed out and began checking Toronto's other Canbank branches. To his mounting annoyance he discovered that not one of the branches had Canshare brochures displayed on their information racks and only a few had display posters in their windows.

That night at the dinner table Arnie related the day's events to his wife. "I honestly believe that the competition from Canbank's own products is worse than the competition Canshare faces from the discount brokerage services of the other banks," Arnie concluded.

What corrective measures should Arnie take to "save" Canshare? Outline, step by step, the strategy Arnie should follow for his next new product to avoid repetition of the problem encountered by Canshare.

3 Gerber Products Company

Andrea Kelly, president of Kelly Research, Inc., wants to develop a research proposal for Gerber Products Company's CEO, David Johnson, who is seriously looking for new product-market opportunities that might make sense for Gerber. As the new CEO, David Johnson has just cleaned out some weak diversification efforts, including trucking, furniture, and toy ventures, that tended to take the company away from its core baby food business. Now he is looking for new opportunities close to the food business. But Mr. Johnson has also made it clear that Gerber may want to move beyond baby foods because only about 4 percent of US households have babies—and the baby food market is *very* competitive.

Mr. Johnson (according to trade press articles) would like new ideas for "premium-quality, value-added products in niche markets." It might be possible, for example, to extend the sales of its baby food products to adults (in general) and/or senior citizens. Some of its current chunky food items are intended for older tots and might be attractive to some adults. They are no-salt, easy-to-chew items. But care may be needed in expanding into these markets. Gerber had troubles in the 1970s with some products that were intended for adult tastes—one was beef stroganoff in a baby food jar. Yet Mr. Johnson now wonders, "How come we can't develop food products that target everyone over the toddler age?"

Recent new Gerber product offerings include a line of applesauce-based fruit cups, bottled water, and shelf-stable homogenized milk. All three of these seem to fit with Gerber's growth plans, offering more premium-quality, value-added products to niche markets. Further growth efforts might include products that will enable the company to get enough experience to understand a market area and be able to pursue joint ventures or acquisitions. This might include activities other than food, or at least baby food—which has become almost a commodity business. The feeling of some Gerber executives is that "opportunities must be better elsewhere—in niches that haven't been worked as hard as baby food." Some market possibilities that have been mentioned in the food-oriented trade press for a company like Gerber are canned or frozen food items for restaurants, military commissaries, gourmet food stores, or specialty departments in chain food stores.

Mr. Johnson's background includes not only domestic but international marketing with major companies that sell cleaning products, health and beauty aids, drug products, and baked goods. So it is likely that he will be willing to consider going quite far from baby foods. And given that Gerber is a major US food processor, with sales over $1 billion, it is clear the company has the production, distribution, and financial resources to consider a good-sized product-market opportunity. But are there any attractive new opportunities—or must Gerber simply copy someone else's earlier developments?

Andrea Kelly wants to develop a research proposal to find and evaluate some new opportunities for Gerber. But she wants to narrow the scope of the search somewhat so she doesn't seem to be "fishing in the whole ocean." She also wants to suggest some attractive-sounding possibilities to catch Mr. Johnson's attention. So she is asking her staff for ideas—to make her proposal more attractive.

Explain how Andrea Kelly should go about selecting possible "attractive opportunities." Suggest five product-market opportunities that might make sense for Mr. Johnson and Gerber Products Company, and explain why.

4 Diego's*

Dr. Albert Collins, a Montreal physician, faced a difficult decision as to whether or not to invest in a new fast food franchise concept specializing in Mexican food. Dr. Collins had made several good business investments and while he thought this was a great opportunity he recognized that there was a chance it wouldn't succeed. He decided to discuss the concept with his friend Jack Timlin, a marketing consultant, who had advised him on a number of earlier ventures. Dr. Collins arranged a meeting and presented the following information to Mr. Timlin.

THE CONCEPT

About six months ago, Dr. Collins had read an article in a major US magazine about a relatively new but already successful fast food franchiser based in Phoenix, Arizona. In operation for less than five years this franchiser had opened 55 locations (some franchised, some corporately owned) in Arizona and several other southwest states and had sold (to one firm) the franchise rights

*This case was written by Mr. Morris Borts, who at the time of its preparation was associated with McGill Univiersty. Copyright 1992 by Marketec Business Consultants Ltd. All rights reserved. No portion of this case may be reproduced by any means without the prior written permission of Marketec, 20 Blue Heron Court, Ottawa, Ontario, K1L 8J7.

for 80 locations in Florida and sold many other, soon to be built, franchises in the midwestern states.

Although Mexican food is very popular in the southern United States, this firm, in all of its advertising and store signs, always uses the phrase "We serve marinated charbroiled chicken and Mexican food" to indicate that it offers a choice of items so that people who don't like Mexican food can also patronize the chain.

On the door of each location is a sticker stating that this restaurant is approved by the American Heart Association as a healthy place to eat away from home. Dr. Collins believed that this endorsement was obtained because of the manner in which the chicken is prepared. First it is marinated in a secret recipe of natural fruit juices and herbs and then it is charbroiled so that the fat drips out of the meat. Chicken prepared this way is lower in cholesterol than fried chicken and is juicier than barbeque (BBQ) chicken. To further enhance its healthy image the chain does not serve french fries but does offer baked potatoes and an assortment of salads.

A quote from the article provided a very strong endorsement from at least one customer: "I do not have a great deal of experience in eating Mexican food, but the dishes were different that what I expected. The chicken was tender and juicy and had a subtle flavour—for my taste it was better than BBQ chicken. The other dishes were very tasty and definitely not spicy. If this is what Mexican food is like, I am a convert."

Dr. Collins investigated further and found out that the recipes could not be protected by patent or copyright. In fact, he learned that the Arizona chain found out how a California chain of chicken restaurants marinated their chicken and then they used the recipe themselves. Dr. Collins then purchased some of the American marinated chicken, had it analyzed by a laboratory and then had a food technologist develop and test the formula and the correct procedures to cook the chicken.

He gathered a group of investors (primarily friends and acquaintances) who liked the concept and were willing to put up most of the money required to open up one or two locations to show that the concept would be successful in Canada. The plan was to sell franchises across the country.

For each location, franchisees would be charged an initial fee plus an ongoing 5 percent royalty on the gross sales of the franchises. In return for these fees the franchisee would have the right to use the trade name, which the investors decided would be Diego's. The franchisee's staff would be trained to prepare the food as per set procedures and the franchisee would purchase the chicken marinade from the franchiser. The franchisee would be assisted in site selection, construction of the restaurant, the purchasing of the required equipment, and would receive ongoing managerial assistance. In addition, the franchisee would benefit from a co-op advertising programme to be funded by a charge of 4 percent of gross sales levied on each location—franchised or corporately owned.

PRELIMINARY RESEARCH

Dr. Collins met with the investment group several times and although nothing was formalized, a considerable amount of preliminary research had been conducted. A location was found for the first Diego's restaurant in a relatively new suburban residential area where most of the homes have been built in the last 10 years. New homes were still being built in the area and there was enough vacant land to more than double the population of the area. Most of the homes sold for $150,000 to $225,000 (compared to the current Montreal average price of $89,500 per home). Census data suggested that the typical home owner in this area was raising a young family and had a managerial job or was a professional with a practice that had not yet developed fully.

Studies have shown that most people will travel about 2.5 to 3.5 km (5 minutes) to go to a fast food restaurant. Since Diego's would be very distinctive, the first few locations probably would draw customers from a slightly larger trading area. Information was obtained from recent census data for the census tracts that would likely constitute the trading area (Table 1).

INVESTOR GROUP MEETING

After the information was collected, the investors held a meeting where a lively debate took place about the proposed image of Diego's, the target market, and other matters.

The investment group couldn't agree what image Diego's should have and what types of customers they should concentrate on satisfying. Some of the members want to concentrate their efforts on attracting and satisfying families with young children (e.g., offering free magic shows on selected evenings and on weekends, offering children free balloons and perhaps offering a special children's menu of items that will appeal to children).

One investor argued that this market segment appeared to be important. A recent newspaper article reported the results of an American study that, in 85 percent of the cases when parents go out to eat with their young children, the children make the final decision on which restaurant the family will go to.

Some of the group argued that children are known as very finicky eaters and maybe they won't like Diego's food. They suggested that Diego's should go after the teenage market or possibly Diego's should concentrate on the adult fast food market.

One member of the investment group had conducted an analysis of the competition in the trading area. He noted that at least two competitors in the trading area, McDonald's and Chi Chi's, had special strategies for attracting children. Two other successful restaurants, St. Hubert B.B.Q. and Swiss Chalet (both specialize in BBQ chicken) have outlets in the area. Another group member provided some data prepared by Statistics Canada that dealt with food purchased from restaurants (Table 2).

One of the members of the investor group was a practising accountant. He estimated that if the average bill at a restaurant of this type was $4.50 (excluding tax) and the actual cost of the food and the packaging was 30 percent of the selling price, the restaurant would need to serve 225,000 meals a year to break even.

Information on traffic flows was also collected. One Thursday, Dr. Collins went to the proposed site and

Table 1 Trading Area Demographic Data

Total population	114,858
Private households	38,500
Total families	31,535
With 1 child at home	6,355
With 2 children at home	8,980
With 3 children at home	3,950
No children at home	12,250
Ages of children	
0 to 4 years	8,860
5 to 9 years	9,035
10 to 14 years	8,425
15 to 19 years	8,975

Source: Statistics Canada, 1986 Montreal CMA census tracts.

Table 2 Weekly Food Purchases from Restaurants, per Family (Canada), 1990

	Food Purchases	Income before Taxes
Average	$27.28	$45,708
1st quintile	12.63	11,808
2nd quintile	22.39	25,333
3rd quintile	32.11	39,453
4th quintile	45.39	55,813
5th quintile	63.51	96,133

Note: The average weekly food purchases from restaurants in the Montreal Metropolitan Area was $33.83.

Source: Statistics Canada, *Family Food Expenditures in Canada—17 Metropolitan Areas*, Cat. 62-554.

between 12:00 noon and 1:00 PM counted 2,000 cars moving in the four directions at the intersection. Between 5:00 PM and 6:30 PM the street heading north in front of the site became a "parking lot" as people headed home. He felt that this was a positive sign in that people could stop on the same side of the street as they were already travelling (and not have to cut across traffic), pick up food for supper, and then continue home.

Related to the decision as to which target market(s) to appeal to, some members wondered if people would be confused if the restaurant was simultaneously promoted as a chicken restaurant and as a Mexican food restaurant. That is, would potential customers perceive the chicken as a Mexican dish or would they consider the chicken to be a suitable alternative to BBQ chicken or fried chicken?

Various members of the investment group then raised the following questions and issues:

- Will consumers recognize the fact that Diego's is really two different restaurants in one and even if a person does not like Mexican food (or is afraid to try it) he or she can order a very tasty chicken or will some stay away because they view Diego's as a Mexican restaurant? Perhaps Diego's is too strong a Mexican name for what we would like to achieve?

- Both images should be positive. Diego's proposed first location is not far from Chi Chi's which exposed the consumer to and expanded the market for Mexican food. According to comparisons made by some of the group, Diego's Mexican dishes taste better and will cost less than the same items at Chi Chi's.

- On the other hand, for many years chicken has been more popular in Quebec than other parts of the country. It may be due to cultural differences or may be the result of the success of the St. Hubert B.B.Q. chain which started in Quebec (Table 3).

- In addition, over the last three or four years the consumption of chicken across Canada has

increased significantly as people switched away from red meats which are higher in cholesterol than chicken. This ties in very nicely with the emphasis that the American chain firmly places on the health aspect of its chicken meals.

Some of the investors debated whether legally they could use an approach similar to the one Americans use and were not convinced that the "healthy" image will be a unique selling proposition that will cause people to pick their restaurant over the competition. They argued that the Canadian laws concerning food advertising were different and more restrictive than the US laws. In Canada the advertising of the cholesterol content of food (with the exception of vegetable oils such as Mazola) is prohibited. In addition, it appears that, even if it wanted to, the Canadian Heart Association would be unable, given the present legal environment, to endorse the restaurant. As well, they argued that many Quebecers are not especially health conscious when it comes to food.

One person had obtained a copy of a research study conducted in Montreal about bakery products. This study concluded that French speaking respondents were less concerned with food additives than the English speaking segment of the population. It was also found that older people were less concerned with this issue than the younger generation. Quebecers consumed large amounts of especially greasy french fries and poutine (French fries, sauce, and melted cheese). In other parts of Canada the preference was for crispier, less oily french fries.

Some research conducted in the Montreal area by one of the group indicated that more than half of the respondents want french fries with their BBQ chicken. Consumers like and expect the combination and that is what the chicken restaurants offer with their meals.

In spite of this information other investors would like to follow the lead of the American firm and not serve french fries but instead offer a choice of baked potatoes or Mexican rice.

One person pointed out that Quebecers love fine food and are receptive to ethnic foods. However, for some reason Mexican food has not caught on in Quebec. Taco Bell, a large US Mexican fast food chain which has opened in Ontario does not, at this time, have any Quebec locations. In Montreal proper, several small Mexican restaurants have opened. None of them appears to be especially successful.

In addition, one of the investment team visited about a dozen supermarkets (some in the area of the proposed location, others in various parts of Montreal and other suburbs). Each store has a small section of packaged Mexican foods. The managers of these stores described the sales of Mexican foods as "slow but steady."

Because there is a lot of money at stake, the investors paid for some basic research. They conducted focus

Table 3 Estimated per Capita Regional Differences in Food Consumption

National average = 100 percent	Chicken	Italian	Chinese	Greek
National	100%	100%	100%	100%
Quebec	125	120	145	130
Ontario	90	75	85	80
Prairies	90	165	35	25
B.C.	90	120	100	85
Atlantic provinces	175	80	55	45

groups in a restaurant setting similar to what is being considered and the respondents had the chance to taste the food. (Table 4 provides a summary of the comments.) The results of the research were interesting in that in two cases the findings go against what the investors thought the consumer might want or accept.

First, it was planned to prepare the food out in the front of the restaurant where it could be seen by people inside and outside. This was intended to show that Diego's had nothing to hide and that the food was prepared under hygienic conditions. In addition, it was hoped that seeing the golden brown chicken on the grill and the aroma of cooking chicken would encourage people to order. According to the focus groups some people viewed this as a strong negative.

Secondly, while travelling through New England, Dr. Collins came across a very successful chain of seafood restaurants which, in order to keep prices low, serves on paper plates and provides plastic cutlery. This makes sense because Harvey's and other fast food chains also use disposables. Again, based on the results of the focus groups, there seems to be resistance in Montreal to eating chicken in this way.

Another research finding was of special interest and requires more study. When respondents were offered a choice between traditional BBQ sauce and salsa, a Mexi-

Table 4 Focus Group Comments

Positive Comments
- The food is delicious.
- Great food.
- I never tasted Mexican food before; it is really good and not at all spicy.
- I am happy that you don't serve french fries. My seven-year-old son just ate nutritious food, not the junk food that he prefers.
- I enjoyed the food. The chicken was moist but not greasy.
- I liked it. I would come back again.
- I hope it opens soon. I am bored and fed up with the traditional fast foods.

Negative Comments
- The chicken looks yellow. What's wrong with it? Is it cheaper quality chicken?
- I don't think French Canadians are ready to eat BBQ chicken on paper plates using plastic cutlery.
- I don't want to see the chicken being cooked. I don't want to know that it was once a living thing.
- The chickens were brought to the grill in a pail. Do they use the same pail to wash the floors?
- For me BBQ chicken and french fries go together. Something is missing and the meal is not enjoyable without french fries.

can sauce, the vast majority opted for the BBQ sauce. Was it because it was something unknown? Was it the fear of something spicy? Or, perhaps, it was just a habit.

THE DECISION

Dr. Collins concluded the presentation to Mr. Timlin with the following comments: "As you can see there is a lot of information to consider. In fact, I am confused as to what I should do. I know that the concept is successful in Arizona but I have also obtained a great deal of information, some of which is not positive, about duplicating this concept in Canada and particularly in Quebec.

"I don't know if I should invest in this project or not. If it succeeds, it will be the chance of a lifetime to make a lot of money. Should I go into it, or not? What, if anything, can be done to improve the concept so that the risk of failure will be reduced?"

What would you recommend that Dr. Collins do? Why?

5 Time to Buy a New Car?*

Robbie and Marisa French lived in a small village located 15 kilometers east of Regina. Marisa helped to organize the village play school and Robbie was marketing manager for one of the Crown corporations in Regina. Both of their children attended school in Regina. Skating, soccer, and swimming necessitated many additional trips into the city in the evening and on weekends. During winter, the highway could become very icy and, in the past eight years, had been closed on three occasions due to bad weather. Robbie's father was a motor mechanic and Robbie had learned to drive when he was 10 years old. Prior to getting married, he had owned an MGB and a Volkswagen Scirocco. Marisa, who had worked for Volkswagen in the United Kingdom, had owned a Ford Escort and a Volkswagen Golf prior to coming to Canada.

The family owned three vehicles: a 1969 Ford half ton, which Robbie used for driving to work during the winter, a 1984 Ford Bronco II, which was driven by Marisa, and a 1986 Ford van. The van had been customized by Triple E Conversions and contained four captain chairs and a sofa bed. It was air-conditioned and used only during summer. The family had purchased this vehicle 18 months earlier after their original van was destroyed by an electrical fire. The fire had occurred when Marisa was driving with their children and their son had been very upset by the incident. The family

*This case was written by Dr. Ed Weymes, who at the time of its preparation was associated with the Faculty of Administration, University of Regina.

intended to use this newer van for summer vacations with the children. In the past two summers, they had only taken two short trips with this van. It was occasionally used by Marisa when she took the children to the beach and by Robbie for commuting to work during summer.

Marisa preferred to drive the Bronco and would only use the van when it was very hot since the Bronco lacked air conditioning. During winter, Marisa preferred the security of the Bronco's four-wheel drive.

The 1987 Saskatchewan budget introduced a 7 cent per liter tax on gas. This tax was to be rebated to Saskatchewan residents and Robbie had just received the forms to claim for his rebate. Between April and December 1987, the French family had purchased just over 3,000 liters of gas. At $0.49 a liter this amounted to a little over $1,500! Robbie now realized why it was becoming so difficult to keep his monthly Visa bill under control. His truck cost him about $20 a week, while the Bronco returned between 22 and 28 miles per gallon and the van about 24 MPG.

In the following days Robbie found himself reading the classified ads and was surprised at the prices being asked for 1984 Bronco's. Most ads sought $12,000 for a "loaded" Bronco. Robbie's wasn't loaded, being only a five-speed with an AM radio. Robbie was also aware that the mid-sized domestic and import cars were capable of obtaining 40 MPG. Robbie decided to phone some dealers for prices of new vehicles.

On Friday evening, Robbie raised the issue of changing the Bronco or the van. Marisa's response was negative; she liked her Bronco's four-wheel drive during winter since this provided her with security when driving their two children into the city. She also thought the van was the ideal vehicle for family vacations. Robbie decided to drop the subject.

At supper on March 21, Marisa informed Robbie that her friend Janie had just purchased a Toyota Tercel. Janie had previously owned a van similar to Robbie and Marisa's. They had purchased the Tercel since their gas costs were becoming excessive. Janie had told Marisa how economical the car was. The French children felt that it would be nice to own the car. Robbie suggested that front-wheel drive cars provided good traction in snow and reminded Marisa that they had owned a Volkswagen Golf when they lived in Northern Ontario.

The following Thursday during dinner, Marisa suggested that the van was collecting dust in the garage and could be sold. Also, she mentioned that Robbie should be driving something better than his 1969 half ton during winter. They decided to advertise the van privately.

The following Saturday, Robbie visited the local Toyota dealer and drove a Tercel. He discussed price and the Ford van's possible trade-in value with the salesman, who indicated that the van was probably worth about $13,500. Robbie thought he could do better with a private sale, having paid $21,500 only 18 months earlier. Robbie then visited the Honda dealer and drove a Civic CX priced at $15,000, which Robbie considered too expensive.

On Tuesday, Robbie called the *Leader Post* and placed an ad for the van. He was informed of the paper's special offer: place an ad for one week and the second week is free. Robbie advertised the van at the same price that he paid for it: $21,500. The upcoming weekend was Easter.

On Thursday, Robbie called the Ford Dealer in Manitoba who'd sold him the van. As a trade Robbie was offered an Escort Wagon DL valued at $14,000. Robbie tried to negotiate for air conditioning and was told that option would cost him less than $1,000. The Saskatchewan Health and Education Tax would add another $1,000 to the investment.

At lunchtime, Robbie visited the Ford dealer in Regina, where his Bronco had received good service. He discussed his requirements with a salesperson and looked at the Sable wagon. Robbie didn't like the car's interior and it was only available in automatic. Robbie wanted a manual five-speed. The salesperson took Robbie to see a Tracer Wagon. Robbie gave the car a quick inspection. Luggage space appeared limited but he was basically impressed with the car. Robbie returned to the showroom and was introduced to the sales manager. They discussed the Wagons that he'd looked at. Robbie said that he was looking to trade his van, but that he'd prefer to sell it privately since he felt he could get a better price.

On Good Friday, Robbie, Marisa, and their two children visited the car dealerships to look at the new vehicles. They selected that day since they wouldn't be bothered by salespeople. They visited the Toyota and Honda lots and also the other Ford dealer who carried the Taurus. Neither Robbie nor Marisa was impressed with the Taurus. They then drove to the Ford dealership to view the Tracer; then to the General Motors dealer where their trip was cut short since one of the children needed to go to the bathroom. Later that evening, Marisa said that she liked all the vehicles that she'd seen but she'd prefer a hatchback and would like air conditioning.

Over the Easter weekend, Robbie placed a For Sale sign in the van and left the vehicle at the end of the drive. On Easter Saturday, Robbie was in a bookstore browsing through a car guide. The section on wagons recommended the Toyota Camry as a "best buy." Over the weekend, there were few phone calls and only one family stopped by to look at the van.

The following Monday, Robbie called Toyota and found that they had a Camry Wagon for $18,000. On Tuesday, Robbie took time off work to visit the Toyota dealer to see the Camry. The salesman told him that a new Camry cost $26,000 and the car described in the phone conversation was a company car with 36,000 kilometers. Robbie didn't drive the car but asked the salesman to give him a price on his van. The salesman asked Robbie what price he'd like for his van. Robbie suggested a trade, indicating that he might be prepared to offer $800 and that he wanted at least $17,000 for his van. The salesman said that he'd take this to the manager, who was out at that time.

Later that morning, the salesman called Robbie to say that the manager wanted to see the vehicle. Robbie agreed to return to the dealership. While his van was being appraised, Robbie and the salesman took the Camry out for a drive. Robbie noticed that one rear tire was worn while the other tires were new. He was suspicious. On the highway, Robbie noticed that the car pulled to the right. The salesman suggested a crosswind but on holding the wheel agreed that the car was pulling.

Back at the dealership, the salesman disappeared to the sales manager's office for 15 minutes. On returning, he informed Robbie that they were a long way apart and the best offer for his van was $11,000. Robbie said the figure was ridiculous and walked away.

The next day, Robbie called the *Leader Post* and dropped his van's price to $17,500. He also received a call from the salesperson who'd showed him the Tracer, inviting him to a Ford promotion where their new luxury cars would be displayed. Robbie declined but asked if he could bring his van over as he would be interested in knowing what price Ford would offer for it.

Robbie declined a drive in the Tracer and sat in the showroom reading a magazine while his van was appraised. Reports in the magazine suggested that the Tracer is good but not as good as the Japanese vehicles. The salesperson returned after 20 minutes, saying that she could trade the Tracer for the van. Air conditioning would be $1,200 and tax about $1,080.

On Saturday, Robbie decided to drive to Indian Head to visit the Ford dealer. As he turned into the village, he noticed a Chrysler dealer and decided to investigate. He was impressed with the Chrysler salesperson, who appeared interested in what Robbie was looking for. He looked at the van and indicated that he would like it on his lot. He invited Robbie to look around.

Robbie was surprised and pleased to see that the Sundance is a hatchback, but then his attention was drawn to a Colt with "Turbo" written on the side. Asking about the price, he was delighted to learn that it cost $16,000 and was a five-speed. It wasn't a hatchback but had air conditioning. Robbie took the car for a test drive and was impressed with the acceleration and handling. Returning to the showroom, he was introduced to the senior partner, who had taken the van for a drive. After discussion between the two salespeople they offered Rob-

bie the Colt for $111 plus tax. Robbie was impressed, as the list on the car was $16,100.

Summarize the events that culminated in the visit to the Indian Head dealership. Identify the different criteria Robbie and Marisa used during their decisions to purchase a new car. Do the criteria differ? Why? Do you think Marisa would have objected had Robbie decided to sell the Bronco instead of the van? Did Marisa's decision criteria change during the buying process? Why didn't Robbie dicker with the Toyota salesman? Do you think the French family traded their van?

6 Boutique Vison*

"It happened again Sunday—Mother's Day," muttered Philip Nephelier, owner of Boutique Vison. A member of the Animal Liberation Front surprised Claire Richmond and sprayed her $25,000 mink coat with paint. Ms. Richmond had just purchased the coat two weeks earlier from the store located in the trendy Queen Street section of Toronto. Over the first four months of 1989, three of Mr. Nephelier's customers had been "attacked" like this and in each case the fur coat was ruined. "It makes me sick to think about this," he said. "I have a right to sell fur coats and my customers have a right to wear them without harassment from fringe elements. Maybe I should sell my store or, barring that, close it down. I'm getting too old to fight back."

THE FUR INDUSTRY IN CANADA

In 1985 (the most recent year for which figures were available), over $100 million of fur pelts were produced in Canada. There were two sources of fur pelts: those taken from animals trapped in the wild and those taken from animals raised on fur farms. In 1985, pelts from trapped animals were worth $49 million while pelts from farm-raised animals were worth $56 million. In total the fur trade in Canada accounted for less than one tenth of 1 percent of the gross domestic product. Even though fur was a luxury product, it was subject to cyclical demand due to economic conditions.

Originally the settlers of Canada relied on wildlife for food and clothing—in some remote parts of the country, Canadians still do. European voyages from England and France brought development of the fur trade which, to a large extent, guided the course of exploration,

---

settlement, and economic development. For two centuries, fur coats were a status symbol and Canadian fur was especially prized. However, demand for fur pelts had been declining over the past 10 years due, in part, to strong antifur sentiments aroused by conservationists and preservationists.

Fur farms (or ranches) were a relatively new industry in Canada. In 1921, the value of farm-bred pelts accounted for only 3 percent of production. By 1937, the value of farm-bred pelts had risen to approximately 40 percent of production. Since then, the value had increased more slowly so that by 1985, fur farms accounted for 53 percent of production. The number of fur farms had fluctuated from 1,083 (during depressed times in the mid-1970s) to 1,584 (in the booming economic period of the early 1980s). Fur farms accounted for 96 percent of the mink pelt harvest and 63 percent of the fox pelt harvest and were located throughout the provinces, though none were located in the Territories. Ontario accounted for 36.8 percent of the fur farm pelt harvest while Nova Scotia (18.5 percent), Quebec (16.3 percent), and British Columbia (13.5 percent) accounted for most of the remainder.

Wild furs were harvested throughout the country. Ontario accounted for 27.0 percent of the wild fur pelt harvest while Quebec (15.8 percent), Alberta (13.4 percent), Saskatchewan (9.9 percent), Manitoba (9.5 percent), British Columbia (9.5 percent), and the Territories (8.9 percent) accounted for most of the remainder. Approximately 250,000 Native Canadians were supported through the wild fur harvest. The federal government estimated that if all trapping were to stop, it would cost taxpayers $36 million to replace lost food sources. Further, the Ministry of the Environment felt that there would be serious harm done to the wilderness by expanded populations of some animals if minimum trapping quotas weren't enforced.

Approximately 275 companies employing 3,000 workers produced fur coats. Two thirds of these firms were located in Quebec with another 30 percent located in Ontario. Employee compensation for wages and benefits averaged $20,200 per person; the total value of fur coats manufactured was $363 million. About two thirds of these coats were exported. In producing a rabbit coat, 15 pelts were required. Sewing, choosing, and handling pelts so that they produced a coat of uniform color and quality was an art that couldn't be easily mechanized. For the most part fur coat manufacturers were small and inconspicuous. They drew little attention from fur protest groups.

There were more than 700 fur retailers operating in Canada with combined retail sales of $300 million. Most establishments operated independently and sold a combination of domestic and imported fur coats. In the United States, a new chain of Jindo fur stores had opened selling Asian pelts, but this company hadn't shown any interest in the Canadian market. Employing approximately 3,500 people, fur retailers and their customers were the favorite target of animal rights groups.

THE ANIMAL RIGHTS LOBBY

In 1980, only a handful of zealous people talked about animal liberation—the inherent "right" of animals to share the planet with humans, as distinct from merely being protected from wanton cruelty. But by 1989, the movement had grown. In the United States, one source estimated that there were 10 million people (7,000 groups) involved with an annual budget of from $200 million to $1 billion. However, when the triple and quadruple counting of names on mailing lists was eliminated and the traditional groups like the Society for Prevention of Cruelty to Animals, voluntary animal shelters and city dog pounds were discounted, the movement was much, much smaller than headlines suggested. A retired US Department of Justice official estimated that the angry, attention-getting fringe amounted to fewer than 10,000 people.

Most of these belonged to radical-sounding groups like "Band of Mercy," "Urban Gorillas" and the "Animal Liberation Front." These were the people who stealthily approached women and spray-painted their fur coats or liberated lobsters from holding tanks in seafood restaurants. Small though their numbers were, their voices were loud, intimidating and unceasing. And in recent years they could be heard clearly through excellent media coverage.

American game show host Bob Barker announced he would no longer host the Miss Universe pageant because fur coats were among the prizes awarded. First Lady Barbara Bush chose not to wear a fur coat to the inauguration. World famous designers Bill Blass, Caroline Herrera, Oleg Cassini and Giorgio Armani decided to stop designing fur clothing. Sears, Roebuck and Company, one of America's largest retailers, announced it would no longer sell fur coats. Even the conservative Humane Society denounced bacon and eggs as "the breakfast of cruelty."

Yet such behavior hardly rated the word *terrorist*, which was how the FBI described one extremist group, the Animal Liberation Front. Indeed, there was not one recorded instance since the inception of the movement in which any animal rights organization had physically hurt anyone.

The core argument of the animal rights movement was well-stated by an anonymous member of the Toronto Humane Society. "I think if people were shown how animals are raised on farms and trapped in the wild, they would be outraged." Animal rights groups argued that modern fur farming techniques meant a cruel existence for animals. They were subjected to cramped conditions and their movements were severely restrained. Only the rampant use of antibiotics allowed animals to survive filthy conditions.

"One of the things we are concerned about is fur farming and trapping in the wild," said Bill Bradley of the Canadian Vegans for Animals Rights group in Toronto. "Vegans" were a radical type of vegetarian who disdained the use of all animal products, be it leather, milk or wool. They were against using animals for entertainment or even as pets (which was seen as confinement). "Our fight and debate is to stop cruelty." Without legislation, he said, there was no incentive for farmers and trappers to do anything other than what was economically expedient. Making money and humanitarianism were not always the same thing. "I don't think the issue will be dealt with until it is legislated," said Schwab.

Fighting by the "official" animal rights groups took many forms—protests, marches, demonstrations, advertising, brochures and speeches. All of it had a very strong message. Consider the following copy from an ad sponsored by "Friends of Animals":

> More than 100 million innocent animals are killed each year by gassing, electrocution, strangulation, neck breaking, clubbing, and leg-hold trapping. All for people to indulge in the beauty of their fur. It's time to stop following the whims of fashion. Instead to set our own standards. To become less callous and more compassionate. Because it's not just our world. It's their world, too.

With this kind of campaign, the antifur lobby had many successes. There was no pretty way to show death and the lobby was able to exploit this on an emotional basis. The European Parliament banned the import of seal pelts, and left-wing members annually proposed banning all fur imports. The Princess of Wales announced she would not wear fur. In the United States more than 300 separate pieces of legislation were introduced at the federal and state levels to restrict trapping. In many cases enactment of regulations took place without the fur industry's participation.

REACTIONS FROM THE FUR INDUSTRY

"The basic problem is that a great many animal welfare groups transpose human feelings to animals. That's not a valid thing to do. Animals aren't human. Just because something would make a human uncomfortable doesn't mean it will be uncomfortable for an animal." So said Sue Johnson, spokesperson for the Ontario Federa-

tion of Agriculture. She believed attempts to promote animal welfare were "thinly disguised efforts to promote vegetarianism." She claimed it wouldn't matter if the farmer or trapper brought his animals into the house, gave them a bed and a bathroom. "The problem from their perspective is that the animals are used for meat, fur and leather in the end."

But the fur industry was beginning to fight back against the forces of "bleeding-heart activism" using the same weapon that had ensnared it in the past: publicity. "Unless the fur industry mounts a significant and effective public awareness program," said Henry Lawson, executive director of the Fur Institute of Canada, "today's young people will be unalterably affected by antifur propaganda."

To guard against that fate, Canada's furriers formed the Fur Industry Public Awareness Committee (FIPAC) in 1985. It enlisted influential organizations representing Canadian native people in the pro-trapping cause. A delegation led by George Erasmus, national chief of the Assembly of First Nations, spent two weeks in Europe presenting the pro-trapping case to politicians, animal activists, and the media. As a result of such representations, both Greenpeace and the World Wildlife Fund agreed to tone down their opposition to trapping.

Through news releases, brochures, and speeches, the fur industry had portrayed itself as more sensitive to the natural environment than many of its city-dwelling critics. One Fur Institute brochure invoked ancient Cree mythology and Albert Schweitzer to make the point that killing animals was part of the natural order of things. "We know that Nature is far crueler than man. It doesn't allow Bambi to sit next to the otter and mink and tell stories at night."

The Institute also stressed that trappers employed humane trapping methods, used the entire animal, and didn't harvest endangered species. They also pointed out that the infamous leg-hold trap was now illegal in most Canadian jurisdictions.

The fur industry believed they were gaining ground against an antitrapping, antifarming lobby that they regarded as increasingly hysterical and misinformed. "There are people out there who believe you shouldn't even kill *rats*," said FIPAC Chairman Joshua Hanson. "You can't deal with people like that on a rational level."

Fur farming had some benefits. Use of modern genetic principles had helped to improve fur farming techniques. New colours of mink were developed which expanded the variety of combinations and styles of fur garments, increasing potential consumption. "Unless an animal is treated in the most humane way, is fed in the best possible manner, and is watched for diseases, we're not going to have a healthy pelt."

The fur industry was also consumer driven. Substitutes for furs did not constitute a threat to the industry.

Antifur activism contributed to the introduction and promotion of imitation furs in the early 1970s but the demand was low. Although they had some effect on sales of the cheapest fur garments, at the time of their introduction, this effect had not persisted. Imitation fur coats were usually purchased by women whose household disposable income was much lower than that of women who bought real fur coats.

While the antifur movement was very strong and effective, a consumer survey showed that only 4 percent of consumers or potential consumers in the core age group of 26 to 35 years old were against killing animals. One third of all women said they either owned or had owned a fur coat. Only 10 percent of this fur-owning group had stopped wearing the coat because of the animal rights issue. Still, one third of the women surveyed said they would never want to own a fur coat. More often, reasons for not planning to purchase a fur coat were lack of interest in furs, allergies to fur, dislike of furs, and, of course, inability to afford a fur coat.

Over the past three years, fur sales had declined in Europe by 40 percent and in North America by 20 percent. Fur retailers blamed the recent mild winters, layoffs (due to mergers and a stock market downturn) in the affluent financial and accounting communities, and increased competition from the Jindo chain.

BOUTIQUE VISON

Philip Nephelier emigrated from France in 1950. As he had experience in the fashion business in Paris, he opened a women's clothing store called La Parisienne on Queen Street near Spadina Avenue in Toronto, Ontario. In his first five years of operation, he experimented with his product mix and soon settled on selling women's coats made of various materials. It wasn't until the 1960s, with the increasing affluence of Canadians in general, and Torontonians in particular, that he specialized further to the field of fur coats and renamed his store Boutique Vison (French for Mink Shop).

"The 1960s were a great time to be selling fur in Toronto. All the women wanted to act like Jacqueline Kennedy. Fashion had been discovered and the height of fashion was owning two or three fur coats for formal occasions. My clientele consisted of older ladies between the ages of 35 and 70. Younger people were more interested in blue jeans and T-shirts."

In the 1970s, Spadina Avenue became home to many retail and wholesale establishments selling furs. Rather than lose business, volumes increased as more and more people traveled exclusively to the area to shop for furs. The businesses that lost sales were located outside the district. "Tastes changed little in the 70s. Women still wanted fox and mink coats. Seal coats declined in popularity. That is when the animal rights groups first had an impact on my business. They passed out their brochures, held a few marches, and focused the media on the seal hunt. I suppose the sight of baby seals being clubbed to death didn't help the matter. But people simply switched from buying seal to something else. They didn't stop buying fur.

"I should have sensed that the animal rights movement wouldn't die out. The success with seals in the 70s gave them strength. In the 80s they demanded that sales of all fur end. They became more militant. One day, in 1985, I found swastikas spray painted on my front windows. After one of my neighbor's stores had been broken into and some of the merchandise shredded with knives and covered in paint, I had iron bars installed on the windows and doors to protect myself. It was like working in a war zone.

"In 1988, it got worse. Periodically small crowds of animal rights activists would gather in front of my store and harass old friends and potential customers. I called the police several times and they did what they could, but the activists were never far away. In late 1988, I came in to the store one Monday morning to find several leg-hold traps filled with stuffed animals chained to the front of my store.

"But then it got worse. In the first four months of 1989, six women had been surprised while walking down the street in fur coats. A group of people, wearing animal masks, sprayed their coats with paint. Three of those people have been loyal customers of mine. True, they weren't injured and their insurance company reimbursed them for the loss. Still, at age 69, I don't know what to do. I don't want to fight a war. I don't have the strength or the determination I once had. The more outspoken furriers, Alan Cherry and Paul Magder, are doing what they can, but it's not enough.

"I'm not a callous person. The treatment of animals touches on our most basic philosophical views. George Bernard Shaw said 'animals are my friends . . . and I don't eat my friends.' Rene Descartes took the opposite view when he said 'Beasts abstract not. I think therefore I am.' I am troubled when animals are subjected to unnecessary harm as in a cock or dog fight. We are upset about pit bulls roaming our streets but we don't do anything about it. There is nothing illegal about selling fur coats and it is no more harmful than having a pit bull.

"I'm getting to the age where I'd like to retire. I had hoped that my nephew Gaston would take over the store but each month he seems to be less interested. Perhaps I can sell my store to someone else. I'm still doing a pretty good business though sales are down 10 percent from a year ago. I would really hate to close the store down, though. I don't want those animal rights people to think they've had a victory."

Should Pierre Gaston agree to purchase Boutique Vison? If he doesn't, what should Philip Nephelier do? Why?

7 Pillsbury's Häagen-Dazs

Assume you're the newly hired product-market manager for Häagen-Dazs, the market leader in the super premium ice-cream market. The company has seen its sales continue to grow during the 1980s, but this market may be on the edge of significant change and very aggressive competition—and you're now responsible for Häagen-Dazs' strategy planning.

Super premium ice-cream sales are slowing down, in part because of competition from other products such as lower-calorie yogurts and ice milk. Some producers' sales, including Häagen-Dazs', are continuing to grow at attractive rates: 10 to 50 percent a year. But other super premium producers are reporting flat sales, and some are going out of business.

There's some evidence, also, that the urge to indulge in super desserts may be giving way to diet and health concerns. Some people are reducing or even eliminating super desserts. And some dessert junkies who want to indulge without too much guilt are turning to soft frozen yogurt and low-calorie ice milk. This has encouraged some super premium ice-cream competitors to offer these products, too. Pillsbury's Häagen-Dazs, International Dairy Queen, Inc., and Baskin-Robbins are selling frozen yogurt. And Kraft, Inc., which makes Frusen Glädjé, and Dreyer's Grand Ice Cream, Inc., are among many other ice-cream makers who are promoting gourmet versions of ice milk. Some producers are even seeking government approval to call such ice milk "light ice cream."

Most ice-cream products are considered economy and regular brands—priced at $2.00 to $3.00 a half gallon. But the higher-priced—and higher-profit—super premium products provided most of the growth in the ice-cream market in the 1980s. The super premium ice-cream category accounted for about 12 percent of total ice-cream sales ($7 billion) in 1989 compared to almost 5 percent in 1980.

Super premium ice cream, with more than 14 percent butter fat (economy ice cream has a minimum of 10 percent) is the ultimate Yuppie product: rich, indulgent, and fashionable. It retails for $2.00 to $2.50 a *pint*, or $8.00 to $10.00 a half gallon.

The rapid growth of the super premium market may be over, however. More and more consumers are becoming concerned about cholesterol—and ice cream is high in cholesterol.

Some of the super premium producers remain optimistic, however. Häagen-Dazs, for example, feels that because "people like to make every calorie count—they want wonderful food." But other competitors are more concerned because they see many close competitors going out of business. Frozen yogurt seems to be a big factor. Also, the easy availability of super premium ice cream in supermarkets has hurt some competitors who sell through ice-cream stores, which specialize in take-out cones, sundaes, and small containers of ice cream.

Many ice-cream producers are turning to frozen yogurt for growth. A fad in the 1970s, frozen yogurt went into a long slump because many people didn't like the tart taste. But now the product has been reformulated and is winning customers. The difference is that today's frozen yogurt tastes more like ice cream.

The yogurt market leader, TCBY Enterprises, Inc., which had sales of only about $2 million in 1983, has risen to over $100 million in sales. Yogurt makers are using aggressive promotion against ice cream. TCBY ads preach, "Say goodbye to high calories—say goodbye to ice cream" and "All the pleasure, none of the guilt." And the ads for its nonfat frozen yogurt emphasize, "Say goodbye to fat and high calories with the great taste of TCBY Nonfat Frozen Yogurt."

Baskin-Robbins has introduced yogurt in many of its stores and has even changed its name to Baskin-Robbins Ice Cream and Yogurt. Häagen-Dazs also offers yogurt in most of its stores.

A new threat to super premium ice cream comes from ice milk. Traditionally, ice milk was an economical product for families on a budget. The butter fat content was at the low end of the 2 percent to 7 percent range. And, in part because of this, it was dense, gummy, and stringy, and had a coarse texture. But the new gourmet ice milk products taste better, due to 6 percent to 7 percent butter fat, less air content, and improved processing. And they still have only about half the calories of ice cream. Some producers of these products find their sales increasing nicely. Dreyer's, for example, is experiencing rapid growth of its Dreyer's Light, which retails for about $4.30 a half gallon.

Other ice-cream producers, including Häagen-Dazs, say they are not planning to offer ice milk under any name. These firms feel their brands stand for high quality and the best ingredients and they don't want to offer a cheap product. As one marketing manager put it, "Ice milk is a failure, and that's why some producers are trying to reposition it as light ice cream."

Evaluate what's happening in the ice-cream market. What should you advise Häagen-Dazs about the apparent leveling off of the super premium ice-cream market and the possible growth of the ice-milk market? Should you plan to have Häagen-Dazs offer an ice-milk product? Why?

8   Wilhelm Van Eyck*

Wilhelm Van Eyck turned his pickup into the lane of Eyckline Farms and stopped at the mailbox. Pulling out the day's mail, he found the usual collection of advertisements, magazines, and personal letters. He noted that his wife would be pleased to get her latest *Chatelaine* and that he had received a letter from cousin Charlie in B.C. Wilhelm and Charlie had corresponded regularly since their immigration to Canada 20 years before. They had gone through public school together and then worked on a local farm while taking evening agricultural courses. Then they left the Netherlands and came to Canada. Charlie settled in B.C. and Wilhelm came to Ontario. Wilhelm had done well for himself and was quite pleased with his operation, which included 50,000 broilers, 100 beef, 500 swine, and 300 acres of crops. He and Charlie spent most of their yearly visits in heated debates about the relative importance of various inputs into their broiler operations, and Wilhelm had little patience with Charlie's belief that he would increase his profits once he found the "magic feed" formula. Wilhelm always answered that no grower would ever have consistently outstanding crops—"too many variables, Charlie. Better to trust your own judgment, not some magic formula. You need healthy chicks and proper management as well as good feed." Charlie never listened, of course. That's what made their yearly visits so interesting.

Wilhelm tossed the mail on the seat beside him and continued down the lane. No doubt about it, he had come a long way in the 20 years since he and Charlie stepped off the boat. He surveyed the orderly spread of Eyckline Farms and admired the new siding on the house and the new chicken house built this year. "Yessir, if you make a dollar you sometimes do well to put it back into the business," he said to himself. He appreciated the advice the building representative had given him on ventilation for the new facility. Of course, it had been a bit extravagant, given Wilhelm's budget, but once he adapted it to his own operation, it had worked out fine. He appreciated good advice. Brushing a speck of dust off the steering wheel of his new pickup, Wilhelm gathered the mail and went into the house, where Polly Van Eyck was preparing lunch. Their sons Harold and Martin were already at the table. Harold, a student at the Ontario Agricultural College, was helping on the farm during the summer as was Martin, a grade 12 student at the local high school.

"Here's your magazine, Polly," Wilhelm said, "and we got a letter from Charlie, too."

"Anything from Guelph, Dad?" asked Harold.

"No, just advertisements. These guys never give up. Wait, here's one from Maple Leaf Mills. I wonder what they want. I just saw old Jim yesterday and he didn't seem to have anything to say—seemed in a hurry, as usual."

Maple Leaf Mills was Van Eyck's current feed supplier for his broiler operation. He had been using their Master Feed for two years despite two price increases. The last price increase had annoyed him somewhat since it seemed designed to cover an increase in extra salespeople services that Van Eyck did not use. However, he had stayed with Master because results were reasonably good. He had to admit that the last crop had not been up to par but he decided he would wait until he got the next results before considering a switch. All the same, he thought, as he looked at the letter, it would have been appreciated if Jim Sellars, the Master salesman, had stopped by to check up on his last results. "I guess he's too busy carting the neighbor's birds to the vet," Wilhelm thought to himself. Since Jim knew Wilhelm preferred to take his own birds to the vet, he rarely stopped by except to take an order.

Wilhelm gave no more thought to the letter from Maple Leaf Mills until after dinner that evening, when he and Harold looked over the accounts in the kitchen. He noticed again the relatively poor returns from the last crop of chicks and the latest price increase of Master Feeds. Harold suggested that they might do better with something less expensive. Then Wilhelm remembered the letter. Opening it, he discovered a form letter explaining MLM's new policy, which required their contract growers to assign proceeds from the processing plant to the feed firm where cost of feed and chicks were deducted. Wilhelm had never contracted with MLM, though he bought both feed and chicks from their companies. He preferred to choose his own processor, and it annoyed him that he should have received a form letter meant only for contract producers. He put down the letter and glanced again at the account book. It was irritating that Jim Sellars had not taken the time to make sure his noncontract customers did not receive the letter. "Too busy giving out expensive advice about medication and high brooder temperatures," muttered Van Eyck. Even more alarming was the policy itself, which seemed almost an insult and further evidence to Wilhelm that the producers who contracted with an integrated firm lost much of their independence. "I don't want anybody telling me what to pay for feed or chicks or when to ship my crop," Wilhelm said to Harold.

The next morning, Van Eyck was on his way to the barn when his neighbor Fritz Lonsdorf stopped by. Lonsdorf was one of the larger broiler producers in the area and Wilhelm enjoyed comparing notes with him. They chatted for awhile about the weather, then Wilhelm mentioned the new MLM policy and their carelessness in

*This case was written by Jane G. Funk and Thomas F. Funk, who at the time of its preparation were associated with the University of Guelph.

sending him the form letter. They had discussed the price increase earlier and Wilhelm's disappointing crop.

Fritz suggested trying his Domar brand; "my birds weighed over 4 lbs. at 7 weeks on the last crop."

"I remembered you telling me," said Wilhelm, lighting his pipe. He also remembered checking with the processor and finding that Fritz's birds had actually been killed at 7 weeks and 5 days and averaged 3.85 lbs. "Nice fellow, Fritz, but you have to take what he says with a grain of salt," Wilhelm told Harold at the time. "Dad," Harold laughed, "You say that about everybody. Fritz does brag a little but you and I both know 3.85 is a darned sight higher than our last average, even with that expensive feed."

He and Fritz continued chatting about John Stern's new farrowing house and the best cure for "bent beak syndrome." Fritz mentioned a new remedy that he had seen advertised in the Poultry Review. Wilhelm remained skeptical: "I wouldn't take a chance, Fritz. I'd get my birds to the vet as fast as I could if I were you. Maybe take them to the university. See what they think of your idea before you try it." Fritz said he would consider it and the two of them made further plans to visit the London Poultry Show later in the month. "Always look forward to seeing the new displays and talking with the other producers," Wilhelm said as Fritz left.

That evening, Wilhelm spread his account books on the kitchen table and noticed again the poor results of the last crop. Not drastic, he thought, but he would hate to see it continue, especially given the high price he paid for MLM feed. Fritz's results kept running through his mind. He thought Master Feed was much the same as other quality feeds but the latest price increase and the poor results made him wonder. He considered the other major variables in his operation to see if they could be responsible for the disappointing performance. His buildings and equipment were the latest design and he handled the management himself with Harold doing most of the work. In the past, Harold had been a little careless—failing to clean the waterer or some other little thing, but lately the boy was really shaping up—"guess they do teach something at the universities after all," thought Wilhelm. Harold often brought home new ideas and Wilhelm enjoyed hearing about the latest university research. No, it wasn't his equipment or management. The chicks, also purchased since he started his operation from MLM-owned Skyline Farms, were top quality. Wilhelm personally rushed them to the University or the lab at the least sign of disease. Lately, Jim Sellars seemed anxious to do this for his customers, but Wilhelm preferred to be right there to give the vet the benefit of his own ideas. He found the vet's advice sound, though he never followed it without first airing his own idea. "Nobody knows my operation as well as I do," he remarked to the vet.

Chicks, management, and equipment were all checked out. That left feed. With the latest price increase, the slightest rise in feed conversion could cause a significant decrease in return per bird. "Beyond a certain price, quality isn't that different," Wilhelm often told cousin Charlie. He looked at the entries in the record book that detailed his feed-purchasing history from the beginning of his operation:

5 years—Starlight Feeds, Milton Milling, Milton.

3 years—Supersweet Feed, Robin Hood Flour Mills Ltd., Milton (purchased Milton Milling).

2 years—A.J. Chance, Hespeler.

1 year— P & H Feeds, Hespeler (purchased A.J. Chance).

3 years—Full-O-Pep Feeds, Quaker Oats Company of Canada Ltd., Guelph.

2 years—Master Feeds, Maple Leaf Mills Ltd., Guelph (purchased Quaker operation).

Wilhelm remembered how he had been quite happy with Milton Milling and stayed with them even after they were purchased by Robin Hood. Soon, Robin Hood discontinued the Starlight brand and tried to switch customers to their Supersweet brand by offering an initial price reduction. Wilhelm had used Supersweet for three years even as the planned price increases were implemented because he was reluctant to switch. Finally, he could not agree that there was a quality difference worth the $8–$10 a ton premium that Robin Hood was charging. When the A.J. Chance salesperson came around and offered $10 a ton less, Wilhelm gave their feed a try and found it was every bit as good as the pricier Supersweet. Not only was it less expensive (about $1,000 less per crop) but more important, the feed conversion and weight both measured up.

Wilhelm stayed with Chance for two years, even after they were purchased by P & H Feeds. Once again, the price started to go up about $2–$3 per crop. "Seems to be the story of my operation," Wilhelm muttered to himself. P & H was now at the same price level as Quaker, and Wilhelm had heard about Quaker results from other growers, so he decided to give it a try. The results with Quaker had been good and Wilhelm stayed with them even after their operation was purchased by Maple Leaf Mills. Soon Maple Leaf Mills phased out the Quaker Line, replacing it with their own Master Feeds. Since Master was competitively priced, Van Eyck made the change and had been satisfied. Then Master began to raise their price. After two price increases, they were one of the most expensive brands in the area, priced in the range of Supersweet. Neither price increase had been announced, and Wilhelm had noticed it only after the feed bills arrived. Though not immediately alarmed,

Wilhelm had become uneasy when his latest crop results had been less than spectacular. "And here I am," Wilhelm said. "Every time one of those big fellows takes over, price goes up and service goes down."

Wilhelm felt he was pretty realistic about his feed expectations, unlike cousin Charlie. He also appreciated that Jim Sellars didn't pressure him to sign a contract but wished he would stop by every now and then for a chat—just to see how things were going. Wilhelm enjoyed chatting with salespeople about market changes, growers' results, disease problems, and so on. But he became annoyed when they brought out their "outstanding grower results." He also disliked paying (through price increases) for services that he did not use. It seemed that Jim Sellars was always too busy running around the country taking birds to the vet and dispensing "free" advice on feeder space, temperature and ventilation, all areas where Wilhelm relied on his own experience. When he wanted advice, he'd ask for it, thank you, and he'd ask somebody who knew what they were talking about.

Wilhelm shut the account books and wandered into the living room. Polly was at the church meeting and Harold and Martin were at the ballgame so he picked up the day's mail, turned on the radio and sat down. Glancing through the Poultry Review, he noticed the ads for A.J. Chance and Purina. Both featured a testimonial by an "outstanding poultry producer," neither of whom was known to Wilhelm. "Sure they get great results," Wilhelm thought. "They probably have $2 million worth of equipment!" An ad for new feeding equipment caught his eye and he made a note to ask Harold what he knew about it. Continuing on, he saw the medication mentioned by Fritz and made another note to ask the vet about it next time he was at the University. Then he heard a car drive in the lane and, looking out, saw Dave Crawford, the salesman for Martin Feeds in Elmira, walking toward the house. Crawford was a pleasant fellow, not much older than Harold. He had been with Martin Feeds for about a year and had been trying to get Wilhelm to consider their Domar brand feeds. It would be pleasant to pass some time with Crawford.

"Hello, Dave. Good to see you. Come on in and have a coffee."

"Thanks, Wilhelm, I was in the neighborhood and thought I'd stop by to give you this article on the new feeding system. I saw it in *Country Guide* and thought you would enjoy reading it."

"That's real thoughtful of you, Dave. I was considering a new system," Wilhelm answered, thinking how Jim Sellars had never even bothered to stop by to see the new chicken house, let alone bring round a bit of unsolicited information.

"My pleasure, Wilhelm, I figured you'd be alone tonight with the women off at the church meeting and the boys at the ballgame. Of course, I also wanted to see that new chicken house. It's the talk of the neighborhood."

They chatted for awhile about local events, latest marketing board activities, and Fritz Lonsdorf's problem with bent beak syndrome. Then Dave said, "Wilhelm, the mill is taking a group of growers to the London Poultry Show and I thought you might be able to join us."

Wilhelm thanked him but explained that he and Fritz had already planned to go. Dave then casually remarked, "I hear Master upped their prices again."

Wilhelm acknowledged that this was so. "Well," Dave went on, "they've got a good feed there, no doubt about it; are you still pleased with their results?"

Wilhelm hesitated, then admitted his last crop was disappointing.

"I can understand your feelings, Wilhelm. I really believe Domar can give you equal or better results. You know our quality and feed conversion ratios are competitive and our price is a good $5 a ton lower. Someone who is as experienced as you are knows we have to offer a quality product to stay in business. Why not let me drop by a ton on Tuesday and you can give us a try?"

"Dave, I'm just not ready to make a change yet, but I sure will give your offer some thought," Wilhelm answered. "I'll let you know in a couple of days."

"Sure, Wilhelm. I understand. I appreciate your considering us. Talk to you later," Crawford said as he rose to go. "Better get on, the women will be home soon."

The next day, Wilhelm took a load of birds to the vet. He drove past the P & H dealer but didn't stop, remembering that their prices were at least as high as Master. Besides, not one of their salespeople had stopped by since he had switched several years earlier. While at the vet, Wilhelm mentioned his dissatisfaction with Master and asked the vet's opinion about Domar. The vet agreed that above a certain price range quality was quite comparable and results would probably be much the same using either feed.

Driving back to Elmira, Wilhelm passed Chuck Hustead, the sales rep for Smith Feeds. Hustead pulled over and asked if Wilhelm had a few minutes to spare. Wilhelm glanced at the birds in the back, but said he could give Hustead a few minutes. Hustead climbed into the truck, dropping his portfolio in the process and scattering papers. Wilhelm sighed and glanced at his watch and the chicks sitting in the sun in the back while Hustead tried to rearrange the papers.

"I was just by your place, Wilhelm. That's some chicken house you have there. I was a little surprised at the ventilation, though."

Wilhelm filled his pipe and looked at Hustead pointedly. "Is that right. Chuck? Well, I did what I thought best."

"Sure, Wilhelm, but I thought those reports I showed you gave some pretty good suggestions," Hustead said.

"They were a little too experimental for me, Chuck. Now what can I do for you?"

"Well, I thought I would stop by and explain our new program. You know we're quality and price competitive, especially after that latest Master price increase."

Wilhelm's pipe went out and the chicks seemed to be getting more restless. Chuck didn't seem to notice as he continued. "Look at these reports! I'll bet you've never seen better results than these."

"My results aren't so bad, Chuck. Besides, I told you before, I don't hold with these consistently outstanding results. You know as well as I do that excellent crops are as much the result of chance and good management as they are of feed."

"Well, have it your own way Wilhelm, but these figures don't lie."

Wilhelm looked at him silently. "Besides, we'll deliver whenever you want and take your birds to the vet so you don't have to waste your time running around," Hustead continued.

Wilhelm's pipe went out again. "Speaking of birds, Chuck, you may have noticed mine are getting nervous so I'd best be getting on."

"Oh—sure, sure! I'll leave these results with you. Once you look them over I'm sure you'll be impressed. By the way, you considered doing business with Fairview Hatcheries? They have good quality chicks. Hardly ever get sick. Probably save you in the long run. Not nearly as nervous as yours."

"See you later, Chuck," said Wilhelm closing the door and driving away.

"I'll be hearing from you soon," shouted Hustead. Wilhelm drove on.

Smith had a good reputation and they were price and quality competitive but Wilhelm was annoyed at Hustead's continual harping on "excellent grower results." It was the same every call. Besides "the ventilation is fine in my new chicken house and it's my business which hatchery I choose!" At least Jim Sellars never pushed him to try a new hatchery! He put the chicks in the chicken house and went into the kitchen, dropping Hustead's reports on the table. Polly came over with the dishes and glancing at the reports said, "Do you need these, Wilhelm?"

"What? Oh, those. No, Polly, throw them away," Wilhelm said as he opened the evening paper.

In the days that followed, Wilhelm continued thinking about his feed situation but made no move to change dealers, as he still had some Master Feed left. He knew he would have to decide soon. Crawford stopped by several times and so did Hustead. Jim Sellars came by once but Wilhelm was out. He left a message to have Wilhelm call if he had any problems. Wilhelm knew there were other feed dealers in the immediate area and he was not opposed to traveling a few miles further, though he thought local feed was probably fresher. Their prices were all pretty competitive with Smith and Domar and the quality similar, at least in his view. There were also several large companies with prices similar to Master and P & H, but he suspected the price difference went into their flashy advertising and not the quality of their feed. "Maybe it isn't worth it to change," he thought. Just then, Jim Sellars passed him on the road and waved. Wilhelm thought he might be coming for a chat but Jim drove on. Wilhelm turned into Eyckline Farms. He had made his decision and would place the call after dinner.

Outline in detail Wilhelm Van Eyck's purchasing decision process. What do you think Wilhelm's decision was? Why? Assuming that Wilhelm is representative of a large group of broiler growers, what marketing implications can be drawn from your analysis? Evaluate the approach and effectiveness of the three sales representatives who called on Wilhelm.

9 Sleepy-Inn Motel

Jack Roth is trying to decide whether he should make some minor changes in the way he operates his Sleepy-Inn Motel or if he should join either the Days Inn or Holiday Inn motel chains. Some decision must be made soon because his present operation is losing money. But joining either of the chains will require fairly substantial changes, including new capital investment if he goes with Holiday Inn.

Jack bought the recently completed 60-room motel two years ago after leaving a successful career as a production manager for a large producer of industrial machinery. He was looking for an interesting opportunity that would be less demanding than the production manager job. The Sleepy-Inn is located at the edge of a very small town near a rapidly expanding resort area and about one-half mile off an interstate highway. It is 10 miles from the tourist area, with several nationally franchised full-service resort motels suitable for "destination" vacations. There is a Best Western, a Ramada Inn, and a Hilton Inn, as well as many "mom and pop" and limited service–lower price motels in the tourist area. The interstate highway near the Sleepy-Inn carries a great deal of traffic since the resort area is between several major metropolitan areas. No development has taken place around the turnoff from the interstate highway. The only promotion for the tourist area along the interstate highway is two large signs near the turnoffs. They show the popular name for the area and that the area is only 10 miles to the west. These signs are maintained by the tourist area's Tourist Bureau. In addition, the state transportation department maintains several small signs showing (by symbols) that near this turnoff one can find gas, food, and lodging. Jack does not have any signs advertising Sleepy-Inn except the two on his property. He has been relying on people finding his motel as they go towards the resort area.

Initially, Jack was very pleased with his purchase. He had traveled a lot himself and stayed in many different hotels and motels, so he had some definite ideas about what travelers wanted. He felt that a relatively plain but modern room with a comfortable bed, standard bath facilities, and free cable TV would appeal to most customers. Further, Jack thought a swimming pool or any other nonrevenue-producing additions were not necessary. And he felt a restaurant would be a greater management problem than the benefits it would offer. However, after many customers commented about the lack of convenient breakfast facilities, Jack served a free continental breakfast of coffee, juice, and rolls in a room next to the registration desk.

Day-to-day operations went fairly smoothly in the first two years, in part because Jack and his wife handled registration and office duties—as well as general management. During the first year of operation, occupancy began to stabilize around 55 percent of capacity. But according to industry figures, this was far below the average of 68 percent for his classification—motels without restaurants.

After two years of operation, Jack was concerned because his occupancy rates continued to be below average. He decided to look for ways to increase both occupancy rate and profitability and still maintain his independence.

Jack wanted to avoid direct competition with the full-service resort motels. He stressed a price appeal in his signs and brochures—and was quite proud of the fact that he had been able to avoid all the "unnecessary expenses" of the full-service resort motels. As a result, Jack was able to offer lodging at a very modest price—about 40 percent below the full-service hotels and comparable to the lowest-priced resort area motels. The customers who stayed at Sleepy-Inn said they found it quite acceptable. But he was troubled by what seemed to be a large number of people driving into his parking lot, looking around, and not coming in to register.

Jack was particularly interested in the results of a recent study by the regional tourist bureau. This study revealed the following information about area vacationers:

1. 68 percent of the visitors to the area are young couples and older couples without children.

2. 40 percent of the visitors plan their vacations and reserve rooms more than 60 days in advance.

3. 66 percent of the visitors stay more than three days in the area and at the same location.

4. 78 percent of the visitors indicated that recreational facilities were important in their choice of accommodations.

5. 13 percent of the visitors had family incomes of less than $20,000 per year.

6. 38 percent of the visitors indicated that it was their first visit to the area.

After much thought, Jack began to seriously consider affiliating with a national motel chain in hopes of attracting more customers and maybe protecting his motel from the increasing competition. There were constant rumors that more motels were being planned for the area. After some investigating, he focused on two national chain possibilities: Days Inn and Holiday Inn. Neither had affiliates in the area.

Days Inn of America, Inc., is an Atlanta-based chain of economy lodgings. It has been growing rapidly and is willing to take on new franchisees. A major advantage of Days Inn is that it would not require a major capital investment by Jack. The firm is targeting people interested in lower-priced motels—in particular, senior citizens, the military, school sports teams, educators, and business travelers. In contrast, Holiday Inn would probably require Jack to upgrade some of his facilities, including adding a swimming pool. The total new capital investment would be between $300,000 and $500,000, depending on how fancy he got. But then Jack would be able to charge higher prices—perhaps $70 per day on the average, rather than the $40 per day per room he's charging now.

The major advantages of going with either of these national chains would be their central reservation system—and their national names. Both companies offer toll-free reservation lines nationwide, which produce about 40 percent of all bookings in affiliated motels.

A major difference between the two national chains is their method of promotion. Days Inn uses little TV advertising and less print advertising than Holiday Inn. Instead, Days Inn emphasizes sales promotions. In a recent campaign, for example, Blue Bonnet margarine users could exchange proof-of-purchase seals for a free night at a Days Inn. This tie-in led to the Days Inn system *selling* an additional 10,000 rooms. Further, Days Inn operates a September Days Club for over 300,000 senior citizens who receive such benefits as discount rates and a quarterly travel magazine. This club accounts for about 10 percent of the chain's room revenues.

Both firms charge 8 percent of gross room revenues for belonging to their chain—to cover the costs of the reservation service and national promotion. This amount is payable monthly. In addition, franchise members must agree to maintain their facilities—and make repairs and improvements as required. Failure to maintain facilities can result in losing the franchise. Periodic inspections are conducted as part of supervising the whole chain and helping the members operate more effectively.

Evaluate Jack Roth's present strategy. What should he do? Explain.

10 O & E Farm Supply*

It was a cool, rainy day in November of 1986 when Len Dow, manager of O & E Farm Supply was sitting in his office looking over the past season's records. He felt he had brought the fertilizer outlet a long way since he purchased it in February of 1985. Volume, which had declined to 7,000 tonnes in 1984 due to poor management, increased to 8,400 tonnes in 1985, and to 10,000 tonnes in 1986 (see Exhibit 1). Profit margins, which were also lower in 1984, had returned to their normal 6 percent level in 1986 due to Len's good managing abilities. In spite of all this, Len was not completely satisfied; he wanted to increase the volume and profitability of the outlet, but was not sure what direction he should take.

THE COMPANY

O & E Farm Supply is located in Goodland, a town centrally located in a major corn and potato–producing area of Ontario. O & E does most of its business within a 5-mile radius of Goodland (60 percent). However, it does have some sales and distribution extending 20 miles from its plant (35 percent), and a very small wholesale market over 100 miles away in Northern Ontario (5 percent). At the present time O & E is involved only in the sale of fertilizers and related services. Dry bulk blends and bagged blends make up the majority of O & E's fertilizer volume (9,000 tonnes) with 28 percent liquid nitrogen making up a much smaller portion (1,000 tonnes). Potato and vegetable farmers purchase almost 60 percent of O & E's production, corn and cereal farmers account for 33 percent, and sod farmers purchase the remaining 7 percent (see Exhibit 2).

---

*This case was prepared by Thomas Funk, Ed Gimpelj, and Ousmane Guindo of the University of Guelph, Guelph, Ontario. All data in the case has been disguised to protect confidentiality. © 1991 by Thomas F. Funk.

Exhibit 1   O & E Fertilizer Sales

Year	Tonnes Liquid and Dry Fertilizers	Tonnes Micronutrients
1982	11,000	—
1983	11,000	—
1984	7,000	—
1985	8,400	10
1986	10,000	100

O & E sells a custom application service for bulk fertilizers and rents application equipment to farmers who wish to apply their own fertilizer. Current equipment consists of two dry fertilizer spreader trucks, two feeder delivery trucks to refill spreader trucks on the farms, and three four-tonne tractor-pulled spreaders which are rented out to customers who spread fertilizer themselves. Since Len purchased the organization he cut the full-time staff from seven to five including himself. One of his newest employees is a young agricultural university graduate who spends most of his time in a sales capacity calling on present and potential customers in the area. Len also spends some of his time making farm calls.

Of O & E's 85 local customers in 1986, five were merchant dealers who resell to farmers. These five dealers accounted for 2,000 tonnes of O & E's business and ranged in volume from 100 to 1,000 tonnes each. For the most part these dealers are located on the fringes of O & E's 20-mile trading area. Of the remaining 80 local customers, Len's records showed that 70 were within five miles of the Goodland plant and 10 were at a greater distance. Almost all of these customers purchased more than 50 tonnes of fertilizer a year from O & E.

O & E sold 10 tonnes of micronutrients in 1985 and over 100 tonnes in 1986. Micronutrients are basic elements that a plant requires in relatively small amounts, compared to the larger amounts of nitrogen, phosphorus, and potassium found in most regular, blended fertilizers. Micronutrients have been proven by university and industry research in the US to improve the quality and yield of crops. Commercial trials carried out in Ontario have indicated similar positive results.

Exhibit 2   O & E Fertilizer Sales by Farm Type, 1986

Farm Type	Percent of Dry Fertilizer Sales	Percent of Acres Served
Potato and vegetable	60%	35%
Corn and cereals	33	60
Sod	7	5

THE MARKET AND COMPETITION

The total market for fertilizers in O & E's trading area has been remarkably stable at approximately 50,000 tonnes for the past several years. This is not expected to change significantly in the future although some shifts in types used are possible. Within five miles of Goodland there are four major fertilizer outlets competing with O & E for approximately 25,000 tonnes of fertilizer business, and within 20 miles there are an additional three fertilizer outlets competing for the remaining 25,000 tonnes. Len estimates that there are approximately 550 farmers within a five-mile radius of Goodland.

Although the market for fertilizer is very competitive, Len feels that he has been able to better his competition by offering excellent service, by remaining open extended hours, by offering advice and timely delivery to his customers, and by knowing how to deal with the large farmer. Len quickly came to realize that farmers placed service ahead of price when deciding where to buy fertilizer as long as the price was close to that of the competition. Len felt that by offering a superior service, he had nurtured a high level of dealer loyalty in his customers which resulted in a lower turnover relative to his competition.

GROWTH OPPORTUNITIES

Although the business had been doing well, Len realized that growth was essential to future success. He therefore had been giving this matter considerable thought the past couple of months. So far, he was able to identify several avenues of growth—now his problem was to evaluate each and arrive at some plan for 1987 and beyond.

Liquid nitrogen

Len had been toying with the idea of getting into 28 percent liquid nitrogen in a bigger way. He estimated that the total current market in his 20-mile trading area was 4,000 tonnes, of which he sold 1,000 tonnes to three corn farmers. This type of fertilizer is of interest mainly to the larger corn farmer because it can be mixed with herbicides for combined application and because of its ease of handling. Although its price per tonne is less than the price per tonne for dry fertilizers, it is comparable in terms of price per unit of actual nitrogen. This is because it usually is less concentrated than other forms of nitrogen such as dry urea which contains 45 percent nitrogen compared to the 28 percent concentration in the liquid form. The product is very corrosive, which means that the farmer must also purchase a stainless steel sprayer costing about $2,000 if he is to use 28 percent liquid nitrogen. This relatively high initial capital outlay restricts use to fairly large farmers. Of the 400 corn farmers in his trading area, approximately 200 have sufficient acreage to be possible 28 percent liquid nitrogen users, and Len estimated that about 20 farmers were using 28 percent liquid nitrogen in 1986. Price is the major purchase criteria since the product is a commodity and little service is involved. Most of the volume of 28 percent liquid nitrogen is sold in December for delivery in the spring (see Exhibit 3 for Costs and Margins). O & E's current holding capacity is 10,000 gallons or 50 tonnes. If output is increased, additional storage and nurse tanks would have to be purchased, as well as another pumping system. A pumping system costs $4,000, storage tanks cost 15 cents per gallon, and a 1,400 gallon nurse tank costs $1,000. Len feels one additional pumping system, one more 10,000 gallon storage tank and two more nurse tanks should allow a large increase in sales. No matter what Len decided to do, he wanted to stay ahead of his competition by at least two years. Because he felt 28 percent liquid nitrogen could be a big thing in the future, he was excited about this possibility. He had seen a new type of potato planter which required only liquid fertilizer. If this type of planter became popular, the potential for liquid fertilizer would increase dramatically. Despite these positive feelings about this market, Len was concerned about a number of things, including the relatively

Exhibit 3   Fertilizer Prices and Margins

| | Dry Fertilizers | | 28 Percent Liquid Nitrogen | | | | Micronutrients | |
| | | | Winter | | Spring | | | |
	$ per tonne	Percent	$ per tonne	Percent	$ per tonne	Percent	$ per tonne	Percent
Average selling price	$248	100%	$138	100%	$170	100%	$700	100%
Cost of sales	203	82	131	95	136	80	595	85
Gross margin	45	18	7	5	34	20	105	15
Estimated fixed costs	$260,000				$20,000		$5,000	

low liquid nitrogen margins and the slow growth of this market in the past. He also wondered whether or not he should consider offering a weed and feed service where O & E would apply liquid fertilizer and herbicides for the farmer all in one operation. Len was not really sure of the demand for this service or what was involved in operating a weed and feed program. He did know that there was no one currently offering such a service in his area.

Micronutrients

Another opportunity confronting Len was to try to expand micronutrient sales in a major way. At the present time, O & E was a dealer for the Taylor Chemical Company which produces and sells a complete line of micronutrients. Included in their line are manganese, zinc, iron, copper, molybdenum, boron, calcium, and sulfur. These materials are sold separately or in various combinations designed to treat specific crops. An example of the latter is the company's vegetable mix which contains magnesium, sulfur, copper, iron, manganese, and zinc in fixed proportions. The individual materials and mixes are sold in two ways: in a dry form for mixing by the dealer with other fertilizer products, and in liquid form for spray application by the farmer on the foliage of the growing crop. Although foliar application is more bother for the farmer and may result in some leaf burning, some farmers prefer it because they can postpone micronutrient application until visible signs of deficiencies occur. Also, there is some research which indicates that micronutrients can be most effective if absorbed through the leaves at the peak growth period of the plant. Despite the apparent advantages of foliar application, Len had not sold any micronutrients in this form during his first two years in this business. If properly applied, he felt liquid micronutrients offered the most value to his customers, yet he noticed a great deal of reluctance and skepticism on the part of even the most progressive farmers in his area to try this product form.

Sales of the dry, mixed micronutrients had grown considerably over the past year and it appeared that the products offered real value to customers. One of Len's customers applied micronutrients to half of a large potato field and treated the other half as he normally did. The treated field yielded 327 hundredweight, whereas the untreated portion only yielded 304 hundredweight. This 23 cwt. gain resulted in a $111.55 higher revenue per acre when computed at the $4.85 per cwt. price to the farmer. Unfortunately, the University of Guelph, which farmers look to for technical information, is not promoting or even recommending the use of micronutrients (see Appendix B). Their soil testing service, which analyzes soil samples for most Ontario farmers and makes fertilizer use recommendations, doesn't even include an analysis for micronutrients. The competition does not want to get involved in this business unless there is a very high demand and they start to lose their other fertilizer business. Of the 100 tonnes sold in 1986, 75 went to six large potato farmers representing 3,500 acres, 10 tonnes went to vegetable farmers, and 15 tonnes went to corn farmers (see Exhibit 4 for rates and costs per acre). Len has been receiving excellent service and advice from the company distributing the micronutrients. He felt that the use of micronutrients was becoming accepted by the farmers using them, and that sales should rise in the future. Len chuckled to himself as he recalled the day two very large potato farmers who were brothers were sitting in his office and the subject of micronutrients came up. One of the brothers, Jack, asked the Taylor sales rep if he thought they should be using micronutrients. The sales rep related all of the advantages of using micronutrients to them, whereupon Jack turned to his brother and asked, "Well, what do you think?" Peter replied, "Yes, I think we should be using them." With that Len landed a micronutrients order worth several thousand dollars.

Len was convinced that micronutrients had potential in his area. His major concern was how he could convince farmers to spend an additional $10 to $15 per acre on a product for which there was no objective basis for determining need.

Northern Ontario

Len was also considering expanding sales in Northern Ontario. Currently he has three dealers selling bagged fertilizer for him in Sault Ste Marie, New Liskeard, and Kenora. O & E's current volume is approximately 500 tonnes of bagged fertilizer only. Several Co-op outlets have most of the market in this area. Prices are very competitive and there appears to be strong dealer loyalty to the Co-ops. There are many small farms in the region with 75–100 acres of workable land per farm. The crop types in the area are mixed grain, barley, hay, and a few hundred acres of potatoes near Sudbury. On the average, farmers in Northern Ontario who use fertilizer purchase 2–3 tonnes of bagged fertilizer per year and do their purchasing in the winter months. Because the retail price of fertilizer in Northern Ontario is similar to that around Goodland, the margin to O & E is reduced by about $17

Exhibit 4 Micronutrient Sales by Crop, 1986

Crop	Tonnes Sold	Acres	Application Rate	Cost per Acre
Potatoes	75	3,500	50# per acre	$15.90
Corn	15	1,300	25# per acre	$ 8.00
Vegetables	10	400	50# per acre	$15.90

a tonne, the sum of the $12 dealer commission and the $5 freight cost. The lower margin is offset to some extent by lower personal selling costs, since dealers are used. Although the growing season is only 2–3 weeks behind that of Goodland, because most sales in the area occur in the winter months, O & E's ability to service the Goodland area in the spring is not affected. One reservation about dealing with the distant Northern Ontario market is that credit could be a problem, particularly because the cost of collection could run very high due to the distance involved. On the more positive side, Len is quite optimistic about the long-run potential growth of this market. He feels that there is an ultimate total industry potential in this market of 50,000 to 60,000 tonnes of dry fertilizer, of which perhaps 10 to 20 percent has been developed at the present time.

Agricultural chemicals

So far, O & E's product line consisted only of fertilizers. Len observed, however, that all of his competitors carried insecticides, herbicides, and fungicides as well, and he wondered if he should be getting into this business too. Len had always believed that concentrating on one line was the way to go. Agricultural chemicals were very competitively priced, leaving small margins in the neighbourhood of 5–10 percent for the dealer. Len felt that farmers in his trading area bought fertilizer and chemicals each on their own merits. Even if a dealer had a hot price on fertilizers, farmers would not buy their chemicals from that dealer unless they were also being offered the lowest price. At any rate, Len sized up his customers as not wanting to buy everything from one dealer, so he was satisfied to receive all of their fertilizer business and to leave the other lines to the other dealers. The set-up costs for carrying chemicals would be approximately $20,000 for an additional warehouse. No other direct costs would be attributable to the chemical line, but Len knew that servicing the line would take valuable time away from servicing and selling the fertilizer line, which could possibly result in lower sales and profits. Len estimated that the average farmer in his trading area spent $3,000 to $5,000 per year on agricultural chemicals.

Dry fertilizers

An alternative Len thought particularly attractive was to expand dry fertilizer sales in his local trading area. Although he had a substantial share of this market already, he felt it would be possible to pick up additional business through aggressive marketing. He was especially interested in this alternative because, no matter what he did, he knew his present plant, which was over 20 years old, would have to be replaced. A new plant could be purchased in two sizes: the smaller size was similar to his present system with a peak-season capacity of 12,000 tonnes and cost $100,000, while the larger size had a peak-season capacity of 15,000 tonnes and cost $160,000. Because of this opportunity to increase his capacity, Len wondered if he shouldn't go with the larger plant and try to sell more dry fertilizer to both his current customers and some new ones in his local trading area. As part of his strategy to do this, he was thinking about adding another person to his staff who would act as a second salesman and develop and offer a comprehensive crop management service to interested farmers. He was also considering the possibility of developing a local advertising program aimed at developing more awareness and interest among farmers outside his immediate 5 mile concentrated area. The total cost of the new sales specialist would be about $35,000 per year, and the local advertising would cost about $10,000 per year.

THE DECISION

Len knew he would have to make a decision soon if he were to make some changes for 1986. Although he had identified what he thought were several good opportunities for future growth, he knew he could not pursue all of them right away and, therefore, he would have to establish some priorities. To help in this assessment, he recently wrote away to the University of Guelph and received a publication entitled "Farmer Purchasing and Use of Fertilizers in Ontario" (see Appendix A for a summary of this 1984 study). With this new information, plus his own size-up of the situation, Len began the process of planning for 1987 and beyond. He knew that economic conditions in 1987 were not expected to be good. This made the necessity of coming up with a successful plan all the more important to Len.

Which of the possible growth opportunities should O & E pursue? Which should not be followed up? On what are you basing your decisions?

APPENDIX A   RESULTS OF FERTILIZER MARKETING RESEARCH STUDY

1. Only 7 percent of total crop acreage in Southern Ontario is not fertilized at the present time. This acreage is almost entirely in soybeans, pasture, and forages.
2. The average fertilizer application rate for Southern Ontario farmers is 384 pounds per acre. Most farmers use soil test recommendations from the University of Guelph to determine the application rate. There is some tendency for farmers to apply

more fertilizer than recommended by their soil tests.

3. The major types of fertilizer used by Southern Ontario farmers are dry bulk blends and liquid nitrogen. Of lesser importance are dry bagged fertilizers, anhydrous ammonia, and liquid mixes (N-P-K). Liquid nitrogen fertilizers are almost exclusively used by very large farmers.

4. Most farmers find the quality and availability of fertilizers to be very good.

5. In Southern Ontario as a whole, a relatively small percentage of farmers purchase a large percentage of the fertilizer products sold. The breakdown is as follows:

	Percent of Farmers	Percent of Purchases
Under 25 tonnes	30%	10%
26–50 tonnes	35	25
51–100 tonnes	20	20
Over 100 tonnes	15	45

6. Over 70 percent of all dry fertilizers are sold to farmers in April and May. This figure is somewhat lower (50 percent) for liquid nitrogen.

7. Thirty percent of Ontario farmers use dealer custom application services, while 75 percent apply the fertilizer themselves using rented dealer application equipment. There is some tendency for larger farmers to be more inclined to want custom application services.

8. In the course of a year, farmers discuss their fertilizer program with a number of parties to get information and advice on various aspects of fertilizer use and dealer selection. The influence groups most widely consulted are the local fertilizer dealer, other farmers, and family members. In addition to these influence groups, fertilizer company representatives, agricultural extension officials, and University scientists are consulted by some farmers. In the case of company representatives and University scientists, proportionately more larger farmers visit these people than smaller farmers.

9. Farmers also obtain fertilizer information from soil test results, various government publications, company sponsored farmer meetings, dealer demonstration plots, and company and dealer displays at farm shows and fairs.

10. Over 60 percent of all farmers contact more than one fertilizer dealer before making a purchase. Larger farmers have a tendency to contact more dealers than smaller farmers.

11. Over 50 percent of all farmers reported receiving an on-farm call by a fertilizer dealer in the last year. Larger farmers reported receiving more dealer calls than smaller farmers.

12. In addition to fertilizers, Southern Ontario farmers purchase, on the average, more than three other products from their fertilizer supplier. Of these, the most common are: herbicides, insecticides, general farm supplies, and seeds. Large farmers are more likely to purchase herbicides and insecticides from their fertilizer supplier than are small farmers.

13. Six dealer services were identified as being essential to all but a very small proportion of farmers: application equipment which is available when needed and in good repair; custom application services; custom fertilizer blending; fertilizer information through a well-informed staff, brochures, newsletters, and farmer meetings; soil testing; and demonstrations.

14. Other dealer services which were reported as being important to smaller groups of farmers were: crop management assistance, help in securing expert assistance with problems, and custom herbicide application.

15. Dealer location, price, and availability of product when needed are the major factors farmers consider when selecting a fertilizer dealer. In general, dealer location and availability of product when needed are more important to smaller farmers, while price is more important to larger farmers.

16. Over 45 percent of all farmers purchase fertilizer from their nearest dealer. On the average, farmers purchase from dealers located less than five miles from their farms.

17. Thirty percent of all farmers purchase from more than one dealer. Larger farmers have a greater tendency to spread their purchases over more dealers than do small farmers.

18. Analysis of dealer switching showed that one-third of the farmers made no dealer changes in the past five years, one-third made only one change, and the remaining one-third made two or more changes. Those farmers making several dealer changes are the larger, younger farmers.

APPENDIX B† NO SUBSTITUTES FOR ROTATION

This past year there has been a lot of interest in Perth and Huron counties about micronutrients. There are numerous plots out this year with different formulations and mixes and ways of application, both on corn and beans. We are sure there will be a lot of discussion this winter about the subject.

Some things are becoming evident about micronutrients, at least we think they are. The first is that you cannot expect dramatic yield increases with individual nutrients on small areas.

Secondly, none of the micronutrient sales staff has been able to explain to us the problem of overapplying micronutrients. They suggest if you put on too much potash you may tie up magnesium. If you put on too much phosphorus, you may need to put on more zinc and manganese. We believe, with our variable soils, in some fields you can put on too much zinc and manganese.

Finally, these micronutrients seem to be most attractive to growers with poor crop rotations. Some of your neighbours have gone to poor crop rotations and their yields have dropped. (You know they are the ones that think Pioneer corn followed by Cargill corn is crop rotation.) Now they are searching for something to pull their yield back to former highs. Micronutrients appear to them to be an answer.

What puzzles us is why some of you are willing to spend large sums of money on products you are not sure will work: shotgun micronutrients. We both know what the problem is. You have to get more crops into the rotation, especially perennial forages. I suppose the bottom line is when you hear your neighbour talking about all the micronutrients he is using. That's just a polite way for him to tell you he has a terrible crop rotation.

11 Different Strokes*

For some time Keith Dahl, a Winnipeg fireman and avid golfer, has considered purchasing and operating a golf

course. An 18-hole, par 3 course located on the outskirts of Winnipeg recently came on the market and Keith was interested. Two years earlier he had inherited a considerable amount of money and was just waiting for an appropriate opportunity to acquire a functioning golf course. Keith had not had a chance to go over the books of the privately owned, but open to the public, Rolling Hills Golf Course although he understood from discussions with other local business people that a couple of problem areas existed. First, the course was too short to provide a real challenge to "serious" golfers. Second, novice players found that a round took "forever" (over 4 hours) to play. And third, it was felt that the present course could not accommodate enough players in a day for the operation to break even. Keith was not sure how he could solve these problems until he happened to be leafing through a recent issue of *Golf Digest* and proclaimed, "I think I've found the answer; the Cayman Ball."

THE CAYMAN BALL

For many years golf ball manufacturers have been devoting their principal research efforts to the development of a longer ball—that is, a golf ball that can be driven further and still meet Golf Association standards. It came as some surprise then when Jack Nicklaus, a living legend in the game of golf, announced the development of a new ball that travelled only half as far as a conventional golf ball.

For several years, Nicklaus, a golfer, course designer, and golf equipment manufacturer, had been considering the concept of a golf ball with regular performance characteristics that would only travel half the regular distance. Convincing the MacGregor Company to begin research and development on the project was no problem—Nicklaus owned the company.

The ball was manufactured by a relatively simple process. It consisted of heating a combination of microscopic glass bubbles and surlyn, and injecting this mixture into the cavity of a mold for a one-piece ball. The ball had a variable density—lighter in the center and heavier toward the outside. Its flight and other characteristics closely resembled those of a conventional ball except for one thing—it floated on water.

The new ball was the same size as a regular ball, 1.68 inches in diameter, but weighed only 40 percent of normal weight, or two-thirds of an ounce. The cost of the ball to the consumer was expected to be similar to that of a conventional ball.

Nicklaus found that using this new ball basically halved the distance he could normally hit with each of his clubs. This translated into a typical shot of approxi-

†This appendix was written by Pat Lynch and John Heard. Mr. Lynch is a soils and crops specialist with the Ontario Ministry of Agriculture and Food. Mr. Heard is an assistant agricultural representative in Perth County. The article appeared in an issue of *Cash Crop Farming*, a publication widely received by Ontario farmers.

*Written by Stephen Tax, MBA, under the supervision of Professor Walter S. Good, as a basis for classroom discussion rather than to illustrate either effective or ineffective handling of an administrative situation. Copyright by the Case Development Program, Faculty of Management, University of Manitoba. Support for the development of this case was provided by the Canadian Studies Program, Secretary of State, Government of Canada.

mately 135 yards with his driver, 100 yards with a 3-iron, and 50 yards with a full wedge. It putted about the same as a regular ball although on longer putts he commented, "you have to hit it a tad harder."

WHY THE NEW BALL?

The basic question asked by many people was why would Jack Nicklaus, affectionately known as the Golden Bear and considered by many to be the greatest golfer of all time, want to change the fundamental structure of the game? The answer was simple; a combination of economics and a desire to introduce new players to the game of golf.

Conventional 18-hole golf courses required a lot of land, could handle relatively few golfers per day, and took what seemed to be an eternity (4 hours or more) to play. For example, a typical par 72 municipal golf course might require 150 acres of land, while a similarly designed par 72 short ball course could be constructed on 50 acres. Nicklaus believed this would be especially appealing in large cities, or countries such as Japan, where land was expensive or in limited supply and the demand to play golf was very high.

He also believed that a 150 acre municipal course that would normally accommodate 200 people in one day could handle 1,600 if it were designed for the short ball. He figured a foursome could play an 18-hole round of golf in two hours on a short ball facility. In effect, golf could be played in half the time, on one-third the land, by eight times as many people. People familiar with the concept also felt the short ball could spawn a number of interesting marketing opportunities for golf entrepreneurs such as lunch-hour golf, backyard golf (MacGregor figured it could also make a ball that would only travel one-quarter the distance of a normal ball), mixed tournaments in which the husband hits the short ball and the wife a conventional ball, and so on. Nicklaus also saw some potential in converting existing par 3 (holes under 250 yards) courses overnight into championship calibre short-ball courses.

CRITICS OF THE CONCEPT

Detractors of the idea contended that the short ball did not have a chance. They felt that no one seriously wanted to only drive a golf ball 100 yards. In contrast, most golfers were combing sporting goods stores and golf course pro shops for balls they could "send into orbit." One golf course architect believed golf traditionalists/purists would resist the short ball just as they resisted Arnold Palmer's ill-fated attempt to introduce 12-hole golf. In addition, the ball was affected more by strong wind conditions than conventional balls. This could be quite frustrating for many golfers and what golfer needed another source of frustration?

INTRODUCTION OF THE IDEA

Once the ball was well along in its development Nicklaus and MacGregor had another decision to make—where to introduce the short ball?

In late 1983, an opportunity arose for Jack to design a golf course as part of a new resort development on Grand Cayman Island. Grand Cayman, a British Crown colony, consisted of 118 square miles of coral with a population of about 18,000 people. It was located in the Caribbean approximately 480 miles south of Miami. Nicklaus believed that this site, being developed by Ellesmere Developments Ltd., of Edmonton, would be perfect for unveiling his new ball.

Despite the fact only 88 acres were available in Grand Cayman to build a golf course, clubhouse, 240 room hotel and marina, plus a number of villas and condominium units, Nicklaus was able to design two 18-hole short ball courses and a conventional, par 35, 9-hole course.

The cost for the design, construction and initial six month growing-in period for the Brittania course was about $4 million. The average cost of a conventional 18-hole course was about $2 million. The annual maintenance budget for Brittania was $550,000, double that of most 18-hole courses. However, these high costs were primarily a function of specific site characteristics such as high labour costs, the difficulty in developing water hazards, and import duties for machinery and materials shipped in from Miami; not the type of golf ball being used.

On February 17, 1985, with Jack Nicklaus in attendance, the Brittania golf course opened for business. Initial golfer reaction was quite positive, although some players found club selection to be a problem. Nicklaus was very enthusiastic about the future of the short ball concept.

CONCLUSION

The Cayman ball appeared to have the potential to solve many of the problems of the Rolling Hills Golf Course in an interesting and unique fashion. "The course could be more challenging, faster to play, and be accessible to more golfers per day using the short ball," exclaimed Keith. "Maintenance costs shouldn't change very much either," he thought. Keith made a note on his calendar to call his lawyer, accountant, and banker to begin negotiations for the purchase of Rolling Hills.

How likely is it that the Cayman ball will gain widespread acceptance? If you were Keith Dahl, would you purchase Rolling Hills and convert it to a Cayman ball golf course? Why or why not?

12 A Chance to Be Self-Employed*

Martine, Chantal, and Philippe, three physiotherapists, were seated at a cafeteria table at Hôpital de Bonne Santé during their lunch break.

"Chantal and Philippe, I've been doing some thinking about my professional future and I'd like to discuss an idea with you," said Martine.

"As I see it, as physiotherapists working in a hospital we're respected, useful members of the medical community, but we're limited in terms of our earnings and chances for advancement. As public sector employees our salaries are negotiated as a group with the government and our earning power is limited. Unless our supervisor leaves or dies, there's no chance for advancement.

"Last night I read an article in an American magazine [*US News and World Report,* June 12, 1989] about the shortage of physios in the States.

"No! No! I'm not thinking of moving to the US. What interests me is that in the States, physios who are self-employed earn an average of 2.3 times as much as those who work in hospitals. I recognize that the American market is different from Quebec and what works in the US may not be successful here, but perhaps there's an opportunity for us here. If you recall the annual report for 1988–1989 of the Presidente Corporation Professionelle des Physiotherapeutes du Québec, it reported that the number of physios in private practice has increased by 500 percent in the past 10 years. [The percentages are misleading because 10 years ago there were very few members of our Corporation in private practice.]

"Although private practice seems to offer significant advantages in terms of career development and earning potential, it has some drawbacks as well. Some clinics have gone bankrupt and the owners have lost their investments. In other cases, the physio-owners earn less than they would if they remained in the public sector.

"The three of us have been friends since our CEGEP (community college) days and I hope that we can agree on staying together as partners in our own clinic. Should we decide to go into private practice, we must do it properly: develop and implement a plan that will help to ensure our success.

"First, we should evaluate the competition that we'll face if we open an office. As I see it, we have three types of competitors: hospitals such as the one where we work, other independent clinics, and for some problems chiropractors (who aren't covered by Medicare). If a patient elects to seek treatment at a hospital, the treatment is free to the patient (i.e., paid by the Régie D'Assurance Maladie), but there's a long waiting list and the start of treatment could be delayed three to six months.

"At private clinics patients are seen in a matter of days, but a fee is charged for each visit. For some people the cost isn't a factor because their treatments are, at least in part, covered by their private health insurance policies. For other people the cost is secondary because of the pain, discomfort, and/or incapacities they're suffering. For some patients the ability to be seen early or late in the day or perhaps even on a Saturday is worth paying for. However, there's still a large part of the market who would like to be treated at a hospital because it's free.

"Although most of a physio's work comes from physician referrals, it is legal, as you know, for us to treat patients who come directly to us without first seeing a physician. If we attempt to cultivate both types of patients we will need to develop a separate plan for direct patient business.

"Because of the necessity of physicians' referrals, private clinics depend on physicians for their patients. Some private clinics are owned, at least in part, by physicians (usually orthopedic surgeons). Other clinics have developed good working relationships with independent physicians. To be successful we must find out what skills and/or features a physician looks for in a clinic before making referrals. Although GPs do from time to time make referrals, the majority of cases originate from a small group of specialists. Based on our experience at this hospital we know some of them, but what about the others who are affiliated with other hospitals in the city?

"In fact, like many other health professionals, we have two types of customers to deal with: the referring physician and the actual user of the service who doesn't have the expertise to accurately evaluate our work. Because patients lack the ability to evaluate the treatment, they often base their evaluation on factors such as: am I getting better, is the person nice to me (friendly,

*This case was written by Mr. Morris Borts, who at the time of its preparation was associated with McGill University. The author acknowledges the assistance of Francine Brock, Pht., and Eva Lessard, Pht., in the preparation of this case. Copyright 1989 by Marketec Business Consultants Ltd. All rights reserved. No portion of this case may be reproduced by any means without the prior written permission of Marketec, 20 Blue Heron Court, National Capital Region, Ontario KIL 8J7.

polite, explains what's happening, etc.), can I get appointments at a convenient time, is the clinic easy for me to get to (location and parking)? Because of our designation, physiotherapists' patients don't usually ask what are our qualifications. Occasionally someone may ask how long we've been working.

"If we decide that we're interested in the work, there are other markets that we could pursue. We could attempt to obtain contracts from two government agencies: the CSST (Workmen's Compensation) and the Régie d'Assurance Automobile du Québec. Both of these agencies pay the clinics directly according to a predetermined fee schedule which tends to be lower than what we'd charge a private patient. However, these agencies can generate a lot of volume. In fact, according to CSST regulations, the patient must go to the clinic and contact the CSST.

"Most clinics have the expertise and equipment to treat almost all types of physio ailment. However it seems that some clinics claim to have a special interest in treating certain types of problems. I don't know if we should be general practitioners or if we should become specialists. I don't know in which area to specialize. If we pick a specialty that's too small, we may find that we won't have enough patients to keep us busy.

"Since I know nothing about business or marketing, I called my good friend Maurice for some advice on how to evaluate the different possible market segments. He gave me some guidelines to use. Since statistical data are limited, he suggested that we'll have to use our expertise and make assumptions. Apparently many business decisions are made using this type of data analysis. Last night when I started thinking about going into private practice, I spent a few minutes looking for some statistical data and I found this. [See Appendices A and B.] I wonder if we spent a little time on research, if we could find other useful data or even articles on the marketing of physiotherapy services.

"For each market segment that we identify, we should determine what special skills or equipment are needed. Are we capable of satisfying these needs? How big is the market? How good a job are our competitors doing in satisfying the need? Will the need grow or diminish over time?

"Since patients are referred by physicians, it won't be necessary for us to have offices that are visible from the street. However we'll have to find out what factors may be important to our clients and pick a location for our office that satisfies these constraints.

"We also must think of how we'll promote our clinic. We must be careful in our promotion. First, the regulations of the Order of Physiotherapists must be respected. Second, we want to maintain our professional image and not undertake promotional activities that could cause negative reactions. Most other medical professionals limit themselves to calling card ads. Oh, you know the type: name, address, phone number, and business hours. Since physician referrals are the key to our profession, what should we do to get doctors to send us patients on a regular basis?

"You think I should stop now? We have enough decisions to make. Unfortunately, opening our own practice is complex, especially for those of us who don't have any formal business training. However there are still at least two more marketing issues that we'll have to deal with.

"One is how to develop our fee schedule for each of our procedures. The other is how do we develop a client-oriented attitude toward our patients. In the future when, hopefully, the clinic becomes too large for the three of us, we'll also have to recruit and train employees who'll accept the client orientation.

"Last night I was so excited about the possibility of being my own boss that I couldn't sleep. I used the time to put together some numbers which may help us to decide if we should proceed or not. I made copies for each of you (see Appendix C) to analyze and I look forward to your comments on these data.

"I just looked at my watch. Our lunch break is just about over and I have a patient scheduled in 10 minutes.

"Why don't the three of us meet Friday evening at my place and try to work on some of the decisions that have to be made. If you can be there about 6:30 we can order a Domino pizza and hope that it's not delivered in 30 minutes and it will be free. On the other hand, if we do have to pay, it may be the first legitimate expense of our new venture.

"I have to run. See you Friday at 6:30."

Should the three physiotherapists leave their jobs at the hospital to set up a private practice? If so, how might they best approach marketing their new venture?

APPENDIX A BREAKDOWN OF PHYSIOTHERAPY SERVICES PROVIDED

Muscular skeletal	47.6%
Medicine	26.0
Neurology	15.0
Arthritis	7.5
Others including fractures and multiple injuries	4.4

Source: Patricia Wells and Eva Lessard, "Analysis of Clinical Experiences of Physical Therapy Students in a Canadian University," *Physio Therapy Canada* 25, no. 2 (March–April 1983), pp. 92–99. Updated information supplied by Eva Lessard.

APPENDIX B   1988 PHYSIOTHERAPY STATISTICS, MONTREAL REGION

1,183,200 patient visits were made to physiotherapists working in Montreal Hospitals (Government of Quebec, Ministère de Santé, vol. 3. *Region de Grand Montréal*).

200,000 private practice patient visits (estimated by E. Lessard).

According to government regulations, a physio working in a hospital should see 15 patients per day.

In 1988, in the Montreal region hospitals there were:

175 full-time physiotherapists.

111 part-time physiotherapists.

36 rehabilitation technicians working under the supervision of a physiotherapist.

APPENDIX C   PRIVATE PHYSIOTHERAPY FACILITY OPERATING COST PROJECTIONS (IN CONSTANT DOLLARS)

Estimated number of working days per year per person: 227 (after statutory holidays, vacation, personal development and sick leave/personal days)

Estimated percent of professional capacity utilized:

Year 1	62 percent
Years 2 and 3	90 percent

Although after year 1, demand will be 100 percent of capacity, in actual fact some people cancel on short notice and other people miss their appointments and actual utilization is estimated at 90 percent of capacity.

Estimated average fee from all types of clients for ½ hour physio consultation = $40 (no GST or PST is charged on physio fees and GST paid by physios on purchases is not recovered).

Based on Quebec medicine hospital norms a physio should see 15 patients per day.

The premises will have four treatment rooms plus an adequate waiting/reception area.

In the first year only the three physio partners will treat patients. In the third year, it is likely that demand will be large enough to employ a fourth physio at a cost of $38,000 per year plus the usual

20 percent fringe costs. Supplies for this additional person are estimated at $40 per week.

After making a few enquiries, I estimate that our operating costs would be:

Rent (2,000 square meters of space)	$30 per meter per year
Business taxes + licenses	$1,500 per year
Insurance (professional and property)	$2,500 per year
Telephone—2 lines	$50 each per month plus GST and PST
Advertising—calling card ads in local paper and mailings to physicians	$600 per month
Promotion meetings	$100 per month
Legal and accounting fees	$200 per month
Supplies (years 1 and 2)	$200 per month
Long-term equipment rentals	$600 per month plus GST and PST
Receptionist/bookkeeper salary	$2,100 per month
Three physio (partners salaries—same as current hospital levels)	$38,000 per year each
Fringe salary costs—UIC, medicine pension plans, vacation, etc.	20 percent of all salaries
Depreciation on leasehold improvements	$4,000 per year
Bank charges, including interest on bank loan	$400 per month

Based on this information, is it worthwhile opening up our own private physio clinic? Is it possible to determine what our profitability would be in each of the first three years of operation?

13 Fileco, Inc.*

Mary Miller, marketing manager for Fileco, Inc., must decide whether she should permit her largest customer to buy some of Fileco's commonly used file folders under the customer's brand rather than Fileco's own FILEX brand. She is afraid that if she refuses, this customer—Natcom, Inc.—will go to another file folder producer and Fileco will lose this business.

Natcom, Inc., is a major distributor of office supplies and has already managed to put its own brand on more

*Adapted from a case written by Professor Kenneth Hardy, University of Western Ontario, Canada.

than 45 large-selling office supply products. It distributes these products—as well as the branded products of many manufacturers—through its nationwide distribution network, which includes 50 retail stores. Now Tom Lupe, vice president of marketing for Natcom, is seeking a line of file folders similar in quality to Fileco's FILEX brand, which now has over 60 percent of the market.

This is not the first time that Natcom has asked Fileco to produce a file folder line for Natcom. On both previous occasions, Mary Miller turned down the requests and Natcom continued to buy. In fact, Natcom not only continued to buy the file folders but the rest of Fileco's lines. And total sales continued to grow. Natcom accounts for about 30 percent of Mary Miller's business. And FILEX brand file folders account for about 35 percent of this volume.

Fileco has consistently refused such dealer-branding requests as a matter of corporate policy. This policy was set some years ago because of a desire (1) to avoid excessive dependence on any one customer and (2) to sell its own brands so that its success is dependent on the quality of its products rather than just a low price. The policy developed from a concern that if it started making products under other customers' brands, those customers could shop around for a low price and the business would be very fickle. At the time the policy was set, Mary Miller realized that it might cost Fileco some business. But it was felt wise nevertheless—to be better able to control the firm's future.

Fileco, Inc., has been in business 25 years and now has a sales volume of $35 million. Its primary products are file folders, file markers and labels, and a variety of indexing systems. Fileco offers such a wide range of size, color, and type that no competition can match it in its part of the market. About 40 percent of Fileco's file folder business is in specialized lines such as files for oversized blueprint and engineer drawings; see-through files for medical markets; and greaseproof and waterproof files for marine, oil field, and other hazardous environmental markets. Fileco's competitors are mostly small paper converters. But excess capacity in the industry is substantial, and these converters are always hungry for orders and willing to cut price. Further, the raw materials for the FILEX line of file folders are readily available.

Fileco's distribution system consists of 10 regional stationery suppliers (40 percent of total sales), Natcom, Inc. (30 percent), and more than 40 local stationers who have wholesale and retail operations (30 percent). The 10 regional stationers each have about six branches, while the local stationers each have one wholesale and three or four retail locations. The regional suppliers sell directly to large corporations and to some retailers. In contrast, Natcom's main volume comes from retail sales to small businesses and walk-in customers in its 50 retail stores.

Mary Miller has a real concern about the future of the local stationers' business. Some are seriously discussing the formation of buying groups to obtain volume discounts from vendors and thus compete more effectively with Natcom's 50 retail stores, the large regionals, and the superstore chains, which are spreading rapidly. These chains—for example, Staples, Office World, Office Max, and Office Square—operate stores of 16,000 to 20,000 square feet (i.e., large stores compared to the usual office supply stores) and let customers wheel through high-stacked shelves to supermarketlike checkout counters. These chains generate $5 million to $15 million in annual business—stressing convenience, wide selection, and much lower prices than the typical office supply retailers. They buy directly from manufacturers such as Fileco, bypassing wholesalers like Natcom. It is likely that growing pressure from these chains is causing Natcom to renew its proposal to buy a file line with its own name.

None of Mary's other accounts is nearly as effective in retailing as Natcom—which has developed a good reputation in every major city in the country. Natcom's profits have been the highest in the industry. Further, its brands are almost as well known as those of some key producers—and its expansion plans are aggressive. And now, these plans are being pressured by the fast-growing superstores—which some expect will knock out many local stationers.

Mary is sure that Fileco's brands are well entrenched in the market, despite the fact that most available money has been devoted to new-product development rather than promotion of existing brands. But Mary is concerned that if Natcom brands its own file folders, it will sell them at a discount and may even bring the whole market price level down. Across all the lines of file folders, Mary is averaging a 35 percent gross margin, but the commonly used file folders sought by Natcom are averaging only a 20 percent gross margin. And cutting this margin further does not look very attractive to Mary.

Mary is not sure whether Natcom will continue to sell Fileco's FILEX brand of folders along with Natcom's own file folders if Natcom is able to find a source of supply. Natcom's history has been to sell its own brand and a major brand side by side, especially if the major brand offers high quality and has strong brand recognition.

Mary is having a really hard time deciding what to do about the existing branding policy. Fileco has excess capacity and could easily handle the Natcom business. And she fears that if she turns down this business, Natcom will just go elsewhere and its own brand will cut into Fileco's existing sales at Natcom stores. Further, what makes Natcom's offer especially attractive is that Fileco's variable manufacturing costs would be quite low in relation to any price charged to Natcom—that is, there are substantial economies of scale, so the "extra" business could be very profitable—if Mary doesn't consider the possible impact on the FILEX line. This Natcom business will be easy to get, but it will require a major change in policy, which Mary will have to sell to Bob Butcher, Fileco's president. This may not be easy. Bob is primarily interested in developing new and better products so the company can avoid the "commodity end of the business."

Evaluate Fileco's current strategy. What should Mary Miller do about Natcom's offer? Explain.

(14) Lucas Foods*

Harold Riley was marketing manager of Lucas Foods, a diversified food manufacturing and wholesaling company based in Calgary. The company had recently had some success with a new product, Gold Medal Crumpettes. Jerry Lucas, the president of Lucas Foods, asked his marketing manager to recommend an appropriate strategy for the new product, which would best capture the available opportunity and support the mission of the company.

THE INDUSTRY

Lucas Foods was in the food manufacturing and wholesaling business, marketing a broad product line that included frozen egg products, shortening, flour, baking mixes, spices, and bulk ingredients. Its primary customers were the five major national food wholesalers, with smaller regional wholesalers and independent grocery stores accounting for a smaller portion of its sales.

Gold Medal Crumpettes was a recent entry in Lucas Foods' bakery products group. It fell into the class commonly known as biscuits. Competitive products in this class included crumpets, scones, English muffins, and tea biscuits. Competition also came from a variety of substitute items such as toast, doughnuts, and muffins. Biscuit producers included such prominent names as Weston Bakeries and McGavin Foods Ltd. domestically, as well as the American firm of S.B. Thomas, which concentrated on English muffins and dominated that market.

Lucas Foods estimated that the product life cycle for specialty bakery goods was from five to seven years. Generally, if a new product was going to be successful, it enjoyed quick acceptance in the marketplace. Introduced in 1984, Gold Medal Crumpettes had had limited distri-

bution. They had been sold in Alberta and Saskatchewan and had been recently introduced in Manitoba, Montana, and Minnesota. Safeway was the only major chain to carry the item in Canada, but sales growth had been steady to date.

HISTORY OF LUCAS FOODS

The company was originally formed under another name over 50 years ago. It specialized in frozen egg products and later diversified into cabbage rolls and frozen meat products. The company was purchased by a major brewery in 1972, but the frozen egg portion of the business was sold back to the original owners six years later. They sold the business to Jerry Lucas in 1979. Since then, sales had doubled to their present annual level of $12 million.

The company followed a "portfolio approach" to its product line, regularly adding or deleting items according to established criteria with respect to the marketing cycle. With the single exception of frozen egg products, no specific product or product family dominated its overall product offering. (An exception was made for frozen egg products because of their unique life cycle and recession-proof qualities.)

In its statement of business mission, Lucas Foods indicated a desire to grow to an annual sales level of $50 million and to become a major national food manufacturer and wholesaler, as well as an exporter. Its major competitive weapons were believed to be its excellent reputation, product knowledge, marketing expertise, and level of customer service.

MARKETING GOLD MEDAL CRUMPETTES

Lucas Foods believed that the consumption of biscuit items was uniform across age groups, seasons, and geographic locations. It is a mature market. The merchandise itself was targeted toward the "upscale buyer." Package design, pricing policy, and product ingredients positioned Gold Medal as high priced and high quality relative to the competition. Therefore, the primary variables for segmenting the market were socioeconomic: Gold Medal Crumpettes were a luxury item.

The Crumpettes were designed to incorporate the taste and texture of scones, English muffins, and biscuits, and could be eaten with or without butter, either toasted or untoasted. They were available in four flavors—plain, raisin, cheese, and onion—and the company had plans to add three more flavors, including pizza. The product could be stored frozen. The name Gold Medal Crumpettes was specifically selected to imply quality.

*This case was written by John Fallows under the supervision of Dr. Walter S. Good, who at the time of this case's preparation was associated with the University of Manitoba.

Since wholesale food distribution in Canada was dominated by relatively few firms, management felt that it had little choice in the distribution of its products. Lucas Foods did not own a large warehouse to store its finished baked goods, but manufactured Gold Medal Crumpettes to order. The merchandise was then transported by common carrier to various customers under net-30-days credit terms.

The goal of the company's promotional efforts was to stimulate and encourage consumer trial of the product. There was some radio advertising when the item was first introduced. Although Lucas suggested the retail price, the distributor, especially in the case of Safeway, did most of the promotion. Typical promotions included:

- Hostesses distributing free samples in supermarkets.
- Crossover coupon promotions with jam companies.
- Mailout coupons to consumers.
- Free products to stores.
- Temporary price reductions for distributors.

So far, $50,000 had been spent on the promotion of Gold Medal Crumpettes. To complement these promotional efforts, Lucas Foods had three salespersons who, along with the marketing manager, regularly called on all major accounts.

Gold Medal's high price was consistent with its positioning and was arrived at after evaluating consumer surveys and the company's production costs. The expected price sensitivity of the market was also considered. A package of eight biscuits retailed for $1.89. The product was sold to supermarket chains in a case of 12 packages, with a factory price of $12 per case. Manufacturing costs, including allocated overhead, were $8.40 per case. This provided a contribution margin of $3.60 per case, or 30 percent. Production capacity was available for up to 16,000 cases per month.

CAPTURING THE OPPORTUNITY

For an estimate of the potential market for Gold Medal Crumpettes, see Exhibit 1. Harold Riley judged that Lucas Foods held a 16 percent share of the Alberta market.

The Alberta consumer had been very receptive to the product, but outside Alberta the company had only a limited reputation and was not well known as a wholesale food supplier. This lack of awareness made it more difficult for the item to obtain the acceptance of retailers. Also, the company faced an almost total lack of consumer awareness outside the province.

Exhibit 1 Total Potential Market for Gold Medal Crumpettes

	Yearly Sales	
	Cases	Volume
Alberta	43,000	$ 520,000
Canada	960,000	$ 11,500,000
United States	9,600,000	$115,000,000

If Gold Medal succeeded in obtaining quick acceptance in new markets, competitors might view the development of a similar product as an attractive proposition. This could be particularly distressing if the competitor taking such an action was a major producer with an existing broad distribution system. Therefore, the speed with which Gold Medal Crumpettes could be introduced and developed into a dominant market position was very important to the long-term survival and profitability of the item. There was also the question of whether or not the degree of consumer acceptance the product had achieved in Alberta could be repeated in other areas.

Pricing research conducted by the company indicated that consumers were not prepared to cross the $2 price level at retail. If production costs were to rise and force an increase in selling price, sales might decline. Also, while the current exchange rate allowed Lucas to be quite competitive in the US market, a strengthening of the Canadian dollar could damage the company's export position.

SELECTING A STRATEGY

Harold Riley had to propose a marketing strategy to Jerry Lucas that he considered would best take advantage of the opportunity available to Gold Medal Crumpettes. He was considering three alternatives:

1. Maintenance of the product's existing market coverage and strategy. This implied limiting distribution and focusing the company's efforts on the Prairie provinces and the states of Montana and Minnesota.

2. Phased expansion. This would involve expanding across Canada, region by region, to become a major force in the Canadian biscuit market and begin selective entry into the US market.

3. Rapid expansion. This approach would involve an attempt to expand rapidly in both countries, to precede and preferably preempt competitive products in all markets, and to seek a dominant position in the North American biscuit market.

During their early discussions, Jerry had pointed out that the company had the financial capacity to undertake any of these options. It was a question of how to best focus the available resources.

Before evaluating his alternatives, Harold drew up the following criteria to guide him in coming to an appropriate decision:

- The alternative should be feasible.
- The alternative should be profitable.
- The market opportunity should be exploited as far as possible while still meeting the first two criteria.
- The alternative should fit into the activities of the company.
- The alternative should be consistent with the mission of the company.
- The alternative should be consistent with Lucas Foods' portfolio management approach concerning return, risk, and diversity.
- There should be early evidence to support the alternative.

Which of the three possible strategies should Lucas Foods follow? Why is that a better choice than the other two possibilities?

(15) West Coast Furniture*

West Coast Furniture is a high-line furniture dealer active in the Vancouver area. The company specializes in expensive luxury furnishings that are purchased by upper-middle to high-income consumers who want fine craftsmanship and quality—and who are prepared to pay for it. West Coast deals in products such as oak burl inlaid coffee tables ($4,000), dining room suites ($10,000–$15,000), bedroom suites ($6,000–$10,000), sofas and couches ($6,000), and executive desks ($8,000).

A slowdown in total company sales began in the mid-1980s. With the onset of the 1990 recession, sales started to deteriorate seriously. This trend became appar-ent to the owners, Stan and Susie, when they reviewed the historical sales of their two main market segments. See Exhibit 1. West Coast had originally relied on its wholesaling operation to other retail furniture dealers, but the company also sold direct to consumers through its own discount retail showroom.

Aside from the difficulties related to declining sales, West Coast was also under pressure from its retail dealers to stop selling direct to consumers. Retail dealers argued that West Coast was supposed to act as their wholesaler and that operating a discount retail showroom made it a direct competitor.

A review of West Coast's performance was definitely in order, so the owners, together with a consultant, examined the firm's two market segments.

WHOLESALE DISTRIBUTION TO RETAIL DEALERS

Product

West Coast's retail distributors concentrated on the low- and mid-range product lines in terms of quality and brand name image. Retailers used a very limited selection of West Coast's luxury name brand product lines to provide an option to those consumers who found the quality and craftsmanship of their regular product lines to be unacceptable. While the retailers carried a good selection of the low- and mid-range product lines in their showrooms (and in immediately available inventory), the brand names distributed by West Coast were available only through catalogue ordering. Retailers followed this policy to minimize their inventory carrying costs for the expensive West Coast product lines.

Price

The retailers' price structures were heavily concentrated in the low and medium ranges. For comparative purposes, a consumer could expect to pay approximately 40 percent more for the cheapest product lines distributed by West Coast than for the most expensive mid-priced products offered by the retailers. This price spread reflected the manufacturing costs and quality of materials

Exhibit 1   West Coast Furniture Sales (in thousands of dollars)

	1984	1985	1986	1987	1988	1989	1990
Wholesale	$1,351	$1,329	$1,304	$1,271	$1,216	$1,137	$1,002
Direct retail	821	831	843	867	905	983	951
Total company sales	$2,172	$2,160	$2,147	$2,138	$2,121	$2,120	$1,953

*This case was written by Dr. Lindsay Meredith, who at the time of its preparation was associated with Simon Fraser University.

used in the furniture. Low- and medium-priced furniture, for example, is made of a thin layer of oak veneer glued to particle board. The brands distributed by West Coast are made from solid oak.

Place

All of the retail dealers were located in the suburban areas of Greater Vancouver. The retailers preferred mall locations in regions where low- to medium-priced townhouses and medium-priced single detached new housing starts were increasing most rapidly. The general consensus in the industry was that these areas of new family formation represented the largest demand for potential furniture sales. Three of West Coast's retailers had declared bankruptcy in 1990. Stan and Susie were left with $18,000 in bad debts.

Promotion

The retailers supplied by West Coast had over recent years begun to rely heavily on advertising their price competitiveness as a means of attracting the young marrieds who comprised the family formation groups. Retail dealers rarely advertised the expensive furniture lines supplied them by West Coast because they didn't wish to scare off potential customers who wanted to avoid high-priced home furnishings.

DIRECT DISCOUNT RETAIL SALES TO CONSUMERS

Product

West Coast's product lines were very high quality with a good assortment of name brand furnishings. Depth of the company's product mix was substantial. Approximately 12 percent of inventory in dining room suites averaged one to two turns per year. (Total 1990 inventory in dining room suites was approximately $300,000.)

Price

West Coast's retail discounting strategy gave customers an approximate 20 percent price advantage over their four major luxury furniture competitors. Prices weren't actually shown on the majority of stock on the showroom floor because Stan and Susie wanted the customers personally to approach the sales staff for help. The sales representatives could then provide price data as well as information about West Coast's fine product quality and competitive value.

Place

West Coast was strategically located in close proximity to three major upscale suburbs in the Greater Vancou-

ver area. Other high-income areas in Vancouver were closer to competitors' locations, but Stan and Susie believed that people who were prepared to spend an average of $8,000 on a home furnishing item were also inclined to spend more search time looking for high quality at good prices.

West Coast's 27,000-square-foot showroom floor was a bit large but necessary to carry its substantial product mix.

Promotion

West Coast relied solely on word of mouth for its advertising. The sales force was by necessity made up of Stan and Susie plus one receptionist/clerk because low cash flows coupled with poor retail sales didn't justify any more help.

The segmental analysis raised a number of questions and concerns regarding West Coast's total operations:

1. While the wholesale operation of the company still accounted for slightly over half of its revenues, what was causing the decrease in West Coast's sales to its retail dealers since 1985? (See Exhibit 1.)

2. Should the company get out of direct selling to consumers since a number of West Coast's retailers didn't like it acting as a competitor? If West Coast chose to remain a wholesaler as well as selling direct to consumers, what could it do about the negative reaction of those retailers who feared direct competition from West Coast?

3. Direct consumer retail sales (see Exhibit 1) indicated a moderate but consistent level of growth over the 1984 to 1989 period. But 1990 sales gave cause for concern. Stan and Susie couldn't understand why they weren't getting a better response from upper-income consumers of luxury home furnishings. After all, the other luxury furniture stores in Vancouver certainly appeared to be getting business. The owners wondered if all of the elements in their marketing mix were operating effectively.

4. Finally, Stan and Susie wondered if they should try advertising, but this involved answering a number of questions: What media should they use: direct mail, newspapers, radio, TV, or magazines? Even if they chose some of these media, where in the newspaper should they advertise, for example? What radio station should they use? If all of the magazines were similar, should they look for the cheapest one? Where would they get the money to pay for the

advertising since poor sales meant that their cash flow was limited?

Would you recommend that West Coast drop its own direct sales program? If not, what changes would you make in that program? What about advertising?

(16) Jenson Company

Frank Jenson, owner of Jenson Company, feels his business is threatened by a tough new competitor. And now Frank must decide quickly about an offer that may save his business.

Frank Jenson has been a sales rep for lumber mills for about 20 years. He started selling in a clothing store but gave it up after two years to work in a lumberyard because the future looked much better in the building materials industry. After drifting from one job to another, Frank finally settled down and worked his way up to manager of a large wholesale building materials distribution warehouse in Hamilton, Ontario. In 1972, he formed Jenson Company and went into business for himself, selling carload lots of lumber to lumberyards in the Niagara Peninsula area.

Frank works with five large lumber mills in British Columbia. They notify him when a carload of lumber is available to be shipped, specifying the grade, condition, and number of each size board in the shipment. Frank isn't the only person selling for these mills, but he is the only one in his area. He isn't required to take any particular number of carloads per month, but once he tells a mill he wants a particular shipment, title passes to him and he has to sell it to someone. Frank's main function is to find a buyer, buy the lumber from the mill as it's being shipped, and have the railroad divert the car to the buyer.

Frank has been in this business for 20 years, so he knows all of the lumberyard buyers in his area very well and is on good working terms with them. He does most of his business over the telephone from his small office, but he tries to see each of the buyers about once a month. He has been marking up the lumber between 4 and 6 percent—the standard markup, depending on the grades and mix in each car—and has been able to make a good living for himself and his family. The going prices are widely publicized in trade publications, so the buyers can easily check to be sure Frank's prices are competitive.

In the last few years, the regional building market slowed down. Frank's profits did, too, but he decided to stick it out—figuring that people still needed housing and that business would pick up again.

Six months ago, an aggressive young salesman set up in the same business, covering about the same area but representing different lumber mills. This new salesman charges about the same prices as Frank but undersells him once or twice a week in order to get the sale. Many lumber buyers—feeling that they were dealing with a homogeneous product—seem to be willing to buy from the lowest-cost source. This has hurt Frank financially and personally—because even some of his old friends are willing to buy from the new competitor if the price is lower. The near-term outlook seems dark, since Frank doubts that there is enough business to support two firms like his, especially if the markup gets shaved any closer. Now they seem to be splitting the business about equally—as the newcomer keeps shaving his markup.

A week ago, Frank was called on by Mr. Talbott of Bear Mfg. Co., a large manufacturer of windows and accessories. Talbott knows that Frank is well acquainted with the local lumberyards and wants him to become Bear's exclusive distributor (sales rep) of residential windows and accessories in his area. Talbott gave Frank several brochures on the Bear product lines. He also explained Bear's new support program, which will help train and support Frank and interested lumberyards on how to sell the higher markup accessories. Talbott explained that this program will help Frank and interested lumberyards differentiate themselves in this very competitive market.

Most residential windows of specified grades are basically "commodities" that are sold on the basis of price and availability, although some premium and very-low-end windows are sold, also. Lumberyards usually do not stock windows because there are so many possible sizes. Instead, the lumberyards custom order from the stock sizes each factory offers. Stock sizes are not set by industry standards; they vary from factory to factory, and some offer more sizes. Bear Mfg. Co., for example, offers many variations in 1/8-inch increments to cater to remodelers who must adjust to many situations. Most factories can deliver these custom orders in two to six weeks—which is usually adequate to satisfy contractors who buy and install them according to architectural plans. This part of the residential window business is well established, and most lumberyards buy from several different window manufacturers—to assure sources of supply in case of strikes, plant fires, and so on. How the business is split depends on price and the personality and persuasiveness of the sales reps. And, given that prices are usually similar, the sales rep–customer relationship can be quite important. One reason Talbott has approached Frank Jenson is because of Frank's many years in the business. But the other reason is that Bear is aggressively trying to expand—relying on its accessories and newly developed factory support system to help differentiate it from the many other window manufacturers.

To give Frank a quick big picture of the opportunity he is offering, Talbott explained the window market as follows:

1. For commercial construction, the usual building code ventilation requirements are satisfied with mechanical ventilation. So the windows do not have to operate to permit natural ventilation. They are usually made with heavy grade aluminum framing. Typically, a distributor furnishes and installs the windows. As part of its service, the distributor provides considerable technical support including engineered drawings and diagrams to the owners, architects, and/or contractors.

2. For residential construction, on the other hand, windows must be operable to provide ventilation. Residential windows are usually made of wood, frequently with light-gauge aluminum or vinyl on the exterior. Lumberyards are the most common source of supply for contractors in Frank's area, and these lumberyards do not provide any technical support or engineered drawings. A few residential window manufacturers do have their own sales centres in selected geographic areas, which provide a full range of support and engineering services, but none are anywhere near Frank's area.

Bear Mfg. Co. feels a big opportunity exists in the commercial building repair and rehabilitation market—sometimes called the retrofit market—for a crossover of residential windows to commercial applications—and it has designed some accessories and a factory support program to help lumberyards get this "commercial" business. For applications such as nursing homes and dormitories (which must meet commercial codes), the wood interior of a residential window is desired, but the owners and architects are accustomed to commercial grades and building systems. And in some older facilities, the windows may have to provide supplemental ventilation for a deficient mechanical system. So, what is needed is a combination of the residential *operable* window with a heavy-gauge commercial exterior "frame" that is easy to specify and install. And this is what Bear Mfg. Co. is offering with a combination of its basic windows and easily adjustable accessory frames. Two other residential window manufacturers offer a similar solution, but neither has pushed its products aggressively and neither offers technical support to lumberyards or trains sales reps like Frank to do the necessary job. Talbott feels this could be a unique opportunity for Frank.

The sales commission on residential windows would be about 5 percent of sales. Bear Mfg. Co. would do the billing and collecting. By getting just 20 to 30 percent of his lumberyards' residential window business, Frank could earn about half of his current income. But the real upside would come from increasing his residential window share. To do this, Frank would have to help the lumberyards get a lot more (and more profitable) business by invading the commercial market with residential windows and the bigger markup accessories needed for this market. Frank would also earn a 20 percent commission on the accessories—adding to his profit potential.

Frank is somewhat excited about the opportunity because the retrofit market is growing. And owners and architects are seeking ways of reducing costs (which Bear's approach does—over usual commercial approaches). But he is also concerned that a lot of sales effort will be needed to introduce this new idea. He is not afraid of work, but he is concerned about his financial survival.

Frank thinks he has three choices:

1. Take Talbott's offer and sell both products.
2. Take the offer and drop lumber sales.
3. Stay strictly with lumber and forget the offer.

Talbott is expecting an answer within one week, so Frank has to decide soon.

Evaluate Frank Jenson's current strategy and how the present offer fits in. What should he do now? Why?

17 YTV*

The mixed expressions on the six faces that greeted Sarah Matthews indicated that not everyone was celebrating last week's licence renewal awarded to YTV in quite the same way. Although successful at their request for increased subscriber rates, everyone knew that the future would be filled with a variety of new competitive challenges.

For this reason, Sarah Matthews, a marketing consultant to the entertainment media industry, was hired to help carve out a plan for the next several years. She took her seat beside Kevin Shea, president and chief executive officer of YTV, and waited for the executive planning meeting to begin.

After she was formally introduced, Sarah explained the procedure she expected to follow for the morning planning session. "I want to emphasize," she continued,

*This case was written by Mr. Brahm Canzer, who at the time of its preparation was associated with John Abbott College and Concordia University.

"that ultimately, all decisions will have to be yours since you will have to implement and monitor them. I'm here to help you better understand where those plans should be headed. I would like to begin by taking a look at the 'big picture' as I see it and then move closer to home and talk about specific strategies for YTV."

She placed a visual aid on the overhead projector, filling the large screen on the wall. "This is a summary of the vital facts we need to remember as we proceed. A set of paper copies of this overhead and others are enclosed in your personal folder, which I'll pass out to you now." The fact sheets appear below.

A BRIEF MEDIA HISTORY AND ENTRY OF YTV

Broadcast television

Television broadcasting began in Canada in the early 1950s with the creation of the Canadian Broadcasting Corporation (CBC). Wholly owned by the Canadian government, it was and remains a highly regulated company in a highly regulated industry.

Because of high start-up costs and technology infrastructure requirements such as studios, equipment, and broadcast antennas, a decade would pass before any national competition in the field would emerge (CTV).

Today, licenses are reviewed by the Canadian Radio and Telecommunications Commission (CRTC), which also grants licenses to radio, television, telephone, cable, and satellite communications companies.

The CRTC strategy has been to balance consumer, industry, and government demands without unduly helping or harming competitors. The CRTC is unlikely to change this approach to the industry.

Due to the perceived power of mass communication media to influence and direct cultural development and public opinion, government involvement and regulations remain an integral part of the business decision-making environment. Most countries, including Canada and the United States, restrict foreign ownership of radio, television, and other communication companies.

Technology

Changing technology continues to interfere with the ability of government or companies to control the selection of programming available to the Canadian market.

In the 1950s, stronger output signals from American border television stations were soon followed by the introduction of cable services in major Canadian city centres. Cable companies first picked up US border station broadcasts with large antennas and redistributed the same programming to their Canadian subscribers. Later, realizing the potential to earn more revenue, these companies began substituting local Canadian advertising in place of the American advertisements.

Furthermore, the signals picked up by the cable companies were not paid for since there was no Canada/US agreement concerning the ownership, copyright, and value of a broadcast signal that could be picked up by any antenna within range. An agreement resulting in cable companies paying for signals would not be reached until the late 1980s.

Specialty television channels

There are now more than 6 million Canadian cable-subscribing households. The expansion of cable services precipitated a new market opportunity for niche programming. The critical mass of viewers targeted with special interest programming first emerged in the United States and Canada in the 1980s. Specialty cable channels now exist for sports, religion, music, education, news, legislature activities, ethnic, and linguistic markets.

Included among these specialty channels is YTV, which began operations in the fall of 1988. Its original licence granted YTV the mandate to distribute a mix of programming for children, with a variety of regulatory strings attached.

The target audiences for YTV were preschoolers during the day, teens during the afternoon, and family in the evening. However, evening programming had to include a major protagonist under 18 years old, a puppet, an animated character, or an animal. With the recent licence renewal, this restriction has been expanded to allow a comic book character, folk hero, super hero, or historical or classical hero. In television, programming determines your audience and thereby your advertising appeal and revenues.

YTV revenue structure

YTV is paid for by subscribers to basic cable service. In other words, no special rate is charged for YTV alone. Instead, a group of channels is provided whether subscribers want them all or not. With the recent rate increase of $.03 more for each subscriber, a total of $.35 per month per subscriber is passed on to YTV by the cable companies.

There is increasing likelihood that subscribers will soon be offered the choice of paying for each channel they receive. The question we must face is not whether but how many subscribers will be lost with this fee structure and how we can price ourselves so as to minimize the loss of subscribers.

Furthermore, the CRTC rate decision implies a greater expectation of revenue growth to come from advertising sales as opposed to cable subscription. The maximum amount of advertising time remains at eight minutes each hour.

YTV programming

YTV has received accolades from CRTC and industry spokespeople for doing a good job of creating new Canadian content programs, awards shows, and socially responsible programming for Canada's youth. In cooperation with several production houses in Canada and abroad, YTV has received recognition for "Tough to Be Young," "Canada's Search for Missing Kids," "Kids and World Crisis," "The Kids Help Phone Benefit Special," "Rights On," "YouthTalk," "YTV Achievement Awards," "StreetNOISE," "YTV Rocks," "YTV Hits," and many others.

YTV will continue to invest 35 percent of revenues on Canadian content shows, increasing from the current 55 hours to 90 hours by 1999 as required by its new licencing agreement.

Future concerns

Besides the likely switch from basic subscription service to separate billing, YTV will likely face increased competition from satellite services, which will bypass cable altogether. This is increasingly becoming an industry that is likely to escape the strict control of government agencies as we have known it for the last 40 years. A home viewer can now point his or her satellite receiving dish at any one of several satellites and pick up a variety of channels from all over the world. Although mainly American-based right now, communications knows no geographic limits.

Furthermore, at this time, a variety of strategies are being tried by the industry to reach wider markets. Turner Broadcasting of Atlanta (TBS) now provides cable companies with a mixture of programming from stations all over the United States. The subscriber in Buffalo may watch a program that originated with a Boston station and then see one from Houston. The geographic source seems to matter little to the viewer.

Also, more specialty channels should be expected. The United States presently has three all-comedy entertainment channels. The limits will be defined by the consumer's willingness to pay and other market forces.

The challenge for us today is to lay out a marketing plan for the near term and develop some sense of where we are likely to be when our license comes up for renewal seven years from now.

How would you expect cable subscribers to respond to the option of separate user fees for each specialty channel received? How much business do you think YTV would lose? How could it make up the revenue loss? What opportunities exist for YTV internationally through satellite broadcasting and marketing programs? What changes will have to be made in order to succeed internationally? What programming suggestions would you make to YTV?

18 Samuel's Furniture (a family affair)*

In 1987, approximately 9.5 million trips were made by British Columbians into the United States. Most of these trips were made via one of the three border crossings that served the Vancouver lower mainland. By 1991, those cross-border trips had risen to around 15.4 million. The majority of the crossings were made through the Peace Arch entry point to Washington State cities such as Bellingham and Seattle.

What caused this marked increase in cross-border travel activity by Canadians? Moe Samuel, his son-in-law Dave Cherry, and his son Elie knew the pretty obvious answer. Canadians were going south in record numbers to buy everything from gas and milk to big ticket durables like appliances and furniture.

Some midmarket Vancouver furniture retailers were badly hurt by this exodus of shoppers to US stores. This was because much of the cross-border purchasing activity was done by consumers who had become extremely price and quality conscious. Experts felt this was caused by the protracted recession and high taxes that were putting a lot of pressure on consumer budgets. In addition, some retail analysts suggested that Canadian consumers were also attracted to US outlets because they perceived that American stores offered a larger assortment of product choices. The ability of American stores to attract Canadian shoppers was not to be taken lightly. The Whatcom County Chamber of Commerce (located in northern Washington State) estimated that 46 percent of the county's total business activity originated in the retail sector, and of that 46 percent, Canadian shoppers generated 40 percent.

In 1991, Moe, Dave, and Elie decided to open a large retail outlet called Samuel's Furniture. It was located approximately 17 kilometers (11 miles) south of the Canadian border just off the US Interstate route 5 (I-5) on exit 262 at a small town called Ferndale. The location was well chosen, especially to intercept Canadians moving south to shop at the Bellis Fair Mall in Bellingham. In fact, for many consumers living in the largest suburbs south of Vancouver (e.g., White Rock, Delta, Richmond, Surrey, and Langley) access to American stores was sometimes more convenient than it was to outlets in the Vancouver city core.

In addition to Canadian trade, Samuel's was, of course, also intended to draw American shoppers from surrounding Whatcom County.

Based on their many years of experience in the Vancouver furniture business, the owners established a positioning strategy for the product, price, and distribution

*This case was written by Dr. Lindsay Meredith, who at the time of its preparation was associated with Simon Fraser University.

components of the Samuel's marketing mix. In addition, part of the promotional mix was also determined.

THE POSITIONING STRATEGY

Product

This element of the marketing mix was centred around two key attributes—quality and assortment. The owners realized that consumers had in recent years become sensitized to the issue of good product quality, especially when it came to big-ticket durables. As a result, they concentrated their product line selection on brand names that were well known for their quality construction and fabrics. Brands like Henredon, Century, Bernhardt, and Gallery, which consumers would recognize as having a good reputation, were given priority in the product mix.

The owners' concern with also offering a wide product assortment was reflected in the full range of home furnishings displayed on their 50,000-square-foot (4,645-square-meter) showroom floor. A display area of this size was considered to be very large in the furniture business, but the consumer drawing power in terms of the product assortment it could hold was felt to be worth the investment. Samuel's carried bedroom, dining room, and living room suites as well as smaller decorating items such as lamps, occasional tables, and art work. In addition, for those customers who wanted even greater selection, they could custom-order direct from manufacturers.

Price

Price ranges reflected the broad spectrum of selection and quality choices that the company felt were necessary to attract consumers in the competitive furniture business. For example, Samuels carried complete dining room suites that varied from a low-end price of $1,165 to a high-end value in the $12,000 range.* For perspective, a medium-priced suite would sell for somewhere in the $3,000 to $5,000 range. In the furniture market, this pricing pattern would place the store in the mid- to very-high-end of the competitive pricing spectrum.

Distribution

Samuel's delivered to both US and Canadian markets. Delivery charges were established at a flat $65. The company also cleared all customs, tax, and import requirements for Canadian buyers at the border. For in-stock items, the average delivery time was three days.

Promotion

Since personal selling as well as quality service were considered by the owners to be important in the sale of mid- to high-end furniture products, a total of eight sales staff and five warehouse employees were used in the Samuel's operation. A high level of product knowledge was required of the staff so that they could clearly explain and demonstrate product quality and features to customers.

A very important part of the promotional mix was incomplete, however. The owners had not decided on what media to use in their introductory advertising campaign. Nor had they decided what media schedule or message content to use in positioning their new store in the minds of Canadian and American shoppers. To complicate matters even more, the Canadian exchange rate was beginning to weaken against the American dollar. Elie, who was to manage Samuel's, was worried that this would drive away the price-sensitive Canadian shopper.

Samuel's had a $200,000 maximum advertising budget for its first year of operation. The owners knew from experience how quickly that could disappear. One weekend of heavy advertising on just BCTV, for example, could cost $4,000. The budget would be spent very quickly if they chose a concentrated campaign. On the other hand, it could be spread out over the entire year with an intermittent campaign. Pulsing or flighting techniques could make the money last longer so that seasonal purchasing patterns could be exploited. Not enough advertising, however, and the whole campaign could fail and jeopardize the store's launch.

Some preliminary information had been collected on possible media sources that might be used in the ad campaign. A number of the media vehicles under consideration, along with comments regarding some of their strengths and weaknesses, are presented in Exhibit 1.

Given the preceding background on Samuel's Furniture and the problems facing Elie, the new manager, address the following questions regarding this real life case: In developing your message content, what attributes do you think should be communicated to consumers about the new store and its products? Which of the various media vehicles facing Elie would you recommend that he choose for his initial advertising campaign? Justify your answer. What are your recommendations regarding media scheduling? Should Samuel's go with a concentrated campaign or an intermittent one? Do you think seasonality would be a factor to consider in scheduling your advertisements?

---

*All dollar values have been converted to Canadian funds.

Exhibit 1 Media and their Characteristics

Television

	Percent Reached*	
BCTV	72% ⎫	Canadian stations covering all of British Columbia, with
CBUT	66	some spillover of TV signal to the United States
CKVU	68 ⎬	
KVOS	53 ⎭	American station in Bellingham covering Whatcom County and Vancouver markets

Radio

CHQM-AM	Older audience/easy listening format
CKNW-AM	Older audience/news and talk show format
CKLG-AM	Teenage–early 20s audience/rock station

The above are Canadian stations with limited spillover signal to the United States.

KGMI-AM	Older audience/news and talk show format—US station with limited spillover to Vancouver market
KISM-FM	Adult aged 35+/soft rock and easy listening format—US station with extensive spillover signal to Vancouver market

Newspapers

Vancouver Sun ⎫	Daily papers covering all of British Columbia; some limited regional edition media buys possible;
Vancouver Province ⎬	no contract rates available for large buys because Samuel's is an American registered company
Delta Optimist ⎫	
Surrey Leader	
White Rock	Community papers covering specific suburbs all south of the Vancouver core; all of these are
Peace Arch News ⎬	published one or two times per week (Monday to Thursday)
Langley Times	
Richmond Review ⎭	
Bellingham Herald	American community paper serving Whatcom County

*Number of viewers × Number of Vancouver market hours watched.

19 CBUR-AM*

Monica Graydon, public relations and promotions director at CBUR-AM (a Burloak, Ontario, radio station) was reading a letter from a disgruntled listener. It was May 1990, and it had been her task, as head of the two-year-old promotion department, to implement a plan to increase the number of station listeners. While her efforts had succeeded in a 40 percent increase in listenership, the letter writer accused the station of abandoning its loyal "alternative" radio audience. With a cup of coffee in one hand and a pencil in the other, she leaned back in her chair and stared out the window. She was reviewing the situation and wondering how she should respond to the listener's complaint.

*This case was written by Marvin Ryder. Case material is prepared as a basis for classroom discussion only. Copyright 1988 by Marvin Ryder, Faculty of Business, McMaster University. This case is not to be reproduced in whole or in part by any means without the express written consent of the author.

THE RADIO INDUSTRY

In the province of Ontario, there were 106 AM and 72 FM stations. Ninety-nine percent of all homes had a radio capable of receiving both AM and FM signals. In Burloak, there were 19 AM and FM radio stations broadcasting. Listeners, however, had a greater choice of stations as signals spilled over from Hamilton, Oshawa, Oakville, Guelph, and Buffalo, New York. Thus the actual number of competing stations in the Burloak market was close to 30.

Of course, many of these stations appealed to small segments of the population. In the FM market, the three biggest stations were CPAL-FM, Z97, and CMOR-FM. CPAL-FM broadcast at 101.3 MHz and was founded on September 10, 1961. It played adult-oriented rock. Z97 (CJKZ-FM) was founded on June 26, 1975. Broadcasting at 97.3 MHz, the station played progressive rock. CMOR-FM opened its doors on October 10, 1963, and broadcast at 103.7 MHz. Its format was contemporary popular and middle-of-the-road music. There were eight FM stations in the Burloak market.

In the AM market, the three biggest stations were CKYK-AM, CPAL-AM, and CBUR-AM. CPAL-AM broadcast at 750 KHz and was founded in 1942. It played top 40 and progressive rock. CKYK-AM was founded on February 28, 1963. Broadcasting at 1230 KHz, the station played top-40 hit music. CBUR-AM, which broadcast at 1510 KHz, was described as having a progressive alternative rock format.

For all radio stations, the only source of revenue was advertising dollars. While a radio station had different rates for different times of the day, length of commercial, and number of commercial time spots purchased, the key factor that determined the amount charged for commercial air time was the size of the listening audience. Exhibit 1 compares advertising rates and audience for the major Burloak radio stations. The more people listening at a given time of day, the more is charged for a commercial to be broadcast at that time. As well, the larger the audience of a radio station, the more potential advertisers there were for that station. In other words, a station with an audience of 100,000 might have 1,000 potential advertisers. A station with an audience of 200,000 might have 3,000 potential advertisers. It was in a station's best interest to increase the size of its audience.

Radio station costs were more or less fixed. A station had to pay 2 percent of its gross revenue to record companies as a royalty for playing their music. All personnel, both on-air and management, were paid a straight salary. All stations had a small advertising/promotion budget which was used to generate awareness for the radio station itself. There were also the standard overhead charges for rent, heat, electricity, and so on. The final cost was maintenance and purchase of equipment. This figure could not be easily projected as technology was rapidly changing in radio. In the past few years, compact disc technology had been introduced. Other as yet undetermined technologies would have to be acquired in the future.

Exhibit 1   Advertising Rates and Audience Size for Selected Burloak Radio Stations

Station	Audience Size	Rate for a 60-Second Commercial*
CPAL-FM	1,200,000	$430
CJKZ-FM (Z97)	800,000	$250
CMOR-FM	650,000	$155
CKYK-AM	1,100,000	$415
CPAL-AM	650,000	$200
CBUR-AM	540,000	$150

*Commercial to be broadcast in peak listener time period of 5 to 10 AM.

COMPANY BACKGROUND

The beginnings of CBUR-AM can be traced to COOL-FM and COOL-AM. COOL-FM, broadcasting at 106.3 MHz, was founded on January 16, 1962. Seven and a half years later, on July 16, 1969, COOL-AM began. In the early days, the station was an almost incidental part of COOL-FM. In fact, it was a single turntable in the FM control room.

By the disco age of 1976, COOL-AM had built a sizable audience around a gimmick: it had only blond announcers. But COOL-AM was going nowhere fast. To hear COOL-AM, you had to live within a mile of the transmitter. Why? Because the 75-foot transmitter was in a valley and the 857-watt signal couldn't escape.

Late in 1976, the station changed its call letters to CBUR-AM and still nothing happened. The big news was in Buffalo, New York, where station WBUF-AM broadcasting at 1530 KHz was eating into the Burloak radio market. The Canadian Radio and Telecommunications Commission (CRTC) didn't welcome the American intrusion so it scouted around for a station broadcasting near the same frequency. It intended to allow that station to broadcast with increased power to block out the Buffalo signal. The closest station was located at 1510 KHz: CBUR-AM.

With permission from the CRTC, the signal was boosted to 5,000 watts and a new 300-foot tower was built in July 1977. A new programming director was hired. He was quoted by the *Burloak Star* as saying, "We'll be playing the music people can't find on the other stations." Thus was born a free-form, alternative format that was to become CBUR's hallmark. In those early days, the music varied from classical to contemporary, from pop to punk, from dirge to dance. But this format worked and soon CBUR-AM had a loyal following that some writers described as a cult.

There still remained one serious problem. As one writer put it, "You could get the signal loud and clear in some parts of the city, but not in others—and never consistently. In my house, on a sunny day and with the wind blowing northeast, CBUR beamed into the kitchen but never into the office adjoining, a mere six feet further east."

To fix that problem, the station needed a further investment from the owners. However the owners were having problems of their own. On May 10, 1980, the owners declared personal bankruptcy. Their holdings, including the radio station, were placed into receivership by the Supreme Court of Ontario. At that time, there was a real danger that the CRTC would revoke the station's license. A plea from one of the announcers for listener support brought in 6,200 letters and 150,000 names on petitions to "save the feeling in radio." CBUR-AM might have been a cult phenomenon but its listeners were as loyal as a family.

Laurentide Corporation (which owned seven radio stations in Alberta, one in Montreal, and a television production company) purchased COOL-FM and CBUR-AM for $2.2 million. The corporation was also willing to invest more money in the company. COOL-FM became CETH-FM and switched from broadcasting disco to ethnic/multicultural programming. As well, the old station headquarters were abandoned for a new location atop a shopping mall. By now, CBUR-AM had an audience of 200,000. While the station appealed to a broad spectrum of people, the typical listener was between the ages of 18 and 34, single or married with no children, well educated, and looking for something different or exciting in music. In fact, one person described them as people "with a look all their own."

Like the previous owners, Laurentide ran into cash problems during the recession of 1981–82. Rumors circulated that CBUR-AM was for sale and that a new programming format was being considered. The newspapers were full of stories: "The station would go country." "A heavy metal format was being discussed." "An oldies programming consultant was brought in." "A group of born-again Christians were on the case." "An all-talk format was a strong likelihood as was a black format."

The eventual purchaser was Scotsman Communications, a media conglomerate. It owned 5 television stations, 10 radio stations, and 5 cable TV services. When Scotsman took over on January 1, 1983, it informed management that it wanted the station to generate more revenue by attracting a larger audience. It was looking for a return on its $3 million investment.

Scotsman's first step was investing more money to have CBUR's signal broadcast from the Railway Tower in Burloak. A 50,000-watt signal coming from the tower increased the station's potential listenership. Almost immediately after going on the Tower on January 1, 1984, ratings doubled. About 400,000 people were tuning into CBUR's signal. Advertising rates were increased somewhat and revenues improved.

In early 1985, CBUR's major competitor, CKYK-AM, went over 1,000,000 listeners. At that moment, CKYK-AM doubled its advertising rate. A staff person explained that "a national advertiser used to buy commercial time on the top three or four stations. In 1985, we were fourth in the market but for some products appealing to our audience we were considered third. When CPAL doubled rates, national advertisers could only afford to buy commercial time on two stations. CBUR was sometimes shut out."

By 1986, revenue for CBUR was growing 2.8 percent per year while revenue for Scotsman Communications was growing 7.7 percent per year. Scotsman made it clear that station revenues would have to increase more. CBUR needed to broaden its listenership. Management felt that it could follow one of two paths. It could modify its blend of music to meet a more mainstream audience or it could develop a promotion department to get more awareness for the station and hopefully more people tuning in. Management chose the latter approach.

A promotion department was set up in 1986. With a limited budget, the department used publicity to generate as much awareness as possible. In the first year, the department was able to get one article per week about the station published in a Burloak newspaper. It also used a promotion vehicle known as the "Rock 'n' Roll Party," a program for high schools, colleges, and universities that brought together an on-air personality with songs for dances or campus pubs. The radio station sponsored a talent search called Ontario Backroads which gave airplay to aspiring new artists.

What little advertising money was available was channeled into TV commercials. Advertising the "Feeling in Radio" that could be found at CBUR, the commercials depicted typical people doing typical things while listening to CBUR. According to Monica, who had been hired to direct the newly formed promotion department, "There was an image that our listeners dressed strangely, had strange hair cuts, did strange things. All we did was show average people enjoying the station."

THE PROBLEM FOR CBUR

The campaign was successful and listenership grew by 40 percent. But then the letter from the listener crossed Monica's desk. The station had made every effort to remain loyal to its basic audience. "Where else could a listener hear Bauhaus, Skinny Puppy, The The, Moev, Comsat Angels, Killing Joke, and The Cure?" she thought to herself. "We may have eliminated some of the extremes in the music we play, but we're still very innovative."

As she thought about the competition, she realized that they had changed their musical programming somewhat in the past year. Other people had told her that CKYK-AM and even CPAL-AM were beginning to play songs that used to be heard only on CBUR-AM. As the more commercial stations began playing new music, CBUR-AM would sound more like them. Monica could understand how a listener would be misled into thinking that the station had become commercial.

The dilemma had always been to increase the number of listeners while not alienating the loyal audience. Was the letter writer correct? In the push to expand the audience, did CBUR-AM abandon its loyal audience? If so, how could it win them back? If it didn't, how could the station change the misperception? After all, there was a rule of thumb that for every 1,000 people who had an opinion, 1 person would write to the station. If more letters came in, there could be a real problem.

Finally, she felt compelled to respond to this letter. What should she say? How should she say it? The coffee cup was empty. Realizing she would have to sleep on the matter, she turned off the light and left her office. Tomorrow she would have to take some action.

How should Monica respond to the listener's complaints? How does she increase audience size without losing devoted fans?

20 Mobay Chemical, Inc.

Mobay Chemical, Inc., is a multinational producer of various chemicals and plastics with plants in Canada, the United States, England, France, and Germany. It is run from its headquarters in Toronto.

Gerry Mason is marketing manager of Mobay's global plastic business. Gerry is reconsidering his promotion approach. He is evaluating what kind of promotion—and how much—should be directed to car producers and to other major customers worldwide. Currently, Gerry has one salesperson who devotes most of his time to the US car industry. This man is based in the Detroit area and focuses on the Big Three—GM, Ford, and Chrysler—and the various molders who supply the car industry. This approach was adequate as long as relatively little plastic was used in each car *and* the auto producers did all of the designing themselves and then sent out specifications for very price-oriented bidding. But now the whole product planning and buying system is changing—and foreign producers in the US are becoming more important.

The new system can be explained in terms of Ford's "program management" approach, developed in 1980 and used on the Taurus-Sable project. Instead of the normal five-year process of creating a new automobile in sequential steps, the new system is a team approach. Under the old system, product planners would come up with a general concept and then expect the design team to give it artistic form. Next, engineering would develop the specifications and pass them on to manufacturing and suppliers. There was little communication between the groups—and no overall project responsibility. Under the new program management approach, representatives from all the various functions—planning, design, engineering, marketing, and manufacturing—work together. The whole team takes final responsibility for a car. Because all of the departments are involved from the start, problems

are resolved as the project moves on—before they cause a crisis. Manufacturing, for example, can suggest changes in design that will result in higher productivity—or better quality.

In the Taurus-Sable project, Ford engineers followed the Japanese lead and did some reverse engineering of their own. This helped them learn how the parts were assembled—and how they were designed. Ford actually bought several Japanese cars and dismantled them, piece by piece, looking for ideas they could copy or improve. Further, Ford engineers carefully analyzed over 50 similar cars to find the best parts of each. The Audi 5000 had the best accelerator-pedal feel. The Toyota Supra was best for fuel-gauge accuracy. The best tire and jack storage was in the BMW 228e. Eventually, Ford incorporated almost all of the best features into its Taurus-Sable.

In addition to reverse engineering, Ford researchers conducted the largest series of market studies the company had ever done. This led to the inclusion of additional features, such as oil dipsticks painted a bright yellow for fast identification and a net in the trunk to hold grocery bags upright.

At the same time, a five-member ergonomics group studied ways to make cars more comfortable and easier to operate. They took seats from competing cars and tested them in Ford cars to learn what customers liked—and disliked. They tested dashboard instruments and controls. Eventually, the best elements in competing models were incorporated into the Taurus-Sable.

Ford also asked assembly-line workers for suggestions before the car was designed—and then incorporated their ideas into the new car. All bolts had the same-size head, for example, so workers didn't have to switch from one wrench to another.

Finally, Ford consulted its suppliers as part of the program management effort. Instead of turning to a supplier after the car's design was completed, the Ford team signed long-term contracts with suppliers—and invited them to participate in product planning. This project was so successful that it appears most auto producers will follow a similar approach in the future.

The suppliers selected for the Taurus project were major suppliers who had already demonstrated a serious commitment to the car industry. They had not only the facilities but the technical and professional managerial staff who could understand—and become part of—the program management approach. Ford expected that these major suppliers would be able to provide the just-in-time delivery system pioneered by the Japanese—and that the suppliers could apply statistical quality-control procedures in their manufacturing processes. These criteria led Ford to ignore suppliers whose primary sales technique was to entertain buyers and then submit bids on standard specifications.

Assuming that the program management approach will spread through the car industry and to other industries as well, Gerry Mason is trying to determine if Mobay's present effort is still appropriate. Gerry's strategy has focused primarily on responding to inquiries and bringing in Mobay technical people as the situation seems to require. Potential customers with technical questions are sometimes referred to other customers already using the materials or to a Mobay plant—to be sure that all questions are answered. But basically, all producer customers are treated more or less alike. The sales rep makes calls and tries to find good business wherever it is.

Usually, each sales rep has a geographic area. If an area like Detroit needs more than one rep, each may specialize in one or several similar industries. But Mobay uses the same basic approach—call on present users of plastic products and try to find opportunities for getting a share (or bigger share) of existing purchases or new applications. The sales reps are supposed to be primarily order getters rather than technical specialists. Technical help can be brought in when the customer wants it.

Gerry now sees that some of his major competitors—including General Electric and Dow Chemical—are becoming more aggressive. They are seeking to affect specifications and product design from the start, rather than after a product design is completed. This takes a lot more effort and resources, but Gerry thinks it may get better results. A major problem he sees, however, is that he may have to drastically change the nature of Mobay's promotion. Instead of focusing primarily on buyers and responding to questions, it may be necessary to try to contact all the multiple buying influences and not only answer their questions but help them understand what questions to raise—and help answer them. Such a process may even require more technically trained sales reps.

Contrast Ford Motor Company's previous approach to designing and producing cars to its program management approach, especially as it might affect suppliers' promotion efforts. Assuming most major producers move in the program management direction, what promotion effort should Gerry Mason develop for Mobay? Should every producer in every geographic area be treated alike—regardless of size? Explain.

21 Bemis Cable, Inc.

Jack Meister, vice president of marketing for Bemis Cable, Inc., is deciding how to organize and train his sales force—and what to do about Tom Brogs.

At its Pittsburgh and Montreal plants, Bemis Cable, Inc., produces wire cable, ranging from .5 inches to 4 inches in diameter. Bemis sells across the United States

and Canada. Customers include firms that use cranes and various other overhead lifts in their own operations—ski resorts and amusement parks, for example. The company's main customers, however, are cement plants, railroad and boat yards, heavy-equipment manufacturers, mining operations, construction companies, and steel manufacturers.

Bemis employs its own sales specialists to call on and try to sell the buyers of potential users. All of Bemis's sales reps are engineers who go through an extensive training program covering the different applications, product strengths, and other technical details concerning wire rope and cable. Then they are assigned their own district—the size depending on the number of potential customers. They are paid a good salary plus generous travel expenses—with small bonuses and prizes to reward special efforts.

Tom Brogs went to work for Bemis in 1981, immediately after receiving a civil engineering degree from McGill University. After going through the training program, he took over as the only company rep in the Quebec district. His job was to call on and give technical help to present customers of wire cable. He was also expected to call on new customers, especially when inquiries came in. But his main activities were to (1) service present customers and supply the technical assistance needed to use cable in the most efficient and safe manner, (2) handle complaints, and (3) provide evaluation reports to customers' management regarding their use of cabling.

Tom Brogs soon became Bemis's outstanding representative. His exceptional ability to handle customer complaints and provide technical assistance was noted by many of the firm's customers. This helped Tom bring in more sales dollars per customer and more in total from present customers than any other rep. He also brought in many new customers—mostly heavy equipment manufacturers in Quebec. Over the years, his sales have been about twice the sales rep average, and always at least 20 percent higher than the next best rep—even though each district is supposed to have about the same sales potential.

Tom's success established Quebec as Bemis's largest-volume district. Although the company's sales in Quebec have not continued to grow as fast in the last few years because Tom seems to have found most of the possible applications and won a good share for Bemis, the replacement market has been steady and profitable. This fact is mainly due to Tom Brogs. As one of the purchasing agents for a large machinery manufacturer mentioned, "When Tom makes a recommendation regarding use of our equipment and cabling, even if it is a competitor's cable we are using, we are sure it's for the best of our company. Last week, for example, a cable of one of his competitors broke, and we were going to give him a contract. He told us it was not a defective cable that caused the break but rather the way we were using it. He told us how it should be used and what we needed to do to correct our operation. We took his advice and gave him the contract as well!"

Four years ago, Bemis introduced a unique and newly patented wire sling device for holding cable groupings together. The sling makes operations around the cable much safer—and its use could reduce hospital and lost-time costs due to accidents. The slings are expensive—and the profit margin is high. Bemis urged all its representatives to push the sling, but the only sales rep to sell the sling with any success was Tom Brogs. Eighty percent of his customers are currently using the wire sling. In other areas, sling sales are disappointing.

As a result of Tom's success, Jack Meister is now considering forming a separate department for sling sales and putting Tom Brogs in charge. His duties would include traveling to the various sales districts and training other representatives to sell the sling. The Quebec district would be handled by a new rep.

Evaluate Jack Meister's strategy(ies). What should he do about Tom Brogs—and his sales force? Explain.

22 Classy Formal Wear*

Stephen Hecht, grandson of Marcus Hecht, the founder of Classy Formal Wear and now executive vice president and chief operating officer of the firm, was considering how his new line of tuxedos, made in Korea but carrying the Yves Saint Laurent label, should be priced. It was June 1987. A large quantity of the new, black, pure-wool tuxedos would be arriving in early 1988 at a cost that would permit a retail price well below any comparable tuxedo in the market. However, a low price might have an unfavorable impact on the firm's marketing image among its most important customers. Stephen Hecht was pondering both the tactical and strategic consequences of alternative prices, in preparation for choosing a price for the new line.

HISTORY AND GROWTH

Marcus Hecht had founded the firm in 1919 as one of the first formal wear rental stores in Canada. At that time, formal wear—tuxedos, full-dress black tailcoat outfits, and morning suits—was worn almost exclusively by well-to-do men. They wore formal attire to such events as weddings, balls, concerts, and school graduations. Hecht felt that the appeal of this type of dress could be broadened if quality formal garments were made available at prices that the growing middle class could afford and, hence, he founded Classy as a formal wear rental company. By renting tuxedos, tailcoats, and morning suits at a fraction of their retail selling prices, Hecht believed that he could attract substantial numbers of new customers who would otherwise not dress in formal wear.

After a slow start, business in Hecht's single store boomed, once Montrealers became aware that they could rent quality formal wear at affordable prices from Classy. Soon Hecht opened a second and a third store. His sons joined the company and even more new stores were opened. Every one of them was a success.

This success did not go unnoticed, especially in other Canadian cities. During this period, other formal wear rental stores were opened in Toronto, Hamilton, Winnipeg, Calgary, Edmonton, and Vancouver, as well as in Montreal. By the late 1940s, Classy had five stores in Montreal and, in anticipation of competitive expansions, the company began opening stores in new cities. An Ottawa store was opened and very quickly it was successful. In the 1950s, the company opened outlets in Toronto and Hamilton and for the first time went head-to-head against other major formal wear specialists. In both of these cities, Classy profitably captured a significant share of the market.

During the 1960s, Marcus Hecht handed the presidency of the company over to his eldest son, Jack, who continued Classy's expansion with the successful opening of stores in Vancouver and Quebec City.

Parallel to the growth experienced in the six cities where Classy now had stores, there were two other important developments. First, the company had built an extensive wholesale network to bring its products to those cities and towns lacking a Classy store. Through this network, Classy would set up a local men's wear store as an agent to represent and rent the company's line of formal wear. Typically, these stores were given a 30 percent commission for performing these functions. Second, Classy began to offer formal wear for sale on a limited scale through their stores and wholesale agents. A narrow range of formal shirts was made available. A small back-up inventory was held in the company's Montreal distribution centre. The product line was widened further by tuxedos being offered for sale on a made-to-order basis only, with an average delivery time of six weeks.

THE MARKET AND COMPETITION

By the 1970s, retail and wholesale sales still accounted for just about 5 percent of total company volume. These sales were basically regarded as an add-on rather than a mainstream contribution to corporate rev-

*This case was written by Dr. V. H. Kirpalani and Mr. Harold Simpkins, who at the time of its preparation were associated with Concordia University.

enues from rentals. Towards the end of the 1970s, two new trends emerged.

The first trend was a leveling off in the number of weddings taking place. This was mainly because the baby boom generation born in the late 1940s and early 1950s had by now moved beyond the early marriage age. Close to 80 percent of formal wear rentals were for weddings, and this stabilization in the number of weddings was not encouraging. The other 20 percent of the market was split about evenly between school graduations and other formal occasions. The second trend was increased competition. In each of the Montreal, Vancouver, and Hamilton markets, Classy had two major competitors, while in Toronto there were four.

In 1978, Jack Hecht died without an heir. His brother Joseph became Classy's president and the trends in the marketplace concerned both him and his son, Stephen, who had been appointed executive vice president and chief operating officer in the early 1980s. A recent MBA graduate from the University of Western Ontario, Stephen brought a pronounced marketing emphasis to Classy's way of doing business. His research and analysis of the formal wear market showed that the leveling off in the number of weddings was being more than offset by an increasing number of weddings "going formal." In other words, although there was no increase in actual weddings, there were more formal weddings. However, he could not be sure how long this trend would continue.

CLASSY'S STRATEGY

Stephen decided to establish two fundamental marketing objectives for Classy. The first was to significantly increase the company's share of the formal wear rental market across the country. The second was to substantially increase the level of Classy's retail and wholesale sales.

One of the key strategic tools that the company used to help it achieve these objectives was the location and design of Classy stores. First, the company opened stores in new cities—namely, Edmonton, Calgary, Winnipeg, and Kitchener. Also, it developed firm plans to open in other major centres. Second, Classy opened additional stores in Vancouver, Toronto, Ottawa, and Montreal. Third, all the new stores were located in prime retail areas, either in downtown cores or in major regional shopping malls. Finally, all of the company's stores, including the older ones, were fitted with retail merchandising fixtures such as suit racks, shirt display units, and point-of-purchase shelving for formal wear accessories.

Another key strategic action Classy deployed was to increase the availability and inventory levels of its retail merchandise. All stores now carried and displayed a basic line of tuxedos priced from $399 to $599, formal shirts from $39 to $49, and bow tie and cummerbund accessory sets priced at $37. By comparison, very few of Classy's competitors carried any retail stock whatsoever, although they all offered used as well as custom-ordered tuxedos for sale.

By late 1987, Classy had 38 retail stores and over 1,000 wholesale agents across Canada and was by far the most dominant formal wear company in the country. Retail sales now accounted for about 10 percent of company revenues. But in Stephen Hecht's assessment, Classy had barely scratched the surface of the potential retail sales market. Moreover, he felt the company was now well positioned to dramatically increase its sales revenues.

PLANNING ITS SALES REVENUES

It was with this in mind that Stephen Hecht developed an aggressive plan to make Classy the leading Canadian formal wear retailer. In early 1987, he visited a number of manufacturers of men's suits in Korea. During his three-week stay in that country, he discovered that the quality of suits being produced there was equal to and, in many cases, better than that of the suits being made in Canada. He also determined that any of the major Korean manufacturers could make quality tuxedos at about 60 percent of the cost of Classy's Canadian suppliers. The same cost structure proved to be the case with the Korean shirt manufacturers. Toward the end of his trip, Stephen Hecht gave an order for 2,000 black pure wool tuxedos to one of the suit manufacturers, for delivery in early 1988. He also placed a substantial order for formal shirts.

On his return to Canada, he actively pursued and secured the exclusive license for the Yves Saint Laurent name and pattern. As a result of this, all of the tuxedos he had ordered from Korea would carry the Yves Saint Laurent label and Classy would be the only formal wear specialist in Canada permitted to sell Yves Saint Laurent tuxedos.

The total landed cost to Classy for these Korean-produced Yves Saint Laurent tuxedos came to $137.50 including licensing fees. To begin the process of developing a pricing strategy for the new tuxedos, Stephen Hecht called a meeting of his three key executives on June 26, 1987. It was a Friday afternoon and so there was less likelihood of interruptions.

MARKETING DECISION TIME

Attending the meeting were Stephen Hecht and Classy's vice presidents of finance, operations, and mar-

Exhibit 1   Competition in the Retailing of Tuxedos

Type of Store	Type of Tuxedos Offered	Designer Labels	Retail Prices
Better Men's Wear Stores	Very high quality 100% wool Italian, German, and American imports	Giorgio Armani Mario Valentino Gianni Versace Hugo Boss Polo by Ralph Lauren	$749–$1,500
Better Department Stores	High quality 100% wool Italian and British imports and Canadian garments	Mani by Giorgio Armani Emmanuel Ungaro Hardy Amies	$ 499–$749
Regular Men's Wear Stores	Good quality polyester/wool blends from Korea and Canada	Private label	$ 295–$349
Discount Men's Wear Stores and Boutiques	Adequate quality polyester/wool blends from Korea and Eastern Europe	Private label	$ 179–$229

keting. Stephen opened the meeting by reviewing the highlights of the plan he had put together. He stated that the company's goal should be to sell 2,000 tuxedos during 1988. He then asked the group for suggestions in regard to a retail selling price for the tuxedos.

The vice president of finance remarked that this purchase of tuxedos by Classy was the largest investment in retail stock that the company had ever made. He went on to say that the company's overall objectives would be best served by recouping this investment as quickly as possible, so that funds for expansion would not be tied up for any appreciable amount of time.

The vice president of operations expressed his agreement with this point of view but was quick to add that in the company's 68-year history, it has never sold more than 500 tuxedos in any one year.

The vice president of marketing added that while the quality and designer name associated with the new tuxedos were inherently attractive, there were three key factors to consider when pricing them. First, consumer research in the United States indicated that the typical tuxedo purchaser was over 35 years of age and was most likely to go to a men's wear or department store, rather than to a formal wear store, for his purchase. Second, most of Classy's current customers were under 35 years of age. Third, within the past two years, there had been strong competition in the retailing of tuxedos. According to the vice president of marketing, competition fell into one of four categoris (see Exhibit 1).

Finally, he pointed out that Classy was not perceived as a formal wear retailer by the 35 and over age group and that in establishing a retail selling price, the average rental price of $85 should be kept in mind. The vice president of operations also reminded the group that the $85 rental price included a shirt, bow tie, cummerbund, or vest, as well as cufflinks and shirt studs.

The next issue that came up at the meeting was the market size. How many men were there who were considering a tuxedo purchase? Should the retail price be set at a low enough level to attract those men who had not as yet considered buying a tuxedo, or should it be set to appeal mainly to those who were already thinking about buying one? Given the company's objective of turning over the 2,000 tuxedos now on order in one year, it was agreed to set a price that would be attractive to both groups.

At this point, the vice president of operations suggested a $299 retail selling price. The vice president of marketing supported this suggestion since it seemed to offer broad appeal to potential consumers and, from an advertising standpoint, could create strong impact. The vice president of finance remarked that the 54 percent markup reflected by this price was slightly above the markup level now being generated by Classy's other retail items. Therefore, he also supported the $299 price.

As the meeting wound down, Stephen Hecht said that the $299 price deserved consideration. But he was going to take a few days to think about it before making a firm recommendation to Joseph Hecht, Classy's president. In Stephen's mind, there were a number of unanswered questions. First was his concern that Classy might be missing a major short-term profit opportunity by not pricing the tuxedos higher, say at $349 or $379 or $399. Given the high-quality pure wool fabrication of the garments, he felt that the market might be willing to pay up to $100 more. Second, if the tuxedos were to be sold to Classy's wholesale agents, the price to them would have to be approximately $150. This would generate a negligible margin to Classy. Although the company could possibly push the majority of sales through its own stores, doing this at a $299 price would effectively close off any wholesale sales opportunity. He was also concerned about supply lines. If the tuxedos sold out very quickly, Classy would be caught in an out-of-stock situation. The lead time for delivery from Korea was six months. The last thing Stephen Hecht wanted was to have to turn away customers because there were no $299 Yves Saint Laurent tuxedos left for sale. On the other hand, he did not want the company holding large quantities of unsold stock at the end of the year. Finally, Stephen Hecht realized that the price would have strategic implications for the kinds of customers that Classy might appeal to, and the image that Classy might create relative to the competition. But he was less sure of the best marketing strategy for Classy to pursue, and how alternative prices might help or hinder the chosen strategy.

Can the new tuxedo line be effectively positioned so as to improve Classy's image? What pricing strategy for the new line is likely to yield maximum profits? What is the extent of the trade-off between higher profits and higher market share in regard to the new line of tuxedos?

(23) Saskatoon Mobile Homes*

Saskatoon Mobile Homes is an independent retailer of mobile homes in Central Saskatchewan. The units are purchased from three factories in Saskatchewan and Alberta and sold primarily within a 200-mile radius of Saskatoon. Mobile homes are fairly uniformly priced within similar lines, so competition is on the basis of the availability of the units and service on and after delivery.

The units are delivered from the factories to the sales lot by a factory truck or a contract carrier. The cost of this is passed on to the dealer on the basis of each individual unit, which is then passed to the purchaser of that unit. There haven't been any undue difficulties in receiving the desired units at the agreed times.

As has been the practice in the industry for some time, delivery of the unit to the customer is paid for by the customer but arranged by the dealer. The method of delivery varies with the dealer and the circumstances. In the past, most dealers have operated their own trucks to deliver the units. However, in the past several years, it has become increasingly common for the dealers to use contract carriers. Now, some dealers use a combination of the two methods, and a few only use contract carriers.

Saskatoon Mobile Homes is currently using a lease operator in addition to its own truck and a contract carrier.[†] It has been using the lease operation for about six months and trying to funnel as many of the deliveries through him as possible. The contract carrier is generally used only when the volume of deliveries can't be handled by the lease operator or the company's own truck. When a delivery is made, the driver is usually required not only to position the unit as the customer desires but also to connect water and sewer facilities. It's becoming evident that within the next several years, customers will also be demanding additional service in the form of leveling and stabilizing the unit at the site.

The possibility of this additional requirement on the present system has led to some concern as to the adequacy of each of the three methods for the future. The owner of the company has requested of Allan Cahoon, the sales manager, an analysis of the current costs of each method and their implications on the future situation both to the dealer and the customer.

Of the three methods of transportation, the sales manager feels the lease operator is currently the least expensive, followed by the operation of the company's own truck. Questions have been raised comparing the contract carrier and a private truck, but the manager feels that any small cost saving that may result from the use of the contract carrier is offset by the additional control he has over one of their own trucks and its driver. Drivers for the contract carrier are becoming reluctant to perform the additional duties associated with the delivery of a mobile home as compared to other types of delivery. As the customers come to expect these additional services in the future, this and the control that can be exercised over the driver will become increasingly important.

At present, when a trip is scheduled with the contract carrier, it can be reasonably assured that a tractor unit will be available on the specified date. But this is based on a very tight timing of previous trips for that

---

*This case was written by Professor Farouk Saleh, who at the time of its preparation was associated with the University of Saskatchewan.

[†]Compared with contract carriers, a lease operator is generally a family operation that's independently owned with fewer available truck units. Lease operators are more readily available on short notice, provide a more flexible schedule of operations and support services, and usually provide cheaper rates due to lower operating costs. Leasing is becoming an increasingly viable alternative to private owning.

Exhibit 1   Costs for Own Truck

Original cost	$6,500.00
Hourly rate per driver	6.00
Yearly maintenance	1,000.00
Oil, gas per year	1,500.00
Tires, 5-year life	700.00
Insurance, license per year	600.00
Permit cost per unit	
14'	25.00
12' and under	10.00

Under the current system, this unit averages about 5,000 miles per year loaded one way; free running miles cost one half as much as loaded miles.
Source: Corporate records.

Exhibit 2   Lease Operator Rates

Mobile Homes—Minimums (short hauls)

	New	Used
Local (up to 5 miles)	$30.00	$40.00
6 to 30 miles	45.00	55.00
31 to 75 miles	60.00	75.00
76 to 100 miles	70.00	85.00

New mobile homes loaded with customer's furnishings and belongings (used rates apply).
Permits and pilot cars are extra.
Tire repairs and/or replacements are extra.

Mobile Homes (per loaded mile)

	New	Used
8', 10', and 12' wide	$ .65	$ .75
14' wide	.75	.85

The above rates are subject to the following extras:

1. B.C. Main highways — $ .05 per loaded mile
2. Gravelled roads (except as noted below) — .10 per loaded mile
   a. B.C.—Fort St. John—North — .40
   b. Alta—High Level–North N/Gravelled portion into Fort McMurray area — .40
   c. Sask.—North of 55th meridian — .40
   d. Man.—North of Thompson — .90
       N/Highways 304 and 373 — .40
3. Hourly rate (waiting, loading, etc.) — $15.00 per hour
4. Hourly rate for winching — $18.00 per hour
5. Mileage charge for use of tires — .05 per mile
6. Mileage charge for use of dollies — .15 per mile

Source: Corporate records and published contract carrier rates.

Exhibit 3   Contract Carrier Rates

Mobile Homes—Minimums (short hauls)

	New	Used
Local (up to 5 miles)	$30.00	$40.00
6 miles to 20 miles	40.00	50.00
21 miles to 40 miles	50.00	60.00
41 miles to 60 miles	60.00	70.00
61 miles to 80 miles	70.00	80.00
81 miles to 100 miles	80.00	95.00

New mobile homes loaded with customer's furnishings and belongings (used rates will apply).
Permits and pilot cars are extra.
Tire repairs and/or replacements are extra.

Mobile Homes (per loaded mile)

	New	Used
8', 10', 12' wide	$ .75	$ .85
14' wide	.80	.95

Twin Wides: Use 14' Wide Rates
Plus additional insurance:

Under 100 miles	$ 50.00 per half
101 miles to 500 miles	90.00 per half
Over 500 miles	140.00 per half

The above rates are subject to the following extras:

1. Permits
   Manitoba: 12' and 14' wide — $ 5.00
   Saskatchewan: 12' wide — 12.00
       14' wide — 27.00
   Alberta: n/a
   British Columbia — 7.00
   Yukon: Delivery in Yukon — 100.00
       Corridor only — 50.00
2. Gravelled roads (per loaded mile)
   a. B.C.—Fort St. John—North — .40
   b. Alta—High Level—North — .40
       Gravelled portion into Fort McMurray area — .40
   c. Sask.—North of 55th meridian — .40
   d. Man.—Highway 304 and 373 — .40
       Certain rough roads will be charged as gravelled roads (e.g., North of Gypsumville and Northeast of The Pass)
3. Hourly rate: waiting, loading, etc. — $15.00 per hour
4. Hourly rate for travel at 25 mph or less — $18.00 per hour
5. Hourly rate for winching — $18.00 per hour
6. Mileage charge for use of tires — .10 per mile
7. Mileage charge for use of dollies — .30 per mile

Source: Corporate records and published carrier rates.

particular unit, and any delays are costly to the dealer in terms of both tied-up inventory and displeased customers.

Of particular concern at the moment is which transportation carrier appears to be best suited to the current situation on short versus long hauls, with some consideration given to factors other than directly measurable costs alone and future implications both from the viewpoint of requirements and potential.

Cost summaries for the private truck, lease operator, and contract carrier are presented in Exhibits 1, 2 and 3, respectively. There's no required lead time for the leased or private trucks other than what is required in scheduling. The contract carrier requires at least one week lead time in addition to this. Data for the private truck costs were taken from company records and are felt to be typical for similar operations. The lease operator rates in Exhibit 2 are the actual rates currently in force; the rates for contract carriers in Exhibit 3 are taken from a current rate schedule of a fairly representative carrier in Saskatchewan but may even be a little cheaper than others.

Of the three alternative transport carriers suggested, which one appears to offer the lowest-cost alternative to the company? What additional factors would have to be taken into consideration before Cahoon can reach a final decision?

(24) AAA Photo Labs, Inc.

Kevin Masters, marketing manager of AAA Photo Labs, is faced with price-cutting and wants to fight fire with fire. But his boss feels that they should promote harder to retailers and/or final consumers and maybe add miniminilabs in some stores to combat the minilab competition.

AAA Photo Labs, Inc., is one of the three major Ontario-based photofinishers—each with annual sales of about $8 million. AAA has seven company-owned plants in five Ontario cities.

AAA does all of its own black-and-white processing. While it has color-processing capability, AAA finds it more economical to have most color film processed by the regional Kodak processing plant. The color film processed by AAA is either off-brand film or special work done for professional photographers. AAA has always given its customers fast, quality service. All pictures, including those processed by Kodak, can be returned within three days of receipt by AAA.

AAA's major customers are drugstores, camera stores, grocery stores, and any other retail outlets that offer photofinishing to consumers. These retailers insert film rolls, cartridges, negatives, and so on, into separate bags, marking on the outside the kind of work to be done. The customer gets a receipt but seldom sees the bag into which the film has been placed. The bag has the retailer's name on it, not AAA's.

Each processing plant has a small retail outlet for drop-in customers who live near the plant. This is a minor part of AAA's business.

The company also does direct-mail photofinishing within Ontario. The Toronto plant processes direct-mail orders from consumers. All film received is handled in the same way as the other retail business.

A breakdown of the dollar volume by type of business is shown in Table 1.

All retail prices are set by local competition, and all major competitors charge the same prices. AAA sets a retail list price and offers each retailer a trade discount based on the volume of business generated. Table 2 shows the pricing schedule used by each of the major competitors in the Ontario market.

All direct-mail processing for final consumers is priced at 33⅓ percent discount off the usual store price. But this is done under the Ontario Prints name—not the AAA name—to avoid complaints from retailer customers. Retail walk-in accounts are charged the full list price for all services.

Retail stores offering photofinishing are served by AAA's own sales force. Each processing plant has at least three people servicing accounts. Their duties include daily visits to all present accounts to pick up and deliver all photofinishing work. These sales reps also make daily trips to the nearby bus terminals to drop off color film to be processed by Kodak and pick up color slides or prints

Table 1

Type of Business	Percent of Dollar Volume
Sales to retail outlets	80%
Direct-mail sales	17
Retail walk-in sales	3
Total	100%

Table 2

Monthly Dollar Volume (12-month average)	Discount (2/10, net 30)
$ 0–$100	33⅓%
$ 101–$500	40
$ 501–$1,000	45
$1,001–above	50

from Kodak. The reps are not expected to call on possible new accounts.

Since the final consumer does not come in contact with AAA, it has not advertised its retail store servicing business to final consumers. Similarly, possible retailer accounts are not called on or advertised to—except that AAA Photo Labs is listed under "Photofinishing: Wholesale" in the Yellow Pages of all telephone books in cities and towns served by the seven plants. Any phone inquiries are followed up by the nearest sales rep.

The direct-mail business, under the Ontario Prints name, is generated by regular ads in the weekend feature and television sections of newspapers throughout Ontario. These ads usually stress low price, fast service, and fine quality. Mailers are provided for consumers to send to the plant. Some people in the company feel this part of the business might have great potential if pursued more aggressively.

AAA's president, Mr. Zang, is worried about the loss of several retail accounts in the $501 to $1,000 monthly sales volume range (see Table 2). He has been with the company since its beginning and has always stressed quality and rapid delivery of the finished products. Demanding that all plants produce the finest quality, Zang personally conducts periodic quality tests of each plant through the direct-mail service. Plant managers are advised of any slips in quality.

To find out what is causing the loss in retail accounts, Zang is reviewing sales reps' reports and talking to employees. In their weekly reports, AAA's sales reps report a major threat to the company—price-cutting. Speedpro, Inc., a competitor of equal size that offers the same services as AAA, is offering an additional 5 percent trade discount in each sales volume category. This really makes a difference at some stores because these retailers think that all the major processors do an equally good job. Further, they note, consumers apparently feel that the quality is acceptable because no complaints have been heard so far.

AAA has faced price-cutting before but never by an equally well-established company. Zang can't understand why these retailer customers would leave AAA because AAA is offering higher quality and the price difference is not that large. Zang thinks the sales reps should sell quality a lot harder. He is also considering a radio or TV campaign to consumers to persuade them to demand AAA's quality service from their favorite retailer. Zang is convinced that consumers demanding quality will force retailers to stay with—or return to—AAA Photo Labs. He says: "If we can't get the business by convincing the retailer of our fine quality, we'll get it by convincing the consumer."

Zang also feels that Kevin Masters should seriously consider the pros and cons of offering AAA's customers the opportunity of installing a miniminilab in their stores—to serve customers who want immediate processing of color film into color prints. Many consumers have gone to one-hour minilab operators in the last decade. In fact, over 30 percent of photofinishing work is now done by such operators—companies like Fotomart and Moto Photo, which are often located in shopping centres. Over 15,000 such minilabs are operating now and have taken almost all of the growth in photofinishing in recent years. As a result, AAA and similar operators have seen flat sales and increasingly aggressive sales efforts as they fight for market share. Zang feels the development of more or less self-service miniminilabs, which can process and print a roll of color film in about 30 minutes, may help AAA succeed in this increasingly competitive market. Zang is thinking of installing one of these $35,000 machines in every logical retail store willing to operate the service along with AAA's present three-day photo service. The machines are the size of a small office copier, and the whole system requires as little as 18 square feet. The machines need no plumbing hookup and little monitoring after a few hours of training (which probably could be done by the sales reps who already call on the stores). Installing these machines in AAA's larger volume stores might win back some of the 30 percent of the market using minilabs—without cutting much into the three-day customer business.

Masters, the marketing manager, disagrees with Zang regarding the price-cutting problem. Masters thinks AAA ought to at least meet the price cut or cut prices up to another 5 percent wherever Speedpro has taken an AAA account. This would do two things: (1) get the business back and (2) signal that continued price cutting will be met by still deeper price cuts. Further, he says: "If Speedpro doesn't get the message, we ought to go after a few of their big accounts with 10 percent discounts. That ought to shape them up."

With respect to installing miniminilabs, Masters has serious reservations. His sales reps might have to become service reps and lose their effectiveness as sales reps. Also, that might slow up the pickup and delivery activity and cause the three-day system to slip into a four-day cycle, which could open AAA accounts to three-day supplier competitors—a disaster! Also, he worries that the stores would have little incentive to promote the use of the machines because it is not their $35,000 machine! Finally, most of AAA's stores, being in outlying areas, don't compete with shopping centres so they have not really felt the impact of the minilabs. But offering an in-store minilab might result in a large shift in business and loss of the present system's production economies of scale. Further, more investment will be required, but it probably won't be possible to raise the retail price much (if at all—the one-hour mini-lab operators usually meet the market price).

Evaluate AAA's present and proposed strategies. What should it do now? Explain.

25 Kelman Mfg., Inc.

Al Kelman, the marketing manager of Kelman Mfg., Inc., wants to increase sales by adding sales reps rather than playing with price, which is how Al describes what Henry Kelman, his father and Kelman's president, is suggesting. Henry is not sure what to do, either. But he does want to increase sales, so something new is needed.

Kelman Mfg., Inc., is a leading producer in the plastic forming machinery industry. It has patents covering over 200 variations, but Kelman's customers seldom buy more than 30 different types in a year. The machines are sold to plastic forming manufacturers to increase production capacity or replace old equipment.

Established in 1952, the company has enjoyed a steady growth to its present position, with annual sales of $50 million.

Some six firms compete in the Canadian plastic forming machinery market. Several Japanese, German, and Swedish firms compete in the global market, but the Kelmans have not seen them in western Canada. Apparently, the foreign firms rely on manufacturers' agents who have not provided an ongoing presence. They don't follow up on inquiries, and their record for service on the few sales they have made is not good. So the Kelmans are not worried about them right now.

Each of the Canadian competitors is about the same size and manufactures basically similar machinery. Each has tended to specialize in its own geographic area. None has exported much because of high labor costs in Canada. Four of the competitors are located in the east, and two—including Kelman—are in the west. The other western Canadian firm is in Calgary, Alberta. All of the competitors offer similar prices and sell FOB their factories. Demand has been fairly strong in recent years. As a result, all of the competitors have been satisfied to sell in their geographic areas and avoid price-cutting. In fact, price-cutting is not a popular idea in this industry. About 20 years ago, one firm tried to win more business and found that others immediately met the price cut—but industry sales (in units) did not increase at all. Within a few years, prices returned to their earlier level, and since then competition has tended to focus on promotion, avoiding price.

Kelman's promotion depends mainly on six company sales reps, who cover British Columbia and the Prairies. In total, these reps cost about $660,000 per year, including salary, bonuses, supervision, travel, and entertaining. When the sales reps are close to making a sale, they are supported by two sales engineers—at a cost of about $120,000 per year per engineer. Kelman does some advertising in trade journals—less than $50,000—and occasionally uses direct mailings. But the main promotion emphasis is on personal selling. Any personal contact outside the western market is handled by manufacturers' agents, who are paid 4 percent on sales—but sales are very infrequent. Henry Kelman is not satisfied with the present situation. Industry sales have leveled off and so have Kelman's sales—although the firm continues to hold its share of the market. Henry would like to find a way to compete more effectively in the other regions because he sees great potential outside of western Canada.

Competitors and buyers agree that Kelman is the top-quality producer in the industry. Its machines have generally been somewhat superior to others in terms of reliability, durability, and productive capacity. The difference, however, usually has not been great enough to justify a higher price—because the others are able to do the necessary job—unless a Kelman sales rep convinces the customer that the extra quality will improve the customer's product and lead to fewer production line breakdowns. The sales rep also tries to sell Kelman's better sales engineers and technical service people—and sometimes is successful. But if a buyer is only interested in comparing delivered prices for basic machines—the usual case—Kelman's price must be competitive to get the business. In short, if such a buyer has a choice between Kelman's and another machine *at the same price*, Kelman will usually win the business in its part of the Western market. But it's clear that Kelman's price has to be at least competitive in such cases.

The average plastic forming machine sells for about $220,000, FOB shipping point. Shipping costs within each major region average about $4,000—but another $3,000 must be added on shipments from western Canada to Ontario or Quebec (and vice versa).

Henry Kelman is thinking about expanding sales by absorbing the extra $3,000 to $6,000 in freight cost that occurs if a customer in eastern Canada buys from his western Canadian location. By doing this, he would not be cutting price in those markets but rather reducing his net return. He thinks that his competitors would not see this as price competition—and therefore would not resort to cutting prices themselves.

Al Kelman, the marketing manager, disagrees. Al thinks that the proposed freight absorption plan would stimulate price competition in the eastern markets and perhaps in western Canada as well. He proposes instead that Kelman hire some sales reps to work the eastern markets—selling quality—rather than relying on the manufacturers' agents. He argues that two additional sales reps in each of these regions would not increase costs too much—and might greatly increase the sales from these markets over that brought in by the agents. With this plan, there would be no need to absorb the freight and risk disrupting the status quo. Adding more of Kelman's own sales reps is especially important, he argues, because competition in the east is somewhat hotter than in the west, due to the number of competitors (including foreign competitors) in the region. A lot of expensive entertaining, for example, seems to be required just to be considered as a potential supplier. In contrast, the situation has been rather quiet in the west—because only two firms are sharing this market and each is working harder near its home base. The eastern competitors don't send any sales reps to western Canada, and if they have any manufacturers' agents, they haven't gotten any business in recent years.

Henry Kelman agrees that his son has a point, but industry sales are leveling off and Henry wants to increase sales. Further, he thinks the competitive situation may change drastically in the near future anyway, as global competitors get more aggressive and some possible new production methods and machines become more competitive with existing ones. He would rather be a leader in anything that is likely to happen—rather than a follower. But he is impressed with Al's comments about the greater competitiveness in the other markets and therefore is unsure about what to do.

Evaluate Kelman's current strategies. Given Henry Kelman's sales objective, what should Kelman Mfg. do? Explain.

26 Fraser Company*

Alice Howell, president of the Columbia Plastics Division of the Fraser Co., leaned forward at her desk in her bright, sunlit office and said, "In brief, our two options are either to price at a level that just covers our costs or we face losing market leadership to those upstart Canadians at Vancouver Light. Are there no other options?" Tamara Chu, Columbia's marketing manager, and Sam Carney, the production manager, had no immediate reply.

Columbia Plastics, based in Seattle, Washington, had been the area's leading manufacturer of plastic molded skylights for use in houses and offices for almost 15 years. However, two years earlier, Vancouver Light, whose main plant was located in Vancouver, British Columbia, Canada, 150 miles to the north of Seattle, had opened a sales office in the city and sought to gain

business by pricing aggressively. Vancouver Light began by offering skylights at 20 percent below Columbia's price for large orders. Now, Vancouver Light had just announced a further price cut of 10 percent.

COMPANY BACKGROUND

The primary business of the Fraser Co., which had recently celebrated the 50th anniversary of its existence, was the supply of metal and plastic fabricated parts for its well known Seattle neighbor, Boeing Aircraft. Until the 1960s, Boeing had accounted for more than 80 percent of Fraser's volume, but Fraser then decided to diversify in order to protect itself against the boom and bust cycle that seemed to characterize the aircraft industry. Even now, Boeing still accounted for nearly half of Fraser's $50 million[†] in annual sales.

Columbia Plastics had been established to apply Fraser's plastic molding skills in the construction industry. Its first products, which still accounted for nearly 30 percent of its sales, included plastic garage doors, plastic gutters, and plastic covers for outdoor lights, all of which had proved to be popular among Seattle home builders. In 1968, Columbia began production of what was to be its most successful product, skylights for homes and offices. Skylights now accounted for 70 percent of Columbia's sales.

THE SKYLIGHT MARKET

Although skylights varied greatly in size, a typical one measured 3 feet × 3 feet and would be installed in the ceiling of a kitchen, bathroom, or living room. It was made primarily of molded plastic with an aluminum frame. Skylights were usually installed by homebuilders, upon initial construction of a home, or by professional contractors as part of a remodeling job. Because of the need to cut through the roof to install a skylight and to then seal the joint between the roof and skylight so that water would not leak through, only the most talented of "do-it-yourselfers" would tackle this job on their own. At present, 70 percent of the market was in home and office buildings, 25 percent in professional remodeling, and 5 percent in the do-it-yourself market.

Skylights had become very popular. Homeowners found the natural light they brought to a room quite attractive and perceived skylights to be energy conserving. Although opinion was divided on whether the heat loss from a skylight was more important to consumers than the light gained, the general perception was quite favorable. Homebuilders found that featuring a skylight

*This case was written by Dr. Charles Weinberg, who at the time of its preparation was associated with the University of British Columbia.

†All prices and costs are in US dollars.

in a kitchen or other room would be an important plus in attracting buyers and often included at least one skylight as a standard feature in a home. Condominium builders had also found that their customers liked the openness that a skylight seemed to provide. Skylights were also a popular feature of the second homes that many people owned on Washington's lakes or in ski areas throughout the northwest.

In Columbia Plastics' primary market area of Washington, Oregon, Idaho, and Montana, sales of skylights had leveled off in recent years at about 45,000 units per year. Although Columbia would occasionally sell a large order to California homebuilders, such sales were made only to fill slack in the plant and, after including the cost of transportation, were only break-even propositions at best.

Four homebuilders accounted for half the sales of skylights in the Pacific Northwest. Another five bought an average of 1,000 each, and the remaining sales were split among more than 100 independent builders and remodelers. Some repackaged the product under their own brand name; many purchased only a few dozen or less.

Columbia would ship directly only to builders who ordered at least 500 units per year, although it would subdivide the orders into sections of one gross (144) for shipping. Most builders and remodelers bought their skylights from building supply dealers, hardware stores, and lumberyards. Columbia sold and shipped directly to these dealers, who typically marked up the product by 50 percent. Columbia's average factory price was $200 when Vancouver Light first entered the market.

Columbia maintained a sales force of three persons for making contact with builders, remodelers, and retail outlets. The sales force was responsible for Columbia's complete line of products, which generally went through the same channels of distribution. The cost of maintaining the sales force, including necessary selling support and travel expense, was $90,000 annually.

Until the advent of Vancouver Light, there had been no significant local competition for Columbia. Several California manufacturers had small shares of the market, but Columbia had held a 70 percent market share until two years ago.

Vancouver Light's entry

Vancouver Light was founded in the early 1970s by Jennifer McLaren, an engineer, and Carl Garner, an architect, and several of their business associates, in order to manufacture skylights. They believed that there was a growing demand for skylights, but there was no ready source of supply available in western Canada. Their assessment proved correct, and their business was successful.

Two years ago, the Canadian company had announced the opening of a sales office in Seattle. McLaren came to this office two days a week and devoted her attention to selling skylights only to the large-volume builders. Vancouver Light announced a price 20 percent below Columbia's, with a minimum order size of 1,000 units to be shipped all at one time. It quickly gained all the business of one large builder, True Homes, a Canadian-owned company. In the previous year, that builder had ordered 6,000 skylights from Columbia.

A year later, one of Columbia's sales representatives was told by the purchasing manager of Chieftain Homes, a northwest builder who had installed 7,000 skylights the previous year, that Chieftain would switch to Vancouver Light for most of its skylights unless Columbia was prepared to match Vancouver's price. Columbia then matched that price for orders above 2,500 units, guessing that smaller customers would value highly the local service that Columbia could provide. Chieftain then ordered 40 percent of its needs from Vancouver Light. Two small builders had since switched to Vancouver Light as well. Before Vancouver's latest price cut had been reported, Tamara Chu, Columbia's marketing manager, projected that Vancouver Light would sell about 11,000 units this year, compared to the 24,000 that Columbia was now selling. Columbia's volume represented a decline of 1,000 units per year in each of the last two years, following the initial loss of the True Homes account.

Columbia had asked its lawyers to investigate whether Vancouver Light's sales could be halted on charges of export dumping—that is, selling below cost in a foreign market—but a quick investigation revealed that Vancouver Light's specialized production facility provided a 25 percent savings on variable cost, although a third of that was lost due to the additional costs involved in importing and transporting the skylights across the border.

THE IMMEDIATE CRISIS

Alice Howell and her two colleagues had reviewed the situation carefully. Sam Carney, the production manager, had presented the cost accounting data, which showed a total unit cost of $135 for Columbia's most popular skylight. Vancouver Light, he said, was selling a closely similar model at $144. The cost of $135 included $15 in manufacturing overheads, directly attributable to skylights, but not the cost of the sales force nor the salaries, benefits, and overheads associated with the three executives in the room. General overheads, including the sales force and executives, amounted to $390,000 per year at present for Columbia as a whole.

Tamara Chu was becoming quite heated about Vancouver Light by this time. "Let's cut the price a further 10 percent to $130 and drive those Canadians right out of the market! That Jennifer McLaren started with those big builders and now she's after the whole market. We'll show her what competition really is!"

But Carney was shocked: "You mean we'll drive her *and* us out of business at the same time! We'll both lose money on every unit we sell. What has that sales force of yours, Tamara, been doing all these years if not building customer loyalty for our product?"

"We may lose most of our sales to the big builders," cut in Howell, "but surely most customers wouldn't be willing to rely on shipments from Canada? Maybe we should let Vancouver Light have the customers who want to buy on the basis of price. We can then make a tidy profit from customers who value service, need immediate supply, and have dealt with our company for years."

Should the Fraser Company match Vancouver Light's prices, undercut that firm, or continue its current pricing policy? Why is your choice superior to the other two courses of action?

27 London Life Insurance Company*

Ralph G. Simmons, Regional Manager at the Toronto Branch of London Life Insurance Company, was reviewing the monthly activity reports for four of his salespeople. It was May 1988, and he was trying to determine what, if any, action was needed to improve the selling performance for the four salespeople. A friend had told him about the three *R*s as applied to sales staff problems—retrain, relocate, replace. He remembered these as he thought about what could be done to help the salespeople achieve their full capabilities.

COMPANY BACKGROUND

Founded in London, Ontario, in 1874, London Life operated, in 1988, in all parts of Canada through a network of regional offices in major cities. Policies were sold and personal contacts were maintained by a sales and management team of over 2,700 professional representatives. This was the largest salesforce among insurance companies in Canada and the field operations were supported by over 2,600 administrative staff members.

London Life sold a comprehensive range of personalized financial security products and services including: life, health, and disability insurance; retirement savings; annuities; and pension policies and contracts. More than 2 million London Life policies and contracts were owned by Canadians, making the company the number one

provider of insurance in the country. They also sold and managed group benefit plans for more than 16,000 businesses coast to coast.

The company was highly computerized with a national network for handling policy applications, processing claims, managing mortgages, loans and investments, and maintaining instant communications among all London Life people to ensure a high level of service to customers.

London Life was a stock insurance company operating under a federal charter. They were a member company of the Trilon Financial Corporation group, and 98 percent of the company's stock was owned by Lonvest Corporation, of Toronto, the insurance arm of Trilon. Through their affiliation with Royal Trust, Royal LePage real estate services, Wellington Insurance for homes and automobiles, Triathlon, a leasing company, Trilon Bancorp and the Holden Group of insurance companies in the United States, they were able to network and develop business referrals of financial services to their customers.

London Life had a very good year in 1987. Total income, for the first time in company history, exceeded $2 billion, double the company's 1981 revenue, while earnings, assets and shareholder income showed healthy increases. With assets of $8.5 billion, they were a major investor in residential and commercial mortgages, real estate, financial markets, and an extensive range of Canadian resource and transportation companies. Their dividend rate to participating policyowners and their level of return to shareholders were among the highest in the industry.

The Corporate Mission Statement was re-written in 1987 to reflect trends in their markets and changing needs of their customers. It now said: "Our Corporate Mission is to be the leader in meeting the needs of Canadians for personalized financial security. We recognize that corporate integrity and superior service are essential in serving our individual and business customers. Everything we do supports our mission."

In the past five years, they had changed their product mix significantly. Sales of savings, investment and retirement products had grown substantially, augmenting strong increases in sales of their traditional individual and group insurance product lines. New technology, much of it in the hands of the sales representatives, was helping to maintain the personalized sales approach which they considered a vital customer service advantage of their company.

*The author gratefully acknowledges the support of the Life Underwriters Association of Canada Research Grant, which funded this work. Copyright © 1988 by Marvin Ryder, Faculty of Business, McMaster University and the Life Underwriters Association of Canada. This case is not to be reproduced in whole or in part by any means without the express written consent of the author.

THE INSURANCE INDUSTRY

At the end of 1987, Canadians owned $819 billion of life insurance, an increase of $79 billion in the past year and nearly seven times the amount owned in 1970. The industry administered 14.2 million individual life insurance policies in Canada and almost 94,000 group life insurance policies, covering 29.4 million certificates at the end of 1987.

Individual life insurance could be broken down into two basic types of protection—whole life (permanent) and term insurance. Whole life insurance offered more than death protection. Unlike term policies, it built cash value that could help families meet financial emergencies, pay for special goals, or provide retirement income. Cash value of whole life insurance policies was a by-product of the level premium system. As the mortality rate increased with age, the cost of life insurance increased. Under the level premium approach, the annual premium remained the same, despite the increased risk of death.

Although the premium charged in a whole life policy's earlier years was higher than the actual cost of the insurance, in later years, it was substantially lower than the actual cost of protection. In the early years, the excess amount of each premium was held in reserve, which, along with interest earned and future level premiums, assured that funds would be available to cover the increased risk of death as the policyholder grew older. The policyholder who decided to give up the protection by surrendering the policy was entitled to a share of the company's reserves. The measure of this share was the cash value plus policy dividends.

Term insurance policies offered protection only and most did not build up cash value. The premiums were initially lower than whole life policies of the same amounts but increased with each renewal of the term policy, reflecting higher mortality rates at older ages.

One form of individual life insurance that had come into use in recent years was mass-marketed insurance. It was sold on an individual basis to members of a group, usually as term life insurance policies with automatic renewal provisions. In contrast, group life insurance was issued in the form of a master policy, under which certificates were issued to the individuals covered.

People bought life insurance for many reasons, but mainly to provide financial protection for their families in the event they themselves should die prematurely. A person created an estate, or added to one, with a life insurance policy, and the future of this estate was protected as the policy was maintained over the years.

During 1987, Canadians purchased $135 billion of life insurance, $14.9 billion more than the amount bought in 1986 and over nine times the 1970 amount. Of that total, 61 percent of new life insurance protection purchased in Canada was bought on an individual basis— that is, by personal or family decision usually through a life insurance agent. Although the market share of individual insurance was down from 1986 when it registered 65 percent, purchases of individual life insurance totalled $83 billion, an increase of 5 percent for the year.

A study of the individual life insurance policies bought by Canadians during 1987 showed that 54 percent were bought by people with incomes under $25,000. Three in four policies were bought by persons aged 15 to 44, one in three by those 25 to 34. Compared to earlier years, more women were buying life insurance. In 1987, 40 percent of policies covered females, compared to 29 percent in 1970. The face amount of these policies on females was 29 percent of the 1987 total, compared to 13 percent in 1970.

There were 169 active life insurance companies in Canada: 80 Canadian incorporated, 67 United States, 10 British, and 12 from Continental Europe. Of the 169 companies, 145 were registered under federal laws and 24 were provincial. Federally registered companies provided 93 percent of the total life insurance in force at the end of 1987. Mutual life insurance companies, which had no shareholders and whose entire boards of directors were elected by their policyholders, provided 55 percent of life insurance in force at the end of 1987. Stock life insurance companies, owned by their shareholders, accounted for 45 percent of life insurance in force.

For over a hundred years, Canadian governments had supervised the life insurance business in Canada to ensure commitments to policyholders were provided for and met. Each year, every life insurance company doing business in Canada had to obtain government certification of its right to continue to do business.

At the end of 1987, 60,600 people were working in the life insurance business in Canada. Of these, 37,100 were engaged in administrative work and 23,500 were in sales. Of the administrative employees, 28,800 were in company head offices and 38,300 worked in branch offices of the companies located throughout the country. Of those in sales, 20,500 were full-time agents and 3,000 were supervisory personnel.

SALES ACTIVITIES AT THE TORONTO BRANCH

There were two sources of salespeople for the Toronto Branch. Each year universities were visited by representatives from the London Life head office. Local managers would join these representatives to conduct first interviews and screen potential candidates. While students in Commerce or Business programs were usually recruited for sales positions, it was not unusual to interview students from Humanities or Social Sciences as well. A second source of salespeople was referral from agents and other managers both from within London Life and from other insurance companies. Some salespeople work better in some environments than in others. Moving people from one branch to another or from one company to another might help them reach their full selling potential. At no time were salespeople solicited through an ad in the newspaper.

When recruiting a potential salesperson, Mr. Simmons looked for seven key factors:

1. An interest in people—concern, caring, being able to relate to someone's feeling, and ability to establish trust;

2. Good, sound judgment—when to act, when to listen;

3. Ability to handle rejection—not consider rejection to be personal when someone isn't interested in a product;

4. Imagination—someone needs imagination to turn the intangible benefits of insurance into something tangible, and good verbal communication skills to express these benefits;

5. Motivation—in some ways this is the spirit of entrepreneurialism yet it should not be "greed" driven—he looked for people who wanted to achieve goals;

6. Intelligence—not measured in grades achieved while taking courses but seen as common sense—"street smart";

7. Ethics/Morals—insurance is a product that people cannot really understand so one needs an agent who will not take advantage of someone's ignorance—as well when people need the product, they are usually facing a crisis and could be easily preyed upon.

Mr. Simmons realized that there was a difference between working for an insurance company and other financial institutions. Insurance involved a personal interaction between the salesperson and the client. It was important that the salesperson understand a client's feelings and interests and then translate these into financial opportunities. It required more than simply "niceness." Salespeople could be nice yet not have someone's basic interests at heart. As Mr. Simmons often said, "An ounce of interest was worth a pound of niceness."

According to Mr. Simmons, salespeople had to keep one overriding objective in mind. London Life existed to help people achieve the financial security or freedom to allow them to do what they want. Mr. Simmons saw this as three basic freedoms: freedom to do; freedom to become; and freedom to belong. Salespeople worked to help clients achieve this freedom on their own terms.

The Toronto branch had approximately 30 salespeople. London Life tried to keep a ratio of one manager for every eight salespeople. This did not imply that a

manager "managed" a specific eight salespeople. "Telling people what to do is not managing them." Rather each of the four managers were specialists in recruiting, training, advancement, and motivation.

All salespeople and managers attended a monthly meeting. Each person's activity report for the month was displayed for the group to see and someone was chosen to make constructive, but critical (if necessary), comments. These comments were not meant to be judgmental—criticism did not help motivate either. While quotas were set by Head Office for each agency, these were not directly translated into quotas for each salesperson. Activity targets were set on a personal basis taking into account each person's strengths and goals.

THE MONTHLY ACTIVITY REPORTS

Mr. Simmons was examining the monthly activity reports for the four salespeople (see Table 1). The first section of the report looked at telephone activity. The first column within the section listed the number of telephone numbers dialed for the month. The next column listed the number of completed calls. From statistical evidence, one of every three calls should be completed. The third and fourth columns listed the number of appointments that were made. "New" appointments were people with whom the agent had no previous contact while with "old" appointments the agent had some previous contact with the people. As a rule of thumb, one of every two completed calls should result in an appointment.

The second section of the report looked at lunchtime activity. After hours selling was frequently associated with this industry but Mr. Simmons did not believe in it. He felt the hours after work belonged to the agent and he or she should spend that time with family and friends. Instead, he suggested that many of the sales contacts should be made at lunchtime. In fact, London Life served lunch in their offices in downtown Toronto. Over some sandwiches and soft drinks, the agents could talk with their contacts.

In this section of the report the first column showed the number of lunchtime appointments (contacts) that were made. Not all contacts were prospective purchasers. Those contacts who were prospective purchasers were called suspects. The second column showed the number of suspects that were determined from the lunchtime meeting. The third column showed the number of fact sheets that were completed. A fact sheet took roughly an hour to complete and listed a lot of personal information about a suspect. The fourth column showed the number of open cases while the fifth column showed the number of closed cases. An open case was a suspect with whom

Table 1   Monthly Activity Reports for the Four Employees

		Telephoning					From Lunches				All Activities				
		Dialed	Reached	New	Old	Number	Suspects	Fact Sheets	Cases Open	Cases Closed	Suspects	Fact Sheets	Cases Open	Cases Closed	Efficiency Points
Roy	January	455	143	30	39	16	11	7	9	10	32	20	30	24	106
Girard	February	401	126	27	31	14	10	8	6	9	28	18	26	26	98
	March	375	130	28	37	13	8	5	6	7	22	17	29	20	90
	April	362	134	25	29	10	7	5	3	6	24	18	24	19	83
Linda	January	500	117	19	26	10	7	4	8	11	28	15	29	30	98
McCallum	February	464	92	15	25	8	5	4	9	10	34	19	27	30	101
	March	525	97	15	27	11	8	6	10	8	36	16	35	28	108
	April	517	102	13	24	8	6	4	12	8	30	19	34	22	98
Donald	January	830	280	91	48	15	12	9	12	13	58	41	51	49	185
Widner	February	793	270	85	55	18	14	11	9	9	66	45	57	51	200
	March	801	265	88	46	16	13	9	13	12	62	39	48	49	180
	April	824	290	86	62	18	15	12	11	11	70	51	62	57	223
David	January	351	108	22	37	15	8	5	11	12	28	13	32	31	105
Southcott	February	275	83	14	30	8	3	3	5	4	36	13	28	28	95
	March	409	130	24	39	16	9	3	11	12	48	14	29	23	106
	April	346	115	21	34	8	6	5	6	1	44	16	30	24	98

the agent had ongoing relations. An open case might mean a suspect was considering the purchase of life insurance, an agent was still putting together a presentation for that person or that they had simply agreed to meet and talk again. A closed case indicated that the agent and suspect had finished their transaction. This might mean that some insurance had been sold or instead that the person had decided not to purchase any insurance.

The next section of the report detailed the same information, summed over all time periods including lunch. In other words, the number of suspects shown under "All Activities" included those suspects "From Lunches." The final section listed an agent's "Efficiency Points." To determine this number, an agent received one point for a lunch appointment, one point for a completed fact sheet, one point for open cases, one point for closed cases and a half point for suspects. As a rule of thumb, an agent should generate 5 efficiency points per working day or roughly 100 efficiency points each month. It should be noted that this was a measure of efficiency and not effectiveness. Effective agents did more than simply "process" suspects and generate sales.

THE FOUR SALESPEOPLE

Roy Girard joined the company eight months ago after graduating with a Bachelor of Commerce degree from the University of Toronto. In the summer of 1987,

he went to Europe and travelled for four months before starting work in September. Roy was very athletic. He played slo-pitch and coached a junior girl's softball team in the summer. In the winter, he played racquetball three times a week and was a forward with a hockey team in a corporate "No-Body-Contact" league. In February, Roy became engaged to his long-time fiancée. She was a public health nurse in London, Ontario. They planned to be married in May 1989.

Linda McCallum joined the company 22 months ago after graduating with a Bachelor of Arts degree in Economics from Queen's University. As far as Mr. Simmons knew, she led a rather quiet life. She was quite fond of the symphony and was also interested in antiques. When she took a vacation in 1987, she travelled through New England. She returned with six new goblets for her early Victorian glass collection. Linda was engaged to be married but Mr. Simmons knew very little about her fiancé or when she planned to be married.

Donald Widner joined the company three years ago after working for two years with an investment company. He had a community college diploma in Marketing and Sales Management. For the past 18 months, Donald had been the top salesperson in the branch. Intensely competitive, he seemed to thrive on the demands of personal selling. He often stated that "he would do whatever it took" to remain number one. Donald was a member of two service clubs (Rotary and Lions) and an elder with his church. His wife was a neurosurgeon at the Hospital for Sick Children in Toronto. They lived in a beautiful penthouse condominium in downtown Toronto and they also had a cabin in northern Ontario, though they did not seem to visit it often. They had no children.

David Southcott was one of the senior salespeople within the company. He joined the company after getting his Bachelor of Commerce degree in 1978 from the University of Toronto. He had been offered promotions to Assistant Sales Manager but he had turned them down as they would have meant leaving the Toronto agency. Many people felt that he was waiting for a vacancy within the agency before accepting a promotion. He was active in the community, serving on the Boards for the United Way and for Big Brothers. He also helped organize the annual corporate fitness challenge which London Life had won last year. His wife had been a public school teacher but she currently chose to stay at home and help raise their three children. David's oldest son had just finished his first season of hockey. David never missed one of his son's games.

THE PROBLEM

The activity reports showed salesperson efficiency. Effectiveness could be measured by the volume of life insurance sold. All four salespeople were candidates for the Million Dollar Round Table. To qualify for membership in the Round Table, a life insurance salesperson had to sell $4 million worth of whole life insurance during the year. For example, a salesperson would qualify for the Round Table if he or she sold 40 people whole life insurance policies with a face value of $100,000 each. The Round Table was an independent organization that promoted the life insurance industry. If an individual qualified for membership, for a fee of $50, he or she could join. Upon joining he or she received a plaque, a magazine, and the opportunity to attend conferences and seminars on such topics as motivation and selling skills. In a given year, approximately 25 percent of the salespeople in the life insurance industry qualified for membership in the Round Table.

Like most companies in the industry, London Life paid their salespeople on the basis of sales performance. The salespeople received a combination of commissions and bonuses and no base salary. The commission rate was 1 percent of the value of a whole life policy. For example, the sale of a $100,000 whole life policy translated into a commission of $1,000. Bonuses were based on the commissions received for the year and increased on a sliding scale from 5 to 15 percent. As shown in Table 2, a salesperson earning $25,000 in commissions received a 5 percent bonus while a salesperson earning commissions of $150,000 (or more) received a 15 percent bonus. While

Table 2   London Life Bonus Structure

Salesperson Commission	Bonus (percent)	Bonus ($)	Total Commission and Bonus
$ 25,000	5%	$ 1,250	$ 26,250
50,000	7	3,500	53,500
75,000	9	6,750	81,750
100,000	11	11,000	111,000
125,000	13	16,250	141,250
150,000	15	22,500	172,500

salespeople earned the 1 percent commission on a new policy, if that policy was renewed by the customer in the next year, the salesperson received a reduced commission on the renewal. The commission structure on renewals was as follows: 0.5 percent of first year renewal, 0.25 percent second year, 0.15 percent third year, 0.12 percent fourth year, 0.08 percent fifth year, and 0.05 percent thereafter.

Mr. Simmons estimated that if the four salespeople continued their current level of sales performance for the year that Roy Girard would receive approximately $39,000 in commissions and bonuses while Linda McCallum would receive approximately $45,000. Virtually all of their commissions and bonuses would be the result of new business. Donald Widner would earn between $75,000 and $80,000 with a small portion of the commission and bonus coming from renewal business. David Southcott would earn about $60,000 for the year with a significant portion of that in renewal commissions.

As Ralph Simmons examined the activity reports he wondered what recommendations, if any, he should make to these salespeople.

Evaluate each of the salespeople based on your knowledge of their background and the activity chart. Should any actions be taken? How effective is the activity chart and its publication as a sales motivation tool? As a sales manager, should a salesperson's private life have any bearing on your evaluation of his or her performance? What should Simmons recommend to each of his four salespeople?

(28) Cutters, Inc.

Tony Kenny, president and marketing manager of Cutters, Inc., is deciding what strategy—or strategies—to pursue.

Cutters, Inc., is a manufacturer of industrial cutting tools. These tools include such items as lathe blades, drill press bits, and various other cutting edges used in the operation of large metal cutting, boring, or stamping machines. Tony Kenny takes great pride in the fact that his company, whose $5.2 million sales in 1991 is small by industry standards, is recognized as a producer of a top-quality line of cutting tools.

Competition in the cutting-tool industry is intense. Cutters competes not only with the original machine manufacturers, but also with many other larger domestic and foreign manufacturers offering cutting tools as one of their many different product lines. This has had the effect, over the years, of standardizing the price, specifications, and, in turn, the quality of the competing products of all manufacturers. It has also led to fairly low prices on standard items.

About a year ago, Tony was tiring of the financial pressure of competing with larger companies enjoying economies of scale. At the same time, he noted that more and more potential cutting-tool customers were turning to small tool-and-die shops because of specialized needs that could not be met by the mass production firms. Tony thought perhaps he should consider some basic strategy changes. Although he was unwilling to become strictly a custom producer, he thought that the recent trend toward buying customized cutting edges suggested new markets might be developing—markets too small for the large, multiproduct-line companies to serve profitably but large enough to earn a good profit for a flexible company of Cutters's size.

Tony hired a marketing research company, Holl Associates, to study the feasibility of serving these markets. The initial results were encouraging. It was estimated that Cutters might increase sales by 65 percent and profits by 90 percent by serving the emerging markets. This research showed that there are many large users of standard cutting tools who buy directly from large cutting-tool manufacturers (domestic or foreign) or wholesalers who represent these manufacturers. This is the bulk of the cutting-tool business (in terms of units sold and sales dollars). But there are also many smaller users all over North America who buy in small but regular quantities. And some of these needs are becoming more specialized. That is, a special cutting tool may make a machine and/or worker much more productive, perhaps eliminating several steps with time-consuming setups. This is the area that the research company sees as potentially attractive.

Next, Tony had the sales manager hire two technically oriented market researchers (at a total cost of $60,000 each per year, including travel expenses) to maintain continuous contact with potential cutting-tool customers. The researchers were supposed to identify any present or future needs that might exist in enough cases to make it possible to profitably produce a specialized product. The researchers were not to take orders or sell Cutters's products to the potential customers. Tony felt

that only through this policy could these researchers talk to the right people.

The initial feedback from the market researchers was most encouraging. Many firms (large and small) had special needs—although it often was necessary to talk to the shop foreman or individual machine operators to find these needs. Most operators were making do with the tools available. Either they didn't know customizing was possible or doubted that their supervisors would do anything about it if they suggested that a more specialized tool would increase productivity. But these operators were encouraging because they said that it would be easier to persuade supervisors to order specialized tools if the tools were already produced and in stock than if they had to be custom-made. So Tony decided to continually add high-quality products to meet the ever-changing, specialized needs of users of cutting tools and edges.

Cutters's potential customers for specialized tools are located all over North America. The average sale per customer is likely to be less than $500, but the sale will be repeated several times within a year. Because of the widespread market and the small order size, Tony doesn't think that selling direct, as is done by small custom shops, is practical. At the present time, Cutters sells 90 percent of its regular output through a large industrial wholesaler—National Mill Supplies, Inc.—which serves the entire area east of the Manitoba-Ontario border and carries a very complete line of industrial supplies (to "meet every industrial need"). Each of National's sales reps sells over 10,000 items from a 910-page catalogue. National Mill Supplies, although very large and well known, is having trouble moving cutting tools. National is losing sales of cutting tools in some cities to newer wholesalers specializing in the cutting-tool industry. The new wholesalers are able to give more technical help to potential customers and therefore better service. National's president is convinced that the newer, less-experienced concerns will either realize that a substantial profit margin can't be maintained along with their aggressive strategies, or they will eventually go broke trying to overspecialize.

From Tony's standpoint, the present wholesaler has a good reputation and has served Cutters well in the past. National Mill Supplies has been of great help in holding down Tony's inventory costs by increasing the inventory in National's 35 branch locations. Although Tony has received several complaints about the lack of technical assistance given by National's sales reps, as well as their lack of knowledge about Cutters's new special products, he feels that the present wholesaler is providing the best service it can. All its sales reps have been told about the new products at a special training session, and a new page has been added to the catalogue they carry with them. So regarding the complaints, Tony says: "The usual things you hear when you're in business."

Tony thinks there are more urgent problems than a few complaints. Profits are declining, and sales of the new cutting tools are not nearly as high as forecast, even though all research reports indicate that the company's new products meet the intended markets' needs perfectly. The high costs involved in producing small quantities of special products and in adding the market research team, together with lower-than-expected sales, have significantly reduced Cutters's profits. Tony is wondering whether it is wise to continue to try to cater to the needs of many specific target markets when the results are this discouraging. He also is considering increasing advertising expenditures in the hope that customers will pull the new products through the channel.

Evaluate Cutters's situation and Tony Kenny's present strategy. What should he do now?

29 KASTORS, Inc.

Rick Moore, marketing manager for KASTORS, Inc., is trying to figure out how to explain to his boss why a proposed new product line doesn't make sense for them. Rick is sure it's wrong for KASTORS, Inc.—but isn't able to explain why.

KASTORS, Inc., is a producer of malleable iron castings for automobile and aircraft manufacturers—and a variety of other users of castings. Last year's sales of castings amounted to over $70 million.

KASTORS also produces about 30 percent of all the original equipment bumper jacks installed in new US-made automobiles each year. This is a very price-competitive business, but KASTORS has been able to obtain its large market share with frequent personal contact between the company's executives and its customers—supported by very close cooperation between the company's engineering department and its customers' buyers. This has been extremely important because the wide variety of models and model changes frequently requires alterations in the specifications of the bumper jacks. All of KASTORS's bumper jacks are sold directly to the automobile manufacturers. No attempt has been made to sell bumper jacks to final consumers through hardware and automotive channels, although they are available through the manufacturers' automobile dealers.

Tim Owen, KASTORS's production manager, now wants to begin producing hydraulic garage jacks for sale through automobile-parts wholesalers to retail auto parts stores. Owen saw a variety of hydraulic garage jacks at a recent automotive show—and knew immediately that his plant could produce these products. This especially inter-

ested him because of the possibility of using excess capacity—now that auto sales are down. Further, he says "jacks are jacks," and the company would merely be broadening its product line by introducing hydraulic garage jacks. (Note: Hydraulic garage jacks are larger than bumper jacks and are intended for use in or around a garage. They are too big to carry in a car's trunk.)

As Tim Owen became more enthusiastic about the idea, he found that KASTORS's engineering department already had a design that appeared to be at least comparable to the products now offered on the market. None of these products have any patent protection. Further, Owen says that the company would be able to produce a product that is better made than the competitive products (i.e., smoother castings, etc.)—although he agrees that most customers probably wouldn't notice the difference. The production department estimates that the cost of producing a hydraulic garage jack comparable to those currently offered by competitors would be about $48 per unit.

Rick Moore, the marketing manager, has just received a memo from Bill Borne, the company president, explaining the production department's enthusiasm for broadening KASTORS's present jack line into hydraulic jacks. Bill Borne seems enthusiastic about the idea, too, noting that it would be a way to make fuller use of the company's resources and increase its sales. Borne's memo asks for Rick's reaction, but Bill Borne already seems sold on the idea.

Given Borne's enthusiasm, Rick Moore isn't sure how to respond. He's trying to develop a good explanation of why he isn't excited about the proposal. He knows he's already overworked and couldn't possibly promote this new line himself—and he's the only sales rep the company has. So it would be necessary to hire someone to promote the line. And this sales manager would probably have to recruit manufacturers' agents (who probably will want 10 to 15 percent commission on sales) to sell to automotive wholesalers who would stock the jack and sell to the auto parts retailers. The wholesalers will probably expect trade discounts of about 20 percent, trade show exhibits, some national advertising, and sales promotion help (catalogue sheets, mailers, and point-of-purchase displays). Further, Rick Moore sees that KASTORS's billing and collection system will have to be expanded because many more customers will be involved. It will also be necessary to keep track of agent commissions and accounts receivable.

Auto parts retailers are currently selling similar hydraulic garage jacks for about $99. Rick Moore has learned that such retailers typically expect a trade discount of about 35 percent off the suggested list price for their auto parts.

All things considered, Rick Moore feels that the proposed hydraulic jack line is not very closely related to the company's present emphasis. He has already indicated his lack of enthusiasm to Tim Owen, but this made little difference in Tim's thinking. Now it's clear that Rick will have to convince the president or he will soon be responsible for selling hydraulic jacks.

Contrast KASTORS, Inc.'s current strategy and the proposed strategy. What should Rick Moore say to Bill Borne to persuade him to change his mind? Or should he just plan to sell hydraulic jacks? Explain.

(30) Grand Foods, Ltd.*

Jessica Walters, marketing manager of Grand Foods, Ltd.—a Canadian company—is being urged to approve the creation of a separate marketing plan for Quebec. This would be a major policy change because Grand Foods's international parent is trying to move towards a global strategy for the whole firm and Jessica has been supporting Canada-wide planning.

Jessica Walters has been the marketing manager of Grand Foods, Ltd., for the last four years—since she arrived from international headquarters in Minneapolis. Grand Foods, Ltd., headquartered in Toronto, is a subsidiary of a large U.S.-based consumer packaged-food company with worldwide sales of more than $2 billion in 1991. Its Canadian sales are just over $350 million—with the Quebec and Ontario markets accounting for 69 percent of the company's Canadian sales.

The company's product line includes such items as cake mixes, puddings, pie fillings, pancakes, prepared foods, and frozen dinners. The company has successfully introduced at least six new products every year for the last five years. Products from Grand Foods are known for their high quality and enjoy much brand preference throughout Canada—including the province of Quebec.

The company's sales have risen every year since Walters took over as marketing manager. In fact, the company's market share has increased steadily in each of the product categories in which it competes. The Quebec market has closely followed the national trend except that, in the past two years, total sales growth in that market has begun to lag.

According to Walters, a big advantage of Grand Foods over its competitors is the ability to coordinate all phases of the food business from Toronto. For this reason, Walters meets at least once a month with her product managers—to discuss developments in local markets that might affect marketing plans. While each manager is free to make suggestions and even to suggest major changes, Walters is finally responsible for all plans.

One of the product managers, Marie LeMans, expressed great concern at the last monthly meeting about the poor performance of some of the company's products in the Quebec market. While a broad range of possible reasons, ranging from inflation and the threat of job losses to politics, were reviewed to try to explain the situation, LeMans insisted that it was due to a basic lack of understanding of that market. She felt not enough managerial time and money had been spent on the Quebec market—in part because of the current emphasis on developing all-Canada plans on the way to having one global strategy.

LeMans felt the current marketing approach to the Quebec market should be reevaluated because an inappropriate marketing plan may be responsible for the sales slowdown. After all, she said, "80 percent of the market is French-speaking. It's in the best interest of the company to treat that market as being separate and distinct from the rest of Canada."

LeMans supported her position by showing that Quebec's per capita consumption of many product categories (in which the firm competes) is above the national average (Table 1). Research projects conducted by Grand Foods also support the "separate and distinct" argument. Over the years, the firm has found many French-English differences in brand attitudes, lifestyles, usage rates, and so on.

LeMans argued that the company should develop a unique Quebec marketing plan for some or all of its brands. She specifically suggested that the French-language advertising plan for a particular brand be developed independently of the plan for English Canada. Currently, the Toronto agency assigned to the brand just translates its English-language ads for the French market. Jessica Walters pointed out that the present advertising approach assured Grand Foods of a uniform brand image across Canada. LeMans said she knew what the agency is doing, and that straight translation into Canadian-French may not communicate the same brand image. The discussion that followed suggested that a different brand image might be needed in the French market if the company wanted to stop the brand's decline in sales.

Table 1 Per Capita Consumption Index, Province of Quebec (Canada = 100)

Cake mixes	107	Soft drinks	126
Pancakes	87	Pie fillings	118
Puddings	114	Frozen dinners	79
Salad dressings	85	Prepared packaged foods	83
Molasses	132	Cookies	123

---

*This case was adapted from one written by Professor Robert D. Tamilia, University of Quebec at Montreal (UQAM).

The managers also discussed the food distribution system in Quebec. The major supermarket chains have their lowest market share in that province. Independents are strongest there—the "mom-and-pop" food stores fast disappearing outside Quebec remain alive and well in the province. Traditionally, these stores have stocked a higher proportion (than supermarkets) of their shelf space with national brands—an advantage for Grand Foods.

Finally, various issues related to discount policies, pricing structure, sales promotion, and cooperative advertising were discussed. All of this suggested that things were different in Quebec—and that future marketing plans should reflect these differences to a greater extent than they do now.

After the meeting, Jessica Walters stayed in her office to think about the situation. Although she agreed with the basic idea that the Quebec market was in many ways different, she wasn't sure how far the company should go in recognizing this fact. She knew that regional differences in food tastes and brand purchases existed not only in Quebec but in other parts of Canada as well. But people are people, after all, with far more similarities than differences, so a Canadian and eventually a global strategy makes some sense, too.

Jessica Walters was afraid that giving special status to one region might conflict with top management's objective of achieving standardization whenever possible—one global strategy for Canada, on the way to one worldwide global strategy. She was also worried about the long-term effect of such a policy change on costs, organizational structure, and brand image. Still, enough product managers had expressed their concern over the years about the Quebec market to make her wonder if she shouldn't modify the current approach. Perhaps they could experiment with a few brands—and just in Quebec. She could cite the language difference as the reason for trying Quebec rather than any of the other provinces. But Walters realizes that any change of policy could be seen as the beginning of more change, and what would Minneapolis think? Could she explain it successfully there?

Evaluate Grand Foods, Ltd.'s present strategy. What should Jessica Walters do now? Explain.

(31) Dalton Olds, Inc.

Bob Dalton owns Dalton Olds, Inc., an Oldsmobile/Nissan dealership in Richmond, British Columbia. Bob is seriously considering moving into a proposed auto mall—a large display and selling area for 10 to 15 auto dealers, none handling the same car brands. This mall will be a few miles away from his current location but easily available to his present customers and quite conve-

nient to many more potential customers. He can consider moving now because the lease on his current location will be up in one year. He is sure he can renew the lease for another five years, but he feels the building owner is likely to want to raise the lease terms, so his total fixed costs will be about $100,000 more per year than his current fixed costs of $650,000 per year. Moving to the new mall will probably increase his total fixed costs to about $1.1 million per year. Further, fixed costs—wherever he is—will probably continue to rise with inflation. But he doesn't see this as a major problem. Car prices tend to rise at about the same rate as inflation, so these rising revenues and costs tend to offset each other.

Bob Dalton is considering moving to an auto mall because he feels this is the future trend. Malls do seem to increase sales per dealership. Some dealers in auto malls have reported sales increases of as much as 30 percent over what they were doing in their former locations outside the mall. The auto mall concept seems to be a continuing evolution from isolated car dealerships to car dealer strips along major traffic arteries to more customer-oriented clusters of dealerships that make it easier for customers to shop.

Bob is considering moving to a mall because of the growing number of competing brands and the desire of some consumers to shop more conveniently. Instead of just the Big Three, now over 30 different brands of cars and 15 brands of trucks compete in the North American market—not including specialty cars such as Lamborghini and Rolls-Royce. Increasing competition is already taking its toll on some domestic and foreign car dealers as they have to take less profit on each sale. For example, even owners of luxury car franchises such as Porsche, Audi, and Acura are having troubles, and some have moved into malls. Dealer ranks have thinned considerably, too. Failures are reported all the time. Recently, some dealers tried to become "megadealers" operating in several markets, but this did not work too well because they could not achieve economies of scale. Now owners of multiple dealerships seem to be going to malls to reduce their overhead and promotion costs. And if customers begin to go to these malls, then this may be *the* place to be—even for a dealer with only one or two auto franchises. That's the position that Bob Dalton is in with his Oldsmobile and Nissan franchises. And he wonders if he should become well positioned in a mall before it is too late.

Bob Dalton's dealership is now selling between 550 and 700 new and used cars per year—at an average price of about $11,000. With careful management, he is grossing about $1,000 per car. This $1,000 is not all net profit, however. It must go towards covering his fixed costs of about $650,000 per year. So if he sells more than 650 cars he will more than cover his fixed costs and make a profit.

Obviously, the more cars he sells beyond 650, the bigger the profit—assuming he controls his costs. So he is thinking that moving to a mall might increase his sales and therefore lead to a larger profit. A major question is whether he is likely to sell enough extra cars in a mall to help pay for the increase in fixed costs. He is also concerned about how his Oldsmobile products will stand up against all of the other cars when consumers can more easily shop around and compare. Right now, Bob has some loyal customers who regularly buy from him because of his seasoned, helpful sales force *and* his dependable repair shop. But he worries that making it easy for these customers to compare other cars might lead to brand switching or put greater pressure on price to keep some of his "loyal" customers.

Another of Bob's concerns is whether the Big Three car manufacturers will discourage dealers from going into auto malls. Now these auto manufacturers do not encourage dealers to go into a supermarket setting. Instead, they prefer their dealers to devote their full energies to one brand in a freestanding location. But as real estate prices rise, it becomes more and more difficult to insist on freestanding dealerships in all markets and still have profitable dealerships. The rising number of bankruptcies or dealerships in financial difficulties has caused the manufacturers to be more relaxed about insisting on a freestanding location.

Evaluate Bob Dalton's present and possible new strategy. What should Bob Dalton do? Why?

(32) Strategic Adventure Park*

In October 1989, Sue and Lisa reviewed the first operating season of their adventure park. Strategic Adventure Park, located 30 miles from a major Maritime city, catered to young adults who enjoyed active war games. The partners were discussing future options and needed to decide what action should be taken because profits fell far short of projected levels.

Sue and Lisa had started an outdoor adventure game called, Capture the Flag. The game was played by two 20-member teams of adults, and the object was to capture the opposing team's flag. Each team's flag was located in a specified area of the playing region; areas could vary from forested hills to open fields. The first team to capture its opponent's flag was the winner.

Team players defended their flag with CO_2-powered paint guns that shot paint balls filled with water-soluble dye. Players tried to shoot members of the opposing team,

and the first team to eliminate all opposing players was declared the winner. Any player hit by a pellet and marked with dye was out of the game. The player then returned to home base and waited 20 to 30 minutes for the next game to start. Home base offered music and refreshments to promote an atmosphere of fun and camaraderie. Camouflage clothing, protective goggles, guns, holsters, and face paint were provided. Each player was required to buy paint balls and CO_2 and to pay a $25 playing fee.

Another adventure game operated in the western part of the province, approximately 150 kilometers from Strategic Adventure Park. A similar game operated in Alberta. The owners of these firms reported that their players were between the ages of 19 and 50. Consequently, Lisa and Sue had directed their research to identifying the population in that age group who lived or worked in Strategic Adventure Park's catchment area. This information was incorporated into a comprehensive business plan.

Because adventure games were relatively unknown in the Maritimes, the owners believed it would be necessary to create awareness and subsequent demand for this type of leisure activity. The primary marketing area was identified as the entire region within one hour's drive from the centre of the city. The marketing section of the business plan originally provided for $2,000 to be spent on advertising before the park opened. Also $400 monthly was provided for advertising after operations had begun. Lisa and Sue hoped to attract the Yuppie and business populations. Their intention was to make personal calls on medium-sized and large businesses and try to promote the idea of setting up inter- and intracompany challenge events. They also prepared a list of individuals whom they intended to telephone, urging them to get a team together to play the adventure game.

In their market research, the owners discovered that the affluent segments of the population tended to buy experiences rather than possessions such as yachts and summer cottages. More and more, they preferred to travel, whitewater raft, sky dive, and so on. This shift in lifestyle would strengthen the Strategic Adventure Park's market position. Because of the proximity of several major military bases, Sue and Lisa also identified military personnel as a potential market, and planned to encourage and attract interunit competitions. They also believed that the several universities in the area, with a combined student population of over 20,000, would provide another source of players. In order to increase business during workdays, Strategic Adventure Park would try to attract company socials and sports teams to play Capture the Flag. In addition, Lisa and Sue planned to set aside certain days for particular groups such as women's groups or stag parties. They would also encour-

*This case was written by Dr. John Kyle, who at the time of its preparation was associated with Mount Saint Vincent University.

age tournament play on slow days. Each of these distinct markets would require a separate advertising thrust.

The market plan was prepared for a period from May 20 to September 30, 1989. This covered the summer operating season. The game could also be played in the winter, with participants wearing white camouflage clothing when ground was snow-covered. This scenario was not included in the initial market plan.

The owners targeted a net profit after taxes of $10,000 but felt this was the minimum profit that they should realize. Two projected income statements were prepared for the business plan. The first was a pessimistic version based on a volume of only 1,200 customers (12.5 percent of capacity). The second statement was based on 35 percent of capacity, which would increase the customer volume to 3,320 for the season. The first scenario produced a profit of $4,943 after taxes and a partial repayment of the company's $12,500 start-up loan. The second scenario resulted in a profit of $39,461 after taxes and full repayment of the bank loan.

The target start-up date of May 20 proved to be overly optimistic. It was hard to locate suitable property. Many areas prohibited the use of air guns, and it was difficult to find terrain suitable for the adventure park. They needed about 40 acres of land with potential for parking. To properly accommodate the game, a combination of wooded and open terrain was needed. Lisa and Sue finally found a site that was within a 45-minute drive of the city. Another factor contributing to the delayed opening was red tape encountered at various levels of government. A building permit was also required for washrooms and food service. Power had to be brought into the site. Then the location needed approximately $1,000 of leasehold improvements and work before opening day. The park didn't start operating until mid July, a delay of almost two months.

It was late June before Strategic Adventure Park finally launched its advertising campaign. To advertise the park, newspapers in three towns near the proposed site were chosen, as well as a metro radio station. Advertising in the metro daily newspaper was ruled out due to cost. Response to the local newspaper and radio advertisements was disappointing.

A delay also affected preparation of a color flyer, which was needed before direct mail advertising could begin. The flyer wasn't ready until mid July. The printers required a telephone number for the brochure, but the telephone company wouldn't issue a phone number until the office trailer was located on the site. Because of the delay in obtaining a suitable site and consequently in setting up the trailer, the direct mailing package to metro businesses was almost two months behind the scheduled date. When finally completed, the direct mailing pro-

duced the greatest response of all advertising. Even so, the number of calls during July and August was small.

When the anticipated minimum volume of players didn't materialize, there was no money left to advertise further. Besides advertising in the media, Lisa and Sue's business plan called for direct telephone selling or another means of reaching potential customers. However, little direct selling was actually undertaken. Lisa discovered that neither she nor her staff had the time to carry out this activity. People who were interested in playing the game telephoned the Strategic Adventure Park number but, unfortunately, were seldom connected with a knowledgeable employee. Commonly during May, and frequently during the rest of the season, staff members were unavailable to answer the telephone because of outdoor work that required their attention. Callers were asked to leave a message on the answering machine. Either the manager or one of the owners would then call the potential customer back to try to make a firm booking. Many telephone callers wouldn't leave their number. This arrangement was unsatisfactory, but sufficient funds weren't available to pay an additional staff member and thus correct the situation. A full-page article in the metro daily newspaper appeared at the end of August. It created a great deal of interest and bookings improved substantially after this. September and October were fully booked.

As the operating season progressed, a pattern developed. Almost without exception, games were played only on weekends. It was found that the optimum number of players per team was 20. (Minimum number of players required was 10.) Because no-shows could result in a game being canceled for lack of sufficient players, a deposit was required to help prevent this from occurring.

During the summer, four more adventure games opened in the catchment area. These games were similar to Capture the Flag. Playing fees and amenities were also similar. However, the Strategic Adventure Park site, by all accounts, was more attractive and challenging to the players. The terrain offered more variety and contributed to a more interesting game. It was difficult to assess whether the new competition had a significant effect on retarding the growth of the business. Nonetheless, the partners were badly demoralized by this turn of events. They didn't attempt to revise the marketing plan.

The original business plan was based on the staff running two games a day. After gaining some experience by operating a few games, it became clear that the same staff couldn't safely run two games in this time period. The owners decided that there wasn't sufficient cash flow to add more staff and that the low volume of players didn't justify the extra expenditure.

Exhibit 1 Projected and Actual Income Statements May 20–September 30, 1989, Budgeted for Only 40 People per Day for 30 Days (1,200 people)

	Projected	Actual
Revenues:		
Fee ($25 pp* × 1,200)	$30,000	$11,125
Pellets ($10 pp × 1,200)	12,000	4,450
CO_2 cartridges ($3 pp × 1,200)	3,600	1,335
Total revenue	$45,600	$16,910
Less variable expenses:		
Pellets ($6 pp × 1,200)	7,200	2,670
CO_2 cartridges ($1.65 pp × 1,200)	1,980	734
Cleaning and repair ($.50 pp × 1,200)	600	223
Part-time staff ($7 × 192 hours)	1,344	1,300
Refreshments ($1 pp × 1,200)	1,200	445
Miscellaneous supplies ($.50 pp × 1,200)	600	110
Delivery costs ($.15 pp × 1,200)	180	1,000
Total variable expenses	$13,104	$ 6,482
Contribution margin	$32,496	$10,428
Fixed expenses:		
Advertising ($400 per mo.)	1,600	400
Utilities ($198 × 4 mo.)	792	800
Office supplies ($75 per mo.)	300	300
Salaries ($10,000 + $6,000)	16,000	4,950
Land rental ($500 per mo.)	2,000	2,000
Trailer rental ($100 per mo.)	500	400
Washroom rental ($100 per mo.)	400	400
Interest expense	125	125
Depreciation expense	125	350
Total fixed expenses	$21,842	$ 9,725
Profit before interest and taxes:	10,654	$ 703
Less taxes (and corporate surtax) payable	2,711	
Less loan repayment of $3,000	3,000	
Net profit (loss)	$ 4,943	

Note: This projected income statement is based on the pessimistic version of future operations.

*pp = per person.

At the end of the season, Sue and Lisa sat down to discuss and evaluate the business. Strategic Adventure Park hadn't attained its target profit of $10,000. The company broke even only by ruthlessly slashing expenses when it was evident that start-up was going to be delayed. For example, the full-time manager's salary was cut in half after the first month's operation. Part-time staff hours were reduced. Advertising expenses were slashed from a projected $1,600 for the season ($400 per month) to an actual $400

for the season. Both owners felt that, as the season ended, it was necessary to identify why operating results had fallen short of projections so that corrective measures could be taken, and to decide whether they should continue operations through the winter. See Exhibit 1.

The issue of the company's longer-term prospects also had to be addressed. Sue and Lisa felt there was cause for some optimism. They believed that because of the game's success on September and October weekends, it was reasonable to assume the 22 weekends of the 1990 May to September season would be fully booked if aggressive marketing was begun before the May start-up. Taking into consideration long weekends, and estimating that an average of 15 players would play each game, the owners forecast that 1,380 players would participate in the 1990 summer season.

All things considered, should Strategic Adventure Park keep operating or should it close? If it keeps operating, what changes should be made for the 1990 season?

33 Lever, Ltd.*

Joe Hall is product manager for Guard Deodorant Soap. He was just transferred to Lever, Ltd., a Canadian subsidiary of Lever Group, Inc., from world headquarters in New York. Joe is anxious to make a good impression because he is hoping to transfer to Lever's London office. He is working on developing and securing management approval of next year's marketing plan for Guard. His first job is submitting a draft marketing plan to Sarah Long—his recently appointed group product manager—who is responsible for several such plans from product managers like Joe.

Joe's marketing plan is the single most important document he will produce on this assignment. This annual marketing plan does three main things:

1. It reviews the brand's performance in the past year, assesses the competitive situation, and highlights problems and opportunities for the brand.
2. It spells out marketing strategies and the plan for the coming year.
3. Finally, and most importantly, the marketing plan sets out the brand's sales objectives and advertising/promotion budget requirements.

In preparing this marketing plan, Joe gathered the information in Table 1.

*Adapted from a case prepared by Mr. Daniel Aronchick, who at the time of its preparation was marketing manager at Thomas J. Lipton, Limited.

Table 1   Past 12-month Share of Bar Soap Market (percent)

	Maritimes	Quebec	Ontario	Manitoba/ Saskatchewan	Alberta	British Columbia
Deodorant segment						
Zest	21.3%	14.2%	24.5%	31.2%	30.4%	25.5%
Dial	10.4	5.1	12.8	16.1	17.2	14.3
Lifebuoy	4.2	3.1	1.2	6.4	5.8	4.2
Guard	2.1	5.6	1.0	4.2	4.2	2.1
Beauty bar segment						
Camay	6.2	12.3	7.0	4.1	4.0	5.1
Lux	6.1	11.2	7.7	5.0	6.9	5.0
Dove	5.5	8.0	6.6	6.3	6.2	4.2
Lower-priced bars						
Ivory	11.2	6.5	12.4	5.3	5.2	9.0
Sunlight	6.1	3.2	8.2	4.2	4.1	8.0
All others						
(including stores' own brands)	26.9	30.8	18.6	17.2	16.0	22.6
Total bar soap market	100.0%	100.0%	100.0%	100.0%	100.0%	100.0%

Joe was somewhat surprised at the significant regional differences in the bar soap market:

1. The underdevelopment of the deodorant bar segment in Quebec with a corresponding overdevelopment of the beauty bar segment. But some past research suggested that this is due to cultural factors—English-speaking people have been more interested than others in cleaning, deodorizing, and disinfecting. A similar pattern is seen in most European countries, where the adoption of deodorant soaps has been slower than in North America. For similar reasons, the perfumed soap share is highest in French-speaking Quebec.

2. The overdevelopment of synthetic bars in the Prairies. These bars, primarily in the deodorant segment, lather better in the hard water of the Prairies. Nonsynthetic bars lather very poorly in hard-water areas—and leave a soap film.

3. The overdevelopment of the "all-other" segment in Quebec. This segment, consisting of smaller brands, fares better in Quebec, where 43 percent of the grocery trade is done by independent stores. Conversely, large chain grocery stores dominate in Ontario and the Prairies.

Joe's brand, Guard, is a highly perfumed deodorant bar. His business is relatively weak in the key Ontario market. To confirm this share data, Joe calculated consumption of Guard per thousand people in each region. See Table 2.

These differences are especially interesting since per capita sales of all bar soap products are roughly equal in all provinces.

A consumer attitude and usage research study was conducted approximately a year ago. This study revealed that consumer "top-of-mind" awareness of the Guard brand differed greatly across Canada. This was true despite the even expenditure (by population) of advertising funds in past years. Also, trial of Guard was low in the Maritimes, Ontario, and British Columbia. See Table 3.

The attitude portion of the research revealed that consumers who had heard of Guard were aware that its deodorant protection came mainly from a high fragrance level. This was the main selling point in the copy, and it was well communicated by Guard's advertising. The other important finding was that consumers who had tried

Table 2   Standard Cases of 3-Ounce Bars Consumed per 1,000 People in 12 Months

	Maritimes	Quebec	Ontario	Manitoba/Saskatchewan	Alberta	British Columbia
Guard	4.1	10.9	1.9	8.1	4.1	6.2
Sales index	66	175	31	131	131	100

Table 3   Usage Results (in percent)

	Maritimes	Quebec	Ontario	Manitoba/ Saskatchewan	Alberta	British Columbia
Respondents aware of Guard	20%	58%	28%	30%	32%	16%
Respondents ever trying Guard	3	18	2	8	6	4

Guard were satisfied with the product. About 70 percent of those trying Guard had repurchased the product at least twice.

Joe has also discovered that bar soap competition is especially intense in Ontario. It is Canada's largest market, and many competitors seem to want a share of it. The chain stores are also quite aggressive in promotion and pricing, offering specials, in-store coupons, and so on. They want to move goods. And because of this, two key Ontario chains have put Guard on their pending delisting sheets. These chains, which control about half the grocery volume in Ontario, are dissatisfied with how slowly Guard is moving off the shelves.

Now Joe feels he is ready to set a key part of the brand's marketing plan for next year: how to allocate the advertising/sales promotion budget by region.

Guard's present advertising/sales promotion budget is 20 percent of sales. With forecast sales of $4 million, this would amount to an $800,000 expenditure. Traditionally such funds have been allocated in proportion to population. See Table 4.

Joe feels he should spend more heavily in Ontario where the grocery chain delisting problem exists. Last year, 36 percent of Guard's budget was allocated to Ontario, which accounted for only 12 percent of Guard's sales. Joe wants to increase Ontario spending to 48 percent of the total budget by taking funds evenly from all other areas. Joe expects this will increase business in the key Ontario market, which has over a third of Canada's population, because it is a big increase and will help Guard "out-shout" the many other competitors who are promoting heavily.

Joe presented this idea to Sarah, his newly appointed group product manager. Sarah strongly disagrees. She has also been reviewing Guard's business and feels that promotion funds have historically been misallocated. It is her strong belief that, to use her words: "A brand should spend where its business is." Sarah believes that the first priority in allocating funds regionally is to support the areas of strength. She suggested to Joe that there may be more business to be had in the brand's strong areas, Quebec and the Prairies, than in chasing sales in Ontario. The needs and attitudes toward Guard, as well as competitive pressures, may vary a lot among the provinces. Therefore, Sarah suggested that spending for Guard in the coming year be proportional to the brand's sales by region rather than to regional population.

Joe is convinced this is wrong, particularly in light of the Ontario situation. He asked Sarah how the Ontario market should be handled. Sarah said that the conservative way to build business in Ontario is to invest incremental promotion funds. However, before these incremental funds are invested, a test of this Ontario investment proposition should be conducted. Sarah recommended that some of the Ontario money should be used to conduct an investment-spending market test in a small area or town in Ontario for 12 months. This will enable Joe to see if the incremental spending results in higher sales and profits—profits large enough to justify higher spending. In other words, an investment payout should be assured before spending any extra money in Ontario. Similarly, Sarah would do the same kind of test in Quebec—to see if more money should go there.

Joe feels this approach would be a waste of time and unduly cautious, given the importance of the Ontario market and the likely delistings in two key chains.

Evaluate the present strategy for Guard and Joe's and Sarah's proposed strategies. How should the promotion money be allocated? Should investment-spending market tests be run first? Why? Explain.

Table 4   Allocation of Advertising/Sales Promotion Budget, by Population

	Maritimes	Quebec	Ontario	Manitoba/ Saskatchewan	Alberta	British Columbia	Canada
Percent of population	10%	27%	36%	8%	8%	11%	100%
Possible allocation of budget based on population (in 000s)	$80	$216	$288	$64	$64	$88	$800
Percent of Guard business at present	7%	51%	12%	11%	11%	8%	100%

(34) E. D. Smith & Sons Limited*

Chris Powell and Lee Ann Jessop of E. D. Smith & Sons Limited reviewed the history of the firm's line of jam and jelly products. As Marketing/Sales Manager—Grocery products and Product Manager, respectively, they determined the company strategic plan for the product line. The hundred-year-old company based in Winona, Ontario, would have to respond to the potential of a free trade agreement with the United States, a recent lack of advertising support for the product line, and trade rumors that shelf space for all jam, jelly, and marmalade products was about to decrease. As they gazed at the lush agricultural lands of the Niagara Escarpment on this warm June day, the plan of action for the remainder of 1988 and 1989 was far from certain.

COMPANY OPERATIONS

The company had kept pace with changing markets and new taste trends by means of a modern, efficient manufacturing capability, progressive management and a dedicated group of over 200 employees. With the exception of sales offices, the entire E. D. Smith company operated from Winona, Ontario. The company continued to handle its own shipping. Products were carried by rail to Atlantic and western Canada, while in Ontario and Quebec the E. D. Smith fleet of transport trailers handled deliveries.

Grocery products accounted for a major proportion of the Food Division business. Not mentioned previously, E. D. Smith marketed chili sauce relish under their own name, H. P. Sauce, and Lea & Perrins. Sales of these products were handled primarily by the 20 person National Grocery Sales Force who worked in all provinces except the Atlantic where a broker was retained.

Although the company's markets were mostly domestic, the firm had limited sales outside North America. Wherever possible, Canadian products were purchased as raw materials. Raspberries from British Columbia, blueberries from the Maritimes, rhubarb in Quebec and apples and cherries from Ontario were examples of Canadian sourcing. In fact, the company was working to establish a Canadian source of strawberries that met its specifications.

People were a key ingredient to E. D. Smith's success. A team spirit was promoted and an open door policy was maintained to ensure good labour relations. Employees were encouraged to participate in "speak-up sessions"

and in the company newsletter—The Homestead—offering a forum for suggestions on maintaining and improving the company's standards. Employees were also encouraged to participate in subsidized courses both on and off the premises.

Automation and innovation had streamlined the production process. Modern methods preserved the products' natural goodness and ensured quality standards while maintaining stable prices. Computers assisted management in controlling operations from receipt of ingredients to order assembly for customer deliveries. While the company was busiest in the fall, production continued year-round with frozen and fresh fruit imported from the United States, British Columbia and Europe. The seasonality and variety of products necessitated a complex scheduling system to ensure maximum efficiency and cost control.

THE JAM, JELLY, AND MARMALADE MARKET

Marketing research indicated that when consumers were asked what image the name E. D. Smith conjured in their mind, the most frequent answer was jam. After all, E. D. Smith was the first company to sell "pure" jam in Canada. Any product called pure jam had to contain a minimum of 45 percent fruit. The remainder of the product could contain sugar and natural preservatives such as citric acid. No additives, no artificial colors, and no chemicals could be added to pure jams.

E. D. Smith sold 80 to 85 percent of its pure jams and jellies in Ontario. Sales in Quebec were negligible due mostly to Quebecers liking sweeter, less thick jams. Likewise sales in Canada's west were nearly negligible. The Maritimes accounted for the remainder of E. D. Smith's jam and jelly sales. Due to the concentration of sales in Ontario, Lee Ann and Chris decided to narrow their focus to this market.

In Ontario, the top six brands of jam, jelly, and marmalade accounted for 50.7 percent of the sales. This was a highly fragmented market with many companies vying for market share. Even foreign companies had some market share though their jams weren't classified as pure jams and were of low quality containing large quantities of pectin (a natural substance used to solidify a jam, jelly, or marmalade). Yet heavy competition was surprising since demand for both jam and jelly hadn't grown in the past five years (annual changes in demand fluctuated between +1 percent and −1 percent) and demand for the marmalade was declining at the rate of 8 percent per year.

Theories to explain the competition were plentiful. Perhaps more and more people weren't eating breakfast (or at least not eating breakfast at home), but breakfast cereal and microwavable breakfast sales were growing.

Perhaps consumers had turned away from jam, jelly, and marmalade in favor of honey, peanut butter, and other breakfast spreads, but these products hadn't shown any appreciable growth in sales. Certainly people hadn't turned to making their own jam. The amount of home-made jam produced in Canada had been on a steady decline for the past 20 years.

The top-selling brand in Ontario was Kraft with 13.7 percent of the market. In fact, it was the best-selling brand in Canada. Typical consumers of Kraft's products were children who used the spread with peanut butter in a sandwich. Kraft was a large, diversified, processed food company which used a family branding approach. It started selling jam, jelly, and marmalade in the 1920s. With a large advertising budget, it was able to establish and maintain the brand name in the consumer's mind. Its position as the only jam, jelly, and marmalade producer was solidified by a product relaunch in 1988. Kraft had changed the packaging (from a round glass jar to a square glass jar) and labelling (giving new emphasis to the fruit).

The number two brand, Laura Secord, had 9.5 percent of the market. Laura Secord only sold pure jams and marmalades. A division of Cattelli Foods, the company started selling jam and marmalade in 1977, making it the newest market entrant. Typical consumers of Laura Secord jams were discriminating shoppers. They were looking for a better product with a better taste. Independent taste tests indicated Laura Secord's flavor was better than Kraft's and equal to E. D. Smith's. The Laura Secord name was also a family brand used for ice cream, chocolate, and pudding products. Rumors were afoot that Cattelli's parent company, John Labatt Ltd., was preparing to sell the Cattelli division. These rumors were reinforced when it was announced that the Laura Secord name had been sold to Nestlé. Nestlé was interested in continuing the chocolate and milk products line, but didn't seem to have any interest in continuing the jam line. Cattelli could soon begin a process of selling the jam production facilities and closing out this business.

The number three brand was Aylmer with 9.3 percent of the market. This company sold mostly pectin jam and apple jelly. The former had far less fruit and far more pectin. Like Laura Secord and Kraft, Aylmer was a family brand spread over several product lines including canned vegetables and soups. Typical consumers of this product were children and the value-conscious buyer.

E. D. Smith was fourth in the market with a 7.6 percent market share. Like Laura Secord, typical E. D. Smith consumers were looking for a better product with better flavor. The diet line of jams, introduced in 1978, accounted for 53 percent of E. D. Smith's market share. The diet jams contained no sugar but were sweetened with Sorbitol, a natural sweetener suitable for use in a low-sugar diet. The diet product line, including apricot, blueberry, raspberry, and strawberry/rhubarb, had recently been reformulated using juice concentrates as sweeteners. The only competition in the diet line was Weight Watchers, but E. D. Smith's market share was 66 percent greater. Overall E. D. Smith sold jam, diet jam, jelly, and a unique lemon spread that was especially popular in the Maritimes.

One quarter of the jam packaged at E. D. Smith used private labelling (the packaging of E. D. Smith product using another firm's jars and labels). Typically, private labelling was done for a grocery store that possessed a house brand (such as Top Valu, Domino, or President's Choice). In recent months, private labels had requested a change in the glass jars from the round shape used by E. D. Smith to a squarer shape similar to that used by Kraft. Kraft had never engaged in any private labelling.

Tied for fifth position were Welch's and Shiriff at 5.3 percent of the market each. Welch's competed in a narrow market niche: grape jams and jellies. In fact, Welch's was the number one seller in that niche. The Welch's family brand extended to grape juice and grape drinks in frozen concentrate, glass jar, and tetra-brick (cardboard box) forms. Shiriff was responsible for the Good Morning product line consisting of marmalades and mint jelly. In 1987, Shiriff Good Morning Marmalade was sold to Smucker's of the United States.

THE SITUATION AT HAND

In 1983, E. D. Smith sold 250,000 cases of jam and jelly in Ontario—a $3.5 million business. By 1988, that figure had declined to 163,000 cases, an annual sales decrease of 11 percent. Without realizing it, E. D. Smith had been milking a cash cow for, at one time, E. D. Smith had been the market leader. The steady decline had been halted only twice during the previous 20 years: with the introduction of diet jam in 1978 and a relaunch of the product in 1974. The relaunch consisted of a change in label design (emphasizing the fruit) accompanied by a couponing campaign on a newspaper/magazine insert. In recent years, the jam line was given no advertising support as E. D. Smith had focused advertising dollars on other product opportunities.

During the recession of the early 1980s, E. D. Smith undertook cost-cutting moves which saw the amount of fruit used in the pure jam reduced to the minimum. Only a small quantity of fruit could be supplied by the E. D. Smith farms so, with purchasing budgets cut back, the quality of the imported fruit also suffered. A final cost-cutting measure saw the substitution of cheaper fructose sugar for glucose sugar for a savings of 36 cents per case of 12 jars. A side effect of using fructose in cooking the jam was a slight browning of the mixture. Glucose sugar improved not only the mixture's color but its flavor as well.

The market was highly price sensitive and E. D. Smith was a price taker or follower. Its strategy was simply to match Kraft's pricing policy, which had been a $2.19 price for the 250-ml container on the retail store shelf. This parity pricing policy was also followed by Laura Secord. Occasionally, to help move a volume of product, one of the three firms used a feature price of $1.99 at the retail store. However it wasn't unusual to find all three brands moving to that price once one took the lead. E. D. Smith expected the regular price, set by Kraft, to increase soon as there had been no price increase during the previous three years.

Chris and Lee Ann were concerned with rumors/suggestions from wholesalers and retailers that the amount of shelf space devoted to jam, jelly, and marmalade in retail stores was about to be reduced. The argument made by the trade was that these products' sales had been declining so they didn't deserve as much exposure as they currently had. This meant that either the number of varieties carried by each store of each type of jam, jelly, and marmalade would be reduced or some brand(s) would have to be eliminated. Both Aylmer and Laura Secord appeared to be vulnerable.

The possible approval of the Free Trade Agreement between the United States and Canada would bring another set of problems. Smucker's, the number one producer of jam, jelly, and marmalade in the United States, had been trying to enter the Canadian market for some time. Though not prohibited from exporting that product to Canada, Smucker's hadn't pursued that Canadian market because of perceived bureaucratic problems. With the Free Trade Agreement in place, a new openness in terms of US investment in Canada, and the acquisition of Shiriff, Smucker's would likely succeed in opening a new Canadian operation.

THE POSSIBILITIES FOR E. D. SMITH

Lee Ann and Chris could take a defensive posture and eliminate some of the varieties of jam and jelly produced by E. D. Smith. Three varieties (strawberry, raspberry, and lemon spread) accounted for nearly 80 percent of sales. These three could be kept in two sizes (250 ml and 500 ml). A different posture would be a flanking maneuver positioning the jam and jelly line as a product used in cooking and baking rather than as a breakfast spread. Jam could be used in cakes as a filling, in jelly rolls, on ice cream, over waffles, in tarts, in dessert treats, in Christmas baking, as a sauce ingredient, or in muffins.

A different flanking maneuver would be to focus on "peculiar" or unique flavors of specialty jam and jellies. At a current average price of $17 per case, a new flavor had to generate sales of at least 4,000 cases to break even. Coupled with this could be a price increase to establish a

premium image. Though sales volume would likely fall, the profit margin on each jar would be greater and, presumably, profits could rise. A more offensive move would be to relaunch or even reformulate the product. In a relaunch, a company could change the packaging, the labelling, or the promotion of the product in such a way that it had a fresh, new image. Reformulation would mean a change in the basic product itself either through a new jam recipe, a change in fruit, or a change in sugar. If a relaunch or reformulation were undertaken, how similar or dissimilar should the packaging, label, promotion, or recipe be to the other products on the market? Should the price be changed? Should E. D. Smith try to become the price leader?

Another offensive move would be to launch the product line in the United States. Informally E. D. Smith liked to concentrate the firm's efforts within an 80-mile radius of Winona. Shipping costs increased price to a nearly noncompetitive level outside of that area. Nonetheless, including the United States, 125 million people lived within an 800-mile radius of Winona.

Twenty years ago, E. D. Smith stopped selling Orange and Three Fruit marmalade. Perhaps the line could be revitalized. The ultimate offensive move would be the launch of a second E. D. Smith jam and jelly line. As with New Coke and Classic Coke, E. D. Smith could have a regular and premium/old-fashioned line of jams and jellies. These two lines would have different price points, packages, labels, and recipes and would require separate promotional support to build awareness and separation in consumers' minds.

THE DECISION

The costing of the many options would have to come later. For now Chris and Lee Ann were screening the alternatives from a strategic viewpoint. Equally of concern was the tactical plan that would have to be developed for any chosen strategies. Chris loosened his tie and Lee Ann took off her jacket. There was plenty of work to be done.

What strategy would you choose for the product lines? Why? What factors are essential to consider?

(35) Canadian Inland*

Inland Manufacturing Corporation, a medium-sized US manufacturer of aluminum products, entered Canada in 1957 by acquiring the assets of two Canadian extrusion†

*This case was written by Professor Peter Banting, who at the time of its preparation was associated with McMaster University.
†Extrusion is the process of forcing aluminum billets under great heat and pressure through dies to form predetermined shapes.

companies. These two companies were then merged into a single Canadian extrusion enterprise with plants in Toronto and Hamilton.

Canadian Inland has two main divisions—industrial and consumer. The industrial division produces semifabricated extrusions that are supplied to manufacturers. The consumer division produces finished aluminum products, such as garden furniture, aluminum ladders, umbrella-type clothes lines, scaffolding, moldings, and cabinet edgings. In addition, Inland owns several aluminum door and window firms. Canadian Inland's sales reached $20 million in 1992.

The parent company's international division looks after all foreign operations. These include plants in France, Germany, Belgium, Spain, Italy, England, and Canada. All subsidiaries operate with a reasonably high degree of autonomy. Of the foreign subsidiaries, however, the Canadian firm is the only one with a consumer products division. It alone has experience, know-how, and marketing knowledge in the consumer area.

Having successfully cultivated the home market, with the prior approval of the parent company the Canadian firm decided to probe foreign markets. The objective was to stimulate demand for Inland's products in the foreign markets and make Inland's other subsidiaries recognize the potential for consumer sales in their respective markets. Sales volume developed by the Canadian company, when sufficiently large, would be turned over for the local subsidiary to expand and ultimately result in the establishment of domestic manufacturing by the sister subsidiary.

On this basis, the Canadian consumer division went "international" in January of 1989. The sales manager, John Foreman, believed that the growing affluence of European workers, their developing taste for leisure, and their lifestyle preferences would permit the company's consumer products to quickly gain market acceptance.

John's first step was to investigate foreign markets. The Ontario Ministry of Industry and Tourism in March 1990 was organizing a trade mission to Europe. After some consultations with members of the department, John accepted their invitation to join this trade mission, which toured Italy, Germany, Holland, France, and England. During the course of the trip, John was officially introduced to leading buyers for department store chains, import houses, wholesalers, and buying groups. The two-week trip convinced John Foreman that there was ample buying power in some of the countries to make the exportation of Canadian-made aluminum consumer products a profitable undertaking.

On his return to Canada, John's next step was to obtain credit references for the firms he considered as potential distributors. To those judged acceptable, he sent letters expressing interest and including samples, prices, and other relevant information.

The first orders received were from a German wholesaler who imported on his own account. Sales in this market totaled $60,000 in 1990. Similar success was achieved in France and England. Italy, on the other hand, did not produce sales. This was attributed to the semi-luxury nature of the company's products. John Foreman concluded that due to the lower level of incomes in Italy, Italians had developed a predisposition toward "making do" with serviceable items, rather than looking for goods and services that would make life easier.

In Canada, Inland distributes through merchant hardware distributors and buying groups, such as cooperatives and hardware chains. In foreign markets, however, there is no recognizable pattern, and channel systems vary from country to country. In one country, sales are made to an individual who stocks goods on his own account. In another, an agent, a buying group, or a hardware wholesaler is engaged. To avoid mixing channels of distribution, Inland has only one account in each country. The chosen distributor enjoys exclusive representation.

In Germany, Inland distributes through a wholesaler based in Hamburg. This wholesaler has a force of five salespeople. The firm specializes in small housewares and has contacts with leading buying groups, wholesalers, and department stores. John Foreman was impressed with the firm's aggressiveness and knowledge of merchandising techniques. He noted that they had won an award from a large American vacuum cleaner firm as its best single foreign representative in 1990, which he considered a good indication of sales ability.

In France, the company sells to a Paris-based buying group of a chain of hardware wholesalers with representation throughout the country. It was felt that this group would provide excellent coverage of the market because of its extensive distributive network.

In Denmark, the Canadian company's line is sold to a buying group representing a chain of hardware retailers. This group recently expanded to include counterparts in Sweden, Finland, and Norway. Together, they purchase goods for about 500 hardware retailers. The buying power of the Scandinavians is quite high, and it is expected that Inland's products will prove very successful in this market.

In the United Kingdom, an importer-distributor, who both buys on his own account and acts as a sales agent, handles the company's line. This firm sells to department stores and hardware wholesalers. The distribution chain in England is quite cumbersome, and the company had found it difficult to attain acceptance in the British market. John Foreman, however, is convinced that this market has the highest potential of all the foreign countries. To date, the do-it-yourself market in Great Britain had brought in a lot of business in aluminum moldings.

The Australian market was established indirectly and successfully. A number of letters were received from Australian merchants who had heard of Inland through the Department of Industry, Trade and Commerce. The supply of garden furniture in Australia was small and prices were high. Prices were quoted and samples sent to the businessmen recommended by the Canadian trade commissioner. The distributor selected is an Australian importer who operates a chain of discount houses and retails on his own account. This firm discovered it could land aluminum furniture in Melbourne at prices competitive with American and Japanese imports.

The Venezuelan market was developed by an American who came to Canada from Venezuela in search of new lines. Inland attributes success in Venezuela to the efforts of this aggressive and capable agent. He has built a sizable trade in aluminum ladders.

In Trinidad and Jamaica, Inland's consumer products are handled by traders who carry such diversified lines as insurance, apples, plums, and fish. They have been successful in selling aluminum ladders.

The sales manager's export strategy is as follows:

1. Product—no product modifications will be made in selling to foreign customers. This might be considered later, after a substantial sales volume has developed.
2. Price—the company will not concern itself with retail prices and will not publish suggested list prices. Distributors add their own markups to their landed cost. Supply prices will be kept as low as possible. This is accomplished by:
   a. Removing advertising expenses and other strictly domestic overhead charges from price calculations.
   b. Finding the most economical packages for shipment (smallest volume per unit).
   c. Bargaining with carriers to obtain the lowest shipping rates possible.
3. Promotion—removal of advertising expenses from price calculations is accomplished because the firm does no advertising in foreign markets. Brochures and sales literature already being used in Canada are supplied to foreign distributors. Inland will continue to promote its consumer products by participating in overseas trade shows. These are staffed by the consumer sales manager. All exhibition inquiries are forwarded to the firm's distributor in that country.
4. Distribution—new distributors will be contacted through foreign trade shows. John Foreman considers large distributors desirable. He feels, however, that they are not as receptive as smaller distributors to a new, unestablished product line. Consequently, he prefers to appoint small distributors. Larger distributors may be appointed after the company has gained a strong consumer franchise.
5. Financing—Inland sees no need to provide financial help to distributors. The company views its major contribution as providing operational products at the lowest possible price.
6. Marketing and planning assistance—John Foreman contends that foreign distributors know their own markets best. Consequently, they are best equipped to plan for themselves.
7. Selection of foreign markets—the evaluation of foreign market opportunities for the company's consumer products is based primarily on disposable income and lifestyle patterns. For example, John fails to see any market in North Africa for his products, which he categorizes as a semiluxurious line. It is his opinion that cheaper products such as wooden ladders (often homemade) are preferred to prefabricated aluminum ladders in regions such as North Africa, Italy, and Spain. Venezuela, on the other hand, he contends is a more highly industrialized market with luxury tastes. Thus, John sees Inland's consumer products as being essentially tailored for a highly industrialized and affluent society.

What do you think of John Foreman's approach to probing foreign markets and to selecting distribution channels? What overseas distribution strategy would you design for Inland?

36 Laskers Foods Limited*

Murray Lasker was wondering what strategy his company, Laskers Foods Limited, ought to follow. It was July 1992 and sales and profits had been on a plateau since 1988. Lasker was thinking of what his next expansionary move should be and the longer-term consequences of such action.

During the late 1800s and early 1900s, many Jewish immigrants from Eastern Europe came to Montreal, bringing several traditionally Jewish ways of preparing and cooking meat. A number of these immigrants soon

---

*This case was prepared by Dr. V. H. Kirpalani and Mr. Harold Simpkins, who at the time of its preparation were associated with Concordia University.

opened delicatessens in the growing Jewish neighborhoods of Montreal. Many of these restaurants specialized in preparing and selling smoked beef briskets for consumption either at home or in the restaurant section of the delicatessen. Each of the delicatessens featuring the briskets added its own unique touch to the curing and smoking process. The various delicatessens became closely identified with the slight but noticeable taste differences that resulted from their individual recipes.

These cured and smoked beef briskets, similar to pastrami and corned beef in appearance, became known as smoked meat, and smoked meat's appeal grew to include virtually every Montrealer. By the 1940s, the hot smoked meat sandwich (thinly sliced steamed smoked meat served on rye bread with mustard) was a Montreal phenomenon. Most of the city's lunch counters and snack bars served smoked meat in this fashion. Since these lunch counters, snack bars, and new delicatessens generally purchased their smoked meat briskets from one or more of the older Montreal delicatessens, many of Montreal's original delicatessens found themselves in the food service business.

One such delicatessen was Laskers Deli, located in Montreal's St. Lawrence Street main district. Jacob Lasker had emigrated from Poland to Canada in the early 1900s. He brought with him a smoked meat recipe his parents had successfully commercialized in his native Warsaw. Within five years of his arrival, Lasker had used smoked meat to make his delicatessen one of the most popular. Laskers Deli was also one of the first delicatessens to sell smoked meat to other restaurants. During the 1930s and 1940s, Jacob Lasker expanded his capacity six times to produce smoked meat briskets. Eventually, Lasker opened a full-scale meat-processing plant behind his St. Lawrence Street delicatessen.

A handful of competitors also set up their own plants. By the 1950s, there were six such operations in Montreal. Because of their size and resultant economies of scale, these plants could produce smoked meat at much lower costs than could individual delicatessen owners. These six plants soon supplied virtually all of the Montreal market, as delicatessen owners gradually stopped making their own smoked meat.

By the early 1960s, Jacob Lasker felt that growth within the smoked meat market had peaked. He decided a complementary product was needed to maintain his company's momentum. Since his four-man sales force was already calling on most Montreal snack bars and lunch counters, and since he had the expertise to produce processed meats in volume, Jacob Lasker decided that hot dog frankfurters would be a logical new product. Lasker believed his company's reputation for manufacturing high-quality smoked meat would facilitate the successful introduction of frankfurters to the food service market.

Furthermore, he felt that Laskers Foods would be able to charge a few cents more per pound for frankfurters because of its reputation as a quality supplier. As a result, he purchased the equipment necessary to produce 4,000 pounds of frankfurters per week.

Selling frankfurters, even to Laskers' smoked meat customers, proved to be much more difficult than was expected. There were many competitors in the frankfurter market and most were larger than Laskers. This market was highly price sensitive; the majority of restaurant and delicatessen owners purchased the cheapest frankfurters available. Profit margins on the frankfurters were small compared to those on smoked meat. As a result, achieving a steady, high-volume sales level was necessary if frankfurters were to be profitable.

When Jacob Lasker died in 1965, his 32-year-old son, Murray, took over the business. Despite the difficulties he'd encountered in trying to sell the company's frankfurters to the Montreal restaurant trade, Murray remained committed to making frankfurters a successful product for Laskers. By the late 1960s, his efforts seemed to have paid off. Laskers' frankfurter manufacturing facilities were at capacity. While smoked meat was still the company's biggest profit contributor, frankfurters rivaled it in terms of sales revenue.

During the late 1960s, Murray Lasker was also moderately successful in expanding the company's distribution through supermarkets. First, he achieved better distribution of the company's smoked briskets through supermarket delicatessen counters. Lasker also introduced two new products to be sold in supermarket self-serve meat sections. One product was sandwich-sliced portions of smoked meat in boil-and-serve plastic pouches. The second product was frankfurters in the traditional 1- and 2-pound packages.

Both the smoked meat and frankfurter products prominently featured the Laskers brand name on their packages, and both achieved distribution in about 25 percent of Montreal's supermarkets. Although no advertising or sales promotion was conducted, their sales were sufficient to warrant their continued stocking by supermarkets. Both the smoked meat pouches and the frankfurters made a significant profit contribution to Laskers Foods Limited.

The late 1960s also saw the takeover of Laskers' three major competitors by multinational packaged goods companies. These large companies believed that Laskers' competitors' brand names and products could be successfully marketed through supermarkets on a local and eventually on a national basis. Also, these multinationals felt that by acquiring these specialty meat producers, they could profitably increase their exposure to the growing food service industry.

The multinationals introduced new products with an emphasis on packaged, presliced meats such as cooked ham, bologna, salami, chicken loaf, bacon, and smoked meat. Also, they expanded retail distribution of their frankfurter brands. Their marketing strategies were supported with high levels of consumer and trade advertising and promotion. At the food service level, they integrated the selling of their existing lines of food products with their newly acquired processed meat lines, thereby offering a more complete range of food service products to both new and existing customers.

These efforts were not all that successful. While the multinationals did achieve high supermarket sales volumes, the profit margins on these sales were much less than anticipated. Consumer price sensitivity had been underestimated and the strength of brand loyalty overestimated. As competition increased, feature or "special" pricing activities became an almost weekly affair, and consumers generally bought the featured brand. Unsuccessful efforts to reduce the level of price sensitivity by substantially increasing expenditures for image-building advertising and promotion dramatically cut into profit margins. On the whole, the multinationals found that profits generated by processed meats at the retail level were much less than satisfactory.

At the food service level, the small and medium-sized processed meat manufacturers responded to the multinationals' expansionary moves by cutting their prices. This action further reduced industry margins and, to a large extent, slowed down the multinationals' growth in the food service markets.

All during this period, Laskers Foods' sales and profits continued their slow but steady growth. This was true despite a dramatic loss to the multinationals of supermarket distribution for their retail self-service smoked meat and frankfurter products. Fortunately, the company had both successfully expanded its distribution of smoked meat briskets in supermarket delicatessen sections and launched its two new products. Also, Laskers Foods opened sales offices in Quebec City, Ottawa, and Toronto, making small inroads into these markets.

By early 1975, Laskers Foods' manufacturing capacity was being fully utilized. The company had no room for expansion in its existing location. Murray Lasker decided continued medium and long-term growth required a larger plant. He also decided to expand the company's product line by adding a full range of processed meats to his smoked meat and frankfurter offerings. The line he ultimately decided on included sausages, salami, bologna, hams, bacon, processed meat loaves, corned beef, pastrami, and smoked poultry. In 1980, construction of Laskers' new manufacturing facilities, in a suburb of Montreal, was completed. At a cost of over $35 million, it featured the most technologically advanced and efficient machinery and production systems available. Total employment at the new plant, including office, sales, and data processing staff, exceeded 250.

From 1981 until 1988, Laskers' sales and profits grew strongly with most of the increases coming from sales of the new products to both existing and new customers. But sales and profits hit an apparent plateau in 1988, staying at about that level until 1991. Exhibit 1 provides more information on relative contribution and market share by product type.

When Murray Lasker analyzed the problems and opportunities represented by his product line, he came to the following conclusions:

1. *Smoked meat*—this was the company's flagship and most profitable product. Laskers Foods could continue to charge a slight premium price within the Montreal food service market. The company was known in the local food service trade as being one of the best, if not the best, smoked meat suppliers. However the Montreal food service market for smoked meat was saturated, and Laskers already held the major share of that market. Major new opportunities involved introducing smoked meat into other geographic areas and expanding the company's supermarket distribution.

2. *Frankfurters*—although Laskers still held a substantial share of the Montreal food service market for frankfurters, this market was becoming increasingly price-oriented. The long-term outlook for frankfurter profit margins was not encouraging.

   At the retail supermarket level, distribution was spotty. Supermarkets favored brands that offered ongoing low prices and frequent feature price promotions. The retail prices charged during these promotions were often at or below manufacturer's cost. Also, the major competitors in the market continued to advertise aggressively. There was no reason to believe this situation would soon change. Murray Lasker felt that the only opportunity for long-term profits in the frankfurter market was in high-volume sales.

3. *Bacon*—Laskers sold bacon at the food service level only, and it was offered in standard 5- and 10-pound boxes. Murray Lasker believed price was the only factor on which buyers differentiated bacon suppliers. The firm with the lowest price would usually get the business. Lasker concluded that bacon was a good door-opener for new food service customers, since they all used it, but that bacon offered no profit growth potential whatsoever.

Exhibit 1   Laskers Foods Limited Contribution by Product and Sales and Estimated Market Shares by City, 1991

Product	Contribution	City	Sales	Estimated Market Share
Smoked meat briskets	14%	Quebec	$ 1,300,000	60%
		Montreal	12,500,000	50
		Ottawa	1,500,000	70
		Toronto	350,000	15
Smoked meat pouches	17	Quebec	40,000	30
		Montreal	260,000	40
		Ottawa	30,000	20
		Toronto	20,000	25
Bulk frankfurters	4	Quebec	1,000,000	9
		Montreal	13,500,000	20
		Ottawa	600,000	6
		Toronto	200,000	1
Prepackaged frankfurters	7	Quebec	100,000	6
		Montreal	400,000	5
		Ottawa	75,000	5
		Toronto	125,000	1
Bulk bacon	3	Quebec	900,000	2
		Montreal	2,000,000	8
		Ottawa	900,000	4
		Toronto	1,000,000	1
Bulk sausages	3	Quebec	200,000	10
		Montreal	900,000	10
		Ottawa	150,000	8
		Toronto	200,000	2
Meat loaves and bologna	4	Quebec	150,000	8
		Montreal	900,000	9
		Ottawa	125,000	7
		Toronto	100,000	1
Ham	5	Quebec	175,000	10
		Montreal	825,000	8
		Ottawa	150,000	10
		Toronto	250,000	2
Smoked poultry	17	Quebec	0	0
		Montreal	250,000	20
		Ottawa	75,000	30
		Toronto	100,000	7
Salami	8	Quebec	100,000	12
		Montreal	800,000	16
		Ottawa	150,000	14
		Toronto	300,000	4

4. *Sausages, meat loaves, and bologna*—Lasker's conclusions about these products were virtually the same as those for bacon. However, he felt that there may be some sales and profit opportunities open to the company by expanding their distribution in the delicatessen section of supermarkets.

5. *Ham*—Laskers' ham offerings were in food service and delicatessen counter sizes and configurations. Except for specialty hams, such as Black Forest Ham, the market was price driven. The long-term outlook for profit margins was for little or no growth.

6. *Smoked poultry*—the market for smoked chicken and turkey seemed limited to certain ethnic groups, particularly Eastern Europeans. Smoked poultry is a specialty product. To increase its

appeal would require a substantial marketing investment.

7. *Salami*—while the market for salami was also somewhat price sensitive, Lasker felt there might still be worthwhile growth potential. The company had obtained good distribution of its salami through supermarket delicatessen sections and restaurants. Lasker also felt that there could be opportunities for a specialty line of salami-type products, including pepperoni, European-style dry sausage, and other delicatessen sausages. The popularity of these kinds of products was increasing as more and more consumers regularly purchased delicatessen-type meats.

In addition to reviewing his product line, Murray Lasker reflected on his company's major strengths and weaknesses. His conclusions follow:

1. *Manufacturing*—Laskers Foods' major strength was manufacturing know-how. The company had state-of-the-art equipment and systems. Its manufacturing costs were among the lowest in the processed meat industry.

2. *Marketing*—the company's only marketing expenses were selling and distribution costs. Laskers Foods didn't have a marketing department, nor did it engage in any advertising or promotion. As a result, its overall cost was almost certainly less than that of major competitors. On the other hand, consumer awareness of and preference for the Laskers brand name, especially outside Montreal, was negligible.

3. *Finance*—Laskers' financial position was strong. The company was privately owned and had no long-term debt. Short-term borrowings were infrequent and for small amounts. Murray Lasker and his family could readily raise $10 million without any outside equity financing.

4. *Personnel*—overall, the quality of Laskers' personnel was above average for the industry. However, the company's organization lacked a marketing department and there was no general sales manager. Instead, sales managers for each of the company's four geographic selling areas all reported directly to Murray Lasker.

After listing the following growth options, Murray Lasker wondered which one or ones would be best for the company at this time:

1. *Expand food service sales regionally*—try to increase penetration of the food service markets in Quebec City, Ottawa, and Toronto to the same level as the company had in Montreal. This option would require that Lasker hire five additional salespeople at a cost of $55,000 per annum each. Additional marketing support costs for this option would be approximately $80,000 in year 1 and $25,000 every year thereafter. Under this approach, Murray Lasker forecasted that sales would rise by $1 million in year 1, $3 million in year 2, and $5 million in year 3.

2. *Increase the company's share of the retail market*—develop, introduce, and support new products to be sold in the self-service sections of supermarkets and/or promote consumer brand insistence for Laskers' existing delicatessen counter products. Self-service sales would require a one-time investment of $150,000 per new product for research and development. Annual advertising and promotion costs were estimated to be $250,000 for each such product. Each new product introduced would be required to break even within two years. Advertising agency personnel with whom Lasker met also insisted that an additional $350,000 in annual media spending would be required to develop consumer brand insistence for the Laskers name at the delicatessen counter.

3. *Expand geographically the smoked meat market*—introduce and support smoked meat in regions outside Montreal. With this option Laskers Foods would need to hire two new salespeople at a cost of $55,000 per annum each. Marketing support costs would be $125,000 in year 1 and $40,000 every year thereafter. Lasker expected annual sales to rise by $1 million in the first year and by $500,000 in each of the next two years if the company followed this approach.

4. *Follow a maintenance strategy*—don't expand, but focus company resources on maintaining current sales of about $40 million with a profit level of 5 percent of sales. However, it would be difficult to maintain sales without a one-time increase in marketing support costs of $325,000.

Develop a long-range strategy for Laskers Foods Limited. Propose a marketing plan for the company for the next 12 months.

37 Health and Welfare Canada*

INTRODUCTION

Jim Mintz, director, and Johanna Laporte, senior marketing officer, Promotion Division, Health Promotion Directorate, Health and Welfare Canada, were meeting to review the results of a psychographic marketing research study they had just received with the view to deciding which market(s) to target and the types of messages that might be most effective in reaching the target markets.

PROGRAM BACKGROUND

The mandate of the Health Promotion Directorate of Health and Welfare Canada is to inform and educate Canadians on issues that may affect their health. This is accomplished through the development and implementation of a wide range of training, research, information, and promotional programs that promote health and encourage the avoidance of health risks. Many of the Health Promotion Directorate's initiatives are implemented in conjunction with provincial and territorial drug agencies and, in some cases, with the assistance of private sector firms and nonprofit organizations.

The Health Promotion Directorate devotes the majority of its efforts to the abuse of legal and illegal drugs, including alcohol, tobacco, prescription drugs, over-the-counter drugs, and solvents.

The abuse of alcohol and other drugs is a societal problem of many dimensions with unacceptable human and economic costs. It results in injury and death on the highways, lost productivity in the work place, and ever-increasing burdens on the law enforcement system and on legal and health care resources. The cost of drug abuse includes the loss of human potential, the destruction of physical and mental health, the breakdown of marriages and families, and personal suffering.

As recently as 15 years ago, the suggestion that marketing could play a role in public health education would have been rejected by health professionals as being unacceptable. In their view, marketing, developed and perfected by profit-oriented firms, was used to encourage the consumption of legal drugs and had no place in the public sector.

*This case was written by Jim Mintz and Johanna Laporte of Health and Welfare Canada and Maurice Borts, who at the time of its preparation was associated with Carleton University.

However, social marketing, which relies on traditional marketing concepts (including the use of marketing research, positioning, planning, distribution, cost-benefit and consumer behavior) has demonstrated its ability to apply marketing tools to help achieve social objectives. That is, social marketing is considered to be a valuable component in a multifaceted approach to achieving social objectives. For example, an article in the *British Journal of Addiction* points out that social marketing can play a major role in developing ways to effectively place alcohol control policies on legislators' agendas, involve desired target groups, and mobilize public support.

The National Drug Strategy "Action on Drug Abuse" launched in 1987 was developed in response to a clearly identified need for a coordinated national strategy that addresses both the demand and supply sides of the drug abuse problem. Health and Welfare Canada was given the lead role in the implementation of the strategy. Close to three-quarters of the $210 million allocated to the initial five-year phase of the program was directed towards education, prevention, and treatment initiatives.

Based on the premise that prevention begins with awareness, the first major undertaking of the Action on Drug Abuse program (June 1987) was a major marketing campaign entitled "Really Me/Drogues pas besoin!" The primary goal of the campaign was to heighten public awareness, both by making information about alcohol and other drug use more accessible and by encouraging public discussion of the issues.

CAMPAIGN BACKGROUND

The development of the "Really Me/Drogues pas besoin!" campaign was based on the review of several research studies that were commissioned by others for their own use. After this secondary data was reviewed, a qualitative research study was commissioned by the Program Promotion Division to identify the attitudes and perceptions of youths 11 to 17 years of age and their parents towards drug use.

Based on this research, two initial target markets were selected.

- Young people 11 to 13 years of age were chosen as the primary group because the research clearly indicated that illicit drug use and alcohol abuse commences at about 14 years of age (this varies slightly from province to province). Young people in this age group begin to start developing strong relationships outside the home. They spend less time with their families and are less dependent on parents for help in decision making. During this period, there is also more questioning of ideas and values as young people begin to test their ability to tackle life's more difficult questions. This is the testing stage.

- Parents of children 11 to 13 years of age were selected as a second target market. The research clearly indicated that communication between parents and their children is an extremely important area. Most parents interviewed perceive that they are communicating with their children on sensitive social issues such as drugs.

The program elements selected to reach the two target audiences (in English and French) included:

- Special events, including:
  A launch press conference.
  A 2-day forum on drug awareness.
  National Drug Awareness Week.
  A one-hour prime time TV special.
  A calendar/magazine included with Hilroy binders—a partnership with a private sector firm.
- Television commercials.
- Radio commercials.
- Buttons, posters, and stickers.
- Magazine ads in family-oriented magazines.
- Really Me booklet—distributed with family allowance cheques at 950 supermarkets across Canada by mail request.

The progress of the Really Me campaign was monitored by a series of tracking surveys conducted at predetermined points in the campaign. The surveys were designed to measure:

- Awareness and public reaction to the campaign.
- Attitudes and social context.
- Behavior, usage, and behavioral intentions.

The research reported high awareness of the campaign:

Age	Awareness
11 to 13 year olds	71%
14 to 17 year olds	76

It was also found that those who used drugs and alcohol on a regular basis (monthly) are as likely to be aware of the campaigns as the rest of the sample, suggesting that those at risk among the target group were reached.

Among those aware of the ads, 70 percent of the primary group (70 percent of 70 percent—i.e., 49 percent of the target) and 81 percent of the secondary group (81 percent of 76 percent—i.e., 61.6 percent of the target group) were able to recall one of several key messages. This data suggests that the ads were not only noted and remembered but also generated a high level of comprehension.

Other research findings include:

- Almost three in four respondents in the primary group felt that the ads would make alcohol and other drugs less popular.
- About half of the respondents were likely to talk to friends about these issues as a direct result of seeing the ads. And about 75 percent of parents felt that the ads would make parents more likely to discuss alcohol and other drug use with their children.
- Based on the detailed research, it was concluded that the campaign has achieved a high level of awareness within the target audience. The target audiences were reached with appropriate, effective messages that they were able to identify with and to which they were receptive.

NEW RESEARCH

In order to build on the success of the "Really Me/Drogues pas besoin!" campaign, the Program Promotion Division commissioned creative research to conduct a new psychographic study in an attempt to identify new potential target markets and to describe the distinctive values and lifestyles of each group. Psychographics attempts to get "inside the consumer's head to find out what he or she is thinking and why." By focusing on major interests, aspirations, beliefs, prejudices, opinions, and spending patterns, not only can meaningful market segments be identified, but the data is of value in painting a picture of the target market, particularly the illustrations and language that will attract the target's attention and help it to relate to the message.

As the result of this research, seven psychographic target markets were identified. Each segment's consumption of the three substances were estimated as is reported in Table 1.

In spite of the desire to tell all youth about the abuse of substances, and because of severe budget constraints and the high cost of preparing commercials and buying media, the Health Promotion Directorate must select and concentrate its efforts on one market segment.

After reviewing the new psychographic data, and the seven identified segments, Jim and Johanna narrowed the list of possible targets down to three segments.

Table 1

Lifestyle Value Segments	13–17-year-olds Percent of Total Youth Market	Smokers	Drinkers		Drug Trial	
			a[†]	b‡	Marijuana	Others
TGIF	24	40*	31	49	25	4
Passive "Luddites"	6	28	21	40	18	2
Concerned moralists	15	15	16	32	9	2
Big city independents	13	10	12	36	8	1
Quiet conformers	18	10	10	25	—	3
Tomorrow's leaders	17	7	15	38	7	2
Small-town traditionalists	7	3	7	19	2	1
Total	100	14	15	38	10	2

*Read as 40 percent of TGIFs smoke (or 40% of 24% = 9.6 of the total youth market).

†Includes respondents who report drinking once a month or more often.

‡Includes respondents who drink less often than once a month.

TGIF—represents not only the largest segment but also contains the heaviest users of tobacco, alcohol, and illicit drugs. This fun-loving segment was labelled TGIF because of its weekend orientation.

Tomorrow's leaders—this relatively large segment consists of light users of the targeted products. However, because these people have strong leadership tendencies, they may act as role models and influence others to reduce their consumption. The name for this segment comes from the trend-setting behavior of the segment.

Passive "Luddites"—although this segment is small, its members are higher-than-average users of all

three types of substances. Because these people are resistant to changes in family structure, morality, and technology, this segment has been called Luddites after a British man named Ludd, who, with his followers, actually resisted the changes of the Industrial Revolution.

Based on the data that appears in the appendix to this case, which segment would you recommend to the Health Promotion Division? Support your decision. Based on the psychographic data for your selected segment, suggest some messages and illustrations that may be effective.

APPENDIX   PROFILE SUMMARIES

	Attitudes	Demographics
TGIF	• Concern is more for today than the future. • No particular work ethic; not ambitious; not disciplined. • Lacking in traditional values and without a strong social conscience. Not quite a "redneck" but pointed in that direction. • Culture of any sort is not a priority. • Not entirely self-sufficient; needs company of others, particularly the opposite sex. • Substance use/abuse a part of the TGIF lifestyle. This includes cigarettes, drugs, and alcohol. • Working is only a means to an end—to enjoy the weekend—self-indulgent. • Spenders, not savers (especially spending on nightclubs and rock concerts).	• Sex—males and females equally. • Socioeconomic—largely middle class. • Geography—modest concentration in Ontario.
Tomorrow's Leaders	• Quite ambitious, with strong leadership tendencies. • A participator; team person; gregarious; outgoing. • Not really traditional; embraces the mores of today; nevertheless, has at least some faith in the system. • Feels a strong social responsibility; supports human rights. • The future is important, and they are optimistic about that future. • Likes to be thought of as fashionable, up-to-date, modern; fitness is important. • Very antismoking. • Heavy owners of high-tech equipment.	• Sex—more males than females. • Socioeconomic—comes from all classes but disproportionately from upper middle. • Geography—across the country.
Passive "Luddites"	• Homebody; family important; traditional family structure. • Universe is close to home. • More old-fashioned views on morality. • More tolerant, if not involved, in substance use/abuse. • Would avoid association with person infected with the AIDS virus. • Claims some degree of independence, but concerned how seen by others. • Not as ready as some to support the disadvantaged. • Lacks optimism; has lower level of ambition. • Jobs are an issue. • Not comfortable with technology. • Financially conservative. • Resents change.	• Sex—more females than males. • Socioeconomic—somewhat above middle; more are upper-middle class. • Geography—more in Quebec and Ontario.

Notes

Chapter 1

1. David Oliver, "Cheer Up," *Report on Business Magazine,* June 1992, pp. 11–12.

2. 1992 World Competitiveness Report, 12th ed.

3. Christopher H. Lovelock and Charles B. Weinberg, *Marketing for Public and Nonprofit Managers* (New York: John Wiley & Sons, 1984); Ruby Roy Dholakia, "A Macromarketing Perspective on Social Marketing: The Case of Family Planning in India," *Journal of Macromarketing* 4, no. 1 (1984), pp. 53–61.

4. Gregory D. Upah and Richard E. Wokutch, "Assessing Social Impacts of New Products: An Attempt to Operationalize the Macro-Marketing Concept," *Journal of Public Policy and Marketing* 4 (1985), pp. 166–78.

5. Malcolm P. McNair, "Marketing and the Social Challenge of Our Times," in *A New Measure of Responsibility for Marketing,* ed. Keith Cox and Ben M. Enis (Chicago: American Marketing Association, 1968).

6. An American Marketing Association committee developed a similar—but more complicated—definition of marketing: "Marketing is the process of planning and executing conception, pricing, promotion, and distribution of ideas, goods, and services to create exchanges that satisfy individual and organizational objectives." See *Marketing News,* March 1, 1985, p. 1. See also Ernest F. Cooke, C. L. Abercrombie, and J. Michael Rayburn, "Problems with the AMA's New Definition of Marketing Offer Opportunity to Develop an Even Better Definition," *Marketing Educator,* Spring 1986, p. 1ff; O. C. Ferrell and George H. Lucas, Jr., "An Evaluation of Progress in the Development of a Definition of Marketing," *Journal of the Academy of Marketing Science,* Fall 1987, pp. 12–23.

7. Northern Telecom, 1991 Annual Report.

8. George Fisk, "Editor's Working Definition of Macromarketing," *Journal of Macromarketing* 2, no. 1 (1982), pp. 3–4; Shelby D. Hunt and John J. Burnett, "The Macromarketing/Micromarketing Dichotomy: A Taxonomical Model," *Journal of Marketing,* Summer 1982, pp. 11–26; J. F. Grashof and A. Kelman, *Introduction to Macro-Marketing* (Columbus, Ohio: Grid, 1973).

9. For a more complete discussion of this topic, see Y. H. Furuhashi and E. J. McCarthy, *Social Issues of Marketing in the American Economy* (Columbus, Ohio: Grid, 1971), pp. 4–6.

10. "The Battle against the Bottlenecks," *Newsweek,* January 27, 1992, p. 31; "Businesses Learn How to Skip Old Laws," *USA Today,* November 5, 1991, p. 1Bff.; "As Socialism Wanes, a Soviet Family Waits in Line, and Worries," *The Wall Street Journal,* October 22, 1991, p. A1ff.; "Capitalism Moscow-Style: Down and Dirty," *USA Today,* October 22, 1991, p. 6A; "Two Moscow Grocery Stores Are Aisles Apart," *USA Today,* September 27, 1991, p. 5A; "Soviet Managers Woo American Investment against Heavy Odds," *The Wall Street Journal,* September 26, 1991, p. A1ff.; "Let's Do Business," *Fortune,* September 23, 1991, pp. 62–68; "After the Soviet Union," *Business Week,* September 9, 1991, pp. 26–38; "Soviet Economy Holds Potential for Disaster as the Union Weakens," *The Wall Street Journal,* September 4, 1991, p. A1ff.; "As Independence Nears, the Baltic States Face Raft of New Challenges," *The Wall Street Journal,* September 3, 1991, p. A1ff.; "Yeltsin's Triumph," *Business Week,* September 2, 1991, pp. 20–29; "The Russian Revolution," *Time,* September 2, 1991, pp. 20–31; "Soviet Upheaval Stirs Worry that USSR Just Might Unravel," *The Wall Street Journal,* August 26, 1991, p. A1ff.; "Rewriting Communism," *Newsweek,* August 5, 1991, pp. 36–38; "Soviets Pin Hopes on Mom 'n' Pop Stores," *The Wall Street Journal,* April 23, 1991, p. A19; "Reawakening: A Market Economy Takes Root in Eastern Europe," *Business Week,* April 15, 1991, pp. 46–58; "The New Russian Revolution," *Fortune,* November 19, 1990, pp. 127–34; "A Day in the Death of the Soviet Union," *Insight,* November 19, 1990, pp. 8–21; Patricia E. Goeke, "State Economic Development Programs: The Orientation Is Macro but the Strategy is Micro," *Journal of Macromarketing,* Spring 1987, pp. 8–21; Jacob Naor, "Towards a Socialist Marketing Concept—The Case of Romania," *Journal of Marketing,* January 1986, pp. 28–39; Coskun Samli, *Marketing and Distribution Systems in Eastern Europe* (New York: Praeger Publishers, 1978).

11. Eric H. Shaw, "A Review of Empirical Studies of Aggregate Marketing Costs and Productivity in the United States," *Journal of the Academy of Marketing Science,* Fall 1990, pp. 285–92; James M. Carman and Robert G. Harris, "Public Regulation of Marketing Activity, Part III: A Typology of Regulatory Failures and Implications for Marketing and Public Policy," *Journal of Macromarketing,* Spring 1986, pp. 51–64; Venkatakrishna V. Bellur et al., "Strategic Adaptations to Price Controls: The Case of the Indian Drug Industry," *Journal of the Academy of Marketing Science,* Winter/Spring 1985, pp. 143–59.

12. Van R. Wood and Scott J. Vitell, "Marketing and Economic Development: Review, Synthesis and Evaluation," *Journal of Macromarketing* 6, no. 1 (1986), pp. 28–48; Robert W. Nason and Phillip D. White, "The Visions of Charles C. Slater: Social Consequences of Marketing," *Journal of Macromarketing* 1, no. 2 (1981), pp. 4–18; Franklin S. Houston and Jule B. Gassenheimer, "Marketing and Exchange," *Journal of Marketing,* October 1987, pp. 3–18; Suzanne Hosley and Chow Hou Wee, "Marketing and Economic Development: Focusing on the Less Developed Countries," *Journal of Macromarketing,* Spring 1988, pp. 43–53.

13. John S. McClenahen, "The Third World Challenge," *Industry Week,"* May 28, 1984, pp. 90–95.

14. Alfred LeBlanc, "Making Inroads in the Japanese Market," June 30, 1992, p. 16.

15. John Saunders and Drew Fagan, "US Trims Softwood Stakes to 6.51%," *The Globe and Mail,* May 16, 1992, p. A1.

16. Telephone call to Canadian Bureau of Industry, Science and Technology, October 16, 1992.

17. William McInnes, "A Conceptual Approach to Marketing," in *Theory in Marketing,* second series, ed. Reavis Cox, Wroe Alderson, and Stanley J. Shapiro (Homewood, Ill.: Richard D. Irwin, 1964), pp. 51–67.

18. Reed Moyer, *Macro Marketing: A Social Perspective* (New York: John Wiley & Sons, 1972), pp. 3–5; see also Roger A. Layton, "Measures of Structural Change in Macromarketing Systems," *Journal of Macromarketing,* Spring 1989, pp. 5–15.

Chapter 2

1. "New Selling Tool: The Acura Concept," *Fortune,* February 24, 1992, pp. 88–89; Black & Decker, 1990 Annual Report.

2. J. David Lichtenthal and David T. Wilson, "Becoming Market Oriented," *Journal of Business Research,* May 1992, pp. 191–208; Caron H. St. John and Ernest H. Hall, Jr., "The Interdependency between Marketing and Manufacturing," *Industrial Marketing Management* 20, no. 3 (1991), pp. 223–30; Regis McKenna, "Marketing Is Everything," *Harvard Business Review,* January–February 1991, pp. 65–79; Sandra Vandermerwe and Douglas Gilbert, "Making Internal Services Market Driven," *Business Horizons,* November–December 1989, pp. 83–89; "Marketing: The New Priority," *Business Week,* November 21, 1983, pp. 96–106; Neal Gilliatt and Pamela Cunning, "The Chief Marketing Officer: A Maverick Whose Time Has Come," *Business Horizons,* January–February 1986, pp. 41–48. For an early example of how the marketing revolution affected one firm, see Robert J. Keith, "The Marketing Revolution," *Journal of Marketing,* January 1960, pp. 35–38. For an overview of some of Procter & Gamble's recent marketing efforts, see "Procter & Gamble Is Following Its Nose," *Business Week,* April 22, 1991, p. 28; "P&G Is Turning Into Quite a Makeup Artist," *Business Week,* April 18, 1991, pp. 66–67ff.; "Health and Beauty Aids: P&G Gives Itself a Makeover," *Sales and Marketing Management,* June 1990, pp. 66–67ff.; "P&G Rewrites the Marketing Rules," *Fortune,* November 6, 1989, pp. 34–36ff.; "Stalking the New Consumer," *Business Week,* August 28, 1989, pp. 54–62; "The Marketing Revolution at Procter & Gamble," *Business Week,* July 25, 1988, pp. 72–73ff. See also Thomas Masiello, "Developing Market Responsiveness Throughout Your Company," *Industrial Marketing Management,* May 1988, pp. 85–94; Robert F. Lusch and Gene R. Laczniak, "The Evolving Marketing Concept, Competitive Intensity and Organizational Performance," *Journal of the Academy of Marketing Science,* Fall 1987, pp. 1–11; "Accountants Struggle as Marketers," *The Wall Street Journal,* July 10, 1989, p. B1. For more on the marketing concept and the academic community, see "Business Schools Revamp to Win Students," *The Wall Street Journal,* August 21, 1991, p. B1ff.; "Ailing College Treats Student as Customer, and Soon Is Thriving," *The Wall Street Journal,* July 17, 1991, p. A1ff. For more on the marketing concept and the medical profession, see William A. Schaffer, "Physician Advertising in United States Since 1980," *International Journal of Advertising* 8, no. 1 (1989), pp. 25–34; "Pediatric Centers Spring Up to Provide Off-Hour Care," *The Wall Street Journal,* February 13, 1989, p. B1. For more on other service industries, see Gary D. Hailey, "The Federal Trade Commission, the Supreme Court and Restrictions on Professional Advertising," *International Journal of Advertising* 8, no. 1 (1989), pp. 1–16; Valarie A. Zeithaml, A. Parasuraman, and Leonard L. Berry, "Problems and Strategies in Services Marketing," *Journal of Marketing,* Spring 1985, pp. 33–46; Paul N. Bloom, "Effective Marketing for Professional Services," *Harvard Business Review,* September–October 1984, pp. 102–10; Betsy D. Gelb, Samuel V. Smith, and Gabriel M. Gelb, "Service Marketing Lessons from the Professionals," *Business Horizons,* September–October 1988, pp. 29–34; Franklin S. Houston, "The Marketing Concept: What It Is and What It Is Not," *Journal of Marketing,* April 1986, pp. 81–87.

3. For more on the marketing concept in the banking industry, see "Despite the Mergers of Many Big Banks, Tiny Ones May Thrive," *The Wall Street Journal,* October 9, 1991, p. A1ff.; "Banking Soft-Sells the Rich," *Adweek's Marketing Week,* June 10, 1991, pp. 24–25; "Mellon Bank Shops for Customers at Local Supermarket," *The Wall Street Journal,* October 5, 1990, p. A4; "Taking a Tip from Retailing, Branch Banks Get Gussied Up," *Insight,* July 16, 1990, pp. 38–39; "Banks Discover the Consumer," *Fortune,* February 12, 1990, pp. 96–104; "Making Change for a Segmented Market, Banks Package Services to Woo Target Groups," *The Wall Street Journal,* November 2, 1989, p. B1ff. For more on the marketing concept and the legal profession, see "Mixed Verdict: Prepaid Legal Services Draw Plenty of Customers and Criticism," *The Wall Street Journal,* August 6, 1991, p. B1ff.; " 'I Love My Lawyer' Ads May Spread to More States," *The Wall Street Journal,* December 7, 1990, p. B1ff.; F. G. Crane, Carolyn Meacher, and T. K. Clarke, "Lawyers' Attitudes towards Legal Services Advertising in Canada," *International Journal of Advertising* 8, no. 1 (1989), pp. 71–78. For more on the marketing concept and the accounting profession, see "Accountants Adopt Pushier Standards," *The Wall Street Journal,* September 17, 1991, p. B1; "Consulting Concerns, Competing Hard, Learn the Business of Selling Themselves," *The Wall Street Journal,* September 27, 1990, p. B1ff.

4. Susan Noakes, "Learning the Marketing Ropes," *The Financial Post,* July 9, 1992, p. 16.

5. Larry C. Giunipero, William Crittenden, and Vicky Crittenden, "Industrial Marketing in Nonprofit Organizations," *Industrial Marketing Management,* August 1990, p. 279; "Profiting from the Nonprofits," *Business Week,* March 26, 1990, pp. 66–74; "Nonprofits Learn How-To's of Marketing," *Marketing News,* August 14, 1989, pp. 1–2; Peter F. Drucker, "What Business Can Learn from Nonprofits," *Harvard Business Review,* July–August, 1989, pp. 88–93; Alan R. Andreasen, "Nonprofits: Check Your Attention to Customers," *Harvard Business Review,* May–June 1982, pp. 105–10; Jeffrey A. Barach, "Applying Marketing Principles to Social Causes," *Business Horizons,* July–August 1984, pp. 65–69; C. Scott Greene and Paul Miesing, "Public Policy, Technology, and Ethics: Marketing Decisions for NASA's Space Shuttle," *Journal of Marketing,* Summer 1984, pp. 56–67; Regina E. Herzlinger and William S. Krasker, "Who Profits from Nonprofits?" *Harvard Business Review,* January–February 1987, p. 93ff.

6. Du Pont, 1990 Annual Report; "Chemical Firms Press Campaigns to Dispel Their 'Bad Guy' Image," *The Wall Street Journal,* September 20, 1988, p. 1ff.; "CFC Curb to Save Ozone Will Be Costly," *The Wall Street Journal,* March 28, 1988, p. 6.

7. "A Matter of Ethics," *Industry Week,* March 16, 1992, pp. 57–62; Michael R. Hyman, Robert Skipper, and Richard Tansey, "Ethical Codes Are Not Enough," *Business Horizons,* March–April, 1990, pp. 15–22; Alan J. Dubinsky and Barbara Loken, "Analyzing Ethical Decision Making in Marketing," *Journal of Business Research,* September 1989, pp. 83–108; John Tsalikis and David J. Fritzsche, "Business Ethics: A Literature Review with a Focus on Marketing Ethics," *Journal of Business Ethics,* September 1989, pp. 695–702; Donald Robin et al., "A Different Look at Codes of Ethics," *Business Horizons,* January–February 1989, pp. 66–73; "Ethics Codes Spread Despite Skepticism," *The Wall Street Journal,* July 15, 1988, p. 17; G. R. Laczniak, R. F. Lusch, and P. E. Murphy, "Social Marketing: Its Ethical Dimensions," *Journal of Marketing,* Spring 1979, pp. 29–36.

8. Mary Anne Raymond and Hiram C. Barksdale, "Corporate Strategic Planning and Corporate Marketing: Toward an Interface," *Business Horizons,* September–October 1989, pp. 41–48; David W. Cravens, "Strategic Forces Affecting Marketing Strategy," *Business Horizons,* September–October 1986, pp. 77–86; Joel E. Ross and Ronnie Silverblatt, "Developing the Strategic Plan," *Industrial Marketing Management,* May 1987, pp. 103–8; Barton A. Weitz and Robin Wensley, eds., *Strategic Marketing: Planning, Implementation and Control* (Boston: Kent, 1984); William A. Cohen, "War in the Marketplace," *Business Horizons,* March–April 1986, pp. 10–20.

9. Carolyn Green, "VIA Acts to Get Back on Track," *Marketing,* April 20, 1992, p. 4.

10. "A Place Called Home," *Royal Bank Reporter,* Fall 1990.

11. Orville C. Walker, Jr., and Robert W. Ruekert, "Marketing's Role in the Implementation of Business Strategies: A Critical Review and Conceptual Framework," *Journal of Marketing,* July 1987, pp. 15–33; Thomas V. Bonoma, "A Model of Marketing Implementation," *1984 AMA Educators' Proceedings* (Chicago: American Marketing Association, 1984), pp. 185–89.

12. Gillette Company, 1990 Annual Report.

13. "And If It Matters, They Also Tell Time," *The Wall Street Journal,* September 20, 1991, p. B1; "High Time for Timex," *Adweek's Marketing Week,* July 29, 1991, p. 24; "Timex Hopes 'True Story' Ads Will Keep Watch Sales Ticking," *The Wall Street Journal,* October 30, 1990, p. B7; "Swatch Says It's Time to Reach Older Crowd," *The Wall Street Journal,* July 2, 1990, p. B1; "Watchmakers Put Emphasis on

Technology," *Advertising Age,* April 3, 1989, p. 28; "Timex, Swatch Push Fashion," *Advertising Age,* July 18, 1988, p. 4.

Chapter 3

1. Michael E. Raynor, "The Pitfalls of Niche Marketing," *The Journal of Business Strategy,* March–April 1992, pp. 29–32; George S. Day and Robin Wensley, "Assessing Advantage: A Framework for Diagnosing Competitive Superiority," *Journal of Marketing,* April 1988, pp. 1–20; Kevin P. Coyne, "Sustainable Competitive Advantage—What It Is, What It Isn't," *Business Horizons,* January–February 1986, pp. 54–61; Michael E. Porter, *Competitive Advantage—Creating and Sustaining Superior Performance* (New York: Free Press, 1986).

2. "Visa, MasterCard Make Inroads Wooing American Express's Corporate Clients," *The Wall Street Journal,* July 3, 1991, p. B1ff.; "Rivalry Rages among Big Credit Cards," *The Wall Street Journal,* May 3, 1991, p. B1ff.; "Visa Explores New Frontiers," *Adweek's Marketing Week,* January 7, 1991, pp. 18–19; "AT&T Tweaks MCI's 'Friends,' " *Advertising Age,* March 2, 1992, p. 4; "MCI, Sprint Ads Hit AT&T Outage," *Advertising Age,* September 23, 1991, p. 3ff.; "Phone Firms Again Spark a Price War," *USA Today,* March 19, 1991, p. 1Bff.; "US Sprint's Troubles Come Amid Ferment in Long Distance Field," *The Wall Street Journal,* July 31, 1990, p. A1ff.; "Long-Distance Battle Shifts to Homes, Small Businesses," *The Wall Street Journal,* December 20, 1989, pp. B1–2; McDonald's Corporation, 1990 Annual Report; "Soviet McDonald's Tastes Success," *USA Today,* November 22, 1991, p. 8B; "McDonald's Beats Lenin 3 to 1," *Fortune,* December 17, 1990, p. 11; "McRisky," *Business Week,* October 21, 1991, pp. 114–22; "McLifestyle," *Adweek's Marketing Week,* September 16, 1991, pp. 4–5; "Play Centers May Be on Menu for McDonald's," *The Wall Street Journal,* August 30, 1991, p. B1ff.; "Pizza Hut Gains Fast-Food Entree to Institutions," *The Wall Street Journal,* November 29, 1991, p. B1ff.; "High-Flying Retail Takes off at Airports," *USA Today,* June 18, 1991, p. 6B; "Consumers in Airports Eat Up Name-Brand Food," *The Wall Street Journal,* May 13, 1991, p. B1; "McDonald's Takes Nip at Supermarkets," *Advertising Age,* March 11, 1991, p. 1ff.; "Microsoft," *Business Week,* February 24, 1992, pp. 60–65; "How Bill Gates Keeps the Magic Going," *Fortune,* June 18, 1990, pp. 82–89; "Will Sony Make It in Hollywood?" *Fortune,* September 9, 1991, pp. 158–66; "Media Colossus," *Business Week,* March 25, 1991, pp. 64–74; "From Walkman to Showman," *Time,* October 9, 1989, pp. 70–71; "A Changing Sony Aims to Own the 'Software' that Its Products Need," *The Wall Street Journal,* December 30, 1988, p. A1ff.

3. "Love Story Has a Lucrative Twist," *USA Today,* February 13, 1992, p. 6B; "Selling Greeting Cards Is No Valentine," *Adweek,* December 9, 1991, p. 10; "Hallmark Cards Get Personal," *Advertising Age,* September 9, 1991, p. 14; "Inside Hallmark's Love Machine," *The Wall Street Journal,* February 14, 1990, p. B1ff.

4. George S. Day, A. D. Shocker, and R. K. Srivastava, "Customer-Oriented Approaches to Identifying Product-Markets," *Journal of Marketing,* Fall 1979, pp. 8–19; Rajendra K. Srivastava, Mark I. Alpert, and Allan D. Shocker, "A Customer-Oriented Approach for Determining Market Structures," *Journal of Marketing,* Spring 1984, pp. 32–45.

5. "The Riches in Market Niches," *Fortune,* April 27, 1987, pp. 227–30.

6. Terry Elrod and Russell S. Winer, "An Empirical Evaluation of Aggregation Approaches for Developing Market Segments," *Journal of Marketing,* Fall 1982, pp. 32–34; Frederick W. Winter, "A Cost-Benefit Approach to Market Segmentation," *Journal of Marketing,* Fall 1979, pp. 103–11.

7. James W. Harvey, "Benefit Segmentation for Fund Raisers," *Journal of the Academy of Marketing Science,* Winter 1990, pp. 77–86; Steven A. Sinclair and Edward C. Stalling, "How to Identify Differences between Market Segments with Attribute Analysis," *Industrial Marketing Management,* February 1990, pp. 31–40; Peter R. Dickson and James L. Ginter, "Market Segmentation, Product

Differentiation, and Marketing Strategy," *Journal of Marketing,* April 1987, pp. 1–10; Russell I. Haley, "Benefit Segmentation—20 Years Later," *Journal of Consumer Marketing* 1, no. 2 (1984), pp. 5–14. See also "The Mass Market Is Splitting Apart," *Fortune,* November 28, 1983, pp. 76–82; Lynn R. Kahle, "The Nine Nations of North America and the Value Basis of Geographic Segmentation," *Journal of Marketing,* April 1986, pp. 37–47.

8. "US Aid Plan for Poor Helps Big Food Firms," *The Wall Street Journal,* March 29, 1991, p. B1ff.; "Breakthrough in Birth Control May Elude Poor," *The Wall Street Journal,* March 4, 1991, p. B1ff.; "American Home Infant-Formula Giveaway to End," *The Wall Street Journal,* February 4, 1991, p. B1ff.; "Selling to Kids," *Adweek,* February 10, 1992, pp. 37–44; "The Littlest Shoppers," *American Demographics,* February 1992, pp. 48–53; "Gatorade for Kids," *Adweek's Marketing Week,* July 15, 1991, pp. 4–5; James U. McNeal, "Planning Priorities for Marketing to Children," *The Journal of Business Strategy,* May–June 1991, pp. 12–15; "Fast-Food Vendors Get Serious with Kids," *The Wall Street Journal,* January 19, 1990, p. B1ff.; "Malt Liquor Makers Find Lucrative Market in the Urban Young," *The Wall Street Journal,* March 9, 1992, p. A1ff.; "Malt Advertising that Touts Firepower Comes under Attack by US Officials," *The Wall Street Journal,* July 1, 1991, p. B1ff.; "Sneaker Makers Face Scrutiny from PUSH," *The Wall Street Journal,* July 19, 1990, p. B1; "Don't Blame Sneakers for Inner-City Crime," *Adweek's Marketing Week,* May 7, 1990, p. 65; "Tobacco Critics See a Subtle Sell to Kids," *The Wall Street Journal,* May 3, 1990, p. B1ff.; "Under Fire from All Sides," *Time,* March 5, 1990, p. 41; "After Uptown, Are Some Niches Out?" *The Wall Street Journal,* January 22, 1990, p. B1ff.

9. Girish Punj and David W. Stewart, "Cluster Analysis in Marketing Research: Review and Suggestions for Application," *Journal of Marketing Research,* May 1983, pp. 134–48; Fernando Robles and Ravi Sarathy, "Segmenting the Computer Aircraft Market with Cluster Analysis," *Industrial Marketing Management,* February 1986, pp. 1–12; Rajendra K. Srivastava, Robert P. Leone, and Allen D. Shocker, "Market Structure Analysis: Hierarchical Clustering of Products Based on Substitution-in-Use," *Journal of Marketing,* Summer 1981, pp. 38–48.

10. Paul E. Green, Donald S. Tull, and Gerald Albaum, *Research for Marketing Decisions* (Englewood Cliffs, NJ: Prentice-Hall, 1988).

Chapter 4

1. "Rubbermaid Turns Up Plenty of Profit in the Mundane," *The Wall Street Journal,* March 27, 1992, p. B4; "The Art of Rubbermaid," *Adweek's Marketing Week,* March 16, 1992, pp. 22–25; "Tupperware Takes Fresh Approach," *USA Today,* March 3, 1992, p. 5B; "Move Over Honda, Cozy Coupe's No. 1," *Adweek's Marketing Week,* December 9, 1991, p. 19; "At Rubbermaid, Little Things Mean a Lot," *Business Week,* November 11, 1991, p. 126; "Little Tikes with a Grown-Up Dilemma," *Adweek's Marketing Week,* September 10, 1991, pp. 18–19; "Rubbermaid Packs an Ecological Lunch," *Adweek's Marketing Week,* September 9, 1991, p. 10; "Rubbermaid Tries Its Hand at Bristles and Wood," *Adweek's Marketing Week,* March 5, 1990, pp. 20–21; Rubbermaid, 1990 Annual Report; "Rubbermaid Moves beyond the Kitchen," *The Wall Street Journal,* February 3, 1989, p. B2.

2. See Peter F. Drucker, *Management: Tasks, Responsibilities, Practices, and Plans* (New York: Harper & Row, 1973).

3. This point of view is discussed at much greater length in a classic article by T. Levitt, "Marketing Myopia," *Harvard Business Review,* September–October 1975, p. 1ff. See also David J. Morris, Jr., "The Railroad and Movie Industries: Were They Myopic?" *Journal of the Academy of Marketing Science,* Fall 1990, pp. 279–84.

4. "Why Inflation Is Not Inevitable," *Fortune,* September 12, 1988, pp. 117–24.

5. "Reichhold Chemicals: Now the Emphasis Is on Profits Rather than Volume," *Business Week,* June 20, 1983, pp. 178–79; Carolyn Y. Woo, "Market-Share Leadership—Not Always So Good," *Harvard Business Review,* January–February 1984, pp. 50–55; Robert Jacobson and David A. Aaker, "Is Market Share All That It's Cracked Up to Be?" *Journal of Marketing,* Fall 1985, pp. 11–22.

6. "Harley-Davidson's U-Turn," *USA Today,* March 2, 1990, p. 1Bff.; "How Harley Beat Back the Japanese," *Fortune,* September 25, 1989, pp. 155–64.

7. "No Air-Bags for Passengers; Ford Stores 3,000 Lincolns," *Automotive News,* March 26, 1990, p. 1ff.; "TRW Says Air-Bag Supply OK Despite Factory Explosions," *Automotive News,* August 7, 1989, p. 4.

8. "Still Battling the Ozone Stigma," *Adweek's Marketing Week,* March 16, 1992, pp. 18–19. For more on the competitive environment, see Klaus Brockhoff, "Competitor Technology Intelligence in German Companies," *Industrial Marketing Management* 20, no. 2 (1991), pp. 91–98; John L. Haverty and Myroslaw J. Kyj, "What Happens When New Competitors Enter an Industry," *Industrial Marketing Management* 20, no. 1 (1991), pp. 73–80; David W. Cravens and Shannon H. Shipp, "Market-Driven Strategies for Competitive Advantage," *Business Horizons,* January–February 1991, pp. 53–61; Roger J. Calantone and C. Anthony di Benedetto, "Defensive Industrial Marketing Strategies," *Industrial Marketing Management,* August 1990, pp. 267–78; Paul N. Bloom and Torger Reve, "Transmitting Signals to Consumers for Competitive Advantage," *Business Horizons,* July–August 1990, pp. 58–66; Fahri Karakaya and Michael J. Stahl, "Barriers to Entry and Market Entry Decisions in Consumer and Industrial Goods Markets," *Journal of Marketing,* April 1989, pp. 80–91.

9. "P&G Wins Lawsuit, Loses Market," *Advertising Age,* September 18, 1989, p. 72.

10. "Most US Companies Are Innocents Abroad," *Business Week,* November 16, 1987, pp. 168–69.

11. CBC Television, "Venture," Sunday February 10, 1991; *The Globe and Mail Report on Business,* January 1991.

12. "The Petro-Crash of the 80's," *Business Week,* November 19, 1979, pp. 176–90. "The Shrinking Standard of Living," *Business Week,* January 28, 1980, pp. 72–78; "Tire Industry Drops into Deep Recession; Gasoline Shortage, Rising Costs Take Toll," *The Wall Street Journal,* October 17, 1979, p. 40.

13. Gerald B. McCready, *Profile Canada: Social and Economic Projections* (Georgetown, Ont.: Irwin-Dorsey, 1977), p. 282.

14. *The Globe and Mail,* February 6, 1991, p. B1.

15. *The Globe and Mail,* November 30, 1990, p. B1.

16. "Cutting Edge: Using Advanced Technology, Gillette Has Managed an Unusual Feat," *The Wall Street Journal,* April 6, 1992, p. R6; "Almost Like Being There: Virtual-Reality Technology Is Finally Moving Out of the Lab," *The Wall Street Journal,* April 6, 1992, p. R10; "Designing Drugs: Computers Promise to Speed up the Development, and Improve the Effectiveness, of New Medicines," *The Wall Street Journal,* April 6, 1992, p. R20; "From Technology to Market—First," *Fortune,* March 23, 1992, p. 108; "The Videophone Era May Finally Be Near, Bring Big Changes," *The Wall Street Journal,* March 10, 1992, p. A1ff.; "Readin', Writin' & Multimedia: Slowly, Teachers Are Turning to a New Tool," *The Wall Street Journal,* October 21, 1991, p. R12ff.; "Get Smart: Everyday Products Will Soon Come with Built-In Intelligence," *The Wall Street Journal,* October 21, 1991, p. R18; "Technology in the Year 2000," *Fortune,* July 18, 1988, pp. 92–98; John D. Ela and Manley R. Irwin, "Technology Changes Market Boundaries," *Industrial Marketing Management,* July 1983, pp. 153–56; Geoffrey Kiel, "Technology and Marketing: The Magic Mix?" *Business Horizons,* May–June 1984, pp. 7–14; Noel Capon and Rashi Glazer, "Marketing and Technology: A Strategic Coalignment," *Journal of Marketing,* July 1987, pp. 1–14. For more on privacy, see "Nowhere to Hide," *Time,* November 11, 1991, pp. 34–40; "Caller ID vs. Privacy: Now There's a Middle Road," *Business Week,* April 1, 1991, p. 87; "Caller ID Service Barred by Pennsylvania Appeals Court," *The Wall Street Journal,* May 31, 1990, p. B1ff.; "Drink Box

Firms to Pay $75,000 to Settle Ad Suit," *USA Today,* August 29, 1991, p. 1B; "Lunch-Box Staple Runs Afoul of Activists," *The Wall Street Journal,* March 14, 1991, p. B1ff.

17. Bruce Gates, "Big R + D Hurdles Still to Clear," *The Financial Post,* April 30, 1990, p. 42.

18. "Consumers: Quality Still Comes First," *USA Today,* March 9, 1992, p. 1Bff.; "Patriotism and the Pocketbook," *USA Today,* March 9, 1992, p. 3B; "Do You Drive an American Car? Don't Be So Sure," *USA Today,* March 2, 1992, p. 1Bff.; " 'Buy American' Is Easier Said Than Done," *The Wall Street Journal,* January 28, 1992, p. B1ff.; "Growing Movement to 'Buy American' Debates the Term," *The Wall Street Journal,* January 24, 1992, p. A1ff.; "Honda, Is It an American Car?" *Business Week,* November 18, 1991, pp. 105–12; "Foreign or Domestic? Car Firms Play Games with the Categories," *The Wall Street Journal,* November 11, 1991, p. A1ff.

19. "As EC Leaders Gather, the Program for 1992 Is Facing Big Problems," *The Wall Street Journal,* December 6, 1991, p. A1ff.; "Now the New Europe," *Fortune,* December 2, 1991, pp. 136–72; "The New Europeans," *The Economist,* November 16, 1991, pp. 65–66; "Tearing Down Even More Fences in Europe," *Business Week,* November 4, 1991, pp. 50–52; Andrew I. Millington and Brian T. Bayliss, "Non-Tariff Barriers and UK Investment in the European Community," *Journal of International Business Studies,* Fourth Quarter 1991, pp. 695–710; Alan Wolfe, "The Single European Market: National or Euro-Brands?" *International Journal of Advertising* 10, no. 1 (1991), pp. 49–58; "Europe Hits the Brakes on 1992," *Fortune,* December 17, 1990, pp. 133–40; Jack G. Kaikati, "Opportunities for Smaller US Industrial Firms in Europe," *Industrial Marketing Management,* November 1990, pp. 339–48; "Europeans Foresee Era of Prosperity, Unity and Growing Power," *The Wall Street Journal,* July 5, 1990, p. A1; "World Business: The Uncommon Market," *The Wall Street Journal,* September 22, 1989, pp. R1–12. See also John R. Darling and Danny R. Arnold, "Foreign Consumers' Perspective of the Products and Marketing Practices of the United States versus Selected European Countries," *Journal of Business Research,* November 1988, pp. 237–48; Sandra Vandermerwe and Marc-Andre L'Huillier, "Euro-Consumers in 1992," *Business Horizons,* January–February 1989, pp. 34–40; James M. Higgins and Timo Santalainen, "Strategies for Europe 1992," *Business Horizons,* July–August 1989, pp. 54–58.

20. Marion Brechin, "The Consumer Movement in Canada," in *Cases and Reading in Marketing,* ed. V. H. Kirpalani and R. H. Rotenberg (Toronto: Holt, Rinehart & Winston of Canada, 1974), pp. 141–46.

21. Muriel Armstrong, *The Canadian Economy and Its Problems* (Scarborough, Ont.: Prentice-Hall of Canada, 1970), pp. 148–49.

22. D. N. Thompson, "Competition Policy and Marketing Regulation," in *Canadian Marketing: Problems and Prospects,* ed. D. N. Thompson and David S. R. Leighton (Toronto: Wiley Publishers of Canada, 1973), pp. 14–15.

23. Seymour Lipset, *Continental Divide: The Values and Institutions of the United States and Canada* (New York: Routledge, 1990).

24. Peter M. Banting and Randolf E. Ross, "Canada: Obstacles and Opportunities," *Journal of the Academy of Marketing Sciences,* Winter 1975, pp. 11–13.

25. "CANDU Report Gets Steam Up in House," *The Financial Post,* May 28, 1977, p. 8; "CANDU's Struggle—Safeguards Competition, Payoffs Take Toll," *The Financial Times of Canada,* March 7, 1978, p. 3.

26. *The Financial Post,* June 25, 1990, p. 37.

27. "Women and Cars," *Adweek's Marketing Week,* February 10, 1992, pp. 14–19; "This Bud's for You. No, Not You—Her," *Business Week,* November 4, 1991, pp. 86–90; "America's Vanishing Housewife," *Adweek's Marketing Week,* June 24, 1991, pp. 28–29; "BMW's 'Feminine Mystique,' " *Adweek's Marketing Week,* February 25, 1991, p. 4; "Marketing Cars to Women," *American Demographics,* November 1988, pp. 29–31.

28. "Farewell, at Last, to Bimbo Campaigns?" *The Wall Street Journal,* January 31, 1992, p. B2; "Women: The Road Ahead," (Special Issue)

Time, Fall 1990; "Grappling with Women's Evolving Roles," *The Wall Street Journal,* September 5, 1990, p. B1; "The Many Faces of Eve," *Adweek's Marketing Week,* June 25, 1990, pp. 44–49; "Mommy vs. Mommy," *Newsweek,* June 4, 1990, pp. 64–67; "Onward, Women!" *Time,* December 4, 1989, pp. 80–89.

29. Frank R. Bacon, Jr., and Thomas W. Butler, Jr., *Planned Innovation,* rev. ed. (Ann Arbor: Institute of Science and Technology, University of Michigan, 1980).

30. Paul F. Anderson, "Marketing, Strategic Planning and the Theory of the Firm," *Journal of Marketing,* Spring 1982, pp. 15–26; George S. Day, "Analytical Approaches to Strategic Market Planning," in *Review of Marketing 1981,* ed. Ben M. Enis and Kenneth J. Roering (Chicago: American Marketing Association, 1981), pp. 89–105; Ronnie Silverblatt and Pradeep Korgaonkar, "Strategic Market Planning in a Turbulent Business Environment," *Journal of Business Research,* August 1987, pp. 339–58.

31. Sara Lee, 1990 Annual Report; Philip Morris, 1990 Annual Report; Richard N. Cardozo and David K. Smith, Jr., "Applying Financial Portfolio Theory to Product Portfolio Decisions: An Empirical Study," *Journal of Marketing,* Spring 1983, pp. 110–19; Yoram Wind, Vijay Mahajan, and Donald J. Swire, "An Empirical Comparison of Standardized Portfolio Models," *Journal of Marketing,* Spring 1983, pp. 89–99; Philippe Haspeslagh, "Portfolio Planning: Uses and Limits," *Harvard Business Review,* January–February 1982, pp. 58–73; Samuel Rabino and Arnold Wright, "Applying Financial Portfolio and Multiple Criteria Approaches to Product Line Decisions," *Industrial Marketing Management,* October 1984, pp. 233–40.

32. "Soviet Breakup Stymies Foreign Firms," *The Wall Street Journal,* January 23, 1992, p. B1ff.; "Some Americans Take the Steppes in Stride," *The Wall Street Journal,* January 23, 1992, p. B1ff.; "Some US Firms Profit in Booming Far East Despite Mighty Japan," *The Wall Street Journal,* January 8, 1992, p. A1ff.; "US Food Firms Find Europe's Huge Market Hardly a Piece of Cake," *The Wall Street Journal,* May 15, 1990, p. A1ff.; "Rewriting the Export Rules," *Fortune,* April 23, 1990, pp. 89–96; "You Can Make Money in Japan," *Fortune,* February 12, 1990, pp. 85–92; "What's Next for Business in China," *Fortune,* July 17, 1989, pp. 110–12; "US Importers Aren't Jumping Ship—Yet," *Business Week,* June 26, 1989, p. 78; "Myth and Marketing in Japan," *The Wall Street Journal,* April 6, 1989, p. B1; Thomas W. Shreeve, "Be Prepared for Political Changes Abroad," *Harvard Business Review,* July–August 1984, pp. 111–18; Victor H. Frank, Jr., "Living with Price Control Abroad," *Harvard Business Review,* March–April 1984, pp. 137–42; Michael G. Harvey and James T. Rothe, "The Foreign Corrupt Practices Act: The Good, the Bad and the Future," in *1983 American Marketing Association Educators' Proceedings,* ed. P. E. Murphy et al. (Chicago: American Marketing Association, 1983), pp. 374–79.

33. Kamran Kashani, "Beware the Pitfalls of Global Marketing," *Harvard Business Review,* September–October 1989, pp. 91–98; "How to Go Global—and Why," *Fortune,* August 28, 1989, pp. 70–76; "Coke to Use 'Can't Beat the Feeling' as World-Wide Marketing Theme," *The Wall Street Journal,* December 12, 1988, p. 35; "Marketers Turn Sour on Global Sales Pitch Harvard Guru Makes," *The Wall Street Journal,* May 12, 1988, p. 1ff.; John A. Quelch and E. J. Hoff, "Customizing Global Marketing," *Harvard Business Review,* May–June 1986, pp. 59–68; Barbara Mueller, "Reflections of Culture: An Analysis of Japanese and American Advertising Appeals," *Journal of Advertising Research,* June–July 1987, p. 51ff.; Subhash C. Jain, "Standardization of International Marketing Strategy: Some Research Hypotheses," *Journal of Marketing,* January 1989, pp. 70–79.

Chapter 5

1. "In the Chips: At Frito-Lay, the Consumer Is an Obsession," *The Wall Street Journal,* March 22, 1991, pp. B1–2; "Frito-Lay Adds High-Tech Crunch," *American Demographics,* March 1991, pp. 18–20; "Frito-Lay Bets Big with Multigrain Chips," *The Wall Street Journal,* February 28, 1991, p. B1ff.; "What the Scanner Knows about You," *Fortune,* December 3, 1990, pp. 51–52; "Hand-Held Computers Help Field Staff Cut Paper Work and Harvest More Data," *The Wall Street Journal,* January 30, 1990, p. B1ff.; "Frito-Lay Shortens Its Business

Cycle," *Fortune,* January 15, 1990, p. 11; PepsiCo, 1990 Annual Report.

2. John T. Mentzer and Nimish Gandhi, "Expert Systems in Marketing: Guidelines for Development," *Journal of the Academy of Marketing Science,* Winter 1992, pp. 73–80; J. M. McCann, W. G. Lahti, and J. Hill, "The Brand Manager's Assistant: A Knowledge-Based System Approach to Brand Management," *International Journal of Research in Marketing,* April 1991, pp. 51–74; A. A. Mitchell, J. E. Russo, and D. R. Wittink, "Issues in the Development and Use of Expert Systems for Marketing Decisions," *International Journal of Research in Marketing,* April 1991, pp. 41–50; "Marketers Increase Their Use of Decision Support Systems," *Marketing News,* May 22, 1989, p. 29; Thomas H. Davenport, Michael Hammer, and Tauno J. Metsisto, "How Executives Can Shape Their Company's Information Systems," *Harvard Business Review,* March–April 1989, pp. 130–34; Martin D. Goslar and Stephen W. Brown, "Decision Support Systems in Marketing Management Settings," in *1984 American Marketing Association Educators' Proceedings,* ed. R. W. Belk et al. (Chicago: American Marketing Association, 1984), pp. 217–21.

3. Nancy J. Merritt and Cecile Bouchy, "Are Microcomputers Replacing Mainframes in Marketing Research Firms?" *Journal of the Academy of Marketing Science,* Winter 1992, pp. 81–86; Michael R. Czinkota, "International Information Needs for US Competitiveness," *Business Horizons,* November–December 1991, pp. 86–91; Lawrence B. Chonko, John F. Tanner, Jr., and Ellen Reid Smith, "Selling and Sales Management in Action: The Sales Force's Role in International Marketing Research and Marketing Information Systems," *Journal of Personal Selling and Sales Management,* Winter 1991, pp. 69–80; Alfred C. Holden, "How to Locate and Communicate with Overseas Customers," *Industrial Marketing Management* 20, no. 3 (1991), pp. 161–68; Naresh K. Malhotra, Armen Tashchian, and Essam Mahmoud, "The Integration of Microcomputers in Marketing Research and Decision Making," *Journal of the Academy of Marketing Science,* Summer 1987, pp. 69–82; Martin D. J. Buss, "Managing International Information Systems," *Harvard Business Review,* September–October 1982, pp. 153–62; Lindsay Meredith, "Developing and Using a Customer Profile Data Bank," *Industrial Marketing Management,* November 1985, pp. 255–68.

4. James G. Barnes and Eva Kiess-Moser, *Managing Marketing Information for Strategic Advantage* (Ottawa: The Conference Board of Canada, 1991).

5. "Focusing on Customers' Needs and Motivations," *Business Marketing,* March 1991, pp. 41–43; James M. Sinkula, "Perceived Characteristics, Organizational Factors, and the Utilization of External Market Research Suppliers," *Journal of Business Research,* August 1990, pp. 1–18; Earl Naumann and Douglas J. Lincoln, "Systems Theory Approach to Conducting Industrial Marketing Research," *Journal of Business Research,* September 1989, p. 151; Bruce Stern and Scott Dawson, "How to Select a Market Research Firm," *American Demographics,* March 1989, p. 44; Bodo B. Schlegelmilch, K. Boyle, and S. Therivel, "Marketing Research in Medium-Sized UK and US Firms," *Industrial Marketing Management,* August 1986, pp. 177–86.

6. For a discussion of ethical issues in marketing research, see "Studies Galore Support Products and Positions, but Are They Reliable?" *The Wall Street Journal,* November 14, 1991, p. A1ff; Ishmael P. Akaah, "Attitudes of Marketing Professionals toward Ethics in Marketing Research: A Cross-National Comparison," *Journal of Business Ethics,* January 1990, pp. 45–54; Ishmael P. Akaah and Edward A. Riordan, "Judgments of Marketing Professionals about Ethical Issues in Marketing Research: A Replication and Extension," *Journal of Marketing Research,* February 1989, pp. 112–20. For more details on doing marketing research, see Harper W. Boyd, Jr., Ralph Westfall, and Stanley F. Stasch, *Marketing Research: Text and Cases* (Homewood, Ill.: Richard D. Irwin, 1988). See also James R. Krum, Pradeep A. Rau, and Stephen K. Keiser, "The Marketing Research Process: Role Perceptions of Researchers and Users," *Journal of Advertising Research,* December 1987–January 1988, pp. 9–22.

7. "The 'Bloodbath' in Market Research," *Business Week,* February 11, 1991, pp. 72–74; "Why Products Fail," *Adweek's Marketing Week,* November 5, 1990, pp. 20–25.

8. Jeffrey Durgee, "Richer Findings from Qualitative Research," *Journal of Advertising Research,* August–September 1986, pp. 36–44; Kathleen M. Wallace, "The Use and Value of Qualitative Research Studies," *Industrial Marketing Management,* August 1984, pp. 181–86. For more on focus groups see "Focus Groups Key to Reaching Kids," *Advertising Age,* February 10, 1992, p. S1ff.; "Focus Group Spurt Predicted for the '90s," *Marketing News,* January 8, 1990, p. 21; Joe L. Welch, "Researching Marketing Problems and Opportunities with Focus Groups," *Industrial Marketing Management,* November 1985, pp. 245–54.

9. Frederick Wiseman and Maryann Billington, "Comment on a Standard Definition of Response Rates," *Journal of Marketing Research,* August 1984, pp. 336–38; Jolene M. Struebbe, Jerome B. Kernan, and Thomas J. Grogan, "The Refusal Problem in Telephone Surveys," *Journal of Advertising Research,* June–July 1986, pp. 29–38.

10. "The 'Bloodbath' in Market Research," pp. 72–74; Tyzoon T. Tyebjee, "Telephone Survey Methods: The State of the Art," *Journal of Marketing,* Summer 1979, pp. 68–77; Nicolaos E. Synodinos and Jerry M. Brennan, "Computer Interactive Interviewing in Survey Research," *Psychology and Marketing,* Summer 1988, pp. 117–38; A. Dianne Schmidley, "How to Overcome Bias in a Telephone Survey," *American Demographics,* November 1986, pp. 50–51.

11. For more detail on observational approaches, see "Kmart Testing 'Radar' to Track Shopper Traffic," *The Wall Street Journal,* September 24, 1991, p. B1ff.; "Targeting the Grocery Shopper," *The New York Times,* May 26, 1991, Sect. 3, p. 1ff.; J. Bayer and R. Harter, " 'Miner', 'Manager', and 'Researcher': Three Modes of Analysis of Scanner Data," *International Journal of Research in Marketing,* April 1991, pp. 17–28; "Using Hidden Eyes to Mind the Store," *Insight,* February 25, 1991, p. 50; "Buy the Numbers," *Inc.,* March 1985; Eugene Webb et al., *Unobtrusive Measures: Nonreactive Research in the Social Sciences* (Chicago: Rand McNally, 1966); "Single-Source Ad Research Heralds Detailed Look at Household Habits," *The Wall Street Journal,* February 16, 1988, p. 39; "Collision Course: Stakes High in People-Meter War," *Advertising Age,* July 27, 1987, p. 1ff.

12. "America's Next Test Market? Singapore," *Adweek's Marketing Week,* February 4, 1991, p. 22; Alan G. Sawyer, Parker M. Worthing, and Paul E. Fendak, "The Role of Laboratory Experiments to Test Marketing Strategies," *Journal of Marketing,* Summer 1979, pp. 60–67; "Bar Wars: Hershey Bites Mars," *Fortune,* July 8, 1985, pp. 52–57.

13. For more detail on data analysis techniques, see Naresh Malhotra, *Marketing Research: An Applied Orientation* (New York: Prentice-Hall, 1993), or other current marketing research texts.

14. See John G. Keane, "Questionable Statistics," *American Demographics,* June 1985, pp. 18–21. Detailed treatment of confidence intervals is beyond the scope of this text but it is covered in most marketing research texts, such as Donald R. Lehmann, *Marketing Research and Analysis,* 3rd ed. (Homewood, Ill.: Richard D. Irwin, 1988).

15. "GM Seeks Revival of Buick and Olds," *The Wall Street Journal,* April 12, 1988, p. 37.

16. Alan R. Andreasen, "Cost-Conscious Marketing Research," *Harvard Business Review,* July–August 1983, pp. 74–81; A. Parasuraman, "Research's Place in the Marketing Budget," *Business Horizons,* March–April 1983, pp. 25–29; Danny N. Bellenger, "The Marketing Manager's View of Marketing Research," *Business Horizons,* June 1979, pp. 59–65.

Chapter 6

1. Daniel Stoffman, *Report on Business Magazine,* November 1990, pp. 78–84.

2. Statistics Canada, *Dictionary of the 1971 Census Terms,* Cat. 12-540 (Ottawa: Information Canada, December 1972).

3. James E. Bell, Jr., "Mobiles—A Possible Segment for Retailer Cultivation," *Journal of Retailing,* Fall 1970, pp. 3–15; and "Mobile Americans: A Moving Target with Sales Potential," *Sales and Marketing Management,* April 7, 1980, p. 40.

4. P. C. Lefrancois and Giles Chatel, "The French-Canadian Consumer: Fact and Fancy," in *New Ideas for Successful Marketing, Proceedings of the 1966 World Congress,* ed. J. S. Wright and J. L. Goldstucker (Chicago: American Marketing Association, 1966), p. 706.

5. See Ron Boychuk, "The Impact of English Media on Francophones," *Marketing,* June 13, 1983, pp. 23–25.

6. The approach, used to answer questions about the French Canadian market, draws heavily on Lefrancios and Chatel, *The French-Canadian Consumer,* but 1981 census figures have been utilized instead of the 1961 census data they employed.

7. "Data Base Offers Consumer Profiles from 'Nine Nations,' " *Marketing News* 18 (May 25, 1984), p. 13.

8. Statistics Canada, *Postcensual Annual Estimates of Population by Marital Status, Age, Sex, and Components of Growth for Canada and the Provinces, June 1, 1982 and 1983,* vol. 1, Cat. 91-2 annual, 1984; 1984–2031: Detailed table, Part II (Ottawa: Minister of Supply and Services).

9. Marina Strauss, "Grocers Miss Hungry Teens," *The Globe and Mail,* April 17, 1991, pp. B1–2.

10. H. Lee Meadow, Stephen C. Cosmas, and Andy Plotkin, "The Elderly Consumer: Past, Present and Future," in *Advances in Consumer Research,* ed. Kent B. Monroe (Ann Arbor, MI: Association for Consumer Research, 1980), pp. 742–47; Betsy Gelb, "Discovering the 65+ Consumer," *Business Horizons,* May–June 1982, pp. 42–46; "What's New in Products for the Aged," *The New York Times,* December 2, 1984; and "The New Old: Where the Economic Action Is," *Business Week,* November 25, 1985, pp. 137–40.

11. This description of Lifestages is adapted from a presentation made to the British Columbia Chapter of the American Marketing Association by George Clements, International Vice President and National Director of Strategic Planning and Research, J. Walter Thompson Canada, November 17, 1992.

International Addendum

1. Based on US Census data, United Nations statistical data, and *The World Market Atlas* (New York: Business International Corp., 1990); "Projected World Population," *USA Today,* October 2, 1991, p. 1A.

2. Based on US Census data, United Nations statistical data, and PCGLOBE software (Tempe, Arizona: PC Globe, Inc., 1990); "We Can Hope It's Getting Wiser, Too," *The Wall Street Journal,* February 28, 1992, p. B1; "Superpowers Lose Population Momentum," *The Wall Street Journal,* April 23, 1990, p. B1; James V. Koch, "An Economic Profile of the Pacific Rim," *Business Horizons,* March–April 1989, pp. 18–25; "Economic and Social Indicators on the Pacific Rim," *Business Horizons,* March–April 1989, pp. 14–15.

3. US Bureau of the Census, *Statistical Abstract of the United States 1991* (Washington, DC: US Government Printing Office, 1991), p. 841; US Arms Control and Disarmament Agency, *World Military Expenditures and Arms Transfers 1990* (Washington, DC: US Government Printing Office, 1991), pp. 35–46; PCGLOBE software (Tempe, Arizona: PC Globe, Inc., 1990); "The Global Economy: Can You Compete?" (Special Report), *Business Week,* December 17, 1990, pp. 60–93; "Markets of the World Unite," *Fortune,* July 30, 1990, pp. 101–20; "Where Global Growth Is Going," *Fortune,* July 31, 1989, pp. 71–92.

4. Raj Aggarwal, "The Strategic Challenge of the Evolving Global Economy," *Business Horizons,* July–August 1987, pp. 38–44; J. S. Hill and R. R. Still, "Adapting Products to LDC Tastes," *Harvard Business Review,* March–April 1984, pp. 92–101; James M. Hulbert, William K. Brant, and Raimar Richers, "Marketing Planning in the Multinational Subsidiary: Practices and Problems," *Journal of Marketing,* Summer 1980, pp. 7–16.

5. "As a Global Marketer Coke Excels by Being Tough and Consistent," *The Wall Street Journal,* December 19, 1989, p. A1ff.;

"American Home Infant-Formula Giveaway to End," *The Wall Street Journal,* February 4, 1991, p. B1ff.; "Three Small Businesses Profit by Taking on the World," *The Wall Street Journal,* November 8, 1990, p. B2.

6. Lee D. Dahringer and Hans Muhlbacher, *International Marketing: A Global Perspective* (Reading, MA: Addison-Wesley Publishing, 1991), p. 182; Philip R. Cateora, *International Marketing* (Homewood, Ill.: Richard D. Irwin, 1990), pp. 387–90 and pp. 468–70; Hana Noor Al-Deen, "Literacy and Information Content of Magazine Advertising: USA versus Saudi Arabia," *International Journal of Advertising* 10, no. 3 (1991), pp. 251–58.

Chapter 7

1. Daniel Stoffman, "Class for the Mass," *Report on Business Magazine,* February 1990, pp. 42–48.

2. K. H. Chung, *Motivational Theories and Practices* (Columbus, Ohio: Grid, 1977), pp. 40–43; A. H. Maslow, *Motivation and Personality* (New York: Harper & Row, 1970). See also M. Joseph Sirgy, "A Social Cognition Model of Consumer Problem Recognition," *Journal of the Academy of Marketing Science,* Winter 1987, pp. 53–61.

3. "What Works for One Works for All," *Business Week,* April 20, 1992, pp. 112–13.

4. Frances K. McSweeney and Calvin Bierley, "Recent Developments in Classical Conditioning," *Journal of Consumer Research,* September 1984, pp. 619–31; Walter R. Nord and J. Paul Peter, "A Behavior Modification Perspective on Marketing," *Journal of Marketing,* Spring 1980, pp. 36–47; James R. Bettman, "Memory Factors in Consumer Choice: A Review," *Journal of Marketing,* Spring 1979, pp. 37–53; Richard Weijo and Leigh Lawton, "Message Repetition, Experience and Motivation," *Psychology and Marketing,* Fall 1986, pp. 165–80.

5. Suanne Kelman, "Consumers on the Couch," *Report on Business Magazine,* February 1991, pp. 50–53.

6. For just a few references, see Alvin A. Achenbaum, "Advertising Doesn't Manipulate Consumers," *Journal of Advertising Research,* April 1972, pp. 3–14; Sharon E. Beatty and Lynn R. Kahle, "Alternate Hierarchies of the Attitude-Behavior Relationship: The Impact of Brand Commitment and Habit," *Journal of the Academy of Marketing Science,* Summer 1988, pp. 1–10; Calvin P. Duncan and Richard W. Olshavsky, "External Search: The Role of Consumer Beliefs," *Journal of Marketing Research,* February 1982, pp. 32–43; M. Joseph Sirgy, "Self-Concept in Consumer Behavior: A Critical Review," *Journal of Consumer Research,* December 1982, pp. 287–300; Joel E. Urbany, Peter R. Dickson, and William L. Wilkie, "Buyer Uncertainty and Information Search," *Journal of Consumer Research,* September 1989, pp. 208–15.

7. Harold H. Kassarjian and Mary Jane Sheffet, "Personality and Consumer Behavior: An Update," in H. Kassarjian and T. Robertson, *Perspectives in Consumer Behavior* (Glenview, IL: Scott, Foresman, 1981), p. 160; H. H. Kassarjian, "Personality and Consumer Behavior: A Review," *Journal of Marketing Research,* November 1971, pp. 409–18; Raymond L. Horton, *Buyer Behavior: A Decision Making Approach* (Columbus, Ohio: Charles E. Merrill, 1984).

8. "Milky Way Light," *Fortune,* February 24, 1992, p. 103; "Labels Lose the Fat," *Advertising Age,* June 10, 1991, p. 3ff.; "Yolkless Dunkin' Donuts," *Fortune,* April 8, 1991, p. 70; "Most Coors Labels Will Drop Claim to Rockies Water," *The Wall Street Journal,* March 15, 1991, p. B3; "FTC Is Cracking Down on Misleading Ads," *The Wall Street Journal,* February 4, 1991, p. B6; "How to Pig Out but Avoid Fat," *Time,* February 5, 1990, p. 65.

9. G. M. Munsinger, J. E. Weber, and R. W. Hansen, "Joint Home Purchasing Decisions by Husbands and Wives," *Journal of Consumer Research,* March 1975, pp. 60–66; George J. Szybillo et al., "Family Member Influence in Household Decision Making," *Journal of Consumer Research,* December 1979, pp. 312–16; Ellen R. Foxman, Patriya S. Tansuhaj, and Karin M. Ekstrom, "Adolescents' Influence in Family Purchase Decisions: A Socialization Perspective," *Journal of Business Research,* March 1989, pp. 159–72; Daniel T. Seymour,

"Forced Compliance in Family Decision-Making," *Psychology and Marketing,* Fall 1986, pp. 223–40; Thomas C. O'Guinn, Ronald J. Faber, and Giovann Imperia, "Subcultural Influences on Family Decision Making," *Psychology and Marketing,* Winter 1986, pp. 305–18.

10. See Gurprit S. Kindra, Michel LaRoche, and Thomas C. Muller, *Consumer Behaviour in Canada* (Scarborough, Ont.: Nelson Canada, 1989), pp. 301–40.

11. George P. Moschis, "Social Comparison and Informal Group Influence," *Journal of Marketing Research,* August 1976, pp. 237–44; James H. Donnelly, Jr., "Social Character and Acceptance of New Products," *Journal of Marketing Research,* February 1970, pp. 111–16; Jeffrey D. Ford and Elwood A. Ellis, "A Reexamination of Group Influence on Member Brand Preference," *Journal of Marketing Research,* February 1980, pp. 125–32; Dennis L. Rosen and Richard W. Olshavsky, "The Dual Role of Informational Social Influence: Implications for Marketing Management," *Journal of Business Research,* April 1987, pp. 123–44.

12. "Survey: If You Must Know, Just Ask One of These Men," *Marketing News,* August 19, 1991, p. 13; James H. Myers and Thomas S. Robertson, "Dimensions of Opinion Leadership," *Journal of Marketing Research,* February 1972, pp. 41–46; Charles W. King and John O. Summers, "Overlap of Opinion Leadership Across Consumer Product Categories," *Journal of Marketing Research,* February 1970, pp. 43–50.

13. Grant McCracken, "Culture and Consumption: A Theoretical Account of the Structure and Movement of the Cultural Meaning of Consumer Goods," *Journal of Consumer Research,* June 1986, pp. 71–84; Walter A. Henry, "Cultural Values Do Correlate with Consumer Behavior," *Journal of Marketing Research,* May 1976, pp. 121–27. See also Lynn R. Kahle, "The Nine Nations of North America and the Value Basis of Geographic Segmentation," *Journal of Marketing,* April 1986, pp. 37–47.

14. "After Early Stumbles, P&G Is Making Inroads Overseas," *The Wall Street Journal,* February 6, 1989, p. B1.

15. This material on time has been condensed from the collected, copyrighted works of Dr. Paul M. Lane and Dr. Carol Felker Kaufman of Western Michigan University and Rutgers University, respectively. It includes works done with coauthors Dr. Jay D. Lindquist and Esther Page-Wood of Western Michigan University, and Gary M. Goscenski of Perspectives Consulting Group.

16. Francois Vary, "Quebec Consumer Has Unique Buying Habits," *Marketing,* March 23, 1992, p. 28.

17. Robert D. Tamilia, "International Advertising Revisited," in *Perspectives in International Business: Readings and Essays,* ed. Harold W. Berkman and Ivan R. Vernon (New York: Rand McNally, 1979).

18. Michael Patterson, "French Agencies Have No Golden Touch—Just a Better Feel for the Quebecois Taste," *Marketing,* October 27, 1975.

19. Robert D. Tamilia, "A Cross-Cultural Study of Source Effects in a Canadian Advertising Situation," in *Marketing 1978: New Trends in Canadian Marketing,* ed. J. M. Boisvert and R. Savitt (Edmonton: Administrative Sciences Association of Canada, 1978), pp. 250–56.

20. P. C. Lefrancois and Giles Chatel, "The French Canadian Consumer: Fact and Fancy," in *New Ideas for Successful Marketing, Proceedings of the 1966 World Congress,* ed. J. S. Wright and J. L. Goldstucker (Chicago: American Marketing Association, 1966), pp. 710–15.

21. C. R. McGoldrick, "The French Canadian Consumer: The Past Is Prologue," speech before the 4th Annual Conference Association of Canadian Advertisers, in *Marketing: A Canadian Perspective,* ed. M. D. Beckman and R. H. Evans (Scarborough, Ont.: Prentice-Hall of Canada, 1972), p. 92.

22. K. S. Palda, "A Comparison of Consumer Expenditures in Quebec and Ontario," *Canadian Journal of Economics and Political Science* 33 (February 1967), p. 26. See also Dwight R. Thomas, "Culture and Consumption Behavior in English and French Canada," in *Marketing*

in the 1970's and Beyond, ed. Bent Stidsen (Canadian Association of Administrative Sciences, Marketing Division, 1975), pp. 255–61.

23. B. E. Mallen, "The Present State of Knowledge and Research in Marketing to the French-Canadian Market," in *Canadian Marketing: Problems and Prospects,* ed. O. N. Thompson and D. S. R. Leighton (Toronto: Wiley of Canada, 1973), p. 105.

24. Jaques Bouchard, "Les 36 Cordes Sensibles du Consommateur Quebecois," unpublished paper, 1973, quoted in *Communication de Masse, Consommation de Masse,* ed. Claude Cossette (Sillery: Le Borial Express, 1975), pp. 257–58.

25. Russell W. Belk, "Situational Variables and Consumer Behavior," *Journal of Consumer Research* 2 (1975), pp. 157–64; John F. Sherry, Jr., "Gift Giving in Anthropological Perspective," *Journal of Consumer Research,* September 1983, pp. 157–68; C. Whan Park, Easwar S. Iyer, and Daniel C. Smith, "The Effects of Situational Factors on In-Store Grocery Shopping Behavior: The Role of Store Environment and Time Available for Shopping," *Journal of Consumer Research,* March 1989, pp. 422–33.

26. Adapted and updated from James H. Myers and William H. Reynolds, *Consumer Behavior and Marketing Management* (Boston: Houghton Mifflin, 1967), p. 49. See also Judith Lynne Zaichkowsky, "Consumer Behavior: Yesterday, Today, and Tomorrow," *Business Horizons,* May–June 1991, pp. 51–58.

27. Wayne D. Hoyer, "An Examination of Consumer Decision Making for a Common Repeat Purchase Product," *Journal of Consumer Research,* December 1984, pp. 822–29; James R. Bettman, *An Information Processing Theory of Consumer Choice* (Reading, MA: Addison-Wesley Publishing, 1979); Richard W. Olshavsky and Donald H. Granbois, "Consumer Decision Making—Fact or Fiction?" *Journal of Consumer Research,* September 1979, pp. 93–100; Lawrence X. Tarpey, Sr., and J. Paul Peter, "A Comparative Analysis of Three Consumer Decision Strategies," *Journal of Consumer Research,* June 1975, pp. 29–37.

28. Raj Arora, "Consumer Involvement—What It Offers to Advertising Strategy," *International Journal of Advertising* 4, no. 2 (1985), pp. 119–30; Don R. Rahtz and David L. Moore, "Product Class Involvement and Purchase Intent," *Psychology and Marketing,* Summer 1989, pp. 113–28; Banwari Mittal, "Measuring Purchase Decision Involvement," *Psychology and Marketing,* Summer 1989, pp. 147–62; James D. Gill, Sanford Grossbart, and Russell N. Laczniak, "Influence of Involvement, Commitment, and Familiarity on Brand Beliefs and Attitudes of Viewers Exposed to Alternative Ad Claims," *Journal of Advertising* 17, no. 2 (1988), pp. 33–43; Marsha L. Richins and Peter H. Bloch, "After the New Wears Off: The Temporal Context of Product Involvement," *Journal of Consumer Research,* September 1986, pp. 280–85.

29. Adapted from E. M. Rogers with F. Shoemaker, *Communication of Innovation: A Cross Cultural Approach* (New York: Free Press, 1968).

30. "3M's Aggressive New Consumer Drive," *Business Week,* July 16, 1984, pp. 114–22.

31. William Cunnings and Mark Venkatesan, "Cognitive Dissonance and Consumer Behavior: A Review of the Evidence," *Journal of Marketing Research,* August 1976, pp. 303–8.

Chapter 8

1. "Japanese Auto Makers Help US Suppliers Become More Efficient," *The Wall Street Journal,* September 9, 1991, p. A1ff.; Toyota, 1990 Annual Report; David L. Blenkhorn and A. Hamid Noori, "What It Takes to Supply Japanese OEMs," *Industrial Marketing Management,* February 1990, pp. 21–30.

2. A. Ben Oumlil and Alvin J. Williams, "Market-Driven Procurement," *Industrial Marketing Management* 18, no. 4 (1989), pp. 289–92; Vithala R. Rao and Edward W. McLaughlin, "Modeling the Decision to Add New Products by Channel Intermediaries," *Journal of Marketing,* January 1989, pp. 80–88; Peter Banting et al., "Similarities in Industrial Procurement across Four Countries," *Industrial Marketing Management,* May 1985, pp. 133–44; John Seminerio, "What Buyers Like from Salesmen," *Industrial Marketing Management,* May 1985,

pp. 75–78; Edward F. Fern and James R. Brown, "The Industrial/Consumer Marketing Dichotomy: A Case of Insufficient Justification," *Journal of Marketing,* Spring 1984, pp. 68–77.

3. John R. G. Jenkins, "Consumer Media as an Information Source for Industrial Products: A Study," *Industrial Marketing Management,* February 1990, pp. 81–86; H. Michael Hayes and Steven W. Hartley, "How Buyers View Industrial Salespeople," *Industrial Marketing Management* 18, no. 2 (1989), pp. 73–80; Barbara C. Perdue, "The Size and Composition of the Buying Firm's Negotiation Team in Rebuys of Component Parts," *Journal of the Academy of Marketing Science,* Spring 1989, pp. 121–28; Erin Anderson, Wujin Chu, and Barton Weitz, "Industrial Purchasing: An Empirical Exploration of the Buy-Class Framework," *Journal of Marketing,* July 1987, pp. 71–86; Rowland T. Moriarity, Jr., and Robert E. Spekman, "An Empirical Investigation of the Information Sources Used during the Industrial Buying Process," *Journal of Marketing Research,* May 1984, pp. 137–47; Joseph A. Bellizzi and Phillip McVey, "How Valid Is the Buy-Grid Model?" *Industrial Marketing Management,* February 1983, pp. 57–62.

4. M. Bixby Cooper, Cornelia Dröge, and Patricia J. Daugherty, "How Buyers and Operations Personnel Evaluate Service," *Industrial Marketing Management* 20, no. 1 (1991), pp. 81–90; Richard Germain and Cornelia Dröge, "Wholesale Operations and Vendor Evaluation," *Journal of Business Research,* September 1990, pp. 119–30; James F. Wolter, Frank R. Bacon, Dale F. Duhan, and R. Dale Wilson, "How Designers and Buyers Evaluate Products," *Industrial Marketing Management* 18, no. 2 (1989), pp. 81–90; Jim Shaw, Joe Giglierano, and Jeff Kallis, "Marketing Complex Technical Products: The Importance of Intangible Attributes," *Industrial Marketing Management* 18, no. 1 (1989), pp. 45–54; "Shaping Up Your Suppliers," *Fortune,* April 10, 1989, pp. 116–22; Vincent G. Reuter, "What Good Are Value Analysis Programs?" *Business Horizons,* March–April 1986, pp. 73–79.

5. Richard F. Beltramini, "Exploring the Effectiveness of Business Gifts: A Controlled Field Experiment," *Journal of the Academy of Marketing Science,* Winter 1992, pp. 87–92; I. Fredrick Trawick, John E. Swan, Gail W. McGee, and David R. Rink, "Influence of Buyer Ethics and Salesperson Behavior on Intention to Choose a Supplier," *Journal of the Academy of Marketing Science,* Winter 1991, pp. 17–24; Scott W. Kelley and Michael J. Dorsch, "Ethical Climate, Organizational Commitment, and Indebtedness Among Purchasing Executives," *Journal of Personal Selling and Sales Management,* Fall 1991, pp. 55–66; Laura B. Forker, "Purchasing Professionals in State Government: How Ethical Are They?" *Journal of Business Ethics,* November 1990, pp. 903–10; "New Jolt for Nynex: Bawdy 'Conventions' of Buyers, Suppliers," *The Wall Street Journal,* July 12, 1990, p. A1ff.; I. Frederick Trawick, John E. Swan, and David Rink, "Industrial Buyer Evaluation of the Ethics of Salesperson Gift Giving; Value of the Gift and Customer vs. Prospect Status," *Journal of Personal Selling and Sales Management,* Summer 1989, pp. 31–38; "Vendors' Gifts Pose Problems for Purchasers," *The Wall Street Journal,* June 26, 1989, p. B1ff; Monroe Murphy Bird, "Gift-Giving and Gift-Taking in Industrial Companies," *Industrial Marketing Management* 18, no. 2 (1989), pp. 91–94.

6. Robert D. McWilliams, Earl Naumann, and Stan Scott, "Determining Buying Center Size," *Industrial Marketing Management,* February 1992, pp. 43–50; Herbert E. Brown and Roger W. Brucker, "Charting the Industrial Buying Stream," *Industrial Marketing Management,* February 1990, pp. 55–62; Robert J. Thomas, "Industrial Market Segmentation on Buying Center Purchase Responsibilities," *Journal of the Academy of Marketing Science,* Summer 1989, pp. 243–52; Ajay Kohli, "Determinants of Influence in Organizational Buying: A Contingency Approach," *Journal of Marketing,* July 1989, pp. 50–65; Melvin R. Mattson, "How to Determine the Composition and Influence of a Buying Center," *Industrial Marketing Management,* August 1988, pp. 205–14; Donald L. McCabe, "Buying Group Structure: Constriction at the Top," *Journal of Marketing,* October 1987; pp. 89–98; W. E. Patton III, Christopher P. Puto, and Ronald H. King, "Which Buying Decisions Are Made by Individuals and Not by Groups?" *Industrial Marketing Management,* May 1986, pp. 129–38; Lowell E. Crow and Jay D. Lindquist, "Impact of Organizational and Buyer Characteristics on the

Buying Center," *Industrial Marketing Management,* February 1985, pp. 49–58; Donald W. Jackson, Jr., Janet E. Keith, and Richard K. Burdick, "Purchasing Agents' Perceptions of Industrial Buying Center Influence: A Situational Approach," *Journal of Marketing,* Fall 1984, pp. 75–83; Michael H. Morris and Stanley M. Freedman, "Coalitions in Organizational Buying," *Industrial Marketing Management,* May 1984, pp. 123–32; Wesley J. Johnston and Thomas V. Bonoma, "The Buying Center: Structure and Interaction Patterns," *Journal of Marketing,* Summer 1981, pp. 143–56.

7. "Relationships: Six Steps to Success," *Sales and Marketing Management,* April 1992, pp. 50–58; "Suppliers Struggle to Improve Quality as Big Firms Slash Their Vendor Rolls," *The Wall Street Journal,* August 16, 1991, p. B1ff.; "Broken Promises," *Inc.,* July 1991, pp. 25–27; "Close Ties with Suppliers Can Pay for Small Firms," *The Wall Street Journal,* April 3, 1991, p. B1; "Service Enables Nuts-and-Bolts Supplier to Be More than the Sum of Its Parts," *The Wall Street Journal,* November 16, 1990, p. B1ff; Randy Myer, "Suppliers—Manage Your Customers," *Harvard Business Review,* November–December 1989, pp. 160–72; Peter W. Turnbull and David T. Wilson, "Developing and Protecting Profitable Customer Relationships," *Industrial Marketing Management* 18, no. 3 (1989), pp. 233–40; David N. Burt, "Managing Suppliers Up to Speed," *Harvard Business Review,* July–August 1989, pp. 127–35; "With Customers, the Closer the Better," *Business Marketing,* July 1989, pp. 68–70; "Machine-Tool Makers Lose Out to Imports Due to Price, Quality," *The Wall Street Journal,* August 17, 1987, p. 1ff; "Detroit Raises the Ante for Parts Suppliers," *Business Week,* October 14, 1985, pp. 94–97.

8. *Ideas for Managers: Newsletter of the National Centre for Management, Research and Development,* University of Ontario, no. 1, pp. 2–3.

9. "Polaroid Corp. Is Selling Its Technique for Limiting Supplier Price Increases," *The Wall Street Journal,* February 13, 1985, p. 36. For other examples, see "Making Honda Parts, Ohio Company Finds, Can Be Road to Ruin," *The Wall Street Journal,* October 5, 1990, p. A1ff.; "Toshiba Official Finds Giving Work to Firms in US Can Be Tricky," *The Wall Street Journal,* March 20, 1987, p. 1ff.

10. Madhav N. Segal, "Implications of Single vs. Multiple Buying Sources," *Industrial Marketing Management,* August 1989, pp. 163–78; Peter Kraljic, "Purchasing Must Become Supply Management," *Harvard Business Review,* September–October 1983, pp. 109–17; Christopher P. Puto, Wesley E. Patton III, and Ronald H. King, "Risk Handling Strategies in Industrial Vendor Selection Decisions," *Journal of Marketing,* Winter 1985, pp. 89–98; John L. Graham, "The Problem-Solving Approach to Negotiations in Industrial Marketing," *Journal of Business Research,* December 1986, pp. 549–66.

11. John W. Henke, Jr., A. Richard Krachenberg, and Thomas F. Lyons, "Competing Against an In-House Supplier," *Industrial Marketing Management* 18, no. 3 (1989), pp. 147–54; Ralph W. Jackson and William M. Pride, "The Use of Approved Vendor Lists," *Industrial Marketing Management,* August 1986, pp. 165–70.

12. For more detail, see "SIC: The System Explained," *Sales and Marketing Management,* April 22, 1985, pp. 52–113; "Enhancement of SIC System Being Developed," *Marketing News Collegiate Edition,* May 1988, p. 4.

13. Canon, 1990 Annual Report; "Can Anyone Duplicate Canon's Personal Copiers' Success?" *Marketing and Media Decisions,* Special Issue, Spring 1985, pp. 97–101.

14. Super Valu, 1990 Annual Report.

15. Robert E. Spekman and Wesley J. Johnston, "Relationship Management: Managing the Selling and the Buying Interface," *Journal of Business Research,* December 1986, pp. 519–32.

16. "Create Open-to-Buy Plans the Easy Way," *Retail Control,* December 1984, pp. 21–31.

17. Safeway, 1990 Annual Report; Food Lion, 1990 Annual Report; Winn-Dixie, 1990 Annual Report; Daulatram B. Lund, "Retail Scanner Checkout System: How Buying Committees Functioned," *Industrial Marketing Management* 18, no. 3 (1989), pp. 179–86; Janet Wagner,

Richard Ettenson, and Jean Parrish, "Vendor Selection among Retail Buyers: An Analysis by Merchandise Division," *Journal of Retailing,* Spring 1989, pp. 58–79; "Supermarkets Demand Food Firms' Payments Just to Get on the Shelf," *The Wall Street Journal,* November 1, 1988, p. A1ff. For a historical perspective on supermarket chain buying, see J. F. Grashof, *Information Management for Supermarket Chain Product Mix Decisions,* PhD thesis, Michigan State University, 1968. For more on wholesaler overload, see Dan Hicks, "MEGA Means Superior Service and Super Selection," *Boise Cascade Quarterly,* August 1985, p. 9.

18. Total investment in farm capital in Canada for 1976 amounted to $48.8 billion. *Quarterly Bulletin of Agriculture Statistics,* April–June 1977, Table 1.

19. "Monsanto Moves into Farmers' Backyard," *Business Week,* February 6, 1965, pp. 60–62. See also "Agricorporations Run into Growing Criticism as Their Role Expands," *The Wall Street Journal,* May 2, 1972, p. 1ff.

20. *Canada Year Book 1976–1977,* p. 516.

21. H. Pellicer, P. Moncrieff, and O. Weaver, *Canadian Agricultural Systems,* 2nd ed. (Department of Agriculture Economics, Toronto McDonald College, 1977).

22. *Policy and Guidelines on Contracting in the Government of Canada* (Treasury Board, Administrative Policy Branch, June 1975); *The Federal Government, Your Client* (Supply and Series, Canada, Ministry of Supply and Services, 1978).

23. Rhéal Séquin, "Rules Must Apply to All, GATT Head Tells Farmers," *The Globe and Mail,* June 2, 1992, p. B4.

24. "How Do You Chase a $17 Billion Market? With Everything You've Got," *Business Week,* November 23, 1987, pp. 120–22; M. Edward Goretsky, "Market Planning for Government Procurement," *Industrial Marketing Management,* November 1986, pp. 287–92; Goretsky, "When to Bid for Government Contracts," *Industrial Marketing Management,* February 1987, pp. 25–34.

25. Pellicer, Moncrieff, and Weaver, *Canadian Agricultural Systems.*

26. World Trade Centre, Vancouver, March 4, 1991.

Chapter 9

1. Bob MacKin, Jr., "Gas Goes 'Green'," *Marketing,* March 16, 1992, pp. 1, 3.

2. "Gurus of Quality Are Gaining Clout," *The Wall Street Journal,* November 27, 1990, p. B1ff.; Ross Johnson and William O. Winchell, *Marketing and Quality* (Milwaukee, WI: American Society for Quality Control, 1989); Joseph J. Belonax, Jr., and Rajshekhar G. Javalgi, "The Influence of Involvement and Product Class Quality on Consumer Choice Sets," *Journal of the Academy of Marketing Science,* Summer 1989, pp. 209–16; Robert Jacobson and David A. Aaker, "The Strategic Role of Product Quality," *Journal of Marketing,* October 1987, pp. 31–44; "Victories in the Quality Crusade," *Fortune,* October 10, 1988, pp. 80–88; John R. Hauser and Don Clausing, "The House of Quality," *Harvard Business Review,* May–June 1988, pp. 63–73; V. K. Shetty, "Product Quality and Competitive Strategy," *Business Horizons,* May–June 1987, pp. 46–52; Jack Reddy and Abe Berger, "Three Essentials of Product Quality," *Harvard Business Review,* July–August 1983, pp. 153–59; Henry J. Kohoutek, "Coupling Quality Assurance Programs to Marketing," *Industrial Marketing Management,* August 1988, pp. 177–88.

3. MCI, 1990 Annual Report; Merrill Lynch, 1990 Annual Report; John Bowen, "Development of a Taxonomy of Services to Gain Strategic Marketing Insights," *Journal of the Academy of Marketing Science,* Winter 1990, pp. 43–50; "America Still Reigns in Services," *Fortune,* June 5, 1989, pp. 64–68; Sak Onkvisit and John J. Shaw, "Service Marketing: Image, Branding, and Competition," *Business Horizons,* January–February 1989, pp. 13–18; "How to Handle Customers' Gripes," *Fortune,* October 24, 1988, pp. 88–100; Leonard L. Berry, A. Parasuraman, and Valarie A. Zeithaml, "The Service-Quality Puzzle," *Business Horizons,* September–October 1988, pp. 35–43; James R. Stock and Paul H. Zinszer, "The Industrial

Purchase Decision for Professional Services," *Journal of Business Research,* February 1987, pp. 1–16; Leonard L. Berry, "Services Marketing Is Different," in Christopher H. Lovelock, *Services Marketing* (Englewood Cliffs, NJ: Prentice-Hall, 1984), pp. 29–37; G. Lynn Shostack, "Designing Services that Deliver," *Harvard Business Review,* January–February 1984, pp. 133–39.

4. Sara Lee, 1990 Annual Report; Avis, 1990 Annual Report; J. B. Mason and M. L. Mayer, "Empirical Observations of Consumer Behavior as Related to Goods Classification and Retail Strategy," *Journal of Retailing,* Fall 1972, pp. 17–31; Edward M. Tauber, "Why Do People Shop?" *Journal of Marketing,* October 1972, pp. 46–49; Christopher H. Lovelock, "Classifying Services to Gain Strategic Marketing Insights," *Journal of Marketing,* Summer 1983, pp. 9–20.

5. Danny N. Bellenger, Dan H. Robertson, and Elizabeth C. Hirschman, "Impulse Buying Varies by Product," *Journal of Advertising Research,* December 1978, pp. 15–18; Dennis W. Rook, "The Buying Impulse," *Journal of Consumer Research,* September 1987, pp. 189–99; Cathy J. Cobb and Wayne D. Hoyer, "Planned versus Impulse Purchase Behavior," *Journal of Retailing,* Winter 1986, pp. 384–409.

6. William S. Bishop, John L. Graham, and Michael H. Jones, "Volatility of Derived Demand in Industrial Markets and Its Management Implications," *Journal of Marketing,* Fall 1984, pp. 95–103.

7. William B. Wagner and Patricia K. Hall, "Equipment Lease Accounting in Industrial Marketing Strategy," *Industrial Marketing Management* 20, no. 4 (1991), pp. 305–10; "Auto Leases in High Gear," *USA Today,* June 6, 1991, p. 1Bff.; Robert S. Eckley, "Caterpillar's Ordeal: Foreign Competition in Capital Goods," *Business Horizons,* March–April 1989, pp. 80–86; M. Manley, "To Buy or Not to Buy," *Inc.,* November 1987, pp. 189–90; Paul F. Anderson and William Lazer, "Industrial Lease Marketing," *Journal of Marketing,* January 1978, pp. 71–79.

8. P. Matthyssens and W. Faes, "OEM Buying Process for New Components: Purchasing and Marketing Implications," *Industrial Marketing Management,* August 1985, pp. 145–57; Ralph W. Jackson and Philip D. Cooper, "Unique Aspects of Marketing Industrial Services," *Industrial Marketing Management,* May 1988, pp. 111–18.

9. Ruth H. Krieger and Jack R. Meredith, "Emergency and Routine MRO Part Buying," *Industrial Marketing Management,* November 1985, pp. 277–82; Warren A. French et al., "MRO Parts Service in the Machine Tool Industry," *Industrial Marketing Management,* November 1985, pp. 283–88.

10. "Alien New Product Strategy Lands on Mars," *Adweek's Marketing Week,* December 10, 1990, pp. 22–23. For more on brand extensions, see "Building on Brand Names: Companies Freshen Old Product Lines," *USA Today,* March 20, 1992, p. 1Bff.; "Multiple Varieties of Established Brands Muddle Consumers, Make Retailers Mad," *The Wall Street Journal,* January 24, 1992, p. B1ff.; "Ultimate Brand Extension: In-Store Bank," *The Wall Street Journal,* November 25, 1991, p. B1ff.; "A New Game of Catch for Rawlings," *Adweek's Marketing Week,* July 15, 1991, p. 24; "Spreading Betty's Name Around," *Adweek's Marketing Week,* March 25, 1991, p. 6; "Elmer's Breaks Out of Its Mold with Color," *Adweek's Marketing Week,* March 11, 1991, p. 8; "Häagen-Dazs Adds Frozen-Yogurt Line," *Adweek's Marketing Week,* February 11, 1991, p. 9; "Swiss Army Swells Ranks," *Adweek's Marketing Week,* June 4, 1990, p. 24; "A Tea in Mr. Coffee's Future," *Adweek's Marketing Week,* May 28, 1990, p. 17. For more on the importance of branding, see "A Lock that's Loaded: Kwikset Keys into a Branded Future," *Adweek's Marketing Week,* May 11, 1992; "Brand Loyalty Steady," *Advertising Age,* March 2, 1992, p. 19; "Brands in Trouble," *Advertising Age,* December 2, 1991, pp. 16–18ff.; "What's in a Name? Less and Less," *Business Week,* July 8, 1991, pp. 66–67; Chip Walker, "What's in a Name?" *American Demographics,* February 1991, pp. 54–56; "Name of the Game: Brand Awareness," *The Wall Street Journal,* January 14, 1991, p. B1ff.; "Brand Names Have Cachet in East Bloc," *The Wall Street Journal,* June 27, 1990, p. B1ff.; Leslie de Chernatony and Gil McWilliam, "The Varying Nature of Brands as Assets: Theory and Practice Compared," *International Journal of Advertising* 8, no.4 (1989), pp. 339–50.

11. "In Pursuit of the Elusive Euroconsumer," *The Wall Street Journal,* April 23, 1992, p. B1ff.

12. The source of this discussion of Canadian trademark policy is B. E. Mallen, V. Kirpalani, and G. Lane, *Marketing and the Canadian Environment* (Toronto: Prentice-Hall of Canada, 1978), p. 137.

13. "Picking Pithy Names Is Getting Trickier as Trademark Applications Proliferate," *The Wall Street Journal,* January 14, 1992, p. B1ff.; "Sweeping Trademark Revisions Now in Effect," *Marketing News,* December 18, 1989, p. 2; "Name That Brand," *Fortune,* July 4, 1988, pp. 9–10; "Putting Muscle into Trademark Protection," *Advertising Age,* June 9, 1986, p. S13; Dorothy Cohen, "Trademark Strategy," *Journal of Marketing,* January 1986, pp. 61–74; George Miaoulis and Nancy D'Amato, "Consumer Confusion and Trademark Infringement," *Journal of Marketing,* April 1978, pp. 48–55; Sak Onkvisit and John J. Shaw, "Service Marketing: Image, Branding, and Competition," *Business Horizons,* January–February 1989, pp. 13–18.

14. "Levi Tries to Round Up Counterfeiters," *The Wall Street Journal,* February 19, 1992, p. B1ff.; "The Patent Pirates Are Finally Walking the Plank," *Business Week,* February 17, 1992, pp. 125–27; "Companies Join Police in Pursuing T-Shirt Bootleggers," *The Wall Street Journal,* September 4, 1991, p. B2; "Whose Bright Idea?" *Time,* June 10, 1991, pp. 44–46; "Trademark Piracy at Home and Abroad," *The Wall Street Journal,* May 7, 1991, p. A22; "How Copycats Steal Billions," *Fortune,* April 22, 1991, pp. 157–64; "Where Trademarks Are up for Grabs," *The Wall Street Journal,* December 5, 1989, p. B1ff.; Ronald F. Bush, Peter H. Bloch, and Scott Dawson, "Remedies for Product Counterfeiting," *Business Horizons,* January–February 1989, pp. 59–65.

15. "Sunkist, a Pioneer in New Product Promotions," *Advertising Age,* November 9, 1988, p. 22ff. For more on licensing, see "Corporate Licensing Grows as Firms Seek 'Risk-Free' Products," *Marketing News,* April 29, 1991, p. 1ff.; "The 1990 Advertising Age Marketer's Resource to Licensing," special supplement, *Advertising Age,* May 28, 1990; "Nestle, Disney Team Abroad," *Advertising Age,* January 15, 1990, p. 1ff.; "Special Report: Licensing," *Advertising Age,* June 6, 1988, pp. S1–6; "What's in a Name? Millions, if It's Licensed," *Business Week,* April 8, 1985, pp. 97–98.

16. "Brand Managers: '90s Dinosaurs?" *Advertising Age,* December 19, 1988, p. 19; "The Marketing Revolution at Procter & Gamble," *Business Week,* July 25, 1988, pp. 72–76; "P&G Widens Power Base—Adds Category Managers," *Advertising Age,* October 12, 1987, p. 1ff.; "P&G Creates New Posts in Latest Step to Alter How Firm Manages Its Brands," *The Wall Street Journal,* October 12, 1987, p. 6; "P&G Makes Changes in the Way It Develops and Sells Its Products," *The Wall Street Journal,* August 11, 1987, p. 1ff.; "Brand Managers Shelved?" *Advertising Age,* July 13, 1987, p. 81.

17. "Drugs: What's in a Name Brand? Less and Less," *Business Week,* December 5, 1988, pp. 172–76; "Ten Years May Be Generic Lifetime," *Advertising Age,* March 23, 1987, p. 76; Brian F. Harris and Roger A. Strang, "Marketing Strategies in the Age of Generics," *Journal of Marketing,* Fall 1985, pp. 70–81; "No-Frills Products: 'An Idea Whose Time Has Gone,' " *Business Week,* June 17, 1985, pp. 64–65; Martha R. McEnally and Jon M. Hawes, "The Market for Generic Brand Grocery Products: A Review and Extension," *Journal of Marketing,* Winter 1984, pp. 75–83.

18. "Supermarkets Push Private-Label Lines," *The Wall Street Journal,* November 15, 1988, p. B1; "Clothing Retailers Stress Private Labels," *The Wall Street Journal,* June 9, 1988, p. 33; "Fighting the Goliaths," *Advertising Age,* August 3, 1987, p. 24ff.; J. A. Bellizzi et al., "Consumer Perceptions of National, Private, and Generic Brands," *Journal of Retailing* 57 (1981), pp. 56–70; Walter J. Salmon and Karen A. Cmar, "Private Labels Are Back in Fashion," *Harvard Business Review,* May–June 1987, pp. 99–106.

19. "Beyond the Pump: A New Crest Dispenser," *The Wall Street Journal,* May 8, 1991, p. B1; "Romancing the Package," *Adweek's Marketing Week,* January 21, 1991, pp. 10–14; "Folgers Puts Coffee in the Bag," *Advertising Age,* January 21, 1991, p. 3ff.; "Pop-Open Packages for a Hurried Populace," *The Wall Street Journal,* April 2, 1990, p. B1; "Special Report: Packaging," *Advertising Age,*

December 12, 1988, pp. S1–4; "Why the Heat-and-Eat Market Is Really Cooking," *Business Week,* June 27, 1988, pp. 90–91.

20. For more on downsizing, see "State AGs Attack Downsized Brands," *Advertising Age,* February 18, 1991, p. 1ff.; "Incredible Shrinking Products," *USA Today,* February 7, 1991, p. 8B; "Critics Call Cuts in Package Size Deceptive Move," *The Wall Street Journal,* February 5, 1991, p. B1ff.; " 'Shrinking' the Brand to Fit the Hard Times," *Adweek's Marketing Week,* November 26, 1990, p. 6. For more discussion on disposable products, see "Disposing of the Green Myth," *Adweek's Marketing Week,* April 13, 1992, pp. 20–21; "The Waste Land," *Adweek,* November 11, 1991, p. 26; "Ridding the Nation of Polystyrene Peanuts," *Adweek's Marketing Week,* October 22, 1990, p. 17; "Convenience Packaging Continues to Pile Up," *The Wall Street Journal,* August 7, 1990, p. B1; "Package Firms Find It's Hard Being 'Green,' " *The Wall Street Journal,* May 25, 1990, p. B1ff. For more on product labelling, see " 'Adjectival' Food Label Gets High Marks," *USA Today,* June 24, 1991, p. 1D; "Group Criticizes FDA Approach on Food Labels," *The Wall Street Journal,* June 7, 1991, p. B3; "Shoppers Value Food's Nutrition Label over Price," *USA Today,* April 11, 1991, p. 1D; "Warning Labels on Alcohol: Just What Is 'Prominent?' " *The Wall Street Journal,* May 4, 1989, p. B1; Dennis L. McNeill and William L. Wilkie, "Public Policy and Consumer Information: Impact of the New Energy Labels," *Journal of Consumer Research,* June 1979, pp. 1–11.

21. J. E. Russo, "The Value of Unit Price Information," *Journal of Marketing Research,* May 1977, pp. 193–201; David A. Aaker and Gary T. Ford, "Unit Pricing Ten Years Later: A Replication," *Journal of Marketing,* Winter 1983, pp. 118–22.

22. "UPC Registers Retailing Impact," *Advertising Age,* April 7, 1986, p. 3ff; "Bar Codes: Beyond the Checkout Counter," *Business Week,* April 8, 1985, p. 90; "Bar Codes Are Black-and-White Stripes and Soon They Will Be Read All Over," *The Wall Street Journal,* January 8, 1985, p. 39; "Firms Line Up to Check Out Bar Codes," *USA Today,* December 4, 1985, pp. B1–2.

23. *Stage 1 Competition Policy—Background Papers,* Section 36(1)(c)—"Misleading Warranties, Etc." (Ottawa: Consumer and Corporate Affairs), p. 42.

24. Arleen N. Hynd, speech delivered to the Association of Canadian Advertisers, Toronto, 1975, p. 9.

25. Joshua Lyle Wiener, "Are Warranties Accurate Signals of Product Reliability?" *Journal of Consumer Research,* September 1985, p. 245f.; Laurence P. Feldman, "New Legislation and the Prospects for Real Warranty Reform," *Journal of Marketing,* July 1976, pp. 41–47; F. K. Shuptrine and Ellen Moore, "Even after the Magnuson-Moss Act of 1975, Warranties Are Not Easy to Understand," *Journal of Consumer Affairs,* Winter 1980, pp. 394–404; C. L. Kendall and Frederick A. Russ, "Warranty and Complaint Policies: An Opportunity for Marketing Management," *Journal of Marketing,* April 1975, pp. 36–43; David L. Malickson, "Are You Ready for a Product Recall?" *Business Horizons,* January–February 1983, pp. 31–35.

Chapter 10

1. Keith Damsell, "Pizza Wars," *The Financial Post Magazine,* July–August 1992, pp. 24–27.

2. George Day, "The Product Life Cycle: Analysis and Applications Issues," *Journal of Marketing,* Fall 1981, pp. 60–67; John E. Swan and David R. Rink, "Fitting Marketing Strategy to Varying Product Life Cycles," *Business Horizons,* January–February 1982, pp. 72–76; Igal Ayal, "International Product Life Cycle: A Reassessment and Product Policy Implications," *Journal of Marketing,* Fall 1981, pp. 91–96; George W. Potts, "Exploit Your Product's Service Life Cycle," *Harvard Business Review,* September–October, 1988, pp. 32–39; Roger C. Bennett and Robert G. Cooper, "The Product Life Cycle Trap," *Business Horizons,* September–October 1984, pp. 7–16; Sak Onkvisit and John J. Shaw, "Competition and Product Management: Can the Product Life Cycle Help?" *Business Horizons,* July–August 1986, pp. 51–62; Mary Lambkin and George S. Day, "Evolutionary Processes in Competitive Markets: Beyond the Product Life Cycle," *Journal of Marketing,* July 1989, pp. 4–20.

3. Jorge Alberto Sousa De Vasconcellos, "Key Success Factors in Marketing Mature Products," *Industrial Marketing Management* 20, no. 4 (1991), pp. 263–78; Paul C. N. Michell, Peter Quinn, and Edward Percival, "Marketing Strategies for Mature Industrial Products," *Industrial Marketing Management* 20, no. 3 (1991), pp. 201–6; "Computers Become a Kind of Commodity, to Dismay of Makers," *The Wall Street Journal,* September 5, 1991, p. A1ff.; "Sales of Major Appliances, TV Sets Gain but Profits Fail to Keep Up: Gap May Widen," *The Wall Street Journal,* August 21, 1972, p. 22; "What Do You Do When Snowmobiles Go on a Steep Slide?" *The Wall Street Journal,* March 8, 1978, p. 1ff; "After Their Slow Year, Fast-Food Chains Use Ploys to Speed Up Sales," *The Wall Street Journal,* April 4, 1980, p. 1ff.; "Home Smoke Detectors Fall on Hard Times as Sales Apparently Peaked," *The Wall Street Journal,* April 3, 1980, p. 1; "As Once Bright Market for CAT Scanners Dims, Smaller Makers of the X-Ray Devices Fade Out," *The Wall Street Journal,* May 6, 1980, p. 40.

4. US Bureau of the Census, *Statistical Abstract of the United States 1991* (Washington, DC: US Government Printing Office, 1991), p. 844.

5. "A Sweet Case of the 'Blahs,' " *Advertising Age,* May 27, 1991, p. 3; "NutraSweet Launches New Ads," *Adweek's Marketing Week,* May 20, 1991, p. 6; "NutraSweet Tries Being More of a Sweetie," *Business Week,* April 8, 1991, p. 88; "NutraSweet Rivals Stirring," *Advertising Age,* June 26, 1989, p. 3ff.; "Calories and Cash: Sugar and Its Substitutes Fight for an $8 Billion Market," *Newsweek,* August 26, 1985, p. 54ff; "Searle Fights to Keep Red-Hot Aspartame Hot for a Long Time," *The Wall Street Journal,* September 18, 1984, p. 1ff.

6. "The Patent Pirates Are Finally Walking the Plank," *Business Week,* February 17, 1992, pp. 125–27; "Is It Time to Reinvent the Patent System?" *Business Week,* December 2, 1991, pp. 110–15; "Software Makers Are Pursuing 'Pirates' around the Globe with Fleets of Lawyers," *The Wall Street Journal,* December 13, 1990, p. B1ff.; Karen Bronikowski, "Speeding New Products to Market," *The Journal of Business Strategy,* September–October 1990, pp. 34–37; "How Managers Can Succeed through Speed," *Fortune,* February 13, 1989, pp. 54–59; "Going on the Offense: US Manufacturers Belatedly Take Steps to Protect Product Lines from Imitators," *The Wall Street Journal,* November 14, 1988, p. R37ff.; "How Xerox Speeds Up the Birth of New Products," *Business Week,* March 19, 1984, pp. 58–59.

7. "Sony Isn't Mourning the 'Death' of Betamax," *Business Week,* January 25, 1988, p. 37; "Sony to Begin Selling VCRs in VHS Format," *The Wall Street Journal,* January 12, 1988, p. 39; Steven P. Schnaars, "When Entering Growth Markets, Are Pioneers Better than Poachers?" *Business Horizons,* March–April 1986, pp. 27–36.

8. "A Big Stretch for Legwear," *Adweek's Marketing Week,* November 2, 1991, pp. 24–25; "Denim Goes Upscale," *Time,* September 2, 1991, p. 71; "The (Sticky) Fad of Summer," *Time,* July 29, 1991, p. 61; "Seller of Velcro Ball and Mitts Hits Homer," *The Wall Street Journal,* July 9, 1991, p. B1; "Soles from the '70s," *Time,* June 24, 1991, p. 41; "Zubaz' Baggy Pant Chic," *Adweek's Marketing Week,* June 10, 1991, p. 22; "The Ultimate Squeeze Play: Girdles Are Back in Style," *Newsweek,* May 13, 1991, p. 63; "Battle of the Bulge Flares Up Anew, Much to the Delight of Girdle Makers," *The Wall Street Journal,* May 10, 1991, p. A5B; "Feelin' Groovy on 7th Avenue: '60s Styles Are Back," *Newsweek,* July 9, 1990, p. 61; George B. Sproles, "Analyzing Fashion Life Cycles—Principles and Perspectives," *Journal of Marketing,* Fall 1981, pp. 116–24; "Fad, Fashion, or Style?" *Saturday Review,* February 5, 1977, pp. 52–53.

9. "Video Games Win Respect as Researchers Adapt Features for Computer Programs," *The Wall Street Journal,* August 29, 1991, p. B1ff.; "Multimedia Goes Mainstream," *Business Marketing,* June 1991, pp. 20–22; "A New Spin on Videodiscs," *Newsweek,* June 5, 1989, pp. 68–69; "Videodisks Make a Comeback as Instructors and Sales Tools," *The Wall Street Journal,* February 15, 1985, p. 25.

10. "Inside Nabisco's Cookie Machine," *Adweek's Marketing Week,* March 18, 1991, pp. 22–23; "Nabisco Unleashes a New Batch of Teddies," *Adweek's Marketing Week,* September 24, 1990, p. 18; RJR Nabisco, 1990 Annual Report; "Making Breakfast Bear-Able," *Advertising Age,* October 16, 1989, p. 3ff.

11. "P&G Unleashes Flood of New Tide Products," *Advertising Age,* June 16, 1986, p. 3ff; "P&G's High Tide Sinks Wisk to No. 2," *Advertising Age,* May 26, 1986, p. 88; "P&G Takes Lead with High-Tech Detergent," *Advertising Age,* April 14, 1986, p. 3ff.;"Industry Is Shopping Abroad for Good Ideas to Apply to Products," *The Wall Street Journal,* April 29, 1985, p. 1ff.; " 'Good Products Don't Die,' P&G Chairman Declares," *Advertising Age,* November 1, 1976, p. 8.

12. Geoffrey L. Gordon, Roger J. Calantone, and C. Anthony di Benedetto, "Mature Markets and Revitalization Strategies: An American Fable," *Business Horizons,* May–June 1991, pp. 39–50; "Teflon Is 50 Years Old, but Du Pont Is Still Finding New Uses for Invention," *The Wall Street Journal,* April 7, 1988, p. 34; William Lazer, Mushtaq Luqmani, and Zahir Quraeshi, "Product Rejuvenation Strategies," *Business Horizons,* November–December 1984, pp. 21–28; "Ten Ways to Restore Vitality to Old, Worn-Out Products," *The Wall Street Journal,* February 18, 1982, p. 25; Patrick M. Dunne, "What Really Are New Products?" *Journal of Business,* December 1974, pp. 20–25.

13. "Smart Toothbrush," *Fortune,* November 4, 1991, p. 168; "Toothbrush Makers Hope to Clean Up with Array of 'New, Improved' Products," *The Wall Street Journal,* October 22, 1991, p. B1ff; "From Making Hearts to Winning Them," *Business Week,* November 16, 1987, pp. 153–56; "Alza Finally Finds a Cure for Losses," *Fortune,* April 28, 1986, p. 80.

14. "Multiple Varieties of Established Brands Muddle Consumers, Make Retailers Mad," *The Wall Street Journal,* January 24, 1992, p. B1ff.; "Do Americans Have Too Many Brands?" *Adweek's Marketing Week,* December 9, 1991, pp. 14–15; "Kimberly-Clark Bets, Wins on Innovation," *The Wall Street Journal,* November 22, 1991, p. A5; "Diaper Derby Heats up as Firms Add Color, Frills," *The Wall Street Journal,* May 9, 1989, p. B1; "Burroughs Welcome Reaps Profits, Outrage from Its AIDS Drug," *The Wall Street Journal,* September 15, 1989, p. A1ff.

15. "New-Product Troubles Have Firms Cutting Back," *The Wall Street Journal,* January 13, 1992, p. B1; "It Costs a Bundle to Get New Items Out," *Insight,* November 19, 1990, p. 45; G. Dean Kortge and Patrick A. Okonkwo, "Simultaneous New Product Development: Reducing the New Product Failure Rate," *Industrial Marketing Management* 18, no. 4 (1989), pp. 301–6; "Firms Grow More Cautious about New-Product Plans," *The Wall Street Journal,* March 9, 1989, p. B1.

16. "The 'Bloodbath' in Market Research," *Business Week,* February 11, 1991, pp. 72–74; "Why New Products Fail," *Adweek's Marketing Week,* November 5, 1990, pp. 20–25; Sharad Sarin and Gour M. Kapur, "Lessons from New Product Failures: Five Case Studies," *Industrial Marketing Management,* November 1990, pp. 301–14; "Diaper's Failure Shows How Poor Plans, Unexpected Woes Can Kill New Products," *The Wall Street Journal,* October 9, 1990, p. B1ff. See also Albert V. Bruno and Joel K. Leidecker, "Causes of New Venture Failure: 1960s vs. 1980s," *Business Horizons,* November–December, 1988, pp. 51–56; Peter L. Link, "Keys to New Product Success and Failure," *Industrial Marketing Management,* May 1987, pp. 109–18.

17. "Suddenly, Hewlet-Packard Is Doing Everything Right," *Business Week,* March 23, 1992, pp. 88–89; "Closing the Innovation Gap," *Fortune,* December 2, 1991, pp. 56–62; "The Racy Viper Is Already a Winner for Chrysler," *Business Week,* November 4, 1991, pp. 36–38; "Deliberately Crude, Models Roar Appeal," *USA Today,* November 1, 1991, pp. 1B–2B; "IBM Bends Its Rules to Make a Laptop," *The Wall Street Journal,* April 15, 1991, p. A9B; "Turning R&D into Real Products," *Fortune,* July 2, 1990, pp. 72–77; "Manufacturers Strive and Slice Time Needed to Develop Products," *The Wall Street Journal,* February 23, 1988, p. 1ff.

18. Adapted from Frank R. Bacon, Jr., and Thomas W. Butler, Jr., *Planned Innovation,* rev. ed. (Ann Arbor: Institute of Science and Technology, University of Michigan, 1980). See also Linda Rochford, "Generating and Screening New Product Ideas," *Industrial Marketing Management* 20, no. 4 (1991), pp. 287–96; "Task Force for New Products," *Business Marketing,* July 1991, pp. 34–36; Robert G. Cooper and Elko J. Kleinschmidt, "New Product Processes at Leading Industrial Firms," *Industrial Marketing Management* 20, no. 2 (1991), pp. 137–48; "Product Development: Where Planning and Marketing Meet," *The Journal of Business Strategy,* September–October 1990, pp. 13–17; Massoud M. Saghafi, Ashok Gupta, and Jagdish N. Sheth, "R&D/Marketing Interfaces in the Telecommunications Industry," *Industrial Marketing Management,* February 1990, pp. 87–95; F. Axel Johne and Patricia A. Snelson, "Product Development Approaches in Established Firms," *Industrial Marketing Management,* May 1989, pp. 113–24; Gordon R. Foxall, "User Initiated Product Innovations," *Industrial Marketing Management,* May 1989, pp. 95–104; David T. Wilson and Morry Ghingold, "Linking R&D to Market Needs," *Industrial Marketing Management,* August 1987, pp. 207–14; G. Urban and J. Hauser, *Design and Marketing of New Products,* 2d. ed. (Englewood Cliffs, NJ: Prentice-Hall, 1993); "Listening to the Voice of the Marketplace," *Business Week,* February 21, 1983, p. 90ff.

19. "How to Let Innovation Happen," *Industry Week,* March 16, 1992, p. 43; "Striking Gold with the Explorer," *Adweek's Marketing Week,* January 14, 1991, pp. 20–21; Shelby H. McIntyre, "Obstacles to Corporate Innovation," *Business Horizons,* January–February 1982, pp. 23–28; "Cutting Costs without Killing the Business," *Fortune,* October 13, 1986, pp. 70–78.

20. "US Companies Shop Abroad for Product Ideas," *The Wall Street Journal,* March 14, 1990, p. B1ff.

21. Eric von Hippel, *The Sources of Innovation* (New York: Oxford University Press, 1988).

22. Marisa Manley, "Product Liability: You're More Exposed than You Think," *Harvard Business Review,* September–October 1987, pp. 28–41; Phillip E. Downs and Douglas N. Behrman, "The Products Liability Coordinator: A Partial Solution," *Journal of the Academy of Marketing Science,* Fall 1986, p. 66ff.; "Gun Dealer Is Held Liable in Accident for Not Teaching Customer Safe Use," *The Wall Street Journal,* June 6, 1989, p. B8; "Liability Waivers Hold Up in More Sports-Injury Suits," *The Wall Street Journal,* November 11, 1988, p. B1; "Lawsuits over Accutane Start to Mount," *The Wall Street Journal,* August 3, 1988, p. 21. "Why Throw Money at Asbestos?" *Fortune,* June 6, 1988, pp. 155–70; "Perils of the Tanning Parlor," *Time,* May 23, 1988, p. 76; T. M. Dworkin and M. J. Sheffet, "Product Liability in the 80s," *Journal of Public Policy and Marketing* 4 (1985), pp. 69–79; "When Products Turn Liabilities," *Fortune,* March 3, 1986, pp. 20–24; Fred W. Morgan, "Marketing and Product Liability: A Review and Update," *Journal of Marketing,* Summer 1982, pp. 69–78; "Marketers Feel Product Liability Pressure," *Advertising Age,* May 12, 1986, p. 3ff.; Ronald J. Adams and John M. Browning, "Product Liability in Industrial Markets," *Industrial Marketing Management,* November 1986, pp. 265–72.

23. "Consumers Start Telling It to the Judge: They're Challenging Japan's Legal Shields," *Business Week,* March 9, 1992, p. 50; "Product Suits Yield Few Punitive Awards," *The Wall Street Journal,* January 6, 1992, p. B1; "The Class Action against Product-Liability Laws," *Business Week,* July 29, 1991, pp. 74–76; Frances E. Zollers and Ronald G. Cook, "Product Liability Reform: What Happened to the Crisis?" *Business Horizons,* September–October 1990, pp. 47–52.

24. "Want Shelf Space at the Supermarket? Ante Up," *Business Week,* August 7, 1989, pp. 60–61; "Grocer 'Fee' Hampers New-Product Launches," *Advertising Age,* August 3, 1987, p. 1ff.

25. "This Bright Idea Could Make GE a Billion," *Business Week,* December 4, 1989, p. 120.

26. Adapted from Frank R. Bacon, Jr., and Thomas W. Butler, Jr., *Planned Innovation,* rev. ed. (Ann Arbor: Institute of Science and Technology, University of Michigan, 1980).

27. "A Smarter Way to Manufacture," *Business Week,* April 30, 1990, pp. 110–17; "Oops! Marketers Blunder Their Way through the 'Herb Decade,' " *Advertising Age,* February 13, 1989, p. 3ff.

28. "The Cutting Edge," *The Wall Street Journal,* April 6, 1992, p. R6; "How the King Maintains His Edge," *The Wall Street Journal,* April 23, 1990, p. A14; "It's One Sharp Ad Campaign, But Where's the Blade?" *Business Week,* March 5, 1990, p. 30; "How a $4 Razor Ends Up

Costing $300 Million," *Business Week,* January 29, 1990, pp. 62–63; "International Ad Effort to Back Gillette Sensor," *Advertising Age,* October 16, 1989, p. 34; "Gillette Readies Sensor," *Advertising Age,* September 18, 1989, p. 1ff.; "At Gillette, Disposable Is a Dirty Word," *Business Week,* May 29, 1989, pp. 54–58; "A Recovering Gillette Hopes for Vindication in a High-Tech Razor," *The Wall Street Journal,* September 29, 1989, p. A1ff.

29. "Oops! Marketers Blunder Their Way Through the 'Herb Decade,' " p. 3ff.

30. "The Company Store: How to Test Market for Fun and Profit," *Inc.,* November 1989, pp. 153–55; "Test Marketing—The Next Generation," *Nielsen Researcher,* no. 3 (1984), pp. 21–23; "Test Marketing Enters a New Era," *Dun's Business Month,* October 1985, p. 86ff.; Steven H. Star and Glen L. Urban, "The Case of the Test Market Toss-Up," *Harvard Business Review,* September–October 1988, pp. 10–27.

31. Peter F. Drucker, "A Prescription for Entrepreneurial Management," *Industry Week,* April 29, 1985, p. 33ff.; E. F. McDonough III and F. C. Spital, "Quick-Response New Product Development," *Harvard Business Review,* September–October 1984, pp. 52–61.

32. Gloria Barczak and David Wilemon, "Successful New Product Team Leaders," *Industrial Marketing Management,* February 1992, pp. 61–68; Don Frey, "Learning the Ropes: My Life as a Product Champion," *Harvard Business Review,* September–October 1991, pp. 46–57; "Brand Managers: The Buck Stops Here," *Food Business,* May 6, 1991, pp. 33–34; "Brand Managing's New Accent," *Adweek's Marketing Week,* April 15, 1991, pp. 18–22; "P&G Keen Again on Ad Managers," *Advertising Age,* September 25, 1989, p. 6; "RJR Trying Brand 'Teams,' " *Advertising Age,* August 14, 1989, p. 1ff.; Robert W. Eckles and Timothy J. Novotny, "Industrial Product Managers: Authority and Responsibility," *Industrial Marketing Management,* May 1984, pp. 71–76; William Theodore Cummings, Donald W. Jackson, Jr., and Lonnie L. Ostrom, "Differences between Industrial and Consumer Product Managers," *Industrial Marketing Management,* August 1984, pp. 171–80; Thomas J. Cosse and John E. Swan, "Strategic Marketing Planning by Product Managers—Room for Improvement?" *Journal of Marketing,* Summer 1983, pp. 92–102; P. L. Dawes and P. G. Patterson, "The Performance of Industrial and Consumer Product Managers," *Industrial Marketing Management,* February 1988, pp. 73–84.

Chapter 11

1. "Goodyear Is Gunning Its Marketing Engine," *Business Week,* March 16, 1992, p. 42; "Gault Turns Goodyear's Debt to Profit" *USA Today,* March 16, 1992, pp. 1B–2B; "Goodyear Plans to Sell Its Tires at Sears Store," *The Wall Street Journal,* March 3, 1992, p. B1ff.; "Goodyear's Go-Getting Gault Just Never Seems to Tire," *The Wall Street Journal,* January 28, 1992, p. B4; "Tire Makers Are Travelling Bumpy Road as Car Sales Fall, Foreign Firms Expand," *The Wall Street Journal,* September 19, 1990, p. B1ff.; "After a Year of Spinning Its Wheels, Goodyear Gets a Retread," *Business Week,* March 26, 1990, pp. 56–58; "Goodyear's Race with Michelin: Burning Rubber to Be No. 1," *Insight,* May 7, 1990, pp. 36–39; Goodyear, 1990 Annual Report; "Goodyear Squares Off to Protect Its Turf from Foreign Rivals," *The Wall Street Journal,* December 29, 1989, p. A1ff.

2. For a discussion of the advantages and disadvantages of direct channel systems, see Bert Rosenbloom, *Marketing Channels: A Managerial View* (Hinsdale, IL: Dryden Press, 1987); Kenneth G. Hardy and Allan J. McGrath, *Marketing Channel Management* (Glenview, IL: Scott, Foresman, 1988). See also David Shipley, Colin Egan, and Scott Edgett, "Meeting Source Selection Criteria: Direct versus Distributor Channels," *Industrial Marketing Management* 20, no. 4 (1991), pp. 297–304; Thomas L. Powers, "Industrial Distribution Options: Trade-Offs to Consider," *Industrial Marketing Management* 18, no. 3 (1989), pp. 155–62.

3. *1988 Direct Selling Industry Survey* (Washington, DC: Direct Selling Association, 1989); Robert A. Petersen, Gerald Albaum, and Nancy M. Ridgway, "Consumers Who Buy from Direct Sales Companies," *Journal of Retailing,* Summer 1989, p. 275ff.

4. Edward L. Nash, *Direct Marketing* (New York: McGraw-Hill, 1986).

5. For a discussion of indirect channel systems, see Louis W. Stern, Adel I. El-Ansary, and James R. Brown, *Management in Marketing Channels* (Englewood Cliffs, NJ: Prentice-Hall, 1989). See also Neil S. Novich, "Leading-Edge Distribution Strategies," *The Journal of Business Strategy,* November–December 1990, pp. 48–53; Donald B. Rosenfeld, "Storefront Distribution for Industrial Products," *Harvard Business Review,* July–August 1989, pp. 44–49.

6. For a classic discussion of the discrepancy concepts, see Wroe Alderson, "Factors Governing the Development of Marketing Channels," *in Marketing Channels for Manufactured Goods,* ed. Richard M. Clewett (Homewood, Ill.: Richard D. Irwin, 1954), pp. 7–9. See also "Distributors: No Endangered Species," *Industry Week,* January 24, 1983, pp. 47–52; "Coke in the Cooler? Fountain Device Targets Small Offices," *Advertising Age,* November 28, 1988, p. B1; "Coke Unveils Compact Dispenser, Hoping to Sell More Soft Drinks in Small Offices," *The Wall Street Journal,* November 17, 1988, p. B1; Louis W. Stern and Frederick D. Sturdivant, "Customer-Driven Distribution Systems," *Harvard Business Review,* July–August 1987, pp. 34–41.

7. "For Video Sales, It's a Green Christmas," *The Wall Street Journal,* December 24, 1991, p. B1f.; "Children's Tapes Help the Sales Market Grow Up," *The Wall Street Journal,* December 24, 1991, p. B1ff.; "After Frantic Growth, Blockbuster Faces Host of Video-Rental Rivals," *The Wall Street Journal,* March 22, 1991, p. A1ff.; "Night of the Living Videos," *Newsweek,* November 12, 1990, p. 59; "Video Stores Try Sharper Focus in Market Glut," *The Wall Street Journal,* July 2, 1990, p. B1ff.; "Meet the King of Video," *Fortune,* June 4, 1990, p. 208.

8. "PC Slump? What PC Slump?" *Business Week,* July 1, 1991, pp. 66–67; "Mail-Order Computers Can Be Bargains, but Some Firms Don't Deliver on Claims," *The Wall Street Journal,* October 4, 1990, p. B1ff.; "A Golden Age for Entrepreneurs," *Fortune,* February 12, 1990, pp. 120–25.

9. Arun Sharma and Luis V. Dominguez, "Channel Evolution: A Framework for Analysis," *Journal of the Academy of Marketing Science,* Winter 1992, pp. 1–16; Teresa Jaworska, "Channel Members' Behavior in Industrial Markets in Poland," *Journal of Business Research,* January 1992, pp. 51–56; B. Ramaseshan and Leyland F. Pitt, "Major Industrial Distribution Issues Facing Managers in Australia," *Industrial Marketing Management,* August 1990, pp. 225–34; Wal-Mart, 1990 Annual Report; N. Mohan Reddy and Michael P. Marvin, "Developing a Manufacturer-Distributor Information Partnership," *Industrial Marketing Management,* May 1986, pp. 157–64; Gul Butaney and Lawrence H. Wortzell, "Distributor Power versus Manufacturer Power: The Customer Role," *Journal of Marketing,* January 1988, pp. 52–63; Bruce J. Walker, Janet E. Keith, and Donald W. Jackson, Jr., "The Channels Manager: Now, Soon or Never?" *Academy of Marketing Science,* Summer 1985, pp. 82–96; Patrick L. Schul, William M. Pride, and Taylor L. Little, "The Impact of Channel Leadership Behavior on Intrachannel Conflict," *Journal of Marketing,* Summer 1983, pp. 21–34; Bert Rosenbloom and Rolph Anderson, "Channel Management and Sales Management: Some Key Interfaces," *Academy of Marketing Science,* Summer 1985, pp. 97–106; Roy D. Howell et al., "Unauthorized Channels of Distribution: Gray Markets," *Industrial Marketing Management,* November 1986, pp. 257–64.

10. Saul Klein, "A Transaction Cost Explanation of Vertical Control in International Markets," *Journal of the Academy of Marketing Science,* Summer 1989, pp. 253–60; "Beer and Antitrust," *Fortune,* December 9, 1985, pp. 135–36; "Car Megadealers Loosen Detroit's Tight Rein," *The Wall Street Journal,* July 1, 1985, p. 6; Wilke D. English and Donald A. Michie, "The Impact of Electronic Technology upon the Marketing Channel," *Academy of Marketing Science,* Summer 1985, pp. 57–71; Robert D. Buzzell, "Is Vertical Integration Profitable?" *Harvard Business Review,* January–February 1983, pp. 92–102; Michael Etgar and Aharon Valency, "Determinants of the Use of Contracts in Conventional Marketing Channels," *Journal of Retailing,* Winter 1983, pp. 81–92; "Why Manufacturers Are Doubling as Distributors," *Business Week,* January 17, 1983, p. 41; Louis W. Stern and Torger Reve, "Distribution Channels as Political Economies:

A Framework for Comparative Analysis," *Journal of Marketing,* Summer 1980, pp. 52−64.

11. "Esprit's Spirited Style Is Hot Seller," *USA Today,* March 25, 1986, p. B5; "Apparel Firm Makes Profits, Takes Risks by Flouting Tradition," *The Wall Street Journal,* June 11, 1985, p. 1ff.; "Is Häagen-Dazs Trying to Freeze Out Ben & Jerry's?" *Business Week,* December 7, 1987, p. 65; "Car Rivals Deal Ads: Convenience vs. New Lines," *Advertising Age,* July 27, 1987, p. 28; "Little Publisher Has Big Ideas on Where to Sell His Books," *The Wall Street Journal,* March 19, 1987, p. 1ff.

12. "This Isn't the Legend Acura Dealers Had in Mind," *Business Week,* November 28, 1988, pp. 106−10; "Car Dealers Mull Going Public at Cost of Independence," *The Wall Street Journal,* May 23, 1988, p. 6; "Retailers Take Tentative Steps as Auto Brokers," *The Wall Street Journal,* December 4, 1987, p. 41; "The New Super-Dealers," *Business Week,* June 2, 1986, pp. 60−66.

13. "Reebok's Direct Sales Spark a Retail Revolt," *Adweek's Marketing Week,* December 2, 1991, p. 7; Reebok, 1990 Annual Report. See also James R. Burley, "Territorial Restriction and Distribution Systems: Current Legal Developments," *Journal of Marketing,* October 1975, pp. 52−56; "Justice Takes Aim at Dual Distribution," *Business Week,* July 7, 1980, pp. 24−25; Saul Sands and Robert J. Posch, Jr., "A Checklist of Questions for Firms Considering a Vertical Territorial Distribution Plan," *Journal of Marketing,* Summer 1982, pp. 38−43; Debra L. Scammon and Mary Jane Sheffet, "Legal Issues in Channels Modification Decisions: The Question of Refusals to Deal," *Journal of Public Policy and Marketing* 5 (1986), pp. 82−96.

14. Gary L. Frazier, James D. Gill, and Sudhir H. Kale, "Dealer Dependence Levels and Reciprocal Actions in a Channel of Distribution in a Developing Country," *Journal of Marketing,* January 1989, pp. 50−69; Allan J. Magrath and Kenneth G. Hardy, "Avoiding the Pitfalls in Managing Distribution Channels," *Business Horizons,* September−October 1987, pp. 29−33; Shelby D. Hunt, Nina M. Ray, and Van R. Wood, "Behavioral Dimensions of Channels of Distribution: Review and Synthesis," *Academy of Marketing Science,* Summer 1985, pp. 1−24; John F. Gaski, "The Theory of Power and Conflict in Channels of Distribution," *Journal of Marketing,* Summer 1984, pp. 9−29; John E. Robbins, Thomas W. Speh, and Morris L. Mayer, "Retailers' Perceptions of Channel Conflict Issues," *Journal of Retailing,* Winter 1982, pp. 46−67; James R. Brown, "A Cross-Channel Comparison of Supplier-Retailer Relations," *Journal of Retailing,* Winter 1981, pp. 3−18; Louis P. Bucklin, "A Theory of Channel Control," *Journal of Marketing,* January 1973, pp. 39−47.

15. See, for example, James H. Barnes, Jr., "Recycling: A Problem in Reverse Logistics," *Journal of Macromarketing* 2, no. 2 (1982), pp. 31−37.

Chapter 12

1. *Toronto Star,* August 8, 1988, p. B1.

2. Brian F. O'Neil and Jon L. Iveson, "Strategically Managing the Logistics Function," *The Logistics and Transportation Review,* December 1991, pp. 359−78; Lloyd M. Rinehart, M. Bixby Cooper, and George D. Wagenheim, "Furthering the Integration of Marketing and Logistics through Customer Service in the Channel," *Journal of the Academy of Marketing Science,* Winter 1989, pp. 63−72; Ernest B. Uhr, Ernest C. Houck, and John C. Rogers, "Physical Distribution Service," *Journal of Business Logistics* 2, no. 2 (1981), pp. 158−69; Martin Christopher, "Creating Effective Policies for Customer Service," *International Journal of Physical Distribution and Materials Management* 13, no. 2 (1983), pp. 3−24; William D. Perreault, Jr., and Frederick A. Russ, "Physical Distribution Service in Industrial Purchase Decisions," *Journal of Marketing,* April 1976, pp. 3−10; Gary L. Frazier, Robert E. Spekman, and Charles R. O'Neal, "Just-In-Time Exchange Relationships in Industrial Markets," *Journal of Marketing,* October 1988, pp. 52−67.

3. Roy D. Shapiro, "Get Leverage from Logistics," *Harvard Business Review,* May−June 1984; pp. 119−26; James E. Morehouse, "Operating in the New Logistics Era," *Harvard Business Review,*

September−October 1983, pp. 18−19; Graham Sharman, "The Rediscovery of Logistics," *Harvard Business Review,* September−October 1984, pp. 71−79.

4. A. Coskun Samli, Laurence W. Jacobs, and James Wills, "What Presale and Postsale Services Do You Need to Be Competitive," *Industrial Marketing Management,* February 1992, pp. 33−42; Richard Germain and M. Bixby Cooper, "How a Customer Mission Statement Affects Company Performance," *Industrial Marketing Management,* February 1990, pp. 47−54; John T. Mentzer, Roger Gomes, and Robert E. Krapfel, Jr., "Physical Distribution Service: A Fundamental Marketing Concept?" *Journal of the Academy of Marketing Science,* Winter 1989, pp. 53−62; Frances G. Tucker, "Creative Customer Service Management," *International Journal of Physical Distribution and Materials Management* 13, no. 3 (1983), pp. 34−50; William D. Perreault, Jr., and Frederick R. Russ, "Physical Distribution Service: A Neglected Aspect of Marketing Management," *MSU Business Topics,* Summer 1974, pp. 37−46.

5. Arthur M. Geoffrion, "Better Distribution Planning with Computer Models," *Harvard Business Review,* July−August 1976, pp. 92−99; David P. Herron, "Managing Physical Distribution for Profit," *Harvard Business Review,* May−June 1979, pp. 121−32; " 'What If' Help for Management," *Business Week,* January 21, 1980, p. 73.

6. Bernard J. LaLonde and P. H. Zinszer, *Customer Service: Meaning and Measurement* (Chicago: National Council of Distribution Management, 1976).

7. For more detail on deregulation of transportation, see Paul D. Larson, "Transportation Deregulation, JIT, and Inventory Levels," *The Logistics and Transportation Review,* June 1991, pp. 99−112; J. J. Coyle, Edward J. Bardi, and Joseph L. Cavinato, *Transportation* (St. Paul, MN: West Publishing, 1986); "Deregulating America," *Business Week,* November 28, 1983. See also James C. Nelson, "Politics and Economics in Transport Regulation and Deregulation—A Century Perspective of the ICC's Role," *The Logistics and Transportation Review,* March 1987, pp. 5−32; Karl M. Ruppentha, "US Airline Deregulation—Winners and Losers," *The Logistics and Transportation Review,* March 1987, pp. 65−82.

8. For a more detailed comparison of mode characteristics, see Roger Dale Abshire and Shane R. Premeaux, "Motor Carriers' and Shippers' Perceptions of the Carrier Choice Decision," *The Logistics and Transportation Review,* December 1991, pp. 351−58; Ronald L. Coulter et al., "Freight Transportation Carrier Selection Criteria: Identification of Service Dimensions for Competitive Positioning," *Journal of Business Research,* August 1989, pp. 51−66; Donald J. Bowersox, David L. Closs, and Omar K. Helferich, *Logistical Management* (New York: Macmillan, 1986); Edward R. Bruning and Peter M. Lynagh, "Carrier Evaluation in Physical Distribution Management," *Journal of Business Logistics,* September 1984, pp. 30−47. See also Paul R. Murphy, Jonathan E. Smith, and James M. Daley, "Ethical Behavior of US General Freight Carriers: An Empirical Assessment," *The Logistics and Transportation Review,* March 1991, pp. 55−72; Edward L. Fitzsimmons, "Factors Associated with Intramodal Competition Reported by Small Railroads," *The Logistics and Transportation Review,* March 1991, pp. 73−90; Phil Ramsdale and Steve Harvey, "Make Freight Cost Control Part of Planning," *The Journal of Business Strategy,* March−April 1990, pp. 42−45.

9. "Railroads Getting in Better Shape for the Long Haul," *The Wall Street Journal,* February 26, 1992, p. B4; "Big Rail Is Finally Rounding the Bend," *Business Week,* November 11, 1991, pp. 128−29; "Comeback Ahead for Railroads," *Fortune,* June 17, 1991, pp. 107−13; "The Road Ahead for Railroads," *Fortune,* May 20, 1991, pp. 13−14; "Trains Double Up to Get Truck Business," *The Wall Street Journal,* July 28, 1989, p. B3; "Railroad Brings Far-Flung Dispatchers Together in Huge Computerized Bunker," *The Wall Street Journal,* May 9, 1989, p. B9; "New Train Control Systems Pass Big Tests," *The Wall Street Journal,* October 26, 1988, p. B6.

10. George L. Stern, "Surface Transportation: Middle-of-the-Road Solution," *Harvard Business Review,* December 1975, p. 82.

11. Statistics Canada, Cat. 52-201, 57-205 (Ottawa: Ministry of Supply and Services Canada, December 31, 1983).

12. "Federal Express Finds Its Pioneering Formula Falls Flat Overseas," *The Wall Street Journal,* April 15, 1991, p. A1ff.; "UPS Challenges Leaders in Air Express," *The Wall Street Journal,* December 20, 1990, p. A5; "Federal Express's Battle Overseas," *Fortune,* December 3, 1990, pp. 137−40; "Can UPS Deliver the Goods in a New World?" *Business Week,* June 4, 1990, pp. 80−82; Gunna K. Sletmo and Jacques Picard, "International Distribution Policies and the Role of Air Freight," *Journal of Business Logistics* 6, no. 1 (1985), pp. 35−53.

13. CSX, 1990 Annual Report.

14. Judith A. Fuerst, "Sorting Out the Middlemen," *Handling and Shipping Management,* March 1985, pp. 46−50; Joseph T. Kane, "Future Shock Is Now for Freight Forwarders," *Handling and Shipping Management,* October 1983, pp. 65−68.

15. C. H. White and R. B. Felder, "Turn Your Truck Fleet into a Profit Center," *Harvard Business Review,* May−June 1983, pp. 14−17.

16. Paul A. Dion, Loretta M. Hasey, Patrick C. Dorin, and Jean Lundin, "Consequences of Inventory Stockouts," *Industrial Marketing Management* 20, no. 1 (1991), pp. 23−28; R. Douglas White, "Streamline Inventory to Better Serve Customers," *The Journal of Business Strategy,* March−April 1989, pp. 43−47; David J. Armstrong, "Sharpening Inventory Management," *Harvard Business Review,* November−December 1985, pp. 42−59.

17. Wade Ferguson, "Buying an Industrial Service Warehouse Space," *Industrial Marketing Management,* February 1983, pp. 63−66; "Warehousing: Should You Go Public?" *Sales & Marketing Management,* June 14, 1976, p. 52; G. O. Pattino, "Public Warehousing: Supermarket for Distribution Services," *Handling and Shipping,* March 1977, p. 59.

18. Kenneth B. Ackerman and Bernard J. LaLonde, "Making Warehousing More Efficient," *Harvard Business Review,* April 1980, pp. 94−102.

19. Tyson Foods, 1990 Annual Report; "Holly Farms' Marketing Error: The Chicken that Laid an Egg," *The Wall Street Journal,* February 9, 1988, p. 44.

20. Shirley J. Daniel and Wolf D. Reitsperger, "Management Control Systems for JIT: An Empirical Comparison of Japan and the US," *Journal of International Business Studies,* Winter 1991, pp. 603−18; "How to Keep Truckin' in the Age of Just-in-Time Delivery," *Business Week,* December 10, 1990, p. 181; "Firms' Newfound Skill in Managing Inventory May Soften Downturn," *The Wall Street Journal,* November 19, 1990, p. A1ff.; Brian Dearing, "The Strategic Benefits of EDI," *The Journal of Business Strategy,* January−February 1990, pp. 4−6; Charles R. O'Neal, "JIT Procurement and Relationship Marketing," *Industrial Marketing Management* 18, no. 1 (1989), pp. 55−64; Prabir K. Bagchi, T. S. Raghumathan, and Edward J. Bardi, "The Implications of Just-in-Time Inventory Policies on Carrier Selection," *The Logistics and Transportation Review,* December 1987, pp. 373−84; "How Just-in-Time Inventories Combat Foreign Competition," *Business Week,* May 14, 1984, pp. 176D−76G.

21. "Circuit City's Wires Are Sizzling," *Business Week,* April 27, 1992, p. 76; "Earning More by Moving Faster," *Fortune,* October 7, 1991, pp. 89−94; "An Electronic Pipeline that's Changing the Way America Does Business," *Business Week,* August 3, 1987, p. 80ff.; "Computer Finds a Role in Buying and Selling, Reshaping Businesses," *The Wall Street Journal,* March 18, 1987, p. 1ff.; "Computers Bringing Changes to Basic Business Documents," *The Wall Street Journal,* March 6, 1987, p. 33.

22. "A Smart Cookie at Pepperidge," *Fortune,* December 22, 1986, pp. 67−74.

23. "As Stores Scrimp More and Order Less, Suppliers Take on Greater Risks, Costs," *The Wall Street Journal,* December 10, 1991, p. B1ff.

24. " 'Green Cars' Are Still Far in the Future," *The Wall Street Journal,* January 13, 1992, p. B1ff.; "Conservation Power," *Business Week,* September 16, 1991, pp. 86−91; "On the Road Again and Again and Again: Auto Makers Try to Build Recyclable Car," *The Wall Street Journal,* April 30, 1991, p. B1; "Clean-Air Proposal Eventually May Add as Much as $600 to Car Sticker Prices," *The Wall Street Journal,* October 11, 1990, p. B1ff.; "Shell Pumps Cleaner Gas in 'Dirtiest' Cities in US," *The Wall Street Journal,* April 12, 1990, p. B1ff.; "Clean-Air Legislation Will Cost Americans $21.5 Billion a Year," *The Wall Street Journal,* March 28, 1990, p. A1ff.; Du Pont, 1990 Annual Report; Matlack, 1990 Annual Report; Shell, 1990 Annual Report.

25. R. F. Lusch, J. G. Udell, and G. R. Laczniak, "The Future of Marketing Strategy," *Business Horizons,* December 1976, pp. 65−74. See also Jonathan R. Copulsky and Michael J. Wolf, "Relationship Marketing: Positioning for the Future," *The Journal of Business Strategy,* July−August 1990, pp. 16−21; John J. Burbridge, Jr., "Strategic Implications of Logistics Information Systems," *The Logistics and Transportation Review,* December 1988, pp. 368−83.

Chapter 13

1. Mark Evans, "Warehouse 'Clubs' Revolutionizing Retail," *The Financial Post,* June 3, 1991, p. 4.

2. *Client's Monthly Alert,* June 1977, p. 3.

3. For additional examples, see John P. Dickson and Douglas L. MacLachlan, "Social Distance and Shopping Behavior," *Journal of the Academy of Marketing Science,* Spring 1990, pp. 153−62; "Penney Moves Upscale in Merchandise but Still Has to Convince Public," *The Wall Street Journal,* June 7, 1990, p. A1ff.; "Can J. C. Penney Change Its Image without Losing Customers?" *Adweek's Marketing Week,* February 26, 1990, pp. 20−24; "Upscale Look for Limited Puts Retailer Back on Track," *The Wall Street Journal,* February 24, 1989, p. B1; "Selling to the Poor: Retailers that Target Low-Income Shoppers Are Rapidly Growing," *The Wall Street Journal,* June 24, 1985, p. 1ff.; "The Green in Blue-Collar Retailing," *Fortune,* May 27, 1985, pp. 74−77.

4. "Specialty Retailing, a Hot Market, Attracts New Players," *The Wall Street Journal,* April 2, 1987, p. 1.

5. "Remaking a Dinosaur," *Newsweek,* February 10, 1992, pp. 38−43; Richard A. Rauch, "Retailing's Dinosaurs: Department Stores and Supermarkets," *Business Horizons,* September−October 1991, pp. 21−25; "Fighting the Tide, Owner Tries to Revive Big Department Store," *The Wall Street Journal,* August 14, 1991, p. A1ff.; Joe Schwartz, "Dump Department Stores?" *American Demographics,* December 1990, pp. 42−43; "Retailing in the '90s: How It Got Here from There," *Marketing News,* June 25, 1990, p. 14ff.; "If May Stores Are Plain Janes, Who Needs Flash?" *Business Week,* January 22, 1990, p. 32; "A Quiet Superstar Rises in Retailing," *Fortune,* October 23, 1989, pp. 167−74; "Why Big-Name Stores Are Losing Out," *Fortune,* January 16, 1989, pp. 31−32; "Stores See Loyal Customers Slip Away," *Advertising Age,* July 11, 1988, p. 12; "How Three Master Merchants Fell from Grace," *Business Week,* March 16, 1987, pp. 38−40; "Department Stores Shape Up," *Fortune,* September 1, 1986, pp. 50−52; "How Department Stores Plan to Get the Registers Ringing Again," *Business Week,* November 18, 1985, pp. 66−67.

6. David Appel, "The Supermarket: Early Development of an Institutional Innovation," *Journal of Retailing,* Spring 1972, pp. 39−53.

7. Statistics Canada, *Retail Trade,* Cat. 63-005, December 1991 (Ottawa: Minister of Supply and Services Canada).

8. "Grocery-Cart Wars," *Time,* March 30, 1992, p. 49; "Selling in the Stores of the Future," *Adweek,* January 20, 1992, pp. 12−13; "How a Terrific Idea for Grocery Marketing Missed the Target," *The Wall Street Journal,* April 3, 1991, p. A1ff.; "Electronic Marketing Enters Supermarket Aisle," *Marketing News,* April 1, 1991, pp. 14−15; " 'Smart Card,' Coupon Eater Targeted to Grocery Retailers," *Marketing News,* June 6, 1988, pp. 1−2; "At Today's Supermarket, the Computer Is Doing It All," *Business Week,* August 11, 1986, pp. 64−65; "Bigger, Shrewder, and Cheaper Cub Leads Food Stores into the Future," *The Wall Street Journal,* August 26, 1985, p. 19.

9. "Catalog Showrooms Revamp to Keep Their Identity," *Business Week,* Industrial/Technology Edition, June 10, 1985, pp. 117−20; Pradeep K. Korgaonkar, "Consumer Preferences for Catalog Showrooms and Discount Stores," *Journal of Retailing,* Fall 1982, pp. 76–88; "Best Products: Too Much Too Soon at the No. 1 Catalog Showroom," *Business Week,* July 23, 1984, pp. 136–38.

10. "Podunk Is Beckoning," *Business Week,* December 23, 1991, p. 76; "Wal-Mart Prepares for Urban Assault," *Adweek,* November 11, 1991, p. 10; "Merchants Mobilize to Battle Wal-Mart in a Small Community," *The Wall Street Journal,* June 5, 1991, p. A1ff.; "Is Wal-Mart Unstoppable?" *Fortune,* May 6, 1991, pp. 50–59; "Wal-Mart Finds New Rivals on Main Street," *Adweek's Marketing Week,* November 19, 1990, p. 5.

11. "Wal-Mart Gets Lost in the Vegetable Aisle," *Business Week,* May 28, 1990, p. 48; "Wal-Mart Pulls Back on Hypermarket Plans," *Advertising Age,* February 19, 1990, p. 49; "Retailers Fly into Hyperspace," *Fortune,* October 24, 1988, pp. 48–52.

12. "Warehouse Clubs Have Big Impact on Grocers," *The Wall Street Journal,* April 6, 1992, p. B1; Shopping Clubs Ready for Battle in Texas Market," *The Wall Street Journal,* October 24, 1991, p. B1ff.; "You Have to Join to Pay," *Newsweek,* August 5, 1991, p. 65; "Bargains by the Forklift," *Business Week,* July 15, 1991, p. 152; "Campbell, Kellogg 'Bulk' Their Brands for Wholesale Clubs," *Adweek's Marketing Week,* April 29, 1991, p. 26; "Corn Flakes, Aisle 1. Cadillacs, Aisle 12," *Business Week,* April 29, 1991, pp. 68–70; Jack G. Kaikati, "The Boom in Warehouse Clubs," *Business Horizons,* March–April 1987, pp. 68–73.

13. "Tandy Bets Big with New Giant Stores," *The Wall Street Journal,* April 16, 1992, p. B1ff.; "There's No Place Like Home Depot," *Nation's Business,* February 1992, pp. 30–35; "This Is a Job for Superstores," *USA Today,* October 8, 1991, p. 4B; "Will Home Depot Be 'The Wal-Mart of the '90s?' " *Business Week,* March 19, 1990, pp. 124–26; "Office Supply Superstores Reshape the Industry," *Marketing News,* January 22, 1990, p. 2; "Born to Be Big," *Inc.,* June 1989, pp. 94–101; "Bookshop 'Super-Store' Reflects the Latest Word in Retailing," *The Wall Street Journal,* February 23, 1987, p. 29; "Hechinger's: Nobody Does It Better in Do-It-Yourself," *Business Week,* May 5, 1986, p. 96; "Electronics Superstores Are Devouring Their Rivals," *Business Week,* June 24, 1985, pp. 84–85.

14. "Some 7-Elevens Try Selling a New Image," *The Wall Street Journal,* October 25, 1991, p. B1ff.; Stop N Go's Van Horn Wants to Reinvent the Convenience Store," *The Wall Street Journal,* February 6, 1991, pp. A1ff.; "In Japan, Conveniences Converge at 7-Eleven," *The Wall Street Journal,* April 6, 1990, p. B1; "Troubled Circle K Is Turning This Way and That," *Business Week,* November 20, 1989, pp. 78–80.

15. Statistics Canada, Cat. 63–21.

16. "Push-Button Lover," *The Economist,* November 16, 1991, p. 88; "Machines Start New Fast-Food Era," *USA Today,* July 19, 1991, pp. 1B–2B; "High-Tech Vending Machines Cook Up a New Menu of Hot Fast-Food Entrees," *The Wall Street Journal,* May 13, 1991, p. B1ff.; "The World's Most Valuable Company," *Fortune,* October 10, 1988, pp. 92–104.

17. "It Helps to Be Cool and Klutzy if You Are Selling on TV," *The Wall Street Journal,* December 31, 1990, p. 1ff.; "Home Shoppers Keep Tuning In—But Investors Are Turned Off," *Business Week,* October 22, 1990, pp. 70–72; "From the Mall to Catalogs to Cable," *Insight,* May 7, 1990, p. 51; "Home Shopping Tries a Tonic for Its Sickly Stock," *Business Week,* April 25, 1988, p. 110; "Home Shopping," *Business Week,* December 15, 1986, pp. 62–69; Joel E. Urbany and W. Wayne Talarzyk, "Videotex: Implications for Retailing," *Journal of Retailing,* Fall 1983, pp. 76–92; George P. Moschis, Jac L. Goldstucker, and Thomas J. Stanley, "At-Home Shopping: Will Consumers Let Their Computers Do the Walking?" *Business Horizons,* March–April 1985, pp. 22–29.

18. "Computer-Ordering Method Helps Newcomer Blossom," *The Wall Street Journal,* January 22, 1991, p. B2; "Electronic Retailing Filling Niche Needs," *Discount Store News,* December 19, 1988, p. 111.

19. "Nabisco Plots Strategy to Sell Oreos with Videos," *Advertising Age,* May 4, 1992, p. 3ff.; "Stores Find Photo Minilabs Quick Way to Process Profit," *Supermarket News,* June 10, 1991, pp. 22–25; "Products No Longer Determine the Selection of Retail Outlet,"

Marketing News, April 1, 1991, p. 9; "Supermarketing Can Be Super Marketing," *ABA Banking Journal,* September 1989, pp. 49–61; Ruth Hamel, "Food Fight," *American Demographics,* March 1989, pp. 36–39ff.; "No Holds Barred," *Time,* August 11, 1988, pp. 46–48; "Special Report: Stores Juggle Space, Specialties," *Advertising Age,* October 12, 1987, p. S1ff.

20. For more on Kmart seeking new markets, see "The Rebirth of Kmart," *Advertising Age,* October 7, 1991, p. 16; "Attention, Shoppers: Kmart Is Fighting Back," *Business Week,* October 7, 1991, pp. 118–20; "Will Kmart Ever Be a Silk Purse?" *Business Week,* January 22, 1990, p. 46. For more on how product-life cycles apply to retailers, see "Rewriting the Rules of Retailing," *The New York Times,* October 15, 1990, Sect. 3, p. 1ff.; "Video Chain Aims to Star as Industry Leader," *USA Today,* July 22, 1988, pp. B1–2; "What Ails Retailing," *Fortune,* January 30, 1989, pp. 61–64; "Don't Discount Off-Price Retailers," *Harvard Business Review,* May–June 1985, pp. 85–92; Ronald Savitt, "The 'Wheel of Retailing' and Retail Product Management," *European Journal of Marketing* 18, no. 6/7 (1984), pp. 43–54; Jack G. Kaikati, Rom J. Markin, and Calvin P. Duncan, "The Transformation of Retailing Institutions: Beyond the Wheel of Retailing and Life Cycle Theories," *Journal of Macromarketing* 1, no. 1 (1981), pp. 58–66.

21. "How Did Sears Blow This Gasket?" *Business Week,* June 29, 1992, p. 38; "An Open Letter to Sears Customers," *USA Today,* June 25, 1992, p. 8A.

22. "Variety Stores Struggle to Keep the Dimes Rolling In," *The Wall Street Journal,* May 7, 1991, p. B2; "Retailers Grab Power, Control Marketplace," *Marketing News,* January 16, 1989, pp. 1–2; Dale D. Achabal, John M. Heineke, and Shelby H. McIntyre, "Issues and Perspectives on Retail Productivity," *Journal of Retailing,* Fall 1984, p. 107ff.; Charles A. Ingene, "Scale Economies in American Retailing: A Cross-Industry Comparison," *Journal of Macromarketing* 4, no. 2 (1984), pp. 49–63; "Mom-and-Pop Videotape Shops Are Fading Out," *Business Week,* September 2, 1985, pp. 34–35; Vijay Mahajan, Subhash Sharma, and Roger Kerin, "Assessing Market Penetration Opportunities and Saturation Potential for Multi-Store, Multi-Market Retailers," *Journal of Retailing,* Fall 1988, pp. 315–34.

23. "Look Who Likes Franchising Now," *Fortune,* September 23, 1991, pp. 125–30; "New Rules for Franchising," *USA Today,* May 6, 1991, p. 11E; "Franchisers and Franchisees Make Some Concessions," *The Wall Street Journal,* February 7, 1991, p. B2; "For US Firms, Franchising in Mexico Gets More Appetizing, Thanks to Reform," *The Wall Street Journal,* January 3, 1991, p. A6; "More Concerns Are Franchising Existing Outlets," *The Wall Street Journal,* December 17, 1990, p. B1ff.; "Flaring Tempers at the Frozen-Yogurt King," *Business Week,* September 10, 1990, pp. 88–90; "Foreign Franchisers Entering US in Greater Numbers," *The Wall Street Journal,* June 11, 1990, p. B2; "Franchisers See a Future in East Bloc," *The Wall Street Journal,* June 5, 1990, p. B1ff.; "Avis Hit by Almost Every Obstacle in Franchise Book," *The Wall Street Journal,* May 3, 1990, p. B2.

24. "Special Report: Mega Malls," *Advertising Age,* January 27, 1992, pp. S1–8; "The Shopping Mall of Dreams," *Newsweek,* December 23, 1991, p. 44; Chip Walker, "Strip Malls: Plain but Powerful," *American Demographics,* October 1991, pp. 48–51; "Developers of Big Shopping Malls Tutor Faltering Tenants in Retail Techniques," *The Wall Street Journal,* April 24, 1991, p. B1; "Japan Becomes Land of the Rising Mall," *The Wall Street Journal,* February 11, 1991, p. B1ff.; "Largest of All Malls in the US Is a Gamble in Bloomington, Minn.," *The Wall Street Journal,* October 30, 1990, p. A1ff.; "When a Mall's Biggest Retailers Fall, Surviving Shops Get an Unpleasant Jolt," *The Wall Street Journal,* October 25, 1990, p. B1ff.; "Going Without: Gap Drops Anchors in Its Plan to Develop Upscale Malls," *The Wall Street Journal,* October 25, 1990, p. B1ff.; Eugene H. Fram and Joel Axelrod, "The Distressed Shopper," *American Demographics,* October 1990, pp. 44–45; "Retailers Use Bans, Guards and Ploys to Curb Teen Sport of Mall-Mauling," *The Wall Street Journal,* August 7, 1990, p. B1ff.; "New Retailers Face Struggle Getting in Malls," *The Wall Street Journal,* July 24, 1990, p. B1ff.; "Rodeo Drive Mini-Mall Is Looking Smart," *The Wall Street Journal,* June 14, 1990, p. B1; Francesca Turchiano, "The (Un)Malling of America," *American*

Demographics, April 1990, pp. 37–39; "Too Many Malls Are Chasing a Shrinking Supply of Shoppers," *Adweek's Marketing Week,* February 5, 1990, pp. 2–3.

25. "Shopper Sightings Reported," *Business Week,* January 13, 1992, p. 81; " 'They're Here to Shop' at Mall Mecca," *USA Today,* December 23, 1991, pp. 1A–2A; "Thriving Factory Outlets Anger Retailers as Store Suppliers Turn into Competitors," *The Wall Street Journal,* October 8, 1991, p. B1ff.; "The Price Is Always Right," *Time,* December 17, 1990, pp. 66–68; John Ozment and Greg Martin, "Changes in the Competitive Environments of Rural Trade Areas: Effects of Discount Retail Chains," *Journal of Business Research,* November 1990, pp. 277–88; "Discount Clothing Stores, Facing Squeeze, Aim to Fashion a More Rounded Image," *The Wall Street Journal,* March 15, 1990, p. B1; "The Wholesale Success of Factory Outlet Malls," *Business Week,* February 3, 1986, pp. 92–94.

26. "Europe Chains in Power Play with Manufacturers," *Supermarket News,* June 3, 1991, pp. 18–19; "Retailing Around the World: Endless Possibilities or Endless Problems?" *Discount Store News,* May 6, 1991, pp. 69–115; "International Intriguing," *Advertising Age,* January 29, 1990, pp. S1–2; Philip R. Cateora, *International Marketing* (Homewood, Ill.: Richard D. Irwin, 1990), pp. 586–93.

27. "Ringing in the Future by Changing the Past," *Insight,* January 8, 1990, pp. 9–17; "Home Banking Gets Another Chance," *The Wall Street Journal,* December 7, 1989, p. B1; "IBM, Sears—Their Gamble May Set Pace for Videotex," *USA Today,* September 20, 1988, p. B1; "Are IBM and Sears Crazy? Or Canny?" *Fortune,* September 28, 1987, pp. 74–79; "Electronic Retailing Goes to the Supermarket," *Business Week,* March 25, 1985, pp. 78–79; "Computer Users Shop at Home over the Phone," *The Wall Street Journal,* February 20, 1985, p. 35.

28. *The Globe and Mail,* August 14, 1990, p. B5.

29. "21st Century Supermarket Shopping," *Adweek's Marketing Week,* March 9, 1992, p. 9; "What Selling Will Be Like in the '90s," *Fortune,* January 13, 1992, pp. 63–65; "The New Stars of Retailing," *Business Week,* December 16, 1991, pp. 120–22; "Retailers with a Cause," *Newsweek,* December 16, 1991, p. 51; "Shop Talk: What's in Store for Retailers," *The Wall Street Journal,* April 9, 1991, p. B1ff.; "The Little Stores that Could," *Adweek's Marketing Week,* February 4, 1991, pp. 16–17; "Retailing: Who Will Survive," *Business Week,* November 26, 1990, pp. 134–44; "Retailing's Winners & Losers," *Fortune,* December 18, 1989, pp. 69–78.

Chapter 14

1. Edward Clifford, "Jean Coutu's US Expansion: So Far, So Good," *The Globe and Mail,* November 1, 1991, p. B7.

2. For a detailed discussion of wholesaling and the operation and management of a wholesale business, see T. N. Beckman, N. H. Engle, and R. D. Buzzell, *Wholesaling,* 3rd ed. (New York: Ronald Press, 1959).

3. Richard Greene, "Wholesaling," *Forbes,* January 2, 1984, pp. 226–28; Lyn S. Amine, S. Tamer Cavusgil, and Robert I. Weinstein, "Japanese Sogo Shosha and the US Export Trading Companies," *Journal of the Academy of Marketing Science,* Fall 1986, pp. 21–32.

4. James D. Hlavacek and Tommy J. McCuistion, "Industrial Distributors—When, Who, and How?" *Harvard Business Review,* January–February 1983, pp. 96–101; Steven Flax, "Wholesalers," *Forbes,* January 4, 1982. See also Roger J. Calantone and Jule B. Gassenheimer, "Overcoming Basic Problems between Manufacturers and Distributors," *Industrial Marketing Management* 20, no. 3 (1991), pp. 215–22; Geoff Gordon, Roger Calantone, and C. A. diBenedetto, "How Electrical Contractors Choose Distributors," *Industrial Marketing Management* 20, no. 1 (1991), pp. 29–42; Nicholas Nickolaus, "Marketing New Products with Industrial Distributors," *Industrial Marketing Management,* November 1990, pp. 287–300; Allan J. Magrath and Kenneth G. Hardy, "Gearing Manufacturer Support Programs to Distributors," *Industrial Marketing Management* 18, no. 4 (1989), pp. 239–44; Donald M. Jackson and Michael F. d'Amico,

"Products and Markets Served by Distributors and Agents, *Industrial Marketing Managment,* February 1989, pp. 27–34; Thomas L. Powers, "Switching from Reps to Direct Salespeople," *Industrial Marketing Management,* August 1987, pp. 169–72; N. Mohan Reddy and Michael P. Marvin, "Developing a Manufacturer-Distributor Information Partnership," *Industrial Marketing Management,* May 1986, pp. 157–64; Michael Levy and Michael Van Breda, "How to Determine Whether to Buy Direct or through a Wholesaler," *Retail Control,* June–July 1985, pp. 35–55.

5. "Sysco Corp.'s Bill of Fare Is Inviting," *USA Today,* August 11, 1989, p. B3; "Dean Foods Thrives among the Giants," *The Wall Street Journal,* September 17, 1987, p. 6; "Food Distribution: The Leaders Are Getting Hungry for More," *Business Week,* March 24, 1986, pp. 106–8.

6. Robert F. Lusch, Deborah S. Coykendall, and James M. Kenderdine, *Wholesaling in Transition: An Executive Chart Book* (Norman, OK: Distribution Research Program, University of Oklahoma, 1990).

7. "Direct Marketing: A Modern Marketing Solution," *Directions* (New York: Direct Marketing Association, 1990); "Special Report: Direct Marketing," *Advertising Age,* September 25, 1990, pp. S1–16.

8. Lusch, Coykendall, and Kenderdine, *Wholesaling in Transition.*

9. "Fruit Fight: Independent Growers Challenge Agribusiness Giants," *Insight,* July 29, 1991, pp. 13–19; "Why Farm Cooperatives Need Extra Seed Money," *Business Week,* March 21, 1988, p. 96; "Independent Farmers Oppose Rules Letting Cartels Decide Output," *The Wall Street Journal,* June 17, 1987, p. 1ff.

10. For more on manufacturers' agents being squeezed, see "Wal-Mart Draws Fire: Reps, Brokers Protest Being Shut Out by New Policy," *Advertising Age,* January 13, 1992, p. 3ff.; "Independent Sales Reps Are Squeezed by the Recession," *The Wall Street Journal,* December 27, 1991, p. B1. For more discussion on wholesaling abroad, see "Japan Rises to P&G's No. 3 Market," *Advertising Age,* December 10, 1990, p. 42; "P&G Rewrites the Marketing Rules," *Fortune,* November 6, 1989, pp. 34–48; " 'Papa-Mama' Stores in Japan Wield Power to Hold Back Imports," *The Wall Street Journal,* November 14, 1988, p. 1ff.; "Campbell's Taste of the Japanese Market Is Mm-Mm Good," *Business Week,* March 28, 1988, p. 42; "Brazil Captures a Big Share of the US Shoe Market," *The Wall Street Journal,* August 27, 1985, p. 35; Jim Gibbons, "Selling Abroad with Manufacturers' Agents," *Sales & Marketing Management,* September 9, 1985, pp. 67–69; Evelyn A. Thomchick and Lisa Rosenbaum, "The Role of US Export Trading Companies in International Logistics," *Journal of Business Logistics,* September 1984, pp. 85–105.

11. "Why Manufacturers Are Doubling as Distributors," *Business Week,* January 17, 1983, p. 41.

12. "Sanyo Sales Strategy Illustrates Problems of Little Distributors," *The Wall Street Journal,* September 10, 1984, p. 33.

13. "It's 'Like Somebody Had Shot the Postman,' " *Business Week,* January 13, 1992, p. 82; "Steel Service Centers: No More Warehouses," *Industry Week,* February 3, 1992, pp. 36–43; Joseph G. Ormsby and Dillard B. Tinsley, "The Role of Marketing in Material Requirements Planning Systems," *Industrial Marketing Management* 20, no. 1 (1991), pp. 67–72; Bert Rosenbloom, "Motivating Your International Channel Partners," *Business Horizons,* March–April 1990, pp. 53–57; Allan J. Magrath, "The Hidden Clout of Marketing Middlemen," *Journal of Business Strategy,* March–April 1990, pp. 38–41; S. Tamer Cavusgil, "The Importance of Distributor Training at Caterpillar," *Industrial Marketing Management,* February 1990, pp. 1–10; "Getting Cozy with Their Customers," *Business Week,* January 8, 1990, p. 86; J. A. Narus and J. C. Anderson, "Turn Your Industrial Distributors into Partners," *Harvard Business Review,* March–April 1986, pp. 66–71; J. J. Withey, "Realities of Channel Dynamics: A Wholesaling Example," *Academy of Marketing Science,* Summer 1985, pp. 72–81; J. A. Narus, N. M. Reddy, and G. L. Pinchak, "Key Problems Facing Industrial Distributors," *Industrial Marketing Management,* August 1984, pp. 139–48.

14. "Cold War: Amana Refrigeration Fights Tiny Distributor," *The Wall Street Journal,* February 26, 1992, p. B2; "Four Strategies Key to Success in Wholesale Distribution Industry," *Marketing News,* March 13, 1989, pp. 22–23. For another example, see "Quickie-Divorce Curbs Sought by Manufacturers' Distributors," *The Wall Street Journal,* July 13, 1987, p. 27; "Merger of Two Bakers Teaches Distributors a Costly Lesson (3 parts)," *The Wall Street Journal,* September 14, 1987, p. 29; October 19, 1987, p. 35; November 11, 1987, p. 33. For yet another example, see "Independent TV Distributors Losing a Starring Role," *The Wall Street Journal,* April 14, 1989, p. B2.

15. "A Few Big Retailers Rebuff Middlemen," *The Wall Street Journal,* October 21, 1986, p. 6; J. A. Narus, N. M. Reddy, and G. L. Pinchak, "Key Problems Facing Industrial Distributors," *Industrial Marketing Management,* August 1984, pp. 139–48; J. A. Narus and J. C. Anderson, "Turn Your Industrial Distributors into Partners," *Harvard Business Review,* March–April 1986, pp. 66–71; J.J. Withey, "Realities of Channel Dynamics: A Wholesaling Example," *Academy of Marketing Science,* Summer 1985, pp. 72–81; "Napco: Seeking a National Network as a Nonfood Supermarket Supplier," *Business Week,* November 8, 1982, p. 70; James A. Narus and Tor Guimaraes, "Computer Usage in Distributor Marketing," *Industrial Marketing Management,* February 1987, pp. 43–54.

Chapter 15

1. Randall Scotland, "Mutual Back Scratching Pays Off," *The Financial Post,* August 13, 1992, p. 13.

2. "Cabbage Patch Campaigner Tells Secret," *The Chapel Hill Newspaper,* December 1, 1985, p. D1.

3. "PR Shouldn't Mean 'Poor Relations,' " *Industry Week,* February 3, 1992, p. 51; "The Great Escape from Kuwait—Pepsi-Style," *Adweek's Marketing Week,* August 13, 1990, p. 7; "Ads Convert Rejection into Free Publicity," *The Wall Street Journal,* July 30, 1990, p. B5; "Wooing Press and Public at Auto Shows," *The Wall Street Journal,* January 8, 1990, p. B1; "Free Association," *Advertising Age,* October 23, 1989, p. 36ff.; Len Kessler, "Get the Most Bang for Your PR Dollars," *The Journal of Business Strategy,* May–June 1989, pp. 13–17; "PR on the Offensive," *Advertising Age,* March 13, 1989, p. 20; Thomas H. Bivins, "Ethical Implications of the Relationship of Purpose to Role and Function in Public Relations," *Journal of Business Ethics,* January 1989, pp. 65–74; E. Cameron Williams, "Product Publicity: Low Cost and High Credibility," *Industrial Marketing Management,* November 1988, pp. 355–60; "Despite Ban, Liquor Marketers Finding New Ways to Get Products on Television," *The Wall Street Journal,* March 14, 1988, p. 31; "More Prime-Time TV Shows Plug Airlines, Hotels in Scripts," *The Wall Street Journal,* May 28, 1987, p. 33; "Small Firms Push Their Own Stock on Cable TV's New 'Infomercials,' " *The Wall Street Journal,* October 3, 1986, p. 31.

4. "Eye-Catching Logos All Too Often Leave Fuzzy Images in Minds of Consumers," *The Wall Street Journal,* December 5, 1991, p. B1ff.; Ronald E. Dulek, John S. Fielden, and John S. Hill, "International Communication: An Executive Primer," *Business Horizons,* January–February 1991, pp. 20–25; Tony Meenaghan, "The Role of Sponsorship in the Marketing Communications Mix," *International Journal of Advertising* 10, no. 1 (1991), pp. 35–48; Kaylene C. Williams, Rosann L. Spiro, and Leslie M. Fine, "The Customer-Salesperson Dyad: An Interaction/Communication Model and Review," *Journal of Personal Selling and Sales Management,* Summer 1990, pp. 29–44; Susan M. Petroshius and Kenneth E. Crocker, "An Empirical Analysis of Spokesperson Characteristics on Advertisement and Product Evaluations," *Journal of the Academy of Marketing Science,* Summer 1989, pp. 217–26; Samuel Rabino and Thomas E. Moore, "Managing New-Product Announcements in the Computer Industry," *Industrial Marketing Management* 18, no. 1 (1989), pp. 35–44; Marc G. Weinberger and Jean B. Romeo, "The Impact of Negative Product News," *Business Horizons,* January–February 1989, pp. 44–50; "High-Tech Hype Reaches New Heights," *The Wall Street Journal,* January 12, 1989, p. B1; "Car Ads Turn to High-Tech Talk—But Does Anybody Understand It?" *The Wall Street Journal,* March 7, 1988, p. 23. For interesting perspectives on this issue, see Jacob Jacoby and Wayne D. Hoyer, "The Comprehension-Miscomprehension of Print Communication: Selected Findings,"

Journal of Consumer Research, March 1989, pp. 434–43. See also Reed Sanderlin, "Information Is Not Communication," *Business Horizons,* March–April 1982, pp. 40–42.

5. "When Slogans Go Wrong," *American Demographics,* February 1992, p. 14; "How Does Slogan Translate?" *Advertising Age,* October 12, 1987, p. 84; "More Firms Turn to Translation Experts to Avoid Costly Embarrassing Mistakes," *The Wall Street Journal,* January 13, 1977, p. 32.

6. "Totally Hidden Video," *Inside PR,* August 1990, pp. 11–13; " 'News' Videos that Pitch Drugs Provoke Outcry for Regulations," *The Wall Street Journal,* February 8, 1990, p. B6; "Public Relations Firms Offer 'News' to TV," *The Wall Street Journal,* April 2, 1985, p. 6.

7. "Reaching Influential Buyers," *Inc.,* May 1991, pp. 86–88; Jagdip Singh, "Voice, Exit, and Negative Word-of-Mouth Behaviors: An Investigation across Three Service Categories," *Journal of the Academy of Marketing Science,* Winter 1990, pp. 1–16; "Selling Software that's Hard to Describe," *The Wall Street Journal,* July 11, 1988, p. 23; Jacqueline Johnson Brown and Peter H. Reingen, "Social Ties and Word-of-Mouth Referral Behavior," *Journal of Consumer Research,* December, 1987, pp. 350–62; Robin A. Higie, Lawrence F. Feick, and Linda L. Price, "Types and Amount of Word-of-Mouth Communications about Retailers," *Journal of Retailing,* Fall 1987, pp. 260–78; Marsha L. Richins, "Negative Word-of-Mouth by Dissatisfied Consumers: A Pilot Study," *Journal of Marketing,* Winter 1983, pp. 68–78; John A. Czepiel, "Word-of-Mouth Processes in the Diffusion of a Major Technological Innovation," *Journal of Marketing Research,* May 1974, pp. 172–80; Leon G. Schiffman and Vincent Gaccione, "Opinion Leaders in Institutional Markets," *Journal of Marketing,* April 1974, pp. 49–53.

8. Meera P. Venkatraman, "Opinion Leaders, Adopters, and Communicative Adopters: A Role Analysis," *Psychology and Marketing,* Spring 1989, pp. 51–68; Mary Dee Dickerson and James W. Gentry, "Characteristics of Adopters and Non-Adopters of Home Computers," *Journal of Consumer Research,* September 1983, pp. 225–35; Everett M. Rogers and F. Floyd Shoemaker, *Communication of Innovations: A Cross-Cultural Approach* (New York: Free Press, 1971), pp. 203–9; Kenneth Uhl, Roman Andrus, and Lance Poulsen, "How Are Laggards Different? An Empirical Inquiry," *Journal of Marketing Research,* February 1970, pp. 43–50; Thomas S. Robertson, "The Process of Innovation and the Diffusion of Innovation," *Journal of Marketing,* January 1967, pp. 14–19.

9. See, for example, "Drug Firms Pitching Consumers Directly," *The Wall Street Journal,* September 4, 1990, p. B9; "Kellogg Shifts Strategy to Pull Consumers In," *The Wall Street Journal,* January 22, 1990, p. B1ff.; "Small Drug Maker Breaks Taboo with Ads Targeted at Consumers," *The Wall Street Journal,* April 20, 1989, p. B1ff.; Alvin A. Achenbaum and F. Kent Mitchel, "Pulling Away from Push Marketing," *Harvard Business Review,* May–June 1987, pp. 38–42; Michael Levy, John Webster, and Roger Kerin, "Formulating Push Marketing Strategies: A Method and Application," *Journal of Marketing,* Winter 1983, pp. 25–34.

10. "Hershey's Sweet Tooth Starts Aching," *Business Week,* February 7, 1970, pp. 98–104; "Big Chocolate Maker, Beset by Profit Slide, Gets More Aggressive," *The Wall Street Journal,* February 18, 1970, p. 1ff.

11. "The Cost of Selling Is Going Up," *Boardroom Reports,* December 15, 1991, p. 15; "An In-House Sales School," *Inc.,* May 1991, pp. 85–86; "Average Business-to-Business Sales Call Increases by 9.5%," *Marketing News,* September 12, 1988, p. 5; "Personal Touch Costs More," *USA Today,* July 27, 1988, p. B1.

12. "What's New in Joint Promotions," *The New York Times,* March 10, 1985; Henry H. Beam, "Preparing for Promotion Pays Off," *Business Horizons,* January–February 1984, pp. 6–13; P. Rajan Varadarajan, "Horizontal Cooperative Sales Promotion: A Framework for Classification and Additional Perspectives," *Journal of Marketing,* April 1986, pp. 61–73.

13. J. F. Engel, M. R. Warshaw, and T. C. Kinnear, *Promotional Strategy* (Homewood, Ill.: Richard D. Irwin, 1988).

14. "Special Report: Sales Promotion," *Advertising Age,* May 4, 1992, pp. 29–36; " 'Recession-Proof' Industry Feels Pinch," *Advertising Age,*

April 29, 1991, pp. 31–38; "Special Report: Marketing's Rising Star, Sales Promotion 1989," *Advertising Age,* May 1, 1989, pp. S1–20; "Special Report: Premiums, Incentives," *Advertising Age,* May 2, 1988, pp. S1–12.

15. For some examples of successful sales promotions, see "Solutions: Hit by the Pitch," *Adweek,* November 11, 1991, pp. 44–45; "The Selling of the Green," *Time,* September 16, 1991, p. 48; "Beyond the Plastic Swizzle Stick," *Adweek's Marketing Week,* May 13, 1991, p. 20; "Helene Curtis' Degree Makes Competitors Sweat," *Advertising Age,* October 29, 1990, p. 20; "Hallmark Gives Away Its Best Cards in an Unusual Promotion," *Adweek's Marketing Week,* July 9, 1990, p. 10; "Audubon Society Hopes Music Videos and Movies Get Its 'Green' Message Out," *The Wall Street Journal,* April 10, 1990, p. B1ff.

16. "The Party's Over: Food Giants Pull Back on Marketing, but Boost Promotion," *Advertising Age,* February 27, 1989, p. 1ff.; "Sales-Promo Surge Has Shops Scrambling," *Advertising Age,* April 14, 1986, p. 114.

17. "Couponing Reaches Record Clip," *Advertising Age,* February 3, 1992, p. 1ff.; "Coupons Maintain Redeeming Qualities," *Direct Marketing,* December 1991, pp. 25–27; "Coupon Vehicles Proliferate," *Adweek's Marketing Week,* November 11, 1991, p. 30; "Get Ready for Global Coupon Wars," *Adweek's Marketing Week,* July 8, 1991, pp. 20–22; Jamie Howell, "Potential Profitability and Decreased Consumer Welfare through Manufacturers' Cents-Off Coupons," *The Journal of Consumer Affairs,* Summer 1991, pp. 164–84; "Clutter Anyone? Marketers Dropped More than 300 Billion Coupons in the Past Year," *Adweek's Marketing Week,* April 8, 1991, pp. 22–25; "ActMedia Rolls Out Coupons," *Adweek's Marketing Week,* February 11, 1991, p. 42.

18. "Marketers Swap More than Goodwill at Trade Show," *Business Marketing,* September 1990, pp. 48–51; "Latest in Corporate Freebies Try to Be Classy instead of Trashy," *The Wall Street Journal,* August 7, 1989, p. B4; Rockney G. Walters, "An Empirical Investigation into Retailer Response to Manufacturer Trade Promotions," *Journal of Retailing,* Summer 1989, pp. 253–72; "Don't Just Exhibit—Do Something," *Business Marketing,* May 1989, pp. 78–79; "Trade Shows Can Pay Off for New Firms," *The Wall Street Journal,* January 1, 1989, pp. B1–2; Ronald C. Curhan and Robert J. Kopp, "Obtaining Retailer Support for Trade Deals: Key Success Factors," *Journal of Advertising Research,* December 1987–January 1988, pp. 51–60; Donald W. Jackson, Janet E. Keith, and Richard K. Burdick, "The Relative Importance of Various Promotional Elements in Different Industrial Purchase Situations," *Journal of Advertising* 16, no. 4 (1987), pp. 25–33; Daniel C. Bello and Hiram C. Barksdale, Jr., "Exporting at Industrial Trade Shows," *Industrial Marketing Management,* August 1986, pp. 197–206; Kenneth G. Hardy, "Key Success Factors for Manufacturers' Sales Promotions in Package Goods," *Journal of Marketing,* July 1986, pp. 13–23.

19. "Trade Promos Devour Half of All Marketing $," *Advertising Age,* April 13, 1992, p. 3ff.; Sunil Gupta, "Impact of Sales Promotions on When, What, and How Much to Buy," *Journal of Marketing Research,* November 1988, pp. 342–55; John A. Quelch, "It's Time to Make Trade Promotion More Productive," *Harvard Business Review,* May–June 1983, pp. 130–36.

20. "IBM Is Offering Workers Prizes to Hawk OS/2," *The Wall Street Journal,* March 27, 1992, p. B1ff.; "3M Distributors Go for the Gold," *Business Marketing,* May 1991, p. 49; "Chain Finds Incentives a Hard Sell," *The Wall Street Journal,* July 5, 1990, p. B1ff.; "Rewards for Good Work," *USA Today,* April 8, 1988, p. B1; Joanne Y. Cleaver, "Employee Incentives Rising to Top of Industry," *Advertising Age,* May 5, 1986, p. S1ff.

21. Donald R. Glover, "Distributor Attitudes toward Manufacturer-Sponsored Promotions," *Industrial Marketing Management* 20, no. 3 (1991), pp. 241–50; Jean J. Boddewyn and Monica Leardi, "Sales Promotions: Practice, Regulation and Self-Regulation Around the World," *International Journal of Advertising* 8, no. 4 (1989), pp. 363–74; Thomas L. Powers, "Should You Increase Sales Promotion or Add Salespeople?" *Industrial Marketing Management* 18, no. 4 (1989), pp. 259–64; "Promotion 'Carnival' Gets Serious," *Advertising Age,* May 2, 1988, p. S1ff.

Chapter 16

1. John Southerst, "Secrets of Sales Superstars," *Canadian Business,* December 1992, pp. 58–62.

2. Philip R. Cateora, *International Marketing* (Homewood, Ill.: Richard D. Irwin, 1990), p. 113; Carl R. Ruthstrom and Ken Matejka, "The Meanings of 'YES' in the Far East," *Industrial Marketing Management,* August 1990, pp. 191–92; John S. Hill and Richard R. Still, "Organizing the Overseas Sales Force—How Multinationals Do It," *Journal of Personal Selling and Sales Management,* Spring 1990, pp. 57–66; Lennie Copeland and Lewis Griggs, *Going International* (New York: Random House, 1985), pp. 111–12; Phyllis A. Harrison, *Behaving Brazilian* (Rowley, MA: Newbury House Publishers, 1983), pp. 23–24.

3. Tom Richman, "Seducing the Customer: Dale Ballard's Perfect Selling Machine," *Inc.,* April 1988, pp. 96–104; Ballard Medical Products, 1987 Annual Report.

4. Thomas R. Wotruba, "The Evolution of Personal Selling," *Journal of Personal Selling and Sales Management,* Summer 1991, pp. 1–12; "Sizing Up Your Sales Force," *Business Marketing,* May 1990; Douglas M. Lambert, Howard Marmorstein, and Arun Sharma, "Industrial Salespeople as a Source of Market Information," *Industrial Marketing Management,* May 1990, pp. 141–48; Michael J. Morden, "The Salesperson: Clerk, Con Man or Professional?" *Business and Professional Ethics Journal* 8, no. 1 (1989), pp. 3–24; George J. Avlonitis, Kevin A. Boyle, and Athanasios G. Kouremenos, "Matching the Salesmen to the Selling Job," *Industrial Marketing Management,* February 1986, pp. 45–54; Kenneth R. Evans and John L. Schlacter, "The Role of Sales Managers and Salespeople in a Marketing Information System," *Journal of Personal Selling and Sales Management,* November 1985, pp. 49–58; "Reach Out and Sell Something," *Fortune,* November 26, 1984, p. 127ff.; James H. Fouss and Elaine Solomon, "Salespeople as Researchers: Help or Hazard?" *Journal of Marketing,* Summer 1980, pp. 36–39; P. Ronald Stephenson, William L. Cron, and Gary L. Frazier, "Delegating Pricing Authority to the Sales Force: The Effects on Sales and Profit Performance," *Journal of Marketing,* Spring 1979, pp. 21–24.

5. "Truck-Driving 'Sales Force' Hauls in Extra Customers," *Marketing News,* May 8, 1989, p. 2.

6. S. Joe Puri and Pradeep Korgaonkar, "Couple the Buying and Selling Teams," *Industrial Marketing Management* 20, no. 4 (1991), pp. 311–18; "P&G Rolls out Retailer Sales Teams," *Advertising Age,* May 21, 1990, p. 18; Frank C. Cespedes, Stephen X. Doyle, and Robert J. Freedman, "Teamwork for Today's Selling," *Harvard Business Review,* March–April 1989, pp. 44–59.

7. John Barrett, "Why Major Account Selling Works," *Industrial Marketing Management,* February 1986, pp. 63–74; Jerome A. Colletti and Gary S. Tubridy, "Effective Major Account Sales Management," *Journal of Personal Selling and Sales Management,* August 1987, pp. 1–10.

8. "Telemarketers Take Root in the Country," *The Wall Street Journal,* February 2, 1989, p. B1.

9. "What Flexible Workers Can Do," *Fortune,* February 13, 1989, pp. 62–64; "Apparel Makers Play Bigger Part on Sales Floor," *The Wall Street Journal,* March 2, 1988, p. 31; David W. Cravens and Raymond W. LaForge, "Salesforce Deployment Analysis," *Industrial Marketing Management,* July 1983, pp. 179–92; Michael S. Herschel, "Effective Sales Territory Development," *Journal of Marketing,* April 1977, pp. 39–43.

10. "Systematizing Salesperson Selection," *Sales and Marketing Management,* February 1992, pp. 65–68; "The Fear Factor: Why Traditional Sales Training Doesn't Always Work," *Sales and Marketing Management,* February 1992, pp. 60–64; Robert C. Erffmeyer, K. Randall Russ, and Joseph F. Hair, Jr., "Needs Assessment and Evaluation in Sales-Training Programs," *Journal of Personal Selling and Sales Management,* Winter 1991, pp. 17–30; Warren S. Martin and Ben H. Collins, "Sales Technology Applications: Interactive Video Technology in Sales Training: A Case Study," *Journal of Personal Selling and Sales Management,* Summer 1991, pp. 61–66; Jeffrey K. Sager, "Recruiting and Retaining Committed Salespeople," *Industrial Marketing Management* 20, no. 2 (1991), pp. 99–104; "The New Deal in Cars," *Adweek's Marketing Week,* August 13, 1990, pp. 18–20; "Two Days in Boot Camp—Learning to Love Lexus," *Business Week,* September 4, 1989; Earl D. Honeycutt and Thomas H. Stevenson, "Evaluating Sales Training Programs," *Industrial Marketing Management* 18, no. 3 (1989), pp. 215–22; Donald B. Guest and Havva J. Meric, "The Fortune 500 Companies Selection Criteria for Promotion to First Level Sales Management: An Empirical Study," *Journal of Personal Selling and Sales Management,* Fall 1989, pp. 47–58; Thomas R. Wotruba, Edwin K. Simpson, and Jennifer L. Reed-Draznick, "The Recruiting Interview as Perceived by College Student Applicants for Sales Positions," *Journal of Personal Selling and Sales Management,* Fall 1989, pp. 13–24; Richard Nelson, "Maybe It's Time to Take Another Look at Tests as a Sales Selection Tool?" *Journal of Personal Selling and Sales Management,* August 1987, pp. 33–38; Thomas W. Leigh, "Cognitive Selling Scripts and Sales Training," *Journal of Personal Selling and Sales Management,* August 1987, pp. 49–56; Barry J. B. Robinson, "Role Playing as a Sales Training Tool," *Harvard Business Review,* May–June 1987, pp. 34–37; Robert H. Collins, "Sales Training: A Microcomputer-Based Approach," *Journal of Personal Selling and Sales Management,* May 1986, p. 71; Wesley J. Johnston and Martha Cooper, "Analyzing the Industrial Salesforce Selection Process," *Industrial Marketing Management,* April 1981, pp. 139–47.

11. "Salespeople on Road Use Laptops to Keep in Touch," *The Wall Street Journal,* April 25, 1991, p. B1; "If Only Willy Loman Had Used a Laptop," *Business Week,* October 12, 1987, p. 137.

12. Bradley S. O'Hara, James S. Boles, and Mark W. Johnston, "The Influence of Personal Variables on Salesperson Selling Orientation," *Journal of Personal Selling and Sales Management,* Winter 1991, pp. 61–68; "Fire Up Your Sales Force," *Business Marketing,* July 1990, pp. 52–55; Richard F. Beltramini and Kenneth R. Evans, "Salesperson Motivation to Perform and Job Satisfaction: A Sales Contest Participant Perspective," *Journal of Personal Selling and Sales Management,* August 1988, pp. 35–42; William L. Cron, Alan J. Dubinsky, and Ronald E. Michaels, "The Influence of Career Stages on Components of Salesperson Motivation," *Journal of Marketing,* January 1988, pp. 78–92.

13. David J. Good and Robert W. Stone, "How Sales Quotas Are Developed," *Industrial Marketing Management* 20, no. 1 (1991), pp. 51–56; James W. Gentry, John C. Mowen, and Lori Tasaki, "Salesperson Evaluation: A Systematic Structure for Reducing Judgmental Biases," *Journal of Personal Selling and Sales Management,* Spring 1991, pp. 27–38; William A. Weeks and Lynn R. Kahle, "Salespeople's Time Use and Performance," *Journal of Personal Selling and Sales Management,* Winter 1990, pp. 29–38; Daniel A. Sauers, James B. Hunt, and Ken Bass, "Behavioral Self-Management as a Supplement to External Sales Force Controls," *Journal of Personal Selling and Sales Management,* Summer 1990, pp. 17–28; "Manage Your Sales Force," *Inc.,* January 1990, pp. 120–22; Jan P. Muczyk and Myron Gable, "Managing Sales Performance through a Comprehensive Performance Appraisal System," *Journal of Personal Selling and Sales Management,* May 1987, pp. 41–52; "High-Tech Sales: Now You See Them, Now You Don't?" *Business Week,* November 18, 1985, pp. 106–7; Douglas N. Behrman and William D. Perreault, Jr., "A Role Stress Model of the Performance and Satisfaction of Industrial Salespersons," *Journal of Marketing,* Fall 1984, pp. 9–21; J. S. Schiff, "Evaluate the Sales Force as a Business," *Industrial Marketing Management,* April 1983, pp. 131–38; Douglas N. Behrman and William D. Perreault, Jr., "Measuring the Performance of Industrial Salespersons," *Journal of Business Research,* September 1982, pp. 350–70.

14. "Chief Executives Are Increasingly Chief Salesmen," *The Wall Street Journal,* August 6, 1991, p. B1ff.; John E. Swan and Richard L. Oliver, "An Applied Analysis of Buyer Equity Perceptions and Satisfaction with Automobile Salespeople," *Journal of Personal Selling and Sales Management,* Spring 1991, pp. 15–26; Joe F. Alexander, Patrick L. Schul, and Emin Babakus, "Analyzing Interpersonal Communications in Industrial Marketing Negotiations," *Journal of the Academy of Marketing Science,* Spring 1991, pp. 129–40.

15. William C. Moncrief et al., "Examining the Roles of Telemarketing in Selling Strategy," *Journal of Personal Selling and Sales Manage-*
ment, Fall 1989, pp. 1–12; J. David Lichtenthal, Saameer Sikri, and Karl Folk, "Teleprospecting: An Approach for Qualifying Accounts," *Industrial Marketing Management,* February 1989, pp. 11–18; Judith J. Marshall and Harrie Vredenburg, "Successfully Using Telemarketing in Industrial Sales," *Industrial Marketing Management,* February 1988, pp. 15–22; Eugene M. Johnson and William J. Meiners, "Selling & Sales Management in Action: Telemarketing—Trends, Issues, and Opportunities," *Journal of Personal Selling and Sales Management,* November 1987, pp. 65–68; Herbert E. Brown and Roger W. Brucker, "Telephone Qualifications of Sales Leads," *Industrial Marketing Management,* August 1987, pp. 185–90.

16. "The New Wave of Sales Automation," *Business Marketing,* June 1991, pp. 12–16; L. Brent Manssen, "Using PCs to Automate and Innovate Marketing Activities," *Industrial Marketing Management,* August 1990, pp. 209–14; Doris C. Van Doren and Thomas A. Stickney, "How to Develop a Database for Sales Leads," *Industrial Marketing Management,* August 1990, pp. 201–8; Michael H. Morris, Alvin C. Burns, and Ramon A. Avila, "Computer Awareness and Usage by Industrial Marketers," *Industrial Marketing Management,* August 1989, pp. 223–32; Al Wedell and Dale Hempeck, "Sales Force Automation: Here and Now," *Journal of Personal Selling and Sales Management,* August 1987, pp. 11–16; Robert H. Collins, "Microcomputer Applications in Selling and Sales Management: Portable Computers—Applications to Increase Salesforce Productivity," *Journal of Personal Selling and Sales Management,* November 1984, p. 75ff.

17. For more on sales presentation approaches, see C. A. Pederson, M. D. Wright, and B. A. Weitz, *Selling: Principles and Methods* (Homewood, Ill.: Richard D. Irwin, 1986), pp. 224–356; Morgan P. Miles, Danny R. Arnold, and Henry W. Nash, "Adaptive Communication: The Adaption of the Seller's Interpersonal Style to the Stage of the Dyad's Relationship and the Buyer's Communication Style," *Journal of Personal Selling and Sales Management,* Winter 1990, pp. 21–28; "Presentations that Spell Pizzazz," *Business Marketing,* February 1989, pp. 86–88; Marvin A. Jolson, "Canned Adaptiveness: A New Direction for Modern Salesmanship," *Business Horizons,* January–February 1989, pp. 7–12.

18. "Did Sears Take Other Customers for a Ride?" *Business Week,* August 3, 1992, pp. 24–25; "An Open Letter to Sears Customers," *USA Today,* June 25, 1992, p. 8A; Joseph A. Bellizzi and D. Wayne Norvell, "Personal Characteristics and Salesperson's Justifications as Moderators of Supervisory Discipline in Cases Involving Unethical Salesforce Behavior," *Journal of the Academy of Marketing Science,* Winter 1991, pp. 11–16; Alan J. Dubinsky, Marvin A. Jolson, Masaaki Kotabe, and Chae Un Lim, "A Cross-National Investigation of Industrial Salespeople's Ethical Perceptions," *Journal of International Business Studies,* Winter 1991, pp. 651–70; K. Douglas Hoffman, Vince Howe, and Donald W. Hardigree, "Ethical Dilemmas Faced in the Selling of Complex Services: Significant Others and Competitive Pressures," *Journal of Personal Selling and Sales Management,* Fall 1991, pp. 13–26; Anusorn Singhapakdi and Scott J. Vitell, "Analyzing the Ethical Decision Making of Sales Professionals," *Journal of Personal Selling and Sales Management,* Fall 1991, pp. 1–12; Rosemary R. Lagace, Robert Dahlstrom, and Jule B. Gassenheimer, "The Relevance of Ethical Salesperson Behavior on Relationship Quality: The Pharmaceutical Industry," *Journal of Personal Selling and Sales Management,* Fall 1991, pp. 39–48; Joseph A. Bellizzi and Robert E. Hite, "Supervising Unethical Salesforce Behavior," *Journal of Marketing,* April 1989, pp. 36–47.

Chapter 17

1. Colin Languedoc "GM Tries to Keep Them for Life," *The Financial Times of Canada,* December 4, 1991, p. B4.

2. Philip R. Cateora, *International Marketing* (Homewood, IL: Richard D. Irwin, 1990); Subhash C. Jain, *International Marketing Management* (Boston: PWS-Kent Publishing, 1990); Lee D. Dahringer and Hans Muhlbacher, *International Marketing: A Global Perspective* (Reading, MA.: Addison-Wesley Publishing, 1991); Courtland L. Bovee and William F. Arens, *Contemporary Advertising* (Homewood, IL: Richard D. Irwin, 1992), pp. 670–97.

3. For some examples of comparative advertising, see "Comparative TV Ad Reviews Criticized," *The Wall Street Journal,* October 23, 1990, p. B6; "Ford Accuses Chevy of Telling Whoppers in Pickup Truck Ads," *The Wall Street Journal,* October 17, 1990, p. B10. See also "Chemical Firms Press Campaigns to Dispel Their 'Bad Guy' Image," *The Wall Street Journal,* September 20, 1988, p. 1ff.; "Spiffing up the Corporate Image," *Fortune,* July 21, 1986, pp. 68–72; Lewis C. Winters, "The Effect of Brand Advertising on Company Image: Implications for Corporate Advertising," *Journal of Advertising Research,* April–May 1986, p. 54ff.

4. "A Comeback May Be Ahead for Brand X," *Business Week,* December 4, 1989, p. 35; "New Law Adds Risk to Comparative Ads," *The Wall Street Journal,* June 1, 1989, p. B6; Steven A. Meyerowitz, "The Developing Law of Comparative Advertising," *Business Marketing,* August 1985, pp. 81–86.

5. John K. Ross III, Larry T. Patterson, and Mary Ann Stutts, "Consumer Perceptions of Organizations that Use Cause-Related Marketing," *Journal of the Academy of Marketing Science,* Winter 1992, pp. 93–98; "Conscience Raising," *Advertising Age,* August 26, 1991, p. 19; "Whales, Human Rights, Rain Forests—and the Heady Smell of Profits," *Business Week,* July 15, 1991, pp. 114–15; "Charity Doesn't Begin at Home Anymore," *Business Week,* February 25, 1991, p. 91; "More Charities Reach Out for Corporate Sponsorship," *The Wall Street Journal,* October 1, 1990, p. B1ff.; "Ads that Work Against the Market," *Insight,* November 27, 1989, pp. 40–41.

6. For more on co-op ads, see "Hard Times Mean Growth for Co-op Ads," *Advertising Age,* November 12, 1990, p. 24; "Co-op Ads Attempt to Look More Like Brand-Name Commercials," *The Wall Street Journal,* July 21, 1989, p. B7; "Co-op: A Coup for Greater Profits," *Marketing Communications,* September 1985, pp. 66–73; "Ad Agencies Press Franchisees to Join National Campaigns," *The Wall Street Journal,* January 17, 1985, p. 29. For more on joint promotions, see "Joint Promotions Spawn Data Swap," *Advertising Age,* October 7, 1991, p. 44; "H&R Block, Excedrin Discover Joint Promotions Can Be Painless," *The Wall Street Journal,* February 28, 1991, p. B3; "Marketers Team in Time of Trouble," *Advertising Age,* February 18, 1991, p. 36.

7. "How Bad a Year for Ads Was '91? Almost the Worst," *Advertising Age,* May 4, 1992, p. 51ff.; *Standard Rate and Data,* April 1992; "What's Right, What's Wrong with Each Medium," *Business Marketing,* April 1990, pp. 40–47; Richard W. Pollay, "The Subsiding Sizzle: A Descriptive History of Print Advertising, 1900–1980," *Journal of Marketing,* Summer 1985, pp. 24–37; Murphy A. Sewall and Dan Sarel, "Characteristics of Radio Commercials and Their Recall Effectiveness," *Journal of Marketing,* January 1986, pp. 52–60; "Special Report: Outdoor Marketing," *Advertising Age,* October 9, 1989, p. 1ff.; "Confused Advertisers Bemoan Proliferation of Yellow Pages," *The Wall Street Journal,* February 27, 1986, p. 23.

8. "No Sexy Sales Ads, Please—We're Brits and Swedes," *Fortune,* October 21, 1991, p. 13; "It's Hot! It's Sexy! It's Drop-Dead Calvin Klein," *Advertising Age,* September 23, 1991, p. 46; "Why Jockey Switched Its Ads from TV to Print," *Business Week,* July 26, 1976, pp. 140–42.

9. "Weighing the Worth of the Super Bowl," *Adweek,* January 14, 1991, p. 16; "Cost of TV Sports Commercials Prompts Cutbacks by Advertisers," *The Wall Street Journal,* January 15, 1985, p. 37; "Study of Olympics Ads Casts Doubts on Value of Campaigns," *The Wall Street Journal,* December 6, 1984, p. 33.

10. "Keep Both Advertiser and the Reader Happy," *Marketing,* July 22, 1974, p. 22.

11. "Ads Head for Bathroom," *Advertising Age,* May 18, 1992, p. 24; "Product Placement Can Be Free Lunch," *The Wall Street Journal,* November 25, 1991, p. B6; "Consumers Seek Escape from Captive-Ad Gimmicks," *The Wall Street Journal,* September 13, 1991, p. B1ff.; "Turner Aims to Line Up Captive Audience," *The Wall Street Journal,* June 21, 1991, p. B1ff.; "Where Should Advertising Be?" *Adweek's Marketing Week,* May 6, 1991, pp. 26–27; "TV Takes on Tabloids at Checkout Line," *American Demographics,* April 1991, p. 9; "In-Store Ads Are Getting Harder to Ignore," *The Wall Street Journal,* October 16, 1990, p. B6; "Turning PCs into Salesmen," *Newsweek,*

March 12, 1990, p. 69; "Video Renters Watch the Ads, Zapping Conventional Wisdom," *The Wall Street Journal,* April 28, 1989, p. B1.

12. How to Spend $1 Million a Minute," *Business Week,* February 3, 1992, p. 34; "An Expensive 30 Seconds," *USA Today,* October 3, 1991, p. 1D; "Prime-Time Rates Take A Tumble," *Advertising Age,* September 16, 1991, p. 6; Darrel D. Muehling and Carl S. Bozman, "An Examination of Factors Influencing Effectiveness of 15-Second Advertisements," *International Journal of Advertising* 9, no. 4 (1990), pp. 331–44.

13. "Now, They're Selling BMWs Door-to-Door—Almost," *Business Week,* May 14, 1990, p. 65; Keith Fletcher, Colin Wheeler, and Julia Wright, "Database Marketing: a Channel, a Medium or a Strategic Approach?" *International Journal of Advertising* 10, no. 2 (1991), pp. 117–28; "Devising Mailing Lists for Every Marketer," *The Wall Street Journal,* May 7, 1991, p. B1; "Warner Tries Target Marketing to Sell Film Lacking Typical Box-Office Appeal," *The Wall Street Journal,* October 3, 1990, p. B1ff.; "Direct Marketing Agency Report," *Advertising Age,* May 21, 1990, pp. S1–10; "Direct Marketing: A Modern Marketing Solution," *Directions* (New York: Direct Marketing Association, 1990); "Special Report: Direct Marketing," *Advertising Age,* September 25, 1990, pp. S1–16; "Breakthrough Direct Marketing," *Business Marketing,* August 1990, pp. 20–29; Robert L. Sherman, *Mailing Lists, Information and Privacy* (New York: Prepared for DMA, June 1989); Lindsay Meredith, "Developing and Using a Data Base Marketing System," *Industrial Marketing Management* 18, no. 4 (1989), pp. 245–58; Gordon Storholm and Hershey Friedman, "Perceived Common Myths and Unethical Practices among Direct Marketing Professionals," *Journal of Business Ethics,* December 1989, pp. 975–80; Steven Miller, "Mine the Direct Marketing Riches in Your Database," *The Journal of Business Strategy,* November–December 1989, pp. 33–36; Frank K. Sonnenberg, "Marketing: Direct Mail–The Right Audience and the Right Message," *The Journal of Business Strategy,* January–February 1989, pp. 60–68; "Special Report: Direct Marketing," *Advertising Age,* January 18, 1988, pp. S1–20; Roger Craver, "Direct Marketing in the Political Process," *Fundraising Management,* October 1987; Rose Harper, *Mailing List Strategies* (New York: McGraw-Hill, 1986); Bob Stone and John Wyman, *Successful Telemarketing* (Lincolnshire, IL: NTC Books, 1986); Pierre Passavant, "Direct Marketing Strategy," *The Direct Marketing Handbook,* ed. Edward L. Nash (New York: McGraw-Hill, 1984). For more on the privacy issue, see "As Phone Technology Swiftly Advances, Fears Grow They'll Have Your Number," *The Wall Street Journal,* December 13, 1991, p. B1ff.; "Firms Peddle Information from Driver's Licenses," *The Wall Street Journal,* November 25, 1991, p. B1; "Equifax to Stop Selling Its Data to Junk-Mailers," *The Wall Street Journal,* August 9, 1991, p. B1ff.; "How Did They Get My Name?" *Newsweek,* June 3, 1991, pp. 40–42; "Amid Privacy Furor, Lotus Kills a Disk," *Adweek's Marketing Week,* January 28, 1991, p. 9.

14. "Benetton Brouhaha," *Advertising Age,* February 17, 1992, p. 62; "Mixing Politics and Separates," *Adweek,* February 17, 1992, p. 30; "Debate Brews over Selling Beer with Sex," *USA Today,* November 15, 1991, pp. 1B–2B; "Controversial Adman Bares His Concept," *USA Today,* July 25, 1991, p. 8B; Prema Nakra, "Zapping Nonsense: Should Television Media Planners Lose Sleep Over It?" *International Journal of Advertising* 10, no. 3 (1991), pp. 217–22; Gary L. Clark, Peter F. Kaminski, and Gene Brown, "The Readability of Advertisements and Articles in Trade Journals," *Industrial Marketing Management,* August 1990, pp. 251–60; "Advertisers See Big Gains in Odd Layouts: Page Position Can Make Ads More Prominent," *The Wall Street Journal,* June 29, 1988, p. 25; Joel Saegert, "Why Marketing Should Quit Giving Subliminal Advertising the Benefit of the Doubt," *Psychology and Marketing,* Summer 1987, pp. 107–20; "And Now, A Wittier Word from Our Sponsors," *Business Week,* March 24, 1986, pp. 90–94.

15. Theodore Levitt, "The Globalization of Markets," *Harvard Business Review,* May–June 1983, pp. 92–102. See also Kamran Kashani, "Beware the Pitfalls of Global Marketing," *Harvard Business Review,* September–October 1989, pp. 91–98; Donald R. Glover, Steven W. Hartley, and Charles H. Patti, "How Advertising Message Strategies Are Set," *Industrial Marketing Management* 18, no. 1 (1989), pp. 19–26.

16. "Special Issue: Agency Report," *Advertising Age,* April 13, 1992, pp. S1–44; "Special Issue: Agency Report Card," *Adweek,* March 23, 1992; "International: World Brands," *Advertising Age,* September 2, 1991, pp. 25–36.

17. "Blame-the-Messenger Mentality Leaves Scars on Madison Avenue," *The Wall Street Journal,* November 20, 1991, p. B4; Brian Jacobs, "Trends in Media Buying and Selling in Europe and the Effect on the Advertising Agency Business," *International Journal of Advertising* 10, no. 4 (1991), pp. 283–92; "Feeling a Little Jumpy," *Time,* July 8, 1991, pp. 42–43; "More Agencies Seek Payment in Advance," *The Wall Street Journal,* May 6, 1991, p. B6; "Big Agency, Small Agency: Which One Is Right for Your Business?" *Business Marketing,* May 1991, pp. 13–15; "DDB Needham 'Results' Plan Draws Yawns," *Advertising Age,* April 1, 1991, p. 3ff.; Ali Kanso, "The Use of Advertising Agencies for Foreign Markets: Decentralized Decisions and Localized Approaches?" *International Journal of Advertising* 10, no. 2 (1991), pp. 129–36; Richard Beltramini and Dennis A. Pitta, "Underlying Dimensions and Communications Strategies of the Advertising Agency-Client Relationship," *International Journal of Advertising* 10, no. 2 (1991), pp. 151–60; "Pursuing Results in the Age of Accountability," *Adweek's Marketing Week,* November 19, 1990, pp. 20–22; "As Ad Research Gains Followers, Agencies Point Out Its Failures," *The Wall Street Journal,* April 5, 1989, p. B11; "Carnation Links Pay, Research," *Advertising Age,* March 6, 1989, p. 1ff.; "More Companies Offer Their Ad Agencies Bonus Plans that Reward Superior Work," *The Wall Street Journal,* July 26, 1988, p. 37; "A Word from the Sponsor: Get Results—or Else," *Business Week,* July 4, 1988, p. 66; Michael G. Harvey and J. Paul Rupert, "Selecting an Industrial Advertising Agency," *Industrial Marketing Management,* May 1988, pp. 119–28; Daniel B. Wackman, Charles T. Salmon, and Caryn C. Salmon, "Developing an Advertising Agency-Client Relationship," *Journal of Advertising Research,* December 1986–January 1987, pp. 21–28.

18. Dahringer and Muhlbacher, *International Marketing: A Global Perspective,* p. 483; *International Werburg,* December 1, 1986, p. 9.

19. "Behind the Scenes at an American Express Commercial," *Business Week,* May 20, 1985, pp. 84–88.

20. "Ads Aimed at Older Americans May Be Too Old for Audience," *The Wall Street Journal,* December 31, 1991, p. B4; "Research Tactic Misses the Big Question: Why?" *The Wall Street Journal,* November 4, 1991, p. B1ff.; "Ads on TV: Out of Sight, Out of Mind?" *The Wall Street Journal,* May 14, 1991, p. B1ff.; "Magazines Helping Advertisers Measure Response to Their Ads," *The Wall Street Journal,* January 16, 1991, p. B5; "TvB Rebuts Prof: Adds Its Voice to Defense of Ads," *Advertising Age,* May 1, 1989, p. 26; "Television Ads Ring Up No Sale in Study," *The Wall Street Journal,* February 15, 1989, p. B6; George M. Zinkhan, "Rating Industrial Advertisements," *Industrial Marketing Management,* February 1984, pp. 43–48; Lawrence C. Soley, "Copy Length and Industrial Advertising Readership," *Industrial Marketing Management,* August 1986, pp. 245–52; David W. Stewart, "Measures, Methods, and Models in Advertising Research," *Journal of Advertising Research,* June–July 1989, p. 54ff.

21. Statistics Canada, *Advertising Expenditures in Canada,* 1965, Cat. 63-216, table 19.

22. *Handbook of Canadian Consumer Markets, 1982,* 2nd ed. (Ottawa: The Conference Board of Canada, February 1982), p. 220. For more detailed information on aggregate expenditures by industry, see Peter Zarry, "Advertising and Marketing Communications in Canada," in *Canadian Marketing; Problems and Prospects,* ed. Donald N. Thompson and David S. R. Leighton (Toronto: Wiley Publishers of Canada, 1973), pp. 230–34. Though the figures given are dated, the relative importance of the industries Zarry mentions has not changed appreciably.

23. Estimate provided by the Canadian Advertising Advisory Board.

24. "Pepsi Challenges Japanese Taboo as It Ribs Coke," *The Wall Street Journal,* March 6, 1991, p. B1ff. For additional examples, see Courtland L. Bovee and William R. Arens, *Contemporary Advertising,* pp. 694–96; Subhash C. Jain, *International Marketing Management,* pp. 559–63; Philip R. Cateora, *International Marketing,* pp. 492–93;

Dahringer and Muhlbacher, *International Marketing: A Global Perspective,* p. 479; Albert Schofield, "International Differences in Advertising Practices: Britain Compared with Other Countries," *International Journal of Advertising* 10, no. 4 (1991), pp. 299–308; Philip Circus, "Alcohol Advertising—The Rules," *International Journal of Advertising* 8, no. 2 (1989), pp. 159–66; Marc G. Weinberger and Harlan E. Spotts, "A Situational View of Information Content in TV Advertising in the US and UK," *Journal of Marketing,* January 1989, pp. 89–94; Jean Boddewyn, "The One and Many Worlds of Advertising: Regulatory Obstacles and Opportunities," *International Journal of Advertising* 7, no. 1 (1988); "Advertisers Find the Climate Less Hostile Outside the US," *The Wall Street Journal,* December 10, 1987, p. 29; Rein Riijkens and Gordon E. Miracle, *European Regulation of Advertising* (New York: Elsevier Science Publishing, 1986); "EEC Media Experts Push for New Limits on Pan-Europe Ads," *Advertising Age,* January 30, 1984, p. 52.

25. *Bill C-227: Proposals for a New Competition Policy for Canada* (Ottawa: Department of Consumer and Corporate Affairs, November 1973), p. 5. See also the complete listing of cases as of that date under the misleading advertising provisions of the Combines Act, found in Appendix C of that publication.

26. S. K. List, "The Right Place to Find Children," *American Demographics,* February 1992, pp. 44–47; "Pediatric Academy Prescribes Ban on Food Ads Aimed at Children," *The Wall Street Journal,* July 24, 1991, p. B8; "Is TV Ruining Our Children?" *Time,* October 15, 1990, pp. 75–76; "Kids' Advertisers Play Hide-and-Seek, Concealing Commercials in Every Cranny," *The Wall Street Journal,* April 30, 1990, p. B1ff.; "NAD Tackles Kids' 900-Number Ads," *Advertising Age,* February 20, 1989, p. 64; "Double Standard for Kids' TV Ads," *The Wall Street Journal,* June 10, 1988, p. 25; "Watchdogs Zealously Censor Advertising Targeted to Kids," *The Wall Street Journal,* September 5, 1985, p. 35; Priscilla A. LaBarbera, "The Diffusion of Trade Association Advertising Self-Regulation," *Journal of Marketing,* Winter 1983, pp. 58–67.

Chapter 18

1. Mark Evans, "Dollar Stores Buck Retail Downtrend," *The Financial Post,* July 30, 1992, p. 11.

2. "Car Makers Seek to Mask Price Increases," *The Wall Street Journal,* August 16, 1989, p. B1.

3. Alfred Rappaport, "Executive Incentives versus Corporate Growth," *Harvard Business Review,* July–August 1978, pp. 81–88.

4. Pricing "in the public interest" is often an issue in pricing government services; for an interesting example, see "Price Policy on Space Shuttle's Commercial Use Could Launch—or Ground—NASA's Rockets," *The Wall Street Journal,* March 21, 1985, p. 64.

5. "Computer Price Cuts Seem Likely Despite Efforts to Hold the Line," *The Wall Street Journal,* September 5, 1985, p. 25.

6. "Harvester Sells Many Trucks below Cost, Citing Need to Maintain Dealer Network," *The Wall Street Journal,* April 19, 1983, p. 8.

7. "Why the Price Wars Never End," *Fortune,* March 23, 1992, pp. 68–78; "Middle-Price Brands Come under Siege," *The Wall Street Journal,* April 2, 1990, p. B1ff.; "Avis, Sidestepping Price Wars, Focuses on the Drive Itself," *Adweek's Marketing Week,* February 12, 1990, p. 24; "Leave the Herd and Leap off the Old Price Treadmill," *Chicago Tribune,* November 11, 1985, Sec. 4, p. 21ff.

8. "Aluminum Firms Offer Wider Discounts but Price Cuts Stop at Some Distributors," *The Wall Street Journal,* November 16, 1984, p. 50.

9. Elliot B. Ross, "Making Money with Proactive Pricing," *Harvard Business Review,* November–December 1984, pp. 145–55; Thomas Nagle, "Pricing as Creative Marketing," *Business Horizons,* July–August 1983, pp. 14–19. See also Subhash C. Jain and Michael B. Laric, "A Framework for Strategic Industrial Pricing," *Industrial Marketing Management* 8 (1979), pp. 75–80; Mary Karr, "The Case of the Pricing Predicament," *Harvard Business Review,* March–April 1988, pp. 10–23; Saeed Samiee, "Pricing in Marketing

Strategies of US and Foreign-Based Companies," *Journal of Business Research,* February 1987, pp. 17–30; Gerard J. Tellis, "Beyond the Many Faces of Price: An Integration of Pricing Strategies," *Journal of Marketing,* October 1986, pp. 146–60.

10. "Ford Expands 'One-Price' Plan for Its Escorts," *The Wall Street Journal,* March 12, 1992, p. B1ff; "18-Month-Old Saturn Walking Tall," *USA Today,* February 24, 1992, p. 1B. For an interesting discussion of the many variations from a one-price system in retailing, see Stanley C. Hollander, "The 'One-Price' System—Fact or Fiction?" *Journal of Marketing Research,* February 1972, pp. 35–40. See also Michael J. Houston, "Minimum Markup Laws: An Empirical Assessment," *Journal of Retailing,* Winter 1981, pp. 98–113; "Flexible Pricing," *Business Week,* December 12, 1977, pp. 78–88; Michael H. Morris, "Separate Prices as a Marketing Tool," *Industrial Marketing Management,* May 1987, pp. 79–86.

11. "Squeezin' the Charmin," *Fortune,* January 16, 1989, pp. 11–12; "Grocers Join Winn-Dixie," *Advertising Age,* November 7, 1988, p. 3; "Grocery Chains Pressure Suppliers for Uniform Prices," *The Wall Street Journal,* October 21, 1988, p. B1; "Grocery Chain Dumps Major Package Goods," *Advertising Age,* October 10, 1988, p. 1ff.

12. "Breakthrough in Birth Control May Elude Poor," *The Wall Street Journal,* March 4, 1991, p. B1ff; "Burroughs Welcome Reaps Profits, Outrage from Its AIDS Drug," *The Wall Street Journal,* September 15, 1989, p. A1ff.

13. Alan Reynolds, "A Kind Word for 'Cream Skimming,'" *Harvard Business Review,* November–December 1974, pp. 113–20.

14. Stuart U. Rich, "Price Leadership in the Paper Industry," *Industrial Marketing Management,* April 1983, pp. 101–4; "OPEC Member Offers Discounts to Some amid Downward Pressure on Oil Prices," *The Wall Street Journal,* November 16, 1984, p. 4.

15. Exchange rates are from the July 17, 1992, issue of *The Wall Street Journal,* but they are available on a daily basis. David N. Hyman, *Economics,* 2nd edition (Homewood, Ill.: Richard D. Irwin, 1992), pp. 82–83; Timothy A. Luehrman, "Exchange Rate Changes and the Distribution of Industry Value," *Journal of International Business Studies,* Winter 1991, pp. 619–50.

16. "Fast-Food Chains Hope Diners Swallow New 'Value' Menu of Higher-Priced Items," *The Wall Street Journal,* March 13, 1992, p. B1ff.; "Value Marketing," *Business Week,* November 11, 1991, pp. 132–40; "Why Chic Is Now Cheaper," *Time,* November 11, 1991, pp. 68–70; "Ford Motor Ventures into 'Value' Pricing," *The Wall Street Journal,* September 18, 1991, p. B1; "Fashion Designers Snip Prices," *Fortune,* May 6, 1991, p. 9; "'Value Pricing' Is Hot as Shrewd Consumers Seek Low-Cost Quality," *The Wall Street Journal,* March 12, 1991, p. A1ff.; Louis J. De Rose, "Meet Today's Buying Influences with Value Selling," *Industrial Marketing Management* 20, no. 2 (1991), pp. 87–90; "A Buyer's Market Has Shoppers Demanding and Getting Discounts," *The Wall Street Journal,* February 8, 1991, p. A1ff.; "'Value' Strategy to Battle Recession," *Advertising Age,* January 7, 1991, p. 1ff.; "'Value' Brands Head for Shelves," *Adweek's Marketing Week,* October 29, 1990, p. 6.

17. For more on quantity discounts, see George S. Day and Adrian B. Ryans, "Using Price Discounts for a Competitive Advantage," *Industrial Marketing Management,* February 1988, pp. 1–14; James B. Wilcox et al., "Price Quantity Discounts: Some Implications for Buyers and Sellers," *Journal of Marketing,* July 1987, pp. 60–70. For more on frequent flier programs, see "Air Miles Program Takes Off," *Direct Marketing,* March 1992, pp. 40–43; "Forget the Green Stamps—Give Me a Ticket to Miami," *Business Week,* February 24, 1992, pp. 70–71; "Frequent Fliers Get New Perks from Airlines," *The Wall Street Journal,* January 5, 1990, p. B1. For more on other frequent buyer programs, see "Frequent Shopper Programs Ripen," *Advertising Age,* August 6, 1990, p. 21; "Clubs Reward Buyers at Bookstore Chains," *Insight,* March 26, 1990, p. 43; "Frequent-Stay Plans Are Best Checked Out," *The Wall Street Journal,* March 20, 1990, p. B1; "Frequent Reader Clubs: A New Book Battleground," *Adweek's Marketing Week,* March 12, 1990, p. 28; "Waldenbooks' Big-Buyer Lure May Mean War," *The Wall Street Journal,* February 27, 1990, p. B1ff. For more on cash discounts, see "Cash Discounts," *Electrical Wholesaling,* May 1989, pp. 90–96.

18. "P&G Plays Pied Piper on Pricing," *Advertising Age,* March 9, 1992, p. 6; "P&G Tries to Build Brand Loyalty with Lower Prices," *The Wall Street Journal,* November 7, 1991, p. B1; "Grocery Price Wars Squeeze Marketers," *The Wall Street Journal,* November 7, 1991, p. B1; "Addiction to Cost Cutting Feeds Slump," *USA Today,* June 5, 1991, pp. 1B–2B; "Store's Concept of 'Sale' Pricing Gets Court Test," *The Wall Street Journal,* May 15, 1990, p. B1ff.; "As Retailers' Sales Crop Up Everywhere, Regulators Wonder if the Price Is Right," *The Wall Street Journal,* February 13, 1990, p. B1ff.; "The 'Sale' Is Fading as a Retailing Tactic," *The Wall Street Journal,* March 1, 1989, p. B1ff.

19. "Getting Around Slotting Fees," *Food Business,* June 17, 1991, p. 12; "Slotting Fees May Get FTC OK," *Advertising Age,* June 18, 1990, p. 4; "P&G 'Teams' Serve Retailers' Needs: Move to Reduce Role of Slotting Fees," *Advertising Age,* August 14, 1989, p. 21; "Want Shelf Space at the Supermarket? Ante Up," *Business Week,* August 7, 1989, pp. 60–61; "Supermarkets Demand Food Firms' Payments Just to Get on the Shelf," *The Wall Street Journal,* November 1, 1988, p. A1ff.

20. For more on coupons, see "Coupon Scams Are Clipping Companies," *Business Week,* June 15, 1992, pp. 110–11; "Pious Town Finds Mighty Temptation in Coupon Clipping," *The Wall Street Journal,* February 21, 1992, p. A1ff.; "Recession Feeds the Coupon Habit," *The Wall Street Journal,* February 20, 1991, p. B1; "Redeeming Feature: Special Printing May Cut Coupon Counterfeits," *Advertising Age,* February 4, 1991, p. 35; "ActMedia Puts the Coupon on the Shelf," *Adweek's Marketing Week,* January 21, 1991, p. 8. For more on rebates, see "Rebate Program Rings Wright Bell," *Advertising Age,* May 21, 1990, p. 44; "Marketers Tighten Rules on Rebate Offers in Effort to Reduce Large Fraud Losses," *The Wall Street Journal,* March 18, 1987, p. 33.

21. "The FTC Redefines Price Fixing," *Business Week,* April 18, 1983, p. 37; "FTC Accuses 6 Title Insurers of Price Fixing," *The Wall Street Journal,* January 8, 1985, p. 8; "Price-Fixing Charges Rise in Paper Industry Despite Convictions," *The Wall Street Journal,* May 4, 1978, p. 2; "Plywood Makers Agree to Settle Antitrust Suit," *The Wall Street Journal,* December 5, 1982, p. 3. See also Mary Jane Sheffet and Debra L. Scammon, "Resale Price Maintenance: Is It Safe to Suggest Retail Prices?" *Journal of Marketing,* Fall 1985, pp. 82–91.

22. For discussion concerning European countries, see *Market Power and the Law* (Washington, D.C.: Organization for Economic Cooperation and Development Publication Center, 1970), p. 206.

23. For a complete summary of all court cases through late 1973 under the Combines Investigation Act, see Appendixes A and B of *Proposals for a New Competition Policy for Canada—First Stage Bill C-227* (Ottawa: Department of Consumer and Corporate Affairs, November 1973).

24. Bruce Mallen, "The Combines Investigation Act: Canada's Major Marketing Statute," in *Cases and Readings in Marketing,* ed. W. H. Kirpalani and R. H. Rotenberg (Toronto: Holt, Rinehart & Winston of Canada, 1974), pp. 169–70. The same source was used in trying to assess the actual impact and the barriers to enforcement of other presently existing Combines Act Trade Practices Provisions.

25. "Jewellery Appraisal Firms and Simpsons Found Guilty of Misleading Advertising," *Canadian Jeweller* 102, no. 9 (September 1981), pp. 7–8.

26. D. N. Thompson, "Competition Policy and Marketing Regulation," in *Canadian Marketing: Problems and Prospects,* D. N. Thompson and David S. R. Leighton (Toronto: Wiley Publishers of Canada, 1973), pp. 14–15; also D. N. Thompson, "Resale Price Maintenance and Refusal to Sell: Aspects of a Problem in Competition of Policy," *University of Toronto Law Journal* 21 (1971), pp. 82–86.

Chapter 19

1. Giles Gherson, "Now the Good News: Much Lower Retail Prices," *The Financial Times of Canada,* August 3/9, 1992, pp. 1, 4.

2. Marvin A. Jolson, "A Diagrammatic Model for Merchandising Calculations," *Journal of Retailing,* Summer 1975, pp. 3–9.

3. Mary L. Hatten, "Don't Get Caught with Your Prices Down: Pricing in Inflationary Times," *Business Horizons,* March 1982, pp. 23–28; "Why Detroit Can't Cut Prices," *Business Week,* March 1, 1982, p. 110; Douglas G. Brooks, "Cost Oriented Pricing: A Realistic Solution to a Complicated Problem," *Journal of Marketing,* April 1975, pp. 72–74.

4. William W. Alberts, "The Experience Curve Doctrine Reconsidered," *Journal of Marketing,* July 1989, pp. 36–49; George S. Day and David B. Montgomery, "Diagnosing the Experience Curve," *Journal of Marketing,* Spring 1983, pp. 44–58; Alan R. Beckenstein and H. Landis Gabel, "Experience Curve Pricing Strategy: The Next Target of Antitrust?" *Business Horizons,* September–October 1982, pp. 71–77.

5. G. Dean Kortge, "Inverted Breakeven Analysis for Profitable Marketing Decisions," *Industrial Marketing Management,* October 1984, pp. 219–24; Thomas L. Powers, "Breakeven Analysis with Semifixed Costs," *Industrial Marketing Management,* February 1987, pp. 35–42.

6. Approaches for estimating price-quantity relationships are reviewed in Kent B. Monroe, *Pricing: Making Profitable Decisions* (New York: McGraw-Hill, 1979). For a specific example, see Frank D. Jones, "A Survey Technique to Measure Demand under Various Pricing Strategies," *Journal of Marketing,* July 1975, pp. 75–77; or Gordon A. Wyner, Lois H. Benedetti, and Bart M. Trapp, "Measuring the Quantity and Mix of Product Demand," *Journal of Marketing,* Winter 1984, pp. 101–9. See also Michael H. Morris and Mary L. Joyce, "How Marketers Evaluate Price Sensitivity," *Industrial Marketing Management,* May 1988, pp. 169–76.

7. Benson P. Shapiro and Barbara P. Jackson, "Industrial Pricing to Meet Customer Needs," *Harvard Business Review,* November–December 1978, pp. 119–27; "The Race to the $10 Light Bulb," *Business Week,* May 19, 1980, p. 124; see also Michael H. Morris and Donald A. Fuller, "Pricing an Industrial Service," *Industrial Marketing Management,* May 1989, pp. 139–46.

8. Thomas T. Nagle, *The Strategy and Tactics of Pricing* (Englewood Cliffs, NJ: Prentice-Hall, 1987), pp. 249–55.

9. For an example applied to a high-price item, see "Sale of Mink Coats Strays a Fur Piece from the Expected," *The Wall Street Journal,* March 21, 1980, p. 30.

10. B. P. Shapiro, "The Psychology of Pricing," *Harvard Business Review,* July–August 1968, pp. 14–24; C. Davis Fogg and Kent H. Kohnken, "Price-Cost Planning," *Journal of Marketing,* April 1978, pp. 97–106.

11. Robert M. Schindler and Alan R. Wiman, "Effects of Odd Pricing on Price Recall," *Journal of Business Research,* November 1989, pp. 165–78; "Strategic Mix of Odd, Even Prices Can Lead to Increased Retail Profits," *Marketing News,* March 7, 1980, p. 24.

12. "Special Report: Marketing to the Affluent," *Advertising Age,* October 19, 1987, pp. S1–32; Peter C. Riesz, "Price versus Quality in the Marketplace," *Journal of Retailing,* Winter 1978, pp. 15–28; John J. Wheatly and John S. Y. Chiu, "The Effects of Price, Store Image, and Product and Respondent Characteristics on Perceptions of Quality," *Journal of Marketing Research,* May 1977, pp. 181–86; N. D. French, J. J. Williams, and W. A. Chance, "A Shopping Experiment on Price-Quality Relationships," *Journal of Retailing,* Fall 1972, pp. 3–16; J. Douglas McConnell, "Comment on 'A Major Price-Perceived Quality Study Reexamined,'" *Journal of Marketing Research,* May 1980, pp. 263–64; K. M. Monroe and S. Petroshius, "Buyers' Subjective Perceptions of Price: An Update of the Evidence," in *Perspectives in Consumer Behavior,* ed. T. Robertson and H. Kassarjian (Glenview, IL: Scott, Foresman, 1981), pp. 43–55; Valarie A. Zeithaml, "Consumer Perceptions of Price, Quality, and Value: A Means-End Model and Synthesis of Evidence," *Journal of Marketing,* July 1988, pp. 2–22.

13. Nagle, *The Strategy and Tactics of Pricing,* pp. 170–72.

14. Daniel T. Ostas, "Ethics of Contract Pricing," *Journal of Business Ethics,* February 1992, pp. 137–46; J. Steve Davis, "Ethical Problems in Competitive Bidding: The Paradyne Case," *Business and Professional Ethics Journal* 7, no. 2 (1988), pp. 3–26; Wayne J. Morse, "Probabilistic Bidding Models: A Synthesis," *Business Horizons,* April 1975, pp. 67–74; Stephen Paranka, "Competitive Bidding Strategy," *Business Horizons,* June 1971, pp. 39–43.

15. For references to additional readings in the pricing area, see Michael H. Morris and Roger J. Calantone, "Four Components of Effective Pricing," *Industrial Marketing Management,* November 1990, pp. 321–30; Valerie Kijewski and Eunsang Yoon, "Market-Based Pricing: Beyond Price-Performance Curves," *Industrial Marketing Management,* February 1990, pp. 11–20; Kent B. Monroe, D. Lund, and P. Choudhury, *Pricing Policies and Strategies: An Annotated Bibliography* (Chicago: American Marketing Association, 1983); "Pricing of Products Is Still an Art, Often Having Little Link to Costs," *The Wall Street Journal,* November 25, 1981, p. 29ff.

Chapter 20

1. "Smart Selling: How Companies Are Winning over Today's Tougher Customers," *Business Week,* August 3, 1992, pp. 46–52; " 'This Is Not a Fun Business to Be in Right Now,' " *Business Week,* July 6, 1992, pp. 68–69; "Dell Computer Battles Its Rivals with a Lean Machine," *The Wall Street Journal,* March 30, 1992, p. B4; "Breaking into European Markets by Breaking the Rules," *Business Week,* January 20, 1992, pp. 88–89; "Computer Superstores Muscle in," *USA Today,* July 8, 1991, pp. 1B–2B; "PC Slump? What PC Slump?" *Business Week,* July 1, 1991, pp. 66–67; "Whatever Happened to the Corner Computer Store?" *Business Week,* May 20, 1991, pp. 131–32ff.; "Mail-Order Computers Can Be Bargains, but Some Firms Don't Deliver on Claims," *The Wall Street Journal,* October 4, 1990, p. B1ff.; "A Golden Age for Entrepreneurs," *Fortune,* February 12, 1990, pp. 120–25; "Can Dell, CompuAdd Broaden Niches?" *The Wall Street Journal,* February 5, 1990, p. B1ff.

2. See most basic statistics textbooks under time series analysis.

3. Checking the accuracy of forecasts is a difficult subject. See "Don't Be Trapped by Past Success," *Nation's Business,* March 1992, pp. 52–54; David L. Kendall and Michael T. French, "Forecasting the Potential for New Industrial Products," *Industrial Marketing Management* 20, no. 3 (1991), pp. 177–84; John T. Mentzer and Roger Gomes, "Evaluating a Decision Support Forecasting System," *Industrial Marketing Management* 18, no. 4 (1989), pp. 313–24; James E. Cox, Jr., "Approaches for Improving Salespersons' Forecasts," *Industrial Marketing Management* 18, no. 4 (1989), pp. 307–12; Ronald D. Michman, "Why Forecast for the Long Term?" *The Journal of Business Strategy,* September–October 1989, pp. 36–41; F. William Barnett, "Four Steps to Forecast Total Market Demand," *Harvard Business Review,* July–August 1988, pp. 28–40; Anthony D. Cox and John D. Summers, "Heuristics and Biases in the Intuitive Projection of Retail Sales," *Journal of Marketing Research,* August 1987, pp. 290–97; Robert H. Collins and Rebecca J. Mauritson, "Microcomputer Applications: Artificial Intelligence in Sales Forecasting Applications," *Journal of Personal Selling and Sales Management,* May 1987, pp. 77–80; Arthur J. Adams, "Procedures for Revising Management Judgments Forecasts," *Journal of the Academy of Marketing Science,* Fall 1986, pp. 52–57; D. M. Georgoff and R. G. Murdick, "Manager's Guide to Forecasting," *Harvard Business Review,* January–February 1986, pp. 110–20.

4. "Monsanto Touts New Sugar Substitute as Sweetest Yet," *The Wall Street Journal,* March 29, 1991, p. B1; Monsanto, 1990 Annual Report, "NutraSweet Rivals Stirring," *Advertising Age,* June 26, 1989, p. 3ff.; "New Sweeteners Head for the Sugar Bowl," *The Wall Street Journal,* February 6, 1989, p. B1; "NutraSweet Sets Out for Fat-Substitute City," *Business Week,* February 15, 1988, pp. 100–103; "NutraSweet May Develop Its Own Simplesse Brands," *Advertising Age,* February 8, 1988, p. 4ff.; "Marketing NutraSweet in Leaner Times," *The Wall Street Journal,* May 7, 1987, p. 36.

5. John E. Smallwood, "The Product Life Cycle: A Key to Strategic Marketing Planning," *MSU Business Topics,* Winter 1973, pp. 29–35;

Richard F. Savach and Laurence A. Thompson, "Resource Allocation within the Product Life Cycle," *MSU Business Topics,* Autumn 1978, pp. 35–44; Peter F. Kaminski and David R. Rink, "PLC: The Missing Link between Physical Distribution and Marketing Planning," *International Journal of Physical Distribution and Materials Management* 14, no. 6 (1984), pp. 77–92.

6. Sam C. Okoroafo, "Modes of Entering Foreign Markets," *Industrial Marketing Management* 20, no. 4 (1991), pp. 341–46; Mike Van Horn, "Market-Entry Approaches for the Pacific Rim," *The Journal of Business Strategy,* March–April 1990, pp. 14–19; Refik Culpan, "Export Behavior of Firms: Relevance of Firm Size," *Journal of Business Research,* May 1989, pp. 207–18; Anthony C. Koh and Robert A. Robicheaux, "Variations in Export Performance Due to Differences in Export Marketing Strategy; Implications for Industrial Marketers," *Journal of Business Research,* November 1988, pp. 249–58; S. Tamer Cavusgil and Jacob Naor, "Firm and Management Characteristics as Discriminators of Export Marketing," *Journal of Business Research,* June 1987, pp. 221–36; Camille P. Schuster and Charles D. Bodkin, "Market Segmentation Practices of Exporting Companies," *Industrial Marketing Management,* May 1987, pp. 95–102; "A Top Japanese Firm in Electronics Finds US Market Difficult," *The Wall Street Journal,* March 25, 1985, p. 1ff. See also "Forest-Products Concerns Urge Using Wood for Latin Houses," *The Wall Street Journal* September 19, 1984, p. 35.

7. "For US Marketers, the Russian Front Is No Bowl of 'Vishnyas,'" *Adweek's Marketing Week,* March 5, 1990; "Learning the Exporting Ropes," *Business Marketing,* May 1989, pp. 80–85; "'Papa-Mama' Stores in Japan Wield Power to Hold Back Imports," *The Wall Street Journal,* November 14, 1988, p. A1ff.; "US Concerns Trying to Do Business in Japan Face Government, Market, Cultural Barriers," *The Wall Street Journal,* July 8, 1985, p. 16; F. H. Rolf Seringhaus, "Using Trade Missions for Export Market Entry," *Industrial Marketing Management,* November 1987, pp. 249–56.

8. John A. Quelch, "How to Build a Product Licensing Program," *Harvard Business Review,* May–June 1985, p. 186ff.

9. "The Steel Deal that Could Boost Big Blue in Brazil," *Business Week,* May 19, 1986, p. 66. See also Robert Porter Lynch, "Building Alliances to Penetrate European Markets," *The Journal of Business Strategy,* March–April 1990, pp. 4–9; D. Robert Webster, "International Joint Ventures with Pacific Rim Partners," *Business Horizons,* March–April 1989, pp. 65–71; Kenichi Ohmae, "The Global Logic of Strategic Alliances," *Harvard Business Review,* March–April 1989, pp. 143–54.

10. "Top US Companies Move into Russia," *Fortune,* July 31, 1989, pp. 165–71; "When US Joint Ventures with Japan Go Sour," *Business Week,* July 24, 1989, pp. 30–31; "More Competitors Turn to Cooperation: Joint Ventures Are Encouraged by Government," *The Wall Street Journal,* June 23, 1989, p. B1; "Your Rivals Can Be Your Allies," *Fortune,* March 27, 1989, pp. 66–76; "How a German Firm Joined with Soviets to Make Good Shoes," *The Wall Street Journal,* February 14, 1989, p. A1ff.; F. Kingston Berlew, "The Joint Venture— A Way into Foreign Markets," *Harvard Business Review,* July–August 1984, pp. 48–55; Robert B. Reich and Eric D. Mankin, "Joint Ventures with Japan Give Away Our Future," *Harvard Business Review,* March–April 1986, pp. 78–86.

11. "Young Managers Learn Global Skills," *The Wall Street Journal,* March 31, 1992, p. B1; "As Costs of Overseas Assignments Climb, Firms Select Expatriates More Carefully," *The Wall Street Journal,* January 9, 1992, p. B1ff.; "Companies in Europe Seeking Executives Who Can Cross Borders in a Single Bound," *The Wall Street Journal,* January 25, 1991, p. B1ff.; Christopher A. Bartlett, "MNCs: Get off the Reorganization Merry-Go-Round," *Harvard Business Review,* March–April 1983, pp. 138–46; James M. Hulbert, William K. Brant, and Raimar Richers, "Marketing Planning in the Multinational Subsidiary: Practices and Problems," *Journal of Marketing,* Summer 1980, pp. 7–16.

12. For further discussion on evaluating and selecting alternative plans, see Francis Buttle, "The Marketing Strategy Worksheet— A Practical Planning Tool," *Long Range Planning,* August 1985,

pp. 80–88; Douglas A. Schellinck, "Effect of Time on a Marketing Strategy," *Industrial Marketing Management,* April 1983, pp. 83–88; George S. Day and Liam Fahey, "Valuing Market Strategies," *Journal of Marketing,* July 1988, pp. 45–57.

13. C. L. Hung and Douglas West, "Advertising Budgeting Methods in Canada, the UK and the USA," *International Journal of Advertising* 10, no. 3 (1991), pp. 239–50; Pierre Filiatrault and Jean-Charles Chebat, "How Service Firms Set Their Marketing Budgets," *Industrial Marketing Management,* February 1990, pp. 63–68; James E. Lynch and Graham J. Hooley, "Industrial Advertising Budget Approaches in the UK," *Industrial Marketing Management* 18, no. 4 (1989), pp. 265–70; "Beat the Budgeting Blues," *Business Marketing,* July 1989, pp. 48–57; Vincent J. Blasko and Charles H. Patti, "The Advertising Budgeting Practices of Industrial Marketers," *Journal of Marketing,* Fall 1984, pp. 104–10; Neil C. Churchill, "Budget Choice: Planning vs. Control," *Harvard Business Review,* July–August 1984, pp. 150–65; Douglas J. Dalrymple and Hans B. Thorelli, "Sales Force Budgeting," *Business Horizons,* July–August 1984, pp. 31–36.

14. William Sandy, "Avoid the Breakdowns between Planning and Implementation," *The Journal of Business Strategy,* September– October 1991, pp. 30–33; Michael MacInnis and Louise A. Heslop, "Market Planning in a High-Tech Environment," *Industrial Marketing Management,* May 1990, pp. 107–16; Bay Arinze, "Market Planning with Computer Models: A Case Study in the Software Industry," *Industrial Marketing Management,* May 1990, pp. 117–30; "Marketing Software Review: Project Management Made Easy," *Business Marketing,* February 1989, pp. 20–27; Thomas V. Bonoma, "Making Your Marketing Strategy Work," *Harvard Business Review,* March–April 1984, pp. 68–76; Barbara J. Coe, "Key Differentiating Factors and Problems Associated with Implementation of Strategic Market Planning," in *1985 American Marketing Association Educators' Proceedings,* ed. R. F. Lusch et al. (Chicago: American Marketing Association, 1985), pp. 275–81.

15. The restaurant case is adapted from Marie Gaudard, Roland Coates, and Liz Freeman, "Accelerating Improvement," *Quality Progress,* October 1991, pp. 81–88. For more on quality management and control, see "Total Quality by Satellite," *Nation's Business,* March 1992, pp. 49–51; "Quality Control from Mars," *The Wall Street Journal,* January 27, 1992, p. A12; "Can American Steel Find Quality?" *Industry Week,* January 20, 1992, pp. 36–39; "The Quality Imperative," *Business Week,* (special issue) October 25, 1991; "Motorola's Baldrige Award-Winning Ways," *Business Marketing,* September 1991, pp. 14–15; "'Q' Tips," *CIO,* August 1991, pp. 26–31; "The Fabric of Quality," *CIO,* August 1991, pp. 34–41.

16. Harvey N. Shycon, "Improved Customer Service: Measuring the Payoff," *The Journal of Business Strategy,* January–February 1992, pp. 13–17; A. Lynn Daniel, "Overcome the Barriers to Superior Customer Service," *The Journal of Business Strategy,* January–February 1992, pp. 18–24; Leonard A. Schlesinger and James L. Heskett, "The Service-Driven Service Company," *Harvard Business Review,* September–October 1991, pp. 71–81; David A. Collier, "New Marketing Mix Stresses Service," *The Journal of Business Strategy,* March–April 1991, pp. 42–45; M. P. Singh, "Service as a Marketing Strategy: A Case Study at Reliance Electric," *Industrial Marketing Management,* August 1990, pp. 193–200; "For Computer Makers, Service Is the Soul of the New Machine," *Adweek's Marketing Week,* May 21, 1990, pp. 20–26; James S. Hensel, "Service Quality Improvement and Control: A Customer-Based Approach," *Journal of Business Research,* January 1990, pp. 43–54; William George, "Internal Marketing and Organizational Behavior: A Partnership in Developing Customer-Conscious Employees at Every Level," *Journal of Business Research,* January 1990, pp. 63–70; Frank K. Sonnenberg, "Marketing: Service Quality: Forethought, Not Afterthought," *The Journal of Business Strategy,* September–October 1989, pp. 54–58; Glenn DeSouza, "Now Service Businesses Must Manage Quality," *The Journal of Business Strategy,* May–June 1989, pp. 21–25; Stephen W. Brown and Teresa A. Swartz, "A Gap Analysis of Professional Service Quality," *Journal of Marketing,* April 1989, pp. 92–98.

Appendix D

Baggaley, J. P. "Developing a Televised Health Campaign: I. Smoking Prevention." *Media in Education and Development* 19, 1986.

Eysenck, M. W. *A Handbook of Cognitive Psychology.* London: Lawrence Erlbaum Associates, 1984.

Health and Welfare Canada. "Making a Difference: The Impact of the Health Promotion Directorate's Social Marketing Campaigns: 1987–1991." Ottawa, 1991.

Ministry of Health Ontario. "Healthy Lifestyles Promotion Program. Social Marketing In Health Promotion: A Communications Guide." Vol. 2M. September 1991.

Kotler, P., and E. Roberto. *Social Marketing: Strategies for Changing Social Behavior.* New York: Free Press, 1989.

Loudon, D., and A. Della Bitta. *Consumer Behaviour: Concepts and Applications.* New York: McGraw-Hill, 1988.

McCarthy, E. J., S. J. Shapiro, and W. D. Perreault. *Basic Marketing: A Managerial Approach,* 6th Canadian ed. Burr Ridge, IL: Richard D. Irwin, Inc., 1992.

Mintz, J. "Social Marketing: New Weapon in an Old Struggle." *Health Promotion,* Winter 1988/89.

Moog, C. *"Are They Selling Her Lips?": Advertising and Identity.* New York: William Morrow and Company, 1990.

Sears, D. O., L. Peplau, and S. Taylor. *Social Psychology.* 7th ed. Englewood Cliffs, NJ: Prentice-Hall, 1991.

Tanguay, C. "Planning Health Promotion." *Health Promotion,* Winter 1988/89.

Tripp, G., and A. Davenport. "Fear Advertising—It Doesn't Work!" *Health Promotion,* Winter 1988/89.

Young, E. "Social Marketing: Where It Has Come From; Where It's Going." *Health Promotion,* Winter 1988/89.

Chapter 21

1. John Southerst, "The Reinvention of Retail," *Canadian Business,* August 1992, pp. 26–31.

2. Bernard J. Jaworski, "Toward a Theory of Marketing Control: Environmental Context, Control Types, and Consequences," *Journal of Marketing,* July 1988, pp. 23–39; Subhash Sharma and Dale D. Achabal, "STEMCOM: An Analytical Model for Marketing Control," *Journal of Marketing,* Spring 1982, pp. 104–13; Sam R. Goodman, *Techniques of Profitability Analysis* (New York: John Wiley & Sons, 1970), especially Chapter 1; Kenneth A. Merchant, "Progressing toward a Theory of Marketing Control: A Comment," *Journal of Marketing,* July 1988, pp. 40–44.

3. Ed Weymes, "A Different Approach to Retail Sales Analysis," *Business Horizons,* March–April 1982, pp. 66–74; D. H. Robertson, "Sales Force Feedback on Competitors' Activities," *Journal of Marketing,* April 1974, pp. 69–71. See also Robert H. Collins, Regan F. Carey, and Rebecca F. Mauritson, "Microcomputer Applications: Maps on a Micro—Application in Sales and Marketing Management," *Journal of Personal Selling and Sales Management,* November 1987, p. 83ff.

4. Robin Cooper and Robert S. Kaplan, "Profit Priorities from Activity-Based Costing," *Harvard Business Review,* May–June 1991, pp. 130–37; Douglas M. Lambert and Jay U. Sterling, "What Types of Profitability Reports Do Marketing Managers Receive?" *Industrial Marketing Management,* November 1987, pp. 295–304; Nigel F. Piercy, "The Marketing Budgeting Process: Marketing Management Implications," *Journal of Marketing,* October 1987, pp. 45–59; Michael J. Sandretto, "What Kind of Cost System Do You Need?" *Harvard Business Review,* January–February 1985, pp. 110–18; Patrick M. Dunne and Harry I. Wolk, "Marketing Cost Analysis: A Modularized Contribution Approach," *Journal of Marketing,* July 1977, pp. 83–94; V. H. Kirpalani and Stanley J. Shapiro, "Financial Dimensions of Marketing Management," *Journal of Marketing,* July 1973, pp. 40–47.

5. See Stewart A. Washburn, "Establishing Strategy and Determining Costs in the Pricing Decision," *Business Marketing,* July 1985, pp. 64–78.

6. Ram Charan, "How Networks Reshape Organizations—For Results," *Harvard Business Review,* September–October 1991, pp. 104–15; "The Personal Computer Finds Its Missing Link," *Business Week,* June 5, 1989, pp. 120–29; "An Electronic Pipeline that's Changing the Way America Does Business," *Business Week,* August 3, 1987, pp. 80–82; "Computer Finds a Role in Buying and Selling, Reshaping Businesses," *The Wall Street Journal,* March 18, 1987, p. 1ff.; "Computers Bringing Changes to Basic Business Documents," *The Wall Street Journal,* March 6, 1987, p. 33; "Networking: Japan's Latest Computer Craze," *Fortune,* July 7, 1986, pp. 94–96; William J. Bruns, Jr., and W. Warren McFarlan, "Information Technology Puts Power in Control Systems," *Harvard Business Review,* September–October 1987, pp. 89–94.

7. Leonard L. Berry, Jeffrey S. Conant, and A. Parasuraman, "A Framework for Conducting a Services Marketing Audit," *Journal of the Academy of Marketing Science,* Summer 1991, pp. 255–68; John F. Grashof, "Conducting and Using a Marketing Audit," in *Readings in Basic Marketing,* ed. E. J. McCarthy, J. J. Grashof, and A. A. Brogowicz (Homewood, IL.: Richard D. Irwin, 1984); Alice M. Tybout and John R. Hauser, "A Marketing Audit Using a Conceptual Model of Consumer Behavior: Application and Evaluation," *Journal of Marketing,* Summer 1981, pp. 82–101.

Chapter 22

1. "Little Is Common beyond Gender?" *Insight,* December 10, 1990, pp. 48–49.

2. "Push-Button Age," *Newsweek,* July 9, 1990, pp. 56–57; "After the Beep: The Message Is Convenience Matters Most," *The Wall Street Journal,* September 19, 1989, pp. B1–2; "Design Is Hot in the Cold Business," *Insight,* September 18, 1989, pp. 44–45; "Will US Warm to Refrigerated Dishes?" *The Wall Street Journal,* August 18, 1989, p. B1; "As 'Fresh Refrigerated' Foods Gain Favor, Concerns about Safety Rise," *The Wall Street Journal,* March 11, 1988, p. 27; "Life in the Express Lane," *Time,* June 16, 1986, p. 64.

3. John P. Robinson, "Your Money or Your Time," *American Demographics,* November 1991, pp. 22–26; "Flood of Information Swamps Managers, But Some Are Finding Ways to Bail Out," *The Wall Street Journal,* August 12, 1991, p. B1ff.; "Fast-Track Kids Exhaust Their Parents," *The Wall Street Journal,* August 7, 1991, p. B1ff.; John P. Robinson, "The Time Squeeze," *American Demographics,* February 1990, pp. 30–33; "Smart Cards: Pocket Power," *Newsweek,* July 31, 1989, pp. 54–55; "How America Has Run Out of Time," *Time,* April 24, 1989, pp. 58–67; Cheryl Russell, "What's Your Hurry," *American Demographics,* April 1989, p. 2; Ruth Hamel, "Living in Traffic," *American Demographics,* March 1989, pp. 49–51.

4. Glenn DeSouza, "Designing a Customer Retention Plan," *The Journal of Business Strategy,* March–April 1992, pp. 24–28; Frank V. Cespedes, "Once More: How Do You Improve Customer Service?" *Business Horizons,* March–April 1992, pp. 58–67; Mary C. Gilly, William B. Stevenson, and Laura J. Yale, "Dynamics of Complaint Management in the Service Organization," *The Journal of Consumer Affairs,* Winter 1991, pp. 295–322; C. Dröge and D. Halstead, "Postpurchase Hierarchies of Effects: The Antecedents and Consequences of Satisfaction for Complainers versus Non-Complainers," *International Journal of Research in Marketing,* November 1991, pp. 315–28; Jagdip Singh, "Industry Characteristics and Consumer Dissatisfaction," *The Journal of Consumer Affairs,* Summer 1991, pp. 19–56; Jerry Plymire, "Complaints as Opportunities," *Business Horizons,* March–April 1991, pp. 79–81; Barbara C. Garland and Robert A. Westbrook, "An Exploration of Client Satisfaction in a Nonprofit Context," *Journal of the Academy of Marketing Science,* Fall 1989, pp. 297–304; A. Parasuraman,

Valarie A. Zeithaml, and Leonard L. Berry, "SERVQUAL: A Multiple-Item Scale for Measuring Consumer Perceptions of Service Quality," *Journal of Retailing,* Spring 1988, pp. 12–40; "Banks Stress Resolving Complaints to Win Small Customers' Favor," *The Wall Street Journal,* December 8, 1986, p. 31; John F. Gaski and Michael J. Etzel, "The Index of Consumer Sentiment toward Marketing," *Journal of Marketing,* July 1986, pp. 71–81; Robert B. Woodruff, Ernest R. Cadotte, and Roger L. Jenkins, "Modeling Consumer Satisfaction Processes Using Experience-Based Norms," *Journal of Marketing Research,* August 1983, pp. 296–304.

5. "Prof: TV Ads Not as Effective as Price and Promotions," *Marketing News,* March 27, 1989, p. 7; "IRI Research Bolsters Value of Advertising," *Advertising Age,* March 6, 1989, p. 71; "Don't Blame Television, Irate Readers Say," *The Wall Street Journal,* March 1, 1989, p. B6; "Television Ads Ring Up No Sale in Study," *The Wall Street Journal,* February 15, 1989, p. B6. For classic discussions of the problem and mechanics of measuring the efficiency of marketing, see Stanley C. Hollander, "Measuring the Cost and Value of Marketing," *Business Topics,* Summer 1961, pp. 17–26; Reavis Cox, *Distribution in a High-Level Economy* (Englewood Cliffs, NJ: Prentice-Hall, 1965).

6. For more on this point, see Robert L. Steiner, "Does Advertising Lower Consumer Prices?" *Journal of Marketing,* October 1973, pp. 19–26; Robert L. Steiner, "Marketing Productivity in Consumer Goods Industries—A Vertical Perspective," *Journal of Marketing,* January 1978, pp. 60–70; see also Robert B. Archibald, Clyde A. Haulman, and Carlisle E. Moody, Jr., "Quality, Price, Advertising, and Published Quality Ratings," *Journal of Consumer Research,* March 1983, pp. 347–56.

7. Arnold J. Toynbee, *America and World Revolution* (New York: Oxford University Press, 1966), pp. 144–45; see also John Kenneth Galbraith, *Economics and the Public Purpose* (Boston: Houghton Mifflin, 1973), pp. 144–45.

8. Russell J. Tomsen, "Take It Away," *Newsweek,* October 7, 1974, p. 21.

9. J. L. Engledow, "Was Consumer Satisfaction a Pig in a Poke?" *MSU Business Topics,* April 1977, p. 92.

10. "Deregulating America," *Business Week,* November 28, 1983, pp. 80–82; E. T. Grether, "Marketing and Public Policy: A Contemporary View," *Journal of Marketing,* July 1974, pp. 2–7; "Intellectuals Should Re-Examine the Marketplace: It Supports Them, Helps Keep Them Free," *Advertising Age,* January 28, 1963; David A. Heenan, "Congress Rethinks America's Competitiveness," *Business Horizons,* May–June 1989, pp. 11–16; Irvin Grossack and David A. Heenan, "Cooperation, Competition, and Antitrust: Two Views," *Business Horizons,* September–October 1986, pp. 24–28; Donald P. Robin and R. Eric Reidenbach, "Identifying Critical Problems for Mutual Cooperation between the Public and Private Sectors: A Marketing Perspective," *Journal of the Academy of Marketing Science,* Fall 1986, pp. 1–12.

11. Frederick Webster, *Social Aspects of Marketing* (Englewood Cliffs, NJ: Prentice-Hall, 1974), p. 32.

12. Robert F. Lusch and Gene R. Laczniak, "Macroenvironmental Forces, Marketing Strategy and Business Performance: A Futures Research Approach," *Journal of the Academy of Marketing Science,*

Fall 1989, pp. 283–96; "The Community's Persuasive Power," *Insight,* December 12, 1988, pp. 58–59; "Companies as Citizens: Should They Have a Conscience?" *The Wall Street Journal,* February 19, 1987, p. 29; John H. Antil, "Socially Responsible Consumers: Profile and Implications for Public Policy," *Journal of Macromarketing* 4, no. 2 (1984), pp. 18–39; James T. Roth and Lissa Benson, "Intelligent Consumption: An Attractive Alternative to the Marketing Concept," *MSU Business Topics,* Winter 1974, pp. 30–34. For more on privacy, see "The $3 Billion Question: Whose Info Is It, Anyway?" *Business Week,* July 4, 1988, pp. 106–7; "Federal Agencies Press Data-Base Firms to Curb Access to 'Sensitive' Information," *The Wall Street Journal,* February 5, 1987, p. 23. For more on shoplifting, see "Marketing Solution Can Cure Shoplifting Problems," *Marketing News,* June 25, 1990, p. 8; "Indelible Color Guard against Shoplifting," *Insight,* June 25, 1990, p. 46; "Chicago Retailers' 'Sting' Aims to Put Shoplifting Professionals Out of Business," *The Wall Street Journal,* June 5, 1990, p. B1ff.; "Retailers Use Hidden Gadgets, High Alertness to Battle Theft," *Insight,* December 18, 1989, pp. 42–43; Warren A. French, Melvin R. Crask, and Fred H. Mader, "Retailers' Assessment of the Shoplifting Problem," *Journal of Retailing,* Winter 1984, pp. 108–15; Robert E. Wilkes, "Fraudulent Behavior by Consumers," *Journal of Marketing,* October 1978, pp. 67–75. For more on ethics, see Joel J. Davis, "Ethics and Environmental Marketing," *Journal of Business Ethics,* February 1992, pp. 81–88; Scott J. Vitell, James R. Lumpkin, and Mohammed Y. A. Rawwas, "Consumer Ethics: An Investigation of the Ethical Beliefs of Elderly Consumers," *Journal of Business Ethics,* May 1991, pp. 365–76; Gene R. Laczniak and Patrick E. Murphy, "Fostering Ethical Marketing Decisions," *Journal of Business Ethics,* April 1991, pp. 259–72; Robert E. Pitts and Robert Allan Cooke, "A Realist View of Marketing Ethics," *Journal of Business Ethics,* April 1991, pp. 243–44; R. Eric Reidenbach, Donald P. Robin, and Lyndon Dawson, "An Application and Extension of a Multidimensional Ethics Scale to Selected Marketing Practices and Marketing Groups," *Journal of the Academy of Marketing Science,* Spring 1991, pp. 83–92; Shelby D. Hunt, Van R. Wood, and Lawrence B. Chonko, "Corporate Ethical Values and Organizational Commitment in Marketing," *Journal of Marketing,* July 1989, pp. 79–90; Dennis E. Garrett et al., "Issues Management and Organizational Accounts: An Analysis of Corporate Responses to Accusations of Unethical Business Practices," *Journal of Business Ethics,* July 1989, pp. 507–20; Donald P. Robin and R. Eric Reidenbach, "Social Responsibility, Ethics, and Marketing Strategy: Closing the Gap between Concept and Application," *Journal of Marketing,* January 1987, pp. 44–58.

13. "Environmental Price Tags," *Nation's Business,* April 1992, pp. 36–41; "It Doesn't Pay to Go Green When Consumers Are Seeing Red," *Adweek,* March 23, 1992, pp. 32–33; "Pollution Prevention Picks Up Steam," *Industry Week,* February 17, 1992, pp. 36–42; "Reach Out and Prod Someone," *Newsweek,* October 14, 1991, p. 50; "Herman Miller: How Green Is My Factory," *Business Week,* September 16, 1991, pp. 54–56; "The Big Muddle in Green Marketing," *Fortune,* June 3, 1991, pp. 91–100; "The Greening of Detroit," *Business Week,* April 8, 1991, pp. 54–60; "Exxon's Army Scrubs Beaches, but Many Don't Stay Cleaned," *The Wall Street Journal,* July 27, 1989, p. 1ff.; "CFC Curb to Save Ozone Will Be Costly," *The Wall Street Journal,* March 28, 1988, p. 6; "Du Pont Plans to Phase Out CFC Output," *The Wall Street Journal,* March 25, 1988, p. 2.

Glossary

Accessories short-lived capital items—tools and equipment used in production or office activities.

Accumulating collecting products from many small producers.

Administered channel systems channel members informally agree to cooperate with each other.

Administered prices consciously set prices aimed at reaching the firm's objectives.

Adoption curve shows when different groups accept ideas.

Adoption process the steps that individuals go through on the way to accepting or rejecting a new idea.

Advertising any *paid* form of nonpersonal presentation of ideas, goods, or services by an identified sponsor.

Advertising agencies specialists in planning and handling mass selling details for advertisers.

Advertising allowances price reductions to firms further along in the channel to encourage them to advertise or otherwise promote the firm's products locally.

Advertising managers managers of their company's mass selling effort in television, newspapers, magazines, and other media.

Agent middlemen wholesalers who don't own (take title to) the products they sell.

AIDA model consists of four promotion jobs: (1) to get Attention, (2) to hold Interest, (3) to arouse Desire, and (4) to obtain Action.

Allowance (accounting term) occurs when a customer isn't satisfied with a purchase for some reason and the seller gives a price reduction on the original invoice (bill) but the customer keeps the goods or services.

Allowances reductions in price given to final consumers, customers, or channel members for doing something or accepting less of something.

Assorting putting together a variety of products to give a target market what it wants.

Attitude a person's point of view toward something.

Auction companies agent middlemen who provide a place where buyers and sellers can come together and complete a transaction.

Automatic vending selling and delivering products through vending machines.

Average cost (per unit) the total cost divided by the related quantity.

Average-cost pricing adding a "reasonable" markup to the average cost of a product.

Average fixed cost (per unit) the total fixed cost divided by the related quantity.

Average variable cost (per unit) the total variable cost divided by the related quantity.

Bait pricing setting some very low prices to attract customers but trying to sell more expensive models or brands once the customer is in the store.

Balance sheet an accounting statement that shows a company's assets, liabilities, and net worth.

Basic list prices the prices that final customers or users are normally asked to pay for products.

Basic sales tasks order getting, order taking, and supporting.

Battle of the brands the competition between dealer brands and manufacturer brands.

Belief a person's opinion about something.

Bid pricing offering a specific price for each possible job rather than setting a price that applies for all customers.

Birthrate the number of babies per 1,000 people.

Brand familiarity how well customers recognize and accept a company's brand.

Branding the use of a name, term, symbol, design, or a combination of these to identify a product.

Brand insistence customers insist on a firm's branded product and are willing to search for it.

Brand managers manage specific products, often taking over the jobs formerly handled by an advertising manager.

Brand name a word, letter, or a group of words or letters.

Brand nonrecognition a brand isn't recognized by final customers at all, even though middlemen may use the brand name for identification and inventory control.

Brand preference   target customers usually choose the brand over other brands, perhaps because of habit or past experience.

Brand recognition   customers remember the brand.

Brand rejection   potential customers won't buy a brand unless its image is changed.

Break-even analysis   an approach to determine whether the firm will be able to break even—that is, cover all its costs—with a particular price.

Break-even point (BEP)   the sales quantity where the firm's total cost will just equal its total revenue.

Breakthrough opportunities   opportunities that help innovators develop hard-to-copy marketing strategies that will be very profitable for a long time.

Brokers   agent middlemen who specialize in bringing buyers and sellers together.

Bulk-breaking   dividing larger quantities into smaller quantities as products get closer to the final market.

Buying centre   all the people who participate in or influence a purchase.

Buying function   looking for and evaluating goods and services.

Capital item   a long-lasting product that can be used and depreciated for many years.

Cash-and-carry wholesalers   like service wholesalers, except that the customer must pay cash.

Cash discounts   reductions in the price to encourage buyers to pay their bills quickly. 2/10, net 30, for example, means that a 2 percent discount off the face value of the invoice is allowed if the invoice is paid within 10 days.

Catalogue showroom retailers   stores that sell several lines out of a catalogue and display showroom, with backup inventories.

Census Metropolitan Area (CMA)   a continuous, 100,000 + labor market.

Central market   a convenient place where buyers and sellers can meet face-to-face to exchange goods and services.

Channel captain   a manager who helps direct the activities of a whole channel and tries to avoid—or solve—channel conflicts.

Channel of distribution   any series of firms or individuals who participate in the flow of goods and services from producer to final user or consumer.

Clustering techniques   approaches used to try to find similar patterns within sets of data.

Combination export manager   a blend of manufacturers' agent and selling agent handling the entire export function for several producers of similar but noncompeting lines.

Combined target market approach   combining two or more submarket segments into one larger target market as a basis for one strategy.

Combiners   firms that try to increase the size of their target markets by combining two or more segments.

Commission merchants   agent middlemen who handle products shipped to them by sellers, complete the sale, and send the money (minus their commission) to each seller.

Communication process   a source trying to reach a receiver with a message.

Community shopping centres   planned shopping centres that offer some shopping stores as well as convenience stores.

Comparative advertising   advertising that makes specific brand comparisons using actual product names.

Competitive advantage   means that a firm has a marketing mix that the target market sees as better than a competitor's mix.

Competitive advertising   advertising that tries to develop demand for a specific brand rather than a product category.

Competitive environment   the number and types of competitors the marketing manager must face, and how they may behave.

Complementary product pricing   setting prices on several related products as a group.

Components   processed expense items that become part of a finished product.

Concept testing   getting reactions from customers about how well a new product idea fits their needs.

Confidence interval   the range on either side of an estimate from a sample that is likely to contain the true value for the whole population.

Consumerism   a social movement that seeks to increase consumers' rights and powers.

Consumer products   products meant for the final consumer.

Consumer surplus   the difference to consumers between the value of a purchase and the price they pay.

Containerization   grouping individual items into an economical shipping quantity and sealing them in protective containers for transit to the final destination.

Contract manufacturing   turning over production to others, while retaining the marketing process.

Contractual channel systems   channel members agree by contract to cooperate with each other.

Contribution-margin approach   a cost analysis approach in which all functional costs are not allocated in *all* situations.

Control   the feedback process that helps the marketing manager learn (1) how ongoing plans are working and (2) how to plan for the future.

Convenience (food) stores   a convenience-oriented variation of the conventional limited-line food stores.

Convenience products   products a consumer needs but isn't willing to spend much time or effort shopping for.

Convenience store   a convenient place to shop—either centrally located downtown or "in the neighborhood."

Cooperative advertising   middlemen and producers sharing in the cost of ads.

Cooperative chains   retailer-sponsored groups, formed by independent retailers, to run their own buying organization and conduct joint promotion efforts.

Copy thrust   what the words and illustrations of an ad should communicate.

(Corporate) chain store   one of several stores owned and managed by the same firm.

Corporate channel systems   corporate ownership all along the channel.

Corrective advertising   ads to correct deceptive advertising.

Cost of sales   total value (at cost) of the sales during the period.

Cues   products, signs, ads, and other stimuli in the environment.

Cultural and social environment   affects how and why people live and behave as they do.

Culture   the whole set of beliefs, attitudes, and ways of doing things of a reasonably homogeneous set of people.

Cumulative quantity discounts   reductions in price for larger purchases over a given period, such as a year.

Customer service level   how rapidly and dependably a firm can deliver what customers want.

Dealer brands   brands created by middlemen.

Decision support system (DSS)   a computer program that makes it easy for a marketing manager to get and use information as she is making decisions.

Decoding   the receiver in the communication process translating the message.

Demand-backward pricing   setting an acceptable final consumer price and working backward to what a producer can charge.

Demand curve   a "picture" of the relationship between price and quantity demanded in a market, assuming that all other things stay the same.

Department stores   large stores that are organized into many separate departments and offer many product lines.

Derived demand   demand for industrial products is derived from demand for final consumer products.

Description (specification) buying   buying from a written (or verbal) description of the product.

Determining dimensions   the dimensions that actually affect the purchase of a *specific* product or brand in a *product-market*.

Direct mail advertising   selling to customers via their mailboxes.

Direct type advertising   competitive advertising that aims for immediate buying action.

Discount houses   stores that sell "hard goods" (cameras, TVs, appliances) at substantial price cuts.

Discounts   reductions from list price that are given by a seller to a buyer who either gives up some marketing function or provides the function himself.

Discrepancy of assortment   the difference between the lines a typical producer makes and the assortment final consumers or users want.

Discrepancy of quantity   the difference between the quantity of goods it's economical for a producer to make and the quantity final users or consumers normally want.

Discretionary income   what's left of income after paying taxes and paying for necessities.

Disposable income   income that's left after taxes.

Dissonance   tension caused by uncertainty about the rightness of a decision.

Distinctiveness stage   a stage in the fashion cycle when consumers seek—and are willing to pay for—products different from those that satisfy the majority.

Distribution centre   a special kind of warehouse designed to speed the flow of goods and avoid unnecessary storing costs.

Diversification   moving into total different lines of business which may include entirely unfamiliar products, markets, or even levels in the production-marketing system.

Diversion in transit   redirection of railroad carloads already in transit.

Door-to-door selling   going directly to the consumer's home.

Drive   a strong stimulus that encourages action to reduce a need.

Drop-shippers   wholesalers that take title to the products they sell but don't actually handle, stock, or deliver them.

Dual distribution   when a producer uses several competing channels to reach the same target market.

Early adopters   the second group in the adoption curve to adopt a new product, these people are usually well-respected by their peers and often are opinion leaders.

Early majority   a group in the adoption curve that avoids risk and waits to consider a new idea after many early adopters have tried it and liked it.

Economic and technological environment   affects the way firms and the whole economy use resources.

Economic emulation stage   a stage in the fashion cycle when consumers want the currently popular fashion but at a lower price.

Economic needs   needs concerned with making the best use of a consumer's limited resources as the consumer sees it.

Economic system   the way an economy organizes to use scarce resources to produce goods and services and distribute them for consumption by various people and groups in the society.

Economies of scale   as a company produces larger numbers of a particular product, the cost for each of these products goes down.

Elastic demand   if prices are dropped, the quantity demanded will increase enough to increase total revenue.

Elastic supply   the quantity supplied increases if the price is raised.

Emergency products   products that are purchased immediately when the need is great.

Empty nesters   people whose children are grown and who are now able to spend their money in ways other than child rearing.

Emulation stage   a stage in the fashion cycle when more consumers want to buy what's satisfying the original users.

Encoding   the source in the communication process deciding what it wants to say and translating it into words or symbols that will have the same meaning to the receiver.

Equilibrium point   the point where the quantity and the price sellers are willing to offer equal the quantity and price that buyers are willing to accept.

Equilibrium price   the going market price.

Exclusive distribution   selling through only one middleman in a particular geographic area.

Expense item   a product whose total cost is treated as a business expense in the year when it's purchased.

Expenses   all the remaining costs that are subtracted from the gross margin to get the net profit.

Experience curve pricing   average-cost pricing using an estimate of future average costs.

Experimental method   a research approach in which researchers compare the responses of groups that are similar except on the characteristic being tested.

Export agents   manufacturers' agents who specialize in export trade.

Export brokers   brokers in international marketing.

Export commission houses   brokers in international trade.

Exporting   selling some of what the firm is producing to foreign markets.

Extensive problem solving   the type of problem solving involved when a need is completely new or important to a consumer—and much effort is taken to decide how to satisfy the need.

Facilitators   firms that provide one or more of the marketing functions other than buying or selling.

Factor   a variable that shows the relation of some other variable to the item being forecast.

Factor method   an approach to forecast sales by finding a relation between the company's sales and some other factor (or factors).

Factors   wholesalers of credit.

Fad   an idea that is fashionable only to certain groups who are enthusiastic about it, but who are so fickle that it's even more short-lived than a regular fashion.

Family brand   a brand name used for several products.

Farm products   products grown by farmers, such as oranges, wheat, sugar cane, cattle, poultry, eggs, and milk.

Fashion   accepted or popular style.

Fashion cycle   three stages in the life of a fashion (the distinctiveness, emulation, and economic emulation stages) that roughly parallel the product life-cycle stages.

Field warehouser   a firm that segregates some of a company's finished products on the company's own property and issues warehouse receipts that can be used to borrow money.

Financing   provides the necessary cash and credit to produce, transport, store, promote, sell, and buy products.

Fixed-cost (FC) contribution per unit   the selling price per unit minus the variable cost per unit.

Flexible-price policy   offering the same product and quantities to different customers at different prices.

Floor planning   the financing of display stocks for car, appliance, and electronics retailers.

FOB   a transportation term meaning "free on board" some vehicle at some point.

Focus group interview   an interview of 6 to 10 people in an informal group setting.

Form utility   provided when someone produces something tangible.

Franchise operation   a franchiser develops a good marketing strategy, and the retail franchise holders carry out the strategy in their own units.

Freight absorption pricing   absorbing freight cost so that a firm's delivered price meets the price of the nearest competitor.

Freight forwarders   transportation "wholesalers" who combine the small shipments of many shippers into more economical shipping quantities.

Full-cost approach   all functional costs are allocated to products, customers, or other categories.

Full-line pricing   setting prices for a whole line of products.

Functional accounts   categories of costs that show the purpose for which the expenditures are made.

General merchandise wholesalers   service wholesalers who carry a wide variety of nonperishable items such as hardware, electrical supplies, plumbing supplies, furniture, drugs, cosmetics, and automobile equipment.

General stores   early retailers who carried anything they could sell in reasonable volume.

Generic market   a market with broadly similar needs and sellers offering various and often diverse ways of satisfying those needs.

Generic products   products that have no brand at all other than identification of their contents and the manufacturer or middleman.

Gross margin (gross profit)   the money left to cover the expenses of selling the products and operating the business.

Gross sales   the total amount charged to all customers during some time period.

Heterogeneous shopping products   shopping products that the customer sees as different, and wants to inspect for quality and suitability.

Homogeneous shopping products   shopping products that the customer sees as basically the same, and wants at the lowest price.

Hypotheses   educated guesses about the relationships between things or about what will happen in the future.

Iceberg principle   much good information is hidden in summary data.

Ideal market exposure   when a product is available widely enough to satisfy target customers' needs but not to exceed them.

Implementation   putting marketing plans into operation.

Import agents   manufacturers' agents who specialize in import trade.

Import brokers   brokers in international marketing.

Import commission houses   brokers in international trade.

Impulse products   products that are bought quickly as unplanned purchases because of a strongly felt need.

Indices   statistical combinations of several time series used to find some time series that will lead the series managers are attempting to forecast.

Indirect type advertising   competitive advertising that points out product advantages to affect future buying decisions.

Individual brands   different brand names used for each product.

Individual product   a particular product within a product line.

Industrial products   products meant for use in producing other products.

Inelastic demand   the quantity demanded would increase if the price were decreased, but the quantity demanded wouldn't increase enough to avoid a decrease in total revenue.

Inelastic supply   the quantity supplied doesn't increase much (if at all) if the price is raised.

Innovation   the development and spread of new ideas and products.

Innovators   the first group to adopt new products.

Inspection buying   looking at every item.

Installations   industrial products that are important capital items such as buildings, land rights, and major equipment.

Institutional advertising   advertising that tries to develop goodwill for a company or even an industry instead of for a specific product.

Intensive distribution   selling a product through all responsible and suitable wholesalers or retailers who will stock and/or sell the product.

Intermediate customers   any buyers who buy for resale or to produce other goods and services.

Introductory price dealing   temporary price cuts to speed new products into a market.

Inventory   the amount of goods that are being stored.

Job description   a written statement of what an employee (for example, a salesperson) is expected to do.

Joint venturing   in international marketing, a domestic firm entering into a partnership with a foreign firm.

Jury of executive opinion   forecasting by combining the opinions of experienced executives—perhaps from marketing, production, finance, purchasing, and top management.

Just-in-time delivery   reliably getting products to the customer *just* before the customer needs them.

Laggards   prefer to do things the way they have done in the past and are suspicious of new ideas; see *adoption curve.*

Late majority   a group of adopters who are cautious about new ideas; see *adoption curve.*

Law of diminishing demand   if the price of a product is raised, a smaller quantity will be demanded; if the price of a product is lowered, a greater quantity will be demanded.

Leader pricing   setting some very low prices on some products to get customers into retail stores.

Leading series   a time series that changes in the same direction but ahead of the series to be forecasted.

Learning   a change in a person's thought processes caused by prior experience.

Licensed brand   well-known brand that sellers pay a fee to use.

Licensing   selling the right to use some process, trademark, patent, or other right for a fee or royalty.

Lifestyle analysis   the analysis of a person's day-to-day pattern of living as expressed in Activities, Interests, and Opinions (which are referred to as AIOs or psychographics).

Limited-function wholesalers   merchant wholesalers who perform only *some* wholesaling functions.

Limited problem solving   when a consumer is willing to put *some* effort into deciding the best way to satisfy a need.

Long-run target return pricing   pricing to cover all costs and over the long run achieve an average target return.

Lower-lower class   (13 percent of the population) consists of unskilled laborers and people in low-paying occupations.

Lower-middle class   (36 percent of the population) consists of small-business people, office workers, teachers, and technicians—the white-collar workers.

Low-involvement purchases   purchases that don't have high personal importance or relevance for the customer.

Macro-marketing   a social process that directs an economy's flow of goods and services from producers to consumers in a way that effectively matches supply and demand and accomplishes the objectives of society.

Mail-order wholesalers   sell out of catalogues that may be distributed widely to smaller industrial customers or retailers.

Management contracting   the seller provides only management skills; the production facilities are owned by others.

Manufacturer brands   brands created by manufacturers.

Manufacturers' agents   agent middlemen who sell similar products for several noncompeting producers for a commission on what is actually sold.

Manufacturers' sales branches   separate businesses that producers set up away from their factories.

Marginal analysis   evaluating the change in total revenue and total cost from selling one more unit to find the most profitable price and quantity.

Marginal cost   the change in total cost that results from producing one more unit.

Marginal profit   profit on the last unit sold.

Marginal revenue   the change in total revenue that results from the sale of one more unit of a product.

Markdown   a retail price reduction that is required because customers won't buy some item at the originally marked-up price.

Markdown ratio   a tool used by many retailers to measure the efficiency of various departments and their whole business.

Market   a group of potential customers with similar needs and sellers offering various products (that is, ways of satisfying those needs) *or* a group of sellers and buyers who are willing to exchange goods and/or services for something of value.

Market development   trying to increase sales by selling present products in new markets.

Market-directed economic system   individual decisions of the many producers and consumers make the macro-level decisions for the whole economy.

Market growth   a stage of the product life cycle when industry sales are growing fast, but industry profits rise and then start falling.

Market information function   the collection, analysis, and distribution of all the information needed to plan, carry out, and control marketing activities.

Marketing audit   a systematic, critical, and unbiased review and appraisal of the basic objectives and policies of the marketing function and of the organization, methods, procedures, and people employed to implement the policies.

Marketing company era   a time when, in addition to short-run marketing planning, marketing people develop long-range plans (sometimes 10 or more years ahead) and the whole company effort is guided by the marketing concept.

Marketing concept   the idea that an organization should aim all its efforts at satisfying its customers at a profit.

Marketing department era   a time when all marketing activities are brought under the control of one department to improve short-run policy planning and to try to integrate the firm's activities.

Marketing information system (MIS)   an organized way of continually gathering and analyzing data to provide marketing managers with information they need to make decisions.

Marketing management process   the process of (1) planning marketing activities, (2) directing the implementation of the plans, and (3) controlling these plans.

Marketing mix   the controllable variables that the company puts together to satisfy a target group.

Marketing model   a statement of relationships among marketing variables.

Marketing orientation   trying to carry out the marketing concept.

Marketing plan   a written statement of a marketing strategy *and* the time-related details for carrying out the strategy.

Marketing program   blends all of the firm's marketing plans into one big plan.

Marketing research   procedures to develop and analyze information to help marketing managers make decisions.

Marketing research process   a five-step application of the scientific method that includes (1) defining the problem, (2) analyzing the situation, (3) getting problem-specific information, (4) interpreting the data, and (5) solving the problem.

Marketing strategy   specifies a target market and a related marketing mix.

Market introduction   a stage of the product life cycle when sales are low as a new idea is first introduced to a market.

Market maturity   a stage of the product life cycle when industry sales level off and competition gets tougher.

Market penetration   trying to increase sales of a firm's present products in its present markets, usually through a more aggressive marketing mix.

Market potential   what a whole market segment might buy.

Market segment   a relatively homogeneous group of customers who will respond to a marketing mix in a similar way.

Market segmentation   a two-step process of (1) naming broad product-markets and (2) segmenting these broad product-markets in order to select target markets and develop suitable marketing mixes.

Markup   a dollar amount added to the cost of products to get the selling price.

Markup chain   the sequence of markups used by firms at different levels in a channel—determining the price structure in the whole channel.

Markup (percent)   the percentage of selling price that is added to the cost to get the selling price.

Mass marketing   the typical production-oriented approach that vaguely aims at everyone with the same marketing mix.

Mass-merchandisers   large, self-service stores that have many departments emphasizing soft goods (housewares, clothing, and fabrics) and that sell on lower margins to get faster turnover.

Mass-merchandising concept   the idea that retailers can get faster turnover and greater volume by charging low prices that will appeal to larger markets.

Mass selling   communicating with large numbers of customers at the same time.

Merchant wholesalers   wholesalers who take title to the products they sell.

Message channel   the carrier of the message.

Micro-macro dilemma   what's good for some producers and consumers may not be good for society as a whole.

Micro-marketing   the performance of activities that seek to accomplish an organization's objectives by anticipating customer or client needs and directing a flow of need-satisfying goods and services from producer to customer or client.

Middleman   someone who specializes in trade rather than production.

Missionary salespeople   supporting salespeople who work for producers by calling on their middlemen and their customers.

Modified rebuy   the in-between process where some review of the buying situation is done, though not as much as in new-task buying or as little as in straight rebuys.

Monopolistic competition   a market situation that develops when a market has (1) different products and (2) sellers who feel they do have some competition in this market.

Multinational corporations   firms that make a direct investment in several countries and run their businesses depending on the choices available anywhere in the world.

Multiple buying influence   the buyer shares the purchasing decision with several people, perhaps even top management.

Multiple target market approach   segmenting the market and choosing two or more segments, each of which will be treated as a separate target market that needs a different marketing mix.

National accounts sales force   salespeople who sell direct to large accounts such as major retail chain stores.

Nationalism   an emphasis on a country's interests before everything else.

Natural accounts   the categories to which various costs are charged in the normal financial accounting cycle.

Natural products   products that occur in nature, such as fish and game, lumber and maple syrup, and copper, zinc, iron ore, oil, and coal.

Needs   the basic forces that motivate a person to do something.

Need-satisfaction approach   a type of sales presentation in which the salesperson develops a good understanding of the individual customer's needs before trying to close the sale.

Negotiated contract buying   agreeing to a contract that allows for changes in the purchase arrangements.

Neighborhood shopping centres   planned shopping centres that consist of several convenience stores.

Net   an invoice term that means that payment for the face value of the invoice is due immediately; see *cash discounts*.

Net profit   what the company earned from its operations during a particular period.

Net sales   sales dollars the company receives.

New product   a product that's new in any way for the company concerned.

New-task buying   when a firm has a new need and the buyer wants a great deal of information.

New unsought products   products offering really new ideas that potential customers don't know about yet.

Noise   any distraction that reduces the effectiveness of the communications process.

Noncumulative quantity discounts   reductions in price when a customer purchases a larger quantity on an individual order.

Nonprice competition   aggressive action on one or more of the Ps other than Price.

Odd-even pricing   setting prices that end in certain numbers.

Oligopoly   a special market situation that develops when a market has (1) essentially homogeneous products, (2) relatively few sellers, and (3) fairly inelastic industry demand curves.

One-price policy   offering the same price to all customers who purchase products under essentially the same conditions and in the same quantities.

Open to buy   a buyer has budgeted funds that he or she can spend during the current time period.

Operating ratios   ratios of items on the operating statement to net sales.

Operating statement   a simple summary of the financial results of a company's operations over a specified period of time.

Operational decisions short-run decisions to help implement strategies.

Opinion leader a person who influences others.

Order getters salespeople concerned with getting new business.

Order getting seeking possible buyers with a well-organized sales presentation designed to sell a product, service, or idea.

Order takers salespeople who sell the regular or typical customers.

Order taking the routine completion of sales made regularly to the target customers.

Packaging promoting and protecting the product.

Penetration pricing policy trying to sell the whole market at one low price.

Performance analysis analysis that looks for exceptions or variations from planned performance.

Performance index a number that shows the relation of one value to another.

Personal needs an individual's need for personal satisfaction unrelated to what others think or do.

Personal selling direct face-to-face communication between a seller and a potential customer.

Phony list prices misleading prices that customers are shown to suggest that the price they are to pay has been discounted from list price.

Physical distribution (PD) the transporting and storing of goods so as to match target customers' needs with a firm's marketing mix within individual firms and along a channel of distribution.

Physical distribution (PD) concept all transporting and storing activities of a business and a channel system should be coordinated as one system that should seek to minimize the cost of distribution for a given customer service level.

Physiological needs biological needs such as the need for food, drink, rest, and sex.

Piggy-back service transporting truck trailers or flat-bed trailers carrying containers on railcars to provide both speed and flexibility.

Pioneering advertising advertising that tries to develop primary demand for a product category rather than a specific brand.

Place making products available in the right quantities and locations when customers want them.

Place utility having the product available where the customer wants it.

Planned economic system government planners decide what and how much is to be produced and distributed by whom, when, and to whom.

Planned shopping centre a set of stores planned as a unit to satisfy some market needs.

Pool car service allows groups of shippers to pool their shipments of like goods into a full rail car.

Population in marketing research, the total group you are interested in.

Portfolio management treats alternative products, division, or strategic business units (SBUs) as though they are stock investments to be bought and sold using financial criteria.

Positioning shows where proposed and/or present brands are located in a market as seen by customers.

Possession utility obtaining a product and having the right to use or consume it.

Prepared sales presentation a memorized presentation that's not adapted to each individual customer.

Prestige pricing setting a rather high price to suggest high quality or high status.

Price what is charged for something.

Price discrimination injuring competition by selling the same products to different buyers at different prices.

Price-fixing sellers illegally getting together to raise, lower, or stabilize prices.

Price leader a seller who sets a price that all others in the industry follow.

Price lining setting a few price levels for a product line and then marking all items at these prices.

Primary data information specifically collected to solve a current problem.

Primary demand demand for the general product idea, not just the company's own brand.

Private warehouses storing facilities owned or leased by companies for their own use.

Producers' cooperatives work almost as full-service wholesalers, with the "profits" going to the producers who are members.

Product the need-satisfying offering of a firm.

Product advertising advertising that tries to sell a specific product.

Product assortment the set of all product lines and individual products that a firm sells.

Product development offering new or improved products for present markets.

Production actually making goods or performing services.

Production era a time when a company focuses on production of a few specific products—perhaps because few of these products are available in the market.

Production orientation an emphasis on making products first and then trying to sell them.

Product liability sellers' legal obligation to pay damages to individuals who are injured by defective or unsafe products.

Product life cycle the stages a new product idea goes through from beginning to end.

Product line   a set of individual products that are closely related.

Product managers   manage products, often taking over the jobs formerly handled by an advertising manager; sometimes called brand managers.

Product-market   a market with very similar needs and sellers offering various close *substitute* ways of satisfying those needs.

Professional services   specialized services that support the operations of a firm.

Profit maximization objective   an objective to get as much profit as possible.

Promotion   communicating information between seller and potential buyer to influence attitudes and behavior.

Prospecting   following down all the leads in the target market.

Psychographics   the analysis of a person's day-to-day pattern of living as expressed in Activities, Interests, and Opinions (sometimes referred to as AIOs or lifestyle analysis).

Psychological pricing   setting prices that have special appeal to target customers.

Publicity   any unpaid form of nonpersonal presentation of ideas, goods, or services.

Public relations   communication with noncustomers, including labor, public interest groups, stockholders, and the government.

Public warehouses   independent storing facilities.

Pulling   getting consumers to ask middlemen for the product.

Purchase discount   a reduction of the original invoice amount for some business reason.

Purchasing agents   buying specialists for their employers.

Pure competition   a market situation that develops when a market has (1) homogeneous products, (2) many buyers and sellers who have full knowledge of the market, and (3) ease of entry for buyers and sellers.

Pure subsistence economy   each family unit produces everything it consumes.

Pushing   using normal promotion effort (personal selling, advertising, and sales promotion) to help sell the whole marketing mix to possible channel members.

Push money (or prize money) allowances   allowances (sometimes called PMs or spiffs) given to retailers by manufacturers or wholesalers to pass on to the retailers' sales clerks for aggressively selling certain items.

Qualifying dimensions   the dimensions that are relevant to a product-market.

Qualitative research   seeks in-depth, open-ended responses.

Quantitative research   seeks structured responses that can be summarized in numbers, like percentages, averages, or other statistics.

Quantity discounts   discounts offered to encourage customers to buy in larger amounts.

Quotas   the specific quantities of products that can move in or out of a country.

Rack jobbers   merchant wholesalers who specialize in nonfood products sold through grocery stores and supermarkets; they often display such products on their own wire or plastic racks.

Random sampling   each member of the research population has the same chance of being included in the sample.

Raw materials   unprocessed expense items (such as logs, iron ore, wheat, and cotton) that are handled as little as is needed to move them to the next production process.

Rebates   refunds to consumers after a purchase has been made.

Receiver   the target of a message in the communication process; usually a customer.

Reciprocity   trading sales for sales; that is, "if you buy from me, I'll buy from you."

Reference group   the people an individual looks to when forming attitudes about a particular topic.

Regional shopping centres   large planned shopping centres that emphasize shopping stores and shopping products.

Regrouping activities   adjusting the quantities and/or assortments of products handled at each level in a channel of distribution.

Regularly unsought goods   products that stay unsought but not unbought forever.

Reinforcement   occurs in the learning process when the consumer's response is followed by satisfaction; that is, reducing the drive.

Reminder advertising   advertising to keep the product's name before the public.

Requisition   a request to buy something.

Research proposal   a plan that specifies what marketing research information will be obtained and how.

Resident buyers   independent buying agents who work in central markets for several retailer or wholesaler customers in outlying areas.

Response   an effort to satisfy a drive.

Response function   a mathematical and/or graphic relationship that shows how the firm's target market is expected to react to changes in marketing variables.

Response rate   the percentage of people contacted in a research sample who complete the questionnaire.

Retailing   all of the activities involved in the sale of products to final consumers.

Return   when a customer sends back purchased products.

Return on assets (ROA)   the ratio of net profit (after taxes) to the assets used to make the net profit, times 100.

Return on investment (ROI) the ratio of net profit (after taxes) to the investment used to make the net profit, multiplied by 100 to get rid of decimals.

Risk taking bearing the uncertainties that are part of the marketing process.

Routinized response behavior mechanically selecting a particular way of satisfying a need when it occurs.

Rule for maximizing profit the firm should produce that output where marginal cost is just less than or equal to marginal revenue.

Safety needs needs concerned with protection and physical well-being.

Sales analysis a detailed breakdown of a company's sales records.

Sales decline a stage of the product life cycle when new products replace the old.

Sales era a time when a company emphasizes selling because of increased competition.

Sales finance companies firms that finance inventories.

Sales forecast an estimate of how much an industry or firm hopes to sell to a market segment.

Sales managers managers concerned with managing personal selling.

Sales-oriented objective an objective to get some level of unit sales, dollar sales, or share of market without referring to profit.

Sales presentation a salesperson's effort to make a sale.

Sales promotion promotion activities—other than advertising, publicity, and personal selling—that stimulate interest, trial, or purchase by final customers or others in the channel.

Sales promotion managers managers of their company's sales promotion effort.

Sales territory a geographic area that is the responsibility of one salesperson or several working together.

Sample a part of the relevant population.

Sampling buying looking at only part of a potential purchase.

Scientific method a decision-making approach that focuses on being objective and orderly in testing ideas before accepting them.

Scrambled merchandising retailers carrying any product lines that they feel they can sell profitably.

Seasonal discounts discounts offered to encourage buyers to stock earlier than present demand requires.

Secondary data information that has already been collected or published.

Segmenters aim at one or more homogeneous segments and try to develop a different marketing mix for each segment.

Segmenting an aggregating process that clusters people with similar needs into a market segment.

Selective demand demand for a specific brand rather than a product category.

Selective distribution selling only through those middlemen who'll give the product special attention.

Selective exposure our eyes and minds seek out and notice only information that interests us.

Selective perception people screen out or modify ideas, messages, and information that conflict with previously learned attitudes and beliefs.

Selective retention people remember only what they want to remember.

Selling agents agent middlemen who take over the whole marketing job of producers, not just the selling function.

Selling formula approach a sales presentation that starts with a prepared presentation outline, gets customers to discuss needs, and then leads the customer through some logical steps to a final close.

Selling function promoting the product.

Senior citizens people 65 and over.

Service wholesalers merchant wholesalers who provide all the wholesaling functions.

Shopping products products that a customer feels are worth the time and effort to compare with competing products.

Shopping stores stores that attract customers from greater distances because of the width and depth of their assortments.

Simple trade era a time when families traded or sold their surplus output to local middlemen, who sold these goods to other consumers or distant middlemen.

Single-line (or general-line) wholesalers service wholesalers who carry a narrower line of merchandise than general merchandise wholesalers.

Single-line (or limited-line) stores stores that specialize in certain lines of related products rather than a wide assortment.

Single target market approach segmenting the market and picking one of the homogeneous segments as the firm's target market.

Situation analysis an informal study of what information is already available in the problem area.

Skimming price policy trying to sell the top of the demand curve at a high price before aiming at more price-sensitive customers.

Social class a group of people who have approximately equal social position as viewed by others in the society.

Social needs needs concerned with love, friendship, status, and esteem—things that involve a person's interaction with others.

Sorting separating products into grades and qualities desired by different target markets.

Source the sender of a message.

Specialty products consumer goods that the customer really wants and is willing to make a special effort to find.

Specialty shop a type of limited-line store; it's usually small and has a distinct personality.

Specialty stores stores for which customers have developed a strong attraction.

Specialty wholesalers service wholesalers that carry a very narrow range of products and that offer more information and service than other service wholesalers.

Standard Industrial Classification (SIC) Codes codes used to identify groups of firms in similar lines of business.

Standardization and grading sorting products according to size and quality.

Staples products that are bought often and routinely without much thought.

Statistical packages easy-to-use computer programs that analyze data.

Status quo objectives "don't rock the boat" pricing objectives.

Stimulus-response model the idea that people respond in some predictable way to a stimulus.

Stockturn rate the number of times the average inventory is sold in a year.

Storing the marketing function of holding goods.

Storing function holding goods until customers need them.

Straight rebuy a routine repurchase that may have been made many times before.

Strategic business unit (SBU) an organizational unit (within a larger company) that focuses its efforts on some product-markets and is treated as a separate profit centre.

Strategic (management) planning the managerial process of developing and maintaining a match between an organization's resources and its market opportunities.

Substitutes products that offer the buyer a choice.

Supermarket a large store specializing in groceries, with self-service and wide assortments.

Superstores stores that try to carry not only foods but all goods and services consumers purchase routinely.

Supplies expense items that don't become a part of a finished product.

Supply curve the quantity of products that will be supplied at various possible prices.

Supporting salespeople salespeople who support the order-oriented salespeople but don't try to get orders themselves.

Target market a fairly homogeneous (similar) group of customers to whom a company wishes to appeal.

Target marketing a marketing mix is tailored to fit some specific target customers.

Target return objective a specific level of profit as an objective.

Target return pricing pricing to cover all costs and achieve a target return.

Tariffs taxes on imported products.

Task method an approach to developing a budget, basing the budget on the job to be done.

Team selling sales reps working together on a specific account.

Technical specialists supporting salespeople who provide technical assistance to order-oriented salespeople.

Technological base the technical skills and equipment that affect the way an economy's resources are converted to output.

Telephone and direct-mail retailing allows consumers to shop at home, usually placing orders by mail or a phone and charging the purchase to a credit card.

Telephone selling using the telephone to find out about a prospect's interest in the company's marketing mix and even to make a sales presentation or take an order.

Threshold expenditure level the minimum expenditure level needed just to be in a market.

Times series historical records of the fluctuations in economic variables.

Time utility having the product available when the customer wants it.

Ton-mile the movement of 2,000 pounds (1 ton) of goods 1 mile.

Total cost the sum of total fixed and total variable costs.

Total cost approach evaluating each possible physical distribution system and identifying *all* of the costs of each alternative.

Total fixed cost the sum of those costs that are fixed in total no matter how much is produced.

Total variable cost the sum of those changing expenses that are closely related to output, such as expenses for parts, wages, packaging materials, outgoing freight, and sales commissions.

Trade (functional) discount a list price reduction given to channel members for the job they're going to do.

Trade-in allowance a price reduction given for used products when similar new products are bought.

Trademark those words, symbols, or marks that are legally registered for use by a single company.

Trading stamps free stamps (such as Green Stamps) given by some retailers with each purchase.

Traditional channel system a channel system in which channel members make little or no effort to cooperate with each other.

Transporting the marketing function of moving goods.

Transporting function the movement of goods from one place to another.

Trend extension extends past experience to predict the future.

Truck wholesalers wholesalers who specialize in delivering products that they stock in their own trucks.

Unfair trade practice acts set a lower limit on prices, especially at the wholesale and retail levels.

Uniform delivered pricing making an average freight charge to all buyers.

Unit-pricing placing the price per ounce (or some other standard measure) on or near the product.

Universal functions of marketing buying, selling, transporting, storing, standardizing and grading, financing, risk taking, and market information.

Universal product code (UPC) special identifying marks for each product that can be "read" by electronic scanners.

Unsought products products that potential customers don't yet want or know they can buy.

Upper class (2 percent of the population) consists of people from old, wealthy families (upper-upper class) as well as the socially prominent new rich (lower-upper class).

Upper-lower class (38 percent of the population) consists of factory production line workers, skilled workers, and service people (the blue-collar workers).

Upper-middle class (11 percent of the population) consists of successful professionals, owners of small businesses, and managers of large corporations.

Utility the power to satisfy human needs.

Validity the extent to which data measure what they are intended to measure.

Value in use pricing setting prices that will capture some of what customers will save by substituting the firm's product for the one currently being used.

Vendor analysis formal rating of suppliers on all relevant areas of performance.

Vertical integration acquiring firms at different levels of channel activity.

Vertical marketing systems a whole channel focuses on the same target market at the end of the channel.

Voluntary chains wholesaler-sponsored groups that work with independent retailers.

Wants "needs" that are learned during a person's life.

Warranty what the seller promises about its product.

Wheel of retailing theory new types of retailers enter the market as low-status, low-margin, low-price operators and then—if they're successful—evolve into more conventional retailers offering more services with higher operating costs and higher prices.

Wholesalers firms whose main function is providing wholesaling activities.

Wholesaling the activities of those persons or establishments that sell to retailers and other merchants and/or to industrial, institutional, and commercial users, but who don't sell in large amounts to final consumers.

Wholly-owned subsidiary a separate firm owned by a parent company.

Zone pricing making an average freight charge to all buyers within specific geographic areas.

Illustration Credits

Chapter 1

Exhibits: *p. 18*, 1–2, adapted from Wroe Alderson, "Factors Governing the Development of Marketing Channels," in *Marketing Channels for Manufactured Products*, ed. Richard M. Clewett (Homewood, Ill.: Richard D. Irwin, 1954), p. 7. *p. 26*, 1–5, adapted from William McInnes, "A Conceptual Approach to Marketing," in *Theory in Marketing*, 2d ser., ed. Reavis Cox, Wroe Alderson, and Stanley J. Shapiro (Homewood, Ill.: Richard D. Irwin, 1964), pp. 51–67. *p. 27*, 1–6, model suggested by Professor A. A. Brogowicz, Western Michigan University.

Photos/ads: Photo of Parliament Buildings courtesy BGM Photo Centre Ltd. *p. 9*, (left) Paul Fusco/Magnum Photos; (right) Courtesy The Hertz Corporation. *p. 13*, (left) P. LeSegretain/Sygma; (right) Courtesy Chiquita Bananas International. *p. 15*, (left) © John Madere 1990 for International Paper annual report; (right) © 1992 by Marianne Barcellona. *p. 19*, Courtesy Banca Serfin/Albert Frank—Guenther Law Advertising Agency. *p. 25*, Courtesy Borden, Inc., photo by David Joel. *p. 28*, (left) Courtesy United Parcel Service of America, Inc.; (right) Courtesy Canadian Yellow Pages/McKim Advertising.

Chapter 2

Exhibits: *p. 41*, 2–3, adapted from R. F. Vizza, T. E. Chambers, and E. J. Cook, *Adoption of the Marketing Concept—Fact or Fiction* (New York: Sales Executive Club, Inc., 1967), pp. 13–15. *p. 46*, 2–4, adapted from discussions of an American Marketing Association Strategic Planning Committee.

Photos/ads: *p. 33*, Courtesy The Black and Decker Corporation. *p. 40*, Scott Wanner/Journalism Services. *p. 52*, (left) Courtesy Promus Companies; (right) Hitoshi Fugo. *p. 57*, (left) Reprint permission granted by Timex Corporation; (right) Courtesy Tissot.

Chapter 3

Exhibits: *p. 82*, 3–2, Igor Ansoff, *Corporate Strategy* (New York; McGraw-Hill, 1965). *p. 106*, 3–15, Russell I. Haley, "Benefit Segmentation: A Decision-Oriented Research Tool," *Journal of Marketing*, July 1968, p. 33.

Photos/ads: *p. 84*, Courtesy Philip Morris Companies. *p. 88*, (left) Courtesy Yashica, Inc./Michael Meyers & Associates, Inc., (right) Courtesy Sony Corporation of America. *p. 95*, Courtesy Heinz U.S.A. *p. 100*, Courtesy Foote Cone & Belding/Orange County. *p. 107*, (left) Courtesy Den-Mat Corporation; (right) Courtesy Colgate-Palmolive Company.

Chapter 4

Exhibits: *p. 129*, 4–3, "Europe: Special Report," *Fortune*, December 2, 1991, pp. 136–72. *p. 144*, 4–7, adapted from M. G. Allen, "Strategic Problems Facing Today's Corporate Planner," speech given at the Academy of Management, 36th Annual Meeting, Kansas City, Missouri, 1976.

Photos/ads: *p. 111*, Courtesy Giant Food Inc. *p. 112*, (left) Courtesy The Little Tikes Company; (right) © John S. Abbot. *p. 117*, (left) Photo courtesy Ball Corporation; (right) Arthur Meyerson Photography. *p. 128*, Courtesy Singapore Airlines, Ltd. *p. 141*, (left) Courtesy McDonald's

Corporation; (right) MIRACLE WHIP is a registered trademark of Kraft General Foods, Inc. Reproduced with permission. *p. 146*, Courtesy Philip Morris Companies Inc. *p. 148*, (right) Courtesy Nissin Foods; (left) Courtesy Ricoh Electronics Inc./Gigante Vaz & Partners.

Chapter 5

Exhibits: *p. 174*, 5–5, adapted from Paul E. Green, Frank J. Carmone, and David P. Wachpress, "On the Analysis of Qualitative Data in Marketing Research," *Journal of Marketing Research*, February 1977, pp. 52–59.

Photos/ads: *p. 153*, © 1989 Jay Brousseau. *p. 156*, (left) Courtesy Urban Decision Systems, Inc.; (right) Courtesy Norand Corporation. *p. 166*, © Steve Smith/Onyx. *p. 170*, Courtesy Colgate-Palmolive Company. *p. 171*, (left) Courtesy Carewell Industries Inc.; (right) Courtesy Nice-Pak Products Inc. *p. 174*, (left) Courtesy SAS Institute Inc.; (right) Courtesy STSC, Inc.

Chapter 6

Photos/ads: *p. 195*, (left) Indy race crowd, *courtesy Molson Indy, Vancouver*; (center) Bike riders, *courtesy Whistler Resort Association*; (right) Old couple playing croquet, no citation; 190 Grand Street Lodge, *courtesy Intercare/Evertt & Assoc.*

Chapter 7

Exhibits: *p. 229*, 7–2, adapted from C. Glenn Walters, *Consumer Behavior*, 3rd ed. (Homewood, Ill.: Richard D. Irwin, 1979). *p. 234*, 7–5, Joseph T. Plummer, "The Concept and Application of Life-Style Segmentation," *Journal of Marketing*, January 1974, pp. 33–37.

Photos/ads: *p. 207*, Courtesy MGTB Ayer. *p. 208*, Courtesy 3M. *p. 210*, Courtesy Forsman & Bodenfors. *p. 216*, (left) Courtesy United Airlines; (right) Courtesy Texas Department of Commerce, Tourism Division. *p. 220*, (left) Chuck Keeler/Tony Stone Worldwide; (right) H. Darr Beiser/USA Today. *p. 221*, (left) Courtesy PPG Industries, Inc.; (right) Frederick Charles/Time Magazine.

Chapter 8

Exhibits: *p. 261*, 8–1, *County Business Patterns—United States, 1989; Statistical Abstract of the United States, 1991; Information Please Almanac, 1992* (Boston: Houghton-Mifflin, 1991). *p. 265*, 8–3, Rowland T. Moriarty, Jr., and Robert E. Spekman, "An Empirical Investigation of the Information Sources Used During the Industrial Buying Process, *Journal of Marketing Research*, May 1984, pp. 137–47.

Photos/ads: *p. 259*, Courtesy Toyota Motor Corporation. *p. 262*, Courtesy Ronalds Printing. *p. 263*, Courtesy Hercules Incorporated. *p. 266*, (left) Courtesy Univex; (right) Courtesy Spring Air. *p. 269*, Courtesy Texaco Inc. *p. 271*, (left) Courtesy Super Valu Stores, Inc.; (right) Steve Smith/Onyx.

Chapter 9

Photos/ads: *p. 293*, (left) Courtesy Toyota Industrial Equipment; (right) Courtesy The Hertz Corporation. *p. 295*, (left) Courtesy Inland Steel

Industries, photo by Archie Lieberman; (right) Courtesy United Parcel Service of America, Inc. *p. 301*, Courtesy Quaker State Corporation. *p. 304*, Courtesy Ryder Trucks Rental Inc. *p. 306*, Reprinted with the permission of Dean Foods Company. *p. 311*, Courtesy CPC International. *p. 318*, Courtesy Lever Brothers Company. *p. 320*, (left) © Eastman Kodak Company; (right) Courtesy Deere & Company.

Chapter 10

Exhibits: *p. 340*, 10–5, adapted from Frank R. Bacon, Jr., and Thomas W. Butler, *Planned Innovation* (Ann Arbor: University of Michigan Institute of Science and Technology, 1980). *p. 343*, 10–6, adapted from Philip Kotler, "What Consumerism Means for Marketers," *Harvard Business Review*, May–June 1972, pp. 55–56.

Photos/ads: *p. 325*, Courtesy of McDonald's Canada. *p. 328*, (left) Gerry Gropp/Sipa Press; (right) Courtesy Tandy Corporation. *p. 331*, Courtesy CLM/BBDO, Paris. *p. 335*, (left) Frank Veronsky; (right) Grant Peterson. *p. 338*, Courtesy Du Pont Company. *p. 341*, Mark Joseph. *p. 344*, Courtesy 3M. *p. 346*, Courtesy Ford Motor Company.

Chapter 11

Exhibits: *p. 365*, 11–2, adapted from D. J. Bowersox and E. J. McCarthy, "Strategic Development of Planned Vertical Marketing Systems," in *Vertical Marketing Systems*, ed. Louis Bucklin (Glenview, Ill.: Scott, Foresman, 1970).

Photos/ads: *p. 353*, Courtesy The Goodyear Tire & Rubber Company. *p. 356*, Courtesy Archer Daniels Midland Co. *p. 358*, (left) © Steven Pumphrey; (right) © 1991 Reid Horn. *p. 360*, Courtesy The Southland Corporation. *p. 363*, Courtesy Sunbrella/Glen Raven Mills, Inc. *p. 367*, Courtesy Colgate-Palmolive Company. *p. 373*, (left) Shigeru Kunita; (right) Paul Chesley/Photographers Aspen.

Chapter 12

Exhibits: *p. 383*, 12–4, adapted from B. J. LaLonde and P. H. Zinzer, *Customer Service: Meaning and Measurement* (Chicago: National Council of Physical Distribution Management, 1976); and D. Phillip Locklin, *Transportation for Management* (Homewood, Ill.: Richard D. Irwin, 1972). *p. 392*, 12–6, adapted from Louis W. Stern and Adel I. El-Ansary, *Marketing Channels* (Englewood Cliffs, N.J.: Prentice Hall, Inc., 1977), p. 150.

Photos/ads: *p. 385*, CN Container ad. *p. 387*, Courtesy Sony Corporation of America. *p. 388*, (left) Photo courtesy Hewlett Packard Company; (right) Courtesy Air France. *p. 390*, © James Schnepf. *p. 394*, All photos used with permission of Mattel, Inc. *p. 395*, Courtesy Emery Worldwide. *p. 397*, (left) Photo courtesy Du Pont; (right) Courtesy Matlock, Inc.

Chapter 13

Exhibits: *p. 405*, 13–2, adapted from Louis Bucklin, "Retail Strategy and the Classification of Consumer Goods," *Journal of Marketing*, January 1963, pp. 50–55.

Photos/ads: *p. 401*, photo by Scott D.J. Graham. *p. 403*, (left) © Bruce Zake 1990; (right) Courtesy Home Shopping Network, Inc. *p. 406*, (left) Robert Wallis/JB Pictures; (right) Burt Glinn/Magnum Photos, Inc. *p. 411*, (left) © Seny Norasingh; (right) Steve Smith/Onyx. *p. 415*, (left) © Reinhold Spiegler; (right) © John McGrail 1992. *p. 417*, (left) Courtesy Kayser-Roth Hosiery, Inc.; (right) Courtesy Golden Valley Microwave Foods, Inc. *p. 424*, Courtesy New England Development. *p. 427*, Courtesy The Great Atlantic & Pacific Tea Co., photo by Steven Begleiter.

Chapter 14

Photos/ads: *p. 433*, Courtesy McLane Company, Inc. *p. 440*, © Steve Niedorf. *p. 441*, (left) Courtesy Cutters Exchange, Inc.; (right) Courtesy R. C. Steele. *p. 442*, Courtesy ARA Services. *p. 445*, Courtesy AT&T. *p. 450*, (left) © Michael Abramson; (right) Courtesy Vons Companies.

Chapter 15

Photos/ads: *p. 457*, Molly Maid logo, Moneysworth & Best logo. *p. 461*, (left) © Seth Resnick; (right) Courtesy Kellogg Company. *p. 462*, Nova Scotia ad. *p. 465*, Courtesy Beckett. *p. 466*, © 1991 FTD. *p. 468*, Courtesy United Parcel Service of America, Inc. *p. 470*, Courtesy Marion Merrell Dow U.S.A.; *p. 473*, Courtesy CLM/BBDO, Paris. *p. 478*, (left) Courtesy Aerostar International, Inc.; (center) Vince Streano/Tony Stone Worldwide; (right) Courtesy Wave Promotions.

Chapter 16

Exhibits: *p. 504*, 16–3, exhibit suggested by Professor A. A. Brogowicz, Western Michigan University.

Photos/ads: *p. 488*, (left) Caroline Parsons/Aria Pictures; (right) Courtesy Toyota Motor Corporation. *p. 493*, (left) Courtesy of AT&T Archives; (right) Terry Husebye. *p. 496*, © William Taufic 1991. All rights reserved. *p. 497* (left) © Joe Stewartson; (right) Courtesy Alcoa; photo by Robert Feldman. *p. 506*, (left) Courtesy Lance; (right) Courtesy Merck & Co., Inc.; photo by Robert Krist.

Chapter 17

Exhibits: *p. 516*, 17–2, adapted from R. J. Lavidge and G. A. Steiner, "A Model for Predictive Measurements of Advertising Effectiveness," *Journal of Marketing*, October 1961, p. 61. *p. 535*, 17–5, based on data from "Special Issue: Agency Report," *Advertising Age*, April 13, 1992, pp. S1-44; "Special Issue: Agency Report Card," *Adweek*, March 23, 1992; "International: World Brands," *Advertising Age*, September 2, 1991, pp. 25–36.

Photos/ads: *p. 515*, Courtesy Nabob Coffee Co. *p. 517*, (left) Courtesy National Dairy Board; Agency: Stricevic O'Connell Advertising Marketing Inc.; (right) Courtesy Hotel Bar Foods, Inc. *p. 519*, Courtesy Tyco Toys, Inc. *p. 521*, Courtesy Michelin Tire Corporation. *p. 526*, Reprinted courtesy Eastman Kodak Company. *p. 528*, Courtesy Dominion Directory. *p. 532*, Courtesy Lawner Reingold Britton & Partners, Boston. *p. 536*, (left) Courtesy Wm. Wrigley Jr. Company; (right) Courtesy General Mills, Inc. *p. 541*, Advertising Agency: TBWA Hamburg; Photos Account Manager: Joachim Schadewaldt; Managing Director: Lutz Kuikuck; Creative Director: Günther Heinrich; Copy: Stephan Chrzeschinski; Art Director: Sven Hillie; Producer: Dorit Bahlburg; Film Producer: What Else; Regisseur and Camera; David McDonald.

Chapter 18

Photos/ads: *p. 545*, Photo by Scott D.J. Graham. *p. 547*, Courtesy Giant Food, Inc. *p. 550*, (left) Courtesy Malt-O-Meal Company; (right) Courtesy Pagano, Schenck & Kay, Inc. *p. 554*, Courtesy United Parcel Service of America, Inc. *p. 563*, Andy Freeberg Photography. *p. 565*, Courtesy of the Quaker Oats Company. *p. 566*, Courtesy Mercedes-Benz of North America, Inc.

Chapter 19

Photos/ads: *p. 587*, photo by Scott D.J.Graham. *p. 589*, Courtesy BCTEL. *p. 590*, Will Van Overbeek. *p. 592*, Courtesy Vons Companies. *p. 595*, (left) Courtesy Geo. Hormel & Company; (right) Kim Steele. *p. 611*, Courtesy Philips Lighting. *p. 614*, (left) Courtesy Severin Montres AG; (right) Courtesy Tiffany & Co. *p. 615*, Courtesy One Price Clothing Stores.

Chapter 20

Exhibits: *p. 652*, 20–10, Marie Gaudard, Roland Coates, and Liz Freeman, "Accelerating Improvement," *Quality Progress*, October 1991, pp. 81–88. *p. 653*, 20–11, Marie Gaudard, Roland Coates, and Liz Freeman, "Accelerating Improvement," *Quality Progress*, October 1991, pp. 81–88.

Photos/ads: *p. 623*, Robb Kendrick/Contact Press Images. *p. 627*, Courtesy International Business Machines Corporation. *p. 636*, Courtesy Groupe Belier Corporate. *p. 640*, Courtesy BDDP, Paris. *p. 641*, Courtesy the Gillette Company. *p. 645*, Courtesy American International Group, Inc. *p. 647*, (left) Courtesy Full Spectrum Graphic Design, Santa Rosa; (right) Courtesy Computer Associates International Inc.

Chapter 21

Photos/ads: *p. 665*, Courtesy Hudson's Bay Company. *p. 667*, Courtesy Quaker State Corporation. *p. 677*, (left) © Philip Saltonstall/Onyx; (right) Courtesy Levi Strauss & Co. *p. 682*, Courtesy Cramer Krasselt.

Chapter 22

Exhibits: *p. 707*, 22–1, adapted from discussions of an American Marketing Association Strategic Planning Committee.

Photos/ads: *p. 695*, John Chiasson/Gamma-Liaison. *p. 697*, (left) Ed Kashi; (right) Melanie Carr/Zephyr Pictures. *p. 699*, Courtesy Du Pont. *p. 701*, (left) © 1991 Binney & Smith Inc.; (right) Ad courtesy Canon U.S.A., Inc., Graphics Systems Division. © 1991 Canon U.S.A., Inc. *p. 703*, (right) Courtesy Sears, Roebuck & Co. *p. 704*, Peter Turnley/Black Star *p. 709*, Courtesy MacLaren: Lintas Inc.

Appendix E

Exhibits: *p. 718*, E–1, adapted and updated from Charles G. Burck, "A Group Profile of the Fortune 500 Chief Executive," *Fortune*, May 1976, p. 172.

Photos/ads: *p. 720*, (left) Kraft, General Foods, and Oscar Mayer are registered trademarks of Kraft General Foods, Inc. Reproduced with permission; (right) Courtesy Colgate-Palmolive Company.

Name Index

Subject Index